Comparative Politics

COMPARATIVE
POLITICS

FIFTH EDITION

EDITED BY
DANIELE CARAMANI

OXFORD
UNIVERSITY PRESS

OXFORD

UNIVERSITY PRESS

Great Clarendon Street, Oxford, OX2 6DP,
United Kingdom

Oxford University Press is a department of the University of Oxford.
It furthers the University's objective of excellence in research, scholarship,
and education by publishing worldwide. Oxford is a registered trade mark of
Oxford University Press in the UK and in certain other countries

First edition 2011
Second edition 2014
Third edition 2017

Impression: 1

Published in the United States of America by Oxford University Press
198 Madison Avenue, New York, NY 10016, United States of America

British Library Cataloguing in Publication Data
Data available

Library of Congress Control Number: 2019955869

ISBN 978–0–19–882060–4

Printed in Italy by
L.E.G.O. S.p.A. Lavis (TN)

Preface

About the book

In designing this textbook on *Comparative Politics*, the ambition was to produce an exciting, authoritative, and up-to-date teaching instrument. We have tried to write chapters of the highest standard in terms of their content, with information presented comparatively and supported by cutting-edge theories and a rigorous methodology. We aimed to provide comprehensive chapters in their substantive coverage of the field, and a worldwide range of countries.

We hope that the fifth edition will speak to comparative politics students at all levels, as well as to teachers who will use it for their classes, as did the first four editions. Our goal was to produce an integrated text with a maximum of cross-references between chapters. At the same time, the modular structure with self-contained chapters should maximize its appeal to lecturers and students, alongside accessible language enhanced by a number of learning features and a similar format throughout. This structure does not require that it is read cover to cover. The book can be used in any order, making it possible to compose courses with a 'variable geometry'. For the same reason, more but shorter chapters have been preferred.

Rationale for the book

The first important feature is that the volume provides a *comprehensive and wide-ranging coverage* of both the *subject areas* of comparative politics and the *geographical spread* of cases. The range of countries includes not only advanced industrial nations, but also developing regions and emerging economies (in post-communist countries, Latin America, Asia, the Middle East, and Africa).

The range of topics is also more comprehensive than in most commonly taught courses in comparative politics. On the one hand, throughout the book attention is given to *theory and methodology*, and three chapters deal specifically with these topics in Section 1 on 'Theories and methods'. As far as possible, all chapters include the most important theoretical approaches in each field of the discipline and present the most recent advances and current debates. No specific approach has been privileged. Methodologically, it is based on rigorous comparative analysis and up-to-date empirical data.

On the other hand, the range of *substantive topics* is reflected in a number of chapters that add to the usual core areas of comparative politics courses. The book devotes a great deal of attention to multi-level institutions and actors (Chapters 11 and 15) and to non-institutional actors such as interest groups, social movements, and media (in Section 4 on 'Actors and processes'). Most importantly, perhaps, the book includes an entire section on 'Public policies' (Section 5)—not only how policies arc made, but also their impact on economies and societies (with a focus on the welfare state and varieties of political economies). This gives a better balance between the 'input' and 'output' sides of the political system. Finally, the book has an entire section (Section 6 on 'Beyond the nation-state') on, first, supranational political systems (such as the European Union) and, second, interactions between political systems internationally. Theoretically, this section deals with major challenges to comparative politics.

The second important feature is the *analytical and comparative* approach of the volume. Information and data are presented thematically rather than country by country, and comparison is carried out on specific political, institutional, and socio-economic phenomena. For us, comparative politics should not be reduced to the one-by-one description of single countries. Case studies (see Appendix 1 'Country profiles') are theoretically useful only if inserted in a broader comparative framework. We understand comparative politics in analytical terms, as a combination of substance (the study of political systems, actors, and processes) and method, i.e. identifying and explaining differences and similarities between cases through the test of hypotheses about relationships—law-like generalizations—between concepts and variables applicable in more than one context. This thematic, analytical, and comparative approach leads to the basic choice of organizing the book around major substantive themes.

The third important feature is that the book presents a large amount of *comparative empirical data*. The analytical approach of the book leads us to present information and data in tables and figures throughout the chapters (as well as in Appendix 2 'Comparative tables' and Appendix 3 'World trends').

Particular attention is given to historical trends, longitudinal data, and time series (see Appendix 3 'World trends'). The book includes a long-term perspective allowing a better appreciation of current changes. It thus combines *time and space dimensions*. There is a specific reason for this. The development of the modern nation-state and mass democracies in the nineteenth century is a unique change that has no previous equivalent. This change involved a totally new political organization—based on principles of individual equality, civil liberties, voting rights—and social organization, in particular with industrialization and the subsequent development of the welfare state. Therefore, an understanding of contemporary society cannot be complete without a long-term perspective highlighting the scope of these changes.

The empirical approach also allows us to provide students with the possibility of *analysing data* themselves. The Online Resources that accompany this book (http://www.oxfordtextbooks.co.uk/orc/caramani5e) include a large amount of *comparative data*, making this not just a learning device, but also a research-oriented data repository. Students can analyse data and lecturers can prepare exercises. Furthermore, a web directory allows students to look for and collect more data in the internet archives of international and national organizations, official and academic data collections, and websites specializing in elections, referendums, or survey data and opinion polls. We believe that comparative politics is an empirical discipline and that theories and methods are of no use if they are not combined with data.

In attempting to achieve these goals, we are aware that we have not produced an 'easy' book. However, we believe that most students are much better, more motivated, and harder working than is often assumed. It is when confronted with challenge and unexplored fields that young people enjoy learning, perform best, and acquire self-confidence. We are convinced that an effort on the part of students will be rewarding and that they will learn from this book and its website. Comparative politics is a broad and fascinating discipline dealing with important current world issues. Studying it will prove a lifetime investment.

Acknowledgements

We very much appreciate that Oxford University Press—our editors in the first four editions, Ruth Anderson, Catherine Page, Martha Bailes and Sarah Iles and Francesca Walker, and the fantastic editors of this fifth edition, Katie Staal and Sarah Iles—shared our approach with strong commitment and encouragement, and supported us substantially, technically, and logistically. From the first steps of the project up to its conclusion, their input has been remarkable and crucial to the successful completion of this volume.

When defining the line-up of contributors and bringing on board new contributors in the second and fourth editions, the criteria were those of excellence. I am very happy that it has been possible to bring together an outstanding group of 'comparativists' from a range of nationalities and academic traditions. All are currently engaged in research, and thus are 'research-minded' and in touch with the most recent advances in their fields of expertise. Building on the success of the previous editions, for this fifth edition I am delighted that it has been possible to bring on board Liesbet Hooghe, Natasha Lindstaedt, Gary Marks, Arjan Schakel, and Dieter Rucht. With these changes, we lose exceptional colleagues from previous editions: Paul Brooker, Hanspeter Kriesi, and John Loughlin. I wish to express grateful thanks on behalf of the whole group for their pleasant collaboration in past editions and for their outstanding scholarly contribution to the textbook. On a personal level, I am honoured that such a prestigious group of scholars has trusted me to lead this endeavour, and very thankful for their professional and collaborative spirit.

I would also like to thank Matt Qvortrup for the numerous comments and corrections on previous editions, and in particular for the constructive critiques received.

Finally, I would like to thank my research assistants over the various editions: Nina Buddeke, Beatrice Eugster, Stephanie Hess, Patrick Lengg, Matthias Meyer-Schwarzenberger, Alexander Schäfer, Siyana Timcheva, and Roman Hunziker for this fifth edition—for the marvellous job they did in preparing the Online Resources, the 'Country profiles', the data for the 'Comparative tables' and 'World trends', and, more generally, for supporting us throughout the project with extreme professionalism and dedication. Their substantial criticisms, too, allowed us to clarify obscure points in several chapters. I am deeply grateful to them for their engagement.

Daniele Caramani

July 2007, September 2010, September 2013, September 2016, September 2019

New to this edition

This fifth edition includes three new chapters, one of which (Chapter 11), by Liesbet Hooghe, Gary Marks, and Arjan H. Schakel, addresses a brand-new topic on 'Multi-level governance', expanding the topic of federalism, decentralization, and subsidiarity to include the supranational level. Furthermore, Natasha Lindstaedt authors a new chapter on 'Authoritarian regimes' (Chapter 6) and Dieter Rucht a new chapter on 'Social movements' (Chapter 16).

This new edition continues to devote more attention to non-Western regions. Thematically, this means first following recent changes in global politics, most notably the backlash against democracy.

- We analyse recent anti-democratic trends in the Arab world, as well as in Turkey, Russia, South Africa, and some countries in Eastern Europe, but also a range of Western countries.

- Democracy promotion is accompanied by themes of autocracy promotion (from countries such as Saudi Arabia, Iran, Russia, China, and Venezuela).

- We devote more attention to hybrid regimes such as competitive-electoral authoritarianism.

- Political culture is analysed also in non-democratic regimes, and the discussion of movements in non-democratic settings such as China has been added. Also, challenges to democracy in Western countries are analysed in changing political cultures.

Second, we continue to analyse the trend against globalization and its consequences, as well as the crisis of supranational integration in Europe with the British 'Brexit' from the European Union. This includes looking at protectionism and other aspects of the downside of globalization, such as trade 'wars'.

Finally, we examine the consequences of the backlash against globalization and of the migration and financial crises on the spectacular rise of populism in Europe, North America, and South America (Brazil and Mexico in particular) and its impact on party systems. Since the third edition (published in 2014), a number of landmark elections and referenda (including the Brexit vote in Britain in 2016) have taken place which have fundamentally altered the political landscape of many countries.

In addition:

- The 'Country profiles' in Appendix 1 have been thoroughly improved and updated with a standardized terminology and categories (such as for electoral systems) and the extension of the section on state formation. Sources have been streamlined and appear in full in the Online Resources. In the fourth edition, eight new countries were added.

- Countries in the 'Comparative tables' in Appendix 2 were increased to sixty in the fourth edition, of which fifty are the same as for the 'Country profiles'.

- The 'World trends' in Appendix 3 are based on new data and new categories, and are based on a better classification of countries in world regions. New 'World trends' graphs have been added on gender, trade, and democracy.

- The bibliography and further reading in each chapter has been updated with the latest literature.

- Data and information have been revised in each chapter (including the latest theoretical contributions in each field; tables, figures, and graphs; web links; and further reading).

Contents in brief

Contents in detail

List of figures

List of boxes

List of tables

Abbreviations

The list of abbreviations does not include the names of political parties, trade unions, social movements, interest groups, or other organizations.

2RS	Two-round (electoral) system
AOC	*Appellations d'Origine Contrôlée*
AV	Alternative vote (electoral system)
CAP	Common Agricultural Policy (European Union)
CDI	Centre for Democratic Institutions (Australia)
CFSP	Common Foreign and Security Policy (European Union)
CIEP	constitutional inter-election period
CIS	Commonwealth of Independent States
CJR	constitutional judicial review
CLRAE	Congress of Local and Regional Authorities of Europe
CMEs	coordinated market economies
CMP	Comparative Manifesto Project
CoR	Committee of the Regions (European Union)
COREPER	Committee of Permanent Representatives of the EU
DG	Democracy and Governance, Directorate General (European Union)
DRG	democracy, human rights, and governance
ECB	European Central Bank
ECJ	European Court of Justice
ECSC	European Coal and Steel Community
EEA	European Economic Area
EEC	European Economic Community
EED	European Endowment for Democracy
EIDHR	European Instrument for Democracy and Human Rights (European Union)
EM–CC	European Model–Constitutional Court
EMU	Economic and Monetary Union
ENEP	effective number of elective parties
ENP	European Neighbourhood Policy (European Union)
ENPP	effective number of parliamentary parties
EP	European Parliament
EPD	European Partnership for Democracy
EPP	European People's Party

ESCS	European Coal and Steel Community
ESDP	European Security and Defence Cooperation (European Union)
ESM	European Stability Mechanism
ESS	European Social Survey
EU	European Union
F	fractionalization index
FAO	United Nations Food and Agriculture Organization
FCO	Foreign and Commonwealth Office (UK)
FDI	foreign direct investment
FPTP	first past the post (electoral system)
GDP	gross domestic product
GEM	gender empowerment measure
GER	gross enrolment ratio
GMO	genetically modified organisms
GNI	gross national income
GNP	gross national product
GPI	gender parity index
GWP	gross world product
HDI	human development index
ICC	International Criminal Court
ICP	International Comparison Programme
ICPSR	Inter-University Consortium for Political and Social Research
ICTs	information and communication technologies
IDEA	International Institute for Democracy and Electoral Assistance
IGO	international governmental organization
ILO	International Labour Organization
INGO	international non-governmental organization
IREX	International Research and Exchanges Board
IRI	International Republican Institute (US)
ISO	International Organization for Standardization
ITU	International Telecommunications Union

LAI	Local Authority Index		QCA	qualitative comparative analysis
LMEs	liberal market economies		QMV	qualified majority voting (European Union)
LSq	least square index			
MDSD	most different systems design		RA	research answer
MEP	Member of European Parliament		RAI	Regional Authority Index
MLG	multilevel governance		RD	research design
MMM	mixed-member majoritarian (electoral system)		RoP	Rules of Procedure (legislatures)
			RQ	research question
MMP	mixed-member proportional (electoral system)		RSS	really simple syndication
			SCJ	justice of the supreme court
MP	Member of Parliament		SES	socio-economic status
MSSD	most similar systems design		SGP	Stability and Growth Pact (European Union)
MZES	Mannheim Centre for European Social Research			
			SIDA	Swedish International Development Cooperation Agency
NAFTA	North American Free Trade Agreement			
NATO	North Atlantic Treaty Organization		SNA	social network analysis
NDI	National Democratic Institute for International Affairs (US)		SMEs	social market economies
			SMO	Social Movement Organization
NED	National Endowment for Democracy (US)		SMP	single-member plurality (electoral system)
NEPAD	New Partnership for Africa's Development		SoP	separation of powers
			STV	single transferable vote (electoral system)
NGO	non-governmental organization			
NIMD	Netherlands Institute for Multiparty Democracy		TIV	trend indicator values
			TNC	transnational companies
NPM	New Public Management		UDHR	Universal Declaration of Human Rights
NSF	US National Science Foundation			
OAS	Organization of American States		UFW	United Farm Workers
OCA	optimal currency area		UN	United Nations
ODA	official development assistance		UNCTAD	United Nations Conference on Trade and Development
OECD	Organisation for Economic Co-operation and Development		UNDP	United Nations Development Programme
OMC	open method of coordination			
OPEC	Organization of Petroleum Exporting Countries		USAID	United States Agency for International Development
OSCE	Organization for Security and Co-operation in Europe		USSR	Union of Soviet Socialist Republics
			WEF	World Economic Forum
PACs	political action committees		WFD	Westminster Foundation for Democracy (UK)
PDA	personal digital assistant			
PPP	purchasing power parities		WHO	World Health Organization
PR	proportional representation (electoral system)		WTO	World Trade Organization
			WVS	World Values Survey
PSTN	public switched telephone network			

List of contributors

Jørgen Goul Andersen is Professor of Political Sociology at the Department of Political Science, Aalborg University, Denmark.

James Bickerton is Professor of Political Science at St Francis Xavier University, Canada.

Peter Burnell is an Emeritus Professor in the Department of Politics and International Studies, University of Warwick, England.

Daniele Caramani is Professor of Comparative Politics at the University of Zurich.

Roland Erne is Professor of European Integration and Employment Relations at University College Dublin.

Frank Esser is Professor of International and Comparative Media Research at the University of Zurich.

Alain-G. Gagnon is Canada Research Chair in Quebec and Canadian Studies at the Université du Québec à Montréal.

Michael Gallagher is Professor of Comparative Politics at Trinity College, University of Dublin.

Simon Hix is Pro-Director (Research) and the Harold Laski Professor of Political Science at the London School of Economics and Political Science.

Liesbet Hooghe is the W. R. Kenan Distinguished Professor of Political Science at UNC-Chapel Hill and Robert Schuman Fellow at the European University Institute, Florence.

Ronald Inglehart is Lowenstein Professor of Political Science and Research Professor at the Institute for Social Research (ISR) at the University of Michigan.

Richard S. Katz is Professor of Political Science at the Johns Hopkins University, Baltimore.

Hans Keman is Emeritus Professor of Comparative Political Science at the Free University of Amsterdam.

Kees van Kersbergen is Professor of Comparative Politics in the Department of Political Science at Aarhus University, Denmark.

Herbert Kitschelt is George V. Allen Professor of International Relations in the Department of Political Science at Duke University, Durham NC.

Christoph Knill is Professor of Political Science at the University of Munich.

Amie Kreppel is a Jean Monnet Chair of EU Politics, the Director of the University of Florida's Center for European Studies (CES), and the Jean Monnet Centre of Excellence in Manchester.

Natasha Lindstaedt is Professor of Government at the University of Essex.

Philip Manow is Professor of Political Science at the University of Bremen, Germany.

Gary Marks is Burton Craige Professor of Political Science at the University of North Carolina, Chapel Hill, and Robert Schuman Fellow at the European University Institute, Florence.

Wolfgang C. Müller is Professor of Democratic Governance at the University of Vienna.

Paul Pennings is Associate Professor of Comparative Political Science at the Free University of Amsterdam.

Aníbal Pérez-Liñán is Professor of Political Science and Global Affairs at the University of Notre Dame, Indiana.

B. Guy Peters is Maurice Falk Professor of American Government at the University of Pittsburgh, PA.

Barbara Pfetsch is Professor of Communication Theory and Media Effects Research at the Freie Universität Berlin and a Director of the Weizenbaum-Institute for the Networked Society in Berlin.

Gianfranco Poggi is Emeritus Professor of Sociology at the University of Virginia, Charlottesville.

Philipp Rehm is Associate Professor in the Political Science Department at the Ohio State University, Columbus, OH.

Bo Rothstein holds the August Röhss Chair in Political Science at the University of Gothenburg in Sweden, where he is co-founder and was the head of the Quality of Government (QoG) Institute 2004–2015.

Dieter Rucht is Emeritus Professor of Sociology at Wissenschaftszentrum, Berlin.

Arjan H. Schakel is Researcher at the Department of Comparative Politics at the University of Bergen, Norway.

Georg Sørensen is Professor Emeritus of Political Science at the University of Aarhus, Denmark.

Alec Stone Sweet is Saw Swee Hock Centennial Professor, Faculty of Law, the National University of Singapore.

Jale Tosun is Professor of Political Science at the Institute of Political Science at Heidelberg University.

Christian Welzel is Chair of Political Culture Research at Leuphana University in Lueneburg, Germany.

Guided tour of learning features

This book contains a number of specially designed learning tools to help you develop the key knowledge and skills you need to study comparative politics.

Reader's guides

Each chapter opens with a reader's guide outlining what you can expect to cover in the chapter, helping you to know what to look for as you read.

> **Reader's guide**
>
> Comparative politics is one of the main disciplines in political scie
> international relations. It deals with internal political structures
> executives), individual and collective actors (voters, parties, social
> processes (policy-making, communication and socialization proces
> goal is empirical: describe, explain, and predict similarities and diffe
> they countries, regions, or supranational systems (such as empires
> be done through the intensive analysis of a few cases (even one cas
> of many cases, and can be either synchronic (b
> not accounting for change over time) or diachr
> politics uses both quantitative and qualitative d
> challenged by interdependence between countri

> **Reader's guide**
>
> Multilevel governance is the dispersion of authority to jurisdictions within and beyo
> Three literatures frame the study of multilevel governance. Economists and pub
> explain multilevel governance as a functionalist adaptation to the provision of publi
> scales. Political economists model the effects of private preferences and moral h
> and political scientists theorize the effects of territorial identity on multilevel g
> approaches complement each other, and today researchers draw on all three t
> over time and across space. The tremendous growth of multilevel governance si

Boxes

Throughout the book, 'Zoom-in' boxes, 'Definition' boxes, and 'For and against' boxes give you extra information on particular topics, define and explain key ideas, and challenge you to weigh up different ideas in order to think about what you have learned.

> **🔍 DEFINITION 1.1**
>
> **'Comparative politics'**
>
> Comparative politics is one of the three main subfields of political science (alongside political theory and international relations) focusing on internal political structures, actors, and processes, and analysing them empirically by describing, explaining, and predicting their variety (similarities and differences) across political systems (and over time)—be they national political systems, regional, municipal, or even supranational systems.

Key points

Each main chapter section ends with key points that reinforce your understanding and help you to assess your own learning.

> **KEY POINTS**
>
> * This chapter addresses the meaning of democracy, types of democracy, the causes of democratization, and the future of democracy.
> * Democracy is the dominant principle of legitimacy in our historical era.
> * The number of democracies in the world expanded in the late twentieth century.

Knowledge-based questions

Knowledge-based

1. What are the main stages of the policy cycle, and how does this concept enhance our understanding of policy-making?

2. Which actors—societal and political—participate in the single stages?

3. What is the role of political institutions in policy-making?

At the end of each chapter, knowledge-based questions allow you to check your progress and then revisit any areas which need further study.

Critical thinking questions

Critical thinking

1. How can we think of policy-making in terms of theory?

2. In which ways are policy typologies related to the policy-making process?

3. Which theoretical concepts cope with the effects of internationalization on domestic policy-making?

Following on from the knowledge-based questions, critical thinking questions allow you to reflect on the subject matter, apply your knowledge, and critically evaluate what you have learnt.

Further reading

FURTHER READING

Classics in European integration and EU politics

Haas, E. B. (1958) [2004] *The Uniting of Europe: Politi Social, and Economic Forces, 1950–1957* (South Bend, University of Notre Dame Press).

Majone, G. (1996) *Regulating Europe* (London: Routledg

Recommendations for further reading at the end of each chapter identify the key literature in the field, helping you to develop your interest in particular topics in comparative politics.

Glossary terms

wise, of weak states. Again, political developme including attempts at **democratization** are deci in an interplay between 'domestic' and 'internatio elements.

The economic basis of sovereign statehood also been transformed. In the modern state, th was a segregated national economy; the major p of economic activity took place at home. In the pe modern state, national economies are much

Key terms appear in bold in the text and are defined in a glossary at the end of the book, identifying and defining key terms and ideas as you learn, and acting as a useful prompt when it comes to revision.

Comparative data section

Country Profile Japan

Japan (Nihon-koku/Nippon-koku)

State formation

The foundation of Japan dates back to 660 BC. A more than 1,000 years of changing empires, Jap became a modern state in 1603. In 1854, Japan forced to open up and sign a treaty with the US,

Extensive empirical data are presented not only to illustrate ideas and concepts, but also for you to use in your own research and analysis, giving you a real sense of how comparative politics works in practice.

In the book you will find different forms of empirical data including:

– twenty **country profiles** (Appendix 1) with information on state formation, forms of government, legal systems, legislature, and electoral systems;

– **world data** on languages, religions, and socio-economic indicators, and **comparative tables** (Appendix 2) to directly compare different countries' statistics across a range of important themes and issues;

– graphs of **world trends** (Appendix 3) on matters from military expenditure to urbanization.

Guided tour of the Online Resources

The Online Resources that accompany this book provide ready-to-use learning and teaching materials for students and lecturers. These resources are free of charge and designed to maximize the learning experience.

www.oup.com/he/caramani5e

FOR STUDENTS

These resources have been developed to help you understand how comparative politics works in practice. Extensive empirical data have been gathered by a team of researchers for you to use in your own research and analysis.

Comparative data sets

Comparative data are available for 200 countries, for use in analysis, essay writing, and lab-based exercises.

Information is taken from official national sources and international organizations, with indicators including: demography; health; human and social rights; gender equality; education; economy and development; communication and transport; geography and natural resources; the environment; and government and security.

Web directory

A web directory points you to databases compiled by international organizations, as well as international and national archives.

Country profiles

An interactive world map presents key information about fifty countries.

Flashcard glossary

A series of interactive flashcards containing key terms allows you to test your knowledge of important concepts and ideas.

Additional material

Additional material to complement the book is provided online, including redundant usage tables and boxes to provide further information and deepen your learning.

Web links

Carefully selected lists of websites direct you to the sites of institutions and organizations that will help you to broaden your knowledge and understanding, and provide useful sources of information in your comparative politics studies.

Review questions

Review questions help you to test your understanding of comparative politics.

FOR LECTURERS

These customizable resources are password protected, but access is available to anyone using the book in their teaching. Complete the short registration form on the site to choose your own username and password.

Test bank

Over 200 multiple choice and true/false questions can be downloaded to virtual learning environments, or printed out for use in assessment.

Figures and tables from the book

All figures and tables in the textbook are available to download electronically.

Seminar activities

Seminar activities are provided as a starting point for student discussion and interaction.

World map

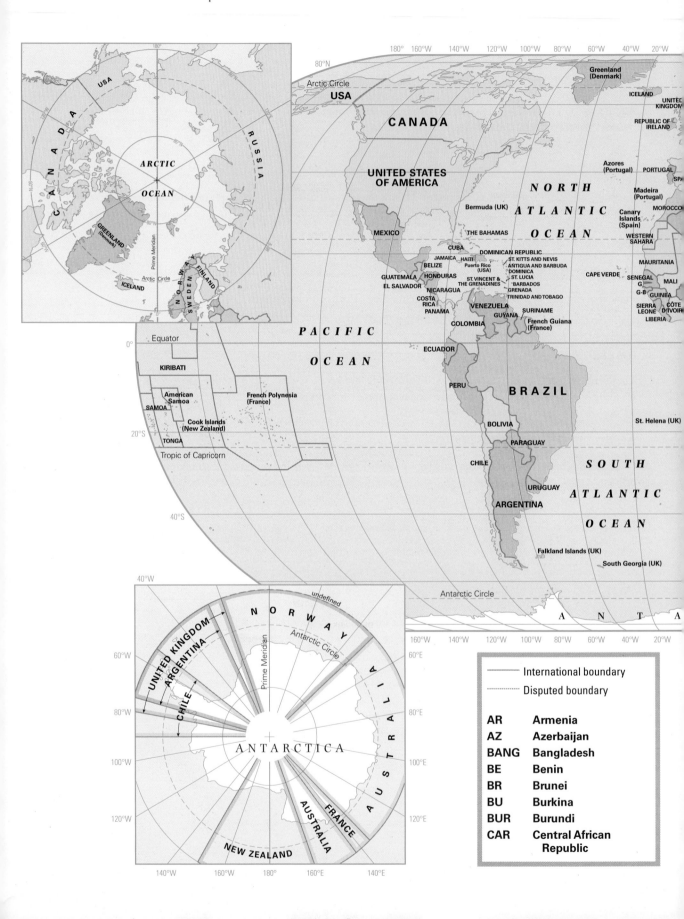

80°N

Arctic Circle

USA

Greenland
(Denmark)

ICELAND

UNITED
KINGDOM

CANADA

REPUBLIC OF
IRELAND

UNITED STATES
OF AMERICA

NORTH

Azores
(Portugal)

PORTUGAL

SPA

ATLANTIC

Madeira
(Portugal)

MOROCCO

Bermuda (UK)

OCEAN

Canary
Islands
(Spain)

MEXICO

WESTERN
SAHARA

THE BAHAMAS

MAURITANIA

CUBA

DOMINICAN REPUBLIC

CAPE VERDE

SENEGAL

MALI

JAMAICA

HAITI

ST. KITTS AND NEVIS
ANTIGUA AND BARBUDA
DOMINICA

G

G-B

GUINEA

BELIZE

Puerto Rico
(USA)

GUATEMALA

HONDURAS

ST. LUCIA

SIERRA
LEONE

CÔTE
D'IVOIR

EL SALVADOR

ST. VINCENT &
THE GRENADINES

BARBADOS

GRENADA

NICARAGUA

TRINIDAD AND TOBAGO

LIBERIA

COSTA
RICA

VENEZUELA

SURINAME

PANAMA

GUYANA

French Guiana
(France)

COLOMBIA

PACIFIC

ECUADOR

OCEAN

PERU

BRAZIL

Equator

0°

KIRIBATI

American
Samoa

French Polynesia
(France)

St. Helena (UK)

SAMOA

BOLIVIA

Cook Islands
(New Zealand)

20°S

TONGA

PARAGUAY

Tropic of Capricorn

SOUTH

CHILE

ATLANTIC

40°S

URUGUAY

ARGENTINA

OCEAN

Falkland Islands (UK)

South Georgia (UK)

Antarctic Circle

A N T A

Inset maps

USA

C A N A D A

R
U
S
S
I
A

ARCTIC

OCEAN

Prime Meridian

GREENLAND
(Denmark)

N
O
R
W
A
Y

S
W
E
D
E
N

FINLAND

ICELAND

Arctic Circle

40°W

undefined

N O R W A Y

60°W

UNITED KINGDOM

ARGENTINA

Antarctic Circle

60°E

Prime Meridian

80°W

CHILE

80°E

A
U
S
T
R
A
L
I
A

A N T A R C T I C A

100°W

100°E

FRANCE

AUSTRALIA

120°W

120°E

NEW ZEALAND

140°W 160°W 180° 160°E 140°E

Legend

	International boundary
	Disputed boundary

AR	**Armenia**
AZ	**Azerbaijan**
BANG	**Bangladesh**
BE	**Benin**
BR	**Brunei**
BU	**Burkina**
BUR	**Burundi**
CAR	**Central African Republic**

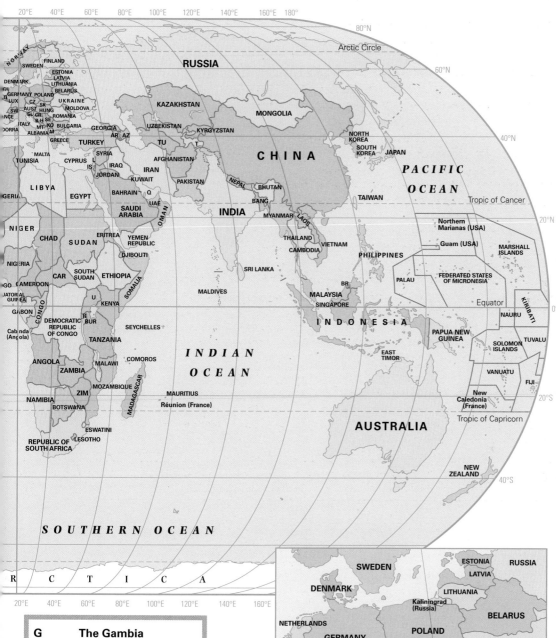

G	**The Gambia**
G-B	**Guinea-Bissau**
IS	**Israel**
L	**Lebanon**
Q	**Qatar**
R	**Rwanda**
T	**Tajikistan**
TU	**Turkmenistan**
U	**Uganda**
UAE	**United Arab Emirates**
ZIM	**Zimbabwe**

World data

World data	The most spoken languages		
Languages	Absolute figures (million)	%	Main geographical areas
Mandarin	1,299.0	19.1	China
Spanish	442.0	6.5	Spain, Latin America
English	378.0	5.5	UK, US, Canada, Australia, New Zealand
Arabic	315.0	4.6	North Africa, Middle East
Hindi	260.0	3.8	India
Bengali	243.0	3.5	Bangladesh
Portuguese	223.0	3.2	Brazil, Angola, Portugal
Russian	154.0	2.2	Russia
Japanese	128.0	1.8	Japan
Lahnda	119.0	1.7	Pakistan
Javanese	84.4	1.2	Indonesia
Turkish	78.5	1.1	Turkey
Korean	77.2	1.1	South Korea
French	76.8	1.1	France, Switzerland, Belgium, Canada
German	76.0	1.1	Germany, Austria, Switzerland
Telugu	74.8	1.1	India
Marathi	71.8	1.0	India
Urdu	69.2	1.0	Pakistan
Vietnamese	68.0	1.0	Vietnam
Tamil	66.7	1.0	India
Italian	64.8	0.9	Italy, Switzerland
Persian	61.5	0.9	Iran, Afghanistan
Malay	60.7	0.9	Malaysia, Indonesia, Thailand

Note: Figures are approximate; the table includes languages spoken as a first language by more than 50 million people.

Source: G. F. Simons and Charles D. Fennig (eds) (2018) *Ethnologue: Languages of the World* (21st edn) (Dallas, Texas: SIL International), http://www.ethnologue.com.

World data 2 Religions in the world

Religious groups	Population 2015 (million)	%
Christians	2,416	32.8
Muslims	1,720	23.4
Hindus	1,007	13.7
Agnostics	687	9.3
Buddhists	516	7.0
Chinese folk-religionists	446	6.0
Ethnoreligionists	267	3.6
Atheists	136	1.8
New religionists	65	0.8
Sikhs	25	0.3
Jews	15	0.2
Spiritists	14	0.2
Daoists	9	0.1
Confucianists	8	0.1
Baha'is	8	0.1
Jains	6	0.0
Shintoists	3	0.0
Zoroastrians	0	0.0
Sum	**7,348**	**100.0%**

Note: Figures are approximate. Christianity includes Roman Catholicism (52.5%), Protestantism (17.6%), Orthodoxy (10.4%), and Anglicanism (3.8%), as well as Pentecostalism, Latter-Day Saints, Evangelicalism, Jehovah's Witnesses, Quakerism, etc. Islam includes Sunnis (83.0%) and Shiites (16.1%).
Source: World Christian Database (http://www.worldchristiandatabase.org).

World data 3 Socio-economic indicators

Indicator	Western Europe	Central and Eastern Europe	Latin America	North America	Middle East and North Africa	Sub-Saharan Africa	Central and Northern Asia	Southeast Asia	Oceania	Total
Population (in millions)	412.5	351.5	514.8	491.0	523.6	1,057.0	3,460.9	648.6	40.9	7,500.8
Population growth (annual %)	0.7	-0.1	0.9	1.0	2.0	2.5	1.3	1.2	1.0	1.3
Life expectancy at birth (years)	81.9	76	75.1	79.4	75	62	73.7	72.6	74	72.5
Urban population (% of total)*	76.3	63.1	67.0	81.1	76.2	43.5	51.6	50.6	59.5	60.5
Labour force participation (% of total population aged 15–64)	75.7	69.3	69.4	71.8	57.4	68.3	68.4	70.2	64.4	68.1
Labour force female (% of female population aged 15–64)	70.6	62.7	58.7	62.8	29.8	62.3	55.0	62.1	58.0	58.1
Unemployment (% of labour force)	6.9	10.0	8.2	4.7	9.6	8.5	4.8	2.5	7.0	7.7
Literacy rate (% of population 15+ years)	96.2	98.9	92.0	94.9	83.6	62.8	83.8	87.3	91.0	82.1
Health expenditure per capita (current US$)	4,485.4	667.1	598.4	4,859.4	776.1	111.0	516.9	391.3	968.4	1,011.6
GDP per capita (current US$)	50,616.4	10,930.0	9,880.8	37,824.7	15,297.2	2,359.5	13,249.2	10,827.9	13,448.8	14,057.7
GINI index (World Bank estimate)**	30.9	31.6	46.1	39.6	35.2	43.6	33.9	36.4	38.4	38.2
Agriculture, value added (% of GDP)	2.9	5.6	6.1	2.0	5.6	20.4	12.4	12.6	15.3	10.5
Industry, value added (% of GDP)	20.6	25.3	24.2	24.7	36.6	23.5	27.3	37.2	15.2	25.4
Services, etc., value added (% of GDP)	67.8	55.9	60.0	68.1	52.2	47.8	53.8	48.1	67.7	55.9
CO_2 emissions (kt)	135,611	124,399	35,204	2,085,860	133,064	15,877	717,564	126,976	29,475	946,092
Energy use (kg of oil equivalent per capita)	4,951.6	2,204.6	1,688.4	5,324	4,037.4	715.3	1,835.3	2,396.8	4,964.5	2,559.9
Forest area (% of land area)	24.7	34.9	41.1	35.3	3.9	30.6	22.2	49.5	50.3	32.0
$PM_{2.5}$ air pollution, mean annual exposure (micrograms per cubic meter)***	10.3	18.9	17.9	11.3	50.1	37.3	39.9	21.6	10.8	27.1

Notes:

*Urban population refers to people living in urban areas as defined by national statistical offices.

**Gini index of 0 represents perfect equality, while an index of 100 implies perfect inequality.

***PM2.5—Particulate matter.

To avoid missing values, the aggregates contain the latest available data between 2010 and 2017 for each country.

Source: World Bank Data.

Introduction to comparative politics

Daniele Caramani

Chapter contents

Reader's guide

Comparative politics is one of the main disciplines in political science, alongside political theory and international relations. It deals with internal political structures (institutions like parliaments and executives), individual and collective actors (voters, parties, social movements, interest groups), and processes (policy-making, communication and socialization processes, and political cultures). Its main goal is empirical: describe, explain, and predict similarities and differences across political systems, be they countries, regions, or supranational systems (such as empires or the European Union). This can be done through the intensive analysis of a few cases (even one case) or large-scale extensive analyses of many cases, and can be either synchronic (based on data collected at only one time point and not accounting for change over time) or diachronic (including a temporal dimension). Comparative politics uses both quantitative and qualitative data. Increasingly, the analysis of domestic politics is challenged by interdependence between countries through globalization.

Introduction

This book is about politics. It is a book about the most important dimensions of political life, not about one specific aspect (such as elections or policies). Furthermore, it is a *comparative* book, meaning that we look at a variety of countries from all over the world. It is not a book about politics in one place only. Also, it is not only about politics today, but rather about how politics changed over time, beginning with the transition to mass democracy in the nineteenth century. In sum, it is a book about the long-term comparative study of politics.

But what, precisely, is politics? Politics is the human activity of *making public authoritative decisions*. They are public because, in principle, they may concern every aspect of a society's life. Political decisions can apply to everyone who is part of a given **citizenship** and/or living in a specific territory (a state) and to every area (religion, environment, economy, and so forth). They are authoritative because the government that makes such decisions is invested with the (more or less legitimate) power to make them binding, meaning that they are supported by the possibility to sanction individuals who do not comply with them. 'Authorities' have the authority—as it were—to force individuals to comply through coercive means.

Politics is thus the *exercise* of the power of making such decisions. However, politics is also the activity of *acquiring* (and maintaining) this power. It is therefore both the *conflict or competition* for power, and its use. Who makes political decisions? How did they acquire the power to make them? Where does the authority to make such decisions come from? What decisions have been taken, why, and how do they affect the life of societies? These are the questions that comparative politics seeks to answer.

It goes without saying that these are important questions. *Which decisions are made* concerns our everyday lives. The decision to increase taxation is a political decision. So are the decisions to cut welfare benefits, introduce military conscription, or carry out military intervention in a foreign country, and invest in renewable energy. But also, *how decisions are made* is important. The way in which public and authoritative decisions are made varies a great deal. In democracies we, as citizens, are directly involved through elections or **referendums**. If we are unhappy with them, we can protest through demonstrations, petitions, or letters, or vote differently at the next election. In other types of government, individuals are excluded (as in authoritarian regimes). And, finally, *who makes or influences decisions* also counts. Many decisions on the maintenance of generous pension systems today are supported by elderly cohorts in disagreement with younger ones who pay for them.

Or, as another example, take the decision to introduce high taxation for polluting industries. Such a decision is heavily influenced by lobbies and pressure groups and by environmental activists. Configurations of power relationships can be very different, but all point to the basic fact that political decisions are made by individuals or groups who acquired that power against others through either peaceful or violent means.

KEY POINTS

- Politics is the human activity of making public and authoritative decisions. It is the activity of acquiring the power of making such decisions and of exercising this power. It is the conflict or competition for power and its use.

- Who decides what, and how, is important for the life of societies.

The definition of comparative politics

A science of politics

Even though the questions addressed in the Introduction above are very broad, they do not cover the whole spectrum of political science. Comparative politics is one of the three main subfields in political science, together with political theory and international relations.[1]

Whereas political theory deals with normative and theoretical questions (about equality, democracy, justice, etc.), comparative politics deals with empirical questions. The concern of comparative politics is not primarily whether participation is good or bad, but rather the investigation of which forms of participation people choose to use, why young people use more unconventional forms than older age groups, and whether there are differences in how much groups participate. Even though comparative political scientists are also concerned with normative questions, the discipline as such is empirical and *value neutral*.

On the other hand, whereas international relations deals with interactions between political systems (balance of power, war, trade), comparative politics deals with *interactions within political systems*. Comparative politics does not analyse wars between nations, but rather investigates which party is in government and why it has decided in favour of military intervention, what kind of electoral **constituency** has

DEFINITION 1.1

'Comparative politics'

Comparative politics is one of the three main subfields of political science (alongside political theory and international relations) focusing on internal political structures, actors, and processes, and analysing them empirically by describing, explaining, and predicting their variety (similarities and differences) across political systems (and over time)—be they national political systems, regional, municipal, or even supranational systems.

supported this party, how strong the influence of the arms industry has been, and so on. As a subject matter, it is concerned with power relationships between individuals, groups and organizations, classes, and institutions within political systems. Comparative politics does not ignore external influences on internal structures, but its ultimate concern is power configurations within systems.

As subsequent chapters clarify, the distinction between disciplines is not so neat. Many argue that, because of globalization and increasing interdependence between countries, comparative politics and international relations converge towards one single discipline. Indeed, the brightest scholars bridge the two fields. What is important for the moment is to understand that comparative politics is a discipline that deals with the very essence of politics where **sovereignty** resides—i.e. in the *state*: questions of power between groups, the institutional organization of political systems, and authoritative decisions that affect the whole of a community. For this reason, over centuries of political thought the state has been at the very heart of political science. Scholars like Aristotle, Machiavelli, and Montesquieu—and many others— were interested in the question, 'How does politics work?'

Being a vast and variegated discipline, comparative politics constitutes a core discipline of political science and, as Peter Hall has asserted, '[n]o respectable department of political science would be without scholars of comparative politics' (Hall 2004: 1).

Types of comparative politics

The term 'comparative politics' originates from the way in which the empirical investigation of the question 'How does politics work?' is carried out. Comparative politics includes three traditions (van Biezen and Caramani 2006).

1. The first tradition is the *study of single countries*. This reflects the understanding of comparative politics in its formative years in the US, where it mainly meant the study of political systems outside the US, often in isolation from one another and involving little comparison. Today, many courses on comparative politics still include 'German politics', 'Spanish politics', and so on, and many textbooks are structured in 'country chapters'. As discussed in Chapter 3 'Comparative research methods', case studies have a useful purpose, but only when they are put in comparative perspective and generate hypotheses to be tested in analytical case studies, such as

> **IMPORTANT WORKS IN COMPARATIVE POLITICS 1.2**
>
> ### Aristotle
>
> Aristotle (350 BC), *Ta Politika (Politics)*
>
> The typologies of political systems presented in this work are based on a data compilation of the constitutions and practices in 158 Greek city-states by Aristotle's students. Tragically, this collection is now lost (with the exception of *The Constitution of Athens*). This work represents the oldest attempt on record of a comparative empirical data collection and analysis of political institutions. Aristotle distinguished three true forms of government: those ruled by one person (kingship); by few persons (aristocracy); and by all citizens (constitutional government), of which the corrupt forms are tyranny, oligarchy, and democracy.

implicit comparisons, the analysis of deviant cases, and proving grounds for new techniques (e.g. synthetic control).

2. The second tradition is *methodological* and is concerned with establishing rules and standards of comparative analysis. This tradition addresses the question of how comparative analyses should be carried out in order to enhance their potential for the descriptive cumulation of comparable information, causal explanations and associations between key variables, and prediction. This strand is concerned with rigorous conceptual, logical, and statistical techniques of analysis, also involving issues of measurement and case selection.

3. The third tradition of comparative politics is *analytical* in that it combines empirical substance and method. The body of literature in this tradition is primarily concerned with the identification and explanation of differences and similarities between countries and their institutions, actors, and processes through systematic comparison. It aims to go beyond merely ideographic descriptions and aspires to identify *law-like explanations*. Through comparison, researchers test (i.e. verify and falsify) whether or not associations and causal relationships between variables hold true empirically across a number of cases. It can be based on 'large-N' or 'small-N' research designs (N indicates the number of cases considered) with either similar or different cases. It can use either qualitative or quantitative data, or 'logical' or statistical techniques, for testing the empirical

validity of hypotheses. But ultimately, this tradition aims at explanation.

This book takes the latter approach.

Like all scientific disciplines, comparative politics is a combination of *substance* (the study of political institutions, actors, and processes) and *method* (identifying and explaining differences and similarities following established rules and standards of analysis). Like all sciences, comparative politics aims to say something general about the world, i.e. formulate generalizations beyond one or a few cases.

What does comparative politics do in practice?

1. To compare means that similarities and differences are *described*. Comparative politics describes the world and, building on these descriptions, establishes *classifications* and *typologies*. For example, we classify different types of electoral systems.

2. Similarities and differences are *explained*. Why did social revolutions take place in France and Russia but not in Germany and Japan? Why is there no socialist party in the US? Why is electoral **turnout** in the US and Switzerland so much lower than in most other democracies? As in all scientific disciplines, we formulate *hypotheses* to explain these differences and use empirical data to test them—to check whether or not the hypotheses hold true in reality. It is through this method that causality can be inferred, generalizations produced, and theories improved.

3. Comparative politics aims to formulate *predictions*. If we know that proportional representation (PR) **electoral systems** favour the proliferation of parties in the legislature, could we have predicted that the change of electoral law in New Zealand in 1996 from first past the post to PR would lead to a more fragmented **party system**?

Why is 'comparative politics' called 'comparative politics'?

Comparative politics as a label stresses the analytical, scientific, and 'quasi-experimental' character of the discipline. It was in the 1950s and '60s that the awareness of the need to carry out systematic comparisons for more robust theories increased. The 'comparative' label before 'politics' was added to make a methodological point in a discipline that was not yet fully aware of the importance of explicit comparison. However, single-case studies can be comparative in an implicit

---

> 📖 **IMPORTANT WORKS IN COMPARATIVE POLITICS 1.3**
>
> ### Machiavelli
>
> Niccolò Machiavelli (written 1513, published posthumously 1532), *Il Principe* (*The Prince*, Florence: Bernardo di Giunta)
>
> This book was novel in its time because it told how principalities and republics are governed most successfully from a realist, or empirical, perspective and not how they should be governed in an ideal world. Machiavelli makes his argument through examples taken from real-world observations compared with one another. In *The Prince*, he compares mainly different types of principalities (hereditary, new, mixed, and ecclesiastic), whereas in *The Discourses on Livy* (*Discorsi Sopra la Prima Deca di Tito Livio*) his comparison between princely and republican government is more systematic.

way, like Tocqueville's *Democracy in America* (1835). As John Stuart Mill noted in his review of the book in 1840, Tocqueville contrasts US specificities with France in a quasi-experimental way. Similarly, books on single countries in the 1960s and early 1970s—on Belgium, Italy, Norway, Spain, Switzerland—not only showed that 'politics works differently over here', but also included systematic, if hidden, comparison with the better-known cases of the US and Britain.

In practice, the label 'comparative' was needed as a battle horse. In an established discipline, this label could and should be dropped. Today, it goes without saying that the analysis of political phenomena is comparative, i.e. entails more than one case. Therefore, we should conclude that—since comparative politics covers all aspects of domestic politics—the discipline of comparative politics becomes 'synonymous with the scientific study of politics' (Schmitter 1993: 171). All the dimensions of the political system can be compared, so all is potentially comparative politics. As Mair noted, '[i]n terms of its substantive concerns the fields of comparative politics seem hardly separable from those of political

---

> **KEY POINTS**
>
> • Comparative politics is an empirical science that studies chiefly domestic politics.
>
> • The goals of comparative politics are: to describe differences and similarities between political systems and their features; to explain these differences; and to predict which factors may cause specific outcomes.

science *tout court,* in that any focus of inquiry can be approached either comparatively (using cross-national data) or not (using data from just one country)' (Mair 1996: 311). The generality of the scope of coverage of comparative politics leads us now to talk about its substance in more depth.

The substance of comparative politics

What is compared?

The classical cases of comparative politics are *national political systems.* These are (still) the most important political units in the contemporary world. However, national systems are not the only cases that comparative politics analyses.

1. First, non-national political systems can be compared: *sub-national regional political systems* (state level in the US or the German *Länder*) or *supranational units* such as (i) regions (Western Europe, Central-Eastern Europe, North America, Latin America, and so on); (ii) empires (Ottoman, Habsburg, Russian, Chinese, Roman, etc.); and (iii) supranational organizations (European Union, the North American Free Trade Agreement (NAFTA), etc.).

2. *Types of political systems* can be compared (e.g. a comparison between democratic and authoritarian regimes in terms of, say, economic performance).

3. Comparative politics compares *single elements* of the political system rather than the whole system. Researchers compare the structure of parliaments of different countries or cabinets, the policies (e.g. welfare state or environmental policies), the finances of parties or trade unions, and the presence or absence of direct democracy institutions and electoral laws.

The various chapters of this book compare the most important features of national political systems. As can be seen in the contents at the beginning of the volume, the variety of topics is large, and comparative politics covers—in principle—all aspects of the political system. It has been argued that precisely because comparative politics encompasses 'everything' from a substantial point of view, it has no substantial specificity, but rather only a methodological one resting on comparison (Verba 1985; Keman 1993a). Yet there is a substantial specificity which resides in the empirical analysis of internal structures, actors, and processes.

It is also true that comparative politics has been through phases in which it focused on particular aspects. This evolution is described in the next two subsections.

From institutions to functions . . .

Comparative politics before the Second World War was mainly concerned with the analysis of the state and its institutions. Institutions were defined in a narrow sense, overlapping with state powers (legislative, executive, judiciary), civil administration, and military bureaucracy. Old institutionalism was formal, using as main 'data' constitutional texts and legal documents. This tradition can be traced back to constitutional authors such as Bodin, Montesquieu, and Constant. The emphasis on the study of formal political institutions focused, naturally, on the geographical areas where they first developed, namely Western Europe and North America.

While the study of state institutions remains important, the reaction against what was perceived as the legalistic study of politics led to one of the major turns in the discipline between the 1930s and the 1960s—a period considered by some to be the 'Golden Age' of comparative politics (Dalton 1991). The **behavioural revolution**—imported from anthropology, biology, and sociology—shifted the substance of comparative politics away from institutions. This tradition can be traced back to the macro-sociology of Spencer, Comte, Marx, Toqueville, and Weber, and led to theories of macro-historical sociology, cultural theories as well as neo-institutionalism, with a much broader conception of norms and their social

---

IMPORTANT WORKS IN COMPARATIVE POLITICS 1.4

Montesquieu

Charles de Secondat, Baron de Montesquieu (1748) *De l'Esprit des Loix (On the Spirit of the Laws,* Geneva: Barrillot et fils)

In this influential book, in which the idea of the separation of powers is presented systematically for the first time, Montesquieu distinguishes between republics, monarchies, and despotic regimes. He describes comparatively the working of each type of regime through historical examples. Furthermore, Montesquieu was really a pioneer of 'political sociology' as, first, he analysed the influence of factors such as geography, location, and climate on a nation's culture and, indirectly, its social and political institutions; and, second, did so by applying an innovative naturalistic method.

meaning, and a stronger emphasis on history. Pioneers of comparative politics such as Gabriel A. Almond, founder of the Committee on Comparative Politics in 1954 (an organization of the American Social Science Research Council), started analysing other aspects of politics than formal institutions, and observing politics in practice rather than as defined in official texts.

What triggered this revolution? Primarily, more attention was devoted to 'new' cases, i.e. a rejection of the focus on the West and the developed world. Early comparativists like James Bryce, Charles Merriam, A. Lawrence Lowell, and Woodrow Wilson—as Philippe Schmitter calls them, 'Dead, White, European Men, but not Boring' (Schmitter 1993: 173)—assumed that the world would converge towards Western models of 'political order' (Fukuyama 2011, 2014). With this state of mind, it made sense to focus on major Western countries. However, the rise of communist regimes in Eastern Europe (and, later, in China and Central America) and the breakdown of democracy where fascist dictatorships came to power—and in some cases lasted until the 1970s, as in Portugal, Spain, and Latin America, and to some extent also in Greece (Stepan 1971; Linz 1978; O'Donnell and Schmitter 1986)—made it clear that other types of political order could exist and needed to be understood. After the Second World War, patterns of decolonization spurred analyses beyond Anglo-Saxon-style liberal democratic institutions. New **patrimonialist** regimes emerged in Africa and the Middle East, and populist ones in South America (Huntington 1968; O'Donnell 1973).

These divergent patterns could not be understood within the narrow categories of Western institutions. New categories and concepts were required, as was greater attention to other actors, such as revolutionary parties and clans under patrimonialistic leadership. The mobilization of the masses that took place in communist and fascist regimes in Europe, as well as under populism in South America, turned attention away from institutions and directed it towards ideologies, belief systems, and communication. This motivated comparativists to ask which were the favourable conditions for democratic stability, and thus to look into political cultures, **social capital**, and traditions of authority.[2]

Finally, the closer analysis of Europe also contributed to a shift away from the formal analysis of institutions. From the 1960s on, European comparative political scientists started to question the supposed 'supremacy'—in terms of stability and efficiency—of Anglo-Saxon democracies based on majoritarian institutions and homogeneous cultures. Other types of democracies were not necessarily the unstable democracies of France, Germany, or Italy. The analyses of

Norway by Stein Rokkan (1966), Austria by Gerhard Lehmbruch (1967), Switzerland by Jürg Steiner (1974), Belgium by Val Lorwin (1966a, b), and the Netherlands by Hans Daalder (1966) and Arend Lijphart (1968a)—most published in Robert Dahl's influential volume *Political Oppositions in Western Democracies* (1966)—as well as Canada, South Africa, Lebanon, and India, all showed that politics worked differently to the Anglo-Saxon model.

Although ethnically, linguistically, and religiously divided, these societies were not only stable and peaceful, but also wealthy and 'socially just' (most remarkably in the case of the Scandinavian welfare states). On the one hand, these new cases showed that *other types of democracies were viable*. Besides the 'Westminster' type of **majoritarian democracy**, these authors stressed the 'consociational' type with patterns of compromise between elites (rather than competition), 'amicable agreement', and 'accommodation'—in short, *alternative practices of politics beyond formal institutions*. On the other hand, these new cases stimulated the investigation of the role of **cleavages** (overlapping vs cross-cutting), as in the case of welfare economies, as well as the role of elite collaboration in the political economy of small countries, which later led to important publications (see e.g. Katzenstein 1985; Esping-Andersen 1990).

What have been the consequences of the broadening of the geographical and historical scope?

First, it increased the *variety of political systems*. Second, it pointed to the *role of agencies* other than institutions, in particular parties and interest groups,

---

📖 **IMPORTANT WORKS IN COMPARATIVE POLITICS 1.5**

Tocqueville

Alexis Charles Henri Clérel de Tocqueville (1835) *De la Démocratie en Amérique* (*On Democracy in America*, Paris: C. Gosselin)

Although this book represents a 'case study'—an analysis of democracy in the US—it is an example of comparison with an 'absent' case, i.e. France and, more generally, Europe. In his implicit comparison, Tocqueville analyses the uniqueness of conditions in American society and geography that were favourable to the development of modern democracy. Tocqueville follows Montesquieu in going beyond public institutions to include social and cultural aspects. He speaks of aristocratic and democratic societies when comparing France with the US. Tocqueville was also strongly influenced by Montesquieu's use of naturalistic methods.

civil society organizations, social movements, and media (Almond 1978: 14). Third, it introduced a *new methodology* based on empirical observation, large-scale comparisons, statistical techniques, and an extraordinary effort of quantitative data collection (see the following section).[3] Fourth, a new 'language', namely **systemic functionalism**, was imported in comparative politics. The challenge presented by the extension of the scope of comparison was to elaborate a conceptual body able to encompass the diversity of cases. Concepts, indicators, and measurements that had been developed for a set of Western cases did not fit the new cases. It also soon became clear that 'Western concepts' had a different meaning in other parts of the world. What Sartori has called the 'travelling problem' (Sartori 1970: 1033) is closely related to the expansion of politics and appears when concepts and categories are applied to cases different from those around which they had originally been developed (see Table I.1).

The emphasis on institutions and the state was dropped because of the need for *more general and universal concepts*. Since the behavioural revolution, we speak of political systems rather than states (Easton 1953, 1965a, b). Concepts were redefined to cover non-Western settings, pre-modern societies, and non-state polities. Most of these categories were taken from the very abstract depiction of the social system by Talcott Parsons (1968). These more general categories could not be institutions that did not exist elsewhere, but their functional equivalents.

Functions dealing with the survival of systems were perceived as particularly important. From biology and cybernetics, David Easton and Karl Deutsch (Deutsch 1966a, b) imported the idea of the *system*—ecological systems, body systems, and so on—and identified 'survival' as its most important function. Similarly, in the 1950s—still in the shadow of the dark memory of the breakdown of democratic systems between the two world wars through fascism and communism—the most important topic was to understand why some democracies survived while others collapsed. Almond and Verba's *The Civic Culture* (1963) is considered as a milestone precisely because it identified specific cultural conditions favourable or unfavourable to democratic stability.

...and back to institutions

It soon also became clear, however, that the price to be paid for encompassing transcultural concepts was that of an excessive level of abstraction. This framework was not informative enough and too remote with regard to the concrete historical context of specific systems. In the 1970s, European comparative political scientists like Rokkan, Lehmbruch, and others (and even more so area specialists from Eastern Europe, Latin America, Africa, and Asia) had already noted that the ahistorical categories of systemic functionalism did not allow the understanding of concrete cases.

The counter-reaction to systemic functionalism starts precisely in 1967 and involves (i) a shift of

Dimensions of analysis	Before	After
Unit	State	Political system
Subject matter	Regimes and their formal institutions	Social and cultural structures, all actors in the process of decision-making
Cases	Major democracies: US, Britain, France; analysis of democratic breakdown in Germany and Italy; authoritarianism in Spain and Latin America	Objective extension of cases (decolonization) and subjective extension with spread of discipline in various countries
Indicators/ variables	West-centric, qualitative categories, typologies	Abstract concepts; empirical universals, quantitatively operationalized variables
Method	Narrative accounts and juxtapositions between cases	Machine-readable data sets and statistics; quasi-experimental comparative method
Data	Constitutional and legal texts, history	Survey (value and attitudes), aggregate (society and economy), and text (actors) data
Theory	Normative: institutional elitism and pluralism; no elaborate conceptualization	Empirical: structural functionalism, systems theory, neo-institutionalism, rational choice, cultural theories

Table I.1 Comparative politics before and after the 'behavioural revolution'

substantial focus; (ii) a narrowing of *geographical* scope; (iii) a change of *methodology*; and (iv) a *theoretical turn*.

Bringing the state back in

The shift of substantial focus consists of a return to the state and its institutions (Skocpol 1985). In recent decades, there has been a re-establishment of the centrality of institutions more broadly defined as sets of rules, procedures, and social norms. In the new-institutionalism theory (March and Olsen 1989; Hall and Taylor 1996; Thelen 1999; Ostrom 2007; Pierson and Skocpol 2002; Przeworski 2004a) institutions are seen as the most important actors, with autonomy and being part of real politics. Institutions, furthermore, are seen as determining the opportunity structures and the limits within which individuals formulate preferences.[4]

Mid-range theories

The excessive abstraction of concepts in systemic functionalism was also countered by a return of attention to varying historical structures, cultural elements, and geographic location, in which the specific context plays a central role (Thelen and Steinmo 1992). Rather than general universalistic theories, mid-range theories stress the advantages of case studies or in-depth analyses of a few countries.

Some authors argue that the reawakening of attention to the state and its institutions is in fact a consequence of this narrowing of geographical scope (Mair 1996). The general language introduced by systemic functionalism—and which nearly discarded the state and its institutions—was needed to encompass a greater variety of political systems. Institutions have recently been re-appreciated because of a closer focus. Systemic functionalism did not forget institutions; they were simply 'absorbed upward into the more abstract notions of role, structure and function' (Mair 1996: 317). A regionally more restricted perspective giving up global comparisons does not require the same level of abstraction of concepts. Therefore, the shift of substantial focus is a consequence of less ambitious theoretical constructions. The change of substantial focus has been favoured by the narrowing of the geographical focus.

Case-oriented analysis

This narrowing of scope also entailed a methodological change. The counter-reaction to large-scale comparisons came from the development of methods based on few cases ('small-N') (see Ragin 1987). They revitalize today a type of comparative investigation that had long been criticized because few cases did not allow the testing of the impact of large numbers of factors—the problem that Lijphart (1971, 1975) named 'few cases, many variables'. This difficulty made the analysis of rare social phenomena, such as revolutions, impossible with statistical techniques. Hence, the great importance of this 'new' **comparative method**. It provides the tool for analysing rigorously phenomena of which only few instances occur historically (see next section 'The method of comparative politics' and Chapter 3 for more details).

Rational choice theory

At the end of the 1980s, another change took place in comparative politics, strengthening further the place of institutions. It was the change given by the increasing influence of rational choice theory in comparative politics, which can be traced back to political economy tradition of Smith, Bentham, Ricardo, and Mill.

Whereas the behavioural revolution primarily imported models from sociology, the change at the end of the 1980s was inspired by developments in economics. In addition, the rational choice change does not revolve around a redefinition of the political, for it applies a more general theory of action that applies equally well to all types of human behaviour, be it in the economic market, the political system, the media sphere, or elsewhere (Tsebelis 1990; Munck 2001).

This theory of action is based on the idea that actors (individuals, but also organizations such as political parties) are rational. They are able to order alternative options from most to least preferred and then, through their choice, seek the maximization of their preferences (utility). For example, voters are considered able to identify what their interest is and to distinguish the different alternatives that political parties offer in their programmes with regard to specific policies. Voters then maximize their utility by voting for the political party whose policy promises are closest to their interests. It is rational for political parties to offer programmes that appeal to a large segment of the electorate, as this leads to the maximization of votes.

It is clear from these premises that the place for 'sociological' factors on which the behavioural revolution insisted—such as socio-economic status and cultural traits—assume a lower key in rational choice models. These models have been crucial to understanding the behaviour of a number of actors.

In the field of party politics, examples include work by Downs (1957), Przeworski (Przeworksi and Sprague 1986), and Cox (1997). Other examples include the work of Popkin (1979) on peasants in Vietnam, Bates (1981) on markets in Africa, Przeworski (1991) on democratization, Gambetta (1993, 2005) on the Mafia and suicide missions, Fearon and Laitin (1996) on ethnicity, and Acemoglou and Robinson (2006) on the origins of political regimes.

Rational choice theory in political science owes a lot to the work of William Riker. He is the founder of the 'Rochester School' (Riker 1990; see also Amadae and Bueno de Mesquita 1999). Today, rational choice theory comes in various forms and degrees of formalization, ranging from 'hard' game-theoretical versions, in which the degree of mathematical formalization is very high, to 'softer' versions in which the basic assumptions are maintained but in which there is no formal theorizing. What is important to note is that the rational choice turn did not lead to a redefinition of comparative politics as a subject matter precisely because it does not offer a meta-theory that is specific to politics. The subject matter did not change under the impulse of rational choice theory. On the contrary, *it has reinforced the pre-eminence of institutions in comparative politics.* Rational choice institutionalism, in particular, sees institutions as constraints of actors' behaviour (Weingast 2002). An example of this approach is the concept of 'veto player' developed by Tsebelis (2002).

At the end of the 1980s, another turn took place in comparative politics, strengthening further the place of institutions. It was the turn given by the increasing influence of rational choice theory in comparative politics.

What is left?

As we have seen, there has been an almost cyclical process.[5] However, comparative politics did not simply return to its starting point.

First, despite the recent narrowing of scope and the tendency to concentrate on 'mid-range theories', the expansion that took place in the 1950s and 1960s left behind an extraordinary variety of topics. A glance at the Contents shows how many *features of the political system* are dealt with in comparative politics.

Second, the great contribution made by the systemic **paradigm** has not been lost. We continue to speak of a political system and use this descriptive tool to organize the various dimensions of domestic politics. In fact, the structure and coverage of the book mirrors the political system as described by David Easton (see Figure I.1 and Box I.6). Easton's work is a monumental theoretical construction of the structural-

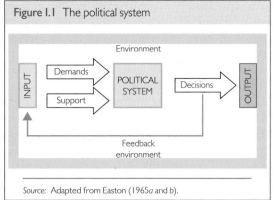

Figure I.1 The political system

Source: Adapted from Easton (1965*a* and *b*).

📖 IMPORTANT WORKS IN COMPARATIVE POLITICS I.6

Easton

David Easton (1953) *The Political System: An Inquiry into the State of Political Science* (New York: Alfred A. Knopf)

This volume is the first of a series of books by Easton on the political system. His work represents the most systematic and encompassing effort on the 'theoretical side' of the behavioural revolution. Scholars like David Easton and Karl W. Deutsch imported the notion of system from other scientific disciplines (biology and cybernetics). This notion soon replaced the formal concept of state and enlarged the field of comparative politics to non-institutional actors. The framework developed by Easton and his colleagues, and its conceptual components (input, output, feedback loop, black box, etc.), are common language today. Easton's work remains the last major attempt to develop a general empirical theory of politics.

---

systemic paradigm, still unrivalled and probably the last and most important attempt to build a general empirical theory including all actors and processes of political systems.

Third, Easton's concepts have marked the minds of political scientists, as well as those of the wider public. His attempt has been an extremely systematic one, with subsequent and cumulative contributors drafted towards one single goal. His concept of *political system*—as a set of structures (institutions and agencies) whose decision-making function is to reach the collective and authoritative allocation of values (*output*, i.e. **public policies**) receiving support as well as demands (*inputs*) from the domestic as well as the international environment which it shapes through outputs in the *feedback loop*—includes all aspects of what is described in this book, from communication to culture, socialization and behaviour, interest articulation through parties, movements or pressure groups, institutions in democratic and authoritarian regimes, decision-making and policies, as well as the interaction with other systems—addressed in Section 6 of this book, 'Beyond the nation-state'.

Fourth, the substantive scope has not ceased to grow, and this trend has continued over the most recent decades. As discussed in Chapter 1 'The relevance of comparative politics', there has been a change in focus from 'input' processes to 'output' processes, namely public policies and policy-making, as well as the outcome and impact of policies. This is the reason why a specific section of this book is devoted to these topics. In particular, recent trends of 'what' is compared include industrial relations, trade, and economic policies (aspects stressed in Chapters 22 'The impact of public policies' and 24 'Globalization and the nation-state'); the reawakening of ethnic, religious, and nationalist movements, trends towards regionalization (aspects stressed in Chapters 11 'Multilevel governance', 15 'Regions', and 17 'Political culture'); and the growing role of pressure groups (see Chapter 14 'Interest groups').

Fifth, new trends also include awareness of the interdependence between national systems (discussed below in the Conclusion more extensively). Chapter 23 'The EU as a new political system' analyses the integration between member-states of the European Union, Chapter 24 'Globalization and the nation-state' addresses the blurring of national boundaries, and Chapter 25 'From supporting democracy to supporting autocracy' shows how states influence others through democratic promotion and peacekeeping.

Finally, in spite of the resurgence of institutions in a narrower sense, other theories maintain their influence and, through more attention to psychological, indeed 'behavioural', factors boosted by experimental methods at the individual level, challenge the assumption of rationality of actors. New institutionalism includes normative, historical, and rational choice varieties. Macro-historical sociology has changed into comparative 'political economy' at both macro- (say, classes) and micro- (individual) levels. Cultural theories maintain their relevance in the study of identities, trust, authoritarian versus liberarian attitudes, etc. What is left is therefore a great variety of theories that today co-exist.

KEY POINTS

- Comparative politics is not limited to the comparison of national political systems, but also includes other units such as sub-national and supra-national organization, single political actors, processes, and policies.

- With the widening of the number of 'cases' (new states or other regions), the need for more general concepts that could 'travel' beyond Western countries led to a focus on functions rather than institutions. In the past three decades, however, a reaction against overly abstract analysis has led back to 'mid-range theories' limited in space and time.

- As for the behavioural revolution, rational choice also aims at a general and unified theory of politics applicable in all times and places. This paradigm was imported into political science from economics and stresses the role of institutions in comparative politics.

- Comparative politics includes as a subject matter all features of political systems and, recently, has turned its attention towards the interaction between them, approaching international relations.

The method of comparative politics

Having discussed the 'what' of comparison, we turn now to the 'how' of comparison.

A variety of methods

Comparative politics does not rely on one specific method only, for four main reasons.

1. Depending on the number of cases included in the analysis (say, 150 or two countries only), the type of data the analysis deals with (quantitative electoral results or qualitative typologies of administrative systems), and the time period covered (the most recent census or longitudinal trends since the mid-nineteenth century), the methods employed are different. *The research method depends on the research question.* We formulate the research question; then we look for the most appropriate data and methods to address it. The choice of cases very often depends on the research question. As explained in Chapter 3 'Comparative research methods', comparative politics may analyse *one single case* (a case study). Research designs can be more or less *intensive or extensive* (depending on the balance between the number of cases and the number of features analysed); they can be *synchronic or diachronic*.

2. The dimensions of comparison can be diverse. It is wrong to suppose that comparative politics is always cross-sectional, i.e. that it involves a spatial comparison between countries or regions. In fact, *spatial (cross-sectional)* comparison is only one of the possible dimensions of comparison. A second dimension of comparison is the *functional (cross-organizational or cross-process) comparison*. Take, as an example, the comparison of the liberal and the nationalist ideologies in Europe. Or the comparison of policy-making of environmental and military policies in, say, the US. Or the comparison of leadership in social movements such as the civic rights movement, the feminist movement, the green movement, and the pacifist movement. The dimension of comparison here is not territorial. A third dimension is the *longitudinal (cross-temporal) comparison*. We can compare institutions, actors, and processes over time as, for example, in the comparison of party organizations in the nineteenth century (**cadre parties**), after the First World War (mass parties), after the Second World War (catch-all parties), and since the 1980s (cartel parties).

3. *Units of analysis* can be diverse. As we have seen, 'what' is compared can be either whole political systems or single actors, institutions, processes, or trends.

4. Comparative research designs can focus on either *similarities* or *differences*. Sometimes we ask questions about similar outcomes, such as, 'Why did social revolutions take place in France, Russia and China?' (Skocpol 1979). To explain similar outcomes, we look for common factors (something that is present in all the cases in which the outcome occurred) in cases which are otherwise very different from each other. As we will see in Chapter 3 'Comparative research methods', John Stuart Mill called this **research design** the **Method of Agreement** (Przeworski and Teune 1970 called it the '**Most Different Systems Design**'). However, sometimes we use the **Method of Difference** (or '**Most Similar Systems Design**'), in which we ask questions about different outcomes, such as 'Why did Britain democratize early and Prussia / Germany late?' (Moore 1966) or 'Why did democracy resist attacks from anti-system forces in some countries and not in others?' (Capoccia 2005). To explain different outcomes, we look at factors that vary (something that is either present or absent in the case in which the outcome either occurred or did not) among otherwise similar cases. We also often combine these two methods.

IMPORTANT WORKS IN COMPARATIVE POLITICS 1.7

Lazarsfeld et al.

Paul F. Lazarsfeld, Bernard R. Berelson, and Hazel Gaudet (1944) *The People's Choice: How the Voter Makes Up His Mind in a Presidential Campaign* (New York: Columbia University Press)

This book is a marvellous example of the use of statistical methods, and multivariate analysis of elections, public opinion, socialization processes, and communication through large data sets and the employment of rudimentary computing techniques. It is an application of the positivist approach to politics and has paved the way for countless studies of the determinants of people's political behaviour: the crucial questions of which groups (classes, professions, age cohorts, gender, and so on) tend to turn out more often, and for which parties they tend to vote. A follow-up volume entitled *Voting* (1954) pursued this line of research. This book is an example of the 'empirical side' of the behavioural revolution.

From cases to variables . . .

Comparative politics prior to the behavioural revolution was typically a discipline that compared few cases. Today, we speak of '*small-N*' *research designs*. As explained earlier in 'The substance of comparative politics', it was thought that the world would converge towards the Anglo-Saxon model of democracy and that, consequently, these were the cases that comparative political scientists should concentrate upon. Therefore, the number of cases ('N') was limited to the US, Britain, France, and a few other cases such as Canada, sometimes Australia and New Zealand, and the 'failed' democracies of Germany or Italy.

The behavioural revolution involved the widening of cases. On the one hand, this involved a much larger effort of *data collection*. Large data sets were created with the help of the development of computer technology. On the other hand, this involved the need for comparability of indicators and, as it turned out, the most general 'language' was that of *quantities*. It is very difficult to establish whether culture, trust, ideology, and identity have the same meaning in different continents. However, it is possible to measure the number of televisions, internet connections, or mobile telephones in all countries of the world. Both factors—the increasing number of cases and the quantification of indicators—led to the development of *statistical techniques*. Therefore, research designs based on a 'large-N' typically employ techniques such as multiple regression and factor analysis (or other statistical techniques) based on coefficients which allow researchers to quantify the strength of the association between political phenomena.

This trend turned attention away from cases and shifted it towards variables. *Intensive* research designs gave way to *extensive* ones: many cases and few variables. Large-N research designs are 'variable-oriented', implying that, with many cases, we ultimately know very little about the context of the countries. Not only did concepts become increasingly abstract in the search for the most general and comparable concepts, but the analysis itself referred increasingly to abstract relationships between variables. We would know that higher literacy levels are associated with higher turnout rates, but we would be ignorant about patterns in single countries.

...and back to cases

More recently there has been a return to 'small-N' and case-oriented research designs and, today, the comparative method is in fact equated with the qualitative techniques based on John Stuart Mill's Methods and on the search for sufficient and necessary conditions. Theda Skocpol (1984), David Collier (1991), and, most prominently, Charles Ragin with his groundbreaking *The Comparative Method* (Ragin 1987), showed that rigorous empirical tests could also be carried out when the number of cases is small (for an overview see Caramani 2009; Schneider and Wagemann 2012).

This methodological shift stresses the intrinsic advantages of the study of few cases. Case-oriented scholars stress that small-N comparisons allow

in-depth analyses in which configurations or combinations of factors are privileged in explanations. Cases are seen as 'wholes' rather than being divided into isolated variables. Constellations of factors represent the explanation rather than the impact of each factor individually.

This is a reaction against the behavioural revolution and its focus on variable-oriented design (e.g. Przeworski and Teune 1970), in which the focus was on parsimonious explanatory designs, i.e. a few key variables whose impact should be tested on as many cases as possible. In two famous articles, Arend Lijphart (1971, 1975) suggested increasing the number of cases (e.g. by selecting several time points) and decreasing the number of variables by focusing on similar cases (thus reducing the number of factors that vary across them).

Such a move implied 'replacing proper names with variables' (Przeworski and Teune 1970), defining concepts able to 'travel' (Sartori 1970), and using 'sets of universals' applicable to all political systems (Almond and Powell 1966; Lasswell 1968). This had led to 'a strong argument against . . . "configurative" or "contextual" analysis' (Lijphart 1971: 690), unable to give rise to generalizing statements. Thirty years later, a large part of the recent debates around methods in the social sciences has focused on the opposite reaction, namely a swing away from the variable-oriented approach towards 'thick' research designs, case studies, and process tracing.

Critiques of case-oriented approaches denounce a return to the past. As John Goldthorpe notes, this represents a revival of holism against which Przeworski and

Teune (1970) had directed their work. In addition, even if one concentrates on 'whole' cases, one still refers to selected features or attributes. Comparison can take place only when one compares cases' values of shared properties or attributes, i.e. variables (Goldthorpe 2000; see also Bartolini 1993). The accusation is that we are going back to holism. And, again, we see a cyclical pattern in the *method* of comparative politics, just as we did for its *subject matter*.

From aggregate to individual data . . .

For a long time, the only available data were those collected as official statistics. The term 'statistics' itself goes back to the seventeenth century and the German School of Statistics. Etymologically, the term means 'science of the state' and its purpose is, as it were, to analyse *state* matters. Statistics started developing during the formation of the modern mercantilist **nation-states** and flourished in the course of the nineteenth century, when the great economic transformations (industrialization) and population movements (urbanization) strengthened the need for states to monitor increasingly complex societies.

The same period saw the development of the liberal nation-state, which, as discussed in Chapters 4 'The nation-state' and 8 'Governments and bureaucracies', increased its intervention in the society and economy, which was accentuated with the **welfare state**. To act, states needed knowledge of the society and economy they were supposed to steer. Democratization also gave a big push towards the development of statistics as governments became accountable; they had to perform, which involved a systematic collection of information. To meet this need, i.e. to increase their 'cybernetic capacity' (Flora 1977: 114), techniques for gathering information greatly improved.

Primarily, statistics were collected for practical reasons linked to the economic and military action of governments. The contents of national statistics relate directly to the activity of the state: security and finance (military and criminal statistics, and statistics relating to income and expense items, taxation, and natural resources). With the growth of welfare states, the transformation of the population and health issues are monitored very closely: birth rates, mortality, health, and mental illness. As far as political statistics are concerned, they were usually included under juridical statistics. However, the presence of political statistics is less common than that of other categories, in particular electoral statistics which are linked to democratization and attempts to legitimize regimes (see Caramani 2000: 1005–15).

The landmarks of this development have been the organization of censuses and the establishment of the annual publication of statistical yearbooks. These often include statistics of neighbouring countries requiring a certain degree of standardization of information to allow for comparisons.

These data are called *aggregate data* because they are available at some territorial level: provinces, regions, countries. Typical aggregate data are election results. We never know how individuals vote because voting is secret. However, we have aggregates: the number of voters and the number of votes for parties and candidates in a constituency. Similarly, we often have data for unemployment rates, population density, and activity in a given sector (e.g. agriculture) for territorial units.

With the behavioural revolution, the approach to data collection changed radically.

1. There is always a risk that official statistics, especially in non-democratic states, may be subject to *manipulation*. This concerns data on elections and all aspects of civil rights, but also data on economic performance. Therefore, the creation of large data sets by university researchers, independent from politics, is an important aspect of the behavioural revolution.

2. Official statistics do not include many variables of interest to researchers. On the one hand, official statistics do not include information on political actors. An example is data on political parties, their members, and their finances. On the other hand, official statistics do not include information on *individuals' values, opinions, attitudes and beliefs, competence and trust in political institutions, and differences between elites and masses in political preferences*. Through official statistics, we would not know whether an individual has authoritarian attitudes or post-material values, and whether he or she is strongly religious. The behavioural revolution introduced *surveys* as a systematic instrument to collect *individual data*. As Chapter 17 'Political culture' shows, political culture cannot be analysed without this type of data, which can be found throughout the world in surveys such as the World Value Survey, Eurobarometers, European Social Survey, Latinobarometers, etc.

3. The collection of individual data involved much larger data sets, as thousands of individuals are included in a survey. This amount of data could be dealt with only through the *computerization of the social sciences*, which began in the 1950s. Certainly, in the past there had been examples of

extraordinary data analysis without computers. Durkheim's *Le Suicide* (1897) is a breathtaking example of comparative multivariate analysis of a huge amount of data presented in tables and figures without the help of computers. Computerization put this type of analysis within the reach of all researchers, first through mainframe systems (usually in a university) and, in the late 1980s, through personal computers and statistical software designed for them. Today, every undergraduate student has Excel, SPSS, R, Stata, or other packages on his or her laptop.

4. Surveys of experts allow establishing the positioning of actors, such as parties, in a multi-dimensional ideological space (see, e.g., the Chapel Hill Expert Survey). Furthermore, new text analysis techniques allow texts such as party manifestos to be analysed (as in the Comparative Manifestos Project), but also newspapers' articles, speeches, press releases, and so on.

The year 1950 proved to be devastating for analysis with aggregate data. This was the year when William S. Robinson published his famous article about 'ecological fallacy' (Robinson 1950). This article undermined the assumption that correlations observed at the level of aggregated units could be inferred at the individual level. Problems of ecological inference arise in the attempt to infer conclusions reached at the level of territorial units down to the individual level. Put simply, what is true on an aggregated level is not necessarily true at the individual level. The effect of this article was disruptive, the term 'ecological fallacy' became popular, and for a long time, analyses based on ecological data were discredited.

...and back to aggregate data

The reaction to this 'shock' began almost immediately, attempting to find solutions to 'ecological fallacy'. Conferences and meetings led to collective publications (see Merritt and Rokkan 1966; Dogan and Rokkan 1969; Berglund and Thomsen 1990; King 1997; King et al. 2004).

Furthermore, international data archives were set up. The most important ones today are the Inter-University Consortium for Political and Social Research (ICPSR) (at the University of Michigan), the Data Archive (at the University of Essex), the Mannheim Centre for European Social Research (MZES), and the Norwegian Data Archive (at the University of Bergen). Data archives developed in all countries are linked together in a global network (see the Online Resources). Such efforts led to major publications of aggregate data collections with documentation, most notably the three editions of the *World Handbook of Political and Social Indicators* (Russett et al. 1964; Taylor and Hudson 1972; Taylor and Jodice 1983), but also other projects (see the 'Yale Political Data Program'; Deutsch et al. 1966). These publications are updated today through the internet resources of the ICPSR.

International organizations such as the United Nations (UN), the World Trade Organization (WTO), the World Bank, the International Monetary Fund (IMF), the World Health Organization (WHO), the Organization for Security and Co-operation in Europe (OSCE), and so forth also contributed to the creation of large comparative data sets with aggregate data in their sectors of competence. The Online Resources provide all the links to these data sets.

But perhaps the main reason for a 'recovery' of ecological data analysis resides in the intrinsic weaknesses of individual-level data. It is more difficult to build long time series with individual data. Only aggregate data that we can collect from the beginning of the nineteenth century allow us to understand topics that need a long-term perspective. This was particularly true during the 1960s and 1970s, when modernization approaches were used to understand newly decolonized countries. Panels—surveys carried out with the same group of respondents over protracted periods of time—are extremely costly (and, anyway, do not allow going 'back' in time). And the use of existing

---

📖 IMPORTANT WORKS IN COMPARATIVE POLITICS 1.10

Rokkan

Stein Rokkan (1970) *Citizens, Elections, Parties* (Oslo: Universitetsforlaget)

This book is a collection of previously published articles and chapters, complemented by unpublished bits and pieces, and conference papers by Stein Rokkan (who never wrote an authored monograph, but preferred to work his writings over and over again). Nonetheless, Rokkan's work provides the most systematic comparative picture of a huge amount of empirical material on similarities and differences between countries in their patterns of state formation, nation-building, democratization, and the structuring of party systems and electoral alignments. In the tradition of 'comparative historical sociology' (with Reinhart Bendix, Otto Hintze, and Barrington Moore, among others), his work encompasses centuries of political development and has inspired generations of scholars, including Theda Skocpol and Charles Tilly.

IMPORTANT WORKS IN COMPARATIVE
POLITICS 1.11

Esping-Andersen

Gøsta Esping-Andersen (1990) *The Three Worlds of Welfare Capitalism* (Cambridge: Polity Press)

This book best illustrates the shift in comparative politics from input to output and public policies. It presents a typology and an explanation of what can be considered the most encompassing of all public policies after the Second World War—the development of the welfare state as the latest stage in the construction of the modern nation-state and citizenship, where social rights complement political and civic rights (as distinguished by T. H. Marshall). This work is a prominent example among other large research programmes, namely on varieties of capitalism (e.g. Susan Strange's work), comparative political economy (e.g. Peter Hall), and welfare states (e.g. Peter Flora).

surveys for comparative purposes is not straightforward. Intelligence services, especially US ones, carried out a number of surveys in Europe after the Marshall Plan to investigate the public's attitudes, its favour of democratic values, and the potential of a communist menace or fascist return. However, these early studies are fragmented, with different questions asked and different groups or respondents.

Therefore, aggregate data have not disappeared and sometimes provide more solid bases than individual-level data for international long-term comparisons.

KEY POINTS

* Comparative politics employs statistical techniques when research designs include many cases and quantitative indicators (variable-oriented large-N studies), or 'comparative methods' when research designs include few cases and qualitative indicators (case-oriented small-N studies). Case studies can also be carried out in a comparative perspective.

* The dimensions of comparison are multiple: spatial, temporal, and functional.

* Research designs aim either to select similar cases and explain their different outcomes (Most Similar Systems Designs, the 'Method of Difference'), or to select different cases and explain similar outcomes (Most Different Systems Designs, the 'Method of Agreement').

* Comparative politics relies on different types of aggregate and individual data.

Conclusion

The variety of comparative politics

The great variety of approaches, methods, and data of comparative politics matches the great variety of the world's societies, economies, cultures, and political systems. In Appendix 2, we have inserted a number of 'Comparative tables' on various indicators. We have also inserted a number of 'World trends' figures in Appendix 3, which show how societies and political systems have changed. Readers will also find 'Country profiles' in Appendix 1, small files on political systems around the world.

The book rests on the principle that *everything is comparable*. Large-scale comparisons through space and time in this book are based on the idea that there are no limits to comparison. Everything—i.e. any case in the world at any point in time—is, in principle, comparable. Analytical comparison never compares cases as such (say, countries) but rather properties (e.g. turnout levels) and their values for each case—whether turnout levels are high or low according to countries. Obviously, turnout applies only where there are democratic elections, so the level of generality and the spatial and temporal scope of the comparison of turnout is limited.

The nineteenth century witnessed what is probably the greatest change in the political organization of human societies with the rise of modern nation-states and democracies. There was no previous experience of mass democracy based on principles of fundamental equality between individuals, civic liberties, political rights, and open participation to the political process and to social welfare. The scope of this change was matched only by the Industrial Revolution during the same period. This is a unique period in our history and we should be aware of its exceptional character, but also of its shortness. Therefore, it is crucial to cover the development of the nation-state and mass democracy over nearly 200 years.

This Introduction has stressed the great variety of what is a huge field of study covering all aspects of domestic politics, with many areas of specialization and subdisciplines which are reflected in the chapters of *Comparative Politics*. The great variety—and the consequent specialization of the field—is the main reason why it is difficult to single out the most important books (see the various boxes scattered through this Introduction). Each subdiscipline has its 'classic' work: in the field of coalition formation, in that of the study of electoral systems, in that of the formation of modern nations, and so forth.

It is not only the broadness of its *substantial focus* of the topics that gives comparative politics a character of great variety. This variety also appears in the *research design* and in the *theoretical frameworks* we apply (see the five 'I's distinguished in Chapter 2 'Approaches in comparative politics'). Today, this variety becomes even larger as comparative politics increasingly 'invades' the discipline of international relations (and vice versa).

From divergence to convergence ...

There would be no comparative politics without this diversity of political systems and their features. The literature up to the 1950s assumed that there would be a *convergence* towards the model of the major Western liberal democracies. On the contrary, there has been *divergence* (in the form of alternative models of political order), and this has led to the actual development of comparative politics.

Is it still like that? Recently, trends towards convergence have been strong. The end of the Cold War in 1989 and the disappearance of the leading superpower that embodied one of the major alternative political models, the 'Third Wave' of democratization (the Arab Spring being its latest manifestation), the pressures towards market economy coming from world trade and globalization, the numerous initiatives to 'export' and 'promote' democracy in Africa and Asia, democratic consolidation in Latin America—these are all patterns of worldwide convergence.

What is the future of comparative politics in a globalized world? Comparative politics—like all 'quasi-experimental' methods—bases its explanations on the covariation between phenomena that leads to a focus on *differences* between cases. Yet, how does such a discipline deal with the existence of *commonalities,* patterns of *homogenization,* and *diffusion* effects? Furthermore, comparative politics was built on the methodological assumption that cases—i.e. national political systems—are independent of each other. It has been less concerned with common aspects and interactions.[6]

As Sørensen notes in Chapter 24 'Globalization and the nation-state', '[t]he standard image of the sovereign nation-state is that of an entity within well-defined territorial borders: a national polity, a national economy, and a national community of citizens', and on this premise researchers thought that they could 'safely ignore what takes place outside the borders of the countries they were studying'. For a long time, the main concern of comparative politics has remained the study of the Westphalian territorial state.

However, it is increasingly difficult to maintain such a position and, indeed, the literature has addressed these issues. In recent years, there has been a resurgence of interest in the so-called 'Galton problem', i.e. the methodological issue raised at the end of the nineteenth century by the polymath Francis Galton concerning associations between phenomena that are, in fact, the result of diffusion and contagion between cases.

Today, most countries are open systems subject to external influences, borrowing and learning from the practices of others, and are part of multilevel **governance** arrangements (see Chapter 11 'Multilevel governance'). For example, it is plausible to suppose that the development of welfare states in various countries (see Chapters 20 'Policy-making' and 22 'The impact of public policies') is affected by diffusion processes through policy transfers and **policy learning**. There is coordination when countries belong to overarching integrating organizations (the European Union, for example, as shown in Chapter 23 'The EU as a new political system'), as well as cases of imposition by conquest, colonialism, and economic dependency (as discussed in Chapter 4 'The nation-state', many current states were part of other states before secession). Finally, our current world, more than ever, experiences migrations (see the 'Comparative Tables' at the end of the volume in Appendix 2).

The risk for comparative politics is—methodologically speaking—that of ending up with 'N = 1'. Already, Przeworski and Teune in their classic book on the comparative method have asked: 'How many independent events can we observe? If the similarity within a group of systems is a result of diffusion, there is only one independent observation' (Przeworski and Teune 1970: 52). Is our methodology fit to analyse common developments, changes without variation between cases, and situations of dependence between them? In an increasingly interdependent world, comparative political scientists realize that social phenomena are not isolated and self-contained, but rather are affected by events occurring within other, sometimes remote, societies. Within a 'shrinking world' the problem is larger today than in the past.

... and back to divergence?

The last section of the book, Section 6 'Beyond the nation-state', addresses precisely these questions, with chapters on integration, globalization, and promotion of democracy in non-Western parts of the world. This is where comparative politics and international relations become contiguous and their efforts, in the future, will increasingly be common efforts.

Nonetheless, today there are also strong signals pointing in divergent directions. The backlash against liberal democracy in many countries relativizes the pattern towards convergence. Both academic literature and public debate increasingly point to countries, even large and long-established democracies, moving away, i.e. diverging, from the liberal democratic regime. This democratic crisis has happened through the rise of right-wing populism, 'illiberal democracy' models, and competitive authoritarianism in some European countries, Turkey, Russia, and the US in the past ten years, but also through left-wing populism in Latin America. Differentiation occurs also at the sub-national level and points to the resurgence of regionalist phenomena, as with the Scottish referendum or the Catalan separatist movement. Also,

supranational integration is called into question by the Trump administration in the US and occurs to different degrees and at different paces as the Brexit referendum in Britain in 2016 has witnessed.

All this is to say that it is difficult to detect patterns in world politics over short periods of time. This is one of the reasons why this book adopts a long-term perspective from the beginning of modern politics—the formation of national states, mass democracies, and industrialization in the nineteenth century. The French expression *'reculer pour mieux sauter'* ('to step backwards in order to jump further') was a favourite of Stein Rokkan, one of the pioneers of comparative politics. To have a firm historical ground for looking into the future fits very well with the philosophy of this book.

FURTHER READING

'Classics' of comparative politics are shown in the boxes in this Introduction. These books should be on every comparative political scientist's shelves.

Overviews of the discipline

Blondel, J. (1999) 'Then and Now: Comparative Politics', *Political Studies*, 47(1): 152–60.

Daalder, H. (1993) 'The Development of the Study of Comparative Politics', in H. Keman (ed.), *Comparative Politics* (Amsterdam: Free University Press), 11–30.

Dalton, R. J. (1991) 'Comparative Politics of the Industrial Democracies: From the Golden Age to Island Hopping', in W. Crotty (ed.), *Political Science* (Evanston, IL: Northwestern University Press), 15–43.

Eckstein, H. (1963) 'A Perspective on Comparative Politics, Past and Present' in H. Eckstein and D. E. Apter (eds), *Comparative Politics: A Reader* (New York: Free Press), 3–32.

Mair, P. (1996) 'Comparative Politics: An Overview', in R. E. Goodin and H.-D. Klingemann (eds), *A New Handbook of Political Science* (Oxford: Oxford University Press), 309–35.

Rogowski, R. (1993) 'Comparative Politics', in A. W. Finifter (ed.), *Political Science: The State of the Discipline* (Washington, DC: American Political Science Association), 431–50.

Schmitter, P. (1993) 'Comparative Politics', in J. Krieger (ed.), *The Oxford Companion to Politics of the World* (Oxford: Oxford University Press), 171–7.

Verba, S. (1985) 'Comparative Politics: Where Have We Been, Where Are We Going?', in H. J. Wiarda (ed.), *New Directions in Comparative Politics* (Boulder, CO: Westview Press), 26–38.

Recent treatments of comparative politics as a discipline

Almond, G. A. (1990) *A Discipline Divided: Schools and Sects in Political Science* (Newbury Park, CA: Sage).

Braun, D. and Maggetti, M. (eds) (2015) *Comparative Politics: Theoretical and Methodological Challenges* (Cheltenham: Edward Elgar).

Chilcote, R. H. (2000) *Comparative Inquiry in Politics and Political Economy* (Boulder, CO: Westview Press).

Landman, T. (2007) *Issues and Methods in Comparative Politics: An Introduction* (2nd edn) (London: Routledge).

Lichbach, M. I. and Zuckerman, A. S. (1997) *Comparative Politics: Rationality, Culture, and Structure* (Cambridge: Cambridge University Press).

Peters, B. G. (1998) *Comparative Politics: Theory and Methods* (Basingstoke: Macmillan).

Wiarda, H. J. (ed.) (2002) *New Directions in Comparative Politics* (3rd edn) (Boulder, CO: Westview Press).

Reference work

Boix, C. and Stokes, S. C. (2007) *Oxford Handbook of Comparative Politics* (Oxford: Oxford University Press).

See also the other titles in the *Oxford Handbooks of Political Science* series. For specific topics see the 'Further reading' section at the end of each chapter.

Scientific comparative politics research publishes results in a number of specialized journals. The most important scientific journals with a focus on comparative politics are the following: *Comparative Politics, Comparative Political Studies, Comparative European Politics, European Journal of Political*

Research, European Political Science Review, and *West European Politics,* among others.

In addition, most countries have political science journals that publish research in comparative politics. Examples include *American Political Science Review, British Journal of Political Science, Revue Française de Science Politique, Scandinavian Political Studies, Politische Vierteljahresschrift, Irish Political Studies, Australian Journal of Politics and History,* and *Swiss Political Science Review.*

Finally, for each subject (elections, parties, communication, etc.) there are specialized journals which include comparative work. Examples are: *Party Politics, Electoral Studies, European Journal of Public Policy, Local Government Studies, Publius: The Journal of Federalism, Journal of Common Market Studies, Journal of Democracy, Democratization, Journal of European Social Policy, Media, Culture and Society,* and *Political Communication.*

ENDNOTES

1. Not all authors would agree with such a division of disciplines, stressing that fields like public administration, policy analysis, political behaviour, and political economy are not part of comparative politics (see, e.g., the titles of the volumes in the *Oxford Handbooks of Political Science* listed in the 'Further reading' section of this Introduction). More importantly, this division into three main disciplines disregards methodology as a separate field. However, opinions diverge as to whether or not methods should be considered within the fields of political science, as they largely overlap with methods in other sciences, such as economics and sociology.

2. In these years, the first studies on political culture were published (see, e.g., Banfield 1958), followed by others stressing the differences in political cultures other than the Anglo-Saxon culture—namely based on clientelism and patronage. For an example of cultural analysis, see Putnam (1993).

3. This involved the creation of data archives, combined with the introduction of computerization and machine-readable data sets. Numbers are a

universal language and thus, from a comparative point of view, the least problematic level of measurement of phenomena in diverse contexts.

4. Within the new-institutionalist theory, different positions have emerged and have been summarized by Hall and Taylor (1996): (1) *historical new-institutionalism* devotes attention to the time dimension and the constraints set by past developments (path dependence), with a strong impact on policy analysis; (2) *sociological new-institutionalism* stresses how institutions model politics and influence preferences by narrowing expectations and orientations; (3) *rational choice new-institutionalism* focuses on how institutions result from the aggregation of individual preferences and on institutions' contribution to solving **collective action** problems.

5. These cycles correspond to what Chilcote (1994) calls traditional, behavioural, and post-behavioural comparative politics.

6. Charles Tilly's critique of Stein Rokkan's model points precisely to Rokkan's failure to genuinely analyse the *interactions* between countries (Tilly 1984: 129).

Visit the Online Resources that accompany this book for additional material, including country profiles, comparative data sets, flashcard glossaries, and web directory.

www.oup.com/he/caramani5e

Section 1
Theories and methods

1

The relevance of comparative politics

Bo Rothstein

Chapter contents

Reader's guide

The issue of the relevance of political science in general, and then also the sub-discipline of comparative politics, has recently received increased attention both in the public debate and within the discipline itself. This chapter considers what comparative politics could be relevant for, such as informing the public debate and giving policy advice. A central argument is that comparative politics has a huge but sometimes underdeveloped potential for being relevant for various aspects of human well-being. Empirical research shows that the manner in which a country's political institutions are designed and the quality of the operations of these institutions have a strong impact on measures of population health, as well as subjective well-being (i.e. 'happiness') and general social trust. One result is that democratization without increased state capacity and control of corruption is not likely to deliver increased human well-being.

Introduction: what should comparative politics be relevant for?

The issue of the relevance of political science in general, and then the sub-discipline of comparative politics, has recently received increased attention both in the public debate and within the discipline itself (Stoker et al. 2015). To answer a question like 'Is comparative politics relevant?' certainly demands that a more basic issue is solved, namely for what, whom, or when should this knowledge be relevant? Many different answers could be given to this question.

First, comparative politics could be relevant for informing the elite: giving advice to parties on how to win election campaigns, how politicians should best act so as to get enough support for their policies in legislative assemblies, how they should interact with strong interest groups such as business organizations and labour unions, and how to best handle factions within their party, to name but a few. In this approach to the issue of relevance, comparative political scientists act as consultants, advisors, or even so-called 'grey eminences' to politicians. This is also where many of those with a degree in political science end up, for example as ministerial advisors or policy consultants, professions which have increased considerably in almost all Organisation for Economic Co-operation and Development (OECD) countries (OECD 2011a,b). Plato ventured into this area some 2,300 years ago with his three famous journeys to Sicily, where he was asked to educate the new King of Syracuse in the noble art of governing. The historical record shows that Plato came to deeply regret his role as teacher to the king. His advice fell on deaf ears and the king became a ruthless tyrant, ruining his country (Lilla 2001).

A well-known formulation in relation to public policy issues is that the researcher's task is to 'speak truth to power' (Wildavsky 1987). The problem is that 'power' may not be that interested, especially if what is spoken comes into conflict with deeply held ideological convictions or specific interests. The extent to which comparative politics is relevant in this respect also depends, of course, on how useful the knowledge is for the policy in question. One problem is that most **public policies** are connected to a specific ideological and/or political orientation, and many argue that science should be about finding out what is the truth and not about supporting any specific ideology or group interest.

A second idea for making comparative political science more relevant is based on informing not the political elite but the general public. This is the comparative political scientist as the public intellectual writing op-ed articles, giving public lectures, and commenting upon current political affairs in the media. The numbers of political events that deserve comment are in principle endless. Why does country X have higher economic growth? Why is gender equality better in some countries than others? Why does nation Z have such a huge **welfare state**? Here, the level of relevance would be determined by the question 'Can political scientists offer something more, deeper, or qualitatively different than what we get from the astute political journalist or pundit that is also intelligible for the general public?' One argument for this approach is that everything else being equal, it cannot be a disadvantage to the quality of debate about **public policies** in a democracy if people with more knowledge choose to participate. An often-heard argument against the 'public intellectual' approach is that the opinions and comments may not always have a good foundation in verified research results.

Politics is a partisan game and that is likely to be one reason why many researchers in comparative politics choose to stay away both from 'speaking truth to power' and from acting as 'public intellectuals'. A fear of being seen as 'normative' seems to hinder many from becoming engaged in issues that many citizens care deeply about (see Box 1.1; Gerring 2015; Stoker et al. 2015). Another problem is, of course, what is known as 'paternalism'. Should the choice of policies in a democracy not be left to the citizens? What rights have the academic elite to tell ordinary people what is best for them? If the experts know which policies are 'best', we could do away with the democratic process. And should we not suspect that behind a shield of objective scientific jargon rests the special interests of the elite?

A way out of this paternalism problem has been suggested by the economist-philosopher and Nobel Laureate, Amartya Sen. His theory of justice, known as the 'capability theory of justice' or 'capability approach', rests on the idea that a just society provides people with 'effective opportunities to undertake actions and activities that they have reason to value, and be the person that they have reason to want to be' (Sen 2010; Robeyns 2011, 2.2). The terminology implies that the problem of justice is not to equalize economic resources or social status as such, but to ensure for all individuals a set of *basic resources* that will equalize their chances to reach their full potential as humans. For this, economic measures like gross national income per capita will not work because (a) economic resources can be very unevenly divided; and (b) economic resources do not always translate into actual capabilities. For example, according to the most recent statistics from the United Nations Development Programme (UNDP), in economic terms South Africa is 60 per cent richer than the Philippines, but has a life expectancy ten years lower.

ZOOM-IN 1.1

Normative theory and empirical research in comparative politics

Institutionally, political philosophy (i.e. 'political theory') is usually kept apart from empirical research in political science. From a policy and relevance perspective this is unfortunate, since without a foundation in normative theory, results from empirical research may be used in ways that stand in sharp conflict with respect for human rights. A strand of literature has pointed to the problem with 'illiberal democracy', implying that majorities may launch policies that are detrimental to civil liberties (King 1999; Zakaria 1997). It is also the case that political philosophers sometimes suggest policies for increased social justice which empirical research has shown are impossible to implement (Rothstein 2017).

due to malnutrition. In addition to the 'hard' objective measures from population health, there is now an abundance of interesting, so-called subjective measures. These include perceptions of the level of corruption in one's country, perceptions of social trust, and whether people report satisfaction with their lives (i.e. 'happiness'). Various research and policy institutions have also produced measures for ranking countries, concerning things like respect for human and civil rights, the rule of law, gender equality, innovativeness, and competitiveness, to name a few. One answer to the question, 'For what is comparative politics relevant?' can thus be '*its potential for increasing human well-being*'.

KEY POINTS

* A discussion of the potential relevance of a discipline such as comparative politics has to start by asking the question 'Relevant for what?'

* Comparative politics can be relevant for informing the public debate and also for giving advice to politicians and government agencies about public policies.

* Comparative politics also has a potential for serving more general goals, such as increased social justice and improved human well-being.

Political institutions and human well-being

Standards for what should be seen as basic resources that increase capabilities include access to high-quality health care and education, basic food and shelter, equality in civil and political rights, equal protection under the law, basic social services and social insurance systems that support people who for various reasons cannot generate enough resources from their own work, support for persons with disabilities, etc. The set of such capabilities enhancing goods and services can, of course, vary, but it is important to realize that equality, as a politically viable concept, has to be about specified things. There is simply no way we—by political means—can equalize the ability to be a skilled musician, to be creative, to be loved, to be an outstanding researcher, a good parent, or a first-rate ballet dancer. What it *is* possible to do by political means is to increase the possibility for those who happen to have ambitions in these (and many other) fields to realize their talents, even if they have not entered this world with the necessary economic endowments to do this. This can be done by giving people access to a certain bundle of goods and services that are likely to enhance their capabilities of reaching their full potential as human beings. In practice, the capabilities approach to justice has been translated to various measures of human well-being, of which many (but not all) are measures of population health. Simply put, a person that dies as an infant due to lack of access to sanitation and safe water, for example, has no possibility of fulfilling whatever potential he or she had. The same goes for a person that dies prematurely due to lack of health care, or who never learned to read and write due to lack of education, or who as a child did not develop her cognitive capacities

It was long taken for granted that the well-being of the population in a country rested on non-political factors such as natural resources, technological and medical inventions, the structural situation of the social classes, or deeply held cultural norms, including religion. The political institutions were seen merely as a superficial reflection or as the 'superstructure' of underlying structural forces, and thus had no or very little impact on the overall prosperity or well-being of a country. This changed in economics, sociology, and political science during the 1990s with what has been termed 'the institutional turn'. The economic historian (and Nobel Laureate) Douglass C. North (1990) was amongst the first to point to the importance of institutions, understood as 'the rules of the game', for explaining why some countries were much more prosperous than others. This became known as 'the new institutionalism' (March and Olsen 1989) and, in comparative politics, as 'historical institutionalism' (Steinmo et al. 1992). Comparing societies with almost identical structural conditions revealed that they could be dramatically different in their ability to produce human well-being, and the scholars in the various institutional approaches could empirically show that what explained the differences was the variation in political, legal, and administrative institutions.

The institutional turn and comparative politics

The implication of this 'institutional turn' for the relevance of comparative politics can hardly be overstated. An example is the issue of access to safe water. The magnitude of the problem can be illustrated by reports from the World Health Organization (WHO), which in 2006 estimated that 1.2 billion people lacked access to enough clean water and that 2.6 billion people lacked adequate sanitation. Figures further reveal that 80 per cent of all diseases in developing countries are waterborne, and that contaminated water causes the death of 2.8 million children every year. A careful estimate by the WHO is that 12,000 people, two-thirds of them children, die every day from water- and sanitation-related diseases (UNDP 2006; Transparency International 2008).

What makes this enormous problem relevant from a comparative politics perspective is that a growing number of experts in the area argue that the problem is not, as was previously assumed, an issue of lack of technical solutions. The acute lack of clean water that affects such a large number of people in developing countries is not due to a lack of technical solutions, such as pumps, reservoirs, or sewers; nor is the problem caused by limited access to natural clean water. Instead, the main problem seems to lie within the judicial and administrative institutions—in other words, in a dysfunctional state apparatus. Developing countries more often than not possess the technical devices needed to provide the population with clean water; the problem is that these technical installations rarely fulfil their functions due to lack of supervision, incompetence, and corruption in the public sector. In many cases, corruption in the procurement process results in extremely low-quality infrastructure being put in place (Rothstein 2011, ch. 1).

The implication is that for comparative politics to be policy relevant, it is not necessary to side with a specific political ideology or special interest group. The capability approach to social justice is, of course, a normative theory, but based on the generally held idea that most people would prefer to live in a country where few newborns die, most children survive beyond their fifth birthday, almost all ten-year-olds can read, people have access to safe water, people live a long and reasonably healthy life, child deprivation is low, few women die when giving birth, the percentage of people living in severe poverty is low, and many report reasonable satisfaction with their lives. More than anything else, an abundance of empirical research shows that the ability to become a 'successful society' in this sense is decided by the quality of the society's political institutions (including the administrative and legal institutions which are inherently political). Simply put, some societies are more successful than others in achieving broad-based human well-being for their populations (Hall and Lamont 2009), and empirically for the most part this turns out to be caused by what can be termed their quality of government (Rothstein 2011). The implication is that the question of whether comparative political science can be relevant becomes different from the consultant/advisor and the public intellectual approaches mentioned in 'Introduction: what should comparative politics be relevant for?' above. Instead, it becomes a question of the extent to which the discipline can contribute to increased human well-being by (a) specifying which political institutions are most likely to increase human well-being' and (b) how such institutions can come about.

Institutions rule—but which?

Not least in research into developing countries, there is now almost a consensus about the importance of institutions and the quality of government in terms of impact on development and human well-being (Rodrik et al. 2004; Acemoglu and Robinson 2012). However, there is little consensus on which particular political institutions matter, how they matter, how they can be created where they are now absent, or how they can be improved if dysfunctional (Andrews 2013; Fukuyama 2014). In addition, as North kept reminding us, the importance of the informal institutions in society should not be overlooked and the importance of formal institutions has often been exaggerated (North 2010). A case in point is Uganda, which, after numerous interventions by the World Bank and many bilateral donors, has established an institutional framework that according to one leading donor organization was 'largely satisfactory in terms of anti-corruption measures' (SIDA 2006). In fact, Uganda's formal institutions of anti-corruption regulation score 99 out of a 100 points in the think tank Global Integrity's index. Thus, while the formal institutions are almost perfect, the informal underbelly is a very different matter. After almost a decade of impressive legislation and a government that rhetorically assured non-tolerance towards corruption, the problem of corruption remains rampant. Uganda ranks as 142 out of 175 countries on Transparency International's Corruption Perceptions Index. One example of an important informal institution that has been shown to have a strong impact on human well-being is the degree of social trust. If people in a society perceive that 'most other people can be trusted', this has a positive impact on overall prosperity and most measures of human well-being (Uslaner 2002). If we knew how to increase the informal institution of social trust within a society, much would be gained. The issue of which institution is not confined to the division between formal and informal. There is also a large discussion about whether the institutions that regulate the *access* to power are more important than the institutions that regulate the *exercise* of power. For example, in a democracy, the former are party and electoral systems and the latter are the rule of law and the capacity of the public administration in general (Holmberg and Rothstein 2012; Fukuyama 2014). These issues will be addressed below.

Table 1.1 Examples of basic institutional variation among representative democracies	
Type of institution	Institutional variations
Electoral system	Proportional vs majoritarian
Legislative assembly	Unicameral vs bicameral
Government structure	Unitarian vs federalist
Central executive	Parliamentarism vs presidentialism
Judicial review	Strong vs weak judicial review
Local governments	Weak vs strong local autonomy
Civil service	Spoils recruitment vs merit-recruitment
Protection of minorities	Strong vs weak protection
Referendums	Regularly used vs not used
Consultation of experts	Routine vs ad hoc

KEY POINTS

- The 'institutional turn' in the social sciences implies a shift away from a focus on structural variables for explaining why some societies are more successful than others in providing human well-being.

- This 'institutional turn' implies an increased relevance for comparative politics since the creation, design, and operations of political institutions are among the central objects of study.

- Institutions, broadly understood as 'the rules of the game', can be both formal and informal. Moreover, they can be located at the 'input side' or at the 'output side' of the political system. This variation opens up an interesting analysis of which institutions are most important for increasing human well-being.

The many faces of democracy

Almost all scholars in comparative politics take for granted that in producing 'the good society', democratic political institutions are to be preferred. Research in **democratization** has been very high on the comparative politics agenda (Teorell 2010). From a capability theory, one problem is that far from all democracies produce high levels of human well-being. This is not only the case if we compare the OECD countries with democracies in the developing world, since there are also huge differences within these groups of countries for most measures of human well-being. One problem is that we tend to speak about democracy as a single political institution, when in fact it is a system that is built on multiple separate institutions. This problem can be illustrated with the following thought experiment. Every representative democracy has to solve a number of issues for which different institutions have been created (or have evolved). For example, the electoral system, the degree of decentralization, the formation of the organizations that are to implement laws

and policies, the way expert knowledge is infused into the decision-making process, and so on. Democratic theory does not provide precise answers to how these institutions should be constructed. There is, to take an obvious example, not a clear answer in democratic theory that tells us if a proportional electoral system (giving rise to a **multiparty system**) is to be preferred or if a first-past-the-post system that usually produces a two-party system would be a better choice. As shown in Table 1.1, at least ten such institutional dimensions can be identified in every representative democracy.

According to the main works in democratic theory, none of the various choices that can be made for the ten institutional dimensions are mutually exclusive. In theory, everything can be combined (even though some combinations are less likely than others). Thus, the result from this thought experiment shows that there are at least 1,024 ways of constructing a representative democracy ($2^{10} = 1,024$). Since many of these dimensions are not dichotomous, but to varying extents gradual (more or less strong **judicial review**, more or less spoils recruitment to the civil service, more or less **decentralization** to local governments, etc.), the possible variation is in fact much larger than '1,024', if not endless. To be concrete, the Swiss, Danish, Brazilian, South African, and British democracies, to just take five examples, are institutionally configured in very different ways. And while it is true that there is some 'clustering' in these dimensions, there are also surprising differences. For example, the relation between the central civil service and the cabinet in Finland and Sweden are very different from how this relation is institutionalized in neighbouring Denmark and Norway. Australia is the only former British colony that has compulsory voting. Another important dimension is how expert knowledge is handled in the decision-making process. Some democracies have developed established routines in the decision-making process to ensure that expert knowledge is used in both the preparation and **implementation** of **public policies**. In other democracies, the use of expert knowledge is more ad hoc. In many policy fields, the demand is not only that decisions about policies are taken in a democratically correct manner, but that especially in areas such as population health, and environmental issues, we also want them to be 'true', or at least in line with the 'best available knowledge'.

Another important institutional variation is the extent of so-called veto points in a democratic system. The argument is that some combinations in the scenario above give rise to many such veto points that can make it difficult for governments to act in a determined and responsible way. If there are many uncoordinated actors (the executive, the courts, the legislative assemblies, the sub-national governments, organized interest groups), the democratic machinery may be unable to produce coherent and effective policies (Tsebelis 2002; Fukuyama 2014).

From the institutionalist-capabilities perspective presented above, we would like to know which institutional configuration of a representative democracy is most likely to produce a high level of human well-being. However, since the number of democratic countries is approximately 100, finding a solution to this '1,024' problem is empirically difficult. Moreover, even if there are some interesting results from this research, changing long-established political institutions may still be a Herculean task.

KEY POINTS

- We often think of democracy in terms of an either/or dimension—a country is either a democracy or (more or less) authoritarian. In reality, democracies turn out to have quite dramatic variation in their institutional configurations.

- The manner in which a democratic political system is organized is often linked to its capability for producing 'valued outcomes' such as economic prosperity, political legitimacy, and social justice.

- Knowledge about the link between the design of political institutions and 'valued outcomes' is therefore essential for the relevance of comparative politics.

Democracy and state capacity

As mentioned above, it has generally been taken for granted, both in comparative politics and in the general public debate, that when it comes to human well-being, the nature of institutions that make up the liberal electoral democracy is the most important factor. Research about democratization has been a huge enterprise in the discipline, with numerous studies of how, when, and why countries shift from various forms of authoritarian rule to electoral representative democracies. There has also been a lot to study since the waves of democracy that have swept over the globe have brought representative democracy to places where it seemed inconceivable fifty, thirty, or even ten years ago. Even though the 'Arab Spring' has not delivered much democratization and there are some recent important set-backs in some parts of the world, the fact is that more countries than ever are now, by the most sophisticated measures used, classified as being democratic, and more people than ever live in democracies (Teorell 2010). While there are many reasons to celebrate this democratic success, if judged from the perspective of capability theory, there are also reasons to be disappointed. One example is South Africa, which miraculously managed to end apartheid in 1994 without falling into a full-scale civil war. As Nelson Mandela said in one of his speeches, the introduction of democracy would not only liberate people, but would also greatly improve their social and economic situation (Mandela 1994: 414). Available statistics give a surprisingly bleak picture for this promise. Since 1994, the country has not managed to improve the average time frame over which children attend school by a single month, economic inequality remains at a world record level, life expectancy is down by almost six years, and the number of women that die in childbirth has more than doubled.[1] Simply put, for many central measures of human well-being, the South African democracy has not delivered many positive results.

Another example has been provided by Amartya Sen, in an article comparing 'quality of life' in China and India. His disappointing conclusion is that on almost all standard measures of human well-being, the communist and autocratic Peoples' Republic of China now clearly outperforms liberal and democratically governed India (Sen 2011). Perhaps the most compelling evidence for the lack of positive effects of democracy on human well-being comes from a recent study on child deprivation by Halleröd et al. (2013). They use data measuring seven aspects of child poverty (access to safe water, food, sanitation, shelter, education, health care, and information) from sixty-eight low- and middle-income countries for no less than 2,120,734 cases (children). The results of this large study show that there is no positive effect of democracy on the level of child deprivation for any of the seven indicators. One argument against this is that it is unrealistic to expect high capacity of new democracies. We should only find a positive effect if we take into account the 'stock' of democracy (Gerring et al. 2012). This argument turns out to be valid in large-n analysis (see Box 1.2), but there are numbers of cases where democratic rule has been established for several decades but where the score is still surprisingly low on measures of human well-being. India became a democracy in 1948, as did the southern regions in Italy. Jamaica has been a democracy since the late 1950s, Ghana has been democratic since 1993, and South Africa since 1994. In short, the picture is this: representative democracy is not a safe cure against severe poverty, child deprivation, high levels of economic inequality, illiteracy, being unhappy or not satisfied with one's life, high infant mortality, short life expectancy, high maternal mortality, lack of access to safe water or sanitation, low school attendance for girls, or low interpersonal trust.

DEFINITION 1.2

Large-n analysis

Large-n study refers to quantitative analyses which employ various statistical techniques of data processing as the main method of inference. Typical data are surveys from representative samples of the population or register data such as measures of infant mortality, wages, taxes, and public spending. Small-n studies use a small number of cases that are analysed by, for example, data collected from archives, interviews with central agents, or participant observation. A common typical approach is tracing the development of public policies over time.

The spectre that is haunting democracy

Why has democratization not resulted in more human well-being? One explanation was given by the noted democratization scholar Larry Diamond in a presentation at *National Endowment for Democracy* in the United States, when the organization celebrated its first twenty-five years of operations:

There is a specter haunting democracy in the world today. It is bad governance—governance that serves only the interests of a narrow ruling elite. Governance that is drenched in corruption, patronage, favoritism, and abuse

of power. Governance that is not responding to the massive and long-deferred social agenda of reducing inequality and unemployment and fighting against dehumanizing poverty. Governance that is not delivering broad improvement in people's lives because it is stealing, squandering, or skewing the available resources.

Diamond (2007: 19)

The implication of Diamond's argument is that representative democracy is not enough for creating human well-being. Without control of corruption (see Box 1.3) and increased administrative capacity, the life situation of citizens will not improve (see Box 1.4).

DEFINITION 1.3

The conceptual 'scale' problem in comparative politics

Research in corruption has until recently not been very prominent in comparative politics. The exception is what is labelled 'clientelism', which is largely about various forms of vote buying. Most corruption, however, occurs in the implementation of public policies and varies a lot in scale and scope, from a minor sum paid to a police officer to avoid a speeding ticket, to gigantic sums paid for arms deals. This variation in scale creates a conceptual problem, since we tend to use the same term for these hugely different types of corruption. However, social science is not alone in having this conceptual 'scale' problem. Biologists, for example, use the same term (bird) both for hummingbirds and condors. The reason is that although there is a huge difference in 'scale', each phenomenon has important things in common.

State capacity, quality of government, and human well-being

If we follow Diamond's idea about the importance of what could be termed 'quality of government' and, instead of having degree of democracy as an explanatory variable, turn to measures of a state's administrative capacity, control of corruption, or other measures of 'good governance', the picture of what public institutions can do for human well-being changes dramatically. For example, the study on child deprivation mentioned in 'Democracy and state capacity' above finds strong effects of measures of the state capacity and administrative effectiveness when it comes to implementation of policies on four out of seven indicators on child deprivation (lack of safe water, malnutrition, lack of access to health care, and lack of access to information), and also when controlling for gross domestic product (GDP) per capita and a number of basic individual-level variables (Halleröd et al. 2013). A study of how corruption impacts five different measures of population health finds similar strong effects, also when controlling for economic prosperity and democracy (Holmberg and Rothstein 2011). Other studies largely confirm that various measures of a state's administrative capacity, quality of government, levels of corruption, and other measures of 'good governance' have strong effects on almost all standard measures of human well-being, including subjective measures of life satisfaction (i.e. 'happiness') and social trust (Ott 2010; Norris 2012). Recent studies also find that absence of violence in the form of interstate and civil wars is strongly affected by measures of quality of government, more so than by the level of democracy (Fjelde and De Soysa 2009; Norris 2012; Lapuente and Rothstein 2014). As shown in Figures 1.1. and 1.2, there is a huge difference in the correlations between one often-used measure of democracy[2] and a measure of 'bad governance' for the **Human Development Index** produced by the United Nations Development Programme.

As can be seen, the correlation between human well-being and the level of democracy is quite low, while the correlation with 'government effectiveness' is substantial. This result is shown to be repeated for a large set of other measures of human well-being and what should generally count as 'successful societies' (Holmberg and Rothstein 2014; Rothstein and Holmberg 2014).

KEY POINTS

- Empirical research indicates that the administrative capacity of the political system in a country is essential for bringing about human well-being.
- Democracy alone seems not to generate human well-being.
- Corruption in the public sector and other forms of low quality of government has a strong negative effect on human well-being.

Does democracy generate political legitimacy?

One counterargument to the lack of 'valued outcomes' from democratization is that the normative reasons for representative democracy should not be performance measures like the ones mentioned above, but political legitimacy. If people have the right to change their government through 'free and fair elections', they will find their system of rule legitimate. In regard to this, empirical research shows even more surprising results, namely that democratic rights or the feeling of being adequately represented by elected officials does not seem to be the most important cause behind people's perception of political legitimacy. Based on comparative survey data, several recent studies show that 'performance' or 'output' measures, such as control of

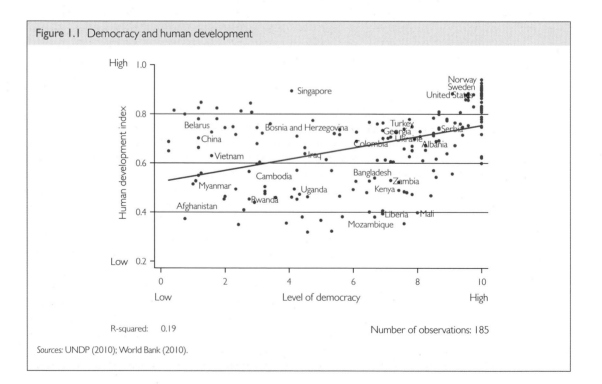

Figure 1.1 Democracy and human development

R-squared: 0.19   Number of observations: 185

Sources: UNDP (2010); World Bank (2010).

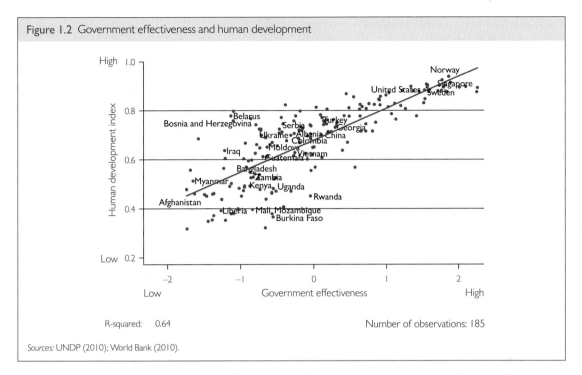

Figure 1.2 Government effectiveness and human development

R-squared: 0.64   Number of observations: 185

Sources: UNDP (2010); World Bank (2010).

Measuring corruption

A large debate exists about the possibility of operationalizing and measuring corruption. Since the practice is usually secret, getting accurate information is problematic. Most measures are based on assessments by country experts, but recently a number of surveys of representative samples of the population has been carried out. These measures correlate on a surprisingly high level, implying that 'ordinary people' and 'experts' judge the situation in the countries they assess in a very similar way. Moreover, a number of related indexes have been constructed, for example measuring the rule of law, government effectiveness, and the impartiality of the civil service. These measures also correlate on a high level with measures trying to capture corruption. Thus, while far from perfect, the measures of corruption that have been launched are now widely used in comparative politics. For an overview, see Charron 2016.

corruption, government effectiveness, and the rule of law, trump democratic rights in explaining political legitimacy (Gilley 2006, 2009). As stated by Bruce Gilley, 'this clashes with standard liberal treatments of legitimacy that give overall priority to democratic rights' (2006: 58). Using a different comparative survey data set, Dahlberg and Holmberg (2014: 515) conclude in a similar vein that 'government effectiveness is of greater importance for citizens' satisfaction with the way democracy functions, compared to factors such as ideological congruence

on the input side. Impartial and effective bureaucracies matter more than representational devices.' Thus, if the relevance of political science is about understanding the causes of political legitimacy, most researchers in this discipline have studied the parts of the political system that are not the most relevant.

One way to theorize about this counter-intuitive result may be the following. On average, one-third of the electorate in democratic elections do not vote. Even fewer use their other democratic rights, such as taking part in political demonstrations, signing petitions, or writing 'letters to the editor'. When a citizen does not make much use of her democratic rights, usually nothing happens. However, if her children cannot get medical care because she cannot afford the bribes demanded by the doctors, if the police will not protect her because she belongs to a minority, if the water is polluted because of the incompetence of the local water managers, if she is denied a job she has the best qualifications for because she does not belong to the 'right' political party, or if the fire brigade won't come when she calls because she lives in the 'wrong' part of the city, these are things that can cause real distress in her life.

It should be underlined that this analysis is not an argument against liberal representative democracy or that people in autocratic regimes should not demand democracy and civil rights. On the contrary, liberal democracy has intrinsic values that are irreplaceable and indispensable. The argument is that if a liberal democracy system is going to produce increased human well-being around the world, quality-of-government factors such as administrative capacity, the rule of law, and control of corruption must be taken into account.

Does democracy cure corruption?

A special problem that so far has not found a persuasive explanation is that in many (but far from all) democracies, the electorate is not punishing corrupt politicians (Chang and Golden 2007). Instead, as shown in Figure 1.3, they are often re-elected, implying that the accountability mechanism in representative democracy does not work as it is supposed to. Some have argued that democracies allow for more political corruption through vote buying and illegal party financing (della Porta and Vannucci 2007). However, this is not a general law. A recent study has shown that political parties in countries in Central and Eastern Europe that mobilize on a 'clean government' agenda have been remarkably successful in elections (Bågenholm and Charron 2015). One may interpret this as a tendency for 'clean governments' in some countries to become a separate political dimension. All in all, as Figure 1.3 indicates, the 'curve' between democracy and corruption is U- or J-shaped, and one important and very relevant issue for comparative politics is to understand why this is so.

KEY POINTS

- Democracy is important for broad-based political legitimacy, but less so than factors related to the quality of government institutions that implement public policies.

- Democracy is not a 'safe cure' against corruption and other forms of low quality of government.

- In many elections, voters are not punishing corrupt politicians. This implies that the accountability mechanisms in representative democracy are not working as intended.

What should be explained?

So far, the argument is that comparative political science, by focusing on institutions that make up the political system, has a huge potential for addressing issues about human well-being, economic prosperity, and social justice that most people care deeply about. In addition, it has been shown that the political institutions that seem to be most important for countries to achieve a high level of human development are those that exist at the 'output' side of the political system. This has two implications for the discussion on how to make comparative politics relevant in relation to the capability theory of justice that underlies this line of reasoning. First, human well-being ought to be the main dependent variable (that we should

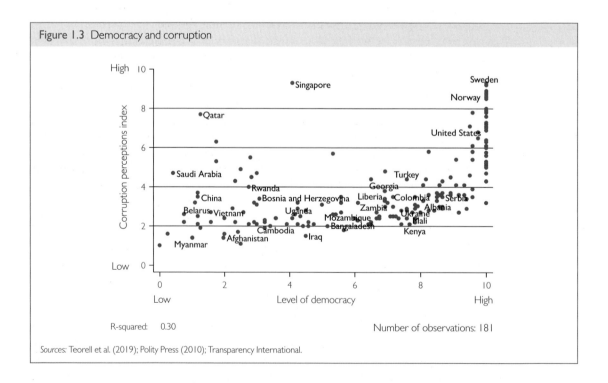

Figure 1.3 Democracy and corruption

R-squared: 0.30   Number of observations: 181

Sources: Teorell et al. (2019); Polity Press (2010); Transparency International.

strive to explain), and the political institutions that operate on the output side of the political system (the quality of the legal system and the public administration) should be central. Second, this approach to relevance to some extent implies a change for the discipline. Instead of just explaining 'politics', more focus needs to be placed on what politics implies for the actual human well-being of the citizens. Questions like, 'Why do different countries have different party systems?', 'Under what conditions do countries democratize?', and 'Why is the relation between business, labour, and state different in different countries?' all need to be complemented by research questions that try to answer *why* there is such a stark variation between countries in the quality of their government institutions and how this can be improved. In general, comparative political science has so far paid relatively little attention to issues about state capacity, control of corruption, and institutional quality (Rothstein 2015).

Statistical significances versus real-life significance

If research and scholarship in an academic discipline is going to be relevant in the sense mentioned above, it is not only necessary to try to explain things that are important for the lives people will have; there is also a normative perspective for the choice of which explanatory variables should be central. I will illustrate this with an example of explanation of the degree of corruption in countries. With the access to large amounts of contemporary and historical data, researches have shown that Lutheran nations, with a large number of settlers from the colonizing country, and nations that are relatively small and ethnically homogeneous, tend to have lower degrees of corruption. Lately, some have added that countries that are islands do well on this account. Most of these explanations are correct and were carried out with scientifically established methods. However, from a relevance perspective, they are of little or no use. To advise a country plagued by systemic corruption to change its history, religion, population, size, and geographical location is meaningless, since these are factors that cannot be changed. Just as a cancer patient is not helped by the advice that he or she should have had other parents, the government in, say, Nepal benefits little from knowing that being landlocked and not being Lutheran have had a negative impact on the country's prospects of development. It is certainly the case that knowledge about such structural factors is of value, but not from a relevance perspective. Variables that have the strongest effects in statistical analysis, for example, may be of little relevance for the improvement of human well-being, since they cannot be changed. As stated by Gerring (2015: 36), researchers 'sometimes confuse the notion of statistical significance with real-life significance'. One conclusion is that there is an argument for focusing the analysis on the types of political institutions mentioned above even if they do not show the strongest effects in the empirical analysis. For example: the way civil servants are recruited, paid, and trained; the manner in which the educational system is accessible for various strata of the population; the possibility of holding people working in the public sector accountable; laws about the right to access public documents; and, of course, the ten institutional dimensions for creating a working democracy pointed out in Table 1.1 are all examples of what can be termed 'institutional devices' that it is possible to change. Changing institutions may certainly be difficult to achieve, but such changes do occur. To sum up, the degree to which comparative politics is relevant is not only decided by the choice of the dependent variables, but also by the choice of the independent variables.

Quality of government, social trust, and human well-being

As mentioned in 'Introduction: what should comparative politics be relevant for?', it is not only formal/legal institutions that have been brought into focus by the 'institutional turn', but also informal ones. One such institution is the degree to which people in a society perceive that 'most other people' can be trusted. This varies dramatically from Denmark, where more than 65 per cent say 'yes' to this survey question, to Romania, where only about 8 per cent answer in the affirmative. What makes this issue important in the discussion of relevance is that social trust tends to be systematically and positively correlated with many measures of human well-being (Rothstein 2013). There are many ways to interpret this question as an informal institution. One is that people are making an evaluation of the moral standard of their society based on their notions of others' trustworthiness (Uslaner 2002). The central question is then what generates high levels of social trust in a society. The most widespread idea has been that social trust is generated 'from below', by people being active in voluntary associations (Putnam 2000). In this approach, the capacity of a society to produce social trust depends on citizens' willingness to become active in broad-based, non-exclusionary voluntary organizations. However, the evidence that associational membership of adults *creates* social trust has not survived empirical testing (Delhey and Newton 2005).

The role of formal and informal institutions

As a response to the failure of the society-centred approach to produce good empirical indicators for its claims about how the causal mechanisms generating social trust operate, the *institution-centred* approach claims that for social trust to flourish it needs to be embedded in and linked to the political context, as well as to formal political and legal institutions. According to this approach, it is trustworthy, uncorrupt, honest, impartial government institutions that exercise public power and implement policies in a fair manner that create social trust and **social capital** (Rothstein 2013). For example, one large-n study concluded that countries in which corruption is low '[seem] to create an institutional structure in which individuals are able to act in a trustworthy manner and can reasonably expect that others will do the same' (Delhey and Newton 2005: 323). Using survey data from twenty-nine European countries, Bjørnskov (2004) concluded that a high level of social trust is strongly correlated with a low level of corruption. Another study, also based on comparative survey data, concludes that 'the central contention . . . is that political institutions that support norms of fairness, universality, and the division of power, contribute to the formation of inter-personal trust' (Freitag and Buhlmann 2005).

Using scenario experiments in low-trust/high-corruption Romania and in high-trust/low-corruption Sweden, Rothstein and Eek (2009) found that persons in both these countries who experience corruption among public health-care workers or the local police when travelling in an 'unknown city and unfamiliar country' not only lose trust in these authorities, but also in other people in general in that 'unknown' society.

To sum up, what comes out of this research is that the major source of variations in social trust is to be found at the output side of the state machinery, namely in the quality of the legal and administrative branches of the state that are responsible for the implementation of public policies. Thus, the theory that high levels of states' administrative capacity and quality of government generate social trust—which makes it easier to create large sets of public goods in a society, and which explains why such societies are more successful than their opposites in fostering human well-being—is currently supported by an extensive amount of empirical research. One conclusion from this is that an important informal institution like social trust can be influenced by the design and quality of the formal and legal institutions.

KEY POINTS

- If the capability approach is to be used as the central metric for relevance of research in comparative politics, a shift of focus in what should be explained (the 'dependent variable') is necessary. The traditional and dominant ambition to explain 'politics' should be complemented by a striving to explain variations in human well-being, broadly defined.

- A focus on what politics can do for increasing human well-being, prosperity, and social justice in the world is also related to the choice of 'independent' variables—that is, factors that can explain the variation in human well-being etc. Variables that have the strongest statistical significance may be less interesting if they are not able to be changed by political means.

- Much research in comparative politics is focused on formal institutions, leaving informal institutions out. One such institution that seems to have a huge impact on human well-being is general social trust. Recent research shows that there is a causal link between how people perceive the quality of formal institutions and their propensity to believe that other people in general can be trusted.

Conclusion

In October 2009, a Senator in the United States Congress from the Republican Party, Tom A. Colburn, proposed an amendment to cut off funding from the US National Science Foundation (NSF) to research in political science. His argument was that research produced by political scientists was a waste of taxpayers' money because it is irrelevant to human well-being. Instead, Colburn argued, NSF should redirect its funding towards research in the natural sciences and engineering that would, for example, produce new biofuels or help people with severe disabilities. While not initially successful, Colburn's attack on funding for political science was approved by the US Congress in 2013, and again in 2015. The argument presented here is that while there may be many reasons to criticize the political science discipline, the argument that it does not have the ability to 'save lives' is patently wrong. Understanding how political institutions operate is the ultimate goal of comparative politics, and it would not be an exaggeration to say that if we today were to summarize human misery in the world, most of it can be explained by the fact that a majority of the world's population live under dysfunctional political institutions. For the most part, it is not a lack of natural resources, financial capital, medical techniques, or knowledge that is the main cause of widespread human misery. Instead, the main culprit is the low quality of the political institutions in many countries. In 2013, the President of the World Bank, Jim Yong Kim, stated that 'in the developing world, corruption is public enemy No. 1'.[3] While corruption certainly has legal, economic, and sociological connotations, it is predominantly an issue about the construction, quality, and ethical standards of the public institutions in a country, which is an issue that should be at the heart of comparative political science.

In addition to the political consultant and public intellectual approaches to the issue of relevance, the argument here has been that comparative politics has a great potential for being relevant for things that most people care about—namely, the level of human well-being of their societies. This is based on connecting the empirical research carried out in the discipline with the normative theory of justice known as the capability approach. This should lead to three consequences that are important for the relevance of the discipline. First, there should be a shift of focus on what should be explained from 'mere politics' to questions that impact on human well-being. The internal operations of the political machine are less interesting than what the machine can, and should, do for people. Second, there should be more focus on variables that both have an explanatory power and that it is possible to change. Third, while not undervaluing the institutions

for representative democracy, more focus ought to be given to the institutions that are related to issues like state capacity. A central issue for increasing the relevance of comparative politics would be to focus on the relation between the '1,024' problem mentioned in 'The many faces of democracy' above and the state's capacity to deliver human well-being. Are some ways of configuring a democratic system more likely to have a positive effect on human well-being than others?

One sometimes hears the argument that research of this type is of lower value because it is seen as 'applied', in contrast to research that is deemed as 'basic'. This distinction may be applicable to the natural sciences, but it is more doubtful whether it is relevant for the social sciences. It should be remembered that the three Nobel Laureates that can be said to be closest to comparative politics—John Nash, Douglass C. North, and Elinor Ostrom—all started out from applied research questions. Nash tried to understand how the superpowers should avoid a devastating nuclear war. North asked the question of why some countries are so much richer than others. Ostrom asked why some local groups managed to handle their common natural resources in a sustainable way while others failed. If starting from applied 'real-world' questions like these can lead to theoretical breakthroughs that deserve a Nobel prize, the distinction in value between 'basic' and 'applied' research cannot apply.

? QUESTIONS

Knowledge-based

1. What does the 'capability approach to social science' state?

2. Why is the design of political institutions relevant for societies?

3. In what ways can democracy reduce corruption?

4. How is corruption related to political legitimacy?

5. What can explain the variations in social trust between countries?

Critical thinking

1. Should comparative politics experts advise politicians?

2. Should comparative politics experts engage in public debates?

3. Is democracy helpful, or even necessary, for societies' well-being?

4. In what ways can knowledge in comparative politics 'save lives'?

5. What would be the optimal way to design institutions in a democracy?

≋ FURTHER READING

Andrews, M. (2013) *The Limits of Institutional Reform in Development: Changing Rules for Realistic Solutions* (Cambridge: Cambridge University Press).

Chayes, S. (2015) *Thieves of State: Why Corruption Threatens Global Security* (New York: W. W. Norton & Co.).

Dahlström, C. and Lapuente. V. (2016) *Organizing the Leviathan: How the Relationship between Politicians and Bureaucrats Shapes Good Government* (Cambridge: Cambridge University Press).

Fukuyama, F. (2014) *Political Order and Political Decay: From the Industrial Revolution to the Globalization of Democracy* (New York: Farrar, Straus & Giroux).

Hall, P. A. and Lamont, M. (eds) (2009) *Successful Societies: How Institutions and Culture Affect Health* (New York: Cambridge University Press).

Holmberg, S. and Rothstein, B. (eds) (2012) *Good Government: The Relevance of Political Science* (Cheltenham: Edward Elgar).

Mungiu-Pippidi A. (2015) *The Quest for Good Governance: How Societies Develop Control of Corruption* (New York, Cambridge University Press).

Norris, P. (2012) *Democratic Governance and Human Security: The Impact of Regimes on Prosperity, Welfare and Peace* (New York: Cambridge University Press).

Rothstein, B. (2011) *The Quality of Government: Corruption, Social Trust and Inequality in a Comparative Perspective* (Chicago, IL: The University of Chicago Press).

Rothstein, B. and Varraich, A. (2017) *Making Sense of Corruption* (Cambridge: Cambridge University Press).

Stoker, G., Peters, B. G., and Pierre, J. (eds) (2015) *The Relevance of Political Science* (New York: Palgrave Macmillan).

ENDNOTES

1. Data from the Quality of Government Data Bank, www.qog.pol.gu.se.

2. The graded measure of democracy is a combination of the average scores of political rights and civil liberties, reported by Freedom House, and the combined autocracy and democracy scores, derived from the Polity IV data set. It has been constructed by Axel Hadenius and Jan Teorell and, as they show, this index goes from 0–10 and performs better, both in terms of validity and reliability, than its constituent parts. A. Hadenius and J. Teorell (2005) 'Cultural and Economic Prerequisites of Democracy: Reassessing Recent Evidence', *Studies in Comparative International Development* 39(4): 87–106.

3. Reuters World Edition, 19 December 2013, http://www.reuters.com/article/us-worldbank-corruption-idUSBRE9BI11P20131219.

 Visit the Online Resources that accompany this book for additional material, including country profiles, comparative data sets, flashcard glossaries, and web directory.

www.oup.com/he/caramani5e

2

Approaches in comparative politics

B. Guy Peters

Chapter contents

Reader's guide

Theories and approaches are crucial in guiding research, and the awareness of what specific perspectives imply is important to make sense of scientific results. The chapter discusses five main approaches in comparative politics that represent important contributions (the five 'I's): old and new institutional analysis, interests and actors' strategies to pursue them through political action, ideas (political culture and social capital), individuals, and the influence of the international environment. The role of 'interaction' is also stressed. The chapter concludes by discussing the importance of looking at political processes, as well as of defining what the 'dependent variables' are.

Introduction

The political world is complex, involving a range of institutions, actors, and ideas that interact continuously to provide **governance** for society. The complexity of politics and government is compounded when we attempt to understand several different political systems, and to compare how these systems function. As comparative politics has moved beyond simple descriptions of individual countries or a few institutions, scholars have required substantial guidance to sort through the huge amount of evidence available, and to focus on the most relevant information. Thus, we need alternative approaches to politics, and particularly to develop approaches that are useful across a range of political systems.

Political theories are the source of these approaches to comparison. At the broadest level, there is the difference between positivist and constructivist approaches to politics (see Box 2.1). At less general levels, a number of different theories enable comparative political scientists to impose some analytical meanings on the political phenomena being observed, and to relate that evidence to more comprehensive understandings of politics. This chapter first discusses some general questions about using theory in comparative political analysis, and then discusses alternative approaches to politics. Each approach discussed provides some important information about politics, but few (if any) are sufficient to capture the underlying complexity. Therefore, the chapter also discusses using multiple approaches, and assesses the ways in which the approaches mentioned interact for more complex explanations.

KEY POINTS

- Given the high complexity of political systems and the wide range of variation between them across the world, it is important to develop approaches that are useful across them all and not simply in single countries.

- Political theories are the main source of such approaches—the division between positivism and **constructivism** being the more general distinction.

Uses of theory in comparison

Although there is an important interaction between theory and **empirical research** in all areas of the discipline of political science, that interaction is especially important in comparative politics. Even with an increasing amount of statistical research in political science, a still significant amount of case research, and a limited amount of experimental research, comparison remains the fundamental laboratory for political science.[1] Without the capacity to compare across political systems, it is almost impossible to understand the scientific importance of findings made in a single country (see Lee 2007), even one as large as the US.[2]

Without empirical political theory, effective research might be impossible, or it certainly would be less interesting. Some questions that are almost purely empirical can and should be researched. It is interesting to know variations in cabinet sizes in European countries, for example, but if the scientific study of politics is to progress, research needs to be related to theory. The information on the size of cabinets can, for example, be related to the capacity of those cabinets to make decisions through understanding the number of 'veto players' in the system (Tsebelis 2002; Koenig et al. 2010).

📢 **FOR AND AGAINST 2.1**

Positivism and constructivism

Most of contemporary political science, and comparative politics, is founded on positivist assumptions. The most basic assumption of positivism is a fact/value distinction, implying that there are real facts that are observable and verifiable in the same way by different individuals. Further, it is assumed that social phenomena can be studied in much the same way as phenomena in the natural sciences, through quantitative measurement, hypothesis testing, and theory formation. For example, the study of political attitudes across political cultures beginning with work such as *The Civic Culture* (Almond and Verba 1963) and extending to more contemporary work such as (Shore 2013) has assumed that there are dimensions of individual political thought that can be measured and understood through surveys and rigorous statistical analysis.

Constructivism, on the other hand, does not assume such a wide gulf between facts and values, and considers facts to be socially embedded and socially *constructed* (see Finnemore and Sikkink 2001). Thus, the individual researcher cannot stand outside political phenomena as an objective observer, but rather to some extent imposes his/her own social and cultural understandings on the observed phenomena. While most positivist research assumes that the individual is the source of social action (methodological individualism), constructivism asserts the importance of collective understandings and values, so that phenomena may not be understood readily in the absence of context. Rather than relying on **variables** to define the objects of research, constructive approaches focus more on dimensions such as scripts or discourses to promote understanding.

Each of these approaches to comparative politics can make major contributions to understanding. The use of the variable-oriented research associated with positivism has added greatly to the comparative understanding of individual-level behaviour, as well as to the understanding of political parties and other mass-based organizations. On the other hand, much of the analysis of formal political institutions and processes of governing still relies on methods that, if not explicitly constructivist, do share many of the assumptions concerning collective understandings and the importance of ideas (see Bevir and Rhodes 2010).

Therefore, comparative political theory is the source of questions and puzzles for researchers. For example, once we understand the concept of **consociationalism**, why is it that some societies have been able to implement this form of conflict resolution and others have not, even with relatively similar social divisions (see Lijphart 1996; Bogaards 2000)? And why have some countries in Africa been successful in implementing elite pacts after civil conflicts (a strategy like consociationalism, involving agreements among elites to govern even in the face of significant ethnic divisions), while other have not (LeVan 2011)? Likewise, political systems that appear relatively similar along a number of dimensions may have very different experiences maintaining effective coalition governments (Müller and Strøm 2000). Why? We may have theories that help explain how cabinets are formed in **parliamentary systems** and why they persist, but the anomalies in and exceptions to these theories are crucial for elaborating the models and enhancing our understanding of parliamentary democracy as an institution (Nikolenyi, 2004).

One crucial function of theory in comparative politics is to link micro- and macro-behaviour. Much of contemporary political theory functions at the micro-level, attempting to understand individual choice. The most obvious example is rational choice, which assumes utility maximization by individuals and uses that assumption about individuals to interpret and explain political phenomena.[3] Likewise, cognitive political psychology is central in contemporary political science (Winter 2013). However, in both cases the individual behaviours are channelled through institutions. Further, there is some reciprocal influence as institutions shape the behaviour of individuals and individuals shape institutions. For example, the institution of the presidency in the US is significantly influenced by the personal style of presidents.

The link between the micro and the macro is crucial for comparative politics, given that one primary concern is explaining the behaviour of political systems and institutions rather than individuals. Variations in individual behaviour and the influence of cultural and social factors on that behaviour are important, but the logic of comparison is primarily about larger structures, and thinking about how individuals interact within parliaments, parties, or bureaucracies. Indeed, one could argue that if a researcher went too far down the individualist route, comparison would become irrelevant and all the researcher would care about would be the individual's behaviour. This problem is perhaps especially relevant for rational choice approaches, which tend to posit relatively common motivations for individuals (but see Bates et al. 2002).

Theory is at once the best friend and the worst enemy of the comparative researcher. On the one hand, theory is necessary for interpreting findings, as well as providing questions that motivate new research. Without political theory, research would simply be a collection of useful information and, although the information would be interesting, it would not advance the analytical understanding of

politics. Further, theory provides scholars with the puzzles to be solved, or at least addressed, through comparative research. Theory predicts certain behaviours, and if individuals or organizations do not behave in that manner, we need to probe more deeply. We should never underestimate the role that simple empirical observation can play in setting puzzles, but theory is a powerful source for ideas that add to the comparative storehouse of knowledge.

As important as theory is for interpreting findings and structuring initial research questions, theory is also a set of blinders for the researcher. After choosing our theoretical approach and developing a **research design** based on that theory, most people find it all too easy to find support for that approach. This tendency to find support for a theory is not necessarily the result of dishonesty or poor scholarship, but generally reflects a sincere commitment by the researcher to the approach and a consequent difficulty in identifying any disconfirming evidence. Most research published in political science tends to find support for the theory or model being investigated, although in many ways negative findings would be more useful.[4]

The difficulties in disconfirming theories is in part a function of the probabilistic methods most commonly used in political science research. More deterministic methods, including case-based methods such as process tracing (Beach and Pedersen 2019), tend to dismiss possible causes for variation in the presumed dependent variable, while probabilistic methods tend to demonstrate varying degrees of contribution to explanation. The use of qualitative comparative analysis (QCA, see Rihoux and Ragin 2009) can also dismiss certain combinations of variables as viable explanations for the outcomes in which we are interested, thus enabling us to reduce the wide range of viable explanations.

Given the tendency to find support for theories, comparative research could be improved by greater use of **triangulation**.[5] If we explore the same data with several alternative theories, or go into the field with alternative approaches in mind, we become more open to findings that do not confirm one or another approach. Likewise, if we could collect several forms of data, substantiating the findings of **quantitative** research with those from **qualitative** methods, then we could have a better idea whether the findings were valid.[6] This type of research can be expensive, involves a range of skills that many researchers may not possess, and may result in findings that are inconclusive and perhaps confusing.

When we discuss comparative political theory, we have to differentiate between *grand theories* and *middle-range theories*, or even analytical perspectives. At one stage of the development of comparative politics, the

Major approaches to comparative politics

Structural functionalism

The purpose of this approach was to identify the necessary activities (functions) of all political systems and then to compare the manner in which these functions were performed. As it was elaborated, it had developmental assumptions about the manner in which governing could best be performed that were closely related to the Western democratic model.

Systems theory

This approach considered the structures of the public sector as an open system that had extensive input (supports and demands) and output (policies) interaction with its environment.

Marxism

Class conflict is an interest-based explanation of differences among political systems. While offering some empirical predictions about those differences, Marxist analysis also posits a developmental pattern that would lead through revolution to a 'dictatorship of the proletariat'.

Corporatism

This approach stresses the central role of state and society interactions in governing, and especially the legitimate role of social interests in influencing policy. Even in societies such as Japan or the US, which have not met the criteria of being corporate states, the identification of the criteria provides a means of understanding politics.

Institutionalism

Although there are several approaches to **institutionalism**, they all focus on the central role of structures in shaping politics and also in shaping individual behaviour. As well as formal institutional patterns, institutions may be defined in terms of their rules and their routines, and thus emphasize their normative structure.

Governance

As an approach to comparative politics, governance has some similarities to structural functional analysis. It argues that certain tasks must be performed in order to govern a society and then posits that these tasks can be accomplished in a number of ways. In particular, scholars of governance are interested in the variety of roles that social actors may play in the process of making and implementing decisions.

Comparative political economy

Comparative political economy is the analysis of how political factors affect economic policy choices. The primary focus has been on how institutions of representation influence policy choices, but political executives and bureaucracies also exert some influences.

---

emphasis was on all-encompassing theories such as structural functionalism (Almond and Powell 1966) and systems theory (Easton 1965b) (see Box 2.2). These theories became popular as comparative politics had to confront newly independent countries in Africa and Asia, and find ways of including these countries in the same models as industrialized democracies. Those grand theories fulfilled their purpose of expanding the geographical concerns, as well as including less formal actors in the political process, but it became evident that by explaining everything they actually explained nothing. The functions of the political system and their internal dynamics discussed were so general that they could not produce meaningful predictions. Since that time, there has been a tendency to rely more on mid-range theories and analysis, although contemporary governance theories have some of the generality of functional theories. The principal exception to that generalization is the development of governance as an approach to comparative politics (Peters and Pierre 2016), emphasizing the need to perform certain key functions to be able to govern any society.

Finally, as we attempt to develop theory using multiple approaches, we need to be cognizant of their linkages with methodologies, and the possibilities for both qualitative and quantitative evidence. Comparative politics is both an area of inquiry and a method that emphasizes case selection as much as statistical controls to attempt to test its theories. Each approach we discuss has been linked with particular ways of collecting data, and we must be careful about what evidence is used to support an approach and what evidence is being excluded from the analysis.

It is also important to note that comparative politics, like the rest of political science, is becoming more experimental. The attempt is, again, to replicate the natural sciences and attempt to use treatment and control groups to ascertain the effects of the treatments on a dependent variable (Nielsen 2016). While these are important methods for attempting to improve the determination of cause-and-effect relationships, they also tend to eliminate context, one of the key features of comparative politics.

Alternative perspectives: the five 'I's

Institutions

The roots of comparative political analysis are in institutional analysis. As far back as Aristotle, scholars interested in understanding government performance, and seeking to improve that performance, concentrated on constitutional structures and the institutions created by those constitutions. Scholars documented differences in constitutions, laws, and formal structures of government, and assumed that if those structures were understood, the actual performance of governments could be predicted. Somewhat later, scholars in political sociology also began to examine political parties as organizations, or institutions, and to understand them in those terms (Michels 1915).

The behavioural revolution in political science, followed by the increasing interest in rational choice, shifted the **paradigm** in a more individualistic direction. The governing assumption, often referred to as *methodological individualism,* became that individual choices, rather than institutional constraints, produced observed differences in governments. It was difficult to avoid the obvious existence of institutions such as legislatures, but the rules of those organizations were less important, it was argued, than the nature of the individual legislators. Further, it was argued that decisions emerging from institutions were to a great extent the product of members' preferences, and those preferences were exogenous to the institutions.

While other areas of political science became almost totally absorbed with individual behaviour,

comparative politics remained truer to its institutional roots. Even though some conceptualizations of behaviour within institutions were shaped by individualistic assumptions, understanding structures is still crucial for comparative politics. With the return to greater concern with institutions in political science, the central role of institutions in comparative politics has at once been strengthened and made more analytical.

The 'new institutionalism' in political science (Peters 2011) now provides an alternative paradigm for comparative politics. This approach assumes that individuals do not act as atomistic individuals, but more on the basis of their connections of institutions and organizations. In fact, contemporary institutional theory provides at least four alternative conceptions of institutions, all having relevance for comparative analysis. *Normative* **institutionalism**, associated with James March and Johan P. Olsen, conceptualizes institutions as composed of norms and rules that shape individual behaviour through developing a 'logic of appropriateness'. Rational choice institutionalism, on the other hand, sees institutions as aggregations of incentives and disincentives that influence individual choice. Individuals would pursue their own self-interest utilizing the incentives provided by the institution. *Historical institutionalism* focuses on the role of ideas and the persistence of institutional choices over long periods of time, even in the face of potential dysfunctionality. Each approach to institutions provides a view of how individuals and structures interact in producing collective choices for society. And some *empirical institutionalism,* to some extent continuing older versions of institutionalism, asks the fundamental question of whether differences in institutions make any difference (Weaver and Rockman 1993; Przeworski 2004a).

Thus, merely saying that institutional analysis is crucial for comparative politics is insufficient. We need to specify how institutions are conceptualized, and what sort of analytical role they play. At one level, the concept of institutions appears formal, and not so different from some traditional thinking. That said, however, contemporary work on formal structures does examine their impact more empirically and conceptually than the traditional work did. Also, the range of institutions covered has expanded to include elements such as electoral laws and their effects on **party systems** and electoral outcomes (Taagapera and Shugart 1989).

Take, for example, studies of the difference between presidential and parliamentary institutions. This difference is as old as the formation of the first truly democratic political systems, but continues to be important. First, the conceptualization of the terms has been strengthened for both parliamentary and presidential (Elgie 1999) systems, and the concept of **divided government** provides a general means of understanding how executives and legislatures interact in governing.[7] Further, scholars have become more interested in understanding the effects of constitutional choice on presidential or parliamentary institutions. Some scholars (Linz 1990*a*; Colomer and Negretto 2005) have been concerned with the effects of presidential institutions on political stability, especially in less developed political systems. Others (Weaver and Rockman 1993) have been concerned with the effects of presidential and parliamentary institutions on policy choices and public-sector performance.

The distinction between presidential and parliamentary regimes is one of the most important institutional variables in comparative politics, but other institutional variables are also useful for comparison, such as the distinction between federal and **unitary states** (and among types of federalism (Hueglin and Fenna, 2015)). Further, we can conceptualize the mechanisms by which social actors such as interest groups interact with the public sector in institutional terms (Peters 2011: Chapter 5). The extensive literature on **corporatism** (see Molina 2007) has demonstrated the consequences of the structure of those interactions. Likewise, the more recent literature on networks in governance also demonstrates the structural interactions of public- and private-sector actors (Sørenson and Torfing 2007).

The preceding discussion concentrated on rather familiar institutional forms and their influence on government performance, but the development of institutional theory in political science has also focused greater attention on the centrality of institutions. Of the forms of institutional theory in political science, historical institutionalism has had perhaps the greatest influence in comparative politics. The basic argument of historical institutionalism is that initial choices shape policies and institutional attributes of structures in the public sector (Steinmo et al. 1992; Fieretos et al. 2016). For example, differences made in the initial choices about **welfare state** policies have persisted for decades and continue to resist change (Pierson 2001*b*). In addition to the observation about the persistence of programmes—usually referred to as **path dependence**—historical institutionalism has begun to develop theory about the political logic of that persistence (see Peters et al. 2005).

Institutional theory has been important for comparative politics, and for political science generally, but tends to be better at explaining persistence than explaining change (but see Mahoney and Thelen 2010*a*). For some aspects of comparative politics, we may be content with understanding static differences among systems, but dynamic elements are also important. As political systems change, especially democratizing and transitional regimes, political theory needs to provide an understanding of this as well as predicting change. While some efforts are being made to add more dynamic elements to institutional analysis (e.g. the 'actor-centered institutionalism' of Fritz Scharpf 1997*c*), institutional explanations remain somewhat constrained by the dominance of stability in the approach.

Historical institutionalism can also be related to important ideas about political change such as 'critical junctures' (Collier and Collier 1991; Capoccia and Keleman 2007), and the need to understand significant punctuations in the equilibrium that characterizes most institutionalist perspectives on governing (see also True et al. 2007). In this approach, change occurs through significant interruptions of the existing order, rather than through more incremental transformations. Much the same has been true of most models of transformation in **democratization** and transition, albeit with a strong concern about consolidation of the transformations (Berg-Schlosser 2008). This view contrasts with the familiar idea of incremental change that has tended to dominate much of political science.

Interests

A second approach to explaining politics in comparative perspective is to consider the interests that actors pursue through political action. Some years ago, Harold Lasswell (1936) argued that politics is about 'who gets what', and that central concern with the capacity of politics to distribute and redistribute benefits remains. In political theory, interest-based explanations have become more prominent, with the domination of rational choice explanations in much of the discipline (Lustick 1997; for a critique, see Green and Shapiro 1994). At its most basic, rational choice theory assumes that individuals are self-interested utility maximizers and engage in political action to receive benefits (usually material benefits) or to avoid costs (see Box 2.3). Thus, individual behaviour is assumed to be motivated by self-interest, and collective behaviour is the *aggregation of the individual behaviours* through bargaining, formal institutions, or conflict.

Rational choice theory provides a set of strong assumptions about behaviour, but less deterministic uses of the idea of interests can produce more useful comparative results. In particular, the ways in which societal interests are represented to the public sector and affect policy choices are crucial components of comparative analysis. The concept of corporatism was central to comparative analysis in the 1970s and 1980s (Schmitter 1974, 1989). The close linkage between social interests and the state that existed in many European and Latin American corporatist societies provided an important comparison for the pluralist systems of the Anglo-American countries, and produced a huge literature on the consequences of patterns of interest intermediation for policy choices and political legitimacy.

The argument of corporatism was that many political systems legitimated the role of interest groups and provided those groups with direct access to public decision-making. In particular, labour and management were given the right to participate in making economic policy, but in return had to be reliable partners, with their membership accepting the agreements (e.g. not striking). These institutionalized arrangements enabled many European and some Latin American countries to manage their economies with less conflict than in pluralist systems such as the UK.

The interest in corporatism also spawned a number of alternative means of conceptualizing both corporatism itself and the role of interests. For example, Stein Rokkan (1966) described the Scandinavian countries, especially Norway, as being 'corporate pluralist', with the tightly defined participation of most corporatist arrangements extended to a wide range of actors. Other scholars have discussed 'meso-corporatism' and 'micro-corporatism', and have attempted to apply the concept of corporatism to countries where it is perhaps inappropriate (Siaroff 1999).

The institutionalized pattern of linkage between social interests and the state implied in corporatism has been eroding and is being replaced by more loosely defined relationships such as networks (Sørenson and Torfing 2007). The shift in thinking about interest intermediation to some degree reflects a real shift in these patterns, and also represents changes in academic theorizing. As the limits of the corporatist model became apparent, the concept of networks has had significant appeal to scholars. This idea is that surrounding almost all policy areas there is a constellation of groups and actors seeking to influence that policy, who are increasingly connected formally to one another and to policy-making institutions. The tendency of this approach has been to modify the self-interested assumption somewhat in favour of a mixture of individual (group) and collective (network or society) interests.

Network theory has been developed with different levels of claims about the importance of the networks in contemporary governance. At one end, some scholars have argued that governments are no longer capable of effective governance and that self-organizing networks now provide governance (Rhodes 1997; for a less extreme view, see Kooiman 2003). For other scholars, networks are forms of interest involvement in governing, with formal institutions retaining the capacity to make effective decisions about governance. Further, the extent of democratic claims about networks varies among authors, with some arguing that these are fundamental extensions of democratic opportunities, and others concerned that their openness is exaggerated and that networks may become simply another form of exclusion for the less well-organized elements in society.

ZOOM-IN 2.3

Rational choice and comparative politics

Rational choice models have made significant contributions to the study of politics and government. By employing a set of simplifying assumptions, such as utility maximization and full information, rational choice models have enabled scholars to construct explanatory and predictive models with greater precision than would be possible without those assumptions. For example, if we assume that individuals act rationally to enhance their own self-interest, then we can understand how they will act when they have the position of a 'veto player' in a political process (Tsebelis 2002). Likewise, if we assume that voters engage in utility maximization, then their choice of candidates becomes more predictable than in other models that depend more on a mixture of sociological and psychological factors (e.g. partisan identification).

By positing these common motivations for behaviour, however, rational choice adds less to comparative politics than to other parts of the discipline of political science. Comparative politics tends to be more concerned with differences among political systems and their members than with similarities (but see Levi, 2009). Comparative politics, as a method of inquiry (Lijphart 1971) rather than a subject matter, relies on selecting cases based on their characteristics and then determining the impact of a small number of differences on observed behaviours. However, if everyone is behaving in the same way, important factors in comparative politics such as political culture, individual leadership, and ideologies become irrelevant. Differences in institutions remain important, or perhaps even more important, in comparison because their structures can be analysed through veto points or formal rules that create incentives and disincentives for behaviours.

Although we tend to think of interests almost entirely in material terms, there are other important interests as well. Increasingly, individuals and social groups define their interests in terms of identity and ethnicity, and seek to have those interests accommodated within the political system, along with their material demands.[8] This concern with the accommodation of socially defined interests can be seen in the literature on consociationalism (Lijphart 1968a). Consociationalism is a mode of governing in which political elites representing different communities coalesce around the need to govern, even in the face of intense social divisions. For example, this concept was devised originally to explain how religious groups in the Netherlands were able to coalesce and govern, despite deep historical divisions.

Like corporatism, consociationalism has been extended to apply to a wide range of political systems, including in Belgium, Canada, Malaysia, Colombia, and India, but has largely been rejected as a solution for the problems of Northern Ireland and Iraq. The concept is interesting for comparative political analysis, but, like corporatism, may reflect only one variation of a more common issue. Almost all societies have some forms of internal **cleavage** (Posner 2004) and find different means of coping with those cleavages. In addition to strictly consociational solutions, elite pacts (Higley and Gunther 1992; Collins 2006) have become another means of coping with difference and with the need to govern. The capacity to form these pacts has been crucial in resolving conflicts in some African countries, and presents hoped-for solutions for some conflicts in the Middle East (Hinnebusch 2006).

Comparative political economy represents another approach to comparative politics that relies largely on interest-based explanations. Governments are major economic actors and their policies influence the economic success of business, labour, and other groups in society. The dynamics of the political economy have gained special importance after the economic crisis beginning in 2008 and the increases in economic inequality that have followed. Therefore, there are significant political pressures to choose policies that favour those various groups in the economy (Hall 1997; Przeworski 2004a). Much of this literature focuses on the role of representation and representative institutions, but the public bureaucracy also plays a significant role in shaping those policies.

Approaches to comparative politics built on the basis of interest tend to assume that those interests are a basis for conflict, and that institutions must be devised to manage that conflict. Politics is inherently conflictual, as different interests vie for a larger share of the resources available to government, but conflict can go only so far if the political system is to remain viable. Thus, while interests may provide some of the driving force for change, institutions are required to focus that political energy in mechanisms for making and implementing policy. Institutional arrangements such as consociationalism and elite pacts can be used to ameliorate, if not solve conflicts that could threaten the viability of a political system (Durant and Weintraub, 2014) And, further, ideas can also be used to generate greater unity among populations that may be divided along ethnic or economic dimensions.

Ideas

Although ideas are amorphous and seemingly not closely connected to the choices made by government, they can have some independent effect on outcomes. That said, the mechanisms through which ideas exert that influence must be specified and their independent effect on choices must be identified (Béland and Cox 2011). In particular, we need to understand the consequences of mass culture, political ideologies, and specific ideas about policy. All these versions of ideas are significant, but each functions differently within the political process.

At the most general possible level, political culture influences politics, but that influence is often extremely vague. Political culture can be the residual explanation in comparative politics—when everything else fails to explain observed behaviours, then it must be political culture (Elkins and Simeon 1979). Therefore, the real issue in comparative analysis is to identify means of specifying those influences from culture, and other ideas, with greater accuracy. As comparative politics, along with political science in general, has moved away from behavioural explanations and interpretative understandings of politics, there has been less analytical emphasis on understanding political culture, and this important element of political analysis has been devalued.[9]

How can we measure political culture and link this somewhat amorphous concept to other aspects of governing? The most common means of measuring the concept has been surveys asking the mass public how they think about politics. For example, in a classic of political science research, *The Civic Culture* (Almond and Verba 1963), the public in five countries were asked about their attitudes towards politics, and particularly their attitudes to political participation. More recent examples of this approach to measurement include Ronald Inglehart's (1997) numerous studies using the World Values Survey, as well as studies that explore values in public and private organizations (Hofstede 2001).

Of course, before surveys for measuring political culture can be devised, scholars must have some ideas about the dimensions that should be measured. Therefore, conceptual development must go along with, or precede, measurement. Lucien Pye (1968) provided one interesting attempt at defining the dimensions of comparative political culture. He discussed culture as the tension between opposite values such as *hierarchy and equality, liberty and coercion, loyalty and commitment,* and *trust and distrust*. Although these dimensions of culture are expressed as dichotomies, political systems tend to have complex mixtures of these attributes that need to be understood to grasp how politics is interpreted within that society.

The anthropologist Mary Douglas (1978) (see also Table 2.1) provided another set of dimensions for understanding political culture that continues to be used extensively (Hood 2000). She has discussed culture in terms of the concepts of *grid* and *group*, both of which describe how individuals are constrained by their society and its culture. Grid is analogous to the dimension of hierarchy in Pye's framework, while group reflects constraints derived from membership in social groups. As shown in Table 2.1, bringing together these two dimensions creates four cultural patterns that it is argued influence government performance and the lives of individuals. These patterns are perhaps rather vague, but they do provide a means of approaching the complexities of political culture.

The trust and distrust dimension mentioned by Pye can be related to the explosion of the literature on social capital and the impact of trust on politics. The concept of social capital was initially developed in sociology, but gained greater prominence with Robert Putnam's research on Italy and the US (Putnam 1993, 2000). This concept was measured through surveys as well as through less obtrusive measures. What is perhaps most significant in the social capital literature is that the cultural elements are linked directly with political behaviour, of both individuals and systems (Hetherington and Huser 2014).

As well as the general ideas contained in political culture, political ideas also are important in the form of *ideologies*. In the twentieth century, politics in a number of countries was shaped by ideologies such as communism and fascism. Towards the end of the twentieth century and into the twenty-first, an ideology of **neoliberalism** came to dominate economic policy in the industrialized democracies and was diffused through less-developed systems by donor organizations such as the World Bank. Within the developing world, ideologies about development, such as Pancasila in Indonesia, reflect the important role of ideas in government, and a number of developing countries continue to use socialist ideologies to justify interventionist states.

Although ideologies have been important in comparative politics, there has been a continuing discussion of the decline—or end—of ideology in political life. First, with the acceptance of the mixed economy welfare state in most industrialized democracies, the argument was that the debate over the role of the state was over (Bell 1965). More recently, after the collapse of the Soviet Union, a similar argument was made concerning the exhaustion of political ideas and the end of political conflicts based on ideas (Fukuyama 1992). However, this presumed end of the role of ideas could be contrasted with the increased importance of conservative ideologies and the increased significance of religion as a source of political conflicts.

A final way in which ideas influence outcomes in comparative politics is through specific policy ideas. For example, while at one time economic performance was considered largely uncontrollable, after the intellectual revolution in the 1930s governments had tools for that control (Hall 1989). Keynesian economic management dominated for almost half a century, but then was supplanted by monetarism and, to a lesser extent, by supply-side economics. Likewise, different versions of the welfare state, for example the Bismarckian model of continental Europe and the Beveridge model in the UK (see Esping-Andersen 1990), have been supported by a number of ideas about the appropriate ways in which to provide social support.

In summary, ideas do matter in politics, even though their effects may be subtle. This subtlety is especially evident for political culture, but tracing the impact of ideas is in general difficult. Even for policy ideas that appear closely related to policy choices, it may be difficult to trace how the ideas are adopted and implemented (Braun and Busch 1999). Further, policy-learning (Sabatier and Jenkins-Smith 1993) and the social construction of agendas and political frames can shape behaviour (see Baumgartner and Jones 2015).

Table 2.1 Patterns of political culture		
Grid	Group	
	High	Low
High	Fatalist	Hierarchical
Low	Egalitarian	Individualist

Source: Douglas (1978).

Individuals

I have already discussed the methodological individualism that has become central to political theory. Although I argued that an excessive concern with individual behaviour, especially when based on an assumption that individual motivations are largely similar, may make understanding differences among political systems more difficult, it is still impossible to discount the importance of individuals when understanding how politics and government work. The importance of political biography and political diaries as sources of understanding is but one of many indications of how important individual-level explanations can be in understanding governing.

Many individual-level explanations are naturally focused on political elites and their role in the political process. One of the more interesting, and perhaps most suspect, ways of understanding elite behaviour is through personality. There have been a number of psychological studies, usually done from secondary sources, of major political figures (Freud and Bullitt 1967; Berman 2006). Most of these studies have focused on pathological elements of personality, and have tended to be less than flattering to the elites. Less psychological studies of leaders, e.g. James David Barber's typology of presidential styles (Barber 1992; see also Simonton 1993), have also helped to illuminate the role of individual leaders (see Table 2.2). Barber classifies political leaders in terms of their positive or negative orientations towards politics and their levels of activity, and uses the emerging types to understand how these individuals have behaved in office.

A more sociological approach to political leaders has stressed the importance of background and recruitment, with the assumption that the social roots of leaders will explain their behaviour. Putnam (1976) remarked several decades ago that this hypothesis was plausible, but unproven, and that assessment remains largely true. Despite the absence of strong links, there is an extensive body of research using this approach. The largest is the research on 'representative bureaucracy' and the question of whether public bureaucracies are characteristic of the societies they administer, and whether this makes any difference (Meier and Bohte 2001; Peters et al. 2015). While the representativeness of the bureaucracy is usually discussed at the higher, 'decision-making' levels, it may actually be more crucial where 'street-level bureaucrats' meet citizens (Hupe, 2019).

The ordinary citizen should not be excluded when considering individuals in comparative politics. The citizen as voter, participant in interest groups, or merely as the consumer of political media plays a significant role in democratic politics, and less obviously in non-democratic systems. The huge body of literature on cross-national voting behaviour has generated insights about comparative political behaviour. Further, the survey-based evidence on political culture already mentioned uses individual-level data to make some (tentative) statements about the system level.

In those portions of political science that deal with government activities, the role of the individual has become more apparent. Citizens are consumers of public services, and the **New Public Management** has placed individual citizens at the centre of public-sector activity (see Chapter 8 'Governments and Bureacracies'). This central role is true for the style of management now being pursued in the public sector. It is also true for a range of instruments that have been developed to involve the public in the programmes that serve them, and also for a range of instruments designed to hold public programmes accountable.

International environment

Much of the discussion of comparative politics is based on analysing individual countries, or components of countries. This approach remains valuable and important. That said, it is increasingly evident that individual countries are functioning in a globalized environment and it is difficult, if not impossible, to understand any one system in isolation. To some extent, the shifts in national patterns are mimetic, with one system copying patterns in another that appear effective and efficient (see DiMaggio and Powell 1991; see also Chapter 24 'Globalization and the nation-state'). In other cases, the shifts may be coercive, as when the European Union has established political as well as economic criteria for membership.

International influences on individual countries, although ubiquitous, also vary across countries. Some,

Table 2.2	Styles of political leaders		
Orientation to politics	Activity	
	Active	Passive
Positive	Bill Clinton	George H. W. Bush
	Tony Blair	Jim Callaghan
Negative	Richard Nixon	Calvin Coolidge
	Margaret Thatcher	John Major

Source: Based on Barber (1992). The role of political elites can also be seen in studies of political leadership (Helms 2013).

such as the US or Japan, have sufficient economic resources and lack direct attachments to strong **supranational** political organizations, and hence maintain much of their exceptionalism. Poorer countries lack economic autonomy and their economic dependence may produce political dependence as well, so their political systems may be influenced by other nations and by international organizations such as the World Bank and the United Nations.

The countries of the European Union present a particularly interesting challenge for comparative politics. While most of these countries have long histories as independent states, and have distinct political systems and political styles, their membership of the Union has created substantial convergence and homogenization. The growing literature on Europeanization (Knill 2001; Schimmelfennig and Sedelmeier 2005; see also Chapter 23 'The EU as a new political system') has attempted to understand these changing patterns of national politics in Europe and the increasingly common patterns of governance. This is not to say that countries with parliamentary democracy and countries with presidential systems will merge entirely, but there is reciprocal influence and some difficulties in sorting out sources of change.

The case of the European Union also points out the extent to which interactions among all levels of government are important for shaping behaviours in any one level. The concept of 'multilevel governance' has been popular for analysing policy-making in the European Union (Hooghe and Marks 2001; Bache and Flinders 2004). For individuals coming from federal regimes, this interaction is a rather familiar feature of governing, and in many cases the sub-national governments have been the principal policy and political innovators. For many European countries, however, multilevel governance is a more distinctive phenomenon that links both **internationalization** and the increasing political power of subnational governments to the national government.

The interaction among countries, and across levels of government, raises an analytical question. When we observe a particular political pattern in a country, is that pattern a product of indigenous forces and national patterns, or is it a product of diffusion? The so-called 'Galton problem' has been present for as long as there have been comparative studies, but its importance has increased as interactions have increased, and as the power of international organizations has increased (Seeliger 1996). Unfortunately, we may never really be able to differentiate all the various influences on any set of observed patterns in the public sector, despite the numerous solutions that have been proposed for the problem (Braun and Gilardi 2006).

While diffusion among countries can be conceived as an analytical problem for social sciences, it can be a boon for governments and citizens. If we conceptualize the international environment as a laboratory of innovations in both political action and policy, then learning from innovations in other settings becomes a valuable source for improving governing. A number of governments have attempted to institutionalize these practices through evidence-based policy-making (Cairney, 2016).

Add a sixth 'I': interactions

Up to this point, I have dealt with five possible types of explanation independently. That strategy is useful as a beginning and for clarifying our thoughts about the issue in question, but it vastly understates the complexity of the real world of politics. In reality, these five sources of explanation interact with one another, so that to understand decisions made in the political process we need to have a broader and more comprehensive understanding. Given that much of contemporary political science is phrased in terms of testing hypotheses derived from specific theories, this search for complexity may not be welcomed by some scholars, but it does reflect political realities.

Let me provide some examples. Institutions are a powerful source of explanations and are generally our first choice for those explanations. However, institutions do not act—the individuals within them act, and so we need to understand how institutions and individuals interact in making decisions. Some individuals who may be very successful in some political settings would not be in others. Margaret Thatcher was a successful prime minister in the majoritarian British system, but her directive leadership style might have been totally unsuccessful in consensual Scandinavian countries, or even perhaps Westminster systems, such as Canada, that also have a more consensual style of policy-making. And these interactions can also vary across time, with a bargainer such as Lyndon Johnson being likely to have been unsuccessful in the more partisan American Congresses of the early twenty-first century.

These interactions between individual political leaders and their institutions raise a more theoretical concern for contemporary comparative politics. Although there is still a significant institutional emphasis in comparative politics, much of contemporary political theory is based on the behaviour of individuals. Therefore, a major challenge for building better theory for comparison is linking the micro-level behaviour of individuals with the macro-level behaviour of institutions. The tendency to attribute relatively common motivations for individuals to some extent simplifies this issue, but in so doing may oversimplify the complexity of the interactions (Anderson 2009).

Another example of interaction among possible explanations can occur between the international environment and institutions. Many of the states in Asia and Latin America have adopted a 'developmental state' model to cope with their relatively weak position in the international marketplace and to use the power of the state for fundamental economic change (Evans 1995; Minns 2006). On the other hand, the more affluent states of Europe and North America have opted for a more liberal approach to economic growth—a model that better fits their position in the international political economy.

The literature on **social movements** provides a clear case for the interaction of multiple streams of explanation (see Chapter 16 'Social movements'). On the one hand, social movements can be conceptualized as institutions, albeit ones with relatively low levels of institutionalization. These organizations can also be understood as reflecting an ideological basis, and as public manifestations of ideas such as environmentalism and women's rights. Finally, some social movements reflect underlying social and economic interests, although again in somewhat different ways than would conventional interest groups. Again, by using all these approaches to triangulate these organizations, the researcher gains a more complete understanding of the phenomenon.

Multiple streams of explanation and their interaction help to emphasize the point made at the outset of this chapter. The quality of research in comparative politics can be enhanced by the use of multiple theories and multiple methodologies when examining the same 'dependent variable'. Any single analytical approach provides a partial picture of the phenomenon in question, but only through a more extensive array of theory and evidence can researchers gain an accurate picture of the complex phenomena with which comparative politics is concerned. This research strategy is expensive, and may yield contradictory results, but it may be one means of coping with complexity.

Much of contemporary political science does not, in fact, cope well with the increasing complexity of their surrounding economies and societies, or indeed of politics itself (see Jervis 1997). Increasing levels of participation and the increasing 'wickedness' of policy problems demands that we develop the means to understand a non-linear world better and have tools to assist in that understanding. Somewhat paradoxically, that may demand the use of (seemingly) relatively simplistic tools such as case studies to begin to understand the dynamics inherent in political processes and their relationships with their environments.

KEY POINTS

- Comparative politics has institutional roots: more than other fields of political science, it stresses the role of institutions in shaping and constraining the behaviour of individuals. However, it is weak in explaining change.

- Rational choice analysis assumes that individuals are self-interested utility maximizers who engage in political action to receive benefits (and avoid costs). As an approach, it is less relevant in comparative politics than in other fields.

- Although cultural explanations are often vague and 'residual', ideas matter, and a great deal of research investigates the impact of cultural traits on political life (e.g. on democratic stability). Recent research stresses factors such as social capital and trust.

- As the last part of this volume stresses, single political systems are increasingly facing international influences because of integration and **globalization**.

What more is needed?

The preceding discussion gives an idea of major approaches to comparative political analysis. These five broad approaches provide the means of understanding almost any political issue (whether within a single country or comparatively), yet they do not address the full range of political issues as well as they might. There are at least two comparative questions that have not been explored as completely as they might have been. We can gain some information about these issues utilizing the five 'I's already advanced, but it would be useful to explore the two questions more fully.

Process

Perhaps the most glaring omission in comparative analysis is an understanding of the **political process**. If we look back over the five 'I's, much of their contribution to understanding is premised on rather static conceptions of politics and governing, and thus issues of process are ignored. This emphasis on static elements in politics is unfortunate, given that politics and governing are inherently dynamic and it would be very useful to understand better how the underlying processes function. For example, while we know a great deal about legislatures as institutions, as well as about individual legislators, comparative politics has tended to abandon concern about the legislative process.

Institutions provide the most useful avenue for approaching issues of process. If we adopt the common-sense idea about institutions, then each major formal institution in the political system has a particular set of processes that can be more or less readily comparable across systems. Further, various aspects of process may come together and might constitute a policy process that, at a relatively high analytical level, has common features. Even if we do have good understanding of the processes within each institution, as yet we do not have an adequate comparative understanding of the process taken more generally.

Outcomes

Having all these explanations for political behaviour, we should also attempt to specify what these explanations actually explain—the dependent variable for comparative politics? For behavioural approaches to politics, the dependent variables will be individual-level behaviour, such as voting or decisions made by legislators. For institutionalist perspectives, the dependent variable is the behaviour of individuals within institutions, with the behaviour shaped by either institutional values or the rule and incentives provided by those institutions. Institutionalists tend to be more concerned about the impact of structures on public-sector decisions, while behavioural models focus on the individual decision-maker and attributes that might affect his/her choices.

As already implied, one of the most important things that scholars need to understand in comparative politics is what governments actually do. If, as Harold Lasswell argued, politics is about 'who gets what', then public policy is the essence of political action and we need to focus more on public policy. As Chapter 1 'The relevance of comparative politics' shows, this was indeed the case. However, policy outcomes are not just the product of politics and government action, but rather reflect the impact of economic and social conditions. Therefore, understanding comparative policy requires linking political decisions with other social, economic, and cultural factors. Unfortunately, after having been a central feature of comparative politics for some time, comparative policy studies appear to be out of fashion. True, some of those concerns appear as comparative political economy, or perhaps as studies of the welfare state (Myles and Pierson 2001), but the more general concern with comparing policies and performance has disappeared in the contemporary literature in comparative politics.

If we look even more broadly at comparative politics, then the *ultimate dependent variable is governance*, or the capacity of governments to provide direction to their societies. Governance involves *establishing goals for society, finding the means for reaching those goals, and then learning from the successes or failures of their decisions* (Pierre and Peters 2000; 2016). All other activities in the public sector can be put together within this general concept of governance. The very generality of the concept of governance poses problems for comparison, as did the structural–functionalist and systems theories (Almond and Powell 1966) popular earlier in comparative politics. Still, by linking a range of government activities and demonstrating their cumulative effects, an interest in governance helps counteract attempts to overly compartmentalize comparative analysis. To some extent, it returns to examining whole systems and how the constituent parts fit together, rather than focusing on each individual institution or actor.

Governance comes as close to the grand functionalist theories of the 1960s and 1970s as almost anything else in recent developments in comparative political analysis (see Box 2.2). Like those earlier approaches to comparative politics, governance is essentially functionalist, positing that there are certain crucial functions that any system of governance must perform, and then attempting to determine which actors perform those tasks, regardless of the formal assignment of tasks by law. While some governance scholars have emphasized the role of social actors rather than government actors in delivering governance, this remains an empirical question that needs to be investigated, rather than merely inferred from the theoretical presumptions of the author.

Governance also goes somewhat beyond the comparative study of public policy to examine not only the outputs of the system, but also its capacity to adapt. One of the more important elements of studying contemporary governance is the role of accountability and feedback, and the role of monitoring previous actions of the public sector. This emphasis is similar to feedback in **systems theory** (see Figure I.1 in the Introduction to this volume), but does not have the equilibrium assumptions of the earlier approach. Rather, governance models tend to assume some continuing development of policy capacity as well as institutional development to meet the developing needs.

KEY POINTS

- One weak point of comparative politics is its focus on the static elements of the political system and a neglect of dynamic political processes. The field of comparative politics, with greater attention to processes, is comparative public policy analysis.

- The dependent variable in comparative politics varies according to approaches; but, perhaps, the ultimate dependent variable is 'governance', i.e. establishing goals for society, finding means to reach those goals, and then learning from the successes or failures of their decisions.

Conclusion

Understanding politics in a comparative perspective is far from easy, but having some form of theoretical or analytical guidance is crucial to that understanding. The discussion in this chapter devotes little time to grand theory; rather, it has focused on analytical perspectives that provide researchers with a set of variables that can be used to approach comparative research questions. These five 'I's were phrased in rather ordinary language, but underneath each is a strong theoretical core. For example, if we take the role of individuals in politics, we can draw from political psychology, elite theory, and role theory for explanations.

Comparative politics should be at the centre of theory-building in political science, but that central position is threatened by the emphasis on individual-level behaviour. Further, the domination of US political scientists in the marketplace of ideas has tended to produce a somewhat unbalanced conception of the relevance of comparative research in contemporary political science. I would still argue that the world provides a natural laboratory for understanding political phenomena. We cannot, as experimenters, manipulate the elements in that environment, but we can use the evidence available from natural experiments to test and to build theory.

 QUESTIONS

Knowledge-based

1. What is the purpose of theory in comparative politics?

2. What is a functionalist theory?

3. What is meant by triangulation in social research?

4. What forms of institutional theory are used in comparative politics, and what contributions do they make?

5. Do institutions make a difference?

Critical thinking

1. Both behavioural and rational choice approaches focus on the individual. Where do they differ?

2. Does political culture help to understand political behaviour in different countries?

3. Do people always act out of self-interest in politics?

4. Will globalization make comparative politics obsolete?

5. Are the policy choices made by political systems a better way of understanding them than factors such as formal institutions or voting behaviour?

≋ FURTHER READING

Basic discussions

Bates, R., Greif, A., Levi, M., Rosenthal, J.-L., and Weingast, B. (2002) *Analytic Narratives* (Princeton, NJ: Princeton University Press).

Braun, D., and M. Magetti (2015) *Comparative Politics: Theoretical and Methodological Challenges* (Cheltenham: Edward Elgar).

Geddes, B. (2002) *Paradigms and Sand Castles: Theory Building and Research Design in Comparative Politics* (Ann Arbor, MI: University of Michigan Press).

Peters, B. G. (2013) *Strategies for Comparative Political Research* (Basingstoke: Palgrave).

Institutional theories

March, J. G. and Olsen, J. P. (1989) *Rediscovering Institutions* (New York: Free Press).

Steinmo, S., Thelen, K. A., and Longstreth, F. (1992) *Structuring Politics* (Cambridge: Cambridge University Press).

Interest-based theories

Sørenson, E. and Torfing, J. (2007) *Theories of Democratic Network Governance* (Basingstoke: Palgrave).

Tsebelis, G. (2002) *Veto Players* (Princeton, NJ: Princeton University Press).

The role of ideas

Beland, D. and Cox, R. H. (2011) *Ideas and Politics in Social Science Research* (New York: Oxford University Press).

Putnam, R. D. (1993) *Making Democracy Work: Civic Traditions in Modern Italy* (Princeton, NJ: Princeton University Press).

Individual theories

Greenstein, F. I. (1987) *Personality and Politics* (Princeton, NJ: Princeton University Press).

Helms, L. (2013) *Oxford Handbook of Political Leadership* (Oxford: Oxford University Press).

The role of the international environment

Cowles, M. G. and Caporaso, J. A. (2002) *Europeanization and Domestic Change* (Ithaca, NY: Cornell University Press).

Pierre, J. (2013) *Globalization and Governance* (Cheltenham: Edward Elgar).

Governance

Peters, B. G. and Pierre, J. (2016) *Governance and Comparative Politics* (Cambridge: Cambridge University Press).

ENDNOTES

1. This classification of research types comes from Arend Lijphart's seminal article (Lijphart 1971).

2. A great deal of political science theory has been developed in reference to the US, given the size and importance of the political science profession there. However, a good deal of that theory does not appear relevant beyond the boundaries of the US (in some cases, not within those boundaries either).

3. This is something of an oversimplification of the assumptions of rational choice approaches, but the central point here is not the subtlety of some approaches but rather the reliance on individual-level explanations. For a more extensive critique of the assumptions see Box 13.5 in Chapter 13 'Party systems'.

4. That is, if we could reject more theories and models, then we could focus on the more useful ones. As it is, we are overstocked with positive findings and theories that have credible support.

5. The classic example of a study that uses triangulation explicitly is Allison (1971). However, this book uses multiple theories, but it does not verify the results through multiple research methods.

6. See, for example, Adcock and Collier (2001), who stress the need for common standards of validity for all varieties of measurement, as well as the interaction of those forms of measurement.

7. Lijphart (1999) has provided a slightly different conceptualization by distinguishing between majoritarian and consensual political systems (see Chapter 5 on 'Democracies'). Some parliamentary systems, such as the Westminster system, are majoritarian, designed to produce strong majority governments that alternate in office. Others, such as in the Scandinavian countries, may have alternation in office, but the need to create coalitions and an underlying consensus on many policy issues results in less alternation in policy.

8. These shifts are to some extent a function of changes in political culture, especially the movement towards 'post-industrial politics' (Inglehart 1990).

9. This is truer for US than for European political science. Discourse theory and the use of rhetorical forms of analysis have been of much greater relevance in Europe than they have in North America, and qualitative methodologies remain more at the centre of European political analysis.

Visit the Online Resources that accompany this book for additional material, including country profiles, comparative data sets, flashcard glossaries, and web directory.

www.oup.com/he/caramani5e

3

Comparative research methods

Paul Pennings and Hans Keman

Chapter contents

Reader's guide

In this chapter, the 'art of comparing' is explored by demonstrating how to relate a theoretically guided research question to a properly founded research answer by developing an adequate research design. First, the role of variables in comparative research is highlighted. Second, the meaning of 'cases' and their selection is discussed. These are important steps in any comparative research design. Third, the focus turns to the 'core' of the comparative method: the use of the logic of comparative inquiry to analyse the relationships between variables—representing theory—and the information contained in the cases—the data. Finally, some problems common to the use of comparative methods are discussed.

Introduction

As the Introduction to this volume stresses, both its substance and its method characterize comparative politics. The method is the 'toolkit' of what, when, and how to compare political systems. In this chapter, the focus is on research methods used in comparative political science: what rules and standards should we adopt to develop a comparative research design?[1] A research design is a crucial step for developing and testing theories and for the verification of rival theories. Hence, as Peters emphasizes, '[t]he only thing that should be universal in studying comparative politics . . . is a conscious attention to explanation and research design' (Peters 1998: 26). Theory development and research design are closely interlinked in comparative politics.

Contrary to everyday practice, where most people are often *implicitly* comparing situations, in comparative politics the issue of what and how to observe reality is *explicitly* part of the comparative method. Dogan and Pelassy (1990: 3), for example, remark '[t]o compare is a common way of thinking. Nothing is more natural than to consider people, ideas, or institutions in relation to other people, ideas and institutions. We gain knowledge through reference.' Yet, the evolution of comparative politics has moved on from implicit comparisons in pre-modern times to explicit ways of comparing political systems and related processes. The major modern development in comparative political science is on linking theory to evidence by means of comparative methods. The particular method to be used depends on the research question (RQ) asked and the research answer (RA) to be given (see also Box 3.1). The actual method chosen is what we label research design (RD), and that is what this chapter is about.

A theory, in its simplest form, is a meaningful statement about the relationship between two real-world phenomena: X, the independent variable, and Y, the dependent variable. According to theory, it is expected that change in one variable will be related to change in the other. The conceptual and explanatory understanding of such a relationship is the point of departure for conducting research by comparing empirical evidence across systems (see also Brady and Collier 2004: 309; Burnham et al. 2004: 57). In more formal terms, a theory posits the *dependent variable* in the analysis—what is to be explained? Additionally, the researcher wishes to know: what are the most likely 'causes' of the phenomenon under investigation? Again, in formal terms: which *independent variables*,

or explanatory factors, can account for the variation of the dependent variable across different systems (e.g. countries) or features of political systems (e.g. parties)? The answer to this question rests heavily on the development of a 'correct' research design. Comparative methods can be considered, therefore, as a 'bridge' between the research question asked and the research answer proposed. This is what we label the 'triad' RQ → RD → RA.

Developing a research design in comparative politics requires careful elaboration. First, the research design should enable the researcher to *answer the question* under examination. Second, the given answer(s) ought to meet the *'standards' set in the social sciences*: are the results valid (authoritative), reliable (irrefutable), and generalizable (postulated) knowledge (Sartori 1994)? Third, are the research design and the methods used indeed *suitable for the research goals* set? This chapter elaborates these issues and attempts to guide the student towards linking research questions to research answers.

KEY POINTS

- The proper use and correct application of methods is essential in comparative politics.

- A correct application implies that the comparative method meets the 'standards' set, in terms of validity, reliability, and its use in a wider sense, i.e. generalizability.

- The relationship between variables and cases in comparative research is crucial in order to reach empirically founded conclusions that will further knowledge in political science.

ZOOM-IN 3.1

The triad RQ → RD → RA

The point of departure is that all research questions are theory guided. The *theoretical* guidance is expressed in relating research questions (RQs) to research answers (RAs) in the shape of *logical* relationships between a dependent variable (Y: what is to be explained) and the independent variables (X: the most likely causes, i.e. factors serving as an explanation). The 'bridge' between RQ and RA is called a research design (RD). Therefore, the comparative method is a *means to an end*: to make choices as to which of the potentially vast mass of relevant empirical data (the evidence) and possible causes (X) explaining variations in Y are valid and reliable in arriving at a research answer.

The role of variables in linking theory to evidence

Since the 1960s, the comparative approach in political science has been considered highly relevant to theory development (see also the Introduction to this volume). Therefore, a research question should always either be guided by theory or itself constitute a potential answer to an existing theoretical argument. The comparative method is about observing and comparing carefully selected information (across space or time, or both) on the basis of a meaningful, if not causal, relationship between variables. A variable is a concept that can be systematically observed (and measured) in various situations (such as in countries or over time). It allows us to understand the similarities and differences between observed phenomena. For example, we can make a difference between democracies and non-democracies or between different types of democracies (e.g. presidential, semi-presidential, and parliamentary). The extent to which the similarities and differences across systems are more or less systematic can tell us more about the plausibility of a theoretical relationship under review. For example, Linz and Stepan (1996), discussing the pros and cons of presidentialism, argued that parliamentary democracies are more enduring than presidential ones. They found that the independent variable—parliamentary versus presidential systems (a dichotomy)—differed considerably in terms of political stability measured in years.

Typologies are often used as a first step in examining the theoretical association between two variables without explicitly arguing a causal relationship. The first step towards a typology is to decide what is to be classified on the basis of a research question. Take, as an example, research on the link between federalism and electoral laws. Different **electoral systems** (e.g. proportional and majoritarian) are distinguished and their significance for territorial structures within a nation (e.g. federal and unitary) is assessed. The major problem of this type of analysis is that miscomparing can lead to misclassification, and therefore to wrongly informed conclusions. However, this can be avoided by checking that all (in this case, four) cells validly include at least a case (inclusiveness), and, further, that one case cannot be placed in more than one cell (exclusiveness). This is called an 'in-between' or hybrid case (see also Braun 2015).

In sum, the comparative method allows us to investigate hypothesized relationships among variables systematically and empirically. In contrast with the methodology of the 'exact sciences', however, the conclusions are drawn from comparisons, *not* experiments. Therefore, the real world of comparative politics provides a *quasi-experimental* workplace for political scientists to examine how the complex world of politics 'turns' by demonstrating in a systematic and rigorous fashion *theoretical relationships among variables*.

An example of how the triad (recall Box 3.1) works and helps to answer a contested issue is the debate, 'Does politics matter?' (see Chapter 21 'The welfare state'). The dependent variable or the outcome (Y) in this example is **welfare state** development, i.e. what the researcher seeks to explain. It is called dependent because we expect that the variation in welfare state provisions across systems also depends on one or more independent variables.[2] As a tentative *answer*, the researcher comes up with a *hypothesis*. In this example, the variation in welfare state development (Y) is dependent on the relative strength of left-wing parties and trade unions in a country (X). This research answer, or hypothesis, is a conjecture about the relationship between the dependent variable and the independent variable and is supposed to explain the outcome, i.e. the development of the welfare state. In a comparative research design, a theoretical relationship is elaborated to account for the differences and similarities in welfare state development (Figure 3.1).

Obviously, any type of 'X–Y' relationship in social science is an abstraction from the complexities of the real world. This is deliberate. By means of hypotheses or explanations (X), those factors are included that can account for the variation in Y. This procedure allows us to establish whether or not a meaningful relationship indeed exists, and whether or not this relationship can be qualified as 'causal' or not (i.e. it is noted as $X \rightarrow Y$).

Causality is a fraught concept in the social sciences and in strict terms is hard to establish. Yet, it is now accepted that if the variation in the dependent variable (Y—here: more or less expansion of the welfare state) is evidently and systematically related to the variation in (one of) the independent variable(s) and a theory as to why this is the case (X_1—socio-economic; and X_2—political indicators), then we can assume causality—at least for the cases included in the analysis. This refers to the idea of 'internal validity' (see Box 3.2).

Our ability to establish causal relationships by means of a comparative research design is considered a major advantage. As we have already stated, comparative analysis is often labelled 'quasi-experimental', meaning that, to a certain extent, we can manipulate reality, enabling the researcher to conduct *descriptive inference* (King et al. 1994: 34ff). This implies that the empirically founded relationship between the independent and dependent variables, based on a number of observations, allows generalization over and beyond the cases under review. Hence, the results of the analysis are considered to be relevant for all political systems where a welfare state is present or emerging (for instance, in Southern and Eastern Europe since the 1990s). In these circumstances, the researcher claims that his/her results are 'externally valid' (see Box 3.2). It is obvious that this 'leap' from the empirical evidence to a more general explanation (the 'theory') is open to criticism (like the occurrence of multi-causality and conjunctural causality; see 'The use of Methods of Agreement and Difference in comparative analysis' below) and drives contesting theories—in this

<table>
<tr><td>🔍</td><td>DEFINITION 3.2</td></tr>
</table>

Internal and external validity in comparative methods

Internal validity refers to the degree to which descriptive or causal inferences from a given set of cases are indeed correct for most, if not all, the cases under inspection. *External* validity concerns the extent to which the results of the comparative research can be considered to be valid for other more or less similar cases, but were not included in the research.

Both types of validity are equally important, but it should be noted that there is a trade-off (Peters 1998: 48; Pennings 2016). The more the cases included in the analysis can be considered as representative, the more 'robust' the overall result will be (*external validity*). Conversely, however, the analysis of fewer cases may well be conducive to a more coherent and solid conclusion for the set of cases that is included (*internal validity*). It should be noted that the concepts of internal and external validity are *ideal-typical* in nature: in a perfect world with complete information, the standards of both internal and external validity may well be met, but in practice this is hard to achieve.

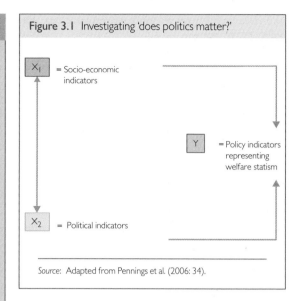

Figure 3.1 Investigating 'does politics matter?'

X_1 = Socio-economic indicators

Y = Policy indicators representing welfare statism

X_2 = Political indicators

Source: Adapted from Pennings et al. (2006: 34).

example, politics does *not* matter but socio-economic developments do—that are developed to disprove or to enhance the theory.

Hence, socio-economic development (represented as X_1 in Figure 3.1) is considered as an important 'cause' explaining the variation in the development and level of welfare statism across Organisation for Economic Co-operation and Development (OECD) countries (e.g. Wilensky 1975). Political variables, such as differences between left- and right-wing parties with respect to how much welfare state is sufficient or the relative strength of these parties in government and the strength of trade unions (X_2 in Figure 3.1), were considered as less relevant (or merely coincidental) to explaining the growth of a welfare state. In other words, the research conducted appeared to prove that 'politics did *not* matter'.

Yet, a major objection concerned the finding that the *non*-political variables (X_1 in Figure 3.1) were insufficiently capable of explaining *why* cross-system differences in welfare statism *differed*, although in many instances the non-political variables X_1 were quite *similar*. The descriptive inference was not homogeneous (i.e. the assumption that a given set of variables always produces the same outcome). This criticism was supported by empirical observations. It appeared that levels of welfare statism tended to become more *divergent* (i.e. more different), whereas the explanatory variables (X_1) would predict otherwise: a *convergent*

(i.e. more similar) development would be expected to occur. Another criticism concerned the **operationalization** of the dependent variable. By examining the various policy components of 'welfare statism' (such as expenditure on social security, education, and health care), it could be demonstrated that the *design* of the welfare state showed a large cross-system variation in the distribution of what was spent on education, health care, and social security within the different countries. Table 22.2 (Chapter 22 'The impact of public policies') shows that change in social expenditures differed considerably between 1980 and 2003. In short, the dependent variable 'welfare statism' could neither exclusively nor causally be linked to non-political factors alone, and nor could political factors be ignored. The comparative analysis conducted demonstrated that political variables appeared to have a considerable (and statistically significant) impact as

KEY POINTS

- Theory comes *before* method and is expressed in its simplest form as the relationship between dependent (Y) and independent (X) variables. The research method follows the research question in order to find the proper research answer.

- Research answers are (tentative) hypotheses that are interpreted by means of descriptive inference on the basis of *comparative* evidence, possibly allowing for causal interpretation.

- The research design is the toolkit to systematically *link* empirical evidence to theoretical relationships by means of comparative methods, *enhancing* the internal and external validity of the results.

well. Hence, the 'new' research answer became: 'Yes, politics does matter'!

Note that the research design not only concerns establishing the $X_2 \rightarrow Y$ relationship, proving that political variables played their role, but is also controlling for the relative impact of 'politics' by including the original explanatory relationship $X_1 \rightarrow Y$ as a rival explanation. The message conveyed here is that research in comparative politics requires a precise and detailed elaboration of a research design—in terms of relationships examined by means of variables and developing corroborating evidence across the cases under review—connecting research questions to research answers that are conducive to causal interpretation by means of descriptive inferences.[3] In the next section, 'Comparing cases and case selection', we turn to selecting the cases suited for **comparison**. This will direct the 'logic' of comparison implied in the research design to be used.

Comparing cases and case selection

Recall that linking theory to evidence always entails the reduction of real-world complexities so as to analyse the (logical) relationship between the X and Y variables. Hence, researchers must make decisions about *what* to compare, i.e. select the cases (the carriers of relevant information), and about *how* this information can be transformed into variables. The key to the development of a proper comparative research design is to decide *which* cases are useful for comparing and *how many* can be selected (see Figure 3.2). The answers to these questions have led to many views, debates, and practical solutions (see Brady and Collier 2004; Braun and Maggetti 2015; Panke 2018; Prescott and Urlacher 2018). An example of a practical solution is a web application called the Case Selector that helps to arrive at a systematic and transparent case selection by identifying most and least similar cases which are most suited for doing case study research (Prescott and Urlacher 2018). Such a tool may help to handle the apparent trade-off between selecting many cases, but with few relevant variables available for analysis, or a few crucial (or contrasting) cases, but with many variables for use. We shall first clarify what a 'case' is.

Cross-case and within-case

The term 'case' has a general meaning in social science methodology, but in comparative methods it is used in a specific manner and is to some extent confusing (Pennings et al. 2006: 34ff). In comparative politics, cases denote the units of observation to be compared.

Often it concerns countries, but one can also compare sub-systems (like regions) or organized entities (like governments or bureaucracies). Yet the level of measurement may be different. Take, for instance, individual voters in several countries: the country is the case compared and determines the level of *analysis*, whereas the voter is the unit of observation (within the case). Conversely, if one compares **party governments** within a country, both the case and the unit of observation—governments—are at the same level of observation. For clarity, we propose to reserve the term 'case' in comparative methods for any type of *system* included in the analysis (recall Note 1). In addition, we refer to *observations* as the values (or scores) of a variable under investigation. For example, if one compares party behaviour of regional parties, then the 'case' is the regional party *within* a system. Conversely, if the welfare state is the focus of comparison, then this concerns the systems to be compared. Public expenditures on social security are the empirical value for each system (see, for instance, Table 22.4). In Box 3.3, cases and variables are discussed in terms of a data matrix (i.e. the organization of the empirical observations by case and by variable). It is important to be precise in this matter because the *number* of observations—large- or small-N—determines what type of (**quantitative** or **qualitative**) analysis is feasible in terms of descriptive inference, given the available variation across the systems, or cases, under review (Pennings et al. 2006: 11; Panke 2018).

The relationship between the cases selected and the variables employed to analyse the research question is a crucial concern. As can be seen from Figure 3.2, the process of case selection is structured as a kind of scale: from one case (often including many variables) to maximizing the number of cases (often with few(er) variables). In addition, it is sometimes suggested that this choice between few or many cases is related to the type of data—quantitative or qualitative—used. This is debatable (see also Brady and Collier 2004: 246–7). For example, the study of welfare states often combines qualitative elements with statistical data (e.g. Kumlin and Stadelmann-Steffen 2016). Or take the study on 'social capital' by Putnam (1993), who combines survey data (reporting attitudes across the population) with a historical analysis of the development of politics and society in Italy since medieval times. Hence, comparative historical analysis can be usefully combined with a cross-sectional quantitative approach.

There is on ongoing discussion on how to combine different types of data. This is called **triangulation**, methodological **pluralism**, or multi-mehod research. In its purest form, it involves cross-case causal inference and within-case causal mechanism analysis and inference (Goertz 2016), but other combinations of methods are also possible. Collier and Elman (2008) distinguish between three types of multi-method research. The first type combines conventional qualitative approaches, such as case study methodologies and interviews. The second type combines quantitative and qualitative methods, for example statistical analysis and process tracing. The third type combines conventional qualitative methods with either constructivist or interpretivist approaches (for more detailed overviews, see: Berg-Schlosser 2012; Giraud and Maggetti 2015; Goertz 2016; Beach 2019). The strength of methodological pluralism is that it helps to overcome the limitations of a single design, for example doing either interviews or statistical analysis. Multi-methods enable the researcher to both explain (using cross-case data) and interpret (using within-case data). It also allows the researcher to address a question or theoretical perspective at different levels, for example both at the individual level and at the country level. This can be useful when unexpected results arise from a prior study. In addition, multi-methods may help to generalize, to a degree, qualitative data. There are also a number of potential weaknesses or risks involved. The results may sometimes be puzzling because different types of data and designs may generate unequal evidence. As Braun and Maggetti (2015) note, there is no 'yardstick' available to judge the extent to which the different methods indeed reinforce the results of the analysis. Hence, before one decides to adopt a multi-method approach these risks should be carefully considered (Creswell 2015; Beach 2018).

These complexities may motivate researchers to stick to one method and keep on improving it instead of combining it with other approaches. One example of an innovative method that is used as a single method is process tracing (see Trampusch and Palier 2016; Beach and Pedersen 2019). This is a qualitative method used to evaluate complex causal processes by means of historical narratives and/or within-case analysis. The main goal of process tracing is to make unit-level causal inferences (i.e. how a given cause affects a single unit like an international organization or a country). It focuses on a causal mechanism by examining how 'X' produces a series of conditions that come together to produce 'Y'. Process tracing is a useful tool for testing hypotheses provided that the causal mechanism under study is well theorized, and not a black-box. It is particularly suited for small-n studies, for example to study why deviant cases diverge from expected trends. Two examples related to the end of the Cold War may illustrate this. Evangelista (2015) uses process tracing in order to assess the contradicting theoretical explanations of why the Cold War ended. This is done by confronting them with the specific political, social, and psychological mechanisms that must come into play for these explanations in order to explain the end of the Cold War comprehensively. He concludes that process tracing cannot prove which explanation is the best one, but it can question the causal claims made by existing approaches by assessing the significant impact of contingent factors, which are mostly neglected in the main paradigms. Gheciu (2005) uses process tracing by combining interviews, participant observation, and discourse analysis in order to demonstrate how the North Atlantic Treaty Organization (NATO) operated after the Cold War as an agent of socialization by introducing liberal-democratic norms into Central and Eastern Europe. The results refute the rationalist assumption that NATO is a military alliance which is irrelevant to processes of constructing domestic norms and institutions. The approach helps to explain how and why the national elites switched from an authoritarian to a liberal-democratic view and conduct.

Comparative historical analysis has returned to the comparative method of late: 'Comparative historical analysis aims at the explanation of substantively important outcomes by describing processes over time using systematic and contextualized comparisons' (Mahoney and Rueschemeyer 2003: 6). Thus, this type of historical analysis is meant to be explanatory, and its mode of analysis is to use time (i.e. change) as the major operationalization of a variable. Processes are studied within the context of historical developments, not in isolation, and historical sequences can be employed to explain the meaning of change. For example, some students employ so-called 'critical junctures' (e.g. the World Wars, or the End of the Cold War) that have transformed the relationship between state and society. Finally, there is the notion of '**path dependence**', meaning that certain political choices made in the past can explain certain policy outcomes at present (see Chapter 22 'The impact of public policies'). The explanation rests, then, on the idea that alternative options for choice were not open any more, or, given the time a policy exists, the 'point of no return' has been definitively passed (Pierson 2000). In short, comparative historical analysis has a lot to offer to the comparative student, either in combination with other approaches or on its own (Keman 2013).

In sum, the selection of cases and variables depends on a deliberate *choice* in relation to the research question and on consideration of the type of approach chosen in view of the explanatory goals set (see also Ragin 2008). Further, the set of cases and variables in

Cases and variables in a comparative data set

In comparative research, the term 'case' is reserved for *units of observation* that are comparable at a certain *level of measurement*, be it micro (e.g. individual attitudes), meso (e.g. regional parties), or macro (e.g. national government). The information in a data set is a two-dimensional rectangular matrix: *variables* in columns (vertical) and *cases* in rows (horizontal). Each cell contains values for each variable, i.e. observations (e.g. levels of GDP, types of governments, or votes for parties), for each case (e.g. countries, regions, or parties). Likewise, variables may represent information *over time* (e.g. points in time, such as years, which are then cases; see Tables 22.1 and 22.2).

use also affects the so-called *ceteris paribus* condition (all other things are considered to be constant for all cases). Therefore, case selection is a crucial step.

Case selection

Cases are the building blocks for the theoretical argument underlying the research design. The number of cases selected in the research design directs the type and format of comparison. This is illustrated in Figure 3.2.

Figure 3.2 shows that there are different options for selection, depending on how many cases and how many variables are involved. *Intensive strategies* are those with many variables and few cases. An example is the analysis of the few consociational democracies that exist. These democracies are Austria, Belgium, the Netherlands, and Switzerland. They are characterized by major internal divisions along religious and/or linguistic lines that divide the population into more or less equally sized minorities. Despite this societal segmentation, which is often regarded as a source of conflict and instability, these countries managed to remain stable due to cooperation between the elites of the segments. *Extensive strategies* are those with few variables and many cases. An example is the analysis of welfare states, as discussed in Chapters 21 'The welfare state' and 22 'The impact of public policies'. Here, many cases, if not all (e.g. all established democracies), are selected, whereas only a few variables are included. If N (number of cases included) is less than ten to fifteen, the strategy is intense. In addition, whether or not 'time' is a relevant factor needs to be taken into account (Pennings et al. 2006: 40–1). This is often the case, in particular when change (or a process development) is a crucial element of the research question (e.g. explaining welfare state developments). This is called *longitudinal* analysis if it is quantitatively organized or *historical* analysis if it is based on qualitative sources. Finally, if statistical analysis is used, as many cases as feasible are required to allow for tests of significance (King et al. 1994: 24; Burnham et al. 2004: 74). Five options for case selection are presented in Figure 3.2.

The single-case study

A single-case study may be part of a comparative research design. But as it stands alone, it is at best implicitly comparative and its external validity is low or absent (see Landman 2003: 34–5). However, it can be used for post hoc validation to inspect whether or not the general findings hold up in a more detailed analysis or to study a *deviant* case (i.e. a case that appears to be an 'exception to the rule'), and can also be used as a *critical* or *crucial* case study (Seha and Müller-Rommel 2016). Another use of a single-case study is as a pilot for generating hypotheses, or confirming or invalidating extant theories (Lijphart 1971: 691).

Time series

Time series or longitudinal analysis can be useful in two ways: first, to compare a specific configuration within a few cases in order to inspect comparative change (which was discussed earlier in 'Cross-case and within-case' in association with comparative historical

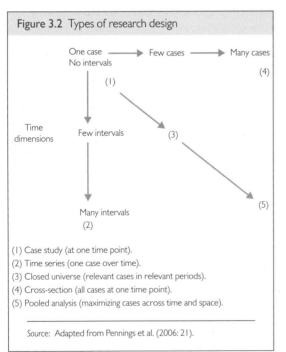

Figure 3.2 Types of research design

One case ⟶ Few cases ⟶ Many cases
No intervals

(1)

Time dimensions — Few intervals   (3)   (4)

Many intervals   (5)
(2)

(1) Case study (at one time point).
(2) Time series (one case over time).
(3) Closed universe (relevant cases in relevant periods).
(4) Cross-section (all cases at one time point).
(5) Pooled analysis (maximizing cases across time and space).

Source: Adapted from Pennings et al. (2006: 21).

analysis). An example is the analysis of new parties that were electorally more successful after the 1990s than before (see Table 12.2). Second, time series can be useful to analyse which factors are (or have become) relevant over time as causes. An example is the comparison of the different waves of **democratization** over time from the nineteenth century up to the present (see Chapter 12 'Political parties'). Another use is to replicate a cross-sectional study by time-series analysis to observe differences in the outcomes (King et al. 1994: 223).

Closed universe

The third option in Figure 3.2 concerns the 'few' cases for comparison at different points of time, taking into account change by defining periodic intervals based on external events (or 'critical junctures'), for instance after a discrete event such as war or an economic crisis. A good example is the developments during the inter-war period when, in some European countries, democracy gave way to dictatorship, whereas in other countries democracy was maintained (see Berg-Schlosser and de Meur 1996). A few(er) cases research design is often called a 'focused comparison' derived from the research question under review.

Cross-section

The fourth option in Figure 3.2 implies that several cases are compared simultaneously. This research design is frequently used. It is based on a selection of those cases that resemble each other more than they differ, and thereby reduce variance caused by other (unmeasured) variables. It implies that the 'circumstances' of the cases under review are assumed to be constant, whereas the included variables vary. This enhances the internal validity of the analytical results. For example, if the focus is on formation of coalition governments, then it follows that we only take into account those democracies where multiparty systems exist.

Pooled analysis

The final option is disputed among comparativists. Although the number of cases can be maximized by pooling cases across time and systems (e.g. twenty rows and twenty columns taken together implies that the N of cases is 400 instead of 20), whereas in a time series data set the years (or other points in time, e.g. periods) are exclusively the cases and in a cross-sectional data set the cases are exclusively the political systems to be compared, the pitfall of pooling is that the impact of time is held constant across all cases (or, at least, changes across cases do not vary (Kittel 1999)).

A possible fallacy is that comparative analysis suffers from the fact that the cases are 'too much' alike and therefore there are no meaningful differences from which to draw conclusions (see King et al. 1994: 202–3). To avoid this, one can include control cases (e.g. analysing EU members in conjunction with non-member states). Another remedy would be to include a 'rival' explanatory variable (as we showed in Figure 3.1: politics versus economics). Pooled analysis is mainly used in sophisticated quantitative approaches and it requires skills in statistical methods at a more advanced level.

All in all, the message is that the range of choice with regard to case selection is larger than is often thought. First, the options available are considerable (in Figure 3.2, options 3 and 5 are often used in combination). Second, the options in developing a research design can be used sequentially. For instance, one could follow up a cross-sectional analysis (option 4) with a critical or a crucial case study (option 1) as an in-depth elaboration of the comparative findings. However, it should be noted that the options for choice as depicted in Figure 3.2 are not completely free. For instance, if industrialization is seen as a *process*, it must be investigated *over time* in order to answer the research question of whether or not this results in a change towards welfare statism.

The main point of this section is not only that case selection is important for how many cases can or should be included in the analysis, but also that the choice is neither (completely) free nor (completely) determined. First, the choice of cases depends on the theoretical relationship under review (X–Y), which defines what type of political system can be selected. Obviously, if one researches the working of democracies, non-democratic systems cannot be included. Second, the type of empirical data available can limit the choice of cases. Third, one should bear in mind that the relationship between cases and variables also determines what type of technique can be used: statistical analysis can only be used if the N is sufficient for tests of significance, whereas a small-N allows for including contextual information or multi-causal analysis (e.g. by means of Fuzzy-Set logic; see 'The use of Methods of Agreement and Difference in comparative analysis'). Finally, if the research question involves a specific phenomenon (like federalism or semi-presidentialism), the N of cases is obviously limited by definition.

Relating the cases and associated information (i.e. data) is the next step in performing comparative analysis. This stage of the research design concerns establishing and assessing the relationship between the evidence (data) collected across the selected cases for the independent and dependent variables in search of a (causal) relationship.

The logic of comparison: relating cases to variables

In comparative methods, there are two well-known research designs that employ a different type of logic: the **Most Different Systems Design** (MDSD) and the **Most Similar Systems Design** (MSSD). These designs relate directly to the type and number of cases under review and to the selection of variables by the researcher in view of the research question and the related (hypothetical) answers. Both have been developed following John Stuart Mill's dictum: *maximize experimental variance—minimize error variance—control extraneous variance* (Peters 1998: 30). In fact, they are 'ideal types'—something to strive for.

Experimental variance

This points to the observed differences or changes in the dependent variable (Y) of the research question, which is supposed to be a function of the independent variable (X). Figure 3.1 is an example of the basic structure of modelling the relationship between a research question and a research answer. The question at stake was whether or not 'politics matters'. A crucial requirement for answering this question and attempting to settle this debate is that the dependent variable (Y = 'welfare statism') indeed varies across cases or over time (or both). Where there is *no* experimental variance, we cannot tell whether or not the independent variables make a difference. Hence, the research design would lead to insignificant results because we cannot tell whether the effect-producing variables (X) account for the observed outcomes (in Y).

Error variance

This is the occurrence of random effects of unmeasured variables. These effects are almost impossible to avoid in the social sciences, given its quasi-experimental nature, which always implies a reduction of 'real-life' circumstances. Even in a single-case study or comparing a few cases, a 'thick' **descriptive analysis** cannot provide full information. However, error variance should be minimized as much as is feasible (in statistical terms, the error term in the equation is then constant or close to zero). One way to minimize error variance would be to increase the number of cases. However, this is not always feasible, as mentioned earlier in the discussion on 'Case selection' (see also 'Conceptual stretching').

Extraneous variance

The final requirement in Mill's dictum is controlling for extraneous variance. If there is no control for other possible influences, the hypothetical relation X–Y may in part be produced by another (unknown) cause. One example of an unknown cause, also called a confounding variable, is the favourable impact of consensus democracy on performance, which could also be caused by economic growth. If the latter is excluded, the analysis may suffer from underspecification, which leads to erroneous results. This is often due to omitted variables and can lead to a *spurious relationship* (a third variable affects both the independent and dependent variables under investigation). There is no 'best' remedy to prevent extraneous variance exercising an influence, other than by having formulated a fully specified theory or statistical significance tests and control variables.[4] One approach is to apply the principles of the Methods of Agreement and Difference. Using these methods, we are in a position to draw causal conclusions by means of logically ordering the *differences* and *similarities* between the dependent and independent variables, based on the empirical evidence available.

The use of Methods of Agreement and Difference in comparative analysis

The logic of comparative enquiry is meant to assess the relationship between the independent variables and the dependent variable in light of the number of cases (many, few, or one) selected for comparison. As we have already seen, case selection has implications for the use of the logics of comparison. Two logics are distinguished:

- Method of Difference;
- Method of Agreement.

The Methods of Difference and Agreement originate from John Stuart Mill's *A System of Logic* (1843). The basic idea is that comparing cases is used to interpret commonalities and differences between cases and variables. Hence, these 'logics' refer to the type of descriptive inference used to examine whether or not there is indeed a causal relationship between X and Y. This assessment is inferred from the empirical evidence (data) collected.

The **Method of Difference** focuses on comparing cases that *differ* with respect to either the dependent variable (Y) or the independent variable (X) but do *not* differ across comparable cases with respect to other variables (the *ceteris paribus* clause). Hence, covariation between the dependent and independent variables is considered crucial under the assumption that the context remains constant. This is the MSSD: locating variables, in particular the dependent variable, that differ across similar systems and accounting for the observed outcomes. An example is the debate on the role of 'politics' as regards the welfare state. We look at the political differences between systems that are similar in terms of their institutional design and examine the extent to which party differences (X) match differences in welfare state provisions (Y). The stronger the match between, for instance, the strength of the left in parliament and government and the 'generosity' of welfare entitlements, on the one hand, and its absence in cases where parties of the right are dominant, the more likely it appears that 'politics matters'. Alternatively, the **Method of Agreement** consists of comparing cases (systems) in order to detect those relationships between X and Y that remain *similar*, notwithstanding the differences in other features of the cases compared. Hence, other variables may be different across the cases except for those relationships that are considered to be causal (or effect-productive). This is the so-called MDSD. An example is Luebbert's analysis investigating the possible causes of regime types during the inter-war period (1919–39). He distinguishes three regime types: liberalism, social democracy, and fascism (Luebbert 1991). The explanatory variable (X) is 'class cooperation' (between the middle class, farmers, and the working class) and regime type is the dependent variable (Y). Luebbert finds that only specific patterns of class cooperation consistently match the same regime type across twelve European countries. Most other variables considered (as possible causes) in the comparative analysis do not match the outcome (regime type) in the same way.

When applying the (quasi-)experimental method to causal problems, one should keep in mind that in social science the degree of control of the independent variables is always limited (Kellstedt and Whitten 2013: 70–88). We cannot control exposure to them because we cannot 'assign' a country a type of regime or a level of social expenditures. In addition, whereas the internal validity of experiments is often high, the external validity (i.e. generalizability) is low. Due to these drawbacks, genuine experiments are rare in comparative politics. Instead, many comparative studies are observational by taking reality as it is, without randomly assigning units of analysis to treatment groups. The major disadvantage of this strategy is that, since we do not control for all possible causes of Y, there is always a chance that some third (confounding) variable is causing Y. This potential problem weakens the internal validity of observational studies. The only way to cope with this problem is to try to identify alternative causes of Y and to present any causal claim in a tentative way. The MSSD- and MDSD-designs are in between the experimental and observational methods and run the risk that they combine the weaknesses of both methods. As a consequence, if one adopts a MSSD- or MDSD-design one should be alert on both the internal and the external validity.

Recently, an alternative approach—*qualitative comparative analysis* (QCA)—has been developed, which attempts to cater for 'multiple causalities' (one of the limits of Mill's logic of comparison) (Schneider 2019). This type of analysis allows for the handling of many variables in combination with a relatively high number of cases simultaneously (recall option 3 in Figure 3.2). Ragin (2008) claims that this type of research design is a way of circumventing the trade-off between many cases/few variables versus few cases/many variables. The logic of comparison employed is based on Boolean algebra, in which qualitative and quantitative information is ordered in terms of *necessary and sufficient* conditions as regards the relationship under investigation. This approach also appears to be well suited to focusing on the variation of comparative variables within cases. Instead of aiming to detect one (at best) effect-producing circumstance (X) by means of a variable-oriented approach, the *homogeneity* of comparable cases directs the process of descriptive inference. An example is the search for the conditions under which economic development is more or less promoted by public policy (Vis et al. 2007). Instead of searching for the strongest or a single relationship, the researcher attempts to find out which *combination* of factors is connected with cases in view of their economic development. This procedure and concomitant logic of comparison has been developed into a 'fuzzy-set logic'.

The many applications and cross-validations of QCA have led to much support, but more recently also to criticisms. Most critics agree that QCA is useful if the goal is to test deterministic hypotheses under the assumption of error-free measures of the employed variables. However, critics argue that most theories are not sufficiently advanced to allow for deterministic hypotheses because causality is a complex phenomenon. In addition, the assumption of error-free measures is an illusion because often scientists have to use proxies or indicators that do not fully represent the original meaning (Hug 2013). Furthermore, as QCA is often used to analyse a relatively small number of cases, it has a problematic ratio of cases-to-variables which may negatively affect the stability of findings (Krogslund and Michel 2014). Several researchers have found that the results are susceptible to minor model specification changes. They argue that the identification of sufficient causal conditions by QCA strongly depends on the values of the key parameters selected by the researcher. They also show that QCA results are subject to confirmation bias because they tend towards finding complex connections between variables, even if they are randomly generated. Others have argued that there is no way to assess the probability that the causal patterns are the result of chance because QCA methods are not designed as statistical techniques. The implication is that even very strong QCA results may plausibly be the result of chance (Braumoeller 2015). If we overlook these criticisms, we can conclude that the main critique of QCA is that it is not robust and often yields erroneous causal connections. On the one hand, these critiques should be taken seriously because they highlight weak spots that should not be overlooked by any researcher that uses QCA. On the other hand, doing causal analysis on a small number of cases by means of QCA should be regarded as a qualitative approach in which interpretation is more important than quantification. If it is purely used as a statistical technique, it may well lead to misleading outcomes because the researcher fully relies on the software to generate causal connections. Applicants of QCA should never do that, and should instead account for all the relevant steps taken during the research and cross-validate the results with alternative sources and interpretations.

A recent development is the combination of QCA and process tracing (Beach 2018; Beach and Rohlfing 2018; Schneider and Rohlfing 2013). This may well be a fruitful combination as far as it combines the strengths of two approaches, namely cross-case comparative analysis and in-depth within-case analysis. This synthesis is an example of multi-method research in comparative politics in which different methodological tools compensate for each other's weaknesses.

KEY POINTS

- The point of departure is a hypothesis concerning the relationship between two or more variables (X–Y) whose empirical validity is to be verified by means of real-world data across a number of cases.

- The Method of Agreement uses MDSD to allow descriptive causal inference. Conversely, the Method of Difference derives its explanatory capacity from MSSD. The shared goal is to eliminate those variables that exemplify no systematic association between X and Y across the cases selected.

- An alternative logic of comparison has recently been developed: QCA/fuzzy-set logic. This approach allows scrutiny of multiple causality across various cases and variables.

- Combining methods like QCA and process-tracing (PT) may help to overcome the weaknesses of both approaches, but only if one succeeds to integrate them into a research methodology that complements these approaches instead of producing contradictory results.

This may potentially allow for more robust causal inferences, but whether this is actually achieved depends on the degree to which the fundamentally different assumptions of in-depth single-case studies match with assumed causal effects across a large set of cases. One major pre-condition to make this work out is to understand the differences between the assumptions being made in case-based and variance-based research approaches and to integrate them into a research methodology that allows these approaches to compensate each other, instead of contradicting each other. That this is a difficult task is argued by Beach (2019), who has shown that several recent attempts at multi-method methodology tend to stay within one approach, thereby also having the same strengths and weaknesses as the overall approach. This implies that there are many practical challenges to be addressed when combining QCA and process tracing without violating their underlying assumptions about the nature of causal relationships (see, for a discussion of those challenges, plus an example which focuses on the congruence between voter views and governmental positions: Beach 2018: 82).

Constraints and limitations of the comparative method

Although the comparative approach in political science is considered to be advantageous in linking theory to evidence, enhancing it as a 'scientific' discipline, there are a number of constraints that limit its possibilities and can impair its usefulness. In this section, we discuss some of these and offer possible solutions. While it is important to be aware of them, it is often difficult for students to find appropriate solutions. Hence, it is wise to seek advice from an experienced researcher or lecturer.

One major concern is that we often have too many different theories that fit the same data. This means that collecting *valid and reliable* data for the cases we have selected to test theoretical relations can turn out to be a daunting task. If this problem is insufficiently solved, it will undermine the quality of the results. More often than not, we are forced to stretch our *concepts* so that they can *travel* to other contexts and increase the number of observations across more cases. However, this may create too large a distance between the stretched concept and the original theoretical concept (Sartori 1970, 1994). If this problem occurs (and it often does), it may well affect the internal *and* external validity of the results (see Box 3.2). In conjunction with this hazard, it has been noted that reliability problems may arise as a result of including (functional) *equivalents* that are used to widen the case selection (and thus increase the number of cases). An example is the concept of the 'federal state'. What defines a federation, and how can such a concept be transformed into measurable entities? Thus, the problem is to what extent a concept transformed into an empirical indicator has the same meaning across different settings or cultures (Van Deth 1998*b*). Finally, some caveats need to be taken into account when interpreting the comparative data available: (i) Galton's problem; (ii) individual and ecological fallacies; and (iii) **overdetermination**.

Conceptual stretching

Conceptual stretching is the distortion that occurs when a concept developed for one set of cases is extended to additional cases to which the features of the concept do not apply in the same manner. Sartori (1970) illustrated this problem by means of the 'ladder of generality'. Enhancing a wider use of a theoretical concept by *extension* (of its initial meaning, i.e. moving from A to B in Figure 3.3) involves a loss of intension (where the observations reflect the original features of the concept, i.e. remain close to B). *Intension* will obviously reduce the applicability of a concept in comparative research across more cases, but it enhances the internal validity of the cases compared. Extension will have the opposite effect, and the question is then whether or not the wider use (i.e. in a higher number of cases to be compared) impairs the claim for external validity of the analytical results. In Figure 3.3,

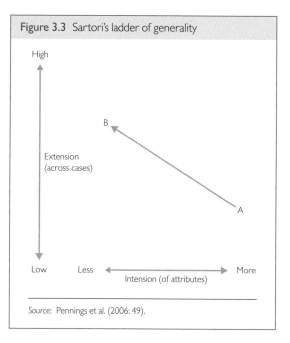

Figure 3.3 Sartori's ladder of generality

Source: Pennings et al. (2006: 49).

this choice is visualized: the more the meaning of a concept moves due to the process of operationalization from position A to B, the less equivalent the information collected for each case may be, and therefore the validity of the results is negatively affected.

The choice to be made and the matter of dispute among comparativists is how broadly or extensively (i.e. from A to B) we can define and measure variables without a serious loss of meaning. There are different opinions on the degree of flexibility that is allowed when 'stretching' concepts to make variables 'travel' across (more) cases. Sartori remarks that *over*stretching is dangerous, and not all concepts can travel all over the world and through all time, like a political party, whereas constitutional design may (Sartori 1994). However, attempts have been made to develop methods to cope with the problem of overstretching and travelling (Braun and Maggetti 2015).

Family resemblance

Some comparativists have suggested another solution by means of 'family resemblance' (Collier and Mahon 1993: 846–8). In its simplest fashion, this method extends the initial concept by adding features which share some of the attributes of the original concept. How far this type of extension can go depends on what the research question is. For example, if we are investigating the behaviour of political parties and define these as any actor that is vote-seeking (= A), office-seeking (= B), and policy-seeking (= C), then the concept of a party can be used in a wider sense. Instead of requiring that all three characteristics are present *simultaneously*, we allow the inclusion of parties that have fewer in common. Examples are electoral democracies, where people can vote (= A), but parties are not allowed to govern (= B), let alone to make policy decisions (= C). This latter type of party often occurs in emerging democracies (see Merkel 2014).

Radial categories

The second option of going up the 'ladder of generality' is the use of *radial* categories. Here, the underlying idea is that each step of extension, thus including new comparable cases, is defined by a *hierarchy* of attributes belonging to the initial concept. In Figure 3.4, this is made visible by defining A as the essential attribute, whereas B and C are considered as secondary. Figure 3.4 demonstrates these two strategies for extension through which the number of cases is to be increased. Family resemblance requires a degree of commonality and this produces three cases in comparison, instead of one under the initial categorization, by sharing two out of the three defining features (AC, AB, BC). The radial method requires that the primary attribute (A) is always included. In Figure 3.4, this means two cases instead of the original single case (A + B and A + C). It is advisable to develop a *typology* first to see empirically how this transformation of a concept may work out.

Equivalence

A related problem of transforming concepts into empirically based indicators concerns the question of whether or not the meaning of a concept stays constant across time and space. Landman and Carvalho (2017: 39-42) argue that this problem is less a matter of whether or not a concept is measured with *identical* results (which is a matter of reliability regarding the measurement). Whatever solution is chosen, at the end of the day it is up to the researcher to convince us whether or not the degree of **equivalence** between measured phenomena is acceptable.

Interpreting results

Galton's problem, ecological and individual fallacies, and over-determination are all hazards that are related to the *interpretation* of the results of the comparative analysis.

Galton's problem

Galton's problem refers to the situation where the observed differences and similarities may well be caused by exogenous factors that are common to all the cases selected for comparison, such as comparing fiscal policy-making across states in Europe after the introduction of the Economic and Monetary Union (EMU) requirements, or the choice for a Westminster-style of parliamentary governance in former British colonies (Burnham et al. 2004: 74). Another example is the process of 'globalization' (see Kübler 2015). Obviously, diffusion will affect the process of descriptive inference because the explanation is corrupted by a common cause that is of similar influence in each case, but is difficult to single out (Lijphart 1975: 17). A possible way to detect such a common cause is either by triangulation or by applying comparative historical analysis.

Individual and ecological fallacies

These fallacies are likewise problematic vis-à-vis the causal interpretation of evidence. An ecological fallacy occurs when data measured on an aggregated level (e.g. at the country level) are used to make inferences about individual- or group-level behaviour. Conversely, individual fallacy is the result of interpreting data measured at the individual or group level as if they represent the 'whole' (e.g. using electoral surveys for party behaviour or national attitudes; see also the Introduction to this volume). This type of fallacy occurs regularly in comparative politics and shows the need for developing a proper level of measurement.

Over-determination and selection biases

Over-determination and **selection biases** are risks that emanate from case selection. In particular, when MSSD is used, the chances are high that the dependent

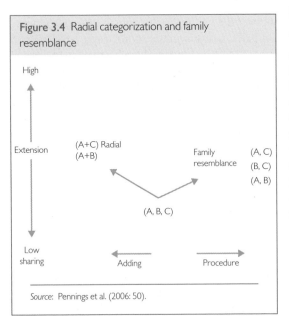

Figure 3.4 Radial categorization and family resemblance

High

Extension

(A+C) Radial
(A+B)

Family
resemblance

(A, C)
(B, C)
(A, B)

(A, B, C)

Low
sharing

Adding   Procedure

Source: Pennings et al. (2006: 50).

variable is over-determined by another difference that is not actually catered for in the research design (Przeworski and Teune 1970: 34). Conversely, if the cases included in the analysis are fairly homogeneous, there is a chance that a selection bias will go unnoticed. As King et al. (1994: 141–2) note, if the similarities among the cases affect the degree of comparative variation of the independent and dependent variables, we cannot draw valid conclusions.

In addition to these constraints and limitations, comparative methods have been criticized for being a-theoretical, empiricist, and solely country-oriented (Newton and van Deth 2016). We may argue that the comparative methods do not offer solutions to all and sundry types of research problems, but help to formulate them and find ways to arrive at plausible answers. Comparison is required to make research insightful and scientifically relevant. The alternative is a single case. However, the comparative approach is developing and learning from these criticisms (Seha and Müller-Rommel 2016). Several new approaches that are related to the 'spatial turn' in comparative politics can help to advance new insights.

One example is multilevel governance (MLG), which criticizes methodological nationalism and other forms of centrism (like Europe or democracies) that often characterize comparative politics. The MLG approach analyses how decision-making competences are shared by policy-relevant actors at different levels of government (i.e. supranational, national, and subnational levels) (Kübler 2015: 63–80). It focuses on the dynamics of cross-level interactions between these actors in one or more policy areas. These interactions often involve forms of **soft power** such as information exchange and persuasion. A second example examines interdependencies, policy diffusion, and policy transfer (Obinger et al. 2013; Jahn and Stephan 2015). This type of research argues that not only developments within nation-states matter, but also relations between nation-states and inter- and **supranational** forms of cooperation and bargaining. Such a relational approach means that policy outcomes are accounted for by multiple interdependencies in conjunction with domestic factors. Policy diffusion and transfer are explained by causal mechanisms such as learning and competition. A related approach is social network analysis (SNA). A network consists of nodes (the agents) and edges (the links or relations between the nodes). The relationships between them represent ways in which actors influence and control each other. Network analysis seeks to describe these (evolving) relationships in order to learn how power structures constrain behaviour and change (for a recent example, see Paterson et al. 2014).

Although these new developments are promising, we have to take into account an important caveat. The existing applications are often rather descriptive and lack explanatory power and generalizability. Hence, they should be regarded as helpful additions to conventional methodologies and not as replacements.

To conclude this section, the constraints and limitations of the comparative method need permanent attention. However, it would be wrong to conclude that—given the complexities and criticisms discussed in this chapter—the comparative approach to politics is therefore misdirected or fallacious. If we accept the fact that most political science is comparative, even if not explicitly so, then it is one of the *strengths* of the comparative method that both the advantages and disadvantages are recognized and discussed in terms of its methodology.

> **KEY POINTS**
>
> * There are many hazards and pitfalls in comparative methods that ought to be taken into account to link theory and evidence in a plausible fashion.
>
> * Conceptual travelling is a sensitive instrument to widen the case selection, as long as overstretching is avoided. The use of 'radial categories' and 'family resemblance' to extend the number of cases can remedy this.
>
> * Interpretation problems are often due to biases like Galton's problem and over-determination, as well as to individual and ecological fallacies. Avoiding these problems as far as possible reduces the probability of drawing invalid conclusions.

Conclusion

Some time ago, Gabriel Almond lamented the lack of progress in political science at large (Almond 1990). His main complaint concerned the lack of constructive collaboration among the practitioners. However, he made an exception as regards the field of comparative politics:

Mainstream comparative studies, rather than being in a crisis, are richly and variedly productive . . . In the four decades after World War II, the level of rigor has been significantly increased in quantitative, analytical, and historical-sociological work.

Almond (1990: 253)

Much of the credit should go to those involved in the further development of the methodology of comparative politics by means of debates on difficult issues in the comparative method. However, new developments, like QCA, process tracing, and the re-emergence of comparative historical analysis, take place and are welcome. This chapter has attempted to demonstrate this. Throughout, we have maintained that comparative politics is a (sub)discipline of political science, where theory development is explicitly linked to empirical evidence by means of a rigorous application of the comparative method. Even if not all the problems—and they do exist—can be solved at this stage, we hold the view that the comparative method is the best way to go forward to further comparative politics within political science at large.

? QUESTIONS

Knowledge-based

1. Why is the 'art of comparing' not only useful for *explicit* comparison, but also an *implicit* part of the toolkit of any political scientist?

2. Can you explain why the comparative method is often called '*quasi*-experimental'? Can you argue *why* this would justify the use of statistics in comparative politics?

3. What exactly is the difference between internal and external validity? Why is this distinction important? Can you give an example of each type of validity?

4. If you examine the debate on 'Does politics matter?', can you describe the research design used? Are you able to develop an alternative one—in terms of variables and cases—to test the same issue of this debate?

5. What is a comparative variable and what is the relation between a concept and an indicator?

Critical thinking

1. What is a case? Can you elaborate what the case is in terms of unit of observation and level of measurement if it concerns a comparative investigation of party government?

2. There are different options as regards the type and number of cases needed to develop a research design. Can you think of a research question that would justify the choice of a single-case study where 'time' is relevant *and* 'inter'-system references are necessary?

3. Globalization is considered not only to grow but also to produce biased results due to diffusion. Can you discuss this problem in relation to the relationship between national policy formation of membership states and the EU?

4. Describe the basic differences between the Methods of Agreement and Difference. Give an example of each, demonstrating this difference.

5. A constraint of the comparative method is 'conceptual stretching' and the solution may lie in extending the number of cases by means of 'family resemblance' or 'radial categories'. Can you think of an example of each to extend the number of valid cases?

≋ FURTHER READING

General literature on methods in political science

Brady, H. D. and Collier, D. (2010) *Rethinking Social Inquiry: Diverse Tools, Shared Standards* (2nd edn) (Lanham, MD: Rowman & Littlefield). This edited volume discusses a wide variety of methodological concerns that are relevant for comparative methods.

King, G., Keohane, R. D., and Verba, S. (1994) *Designing Social Inquiry* (Princeton, NJ: Princeton University Press). This is a contemporary classic in social science methods, written by three political scientists. It is an introduction and uses much material taken from comparative politics.

Kellstedt, P. M. and Whitten, G. D. (2018) *The Fundamentals of Political Science Research* (Cambridge: Cambridge University Press). This book presents an accessible approach to research design and empirical analyses in which researchers can develop and test causal theories.

Keman, H. and Woldendorp, J. (2016) *Handbook of Research Methods and Applications in Political Science* (Cheltenham: Edger Elgar). Representing an up-to-date state of affairs for approaches and methodologies in use, including much hands-on information, discussing different approaches and applying methods in political science.

Landman, T. and Carvalho, E. (2017) *Issues and Methods in Comparative Politics: An Introduction* (4th edn) (Abingdon and New York: Routledge). This introductory text discusses various fields within comparative politics, focusing on different research designs by means of one, few, and many cases.

Specific literature on comparative methods

Beach, D. and Pedersen, R. B. (2016) *Causal Case Studies: Foundations and Guidelines for Comparing, Matching and Tracing* (Ann Arbor, MI: University of Michigan Press). This book delineates the ontological and epistemological differences among causal case study methods, offers suggestions for determining the appropriate methods for a given research project, and explains the step-by-step application of selected methods.

Braun, D. and Maggetti, M. (eds) (2015) *Comparative Politics: Theoretical and Methodological Challenges* (Cheltenham: Edward Elgar). A profound and thorough discussion of the contemporary challenges for comparative politics regarding multilevel analysis, concept formation, multiple causation, and complexities of descriptive inference.

Mahoney, J. and Rueschemeyer, D. (eds) (2003) *Comparative Historical Analysis in the Social Sciences* (Cambridge: Cambridge University Press). This reader contains many different views on developing qualitative types of comparative research, with an emphasis on history and the use of case studies.

Pennings, P., Keman, H., and Kleinnijenhuis, J. (2006) *Doing Research in Political Science: An Introduction to Comparative Methods and Statistics* (2nd edn) (London: Sage). This is a course book intended for students. It is an introduction to the use of statistics in comparative research and contains many examples of published research.

Ragin, C. (2008) *Redesigning Social Inquiry. Fuzzy Sets and Beyond* (Chicago, IL: University of Chicago Press). The book centres on the 'fuzzy-set' approach as an alternative to other comparative methods, as discussed in this chapter (see also Box 3.3) and discusses the advantages of this approach in comparison with extant practices.

ENDNOTES

1. In comparative politics the term 'cross- national research' is often used to depict the cases for comparative analysis (e.g. Landman 2003). Here, I use the term 'cross-system analysis' to avoid the idea that only 'nations' are cases in a comparative politics (Lijphart 1975: 166).

2. There are many names in use for independent variables: exogenous, effect-producing, antecedent variables, etc. They all have in common that a change in X affects Y. In this chapter, we use the term dependent (Y) and independent (X) variables.

3. Another way of developing a causal argument is counterfactual analysis, asking what happens if a variable is omitted from the equation. In this example: what if 'politics' does not play a role?

4. Figure 3.1 is a way to handle spuriousness: by controlling for social and economic factor X_1, one could estimate the relative influence of politics X_2 in terms of a direct relationship.

Visit the Online Resources that accompany this book for additional material, including country profiles, comparative data sets, flashcard glossaries, and web directory.

www.oup.com/he/caramani5e

Section 2
The historical context

4

The nation-state

Gianfranco Poggi

Chapter contents

Reader's guide

The most significant political units of the modern world are generally referred to as 'states' or 'nation-states'. It is within and between states that contemporary political business is carried out. This chapter explains how this particular kind of political unit came into being and how it became dominant. It provides the conceptual and historical background for the study of many themes of comparative politics. We suggest that this chapter is read in combination with Chapter 24 on 'Globalization and the nation-state', which discusses some recent challenges to the dominance of this political unit.

Introduction

The comparative analysis of the arrangements under which political activity is carried out considers chiefly a multiplicity of interdependent but separate, more or less autonomous, units—let us call them polities. Polities differ among themselves in numerous significant respects, and entertain with one another relations—friendly or antagonistic—which reflect those differences. These exist against the background of considerable similarities. The most important of these qualify the polities making up the modern political environment for being called 'states'.

The expression 'state' has been applied by scholars to polities which have existed in pre-modern contexts—say, to ancient Egypt, or imperial China. Here we suggest that 'state' is more appropriately used to designate the polities characteristic of the *modern political environment,* which came into being in Western Europe at the end of the Middle Ages, roughly between the thirteenth and the fifteenth centuries.

First, this chapter offers a general and streamlined portrait of the state—a concept that sociologists inspired by Max Weber might call an ideal type.

It comprised a set of traits embodied in most states to a greater or lesser extent. Some significant contemporary developments within the modern political environment have brought into being polities to which some features of the portraits—for instance, **sovereignty** (see Chapter 24 'Globalization and the nation-state')—apply poorly, if at all. On this account, particularly in certain parts of the world, some polities are designated, both in scholarly and in public discourse, as *failed states*.

The conceptual portrait that follows privileges what *proper states* are like. But even these embody to a different extent the portrait's features, having acquired them through diverse historical processes.

KEY POINTS

- Most contemporary political units (polities) share features which justify calling them 'states'.

- To that extent, they all constitute present-day embodiments of a kind of polity which first developed in the modern West. But such embodiments are realized in them to different extents and in different manners.

- Comparative politics considers both the constitutive features of the 'state' and the major steps in its development.

A portrait of the state

Monopoly of legitimate violence

States are, in the first place, polities where a single centre of rule has established (to a variable extent and manner) its exclusive entitlement to control and employ the ultimate medium of political activity—organized violence—over a definite territory. Individuals and bodies operating within that territory may occasionally exercise violence, but if they do so without mandate or permission from the centre of rule, the latter considers that exercise illegitimate and compels them to 'cease and desist'.[1]

Territoriality

To qualify as a state, the polity must not only effectively 'police' a given portion of the earth by overwhelming any internal challenges to its own monopoly of legitimate violence, but it must also claim that portion, against all comers, as exclusively its own: must be able and disposed to defend it, patrol its boundaries, confront and push back any encroachment by other states upon its territory's integrity, and prevent any unauthorized

exploitation of its resources. Once more, the ultimate medium of such activities is organized violence.

The territory is not simply a locale of the state's activities (violent or other), or its cherished possession. Rather, it represents the physical aspect of the state's own identity, the very *ground* (this expression is itself a significant metaphor) of its existence and of its historical continuity. The state does not so much *have* a territory; rather, it *is* a territory (Romano 1947: 56).

Sovereignty

With reference to its territory, furthermore, the state establishes and practices its sovereignty—that is, holds within it (and thus over its population) ultimate authority. Each state recognizes no power superior to itself. It engages in political activity on nobody's mandate but its own, commits to it resources of its own, operates under its own steam, at its own risk. It is the sole judge of its own interests and bears the sole responsibility for defining and pursuing those interests, beginning with its own security. Sovereignty also means that each state accepts no interference from others in its own domestic affairs.

Plurality

Thus, the modern political environment presents a plurality of territorially discrete, self-empowering, self-activating, self-securing states. Each of these presupposes the existence of all others, and each is in principle their equal, for it shares with them its own characteristics—sovereignty in particular. Since there does not exist a higher layer of authority over the states (an overarching political unit endowed with its own resources for violence, entitled to oversee and control the states themselves), these necessarily tend to regard each other as potentially hostile, as constituting possible threats to their own security, and enter into relations with one another, aiming in the first instance to neutralize those threats.

Relation to the population

States exercise rule over people and pursue policies binding on people. But states, though they sometimes project themselves as self-standing personified entities, are themselves *made of* people and operate exclusively within and through the activities of individuals. Thus, the existence itself of states involves a form of social inequality, a more or less stable and pronounced asymmetry between people exercising rule (a minority) and people subject to it (the great majority).

Such asymmetry is to an extent bounded and justified by the sense in which both parts to it belong together, and collectively constitute a distinctive entity—a *political community*. For this community, the activities of rule represent a medium for coming into being, for achieving and maintaining a shared identity, for pursuing putatively common interests. As is the case for the territory, the relationship between the state and its population is not purely factual; the population is not perceived as a mere demographic entity, but as a people (or, as we shall see, as a nation). As such, it entertains a constitutive relation with the state itself.

All this, of course, lends itself to much ideological mystification. For instance, it induced Marx to speak of the nation as an 'illusory' community and to reject the view of the people or the nation as the source and/or carrier of the state's sovereignty. But how illusory can you call a commonality in the name of which feats of great magnitude and significance have been accomplished (for good or for evil) throughout modern history?

KEY POINTS

- Internally, states possess a single centre of power that reserves for itself the faculty of exercising or threatening legitimate violence.

- A state does not respond to any other power for the uses to which it puts that faculty and others.

- The state uses organized violence to protect one portion of the earth which it considers its own territory. It claims exclusive jurisdiction over the population inhabiting that territory and considers itself as solely entitled to define and to pursue its interests.

- Externally, each state exists side by side with other states, all endowed with the same characteristics, and considers them as potential contenders, allies, or neutral parties.

A more expansive concept

A definition of the state in Weber's *Economy and Society* stresses what I have said so far and introduces the points to be made in this section.

The primary formal characteristics of the modern state are as follows: it possesses an administrative and legal order subject to change by legislation, to which the organised activities of the administrative staff, which are also controlled by regulations, are oriented. This system of order claims authority, not only over the members of the state, the citizens, most of whom have obtained membership by birth, but also to a very large extent over all action taking place in the area of its jurisdiction. It is thus a compulsory organisation with a territorial basis. Furthermore, today, the use of force is regarded as legitimate only so far as it is permitted by the state or prescribed by it.

Weber (1978: 56)

This definition points to additional features of states active in the nineteenth and twentieth centuries—though, of course, individual states display them to a different extent and in different ways. This *diversity* is the main theme of the study of comparative politics.

The role of law

We begin by noting that *law*, understood as a set of general enforceable commands and prohibitions, has played a significant role in the construction and management of states. In all societies, law so understood has chiefly performed two functions: first, to repress antisocial behaviour; second, to allocate between groups or individuals access to and disposition over material resources. In the West, however, law has been put to further uses: *establishing polities, deliberating and pursuing policies, instituting public agencies and offices, and activating and controlling their operations.*

These uses of law developed first in the Greek *polis*, then in the Roman Republic and Empire. Subsequently, European polities maintained a connection with the realm of law: rulers were expected to serve justice, observe it in their own conduct, and enforce it in adjudicating disputes and punishing crimes. But for a long time, the commandments in question were understood to express folkways and the moral values of religion. Local judges and juries were said to *find* the law, and were not meant to *make* it. Much less did the rulers do so. Instead, they mostly enforced the verdicts of judges and juries.

This arrangement subsequently changed. Rulers undertook to play a more active legal role. Increasingly assisted by trained officials, they began to codify local vernacular sets of customs and usages and to enforce them uniformly over the territory. Above all, they asserted themselves as the source of a new kind of law— *public* law. This regulated the relations on the one hand between the organs and offices of the state itself, and on the other between the state and various categories of individuals and groups, generally asserting the supremacy of the former's interests over those of the latter.

Two later developments counterbalanced one another. On the one hand, it was increasingly asserted that *all law was such only in so far as it was produced by the state*, through special organs and procedures. Law had become, so to speak, the exclusive speech of the state. On the other hand, *the state declared itself bound by its own laws*. The activities of its organs and the commands of state officials were considered valid only if their content or, more often, the ways in which they were produced, conformed with some express legal principles, such as those contained in **constitutions**.

To an extent that varied in time and from region to region, the state—without ceasing to assert its own grounding in sheer might—became involved in producing and implementing (and, by the same token, complying with) arrangements expressed in legal instruments of diverse kinds: constitutions, statutes, decrees, judgements, ordinances, and by-laws.

Centralized organization

These instruments make up a more or less explicit and binding hierarchy of legal sources. Typically, the constitution lies at the top, by-laws stand lower than statutes, and so on. This is so in three closely related senses.

1. Higher sources authorize and place boundaries upon lower ones.

2. The products of lower sources can change without altering the content of higher ones, but can articulate and specify them in different and variable ways.

3. The verified contrast between the content of a higher source and that of a lower one invalidates the lower one. Special judicial organs are empowered to issue judgements of different scope or gravity. Higher ones may review and nullify or revise the judgements of lower ones.

Other aspects of the state reveal a preoccupation with unity and coherence, and express it through hierarchy. For instance, the monopoly in the exercise of violence has a legal aspect (Max Weber speaks of 'legitimate force'). But much more significant are its organizational components, summarized in the contemporary expression 'command, communication, and control', without which that monopoly cannot be secured.

Those components have sometimes a very loose relationship (if any) to legal constraints. The organizational blueprint of the state mostly reveals a *managerial rather than a legal* rationality. It is chiefly intended to make the operations of all state agencies as responsive as possible to the directives of the political centre, and to render them uniform, prompt, predictable, and economical.

The distinction between state and society

The distinction between 'state' and '(civil) society', theorized by Hegel among others, is more or less expressly reflected in the constitution of several Western states. The state, in principle, is an ensemble of arrangements and practices which address *all and only* the political aspects of the management of a territorially bounded society. It represents and justifies itself as a realm of expressly political activities (legislation, jurisdiction, police, military action, public policy) complementary to a different realm—society—comprising diverse social activities not considered political in nature, which the state organs do not expressly promote and control. Individuals undertake those activities in their private capacities, pursue values and interests of their own, and establish among themselves relations which are not the concern of public policy.

Religion and the market

At the centre of society stand two sets of concerns which for a long time the state had considered very much as its own, but subsequently released from its control.

First, the state became increasingly secular. That is, it progressively dismissed any concern with the spiritual welfare of individuals, which previously it had fostered, mostly by privileging (and professing) one religion and associating itself with one church. (A critical reason for this development was the breakdown of the religious unity of the West caused by the Reformation.) Second, the state progressively entrusted to the two central institutions of private law—*property* and *contract*—the legal discipline of the activities which relate to the production and distribution of wealth, and which increasingly take place via the *market*.

However, one meaning of sovereignty is that the state's specific concern with external security and public order may override those of private individuals, especially in confronting emergencies. Furthermore, private activities are carried out within frameworks of public rules, which the state is responsible for enacting and enforcing.

However, it is the state's prerogative to fund its own activities by extracting resources from the economy. Typically, the modern state is a 'taxation state': it extracts resources from the society's economic system chiefly by regularly levying moneys from stocks and flows of private wealth. Such levies, authorized by law and carried out by public officials, are compatible with the security of private property and with the autonomous operations of the market. The name itself of another subsidiary form of extraction, the *public debt*, again suggests that compatibility: private individuals become creditors of the state. The significance of these phenomena, which are often the subject of controversy, has been argued by Stasavage (2011).

Various aspects of the *interaction* between the state's economic interests and the society's political interests are a constant component of modern social dynamics, often characterized by such expressions as *politics and the market*. What is characteristic of many *failed states* is the frequency and the extent to which the occupants of significant positions in the political system misappropriate, and put to their own advantage, enormous amounts of economic resources officially destined for public use. Sometimes its critics label this phenomenon—particularly evident in some parts of Africa—*kleptocracy*: that is, rule by thieves. But the phenomenon is present in other parts of the world. For example, in 2015, at the end of Cristina Kirchner's tenure of the presidency of the Argentinian Republic, it was calculated that over its twelve-year duration her family's patrimony had increased eight-fold.

In the modernization of different societies, the distinction between state and society is accompanied by further processes of differentiation taking place within both realms. For instance, within the civil society there emerges a domain—science—which attends expressly and exclusively to the production and distribution of secular knowledge about nature, autonomously from religious authorities. Within the state itself, the so-called 'separation of powers' between the legislature, the judiciary, and the executive constitutes the outcome of a process of differentiation. The process also produces its effects in the context of the executive, with the development of bureaucratic systems of administration (see also Chapter 8 'Governments and bureaucracies'). As a result, the state increasingly presents itself as a complex of purposely differentiated and coordinated parts, each designed to perform a specific task.

The public sphere

Behind these aspects of political modernization lies a further phenomenon—the formation of the '**public sphere**' as a kind of hinge between state and society. As if to balance and complement the extent to which the state monitors and assists the processes of the civil society, the subjects active in it acquire a capacity first to observe the activities of the state, then to communicate with one another about them, to criticize them, and finally to make significant inputs into them. This is only possible, at first, for the narrow portion of the population possessing the leisure and the necessary material and cultural resources.

But over time this portion grows, availing itself of such arrangements as the freedom of speech, of the press, of petition, of **assembly**, of association; of rules that require some state organs to conduct their activities in public, exposing them to legitimate debate and criticism; above all, of the institutions of 'representative' government. Due to these in particular, the selection of the small minorities who directly and continuously operate some state organs comes to depend on registering the preferences periodically expressed by the much larger numbers of people making up the electorate.

At first, only a narrow minority within the population can form and express such preferences. Even as that minority grows, with the progress of **liberalism**, for a long time its rights remain limited by two qualifications: (i) material possessions (*census voting*); and (ii) cultural attainments (*capacity voting*) (see also Chapter 5 'Democracies'). We can characterize the progress of *democracy* as the progressive lowering and then elimination of these barriers. In the long run, the great majority of the adult population (mostly, until relatively recently, excluding women) acquires, through suffrage, an equal (though minimal) capacity to express political preferences and to impinge on the selection of governing elites and, via these, the formation and execution of public policy.

The new 'entrants into politics' are mobilized by expressly formed organizations—political parties (see Chapter 12 'Political parties')—which compete in order to determine directly who at a given time has the decisive say in legislative and executive organs, and indirectly the content of their activities. In this manner, public policy is increasingly the product of 'adversary politics', of a periodic, legitimate contest between parties for electoral support. The party which has failed in a given contest can publicly criticize the policies of the successful party, elaborate alternative policies, and seek success in the next contest.

The burden of conflict

Although we generally think of political participation chiefly as entailing a *vertical* flow of influence from the society at large towards its political summit, we should not forget the etymological meaning of 'participation'—*taking sides*—that points instead to a *horizontal* split, a division within the society itself. Put otherwise: through the public sphere, the contrasts of opinion on political matters formed within the society map themselves onto the state, affecting the operations of its legislative organs and of those charged with the formation and **implementation** of policy.

Political alignments such as parties often derive their conflicting policy orientations from deep and long-standing *social cleavages* within the population (see Chapter 13 'Party systems'). Some **cleavages** do not just represent different orientations of opinion concerning single issues, but also reflect serious cultural differences (say, between religious or linguistic groups), tensions between a country's centre and its periphery, ethnic differences, or sharp class antagonisms. In the modern political vocabulary, the significance of such a threat is evident in such negative expressions as 'sectionalism', 'factionalism', 'partisanship', or 'interest', and in the contrasting emphasis on the necessity of protecting the state's 'unity' from such phenomena, appealing instead to the generality's 'loyalty', 'discipline', and 'spirit of sacrifice'.

Citizenship and nation

In most modern states, this threat is countered by two different, and to an extent complementary strategies: **citizenship** and the nation.

Citizenship

The first strategy consists in the institution of citizenship, which finds its primordial expression in the dictum that *all citizens are equal before the law*. Eventually, the principle came to signify the progressive inclusion of all individuals making up the people into a formally equal relationship to the state itself. Individuals placed under the same obligations and enjoying the same entitlements vis-à-vis the state were made to feel more equal to one another. Furthermore, their activities relating to the public sphere were put at the service of a new principle of equality, associated with the progress of democracy, and originally phrased as *'one man, one vote'*.

Under this principle, as we have seen, broader and broader masses of individuals entered the political process and made inputs into the state's activities via the electoral competition between parties. Those supported chiefly by economically disadvantaged strata promoted public policies that added to citizenship new entitlements towards the state. These, to an extent, reduced, or compensated for, economic inequalities generated among individuals by market processes and the resultant class cleavage.

However, this happened by mobilizing class contrasts, by making the processes of creation and distribution of wealth an object of public contention and of policy, no longer shielded from the state by the separateness of the economic realm and the autonomy of the market. The state acknowledged the significance of socio-economic cleavages and expressly worked to reduce it via the increasing operations of the **welfare state**. To this end, it extracted from the economy greater and greater resources, and entrusted them to expressly created public organs, charged with both redistributing some of those resources and assisting the economy in producing further ones. This process, however, also produced negative effects, at any rate from the standpoint of the elites privileged by the workings of the economy—although often also elites, these variously benefitted from the growing involvement of the state in economic affairs.

Nationhood

The second strategy seeks to generate in the whole society, across the classes, a shared sense of solidarity grounded on nationhood. The political community typical of modern states understands itself as a *nation*. Most of the polities with which this book deals define themselves as nation-states; the relations of states with one another make up international politics; the pursuit of the national interest by each state is supposed to be the key rationale of those relations. Finally, **nationalism** is widely seen (for better or for worse) as a most significant determinant of political activity.

For all this, the concept of nation is notoriously hard to define. The etymology of the expression hints at a nation's origins in a shared biological heritage, for it has the same root as 'nature' and *nasci* (Latin for 'to be born'). And indeed, some contemporary accounts of the concept, sometimes labelled 'ethnic', emphasize similarity (and continuity) of blood, attributing to the phenomenon of nationhood a primordial, biological origin. Although this emphasis is echoed in the ideologies of many political movements, it does not accord well with the fact that the reference to nationhood as a political value and the corresponding 'consciousness of kind' are by and large modern phenomena.

Reflecting this, most contemporary scholarly understandings of nationhood treat it as a response to, or a component of, other modern phenomena, such as industrialization, the diffusion of literacy, the emergence of media of communication addressing broader and broader publics, and indeed the state's need to generate at large a sense of identification with itself and of commitment to its interests. This view found exemplary expression in a statement the Italian statesman Massimo D'Azeglio made in 1861: 'We have made Italy, now we must make the Italians.' On this account, nations have recently been characterized as *imagined and socially constructed* communities (Anderson 1983) (see Box 4.1).

In this view, most nations have been brought into being by protracted, intense, diffuse communication processes, mostly activated by the state itself and carried out on its behalf, funded from the public purse, and carried out by modern intellectuals (historians, journalists, poets, musicians, teachers, political leaders). Their products are diffused by public education systems (whose audiences are to a various extent recruited through compulsion), and by symbolic practices promoted by the state (such as monuments, street names, public festivities, commemorations, and military parades). To the extent of its success, this operation sustains in the members of the public a sense of trust, mutual belonging, pride, and solidarity.

As a result of such socialization processes, a people who had lived for generations within the same framework of rule may come to share a value-laden, emotionally compelling image of its history and its destiny, a sense of its own uniqueness and superior value. It comes to perceive itself as a distinctively significant, binding, active, collective entity. It generally identifies closely with the territory of the state, which it considers its own cradle and the material ground of its identity. Alternatively, it aspires to make the territory on which it resides the seat of a new self-standing state, intended to give political expression to its unity, to redeem its population from its painful and demeaning subjection to a state governed by foreigners. It may then happen that the emergence of a nation as a cultural entity *precedes* the formation of a state, intended to become the nation's own institutional container and give it political expression.

The emphasis on nationhood counteracts the tendency of the public sphere to project into the political realm divisions arising from the diverse, often conflicting, interests which motivate the activities of

private individuals in the civil society. But the appeal to nationhood has also a more positive significance, which relates it to citizenship and the trend towards widening and enriching its significance.

Earlier in this section, I considered citizenship as a set of arrangements for reducing the economic under-privilege of large social groups, and thus their material distance from privileged groups. But the effort to reduce greater socio-economic inequality can also impart more significance to nationhood itself. In the historical career of citizenship, the rhetoric of 'one nation' has played at least as great a role as that of 'social justice'. In fact, the earliest modern state-wide 'welfare' policies, initiated by Bismarck in nineteenth-century Germany, were probably inspired more by the first concern than by the second. And one may detect a connection between the burden and suffering that the state's military ventures imposed on a people, supposedly on behalf of the national interest, and the state's attempt to ease those burdens or compensate for those sufferings through *welfare* initiatives.

Although it is argued that political power maintains its ultimate grounding in the exercise or the threat of organized violence, the latter ceases to manifest itself openly and harshly in everyday experience. Most of the people professionally involved in (so to speak) the business of politics no longer differ markedly (as they did in earlier stages of state development) in their attire, their posture, their speech, the ways they relate to one another and to other people, from individuals involved in commerce, management, or the liberal professions.

Today, most kinds of political and administrative activity are carried out in peaceable and orderly sites (legislative bodies, courts, public agencies of various kinds), where people generally talk politely to one another, consult and refer to documents, argue about solutions to problems, negotiate arrangements, express reasons for their preferences, put forward proposals. Even when superiors expressly give binding orders to their subordinates, they refer at most in an implicit, covert manner to the sanctions which would follow from disobedience, and those sanctions rarely entail the exercise or the threat of violence. The highest and most general legal commands—say, statutes—are expressed in highly codified sophisticated language. Lower-level commands (say, a fine or an order to pay tax) are only valid and binding if they refer to higher-level ones.

This does not mean that political activity has lost its ability to threaten or exercise violence. However, the personnel routinely involved in it are generally (not in times of war) a minority among the multitude of people carrying out the manifold political activities that were characteristic of a developed state.

DEFINITION 4.1

Imagined communities

The nation is an 'imagined' political community.

- It is *imagined* because the members of even the smallest nation will never know most of their fellow members, meet them, or even hear of them, yet in the minds of each lives the image of their communion.

- It is imagined as *limited* because even the largest of them, encompassing perhaps a billion human beings, has finite, if variable boundaries, beyond which lie other nations.

- It is imagined as *sovereign* because the concept was born when enlightenment and revolution destroyed the legitimacy of the divinely ordained hierarchical dynastic realm.

- It is imagined as a *community* because, regardless of the actual inequality and exploitation that may prevail/in each, the nation is always conceived of as a deep horizontal comradeship.

Adapted from Anderson (1983: 6–7)

Generally, only people serving in the police and the armed forces are authorized and expected to bear arms, to wear uniforms. *They* belong to bodies where an imperious chain of command obtains; harsh sanctions may be promptly inflicted on those members who disobey or disregard orders. Thus, the threat or exercise of violence is entrusted to specialized personnel and separated from the normal practices of political authority, both materially (for instance, soldiers reside in barracks) and symbolically (consider again the uniforms worn by members of the army and the police, their visible markers of rank).

Punishment is no longer inflicted on miscreants in public places, or in a particularly visible, dramatic, cruel manner. The most common among serious punishments—imprisonment—is mostly carried out in a routinized, silent, invisible manner, in separate buildings, often out of the public eye. And the decision to bring to bear the means of violence on criminals or on enemies belongs in principle to political personnel not themselves directly involved in practising violence—judges, members of representative bodies, and top political officials.

This kind of 'civilianized' arrangement typically does not diminish the state's capacity for organized violence, but increases it. Paradoxically (but this effect had already been theorized by Hobbes) the increase in the *potential* for violence is typically accompanied by a decrease in the entity of *actual* exercise of violence. As they go about the ordinary business of their lives, individuals may be spared the experience of fear by the very fact that the potential violence monopolized by the state becomes more, not less, fearsome.

The conceptual portrait recapped

The modern political environment is composed of a plurality of states sharing some formal characteristics. Thanks to its monopoly of legitimate organized violence, each state exercises sovereign power over a population which inhabits a delimited territory, and constitutes a political community, often referred to as a nation. The interactions between states are normally peaceable, but since they are not overseen and regulated by a superior power capable of imposing sanctions, they ultimately depend on the armed might that each state can bring to bear in order to contrast or overwhelm other states pursuing interests opposed to its own. Thus, those interactions are highly contingent and may periodically be adjusted by the threat or exercise of military action between the states involved.

Over the course of the past two or three centuries, many states have, to a greater or lesser degree, acquired additional traits. Their internal structure is generally designed and controlled by the laws each state produces and enforces, which in turn regulate its own activities. These are very diverse, and are generally carried out by a number of organs and specialized agencies. They deal directly with matters the state considers to be of public significance, viewing other matters as the primary concern of (civil) society, pursued on the initiative of individual citizens.

However, some state activities, including the making of laws and their enforcement, lay down frameworks for the pursuit by individuals of their own private concerns. Furthermore, the institutions of the public sphere may empower individuals to form and communicate opinions on state policies, and to organize themselves in parties which represent the diverse (and often contrasting) interests within the society, select the personnel of various state organs, and mandate their policies.

In the course of the past two centuries, most states have conferred on the individuals within their populations a variable set of citizenship entitlements, beginning with those relating to the public sphere, and comprising claims to various benefits and services provided by the state, ultimately funded from the proceeds of the state's fiscal activities. The advance of citizenship has often entailed making a public issue of socio-economic differences between individuals, and committing state policy to their moderation. For this reason, it has often been contested. One may consider the appeal to nationhood, and the state's positive efforts to 'push' that appeal, as a way of curbing the divisive effects of the contests over the reach and content of citizenship entitlements.

Q   DEFINITION 4.2

Citizenship

So far, my aim has been to trace in outline the development of citizenship in England to the end of the nineteenth century. For this purpose, I have divided citizenship into three elements: civil, political, and social. I have tried to show that civil rights came first, and were established in something like their modern form before the first Reform Act was passed in 1832. Political rights came next, and their extension was one of the main features of the nineteenth century, although the principle of universal political citizenship was not recognized until 1918. Social rights, on the other hand, sank to vanishing point in the eighteenth and early nineteenth centuries. Their revival began with the establishment of public elementary education, but it was not until the twentieth century that they attained equal partnership with the other two elements of citizenship.

Marshall (1950: 27–8)

KEY POINTS

- States differentiate between their political activities and those of the civil society (the pursuit of private economic interests and the expression of personal beliefs and values). They articulate themselves through legal instruments (constitutions, statutes, decrees, various kinds of rulings) into units operated by distinct bodies of personnel. In particular, they have entrusted practices concerning internal order and external defence to the police and the military.

- In the democratic state, decisions over state policies are the products of the peaceable competition between parties seeking to maximize their electoral support in order to occupy the top positions in various state bodies and to promote the interests of their supporters.

- Policies pursued by states since the middle of the nineteenth century have sought to moderate inequalities by assigning individual members of the population civil, political, and social rights—i.e. citizenship (see Box 4.2).

- To counter divisive tendencies between groups, states have undertaken policies intended to generate a sense of commonality—chiefly, a sense of national belonging.

State development

The features of the state presented in the preceding section, 'A more expansive concept', are the outcomes of complex historical events (see Box 4.3). These differed not just in their location in space and time, but also in (i) the sequence in which they occurred; (ii) the degree to which their protagonists expressly sought to produce those outcomes; (iii) the extent to which the features agreed or conflicted with one another; and (iv) the impact they had on the patterns of political activity of each state, its relations to the civil society, and its capacity to respond to new challenges.

Furthermore, as we have seen, all states-in-the-making operated in the presence of one another, which led some states to imitate some aspects of others, or, on the contrary, to emphasize their differences. This further complicated the historical processes. For instance, some states previously unified by the successful efforts of royal dynasties sought to strengthen their unity by promoting a sense of nationhood. Later, other states imitated such a nation-building project. Furthermore, populations which, despite being ruled over by foreign powers, had somehow acquired a sense of themselves as 'nations without states' sought to build states of their own. Thus, in some cases **state-building** preceded nation-building; in other cases, it was the opposite.

The study of comparative politics necessarily simplifies these complex phenomena, for instance by stressing either differences or similarities between units. It contrasts states built early, in late medieval or early modern Europe (for instance, England or France), with others built during later stages of modernization (for instance, in the second half of the nineteenth century, as in the case of Germany or Italy). It distinguishes states built upon successful conquest (for instance, England) from those owing their existence to the breakdown of larger polities (for instance, contemporary Serbia or Ukraine).

This section of the chapter distinguishes three main phases within the story of state formation and development, which unfolded first in Europe, then extended to polities established elsewhere by European powers (for instance, North America), and later encompassed other parts of the world. However, the way in which it is narrated here chiefly reflects the European experience. Even in this context, the succession of phases suggested purposely abstracts from a huge variety of events, incidents, and episodes which a properly historical treatment would have to reconstruct.

Consolidation of rule

We can label the first phase, which takes place largely between the twelfth and the seventeenth centuries,

Q DEFINITION 4.3

Patterns of state formation

We can distinguish at least five paths in state formation.

1. Through *absolutist kingship*, which obtained independent power by building up armies and bureaucracies solely responsible to monarchs (e.g. France, Prussia).

2. Through *kingship-facing judges and representative bodies* (and, within them, eventually political parties), which developed sufficient strength to become independent powers (e.g. England, Sweden).

3. State formation from below through *confederation or federation*, intended to preserve some degree of autonomy for the constituent 'states' and a general emphasis on the division of power within the centre through 'checks and balances' (e.g. Switzerland, US).

4. State formation through *conquest and/or unification* (e.g. Germany, Italy).

5. State formation through *independence* (e.g. Ireland, Norway, and cases of break-up of empires: Habsburg and Ottoman empires).

Adapted from Daalder (1991: 14)

'consolidation of rule'. During this phase, with different timings in different countries, a decreasing number of political centres each extend their control over a larger and larger portion of Europe. Each typically broadens the territorial reach of its own monopoly of legitimate violence and imposes it on other centres. The political map of the continent becomes simpler and simpler, since each centre now practises rule, in an increasingly uniform manner, over larger territories. Furthermore, these tend to become geographically more continuous and historically more stable—unless, of course, they become themselves objects of further processes of consolidation.

Sometimes these are peaceful. For instance, the scions of two dynasties ruling over different parts of Europe marry, and the territorial holdings of one spouse become welded to those of the other. However, consolidation is mostly the outcome of open conflicts between two centres over which one will control which territory. Such conflicts are mostly settled by war, followed by the winner conquering and forcibly annexing all or part of the loser's territory. 'States make war', as someone memorably put it, 'and wars make states' (Tilly 1990: 42).

However, waging war requires a financial capacity to muster resources—troops, officers, hardware—and deploy them against opponents, making them prevail in the clash of arms against the resources wielded by the enemy. Very often, military innovation confers an advantage to larger armies and fleets, which can wage war over more than one front, and become internally differentiated into 'services' performing distinct complementary military tasks. But such armies and fleets can only be afforded by rulers who marshal larger resources, which in turn requires raising troops from larger populations, tapping the wealth produced by larger territories. This premium on size is a strong inducement to consolidation.

But the recourse to war, however frequent throughout European history, is intermittent. When weapons are silent, however temporarily, resources of a different nature come into play. Often, political centres intent on consolidating rule do this in response to an appeal for peace, which recurs most frequently in European history, often voiced by religious leaders. Each centre seeks to prove itself by establishing its control over a larger territory, thus putting an end to rivalries between lesser powers which would otherwise occasion war. This does not always involve prevailing over those powers in battle. Diplomatic action, alliances and coalitions, the ability to isolate opponents or to make them accept a degree of subordination, and sometimes the recourse to arbitration by the empire or the papacy also play a role.

Besides, military activity itself requires and produces rules of its own, the very core of an emerging body of law seeking to regulate, more or less successfully, aspects of the relations between states. Another significant part of such law makes conflict over territory less likely by laying down clear principles for succession into vacant seats of power, which generally make the exclusive entitlement to rule dependant on legitimate descent. Other developments contribute to the same effect, which we might call 'pacification'. In particular, advances in geography, in the measurement of terrain, and in cartography allow the physical reach of each centre of rule to be clearly delimited by geographical borders, often determined by features of the terrain. It remains true, as Hobbes put it, that states maintain towards one another, even when they are not fighting, 'a posture of warre'. But they partition the continent of Europe, and later other continents, in a clear and potentially stable manner.[2]

Rationalization of rule

There is often an overlap between the processes of consolidation in the first phase of state formation and development, and the processes of a second phase, which I label the 'rationalization of rule'. Consolidation, we have seen, produces larger, more visible, and stable containers of state power; **rationalization** bears chiefly on the ways in which such power is exercised. We can characterize such ways by distinguishing in turn three aspects of it: (i) **centralization**; (ii) hierarchy; and (iii) function. Let us take them in turn.

Centralization

In consolidating and then exercising rule, rulers largely availed themselves of the cooperation of various subordinate but privileged power-holders— chiefly, aristocratic dynasties, towns and other local or regional bodies, bishops, and other ecclesiastical officials. Often that cooperation was granted only after the subordinate powers had been forced to renounce some of their privileges—in particular, especially as concerns aristocrats, that of waging private wars.

All the same, their later cooperation generally had to be negotiated, since the privileged powers maintained a degree of autonomous control over various resources, and managed them in the first instance on their own behalf. They could be induced to do so on the ruler's behalf only under certain conditions, sanctioned by tradition or by express agreements between themselves and the ruler. For instance, the cooperating lesser powers would extract economic resources from the local population under their jurisdiction in order to convey them to the ruler. But they would do so only if they had given their consent to the purpose to which the ruler intended to commit those resources. They often kept a fairly large part of those resources for themselves, and controlled locally the ways in which the remainder of them were managed and expended in their respective part of the territory.

Obviously, such arrangements considerably limit the rulers' freedom of action, their ability to lay down policy for the state as a whole and have it promptly, reliably, and uniformly implemented over the whole territory. They make the conduct of political and administrative business discontinuous and sometimes erratic, since who is charged with it at a given time—in particular, qua head of an aristocratic lineage—depends on the vagaries of hereditary succession, and often has no particular inclination or capacity for that business. Even the cooperation granted, as we have seen, by constituted collective bodies (the so-called 'estates') tends to give priority to their particular interests, and thus to preserve traditional arrangements, beginning with their autonomy. This makes it difficult for the ruler to coordinate and render predictable the practices of the several powers interposed between himself at the top and, at the bottom, a territory made larger by consolidation and its population.

To remedy this situation, rulers progressively dispossess the existent individuals and bodies of their faculties and facilities they had employed in their political and administrative tasks.[3] They put in place alternative arrangements for performing both those tasks and those required by new circumstances. Instead of relying on their former cooperators, they choose to avail themselves of *agents and agencies*, i.e. individuals and bodies which the rulers themselves select, empower, activate, control, fund, discipline, and reward. In other terms, rulers build *bureaucracies* (see Box 4.4).

In principle, this process could greatly increase the hold upon social life at large of the political centre, enable the ruler to exercise power in an unbounded, arbitrary, and despotic fashion, and expose all those subject to it to extreme insecurity. In fact, the previous cooperators who objected to the ruler's new arrangements often raised complaints to that effect, sometimes with considerable justification. But more often, their objections simply reflected their attachment to their previous privileges. We would not characterize this phase as 'rationalization of rule' if its chief import had been solely to unbind rule.

It is a feature of 'the European miracle'—the title of the book by Jones (1981)—that this phase of state-building has two apparently contrasting aspects. Rulers do come to oversee, control, and to an extent manage social life at large in a more and more intense, continuous,

---

ZOOM-IN 4.1

The bureaucratic state

Where the rule of law prevails, a bureaucratic organization is governed by the following principles.

1. Official business is conducted on a continuous basis.

2. There are rules in an administrative agency such that (i1) the duty of each official to do certain types of work is delimited in terms of impersonal criteria; (ii) the official is given the authority necessary to carry out his/her assigned functions; and (iii) the means of compulsion at his/her disposal are strictly limited.

3. Official responsibilities and authority are part of a hierarchy.

4. Officials do not own the resources necessary for the performance of their functions, but are accountable for their use. Official and private affairs are strictly separated.

5. Offices cannot be appropriated by their incumbents in the sense of private property that can be sold or inherited.

6. Official business is conducted on the basis of written documents.

Source: Bendix (1960: 418–19).

---

systematic, purposive, and pervasive manner. However, to be legitimate, rule must appear to be oriented to interests acknowledged as general, and be exercised in a more and more impersonal and formal manner. The notion of *raison d'état* conveys both aspects. It asserts that the might and security of the polity are a general and paramount interest whose pursuit may occasionally override all others. But that interest is to be sought through self-conscious deliberation, grounded on an assiduous, detached monitoring of circumstances.

In fact, the rationalization of rule itself is part of a broader process of rationalization of social existence at large. Each major sphere of society (beginning with the three already mentioned: politics, economy, and religion) becomes the exclusive concern of a different institutional complex—a distinctive ensemble of arrangements, personnel, resources, principles, and patterns of activity. This allows (and perhaps demands) each concern to be pursued in such a way as to maximize a distinctive goal: respectively, the might and security of the state, the profitability of economic operations, and the individual's prospects of spiritual salvation.

Hierarchy

In the political context, rationalization changes the basis of the routine exercise of power: the public understanding of its nature, its objective, its boundaries.

As we have seen, that basis was traditionally constituted by the *rights and perquisites* of a number of privileged individuals and bodies (see Chapter 8 'Governments and bureaucracies'). The new basis consists in the *duties and obligations* of individuals (we may label them 'bureaucrats' or 'officials') appointed purposefully to established offices. Their political and administrative activities can be programmed from above by means of express commands. Those issuing such commands can reward those to whom they are issued if they comply with them, and punish them if they do not. The commands themselves have two critical characteristics: (i) they tend to be general, i.e. they refer in abstract terms to a variety of concrete circumstances; (ii) their content can legitimately change, and thus respond to new circumstances (see Box 4.4).

For this to happen, the new ensembles of individuals who carry out political and administrative activities—the bureaucratic units—must be hierarchically structured. At the bottom of the structure, even lowly officials are empowered to impart commands (issue verdicts, demand tributes, conscript military recruits, deny or give permissions) to those lying below the structure itself. However, those officials themselves are supposed to do so in compliance with directives communicated to them by superiors. These monitor the activity of their direct subordinates, verify their conformity with directives and, if necessary, override or correct their orders. This arrangement, replicated at various levels within the whole structure, establishes an ordered array where higher offices supervise, activate, and direct lower ones. In a related hierarchical arrangement, lower offices *inform* higher ones—make suggestions on how to deal with situations—and higher ones *make decisions* and transmit them downwards to lower ones for implementation.

As already indicated, law plays a significant role in structuring these arrangements for rule. First, as we have seen, law itself is a hierarchically structured set of authoritative commands. Second, law can be taught and learned, and the knowledge of it (at its various levels) can determine, to a greater or lesser extent, the content of the agents' political and administrative operations.

This second aspect of the law points to a broader aspect of the rationalization of rule—the growing role of *knowledge* in the government and administration of the state. As rulers increasingly dispense with the cooperation of privileged individuals and bodies, the agents who replace them are largely chosen on account of what they know, or are presumed to know, and by their having earned academic degrees and passed selective tests. Agents are expected to orient their practices of rule less and less to their own individual preferences or to local particular tradition and lore,

and more and more to expressly imparted and learned systematic knowledge. Legal knowledge is the prototype of this, especially on the European continent, but it is increasingly complemented and supplemented by different kinds of knowledge—for instance, those relevant to equipping armies and waging war, building roads and bridges, charting the country, collecting statistical data, keeping financial accounts, minting money, policing cities, and safeguarding public health.

Function

Another principle structuring the centralized system of offices is *function*: the system is internally differentiated in order to have each part deal optimally with a specific task. To this end, the system parts must possess materially different resources—not only various bodies of knowledge, acquired and brought to bear by appropriately trained and selected personnel, but artefacts as diverse as weapons at one end and printing presses at the other.

For all its diversity, the whole structure is activated and controlled not only by knowledge but also by *money*, another public reality distinctly connected with rationality, chiefly acquired through taxation. Traditional power holders had usually engaged in collaborating with rulers' material and other resources from their own patrimony; their collaboration was self-financed and unavoidably self-interested. Now, agencies operate by spending public funds allocated to them by express periodic decisions (budgets) and are held accountable for how those funds are spent. Office holders are typically salaried, manage resources that do not belong to them but to their offices, and, as they comply with their duties, are not expected to seek personal gain, except through career advancement.[4]

To the extent that it is rationalized, the exercise of rule becomes more compatible with the individuals' pursuit of their interests within the civil society. From the perspective of those individuals, rule exercised by officials appears more regular and predictable, and occasional deviations from rules can be redressed. Rulers are interested in increasing the resources available to the society as a whole, if only to draw upon them in funding their political and administrative activities. But to this effect they must respect the requirements of the country's economic system, at best protect, or indeed foster, its productive dynamic, which rests increasingly on the market. To this end, again, the extraction from the economy of private resources by the state increasingly takes place chiefly by means of taxation.

The security of those resources and of their employment must be sustained by guaranteeing, through appropriate legislation and the machinery of law enforcement, the institutions of private property and contract. But other social interests and cultural concerns, not just economic ones, also benefit from the limits that rationalized rule sets on its own scope and from the arrangements it makes in order to recognize and protect the autonomy of civil society.

The expansion of rule

In the third phase, states display a dynamic which we may label the 'expansion of rule'. For centuries, the activities of each state had been oriented to two main concerns:

1. On the international scene, it sought chiefly to secure itself from encroachments on its territory by other states and on its ability to define and pursue its own interests autonomously.

2. Within its territory, it was committed to maintaining public order and the effectiveness of its laws.

In the second half of the nineteenth and through much of the twentieth century, however, states brought their activities of rule to bear on an increasingly diverse range of social interests.

Essentially, the state no longer simply *ordains* through legislation the autonomous undertakings of individuals and groups or *sanctions* their private arrangements through its judicial system. Increasingly, it *intervenes* in private concerns by modifying those arrangements or by collecting greater resources and then redistributing them, more to some parties than to others. Also, it seeks to *manage* social activities according to its own judgements and preferences, for it considers the outcome of those activities as a legitimate public concern, which should reflect a broader and higher interest (such as the promotion of industrial development, social equity, or national solidarity).

The expansion of rule modifies deeply the relationship between state and society of the previous phase. On this account, we can classify most of its explanations according to whether they locate the main source of the drive to expand in the state itself or in society.

The former accounts occur in various versions:

1. First, they impute to the state's administrative machinery an inherent tendency to grow, to avail itself of more resources, to take charge of more tasks, and to address more numerous and diverse social interests, instead of leaving them to the market or to the autonomous pursuits of individuals and groups (see Box 4.5).

2. Or, second, they may see the main reason for state expansion in the dynamics of representative democracy and of adversary politics. Putting it

ZOOM-IN 4.2

Wagner's law

Consider the following scattered indication of the validity of Wagner's law, according to which government spending tends to rise faster than the growth of the national economy as a whole. In the UK, government spending accounted over time for the following percentages:

Year	%
1890	8.9
1920	20.2
1938	30.0
1960	36.4
1970	43.0
1981	50.3
1983	53.5

Similarly, in the US the amount of government (federal, state, and local) spending as a proportion of the net national product almost tripled between 1926 and 1979. For all OECD countries over the period 1953–73, the average of the national product accounted for by government spending rose from 34 to 39 per cent.

Source: Poggi (1999: 109).

simply, it pays for a party out of power to increase its support by promising, if voted into power, to devote more public resources to this or that new state activity, and thus advance the interests of social groups responding to its appeal. Typically, it is parties of the left which have successfully played this card, and made new use of state activity and state expenditure to reduce the disadvantages inflicted on their supporters by market processes.

3. This interpretation fits closely with a third one, which imputes the expansion of the state chiefly to phenomena located in the society side of the state–society divide. Here, underprivileged groups stand to gain most by state expansion, and thus invoke it and favour it, through their suffrage or by other forms of **mobilization**.

4. However, according to a fourth interpretation, many aspects of state expansion support directly or indirectly, rather than correct and counteract, the workings of the market economy in the interest primarily of firms and employers. For instance, some colonial ventures of European

states favoured major economic forces seeking privileged access to the raw materials, manpower, and market opportunities that they saw in foreign lands, or seeking profit from the supply to the state of military and naval hardware. Furthermore, for over a century now, many public resources have been committed to educational activities, which deliver to the labour market employees equipped with the diverse qualifications and skills the economy needs. In the second half of the twentieth century, the state often underwrote, on behalf of firms and thus primarily of employers, substantial research and development costs to sustain advanced and profitable production processes and to fund innovation in them.

More widely, this fourth interpretation attributes much state expansion to the fact that, left to itself, the market often does not generate enough demand for industrial products to sustain capital investment, a reasonable level of employment, and thus domestic demand for industrial products. From this perspective, the main beneficiaries of state expansion are, in the end, the more established and privileged social groups.

In fact, the frequently evoked imagery of states expanding by considering as their own social tasks previously performed by autonomous social forces, and usurping society, is sometimes misleading. Many of the activities carried out, well or otherwise, by the expanding state, respond to *novel* needs, potentialities, and opportunities generated by ongoing social developments, such as the demographic explosion, urbanization, increasing literacy, mass motorization, further industrialization, and growing complexity of society itself. Even at the end of the nineteenth century, Durkheim had argued, in opposition to Spencer, that in the process of modernization the development of the private realm also requires the development of the public one.

Whatever the reasons for it, state expansion entails a growth in three interdependent aspects:

- the *fiscal take*, i.e. the portion of a country's yearly product extracted and managed by the state;
- the degree of *internal differentiation* of the organizational machinery of the state;
- the *total number of individuals* whom those units employ, and who possess increasingly varied qualifications and skills.

The last two phenomena not only displace the line between state and society, but also affect deeply the state itself, which increasingly resembles an ever-growing poorly coordinated ensemble of increasingly diverse units. The ordinary political processes—the articulation of collective interests via the parties and their periodic electoral competition, the determination of the executive by majorities, and the formation of policies through the interplay between the executive and parliaments—can less and less effectively activate and steer an administrative machinery so vast, expensive, complex, and diverse.

Much in political decision-making and in the subsequent administrative activity responds to the interests of the units themselves, or those of the specific, often narrow, sections of society they cater to, rather than expressing a political project reflecting a comprehensive view of the society as a whole. Thus, the administrative machinery becomes *overloaded* by multiple, ever-changing, conflicting demands. Furthermore, components of it are 'captured' by powerful and demanding social forces, and serve their needs rather than those of the public at large. All these phenomena make it more and more difficult for the political elites themselves to design and put into effect the policies for which the electorate has expressed a preference.

These phenomena manifest themselves in most contemporary states, but they do so to a different extent and in diverse ways. As the subsequent chapters show, one of the major tasks of the study of comparative politics is to establish empirically, and to account for, the variations present in the contemporary political environment, both in those manifestations and in the responses they find in the political authorities, the parties, and the **social movements**.

KEY POINTS

- One can distinguish, within the historical career of the modern state, three main phases which different European states have followed in somewhat varying sequences.

- *Consolidation of rule*: within each larger part of the continent (beginning with its Western parts) one particular centre of rule asserted its own superiority, generally by defeating others in war, subjecting the respective lands to its own control, and turning them into a unified territory.

- *Rationalization of rule*: each centre of rule increasingly relied on functionaries selected and empowered by itself, expressly qualified for their offices, and forming hierarchically structured units, within which their careers would depend on the reliability and effectiveness of their actions.

- *Expansion of rule*: states progressively took on broader sets of functions, in order both to confront social needs generated by ongoing processes of economic modernization and to respond to demands for public regulation and intervention originating from various sectors of society. They added new specialized administrative units and funded their activities by increasing their 'fiscal take' from the economy.

Conclusion

It can safely be assumed that the vast majority of this book's readers live in a political environment which resembles more or less closely the portrait of 'the state' given in this chapter, and whose institutions and practices bear traces of the developments sketched in the last section on 'State development'. For this reason, those readers—whatever their feelings about the state of which they are citizens, and however they position themselves vis-à-vis the particular govern-ment which runs it—may take for granted its main features, including the fact that they are able, among other things, to study scientifically that state itself and to compare it with others. However, this chapter, and others in this book, are intended to challenge the assumption that such matters can indeed be taken for granted.

The following statement by a notable German social theorist, Heinrich Popitz (1925–2002), entails such a challenge.

The history of society shows only rare instances where the question 'how can one lay boundaries around institutionalized violence?' has been confronted in a positive and viable manner. Essentially, this has happened only in the Greek *polis*, in the Roman republic and a few other city states, and in the history of the modern constitutional state. And the answers given to that question have been astonishingly similar. The principle of the supremacy of the law and of the equality of all before the law (the Greeks named it *isonomia*). The notion that the making of norms by the state encounters limitations (fundamental rights). Norms assigning different competences to various political organs (division of powers, federalism). Procedural norms (decisions by collective bodies, their public nature, appeals to and review by higher organs). Norms on the occupancy of offices (turn-taking, elections). Finally, norms concerning the public sphere (freedom of opinion, freedom of association and assembly). The similarity, or indeed the commonality among such answers suggests that there are systematic solutions of the problem, how to limit institutionalized power and violence, and that these solutions, although they presuppose certain premises if they are to hold, can to an extent hold across different contexts—as different, say, as city states and those ruling over extensive territories.

Popitz (1992: 65)

Popitz's statement suggests some comments.

1. Although I have treated 'the state' as essentially a modern phenomenon (and its development as the chief political dimension of the broader phenomenon of modernization), some of its distinctive institutional arrangements had already manifested themselves in antiquity, as well as in the Middle Ages.

2. Both the earlier and the later (modern) arrangements appear at first as part of a distinctive Western story, for they originated in Europe and were subsequently transposed to parts of the rest of the world conquered and colonized by European powers, especially in North America and Australia. (However, the US was the first place where a peculiar arrangement, federalism, was more expressly and successfully experimented with, and it served as a model for further experiments—see Chapter 11 'Multilevel governance'.) Since then, some arrangements of this nature have become common to polities operating across the globe, although in different modes of interpretation and **implementation**. Sometimes these modes superficially imitate those of the more established states, but actually characterize the political units employing them as *failed states*.

3. The arrangements mentioned by Popitz, singly and together, succeed in an intrinsically difficult job—limiting, constraining, and 'taming' institutionalized political power.

This last point suggests a further consideration, left implicit in Popitz's statement. Such success cannot be taken for granted. It is a matter of degree, for it requires overcoming a built-in tendency of politi-cal power to grow upon itself, to escape limits and constraints, to 'go wild' as it were—a tendency that can manifest itself in many circumstances and in many ways. In fact, some states which shared the character-istics mentioned in the first section of this chapter, 'A portrait of the state', have not presented all those mentioned in the second section, 'A more expansive concept', which have appeared in later phases of polit-ical modernization and which (in the author's judge-ment) go a long way towards 'civilizing' the state itself.

For instance, the Tsarist Empire refused to endorse many characteristic institutions of the constitu-tional, liberal, democratic states of Western Europe. Worse, even states which at a given point exhibited all those characteristics subsequently veered away from constitutionalism, **liberalism**, and democracy, and underwent institutional changes generally associated with the notion of 'totalitarianism'—as happened in the twentieth century in Italy and Germany (see Chapter 6 'Authoritarian regimes'). And even some of the constitutive features of states listed in the first section, such as 'sovereignty', are currently put under stress by a number of developments—for example, those associated with 'globalization' or with the formation of transnational polities (see Chapter 24 'Globalization and the nation-state').

Even apart from such dramatic developments, the liberal–democratic states themselves differ from one another in many relevant respects. For instance, some impart a centralized and some a federal structure to the relations between the state's political centre and its political periphery. States differ in the extent to which they have broadened and enriched the entitlements of citizenship, or in the extent to which and the manner in which a given state seeks through its policies to support and plan the development of its national economy, as against leaving such development entirely to the workings of the market. The size of the so-called 'public sector' of the economy, and the way in which it has been managed, again have differed from state to state, as have their respective taxation policies.

These and other issues have often been fought over in significant lasting confrontations between parties and between sectors of opinion, and their settlement has been more or less stable, creating affinities or contrasts between states. Besides being the themes of public life, those issues constitute the main topics of the scholarly study of politics, whether focused on a particular state or on the diversity and similarity between states. The latter, of course, is the main concern of this book as a whole.

? QUESTIONS

Knowledge-based

1. What is civil society?

2. Do nations create states or vice versa?

3. What is meant by 'sovereignty'?

4. What part did military force play in the making of European states?

5. How do states typically acquire the economic resources they use?

Critical thinking

1. How can one explain the fact that members of a state's population progressively acquired rights vis-à-vis the state?

2. What part did law play in the development of the modern state?

3. For what reasons did rulers establish bodies of officials appointed and empowered by themselves?

4. What is meant by 'consolidation of rule'?

≋ FURTHER READING

Elias, N. (2000 [1938]) *The Civilizing Process: Sociogenetic and Psychogenetic Investigations* (1st edn) (Oxford: Blackwell). The second large volume of this impressive work deals with the 'sociogenesis of the state'.

Lachmann, R. (2010) *States and Power* (Cambridge: Polity Press). A valuable interpretation of many phenomena considered in this chapter, mostly from a perspective at some variance from that adopted here.

Poggi, G. (1978) *The Development of the Modern State: A Sociological Introduction* (Stanford, CA: Stanford University Press). A compact and accessible statement, ranging from the Middle Ages to the contemporary era.

Tilly, C. (ed.) (1975) *The Formation of National States in Western Europe* (Princeton, NJ: Princeton University Press). A very influential collection of major contributions to its theme, including its military, fiscal, and economic aspects.

Weber, M. (1994 [1919]) 'Politics as a Profession and Vocation', in P. Lassman and R. Speirs (eds), *Weber: Political Writings* (Cambridge: Cambridge University Press) 309–69. A compact but most illuminating and provocative discussion of the nature of politics and the modern state by one of the most significant modern social theorists.

ENDNOTES

1. One often speaks, today, of 'failed' states (see Chapter 25 'From supporting democracy to supporting autocracy').

2. The same rules of delimitation apply to the sea.

3. However, they mostly do that without depriving those individuals and bodies of their private resources and their status advantages.

4. Since not only more significant faculties and responsibilities correspond to higher offices, but also greater material and status rewards, the hierarchical structure we have talked about also constitutes a career system. It is a ladder which office-holders can climb to satisfy their legitimate ambitions.

Visit the Online Resources that accompany this book for additional material, including country profiles, comparative data sets, flashcard glossaries, and web directory.

www.oup.com/he/caramani5e

5

Democracies

Aníbal Pérez-Liñán

Reader's guide

Democracy is the most legitimate form of government in our contemporary era, but the meaning of democracy is still highly contested. This chapter explores the defining elements of modern democracy and traces the origins of this form of government. It also describes different models of democracy (presidential and parliamentary, democracies oriented towards consensus or majoritarian rule), and it analyses the conditions—economic and political, domestic and international—that allow some countries to become democratic but preserve others under the rule of dictatorships. It finally discusses the future of democracy, and the challenges that lie ahead for new generations of citizens.

Introduction

What is democratic rule? Are all democracies equal? Why can some societies achieve democracy while others cannot? How shall democracies evolve in the twenty-first century? These questions shape policy debates throughout the world, from pubs and coffee shops to parliaments and international organizations. These questions defy any simple answers, but we cannot ignore them. Democracy is the dominant principle of legitimacy for governments in our historical era, and rulers everywhere—even the most despotic ones—claim democratic credentials as justification for their power.

In this chapter, we address four crucial issues. First, what do we mean by democracy in the field of comparative politics? Contemporary democracy is an amalgam of political institutions and practices that originated in different historical periods and regions of the world. Moreover, the term 'democracy' describes an ideal as much as the reality of certain forms of government; for this reason, democratic practices are permanently evolving.

Second, we explore the diversity of democratic regimes. Although all democratic systems share some common characteristics, democracies differ in important ways—and some democracies arguably work better than others. The diversity of this family of regimes has increased over time, as the number of democracies expanded in the late twentieth century. By 1974, only thirty-five countries in the world (about 26 per cent of all independent states) could consider themselves democratic; by 2018, some ninety-nine countries (57 per cent of all states) displayed democratic characteristics.

The expansion in the number of democracies prompts our third topic: what variables facilitate the **democratization** of dictatorships, and what factors place democracies at risk of becoming authoritarian regimes? The question of regime change—how dictatorships transit into democracy, and vice versa—connects this chapter with the discussion of authoritarian systems in Chapter 6 'Authoritarian regimes'.

Finally, if the survival of democracy is not guaranteed, we are forced to address the future of our favourite form of government. What are the main problems of contemporary democracy? How can democracy be reformed without being endangered in the process? These are the great challenges for generations to come.

KEY POINTS

- This chapter addresses the meaning of democracy, types of democracy, the causes of democratization, and the future of democracy.

- Democracy is the dominant principle of legitimacy in our historical era.

- The number of democracies in the world expanded in the late twentieth century.

What is democracy (and who created it)?

The term 'democracy' is used in daily life with multiple meanings. Democracy is, first and foremost, an ideal for social organization, a desired system in which—depending on who is speaking—social equality is pursued, freedoms are treasured, justice is achieved, and people respect each other. 'Government of the people, by the people, for the people', famously asserted US President Abraham Lincoln, commemorating the battle of Gettysburg in 1863. When used in this way, the term becomes an 'empty signifier', a carrier for our normative desires and concerns for the political system. This flexibility in meaning has allowed **social movements** to push the boundaries of democracy for over two hundred years (Markoff 1996). But this expansive use also implies that different people will invoke democracy to highlight different dreams and demands at different times. We shall return to this issue in the conclusions of this chapter, 'The future of democracy'.

There is also a historical meaning, since the term—combining the Greek words for 'people' and 'power'—originated in Athens in the sixth century before the Christian era. Athenian democracy would be a strange form of rule for any modern observer: it was *direct* democracy, in the sense that major decisions were made by citizens meeting at a popular **assembly**; only a very small minority of the city's population was granted **citizenship** (women, slaves, former slaves, foreigners, and minors were excluded), there was no constitutional protection of individual rights, and all citizens were expected to participate in the assembly. As a result, the system did not scale up well beyond the size of an independent city, and popular decisions were often arbitrary and inconsistent. Ancient commentators criticized the Athenian regime as the rule of an uninformed mob and argued in favour of 'mixed' forms of government combining principles of monarchy, aristocracy, and democracy (an inspiration for later ideas about separation of powers). The term 'democracy' thus carried a negative connotation for most educated readers until well into the eighteenth century.

The third and most common usage refers to 'really existing' democracies, the political regimes that rule in many contemporary societies. This form of government, which emerged during the nineteenth and twentieth centuries, can be best described as a *mass liberal republic*. Modern democracies are built on republican arrangements: most policy decisions are not made directly by citizens, but they are delegated to representative legislatures (Chapter 7 'Legislatures') and executive leaders (Chapter 8 'Governments and bureaucracies'), who are accountable to the electorate. Moreover, modern democracies are built on the liberal principles of the eighteenth century. Political rights are recognized for all citizens; social and human rights are recognized for non-citizens as well. The government is expected to respect such rights and to protect individuals when their rights are threatened by other actors, such as criminals or corporations (Chapter 9 'Constitutions, rights, and judicial power').

Liberal republics already existed before the industrial era, often under the guise of a constitutional monarchy, to represent the interests of a small aristocratic minority. For example, political scientist Samuel Finer described Great Britain in the eighteenth century as a 'crowned, nobiliar, republic' (Finer 1997: 1358). However, the past two centuries have witnessed an enormous expansion in the scale of political systems—both democratic and non-democratic—to incorporate large segments of the population into the political process. Modern societies achieved this mostly by progressively expanding the right to vote to men without property, to women, to excluded ethnic groups, and to younger adults. Today, over eight hundred million people are eligible to vote in any Indian election, an impressive feat considering that this number of eligible voters is larger than the total population of Europe and more than two-and-a-half times the population of the US.

The historical result of this process is the familiar system of government commonly called 'Western democracy', 'liberal democracy', or plainly 'democracy' in our daily parlance. As the system evolved during the twentieth century, social scientists struggled to understand its defining characteristics. In 1942, economist Joseph Schumpeter argued that modern democracy is the 'institutional arrangement for arriving at political decisions in which individuals acquire the power to decide by means of a competitive struggle for the people's vote' (Schumpeter 1943 [1947]: 269). This definition emphasizing competitive elections has been praised for its simplicity, but also criticized for its limited understanding of the democratic process. In 1971, Robert Dahl extended this idea to argue that modern democracy is defined by the combination of open contestation for power and inclusive political participation. Dahl renamed this system as 'polyarchy' (the government of the many) to distinguish really existing democracies from any abstract democratic ideal. Dahl argued that this system requires a minimum set of procedures and guarantees to work, namely: (i) freedom of organization; (ii) freedom of expression; (iii) the right to vote; (iv) eligibility for public office; (v) the right of leaders to compete for support; (vi) alternative sources of information; (vii) free and fair elections; and (viii) institutions that make policies dependent on voters' preferences (Dahl 1971).

Schumpeter's 'minimalist' definition and Dahl's conception of polyarchy have shaped in one way or another most definitions of democracy currently used in comparative politics. Those definitions vary in their details, but they generally acknowledge four principles identified in Box 5.1: free and fair elections, universal participation, respect for civil liberties, and responsible government. All conditions must be simultaneously present for a country to be called democratic; if one of the conditions is conspicuously absent, the political system will fail—for one or another reason—to meet contemporary standards of democratic rule.

The four general conditions presented in Box 5.1 may be implemented in practice through diverse institutional arrangements. Two implications follow from this. The first one is that, if we look at their specific features, modern democracies can be quite different from each other. This topic will be explored in the next section of the chapter, 'Types of democracy'. The second implication is that no society has truly 'invented' modern democracy. Existing democracies combine institutions that originated in different countries and historical periods. John Markoff (1999) has shown that democratic innovations often emerge in peripheral countries that are not the great powers of the era. For example, the idea that political parties are necessary for democratic life—and not just selfish factions—had probably gained root in the US by the early 1820s. The requirement that voting is conducted in secret using a standard ballot was first adopted by British colonies in Victoria and South Australia in the mid-1850s. By 1825, most states in the US allowed all white men to vote without imposing property requirements; Switzerland eliminated income requirements for voters at the national level in its 1848 constitution, and several Latin American nations did so during the nineteenth century. New Zealand was the first democracy to guarantee women the right to vote in national elections by 1893. These innovations were progressively embraced by other societies, and today they are part of our standard repertoire of democratic practices.

How do we know if a country is democratic?

A working definition of democracy is crucial for research in comparative politics. We may want to establish, for example, whether the economy grows faster in democracies or in dictatorships, whether democracies invest more in health or education than authoritarian regimes, of whether democratic countries are less likely to experience terrorism or other forms of political violence. These questions require an operational definition of democracy precise enough to classify specific countries as we observe them during particular historical periods. Such definition should be able to capture the traits described in Box 5.1 without conflating the concept of democracy with the

---

DEFINITION 5.1

Four defining attributes of modern democracy

1. **Free and fair elections**. National government is exercised by a legislature—parliament, congress, or assembly—and by an executive branch typically led by a prime minister or president. The legislature (at least a significant part of it) is elected by the people, while the head of the government can be elected by the people or selected by the majority in parliament. The electoral process leading to the formation of new governments is recurrent (elections take place every few years), free (candidates are allowed to campaign and voters to participate without intimidation), and fair (votes are counted without fraud, and the government does not create an unequal playing field against the opposition).

2. **Universal participation**. The adult population enjoys the rights to vote and to run for office without exclusions based on income, education, gender, ethnicity, or religion. Modern democracies may exclude some adults from participating based on their place of birth (foreigners are not allowed to vote in most elections) or their criminal record (although many countries allow incarcerated populations to vote). Moreover, all democracies exclude minors from participating. Standards of inclusion have expanded over time: most 'democracies' did not allow women to vote until well into

the twentieth century, and the age for active citizenship has declined over time from twenty-one to eighteen, and even sixteen years in many countries.

3. **Civil liberties**. Democratic governments do not commit gross or systematic human rights violations against their citizens, do not censor critical voices in the mass media, and do not ban the organization of legitimate political parties or interest groups (with 'legitimate' understood in a broad sense). Modern democracies usually codify citizen rights and government authority in a written constitution, and rely on an independent judiciary and other institutions of accountability (such as constitutional courts, independent comptrollers, and investigative agencies) to protect citizens' rights against government encroachment.

4. **Responsible government**. Once elected, civilian authorities can adopt policies unconstrained by the monarch, military officers, foreign governments, religious authorities, or other unelected powers. To protect civil liberties, some decisions may be overturned by a constitutional court. Interest groups intervene in the policy-making process, but executive leaders respond for their actions to the elected representatives in the legislature, and both executive leaders and elected representatives are ultimately responsible to voters for their policies.

Adapted from Mainwaring et al. (2007)

---

outcomes that we want to explain (i.e., the 'dependent variables'; see Chapter 3 'Comparative research methods'), such as economic prosperity, social welfare, or political stability.

Some scholars have approached this task by creating a *dichotomous* measure of democracy. Przeworski et al. (2000), for example, identified four basic features of democracy (the chief executive must be elected, the legislature must be elected, multiple parties must compete for office, and alternation in power must be possible), and collected information to document these features in 141 countries every year between 1950 and 1990. Countries matching these four conditions by 31 December were classified as democracies during that year, and those missing at least one condition were classified as dictatorships.

Most scholars, however, have embraced an understanding of democracy as a *continuous* variable. Because the four conditions introduced in Box 5.1 can be present to different degrees, societies may become more or less democratic over time. Implicit in this approach is the idea of a continuum ranging between situations of blatant dictatorship, on one pole of the spectrum, and full democracy, on the other, with several intermediate stages (e.g. 'semi-democracies')

in between those extremes. Some **threshold** along this imaginary continuum marks the point above which countries can be considered fully democratic.

Several research projects have created continuous measures of democracy for multiple countries over time. The Polity project (initiated by Ted Robert Gurr in the 1960s) provides an annual score ranging between –10 (institutionalized autocracy) and 10 (institutionalized democracy) for all countries with a population greater than half a million since 1800. Freedom House, an organization based in New York, has created yearly ratings for Civil Liberties and Political Rights for 195 countries and fifteen territories since 1972. Each rating ranges between 1 (most democratic) and 7 (least democratic). The Varieties of Democracy (V-Dem) project, based at the University of Gothenburg in Sweden and the University of Notre Dame in the US, provides annual measures for different understandings of democracy (Electoral, Liberal, Egalitarian, Participatory, Deliberative) ranging between 0 (least democratic) and 1 (most democratic) for 202 countries and territories since 1789. The information generated by these projects is open to the public and easily available online.

Although the specific definitions of democracy vary in each case, these projects follow a common strategy: they disaggregate the meaning of democracy into sub-components or dimensions (e.g. civil liberties and political rights), they score country-years on each dimension based on the information provided by country experts (Freedom House and V-Dem) or trained coders (Polity), and then combine the information for these components to create an aggregate democracy score for each country-year (Munck and Verkuilen 2002). This approach is particularly useful to understand controversial countries: it is easy to classify extreme cases such as Switzerland or North Korea using a dichotomous scale, but complex cases such as Hungary under Viktor Orbán, Turkey under Recep Tayyip Erdoğan, or Venezuela under the late Hugo Chávez resist a binary classification and require a more nuanced understanding of democracy.

Hybrid regimes

To conceptualize political regimes that fall 'somewhere in between' full democracy and overt dictatorship, scholars have used a wide range of categories. For example, based on its ratings for Civil Liberties and Political Rights, Freedom House classifies countries every year as Free, Not Free, and Partly Free.[1] David Collier and Steven Levitsky identified hundreds of diminished subtypes employed by scholars to describe imperfect democracies, labels such as 'oligarchical democracy', 'restrictive democracy', or 'tutelary democracy' (Collier and Levitsky 1997). Diminished subtypes paradoxically add an adjective (e.g. 'oligarchical') to indicate that one of the defining attributes of democracy (e.g. universal suffrage) is weak or partly missing.

Some of these labels refer to regimes that generally meet the basic attributes of democracy presented in Box 5.1, but display a distinctive weakness. For example, Guillermo O'Donnell coined the term 'delegative democracy' to describe a type of democratic regime in which the executive branch concentrates excessive power and is hardly accountable to other branches of government such as the legislature or the judiciary. 'Delegative democracies rest on the premise that whoever wins election to the presidency is thereby entitled to govern as he or she sees fit, constrained only by the hard facts of existing power relations and by a constitutionally limited term of office' (O'Donnell 1994: 59). Other labels refer to 'democracies' in which some constitutive attributes are so weak that it is dubious whether the regime truly meets the requirements presented in Box 5.1. For instance, Fareed Zakaria used the term 'illiberal democracy' to describe regimes that display multiparty elections and universal participation, but generally fail to respect civil liberties and the rule of law (Zakaria 2007).[2]

KEY POINTS

- References to modern democracy, intended to describe a contemporary form of government, must be distinguished from normative uses of the term intended to denote an ideal and from references to government in classical Athens.

- Empirical definitions of democracy used in comparative politics usually connote free and fair elections, universal suffrage, civil liberties, and responsible government.

- No single society created democracy; representative and participatory institutions emerged in multiple places and disseminated during the nineteenth and twentieth centuries.

- The most commonly used measures of democracy—by Freedom House, Polity, and the V-Dem projects—provide yearly scores for a large number of countries.

- Defective democracies are often characterized with labels such as delegative democracy or illiberal democracy.

Types of democracy

In contrast to the 'diminished' subtypes discussed in the previous section, 'What is democracy (and who created it)?', fully democratic regimes always display the four attributes presented in Box 5.1. However, the fact that all democracies share these fundamental characteristics does not mean that all democracies look alike. Democratic systems can be quite different in many regards. What are their main differences? Are some democracies *better* than others?

Parliamentary or presidential?

The most important difference among democracies involves the distinction between parliamentary and presidential systems. **Parliamentary democracies** emerged from the historical transformation of absolutist monarchies into democratic regimes. Their characteristic features are the indirect election of the chief executive, limited separation of powers but a clear separation between the heads of government and state, and flexible terms in office.

In parliamentary systems, citizens vote to elect members of the legislature (parliament), and the majority in parliament in turn determines who becomes the head of the government (i.e., the prime minister or chancellor). If no party has a majority in parliament, multiple parties must form a coalition to appoint the new government. This usually requires that several parties craft an agreement about future policies and share the ministerial positions in the cabinet (see Chapter 8 'Governments and bureaucracies').[3]

The prime minister and other ministers in the cabinet are, in most parliamentary systems, members of parliament as well. Even though there is a clear separation of functions between the executive and the legislature, there is no explicit separation of powers among these individuals.

Because parliamentary democracies emerged from the transformation of monarchies, there is a separation between the head of the government (the prime minister) and the head of state (the monarch). The principle of responsible government (Box 5.1) implies that the elected prime minister commands the administration; the political role of monarchs in modern parliamentary democracies is weak and oriented towards the preservation of national unity. Although Belgium, Japan, the Netherlands, Spain, the UK, and other democracies officially preserve—and love—their monarchs to this day, these regimes are effectively republics in disguise. Some parliamentary countries, such as Germany, India, and Italy, have adopted an explicitly republican constitution and appoint a president to perform the duties of head of state. This president is elected indirectly, by parliament or by an electoral college. For instance, the head of state is appointed by a college formed by the lower house of parliament and delegations of the states in Germany, by the two houses of parliament and state legislatures in India, and by both houses of parliament and delegations of the regions in Italy. Irrespective of the election procedure, these presidents are politically weak figures.

Finally, although parliamentary systems are mandated to call elections at certain intervals (for instance, every five years in the UK), an election can take place sooner than expected if the prime minister clashes with parliament. In agreement with the head of state, the prime minister can, in most cases, request the dissolution of parliament and call for a new election in the middle of the term. Alternatively, the majority in parliament can support a vote of no-confidence against the government, forcing the prime minister and the cabinet to resign. If the government considers a particular policy crucial for its legislative agenda, it can also present a motion of confidence to parliament. If parliament votes against the government's motion of confidence, the prime minister and the cabinet must resign; parliament must then appoint a new administration, or the head of state must schedule a new election.

Presidential democracy originated in the efforts of the US to create a continental republican government in 1787. This constitutional model spread to Latin America in the nineteenth century and to parts of Africa (e.g. Ghana, Zambia) and Asia (South Korea, the Philippines) in the twentieth century. Under presidential systems, there is a popular election of the chief executive, clear separation of powers but no separation between head of state and head of the government, and fixed terms in office.

In presidential democracies, voters participate in separate electoral processes to elect members of the legislature (congress) and the head of the government (president). These elections may happen concurrently on the same day, but they are separate contests. Popular votes cast for congress members are typically tallied and aggregated at the local level, to elect representatives for particular districts; votes cast for the president are typically tallied and aggregated at the national level, to elect the country's chief executive.[4]

The president and (in most presidential regimes) the members of the cabinet are not members of congress. This creates a strict **separation of powers** between the two elected branches. Coordination among the executive and the legislature is achieved only to the extent that the president and some members of congress belong to the same political party, or if the president is able to form a coalition with members of other parties. However, the elected president plays the role of head of the government and head of state simultaneously.

Finally, in presidential democracies the president and members of congress are expected to serve in office for a fixed period. The president has no constitutional power to dissolve congress and congress cannot issue a vote of no-confidence against the president.[5] Executive re-election is usually constrained. In the US, for example, the president's term lasts four years, with a single possibility of immediate re-election. Representatives (members of the lower house of congress) last in office for two years, and senators for six years, with the possibility of indefinite re-election. In Uruguay, the president's term lasts five years but immediate re-election is banned—the person may return to the presidency only after a period out of office. Uruguayan representatives and senators are elected for a period of five years, concurrent with the president's term. Legislative re-election is allowed, but while more than 80 per cent of incumbent US congress members return to office in any given election, only 50–70 per cent of Uruguayan legislators are typically re-elected (Altman and Chasquetti 2005).

Some countries have institutional arrangements that blend elements of presidentialism and parliamentarism. **Semi-presidential regimes** combine a directly elected president, who serves in office for a fixed term, and a prime minister, who is responsible to parliament (Elgie 1999). Such arrangements are common in Western Europe (e.g. Austria, France, Ireland, Portugal), Eastern Europe (e.g. Bulgaria, Poland, Romania, Ukraine), Africa (e.g. Cape Verde,

Mali), and Asia (e.g. Mongolia, South Korea, Taiwan). However, the powers accorded to the president in such regimes vary considerably. Some semi-presidential regimes, such as Austria or Ireland, have very weak presidents and effectively operate as **parliamentary systems**. Others, like South Korea or Taiwan, grant considerable authority to the head of state and effectively function as presidential systems (Schleiter and Morgan-Jones 2009).

The literature in comparative politics sometimes refers to these as hybrid constitutions, but this concept of 'hybridity', used to depict a democracy that is in part parliamentary and in part presidential, must be clearly distinguished from the concept of hybrid regimes discussed in the previous section, 'What is democracy (and who created it)?', intended to describe regimes that are in part democratic and in part authoritarian. Hybrid constitutions are discussed more extensively in Chapter 8 'Governments and bureaucracies'.

Which constitutional arrangement is better for democracy? Not surprisingly, people disagree about this. About three decades ago, Juan Linz argued that presidential constitutions make the political process 'rather rigid'. Three institutional features of presidentialism are, in this view, dysfunctional for democracy. First, presidential elections are winner-take-all contests in which the prize (the president's seat) cannot be shared by multiple parties. As a result, electoral competition encourages political polarization. Second, because the president simultaneously serves as head of state and head of the government, he or she may claim to be the only true representative of the people, embrace a 'plebiscitarian' style of government, and dismiss all criticisms by the opposition. Finally, because the president and congress members are both elected independently and serve

for fixed terms in office, disagreements between the two branches of government may lead to paralysis in the policy-making process. Without the possibility of anticipated elections or a vote of no confidence, presidential constitutions create a system of dual legitimacy (Linz 1990*a*).

Challenging this view, Scott Mainwaring and Matthew Shugart argued that, despite some of these problems, presidential systems offer important advantages to voters. Presidentialism gives citizens the choice to support different parties in the legislative and in the presidential election. It also strengthens government responsibility (see Box 5.1). Many parliamentary regimes have coalition governments in which responsibility is shared by multiple parties and therefore blurred across party lines. In a presidential regime, where the head of the government is also head of state, by contrast, voters clearly know which party is in charge of the executive branch, and they can reward the party or vote against it at the next election, depending on its performance in office. Finally, legislators have greater independence under presidentialism. Because presidential regimes do not have confidence votes, legislators of the ruling party may oppose the president's policies without fearing the fall of the administration. Similarly, legislators of the opposition may challenge the president's policies without fearing the dissolution of congress (Mainwaring and Shugart 1997). Box 5.2 provides a comparison of the arguments in favour and against presidential constitutions.

Majoritarian or consensus?

A second set of differences among democratic systems involves the distinction between majoritarian and consensus democracies. This classification originates

---

◁ FOR AND AGAINST 5.2

Some arguments for and against presidentialism

Characteristics of presidentialism	Advantages	Disadvantages
The head of the government is elected by a popular election.	Voters have greater choice.	Winner-takes-all election induces political polarization.
President is head of state and head of the government.	Voters have more clarity about who controls the executive. Better government accountability.	President may adopt 'plebiscitarian' style and claim to be the only true representative of the people.
President and legislators have fixed terms in office.	Legislators have greater independence; they do not fear dissolution of parliament.	Dual legitimacy; executive–legislative deadlock.

Sources: Mainwaring and Shugart (1997); Linz (1990*a*); Elgie (2008*b*).

in the work of Arend Lijphart (1984, 1999, 2012), who argues that some democratic regimes are organized to facilitate majority rule, while others are designed to protect minorities (and thus promote decision-making by consensus). Such different conceptions of the democratic process effectively translate into unique constitutional features. For example, **majoritarian democracies** have several features that typically produce government by a single party (rather than a coalition), and limited autonomy for local governments (rather than federalism).

Majoritarian democracies adopt a disproportional electoral system for the election of legislators. Voters in the UK or in the US, for instance, elect only one legislator (the candidate with the largest number of votes) to represent each district. Such an electoral system discourages voters from supporting smaller parties, and it makes it easier for the largest party to win a majority of seats in the parliament or congress, even when the largest party does not win a majority of the vote at the national level. For example, in the 2015 British election, the Conservative Party obtained 37 per cent of the national vote and 51 per cent of the seats in parliament. Chapter 10 'Elections and referendums' provides a more detailed explanation of how majoritarian electoral systems work. Unwilling to 'waste' their votes on smaller parties with little chance of winning, voters will concentrate their support on the two largest parties, sustaining a **two-party system** (see Chapter 13 'Party systems').

Under a two-party system, it is very likely that the party winning the election will have a majority in the legislature. Moreover, if the country has a parliamentary constitution, the majority party will have no need to form a coalition in order to appoint the new government. Therefore, governments in majoritarian democracies are typically run by single-party cabinets (see Chapter 8 'Governments and bureaucracies').

If the executive branch is controlled by a single party which also has a majority in parliament (or congress), and if the head of the government is the main leader of this party, it is likely that the executive branch will dominate the legislature due to the influence of party leadership on most legislators.

In addition to these traits that define the balance of power between the executive branch and the legislative parties, majoritarian democracies also have distinctive characteristics that define the relationship between the central government (representing the national majorities) and the local governments (representing sub-national minorities).

Majoritarian democracies tend to have unitary and centralized government, such that the institutions representing the majority at the national level will decide on policies at the local or regional level (see Chapters 11 'Multilevel governance' and 15 'Regions'). Because local governments are weak and unable to demand equal representation in the legislature, a federal senate is typically not included in the constitution. Thus, legislatures are more likely to be **unicameral** (Chapter 7 'Legislatures').

Because the will of the majority at the national level is expected to define the organization of government at the national and the local levels, the constitution is flexible—that is, relatively easy to change. An extreme example of constitutional flexibility, the UK does not even have a written constitution; legislative majorities can therefore eliminate or create new institutions—such as the Supreme Court of the United Kingdom, inaugurated in 2009—through a simple act of parliament.

Since the constitution is flexible, legislative majorities are rarely constrained by the legal interpretation of the constitution exercised by courts. Majoritarian democracies typically have limited **judicial review** (see Chapter 9 'Constitutions, rights, and judicial power').[6]

In contrast to this set of arrangements, **consensus democracies** are designed to protect the power of partisan and regional minorities. Therefore, they embrace coalition governments to favour national agreements, and federalism to preserve local autonomy.

Consensus democracies adopt **proportional electoral systems** that translate the percentage of votes obtained by each party into a very similar proportion of seats in the legislature. For example, in the 2014 Belgian election the incumbent Socialist Party obtained about 13 per cent of the national vote and gained 15 per cent of the seats in the lower house of parliament.

Because votes count even when citizens support a small party, electoral rules will sustain a **multiparty system**. For instance, even though the outcome of the 2015 Swiss election was described by the media as a 'landslide victory' for the Swiss People's Party, more than ten parties won seats in the lower house of the Swiss Federal Assembly. The successful Swiss People's Party captured only 29 per cent of the vote at the national level, and about 32 per cent of the seats in the lower house.

With a large number parties represented in the legislature it is unlikely that any single organization will control a majority of the seats. In countries with parliamentary constitutions, several political parties will need to form a coalition to appoint a new government. And in order to achieve broad consensus about future policies, these government coalitions will often include a large number of partners—even small party blocs that are not strictly necessary to form a legislative majority. Since coalition governments depend on the agreement of all partners in the legislature to preserve their unity and avoid a vote of no confidence, consensus democracies provide a balanced relation between the executive and the legislature.

These features make consensus democracy the best option for plural societies, nations divided along ethnic, linguistic, or religious lines. In order to protect regional minorities from the dictates of nationwide majorities, consensus democracies also have a federal system with decentralized government, such that local governments (e.g. states in the US, cantons in Switzerland) enjoy extensive authority to shape policies at regional level.

Since local communities demand balanced representation in the national legislature, the constitution usually provides for an upper house, such as the US Senate, the German Bundesrat, or the Swiss Council of States. Thus, legislatures are likely to be **bicameral**.

To guarantee the autonomy of local communities embedded in the constitution, constitutional reforms require large majorities (e.g. two-thirds of the votes in the legislature) and additional ratification (e.g. public support in a referendum, or approval by a majority of state legislatures). Constitutional rigidity thus discourages national majorities to alter the constitution without extensive consultation. Moreover, since the constitution is rigid, proper interpretation of the constitution is crucial for the political process. Consensus democracies typically have powerful supreme courts or constitutional tribunals that exercise strong **judicial review**.

Box 5.3 summarizes the main attributes of majoritarian and consensus democracies. These are ideal types, never found in pure form among really existing regimes. Real democracies usually involve some combination of majoritarian and consensus elements. The US, for example, looks majoritarian regarding the first set of features, but it operates as a consensus democracy for the second set of features. Some countries, however, are very close to one of the two ideal types. The UK generally matches the characteristics of a majoritarian democracy—in fact, this model is also discussed in the specialized literature as the Westminster model of democracy, in a reference to the palace housing the British parliament. By contrast, Belgium and Switzerland are very close to the consensus model.

As in the case of parliamentary and presidential constitutions, scholars have debated the advantages and disadvantages of these models of political organization. Majoritarian democracies are *decisive*: they can make policy changes quickly and effectively, but they are potentially volatile, since policies will shift with the whims of the majority. Consensus democracies, by contrast, are *resolute*: they will agree on major policies and sustain them based on broad agreements (Cox and McCubbins 2001). Decades ago, scholars feared that democratic systems with too many parties would be prone to political unrest, and thus favoured the two-party systems characteristic of majoritarian democra-

---

↘ ZOOM-IN 5.3

Majoritarian and consensus democracies

	Majoritarian	Consensus
Electoral system	Disproportional	Proportional representation
Party system	Two-party	Multiparty
Government	Single-party	Coalitions
Inter-branch balance	Executive dominance	Balanced power
Interest representation	Pluralism	Corporatism
Local government	Unitary	Federal
Legislature	Unicameral	Bicameral
Constitution	Flexible	Rigid
Judiciary	Weak or no judicial review	Strong judicial review
Central bank	Dependent on executive	Independent
Optimal for	Homogeneous societies	Plural societies

Source: based on Lijphart (2012).

cies, or at least moderate forms of multipartism (Sartori 1976). More recently, George Tsebelis argued that institutions designed to empower minorities create multiple 'veto players' and encourage policy paralysis (Tsebelis 2002). However, Arend Lijphart has argued that consensus democracies perform at least equally well, and often much better than majoritarian systems when we consider macroeconomic outcomes, social unrest, voter turnout, women's participation in politics, and other indicators of democratic quality (Lijphart 2012).

KEY POINTS

- Parliamentarism involves the election of the chief executive by parliament, separation between head of government and head of state, and the possibility of a vote of no confidence or anticipated elections.

- Presidentialism allows for popular election of the chief executive, a unified head of state and government, and fixed terms in office.

- Majoritarian democracies involve disproportional elections, two-party systems, and single-party governments; unitary government, unicameralism, flexible constitutions, and weak judicial review.

- Consensus democracies involve proportional elections, multiparty systems, and broad coalition governments; federalism, bicameralism, rigid constitutions, and strong judicial review.

- Scholars have articulated arguments in favour of parliamentarism over presidentialism, and of consensus over majoritarian systems, but there is no agreement regarding the 'best' form of democracy.

Why some countries have democracy and others do not

For many people in the world today, the fundamental question is not what kind of democracy is better, but how to achieve any democracy at all. About half of the world's population still lives under regimes that cannot be considered democratic. This begs an important question: what factors facilitate the process of democratization? How can democracy be established and preserved? For scientific purposes, this issue can be disaggregated into two separate analytical problems. First, countries that suffer a dictatorship may, under the right circumstances, adopt a democratic regime. We call this process a *transition* to democracy. Second, countries that have a troubled democratic regime may, in unfortunate circumstances, slide back into dictatorship. We call this process a democratic *breakdown*.[7]

This analytic distinction is relevant whether we treat democracy as a continuous or a discrete variable. If we conceptualize political regimes as located in a continuum between full authoritarianism and full democracy, a transition means 'moving up' along this continuum, while a breakdown means 'sliding back' from the democratic into the authoritarian region. If we conceptualize regime types in a dichotomous way (democracy vs dictatorship), dictatorships constitute a set of political regimes exposed to the probability of democratic transition, while democracies constitute a set of regimes exposed to the risk of breakdown. Explaining the survival of a democratic regime is equivalent to understanding why a breakdown does *not* occur.

No single explanation can account for why some countries enjoy democracy while others do not. In general, theories seeking to explain the causes of democracy—and its downfall—have emphasized four types of variables: structural (social and economic) factors; institutional conditions; the role of political actors (leaders, organizations, and social movements); and international forces.[8] Some theoretical explanations discussed in this section claim to account for transitions as well as breakdowns, while others only seek to explain one of the two outcomes.

Structural factors

Among social and economic explanations, two have received distinctive attention among scholars. The first one relates to the role of **economic development** as a precondition for democratization. In a classic article published in 1959, sociologist Seymour Martin Lipset claimed that 'the more well-to-do a nation, the greater the chances that it will sustain democracy' (Lipset 1959: 75). Lipset was perhaps the most influential of modernization theorists, a group of scholars that emphasized how the social transformations produced by long-term economic development—transformations leading to better living standards, greater urbanization, higher levels of literacy and technical education, the emergence of a middle class, a greater role of industrial activities vis-à-vis traditional agriculture—create conditions that facilitate the emergence of modern democratic politics. Later scholars seeking to test this hypothesis found a strong correlation between economic development and levels of democracy (Cutright 1963; Needler 1968; Jackman 1973), a correlation which is mostly driven by the fact that wealthy countries almost always have democratic regimes. By contrast, poor countries can be democratic or authoritarian—although very poor nations have a greater propensity

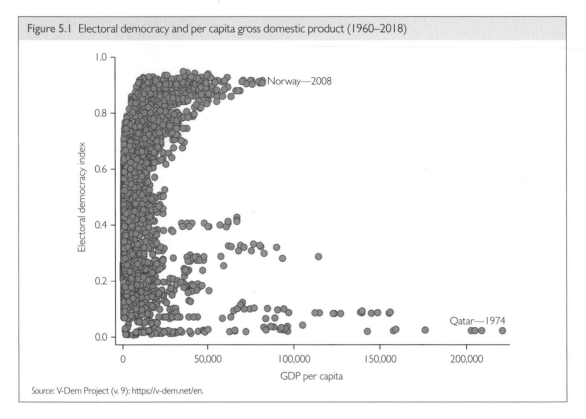

Figure 5.1 Electoral democracy and per capita gross domestic product (1960–2018)

Source: V-Dem Project (v. 9): https://v-dem.net/en.

towards authoritarianism. This pattern is depicted in Figure 5.1, which plots country-years between 1960 and 2014 according to per-capita gross domestic product (in the horizontal axis) and V-Dem's Electoral Democracy Score (ranging between 0 and 1).

Figure 5.2 noticeably displays a few countries with annual incomes above $100,000 dollars per capita which are surprisingly undemocratic (with values close to zero in the vertical axis). These points in the plot correspond to Qatar and Saudi Arabia, major hydrocarbons exporters in the Middle East, for several years after the oil boom of 1973. Michael Ross argues that authoritarian rulers can employ extraordinary revenues from oil exports to expand patronage, reduce taxation, and strengthen repressive security forces, preventing challenges from democratic groups (Ross 2001). In turn, Kevin Morrison claims that oil revenues stabilize any regime, democratic or authoritarian, because they minimize the need to collect unpopular taxes (Morrison 2014).

Even during the heyday of modernization theory in the 1960s, some scholars questioned the optimistic view linking development and democracy. Samuel Huntington warned that, in the absence of solid institutions, fast social and economic transformations can cause political turmoil and violence (Huntington 1968); in turn, Barrington Moore noted that in some countries modernization produced fascist or communist dictatorships (Moore 1966). More recently, Przeworski et al. claimed that the correlation between development and democracy is not driven by a greater rate of *transitions* among wealthy dictatorships, but by a low rate of *breakdowns* among wealthy democracies. In other terms, authoritarian regimes may democratize for a number of reasons, but once democracy is established in a wealthy country, it is very unlikely to backslide into authoritarian rule (Przeworski et al. 2000). Moreover, most economists argue that this correlation reflects the reverse causal relationship: development does not cause democracy, but better institutions facilitate economic growth (Acemoglu et al. 2008).

A second structural condition presumed to influence democratization is the level of social inequality. Proponents of this theory assert that in societies where wealth is very unequally distributed, economic elites resist democratization because democratically elected governments will redistribute income in favour of the poor. The reason for this expectation is that, if a majority of voters are poor, they should demand redistributive policies—that is, higher taxes for the rich and more generous social policies for the poor—in exchange for their electoral support. Based on these assumptions, Carles Boix has argued that, in dictatorships with high levels of inequality, transitions to democracy will be unlikely because powerful elites will resist them. And if democracy is ever established, a democratic break-

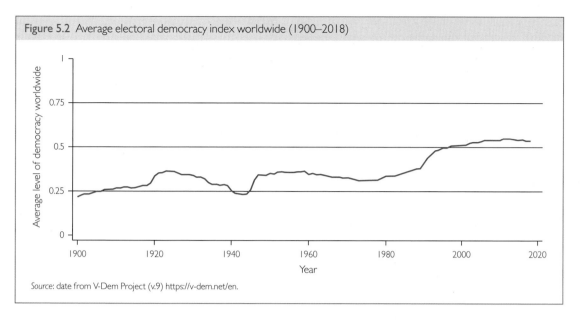

Figure 5.2 Average electoral democracy index worldwide (1900–2018)

Source: date from V-Dem Project (v.9) https://v-dem.net/en.

down will be likely unless wealthy elites can avoid taxes by taking their assets out of the country (Boix 2003). In a more sophisticated argument, Daron Acemoglu and James Robinson claim that transitions to democracy are unlikely in dictatorships that are highly unequal, because wealthy elites fear democracy, and in those that display very low levels of income inequality, because the poor do not push for democratization (Acemoglou and Robinson 2006).

These arguments have faced criticism for being excessively simplistic. Land inequality, which empowers landowners in the countryside, may have very different effects on democracy than income inequality, which sometimes results from processes of economic modernization (Ansell and Samuels 2014). Moreover, not all dictatorships favour the rich, and not all democracies favour the poor (Levitsky and Mainwaring 2006). Consider, for example, the Soviet Union, Mao Zedong's China, or Fidel Castro's Cuba. Although undemocratic, those regimes redistributed wealth extensively in favour of the poor. By contrast, even though some democracies have reduced social disparities in the developing world (Huber and Stephens 2012), income inequality has been growing among advanced industrial democracies since the 1970s (Piketty 2014).

Institutions

The nature of some democratic institutions may also facilitate authoritarian backsliding. Almost three decades ago, Juan Linz argued that presidential democracies are more likely to break down than parliamentary ones because presidential elections encourage political polarization, foster a 'plebiscitarian' style

of government, and facilitate deadlock between the executive and the legislature (see Box 5.2) (Linz 1990a). Scholars testing this hypothesis with statistical data found that, indeed, presidential systems face a greater risk of breakdown than parliamentary ones (Stepan and Skach 1993). But other studies qualified this finding by noting that not all presidential regimes are equally exposed to the risk of authoritarian reversion. They argued that presidential democracies are more fragile when the constitution gives presidents greater powers over legislation, discouraging negotiations with congress (Shugart and Carey 1992); when the party system is fragmented, such that the president's party is consistently unable to have a majority in congress (Mainwaring 1993); and when military officers have a tradition of political intervention (Cheibub 2007). Recent studies have shown that presidential democracies are brittle when the executive controls the legislature and the judiciary. Without checks, the government is tempted to encroach on the rights of the opposition (Pérez-Liñán et al. 2019).

Just as some democratic institutions may produce fragile democracies, some authoritarian institutions may also produce fragile dictatorships. Military regimes are more likely to democratize than other types of dictatorship because military officers—unless they anticipate trials for human rights violations—can always return to the barracks and pursue a military career after civilian rulers regain power. Moreover, generals want to preserve military unity and often dislike the factionalism introduced in the armed forces by the exercise of day-to-day government (Geddes 2003). By contrast, authoritarian regimes with stronger 'representative' institutions, such as political parties or legislatures, create a stronger base of mass support, coordinate the ambitions of authoritarian elites, and delay transitions to democracy (Magaloni 2006; Gandhi 2010; Svolik 2012).

Actors and agency

Theories based on structural factors or institutional conditions can offer frustrating lessons for advocates of democracy. Structural factors like economic modernization or income inequality change slowly and over the long term; political institutions can be modified by constitutional reforms and other forms of human action, but institutions tend to be quite enduring and change at a slow pace (Krasner 1984; Mahoney and Thelen 2010b). However, these conditions cannot fully explain the dynamics and the timing of regime change. Within the boundaries imposed by structures and institutions, regime change is ultimately triggered by political actors exercising moral choices—that is, agency.

The role of leaders, organizations, and social movements in democratic transitions has been a matter of scholarly concern for decades. Almost fifty years ago, Dankwart Rustow claimed that democracy emerges when leaders of contending factions realize that it is impossible to impose their views unilaterally, and they voluntarily establish an institutional arrangement for sharing power like the one described in Box 5.1 (Rustow 1970). In a similar vein, O'Donnell and Schmitter noted that transitions to democracy occur when the coalition of actors supporting an authoritarian regime faces internal divisions, and democratic leaders engage in a series of pacts to strengthen the project represented by a democratic coalition (O'Donnell and Schmitter 1986).

Seeking to understand the breakdown of democratic regimes, Juan Linz argued that democracies become easy targets of authoritarian forces when moderate leaders abdicate their responsibilities and let 'disloyal' politicians—those who use the rules of democracy to pursue authoritarian goals—polarize the electorate (Linz 1978). A similar conclusion was reached by Nancy Bermeo, who showed that social conflict and polarization preceding democratic breakdowns in Europe and Latin America were driven by political elites, not by ordinary people (Bermeo 2003). In turn, Giovanni Capoccia claimed that democracy survived in inter-war Europe where key parties supported a legal strategy to repress extremist leaders and to incorporate their followers to democratic life (Capoccia 2005).

Recent works have also emphasized the importance of political actors and their choices. Mainwaring and Pérez-Liñán showed that authoritarian regimes are more likely to democratize, and democracies are less likely to collapse, when political leaders express normative commitments to democracy (Mainwaring and Pérez-Liñán 2013). In turn, Chenoweth and Stephan argued that the use of nonviolent strategies by social movements—such as protests, boycotts, and civil disobedience—is more likely to trigger a transition to democracy than violent resistance against authoritarian rule. Once established, the new regime will be less likely to suffer a civil war than democracies emerging from violent transition processes (Chenoweth and Stephan 2012).

International forces

Explanations based on structural factors, institutions, or local actors focus on domestic variables to understand regime change. But some important forces driving (or hindering) the emergence and survival of democracy originate outside of the country. Chapter 25 'From supporting democracy to supporting autocracy' shows that the US, the European Union, and some new democracies such as Poland or the Czech Republic have been active promoters of democracy across the world in recent years.

There is a simple way to visualize the contribution of international factors in processes of democratization. Figure 5.2 shows the average level of democracy for all independent countries in the world between 1900 and 2014, using V-Dem's Electoral Democracy Index. The series show that the average level of democracy in the world has grown since 1900, but not at a constant pace. During some historical periods, consecutive countries adopt democratic practices, and worldwide levels of democracy grow considerably in a relatively short span. In other historical periods, democracy recedes concurrently in multiple places, and the global average declines.

Decades ago, Samuel Huntington described historical cycles of democratic expansion as 'waves' of democratization (Huntington 1991). At least three such waves are visible in Figure 5.2. The first one started in the nineteenth century (although data for the figure is available from 1900), when North American, most Western European, and some South American and Pacific countries embraced democratic principles, and lasted until about 1920, when European democracies confronted the threat of fascism. The second wave took off at the end of World War II, when most of Western Europe re-established democratic practices, India became independent, and some Latin American societies toppled their dictators. It lasted until about 1960, when democracies in Latin America and other regions were challenged by military intervention and fragile democracies broke down in Africa. The third wave of democratization started slowly in the mid-1970s, as Portugal, Spain, and Greece overcame their dictatorships; it took off in the 1980s, as Latin American countries overcame military rule; and accelerated in the 1990s, when the decline of the Soviet Union allowed for democratization in Eastern Europe and democracy spread to important parts of Africa and Asia.

These 'waves' of democratization are hard to explain if we focus exclusively on domestic explanations for regime change. Multiple countries would have to experience similar changes in their internal conditions simultaneously (e.g. changes in levels of economic development, income inequality, institutions, or actors' orientations) to account for convergent patterns of regime change in a short historical period. Because countries—even those located in the same geographic region—can be quite different, this is a rather implausible explanation for most waves of democratization.

A more plausible explanation is that democratization in one country will influence the perceptions and expectations of actors in other countries, triggering democratic 'contagion'. Several studies have documented processes of democratic diffusion among neighbouring countries, or even across geographic regions (Gleditsch 2002; Brinks and Coppedge 2006; Wejnert 2014).[9]

External actors can play important roles in domestic democratization in several ways. Jon Pevehouse has documented that regional organizations, such as the Organization of American States, can oppose authoritarian reversions and promote democracy 'from above' (Pevehouse 2005). Finkel et al. established that wealthy democracies can promote democratization through foreign aid programmes oriented towards this purpose (Finkel et al. 2007). Chapter 25 'From supporting democracy to supporting autocracy' addresses international support for democracy in greater detail.

However, it is important to keep in mind that external influences ultimately operate through domestic coalitions. John Markoff has shown that social movements play a key role in the process of democratic diffusion (Markoff 1996). Kurt Weyland warns that successful movements against dictators may spread to other countries very fast, but they fail when there are no political organizations able to direct (and moderate) their struggle. This partly explains the disappointing outcomes of the 'Arab Spring' in the Middle East after 2011 (Weyland 2014). In the end, external influences can have limited impact in the absence of domestic actors committed to foster a democratic transformation (Mainwaring and Pérez-Liñán 2013).

KEY POINTS

- To understand the presence of democracy in some countries (and its absence in others) we need to account for the establishment of democracy (democratic transitions) and its survival (i.e. avoidance of democratic breakdowns).

- Structural explanations: modernization theory claims that economic development promotes democratization; theories of inequality underscore that social inequities hinder it.

- Institutional explanations: critics of presidentialism argue that presidential democracies are more likely to break down than parliamentary ones. Students of authoritarian regimes claim that dictatorships with parties and legislatures are more resilient than military regimes.

- Political actors: individuals and organizations exercise agency in the transformation of political regimes. Leaders committed to democracy foster transitions and resist breakdowns.

- International forces: external factors influence domestic democratization through contagion (diffusion), through the diplomatic action of international organizations, and because established democracies can use foreign aid to support domestic democratic groups.

Conclusion: the future of democracy

Democracy is a reality as much as it is an ideal. For this reason, democratic regimes are always in flux. The gap between the experience of existing democracy as it *is* and our expectations for democracy as we would *like it to be* inspires political action in rich and in poor countries, in old as well as in new democracies. The future of democracy will result from the ability of new political actors to expand the frontiers of democratization without undermining the democratic achievements of past generations.

Democratic regimes will be tested by important challenges in the decades to come. Among those challenges are the limits imposed by supranational institutions (Chapter 23 'The EU as a new political system') and globalization (Chapter 24 'Globalization and the nation-state'), the resurgence of intolerant nationalism, and the temptation to limit civil liberties in the name of national security. The rise of leaders—both on the left and on the right of the ideological spectrum—who embrace populist and anti-liberal discourses, has created new anxieties about the future of democracy in countries as diverse as Bolivia, Brazil, Hungary, the US, the Philippines, and Poland. New studies claim that political parties have a crucial responsibility to prevent the nomination of such leaders, and that opposition forces must employ the institutional resources of democracy to limit their power once they come to office (Levitsky and Ziblatt 2018).

Beyond those issues, crucial for the survival of existing democratic systems, future generations will struggle to redefine the meaning of democracy itself. The contemporary definition presented in Box 5.1 focuses on electoral procedures and civic liberties. Yet, more ambitious conceptions of democracy call for the enrichment of these minimum requirements with additional criteria such as substantive equality (egalitarian democracy), citizen engagement (participatory democracy), and respectful and reasonable dialogue (deliberative democracy) (Coppedge et al. 2011).

Moreover, the history of modern democracy entails the progressive expansion of citizenship to groups previously excluded from the political process. This expansion is always contested because it is not obvious that new groups should have the right to enjoy citizenship. After the process is completed, however, the boundaries of citizenship shift and a new definition of 'the people' becomes entrenched. In the early nineteenth century, most republics considered property and literacy as 'natural' requirements to grant men the right to vote. In the early twentieth century, most democracies still excluded women and ethnic minorities from the electoral process. Such restrictive definitions of the people were widely accepted at the time, but are morally unacceptable for our contemporary observers.

It is certain that the future of democracy will bring the expansion of rights to new groups, but it is hard for us—as it was for any society in the past—to anticipate who the people will be in the future. One possibility is that young individuals, now considered dependent minors, will acquire greater rights. Throughout the twentieth century, democracies reduced the minimum age to participate in politics—from twenty-one to eighteen, and later to sixteen years of age in many countries—but it is still unclear when individuals should be considered mature enough to exercise full citizenship. Consider, for example, the case of the US: individuals are considered responsible enough to drive at the age of sixteen; to vote, join the army, and own handguns at the age of eighteen; and to drink alcohol only at the age of twenty-one.

Another possibility is that migrants will acquire increasing political rights. Our traditional understanding of democracy assumes that the people were born and raised in a given territory, but human populations are increasingly mobile. By 2015, 244 million people— more than 3 per cent of the total world population— lived outside their countries of origin (United Nations Population Division 2015). This poses two parallel challenges. The first one is to allow greater political participation by citizens who are physically located outside their national territories. A 2007 report by the International Institute for Democracy and Electoral Assistance showed that 115 countries and territories currently allow their expatriates to vote from abroad, in most cases with little restrictions (Ellis et al. 2007). The second—and more controversial—challenge is to grant representation to foreign residents who are active community members in their host countries. According to David Earnest, at least twenty-four democracies have allowed foreign residents to participate in elections since 1960. Earnest showed that a majority of such democracies grant voting rights to non-citizen aliens only at the local level; just a very small group (eight nations) allows non-citizens to vote at the national level, and in all but two cases— New Zealand and Uruguay—the right to participate in national elections is restricted to migrants from preferred countries (Earnest 2006).

Even more puzzling is the possibility that some kinds of democratic rights will be extended beyond human populations in the future. In June 2008, for example, the Environmental Committee of the Spanish Parliament approved a resolution to grant basic rights to the great apes—orangutans, gorillas, chimpanzees, bonobos, and humans—including the rights to life, individual liberty, and the prohibition of torture. Similar bills were introduced in the US House of Representatives in 2008 and reached the Senate in 2010. Advocates of animal rights, however, argue that even this radical expansion of legal rights would be insufficient to prevent the massive abuse and slaughter of animals raised for human consumption in factory farms (Wolfe 2013: 104–11).

Irrespective of future trajectories, which are hard to anticipate, any real expansion of democratic rights will require building on the foundation of existing democratic achievements. Because of this, readers should remember that modern democracy is a fledgling form of government, with roots that barely extend two hundred years into the past. The Roman Republic lasted for almost 500 years before giving way to imperial rule, the Byzantine Empire survived for 1,100 years before falling to the Ottoman Empire, and the Ottoman Empire in turn lasted for more than 600 years before giving birth to modern Turkey. Such successful regimes—long gone after their heyday— remind us that modern democracy is just a newcomer to the history of political systems; it cannot be taken for granted, and it should be carefully nurtured if it is going to survive and thrive.

? QUESTIONS

Knowledge-based

1. What are the four traits that define modern democracy? Can a regime be democratic if only one attribute is missing?

2. What are the main differences between the president of a parliamentary democracy and the president of a presidential democracy?

3. Which features distinguish a majoritarian democracy from a consensus democracy?

4. Are theories explaining transitions to democracy also useful to explain democratic breakdowns?

5. Why do democracies emerge in 'waves'?

Critical thinking

1. Is presidential or parliamentary democracy a better choice for newly democratic regimes?

2. What are the advantages and disadvantages of consensus vis-à-vis majoritarian democracy?

3. Which configuration of conditions (economic, social, institutional, political, and international) would create the most adverse historical context for the survival of a democratic regime?

4. Which of those conditions would be, in your opinion, the most important factor for the survival of democracy?

5. Provide three reasons for why resident aliens should be granted the right to vote, and three reasons for why they should not be granted the right to vote in a democratic country.

≋ FURTHER READING

Bermeo, N. (2016) 'On Democratic Backsliding', *Journal of Democracy*, 27(1), 5–19.

Levitsky, S. and Ziblatt, D. (2018). *How Democracies Die.* (New York: Crown).

Lijphart, A. (2012) *Patterns of Democracy: Government Forms and Performance in Thirty-Six Countries* (2nd edn) (New Haven, CT: Yale University Press).

Markoff, J. (1999) 'Where and When was Democracy Invented?' *Comparative Studies in Society and History*, 41(4), 660–90.

Munck, G. L. and Verkuilen, J. (2002) 'Conceptualizing and Measuring Democracy—Evaluating Alternative Indices', *Comparative Political Studies*, 35(1), 5–34.

🖹 ENDNOTES

1. Freedom House's ratings for Civil Liberties and Political Rights range between 1 (most free) and 7 (least free). After taking the average for both ratings, the organization classifies countries as Free (if the average rating is between 1 and 2.5), Partly Free (3–5), or Not Free (5.5–7).

2. For countries below this threshold, students of comparative politics also use similar labels to describe authoritarian regimes that display some democratic attributes, for example 'electoral authoritarianism' (Schedler 2013) or 'competitive authoritarianism' (Levitsky and Way, 2010). For a discussion of this topic, see Chapter 6 'Authoritarian regimes'.

3. After the election, the head of state (monarch or president) usually 'invites' the leader of the largest party in parliament to form a new government.

Many parliamentary systems also require that the parliamentary majority formally supports the new government in a 'vote of investiture' before the new cabinet takes office.

4. The US is the only presidential democracy that still preserves an Electoral College to elect the president. Under this indirect procedure, designed in the eighteenth century, votes are tallied and aggregated at the state level in order to appoint a certain number of 'electors' from each state, who then cast their votes for particular presidential candidates. Nowadays, electors pre-commit to support specific candidates and they have no autonomy once appointed. Therefore, the Electoral College is simply an intermediate source of 'noise' between the popular vote and the final selection of the US president.

5. Few constitutions empower the president to dissolve congress, and they do so only under very restrictive circumstances. More constitutions grant congress special powers to impeach the president, but this action requires evidence that the president has committed serious misdemeanours in office (Pérez-Liñán 2007).

6. Lijphart also identifies two additional traits of majoritarian democracies: a pluralist system of interest representation, and a central bank dependent on the executive (as opposed to corporatist representation and more independent central banks in consensus democracies), but these characteristics are less clearly related to the other institutional features described in the chapter.

7. When changes towards authoritarianism occur at a slow pace—sometimes over several years—scholars also refer to *democratic erosion* or *democratic backsliding* to describe the process (Bermeo 2016).

8. A fifth set of theories emphasizes the role of political culture as an explanatory factor. Those arguments are discussed in detail in Chapter 17 'Political culture'.

9. Besides multilateral diffusion, international powers may in extreme circumstances impose unilateral regime change. For example, domestic political conditions changed abruptly in Western Europe with the expansion of Nazi Germany, and again after the Allies prevailed in World War II.

Visit the Online Resources that accompany this book for additional material, including country profiles, comparative data sets, flashcard glossaries, and web directory.

www.oup.com/he/caramani5e

6

Authoritarian regimes

Natasha Lindstaedt

Reader's guide

For many years, the concept of an authoritarian regime was considered to be one large category, with little understanding of how these regimes differed. The study of authoritarian regimes has come a long way since. Though all authoritarian regimes share in common that there is no turnover in power of the executive, there are considerable differences that distinguish autocracies. Authoritarian regimes today are increasingly attempting to use 'democratic' institutions to prolong their rule. This has led to a rise in competitive authoritarian regimes, or hybrid regimes. In spite of these changes, authoritarian regimes are more robust than ever. This chapter explains the different ways in which authoritarian regimes are categorized. The chapter then explains how the different types of authoritarian regimes perform, and what factors make them more durable. As the chapter demonstrates, autocratic regimes have become increasingly better equipped to maintain themselves.

Introduction

Most scholarly work in comparative politics has focused on defining democracy, measuring democracies, and theorizing the various models of democracy. In contrast, for many years, authoritarianism was thought to be a residual category of what democracy is not. Any regime that was not democratic was simply labelled 'authoritarian'. More work in the past two decades has now uncovered the mystery that used to surround authoritarian regimes (Geddes 2003; Hadenius and Teorell 2007; Gandhi 2008; Svolik 2012). Authoritarian regimes not only differ from democracies, but they also differ from each other. There are authoritarian regimes like Singapore that, while never seeing turnover in power of the ruling party, enjoy high living standards and low levels of corruption. There are also authoritarian regimes like Chad, which are deeply impoverished, with citizens living under high levels of repression and arbitrary laws.

Generally, authoritarian regimes are defined as regimes that have no turnover in power of the executive. They do not have meaningful elections and the government only represents the preferences of an elite and privileged part of the population. Authoritarian regimes are the result of a 'theft of public office and powers' (Brooker 2014, 3). Though authoritarian regimes all generally share these features in common, as this chapter discusses, authoritarian regimes are not one and the same, and the structural differences between them are vast.

An authoritarian style of rule was the dominant form of rule for many centuries, but one of the most extreme forms of authoritarianism, totalitarianism was popularized in the 1920s and 1930s. Scholars developed these theories on totalitarianism to take account of the new type of authoritarian rule that emerged in countries such as Germany under Adolph Hitler and the Soviet Union under Josef Stalin. Thus, the conceptualization of totalitarianism represents one of the earliest efforts to disaggregate authoritarian regimes. Political science research has built on these early efforts and researchers have developed a number of ways to distinguish between different types of authoritarianism.

More contemporary studies of authoritarian regimes were inspired by the original typological work on authoritarian regimes. Contemporary typologies of authoritarian regimes offer a framework for understanding the differences across autocracies. These research strains can broadly be grouped into two categories: continuous and categorical. While continuous typologies can illustrate the degree of authoritarianism, categorical typologies can be used to differentiate between authoritarian regimes. Categorical typologies are particularly important in understanding who rules, and how that may impact the longevity of the regime and its performance.

In particular, understanding what explains authoritarian stability is a key area of inquiry for both political scientists and policy-makers. Early studies of authoritarian rule focused on the importance of controlling the masses and gaining legitimacy. Authoritarian regimes repressed their citizens on a wide scale to ensure compliance, while schools and media propaganda penetrated the minds of the public to promote the virtues of the regime. More recent studies of authoritarian systems argue that elites are far more important to regime survival (see Geddes 2003; Svolik 2012). These studies demonstrated how leaders co-opted and purged elites in order to prevent coups and removals. More recent studies of authoritarian regimes have also looked at the role of institutions, such as elections and parties (Gandhi and Przeworski 2007; Wright and Escriba-Folch 2012). Paradoxically, 'democratic' institutions are used by authoritarian regimes to prolong their rule, and do not signal that a regime is democratizing. The adoption of these democratic institutions is just one tool of many that dictatorships use to survive.

KEY POINTS

- Authoritarian regimes are regimes that have no turnover in power of the executive.

- Studies of authoritarian rule have noted that there are vast structural differences between authoritarian regimes that can affect regime longevity.

- Understanding what explains authoritarian stability is a major area of inquiry for both political scientists and policy-makers.

Totalitarian regimes

Early work seeking to understand variation across autocracies focused on defining differences between authoritarianism and totalitarian regimes (Friedrich and Brzezinski 1956; Linz, 1964, 2000). Following World War II, the concept of totalitarianism gained traction in political science, probably due to the increased international prominence of regimes like Germany under Adolf Hitler and the Soviet Union under Josef Stalin. One of the foundational works on totalitarianism is Hannah Arendt's work *The Origins of Totalitarianism* (1973). Arendt highlights the uniqueness of totalitarianism, calling it a new and extreme form of dictatorship. Relying heavily on the cases of Hitler and Stalin, Arendt argues that the common thread among all totalitarian regimes is that the leadership wants to transform human nature, by providing a complete road map for the organization of human life. In contrast to other dictatorships that only seek enough power required to keep them in office, totalitarian leaders seek to exert full control over society. As Arendt argues, these systems strive to permanently dominate every individual in every aspect of their lives, subjecting citizens to omnipresent terror as a means of ensuring compliance. A charismatic leader, a party, and the secret police were often critical to maintaining such a tight grip over society.

To achieve such total control, totalitarian regimes resort to high levels of repression. Historically, these regimes have used the massive and/or arbitrary use of terror—as seen in the concentration camps, purges, and show trials—to force citizen and elite compliance. In Cambodia, for example, Pol Pot and the Khmer Rouge (1975–79) killed over one-third of the country's 8 million people. The Khmer Rouge sought to revolutionize society by implementing collectivization. To this end, the regime pursued policies including the forcible depopulation of cities and agricultural reform. Many people were tortured or arrested, and all ethnic Chinese, Vietnamese, Buddhists, and Muslims were killed or targeted (all religions were banned). The regime wanted to create a new society, by forcing urban dwellers to the countryside to work on collective farms. To focus on agricultural communism, teachers, merchants, and almost the entire intellectual elite of the country were murdered. The regime burned books, closed schools, shut down hospitals, and abolished money. The regime all but eliminated individual freedom and personal privacy. People were not free to travel, married couples could only communicate on a limited basis, and the regime banned family members from speaking to each other. People were not allowed to eat in private and were required to eat in the commune. There was also no post or telephones (Kiernan 2002).

Totalitarian regimes also rely heavily on ideology and propaganda to create an undyingly loyal citizenry and foment legitimacy for the regime. To do so, totalitarian regimes indoctrinate their citizens to be loyal towards their regimes and subjects are infused with ideological messages at schools and universities, and through the media and the arts. In contrast, authoritarian regimes put less emphasis on ideology, preferring to foster authoritarian mentalities that are obedient and unquestioning of the status quo. In authoritarian regimes, ideology is either unimportant to the regime or it gradually becomes less and less important with time. Authoritarian leaders are so careless with ideologies that they are often able to change allegiances and switch doctrines and principles with ease. For example, Idi Amin (1971–79) of Uganda initially had a strong relationship with Western powers and Israel, and then changed his mind, declared his commitment to Islam, and pursued relationships with countries such as Libya.

The participatory nature of totalitarian regimes—including mass membership in the party and party-controlled organizations—is another key distinguishing factor between totalitarian and authoritarian systems. In autocracies, the regime often relies on a narrow set of backers to maintain control, and citizens have limited opportunities to actively participate in the society and state. In totalitarian systems, the party and other mobilizing organizations activate the public on a significant scale to take part in achieving the objectives of the state. This mass mobilization allows these regimes to carry out important changes. Totalitarian regimes also aim to completely reconstruct society and transform human nature, whereas authoritarian regimes prefer to demobilize and depoliticize their citizens. In contrast, authoritarian regimes want the public to be apathetic and uninterested in challenging the status quo. Authoritarian regimes also allow for some degree of pluralism, such as allowing elections to take place where there is a small degree of competition. Later in the chapter, in the section 'What makes authoritarian regimes durable?' we will explain why they may choose to do so.

Today, there are very few truly totalitarian regimes. North Korea remains one of the last. While regimes in Eastern Europe and the Soviet Union eventually fell, North Korea has refused to buckle, and has been determined to maintain an activated citizen public that is fully committed to the regime. The regime facilitated mass mobilization on this scale through one of the most penetrating personality cults in the world. North Koreans are constantly indoctrinated to believe the ideological tenets of the regime, known as *juche* or self-reliance. The ideology of the regime serves to unite the public and subordinate it under the will of the state. The ideology provides guidelines for all areas of human endeavour, such as literature, songs, farming, and architecture. The regime has complete ownership over the media and other propaganda machines. Citizens are required to listen to state-run radio at all times, though they are permitted to lower the volume.

North Koreans are also one of the most repressed people in the world. They are severely punished if they try to leave the country. Any sign of dissent could have them killed or sent to a gulag. The state exercises such total control over society that no one is exempt from investigation and everyone is constantly watched. Andrew Scobell writes that 'the climate of terror is instilled not just by the visible elements of the coercive apparatus … but also by a fear of being informed on by a colleague, friend or even a loved one' (Scobell 2006, 34). Freedom of movement is also severely restricted inside North Korea. There are no civil liberties or political rights.

Eritrea also rules over its citizens in a totalitarian manner. Eritreans enjoy no political rights, no civil liberties, and face constant control over their freedom of movement. Rarely are Eritreans under the age of fifty given permission to go abroad. Those who travel without approval will face imprisonment or death.

Family members of those who flee are either heavily fined or detained. Citizens are also forced to go into the military and then into compulsory labour for enterprises that are controlled by the regime. Non-compliance results in being rounded up by the police and executed on the spot. There is no academic freedom and citizens censor themselves in discussions, even in private.

Returning to the example of Cambodia, we can see that there are vast differences between Cambodia today and Cambodia under the Khmer Rouge. For over three decades, the Cambodia's People's Party led by Hun Sen has run Cambodia. Similar to many other authoritarian regimes, regular elections are held in which the opposition can take part. In the 2013 elections, the opposition gained a substantial number of seats. In spite of high levels of political repression and infringement on press freedom, people have freedom of movement, and are free to associate with whom they choose. Instead of constant surveillance of the public and use of brutal repression, the regime sustains its power by giving handouts to cultivate a loyal following, particularly in the rural areas (for more on this see Box 6.3), where Hun Sen has most of his support. The regime has made no effort to indoctrinate and activate the public and the ideology of the regime has mostly lost its meaning.

KEY POINTS

- Totalitarian regimes are an extreme form of authoritarian regime that was popularized in the 1920s and 1930s, but is very rare today.

- Totalitarian regimes exercise considerable power over their citizens by using the party and secret police.

- Totalitarian regimes aim to repress and fully indoctrinate their citizens.

Beyond totalitarianism: understanding authoritarian regimes

Multiple research strains have spawned from the original typological work on authoritarian regimes. These research strains can broadly be grouped into two categories: continuous and categorical. The continuous typologies of authoritarian regimes disaggregate regimes based on how 'authoritarian' they are, whereas the categorical typologies of authoritarian regimes view all autocracies as equally authoritarian, ignoring the degree of authoritarianism. Instead, they focus on the heterogeneity that exists within the world of authoritarian regimes.

Categorical typologies

The contemporary literature on categorical typologies of dictatorship is quite extensive. These typologies use minimalist definitions of democracy (the absence of turnover in power) to distinguish between democracies and authoritarian regimes. They then disaggregate authoritarian regimes based on meaningful ways in which dictatorships vary from one another. Within this research tradition, classifications of authoritarian regimes either emphasize the strategy the authoritarian leader uses to stay in power or the structure of the authoritarian regime.

Work by Barbara Geddes has looked at how autocracies vary with respect to their institutional structures. She identifies which groups in authoritarian regimes hold political power and control policy, examining post-World War II regimes lasting three years or longer. Authoritarian regimes are grouped according to whether they are personalist, single-party, military, or hybrids of these three. These categorizations are based on whether access to political office and influence over policy are controlled by a single individual (as in personalist regimes), a hegemonic party (as in single-party regimes), the military as an institution (as in military regimes), or a royal family (as in monarchies).

Personalist dictatorships are perhaps the most notorious and fascinating form of authoritarianism. Leaders of personalist dictatorships exercise power with little restraint. The leader deliberately weakens and de-professionalizes the military so that it will pose little threat to the dictator's power. The leader also diminishes the legislature to the point where it has no meaning; it simply acts as a rubber stamp on executive decisions. Political parties, if they exist, are also simply a vanity organization to help prop up a leader. The leader also politicizes the judiciary and uses it as a tool for thwarting regime opposition, while the media remains completely under the dictator's control.

Personalist dictators usually do not espouse an ideology. When they do, the ideology is based on the personalist leader's own thoughts, such as 'Mobutuism'—the eclectic ideology of dictator of Zaire, Joseph Mobutu. Personalist leaders often try to foster a personality cult, or an idealized and messianic image of the leader. Due to the limited checks on their power, personalist dictators rule at their own discretion and are unencumbered by rules. As a result, it is difficult to distinguish between the state and the dictator. The dictator is also usually surrounded by an entourage of sycophants who are eager to tell the dictator what they want to hear, with policies often reflecting the personal whims and impulses of decision-making that take place without advice or restraint. Muammar al-Qaddafi of Libya, for example, replaced the Gregorian calendar with a solar calendar, changing all of the months with names that he invented himself and ordered all citizens to own chickens. Russia under Vladmir Putin, Chad under Idriss Déby, and Belarus under Alexander Lukashenko are all examples of personalist rule today, while notable personalist leaders of the past include Idi Amin of Uganda, Saddam Hussein of Iraq, and Ali Abdullah Saleh of Yemen.

Personalist regimes tend to very durable, as personalist dictators tend to use a variety of tactics to stay in power for an extended length of time (see Table 6.1—with the exception of Iran, all of the regimes are personalist). As stated previously, personalist leaders usually only surround themselves with those who are undyingly loyal and non-threatening. However, just being loyal is sometimes not enough. Dictators may regularly reshuffle high-level government officials to ensure that no one individual is able to establish a personal following or base of support. This practice also enables leaders to breed loyalty among their inner circle. By creating a system characterized by uncertainty and vulnerability, elites realize that they are completely dependent on the dictator. This was a favoured tactic of Zaire's Mobutu, who would shuffle cabinet members around. Mobutu would put a member of his inner circle in jail one day, only to later release him from jail and promote him. These erratic actions kept everyone on their toes, but also ensured that the elites remained loyal in case the dictator's mind changed and they were within their good graces again. Divide-and-rule tactics are also used to prevent a cohesive challenge to the regime. Many leaders, such as Siad Barre of Somalia, Mobutu of Zaire, and Libya's Muammar Qaddafi pitted tribal groups against one another to maintain their power. In addition to exacerbating existing divisions, authoritarian leaders also seek to manufacture them, where they do not exist.

Personalist dictatorships are also the most unpredictable. They are less likely to democratize after the dictator falls and the mode of exit tends to be long, protracted, and bloody. Because their leaders conflate themselves with the state, they cannot see a life for themselves after being in power. They become increasingly delusional over time about their power, control, legitimacy, and popularity. They usually refuse to give up power, such as was the case with Qaddafi and Hussein. The aftermath of their rule is usually a period of confusion and chaos, since the leader deliberately hollowed out the institutions of the state and the key power holders in the regime were often incompetent, inexperienced, and ineffective. The institutional void also explains why personalist regimes have the lowest likelihood of democratizing after the regime breaks down (Ezrow and Frantz 2011).

Single-party regimes are regimes in which policy-making control and political offices are in the hands of a single party. Other parties may be allowed to operate, compete in elections, and hold political posts, but their hold on power is minimal. In these systems, the party continues to exert influence because it is well organized and autonomous, which prevents the leader from taking personal control over policy decisions and the selection of regime personnel (Geddes 2003). The leader of the regime is typically the head of the party, and is selected to this post by the party's central committee or politburo or via some sort of electoral process controlled by the party. Examples of single-party dictatorships in power today include China, Laos, and Vietnam, and in most of Eastern Europe during the Cold War.

In single-party regimes, the party controls nearly all of the state institutions and dominates most aspects of the political sphere, such as local government, civil society, and the media. Even the military is subordinate to the party. Within single-party regimes, we can distinguish between those that prohibit opposition parties' participation in elections (e.g. China or Vietnam today), and what scholars have called dominant-party regimes, which permit the opposition to compete in multiparty elections that usually do not allow alternation of political power (e.g. Tanzania and Mexico before 2000).

Single-party regimes are the most institutionalized of all authoritarian regimes and can appear quite similar to democracies, as most have elections and legislatures and most emphasize the importance of public participation in the political process. Some even impose term limits on leaders and elites and have rules that dictate how key political posts are filled. Single-party dictatorships differ from democracies, however, in that legislatures are nearly always filled with party supporters, enabling them to change the rules of the game continuously in the party's favour. Likewise, opposition parties (if they are not banned) face institutional disadvantages and/or constant threats and harassment. Mexico's long-running Institutional Revolutionary Party (PRI) was able to use its hegemonic status to weaken and discourage the opposition by orchestrating huge electoral victories. This signal of party invincibility reinforces elite loyalty to the party and dissuades other actors such as the military from supporting the opposition.

Of all the regime types, single-party regimes tend to be the longest lasting, experience the fewest coups, and enjoy higher economic growth and more measured foreign policy than other authoritarian regime types. Because there are more veto players and decision-making usually revolves around discussion and consultation, policy output is predictable and pragmatic, which contributes to their longevity and relatively strong economic performance.

Military regimes are regimes where military officers exercise political power and control over policy and the security forces. Military regimes often create a token political party, but the party is subordinate to the military. Military regimes are not regimes where someone from a military background has won an open election. There are many democracies around the world where a military leader was democratically elected. Instead, military regimes are cases where the military has seized power and has taken control of the executive (Finer, 2017). Military regimes are also not regimes that are simply ruled by a man in uniform who has coup-proofed the military. Colonel Muammar Qaddafi seized power of Libya in 1969, but Libya was not a military regime. General Idi Amin of Uganda also had a military background when he staged a coup in 1971, but Uganda was also not a military regime. Military regimes were most common in Latin America during the Cold War, such as Argentina (1976–83) and Peru (1968–80). Thailand is a current example, and up until recently so was Algeria.

Military regimes may have a chief executive that is a civilian (as in the case of Uruguay in 1976), but true power lies in the hands of the military. Military dictatorship, therefore, is a more collegial form of autocracy than personalist dictatorship, because members of the ruling junta make decisions jointly. During the Brazilian dictatorship (1964–85), for example, consultation among military officers remained important through the many years of military control, most visibly during negotiations over planned presidential successions every few years (Stepan 2015). The case of the Brazilian military regime ruling for twenty-one years is somewhat of an anomaly. Most military regimes last only a few years, as splits within the military can take place once the military enters politics, which incentivizes military regimes from going back to the barracks in a timely fashion to preserve their unity and legitimacy (Geddes 1999). Possibly because military rule is so short lived, after the military leaves power, the chances of democratizing are higher than for other types of authoritarian rule (Geddes et al. 2014).

Monarchies—and more specifically absolute monarchies—are systems where a person of royal descent inherits the position of head of state in accordance with accepted practice or the constitution (Hadenius and Teorell 2007). Inherited positions are not always automatically based on primogeniture, as some monarchies manage leadership succession by having the ruling family or monarch select a successor from the family. To be a monarchical dictatorship, the monarch and members of the ruling family occupy key positions of power and exercise control over the military and security services, access to political office, and control domestic and foreign policy. Historically, most authoritarian regimes of the past were hereditary monarchies. Today, all of the monarchies are located in the Middle East and North Africa, with the exception of Brunei (1959–present) and Eswatini (formerly Swaziland) (1968–present). Monarchies had largely been understudied, but the Arab Spring led to a surge in research seeking to understand why the monarchies proved to be so resilient relative to other forms of autocracy that were toppled by protest in Tunisia, Egypt, Libya, and Yemen.

Like single-party regimes, monarchies tend to be particularly durable. Large ruling families create a long list of veto players that serve to temper the whims of the monarch in the decision-making process and ensure that policies are stable and sound. Also, like single-party regimes, monarchies also often have institutionalized leadership transitions. The process of selecting a leader from among the family ranks requires aspiring rulers to build consensus and bargain among various family factions. Members of the ruling family who are not in line to compete for the throne tend to support the new monarch and are often given a key position within the state bureaucracy to keep them happy (Herb 1999).

Some scholars have suggested that it is the traditional religious and tribal legitimacy that these regimes enjoy that induces strong citizen support (Hudson 1977; Kostiner 2000). For example, historical-religious claims to legitimacy are important in Jordan, where the Hashemite House of Jordan claims descent from Muhammad himself. The dynastic families ruling Bahrain, Kuwait, Oman, Qatar, Saudi Arabia, and the United Arab Emirates also command respect among the tribal confederations in their societies. In addition to traditional sources of legitimacy, authoritarian monarchies benefit from the ability of the ruling family to penetrate society and mobilize diverse networks of support, similar in many ways to the role ruling parties play in single-party dictatorships. Compared to republics, monarchies are closer to the

Table 6.1	Longest serving dictators
Cameroon	Paul Biya (1975–)
Equatorial Guinea	Teodoro Obiang (1979–)
Iran	Ali Khameini (1981–)
Republic of Congo	Denis Sassou Nguesso (1979–1992; 1997–)
Cambodia	Hun Sen (1984–)
Uganda	Yoweri Museveni (1986–)
Chad	Idriss Deby (1990–)
Kazakhstan	Nursultan Nazarbayev (1991–)
Tajikistan	Emomali Rahmon (1992–)
Eritrea	Isaias Afwerki (1993–)

societies they govern because their traditions generate high levels of respect and admiration. Monarchies have also been adept at bestowing upon their subjects 'gifts' which come in the form of economic payments or patronage (jobs).

Continuous typologies

Many scholars claim that there is a grey zone that lies between democracies and authoritarian regimes (Levitsky and Way 2010). Continuous typologies of authoritarianism emphasize the various gradients of authoritarian regimes. They identify the extent to which regimes are democratic or authoritarian and place regimes along a democratic–autocratic scale. For the purposes of this chapter, we will not focus on democracies with adjectives, such as flawed democracies, weak democracies, or illiberal democracies. Instead, we focus on frameworks that are used to understand and differentiate regimes according to the degree to which they are authoritarian.

There are several authors that focus on authoritarian regimes that hold elections with a small degree of uncertainty. These regimes are referred to as **hybrid regimes, electoral authoritarian regimes**, or **competitive authoritarian regimes**. We highlight the main components of hybrid regimes and how they fail to fulfil the minimum requirements to be considered democratic. In hybrid regimes, democratic institutions are used to exercise political authority, but incumbents violate the rules often enough that the 'regime fails to meet conventional minimum standards for democracy' (Levitsky and Way 2002, 52).

Though hybrid regimes hold elections in which the opposition is able to meaningfully challenge incumbents, the electoral 'playing field' is not fair as it is in democracies. Instead, incumbents have access to a variety of state resources that can help them steer the election's outcome in their favour. They can deny the opposition adequate media coverage, harass and threaten opposition candidates and/or supporters, and manipulate the electoral rules and results in ways that disadvantage opposition candidates.

These regimes are not fully autocratic, however, in that electoral institutions not only exist, but could lead to turnover in power. Thus, in spite of the dominance of the ruling group or party, elections are not entirely predetermined in competitive authoritarian regimes, as they are in 'pure' forms of dictatorship. Though there are multiple advantages given to incumbents, as discussed above, elections in hybrid regimes are generally free of massive fraud. In pure authoritarian regimes, by contrast, elections are either non-existent or the outcome is already decided well before the date of the election.

Hybrid regimes differ from pure authoritarian regimes in other ways, as well. In pure authoritarian regimes, legislatures either do not exist or are controlled by a single ruling party, the judiciary has little independence or political power apart from the ruling group or party, and most forms of media are state owned and closely censored. In comparison, in hybrid regimes, though legislatures are weak, there is occasional activity that takes place there. The judiciary is not totally powerless, but it is coerced through bribery and extortion. An independent media can operate, but is severely restricted. For example, in Nicaragua under Daniel Ortega, the media can operate but is limited in what it can say. Elections are held, but the outcome is tilted heavily in favour of Ortega and his Sandinista Party. The judiciary also faces political interference (Thaler 2017).

The strength of continuous typologies is that they acknowledge that most regimes may not be fully democratic or fully autocratic. It is likely that these grey zone regimes differ from their authoritarian counterparts in meaningful ways, particularly in terms of the civil and political liberties enjoyed by their citizens, and the level of uncertainty in the electoral processes. The weakness of continuous typologies is that they imply that as regimes become less authoritarian, they become closer to being democracies. This may not be true, however as regimes may employ democratic institutions but may not be democratizing. The likelihood of democratization may be independent of how authoritarian a regime is, or appears to be. Continuous typologies are also, by definition, restricted to differentiating regimes along a single dimension, which is typically the level of competitiveness of the regime. Continuous typologies also do not capture more of the complexities and differences between authoritarian regimes.

KEY POINTS

- Scholars today differentiate authoritarian regimes either by category or degree of authoritarianism.

- Personalist dictatorships perform poorly on nearly every dimension compared to other forms of authoritarian rule.

- Military dictatorships do not tend to last very long and prefer to negotiate their exits, while monarchies and single-party regimes are very durable.

- Competitive authoritarian regimes are authoritarian regimes that hold elections that have some degree of uncertainty, but where the odds are heavily stacked in their favour.

What makes authoritarian regimes durable?

Foundational work on the survival of authoritarian regimes frames the central political issue in these regimes as one between the authoritarian elite and the much larger population. This was the focus of the now classic literature on totalitarianism by authors such as Hannah Arendt, Carl Friedrich, and Zbigniew Brzezinski. Thus, the assumption from the early literature on authoritarian regimes was that the biggest threat to the survival of authoritarian rule came from the masses. Early literature focused on how authoritarian regimes were able to prevent the masses from toppling the regime in a revolution, through a combination of repression, indoctrination, and legitimation. The literature from the past decades looks at how regimes must manage elites to prevent coups from taking place. The most recent work on authoritarian rule acknowledges that the masses have become more important to regime survival, illustrated by a spike in revolutions and a decline in military coups. Unlike authoritarian regimes of the past, today's autocrats are using sophisticated technology and social media to reach their intended audience, to ensure that citizens continuously hear a pro-regime message.

Repression

Dictators have to repress their citizens, to varying degrees, to maintain control. There are early examples of massive purges and executions that have taken place under Josef Stalin, Kim Il Sung, Saddam Hussein, and so on. Early work by the likes of Juan Linz claimed that repression was the most common tool that dictators use to maintain power and is a central element of regime stability. More recently, studies have argued that repression may be more selective, or more of a last resort used to re-stabilize a critical situation (Svolik 2012). Studies have shown, however, that the more repressive an authoritarian regime was, the longer the regime survived (Escribà-Folch 2013; see also Bellin 2004).

Though high levels of repression raise the risks of gaining negative international attention and may breed popular discontent, regimes can reduce threats to their power simply by eliminating the opposition, through imprisonment, disappearances, and executions. The costs of opposing the regime rise when there are high levels of repression. Saudi Arabia's regime is so repressive, that it has virtually no opposition inside the country (though there is an opposition living in exile). No second revolution took place in Iran during protests in 2009 because the government responded to the protests by killing over seventy people and arresting 4,000. Citizens believe that they have no choice but to obey the regime or risk their lives. Repression also makes it more difficult for the opposition to organize themselves. It is more risky for individuals to publicize their opinions, making it difficult for any opposition to orchestrate collective action. As such, more repressive authoritarian regimes experience fewer protests relative to regimes that are more permissive (Kricheli et al. 2011).

In spite of this, repression does carry some risks for authoritarian regimes. Authoritarian regimes that are highly repressive lack accurate information about how their citizens truly feel about the regime. Repressive regimes also have to grant the security forces high levels of power to execute these actions, and this additional power can eventually lead to the security forces turning against civilian-led regimes. It is also true that some authoritarian regimes cannot afford to execute high levels of repression against their citizens.

In cases where regimes have the capacity to repress, purging (such as imprisonment, executions, and disappearances) is a specific tactic used to eliminate political enemies that threaten an autocrat's power. **Purges** send a clear message to anyone who dares to challenge the regime: you will likely end up dead. In order to set the right tone of just how ruthless the regime is, it is common that elite purges take place during the early stages of a regime, or during the process when the leader is consolidating power. Saddam Hussein, for example, executed most members of his elite support group in 1979, replacing them with new supporters (Ezrow and Frantz 2011). The great purge in the Soviet Union in the 1930s saw hundreds of potentially threatening government officials purged in order to eliminate challenges to Stalin's rule. Early purges took place in Uganda under Idi Amin, in Zimbabwe under Robert Mugabe, in China under Mao Zedong, and more recently in North Korea under Kim Jong-un. An exception to this is the recent dismissal of more than 140,000 Turkish workers in July of 2016, in response to the attempted coup against Prime Minister Recep Erdoğan.

Legitimacy

In order to mitigate the problem of relying on repression alone, authoritarian regimes also need to ensure that they have high levels of legitimacy. Not surprisingly, authoritarian regimes that enjoy some level of legitimacy tend to last longer than those that do not (for more on this, see Box 6.1 on authoritarian nostalgia) (Gerschewski 2013). This helps to explain why the Arab monarchies were more resistant to breakdown compared to some of their republican counterparts in the Arab Spring. Monarchies, as we explained in 'Categorical typologies' earlier in the chapter, enjoy some level of legitimacy based on their historical-religious claims.

Authoritarian regimes can also earn legitimacy when they can claim credit for a strong economic performance. Modernization theory held that authoritarian regimes that grew economically, leading to the formation of an educated middle class, would eventually democratize, as was the case in Taiwan and South Korea. More recent scholarship, however, has argued that economic growth can have a stabilizing effect in authoritarian regimes. Though economic growth is stabilizing to democracies, impressive economic performance can be equally stabilizing to authoritarian regimes. Work by Adam Przeworski and Fernando Limongi (1997) have found that authoritarian regimes that enjoy consistent economic growth are able to remain stable. Singapore and Vietnam point to high levels of economic growth as evidence that authoritarian rule is benefiting and not harming their countries. In the case of China, since Mao Zedong died, the regime has been able to lift 500 million people out of poverty and has achieved double-digit growth rates for several decades.

Authoritarian regimes can legitimize their rule by using propaganda to inculcate ideological principles or ideas. This is important to attaining full compliance of the population to an authoritarian regime. It may help to convince individuals that there is a need for some suffering to achieve the mission of the regime. Attempts to legitimize a regime's rule through the inculcation of an ideological agenda usually takes place through the mass media, but can also take place through the educational system, where students are taught to accept the message of the regime uncritically, while closing down alternatives to different views. More recent studies have shown how introducing new pro-regime content in the curriculum in China has led to higher trust in government officials

---

BOX 6.1

Authoritarian nostalgia

Authoritarian nostalgia refers to sentiments among the public that romanticize past periods of authoritarian rule. Nostalgia refers to the loss of an idealized past or a desire to re-experience the past. It typically emerges in situations of transition and uncertainty. It is also more likely to surface when there is a current dissatisfaction with the present. With nostalgia, the disappointing present is contrasted with an idealized conception of the past.

Individuals socialized under authoritarian rule may view authoritarian forms of government as more legitimate to democracy. These political attitudes that are acquired in early adulthood tend to remain stable for years to come. For this reason, authoritarian nostalgia is particularly noticeable in Eastern Europe, which endured long spells of authoritarianism. Studies have revealed that Eastern Europeans who endured years of communist policies and indoctrination are more likely to be nostalgic about this period (Neundorf et al. 2017). Cohorts that were indoctrinated with communist propaganda during their impressionable years (childhood to young adulthood), are more likely to be nostalgic for communism compared to both older and younger generations, which were not indoctrinated during their impressionable years. Overall, socialization under authoritarian rule tends to suppress the development of democratic attitudes.

and a re-alignment of views on political participation and democracy with those promoted by the authorities (Cantoni et al. 2014).

Co-optation of citizens and elites

In addition to indoctrinating citizens, leaders seek to prolong their political survival by co-opting support for their regime. Co-optation refers to a regime's efforts to engender loyalty, often by tying strategically relevant actors or groups to the regime elite. By co-opting the opposition and providing them with jobs, payments, and other benefits, this ensures that the opposition has a vested interest in the regime. Using co-optation instead of repression avoids the risk of fostering social discontent. By creating these relationships and permitting the opposition (or pseudo-opposition) to exist, authoritarian regimes can create a façade of competition, while also preventing the opposition from coalescing to mount a significant challenge against the regime.

It is not just the opposition that can be co-opted, but also the elite. Thus far in the chapter we have yet to introduce that most scholars (in contrast to early works on totalitarianism) view the biggest threats to the regime as coming from within, with coups (orchestrated by the military or elites) remaining the most likely mode of exit for authoritarian leaders. Given that authoritarian regimes must make sure that elites are happy, buying the support of the elites is critical to preventing a fall from power. In addition to offering financial incentives to elites, authoritarian regimes can use institutions such as political parties and legislatures to purchase elite loyalty. Financial gifts alone are not enough, as loyalty can shift quickly and an economic downturn may make it difficult to maintain high rates of financial rewards. Elites are offered important roles in parties and legislatures as a way of keeping them happy and more reluctant to challenge the regime.

Use of 'democratic' institutions

Contemporary work on authoritarian regimes has acknowledged that modern authoritarian regimes now utilize democratic institutions such as political parties and legislatures to prolong their rule (Gandhi and Przeworski 2007; Gandhi 2008). Counterintuitively, elections have become the norm in contemporary autocracies (for more on how elections coincide with increasing autocratization, see Box 6.2). In 1970, only 59 per cent of autocracies regularly held elections (one at least every six years). As of 2008, that number had increased to 83 per cent (Kendall-Taylor

---

BOX 6.2

Autocratization in Venezuela and Turkey

The process of states becoming increasingly autocratic is known as autocratization. (When this happens to a democracy, it is referred to as democratic backsliding.) As many regimes around the world are seeing their democratic institutions erode as the result of a slow process and not due to a sudden seizure of power, such as a coup (referred to as an authoritarian reversal), the term 'autocratization' is more commonly used. There are two notable forms of autocratization: executive aggrandizement, or the increasing power of the executive vis-à-vis the other branches of government, and electoral manipulation. Below, we show examples of autocratization in Venezuela under Hugo Chávez (1999–2013) and Turkey under Recep Tayyip Erdoğan (2003–).

Examples of *executive aggrandizement* in Venezuela under Hugo Chávez:

- The constitution was amended to give Chávez power to rule by decree.
- Chávez eliminated the Senate and created a twenty-one-person unelected council that was loyal to him.
- He added an additional twelve seats to the Supreme Court, to ensure that the now thirty-two-seat tribunal was filled

with government supporters that had to pledge a commitment to Chávez's agenda.

Examples of *electoral manipulation* in Venezuela under Hugo Chávez:

- The National Electoral Commission was placed under Chávez's control and filled with regime loyalists.

Examples of *executive aggrandizement* in Turkey under Recep Tayyip Erdoğan:

- Erdoğan transformed Turkey into a presidential system.
- He removed as many as 3,000 sitting judges.
- He provided the National Intelligence Organization (headed by a presidential appointee) with the power to collect all/any information from any entity in Turkey without having to seek judicial permission or submit to judicial review.
- Erdoğan was given the power to name fourteen of the seventeen Constitutional Court judges.

Examples of *electoral manipulation* in Turkey under Recep Tayyip Erdoğan:

- A referendum revised term limits for Erdoğan, giving him the ability to stay in power until 2029.

and Frantz 2015). Authoritarian elections serve several functions that enable incumbent regimes to solidify their support among the elite, opposition, and public.

Authoritarian elections enable dictators to deter potential rivals by signalling the dominance and authority of the regime. As mentioned previously, elections can also be used to maintain elite cohesion by institutionalizing competition for power and resources, which helps damper potentially destabilizing elite rivalries. Elections can also weaken the opposition because the regime can pursue a divide-and-rule strategy. While some opposition parties are permitted to compete, others are disqualified, while some regimes also opt to have a strict vetting process in place (as is the case in Iran) to ensure that no threatening opposition candidates have a chance to run.

Authoritarian regimes also use elections to boost public support. Many authoritarian regimes increase public spending just prior to elections in order to mobilize popular support and secure mass votes for their regimes. Elections can also provide authoritarian regimes with important information on how well their policies are working and how popular or unpopular different candidates are. Authoritarian regimes can respond to this information in ways that prevent discontent from snowballing. In Mexico, the PRI used electoral results to identify where the party lacked support and needed to focus additional resources to win votes (Magaloni 2008). Singapore, under the People's Action Party, uses elections to gauge how popular and effective its policies are.

Political parties and legislatures are also common features of contemporary autocracies. Although the vast majority of authoritarian regimes have long incorporated at least one political party, these regimes have increasingly adopted multiple political parties and legislatures since the end of the Cold War. As of 2008, 84 per cent of autocracies allowed multiple political parties and a legislature (Kendall-Taylor and Frantz 2015). As with elections, political parties and legislatures also prolong the durability of autocracies (Geddes 2005). Since the end of the Cold War, dictatorships with multiple political parties and a legislature lasted fourteen years longer in office than those without these institutions (nineteen years versus five, on average) (Kendall-Taylor and Frantz 2015).

Parties are used in authoritarian regime not only to spread the regime's ideology (if it exists), but also to distribute benefits to loyal citizens in areas that may extend beyond the regime's reach. Before Malaysia saw the opposition win its first victory in 2018, Malaysia's dominant United Malays National Organisation (UMNO) party was a massive machine to distribute benefits such as financial assistance and electronic equipment to rural voters. Authoritarian regimes are effective in gaining the loyalty of their rural constituencies, and they use parties to transfer benefits to these areas. Parties also provide members with a host of different benefits including jobs, preferential access to schooling for their children, and access to lucrative government contracts. Parties can also help organize public rallies in support of the regime and can help monitor citizen behaviour.

Legislatures also help prolong authoritarian regimes because they incentivize the opposition to participate in the system instead of fighting to take down the regime. The opposition, when it can gain some seats, is less likely to resort to violence and mobilize their constituents. The Muslim Brotherhood has been allowed to operate in Jordan and has been delegated some influence over education and social policies. In return, the Muslim Brotherhood in Jordan respects the king and the monarchy.

> **KEY POINTS**
>
> * Most authoritarian regimes today hold elections and use other 'democratic' institutions to prolong their rule.
>
> * Authoritarian regimes of the past were more repressive; authoritarian regimes of today are more apt to use co-optation, and some authoritarian regimes enjoy genuine support.
>
> * Authoritarian regimes are more likely to emerge slowly over time, and not from a sudden seizure of power by the military.

How do authoritarian regimes perform?

There was a moment in comparative politics when scholars saw the phenomenal success of the Asian tigers, and attributed this success to advantages of authoritarian rule. Authoritarian regimes are able to pursue policies that are sound and effective, but that might not be popular with citizens. Authoritarian regimes are also more insulated from particularistic interests that could lead to policies that favour certain groups at the expense of the rest of the country. As mentioned in 'Beyond totalitarianism: understanding authoritarian regimes' earlier, the success of China, Vietnam, Malaysia, Hong Kong, Taiwan, South Korea, Singapore and Chile gave scholars pause to consider the economic benefits of authoritarian rule.

In spite of this optimism about the benefits of authoritarian rule, generally speaking, authoritarian regimes do not consistently perform well compared to consolidated democracies (for more on this see Table 6.2 and Box 6.3). Moreover, there is more variation within authoritarian regimes in terms of their performance. For every Singapore and Qatar, you also have the Democratic Republic of Congo, Central African Republic, Venezuela, South Sudan, and Chad. Most of the poorest regimes in the world are concurrently authoritarian, and the few wealthier authoritarian regimes tend to be rich in oil.

The variance in performance levels in authoritarian regimes is in part due to the different types of authoritarian regimes. Here it is useful to recall the Geddes typology mentioned earlier in the chapter to demonstrate the relationship between regime type and growth. Accordingly, studies have shown that one-party states have been solid economic performers compared with personalist regimes, with military regimes falling in the middle (Frantz and Ezrow, 2011). What is the reason for this?

Table 6.2 Average nominal GDP per capita	
Authoritarian regimes	$ 6,525
World average	$11,355
Democracies	$25,307

Source: IMF (2018).

Personalist regimes have few checks on their power compared to single-party regimes, which have the most people involved in regime decision-making. Independent state institutions can constrain dictators from enriching themselves or pursuing bad policies. Personalist dictatorships are freer to make poor decisions that lead to policy instability and poor economic performance. They are free to rule by decree, without much consultation or discussion. Personalist dictators may also divert much of their spending towards their own personal goals or towards the repressive apparatus. In contrast, other authoritarian regimes have more checks and balances on their leadership, which may prevent the implementation of predatory policies. In fact, studies show that the existence of parties and legislatures in dictatorships enhances economic growth (Gandhi 2008; Wright 2008).

As personalist dictatorships are unlikely to have institutionalized succession, the goal of personal survival trumps regime survival. The personalist leader will pursue policies that are inimical to growth because they do not want to encourage the formation of a thriving middle class that could pose a threat to them. Personalist regimes have fewer checks on their power, giving them the freedom to engage in kleptocratic behaviour, or stealing millions—if not billions—from the state. Single-party leaders know that there

---

BOX 6.3

Corruption and clientelism

On average, authoritarian regimes also tend to exhibit higher levels of corruption (or the abuse of power for illegitimate private gain) compared to democracies (Chang and Golden 2010). A particular form of corruption that is critical to the survival of an authoritarian system is clientelism or patron-clientelism. Though not every form of clientelism is corrupt, the persistence of clientelist networks does undermine democracy and accountability. Clientelism refers to the personal relationships that are formed between citizens (clients) and the government (patrons) that repeatedly revolve around an exchange of resources (Hicken 2011). Citizens offer their loyalty and support for the regime in exchange for various types of particularistic benefits from the government, such as jobs, financial assistance.

Clientelist states structure their networks in ways that allow patrons to target benefits to individuals and to monitor their political support. For example, in the 1980s, the Singapore government changed its vote-counting system to allow the government to count and report votes at the ward level, which in Singapore roughly equates to an apartment block. As the vast majority of

Singaporeans live in public housing estates, the change gave the government access to detailed data about the distribution of its support. The ruling People's Action Party subsequently tied housing services to support for the regime. Apartment complexes that supported the opposition could expect to be last on the list for upgrades and improvements (Tremewan 2006).

Clientelism differs to some degree with **rentierism**, or when resource-rich authoritarian regimes use rents to buy political support. The key difference is that the benefits are less particularistic. For example, all citizens may be the beneficiary of no taxation. As such, citizens in these countries have a greater incentive to turn a blind eye to the repressiveness of the regime. Not surprisingly, during the Arab Spring, oil-rich monarchies were better able to stave off widespread discontent. Saudi Arabia, for example, announced an $80 billion package of public sector wage increases, greater unemployment payments and college stipends, along with other investments in low-income housing (Brownlee et al. 2013). Many citizens in the oil-rich Gulf work directly for the state and are completely dependent on the regime for their livelihood, which helps to explain why these regimes have been so stable.

are checks on their decision-making and that leadership succession has been established. Therefore, the regime has a greater incentive to focus on economic performance to maintain legitimacy, rather than counter-productive leadership survival strategies.

While there is wide variation in authoritarian regimes when it comes to economic growth, authoritarian regimes have performed poorly compared to democracies when it comes to preventing famines. In fact, famines have only taken place in authoritarian regimes. The most notable famine was caused by the Great Leap Forward in China from 1958–61, where as many as 30 million people died, due to faulty government policies that were not corrected for three years, with government cover-ups (Sen 1999). Authoritarian regimes lack an independent media to highlight that the famine is taking place. There are no opposition parties in the legislature to voice outrage and no free speech so that citizens can also declare their disgust. Reports in the news and public protests carry

information that authorities need to know in order to resolve the problem. These actors can also pressurize and compel regimes to take action. Authoritarian regimes tend to want to cover up any negative news story, even if it comes at the expense of their own people.

> ### KEY POINTS
>
> - Authoritarian regimes do not perform as well economically as democracies do, and there is a wide variance in performance levels.
> - Personalist regimes are the most corrupt and usually perform poorly, while single-party regimes generally perform the best.
> - Though there are still more democracies in the world than authoritarian regimes, the international environment is more favourable to authoritarianism than it was after the Cold War ended.

Conclusion

Authoritarian regimes form an area of comparative politics that is increasingly studied, and as such, more is understood about how autocracies function than ever before. Previously, there was an assumption that all authoritarian regimes were controlled by a strongman. The image of Idi Amin of Uganda and Saddam Hussein of Iraq fit this depiction. And though strongmen certainly exist, there are also regimes that have been led by just one party, such as Vietnam or run by a military junta, as was the case in Brazil for several decades. As Barbara Geddes concluded, 'different kinds of authoritarian regimes differ from each other as much as they differ from democracy' (1999, 121). There is considerable variation across dictatorships, which has resulted in the classification of authoritarian regimes into different categories based on who holds power. This framework helps to understand how authoritarian types explain a host of different outcomes such as economic performance and mode of exit.

There is also variation across dictatorships in terms of how authoritarian dictatorships are. Authoritarian regimes of the past were all considered to be repressive and controlling of their publics. But today's dictatorships are savvy enough to employ democratic institutions, not as a way to ensure representation and turnover in power, but as a means to safeguard their survival. The varying degrees of pluralism and usurpation of democratic institutions, such as legislatures and elections, has led to the rise of hybrid regimes, or authoritarian regimes that have some democratic

features. In some cases, there is almost no uncertainty about the outcomes, and the institutions are merely pseudo institutions. In other cases, the institutions allow for more liberty, voice, and representation comparatively speaking. Due to the variance in degrees of authoritarianism, continuous measures of authoritarian regimes help us understand different levels of repressiveness.

The variance in the degree of authoritarianism is reflective of the fact that regimes of today use a wider range of tools to maintain themselves in power. While authoritarian regimes are still repressive, that is not the only mode of control. The literature of the past few decades has revealed that the biggest threats to regimes' power are elites. As such, co-optation strategies are used to ensure that elites will not threaten the incumbent's power. As authoritarian regimes live under constant threat that their rule will be overturned (and possibly in a violent manner), hedging against this risk also extends to shaping the hearts and minds of the public.

To conclude, though authoritarian regimes have toppled in many countries around the world, the climate for authoritarian regimes is more favourable than it has been for some time. Since the Cold War ended, many democracies have experienced authoritarian reversals, while authoritarian regimes have resisted democratization. Clearly, the authoritarian regimes of today have become even shrewder than their predecessors in masking their authoritarian behaviour and prolonging their survival.

QUESTIONS

Knowledge-based

1. What is the difference between an authoritarian regime and a totalitarian regime? What makes North Korea totalitarian and not authoritarian?

2. How important are different forms of repression in maintaining authoritarian rule? Why is repression alone not enough? Are there any authoritarian regimes around the world that do not use repression?

3. Why are monarchies and single-party regimes so resilient? What do these two regimes share in common? Does this help explain why the monarchies were more resilient than the republics during the Arab Spring?

4. Why are more and more authoritarian regimes holding elections? When does holding elections backfire for authoritarian regimes?

5. Why are military coups less frequent today than in the past? Is military rule unpopular?

Critical thinking

6. Today personalism in leadership is on the rise. Is that a concern? Why, or why not?

7. Do you agree that it is important to differentiate between authoritarian regimes that hold elections that have some degree of pluralism and those that do not? Does this make Russia under Vladmir Putin less authoritarian than China under Xi Jinping?

8. Can an authoritarian regime be legitimate?

9. Are there cases where people are better off living in authoritarian regimes than democracies?

10. Why have authoritarian regimes been allocated only one chapter in this book?

FURTHER READING

Brooker, P. (2014). *Non-Democratic Regimes* (Basingstoke, UK: Palgrave Macmillan).

Brownlee, J. (2007). *Authoritarianism in an Age of Democratization* (Cambridge: Cambridge University Press).

Diamond, L., Plattner, M. F., and Walker, C. (eds) (2016). *Authoritarianism Goes Global: The Challenge to Democracy* (Baltimore, MD: JHU Press).

Ezrow, N. M. and Frantz, E. (2011). *Dictators and Dictatorships: Understanding Authoritarian Regimes and their Leaders* (New York City, NY: Bloomsbury Publishing).

Gandhi, J. (2008). *Political Institutions under Dictatorship* (Cambridge: Cambridge University Press).

Geddes, B. (2003). *Paradigms and Sand Castles: Theory Building and Research Design in Comparative Politics* (Ann Arbor, MI: University of Michigan Press).

Herb, M. (1999). *All in the Family: Absolutism, Revolution, and Democracy in Middle Eastern Monarchies* (Albany, NY: SUNY Press).

Linz, J. J. (2000). *Totalitarian and Authoritarian Regimes* (Boulder, CO: Lynne Rienner Publishers).

Svolik, M. W. (2012). *The Politics of Authoritarian Rule* (Cambridge: Cambridge University Press).

Visit the Online Resources that accompany this book for additional material, including country profiles, comparative data sets, flashcard glossaries, and web directory.

www.oup.com/he/caramani5e

Section 3
Structures and institutions

7

Legislatures

Amie Kreppel

Chapter contents

Reader's guide

This chapter addresses the political roles and powers of legislatures. The first step is to define different types of legislatures on the basis of their functions and the character of their relationship with the executive branch. The analysis then turns to an examination of the roles of legislatures within the political system as a whole, as well as several critical aspects of the internal organizational structures of legislatures. Finally, the relationship between the political power and influence of a legislature and the structure of the broader political and party system is discussed. Throughout the chapter, the focus is on legislatures within modern democratic political systems, although many points apply to all legislatures regardless of the nature of the regime in which they exist.

Introduction

The role of legislatures within the broader political system is far from straightforward. Different scholars have come to very different conclusions about the political power and policy influence of legislatures. General evaluations vary depending on the cases that are studied, the theoretical framework employed, the historical period under examination, and the precise understanding of 'power' and 'influence' invoked.

This chapter examines the influence and importance of legislatures across a variety of different 'core' tasks, including representing and linking citizens and government, providing oversight of the executive, and, of course, policy-making. The importance of these tasks, and the variation that exists between legislatures in their performance, make the understanding of legislatures a critical component of any attempt to comprehend politics more generally. Legislatures exist in nearly every country on the planet, and have the potential to play an important political role, even in non-democratic systems.

KEY POINTS

- Legislatures are present throughout the world and play a central role in almost all political systems.
- However, variations in their powers and structures are large.

What is a legislature?

The variety of terms such as 'assembly', 'congress', or 'parliament' that are often used interchangeably with the term 'legislature' increases uncertainty about the roles and powers of legislatures. Before we can examine the types of legislature that exist, it is necessary to define what a legislature is. The exact meaning of these terms is not as clear as one might expect. Definitions of 'assembly', 'legislature', 'parliament', and 'congress' provided in dictionaries do not always differentiate between these terms (see Box 7.1). All four are defined as 'a legislative body' or 'a body of persons having the power to legislate', making efforts to clearly distinguish between them difficult. Yet most would agree that the terms are not interchangeable.

Of these four terms, 'assembly' is the most general. Additional definitions of the word (uncapitalized) refer simply to the coming together of a group of people for some purpose—for example, a school assembly. It is only when we add the qualifier 'political'

or 'legislative' that we think of assemblies in the same context as legislatures, parliaments, and congresses. Parliaments and congresses, generically, can best be understood as two types of legislatures. This interpretation of these four terms creates a hierarchy of institutions from the most general (an assembly) to the most specific (congresses and parliaments) that are types of the mid-level category of 'legislatures' (see Figure: 'A hierarchy of institutions', in the Online Resources).

Assemblies and legislatures

If we begin with the broadest definition of an **assembly** as 'a group of persons gathered together, usually for a particular purpose, whether religious, political, educational, or social', we can then designate **legislatures** as those assemblies for which the 'particular purpose' in question is political and legislative (*American Heritage Dictionary*, 4th edn). This definition of legislatures is expansive enough to include a wide array of very different institutions, while still distinguishing between legislatures and other types of assemblies organized for religious, educational, or social purposes.

Precisely because of its inclusiveness, the term 'legislature' is too broad to help us distinguish between different types of legislative institutions. To accomplish this task, we must move beyond dictionary definitions and concentrate on the structural characteristics of the political system in which a legislature is situated. Regardless of whether or not a political system can be categorized as democratic, *if there is a legislature in addition to an executive branch, the relationship between the two will determine the core characteristics of the legislature.* The central characteristic of significance is the relative level of interdependence between these two branches of government.

DEFINITIONS 7.1

Assembly: a legislative body; specifically, the lower house of a legislature.

Legislature: a body of persons having the power to legislate; specifically, an organized body having the authority to make laws for a political unit.

Parliament: the supreme legislative body of a usually major political unit that is a continuing institution comprising a series of individual assemblages.

Congress: the supreme legislative body of a nation, and especially of a republic.

Merriam-Webster online (http://www.m-w.com).

Parliaments

In what are commonly referred to as '**parliamentary systems**' the executive branch is selected by the legislature, usually from among its own members. The executive branch or 'government' is formally responsible to the legislature throughout its tenure. This means that it can be removed from office at any time should a majority within the legislature oppose it, regardless of the electoral cycle. In turn, removal of the executive by the legislature may be accompanied by early legislative elections. Because there is a high degree of mutual dependence between them, these types of system are known generically as **fused-powers systems**.

Legislatures in **parliamentary systems** are generally referred to as '**parliaments**', regardless of their formal title. This name reflects not only the type of system in which the legislature resides, but also its central task. The word 'parliament; is derived from the French verb *parler*, to speak.[1] The name is well chosen, as the institutional and political constraints on parliaments generally serves to focus their activities on debate and discussion.

Congresses

A different type of legislature, known as a '**congress**', exists within what are popularly referred to as presidential systems. Presidential systems are considered separation-of-powers (SoP) systems. The legislative and executive branches are selected independently, and neither has the ability to dissolve or remove the other from office (except in the case of incapacity or significant legal wrongdoing). The best-known SoP system is that of the US. The fact that the official name of the legislature of the US is 'the Congress' is neither an accident nor a reason to avoid using the term 'congress' to refer to this type of legislature more generally.

The word '**congress**' is derived from the Latin *congressus*, 'a meeting or [hostile] encounter; to contend or engage' (Harper 2001). The use of congress to denote legislatures within SoP systems in general is justified by the policy-making focus of their activities, as well as the increased likelihood of a more conflictual relationship with the executive branch when compared with fused-power systems because they need not share partisan majorities. Examples of both types of system can be found in Table 7.1.

KEY POINTS

- The words '**assembly**', '**legislature**', '**parliament**', and '**congress**' are not interchangeable and care should be taken to use the right word to avoid confusion and/or a lack of precision.
- **Parliaments** exist in fused-powers (usually parliamentary) systems.
- **Congresses** exist in separation-of-powers (usually presidential) systems.
- Both parliaments and congresses are types of **legislature**, meaning that they are political assemblies with some legislative tasks.

Table 7.1 'Parliament'- and 'Congress'-type legislatures (a selection)

Country	Lower chamber	Legislature type	Regime
Argentina	Chamber of Deputies	Congress	SoP
Austria	National Council (Nationalrat)	Parliament	Fused
Belarus	Chamber of Representatives		Non-democratic
Belgium	House of Representatives	Parliament	Fused
Bhutan	Tsgogdu		Non-democratic
Bolivia	Chamber of Deputies	Congress	SoP
Brazil	Chamber of Deputies	Congress	SoP
Canada	House of Commons	Parliament	Fused
Chile	Chamber of Deputies	Congress	SoP
China	National People's Congress		Non-democratic
Colombia	Chamber of Representatives	Congress	SoP
Czech Republic	Chamber of Deputies	Parliament	Fused
Denmark	Folketing	Parliament	Fused
Finland	Eduskunta	Parliament	Fused
France	National Assembly	Parliament	Fused
Germany	Federal Council	Parliament	Fused
Greece	Vouli	Parliament	Fused
Guyana	National Assembly	Parliament	Fused

(continued)

Table 7.1 'Parliament'- and 'Congress'-type legislatures (a selection) (continued)

Country	Lower chamber	Legislature type	Regime
India	Lok Sabha	Parliament	Fused
Iran	Islamic Consultative Assembly		Non-democratic
Israel	Knesset	Parliament	Fused
Italy	Chamber of Deputies	Parliament	Fused
Japan	House of Representatives	Parliament	Fused
Korea, South	Kukhoe	Congress	SoP
Mexico	Chamber of Deputies	Congress	SoP
New Zealand	House of Representatives	Parliament	Fused
Pakistan	National Assembly	Parliament	Fused
Peru	Congress	Congress	SoP
Poland	Sejm	Parliament	Fused
Romania	Chamber of Deputies	Parliament	Fused
Russia	State Duma	Parliament	Fused
Singapore	Parliament		Non-democratic
Slovakia	National Council	Parliament	Fused
Spain	Congress of Deputies	Parliament	Fused
Switzerland	National Council	Congress	SoP[a]
Taiwan	Legislative Yuan	Congress	SoP
Tanzania	Bunge	Parliament	Fused
Turkey	Grand National Assembly	Parliament	Fused
UK	House of Commons	Parliament	Fused
US	House of Representatives	Congress	SoP
Venezuela	Chamber of Deputies	Congress	SoP

[a] The executive in Switzerland is unique in that it is collegial (seven members) and indirectly elected by the legislature, but it is not responsible to the legislature, nor can it dissolve the legislature.

The role of legislatures

Although the activities and roles that legislatures perform will vary significantly according to the political environment in which they exist, they can be loosely organized into three categories: (i) linkage and representation; (ii) oversight and control; and (iii) policy-making.

When fulfilling the first task, legislatures serve as the 'agents' of the citizens they represent and are expected to act in their interests. In the second case, legislatures become the 'principals' and are tasked with the monitoring and collective oversight of the executive branch (including the bureaucracy). Finally, when pursuing the third type of activity, legislatures engage in legislating and may be acting as agent, principal, or both, but the task is specifically focused on

the policy process. *What differentiates legislatures is not which of these roles they play, but the degree to which their activities emphasize some roles over others.*

An '**agent**' is an actor who performs a set of activities and functions on behalf of someone else (the **principal**). The standard 'principal–agent problem' revolves around the fact that agents are likely to have both incentives and opportunities to shirk their duties and still receive the benefits associated with having done them. Thus, the principal has an incentive to devise some form of oversight to ensure that the agent is performing its tasks.

In the political realm, legislatures serve as agents and principals in relation to the electorate and the executive respectively. Thus, the electorate (citizens) must act to control the legislature and the legislature must seek to control the executive branch.

Legislature as agent: linkage, representation, and legitimation

Linkage

Linking citizens to the government is one of the most fundamental tasks that a legislature performs. It serves 'as an intermediary between the **constituency** and the central government' (Olson 1980: 135). In this context, legislatures act as a conduit of information allowing demands at a local level to be heard by the central government and the policies and actions of the central government to be explained to citizens. The ability of legislatures to serve as *effective* tools of communication varies, as does the *relative importance* of this role.

The degree to which a legislature is able to serve as an effective means of communication between citizens and government depends critically on the level of regularized interaction between the members of the legislature and their constituencies, as well as the type and frequency of opportunities to convey information to the executive branch. In general, individual legislators will spend more time and be more actively engaged with their constituents when they are elected in single-member districts as opposed to multi-member districts (see Chapter 10 'Elections and referendums'). This is because they are the sole representatives of the citizens in their constituency (the citizens within their district) at the national level.

The linkage role will be more important in political systems in which citizens do not elect the executive directly. Thus, in parliamentary **fused-powers systems**, the linkage function of the parliament-type legislature is likely to be more of central importance because it may be the only mechanism of communication between citizens and the central government.

Representation

The individual members of a legislature are also expected to *represent* their constituents and work to protect their interests. Legislators are responsible for advocating for their constituents in their stead, ensuring that the opinions, perspectives, and values of citizens are present in the policy-making process (Pitkin 1967).

However, there are different interpretations of the representative responsibility of legislators, depending on whether they are understood to be *delegates* or *trustees*. In the former case, members of legislatures are expected to act as mechanistic agents of their constituents, unquestioningly carrying messages and initiatives from them to the central government. In contrast, if members of the legislature are viewed as trustees, the expectation is that they will serve as an interpreter of their constituents' interests and incorporate the needs

of the country as a whole, as well as their own moral and intellectual judgement, when acting within the political, and especially policy, realm.

Debating

The plural characteristic of legislatures also enables them to serve as public forums of debate, in which diverse opinions and opposing views can directly engage with one another with the goals of informing citizens, as well as influencing public opinion and policy outcomes. In general, the debate function will be a more central and important activity in those legislatures with limited direct control over the policy-making process, which includes most non-democratic systems.

By fostering debate and discussion, legislatures can serve as important tools of compromise between opposing groups and interests within the society. The capacity of a legislature to effectively serve as a public forum of debate will be more important in heterogeneous societies in which there are significant policy-related conflicts between groups. Even when compromises are not achieved, the opportunity for minority or oppositional groups to openly and publicly express their views within the legislature may serve to limit conflict to the political realm, avoiding the much more detrimental effects of social unrest and instability.

Legitimation

Ultimately, the ability of a legislature to create links between citizens and government by providing adequate representation to critical groups and minority interests, and fostering public debate, will determine both its institutional legitimacy, and its ability to provide legitimacy for the political system as a whole. The ability to mobilize public support for the government as a whole is an important aspect of a legislature's performance. In fact, even if legislatures 'are not independently active in the development of law, and even if they do not extensively supervise the executive branch, they can still help obtain public support for the government and its policies' (Olson 1980: 13). This legitimizing function of legislatures is fundamentally a reflection of their linkage and representational activities (Mezey 1979).

Legislature as principal: control and oversight

Control

The ability of the governed to control the government is one of the foundational tenets of representative democracy. The primary tool used to achieve this goal is regularly scheduled free and fair elections. The type of executive oversight and control practised by the legislature is directly linked to the nature of the relationship between voters and the executive branch *and* between the legislature and the executive branch.

Democratic political systems have two different 'principals' monitoring the executive branch, each of which has a different set of tasks. Voters directly or indirectly select the executive during elections. However, citizens often lack sufficient time, information, and the technical skills needed to effectively oversee the details of the political activity of the executive branch. It is the task of the legislature to fill this lacuna. In this context, there is a greater degree of difference between presidential (SoP) and parliamentary (fused-powers) political systems.

1. The control functions of congress-type legislatures in SoP systems are more limited than those in fused-powers systems. The critical difference is the extent to which policy initiatives are a legitimate subject of control and oversight by the legislature. In SoP systems, the policy agenda of the executive branch is not subject to legislative control or oversight. The executive cannot be removed from office because a majority in the legislature disapproves of its policies. In fact, the legislature's ability to remove an executive from office in SoP systems is usually restricted to cases of illegal activity and/or physical or mental incapacity. This type of formal *impeachment* of the executive is a rare and generally complex legal process.

2. Parliament-type legislatures in fused-powers systems are explicitly tasked with policy-related control of the executive branch. Executives are responsible to the legislature for their policy agenda and can be removed from office if their policy goals are deemed unacceptable by a majority in the legislature. Removal of the executive in fused-powers systems is accomplished through a *motion of censure* or a *vote of no confidence*. This does not imply any legal wrongdoing. As a result, in most fused-powers systems the removal of the sitting executive by the legislature does not result in a crisis or systemic instability.[2]

The significant difference between fused-powers and SoP systems in the policy-related control activities of legislatures is a function of the broader political system. More specifically, it is a result of the character of the legislative–executive relationship. In SoP systems, voters select their legislature and executive independently from one another. In fused-powers systems, voters cast votes only for the legislative branch. Selection of the executive occurs indirectly through the legislature. This difference is significant for two reasons.

First, the independent election of the executive and legislative branches makes it far more likely that there will be *substantial differences in their respective ideological or partisan identities*. For example, in the US the election of a president from one party and a congressional majority from the other is a relatively common occurrence (**divided government**). In fused-powers systems, however, it is impossible for the majority in the parliament and the executive branch to be from wholly distinct and opposing parties or coalitions. All governments in fused-powers systems *must* have the implicit or explicit support of a majority of members within the legislature to remain in office. The executive branch (prime minister and the cabinet ministers) are elected by the legislature. This process reduces the likelihood of policy-related conflict between the legislature and the executive.

The second reason for the difference in the control function is tied to the requirements of the democratic process. Representative democracy requires that elected officials be responsible to those who elected them. In SoP systems, voters elect the executive, and therefore only voters have the power to change or remove the executive. If a congress could remove a popularly elected president though a vote of censure or a similar mechanism on the basis of policy disagreement, it could easily undermine the democratic process as a whole.

Oversight

Legislatures in both SoP and fused-powers systems play a critical role in ensuring proper oversight of both the budgetary implications of policies and their implementation. Legislatures may be able to exercise some oversight and control functions in non-democratic systems, even if they are unable to effectively control the executive branch as a whole.

Legislative oversight of the executive branch is generally quite broad, entailing the development and passage of policies, as well as the monitoring of executive agencies tasked with the implementation of those policy decisions. Although most legislatures engage in both types of oversight, in general the former task is of greater significance in fused-powers systems, while the latter takes precedence in SoP systems.

Question time, inquiries, hearings, and investigative committees are frequently used by legislatures to gather information and, if necessary, to hold various actors and agencies within the executive branch accountable. Legislatures have increased their executive oversight activities over time, largely in response to the growing complexity of government and the need to delegate activities to other agencies.

1. *Question time* is used in parliaments and provides a regularly scheduled opportunity for members

of the legislature to present oral and written questions to members of the government, including the prime minister and other cabinet members.

2. In contrast, *special inquiries* and *hearings* are organized on an ad hoc basis to investigate specific topics or issues that are considered important by some legislators.

3. *Investigative committees* are similar, but are more formalized, tend to address higher-order issues, and often have a longer duration.

4. In addition, legislatures may request or require that the executive and/or its bureaucratic agencies provide it with *reports on specific issues* of concern, make presentations to the full legislature or relevant committees, or respond to specific inquiries in hearings.

Budget control

Legislatures may also engage in indirect oversight of executive policy initiatives through their control over the budgetary process. The earliest forms of legislatures were little more than groups of aristocratic lords called together by the king to approve new taxes and levies. Although monarchs had access to vast resources, they were often in need of additional funds to pay for the armies necessary to wage war and quell uprisings (see Chapter 4 'The nation-state'). This practice established the nearly ubiquitous norm of legislative control over the *power of the purse*. The result is that most political systems require legislative approval of national budgets and tax policies.

Control and oversight of expenditure, even if limited by entitlements and other political artifices, is a powerful tool that can provide even the weakest of legislatures the opportunity to influence policy decisions.[3] There are few policy goals that can be achieved without some level of funding. As a result, the ability of the legislature to withhold or decrease funding for initiatives supported by the executive branch can become a useful bargaining tool. In fact, the need to obtain legislative approval for spending initiatives can even provide legislatures with the potential to influence decision-making in policy arenas traditionally reserved for the executive branch, such as foreign and security policy.

Legislature as legislator: policy-making vs policy-influencing

There are a number of ways that legislatures can be directly involved in the policy-making process, ranging from simply giving opinions to making significant amendments, and from initiating independent proposals to vetoing the proposals of the executive branch. However, as already discussed earlier in the section, there are a broad variety of tasks regularly accomplished by legislatures, and in many cases, legislating is not one of the most important (see Table: 'Legislative powers of legislatures', in the Online Resources).

Consultation

The most basic, and generally least influential, type of legislative action is consultation. This power grants the legislature the authority to present an opinion on specific legislation, a general plan of action, or broad policy programme. Consultation in no way guarantees that the executive branch will abide by the opinion of the legislature. Yet, the ability to present an opinion and to differentiate the views of the legislature from that of the executive can be important in many contexts. In particular, legislative opinions that are in conflict with the proposals put forward by the executive branch and are public in nature may provide important information to the public, as well as serving as a tool of linkage and representation.

Delay and veto

A common ability among even comparatively weak legislatures is the power to delay legislation. This is a 'negative power' in that the legislature can only slow down the process, not provide positive input or substantive change directly. Despite this, the ability to delay passage of a proposal can be an effective bargaining tool when the executive branch prefers rapid action.

In its most extreme incarnation, the power of delay becomes the power of veto. Legislatures with veto power can definitively and unilaterally block policies from being adopted. Like the power of delay, veto power is negative. As a result, it will only be an effective bargaining tool for the legislature when the executive branch has a strong interest in changing the status quo.

Amendment and initiation

The most important *positive* legislative tools are the power to amend and initiate proposals. The ability to amend bills allows the legislature to change aspects of the executive branch's proposal to achieve an outcome in line with the preferences of a majority of its members. Frequent restrictions to amendment power include limitations on the stage in the process at which amendments can be introduced (Spain), the number of amendments that can be introduced (Austria), or the ability of the legislature to make changes that would incur additional costs (Israel).

An independent power of initiative grants individuals or groups within the legislature the right to introduce their own policy proposals independent of the executive branch. In some legislatures, all proposals must formally be initiated by the legislature (the US), while in others the legislature has no formal ability to initiate proposals independently (the European Union). Most political systems fall somewhere between these two extremes.

In most fused-powers systems, few independent-member initiatives are adopted, while the executive tends to have very high rates of legislative success (Diermeier and Vlaicu, 2011). In West European countries, for example, 80–90 per cent of successful proposals are initiated by the executive branch. In some cases, such as Israel, private-member bills are estimated to account for less than 9 per cent of adopted proposals (Mahler 1998). In Belgium between 1971 and 1990, a total of 4,548 private-member bills were initiated, but just 7.3 per cent were ultimately adopted (Mattson 1995).

The centrality of the policy-making function of government has led to the development of a number of different attempts to categorize legislatures on the basis of their policy influence (see Table: Major classification of legislatures, in the Online Resources). Thus, we can differentiate in a dichotomous way between *transformative legislatures* that have a high degree of direct policy-making influence and *arena-type legislatures* that are more engaged in the linkage and oversight functions, with little direct policy influence (Polsby 1975). Alternatively, legislatures can be understood in terms of their 'viscosity' or capacity to slow down, and even block, the executive in its attempts to make policy decisions (Blondel 1970).

KEY POINTS

- Legislatures engage in a variety of tasks, including providing a link between citizens and the central government, representing citizen interests, executive oversight, and participating in the policy-making process.

- While most legislatures in democratic systems perform all of these roles to some extent, the emphasis placed on the various roles and tasks will vary between legislatures.

- The very different character of the relationship between the executive branch and the legislature in fused-powers and **separation-of-powers systems** influences which roles and tasks are emphasized by a legislature.

- There are a number of different tools that a legislature may employ within the policy-making process, including consultation, delay, veto, amendment, and initiation. While the powers of delay and veto are 'negative' in that they delay or block policies, amendment and initiation are 'positive' powers.

The internal organizational structures of legislatures

Legislatures are likely to be ineffective if they do not have an internal structure that allows for an efficient division of labour, specialized expertise, access to independent sources of information, and other basic organizational and operational resources. An analysis of the internal structures and resources of a legislature can often provide a more accurate assessment of its general level of activity and influence than a review of the formal powers granted to it in the **constitution**.

Number and type of chambers

In most cases, legislatures have either one chamber (unicameral) or two (bicameral). Multi-chamber legislatures are generally created to ensure adequate representation for different groups within the political system. The lower (and usually larger) chamber provides representation for the population as a whole, while the upper chamber represents specific socially or territorially defined groups. These can be the political subunits such as states (US), *Länder* (Germany), or cantons (Switzerland), or different groups of citizens such as aristocrats (UK) or ethnicities (South Africa under apartheid).[4] **Unicameral legislatures** are more likely to be found in unitary political systems with comparatively homogeneous populations (e.g. Denmark).

More important than the actual number of legislative chambers is the relationship between them. In unicameral systems, all the powers of the legislative branch are contained within the single chamber. However, in bicameral systems these powers may be (i) *equally shared* (both chambers can exercise all legislative powers); (ii) *equally divided* (each chamber has specific, but more or less equally important, powers); or (iii) *unequally distributed* (one chamber has significantly greater powers than the other). The first two cases are considered to be *symmetric bicameral* systems, while the latter are *asymmetric bicameral* systems. Table 7.2 provides some examples.

Knowing how many chambers a legislature has and understanding the relationship between them (symmetric or asymmetric) is important because these attributes impact on the broader policy-making process. For example, if the chambers within a symmetric bicameral legislature have significantly different or opposing ideological majorities, it may delay the legislative process, as a proposal acceptable to the majority of both chambers must be developed. Such a situation may also force increased political compromise and ensure a higher level of representation for minorities or territorial groups. However, failure to reach a compromise can block the policy process as a whole, or force the executive branch to attempt to govern without the legislature (through decrees, for example). In the worst-case scenario, such a blockage might even threaten the stability of the political system itself if the necessary policies cannot be adopted.

Number, quality, and consistency of members

By their nature, legislatures bring together a comparatively large number of people. The legislature is usually the most numerous and most diverse of the primary branches of government. Thus, the tools and structures it uses to organize itself are particularly critical and often quite informative in assessing the effective roles of the legislature within the broader system.

Size

A few basic descriptive statistics can reveal a good deal about the character and political role of a legislature. For example, the number of members relative to the size of the general population, the number of days per year the legislature is in session, the extent to which members are 'professional' legislators or maintain additional external employment, the rate of member turnover from one election to the next, and the general 'quality' of members can all provide information on the likely level of political influence that a legislature has within the political system and the policy-making process (see Table: The impact of general characteristics on legislative influence, in the Online Resources).

The relationship between these characteristics and the roles of the legislature is relatively straightforward in most cases. The size of the legislature is telling

Table 7.2 Representation and role/asymmetry of upper chambers

Country	Federal (Y/N)	Upper chamber	Size	Basis of representation	Mode of selection	Symmetric (Y/N)
Argentina	Y	Senate	72	Provincial	Directly elected	Y
Austria	Y	Bundesrat	64	*Länder*	Indirect election by provincial legislature by PR	N
Belarus	N	Council of the Republic	64	Regions	Indirectly elected, eight appointed by president	Y
Belgium	Y	Senate	60	Regions	Indirectly elected by community and regional parliaments (50) and co-opted (10)	N
Bolivia	N	Senate	27	Departments	Directly elected—top two parties (2/1) three seats per admin. dept.	Y
Brazil	Y	Senate	81	States	Directly elected—simple majority, three seats per state	Y
Canada	Y	Senate	105	Regions	Appointed—by government on a regional basis	N
Chile	N	Senate	38	Regions	Directly elected in nineteen senatorial districts	Y
Colombia	N	Senate	102	National	100 directly elected in a single national constituency, plus two from special district for indigenous communities	Y
Czech Republic	N	Senate	81	National	Directly elected—simple majority 1/3 every two years	N
France	N	Senate	348	Departments	Indirect election by electoral colleges in each department	N
Germany	Y	Bundesrat	69	*Länder*	Indirectly selected by *Länder* governments	N
Grenada	N	Senate	13	National	Appointed—by governor general (on advice of prime minister)	N
India	Y	Rajya Sabha	245	States/territories	Indirectly elected (233), appointed by president (12)	N

(continued)

Table 7.2 Representation and role/asymmetry of upper chambers (continued)

Country	Federal (Y/N)	Upper chamber	Size	Basis of representation	Mode of selection	Symmetric (Y/N)
Italy	N	Senate	315	Regions	Directly elected—PR and majority bonus within regions	Y
Japan	N	House of Councillors	252	National and prefecture	Directly elected—nationally (100) and within prefectures (152)	N
Mexico	Y	Senate	128	States	Directly elected—modified majority (one per state to second party)	Y
Pakistan	Y	Senate	87	Provincial and tribal areas	Indirectly elected (four per province + eight per tribal areas + three per capital territory)	N
Poland	N	Senate	100	Districts	Directly elected—simple majority, two or three per district	N
Romania	N	Senate	143	National	Directly elected—two-ballots majority	Y
Russia	Y	Council of Federation	178	Federal units	Indirectly selected (two per republic, oblast, krais, okrug, and federal city)	N
St Lucia	N	Senate	11	National	Appointed by Governor General: prime minister selects six and opposition three	N
Spain	N	Senate	257	Regional	Directly elected (208)—majority indirectly elected (49)	N
Switzerland	Y	Council of States	46	Cantons	Directly elected—simple majority	Y
UK	N	House of Lords	731	Class	Hereditary and by appointment	N
US	Y	Senate	100	Federal units	Directly elected—simple majority	Y

Source: Compiled by the author from Kurian et al. (1998). Updated from official national legislative websites and Inter-Parliamentary Union online database (2018).

because of the difficulty that large diverse groups generally have in reaching coherent decisions. The more members a legislature has, the more time each decision is likely to require (as a result of the need to allocate speaking time to all members, for example). More members are likely to lead to more complex mechanisms of internal organization and more thinly spread institutional resources. However, membership numbers must be interpreted in context, as very small countries will naturally tend to have much smaller legislatures, while more populous countries will on average have larger legislatures (see Table 7.3).

Time

The amount of time that legislators spend attending to legislative tasks is also a useful indicator of the broader role of the legislature. At one extreme are legislatures that are formally or functionally 'in session' year-round. On the other end of the spectrum are 'part-time' legislatures that meet for only a few days each year (see Table 7.4).

The length of the annual session of a legislature is often directly tied to the type of members it attracts.

Part-time legislatures that are in session only for short periods of the year not only provide the opportunity for their members to engage in other professional activities, but they often make it a functional requirement. The average annual salary of a legislator is more likely to constitute a 'living wage' when the task performed constitutes a full-time job. Of course, there are also legislatures that are formally 'full-time' that nonetheless fail to provide members with a sustainable salary.[5]

The need for legislators to maintain additional external employment reduces the amount of time and effort they can dedicate to their legislative tasks. In some cases, the role of the legislature is so limited that this is not a concern. In others, however, it will not only reduce the effectiveness of legislators, but will also impact the type of individuals who join the legislature. This can impact both the quality of members and the rate of membership turnover from one election to the next. When legislative wages are low, it can serve to restrict membership to those with alternative sources of wealth and keep the most qualified individuals from considering the legislature as a career option.

Table 7.3 Population and size of lower chamber in forty-one countries

Country	Lower chamber	Population	Size	Reps/citizens
Argentina	Chamber of Deputies	43,847,277	257	170,612
Austria	National Council (Nationalrat)	8,569,633	183	46,219
Belarus	Chamber of Representatives	9,481,521	110	86,006
Belgium	House of Representatives	11,371,928	150	67,800
Bhutan	Tsgogdu	784,103	150	4,805
Bolivia	Chamber of Deputies	10,888,402	130	80,201
Brazil	Chamber of Deputies	209,567,920	513	378,064
Canada	House of Commons	36,286,378	301	116,287
Chad	National Assembly	14,496,739	125	90,193
Chile	Chamber of Deputies	18,131,850	120	138,104
China	National People's Congress	1,382,323,332	2978	452,435
Colombia	Chamber of Representatives	48,654,392	163	287,620
Czech Republic	Chamber of Deputies	10,548,058	200	52,566
Denmark	Folketing	5,690,750	179	31,283
Egypt	People's Assembly	93,383,574	454	184,537
Finland	Eduskunta	5,523,904	200	27,144
France	National Assembly	64,668,129	577	113,752
Germany	Federal Diet (Bundestag)	80,682,351	598	136,995
Greece	Vouli	10,919,459	300	36,051
India	House of the People (Lok Sabha)	1,326,801,576	545	2,220,538
Iran	Islamic Consultative Assembly	80,043,146	270	285,489
Israel	Knesset	8,192,463	120	66,403
Italy	Chamber of Deputies	59,801,004	630	96,620
Japan	House of Representatives	126,323,715	500	255,040
Korea, South	Kukhoe	50,503,933	299	167,239
Mexico	Chamber of Deputies	128,632,004	500	224,673
New Zealand	House of Representatives	4,565,185	120	37,108
Pakistan	National Assembly	192,826,502	217	837,876
Peru	Congress	31,774,225	120	251,132
Poland	Sejm	38,593,161	460	83,779
Romania	Chamber of Deputies	19,372,734	341	55,847
Russia	State Duma	143,439,832	450	318,444
Singapore	Parliament	5,696,506	83	64,005
Slovakia	National Council	5,429,418	150	36,302
Spain	Congress of Deputies	46,064,604	350	133,760
Switzerland	National Council	8,379,477	200	40,070
Taiwan	Legislative Yuan	23,395,600	164	142,104
Tanzania	Bunge	55,155,473	275	163,378
Turkey	Grand National Assembly	79,622,062	550	135,862
UK	House of Commons	65,111,143	659	95,875
Venezuela	Chamber of Deputies	31,518,855	165	175,431

Source: Compiled by the author from Kurian et al. (1998), national websites and the Inter-Parliamentary Union online database (2016).

Table 7.4 Comparison of annual session duration

Country	Lower chamber	Annual session(s)	Meeting days (sittings)
Argentina	Chamber of Deputies	Annual session from 1 March to 30 November	
Austria	National Council (Bundesrat)	Annual session from mid-September to mid-July	
Belarus	Chamber of Representatives	Variable	170 days
Belgium	House of Representatives	Annual session from second Tuesday in October to 20 July	Minimum of forty days per session
Bhutan	Tsgogdu	Must meet at least once per year (May–June or October–November)	
Bolivia	Chamber of Deputies		Ninety days (possible to extend to 120)
Brazil	Chamber of Deputies	Two sessions annually: 1 March–30 June and 1 August–5 December	
Canada	House of Commons		
Chad	National Assembly	Two sessions annually in April and October	Ninety days in session
Chile	Chamber of Deputies	One annual session, 21 May–18 September	
China	National People's Congress	Once per year (usually in March)	Fourteen days
Colombia	Chamber of Representatives	Two sessions annually: 20 July–16 December and 16 March–20 June	
Denmark	Folketing	Annual session, October–October (no meetings in July, August, and September)	Approximately 100 plenary meetings per year
Finland	Eduskunta	Spring and autumn sessions (recess December–January and summer)	
France	National Assembly	Annual session, October–June	
Greece	Vouli	Annual session from first Monday in October (for not less than five months)	
India	House of the People (Lok Sabha)	Three sessions per year: February–May, July–August, November–December	
Italy	Chamber of Deputies	Year-round (official vacations: one week for Easter, two weeks for Christmas, and August)	
Japan	House of Representatives	Ordinary session January–May (extraordinary sessions summer–autumn)	150 days/ordinary session (extraordinary ones vary)
Korea, South	Kukhoe	Regular session may not exceed 100 days (special session not to exceed thirty days)	Average of forty-five days per year in plenary session
Mexico	Chamber of Deputies	Two sessions annually: 1 September–15 December and 15 March–30 April	
New Zealand	House of Representatives	Session runs for full calendar year, generally no sittings in January	
Pakistan	National Assembly	Two annual sessions. Must not remain in recess for more than 120 days at a time	
Poland	Sejm	Continuous, sittings determined by Presidium	Twenty-six sittings per year (1–4 days each) October 2001–October 2005

Table 7.4	Comparison of annual session duration (continued)		
Romania	Chamber of Deputies	Two sessions annually: February–June and September–December	
Russia	State Duma	Two sessions annually: mid-January–mid-July and beg. October–end of December	Generally two days per week, three weeks per month in session
Singapore	Parliament	No set calendar, one sitting per month Six months maximum between sessions	
Slovakia	National Council	Two annual sessions (spring and autumn)	
Spain	Congress of Deputies	Two sessions annually: February–June and September–December	
Switzerland	National Council	Four times per year (every three months), extraordinary sessions are allowed	Three weeks/ordinary session, one week/extraordinary session
Taiwan	Legislative Yuan	Two sessions annually: February–May and September–December	Two sittings per week while in session
Tanzania	Bunge	Variable number of sessions lasting between four days and two weeks	Twenty-five–thirty days per year on average
Turkey	Grand National Assembly	Annual session: 1 October–30 September, may recess for a maximum of three months	Meets Tuesday–Thursday in session
UK	House of Commons	Full year, adjourns for Christmas (three weeks), Easter (one week), and summer (ten weeks)	Four–five days per week while in session
Venezuela	Chamber of Deputies	Ordinary sessions: early March–early July and early October–late November	

Source: Based on Kurian et al. (1998), updated from official national government and legislative websites (2018).

Committees

Almost without exception, legislatures organize internally on the basis of committees. However, the variations that exist between these committees can be enormous. Legislatures may have few or many committees and they may be created on an ad hoc basis or permanently established. In addition, there may be highly specialized subcommittees and/or temporary committees of inquiry created to address specific crises or questions. In some cases, committees are responsible for reviewing and amending proposals before the full plenary discusses them; in others, they are in charge of implementing the changes decided by the full plenary. These relationships are outlined in the Table: The impact of committee characteristics on legislative influence, in the Online Resources.

Permanency and expertise

One of the most important aspects of committees is their permanency. Committees that are created on an ad hoc basis not only tend to be less efficiently organized, but their members lack the opportunity to develop area-specific expertise, or the contacts with external actors that facilitate independent and informed decision-making. Given the size of most legislatures, committees often serve as the forum for most legislative activity, including bargaining and coalition-building between political parties. The smaller size and less public nature of committees increase their utility as a forum for these types of activity. However, if the committees are not permanent, they are unlikely to provide the necessary level of stability and expertise.

Specialization

Committees within influential legislatures also mirror the organization of the executive branch, with distinct committees for each cabinet portfolio. The association of specific committees with cabinet ministries can foster relationships between the members and staff of the legislature and the executive branch, which can improve inter-institutional cooperation.

Subcommittees and temporary committees

The potential for additional flexibility and specificity can be added through the incorporation of subcommittees and temporary investigative committees (sometimes referred to as committees of inquiry). These allow for still greater levels of specialization and permit the legislature to react to significant events or crises in a timely fashion.

One of the surest indicators of the role of committees, and through them the policy influence of the legislature, is the order in which proposals move between the plenary and the committees. If legislation is fully vetted in plenary *prior* to being sent to committee, committees are unlikely to play a substantial role in policy-making. Given the hurdles to engaging in a thorough analysis of policy proposals in plenary, this process of vetting bills indicates a comparatively small policy role for the legislature. In contrast, when bills are reviewed and amended within the committees first, the legislature is more likely to have a substantial influence on policy outcomes.

Hierarchical structures and internal decision-making

Within every legislature there is a variety of internal positions of authority and power, even if the institution itself is relatively weak. At the level of the legislature there is generally a president, one or more vice-presidents, and in some cases questors or other secretarial/administrative positions. In addition, most legislatures will also have leadership positions within organized subunits—for example, chairs of committees, subcommittees, and/or specialized delegations and/or working groups.

The most fundamental difference between legislatures in terms of internal organization is between those that distribute internal positions of authority proportionally amongst all the groups (usually political parties) represented, and those that use a 'winner-takes-all' system, assigning leadership positions only to members of the majority (party or coalition). In the former case, cooperation and compromise between government and opposition groups is facilitated by the requirements of working within an institution with clear power-sharing structures. In contrast, winner-takes-all systems are more likely to foster ideological polarization.

Majoritarian or winner-takes-all systems discourage compromise. As a result, these types of legislature will function well only when the majority in charge is reliable, either because of a high degree of party discipline or because of significant numerical superiority over the opposition. When parties are weak or undisciplined, and/or majorities are slim, individual member defections can lead to the defeat of majority proposals. On the other hand, when majorities are large and/or parties are disciplined, decision-making

is likely to be more efficient and policy innovation easier to achieve.

In contrast, legislatures that distribute leadership positions among the parties and groups of both the majority and the opposition are more likely to experience cross-party agreements and compromises, and in some cases, this may even be a requirement, given the proportional distribution of positions of power. This type of policy process is less likely to suffer significant negative consequences from individual member defections on particular issues. At the same time, however, this approach to policy-making is likely to be more time-consuming and to lead to incremental policy reform based on compromises between opposing groups rather than sweeping ideologically informed policy innovations.

These are the two most extreme scenarios and there are, of course, a number of intermediate alternatives. For example, the majoritarian system is used to distribute internal positions of power in the US legislature; however, there is also a comparatively low level of party discipline. As a result, a number of different outcomes are possible, depending on the size of the majority held by the largest party and the level of bipartisan cooperation possible on a given issue. In general, however, legislatures that share internal positions of authority proportionally *tend* to be more consensual in character than those that use a winner-takes-all system.

KEY POINTS

- Understanding the internal organizational structures, membership, and resources of legislatures is a critical component of evaluating their overall influence and role within the broader political system.

- Most legislatures have one or two chambers. In the case of bicameral legislatures, it is critical to understand both the representative function of each chamber and the relative distribution of power between them.

- The relative level of '**professionalization**' of a legislature (including the amount of time it is in session each year), the character of its committees and other internal organizational structures, the type of members it attracts, and the resources they have at their disposal are generally an accurate indication of its influence and power within the policy process and the broader political system.

Assessing a legislature's power

All legislatures, democratic or not, claim to fulfil the central representative/linkage, oversight, and legislative roles discussed in 'The role of legislatures' above.

Yet, there are vast differences between legislatures in terms of the emphasis and centrality they ascribe to these roles and, as a result, to the function they perform within the political system. There are legislatures for which the linkage and oversight functions are clearly pre-eminent (as in the UK, Greece, and Chile), while others place more emphasis on their legislative function (the US, Italy, Germany, and the Netherlands). The next task is to understand the systemic characteristics that lead to these variations.

The underlying cause of the differences between legislatures is surprisingly simple, at least conceptually. Fundamentally, the extent to which a legislature is an active and effective participant in the legislative process versus assuming a more passive legislative role (focusing instead on oversight and linkage) is directly tied to the *degree of autonomy* it enjoys. More specifically, there are two aspects of a legislature's relative autonomy that are important:

- the independence of the institution as a whole;
- the independence of its members individually.

Institutional independence: executive–legislative relations

The institutional autonomy of a legislature is a function of its formal structural interaction with the executive branch. As seen in 'What is a legislature?' above, fused-powers systems centralize legislative authority in the executive; while SoP systems tend towards decentralized legislative decision-making, increasing the role of the legislature (see also Chapter 8 'Governments and bureaucracies').[6]

Fused-powers systems are structured hierarchically insofar as voters elect the members of the legislature, and the members of the legislature, in turn, select the executive branch. In contrast, in SoP systems both the leader of the executive branch and the members of the legislature are elected by citizens (see Figure 7.1). The difference in the method of choosing the executive branch is of critical importance. The selection of the executive branch by the legislature has significant implications for the latter's relative institutional autonomy. Perhaps counter-intuitively, the power to elect and dismiss the executive branch serves to *reduce* the autonomy and independent policy influence of a legislature.

In a SoP system, elections for the legislative and executive branches are not necessarily linked to each other in timing or, more importantly, outcome. This means that there is no guarantee that the result will be a similar partisan distribution. In contrast, in a fused-powers system the elections of the two branches are integrally connected because following each legislative election the new legislature must select the executive branch. In fused-powers systems, the need for the executive to be selected by, and maintain the support of, a majority within the legislature requires a partisan link between the two branches. Even in systems with frequent **minority governments**, the implicit support (or lack of opposition) of a majority of the legislature is necessary to maintain the government in office.

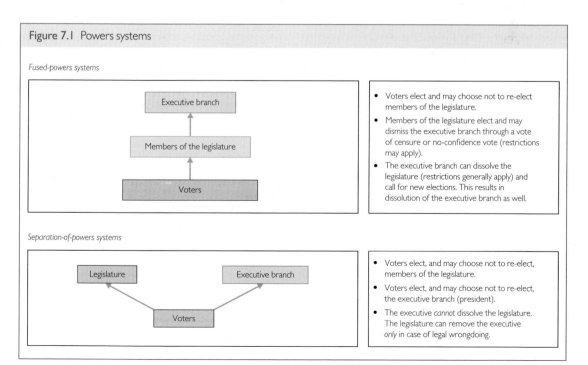
Figure 7.1 Powers systems

In contrast, in SoP systems the executive and legislative branches are selected independently, even when election occurs simultaneously. Citizens are given the opportunity to cast separate and distinct votes for each branch, despite the fact that these votes are often cast on a single ballot. By decoupling the two votes, SoP systems impose no restrictions on the partisan or ideological relationship between the two branches, and any partisan distribution of partisan majorities is possible. The absence of a partisan link between the executive and legislative branches, in combination with their structural independence, is essential in ensuring that the legislature has the potential to play an influential role in the policy-making process.

The impact of the interdependent relationship that exists between the executive and the legislature in fused-powers systems is particularly important. The responsibility of the legislature for both installing and maintaining the executive branch severely constrains its ability to pursue independent legislative action. Majorities must remain comparatively stable in their support for the executive and, by extension, the executive's policy initiatives. In many cases, the defeat of an executive initiative of even moderate significance is considered a de facto vote of 'no confidence' with the potential to force the resignation of the government. The resulting instability, including the potential for new legislative elections, makes such actions risky for legislatures in fused-powers systems.

SoP systems do not place any of these restrictions on the legislature. Because the executive branch is wholly distinct, there is no need for the legislature to maintain any form of support for it. The defeat of a policy proposal from the executive branch in the legislature has no capacity to impact the tenure of the executive branch or the timing of legislative elections.

The fixed terms of office for both the legislative and the executive branches frees the legislature from the burden of maintaining the executive in office. At the same time, it liberates both branches from any need for ideological affinity or policy consensus.

Member independence: the role of political parties

The ability of legislatures to take full advantage of the possibilities offered by a SoP system, as well as the degree to which those in fused-powers systems are able to make the most of their more limited legislative prospects, also depends on a less formal aspect of the political system. The character of the party system, and in particular the relative level of autonomy individual members of the legislature enjoy vis-à-vis their parties, can significantly affect the ability of the legislature as a whole to influence policy outcomes.

Unlike institutional independence, which is largely a function of the constitutionally defined structures of the political system, partisan autonomy depends on the characteristics of the party system. There are some elements of the party system that are especially important. These can be divided into two categories: (i) party-specific characteristics; and (ii) systemic attributes of the party system. Examples of each type of variable are provided in Table 7.5. The underlying question addressed by each of these variables is fundamentally the same in all cases: to what extent is the political future of an individual member of the legislature controlled by his/her political party?

For most legislators, there are two primary concerns or goals: (i) election/re-election; and (ii) the achievement of some set of policy outcomes (Fiorina 1996; Kreppel 2001). Both are intrinsically related

Table 7.5 Party and system characteristics related to member autonomy

Party characteristics	
Candidate selection	Centralized vs decentralized selection by local units and/or activists, existence of leadership veto, self-nomination, etc.
Internal organization of political party	Hierarchical vs decentralized party structures, role of legislative leadership in party structures (sharing of leaders)
Party system characteristics	
Electoral system	Party-centred (i.e. party lists with or without preference votes), candidate-centred (usually single-member districts)
Sources of party and campaign funding	Existence of, and rules regulating, state financing, presence of fixed donor groups (labour), private resources, etc.

to each other and central in determining legislator behaviour, regardless of the broader political system.[7] Secondary concerns often include the attainment of internal party or institutional positions of power such as a committee chairmanship or a party leadership role. Both the candidate selection mechanisms and the internal organizational structure of political parties deeply impact the ability of members to achieve these goals if they lose the support of their party leadership.

Party organization

If re-election is important to legislators, then their autonomy is reduced to the extent that their re-election is controlled by their party leaders' influence over the electoral process. If the party leadership controls candidate selection, or the ordering of the party lists is controlled by the party elite, those wishing to be re-elected must maintain their support, and this usually means supporting the party position within the legislature (on **electoral systems** see Chapter 10 'Elections and referendums'). On the other hand, in parties that allow local party organizations to select candidates or in which the ordering of the party lists is predetermined or decided by party members, individual legislators will enjoy a comparatively high level of partisan independence. In other words, the greater the party leadership's control over a member's re-election, the lower the member's autonomy.

The impact of the centralization of a political party on member autonomy is less direct, but equally important. The more centralized a political party, the fewer opportunities there are for independent decision-making by members. In decentralized parties, there may be multiple centres of decision-making, offering individual members both more opportunities to influence decisions and a broader array of policy outcomes supported by some portion of the party. Decentralized parties are also less likely to issue vote instructions, freeing members to vote in accordance with their personal or constituency preferences (linkage and representation).

The relationship between organized party leadership within the legislature and the leadership structures that govern the 'electoral party' is also important. Although ostensibly the party in the legislature is simply a subset of the larger electoral party, there are many cases in which the two-party organizations clash, creating opportunities for members to act independently. It is not an uncommon phenomenon for the compromises required by the policy-making process within the legislature to cause alarm amongst party activists and leaders outside the legislature. Parties that employ a single unified leadership structure within and outside the legislature are less likely to

face this type of intra-party strife, effectively decreasing opportunities for members to act independently.

Electoral laws

While the different scenarios discussed above can vary between political parties within a political system, there are other elements that will generally affect all parties equally (and thus all individual members of a legislature) in a similar manner. Two of the most important systemic variables are (i) the electoral system; and (ii) the rules regulating campaign funding.

Electoral systems influence member independence directly and profoundly by determining the nature of the voters' choices. In single-member districts, voters are asked to select between individual candidates, while in proportional representation systems the choice is between political parties. The latter method highlights the importance of parties and reinforces their primacy in mediating the citizen–government relationship. In contrast, in candidate-centred elections the political and personal attributes of the individual candidate are primary, and in some cases may even overshadow the significance of party affiliation.

Thus, the relative autonomy of individual members of a legislature will increase as the electoral system offers opportunities for them to win re-election as a result of a high level of personal voter support. Elections that focus exclusively or even primarily on political parties significantly reduce the capacity of members to compete in the face of opposition or even indifference from their party's leadership. As important as electoral opportunity is, however, without access to sufficient financial resources no candidate will be competitive.

The most important aspect regarding finance is the presence (or absence) of state funding and the rules that govern access to these funds (on party finances, see Chapter 12 'Political parties'). Where state funding for electoral campaigns is the primary source of funds, easily accessible state financing for parties and campaigns increases the possibilities for new parties to form and/or independent candidates to compete. As a result, the costs to members of leaving their party to run for election independently or to form a new party are reduced and political independence is increased. Even if members rarely choose to pursue either of these opportunities, the fact that they exist is enough to diminish the capacity of the party to act against members for failing to follow the party line.

Summing up, the combination of individual and institutional autonomy defines the extent to which a legislature can effectively shape the policy process and help to determine legislative outcomes. These underlying relationships between the executive and the

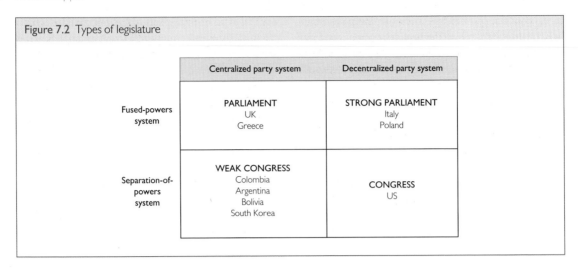

Figure 7.2 Types of legislature

	Centralized party system	Decentralized party system
Fused-powers system	**PARLIAMENT** UK Greece	**STRONG PARLIAMENT** Italy Poland
Separation-of-powers system	**WEAK CONGRESS** Colombia Argentina Bolivia South Korea	**CONGRESS** US

legislature and between the political parties and their members within the legislature create the broad structural constraints within which all the other elements we have discussed operate. At one extreme are legislatures that are dominated by the executive branch (parliaments), with individual members largely controlled by their political parties. At the other extreme are legislatures that are formally independent from the executive branch (congresses) within political systems in which political parties are weak or decentralized and unable to effectively control the members of the legislature. These variables can be condensed into a simple 2 × 2 table such as Figure 7.2.

KEY POINTS

- The institutional autonomy of the legislature (from the executive branch) and the individual autonomy of its members (from political parties) are the most fundamental variables affecting the policy influence of a legislature.

- Institutional autonomy is largely dependent on the formal political structures. In fused-powers systems in which the legislature selects the executive, the two branches are mutually dependent and the institutional autonomy of the legislature is reduced. In separation-of-powers systems, the legislature and the executive are both selected by the voters and the institutional autonomy of the legislature is increased.

- The autonomy of individual members of the legislature is a function of their dependence on political parties to achieve their electoral and policy goals. Individual members will have less autonomy in party-centred PR electoral systems.

- Additional factors influencing the relative independence of individual members include the availability of state funding for electoral campaigns.

Conclusion

In the end, what difference does it make if a legislature is powerful or not? Why does it matter if the legislature has the capacity to independently affect policy outcomes? Is a strong legislature better or worse than a weak one? Ultimately, there is no 'best' type of legislature, nor is there any reason that a more powerful legislature should be considered 'better' than one that is less influential. However, it is important to understand what type of legislature exists, particularly if there are concerns about key aspects of the political process, such as its representativeness, its efficiency, or the quality of the policy outputs it produces.

The primary difference between the two general types of legislatures (parliamentary or congressional) and the variations of each presented in Table 7.1 is the relative importance of the core tasks performed by all legislatures—representation, linkage, oversight, and policy-making—in terms of the legislature's workload.

That said, the ability of the legislature to independently affect policy outcomes does have the potential to change the character of the political system by shifting the balance of power between the executive and legislative branches, and this carries with it significant repercussions. For example, political systems with parliament-type legislatures that are focused primarily on their linkage and oversight functions will tend to have a more hierarchically structured policy-making process in which power is concentrated within the executive branch (and often within the political party hierarchy). This will generally lead to more *efficient* decision-making because fewer actors are involved in the process. However, the restricted level of access may result in the exclusion of key social groups from the policy-making process or may lead to large policy swings when a new government enters office.

In contrast, political systems that disperse power and facilitate the participation of a strong congressional-type legislature in the policy process are likely to be less efficient in terms of decision-making speed, but more *inclusive*. Because both the executive and the legislature participate in the policy process, more coordination and compromise is necessary. This will certainly be the case when different political parties control these institutions (and/or when party control over individual members is weak). The likely result is a slower decision-making process with outcomes that represent broad compromises. Large policy swings are less likely and incremental change more common. However, because of this there is less likelihood that significant minority groups in society will be wholly excluded from the policy-making process or violently opposed to the resulting policy outcomes.

Understanding the type of legislature that exists within a given political system, including both its formal relationship to the executive and less formal links to the political parties, can provide a good deal of information about the political system itself. Additional information about the legislature's internal organizational structures, the strength of its committee system, the quality of its members, and its access to resources will all provide significant additional clues about the type and relative policy influence of the institution as a whole.

QUESTIONS

Knowledge-based

1. What are the differences between an assembly, a legislature, a parliament, and a congress?

2. What are the core tasks of a legislature in a democratic society?

3. What are separation-of-power systems and fused-power systems?

4. How are the oversight and control functions of legislatures different in fused-powers and separation-of-powers systems?

5. What are the five possible tools that legislatures may have at their disposal to influence the policy-making process? Which are 'negative' and which are 'positive'?

6. What is the difference between a symmetric and an asymmetric bicameral legislature? Why is it important?

Critical thinking

1. Why are legislatures generally better able to represent the interests of citizens than the executive branch?

2. Why are the structure and role of the committee system a good indicator of the policy-making influence of the legislature?

3. Why are political parties influential in determining the autonomy of a legislature?

4. What are the broader implications of having a strong legislature that is able to independently influence policy outcomes?

FURTHER READING

Döring, H. (ed.) (1995) *Parliaments and Majority Rule in Western Europe* (Frankfurt-am-Main: Campus).

Döring, H. and Halleberg, M. (eds) (2004) *Patterns of Parliamentary Behaviour: Passage of Legislation Across Western Europe* (Aldershot: Ashgate).

Fish, S. and Kroenig, M. (2009) *The Handbook of National Legislatures: A Global Survey* (Cambridge: Cambridge University of Press).

Inter-Parliamentary Union (1986) *Parliaments of the World: A Comparative Reference Compendium* (2nd edn) (Aldershot: Gower House).

Loewenberg, G., Patterson, S., and Jewell, M. (1985) *Handbook of Legislative Research* (Cambridge, MA: Harvard University Press).

Martin, S., Saalfeld, T., and Strom, K. (eds) (2014) *The Oxford Handbook of Legislative Studies* (Oxford: Oxford University Press).

McKay, W. and Johnson, C. (2012) *Parliament and Congress: Representation and Scrutiny in the Twenty-First Century* (Oxford: Oxford University Press).

Norton, P. and Ahmed, N. (eds) (1999) *Parliaments in Asia* (London: Routledge).

Squire, P. and Hamm, K. (2005) *101 Chambers: Congress, State Legislatures, and the Future of Legislative Studies* (Columbus, OH: Ohio State University Press).

ENDNOTES

1. The term is also related to the Anglo-Latin 'parliamentum', although the French *'parlement'* predates this construction (Harper 2001).

2. There is a number of institutional structures that can increase or decrease the ease with which a legislature can successfully adopt a motion of no confidence, such as the requirement for all such motions to include a simultaneously adopted motion for the investiture of a new executive (the German **constructive vote of no confidence**). In some parliamentary systems use of censure votes is very rare (Germany, the UK), in others it occurs more regularly (France), while in still others use of the mechanism is so common as to cause concern for the system as a whole (Italy pre-1994).

3. Entitlements, as opposed to discretionary funds, are pre-existing financial commitments that cannot be withdrawn or decreased.

4. For example, under the previous apartheid regime South Africa had a tripartite legislature, with each chamber's membership drawn from a distinct racial group.

5. The British House of Lords is a well-known example.

6. This dichotomy ignores the existence of hybrid systems such as the French semi-presidential model.

7. Even in the case of a venal pursuit of power, within a democratic system policy outcomes will become important to the extent that they influence the probability of re-election. Thus, the two goals are inextricably linked.

Visit the Online Resources that accompany this book for additional material, including country profiles, comparative data sets, flashcard glossaries, and web directory.

www.oup.com/he/caramani5e

8

Governments and bureaucracies

Wolfgang C. Müller

Chapter contents

Reader's guide

This chapter looks at decision-making modes of governments and their capacities to govern. Special attention is given to the relationship between the political and administrative parts of government. The chapter begins by addressing definitions and distinguishing what constitutes government under different regimes. The chapter presents different modes of government that reflect the internal balance of power: presidential, cabinet, prime ministerial, and ministerial government. Then it addresses the autonomy of government, in particular from political parties and the permanent bureaucracy. Next, the chapter discusses the political capacity of governments, the relevance of unified versus divided government, majority versus minority government, and single-party versus coalition government. Finally, the chapter highlights the bureaucratic capacities of government, addressing issues such as classic bureaucracy, the politicization of bureaucracies, and the New Public Management.

Introduction

The term 'government' has several meanings. In the broadest sense, it refers to a hierarchical structure in any organized setting, including private clubs, business firms, and political institutions. Within politics, a broad definition of government includes all public institutions that make or implement political decisions and that can be spread over several tiers, which are called federal, state, and local government. That general understanding of government includes the executive, legislative, and judicial branches. Most common, however, is to refer to a country's *central political executive* as 'the government', and that is how this term will be used in this chapter.[1]

The job of the government is to govern the country. Governing means ruling. It is not, as the term 'executive' might suggest, just implementing laws passed by the legislature. Rather, governing means the government having a strong imprint on the laws passed during its reign and more generally exercising overall control over a country and determining its direction. As we shall see, governments are not always able to live up to very strong expectations about their ability to dominate political decision-making. Yet, even weak governments tend to be the political system's most important single political actor. This is a major reason why individuals and political parties mostly want to be in government. And because government is so important, positions in the central political executive tend to come with other goods that make them even more attractive: social prestige, decent income, public recognition, and privileged access to other powerful and/or famous people. The chance to govern the country and to enjoy these privileges is meant to motivate the best people to compete for government office. In democracies, such competition for government office is ultimately tied to elections. Either the government is directly elected or it is responsible to a parliament that results from general elections.

A few men and (increasingly also) women (Bauer and Tramlay 2011), distinguished and carefully selected as they may be, cannot run a country. Therefore, governments have bureaucracies to support them in their tasks of ruling and administrating the country. Thus, in functional terms, governing is not the exclusive task of the government. This has given rise to the notion of the *core executive*, which comprises 'all those organizations and procedures which coordinate central government policies, and act as the final arbiters of conflict between different parts of the government machine' (Rhodes 1995: 12). This implies that it is difficult to pin down the precise composition of the core executive. While the government in the narrow sense constitutes its centre, the core executive also comprises top civil servants, the key members of ministers' private cabinets, and a list of actors which varies over time and space. Realistically, the demarcation line between what constitutes the core and what belongs to the remaining parts of the executive also depends on the analyst's perspective and judgement. At the same time, the core executive focus emphasizes coordination and negotiation rather than hierarchical relations among the units that constitute the core executive (Rhodes

and Dunleavy 1995; Smith 1999). This perspective has become more important over time, due to the increasing complexity of governing in the modern world and in the context of **supranational** government, in particular in the European Union (EU) (Levi-Faur 2012).

KEY POINTS

- The term 'government' has several meanings. The most common refers to the country's central political executive.

- Governing means ruling, exercising overall control over a country, and determining the course it will take.

Types of government

Government and the separation of powers

Today's governments emerged through the piecemeal splitting-off of state functions from a traditionally undivided central government (usually a monarch) (King 1975; Finer 1997). In order to limit the government's power, judicial functions were transferred to courts and legislative functions to parliaments. This process began in twelfth- and thirteenth-century England. It had many national variations and, in Europe, was not completed before the twentieth century. The constitutional doctrine of the separation of powers—as developed first and foremost by the political philosophers Locke, Montesquieu, and Madison—provides a normative justification for the separation of institutions (Vile 1967; see also Chapters 7 'Legislatures' and 9 'Constitutions, rights, and judicial power').

In practice, state functions were never as neatly separated as envisaged by political philosophers. The executive has retained important legislative functions, in particular drafting legislation and issuing government decrees and ordinances (Carey and Shugart 1998). With political parties establishing themselves as the main mechanism to structure elections and to coordinate incumbents, executives have gained an almost de facto monopoly in law-making in **parliamentary systems**. In presidential systems, this is not true to the same extent, but executives also exercise a large influence on legislation.

The normative foundations of democratic government rest on two premises: the government must be connected to the electoral process and must work under constitutional constraints. Within these confines, government can be organized in many ways. Three are quite common: *parliamentarism*, *presidentialism*, and *semi-presidentialism*. Another is connected with the successful Swiss model and deserves a mention: the *directorial* form of **cabinet government**. Finally, government with a directly elected prime minister, which may appear as a 'natural' democratic improvement on parliamentarism, has failed in its only real-world test in Israel. Box 8.1 and Figure 8.1 show how these regime types can be distinguished.

In presidential systems, the executives are not politically accountable to the legislatures, but the legislatures do play a significant role in holding presidents accountable for judicial offences such as treason or bribery. However, often the decision to investigate such offences and to proceed with the impeachment of the president is primarily political (Pérez-Liñán 2007). Typically, it involves actors from both chambers of the legislature and qualified majorities to do so.

The government under different democratic regime types

What constitutes the government depends on the regime type. Presidentialism constitutionally provides for a one-person executive, but including his cabinet under the label of 'government' may be a useful working definition. Although the relations between the president and the cabinet are fundamentally different under fully fledged semi-presidentialism, both can be considered as constituting the government. Yet, semi-presidential regimes offer a wide range of different

---

ZOOM-IN 8.1

Government creation and accountability under different regime types

Presidentialism

- Direct or quasi-direct popular election of the president for a fixed period.

- The head of state is identical to the head of government.

- The president is not politically accountable to the legislature.

- Government members are appointed by the president (mostly with the consent of the legislature).

Parliamentarism

- The head of government (prime minister, chancellor, etc.) is different from the head of state (monarch or president).

- Most parliamentary systems allow for parliamentary dissolution by the head of state (typically on the prime minister's or government's proposal).

- The prime minister is elected by parliament in some countries (e.g. Germany, Spain), appointment by the head of state (e.g. Italy, Ireland) or speaker of parliament (Sweden), with subsequent vote of confidence and appointment by the head of state without an obligatory vote of confidence in another set of countries (e.g. UK, the Netherlands).

- The prime minister and the cabinet are politically accountable to the parliament, i.e. they can be removed from office by a vote of no confidence at any time for no other reason than that the parliament no longer trusts the government. Some countries (Germany, Spain, Belgium, Hungary) require a *constructive* no-confidence vote, i.e. parliament must replace the sitting government with an alternative government with the same vote.

Directorial government

- Currently, only Switzerland works with directorial government. The Bundesrat or Conseil Fédéral (Federal Council) consists of seven individuals who are elected individually by parliament (the joint meeting of both chambers) for the entire term of parliament.

- The federal president is head of government and head of state. This is inspired by US presidentialism, but the country's linguistic and religious diversity have required collegial government—the cabinet members rotate the presidency between them on an annual basis.

- The government is not politically accountable to parliament.

Directly elected prime minister

- Only Israel practised this system from the elections between 1996 and 2003. The prime minister was popularly elected with absolute majority (in two rounds, if necessary) at the date of each parliamentary election and when the office of prime minister was vacant.

- The cabinet was nominated by the prime minister, but required a parliamentary vote of confidence to take office.

- The prime minister was politically accountable to parliament. However, a successful vote of no confidence also triggered the dissolution of parliament and hence led to new elections.

Semi-presidentialism

- The president is directly (or quasi-directly) elected.

- The president appoints the cabinet.

- The cabinet is politically accountable to parliament.

- The president can dismiss the cabinet and/or dissolve parliament.

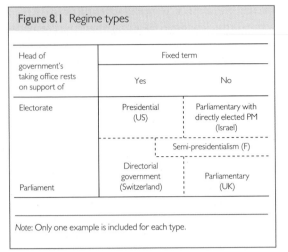

Figure 8.1 Regime types

Head of government's taking office rests on support of	Fixed term	
	Yes	No
Electorate	Presidential (US)	Parliamentary with directly elected PM (Israel)
		Semi-presidentialism (F)
Parliament	Directorial government (Switzerland)	Parliamentary (UK)

Note: Only one example is included for each type.

working modes (Elgie 1999). Sometimes the president acts as the real head of government, relegating the prime minister to a mere assistant and occasionally the scapegoat for things that do not go well, sometimes the holders of these two offices work together or against each other in complex power-sharing arrangements, and sometimes the president is little more than a powerful head of state in reserve for crisis situations. The archetypical case of semi-presidentialism, France, has seen the two former variants, while other countries (e.g. Austria) resemble the latter and combine a semi-presidential constitution with a parliamentary working of the system.

Parliamentarism in many ways is a simple form of government: the cabinet is the government (Strøm et al. 2003). And although the mechanisms of creation and accountability are fundamentally different, the cabinet also constitutes the government in systems with a directly elected prime minister (Israel) and in systems with directorial government (Switzerland).

KEY POINTS

- Today's governments constitute what remains of absolute monarchs, after splitting-off of judicial and legislative functions.

- Notwithstanding the separation-of-powers doctrine, state functions are not fully separated. The government has retained important legislative powers, although differences exist between different regime types.

- Different regime types also distinguish themselves by the definition of government. Constitutionally, one-person executives and collective bodies can be distinguished. Some governments include the head of state, while others have a separate head.

The internal working of government

Constitutional texts are typically silent about the internal working and decision-making of government, and much is left to the political actors. Over time, conventions may establish themselves. Conventions are normative rules that are generally respected. Although they are not backed up by law, breaking conventions typically is not cost-free for the breaker. Nevertheless, the more a mode of governing rests on formal rules, the more difficult it is to introduce change.

Political science has established a number of descriptive models of government. These models are partly derived from the constitutional order, but try to highlight how government actually works and arrives at decisions. Models capture which actors are typically able to leave their imprint on the outcome of the government decision-making process to a greater extent than other participants. They were developed with the background of the archetypal cases of presidential and parliamentary government—the US and the UK—and subsequently applied to other cases.

Presidential government

The principle of presidential government is to vest all executive power in a single, directly elected politician for a fixed term (i.e. the president is not politically accountable to the legislature). As Article II of the US Constitution puts it, 'The executive Power shall be vested in a President of the United States of America.' Lijphart (1992) lists 'a one-person executive' among the defining principles of presidentialism. More realistically, the 'elected executive names and directs the composition of the government' (Shugart and Carey 1992: 19). Thus, within the executive domain, the president is sovereign. Different US presidents have developed their own styles. Some have used their cabinet members mainly for executing their orders while others have used them as advisers, but a collective decision-making system has never been established (Warshaw 1996).

Cabinet government

Cabinet government represents the operating mode of the parliamentary system as it emerged in Britain in the first half of the nineteenth century. Then the cabinet discussed and decided the important issues collectively. The prime minister was a first among equals (*primus inter pares*), not the boss of the other ministers. The background to that was the limited role of the state and the fact that initially the cabinet was the monarch's creation. A slim state kept the cabinet agenda manageable. The cabinet being the monarch's creation had three implications.

1. In many ways the monarch was his own 'prime minister', dealing with his ministers on an individual basis.
2. The ministers objected to a strong prime minister undermining their direct link to the monarch.
3. So did parliament, which was keen to avoid individual ministers' accountability being obscured by cabinet hierarchy (Mackintosh 1977: 56). Cabinet government continued to prevail when electoral reform gradually loosened the cabinet's tie with the monarch while strengthening that with the House of Commons (Mackintosh 1977: 155–8, 257–343).

However, with the gradual increase of government tasks, more and more issues needed to be handled and decided. While their number clearly exceeded what a cabinet could handle as a collective body, at the same time many issues became too technical to allow a meaningful discussion between non-specialists. This had two consequences. First, the proportion of government decisions going though cabinet declined. Second, many cabinet decisions became formal, only ratifying what was 'precooked' before the cabinet meeting within and between the ministries (Burch and Holliday 1996; James 1999; Smith 1999). Thus, classical cabinet government is a thing of the past. Yet this has not made the cabinet an empty vessel, making decisions only in name but not in substance. A number of authors have identified important issues that are still decided by the cabinet in substance and have stressed the role of the cabinet 'as court of appeal for *both* ministers radically out of sympathy with a general line, *and* for a premier confronted by a ministerial colleague who insists on ploughing her or his furrow' (Dunleavy and Rhodes 1990: 11). If a cabinet fulfils these functions (i.e. deliberates and decides important issues and also functions as court of appeal), then we can speak of *post-classical cabinet government*.

Prime ministerial government

Since the early 1960s, a transformation of the operating mode of British cabinets has been noted. Richard Crossman coined the term **prime ministerial government** (Crossman 1963, 1972). In this model, collective deliberation and effective decision-making in and by the cabinet have been replaced by monocratic decision-making by the prime minister. Authors writing about other European states that experienced long stretches of single-party government, in particular Greece and Spain, have echoed the British diagnosis: cabinet government has given way to prime ministerial government.

There are three different modes of prime ministerial government: (i) a generalized ability to decide policy *across all issue areas* in which the prime minister takes an interest; (ii) by *deciding key issues* which subsequently determine most remaining areas of government policy; and (iii) by defining a *governing ethos*, 'atmosphere', or ideology which generates predictable solutions to most policy problems, and hence constrains other ministers' freedom of manoeuvre so as to make them simple agents of the premier's will (Dunleavy and Rhodes 1990: 8).

Prime ministerial government suggests monocratic decision-making and hence resembles presidential government. The difference is that presidents have a constitutional right to do so, while prime ministers need to go beyond their constitutional role. Also, presidents are unassailable, as their term is fixed, while in principle prime ministers can be forced out of office. Such involuntary departure from office is not just a hypothetical possibility, as the most powerful British post-war prime minister, Margaret Thatcher, experienced in 1990 when she was ousted by her party.

Ministerial government

Finally, the transformation of cabinet government is seen to have occurred in the opposite direction. Rather than concentrating power in the prime minister, it has dispersed among the individual cabinet members. This is **ministerial government** or, in Andeweg's (1997) terminology, 'fragmented government'. Decisions ending up in the cabinet typically are ratified only. Ministers are overworked and primarily concerned about getting their own act together. They are inclined to interfere in the business of other ministers only if the decisions concerned would produce negative fallout for their own department. Otherwise, ministers respect a tacit rule of mutual non-intervention. As non-intervention is mutual, this rule helps them to get cabinet support for their own policies, and it is the success or failure in directing their respective ministry that is crucial for the conduct of their careers. Recognizing this development, Laver and Shepsle (1990, 1996) have described ministers as 'policy dictators' within their own domain as the founding assumption for their coalition theory.

Models of government and cabinet coalitions in parliamentary systems

Thus far, party has been absent from the government modes presented here. The implicit assumption is that no party line of division runs through government, though party bonds may be important to overcoming other **centrifugal** forces (such as conflicting departmental interests). Indeed, cabinets consisting of more than a single party are unlikely to approach either full-blown prime ministerial or ministerial government.

To begin with, in the former the prime minister's dominance is partly due to his/her role as electoral leader—and indeed victor—when coming to office. The ministers' submission to the prime minster partly rests on his role as a party asset that is not to be damaged by internal challenges. Coalition governments can come close to prime ministerial government when one party is dominant and the coalition builds on an electoral alliance which ties together the cabinet parties. Yet, in most cases the analogy to prime ministerial government in coalition governments is the establishment of an oligarchic leadership, consisting of the leaders of the coalition parties, with each party leader being on the one hand a 'prime minister' of his/her party team in government, and on the other hand deciding critical issues together with the other party leader(s). Note, however, that there are limits to collective leadership and 'sharing' the prime minister's powers. Party leaders cannot attend international summits—which are often the place where important decisions are made (e.g. on the management of the recent Euro crisis)—in tandem. Nor can constitutional powers be formally shared. Thus, in the case of conflict, the prime minister can always invoke whatever powers the constitution has endowed the office.

In strict terms, ministerial government in coalition regimes would mean that 'the cabinet is not simply a *collection* of coalition partners, but instead it is a *distribution* of specific powers over **policy formulation** and **implementation** among those partners' (Laver and Shepsle 1996: 282). In other words, each government party would implement its own policy in its departments and exercise no influence on the departments held by its partner or partners. This assumption underlies the coalition theory of Laver and Shepsle (1990, 1996; for a critique see Dunleavy and Bastow 2001), which predicts the formation of the government that allows each of the government parties full control over its most preferred policy dimension.

Nowhere does coalition government work strictly according to the ministerial government model (see the contributions in Laver and Shepsle (1994)). At least some policies are agreed between the parties before the coalition is set up. These deals are often fixed in coalition agreements. Moreover, coalition governance mechanisms such as coalition committees, watchdog junior ministers, and other scrutiny mechanisms are established to guarantee that the deals are being observed by the coalition partners (Müller and Strøm 2000; Thies 2001; Timmermans 2003, 2006; Martin and Vanberg 2004, 2011; Strøm et al. 2008; Strøm et al. 2010). Yet, within these important confines, even coalition governments can display a tendency to work according to the ministerial government mode (Bergman et al. 2019).

Variability of government modes

Government modes are not fixed once and for all. The preceding discussion of the transformation of cabinet government into prime ministerial government and/or ministerial government already suggests some long-term change. Yet, government modes also vary according to political conditions and issues (Andeweg 1997). Thus, single-party governments are more likely to become prime ministerial than coalition cabinets. At the same time, each cabinet is likely to handle issues differently, depending on their relevance and potential for causing damage to the government.

KEY POINTS

- Constitutions are silent about the internal working and decision-making of government, leaving much to the political actors who adapt the government modes to changing circumstances.

- Presidential systems provide for presidential government (with its internal variations). Parliamentary systems offer a broader range of decision modes: cabinet government, prime ministerial government, and ministerial government.

- Coalition governments in parliamentary systems typically have developed more complex decision modes.

The autonomy of government

In the previous section, 'The internal working of government', when political parties were mentioned the assumption was that there is no difference whatsoever between government members and their parties. Yet political parties are complex entities. They consist of (i) the mass organization (the 'party on the ground'); (ii) the parliamentary party; and (iii) the party team in government (the latter two are also referred to as 'party in public office'). To make it more complicated, the 'party in the electorate' also exists. Although this layer lacks organization, and therefore the quality of a political actor, it is a highly relevant reference point for politicians.

Thus, understanding governments requires exploring the autonomy these layers have from other actors or providers of essential resources, without which they would not be able to govern. This section discusses political parties and, more briefly, the bureaucracy. Parties are essential for getting a government into office and maintaining it there, and without the permanent bureaucracy the government could not govern.

Government autonomy: the party dimension

It is the electoral connection which makes government democratic, and it is political parties which play a crucial role in structuring elections, even when the electoral system allows the choice of individual candidates (Katz 1997). Modern democracies, therefore, have **party government** in a general sense (Müller and Narud 2013). Yet, this understanding of party government can be contrasted with a more specific one. According to Richard Rose:

> . . . party government exists only in so far as the actions of office-holders are influenced by values and policies derived from the party. Where the life of party politics does not affect government policy, the accession of a new party to office is little more significant than the accession of a new monarch; the party reigns but does not rule.
>
> Rose (1976: 371)

What role parties have after the elections is subject to normative and empirical discussions. It is sufficient here to say that conflicting normative theories suggest both the full autonomy of elected officials from their party and, conversely, a strong role of the party in determining the course steered by the government. The former position can be associated with constitutional theory and liberal and conservative thinkers, and the latter one with much of constitutional practice and mostly socialist ideas (Birch 1967). The remainder of this section explores the issue empirically.

Thus, the key question is to what extent political parties can control the behaviour of their government teams. Three means of control are of particular importance (Rose 1976; Katz 1986; Müller 1994; Blondel and Cotta 2000).

Party programmes

Party control of the cabinet will be enhanced in situations where party programmes not only clearly state the intentions of the party, but also specify appropriate means to the desired ends. In such circumstances, ministers will have clear targets, whilst the party will have a yardstick for measurement of their performance.

Selection of cabinet members

Party control of the cabinet will be enhanced where cabinet ministers have internalized and acted upon party values. The internalization of party values is hard to measure, but holding high party office is certainly a plausible indicator. Note that ministers who have good intentions of serving their party still need to be skilled executives in order to succeed.

Permanent control of the party over the cabinet

While the above conditions increase the likelihood of 'partyness of government' (Katz 1986), they do not guarantee the implementation of party policies. Therefore, parties may want to exercise permanent control over their ministers. Naturally, the less these two conditions are fulfilled—for instance, because of the need to appoint technical experts rather than party leaders—and the more changed circumstances (such as international crises und unexpected economic developments) have dated the party programmes, the more important such control can be considered.

Empirical studies of party programmes and their relevance to government policy have a long tradition, though most of them confine themselves to single countries and cabinets. In one of the few comparative and comprehensive studies, McDonald and Budge (2005) took a highly aggregated approach and compared party ambitions (programmes) in twenty-one countries with government ambitions (government declarations) and actual outputs in terms of budget priorities. This study did not find relevant party impact on government in a short-term perspective. The inertia of public policy is simply too strong. In the words of McDonald and Budge (2005: 180): 'The reason is not that changes are not made but that they are slow, because of preexisting budgets, contracts, commitments, and entitlements in the field of expenditures; time constraints, due process, legislative and social opposition, and administrative bottlenecks in the field of legislation.'

Only when a party manages to hold on to government for a long time—McDonald and Budge list the New Deal Democrats in the US, the Thatcher–Major Conservatives in the UK, and the Scandinavian Social Democrats—will a party imprint on public policy be clearly visible.

Blondel, Cotta, and associates chose a less aggregated approach (Blondel and Cotta 1996, 2000).

Conceptually, they considered both directions of influence: party on government and government on party. Three ideal types of party–government relations can be distinguished:

- dominance—one of the two dominates the other;
- autonomy—government and government parties coexist without exercising influence on each other;
- fusion—party and government become politically indistinguishable.

Empirically, this research was concerned with appointments (to the cabinet and the party executive), government patronage, and fifty policy decisions in a set of West European countries. Unlike the McDonald and Budge (2005) study, which extracted general policy concerns of parties from their manifestos and the general direction of government policies from budget domains, this research was concerned with specific pledges and specific government policies. The aim was to establish to what extent government behaviour has a party origin and in what direction, if any, top-level recruitment takes place—from the party to the government (as the party government model suggests) or in the opposite direction.

The more exploratory study by Blondel and Cotta (1996, 2000) suggests that the ideal-typical picture of party government—with the party taking over government—needs correction. Specifically, following an initial period of *fusion* after a party enters government, new government appointments lead to increasing *autonomy* of the two, though 'fast-track' appointments of government members to high party office suggest even a tendency towards *dependence* of the party. With regard to policy, the government is not just the technocratic executor of party policy. Rather, the government plays a significant role in shaping policies originating from the party and initiating its own ones. Patronage, it seems, is used to compensate the party for its desired policies which the government cannot deliver or does not want to deliver.

Presidentialization?

One recent attempt to capture the strengthening of the executive vis-à-vis political parties is the concept of presidentialization. Specifically, it means the strengthening of the chief executive. Although the term 'presidentialization' has been used earlier in studies of the British prime minister (Foley 1993, 2000; Pryce 1997), the most systematic comparative attempt has been made by Poguntke, Webb, and collaborators (Poguntke and Webb 2005). They associate presidentialization—in all regime types—with '(1) increasing

leadership power resources and autonomy within the party and the political executive respectively, and (2) increasingly leadership-centred electoral processes' (Poguntke and Webb 2005: 5). In their analysis, this process affects the internal working of the executive, the running of political parties, and the functioning of the electoral process.

Presidentialized government represents one ideal type of government. The 'partyfied' type of government occupies the opposite end of the continuum. The key question then is what is the role of individual leaders and of collective actors? Poguntke and Webb note that different regime types—parliamentarism, semi-presidentialism, and presidentialism—provide the actors with different power resources and hence constrain the place a specific government can take on the continuum. Thus, a parliamentary system under a strong prime minister can be more 'presidentialized' than a presidential system under a weak president, but never more so when the president is strong.

In their fourteen-country empirical analyses Poguntke, Webb, and associates identify an almost uniform trend towards presidentialism. Specifically, they recognize shifts in intra-executive power to the leader, increasing autonomy of the executive leader from the party, shifts of intra-party power to the leader, the leader's increasing autonomy from other party heavyweights, a growth of the leader's media coverage, increasing focus on the leader in electoral campaigns, and growing leader effects on voting behaviour. In combination, these developments indeed suggest a major shift away from the 'partyfied' type of democracy.

Government autonomy: bureaucratic government?

The number of people who enter or leave government after elections (i.e. elected leaders and political appointees) differs from system to system. Yet, in most systems their numbers are tiny compared with those of bureaucrats, even when lower-rank civil servants are not considered. In many parliamentary systems in the first post-war decades, little more than two dozen posts changed hands when a wholesale government turnover occurred.

The idea of bureaucratic government (Rose 1969) rests on the assumption that a small group cannot run the whole show and critically depends on the permanent bureaucracy. Bureaucrats can set the agenda of their political masters by identifying problems that need to be addressed; they can limit political choices by presenting a narrow set of alternatives and by undermining the viability of ideas that run counter to the department's common wisdom. Such ideas are labelled, for instance, as not workable, too expensive, having huge undesirable side effects, conflicting with higher-level rules (such as the Constitution or EU rules), having already failed in earlier attempts, etc. More so than any other mode of government, bureaucratic government remains—and needs to remain—invisible. Thus, politicians continue to dominate the public stage. They may even make consequential decisions (according to one of the above modes). Yet these decisions can be compared to choosing the flag to fly on a ship sailing on the ocean, while it is bureaucrats who determine its course. Moreover, most administrative decisions escape the politicians' attention altogether.

KEY POINTS

- Party government means that government actions are strongly influenced by the values and policies of the government party or parties.

- Political parties control their teams in government by the means of party programmes, the recruitment of party leaders into government office, and permanent oversight and control of the government.

- Empirical studies mostly demonstrate that parties have only a limited impact on government. Initial fusion of party and government often gives way to government autonomy, and occasionally party dependence on the government.

- Individual leaders tend to gain weight relative to the parties ('presidentialization').

The political capacity of government

Modern governments of rich nations can achieve much. They can maintain law and order, provide essential services to their citizens, strengthen the economy, and send men and women into orbit or to explore outer space. Yet, whether governments can indeed do what is in the capacity of modern states depends largely on the political conditions that prevail during their reign. This section can discuss only a few selected topics. It leaves aside much of the often very consequential nitty-gritty details of institutional rules (see e.g. Weaver and Rockman 1993; Strøm et al. 2003). Nor does it discuss systematically the reactions of citizens, interest groups, and the economy to government policy that at times have brought governments to their knees. It is sufficient here to refer to a few examples: the 2006 riots in the French *banlieues* (suburban housing complexes) which led the government to partly reverse its reform of the labour law; the mass strikes of the British trade unions that brought down the Heath government in 1974; and the less visible but much more common influence exercised by the investment decisions of firms in a globalized economy that have considerably constrained national governments' freedom of manoeuvre.

Unified versus divided government

The concepts of unified and divided government were invented in the US. **Divided government** means that the presidency is held by one party and at least one chamber of Congress is controlled by the other party; **unified government** is when all three are under the control of the same party (see also Chapter 7 'Legislatures'). The concepts of unified and divided government transfer easily to other presidential systems, although the multiparty nature of some of them requires some modification. Leaving aside non-partisan presidents, the (one-person) presidency by necessity must be under the control of one party and one party only. In contrast, no single party may control a majority in the legislature.

Yet a legislature passing a great number of detailed laws could make the president its mere servant. This could indeed be the case if no further provision were added to the definition of presidential government—some law-making authority of the president (Shugart and Carey 1992).

The US presidency represents the archetypal case of presidentialism. The formal law-making capacity of the president is negative: the president can veto any law passed by Congress. As long as no vote in both the House of Representatives and the Senate overrides the veto with a two-thirds majority, the law is rejected and the status quo prevails. The US has seen divided government for most of the post-war period. Yet empirical studies suggest that this was not very consequential, as open battles between the Congress and the president resulting in vetoes and occasional overrides have been very limited (Mayhew 1991; Binder 2003). Note, however, that actors anticipating defeat may avoid such battles. While many studies of the US highlight the factors that prevent legislative immobilism, a comparative perspective can be particularly useful as it brings out many of the same factors more sharply and adds additional ones.

In Latin America, the most powerful presidents enjoy a much richer set of legislative instruments than their US counterparts. Veto power can take the form of the line veto, enabling the president to veto specific clauses in legislation but accepting the rest, and most presidents also enjoy decree power, the right of legislative initiative, and some procedural power in Congress (Mainwaring and Shugart 1997a; Morgenstern and Nacif 2002). At the same time, these systems are multiparty. Hence, the chances of a president finding his party endowed with a legislative majority are often modest or non-existent. One influential study (Linz 1990a, 1994) has identified the main reason for the frequent breakdowns of democracy in Latin America in the institutional 'rigidity' of presidentialism—with fixed terms of both the president and the legislature. This, in turn, causes long periods of legislative gridlock followed by short periods of legislative overproduction. Both encourage frustrated political actors to resort to non-democratic means. Yet the specific assumptions about the behaviour of actors underlying Linz's theory have not withstood empirical scrutiny (Cheibub 2007; Mainwaring and Shugart 1997b; Llanos and Marsteintredet 2010). While it is true that democracy has had a rough life in Latin America, this is not just down to divided government. Presidents have found ways to cope with it, as Cox and Morgenstern (2002) demonstrate (see Table 8.1).

Depending on their own strength in terms of institutional empowerment and party support in the legislature (Martínez-Gallardo 2012), presidents employ four different strategies. I consider first the two extreme categories. The president uses unilateral powers if the legislature is hostile (*recalcitrant*). He uses presidential decrees to push forward his own policies (rather than making legislative proposals to the assembly) and vetoes laws passed by the legislature that run counter to his policy ambitions. In Cox and Morgenstern's typology, this is the *imperial* president. This was the behavioural pattern of Chile's President Allende before General Pinochet's tragic military coup in 1973.

At the opposite end of the spectrum, if the president is sure that the assembly will follow his lead, he dictates his terms in the form of legislative initiative. Such a *dominant* president could be found in Mexico in the years of the Party of the Institutionalized Revolution (PRI) single-party dominance.

The two intermediate cases require the president to engage in give-and-take relations with the assembly. For the president, this is more rewarding than unilateral action, as he does not need to push his powers to the very limits of constitutionality (or beyond) and because legislation is harder to overturn than presidential decrees. If the president meets a legislature that is *workable*, he engages in legislative coalition-building. This requires policy deals (substantive compromises) and perhaps appointments from the coalitional parties to cabinet office. According to Cox and Morgenstern (2002), presidents in post-dictatorial Chile have followed that strategy. Recent research suggests that the president's policy objectives may be better served by confining their strategy to making policy compromises (if necessary) with the assembly but remaining in full control over cabinet appointments (Martínez-Gallardo and Schleiter 2015).

Finally, if the president meets a legislature that largely consists of constituency-bound representatives who need to bring home immediate benefits for the purpose of their re-election, the president offers pork and large-scale patronage rather than policy concessions. Elected representatives then sell their policy-making powers for goods and services that, in turn, they can allocate in their districts to secure their re-election. Probably much of Brazil's recent history provides a good example of the relevance of a *parochial* strategy (Ames 2002).

Table 8.1 President–assembly relations under presidentialism

Presidential strategy	Assembly strategy			
	Reject	Bargain	Demand payments	Acquiesce
Undertake unilateral action	Imperial president, *recalcitrant assembly*			
Bargain		Coalitional president, *workable assembly*		
Pay-off			Nationally oriented president, *parochial assembly*	
Dictate				Dominant president, *subservient assembly*

Source: Cox and Morgenstern (2002: 455).

As Cox and Morgenstern (2002) make clear, the same forces are at work in the US as in the two intermediary cases. Clearly, the office of the US president is not endowed with the institutional powers of imperial presidents in Latin America and elsewhere. But different presidents were in different situations with respect to party support in Congress and other resources and chose their strategies accordingly. The record suggests that they were quite successful, although less so in more recent situations of divided government (Mayhew 1991; Binder 2003).

Attempts have been made to apply the concepts of unified and divided government to other regime types than presidentialism (Elgie 2001; Laver and Shepsle 1991). Accordingly, semi-presidential systems are treated as a close analogy to presidential ones. The only difference is that the division line does not run between the executive and the legislature but between the legislature plus the cabinet on one side and the president on the other. With regard to parliamentary systems, the authors identify minority governments as cases of 'divided government'. Here, the division line runs between the cabinet (supported by a parliamentary minority) and the parliamentary majority. Without doubt, these situations replicate some characteristics of divided government as it has emerged in presidential systems. Yet the very fact that the survival of government is not at stake in the latter while it is in the two former makes the analogy less than perfect and perhaps a case of 'conceptual stretching' (Sartori 1970; see also Chapter 3 'Comparative research methods').

Majority versus minority government

Governments that enjoy majority support—at least 50 per cent of the seats plus one—in parliament can not only survive in office but also enact their political programme. For a long time, **minority governments**—governments comprising parties that collectively miss that mark—were considered an anomaly. They were considered as unwanted crisis symptoms, coming to power when no **majority government** could be formed. Such situations are also referred to as *immobiliste*, as they will be unable to produce political decisions (Laver and Schofield 1990: 72). Yet, as Strøm (1990) demonstrated, and more recent studies confirmed, minority governments are neither rare nor particularly unstable. This result is not driven by governments that have a *formal* minority status but can rely on a legislative (rather than government) majority coalition.

What is the rationale of minority governments? Laver and Schofield (1990: 77–81) suggest that minority

governments occupying the ideological centre or, more technically, that hold the median legislator, are 'policy viable'. This means that they can divide the opposition by policy proposals at the centre of the policy space. Although the left opposition will consider them too much to the right and the right opposition will find them too much to the left, these parties cannot join forces to bring down the government and enact alternative policies.

Of course, effective government by minority cabinets suggests that policy is the only or overwhelming motive that drives political parties. If office were dominant, parties left and right of the government would join forces to bring down any minority cabinet, as any new government would at least increase their chances for government office. In practice, most parties are indeed interested in government office in its own right (Müller and Strøm 2000). Yet, their behaviour is constrained by the anticipated reaction of their voters. The bringing down of a social democratic minority cabinet by parties further to the left in alliance with right-wing parties may not be well received by left voters, particularly when it results in a new government more to the right than the one replaced. Anticipated voter reactions also matter in another sense: governing often results in electoral costs which some parties have good reasons to avoid (Strøm 1990). Indeed, as Narud and Valen (2008) show, there has been a monotonic and strong trend for government parties to lose votes since the 1980s. This trend is even stronger in Central and Eastern Europe (Bergman et al. 2019). More dramatically, most European governments have not been returned to office in the years immediately following the outbreak of the current financial crisis.

Table 8.2 provides a broad overview of the frequency of government types in democracies worldwide. The upper part of the table shows that minority situations—situations where no single party commands a parliamentary majority—are frequent, though more so in parliamentary than in presidential systems. The lower part suggests that about 45 per cent of these situations produce minority government in parliamentary systems and close to 78 per cent in presidential systems. More recently, the postwar or post-democratization record of twenty-eight European countries shows a similar picture: the breakdown of 610 cabinets is 12 per cent majority and 30 per cent minority single-party and 54 per cent majority and 15 per cent minority coalition cabinets (Bergman et al. 2013).

Overall, majority cabinets enjoy a longer life than minority cabinets. Yet minority governments have a similar or even longer duration in some Western countries, particularly in those where they are a

Table 8.2 Coalitional status of governments under parliamentarism and presidentialism (1945–2002)

	Parliamentary regimes		Presidential regimes	
	N	%	N	%
Majority situations	215	43.2	121	55.5
Minority situations	283	56.8	97	44.5
Total	**498**	**100.0**	**218**	**100.0**
Government types in minority situations				
Majority coalitions	175	54.2	31	22.3
Single-party minority governments	83	25.7	49	47.6
Minority coalitions	65	20.1	31	30.1

Notes: The upper part of the table identifies government formation situations by counting the number of legislative seat distributions. Changes in the seat distribution are triggered by elections and by splits and mergers of parties. The lower part records the government *type* that was formed in minority situations. Changes in the composition of government that did not affect its type (e.g. the switch from one majority coalition to another in a sitting parliament) are not registered. The number of government types exceeds that of minority situations because different government types were subsequently formed under the same seat distribution.
Source: Cheibub et al. (2004: 573–5).

regular outcome of government formation. Thus, in most cases minority cabinets are clearly more than temporary solutions between two 'regular' majority governments.

As we have seen, minority governments can be helped by their central location in the policy space. Institutional mechanisms such as presidential powers (already discussed in the context of divided government in 'Unified versus divided government') can also increase their capacity. The French government is particularly lucky as the prime minister can draw on an arsenal of procedural rules which help to force through government policy. The strongest instrument is Article 49.3 of the Constitution. It allows the government to turn any decision about legislation into a confidence issue, shifting the burden of proof to its opponents. Legislative proposals introduced under Article 49.3 are automatically adopted—without a vote on the proposal itself—as long as no no-confidence vote (requiring a majority of *all* MPs) unseats the government (Huber 1996). While this instrument is used frequently in France, most governments lack such strong instruments. Therefore, in order to survive and get policies passed, minority cabinets need to engage in negotiations with the opposition. This limits their capacities, as is also reflected in government durations (Table 8.3). Overall, majority cabinets enjoy a longer life. In aggregate, they outlive minority cabinets by eight months. Yet, this is not true in every case.

Single-party versus coalition government

Single-party governments have the distinctive advantage that no party line of division runs through the government. This implies that the government goals will be relatively uncontroversial internally. Any remaining differences are likely to be suppressed, given the common goal of survival in office. Parties holding government office as a result of their strong position—commanding a parliamentary majority or occupying a strategic position in the party system—are also likely to have strong leadership that can overcome internal difficulties. Hence, with everything else equal, governments consisting of a single party can be considered homogeneous. This implies that they can make decisions quickly, avoid disagreeable compromises, and maintain a common front.

Coalition governments, in turn, need to satisfy at least some of the ambitions of each of the government parties. Even in the unlikely case of (almost) complete a priori agreement between the coalition partners about government goals, the fact remains that office-sharing means that the personal ambitions of some would-be ministers in the parties must be frustrated. This, in turn, may result in only half-hearted support of the government (Sartori 1997). In most cases, some of the party's policy ambitions will be compromised. This typically lengthens the internal decision-making process and often exposes internal divisions to the

Table 8.3 Absolute and relative cabinet duration in twenty-eight European democracies (1945–2011)

Country	Period	Absolute duration			Relative duration		
		Mean	Standard deviation	No. of cabinets	Mean	Standard deviation	No. of cabinets
Austria	1945–2011	911	401.35	25	0.71	0.26	24
Belgium	1946–2011	544	519.28	40	0.45	0.36	40
Bulgaria	1990–2011	728	556.58	10	0.54	0.38	9
Czech Rep.	1992–2011	605	462.64	11	0.61	0.37	10
Denmark	1945–2011	680	337.83	35	0.55	0.26	35
Estonia	1992–2011	536	296.45	12	0.58	0.36	12
Finland	1945–2011	457	415.36	50	0.53	0.34	50
France	1959–2011	660	466.76	29	0.58	0.29	28
Germany	1949–2011	762	505.48	29	0.65	0.37	28
Greece	1977–2011	822	517.38	15	0.62	0.36	14
Hungary	1990–2011	760	456.04	10	0.83	0.24	9
Iceland	1944–2011	747	487.06	32	0.61	0.35	31
Ireland	1944–2011	958	450.60	25	0.59	0.25	25
Italy	1945–2011	390	347.46	55	0.34	0.31	54
Latvia	1993–2011	323	179.44	19	0.43	0.31	18
Lithuania	1992–2011	559	431.16	12	0.58	0.40	11
Luxembourg	1945–2011	1239	652.71	19	0.86	0.24	18
Malta	1987–2011	1279	552.48	7	0.75	0.37	6
Netherlands	1945–2011	773	541.73	28	0.65	0.34	27
Norway	1945–2011	793	409.17	30	0.76	0.31	29
Poland	1991–2011	429	354.09	16	0.45	0.37	16
Portugal	1976–2011	629	530.17	19	0.50	0.34	19
Romania	1990–2011	446	275.95	17	0.53	0.36	16
Slovakia	1992–2011	686	593.49	10	0.59	0.37	10
Slovenia	1992–2011	614	408.32	12	0.74	0.27	12
Spain	1977–2011	1111	330.45	11	0.82	0.21	11
Sweden	1945–2011	829	434.47	29	0.82	0.29	28
UK	1945–2011	997	509.99	24	0.66	0.30	23
All 28		687	490.54	631	0.59	0.34	613

Note: Absolute duration is in days, relative duration in percentage of the time until the end of the constitutional inter-election period (CIEP).
Sources: Saalfeld (2013) (calculated from Andersson and Ersson (2012)).

public, with the consequence that the government appears divided, and therefore weak. The alternative of one party quietly submitting would allocate the costs of coalition one-sidedly; that party would be considered by its activists and voters to be selling out to its coalition partner. These problems tend to remain modest in ideologically homogeneous coalitions but accelerate in heterogeneous ones. And they tend to be particularly tricky when they are fuelled not only by party policy ambition but also by office ambition. Whenever the most prestigious office—that of prime minister—is at stake *between* the coalition partners, coalitions tend to be seriously hampered by internal rivalry and conflict.

According to Table 8.2, in minority situations coalition governments are the dominant outcome in parliamentary regimes and still result in more than half of such situations in presidential regimes. A wealth of research shows that the overall picture is remarkably balanced between single-party and coalition cabinets. In the aggregate, single-party governments do not last significantly longer than coalition governments. Yet, this similarity should not prevent us from seeing that very different forces are at work here. Coalition governments that do not reach the maximum possible duration generally terminate over internal conflict and unbridgeable differences between the partners. In contrast, single-party governments tend to shorten their term because they feel strong and early elections are likely to return them to government (Strøm and Swindle 2002). In East-Central Europe the picture is remarkably similar, particularly given the lack of consolidation of both parties and party systems in most of the countries (Nikolenyi 2004; Conrad and Golder 2010).

KEY POINTS

- The political capacities of governments differ widely, depending on the government's support base in the political institutions and the society.

- In presidential regimes, 'unified government' suggests greater capacities. 'Divided government' requires the president to use institutional prerogatives, bribe members of the legislature, or compromise with legislative parties.

- In parliamentary regimes, single-party majority governments normally have the greatest political capacity.

Bureaucratic capacities

No government can achieve its goals, limited as they may be, without many helping hands. The modern state has developed the permanent bureaucracy as the prime instrument for that purpose (see Chapter 4 'The nation-state'). In order to fulfil the bureaucracy's mission, its members—the bureaucrats—need to be able and willing to do their job. In addition, the internal organization of tasks and processes can exercise a major influence on bureaucratic capacities.

Working from an idealization of the Prussian bureaucracy, Max Weber (1947) outlined the key characteristics of bureaucratic organization.

Personnel

Formal lifelong employment of bureaucrats who receive a fixed salary and earn pension rights in return for their service and who are promoted largely on the basis of their seniority (the length of their service).

Organization

Specialization, training, functional division of labour, well-defined areas of jurisdiction, and a clear hierarchy among the bureaucrats.

Procedure

Impersonal application of general rules (mostly laws and government decrees); business is conducted on the basis of written documents, bureaucratic decisions are recorded, and the relevant documents carefully stored.

Each of these features has a specific function in making the bureaucratic organization an effective instrument. Indeed, Weber suggested that it is not only *effective* (i.e. gets things done) but, indeed, 'capable of attaining the highest degree of *efficiency*' (i.e. gets things done with a minimum of cost) (1947: 337). Lifelong employment and career perspectives allow the administration to attract and retain qualified staff. Personnel stability, in turn, is one condition for a smooth working of the administrative machine that builds on division of labour and specialization. Well-trained bureaucrats who work on clearly defined issues and who are part and parcel of an unambiguous command chain are able to produce 'standardized' decisions. This means that, when confronted with the same case, different bureaucrats would arrive at identical decisions derived from the general rules. Paying the bureaucrats a fixed salary and having strong rules of incompatibility aim to prevent personal interest intervening in their decisions. Finally, the requirement that decisions are fully documented and hence can be checked at any time helps to keep bureaucrats on track.

A cornerstone of the bureaucratic system is **merit system** recruitment. Accordingly, access to the administration is not restricted to particular segments of society; selection and promotion aim at appointing the best-qualified individuals. With regard to promotion, in the case of equal qualifications seniority is decisive. Clearly, in such a system political affiliation and attitudes of job applicants and members of the bureaucracy do not play any role. Such considerations would not only be inappropriate but also unnecessary, as the bureaucracy is considered a neutral instrument.

Within the confines of laws and regulations, the merit bureaucrats serve every government loyally.

Problems of bureaucracy

To be sure, Max Weber's appraisal of bureaucracy rested on its comparison with pre-modern types of organization (including patrimonial systems where offices were sold and, in turn, generated income for their holders). He was quick to add that real-life bureaucracies become inefficient when decisions need to take into consideration the individual characteristics of the cases to be decided. Indeed, the term 'bureaucracy', and even more so the adjective 'bureaucratic', in ordinary language implies excessive rules and complicated procedures, formalism, and rigidity in their application—hence delay and inefficiency in making decisions and consequently the waste of public money. It is true that each of the principles of bureaucratic organization can be overdone. The rule of law then degenerates to rigidity and inertia in procedures and over-regulation, specialization of bureaucrats leads to civil servants who perform acts without understanding their consequences, and personnel stability and arcane internal rules create a closed system out of touch with its environment. One possible consequence of the latter is groupthink. Groupthink means the unconscious minimizing of intra-organizational conflict in making decisions at the price of their quality, which can lead to disaster (Janis 1972; 't Hart 1990). A famous case of groupthink was the Kennedy administration's Bay of Pigs invasion, and perhaps the same can be said about the more recent Iraq war planning of the Bush administration.

Theories of bureaucracy have been concerned with such phenomena but more often with less spectacular developments. Parkinson's Law is a famous formula for the creeping but consequential growth of the bureaucracy. Parkinson (1958) suggested that in a bureaucratic organization 'work expands to fill the time allotted'. Consequently, the development of bureaucratic organizations, such as the British Colonial Office, does not reflect its objective function. Indeed, that office increased its staff size considerably as the British Empire declined.

As we have seen earlier in this section, the principles of bureaucratic organization aim to separate the private interest of bureaucrats from the decisions they have to make. Yet to assume that human beings will ever be able and willing to separate completely their private preferences from their behaviour as officials would be naive. Bureaucrats do have private interests and political preferences. They want to boost their income and prestige by climbing up the career ladder, and will probably take account of their own political preferences when preparing or making decisions.

Let us consider first the growth of bureaucracy. Parkinson (1958) noted that officials want to 'multiply subordinates, not rivals'. The Public Choice School made the private interests of bureaucrats their starting point. Within this approach, the work of Niskanen (1971) has been the most influential. His theory builds on the simple assumption that bureaucrats have the goal of increasing their budgets. This is because most of the bureaucrats' personal incentives—salary, reputation, power, policy-making capacity—are positively related to the size of their organization's budget. The push of the bureaucrats is met by the pull from societal groups and their representatives who make increasing demands on government. Two reasons make it difficult to keep the growth of government at bay.

1. It is often hard or impossible to measure objectively the 'final outputs' of bureaucracies. With regard to many outputs it is hard to say when an optimal level is reached and to avoid overproduction. The many times overkill capacity built up by the superpowers during the Cold War is a case in point.

2. Specific bureaucracies tend to be the only suppliers of particular (public) goods (e.g. defence or public health). This avoids wasteful duplication but also frees the bureaucracies from competitive pressure (which has negative effects on efficiency) and deprives the politicians of alternative sources of information. All this contributes strongly to the growth of government.

Niskanen's theory is difficult to test. When confronted with empirical data, the evidence has been mixed. While some have found very little evidence conforming to the theory (Blais and Dion 1991), other studies remain sceptical about the power of bureaucrats to set the agenda in a way that results in ever-increasing budgets, but marshal impressive empirical evidence that production of services by private-sector firms is considerably cheaper than that by bureaucrats (Mueller 2003: 371–80). In any case, with Niskanen serving on the Board of Economic Advisers under President Reagan and having inspired this president's thinking, his theory has been quite important for the efforts at rolling back the state since the 1980s.

I now turn to the effort that bureaucrats bring to their job and to the question of whether they diverge from the directions given by political officials. In recent years, several studies have employed the principal–agent framework of micro-economics to address these issues (see also Chapters 7 'Legislatures' and

9 'Constitutions, rights, and judicial power'). Brehm and Gates (1997: 50) have nicely summarized the set of options that bureaucratic agents have.

1. They may either work in the interest of their principal (no agency problem) or engage in leisure-shirking, dissent-shirking, or sabotage.

2. In the case of *leisure-shirking*, bureaucrats simply do not work as much as they are expected to do (and are paid for). They may have a late start in the morning, enjoy an extended lunch break, and 'compensate' for this by leaving their office early, as a widespread stereotype of civil servants suggests (for an empirical example see Putnam (1993: 5)).

3. *Dissent-shirking* means that bureaucrats do not do their best to implement the policies desired by their principals because they themselves have different preferences. This either means that the status quo is preserved or that the incumbent minister experiences an improvement from the status quo, but not enough to satisfy his/her ambitions.

4. While shirking leads to insufficient or no policies, *political sabotage* means the production of negative outputs. In this case, civil servants actively work against the interests of their principal.

Note, however, that it is not necessarily the fault of bureaucrats if politicians are not satisfied with their services. Simply, sometimes politicians demand more than a Weberian (neutral) bureaucrat can give: privilege the minister's constituency, help acquaintances of the minister obtain government permits to which they are not entitled, twist a public tender to benefit a sponsor of the minister's party, help mislead the opposition when preparing answers to parliamentary questions, and obstruct investigations of the Audit Court, parliamentary investigation committee, or public prosecutor. Indeed, there are plenty of cases where members of government have suggested such behaviour to their civil servants. Of course, we know only those that eventually were exposed to the public, mostly ending with ministerial resignation. Yet it may be safe to assume that these cases constitute only the tip of the iceberg.

Politicians have responded in two ways to their uneasiness with the bureaucracy by: (i) establishing spoils systems; and (ii) introducing New Public Management.

Spoils systems

In a **spoils system** the victorious party is free to appoint large layers of the administration after each election, with the jobs going to the party faithful. Thereby the party rewards them for their work towards victory, either by providing their labour or by making important financial contributions. An open spoils system was practised in the US in the nineteenth century, with President Andrew Jackson (1829–37) being crucial in its introduction. The claim was that the spoils system would be democratic in two ways.

1. It would allow the victor of the democratic contest to work with an administration that shares his political philosophy, and hence would help him to live up to the promises made in the campaign.

2. It was radically democratic as it entrusted ordinary Americans rather than a closed elite of professional bureaucrats with the business of government.

In the second half of the nineteenth century, the spoils system came under attack. Eventually, the Pendleton Civil Service Act (1883) established a merit system that was gradually introduced for the bulk of government positions. Only senior government jobs remained up for grabs for the victor. Yet, compared with most other systems, the US maintained a large degree of open politicization. Each change in the office of president is accompanied by the replacement of thousands of government employees by people more akin to the new incumbent and his party.

The major advantage of open spoils systems is that they provide the politicians with administrators who are committed to the government goals. Hence, if political faith would suffice to move mountains, the government would be enabled to achieve its goals. The disadvantage of bringing in cohorts of new people, often with little prior experience in public administration, is that the appointees do not know enough about their organization and its environment. Nor do they know each other, resulting in a 'government of strangers' (Heclo 1977). Moreover, political appointees often do not stay long enough to compensate for these disadvantages by learning 'on the job'.

While open spoils systems are rare, covert ones are more frequent. These are merit systems only in name, with the jobs in the civil service and more broadly in the public sector being allocated among party candidates. To provide just a few examples, such practices were widely applied in Austria, Belgium, and Italy for much of the post-war period, they have been reinvented in some of the post-communist systems, including Slovakia and Poland (O'Dwyer 2006: Chapter 3 'Comparative research methods'), and they are endemic in Latin America and in the Third World in general. Party politicization affecting exclusively the top layers of the bureaucracy has been practised even more widely, for example in France, Germany, and Spain (Page and Wright 1999, 2007; Suleiman 2003).

As bureaucracies are formally merit systems, bureaucrats appointed as political trustees of a specific party stay on even when the government changes.

The disadvantages are obvious: elected leaders have to work with bureaucrats who are not politically neutral but oppose the goals of the government and may indeed engage in dissent-shirking or political sabotage. Thus, while the problem of the bureaucrats' willingness can be resolved for those politicians who make the appointments, it may make things worse for their successors from different parties. One possible 'way out' for them is to strip the alien partisans of their most important functions, cut them off from politically critical communication, and hence make them 'white elephants', and hire another layer of partisans. The consequence will be an oversized bureaucracy for which the taxpayer will have to settle the bill.

New Public Management systems

New Public Management (NPM) systems represent a more fundamental challenge to the classic bureaucratic system than the undermining of merit recruitment. They aim to resolve the problems of both the willingness and efficiency of bureaucrats. Moreover, the proponents of NPM systems claim that establishing these systems can reverse the growth of the state.

NPM systems were first introduced in the US under the Reagan presidency in the 1980s. They were soon imported by the UK and New Zealand, and later diffused throughout the Western world. NPM builds on transferring methods from the market economy to the public sector.

Personnel

Top positions in the public sector are open to outside candidates who are hired on a fixed-term basis (rather than lifelong employment). Consequently, salaries for public-sector managers match those of the private sector and payment is tied to performance.

Organization

NPM methods aim to create 'internal markets' in the public sector. This implies splitting large bureaucratic units into smaller ones and allowing for—indeed encouraging—competition between different public-sector units (e.g. schools) and, where possible, between public- and private-sector units (e.g. agencies and firms). In other words, NPM aims to create an environment that makes profit-seeking the survival strategy.

Procedure

According to NPM doctrine, it is no longer sufficient for a civil servant to observe administrative regulations in every detail, to follow the specific instruction of his/her superiors, and not to steal public money. Rather, accountability is based on the civil servant's performance in attaining the agency's goals. Thus,

public-sector managers are expected to engage in managerialism and entrepreneurship (Peters and Pierre 2001; Suleiman 2003).

NPM schemes greatly enhance the potential for political control over the bureaucracy. Politicians (i.e. people whose positions are ultimately tied to the electoral process) control more financial and career incentives and can—by tying rewards to outcomes—more effectively align the preferences of civil servants with their own. Interestingly, the parliamentary accountability of ministers has not been enhanced in the sense of making them more directly responsible for the acts of their civil servants. Thus, one of the side effects of NPM schemes is the shoring up of politicians against scrutiny (Strøm et al. 2003). Critics of the NPM revolution focus on the deprofessionalization and politicization of the bureaucracy. As Suleiman (2003: 17–18) has put it: 'Political affiliation has once again become a determining criterion in appointments to top-level positions', with the tendency to view the bureaucracy 'as the instrument of the government *of the day* rather than of the government *of the state*'. Critics also suggest that the goal of the state organized along NPM lines 'is no longer to protect society from the market's demands but to protect the market from society's demands' (Daniel Cohen, quoted in Suleiman 2003: 16).

The quality of governance

Finally, let us take a look at the performance of the bureaucracy. Table 8.4 reports the World Bank's government effectiveness index for selected countries for the earliest and most recent years available. With regard to the developments outlined previously, 1996 is the year when most Western administrations had been affected by some NPM reforms, while they had already had a profound impact on the administrations of the pioneer countries—the US, the UK, and New Zealand. As noted earlier in 'Problems of bureaucracy', the performance of bureaucracies is difficult to measure, and this index is the most ambitious attempt to do so to date. It draws on a wealth of cross-country data, mostly measures of the perceptions of the clients of government agencies and professional observers, such as rating agencies. Governance is conceptualized as an overall measure of the quality of the public services and civil service, the degree of the civil service's independence from political pressure, the quality of policy formulation and implementation, and the credibility of the government's commitment to such policies. The data employed and the index construction is carefully documented in the paper cited at the bottom of Table 8.4 and a number of earlier papers that are available on the World Bank's webpage.

Table 8.4 shows that the quality of governance differs considerably between regions and countries

Table 8.4 Government effectiveness index (1996–2018)

	1996	2005	2014	2017
Non-European democracies				
Australia	1.80	1.75	1.61	1.54
Canada	1.74	1.89	1.76	1.85
India	−0.11	−0.11	−0.21	0.09
Israel	0.77	1.04	1.21	1.39
Japan	0.91	1.29	1.81	1.62
New Zealand	1.77	1.75	1.93	1.77
US	1.52	1.54	1.47	1.55
Western Europe				
Austria	1.73	1.68	1.57	1.46
Belgium	1.71	1.71	1.38	1.18
Denmark	1.76	2.12	1.82	1.80
Finland	1.72	2.13	2.00	1.94
France	1.25	1.67	1.40	1.35
Germany	1.72	1.51	1.73	1.72
Iceland	1.86	1.97	1.49	1.45
Ireland	1.67	1.74	1.60	1.29
Italy	0.84	0.56	0.37	0.50
Luxembourg	1.96	1.78	1.65	1.68
Netherlands	1.94	1.94	1.82	1.85
Norway	1.95	1.86	1.83	1.98
Portugal	1.27	1.06	0.99	1.33
Spain	1.62	1.51	1.16	1.03
Sweden	1.92	1.89	1.80	1.84
Switzerland	1.76	1.85	2.11	2.06
UK	1.88	1.77	1.63	1.41
Post-Soviet systems				
Bulgaria	−0.04	0.18	0.08	0.26
Czech Republic	0.62	0.93	1.02	1.02
Estonia	0.61	0.96	1.02	1.12
Hungary	0.86	0.77	0.53	0.51
Latvia	0.49	0.57	0.96	0.90
Lithuania	0.53	0.78	0.98	0.98
Poland	0.68	0.48	0.83	0.63
Romania	-0.29	-0.31	-0.03	-0.17
Russia	-0.45	-0.50	-0.11	-0.08
Slovak Republic	0.46	0.93	0.88	0.81
Slovenia	0.89	0.89	1.01	1.17
Latin America				
Argentina	0.17	−0.12	−0.16	0.16
Brazil	−0.14	−0.10	−0.14	−0.29
Chile	1.34	1.24	1.16	0.85
Mexico	0.23	0.07	0.20	−0.03

Note: The World Bank's government effectiveness index, Kaufmann et al. (2006), includes measures of the quality of the public services and civil service, the degree of the civil service's independence from political pressure, the quality of policy formulation and implementation, and the credibility of the government's commitment to such policies. The mean of 213 countries is zero, and virtually all scores lie between −2.5 and 2.5. Higher scores indicate better outcomes.

Source: http://www.data.worldbank.org/data-catalog/worldwide-governance-indicators.

(higher scores indicate better outcomes). Given that the more recent data include more variables, not too much should be made out of small changes in the absolute values. What is more reliable is the relative placement of countries. Comparing the regions, we see that the Anglo-Saxon settler democracies and the countries of Western Europe can pride themselves on good governance, while the other established democracies (Israel, Japan, and India), the more recent democracies in Latin American, and the Central and East European post-Soviet systems are clearly lagging behind. In Western Europe, we observe a clear North–South decline of good governance. In Latin America, Chile, the country with the longest democratic tradition, also provides the best governance. The positive development in the post-Soviet states is that the quality of governance has improved considerably over the past decade.

Notwithstanding the care and effort that went into this index, it constitutes a beginning rather than an end of conceptual work and actual measurement (Rothstein 2011). The quality of governance can be seen as part and parcel of a much broader theme: the quality of government in the sense of the state's impartial provision of essential services that crucially influence the life chances of citizens.

KEY POINTS

- A government's capacity to implement its decisions depends critically on the ability and willingness of bureaucrats and the structures and processes of the public administration.

- Classic bureaucracy aims to make the civil service a neutral instrument. In practice, the inclusion of individual political preferences by bureaucrats can lead to agency loss; bureaucratic career concerns foster the growth of the state.

- The establishment of spoils systems and New Public Management methods can provide governments with greater grip on their bureaucrats. Yet both methods have their own problems.

Conclusion

Governments are key institutions in democratic states. Who occupies government normally determines the direction a country will take. This is particularly true where cohesive political parties allow the fusion of executive and legislative power. This chapter has been concerned with three important and interrelated questions: (i) how government decisions are made; (ii) how autonomous governments are from the providers of key resources; and (iii) what capacities governments have to rule the country.

Government decision-making depends on basic regime characteristics, but within such confines can take different forms such as cabinet, prime ministerial, and ministerial government under parliamentarism. The modes of government change with functional requirements and according to the prevailing political conditions (e.g. single-party vs coalition government).

Government autonomy vis-à-vis the parties that bring governments to office is controversial from a normative point of view. The party government model denies autonomy, while constitutional theory prescribes it. Empirically, government autonomy from parties has enormously increased. Part and parcel of that process is the tendency towards presidentialization—the vesting of more power in the chief executive.

Government capacities are high in situations of unified or majority single-party government, and they are considerably constrained in situations of divided or minority government and when the government is a coalition. Institutional rules can partly compensate for the lack of party support. Governments depend critically on support from their bureaucracies. The classic model of a neutral bureaucracy, which serves any government equally well, has come under attack from two sides: one focuses on the self-interest of bureaucrats, and one denies the bureaucracy's neutrality or demands its 'democratization' so that politicians have an instrument in tune with their preferences.

QUESTIONS

Knowledge-based

1. Which different meanings does the term 'government' carry?

2. What distinguishes prime ministerial government from cabinet government?

3. What distinguishes divided and unified government?

4. What are spoils systems and which forms exist?

5. What distinguishes classic bureaucracy from New Public Management bureaucracy?

Critical thinking

1. How can parties provide party government?

2. Why can minority governments survive?

3. What are the problems of coalition governance?

4. What are the problems of bureaucracy?

5. What is the presidentialization of politics?

FURTHER READING

Important texts on government not cited in this chapter

Edwards, G. C. and Howell, W. C. (eds) (2011) *The Oxford Handbook of the American Presidency* (Oxford: Oxford University Press).

Hayward, J. and Wright, V. (2002) *Governing from the Centre: Core Executive Coordination in France* (Oxford: Oxford University Press).

Peters, B. G., Rhodes, R. A. W., and Wright, V. (eds) (2000) *Administering the Summit: Administration of the Core Executive in Developed Countries* (Basingstoke: Macmillan).

Rhodes, R. A. W., Wanna, J., and Weller, P. (2009) *Comparing Westminster* (Oxford: Oxford University Press).

Rose, R. (2001) *The Prime Minister in a Shrinking World* (Cambridge: Polity Press).

Rose, R. and Suleiman, E. N. (eds) (1980) *Presidents and Prime Ministers* (Washington, DC: American Enterprise Institute).

Rothstein, B. (2011) *The Quality of Government: Corruption, Social Trust, and Inequality in International Perspective* (Chicago, IL: University of Chicago Press).

Scartascini, C., Stein, E., and Tommasi, M. (eds) (2010) *How Democracy Works* (New York: Inter-American Development Bank).

ENDNOTE

1. Another meaning of 'government' refers to the political science sub-discipline that takes its name from the subject of its study, i.e. government in its broadest meaning. Thus, this chapter is a contribution to 'comparative government'.

Visit the Online Resources that accompany this book for additional material, including country profiles, comparative data sets, flashcard glossaries, and web directory.

www.oup.com/he/caramani5e

9

Constitutions, rights, and judicial power

Alec Stone Sweet

Reader's guide

This chapter examines the evolution of systems of constitutional justice since 1787. After introducing and defining key terms, it surveys different kinds of constitutions, rights, models of constitutional review, and the main precepts of 'the new constitutionalism'. The chapter then presents a simple theory of delegation and judicial power, focusing on why political elites would delegate power to constitutional judges, and how to measure the extent of power, or discretion, delegated. The evolution of constitutional forms is then presented. Beginning in the 1980s, the 'new constitutionalism' took off, and today has no rival as a model of democratic state legitimacy. As constitutional rights and review has diffused around the world, so has the capacity of constitutional judges to influence, and sometimes determine, policy outcomes.

Introduction

This chapter provides an overview of the emergence, diffusion, and political impact of systems of constitutional justice. By *system of constitutional justice*, I mean the institutions and procedures, established by a constitution, for the judicial (third-party) protection of fundamental rights. In 1787, when the fully codified, written constitution was just emerging as a form, no such system existed anywhere in the world.

At the dawn of the twenty-first century, one finds that virtually all new written constitutions include a charter of rights that is enforceable by a constitutional or supreme court, even against legislation. With very few exceptions, legislative sovereignty has formally disappeared. The 'new constitutionalism' killed it, paradoxically perhaps, in the name of democracy.

The salience to comparative politics of constitutions and rights exploded in the 1990s, in waves of **democratization** that swept away authoritarian and one-party regimes in Central and Eastern Europe, the Balkans, Central and South America, Africa, and Asia. As we will see, virtually all new constitutions written since 1985 contain a charter of rights and a judicial mode of protecting those rights. That is, they established new systems of constitutional justice. Law and courts have also become a significant component of international politics (Alter 2014) led by the courts of the European Union, the European and Inter-American Conventions on Human Rights, and the World Trade Organization (WTO) (Stone Sweet and Brunell 2013). Virtually non-existent in 1980, comparative judicial politics is a growing and important field today.

The chapter proceeds as follows. The first section, 'Key concepts and definitions' presents basic concepts and defines key terms. In the next section, Delegation and judicial power', I discuss the institutional determinants of judicial power within any system of constitutional justice. The third section, 'The evolution of contributional review', charts the diffusion of institutional forms associated with contemporary constitutionalism—the written constitution, the charter of rights, and constitutional **judicial review**—from 1787 to the present. In the fourth section, , 'Effectiveness', I discuss some of the empirical findings of those who have studied the impact of rights adjudication on the greater political system, and the final section concludes.

Key concepts and definitions

There is no consensus on how to define concepts such as 'constitution', 'constitutionalism', and 'rights'. My aim is to provide useful definitions of these and other terms to readers of this book (students of comparative politics), not to fix authoritative meanings. Students should note the discussion of alternative views and debate them; and they should remember that, in this field at least, virtually any attempt to carefully define concepts will be controversial.

Let's start with the word 'constitution'. I prefer a broad, generic definition: a constitution is a body of hierarchically superior, meta-norms, those higher-order legal rules, principles, and procedures that specify how all other legal norms are to be produced, applied, enforced, interpreted, and changed. Meta-norms *constitute* political systems, as written constitutions do for the modern **nation-state**. In England (later the UK), whose constitution has evolved over centuries and remains uncodified, well-understood principles and conventions provide a simplified representation, or model, of how the political system is expected to function.

In today's world, written constitutions are the ultimate, formal source of state authority: they establish governmental institutions (legislatures, executives, courts), and grant them the power to make, apply, enforce, and interpret laws. Constitutions tell us how lower-order legal norms are to be made, especially statutes. They lay down legislative procedures; and they tell us how legislative authority is constituted (through elections, for example), and what the legislature can do (through enumerating powers). Constitutions also indicate how the various institutions are expected, if only ideally, to interact with one another (through 'separation-of-powers' doctrines). Most new constitutions written over the past sixty years also contain a charter of *rights*, which are, by definition, substantive constraints on the law-making of state officials. And most also established a supreme or constitutional court to protect these rights against unlawful governmental incursion.

I use 'constitutionalism' in two ways. While the concept of a constitution is reasonably straightforward, 'constitutionalism' is more contested. We use the term primarily to denote the commitment, on the part of any given political community, to work within the rules established by the constitution. The commitment to respect and to live under a constitution, and the degree to which public officials, political parties, interest groups, and other elites mobilize to undermine or destroy it, varies cross-nationally, and within any polity over time.

A second way to conceptualize constitutionalism is as a cultural or ideological construct, such that one can speak of 'Canadian' or 'Taiwanese' constitutionalism, for example. 'Constitutionalism is the set of beliefs associated with constitutional practice', Neil Walker (1996: 267) suggests, embodying the fundamental notions of how 'we', in 'our' political system organize the state (federal or unitary), constitute our government (centralization or checks and balances), provide for representation and participation (elections and referenda), protect minorities and fundamental freedoms (rights and judicial review), promote equality (taxation and social welfare regimes), and so on. This type of 'constitutionalism' will vary in different places, not only in its content, but in its strength and coherence. A robust constitutionalism expresses the self-understanding of a political community— its values, aspirations, and idealized essence—and provides a wellspring of legitimizing resources for the body politic, helping it to evolve as circumstances change (Rosenfeld 2010). In contrast, a weak constitutionalism fails to represent collective identity, and times of crisis will challenge the legitimacy of the constitutional order.

It is worth noting other definitions. For the political scientist, Carl Friedrich (1950: 25–8, 123), constitutionalism refers to 'limited government', situations wherein the constitution 'effectively restrains' those who control the coercive instruments of the state. Michel Rosenfeld (1994: 3) notes that 'there appears to be no accepted definition of constitutionalism', and then states that 'modern constitutionalism requires imposing limits on the powers of government, adherence to the rule of law, and the protection of fundamental rights'. We will return to the 'limited government' formulation shortly, but for now it is enough to note that constitutions do not just limit state power, they constitute and enable it.

Constitutional forms and the 'new constitutionalism'

Most notions of constitutionalism emphasize the good and proper functions that one expects a constitution to perform: to enable self-governance, to constrain the abusive capacities of the state, to embody political ideals, and to express and maintain collective identity within democratic arrangements over time. I define a constitution as a body of meta-norms, those legal rules and principles that tell us how all other lower-order legal norms are to be produced, applied, and interpreted. Where we see meta-norms, we observe a constitution. Constitutionalism refers to the commitment of a polity to govern itself in conformity with the meta-norms, but this commitment may be absent in some places, at some times. A constitution can be 'bad' for democracy. Meta-norms could establish dictatorship and deny the People any say in their own governance; and a polity's 'constitutionalism' could help to legitimize authoritarianism. In world history, there are far more examples of constitutional regimes that have failed to sustain limited government and participatory democracy than there are examples of success.

Constitutions vary in their capacity to constrain the authority of those who make and enforce the laws. Consider the following simple typology of constitutional forms that have existed since 1789, the year in which the first fully codified constitution, of the US[1] entered into force.

Type 1: the absolutist constitution

In this model, the authority to produce and change legal norms, including the constitution, is centralized and absolute. The controlling meta-norm is the fact that the rulers are 'above the law'. In such systems, the meta-norms reflect, rather than restrict, the absolute power of those who govern. The type 1 constitution typically rejects popular **sovereignty**, rights, and separation of powers. The archetype of the type 1 constitution in Europe is the French Charter of 1814, which other monarchies, especially in the Germanic regions, widely imitated. In the twentieth century, many constitutions read as if they were full-scale constitutional democracies, but in fact functioned as single-party or one-man dictatorships. Examples include the USSR and many Central European states under Communist Party control, and situations resulting after military coups in Asia, Africa, and Central and South America. Although less prevalent in recent decades, there have been a few constitutions since 1980 that expressly enshrined one-person or one-party rule (Sri Lanka, Togo, and Niger, among others).

Type 2: the legislative supremacy constitution

In this form, the constitution provides for a set of governmental institutions and elections to the legislature; elections legitimize legislative authority, and legislative majorities legitimize statutes. The classic parliamentary sovereignty model is defined by three basic meta-norms. First, the constitution is not *entrenched*; that is, there are no special, non-legislative procedures for revising it. No parliamentary act can bind a future parliament, and parliament can revise the constitution through a majority vote (a rule of change). To take a dramatic example, by way of an ordinary statute, the British House of Commons abolished the power of the House of Lords to veto legislative proposals in 1911, removing the last important constraint on the Commons' primacy. Second, any legal norm that conflicts with parliamentary legislation is itself invalid (a criterion of validity). Judicial rulings are subject to this rule, hence the prohibition of judicial review of statute (a rule of adjudication). In the case of a conflict between two statutory provisions, the one adopted later in time trumps, under the doctrine of implied repeal (a rule of change that determines validity). Third, the constitution contains no body of substantive constraints on legislative powers. Public liberties, whether granted by the legislature through statutes or the courts through case law, can be rescinded by a legislative act. The French Third (1875–1940) and Fourth (1946–1958) Republics, and the UK, until recently, are relatively pure examples of legislative sovereignty regimes.

Type 3: the higher law constitution

Both models 2 and 3 organize representative, democratic governance: meta-norms establish (or recognize) the authority of governmental institutions, and then link these arrangements to the People, via elections and other procedures. The higher law constitution provides for a system of constitutional justice: it adds a charter of rights that binds the legislature, and establishes an independent, judicial means of enforcing those rights. Further, the constitution is entrenched: explicit rules of change govern the amendment of the constitutional text, through procedures that, typically, are more onerous than those in place for legislating. Thus, in contrast to models 1 and 2, the type 3 constitution prioritizes rights protection, rejects legislative sovereignty, and makes overriding (through constitutional amendment) the constitutional rulings of high courts difficult.

The type 1 constitution no longer exists as a viable form in the world today, though constitutionalism, as I have defined it, may be largely absent in many authoritarian regimes that otherwise possess a type 3 constitution. These are the so-called 'sham constitutions' (Law and Versteeg 2013), which have little or no actual influence on politics. With a polite bow to the British and the French for their historic contributions, and a nod to an important holdout—Australia— we can declare the classic form of the type 2 model extinct, partly replaced by the 'new commonwealth model', discussed below. In contrast, the domination of the type 3 form is today nearly complete. Type 3 constitutions vary significantly; it is a fact that no two are identical. Nonetheless, one of the most remarkable developments in global politics over the past fifty years has been the broad convergence on the view that only type 3 constitutions are considered to be 'good' constitutions. This convergence has been called the 'new constitutionalism' (Shapiro and Stone Sweet 1994).

The precepts of this 'new constitutionalism' are as follows: (i) institutions of the state are established by, and derive their authority exclusively from, a written constitution; (ii) this constitution assigns ultimate power to the People by way of elections or referenda; (iii) the use of public authority, including legislative authority, is lawful only insofar as it conforms with the constitutional law; (iv) the constitution provides for a catalogue of rights, and a system of constitutional justice to defend those rights; and (v) the constitution itself specifies how it may be revised.

The new constitutionalism has also significantly infected the remaining type 2 systems. While rejecting proposals to establish a charter of rights at the constitutional level, New Zealand (1990) and the United Kingdom (1998) nonetheless adopted statutes on human rights that are special in that they are not subject to implied repeal. Under the 1998 Human Rights Act (incorporating the European Convention on Human Rights), British high courts are empowered (i) to interpret statutes (and all other public acts), as far as possible, in conformity with rights; and (ii) to declare statutory provisions' incompatibility with rights, when a rights-conforming interpretation is impossible. Since Parliament is not bound by such a declaration, legislative sovereignty remains formally intact. The New Zealand courts, too, are under a duty to interpret statutes in rights-conforming ways, but Parliament has the 'last word'. In type 3 systems, constitutional judges typically have the 'last word' on constitutionality, subject only to override through constitutional amendment. In the so-called 'Commonwealth model' (Gardbaum 2013), the legislature can ignore (Great Britain, New Zealand) or legislatively set aside (Canada, a type 3 system) judicial decisions on rights (Hiebert 2011). Australia is now actively debating whether to adopt a statutory bill of rights, as the federated Australian state of Victoria did in 2006.

Rights

Constitutions establish the procedures to be followed for producing various forms of law. These are *procedural* constraints: if the procedure is not followed, then the legal norm produced (statute, administrative determination, judicial decision) is not constitutionally valid. Rights are a different type of meta-norm, in that they impose *substantive* constraints on the exercise of public authority. When state officials make, interpret, and enforce law, they must respect rights, or their acts may be invalidated, as law.

It is not enough to define rights simply as 'substantive constraints on law-making'. The structural properties of rights vary along a number of dimensions, two of which deserve special attention. The first concerns the hierarchical relationship between a rights provision, on the one hand, and the purposes for which public authority is exercised, on the other. A right might be conceived as more or less absolute: when an act of government violates the right, that act is unconstitutional. The right, being hierarchically superior, trumps any norm in conflict with it. Rights might also be conceived as relative values, to be *balanced* against other constitutional values, including the government's various duties to act in the public interest (Stone Sweet and Mathews 2019). Because the constitution grants powers to government to do certain things—to secure the country's defence, regulate the economy, and provide social security and welfare assistance, for example—these purposes rise to constitutional status, alongside rights. *Balancing* is a basic technique that judges use to resolve tensions between a right and a state purpose, once judges have determined that a right is not absolute. The balancing judge weighs the marginal cost of infringement of the right against the marginal social benefits of the law in question, and then decides which value will prevail, in light of the facts of the case. When the state decides to build a new airport on existing farmland, for example, the property rights of the farmers whose land is to be expropriated may be outweighed by the 'public' or 'general' interest in the project.

The second dimension of variance concerns the nature of the obligation imposed on public authority by rights provisions. A right may impose a *negative* obligation on the state: (i) the state may not infringe upon the right (an absolute version of rights); or (ii) the state may not infringe upon the right more than is necessary to achieve a legitimate public purpose (a balancing version of rights). In some countries, rights provisions may impose duties on the part of government, for example, to take measures to facilitate the enjoyment of a particular right (Fredman 2008). Or a right might entitle citizens to certain benefits—adequate health care, employment, and housing, for example. One classic typology categorizes rights as *negative* or *positive*: the former constrains government *not* to do certain things; the latter encourages (or requires) government to act to accomplish certain goals. India, South Africa, and Colombia are examples of legal systems whose high courts routinely supervise if and how well the government performs their duties under the dictates of positive rights. Older constitutions rarely contain positive rights; newer constitutions almost always do.

Constitutional review

Once a polity commits to govern itself under a type 3 constitution, the problem of how to guarantee the constitution's normative supremacy arises. The type 3 constitution solves this problem by establishing a system of 'constitutional review': a 'judicialized' (third-party) mechanism for assessing the constitutional legality of all other legal norms. Two modes of constitutional review are dominant in the world today. The first is called 'judicial review', the archetype of which is found in the US. American review is 'judicial' in that it is performed by the judiciary, in the course of resolving litigation. In the second mode, which has its origins in Austria and Germany but has spread to Latin America, Africa, and Asia, the powers of constitutional review are exercised by a special court—a constitutional court—while the ordinary (non-constitutional) courts are denied the

authority to void legal norms, like statutes, when they conflict with the constitution.

At this point, we confront radically different notions of separation of powers, which are constitutional conceptions of how the various state institutions, or branches of government, should function and interact with one another. Simplifying, in judicial review systems, the courts are understood to comprise a separate but co-equal branch of government, within a system of 'checks and balances'. The duty of US courts (their 'judicial function') is to resolve legal disputes: 'cases or controversies' that arise under 'the laws of the US'. The Constitution is one of 'the laws'. If litigants can plead the constitutional law before the courts, American judges will need to possess the power of judicial review in order to resolve the dispute—that is, in order to do their jobs. Such is the logic of *Marbury* v. *Madison* (1803), the Supreme Court decision that established constitutional review authority in the US (*Marbury* v. *Madison*. 5 US 137, 1803). The 'American model' of judicial review is also called the 'decentralized model', since review powers are held by all courts, not just the Supreme Court.

As we will soon see, giving review powers to all courts is not as popular as concentrating review authority in a specialized jurisdiction (Stone Sweet 2012). Constitutional courts are favoured in countries where *judicial* review has traditionally been prohibited. Those who wrote new constitutions wished to enable rights protection while, at the same time, preserving legislative sovereignty as much as possible. In such polities (most of Europe and Latin America, for example), separation of powers doctrines take great pains to distinguish the 'political function' (to legislate, to make law) from the 'judicial function' (to resolve legal disputes according to legislation). The American checks and balances system appears to create a 'confusion of powers', since it permits the courts to participate in the work of the legislature. Because this system or review emerged in Europe and later spread globally, it is often called the 'European' or the 'centralized model'. The main features of these two models are contrasted in Boxes 9.1 and 9.2.

We can break down the 'centralized model' of constitutional review into four constituent components. First, constitutional courts enjoy exclusive and final constitutional jurisdiction. Constitutional judges alone may invalidate a law or an act of public authority as unconstitutional, while the 'ordinary' courts (i.e. the judiciary—the non-constitutional courts) remain prohibited from doing so. In the US, review authority inheres in judicial power, and thus all judges possess it. Second, constitutional courts only settle constitutional disputes. In contrast, the

> 📣 **FOR AND AGAINST 9.1**
>
> ## The American vs the European models of judicial review
>
> | American judicial review | European constitutional review |
> | --- | --- |
> | Constitutional judicial review authority is *decentralized*: all judges possess the power to void or refuse to apply a statute on the grounds that it violates the constitution law. | Review authority is *centralized*: only the constitutional court may annul a statute as unconstitutional. Judicial review of statute is prohibited. |
> | The Supreme Court is a court of 'general jurisdiction': it is the highest court of appeal in the legal order, for all issues of law, not just constitutional issues. | The Constitutional Court's jurisdiction is restricted to resolving constitutional disputes. The ordinary courts handle civil suits and criminal matters. |
> | Judicial review is defensible under prevailing separation of powers doctrines to the extent that it is 'case or controversy' review. Judges possess review authority because their legal duty is to resolve legal 'cases', some of which will have a constitutional dimension. | Review powers are defensible under separation of powers doctrines to the extent that it is not exercised by the judiciary, but by a specialized 'constitutional' organ, the constitutional court. |
> | Judicial review is understood to be 'concrete', in that it is exercised pursuant to ordinary litigation. Abstract review decisions look suspiciously like 'advisory opinions', which are prohibited under US separation of powers. | Constitutional review is typically 'abstract': the review court does not resolve 'concrete cases' between two litigating parties, but answers constitutional questions referred to it by judges or elected officials. Judicial review looks like a 'confusion of powers', since the judges participate in the legislative function. |

US Supreme Court is the highest court of appeal for almost all disputes about rights in the American legal order. Constitutional courts do not preside over litigation, which remains the function of the ordinary judges. Instead, they answer *constitutional questions* referred to them. Third, constitutional courts have links with, but are formally detached from, the judiciary and legislature. They occupy their own 'constitutional' space, a space neither clearly 'judicial' nor 'political'. Fourth, some constitutional courts are empowered to review legislation before it has been enforced; that is, before it has actually affected any person negatively, as a means of eliminating unconstitutional legislation and practices *before* they can do harm. Thus, in the centralized model of review, the judges that staff the ordinary courts remain bound by the supremacy of statute, while constitutional judges are charged with preserving the supremacy of the constitution.

Modes of review: abstract and concrete

The two models of review differ with respect to the pathways through which cases come to the judges. In the US, rights review is activated when a litigant pleads a right before a judge—any judge. In countries with constitutional courts, there are three main procedures that activate review, although not all constitutions establish all three procedures.

The first is called **abstract review**. Abstract review is the pre-enforcement review of statutes. Some systems enable the statute to be reviewed before it enters into force (a priori review), others after promulgation but before application (a posteriori review). Abstract review is also called 'preventive review', since its purpose is to filter out unconstitutional laws before they can harm anyone. Typically, executives, parliamentary minorities, and regions or federated entities in federal states, possess the power to refer laws to the court.

The second mode is called **concrete review**, which is initiated by the judiciary in the course of litigation in the courts. Ordinary judges activate review by sending a constitutional question—is a given law, legal rule, judicial decision, or administrative act constitutional?—to the constitutional court. The general rule is that a presiding judge will go to the constitutional court if two conditions are met: (i) that the constitutional question is material to litigation at bar (who wins or loses will depend on the answer to the question); and (ii) there is reasonable doubt in the judge's mind about the constitutionality of the act or rule in question. Referrals suspend proceedings pending a review by the constitutional court. Once rendered, the constitutional court's judgment is sent back to the referring judge, who then decides the case on the basis of the ruling. In such systems, ordinary judges are not permitted to determine the constitutionality of statutes on their own. Instead, aided by private litigants, they help to detect unconstitutional laws and send them to the constitutional court for review.

The third procedure—the 'constitutional complaint'—goes by a variety of designations, including the *amparo* throughout Latin America (Brewer-Carias 2014). It brings individuals into the mix. Individuals or an ombudsman are authorized to appeal directly to the constitutional court when they believe that their rights have been violated.

Abstract review is 'abstract' because the review of legislation takes place in the absence of litigation, in American parlance, in the absence of a concrete 'case or controversy'. Concrete review is 'concrete' because the review of legislation, or other public acts, constitutes a stage in ongoing litigation in the ordinary courts. In individual complaints, a private individual alleges the violation of a constitutional right by a public act or governmental official, and requests redress from the court for this violation. In American judicial review, all review is (at least formally) 'concrete', in that it is embedded in a concrete 'case'.

To summarize, this section defines and discusses three basic concepts, that of the *constitution*, *rights*, and *constitutional review*, and of various modes of review. Each of these is a constituent component of any 'system of constitutional justice', whose diffusion and impact is the topic of the rest of the chapter.

KEY POINTS

- A *constitution* is a body of legal norms—*meta-norms*—that governs the production and application of all other legal norms. *Constitutionalism* refers to a polity's commitment to abide by the constitution, and to the main principles found in any polity's constitution.

- A *system of constitutional justice* is a central component of the *type 3 constitution* and of *the new constitutionalism*. Such systems combine a written, entrenched constitutional text, *rights*, and a judicial mechanism—*constitutional review*—for the protection of rights.

- There are two main models of constitutional review today: the *American model* of diffuse judicial review, and the *European model* of concentrated review performed by a constitutional court. The models rest on different notions of *separation of powers*. American judicial review is expected to be fundamentally *concrete*, whereas European constitutional review is often *abstract*.

Delegation and judicial power

The power of constitutional judges is *delegated* power (Thatcher and Stone Sweet 2002): a written constitution expressly confers upon the judges review authority and indicates how it may be used. In this section, I respond to a basic question: why would political elites, those who draft a constitution and will live under it, choose to grant review authority to constitutional judges—that is, why should they choose to constrain themselves? I then then discuss some of the consequences of this choice from the perspective of delegation theory, focusing on issues of agency and control. In doing so, I respond to a second question: to what extent can we expect political elites to remain 'in charge' of the evolution of the polity after delegating review powers?

The constitution as incomplete contract

People contract with each other in order to achieve benefits that they could not expect to realize on their own. Modern democratic constitutions can be conceived as contracts. They are negotiated by political elites—typically as representatives of political parties or associations—who seek to constitute a new political system to replace the old order. In establishing a democracy, each contracting party knows that it will be competing with others for political power, through elections. Constitutional contracting also yields another crucial benefit: to constrain one's opponents when they are in power (Stone Sweet 2000: ch. 2; Ginsburg 2003: ch. 2). The constitution thus produces two important common goods for the parties, in the form of a set of enabling institutions and a set of constraints.

Constitutional contracting, like all contracting, generates a demand for third-party dispute resolution and enforcement. Indeed, the social logic of contracts provides a logic of courts, more generally. The move to constitutional review is one way to deal with commitment problems associated with constitutional contracting, especially when it comes to protecting rights.

Take the following simplified scenario which has, in fact, occurred in many places since 1945. Once the contracting parties (political elites) decide to include a charter of rights in their constitution, not least to constrain their future opponents when the latter are in power, they face two tough problems. First, they disagree about the nature and content of rights, which threatens to paralyse the drafting process. The left-wing parties favour positive social rights, and limits on the rights to property. The right-wing parties prefer to privilege negative rights, and do not want strong property rights. They compromise, drafting an extensive charter of rights that (i) lists most of the rights that each side wants; (ii) implies that no right is absolute

> ↘ **ZOOM-IN 9.2**

Modes of constitutional review

The American model and judicial review

A legal 'case'—defined as a legal dispute brought to a court as litigation between two parties who have opposed interests—activates review once one of the parties pleads the constitution, such as a right. Any court can, at the behest of either party, void a law as unconstitutional if that court determines that the statute violates the constitution.

The European model and abstract review

Abstract review is initiated when elected officials—typically the parliamentary opposition, the executive, or the government of a regional of federated state—refer a law for review after the law has been adopted by the legislature, but before it has been enforced. This mode of review is called 'abstract' because it proceeds in the absence of a concrete judicial case, since the law has yet to be applied. The review court compares the constitutional text and the statute, in the abstract, to determine whether the latter conforms to the former. Abstract review is also called 'preventive review', since it allows the system to filter out unconstitutional laws before they can harm people.

The European model and concrete review

Concrete review is initiated when an ordinary judge, presiding over litigation in the courts, refers a constitutional question—for example, is law X, which is normally applicable to the dispute at bar, unconstitutional?—that the constitutional court must answer. The referring judge then resolves the dispute with reference to the constitutional court's ruling. This mode of review is called 'concrete', since it is related to a concrete case already underway in the ordinary courts. In comparison with American judicial review, however, concrete review still looks more 'abstract', in that the constitutional court does not preside over, or settle the case, which remains the responsibility of the referring judge.

The European model and the constitutional complaint

Individuals may activate the constitutional court directly by sending to the judges a constitutional complaint, which alleges that their rights have been violated by a public authority, after judicial remedies have been exhausted or are not available. Most constitutional complaints are, in effect, appeals of judicial decisions. In many Latin America countries, a version of this procedure—called an *amparo*—exists.

or more important than another; and (iii) is vague about how any future conflict between two rights, or a right and a legitimate governmental purpose, will be resolved. Second, they have to decide how rights will be enforced. Delegating rights review authority to a constitutional court helps them deal with both problems. In agreeing to allow constitutional judges to decide how rights will be interpreted and enforced, they are able to move forward.

In this account, courts are (at least partly) an institutional response to the fact that most contracts are 'incomplete', and the new constitution, too, is an incomplete contract. Contracts can be said to be 'incomplete' to the extent that there exists meaningful uncertainty as to the precise nature of the commitments made (the rights and obligations of the parties under the contract), over time. Due to the impossibility of negotiating specific rules for all possible contingencies, and given that, as time passes, conditions will change and the interests of the parties to the agreement will evolve, all contracts are incomplete in some significant way.[2]

Type 3 constitutions—complex instruments of governance designed to last indefinitely, if not forever—are paradigmatic examples of incomplete

bargains. Much is left general, even ill-defined and vague, as in the case of rights. Generalities and vagueness may facilitate agreement at the bargaining stage. But vagueness, by definition, is legal uncertainty, and legal uncertainty threatens to undermine the reason for contracting in the first place. The establishment of constitutional review is an institutional response to the incomplete contract—that is, to the problems of uncertainty and enforcement. Each party to it has an interest in seeing that the other parties obey their obligations when they are in power, and that they will be punished for non-compliance. As important, judicial review functions to clarify the meaning of the constitution over time, and to adapt it to changing circumstances.

Principals, agents, trustees

Across the social sciences, as well as in the law and economics tradition, scholars use the 'Principal–Agent' [P–A] framework to depict or model authority relations constituted by delegation (see Chapter 7 'Legislatures'). The framework focuses on the relationship between those who delegate, who are called 'Principals', and those to whom power is delegated, called 'Agents'. Assume that the Principals are those who govern a political system, and that they will create an Agent, and give to the Agent discretionary powers to make law, when they believe that doing so will help them govern more efficiently and effectively.

Consider the following simple P–A model of a type 2 system. Given the rules of legislative sovereignty, the courts are Agents of their Principal—the elected Parliament, which is itself an Agent of the electorate. In such a regime, the judges' task is to enforce statutory provisions, and review of the lawfulness of statutes is prohibited. In order to perform their task properly, judges will need discretion powers to interpret legislation. But because interpretation is itself a form of law-making, the question of the Agent's fidelity to the Principal's preferences inevitably arises. We know that the more the law is litigated, the more judges will determine what parliament's law actually means, in practice. Yet, even in the face of extensive judicial law-making, the Principal remains in charge. Insofar as the legislator can identify judicial 'errors', it can correct them, since the decision rule governing override—a majority vote of the Parliament—facilitates the legislator's control. The decision rules governing the Principal's capacity to override the decisions of an Agent are crucial, but they are never the whole story. A parliament that is unable to muster a majority vote to override remains sovereign, as a formal matter, but its actual capacity to control the courts is in doubt.

The traditional P–A framework loses much of its relevance when it comes to systems of constitutional justice. It is more appropriate to apply a model of 'constitutional trusteeship' to situations wherein the founders of new constitutions confer expansive powers on a review court (Stone Sweet 2002). In systems of constitutional trusteeship, political elites—the political parties, the executive, members of parliament—are *never* Principals in their relationship to constitutional judges. Depending upon the relevant decision rules in place, these officials may seek to overturn constitutional decisions, or restrict the constitutional court's powers, but they can usually only do so by working to amend the constitution. Yet, as we have seen, the decision rules governing constitutional revision processes are typically more restrictive than those governing the revision of legislation; in many countries, amendment is a practical impossibility, especially when it comes to rights provisions.

Elected officials also typically perform some of the functions usually associated with Principals. Politicians can and do influence constitutional and supreme courts through appointments,[3] for example. Nonetheless, if the founders of new constitutions, establish (i) the primacy of rights; (ii) judicial review to defend rights; and (iii) restrictive procedures for constitutional amendment, they have shifted power away from themselves and to constitutional judges. As members of political parties, they will compete with each other in order to be in the position to govern, and, once in power, they legislate—but under the supervision of the constitutional judge.

The zone of discretion

The points just made can be formalized in terms of a theoretical *zone of discretion*—the strategic environment—in which any court operates (see Stone Sweet 2002, 2012). This zone is determined by (i) the sum of powers delegated to the court, and possessed by the court as a result of its own accreted rulemaking; minus (ii) the sum of control instruments available for use by non-judicial authorities to shape (constrain) or annul (reverse) outcomes that emerge as the result of the court's performance of its delegated tasks. In situations of trusteeship, wherein the agent exercises fiduciary responsibilities, the zone of discretion is, by definition, unusually large. In some places and in some domains, the discretionary powers enjoyed by constitutional courts are close to unlimited.

We can compare the zone of discretion across courts and countries. As we have just seen in 'The constitution as incomplete contract', the ordinary judge operating in a type 2 system of legislative sovereignty is an Agent whose zone of discretion is highly restricted. In Britain and New Zealand, where human rights statutes have been adopted, judges possess relatively more power, but legislators retain the 'last word'. In type 3 constitutions, high courts operate in much larger zones of discretion, as Trustees of the constitution. The authority to review the constitutionality of legislation is a vast power, which varies in particulars across systems. Where the 'centralized' model of protecting rights reigns supreme, the widest zone of discretion will be found in a country where (i) the constitutional court has been delegated abstract and concrete review powers, as well as the authority to process individual complaints; and where (ii) it is relatively difficult or impossible to amend rights provisions. Most powerful constitutional courts benefit from such a situation.

However conceptualized, it is relatively easy for students of comparative constitutional politics to, first, read new constitutions, and then construct an account of a review court's zone of discretion, and to compare zones across countries (see Box 9.3). Tushnet (2009), for example, proposes a classification scheme in which systems of review are either 'strong' or 'weak' when it comes to rights protection. An absence of judicial supremacy characterizes the weak form with the Commonwealth model (Gardbaum 2013); in Canada, as noted above in 'Key concepts and definitions', Parliament can re-enact a statute declared to be unconstitutional by the Court under the Charter of Rights.

Mapping a zone of discretion cannot tell us what constitutional courts will actually do with their powers, or how those who can change the constitution will react. The best we can do is to predict that, other things equal, constitutional judges operating in a relatively larger zone will come to exercise more influence over the evolution of the polity than those operating in relatively smaller zones. We should not expect our predictions to be accurate, since zone-of-discretion analysis on its own does not take into account many factors that will be important in particular contexts.

In situations in which elected officials would seek to weaken or destroy a system of justice, degrees of constitutional entrenchment matter a great deal. A case in point is the recent experience of Hungary. Beginning in the mid-1990s, the Hungarian court made itself one of the most powerful and effective constitutional courts in Central and Easter Europe, indeed, in the world. In 2011, however, a coalition government led by Prime Minister Viktor Orban obtained more than the two-thirds of the seats necessary to amend the constitution. In direct response to a series of constitutional court rulings, the coalition moved to override the court through amending the constitution, as well as to strip it—and the judiciary more generally—of some of its most important powers (Varju and Chronowski 2015). In 2015, a new political majority in Poland initiated a similar process of curbing the court, albeit without formally revising the constitution, which has provoked a deep crisis in Polish constitutionalism (Sadurski 2019). Thus, in constitutional regimes that locate the amending authority in the parliament, a court's zone of discretion could expand or contract depending upon election results.

Other logics

This section helps to explain the delegation of authority to constitutional judges, presupposing that the elites want, in good faith, to establish a system of constitutional justice. This theory does not work very well at explaining why, in today's world, autocratic rulers, too, write constitutions with rights and review, despite having no commitment to building an open, democratic competition for power with opponents. Nonetheless, authoritarian rulers too find uses for constitutions and courts (Ginsburg and Simpser 2014). Litigation may comprise a relatively cheap means of

monitoring what police and the lower echelons of the bureaucracy are doing on the ground; and courts can help rulers enforce new policy in the face of resistance, or remove challengers to their power altogether. Rulers also institute review in order to achieve a measure of international respectability, and to attract investment, never doubting their capacity to control their courts.

The evolution of constitutional review

In 1789, no system of constitutional justice existed anywhere on earth. After 1950, 'the new constitutionalism' emerged and then, in the 1990s, exploded into prominence. Between 1789 and 1950, the institutional materials that would solidify into the current 'models' of review were beginning to take shape, in the US, France, Austria-Germany, and Scandinavia. I will briefly examine each of these cases in turn.

1789–1950

In the Americas, the Federal Constitution of the US (1787) replaced the Articles of Confederation (1781), one of the first written constitutions of any modern nation-state. The new constitution established a Supreme Court and the judiciary as a separate branch of government, but the document neither contained a charter of rights nor expressly provided for the judicial review of statutes. The Court's main purpose was to manage federalism, in particular, to secure national supremacy with regard to interstate commerce and finance. In 1791, the Bill of Rights was added to the text, as amendments, and constitutional review was added in 1803 through the *Marbury* decision. Only in the 1880s did rights review begin to emerge. In its most important decisions during this period, the Court defended the property rights of merchants and firms against state laws designed to regulate their commercial activities. During the World War I period, the Court began to deal with civil and political rights, but it actually did very little to protect them. In 1937, the Court abandoned its opposition to market regulation of economic rights, after successive elections had cemented the power of New Deal Democrats, and in the face of President Roosevelt's threat to 'pack the Court'.

By the end of World War II, it would have been difficult to argue that constitutional experience in the US provided a respectable example of an effective 'system of constitutional justice', at least by today's standards. The Constitution, after all, had formally

↘ **ZOOM-IN 9.3**

The structural determinants of judicial power

The zone of discretion

The zone of discretion is a theoretical understanding of the strategic environment in which any court operates. The size of the zone is determined by (i) the sum of powers delegated to the court, and possessed by the court as a result of its past rulings; minus (ii) the sum of control instruments available to overrule or otherwise constrain the court by, for example, political elites who do not like the court's decisions. The zone varies across countries, and it will vary across time in the same country, depending upon how the court interprets the constitution and its role in enforcing it.

France and Germany

The German Federal Constitutional Court enjoys one of the largest zones of discretion of any court. It possesses wide jurisdiction over all constitutional issues, defends both rights and federal arrangements, exercises abstract and concrete review, and receives constitutional complaints. In its case law, the court has made it clear that the German legislative authority must be exercised to enhance rights protection, wherever possible, given other constitutional values. Control instruments are extraordinarily weak. The German constitution does not allow an amendment to weaken rights provisions which, in practice, means that the court's decisions on rights are irreversible, except by the court itself. Because most important political issues make it to the court through one procedure or another, German politics has become highly judicialized.

The French Constitutional Council exercises the abstract review of statutes adopted by parliament, prior to their entry into force. The council radically expanded its own zone of discretion in the 1970s when it incorporated, against the founder's wishes, a charter of rights into the constitution. Compared with the German case, however, the council's zone is quite restricted. It does not handle referrals from the courts or individuals, thus reducing its capacity to control policy outcomes beyond legislative space. As important, the decision rules governing constitutional revision are more permissive than in the German situation: the constitution can be revised by a 3:5 vote of deputies and senators in a special session. Two council decisions have been overruled in order (i) to permit the right-wing majority to tighten immigration policy (amendment

of 1993), and (ii) to allow the left-wing majority to develop affirmative action policies for women (amendment of 1999).

European countries with Kelsenian courts operate in large zones of discretion, given that (i) the courts possess broad powers to protect charters of rights, most of which are more extensive than in the German situation; and (ii) it is almost impossible to amend constitutional rights provisions.

The US and Canada

In the US and Canada, all courts may exercise the judicial review of statutes.

The US Federal Constitution provides for a short list of negative rights, although the Supreme Court has 'discovered' a longer list of rights, such as privacy, thereby expanding its own zone of discretion. It is difficult to amend the US Constitution—readers should check out Article V! In practice, this means that the Court's case law on constitutional rights can only be changed if the Supreme Court changes its mind.

In 1982, Canada became fully independent from the UK, when it 'repatriated' its constitution and supplemented it with an extensive Charter of Rights and Freedoms. Repatriation radically expanded the judiciary's zone of discretion. The 'Notwithstanding Clause' of the charter permits the federal and provincial parliaments to 'override' a right for a period of five years, renewable thereafter. Thus, there is no de facto judicial supremacy when it comes to rights, as there is in much of Europe and the US. Canadian legislators can choose to violate a right, but their responsibility for doing so is complete. The Canadian Parliament has never chosen to do so, although some provincial legislatures have voted overrides.

Students should consider this question, to which there may not be a clear answer: is the zone of discretion of the US Supreme Court greater or smaller than that of the Canadian Supreme Court? On the one hand, the Canadian Constitution gives a privileged place for the Charter of Rights and Freedoms, which is a richer text than the American Bill of Rights. On the other hand, a Canadian Supreme Court's ruling on rights can be more easily set aside. But as this chapter emphasizes, the zone of discretion does not tell us what a court will actually do with its discretionary authority. Might a 'Notwithstanding Clause' encourage a court to be a more aggressive rights protector if it knows that it does not have the last word on a statute's constitutional legality?

---

sanctioned slavery. The Civil War led to slavery's abolition, and to the adoption of the 13th, 14th, and 15th Amendments (1865–70). Prior to 1950, the Court made little of the 14th Amendment, which guarantees 'equal protection under the laws', for the purposes for which it was designed: to combat institutionalized racism

and other forms of discrimination. Instead, the Court, and therefore the Constitution, was complicit in systematic rights abuses of the worst kind. In 1883, the Court had struck down as unconstitutional a Congressional statute banning discrimination against former slaves in hotels, railroads, theatres, and so on; and in

1896, it bestowed constitutional legitimacy on the official apartheid that many Southern states had instituted after Reconstruction.[4] Apartheid would remain an important element of American constitutional law until well after World War II.

Although the American experience is increasingly irrelevant to global constitutionalism, it has had an impact. The US produced a model of judicial review, and this model has been adopted by other polities. Further, the Supreme Court demonstrated to the world that constitutional review could survive, and even prosper, not only through supervising federalism, but through protecting rights. In the 1950s, the Court gradually moved to protect civil rights, especially freedom of speech and assembly, voting rights, 14th amendment protections, and the rights of defendants in criminal cases. Indeed, by the end of the 1960s, the Court had transformed itself into a formidable rights protector. This posture helped to create and sustain a rights-based, litigation-oriented politics in the US (Epp 1998), a politics that remains vibrant today. As important, Americans occupied post-World War II Germany and Italy, and they insisted that these countries write constitutions that included a charter of rights and a review mechanism, thus helping to provoke the move to the 'new constitutionalism' in Europe.

In 1803, when *Marbury* v. *Madison* was rendered, the French were completing the destruction of independent judicial authority. That process began with the Great Revolution of 1789. In 1790, the legislature prohibited judicial review of legislation, and that statute remains in force today. By 1804, a new legal system had emerged. It was constructed on the principle—a corollary of legislative sovereignty—that courts must not participate in the law-making function. The judge

was cast as a 'slave' of the legislature—more precisely, of the code system. The codes are statutes which, in their idealized form, purport to regulate society in a comprehensive way, not least in order to reduce judicial discretion to nil. Through imitation, revolution, and war, the code system and the prohibition of judicial review spread across Europe during the nineteenth century (the British Isles and the Nordic region being the most important exceptions). Although the nineteenth century witnessed momentous regime change, a relatively stable constitutional orthodoxy nonetheless prevailed. In this orthodoxy, constitutions could be revised at the discretion of the lawmaker; separation-of-powers doctrines subjugated judicial to legislative authority; and constraints on the lawmaker's authority, such as rights, either did not exist or could not be enforced by courts.

Curiously, the French Revolution did produce the first modern charter of rights. In 1789, the Constituent Assembly adopted the *Declaration of the Rights of Man and of the Citizen* before it completed its task of drafting the Constitution of 1791. Since 1791, the French have lived under fifteen different written constitutions, but none provided for rights review, and none made the Declaration judicially enforceable. Constitutional review powers were periodically conferred on specialized state organs (never courts) in order to police the boundaries between executive and legislative authority, not to protect rights from legislative infringement. In the 1970s, the Constitutional Council incorporated the Declaration into the Constitution of the Fifth Republic (1959–present), against the express wishes of the founders (Stone 1990).

The founders of the Fifth Republic established the Constitutional Council to help ensure the dominance of the executive (the Government, named by the President) over the parliament (National Assembly and Senate) in legislative processes. Its role was transformed by two constitutional changes. First, as mentioned, the Council incorporated a bill of rights into the constitution, where none previously existed, a process completed by 1979. The decision expanded the Council's zone of discretion considerably. Second, in 1974 the power to refer statutes adopted by parliament *before* their entry into force was given to any sixty National Assembly deputies or sixty senators—that is, to opposition parties. The Council exercises only politically initiated, pre-enforcement, abstract review of statutes. Once a statute has entered into force, it is no longer subject to constitutional review of any kind: legislative sovereignty thus remains formally intact.

The French experience is important for two main reasons. First, its code system and its conception of legislative sovereignty and separation of powers spread across Europe, and would later take hold in Africa and Latin America, through the influence of French and Spanish colonialism. Second, like the Germans, the French experimented with models of non-judicial, politically activated, constitutional review in the form of specialized state organs. These experiments are cousins of the modern constitutional court, and a number of states use the 'constitutional council' model today.

In the area now comprised of Austria, Germany, and Switzerland, specialized state organs became a common feature of government in various federal polities during the nineteenth century. These bodies dealt primarily with jurisdictional disputes between state institutions, or among levels of government. The modern constitutional court is the invention of the Austrian legal theorist, Hans Kelsen, who developed the European model of constitutional review partly from these experiences. Kelsen drafted the constitution of the Austrian Second Republic (1920–34), and he included a constitutional court among its most important state institutions. He was also a legal theorist, whose writings and teachings turned out to be extraordinarily influential after World War II. As discussed below in 'The diffusion of higher law constitutionalism', one sees that the 'Kelsenian' court, which is at the heart of the European model, is now the most popular institutional form of review in the world.

Some scholars speak of a 'Scandinavian Model' of review, and note that it is one of the world's oldest (Husa 2000). In Norway, the power of the judiciary to invalidate law as unconstitutional has been asserted since at least the 1860s, although the question of whether this power extended to judicial review of statutes was not definitively resolved until a Supreme Court decision of 1976 suggested that the answer was yes. Simplifying, the Danish Constitution of 1849 expressly provides for rights but not for review, and the Swedish Constitution (elements of which have been in place since 1809) provided for review but not for rights (until 1974). None of the courts in the region ever used review authority to any noticeable effect. Indeed, even today, these courts do little constitutional judicial review of any political consequence, and deference to the legislature is the rule (Husa 2000; Hirschl 2011).

The diffusion of higher law constitutionalism

During the inter-war period (roughly 1918–38), constitutional review was established in Czechoslovakia (1920), Liechtenstein (1925), Greece (1927), Spain (1931),

and Ireland (1937); further, the German Supreme Court of the Weimar Republic also flirted with review (Stolleis 2003). Of these, only the Irish Supreme Court actually did much review, and only the Irish Court survived World War II. It is today one of the world's most effective review courts.

After World War II, review courts were established in Europe in successive waves of constitution-making, following the end of fascism in Greece, Spain, and Portugal in the 1970s, and then the fall of communism in Central and Eastern Europe after 1989. Apart from the Greek 'mixed' system, every country adopted the Kelsenian constitutional court. The American model was rejected. Kelsenian courts were established in Austria (1945), Italy (1948), the Federal Republic of Germany (1949), France (1958), Portugal (1976), Spain (1978), Belgium (1985), and, after 1989, in the post-communist Czech Republic, Hungary, Poland, Romania, Russia, and other post-Soviet states, Slovakia, the Baltics, and in the states of the former Yugoslavia. The exception is Estonia, whose system mixes elements from the two models.

The American model is found in Africa, Asia, and the Caribbean, especially in those countries that had been colonized by Great Britain, or are part of the Commonwealth. In moving to rights and review, these systems, in effect, 'constitutionalize' the basic common law legal order. Judicial review is also found in countries that were under US occupation or influence after 1950, such as Japan and parts of Central and South America.

With decolonization, the number of states in the world expanded steadily throughout the 1950s and 1960s. Many of these new states were not very stable. Beginning in the 1970s, many post-colonial states in the developing world began to experiment with different constitutional forms. Written constitutions proliferated, most of which did not last, but they were almost always replaced with new written constitutions. By the 1990s, the basic formula of the new constitutionalism—(i) a written, entrenched constitution; (ii) a charter of rights; and (iii) a review mechanism to protect rights—had become standard, even in what most of us would consider non-democratic, authoritarian states.

There are at least three important reasons for the diffusion of systems of constitutional justice. First, in episodes of transition from authoritarian rule, there is simply no better way for constitution-makers to distinguish a new, democratic regime from the old, authoritarian one than to entrench a system of constitutional justice. Where the old regime is viewed as perpetrating massive and systematic rights abuses, few will see a contradiction between democracy and rights protection. Second, the framers of new constitutions copy forms perceived to be successful to prior transitions. The German experience, after the horrors of the Holocaust, directly influenced the design of new constitutions in Spain and Central and Eastern Europe, but also Colombia and South Korea. Third, since the 1990s in particular, international organizations have heavily promoted constitutional reform, emphasizing rule of law as basic to peace and development, and rights protection as basic to rule of law. The International Monetary Fund, the World Bank, and other development organizations partly conditioned development aid and other resources in congruence with international standards. In the 1990s, following the collapse of communism in Europe, the EU and the Council of Europe (the centrepiece of which is the European Convention on Human Rights) required that framers of new constitutions provide for constitutional justice as a prerequisite for membership and support programmes.

Systems of constitutional justice in the twenty-first century

We can now survey the state of the world, as regards systems of constitutional justice. The written constitution is the norm. There are 194 states in a recent data set compiled on constitutional forms,[5] 191 of which have written constitutions. Israel, New Zealand, and the UK do not have fully codified, entrenched constitutions. Israel nonetheless possesses a powerful Supreme Court that protects rights as part of the higher law (Gross 1998). As discussed in Box 9.3, New Zealand (1990) and the UK (1998) adopted charters of rights in the form of statutes, but courts may not enforce these rights against the will of Parliament. Constitutions are currently suspended in a handful of states, including Thailand and Somalia.

Second, the constitutions of 183 out of the 194 states in the data set contain a charter of rights. Most include not only traditional civil and political rights, but positive or social rights. There have been 114 constitutions written since 1985 (not all of which have lasted), and we have reliable information on 106 of these. All 106 of these constitutions contain a catalogue of rights. It seems that the last constitution to leave rights out was the racist 1983 South African constitution—hardly a model to emulate.

We also compiled information on the establishment of review mechanisms since 1985. Of the 106 constitutions written since 1985 on which we can reliably report, all but five established constitutional review: those of North Korea, Vietnam, Saudi Arabia, Laos, and Iraq (in its 1990 constitution).

Table 9.1 Regional distribution of models of constitutional review

	CJR	EM–CC	Mixed*	Other**	None
Europe	5	31	3 (1)	1	2
Africa	12	29	1	6	3
Middle East	2	5	0	3	1
Asia and SE Asia	18	13	2	11	0
North America	2	0	0	0	0
Central America	3	3	3 (1)	0	0
South America	3	4	5 (3)	0	0
Caribbean	8	0	0	1	0
Totals	**53**	**85**	**14**	**22**	**6**

Note: CJR: Constitutional judicial review (the American model). EM–CC: European Model–Constitutional Court. Mixed: systems that mix elements of the American and European models.

*The number in parentheses refers to systems with European model constitutional courts, such as Portugal, but which also give review authority to ordinary judges. I have deferred to Dr Mavčič's classification, though I would normally count these states under the EM–CC column.

**Review mechanisms, often unique, that are unclassifiable.

Source: Presentation based on data compiled by Dr Arne Mavčič, http://www.concourts.net, last updated in October 2005. French Council-based systems were counted under the 'EM–CC' column, and Saudi Arabia, which is not included in the Mavčič data set, was counted under the 'None' column.

Table 9.1 presents data on the regional distribution of the various review mechanisms. The European model is clearly ascendant. Moreover, with few exceptions, the most powerful review courts in the world are Kelsenian courts. The spread of the European model has also meant the diffusion of abstract review. Mavčič (http://www.concourts.net) examined modes of review in 125 constitutions currently in force, and determined that seventy of them conferred abstract review authority on judges. Most of these also provide for individual, constitutional complaints. The American 'case or controversy' model is moribund, with little chance of being revived.

Effectiveness

Many political scientists will not be interested in these developments if systems of constitutional justice do not influence broader political processes: the development of the constitution, the making of public policy, inter-branch conflicts, and competition among political elites. To the extent that constitutional review is *effective*, it will be central to these and other processes.

Constitutional review will be *effective* to the extent that (i) important constitutional disputes arising in the polity are brought to the review authority on a regular basis; that (ii) the judges who resolve these disputes give reasons for their rulings; and that (iii) those who are governed by the constitutional law accept that the court's ruling has some precedential effect. Effectiveness varies across countries and across time in the same country.

Most review systems throughout world history have been relatively ineffective, even irrelevant. In weak systems, important political disputes may not be sent to constitutional judges for resolution, and decisions that constitutional judges do render may be ignored. Political actors may seek to settle their disputes by force, rather than through the courts, sometimes with fatal consequences for the constitutional regime. Put simply, elites may care much more about staying in power at any cost, or enriching themselves, or rewarding their friends and punishing their foes, or achieving ethnic dominance, then they care about building constitutional democracy. Constitutional regimes may also be overthrown by force. In some countries, the military coup d'état remains a constant threat. In the 2006–15 decade, at least forty coups were attempted in these areas, and at least nine were successful, including in Egypt, Fiji, Guinée-Bissau, Mali, Mauritania, Niger, Thailand, and Yemen. None of these proceeded with respect to constitutional principles. Nonetheless, despite the odds, some courts and constitutions have operated as constraints even on military dictatorship, as in Pinochet's Chile (Barros 2002), or Sadat's Egypt (Moustafa 2007).

Where constitutional review systems are relatively effective, constitutional judges manage the evolution of the polity through their decisions. There are several necessary conditions for the emergence of effective review systems; each is related to the court's 'zone of discretion'. First, constitutional judges must have a case load. If actors, private and public, conspire not to activate review, judges will accrete no influence over the polity. Second, once activated, judges must resolve these disputes and *give defensible reasons* in justification of their decisions. If they do, one output of constitutional adjudication will be the production of a constitutional case law, or *jurisprudence*, which is a record of how the judges have interpreted the constitution. Third, those who are governed by the constitutional law must accept that constitutional meaning is (at least partly) constructed through the judges' interpretation and rule making, and use or refer to relevant case law in future disputes.

Why only some countries are able to fulfil these conditions is an important question that scholars have not been able to answer. The achievement of stable type 3 constitutionalism depends heavily on the same macro-political factors related to the achievement of stable democracy, and we know that democracy is difficult to create and sustain. Among other factors, the new constitutionalism rests on a polity's commitment to: elections; a competitive party system; protecting rights, including those of minorities; practices associated with the 'rule of law'; and a system of advanced legal education. Each of these factors is also associated with other important socio-cultural phenomena, including attributes of political culture, which may be fragmented. Constitutional judges can contribute to the building of practices related to higher law constitutionalism, but there are limits to what they can do if they find themselves continuously in opposition to powerful elites, institutions, and cultural biases in the citizenry.

It is therefore unsurprising that one finds relatively effective review mechanisms in areas where one finds relatively stable democracy, which now includes the post-Communist countries of Central Europe. Ranked in terms of effectiveness, I would place the systems of (i) Canada and the US in the Americas; (ii) Germany, Ireland, and Spain in Western Europe; and (iii) the Czech Republic and Slovenia in Central Europe on top of the list. As noted, Hungary and Poland have now fallen off the list. Outside of these regions, there are four courts operating in difficult environments that would also make this list: Colombia, India (Verma and Kumar 2003), Israel, and South Africa. In Asia, the constitutional courts of Indonesia, South Korea, and Taiwan are building effectiveness quite rapidly.

The impact of constitutional review

There has been no systematic research or data collection on constitutions, rights and rights protection, or on the politics of constitutional review. However, since 1990, scholars have produced a mountain of single-case studies, and a handful of comparative treatments on these topics. I will not summarize all of this work here. Instead, I will focus on the impact of new review systems on politics in the two areas that have attracted the most attention.

Transitions to constitutional democracy

Since 1950, type 3 constitutions, rights, and review have been crucial to nearly all successful transitions from authoritarian regimes to constitutional democracy. Indeed, it appears that the more successful any transition has been, the more one is likely to find an effective constitutional or supreme court at the heart of it (Japan being the most important exception). Review performs several functions that facilitate the transition to democracy. It provides a system of peaceful dispute resolution, under the constitution, for those who have contracted a new beginning, in light of illiberal or violent pasts. It provides a mechanism for purging the laws of authoritarian elements that have built up over many years, given that the new legislature may be overloaded with work. And a review court can provide a focal point for a new rhetoric of state legitimacy, one based on respect for rights and other values of the new constitution, and on the rejection of old rhetorics (fascism, one-party rule, legislative sovereignty, the cult of personality, and so on).

The most extensive research on the role of new systems of constitutional justice in consolidating democracy has focused on post-Apartheid South Africa (Klug 2000), and Asia (Ginsburg 2003), as new courts in Indonesia, South Korea, and Taiwan steadily built effectiveness through patrolling the boundaries between legislatures and executives, pushing political leaders into dialogues with one another, and ensuring that electoral law is respected (Lin 2017; Yap 2017).

The 'judicialization' of politics

A second important strain of research focuses on the impact of review on policy processes and outcomes (see Box 9.1). Most studies of judicialization proceed by conceptualizing constitutional review and rights adjudication as an extension of the policy process, and then observing and evaluating the impact of review on final outcomes and subsequent policy-making in the same area. The classic work in this vein is Martin Shapiro's *Law and Politics in the Supreme Court* (1964), but the basic theory (Stone Sweet 1999) and approach has been applied to: Western (Shapiro and Stone Sweet 1994; Stone Sweet 2000) and Central and Eastern Europe (Sadurski 2013), the Commonwealth model countries and Canada (Hiebert 2011), Latin America (Sieder et al. 2005), and Asia (Stone Sweet and Mathews 2017; Yap 2015; 2017), as well as many other specific countries.

It is easier to study the impact of rights review on legislative activity in centralized review systems than in decentralized systems, because constitutional judges and legislators interact with one another directly, through abstract review referrals and decisions. I have developed a theory of the constitutional judicialization of politics in Western Europe (Stone Sweet 2000). I show, among other things, that the impact of rights and the court on legislative activity will vary as a function of three factors: the existence of abstract review, the number of veto points in the policy process, and the content of the court's case law. The more centralized is the policy process—the greater the parliamentary majority, the more that majority is under the control of a unified executive, and the fewer veto points there are in legislative procedures—the more the opposition will go to the constitutional court to block important policy initiatives. Abstract review referrals are the most straightforward means of doing so. In many policy domains, legislative politics have become highly 'judicialized'.

DEFINITION 9.4

The judicialization of politics through rights adjudication

The phrase 'judicialization of politics' refers to the process through which the influence of courts on legislative and administrative power develops over time. In some places, in some sectors, policy is highly judicialized; in others, it may not be judicialized at all.

Rights review leads to the judicialization of legislative politics to the extent that (i) constitutional rights provisions have a legal status superior to statutes; (ii) the review court receives important cases in which statutes are alleged to have violated rights; and (iii) the court sometimes annuls statutes on the basis of rights, and gives reasons for doing so. In judicialized settings, legislators worry about and debate the constitutionality of bills during the legislative process, and they will draft and amend their bills in order to insulate them from constitutional censure. In judicialized settings, constitutional courts routinely take decisions that serve both to construct the constitutional law and to amend legislation under review.

Some of the more controversial examples of highly judicialized politics around the world concern attempts to combat racial and gender discrimination, to liberalize and regulate abortion, and to criminalize 'hate speech', obscenity, and pornography.

In policy domains that are highly judicialized, courts and judicial process are part of the greater policy process. If political scientists do not pay close attention to courts, they will miss a large part of the action.

KEY POINTS

- Systems of constitutional review are *effective* insofar as constitutional judges are able to influence the development of the constitutional law and public policy through their interpretations of rights and other constitutional provisions. We do not find much effectiveness in countries that are not relatively stable democracies.

- In some places, including South Africa and Central and Eastern Europe, constitution courts have been important to processes of democratization.

- In countries where review is highly effective, constitutional judges have become powerful policy-makers. Examples are mainly found in North America and Western Europe, although the courts of Colombia, Israel, and South Africa deserve mention.

The web of constitutional constraints facing legislators has grown and become denser, as constitutional courts have processed a steady stream of cases, and built a policy-relevant jurisprudence. This orientation is also applicable to Central Europe (Sadurski 2013), Canada, New Zealand, and the UK (Hiebert 2011), and South Korea and Taiwan (Lin 2017; Yap 2017). In addition, high levels of judicialization tend to raise the classic normative debates about the political legitimacy of rights protection noted in Box 9.2.

FOR AND AGAINST 9.5

A normative debate: is rights review democratic?

Con	Pro
Rights review subverts majority rule, by allowing constitutional judges to substitute their policy choices for those of legislators.	Democracy does not simply mean the domination of the majority over everyone else. It also means basic standards of good governance, which must include the protection of rights.
Rights provisions are vague and ill-defined. In a good democracy, elected officials will determine how rights should be protected in law.	It is precisely because rights provisions are not expressed as clear rules that we need judges to interpret them. Good constitutional rulings will lead legislators to care more about rights.
Judges can interpret rights in any way they wish, without being held democratically accountable for their decisions. We can expect an effective system of constitutional review to subvert, routinely, the will of the elected representatives of the People.	Rights are too important to be left to the protection of elected politicians. Judges are relatively more insulated from short-term political calculation, and are thus more likely to protect rights better than elected politicians.
The judicialization of politics through rights adjudication reduces the centrality of legislative debate, and therefore reduces the political responsibility of legislative majorities for their policy decisions. Such responsibility is basic to democratic legitimacy.	Judicialization means that legislatures govern, in dialogue with judges, in order to make rights protection effective. The legitimacy of the regime depends, in part, on how legislators and judges interact with one another to protect rights.

Conclusion

Constitutional law is political law: it is the law that constitutes the state and governs acts of authority made in the name of the polity. Since the 1950s, the new constitutionalism has been consolidated as an unrivalled standard. Though we find provision for rights review virtually everywhere today, not all systems of constitutional justice are equally effective. Indeed, in many places they are irrelevant. Judges help to govern through two linked processes.

First, they adapt the constitution to changing circumstances, on an ongoing basis, through interpretation. Second, in applying their constitutional interpretations to resolve rights disputes, the judges will make policy, including legislative policy. The more effective is any system of review, the more judges will, inevitably, become powerful policy-makers. Both outcomes inhere in a simple legal fact, made real through effective review: the constitution is higher law, and therefore binds the exercise of all public authority.

? QUESTIONS

Knowledge-based

1. What are the main differences between a type 2 and a type 3 constitution?

2. What is 'the new constitutionalism' and what does it have to do with politics?

3. What is the difference between a court that is 'an agent of the legislature' and a court that is a 'trustee of the constitution?'

4. How does the American model of review differ from the European model?

5. Why is the zone of discretion, in part, determined by constitutional provisions that specify how the constitution is to be revised?

Critical thinking

1. In what ways does a constitution *constitute* the state and the political system?

2. Do you think it is good for a country to have a big catalogue of rights and an effective system of review?

3. Would you rather live in a country whose politics are relatively more, or relatively less, constitutionally 'judicialized'?

4. Why do you think that an authoritarian dictator might draft a constitution with rights and review?

5. Which are the most effective courts?

≋ FURTHER READING

Comparative treatments of the politics of constitutional judicial review published since 2000 include:

Ginsburg, T. and Simpser, A. (eds) (2013) *Constitutions in Authoritarian Regimes* (Cambridge, MA: Harvard University Press).

Rosenfeld, M. and Sajo, A. (eds) (2012), *Oxford Handbook of Comparative Constitutional Law* (Oxford: Oxford University Press).

Sadurski, W. (2013) *Rights Before Courts: A Study of Constitutional Courts in Postcommunist States of Central and Eastern Europe* (Dordrecht: Springer).

Sieder, R., Schjolden, L., and Angell, A. (2005) *The Judicialization of Politics in Latin America* (New York: Palgrave Macmillan).

Stone Sweet, A. (2000). *Governing with Judges: Constitutional Politics in Western Europe* (Oxford: Oxford University Press).

Stone Sweet, A. and Mathews, J. (2019). *Proportionality Balancing and Constitutional Governance* (Oxford: Oxford University Press).

Yap, P.-J. (2017). *Courts and Democracies in Asia* (Cambridge: Cambridge University Press).

See also the research listed in References at the end of the volume and quoted in this chapter. The *International Journal of Constitutional Law* is the leading journal devoted to research on constitutional law and courts, though it only rarely publishes articles written by social scientists.

ENDNOTES

1. I exclude the Articles of Confederation (1777–88), which functioned as the first constitution uniting the American colonies after the 1776 Declaration of Independence. The Articles provided for a legislature, but no federal president or judiciary.

2. A 'complete' contract 'would specify precisely what each party is to do in every possible circumstance and arrange the distribution of realized costs and benefits in each contingency so that each party individually finds it optimal to abide by the contract's terms' (Milgrom and Roberts 1992: 127).

3. In this chapter, I do not discuss the extent to which appointment procedures and the partisan affiliation of judges have influenced the development of constitutional law around the world. These factors have surely mattered, but how much remains a mystery. To date, no sophisticated comparative work on the topic has been produced.

4. Civil Rights Cases, 109 US 3 (1883); Plessy v. Ferguson, 163 US 537 (1896).

5. The data set was compiled by Christina Andersen and Alec Stone Sweet. It includes 196 states, but we were unable to find adequate information on two (Brunei and the Central African Republic), so we do not count them here.

Visit the Online Resources that accompany this book for additional material, including country profiles, comparative data sets, flashcard glossaries, and web directory.

www.oup.com/he/caramani5e

10

Elections and referendums

Michael Gallagher

Chapter contents

Reader's guide

This chapter covers the two main opportunities that people have to vote in most societies: elections and referendums. Elections are held to fill seats in parliaments or to choose a president, while at referendums citizens decide directly on some issue of policy. Elections are the cornerstone of representative democracy, in that the people elect others to make decisions. Referendums are sometimes perceived as the equivalent of 'direct democracy', but in practice they are deployed only as a kind of optional extra in systems of representative democracy, with hardly anyone suggesting that all decisions should be made by referendum. The chapter explores the variety of rules under which elections are held, and examines the consequences of this variation. It then looks at the use of the referendum and assesses its potential impact on a country's politics.

Introduction

We saw in Chapters 7 'Legislatures' and 8 'Governments and Bureaucracies' that parliaments and governments have the potential to be important actors. In this chapter, we look at how governments and parliaments come into being in the first place. The process of election is an essential requirement of any political system that hopes to be regarded as possessing democratic credentials. The election is the main mechanism by which the people are able to express their views about how their country should be governed.

However, not all elections are the same. Elections are governed by rules that determine what kind of choices people can make when they turn out to vote and how those choices are converted into seats in parliament or the election of a president. Identical sets of voter preferences in two adjacent countries might have to be expressed differently if the electoral rules are different, or, even if the ballot papers capture their preferences in the same way, the counting rules might deliver different results. Hence, it is important to understand what kinds of rules are used and what consequences different rules have.

Governments and parliaments, produced by elections, make most of the political decisions facing a country, albeit within the constraints imposed by some of the other actors studied in this book, such as courts and interest groups (see Chapters 9 'Constitutions, rights, and judicial power' and 14 'Interest groups', respectively). However, some decisions are taken not by these elected authorities but, rather, by the people themselves in referendums on specific issues. Whereas the use of elections is universal among democracies, the use of referendums varies enormously.

This variation is itself intriguing, as is the question of why some issues are put to referendums while others are not. The chapter examines the different kinds of referendums that are held or are provided for in countries' constitutions, and the kinds of issues that tend to be the subject of referendums. It looks at the reasons advanced for their use and at the concerns expressed by critics. There has been some dispute as to whether voters in referendums take much notice of the question supposedly at issue, and the chapter reviews the evidence before assessing the impact of referendums.

Elections and electoral systems

Elections are a virtually universal feature of modern politics. Even regimes that cannot be considered democracies in any sense of the word, and that provide voters with little or no freedom of choice when they arrive at the polling station, have felt there might be some kind of legitimacy to be derived from holding elections.

In modern liberal democracies, elections are the central representative institution that forms a link between the people and their representatives. For the most part, the decisions that affect us all are taken by a tiny handful of individuals, such as members of parliament, government ministers, or presidents, sometimes known collectively as the 'political class'. The reason why we regard this state of affairs as legitimate rather than as an appalling usurpation of our rights is that the members of the political class are not simply imposed upon us but, rather, are elected by us to be our political representatives. Moreover, they face re-election and therefore can be voted out at the next election if they fail to satisfy us. This mechanism of achieving representation and accountability is central to the concept of modern democracy (see Chapter 5 'Democracies'). A regime whose leaders are not elected and are not subject to the requirement of regular re-election cannot be considered democratic.

By an **electoral system** we mean the set of rules that structure how votes are cast at elections and how these votes are then converted into the allocation of offices. We look first at electoral regulations (the rules governing the breadth of the franchise, ease of **ballot access**, and so on) and then specifically at electoral systems.

Electoral regulations

Among modern democracies, variations in the extent of the franchise are matters of detail rather than of principle (for an overview, see Caramani 2000: 49–57). Generalizing somewhat, in the first half of the nineteenth century the male landed gentry constituted the bulk of the *electorate* (those who are entitled to vote), but from the middle of the century the franchise was gradually extended to the male section of the growing middle class. Around the turn of the century, further advances meant that the male working class had the vote by the time of World War I (1914). The struggle to secure the same rights for women took longer and, particularly in some mainly Catholic countries such as France and Italy, women did not get the vote on the same basis as men until after World War II (1945). The voting age was reduced steadily throughout the twentieth century, and in most countries these days stands at eighteen (Caramani 2000: 56–7). There are pressure groups in many countries seeking further reduction, achieving some success in Argentina, Austria, Brazil, Ecuador, and Malta (voting age of sixteen), and Greece and Indonesia (seventeen), though in a 2015 referendum, voters in Luxembourg heavily rejected lowering the age from eighteen to sixteen. Voting is generally voluntary, though in a few countries such as Australia and Belgium it is compulsory. Given that **turnout** in most countries is related to socio-economic status (SES), it has been argued that making voting compulsory would help eliminate the 'yawning SES voting gap' (Hill 2006; Umbers 2018) (see Box 10.1).

The ease of access to the ballot varies across countries and can be an important factor in determining whether new candidates or parties take the plunge and stand at an election. Most states impose some kind of requirement, such as a financial deposit, demonstrated support from a number of voters, or the endorsement of a recognized party. The requirements are typically more demanding in candidate-oriented systems than in party-oriented ones (see Katz 1997: 255–61). Onerous access requirements can be a significant deterrent for small parties or independent candidates.

Generally, the term of presidents is fixed, while for parliaments constitutions specify a maximum period but not a minimum. The president of the US has a four-year term, while the French president has five years. The term of some parliaments is fixed: for example, those of Norway, Sweden, and Switzerland have a four-year lifespan, while members of the US House of Representatives serve terms of only two years, which means that they operate in pretty much perpetual campaign mode. Senators in the US, by contrast, have six years to savour the fruits of election. However, most parliaments do not have a fixed term; instead, the government (or prime minister, or in some cases the head of state) of the day has the power to dissolve parliament, and characteristically uses this power to call the election at the time most advantageous to itself. The maximum time between elections is usually four years, though in a few countries (including Canada, France, Italy, and the UK) it is five years, while in Australia and New Zealand it is an exceptionally short three years.

Electoral systems

The precise rules governing the conversion of votes into seats may seem a rather technical matter, yet electoral systems matter. They can have a major impact upon whether a country has a **two-party** or a **multiparty system**, whether government is by one party or a coalition of parties, whether voters feel personally represented in a parliament, and whether women and minorities are heavily under-represented in parliament.

📢 **FOR AND AGAINST 10.1**

Should voting be compulsory?

Arguments for compulsory voting	Arguments against compulsory voting
Our forebears struggled and died in order to win the right to vote, so people today have a duty to vote.	It is perfectly legitimate to take no interest in politics, or not to vote for whatever reason.
Politicians have a strong incentive to skew their policies towards those who will punish or reward them, depending on their record in office, and to neglect those who are unlikely to vote. When voting is optional, the better off are much more likely to vote than the poor, so policy outputs will favour the better off.	If everyone is compelled to vote, the votes of those who actually care about the outcome of an election are diluted by the votes of those with no interest in the outcome and who may be voting on a virtually random basis.
The role of money in politics is reduced, since parties no longer need to motivate their supporters to turn out.	The onus should be on parties and candidates to persuade citizens that there is some reason why they should vote, rather than being able to rely on the state to compel them to do so.
All citizens have an incentive to inform themselves about the issues and about the performance of politicians, making for a better-informed electorate.	Even those with no real interest in the election have to vote, so politicians have even more of an incentive than under optional voting to engage in attention-catching stunts to try to impress those who know nothing about the issues.
Compulsion is not a breach of principle; for example, everyone has to pay taxes, whether they want to or not. People have an obligation to contribute towards the democracy whose benefits they enjoy and should not be allowed to free-ride on the contributions of others.	Freedom of choice implies the right not to turn out if you don't wish to, and this would be infringed by compelling people to turn out.

This is not the place to supply a complete account of how the entire world's electoral systems work (see Reynolds et al. 2005; Gallagher and Mitchell 2008: appendix A; Farrell 2010). However, we can sketch the main categories and the dimensions of variation, before moving on to examine the consequences of different configurations.

The main categories of electoral systems

There are many ways in which to categorize electoral systems, the most straightforward of which relates to the magnitude of the constituencies in which seats are allocated (a **constituency** is the geographic area into which the country is divided for electoral purposes; this is referred to as a 'district' in the US). We may begin with the distinction between systems based on *multimember constituencies*, in which the seats are shared among the parties in proportion to their vote shares, and those based on *single-member constituencies*, in which the strongest party in each constituency wins the seat. The former are often termed **proportional representation** (PR) systems, while the latter are termed **majoritarian** systems.

Single-member plurality

The simplest system of all is single-member plurality (SMP), also known as 'first-past-the-post' (FPTP). Voters simply make a mark, such as placing a cross, beside their choice of candidate, and the seat is then awarded to the candidate who receives most votes (i.e. a plurality). This is used in some of the world's largest democracies, such as India, the US, the UK, and Canada; over 40 per cent of the world's population, and over 70 per cent of those in an established democracy, live in a country employing this system (Reynolds et al. 2005: 30; Heath et al. 2008; Mitchell 2008; Massicotte 2008).

Alternative vote

Under the alternative vote (AV), voters are able to rank order the candidates, placing a '1' beside their first choice, '2' beside their second, and so on (Farrell and McAllister 2008). The counting process is a little more complicated. If one candidate's votes amount to a majority of all votes cast, that person is deemed elected. If not, then the lowest-placed candidate is eliminated from the count and his/her ballots are redistributed according to the second preference expressed on them. Supporters of this candidate are in effect asked, 'Given that your first choice lacked sufficient support to be elected, which candidate would you like to benefit from your vote instead?' The counting process continues, with successive eliminations of the bottom-placed candidate and transfers of their votes to the remaining candidates, until one candidate does have an overall majority of the votes. In consequence, AV is regarded as a majority system, given that the winner requires an absolute majority of the votes at the final stage, whereas under SMP a plurality suffices. AV is employed in Australia but scarcely anywhere else; in May 2011, the people of the UK voted heavily (68 per cent to 32 per cent) against adopting it for elections to the House of Commons (Whiteley et al. 2012).

Two-round system

Another way of filling a single seat is by the two-round system (2RS): if no candidate wins a majority of votes in the first round, a second round takes place in which only certain candidates (perhaps the top two, or those who exceeded a certain percentage of the votes) are permitted to proceed to the second round, where whoever wins the most votes is the winner. This is employed to elect parliaments in more than twenty countries, including France, Iran, and several former French colonies, and is widely used to elect presidents (Elgie 2008a; Blais et al. 1997).

These three systems—SMP, AV, and 2RS—thus differ, yet they have much more in common than differentiates them, because they are all based on single-seat constituencies.

Proportional representation

Proportional representation is a principle, which can be achieved by any number of different methods, all of which have the aim, with some qualifications as we shall see, of awarding to each group of voters its 'fair share' of representation—or, putting it another way, of allocating to each party the same share of the seats as it won of the votes. The simplest way of achieving this is to treat the whole country as one large constituency, as happens in Israel, the Netherlands, and Slovakia; then it is a straightforward matter to award, for example, twenty-four seats in a 150-member parliament to a party that receives 16 per cent of the votes (Rahat and Hazan 2008; Andeweg 2008). That guarantees a high level of **proportionality**, by which we mean the closeness with which the distribution of seats in parliament reflects the distribution of votes ('disproportionality' refers to the degree of difference between these two distributions). At the same time, it might leave voters feeling disengaged from the political system, as they do not have a local MP. More commonly, then, the country is divided into a number of smaller constituencies, each returning on average perhaps five, ten, or twenty MPs. Now the seats are awarded proportionally within each constituency, but it cannot be guaranteed that the overall level of proportionality will be quite as high as when there is just one national constituency. Brazil, Finland, Indonesia, and Spain all exemplify this approach (Hopkin 2008; Raunio 2008).

There are different methods of awarding seats proportionally within each constituency, which are based on slightly different conceptions of what constitutes 'perfect proportionality'. Some methods are even-handed between large and small parties, while others, such as the widely used D'Hondt method, give the benefit of any doubt to larger parties. (For an explanation of the technical details, see Gallagher and Mitchell (2008: appendix A); see also Chapter 13 'Party systems'.)

The systems outlined above are known as **list systems**, because each party presents a list of candidates to the voters. While list systems are still the most common form of electoral system in the world (Reynolds et al. 2005: 30), in recent years a few countries have adopted what are usually termed **mixed systems**. Here, the voter casts two votes: one for a local constituency MP and one for a party list. A certain proportion of MPs are elected from local (usually single-member) constituencies and the rest from party lists; in Germany, the archetype of this category, the proportions are half and half, though in other countries the balance might tilt this way or that. The constituency seat is usually allocated under SMP rules.

The allocation of the list seats under mixed systems depends on whether the constituency part and the list part of the election are integrated or separate (on mixed systems see Shugart and Wattenberg 2003). In the first case, the system is known as a *compensatory* **mixed system** (sometimes the word 'compensatory' is replaced by 'corrective' or 'linked', and the system is also known as mixed-member proportional (MMP)). The list seats are awarded in such a way as to rectify the **under-representations** and **over-representations** created in the constituencies, ensuring that a party's overall number of seats (not just its list seats) is proportional to its vote share. Typically, small parties fare badly in the single-member constituencies, winning hardly any seats, but are brought up to their 'fair share' overall by receiving the appropriate number of list seats, while the larger parties, which usually win more than their 'fair share' in the constituencies, are awarded few or none of the list seats because their constituency seats alone bring them up to or close to the total number to which they are entitled. Compensatory mixed systems can thus result in highly proportional outcomes, though they are easy for parties to manipulate so as to produce distorted outcomes. Germany and New Zealand are examples of this system (Saalfeld 2008; Vowles 2008).

If the list part and the constituency part of the election are separate, though, we have a *parallel mixed system* (sometimes termed mixed-member majoritarian (MMM)). Now, the list seats are awarded to parties purely on the basis of their list votes, without taking any account of what happened in the constituencies. This benefits large parties, which retain the over-representation they typically achieve in the constituencies, and offers less comfort to smaller ones than a compensatory system would. Parallel mixed systems are more widely employed than compensatory ones, with Japan, Mexico, Russia, and Venezuela among the users (Reed 2008).

While virtually all PR systems use party lists somewhere along the line, the *single transferable vote* (STV) in multi-member constituencies (PR-STV) dispenses with them. This takes the logic of the alternative vote and applies it to multimember constituencies. That is, as under AV, voters are able to rank all (or as many as they wish) of the candidates in order of their choice and yet, as under any other kind of PR system, the results will reflect a high degree of correspondence between the votes cast for a party's candidates and its share of the seats. Any explanation of how the votes are counted under PR-STV tends to make the system sound more complicated than it actually is, and examining a specific example is the best way to understand the mechanics (examples are given in Gallagher and Mitchell 2008: 594–6; Farrell and Sinnott 2018: 92–100). In brief, if a voter's top-ranked candidate is so popular that he/she does not need the vote, or so unpopular that he/she cannot benefit from the vote, the vote is transferred to the candidate ranked second by the voter. Typically, because voters are party-oriented, they give their second preference to another candidate from the same party as their first-choice candidate.

PR-STV differs from list systems not only in voters' power to rank but also in that it does not presuppose the existence of parties or their salience in voters' minds: voters may rank candidates on the basis of whatever factor is most important to them, which might be (and in parliamentary elections usually is) party affiliation, but could also be views on a particular issue that cuts across party lines, perceived parliamentary or ministerial ability, gender, locality, and so on. Thus, voters can convey a lot of information about their attitudes towards the candidates, rather than having, in effect, to say 'yes' to one and 'no' to the rest as under most systems. The 'discreet charm' of PR-STV lies in the paradoxical combination of its popularity among students of electoral systems (see below in 'Consequences of electoral systems') but its far from widespread use; only Ireland and Malta employ it to elect their national parliaments (Gallagher 2008a).

Dimensions of variation

There are many different electoral systems, but they vary in a limited number of dimensions. Three are particularly important. The first is *district magnitude*, by which is meant the number of MPs elected from each constituency. A second is the degree of *intra-party choice*, the extent to which voters are able to decide which of their party's candidates take the seats that the party wins. A third concerns the difficulty of winning seats, expressed through the idea of **thresholds**.

District magnitude

District magnitude varies from one in countries that employ single-member constituencies up to the size of the parliament when the whole country constitutes a single large constituency. The higher the average district magnitude, the more proportional we can expect the election result to be (Shugart and Taagepera 2017: 69–70). When there are more seats to share out, it is easier to achieve a 'fair' distribution, whereas when there is only one seat the largest party in the constituency takes it and the other parties receive nothing.

Intra-party choice

Much of the discussion so far has been about how seats are shared among parties, but some voters may be at least as interested in which particular individuals fill those seats. How much intra-party choice among candidates is provided by the electoral system? Under single-member constituency systems there is no intra-party choice for the simple reason that no party runs more than one candidate; if a voter likes a party but not its candidate, or likes a candidate but not her party, he simply has to grit his teeth and accept an unpalatable option.

Under PR systems, the degree of choice varies. Some list systems offer no intra-party choice; these are based on what are termed *closed lists*, where the party determines the order of its candidates' names on the list and the voters cannot overturn this. Under such a system, if a party wins, say, five seats in a constituency, those seats go to the first five names on its list, as decided by the party, whatever the voters think of those individuals. Closed lists are used in Israel, Italy, South Africa, and Spain, and in the overwhelming majority of countries that have mixed systems.

Other list systems, though, use preferential or open lists, in which the voters can indicate a preference for an individual candidate on their chosen party's list. In some cases, the voters' preference votes alone determine which candidates win the seats; in others, it needs the preference votes of a certain number of voters to earn a candidate a seat ahead of someone whom the party placed higher on the list (Shugart 2008: 36–50). Brazil, Chile, Indonesia, and Poland are examples of countries where the voters have an effective voice in determining which of their party's candidates become MPs. In PR-STV, the voters have complete freedom to award rank-ordered preferences for any candidate, not just within parties but also across party lines.

Thus, under closed-list systems the key intra-party battle takes place at the candidate selection stage, since, in order to have a chance of election, aspiring MPs must ensure that the party gives them a high position on the list. Under preferential list systems and PR-STV, candidate selection is important but not all-important, because the voters decide which of the selected candidates are elected. The trend in Europe since 1990 has been towards allowing voters greater power to decide which individual candidates are to represent them in parliament (Renwick and Pilet 2016: 48).

Thresholds

Usually, electoral systems contain some inbuilt feature designed to prevent very small parties from winning seats; this may be justified on the grounds that it is desirable to prevent undue fragmentation of parliamentary strength and to facilitate the formation of stable governments, though of course it can also be motivated simply by the desire of larger parties to discriminate against smaller ones.

A good example of a threshold is that employed in Slovakia, which, as mentioned earlier in 'Proportional representation', has just one, national, constituency. This would make possible a very high degree of proportionality—except that the country also applies a 5 per cent threshold, meaning that no party that receives fewer votes than this wins any seats at all. At Slovakia's 2016 election, 13 per cent of voters cast a ballot for a party that did not reach the threshold, and so they were unrepresented in parliament. Thresholds in the range of 3–5 per cent are common; that of the Netherlands is unusually low (0.67 per cent) and Russia's threshold between 2003 and 2016, at 7 per cent, is unusually high.

Origins of electoral systems

Despite parties' obvious vested interest in electoral system choice, not all the electoral systems that countries use today result from a partisan battle. Some do, of course. For example, Australia's alternative vote electoral system was chosen in 1918 by the two centre-right parties, since it enabled them to continue as separate entities without splitting the centre-right vote and allowing the Labor party to win. In other countries, such as France, Greece, and Italy, the electoral system is periodically changed by the party in power with the aim of benefiting itself and damaging its opponents.

In other countries, though, there was a degree of consensus behind the initial selection of an electoral system, and partisan motives alone do not always determine the stances taken by parties on adoption or reform of the electoral system (Rahat 2011; Renwick 2010). This is true of Denmark and Finland, for example, and helps to explain why the electoral systems of both countries have lasted since the early twentieth century. In other countries again, the electoral system was never consciously 'chosen'; in the US and the UK, for example, it evolved and became the electoral system at a time when there was no awareness of the options that could have been considered. If there is a long-term trend, it is in the direction of a move, especially pronounced in Europe, away from majoritarian systems and towards PR (Caramani 2000: 48, 58–63).

Consequences of electoral systems

The most widely studied aspect lies in the impact of electoral systems upon party systems (Lijphart 1994). Both electoral and parliamentary strength are more fragmented under PR systems than under non-PR systems (Shugart and Taagepera 2017: 67). In the 1950s, the French political scientist Maurice Duverger coined what has become known as 'Duverger's law'. In essence, he argued that the single-member plurality system was associated with a two-party system and that PR was associated with multiparty systems (for fuller discussion see Box 13.3); of course, any impact may be visible only over the course of several elections (Best 2012). As many people, including Duverger, have observed, the causal relationship also runs the other way round; that is, the parties in a two-party system may retain the existing SMP system in order to pre-empt the growth of rivals, while if a multiparty system emerges under SMP, as happened in several European countries in the early twentieth century, they may agree to move to PR in order to produce mutually assured survival.

The impact upon party systems has a knock-on effect upon government formation. When disproportionality is low and parliamentary strength is fragmented, as typically occurs under PR systems, the likelihood of any one party winning an overall majority is lower than under a non-PR system. Consequently, under archetypal PR systems, such as those in Belgium or Finland, the prospect of single-party government, let alone single-party majority government, is unthinkable.

Other consequences of electoral systems are not so easy to quantify. Proponents of PR argue that it tends to produce parliaments that are more representative socio-demographically, as well as politically, than other parliaments. This is partly because under PR parties need to nominate a 'ticket' or list containing a number of candidates, and they normally take good care to ensure that this is a balanced ticket so as to ensure its wide appeal. Gender representativeness is the easiest aspect to measure, and on average there are more female MPs in PR countries than in non-PR countries (Norris 2004). However, there can be wide variation among countries with similar electoral systems, highlighting the role of other factors. Renwick and Pilet (2016: 271), studying the aftermath of reforms in a number of countries that increased the ability of voters to decide which individual candidates should represent them, did not detect any impact, either positive or negative, on the share of female MPs, or indeed on voters' broader levels of satisfaction with democracy.

Electoral systems might also have an impact on the way in which MPs behave, as was discussed in Chapter 7 'Legislatures'. Here, we can expect the main variation to be not between PR and non-PR systems, but between those systems under which voters do and do not have a choice of candidate from their preferred party. In the former (open-list PR or PR-STV) candidates of each party are, in effect, competing with each other for preference votes from the electorate. In the latter (closed-list or single-member constituency systems), voters are unable to express a view on individual candidates but simply have to take the list (a one-person list in single-member constituency systems) as the party offers it to them. Thus, we would expect MPs in the first category to pay more attention to constituency service than those in the second. There is some evidence of this and, in addition, the proportion of locally born and presumably locally oriented MPs is higher in open-list and PR-STV countries than in closed-list countries (Gallagher 2008a: 557–62; Shugart et al. 2005). At the same time, though, political culture also plays a part in determining the behaviour of MPs; for example, MPs in Britain and France, as well as their voters, see constituency work as an important part of the MP's role and accordingly engage in it extensively, even though they are not subject to competition with running mates for votes.

Which system is best depends, of course, on what we want from an electoral system (Katz 1997: 278–310; Gallagher 2008a: 566–75). The main choice any electoral system designer has to make is between a PR and a non-PR system. PR systems are usually supported on the grounds that they produce a parliament that accurately represents the people's preferences: can elections really be considered democratic unless the distribution of seats among parties closely reflects the way people voted? PR ensures that no party will be hugely over-represented and that no significant group of voters will be left under-represented. Any danger of excessive fragmentation can be averted by adjusting variables such as the threshold or the district magnitude.

Supporters of non-PR systems stress the greater likelihood that these will lead to a two-party system and argue the merits of this (see Box 13.2), such as stable effective government rather than multiparty coalition and the opportunity for voters to eject a government from office. Those who study electoral systems tend to prefer mixed systems or PR-STV (Bowler et al. 2005)—but the political actors who choose electoral systems may not seek advice from academics.

Referendums

Government today is representative government, meaning that the great majority of political decisions in all countries are taken by elected officials rather than directly by the people themselves. Nonetheless, some countries employ the device of the referendum, in which the people are able to vote on some issue.

We should be clear that this does not amount to 'direct democracy', a much-used but vague term. Rather, it is simply a question of whether a given country's system of basically representative government does or does not include provision for the referendum (Hug 2009). The term 'direct democracy' has its roots in the idea that, under the institutions of representative government, the people's role in decision-making is only indirect, in that they elect representatives, who then make the decisions. When the referendum is used, it seems that the people are making the decisions themselves. However, 'direct democracy' has many connotations, both positive and negative, so scholars tend to give the phrase a wide berth and instead analyse the referendum as an institution within the framework of representative democracy.

Types of referendum

In a referendum, as Butler and Ranney (1994: 1) usefully define the term, 'a mass electorate votes on some public issue'. The most useful typology designed to impose some order upon the potential chaos of a large number of referendums is that of Uleri (1996; 2003: 85–109). While we do not have space to elaborate the full typology, three of the dimensions it identifies are particularly important.

First, a referendum might be mandatory in the circumstances, or optional. For example, the referendums in Denmark and Ireland in 1972 on whether to join the European Community were mandatory because both countries' constitutions specified the necessity for a referendum on an issue with such major implications for sovereignty, whereas the French and Dutch referendums of 2005 on the proposed EU constitution and the UK 'Brexit' referendum of June 2016 were optional in that it was not legally or constitutionally necessary that a referendum be held. When referendums are optional, the device is open to partisan manipulation, for example by a government that decides to put an issue to a referendum in the hope of boosting its position or dividing the opposition.

Second, the referendum may take place at the request of either a number of voters, in which case we term it the **initiative**, or a political institution. The distinctive feature of a people's initiative is clear: it enables a set number of voters to bring about a popular vote. The initiative is conspicuous by its rarity in the world's constitutions, though those few states that employ it do so on a large scale. Switzerland leads the way here, with most of its popular votes being initiated by voters; if a prescribed number (which varies from 50,000 to 100,000 depending on the nature of the proposal) sign a petition calling for a vote on amending the constitution or rejecting a bill recently passed by parliament, such a vote must take place.

Italy was for long the only other West European country to allow the initiative, and while the engaged citizenry brought about many popular votes in the 1980s and 1990s, the use of this weapon against the political class—for that was how many of these initiatives were perceived—has since declined. More recently, the Netherlands introduced a provision under which 300,000 voters could demand a non-binding popular vote, and in 2016 this resulted in a vote on the rather abstruse topic of Dutch ratification of a treaty between the EU and Ukraine. A number of post-communist countries have provision for the initiative in their constitutions, but the difficulty of mobilizing the population in most of these countries means that the initiative has not become significant. The initiative is also a prominent feature of state-level politics in parts of the US, especially the south-west.

Third, there is a distinction between *decision-promoting* and *decision-controlling* referendums. Provision for the former is rare; so-called 'plebiscitarian' referendums, where an authoritarian leader makes a proposal and then calls a popular vote to endorse this, belong in this category, examples being the referendums held in France by Napoleon and Louis Napoleon, or more recently in some authoritarian regimes such as Belarus, Rwanda, and Turkmenistan on extending the rule of the incumbent president. Decision-controlling referendums, where an actor opposed to some proposal may invoke the people as a potential veto player, are more common. Here we may distinguish between abrogative referendums or initiatives (which aim to strike down an existing law or constitutional provision) and rejective ones (which aim to prevent some proposal from passing into law or the constitution). Switzerland has a widely used provision for the rejective initiative, under which, within ninety days of parliament's approval of a bill, 50,000 citizens may launch a challenge to it by calling a popular vote. Italy provides for the abrogative initiative, allowing citizens to call a vote on any existing law. In some other countries, a minority of parliamentarians (as in Denmark or Spain) or a number of regional councils (as in Italy) may call a rejective referendum on certain proposals.

The rationale of the referendum

Why use referendums? There are, of course, cases for and against, yet on the whole the evidence is strangely inconclusive and suggests that neither supporters nor sceptics are on secure ground when they try to make a general case about referendums. We can categorize the arguments as related to process or to outcome. Process-related arguments suggest that, regardless of the decisions reached, the very fact that they have been reached through a referendum is important in itself, while outcome-related arguments suggest that the quality of decisions may be affected by the direct involvement of the voters (see Box 10.2). On the whole, supporters of referendums are more likely to invoke process-related arguments, while opponents tend to emphasize the impact on outcomes.

Process-related arguments

The two main process arguments are, first, that certain policies can be fully legitimated only by their endorsement in a referendum and, second, that participation in a referendum is good in itself and also educates voters about issues.

The legitimation argument rests on the fact that at elections individual voters are influenced by many factors. We cannot conclude that, just because a party includes a particular policy promise in its manifesto, anyone who votes for a candidate of this party necessarily wants to see that policy implemented. The policy may not have affected their vote at all, or they may have voted for the party despite, rather than because of, this particular policy. Consequently, opponents of a policy might claim that the government has no explicit mandate for it.

Hence, it is argued, we can only be sure that the people are in favour of a particular policy if they have actually endorsed it in a referendum. While no one except a referendum fanatic would suggest that this kind of validation process is needed for every piece of legislation or government decision, the argument has special force in the case of major choices facing a society: whether to join or leave a transnational body such as the European Union (EU), whether to secede from an existing state and become independent, or whether to make a significant change to the political institutional regime or to the moral ethos of society. In these cases, many voters may feel that elites do not have the right to make such decisions on their behalf. The case for a referendum is even stronger if the proposal is one that did not feature prominently in the preceding election or that, if implemented, would be more or less irreversible.

For example, fourteen of the nineteen countries that joined the EU between 1973 and 2004 held a referendum to decide whether to join, while Norway's people decided against joining in two referendums. Britain voted twice (in 1975 and 2016) on whether to leave. The secessions of Norway from Sweden in 1905, Iceland from Denmark in 1944, East Timor from

FOR AND AGAINST 10.2

Referendums: arguments for and against

Arguments for the referendum	Arguments against the referendum
The referendum enhances democracy by enabling more people to become directly involved in decision-making.	Elected politicians have an expertise in policy-making that ordinary people do not, so taking decision-making out of the hands of political representatives is likely to lead to lower-quality decisions.
Because of the way policies are bundled together at elections, only by holding a referendum on an issue is it possible to get a clear verdict from the people on that issue.	In practice, many people decide how to vote in a referendum on the basis of extraneous factors, so we cannot draw inferences about policy preferences from voting behaviour in a referendum.
A decision made by the people directly has more legitimacy than one made by the political class alone, especially if the issue is a fundamental one for the future of society.	Referendums give insensitive or prejudiced majorities an opportunity to ride roughshod over minority rights.
The referendum process creates a more informed electorate, as people are exposed to arguments on either side of the issue.	Those most likely to vote in a referendum are those who feel most strongly on an issue and the better off, so referendums work against the interests of moderates and the less well off.
All the evidence suggests that the referendum, sensibly used, can enhance representative democracy.	The use of referendums opens the door to the prospect of a 'direct democracy' in which people cast votes on the 'issue of the day' without taking the trouble to inform themselves, thus trivializing the decision-making process.

Indonesia in 1999, Montenegro from Serbia in 2006, and South Sudan from Sudan in 2011 were all put to, and approved in, referendums, while the people of Scotland narrowly voted against leaving the UK in a referendum in 2014. The proposed adoption or fundamental alteration of a new constitution is sometimes decided by referendum, as in France (1958), Kenya (2010), and Spain (1978). In Catholic countries in particular, referendums have been thought appropriate to decide moral issues: divorce in Ireland, Italy, and Malta; abortion in Ireland, Italy, and Portugal; same-sex marriage in Ireland.

The second process-related argument is that the opportunity to vote in referendums increases political participation, which is inherently a good thing. The use of referendums might be able to reduce feelings of disengagement from the political process by involving people directly in decision-making. Citizens may respond to this empowerment by educating and informing themselves about the subject, thus raising the level of political knowledge in society (Tierney 2014). Yet, it would be facile to imagine that unleashing a tranche of referendums on an indifferent populace will somehow create an engaged citizenry. Unless electors regard the issues at stake as important, they are unlikely to make the effort to vote.

Outcome-related arguments

Giving people more chances to take part in decision-making is cited as an argument in favour of referendums, but there is also a counterargument. As Papadopoulos puts it, increasing the number of opportunities to participate also increases the opportunities for exclusion, and hence the use of referendums may lead to worse outcomes than purely representative democracy (quoted in Uleri 1996: 17).

Another outcome-related argument is the claim that, because the referendum is an inherently majoritarian device, it might result in infringement of the rights of minorities. Legislators, it is argued, are aware of the need for balance and for toleration, even of groups whose behaviour they personally disapprove of. In contrast, the mass public, which bases its opinions on information fed to it by partisan sources or gleaned via the simplistic coverage of the tabloid press and their broadcasting equivalents, has no inhibitions about giving free rein to its prejudices in the privacy of the ballot box. As James Bryce summed up this line of thought over a century ago, parliamentarians 'may be ignorant, but not so ignorant as the masses' (quoted in Gallagher 1996: 241). The Swiss referendum of November 2009, when the people voted by 57 to 43 per cent to ban the building of any more minarets in Switzerland, might be cited as an example by proponents of this view. Similarly, in 2016 voters in Hungary overwhelmingly opposed accepting migrants even if there was EU pressure on the country to do this, while in 2018 Romanian voters expressed their opposition to same-sex marriage—though both of these votes failed to reach a turnout threshold and hence were not binding upon parliament. Likewise, a peace agreement painstakingly negotiated between the Colombian government and the rebel group FARC was narrowly rejected by the electorate in 2016 (a slightly amended version was later ratified by parliament and not put to a referendum). A similar if rather elitist point, to the effect that referendums transfer the resolution of a question from those with some expertise to those with little or none, was heard in the aftermath of the 'Brexit' referendum of June 2016, when the people of the UK voted by a 52–48 majority to leave the EU. Most MPs were opposed to Brexit as, among the electorate, were those with more than the minimum level of education and those under fifty.

However, empirical evidence from the US suggests that, at least when it comes to minority protection, the key factor is not the mode of decision-making but the size of the unit making the decision: minority rights receive less protection in small, local units than at state level (because the former are more likely to be homogeneous), regardless of whether the decision is made by referendum or by elected representatives, but there is no sign that referendums per se discriminate against minorities (Donovan and Bowler 1998: 264–70).

Moreover, there is often room for normative debate as to whether a particular decision amounts to unfair and discriminatory treatment of a minority or whether it is simply a perfectly legitimate, albeit contentious, choice by a majority of the voters. As defenders of the latter position are wont to say, majorities have rights too. Representative government is often criticized for being unduly responsive to pressure from well-organized and sometimes well-resourced minorities, who secure concessions at the expense of the public weal, and referendums could help to counter this. Still, unbridled use of the referendum does have the potential to upset what may be a delicate balance within society, and, consequently, in most states employing it, there are devices to curb the danger of majoritarianism.

1. In most countries, access to the referendum is highly restricted. Usually, it is the legislature that decides whether, and on what proposal(s), a vote is to take place, so it has control over the items that get onto the referendum agenda in the first place.

2. In countries that provide for the initiative, where a certain number of voters themselves can trigger a public vote without needing the consent of parliament, a judicial body such as a constitutional court frequently has a veto role. Such bodies have been active in Italy and in a number of post-communist countries. Courts also play an important role in the US, possessing the power (regularly used) to strike proposals from the ballot paper or, *post hoc*, to nullify the outcome of a vote on the basis that its implementation would be contrary to the state or federal constitution (Magleby 1994: 235–6; Tolbert et al. 1998: 50–3).

3. In federal countries, a 'double majority' is a common requirement: a proposal requires the support of a majority of voters and also a majority within at least half of the federal units (Australia, Switzerland).

The outcome-related arguments, then, are largely critical of the referendum, but for the most part they are not convincing. The process-related arguments tend to be cited primarily by advocates of the referendum, but here too there is plenty of room for debate. The fact that it is impossible to point to clinching arguments on one side or the other helps to explain why there is such variation across the world in the use of the referendum, as we shall now see.

Empirical patterns

The use of referendums is widespread, albeit uneven. Legal and constitutional provision increased somewhat in the last three decades of the twentieth century (Scarrow 2003: 48), and the frequency of referendums is also increasing over time (LeDuc 2003: 21). Even so, we should not exaggerate their use. Most democratic states hold at most one referendum per decade on average. Switzerland holds many more referendums than any other country, on average around seven annually; its tiny neighbour Liechtenstein sees around one per year on average, and other relatively heavy users of the device are Italy, New Zealand, Ireland, Australia, and Uruguay.

Indeed, the variation in the frequency of referendums is striking. Some established democracies have held no national referendums at all (post-war Germany, India, Japan, the US) or very few (Netherlands, Spain, the UK). In some others, such as Australia, Denmark, France, Ireland, and New Zealand, the referendum has become established as a means by which the country reaches decisions on major questions. In others again, a large and disparate range of issues, some major and some more or less trivial, have been put to a vote of the public; Switzerland and, to a lesser extent, Italy and Liechtenstein epitomize this pattern.

Explaining the variations is not easy. Worldwide, the largest countries make little use of the referendum, but within Europe large countries such as France and Italy are regular users. Some federal countries eschew the referendum, while others such as Australia and Switzerland embrace it. There are apparent cases of diffusion, or common roots, of patterns between neighbouring countries, such as Switzerland and Liechtenstein, yet there is significant variation among the Scandinavian countries, which generally keep a close eye on each other's experiences.

The dramatic contrast between Switzerland and every other country represents a qualitative as well as a quantitative difference. Elsewhere, democracy is fundamentally representative in nature, and the referendum is a kind of 'optional extra' that modifies, to a greater or lesser degree, the way in which the political process functions. In Switzerland, in contrast, the referendum is woven deep into the fabric of democracy, and, far from constituting an occasional 'shock to the system' it is an inherent part of that system (Serdült 2014).

Referendum subjects, outside Switzerland, do not usually cover the full range of political issues. In particular, conventional left–right issues such as the familiar tax-versus-spending trade-off, which usually underlie the party system, rarely feature on referendum ballots. More characteristically, as already mentioned, referendum votes concern sovereignty-related questions such as independence, secession, or membership of (or closer integration within) the EU. The rationale is that these are non-partisan issues that transcend the day-to-day political warfare between parties and that the parties do not have the right to decide on the people's behalf.

Voting behaviour at referendums

A central argument in favour of referendums is that they allow the people to decide directly on the resolution of some important issue. This argument would be weakened if it were to transpire that, in practice, many people's voting behaviour is determined not by their views on the issue at stake but by peripheral or extraneous questions. Allegations to this effect were heard in the summer of 2005, when the people of France and the Netherlands rejected the proposed EU constitutional treaty, and in 2016, when Dutch voters voted against ratification of a treaty between the EU and Ukraine. Critics of the referendum suggested that many of the 'No' voters had not been voting on the

substantive issues at all but had allowed themselves to be swayed by irrelevancies or had simply taken the opportunity to strike a blow at the unpopular political establishment by rejecting one of its most cherished proposals.

More broadly, the academic literature in this area has implied two 'ideal-type' interpretations of referendum voting behaviour. According to one point of view, sometimes termed the *issue-voting perspective*, voters decide mainly on the basis of the issue on the ballot paper. According to the other, sometimes termed the *second-order election perspective*, voters take little notice of that issue and instead cast a vote according to what really matters to them, i.e. their evaluation of the actors on each side, especially the government; if they dislike the government of the day, they will vote against pretty much any proposition that it puts to a referendum.

The reality, as most people would expect, is somewhere between the two ideal-type interpretations. That is to say, voters take into account a range of factors: they do assign a lot of importance to the substantive issue itself, but they are also interested in knowing about who its proponents and opponents are. Other things being equal, a proposal advocated by a popular government will, of course, fare better than one advanced by an unpopular one, but that is not to say that voters do not give primacy to the question on the ballot paper. The role of campaign finance is also uncertain, and there is surprising variation in the extent to which this is regulated cross-nationally (Gilland Lutz and Hug 2010).

Whether this adds up to an argument for holding more referendums on the EU, or for holding none at all, is a question that divides students of the EU. It is difficult to answer many of the questions to which we would like to know the answers, such as whether the pace of European integration would have been more rapid if there had been fewer referendums on the subject (Binzer Hobolt 2009: 242–8)—and if we did know the answer to that, it would simply raise the normative question of whether this should be seen as an argument for or against the use of referendums on European integration.

Referendum turnout is usually lower than in parliamentary elections, but it varies quite markedly, depending mainly on how important the issue is (Kobach 2001; LeDuc 2003: 169–72). For example, in New Zealand, 83 per cent of voters turned out in a 1993 referendum on changing the electoral system, whereas two years later only 28 per cent voted on a question concerning the number of firefighters who should be employed. General election turnout, in contrast, is much more stable.

Similarly, campaign effects can be much greater in referendums than in general elections. If the issue is of low salience for most voters and has not been extensively politicized before the campaign begins, the campaign has scope to make a major impact and we may see large shifts of opinion as it proceeds. When the reverse applies, there is typically no more volatility than during an election campaign. If a large swing occurs, it is likely to be in a negative direction (Renwick 2014). Characteristically, the process is one whereby voters initially incline to a 'soft Yes' (in other words, they like the sound of the proposal in principle), but opponents are able to conjure up the 'fear of the abyss' (Darcy and Laver 1990). They raise a host of objections and doubts, so even if voters are by no means sure that the dire warnings really are valid, they still feel it would be safer to maintain the status quo for the time being.

The impact of referendums

Referendums might make a significant difference to politics in a number of ways, most obviously to policy outcomes. Here we could expect them to have a conservative impact, in that the people are brought into the decision-making process as an additional 'veto player'. A policy change agreed by the elite can potentially be prevented unless the people also approve it. Therefore, critics warn of the danger of policy immobilism if the referendum is too readily available as a blocking mechanism, asking whether any of the main advances of the past, such as extending the franchise to those with little property and to women, or the establishment of religious freedom, would have occurred had the eligible voters of the day been able to prevent it by a direct vote on the issue. Defenders argue that this is exaggerated, and that the endorsement of the voters is 'a powerful legitimiser of political decisions', depriving the outvoted minority of any sense that they have a valid grievance (Setälä 1999: 161). Major decisions involving sovereignty, or the allocation of values within a society, might not be regarded as fully legitimate by opponents if they are taken solely by the political class. Testing these propositions empirically—that policy innovation is slower in countries that employ the referendum, and that decisions made by a referendum enjoy greater legitimacy than those made by representative institutions alone—would, of course, be a challenge.

Where the initiative is available, the danger is of too much rather than too little policy innovation. Minorities might be able to get their superficially attractive but essentially populist schemes approved by a public that does not take the trouble to scrutinize them thoroughly or to ask how they will be funded, whereas elected parliamentarians would not be so gullible. This is a particular concern of elite theorists of democracy such as Giovanni Sartori, who refers to the 'cognitive incompetence' of most citizens, and of others who attribute great power to those who control the media and see referendums as merely 'devices for the political mobilization of opinion-fed masses by the elite' (Sartori 1987: 120; Hirst 1990: 33). Such arguments were aired in the aftermath of the UK's 2016 Brexit referendum. However, some of the arguments against allowing ordinary people to make decisions through referendums virtually amount to arguments against allowing people to vote at all. Moreover, the picture of voter incompetence can be disputed; even if voters do not possess comprehensive information about the case for and against the referendum issue, they may have acquired as much information as they actually need (Lupia and Johnston 2001).

Finally, what about the impact of referendums on the quality of democracy? As indicated earlier in the section, it is possible to construct plausible arguments to the effect that the use of the referendum will greatly enhance, or greatly damage, the functioning of democracy. Yet the final verdict is that the quality of democracy seems to be little affected one way or the other by the incidence of referendums. The standard of democracy does not seem to differ so very much between Denmark (with nineteen post-war referendums) and Finland (one), or between France (fifteen) and Germany (zero). It is difficult to find countries whose people feel their quality of democracy has been ruined by either the existence or the non-existence of referendums. Public attitudes, as far as we can tell, are broadly supportive (Dalton 2004: 182–4; Donovan and Karp 2006).

The referendum, then, is entirely compatible with the institutions of representative government. It is not an essential feature of a system of representative democracy but is, rather, an 'optional extra'. In the minds of some of its more fervent proponents and opponents, it might become the cornerstone of **governance**, transforming representative democracy into direct democracy, with citizens texting in their votes on the 'issue of the day' as they might for the winner of a TV talent show. This is not a realistic vision. Representative government has established itself across the developed world, and the evidence suggests that the referendum can play a significant role within it.

Conclusion

In this chapter, we have looked at the two main voting opportunities in modern democracies: elections and referendums. Elections are central to any political system that claims to be democratic, while referendums, in contrast, are used extensively in some countries yet rarely or never in others.

Electoral regulations, the set of rules governing the holding of elections, tend to be quite similar among democracies, though there are some variations when it comes to the age at which one can vote or be a candidate, the ease of access to the ballot, and the term of office of elected representatives. The franchise was broadened steadily during the nineteenth and twentieth centuries, and the main debate now concerns not whether certain categories of citizens should be allowed to vote but, rather, whether people should be compelled to vote. Some argue that compulsory voting leads to more equitable policy outputs; others see it as an infringement of personal rights.

Electoral systems, the set of rules that structure how votes are cast at elections and how these votes are then converted into the allocation of offices, have the potential to play a significant role in influencing a country's political system. While there is a good deal of variation across countries, we have seen that elec-

toral systems can be grouped into two main categories, PR and non-PR. Proportional representation systems provide a closer relationship between the distributions of votes and of seats, and are associated with multiparty systems; non-PR systems are more likely to produce single-party governments and something approaching a two-party system.

When we look at referendums, we find a good deal of variation, not only in the frequency of use but in the kind of referendum. Some are initiated by the voters themselves, others by governments or parliaments. Some are held because the country's constitution prescribes that a referendum is necessary before a particular step can be taken; others are held at the whim of a government that hopes to derive some partisan advantage from the vote. Some are decisive, others merely advisory. While referendum issues can also cover a wide range, certain issues do seem to be regarded as especially suitable for popular votes: those concerning sovereignty, for example, or moral issues that cut across party lines.

The merits and demerits of referendums have been vigorously argued for many decades. One line of criticism casts doubt on voters' competence to reach a conclusion on the issues placed before them, suggesting that they are easily manipulated and tend to vote primarily on the basis of their attitude to the government of the day. The evidence does not support this, though undoubtedly voters' behaviour is affected by their evaluations of those arguing the case for and against the referendum issue. Referendums undoubtedly increase participation in the decision-making process, though proponents and opponents disagree as to whether this a good thing; for the former, it results in a more informed electorate, while for the latter, it places decisions in the hands of those ill-equipped to make them. Proponents argue that a vote by the people legitimizes a decision in a way that a vote by parliament never could; opponents are concerned about the dangers of intolerant majorities trampling over the rights of minorities. The available evidence suggests that the hopes of proponents and the fears of opponents may both be exaggerated.

The two institutions are linked in that the significance of elections may be reduced when referendums are available to opponents of government measures. When there are no referendums, elections have a greater potential to be a decisive arena, since they produce governments whose proposals cannot be blocked by a popular vote. In a country where major issues must be put to the people in a referendum, in contrast, elections settle less; the people retain veto power in certain areas regardless of the wishes of the government or parliament. If the opposition has the power to trigger a rejective referendum, the government has a strong incentive to make whatever concessions are necessary to prevent this from happening.

Where there is provision for the initiative, the opposition has a further weapon to block the government, and the link between 'winning' an election and being able to impose one's policy preferences becomes even weaker.

? QUESTIONS

Knowledge-based

1. What are the main consequences of electoral systems?

2. Taking any country as an example, what difference would we expect to see in its politics if it changed from a PR electoral system to a non-PR system, or vice versa?

3. Are there certain subjects that are especially suitable, and certain subjects that are especially unsuitable, to be put to the people for decision by referendum?

4. Why is the referendum widely used in some democracies and rarely or never used in others?

5. How real is the danger that referendums will result in majorities infringing the rights of minorities?

6. Should the power of a sufficient number of ordinary citizens to initiate public votes, which at present is confined to a few countries, be given to people in every country?

Critical thinking

1. Should voting be made compulsory in modern democracies? What would be the main consequences of compulsory voting?

2. Do electoral systems shape party systems, or do the dominant actors in party systems choose the electoral system that suits them?

3. Does the use of the referendum result in better policies than would be made without it?

4. Does the use of referendums threaten representative democracy, enhance it, or have little impact either way?

≋ FURTHER READING

Altman, D. (2011) *Direct Democracy Worldwide* (Cambridge: Cambridge University Press).

Colomer, J. (ed.) (2004) *Handbook of Electoral System Choice* (Basingstoke: Palgrave Macmillan).

Farrell, D. M. (2010) *Electoral Systems: A Comparative Introduction* (2nd edn) (Basingstoke: Palgrave Macmillan).

Gallagher, M. and Mitchell, P. (eds) (2008) *The Politics of Electoral Systems* (Oxford: Oxford University Press).

Gallagher, M. and Uleri, P. V. (eds) (1996) *The Referendum Experience in Europe* (Basingstoke: Macmillan).

LeDuc, L. (2003) *The Politics of Direct Democracy: Referendums in Global Perspective* (Peterborough, Ontario: Broadview Press).

Lijphart, A. (1994) *Electoral Systems and Party Systems: A Study of Twenty-Seven Democracies, 1945–1990* (Oxford: Oxford University Press).

Renwick, A. and Pilet, J.-B. (2016), *Faces on the Ballot: The Personalization of Electoral Systems in Europe* (Oxford: Oxford University Press).

Shugart, M. S. and Taagepera, R. (2017), *Votes from Seats: Logical Models of Electoral Systems.* Cambridge: Cambridge University Press.

Tierney, S. (2014) *Constitutional Referendums: The Theory and Practice of Republican Deliberation* (Oxford: Oxford University Press).

 Visit the Online Resources that accompany this book for additional material, including country profiles, comparative data sets, flashcard glossaries, and web directory.

www.oup.com/he/caramani5e

11

Multilevel governance

Liesbet Hooghe, Gary Marks, and Arjan H. Schakel

Reader's guide

Multilevel governance is the dispersion of authority to jurisdictions within and beyond national states. Three literatures frame the study of multilevel governance. Economists and public policy analysts explain multilevel governance as a functionalist adaptation to the provision of public goods at diverse scales. Political economists model the effects of private preferences and moral hazard. Sociologists and political scientists theorize the effects of territorial identity on multilevel governance. These approaches complement each other, and today researchers draw on all three to explain variation over time and across space. The tremendous growth of multilevel governance since World War II has also spurred research on its effects. Multilevel governance has gone hand in hand with subnational and supranational elections, and has greatly diversified the arenas in which citizens can express their preferences. The effects of multilevel governance for ethno-territorial conflict are debated. Does it fuel and dampen demands for regional self-rule? On the one hand, multilevel governance provides resources for separatist movements; on the other, it opens the possibility for accommodation through shared rule. Finally, multilevel governance leads to greater subnational variation in social policy, yet also makes it possible for central and regional governments to coordinate policy.

Introduction

Authority—the competence to make binding decisions that are regarded as legitimate—has been dispersed from the central state upward and downward over the past seventy years. Multilevel governance has become the new normal. This process has been two-sided. Authority has shifted both to subnational jurisdictions and to international institutions (Hooghe and Marks 2003).

Europe is an example of the two-sided character of multilevel governance. Europe has experimented with scaling up to the supranational level, chiefly to the European Union, to gain the benefits of scale in providing public goods. The Union encompasses countries and their regions in a continental system of economic exchange, individual mobility, dispute resolution, fundamental research, and external representation. Scale enhances efficiency in each of these endeavours because it makes sense to co-determine the policy for all the people affected by a policy, rather than just one segment, and because the cost of providing a public policy is lower if it is shared across a very large number of people. In addition, the economic size of the Union makes it a great power in global economic, financial, and environmental governance. At the same time, Europe has been at the forefront of decentralizing authority within states (Marks et al. 2008a; Tatham 2014). Since the 1960s, new tiers of subnational government have been created in twenty-two European countries, and self-rule has been extended to several regions with distinctive communities, including the Azores, the Basque country, Catalonia, Corsica, Flanders, Scotland, South-Tirol, and Wales.

This chapter is concerned with subnational authority, but to understand sources and effects it is useful to begin with the wider backdrop of multilevel governance. We then narrow the focus to multilevel governance within states. What form has multilevel governance taken, and how does it vary across countries? We next turn to the effects of multilevel governance. How does multilevel governance affect the structure and functioning of party systems, ethnoterritorial conflict, and social policy?

KEY POINTS

- Multilevel governance is the dispersion of authority within and beyond national states.
- Authority is the competence to make binding decisions that are regarded as legitimate.

Two logics

Two logics underpin multilevel governance. One is a functionalist logic that conceives governance as an instrument for the efficient delivery of goods that individuals cannot provide for themselves. The other, no less powerful, logic is the demand for self-rule by those living in distinctive communities.

The premise of the functionalist logic of multilevel governance is that every public good has an optimal spatial scale. Where the benefits and costs of providing a public good are contained within the local community, as for parks, public libraries, or elementary schools, it is best to let local government decide because they have better information on local tastes and conditions.

Where a public good has broad externalities or economies of scale, as in health care, pensions, or regulating income inequality, national government should be responsible.

Public goods with externalities that extend beyond national borders, for example facilitating international trade or combating highly infectious disease, call for governance at the continental or global level (see Box 11.1).

The optimal design is then to bundle policies in a limited number of widely spaced tiers of government. The result is a Russian Doll arrangement, where local governments are nested in regional governments, which are nested in national governments, and so on up to the globe as a whole. The overall pattern is unplanned, but it has a rational structure of roughly equally spaced tiers at exponentially increasing population levels. When one plots the average population of each tier of government on a log scale, as in Figure 11.1, the result is a linear progression of nested tiers—a ladder of governance.

States can exist at different population scales within the ladder. A small state, e.g. Luxembourg at b in Figure 11.1, has just one level within it and several levels beyond, including Benelux, the European Union, and a panoply of cross-regional and global organizations. A state at d in the Figure (say Brazil) has several levels within it and only two levels above. For Brazil, this is Mercosur at the regional international level and the United Nations system of international organizations at the global level.

Hence, the larger the population of a state, the greater the number of levels of government within it and the fewer above it (Hooghe and Marks 2009; Hooghe et al. 2016b). Box 11.2 illustrates this for four countries with widely divergent population sizes.

The second logic that drives multilevel governance is an identity logic that conceives governance

---

BOX 11.1

Concepts of a functional logic

Public good

A public good is a policy or service provided by government that is non-excludable and/or non-rivalrous, i.e. individuals cannot be excluded from using the good and the use by some does not reduce its availability to others. Examples are clean air, trade, rule of law.

Externality

An externality occurs when a policy or service provided in one jurisdiction affects another jurisdiction. For example, an industrial plant in region A may cause pollution in region B (*negative* externality) or individuals educated in region A may live and pay taxes in region B (*positive* externality).

Economies of scale

Economies of scale occur when the marginal cost of one unit of a policy or service decreases as the number of units increases. For example, a region of one million residents can provide specialist hospital care at a lower cost/taxpayer than a municipality of a 100,000 people.

Optimal jurisdictional design

A jurisdictional design is optimal when public goods are allocated across levels of government so that externalities are internalized and scale benefits maximized.

Figure 11.1 The ladder of governance

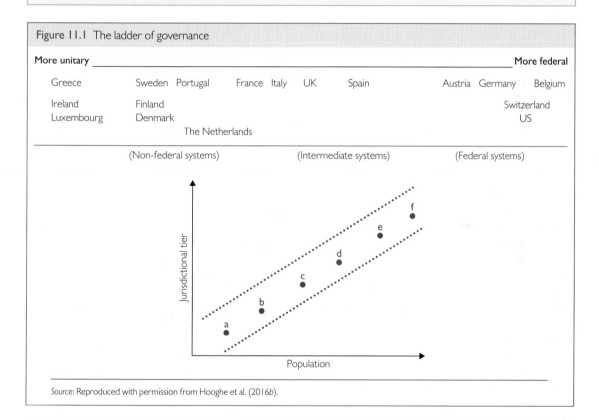

Source: Reproduced with permission from Hooghe et al. (2016b).

BOX 11.2

Is there an underlying structure of governance?

The relationship between government tiers and population size reveals an elegant ladder of governance across a vast range of scale in countries as different as China, Luxembourg, Argentina, and the US. The Y-axis in each figure arrays government levels in order of population size. The X-axis estimates the population of each level on a logarithmic scale. We describe the fitted line in each figure as a jurisdictional axis. The alignment of jurisdictions along the axis suggests that the

BOX 11.2 (continued)

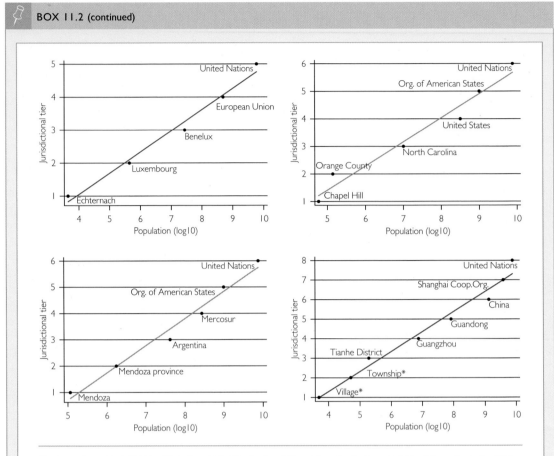

Note: Luxembourg (top left), United States (top right), China (bottom left), and Argentina (bottom right). Population estimates for 2010; population numbers for village and township in China are averages for the Tianhe District.

structure of government has a functional logic which maximizes scale flexibility in policy provision but minimizes the number of jurisdictional tiers.

One implication is that the larger the population of a country, the greater the benefit of subnational jurisdictions that can deliver policy at the appropriate level.

as an expression of the desire for self-rule by a group that sees itself as a distinct community. Demanding self-rule is quite different from demanding a particular package of public goods. Individuals living in such communities may have exclusive identities with their region or country. They may insist on self-rule, even if this hurts economic growth.

From an identity perspective, the structure of governance should follow the boundaries of communities. One result is that the population of jurisdictions at a given subnational level can vary widely. Consider Spain's seventeen autonomous communities, the highest subnational tier established in the years after Spain's transition to democracy following Franco's death in 1976. The median population of an autonomous community is just over two million, but the range is wide. Navarre, Rioja, and Cantabria have

fewer than 700,000 inhabitants, whereas Catalonia and Andalusia have more than seven million. The Spanish constitution of 1978 recognizes that identity—not scale—sets the boundaries of its 'automous communities', which include the special historical nationalities of the Basque Country, Catalonia, Galicia as well as the chartered rights of Navarre. It mandates that an 'autonomous community' can be constituted by a single province with 'a historical regional identity', or by adjacent provinces with 'common historical, cultural, and economic characteristics', or by a region having a distinct territory. Jurisdictional design in Spain, as in many countries in Europe and across the world, reflects the history and identity of its regional peoples.

Where distinctive communities such as the Azores or Quebec demand self-rule, they seek to gain

DEFINITIONS 11.3

Multilevel governance

Multilevel governance is the dispersion of authority within and beyond national states.

Decentralization

Decentralization is the shift of authority (fiscal, political, administrative) from the centre to regional or local governments within a country.

Federalism

Federalism is practiced where government functions within a country are shared between the central government and regional governments so that neither the centre nor the regions may unilaterally change the system.

Unitary government

A unitary government is where the central government may share authority with local and regional governments, but the central government can change the system unilaterally.

Self-rule

Self-rule is the extent to which a regional government exercises authority in its territory.

Shared rule

Shared rule is the extent to which a regional government co-exercises authority within the country as a whole.

Confederation

A confederation is where the central government is constituted by sovereign units that may unilaterally change the association. Common policies are often limited to defence, foreign policy, and currency.

Devolution

Devolution is the process of granting legislative autonomy to one or several regions within an overall unitary framework.

Home rule

Home rule is where the region has extensive self-rule so that it exercises some key functions of a sovereign state.

authority in ways that break the uniformity of authority across a country. The result is *differentiated governance*, in which one or more regions in a country have authoritative competences that distinguish them from other regions in the same country. The demands of minority communities for self-rule can set them apart from other territories within the state, and central governments may decide to accommodate them. Scotland has long had a distinctive legal status within the UK, with Wales following from 1964. Yet the concept of differentiation travels well beyond Britain. Many countries have some form of differentiated governance, and the incidence has been growing in recent years, as we explain in the next section on 'Concepts and definitions'.

KEY POINTS

- Multilevel governance is a response to functionalist pressures for the efficient provision of public goods from the local to the global levels.
- Multilevel governance is a response to the demand for self-rule by a group that sees itself as a distinct community.

Concepts and definitions

Multilevel governance describes the dispersion of authority whether this is within a state or beyond it. So, it ties together comparative politics and international organization to encompass the EU and the decentralization of its member states. Most of the concepts that had previously been used to describe the dispersion of authority apply exclusively within states (Box 11.3).

Of these concepts, *decentralization* is the most commonly used. It refers to the shift of authority towards regional or local government and away from central government. This can be political (e.g. setting up regional elections), fiscal (e.g. granting tax or spending powers), or administrative (e.g. the power to hire personnel) (Rodden 2004; Falleti 2005; Wibbels 2006). A limitation of the concept of decentralization is that it does not distinguish between local or regional government. Knowing whether a state is more or less centralized does not tell one which tier does what. Measures of decentralization focus on the central state and consider all levels of subnational governance as 'the other', the non-central state (Hooghe et al. 2016a). Hence, if a country is described as highly decentralized, we do not know a priori whether it has strong regions or strong local governments (Marks et al. 2008a).

A standard way of conceiving the territorial structure of authority is as a choice between a *federal* or *unitary* system of government (Elazar 1991; Watts 1998). The chief difference is that under federalism the centre cannot change the structure unilaterally, whereas in a unitary state it can. A federal system is partitioned in regional units, whereas a unitary system may or may not have regional units. Hence in a federal system, government functions are divided and sometimes shared between the central government and regional governments, and this dual sovereignty is constitutionally protected against change by either the centre or the regions acting alone (Riker 1964). Classical examples of federations are Australia, Brazil, Canada, Germany, India, Nigeria, and the US.

A *confederation* is looser than a federation in that the central government is less important, and often subordinate to, the constituent units. Its basis is often a treaty, its powers are usually confined to foreign affairs, defence, and perhaps a common currency, and the units retain the right to secede. Confederations are less common than federations. The US from 1781–89, Switzerland from 1815–48, Germany from 1815–66, and the short-lived confederation of Serbia-Montenegro (2003–06) are examples. Some would also categorize the EU as a confederation (Watts 1998).

In a unitary government, ultimate authority resides with the central government. However, this says nothing about the existence or authority of regional governments. Some unitary states have no regional level, whereas others have regional governments with extensive autonomy. That autonomy may be nearly as wide-ranging as in federal states, but in contrast to federations, the central government can modify the structure of government unilaterally. This idea is expressed in another oft-used term, *devolution*, which refers to the statutory delegation of legislative powers from the central government to regional or local governments. The concept of delegation implies that any transfer of authority is conditional upon the centre's consent. The transfer of authority to Scotland and Wales has been described as devolution to signal that this did not turn the UK into a federation because the devolved powers can, in theory, be revoked by the UK central government.

A unitary state may grant extensive autonomy to a region, making it virtually a self-standing state. The term for this is *home rule*. The remaining link between the region and the country may become very thin, as for example between the Farøer Islands and Denmark, or between the Åland Islands and Finland. Ireland had home rule within the UK until it broke away in 1922.

The federal/unitary distinction brings out the tension between *self-rule* and *shared rule*. Self-rule is the authority that a subnational government exercises in its own territory. Shared rule is the authority that a subnational government co-exercises in the country as a whole. The distinction is familiar in the study of federalism. It is particularly useful because self-rule and shared rule encompass the concept of authority, yet take us an important step closer to the ground—that is, to institutional characteristics that can be empirically evaluated (Elazar 1987; Marks et al. 2008b).

Self-rule enables communities smaller than the state to practice autonomy, which can help them preserve distinctiveness or tailor policies to local needs. Yet sharing rule with other regions and the central government in a larger state provides access to the benefits of scale in security, trade, and insurance against external shocks, such as a flood or earthquake. Federal systems institutionalize a trade-off between self-rule and shared rule, but with deepening regional authority in many unitary systems, this trade-off has become a live issue there too. It is not possible for a region to have both complete self-rule and extensive shared rule. If the Flemish government seeks full control over who can immigrate into Flanders, it cannot also hope to codetermine rules that apply to other Belgian regions. Shared rule ties a region to the country as a whole in return for a seat at the table that sets national policy.

Students of local government have developed their own ways to categorize countries (Page and Goldsmith 2010). The chief difference with regional authority is that, for local government, shared rule—institutions that empower local government to routinely co-determine national policy—is typically not on the cards. Local authority is mostly about variation in self-rule, and experts find it useful to break this down in political discretion over policy-making and the extent to which central rule-making can constrain this, financial authority to raise and spend money, and the extent to which local populations can elect (select) their own local government. In a recent comprehensive study, Ladner et al. (2019) array forty European countries from having the most authoritative local authorities in the Nordic countries and Germany to the least authoritative in Georgia, Malta, Moldova, Turkey, and the UK.

Classifications are often inadequate for capturing the complexities of state organization. In the next section, 'What are the chief trends?', we employ measures that conceive regional and local authority as a continuum. It makes sense to conceive of regional and local authority as a continuous dimension rather than in categorical terms, and the concepts of multilevel governance, self-rule, and shared rule can help us unpack the variety of levels at which subnational authority is exercised.

KEY POINTS

- The standard way of conceiving the territorial structure of government is as a basic choice between a federal or unitary constitution. Under a federal constitution, the centre cannot alter the structure unilaterally, whereas under a unitary constitution it can.

- An alternative approach is to conceive regional authority and local authority as continuous dimensions.

- When estimating authority as a continuous dimension, it helps to distinguish between self-rule—the authority that a subnational government exercises in its own territory—and shared rule—the authority that a subnational government co-exercises in the country as a whole.

What are the chief trends?

The growth in multilevel governance within states since World War II amounts to a quiet revolution. It is quiet because it is rarely constitutionalized and almost never catapults countries into full-blooded federalism. In Europe, just one country—Belgium—has become federal, and worldwide the number of countries that have crossed the federal-unitary boundary can be counted on the fingers of one hand. Yet the growth of multilevel governance has affected almost every non-federal country that is middle-sized or larger.

This calls into question a conventional conceptualization of state authority that has long held sway in comparative politics: namely that a country is either federal, in which authority is divided between regional governments and a central government so that each has the final say over some decisions, or unitary, in which the central government monopolizes authority. Multilevel governance transcends the divide because it reveals that unitary states may have multiple levels of government, directly elected regional assemblies, and strong regional or local executives. In this respect, the dichotomy between federal and unitary countries is better conceptualized as a continuum. However, unlike federations, this dispersion of authority is usually not anchored in the constitution.

The Regional Authority Index (RAI) estimates regional and intermediate subnational government in eighty-one countries in the Americas, Europe, Southeast Asia, and the Pacific from 1950–2010 (Hooghe et al. 2016a and b), while the Local Authority Index (LAI) covers local government in thirty-nine European countries from 1990–2014 (Ladner et al. 2016, 2019). Both indices break authority down in administrative, political, and fiscal components.

Three trends have been particularly important. First, there has been a marked rise in both regional and local authority. The RAI has increased in Europe by 7 per cent since 1990, and the LAI has increased by 6 per cent. These are notable trends considering that government institutions tend to be very sticky.

These decades have seen a whirlwind of regional reform in Central and Eastern Europe. Eight countries created new regional tiers: Albania, the Czech Republic, Croatia, Hungary, Latvia, Lithuania, Romania, and Slovakia. Poland comprehensively revamped its existing tier. The reforms responded to twin pressures: a desire for greater subnational democracy after the collapse of authoritarianism, and a functional need to have accountable institutions in place to allocate EU developments funds after EU accession. Several Western European countries reformed subnational government. Finland, Greece, and Ireland introduced a new self-governing tier, and regions in Germany, Italy, Switzerland, and Spain gained new competences. The most dramatic changes took place in Belgium and the UK as a response to the mobilization of territorial identity. Belgium became federal in 1995 in an effort to stabilize Flemish–Francophone relations. The UK government devolved special powers to Scotland, Wales, Northern Ireland, and London. In federal countries, the quiet revolution has been mostly centripetal, drawing constituent units into joint decision-making. In non-federal countries, it has been mostly centrifugal, giving regions greater self-rule without compensating reforms that give them greater responsibility for the country as a whole.

The changes in local government have also been most marked in Central and Eastern Europe. This reflects a catch-up process with Western Europe. As former communist societies become more democratic, so multilevel governance deepened. Just nine counties saw some weakening of local governance, while twenty-six countries experienced some strengthening. Overall, local governments gained in authority across the board, with one exception: the authority to borrow money. This was constrained in many countries in response to the financial crisis that hit Europe from 2008.

By 2010, every European country had authoritative local government or authoritative regional government, or both, as Figure 11.2 reveals. The dark bars show the extent of regional authority and the light bars show the extent of local authority, with countries arrayed from highest to lowest regional authority. Most European countries (nineteen of thirty-five) deepened both regional authority and local autonomy over the past two decades. Fifteen increased either local or regional authority. Just one country (Denmark) scaled back both regional and local authorities.

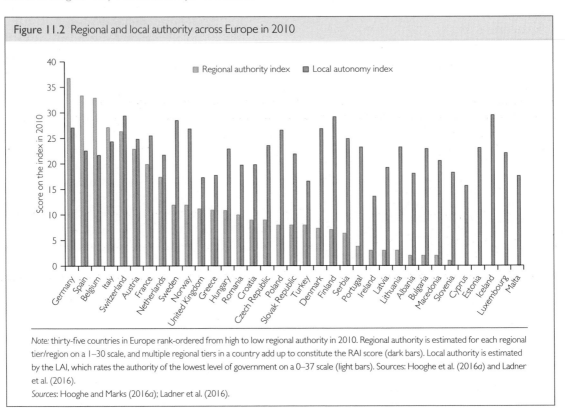

Figure 11.2 Regional and local authority across Europe in 2010

Note: thirty-five countries in Europe rank-ordered from high to low regional authority in 2010. Regional authority is estimated for each regional tier/region on a 1–30 scale, and multiple regional tiers in a country add up to constitute the RAI score (dark bars). Local authority is estimated by the LAI, which rates the authority of the lowest level of government on a 0–37 scale (light bars). Sources: Hooghe et al. (2016a) and Ladner et al. (2016).

Sources: Hooghe and Marks (2016a); Ladner et al. (2016).

The top five countries with respect to regional authority are Germany, Spain, Belgium, Italy, and Switzerland. Three are fully fledged federations, and Spain and Italy might be described as 'quasi-federal' because they have devolved extensive self-rule and some shared rule to their regions. Five countries (Cyprus, Estonia, Iceland, Luxembourg, and Malta) have no authoritative regions. These countries have small populations, and there is little functional rationale for a regional government between the local and the national.

While regional authority varies widely across Europe, the range in local autonomy is narrower. Every contemporary European country requires local governments to provide local public goods related to infrastructure and local services. Interestingly, the five countries without regions have higher than average local authority. Authoritative local governments pick up tasks there that in other countries are handled at the regional level.

Figure 11.3 shows how regional authority developed for eighty-one countries in five world regions from 1950. The trend is upwards, but note the pronounced dips in Latin America and in Southeast Asia in the 1960s and 1970s. These coincide with authoritarianism. The downward trends were reversed once these world regions democratized. A chief driver of multilevel governance, as Box 11.4 notes, is democracy.

While authoritarian rulers are suspicious of multilevel governance because it can provide opponents with an alternative power centre, democratic rulers let the chips fall where they may: decentralization is desirable if it can firm up political support, or it may not be.

A second trend is differentiated governance, in which governments at the same territorial level have divergent political, administrative, or fiscal powers. In 1950, sixteen of the forty-eight countries we track between 1950 and 2010 had one or more regions that meet this criterion. By 2010, as Figure 11.4 illustrates, this had increased to twenty-nine countries. No country with differentiated regional governance has become uniform; thirteen countries have become differentiated, chiefly in response to the demand for self-rule on the part of those claiming to represent distinct ethnic communities.

Historically, differentiation was introduced to appease territories with distinctive identities. Quebec, the only predominantly French-speaking region on the North American continent, controls immigration. Aceh and Scotland have their own legal orders within their respective states. Bolivia's indigenous communities can elect their representatives according to their own rules. The Basque provinces collect their own taxes, while the central government collects taxes on behalf of the other Spanish comunidades. The Åland Islands can exclude non-resident Finnish citizens from

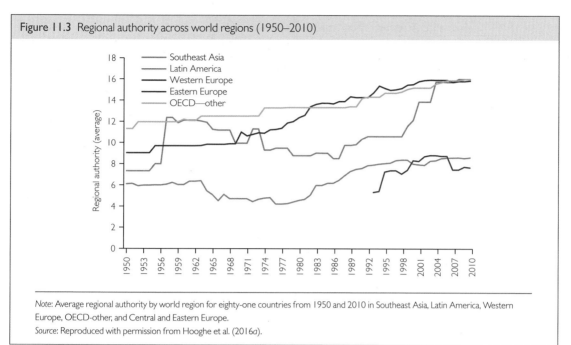

Figure 11.3 Regional authority across world regions (1950–2010)

Note: Average regional authority by world region for eighty-one countries from 1950 and 2010 in Southeast Asia, Latin America, Western Europe, OECD-other, and Central and Eastern Europe.

Source: Reproduced with permission from Hooghe et al. (2016a).

buying land. Greenland and the Farøer Islands are exempt from Denmark's membership of the EU.

Other arrangements tailor authority to the unique governance challenges of national capitals. In authoritarian regimes, capital cities often have less authority than other regions because rulers want to keep close tabs on potential opposition. Kuala Lumpur, Caracas, and in times past, Asunción, Bogota, Mexico City, and Jakarta,

have been directly governed from the centre. The driving force in differentiated governance is identity, though functionality can also play a role. In recent years, differentiation has allowed regional and local governments to experiment with policies, accommodate the demands of distinctive territories, or address the metropolitan governance challenges of large-scale urban areas. Hence the logic can be functional, as well as identity-based.

BOX 11.4

Drivers of multilevel governance

Ethno-territorial identity

The demand for self-rule by territorially concentrated groups pressures central states to decentralize authority. If one region gains self-rule, other regions may demand the same.

Democracy

Democracy diminishes the cost of political mobilization on the part of those who desire self-rule and multiplies the points at which they can access decision-makers. Whereas autocrats rule by denying authority to others, democratic leaders can retain rule by shifting authority out of their own hands if that wins them support.

Interdependence

As people trade, travel, and migrate across national borders, so national states become too small to tackle large-scale

externalities such as regulating trade or climate change and too large to address the cultural and economic effects of mobility on neighbourhoods, towns, and regions.

Affluence

The more affluent a society, the greater the demand for public goods that are best provided closer to the citizen. These include health, education, infrastructure, and a sustainable environment. Regional and local governments can tailor these policies to local circumstances.

Peace

Interstate war drives national centralization; peace allows central governments greater latitude to allocate authority to regional, local, and international jurisdictions.

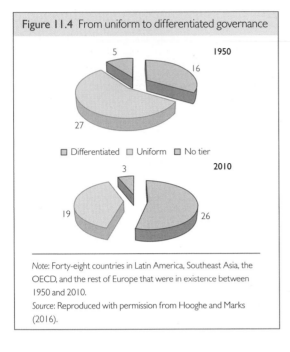

Figure 11.4 From uniform to differentiated governance

Note: Forty-eight countries in Latin America, Southeast Asia, the OECD, and the rest of Europe that were in existence between 1950 and 2010.

Source: Reproduced with permission from Hooghe and Marks (2016).

The upshot is that the territorial structure of governance in Europe has been transformed, reversing a centuries-long process of centralization. The development of the national state from the twelfth century was a long, zig-zag process, in which central states claimed and gradually gained a monopoly of legitimate coercion, creating national armies, national courts, national taxation systems, national health, national education, and national welfare (Tilly 1990). Centralization reached its peak in the first half of the twentieth century. It has been superseded by an era of multilevel governance that began in the second half of the twentieth century (Hooghe and Marks 2016). However, we very much doubt that this is the end of the history of jurisdictional design. The forces that underpinned central state building in Europe—war, nationalism, authoritarianism—have not left the stage. Should any or several return, the result would be to weaken international and subnational governance and compress authority to the national level.

A third trend is the scaling up of subnational government—that is, the concentration of populations and resources in fewer, larger units. The median size of regional units has increased, especially in Europe. Denmark replaced its fifteen counties with five regions in 2007; France reduced the number of regions from twenty-two to thirteen in 2016; Greece abolished its fifty-two prefectures and empowered thirteen larger-scale regions in 2011. The scale of local government has always been, and remains, hugely different across Europe—from an average size in 2014 of under 2,000 people in Slovakia, France, and the Czech Republic to over 50,000 residents in Turkey, Denmark, Ireland, and the UK. Some countries such as Greece, Denmark, Latvia, and Ireland, have drastically reduced the number of municipalities in the past two decades, and others such as the Czech Republic, Croatia, or Slovenia have multiplied them (Ladner et al. 2019).

Scaling up at the local level has come in two forms. One is the proliferation of inter-municipal cooperation arrangements (Allain-Dupré 2018). The other is the creation and empowerment of metropolitan areas. About half of the population in the Organization for Economic Cooperation and Development (OECD) lives in a metropolitan area of half a million people or more, and by 2015 around two-thirds of these areas had acquired their own government. A study by the OECD counts 178 governance arrangements in existence in 2015 (Ahrend et al. 2014; Allain-Dupré 2018). The majority were created in the past two decades, and there has been a pronounced acceleration from 2000.

KEY POINTS

- Subnational authority has deepened in most countries around the world.

- Subnational governance has become more differentiated as individual regions or localities acquire distinct powers.

- The scale of subnational governance has increased as larger regions have replaced smaller regions and in response to the particular demands of governing metropolitan centres.

- The chief drivers of multilevel governance are ethno-territorial identity, democracy, interdependence, affluence, and peace.

Three literatures

Distinct literatures motivate an understanding of decentralization and multilevel governance. The theory of fiscal federalism sets out normative guidelines for assigning tasks to levels of government (Box 11.5). Wallace Oates' (1972) decentralization theorem summarizes a golden rule of multilevel governance: 'decentralize where you can and centralize where you must'. So which policies are best provided at the local or regional level, and which are best provided nationally? Oates identifies several conditions that can tip the balance in one direction or the other.

- *Economies of scale.* Can a local/regional government provide the policy as cheaply as the central government?

- *Inter-regional externalities.* Does the policy affect other regions?
- *Heterogeneity of preferences.* Do citizens in different parts of the country want different policies?
- *Information asymmetry.* Are subnational governments better informed about what their constituents want?

This approach promises a 'perfect mapping', where each public good is provided at the appropriate scale (Olson 1986). However, this assumes that government operates as a distinterested custodian of the public interest. There is no politics here, no self-interested actors, and no problems that arise from getting those who exercise power to act in the public interest.

Scholars began to question these assumptions from the 1990s (Weingast 1995; Inman and Rubinfeld 1997; Besley and Coate 2003). Instead of assuming that public decision-makers are detached social planners, second-generation literature models political actors as self-interested utility maximizers (Treisman 2007). Bureaucrats may be chiefly interested in maximizing their budget, even if this hurts general welfare. Politicians may centralize authority in an effort to increase their chances for re-election. Local or regional governments may run up debts in the expectation that the national government will bail them out.

Jonathan Rodden (2006) documents how decentralized finance poses a moral hazard for countries in which subnational governments are funded primarily through revenue sharing and grants. If those subnational governments can take on debt to supplement their grants, the central government often ends up paying the bill, and these central bailouts can have serious country-wide effects. Hence Brazil's state-level debts in the 1980s and 1990s led to macroeconomic instability and hyperinflation. Germany's regional debt accumulated after unification, but the federal government was able to leverage Eurozone membership to extract new fiscal rules that prohibit regional net borrowing as of 2020. Voters may freeride too; they may try to have their cake and eat it by accessing public goods while evading taxes. While this second-generation literature builds on the first-generation approach, it regards jurisdictional outcomes as motivated chiefly by economic self-interest on the part of rulers, groups, and voters.

Third-generation literature examines the effects of territorial identity and the demand for self-rule to help explain the structure of government (Banting and Kymlicka 2017; Hooghe and Marks 2016; Moreno and Collino 2010). In addition to distributional competition about 'who gets what', this literature raises the *Who Question*—conflict over who should have the right to rule themselves. This extends the analysis beyond the pressures for functionally efficient governance and economic self-interest. At stake are the boundaries of jurisdictions, as well as the allocation of tasks across levels (Rokkan 1983).

Many national states encompass distinctive communities, and when mobilized, they care more about self-rule than about optimal task allocation. When such communities demand self-rule, they are claiming a collective right to exercise authority. The demand is not derivative from a preference over policy. By asserting the right of a community to govern itself, it expresses a *polity* preference rather than a *policy* preference. When identity becomes politicized, it tends to narrow the scope for cost–benefit considerations, and in some instances, can overwhelm it.

Within states, peripheral groups are most liable to demand self-rule. Geographical isolation, linguistic distinctiveness, and a history of independence can lead members of a group to see themselves as a people

---

📌 **BOX 11.5**

Approaches to decentralization and multilevel governance

First Generation	Second Generation	Third Generation
• Government as a custodian of the public interest	• Government as an instrument for self-interested actors	• Government as an expression of community
• Costs and benefits of decentralization	• Social optimality versus group interest	• Functional pressures versus group identity
• Optimal task allocation	• Who gets what?	• Who gets self-rule?

entitled to self-rule. Some peripheral communities divide the world into 'them' and 'us' and resent the rule of those they regard as foreign. The geo-historical bases for such identities are especially strong in Europe and Asia. Territorially concentrated ethnic minorities are less common in Latin America, though in recent decades Bolivia, Colombia, Ecuador, Nicaragua, Panama, and Venezuela have seen the mobilization of indigenous communities demanding self-rule.

Such regions have systemic effects for the countries in which they are located. The transformation is sharp in Britain, once a bastion of democratic class struggle. As the bases of traditional class conflict have eroded, territorial issues have become more salient. The motive force is Scottish nationalism, and it has shaken up Britain as a whole. English nationalism has come to the fore not just in opposition to Europe, but in a preference for expressly English political institutions, including most recently an English national anthem. Support for beefing up the Welsh assembly has also grown over the past decade, and recently regionalism also emerged within England (e.g. the Yorkshire Party and the Wessex Regionalist Party). Diagnosing an 'ever looser union', Charlie Jeffery (2013: 326) observes that 'broad-based discontent over current governing arrangements signifies the emergence, in nascent and as yet rather unfocused form, of an English political community'.

When community comes into play, regional governance involves not just public policy, but also the underlying structure of contestation. Mobilization for self-rule on the part of a distinctive region can affect which issues come to the surface in the society as a whole. Regional governance raises communitarian issues that are associated with a dimension of contestation hinging on nationalism, territorial governance, and immigration. These issues are only weakly related to left-versus-right conflict concerning the distribution of income, welfare, and the role of the state. Whereas class conflict divided society along functional lines, regional governance divides society along territorial lines (Lipset and Rokkan 1967). Whereas class conflict was instrumental in constructing national states, conflict over regional self-rule can fragment national states.

Each of these approaches starts from a distinct conception of governance: governance as a custodian of the public interest; governance as an instrument for private gain; governance as an expression of community. It is possible to use these approaches as alternative lenses, but it makes sense to conceive them as complementary. The sections to come survey research on democracy, ethno-territorial conflict, and social policy to illustrate how multilevel governance may affect social and political phenomena.

KEY POINTS

Scholarship on multilevel governance can be organized in three broad approaches. We conceive these approaches as complementary, rather than competing.

- A functionalist approach predicts that the structure of authority reflects that each policy has its optimal spatial scale.
- An economic approach predicts that jurisdictional design reflects economic self-interest on the part of rulers, groups, and voters.
- An identity approach predicts that territorial identity and the demand for self-rule shape the structure of governance.

The effects of multilevel governance

The rise of multilevel governance has spurred researchers to examine its effects. This section reviews scholarship on multilevel governance and democracy, the management of ethno-territorial conflict, and social policy.

Democracy

Multilevel governance and democracy engage entirely different questions. Multilevel governance responds to the *Who Question*: who gets to form a polity? Democracy responds to the *How Question*: how are decisions made in a polity? Democracy says nothing about the territorial structure of governance; multilevel governance says nothing about how decisions are made within regions or localities. Yet multilevel governance has extended the reach of democracy over the past half-century. When authority is conveyed to subnational institutions in a democracy, there is a presumption that citizens should have some say.

The incidence of regional elections has grown in recent decades and is now almost universal. Eighteen European states have introduced regional elections over the past half-century. Today, 83 per cent of EU citizens can vote in a regional as well as local and national elections (Schakel 2019). Beyond Europe, federal countries have always had regional elections, but until the decades around the turn of the twentieth century this was unusual in unitary countries. As unitary countries deepened regional governance, so they have introduced elections. Today four in five countries with a population greater than ten million have regional as well as national elections. Populous countries—such as Indonesia or India—have several directly elected intermediate tiers (Schakel and Romanova 2018).

Multilevel elections provide opportunities for vote switching where a person votes for one party in a national election and a different party at the regional level. This raises the possibility of systemic divergence between regional and national party systems (Dandoy and Schakel 2013; Schakel 2017; Swenden and Maddens 2009). Are we seeing the reversal of a century-long process of nationalization of party systems (Caramani 2004)?

We find limited evidence for this. Figure 11.5 displays average vote shares for regional parties in national and regional elections since the 1970s in twenty-three European democracies. Regional political parties in distinctive regions have gained an increasing share of the vote from the 1970s to the 2000s. A distinctive region is a region with a prior history of statehood, a region that is located on an island, or a region in which a majority of the population speaks a language that is different from the national language. Around one in twelve regions is distinctive in one of these ways, and Figure 11.5 reveals that the vote share for regional parties in such places is unusually high. However, it is still only 13–15 per cent on average. In the remaining regions, there is scant evidence of regionalization: the average vote share for regional parties in standard regions ranges between only 2 and 3.5 per cent in

the 2000s. After four decades of regional elections, national party systems continue to structure party competition throughout much of Europe.

A core first-generation claim is that decentralization brings governance closer to the citizen. This notion has roots in the writings of Mills, Montesquieu, and de Tocqueville (Faguet 2014), and its modern variant is succinctly expressed by Wallis and Oates (1988: 5): decentralization makes government more responsive by 'tailoring levels of consumption to the preferences of smaller, more homogenous, groups'.

Information is at the heart of this. Subnational government can respond better to citizens because it has access to fine-grained knowledge about citizens' preferences. Should the community expand and upgrade an existing primary school, or should it open a new primary school in a different part of town? Should the region subsidize home care for the elderly, build more retirement homes, or let the market service seniors? What kind of inward investment should the region attract to best take advantage of the region's workforce, schools, and local market? The information needed to make these kinds of decisions is called 'soft' because it is difficult to standardize, resistant to batching, and expensive to pass up a hierarchy (Arrow 1991: 5; Hooghe and Marks 2013).

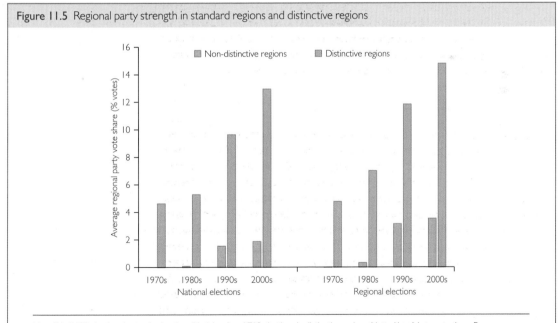

Figure 11.5 Regional party strength in standard regions and distinctive regions

Note: N = 2,192 elections in standard regions (dark bars) and 710 elections in distinctive regions (dotted bars) in twenty-three European countries. The bars show average regional party vote share by decade. The left panel displays regional party votes in national elections and the right panel displays regional party votes in regional elections. A distinctive region has one or more of the following characteristics: a majority speaks a different language from the dominant national language; the region has a history of at least thirty years of sovereign statehood between 1200 AD and 1950; the region is an island or archipelago 30 km or more from the mainland.

Sources: Dandoy and Schakel (2013); Hooghe et al. (2016a); and Schakel (2017).

The upshot is that multilevel governance makes government more responsive to citizens, and thereby strengthens democracy.

However, multilevel governance can blur responsibility when voters lose sight of which governmental level is responsible for what. This becomes ever more problematic as policies require coordinated action by local, regional, national, and international governments (Léon 2010, 2018). The problem is two-sided. For voters to be able to hold politicians accountable, they must be able to link outcomes with politicians' actions. Hence, they need to know not only the relevant actors but also the distribution of powers in the areas they care most about. Otherwise, they may punish or reward the wrong level of government. Is it possible for citizens to distinguish who is responsible for what? The second problem is strategic. When policies are shared among governments at different levels, politicians may intentionally blur responsibility. They may blame other governments for bad policy outcomes, or they may claim credit for good outcomes, even if they had little to do with them.

Blurring of responsibility appears to be partisan. Comparing data from the twenty-eight countries in the 2014 European Election Study (EES), Däubler and colleagues (2018) find that voters in federal Austria, Belgium, Germany, and Spain are no worse in pinpointing which level of government is responsible for the most important problem than are voters in non-federal France, Estonia, or Portugal. What differs is how voters arrive at this decision. In multilevel systems, voters are more partisan in their assessment. Using the same EES data, Léon and her colleagues (2018) show that in federal states, partisans of the national government are much more likely to attribute responsibility for poor economic performance to the regional government. By contrast, in non-federal states, partisan and non-partisan voters do not differ much.

The most effective way in which responsiveness can be blunted is by constraining political competition (Faguet 2014). In principle, dispersing authority across multiple levels of government should increase the opportunities for access, but national and subnational politicians may try to restrict competition. This is apparent in Argentina, where collusion between the federal government and provincial barons has stunted economic development in the poorer parts of the country. Federal governments in Buenos Aires buy provincial legislative support with fiscal hand-outs that provincial barons use to buy off potential challengers (Gervasoni 2010). Money is diverted to rent seeking, and as a result, public policy is inferior in the affected provinces (Ardanaz et al. 2014). A hegemonic party can stifle responsiveness. Studying subnational politics in the Tigray regional state of Ethiopia, Mezgebe (2015) finds that one-party dominance distorts the incentive structure for politicians seeking power: rather than responding to local demands in a bid for electoral support, they invest in intra-party politics to improve their chances for office.

In Western democracies, blurring tends to be more subtle. Politicians may seek to exploit multilevel decision-making to blame external actors. In a case study of the 2015 EU directive on genetically modified organisms (GMO), Tosun and Hartung (2018) document how the European Commission avoided blame for an unpopular policy by authorizing GMOs for cultivation, food, and feed in principle, while allowing member-states and regions to opt out. In Germany, federal and regional governments further blurred responsibility by making opt-out conditional on the consent of regional and federal veto players.

None of this negates the basic thrust that decentralization brings governance closer to the people. This has transparent informational benefits, but as third-generation scholars find, it has additional benefits. For many citizens, government is an expression of community as much—or more—than an instrument for policy delivery. This is the chief conclusion of a comparative survey conducted in fourteen regions across Austria, France, Germany, Spain, and the United Kingdom, which shows that large majorities want a stronger regional government but *less* interregional variation in policies such as tuition fees, dealing with young offenders, old age care, and unemployment benefits. The drivers of support for regional autonomy do not appear to be heterogeneity of preferences, but identity and a desire for self-rule (Henderson et al. 2013). The role of identity is apparent also in Bolivia in the late 1990s, where a radical decentralization of powers and money to local communities transformed political competition. As Faguet (2019) remarks, 'For the first time in 500 years, members of Bolivia's ethnic and cultural majority ran for public office in large numbers, were elected, and proceeded to wield (local) power.' Hundreds of new indigenous political parties sprung up that shared a programmatic agenda rejecting capitalism for pre-Columbian forms of collective property, community self-government, and indigenous representation and decision-making. They would become the foundation stones for Evo Morales' MAS party, which took power in 2006. A centuries-old creole establishment collapsed.

Ethno-territorial conflict

Does multilevel governance mitigate or exacerbate ethno-territorial conflict? On the one hand, multilevel governance gives regionalists some of what they want, and this may weaken their appeal. On the other hand, multilevel governance can transform national minorities into regional majorities with the institutional capacity to intensify autonomy demands. Hence, multilevel governance may provide a check on separatism, or it may fuel it by institutionalizing identity politics.

The fragility of national institutions in multi-ethnic societies is a live topic among scholars of multilevel governance. A second-generation approach is to model the likelihood of secession as an economic trade-off between the costs of independence versus union for those living in a region. On the one side are the costs of insufficient scale in the provision of public goods, including security, law, and taxation. In William Riker's analysis (1964), these costs can be great enough to induce separate polities to combine in a federal regime. On the other side, centralized taxation may exploit those living in a region. Buchanan and Faith (1987) hypothesize that a region may break away if its loss from interregional transfers exceeds the benefits of economic union. Bolton and Roland (1997) contend that secession can derive simply from differences in regional tastes. They refer to Belgium as a case where territorial differences in the desired level of redistribution could produce majorities in both Flanders and Wallonia for secession.

Third-generation scholars argue that demands for secession may arise from territorially concentrated minorities who demand self-rule to sustain the distinctiveness of their laws, language, or social norms. This raises the possibility that a region may secede even if independence is more economically costly than union. This line of analysis highlights the *Who Question*—'Who should have the right to rule themselves?' To engage this question, one must extend the analysis beyond economic self-interest and optimal policy provision to conceptions of identity and minority nationalism.

Whether differentiated governance moderates or intensifies minority nationalism is hotly debated (McGarry and O'Leary 2009; Roeder 2009; Weller and Nobbs 2010; Stepan et al. 2011). The thrust of differentiated governance has been to adjust jurisdictional boundaries in line with a concentrated minority community. This minimizes interaction between an ethnic group and the rest of the country, but does this stabilize ethno-territorial conflict? Opponents point at the increased risk of intra-regional ethnic conflict as minorities in the region experience discrimination. When in 1980, and again in 1995, the Quebec government called a referendum for an independent Quebec, the threat of secession mobilized the English-speaking minority in Montreal, along with Inuit and First Nations communities across the province. In the end, Quebec voted against secession and the counter-mobilization subsided, though the potential for communal conflict within Quebec remains. Extensive autonomy may also embolden separatist leaders who have procured the legitimacy of a popular mandate and, if in government, can use newly acquired state resources to establish de facto independence. Also, extensive autonomy raises the stakes in party competition, which may induce political parties to outbid one another with radicalizing demands (Zuber 2011). Ultimately, the success of multilevel governance in mitigating conflict depends on whether accommodation strengthens or weakens exclusive conceptions of community among voters and elites.

A different approach is to give regions across the board a role in decision-making in the country as a whole. This is the federal cure for minority nationalism. Regions can be represented directly in a national chamber or they can participate in intergovernmental arrangements in which they negotiate with the central government. In Belgium, both strategies were used in an effort to contain Flemish nationalists, culminating in the leap to federalism in 1995. The senate became a chamber composed of the regional and community representatives, and inter-ministerial conferences with regional input covered the range of national policy. While these conferences have no formal decision power, they are a venue for binding cooperation agreements. None of this eliminates territorial conflict, but it engages autonomist elites in national policy-making and gives them a greater stake in the overarching polity. The idea is that the centrifugal effects of self-rule are offset by centripetal effects of shared rule.

There are many paths to this goal (Amoretti and Bermeo 2004). Regions and ethnic minorities can be granted special representation in national institutions or receive veto rights on certain types of legislation. For example, the sparsely populated Åland Islands have a guaranteed seat in the Finnish parliament, and more importantly, the parliament is required to obtain an opinion from the Åland government on any act of special importance to the islands. The Åland government can also participate in the preparation of the Finnish negotiating position in the EU on matters within its powers, and the Åland parliament must give its consent to international treaties. Electoral laws can set aside seats for representatives of certain ethnic groups or regions (Lublin 2014). For example, the Maori population in New Zealand has reserved seats in parliament. Slovenia sets aside one seat for its Italian minority in Istria and one for its Hungarian minority in Prekmurje. The chief objective of these measures is to build trust between the minority and the rest of the country.

Territorial identity politics is almost always mediated by political parties. In some cases, regionalist parties predate regional elections and use national elections as a platform for their demands, while in others they emerge following the opportunity for regional representation (Brancati 2006). Some regionalist parties lose votes after the region has received autonomy, while other parties capitalize on unmet demands. Rarely do ethno-nationalist parties dominate political discourse in a region. In Scotland, the Scottish National Party competes with the British-wide Labour and the Conservative parties. In Catalonia, pro-autonomist parties contend with pro-Spanish opposition parties. And while there are no longer any all-Belgian parties competing in Flemish elections, just two of the six major parties run on a predominantly autonomist-separatist platform.

The causality between multilevel governance and ethno-territorial conflict runs both ways. Multilevel governance bolsters territorial identities while it routinizes regional demands. Separatist political parties are empowered in distinctive regions, but they have to compete with unionist parties. Multilevel governance supplies opportunity for separatist movements and at the same time opens the possibility for accommodation. Our evidence provides many cases of regional empowerment, but no case of complete separation in a consolidated democracy. Several democracies contain regions in which there is considerable support for full independence. These include Aceh, the Basque Country, Catalonia, Flanders, Greenland, Mindanao, Puerto Rico, Quebec, and Scotland. But even if several of these regions were to break away, it would still be true to say that consolidated democracies commonly disperse territorial authority, but rarely break apart.

Social policy

The development of social policy in multilevel systems illustrates how a functional approach to social policy can be overshadowed by political interest, institutional incentives, and identity.

Original thinking on social provision was deeply influenced by the idea that redistributive taxation should be centralized (Musgrave 1959). If decentralized taxation triggers race-to-the-bottom competition among governments to attract capital, the result will be less redistribution than is optimal from a national perspective. However, spending should be decentralized if those living in different regions have different tastes concerning, for example, social assistance, public housing, health, or education. Hence the result according to Oates' theorem (1972) is to collect revenue for redistribution centrally but spend it locally.

There is evidence that it makes sense to adjust social policy provision to the preferences and conditions of those living in particular corners of the country. For example, Bunte and Kim (2017) find that decentralization reforms in Nigeria effectively led local politicians to align education, health, infrastructure, and agriculture spending with local demands. However, scholars have also investigated how multilevel governance can distort social spending. Political decentralization can give regional actors the opportunity to target social spending at their clients and time their spending prior to elections. In a study of educational spending in fourteen OECD countries, Kleider et al. (2018) show that regional governments having the same ideological or party make-up as the central government systematically receive a disproportionate share of central funding. Comparing national social programmes in Argentina and Brazil, Niedzwiecki (2016) finds that subnational governments run by the opposition actively hinder the implementation of national policies. Explaining the wide variation in welfare services in India, Tillin et al. (2015) demonstrate that welfare performance is erratic in pro-business states, in states where clientelistic political parties target services to their supporters, and in predatory states where public office is a channel to private gain. In Ecuador, Mejia Acosta and Menendez (2019) find that mayors concentrate public spending immediately before elections.

Much second-generation research focuses on the systemic effects of multilevel governance (Leibfried and Pierson 1995a). A key question is whether decentralization leads to a race to the bottom as regions reduce welfare provision to lower taxes (Pierson 1995). Regions that finance social policy out of their own revenues are liable to limit welfare in an effort to attract external investment (Meija Acosta and Tillin 2019). However, there is also evidence that some regions increase social spending, particularly in education or health, to attract firms that need a dense pool of highly educated workers. A recent longitudinal study of fourteen OECD countries finds diverse regional outcomes rather than a uniform race to the bottom (Kleider 2018).

One finding on which there is impressive consensus is that decentralization leads to greater variation within a country. Whether a region invests in social policy can then depend on a range of region-specific factors: a region's affluence, its bureaucratic capacity, its government's pro-social ideology, and, as recent work shows, a region's distinctive identity. This raises the question of how to mitigate such regional inequality. One possible solution is shared rule, which gives regions a stake in the country as a whole. Whereas self-rule produces variance among regions, shared rule allows the central government and regional governments to develop joint policies that increase economic convergence. Shared rule can take the form of a second chamber composed of regional representatives as in Germany, or it can consist of intergovernmental coordination as in Spain, Belgium, and Italy, or more indirectly, it can be sustained by centralized political parties, as in France and Austria.

Recent literature on social policy investigates the effects of territorial identity for social policy provision. Social identity theory predicts that strong attachment to a territorial community can lead citizens to prefer more social welfare, education, and health services.

In a comparison of Kerala and Uttar Pradesh in India, Singh (2015) demonstrates that Kerala's elites drew on the state's overarching linguistic identity to mobilize support for investment in education, health, and welfare. By contrast, Uttar Pradesh, which is larger and richer, lacks a subnational identity that can motivate regional social policy. Uttar Pradesh was closely associated with Gandhi's nationwide Congress Party, and following the decline of the Congress Party from the 1980s, elite and popular support shifted to diverse religious and caste identities that divide the region. The upshot is that Uttar Pradesh has had a relatively weak commitment to collective educational, health, and social policies. Similarly, the lack of social solidarity has been hypothesized to constrain support for European-wide redistribution. Examining weak public support for European bailout programmes, Kuhn and Stoeckel (2014) find that the most important factor is not economic interest, but whether citizens conceive of themselves as Europeans.

KEY POINTS

Multilevel governance has had three major effects.

- It extends democracy by introducing elections at the subnational and supranational levels.

- It creates opportunities for accommodating territorial minorities.

- It generally leads to greater variation in social policy within a country.

Conclusion

Over the past seven decades, the territorial structure of governance has become multilevel. Authority has been dispersed away from central government to regional and local governments, as well as to international organizations. This chapter looks at developments within states, but it is instructive to conceive this as one side of the coin.

Comparative data on regional and local authority allows us to identify some broad trends. First, regional and local governments have gained authority. Nearly all countries now have subnational governments that exercise authority over diverse policies including education, urban planning, health, and economic development. Correspondingly, subnational governments spend a substantial share of the government budget. In addition, most subnational governments are elected and accountable to their constituents rather than to the central government.

At the same time, there has been a trend to differentiated governance in which some subnational governments exercise special political, administrative, or fiscal powers that distinguish them from other regions in their tier. This relaxes the principle that rights and obligations are uniform across the national territory.

To explain these developments and their effects on democracy, ethno-territorial conflict, and social policy, it is helpful to begin with a functionalist perspective in which the structure of authority reflects the diverse scales at which public goods are best provided. A second perspective suggests that the structure of government is motivated by economic self-interest on the part of rulers, groups, and voters. Third-generation theory introduces identity and the demand for self-rule on the part of regional communities and ethnic minorities. This extends the analysis beyond pressures for functionally efficient governance and economic self-interest, and it problematizes the boundaries of jurisdictions. When one combines these perspectives, governance is shaped both by 'who should have the right to self-rule' and 'who gets what'.

? QUESTIONS

Knowledge-based

1. What is multilevel governance?

2. What is the difference between a federal and unitary system?

3. What is self-rule? What is shared rule? Why are these useful ways to conceive of subnational authority?

4. What is differentiated governance?

5. What are three important drivers of multilevel governance?

Critical thinking

1. Explain the assumptions underlying Oates' decentralization theorem.

2. What does a conception of government as a custodian of public interest get wrong when considering the effects of multilevel governance?

3. Does multilevel governance deepen or weaken democracy?

4. Does decentralization lead to a race to the bottom in social policy provision?

5. Why and how does identity constrain social policy provision?

FURTHER READING

Classics

Elazar, D. J. (1987). *Exploring Federalism* (Tuscaloosa, AL: University of Alabama Press).

Oates, W. E. (1972). *Fiscal Federalism* (New York: Harcourt Brace Jovanovich).

Riker, W. H. (1964). *Federalism: Origin, Operation, Significance* (Boston, MA: Little, Brown).

Rokkan, S. (with D. Urwin) (1983). *Economy, Territory, Identity: Politics of West European Peripheries* (London: Sage).

Reference works on regional and local authority

Hooghe, L., Marks, G., Schakel, A. H., Niedzwiecki, S., Chapman Osterkatz, S., and Shair-Rosenfield, S. (2016) *Measuring Regional Authority: A Postfunctionalist Theory of Governance, Vol. I* (Oxford: Oxford University Press).

Ladner, A., Keuffer, N., Baldersheim, H., Hlepas, N., Swianiewicz, P., Steyvers, K., and Navarro, C. (2019) *Patterns of Local Autonomy in Europe* (London: Palgrave Macmillan).

Loughlin, J., Hendriks, F., and Lidström, A. (eds) (2013) *The Oxford Handbook of Subnational Democracy in Europe* (Oxford: Oxford University Press).

Page, E. C. and Goldsmith, M. J. (eds) (2010) *Changing Government Relations in Europe: From Localism to Intergovernmentalism* (London: Routledge).

Watts, R. L. (2008) *Comparing Federal Systems* (Kingston: Institute of Intergovernmental Relations).

Additional reading

Giraudy, A., Moncada, E., and Snyder, R. (eds) (2019) *Inside Countries: Subnational Research in Comparative Politics* (Cambridge: Cambridge University Press).

Hooghe, L. and Marks, G. (2016) *Community, Scale and Regional Governance: A Postfunctionalist Theory of Governance, Vol. II* (Oxford: Oxford University Press).

Leibfried, S. and Pierson, P. (eds) (1995) *European Social Policy: Between Fragmentation and Integration* (Washington D.C.: Brookings Institution).

Oates, W. (2005) 'Toward a Second-Generation Theory of Fiscal Federalism', *International Tax and Public Finance*, 12: 349–74.

Rodden, J. (2006) *Hamilton's Paradox: The Promise and Peril of Fiscal Federalism* (Cambridge: Cambridge University Press).

Treisman, D. (2007) *The Architecture of Government: Rethinking Political Decentralization* (Princeton, NJ: Princeton University Press).

Zuber, C. I. and Szöcsik, E. (2019) 'The Second Edition of the EPAC Expert Survey on Ethnonationalism in Party Competition—Testing for Validity and Reliability', *Regional and Federal Studies*, 29(1): 91–113.

 Visit the Online Resources that accompany this book for additional material, including country profiles, comparative data sets, flashcard glossaries, and web directory.

www.oup.com/he/caramani5e

Section 4
Actors and processes

12
Political parties

Richard S. Katz

Reader's guide

Political parties are among the central institutions of modern democracy. But what is a political party? Why are parties central to democracy, and how are they organized? This chapter considers the definition, origins, and functions of parties. What role do parties play in the working of democracy? And what benefits do parties provide for those who organize them? The chapter then considers the ways in which parties are organized, regulated, and financed. It concludes with brief discussions of the role of parties in the stabilization of democracy in the late twentieth and early twenty-first centuries, and of challenges confronting parties in the current millennium.

Introduction

Organizations identified as 'political parties' are among the central actors in politics. Whether or not in power as the result of victory in free and fair elections, the governments of most countries have effectively been in the hands of party leaders: Winston Churchill as leader of the British Conservative Party; Indira Gandhi as leader of the Indian National Congress; Adolf Hitler as the leader of the German Nazi Party;

Xi Jinping as General Secretary of the Communist Party of China; Ahmed Sékou Touré as leader of the Parti Démocratique de Guinée-Rassemblement Démocratique Africain.

When governments were not in the hands of party leaders, most often because **party government** was interrupted by a military takeover, the resulting **juntas** (see Chapter 6 'Authoritarian regimes') usually announced that their rule would be only temporary—until a regime of legitimate or honest or effective parties can be restored. And if, at the beginning of the twenty-first century, there are occasional suggestions that **social movements** and **governance** networks might supplant parties as the leading institutions channelling political participation and structuring government, experience to date offers little reason to suspect (or hope) that this will happen any time soon.

KEY POINTS

- Political parties are the central actors in democratic politics, as well as in many authoritarian and totalitarian regimes.

- It is unlikely that social movements or governance networks will replace the parties' many roles.

Definitions of party

Given their ubiquity, one might think that the definition of political party would be straightforward, but quite the reverse is true. Parties like the American Democrats, the Italian Fascists, or the Kenyan African National Union (KANU)—not to mention the myriad smaller parties like the Polish Beer Lovers or the British Official Monster Raving Loony Party—are so different in motivation, organization, behaviour, and relevance as to raise the question of whether a single umbrella category can encompass them all. Indeed, there are many scholars who would argue that some of these 'parties' should not be included.

Although it is only one among many possible definitions of party (see Box 12.1 for more examples), it is instructive to unpack Huckshorn's (1984: 10) definition—'a political party is an autonomous group of citizens having the purpose of making nominations and contesting elections in the hope of gaining control over governmental power through the capture of public offices and the organization of the government'—in order to highlight the issues involved. Huckshorn explicitly combines four elements common to many definitions, and implicitly adds another.

The first explicit element concerns the *objective of parties*: 'gaining control over governmental power through the capture of public offices and the

organization of the government'. However, there has been considerable disagreement concerning the underlying motivation for this pursuit of power. For some (Lasswell 1960), the pursuit of power reflects psychopathology; others (Downs 1957; Schumpeter 1950; Schlesinger 1991) emphasize the pursuit of office essentially as an employment opportunity. From a more public-regarding perspective, one finds Edmund Burke's (1770) classic definition, as quoted in Box 12.1.

The second explicit element concerns *methods*: 'making nominations and contesting elections . . . and the organization of the government'. This points to two separable arenas in which parties operate: the electoral and the governmental. As will be noted in the section on the 'Origins of Parties', one significant question is: which came first?

The third explicit element of Huckshorn's definition is *competition*, expressed in the 'contesting' of elections and the 'hope [as opposed to the certainty] of gaining control'. But does the contesting of elections require free and fair competition among independent competitors, or merely that the form of elections is observed? This is related to the fourth element, that the group of citizens be *autonomous*. At the extreme, these criteria appear to disqualify the parties of 'one-party' states, although on the other side these parties may claim to be facing real, if clandestine and illegal, opposition from 'counter-revolutionary forces'. Moreover, these parties' structures may also play a significant role in the organization and control of the government, more conventionally understood.

The implicit element of Huckshorn's definition is that the group of citizens has some level of coherence that allows them to coordinate their actions and to maintain an identity over time. While this does not require a formal organization, it certainly is facilitated by one, so that both some minimal level of organization and some minimal level of unity have become part of the definition of party.

While these issues are important for political science, they are also important in law, because organizations that are legally recognized as parties are frequently accorded special privileges (such as public subventions) and obligations (such as enhanced requirements for transparency). One particularly vexing question is what happens if a recognized party falls below the **threshold** for initial recognition: does it retain its privileged status anyway, lose its special status but remain in existence as a non-party political organization, or is it dissolved altogether?

DEFINITION 12.1

Definition of party

David Hume (1741)	'Factions may be divided into personal and real; that is, into factions, founded on personal friendship or animosity among such as compose the contending parties, and into those founded on some real difference of sentiment or interest . . . . though . . . parties are seldom found pure and unmixed, either of one kind or the other.'
Edmund Burke (1770)	'[A] party is a body of men united, for promoting by their joint endeavours the national interest, upon some particular principle in which they are all agreed.'
Walter Bagehot (1889)	'The moment, indeed, that we distinctly conceive that the House of Commons is mainly and above all things an elective assembly, we at once perceive that party is of its essence: there never was an election without a party.'
Max Weber (1922)	'"[P]arties" live in a house of "power". Their action is oriented toward the acquisition of social "power," that is to say toward influencing communal action no matter what its content may be.'
Robert Michels (1911)	'The modern party is a fighting organization in the political sense of the term, and must as such conform to the laws of tactics.'
Joseph Schumpeter (1950)	'A party is not . . . a group of men who intend to promote the public welfare "upon some particular principle on which they are all agreed". A party is a group whose members propose to act in concert in the competitive struggle for political power.'
Anthony Downs (1957)	'In the broadest sense, a political party is a coalition of men seeking to control the governing apparatus by legal means. By coalition, we mean a group of individuals who have certain ends in common and cooperate with each other to achieve them. By governing apparatus, we mean the physical, legal, and institutional equipment which the government uses to carry out its specialized role in the division of labor. By legal means, we mean either duly constituted or legitimate influence.'
V. O. Key Jr (1964)	'A political party, at least on the American scene, tends to be a "group" of a peculiar sort . . . Within the body of voters as a whole, groups are formed of persons who regard themselves as party members . . . In another sense the term "party" may refer to the group of more or less professional workers . . . At times party denotes groups within the government . . . Often it refers to an entity which rolls into one the party-in-the-electorate, the professional political group, the party-in-the-legislature, and the party-in-the-government.'
William Nisbet Chambers (1967)	'[A] political party in the modern sense may be thought of as a relatively durable social formation which seeks offices or power in government, exhibits a structure or organization which links leaders at the centers of government to a significant popular following in the political arena and its local enclaves, and generates in-group perspectives or at least symbols of identification or loyalty.'
Joseph Schlesinger (1991)	'A political party is a group organized to gain control of government in the name of the group by winning election to public office.'
John Aldrich (1995)	'Political parties can be seen as coalitions of elites to capture and use political office. [But] a political party is more than a coalition. A political party is an institutionalized coalition, one that has adopted rules, norms, and procedures.'
Elections Canada Act	'[P]olitical party means an organization one of whose fundamental purposes is to participate in public affairs by endorsing one or more of its members as candidates and supporting their election. [R]egistered party means a political party that is registered in the registry of political parties referred to in section 394 as a registered party.'
'UCLA school'	'A political party is a coalition of intense policy demanders.'

Origins of parties

The origins of modern parties lie first in the representative assemblies of the sixteenth to nineteenth centuries, and second in the efforts of those who were excluded from those assemblies to gain a voice in them. In both cases, parties arose in response to the fact that coordinated action is likely to be more effective than action taken by isolated individuals, even if they are in perfect agreement.

The earlier parties were *parties of intra-parliamentary origin*, evident, for example, in the British parliament in the seventeenth century—and even then, the novelty was not the existence of factions but rather acceptance of the ideas that disagreement was not synonymous with disloyalty and that organization was not synonymous with conspiracy. Over time, these parties developed recognizable leadership cadres and became active in electoral campaigns. Their most significant contribution to the development of modern politics, as well as the greatest reinforcement of their own strength, was to wrest control of the executive from the hands of the monarch and replace that control with responsibility to parliament, which ultimately meant that ministers would in fact be chosen by, and be responsible to, the parties (and especially their leaders) that controlled a majority of the parliamentary seats.

The rise of parliamentary government was far from equivalent to **democratization**, because well into the nineteenth century, and generally into the twentieth, the right to participate in political life, including the right to vote, was highly constrained by a variety of economic, religious, and gender restrictions. The need to mobilize and organize large numbers of those excluded from legitimate participation to support leaders advocating for reforms—including the extension of political rights—gave rise to development of *parties of extra-parliamentary origin*. The ultimate success of these

parties in inducing the parties of the *régimes censitaires* to broaden the suffrage was instrumental in converting the liberal regimes of the nineteenth century into the liberal democracies of the twenty-first century. Indeed, as Schattschneider (1942: 1) famously remarked, 'the political parties created democracy, and modern democracy is unthinkable save in terms of the parties'.

The distinction between parties of intra- and extra-parliamentary origin (Duverger 1954) is not only a matter of timing, with parties of internal origin generally coming earlier. Especially at their origins, they often differ substantially in their organizations as well, and these 'genetic' differences tend to persist for many decades after parties of external origin win parliamentary representation, or parties of internal origin build membership organizations 'on the ground' (see Panebianco 1988).

Parties of internal and external origin have also tended to differ with respect to their social bases, with those originating in parliament representing the 'establishment' of the upper and upper middle classes (or earlier, the nobility and gentry, and more recently, particularly in 'pacted' transitions to democracy in the former Soviet bloc, the clientele of the old regime), while those of external origin represent the middle, lower middle, and working classes, sometimes the adherents of dissenting religions, speakers of marginalized languages, opponents of the old regime, etc.

In the late twentieth century, a new type of externally originating party appeared in a number of countries—most notably and successfully in Italy. In these cases, a rich entrepreneur used his wealth in effect to create (or 'buy') a party in much the same way as he might create a chain of retail stores (Hopkin and Paolucci 1999). Although created outside parliament, these parties tend to look more like older parties of internal origin, both in their balance of power between the central party organization (dominated by the entrepreneur through party officials who are in reality his employees) and ordinary members (if any), and in their conservative, or at least pro-business, policy profile. In particular, they are created to be 'cheerleaders' for an already established leader, who has little interest in or need for input of ideas or resources from below. Like the earlier parties of internal origin, and unlike most leader-centred parties of external origin, they depend on the material resources that the leader can mobilize, rather than on his/her personal charisma. Even more recently, there have been attempts to create 'virtual parties' through the internet, with discussion groups and e-mail lists replacing party meetings.

- Some parties originated within parliaments, while others originated outside parliaments with the objective of getting in.
- The subsequent power relations of a party generally favour leaders whose positions in public office, or in an external party organization, are analogous to the positions of the leaders who originally built the party.

The functions of parties

Political parties perform a number of functions (see Box 12.2) that are central to the operation of modern democracies. Indeed, as already observed, parties are often defined at least in part by the performance of these functions. It should be recognized, however, that these are not the only things that parties do (for example, parties may serve as social outlets for their members), nor do all parties effectively perform (or even attempt to perform) all of these functions.

Coordination

Historically, the first function of political parties, and still one of the most important, is that of coordination within government, within society, and between government and society at large. Particularly, the function of connecting society and the state is frequently identified as 'linkage'.

Coordination within government

Coordination within government (the 'party in public office') takes place in many venues. Most obviously, the coordination function is manifested in party caucuses (or groups, clubs, or *Fraktionen*) in parliaments, with their leaders, whips (party officials in charge of maintaining discipline and communication within the party's parliamentary membership, and 'newsletters' informing members of the expectations of their leaders), policy committees, etc. Parliamentary party groups also structure the selection of committee members and the organization of the parliamentary agenda. Whether in a system of formal separation of powers, like the US, or more pure parliamentary government, like New Zealand, parties provide the bridge between the legislative and executive branches. They also structure coordination between different levels (national, regional, etc.) of government. To the extent that parties perform this function comprehensively and effectively, it becomes reasonable to regard parties, rather than the individual politicians who hold office in their name, as central political actors.

Coordination within society

Political parties are among the institutions (along with interest groups, non-governmental organizations (NGOs), and the like) that organize and channel the political activity of citizens. Even in the absence of a formally organized 'party on the ground', party names and histories serve as points of reference and

---

ZOOM-IN 12.2

Functions of parties

Coordination	Maintaining discipline and communication within the parliamentary caucus.
	Coordinating action of the parliamentary caucus in support of, or opposition to, the cabinet.
	Organizing the political activity of like-minded citizens.
	Patterning linkage between representatives in public office and organized supporters among the citizenry.
Conducting electoral campaigns and structuring competition	Providing candidates, and linking individual candidates to recognizable symbols, histories, and expectations of team-like behaviour.
	Developing policy programmes.
	Recruiting and coordinating campaign workers.
Selection and recruitment of personnel	Selection of candidates for elections.
	Recruitment and/or selection of candidates for appointed office.
	Recruitment and socialization of political activists and potential officeholders.
Representation	Speaking for their members and supporters within or in front of government agencies.
	Being the organizational embodiment in the political sphere of demographically or ideologically defined categories of citizens.

identification for citizens. Where there are more formal organizations, these provide venues for political education, discussion, and the coordination of **collective action**.

Coordination between government and society

Parties also link the party on the ground as a group of active citizens supporting a particular political tendency and the party in public office as a group of officials claiming to represent the same tendency. Within party organizations, this function is often performed by a party central office. Whether this linkage takes, or is supposed to take, the form of control over the party in public office on behalf of the party on the ground, or direction of the party on the ground as an organization of supporters of the party in public office varies among parties, as indeed does the effectiveness of the linkage whichever way it runs, and the level of coordination and discipline within either the party on the ground or the party in public office.

Contesting elections

A second major defining function of political parties is the conduct of electoral campaigns, and of political competition more generally. Parties provide most of the candidates in elections, and an even larger share of those who are elected. In many political systems, parties are the formal contestants of elections—the ballot clearly identifies parties as the things among which the citizen is asked to choose—but even when the object of choice formally is individual candidates, the most relevant characteristic of those candidates is usually their political party affiliation. Ordinarily (the US, in which the organization and funding of campaigns is based primarily on individual candidates, being a notable exception), most of the funds required for a political campaign are raised and spent by parties, whether nationally or at the **constituency** level, and campaign workers are recruited and directed by parties. The policy positions advocated in a campaign are generally those that were formulated and agreed to within parties. Between elections as well, parties generally act as the primary protagonists in political debates.

Recruitment

A third major function of parties is the recruitment and selection of personnel, with the balance between recruitment (finding someone willing to do the job) and selection (choosing among multiple aspirants) depending both on the party and the nature of the

position to be filled. The selection function is most significant with regard to candidacies for important offices and within parties whose candidates have a high probability of success. For minor offices (especially those that are unpaid), hopeless constituencies, or positions at the bottom of a party list of candidates, the primary function often is recruitment—avoiding the embarrassment of not being able to fill the position (Sundberg 1987).

Taken together, these three functions of coordination (especially within the party in public office), conducting electoral campaigns (especially the formulation and presentation of policy programmes, platforms, or manifestoes), and recruitment of candidates for both elective and appointive office, to the extent that they are performed in a coordinated way, and to the extent that party elected officials effectively control the state, make the parties the effective governors, and give rise to the idea of 'democratic party government' (Rose 1976; Castles and Wildenmann 1986). Of course, not all democratic governments are democratic in this way. In the US, for example, the coherence of parties has been much lower than in most other democracies, making individual politicians rather than their parties the real governors. In Switzerland, the **referendum** makes the citizens, and the variety of groups (including but by no means limited to parties) that can organize petitions demanding a referendum, the ultimate deciders of individual questions at the expense of party government.[1]

Representation

Finally, parties perform a variety of functions that may be classified as representation. First, parties speak and act for their supporters, in electoral campaigns, in the corridors of power, and in the media and other public fora of discussion. Parties serve as **agents** of the people, doing things that the people do not have the time, the training and ability, or the inclination to do for themselves. Parties also represent citizens in the sense of being the organizational embodiment in the political sphere of categories of citizens, as with a labour party, a Catholic party, the party of a language group or region, or even possibly a women's party.[2] Parties may, by analogy, represent the organizational embodiment of ideologies.

In another common categorization of the functions of parties (Almond and Powell 1966: 14–15), these are grouped as *interest articulation* (the expression of demands), *interest aggregation* (the formulation of policy packages and the construction of coalitions), and *rule-making and application* (actually governing).

KEY POINTS

- Political parties play a central role in coordinating among public officials, among citizens with common political preferences, and between citizens and officials.

- Political parties are generally the central participants in elections, responsible for both the candidates and the issues among which voters will choose.

- Political parties are central participants in the recruitment of political personnel, both for elective and appointive office.

- Political parties serve as representatives of both social groupings and ideological positions.

Models of party organization

Types of party

Models of parties are summarized in Table 12.1.

Cadre or elite parties

The earliest 'modern' parties were the **cadre** (or elite or caucus) parties that developed in European parliaments. Because, particularly in an era of highly restricted suffrage, each of the MPs who made up these parties generally owed his election to the mobilization of his own personal clientele or the clientele of his patron, there was little need for a party on the ground, and certainly not one organized beyond the boundaries of individual constituencies. Hence, there was also no need for a party central office. Within parliament, however, the advantages of working in concert both to pursue policy objectives and to secure access to ministerial office led to the evolution of parliamentary party organizations, frequently cemented by the exchange of patronage.

As electorates expanded, elite parties in some places developed more elaborate local organizations—most famously the 'Birmingham caucus' of Joseph Chamberlain—and some greater coordination (frequently taking the form of centrally prepared 'talking points' and centrally organized campaign tours by nationally known personalities) by a central office, but the heart of the organization remained the individual MP and his/her personal campaign and support organization. At the level of the electorate, the concept of 'party membership' remained ill-defined. In the twenty-first century, parties that approximate the caucus format remain significant in the US and to a certain extent in Japan (the Liberal Democratic Party) and on the right in France.

Mass parties

The **mass party** developed from the second half of the nineteenth century. In contrast with the intra-parliamentary origins of the caucus party, the 'genetic myth' of the mass party identifies it as a party of extra-parliamentary origin.[3] In the initial absence of either elected officials (a party in public office) or a network of local organizations (a party on the ground), the mass party begins with a core of leaders who organize a party central office with the aim of developing a party so as to be able to win elections and ultimately gain public office.

In contrast to the cadre party, which generally claimed to be speaking for the 'national interest' (although often based on a highly truncated view of who constituted 'the nation'), mass parties claimed to represent the interest only of a particular group (most often a social class),[4] and frequently built on the pre-existing organizations of that group (e.g. trade unions). Their primary political resource was numbers, with many small contributions of labour and money substituting for the few, but large, contributions available to elite parties. Both as a reflection of their subcultural roots and as a way of mobilizing their supporters, mass parties often pursued a strategy of 'encapsulation', providing a range of **ancillary organizations** (women's groups, after-work clubs, trade unions) and services (a party press, party-sponsored insurance schemes), which both helped isolate supporters from countervailing influences and made party support a part of the citizen's enduring personal identity rather than a choice to be made at each election.

Naturally, all of this required extensive organization. The archetypal mass party is organized on the ground in branches composed of people who have applied for membership, have been accepted (and potentially are liable to expulsion), and have certain obligations to the organization (most commonly including the payment of a subscription or fee) in exchange for which they acquire rights to participate in the organization's governance, especially by electing delegates to the party's national congress (or convention or conference).

In principle, the national congress is the highest decision-making body of a mass party, but as a practical matter it can only meet for a few days every year (if that often), and therefore elects a party executive committee and/or chairman or president or secretary who is effectively at the top of the party hierarchy. The executive also manages the staff of the party central office. Again in principle, the representatives elected to public office under the party's banner are agents of the party, on the presumption that voters were choosing among parties and not individual candidates, and so are subject to the direction of the party congress and executive, which are also responsible for formulating the party's political programme.

The reality is often rather different, with, as indicated by Michels' **'iron law of oligarchy'** (Michels 1915),

Table 12.1 Models of parties

	Elite, caucus, or cadre party	Mass party	Catch-all party	Cartel party	Business-firm party
Period of initial prominence	Rise of parliamentary government to mass suffrage	Drive for mass suffrage	1950s and 1960s	1980s to present	1990s to present
Locus of origination	Parliamentary origin	Extra-parliamentary origin	Evolution of pre-existing parties	Evolution of existing parties	Extra-parliamentary initiative of political entrepreneurs
Organizational structure	Minimal and local	Members organized in local branches	Members organized in branches, but marginalized in decision-making	Central office dominated by party in public office, and largely replaced by hired consultants	Minimal formal organization, with hierarchical control by the autonomous entrepreneur and his/her employees
	Party central office subordinate to party in public office	Central office responsible to an elected party congress	Central office subordinate to party in public office	Decisions ratified by plebiscite of members and supporters	
Nature and role of membership	Elites are the only 'members'	Large and homogeneous membership	Heterogeneous membership organized primarily as cheerleaders for elites	Distinction between member and supporter blurred	Membership minimal and irrelevant
		Leadership formally accountable to members		Members seen as individuals rather than as an organized body	
Primary resource base	Personal wealth and connections	Fees from members and ancillary organizations	Contributions from interest groups and individuals	State subsidies	Corporate resources

Source: Adapted in part from Katz and Mair (1995) and Krouwel (2006).

the very structures of internal party democracy leading to the domination of the party by its elite—a result that is less surprising when one remembers that the extra-parliamentary elite were initially the creators of the party. Moreover, in many parties that approximate the ideal type of mass party, ancillary organizations as well as the parliamentary party and the central office staff are guaranteed representation in the national congress and/or the national executive, increasingly making the question of whether authority in the mass party flows from the bottom up or from the top down an open one.

Catch-all parties

The mass party originated primarily as the vehicle of those groups that were excluded from power under the *régimes censitaires*. However, it proved highly effective, first in securing broader rights of participation for its clientele groups and then in winning elections under conditions of broadly expanded suffrage, and in many cases, this forced the cadre parties to adapt or risk electoral annihilation.[5] Simply to become mass parties was not appealing, however. In general, the social groups that they would represent were not large enough to be competitive on their own under mass suffrage and thus they had to be able to appeal across group boundaries. Moreover, the party in public office did not find the idea of ceding ultimate authority to a party congress and executive, even if in name only, attractive. The result was to create a new party model, with much of the form of the mass party (members, branches, congress, executive), but organized as the *supporters* of the party in public office, rather than as its masters.

At the same time, many mass parties were forced to change, both by pressure from a party in public office increasingly able to claim responsibilities and legitimacy based on a direct relationship with the electorate rather than one mediated by the external party organization, and by changes in society (e.g. breakdown of social divisions, spread of mass media) that made the strategy of encapsulation less effective and the resources provided by the parties' *classes gardées* less reliable and less adequate.

The result was (i) a reduction in the role of members relative to professionals; (ii) a shedding of ideological baggage; (iii) a loosening and ultimate abandonment of the interconnection of party and a privileged set of interest organizations (again, particularly unions); and (iv) a strategy that reached across group boundaries for votes and resources. Particularly looking at these changes in mass parties of the left, Kirchheimer (1966) identified this new type as the **catch-all party**. In fact, however, in both strategy and organization, Kirchheimer's catch-all party looks very much like that just described as the adaptation of the old cadre parties. As the catch-all party developed, it became increasingly reliant on political professionals—pollsters, media consultants, etc. (see Chapter 19 'Political communication')—leading to the idea of the electoral-professional party as an alternative to, or simply a variant of, the catch-all model (Panebianco 1988). Although most electoral-professional parties have formal membership organizations, the emphasis has shifted so much towards the party in public office and the central office (or hired consultants) that the membership is effectively superfluous, or maintained primarily for cosmetic reasons (i.e. the belief that having a membership organization will make the party look less elitist or oligarchic).

Cartel parties

By the last quarter of the twentieth century, even the catch-all model was under considerable pressure. Increasing public debts confronted ruling parties, with a choice between dramatic increases in taxes and dramatic cuts in welfare spending. Globalization reduced the ability of governments to control their economies. All this was exacerbated by the financial crises, beginning around 2007. Increases in education and leisure time, along with the growth of interest groups, NGOs, etc., gave citizens both the abilities and the opportunities to bring pressure to bear on the parties themselves, and on the state without requiring the intermediation of the parties. Party loyalties, and memberships, began obviously to erode. Shifts in campaign technology increased the cost of electoral competitiveness beyond the willingness of members and other private contributors to provide—at least without the appearance, and often the reality, of corruption which, when revealed, made parties even less popular.

These developments have inspired a number of adaptations and other initiatives. Katz and Mair (1995) have suggested that in many countries catch-all parties moved in the direction of what they call the 'cartel party'. This involves at least four major changes in the relationships among the parties, the citizenry, and the state, and between parties and their members.

1. The mainstream parties—i.e. those that are in power, or are generally perceived to have a high probability of coming to power in the medium term—in effect form a *cartel to protect themselves both from electoral risks* (e.g. by shifting responsibility away from politically accountable agencies so that they will not be held responsible for them or by minimizing the difference in rewards to electoral winners and electoral losers) *and to supplement their decreasingly adequate resources with subventions from the state* (justified in terms of the parties' centrality to democratic government or of insulating parties from corrupt economic pressure).

2. The parties reduce the relevance of their role of representation, in favour of a part of their role as governors, defending policies of the state (including those made by bureaucrats, 'non-political' agencies like central banks, and even previous governments made up of other parties), in effect becoming *agencies of the state rather than of society*.

3. Cartel parties tend to increase the formal powers of party members, and indeed in some cases to allow increased participation by supporters who are not formal members. However, they do this as a way of *preserving the form of internal democracy while disempowering party activists*, who are perceived to be less willing to accept the limitations implicit in a cartel.

4. In part, simply by extending the trends evident in the catch-all party, cartel parties also tend to replace the staff of the party central office with hired consultants, both *further privileging professional expertise over political experience and activism* and *removing another possible source of challenge* to the leaders of the party in public office.

Anti-cartel parties

Although both Duverger (the principal elaborator of the idea of the mass party) and Kirchheimer (the elaborator of the idea of the catch-all party) presented their models as somehow representing an end-state of party development, each of the models has generated its own challenger. In the case of the cartel party, Katz and Mair identify what they call the anti-party-system party as the cartel party's challenger. Parties of this type have also been identified as 'left-libertarian', 'new right', or 'populist' parties, or as 'movement parties'. They tend to expect a much deeper commitment from their members than either catch-all or cartel parties, and in this way are similar to the mass party, but they are organized around an idea rather than a social grouping (although the idea may be differentially attractive/popular among different groups). However, two of their primary appeals are simply to a sense of frustration that substantive outcomes appear to change little, if at all, regardless of which of the mainstream parties wins an election, and to a sense that all the mainstream parties are more interested in protecting their own privileges than in advancing the interests of ordinary citizens.

Recent examples include AfD in Germany, MoVimento Cinque Stelle in Italy, and Podemos in Spain. In the aftermath of its electoral victory in Greece in 2015, Syriza became the most successful anti-cartel party, but also a prime example of the dilemma faced by a successful anti-cartel party: that it is difficult to be an outsider and in government at the same time.

Niche parties

In recent decades, scholars have identified a second type of party that stands outside of the political mainstream. Identified as 'niche parties' (Meguid 2005, 2008), these parties focus on issues other than those (generally economic) issues emphasized by the major parties and on the representation of minority groups (such as the ultra-religious in Israel). Some scholars also include small parties of the extreme left and extreme right in this category.

Like niche firms in economic markets, niche parties do not try to broaden their appeal, but rather try to monopolize a limited segment of the electorate. Because their primary concerns are off the major axis of competition, a niche party can sometimes play the role of 'king-maker' in an evenly divided parliament, willing to tip the balance either way in exchange for major concessions on the issues about which it cares most. The primary threat to a niche party is that one or more of the mainstream parties will invade its market by adopting similar positions on the niche party's issues.

Business-firm parties

An alternative form of challenger to established parties is represented by what Hopkin and Paolucci (1999) have called the 'business-firm party'. The prototypical example is Forza Italia, a 'party' created by Silvio Berlusconi—a businessman who became prime minister in Italy—essentially as a wholly owned subsidiary of his corporate empire and staffed largely by its employees. While there may be an organization on the ground to mobilize supporters, it is only 'a lightweight organisation with the sole basic function of mobilising short-term support at election time' (Hopkin and Paolucci 1999: 315). Although Forza Italia developed from a previously existing firm, Hopkin and Paolucci argue that essentially the same model will typify 'purpose-built' parties in the future.

Parties in the US

Parties in the US present yet another model. From a European perspective, they appear to have much in common with the nineteenth-century cadre party, and Duverger famously identified them as a case of 'arrested development'. What they have in common with the cadre party is (i) a weak central organization; (ii) a focus on individual candidates rather than enduring institutions; and (iii) the absence of a formal membership organization. Where they differ profoundly, however, is in being extensively regulated by law, to the extent that Epstein (1986) could reasonably characterize them as 'public utilities', and in allowing the mass 'membership' (see later in this section for an explanation of the quotation marks) to make the most important decision:

that of candidate selection. Although US parties are ubiquitous, they are also extremely weak as organizations. This ordinarily leaves them extremely sensitive to the 'intense policy demanders' who control the money required for successful campaigns, and always liable to 'capture' by insurgents—who may have little prior connection to the party at all. This was clearly illustrated by the 2016 presidential election, in which Donald Trump, who had never run for any public office, and in 2004 had told a reporter, 'In many cases, I probably identify more as Democrat', secured the Republican party nomination for president over the opposition of virtually the entire Republican establishment and then went on to win the election. It also explains why populist challenger parties have been unable to gain traction in the US, notwithstanding levels of popular discontent that have fuelled such parties in other places.

Reflecting the federal nature of the country, the basic unit of party organization is the state party. The national committees of the two parties, which control the national party central offices and elect the national chairmen, are made up of representatives of the state parties. The national conventions are not policy-makers, even in form; they are called for the purpose of selecting—and effectively since the 1950s merely confirming the selection of—presidential candidates. Moreover, reflecting the separation of powers in the US constitution, both parties have separate organizations in each house of the Congress, which not only serve as the equivalent of parliamentary party caucuses but also maintain their own independent fundraising and campaign-mounting capacity, almost as if they were separate parties.

The three key features of the US legal system of party regulation are (i) the use of primary elections; (ii) the vacuous definition of party membership; and (iii) the candidate-centred nature of party regulation. In the decades around the turn of the twentieth century, reformers intent on breaking what they saw as the corrupt and excessive power of party bosses 'democratized' the parties by putting power into the hands of ordinary party members (whom they identified as party voters) through the use of primary elections (see Box 12.3).

Virtually all of the party's candidates for public office, as well as the vast majority of delegates to its national nominating convention, are also chosen in primary elections. Unlike so-called primaries in other countries, these are public elections, run by the state and structured by public law, rather than party rules. The second element of these reforms was to deny the parties the right to define or control their own memberships. Rather than having formal members, US parties only have 'registrants', i.e. voters who have chosen to affiliate with one of the parties in the process of registering to vote. But while this might suggest widespread participation in candidate selection, in fact voter turnout in primary elections is usually quite low, often leaving the decision in the hands of each party's most extreme and intransigent 'members'.

American law generally treats registrants as if they were members in a more substantive sense, but the party has no control over who registers as a 'member', and the member takes on no obligation by enrolling. Moreover, some states do not have partisan registra-

ZOOM-IN 12.3

Types of American primary

Closed primary	Only those who have registered in advance as 'members' of the party may participate.
Modified primary	Those who have registered as 'members' of the party, and—at the party's discretion—those who are registered as 'independent' or 'non-affiliated' voters may participate.
Open primary	All registered voters may participate in the primary election of the one party of their choice.
Blanket primary	All registered voters may participate, choosing if they wish among the candidates of a different party for each office. The candidates of each party with the most votes become the nominees.
Louisiana 'primary'	All registered voters may participate, choosing among all of the candidates for each office. If a candidate receives an absolute majority of the votes, that person is elected, and the 'primary' in effect becomes the election for that office. Otherwise, the two candidates with the most votes, regardless of party, become the candidates for the (run-off) general election.
Top two primary	All registered voters may participate and all candidates are listed together. The two candidates with the most votes, regardless of party, compete in the general election.

tion, and even in some states that do have partisan registration, any voter can claim the right to participate in a party's primary elections (open primary) without even the pretence of prior registration in it. Generally, the choice between open and closed (only party registrants may participate) primaries is determined by state law, although the parties have won (in court) the right to determine for themselves whether to allow voters who are not registered as 'members' of any party to participate in their own primary. Finally, even when ostensibly dealing with parties, US legal regulations focus on candidates as individuals. The overwhelming majority of the money spent in US campaigns is controlled by the candidates' own committees or by ostensibly non-partisan groups, and in general the parties are regarded merely as a privileged class of 'contributor'.

Membership

Although the original parties of intra-parliamentary origin had no members other than the MPs who aligned themselves with a party caucus, most modern parties claim to have a membership organization. However, the modes of acquiring membership, the role played by members both in rhetoric and in practice, and the size of the membership organization vary widely among parties.

As suggested previously in 'Mass parties', the prototypical membership-based party is the mass party. In its simplest form, the members of a mass party are individuals who have applied and been accepted as members of local branches or sections. In some parties, this form of direct individual membership is, or was, supplemented by indirect membership acquired as part of membership in an affiliated organization. Most commonly, these were trade unions affiliated to social democratic parties, such as the British Labour Party.

Affiliated membership might come automatically and inescapably as part of union (or other group) membership, or it might require an explicit choice by the potential member either to acquire party membership ('contracting in') or to decline party membership ('contracting out'); membership rights, such as voting for members of the party executive, might be exercised by the individual or indirectly through representatives of the affiliated organization. With the development of the catch-all party model and the weakening of social class as the basis of party politics, affiliated memberships have been dropped by some parties (e.g. the Swedish Social Democrats), leaving only individual membership.

Membership remains important to the self-understanding of many parties, and the idea that party leaders should be responsible to a membership organization has been widely embraced as a necessary element of democratic governance, although there are prominent dissenters from this view (e.g. Sartori 1965: 124).

Despite its perceived importance, party membership has generally been declining, often in absolute terms but almost always relative to the size of the electorate (see Table 12.2 for examples). Although some scholars (e.g. Katz 1990) argue that members may cost a party more than they are worth—and that the value to a citizen of being a party member may also be exceeded by its cost—this has commonly been regarded as a problem, for which, however, no real solution has yet been found.

In recent years, some parties have attempted to address the problem of declining membership by introducing forms of affiliation short of full membership. In the limiting case, the Canadian Liberal Party has moved to replace dues paying membership with free registration on their website.

Regulation

Whether or not they reflect the merging of parties with the state, an increasing number of countries have enacted special 'party laws', either supplementing or replacing legal regimes that treated parties as simply one more category of private association. In some cases, these laws are embedded in the national constitution, while in others they are ordinary statutes or bodies of regulations.

Justifications of special party laws can generally be categorized into three groups. The first is the *centrality of parties to democracy*. In several cases (Germany, France, Spain, Portugal, Greece, Italy), this is specifically acknowledged in the national constitution, while in others it has been acknowledged either in the law or in the parliamentary debates when the law was enacted. In general, this has justified giving parties special rights, protections, or privileges beyond those that would normally be granted to an 'ordinary' private association.

The second, albeit closely related, justification is the *power of parties*. Because of their central position in democratic government, a party that is anti-democratic or corrupt may pose a particularly serious threat to democracy. Hence, if their importance justifies special privileges, the dangers they pose justify special oversight and restrictions.

Third, a party law may be justified as a matter of administrative convenience or necessity. Most commonly, this justification has revolved around the twin problems of **ballot access** (the right to place

Table 12.2 Party membership

Country	Membership/electorate (%)			
	Time 1	%	Time 2	%
Austria	1980	28.48	2008	17.27
Belgium	1980	8.97	2008	5.52
Czech Republic	1993	7.04	2008	1.99
Denmark	1980	7.30	2008	4.13
Finland	1980	15.74	2006	8.08
France	1978	5.05	2009	1.85
Germany	1980 (West only)	4.52	2007 (whole)	2.30
Greece	1980	3.19	2008	6.59
Hungary	1990	2.11	2008	1.54
Ireland	1980	5.00	2008	2.03
Italy	1980	9.66	2007	5.57
Netherlands	1980	4.29	2009	2.48
Norway	1980	15.35	2008	5.04
Portugal	1980	4.28	2008	3.82
Slovakia	1994	3.29	2007	2.02
Spain	1980	1.20	2008	4.36
Switzerland	1977	10.66	2008	4.76
UK	1980	4.12	2008	1.21

Sources: Mair and Biezen (2001); Biezen et al. (2012).

candidates on the ballot) and control over the party's name or symbols (particularly on the ballot), although the related question of the right to form a parliamentary group may also be involved. (Alternatively, this may be regulated by the parliament's own Rules of Procedure—see Chapter 7 'Legislatures'.)

Where there is a party law, one of the first issues to be dealt with is the definition of party—to determine whether a group is entitled to the privileges and subject to the regulations of the law. Unlike the definitions discussed earlier in 'Definitions of party', legal definitions are generally procedural and organizational, and may indeed distinguish between parties in general and parties that are entitled to special treatment. For example, while the Canada Elections Act defines a party simply as 'an organization one of whose fundamental purposes is to participate in public affairs by endorsing one or more of its members as candidates and supporting their election', the 'real' definition is that of a 'registered party'. To be a registered party, an organization must file an application declaring that it meets the definition of a party just quoted, but also declaring its full name, a short-form name or abbreviation (that will appear on the ballot), its logo (if any), and the names, addresses, and signed consent of the party's leader,

officers, auditor, chief agent, and 250 electors. Finally, it must endorse at least one candidate.[6] In other countries, official recognition may require that the party 'offer sufficient guarantee of the sincerity of their aims' (German Law on Political Parties of 1967, Section 2(1)), and/or adhere to prescribed norms of internal democracy.

Continuing with the Canadian example, once a party is registered it acquires a number of privileges, including the following: (i) contributions to the party become eligible for tax credits; (ii) the party's name appears on the ballot; (iii) if it has received at least 2 per cent of the valid votes nationally or 5 per cent of the valid votes in the districts in which it had candidates, half of its election expenses can be reimbursed by the federal treasury, and until 2015 the party could receive a quarterly subvention based on its vote at the previous election. The requirements for ballot access in Canada are the same for party and non-party candidates (except that a candidate wishing to have a party designation on the ballot must submit a letter of endorsement from the party leader in addition to the required signatures and deposit), but in some countries the candidates of a registered party, or a party that already has some level of representation in parliament, may be given a place on the ballot without having to satisfy the requirements imposed on non-party or new party or very minor party candidates.

On the other hand, acquiring official status often also subjects a party to a number of obligations. Canadian registered parties, for example, are required to submit frequent, and audited, financial reports. German law requires membership participation in the selection of party leaders and that candidates be selected by secret ballot, requirements that are not imposed in equivalent detail on other private associations.

Finance

One field in which state involvement in the affairs of parties has been particularly prominent is that of finance. Traditionally, this has taken the form of regulation, and most specifically of prohibitions, against taking money from certain sources, or using it for certain purposes. Although they were directed at candidates rather than parties per se (which the law did not explicitly recognize), the British Corrupt Practice Prevention Act of 1854 and the Corrupt and Illegal Practices Prevention Act of 1883 were early examples. Often these were supplemented by requirements of public disclosure of sources of income, objects of expenditure, or both. In recent decades, these regulatory regimes have been supplemented in many countries by programmes of state support for parties. Some of these take the form of 'tax expenditures', while in other cases parties receive either partial reimbursement of expenses or subventions directly from the state, frequently accompanied by even more invasive regulations justified as monitoring the use of public money.

Regulation of spending

Regulation of party spending has been more or less synonymous with regulation of *campaign* spending—although, of course, parties spend money on many things that are at best indirectly related to campaigns (e.g. social events that help cement member commitment but have no overt connection to a campaign). These regulations take three general forms: bans on particular forms of spending, limitations on total spending, and required disclosure of spending.

Aside from bans on such obviously corrupt practices as vote buying or bribery, the most significant prohibition (or limitation) of a specific form of expenditure concerns the buying of advertising time in the broadcast media. Limitations on total spending are generally based on the size of the electorate and the type of office involved. Expenditure reports are frequently required, and provide some element of transparency, but differ widely among countries with regard to the categories of expenditure that are reported, the degree of detail (e.g. specific recipients or only category totals), the frequency and currency of reports, and the degree to which reports are audited or otherwise subject to independent verification.

Beyond these questions of reporting, all forms of regulation of party spending confront a number of interrelated problems concerning exactly whose spending is to be controlled. Is it parties as organizations, or candidates as individuals, or everyone, including those without formal ties to either candidates or party organizations? To exclude parties (or to include national party organizations but not their local affiliates) is likely to make regulation nugatory, but to include them requires a level of official recognition that until recently was rare in countries with single-member district electoral systems. To include everyone may be seen as an unacceptable limitation on the political speech rights of citizens, but to include only formal party organizations and their candidates risks the explosion of spending by organizations that are effectively the party in another guise, but now unregulated, or less regulated.

Once party and campaign spending are equated, a further problem becomes the definition of the campaign. This involves two questions. First, when does the campaign begin? If the regulated campaign period is too short, its regulation may be of little consequence. Japan, for example, has a very short formal campaign period, during which virtually everything is prohibited, but it is preceded by a real campaign subject to very little regulation. Second, what activity is campaign activity? As with the question of regulating non-party spending, an excessively broad definition of campaigning may subject all political speech to burdensome regulation, but an excessively narrow definition, such as the US 'magic words' doctrine (only messages containing words or phrases like 'vote for', 'elect', 'Smith for Congress', 'vote against', and 'defeat', and referring to a specific candidate, count as campaigning) may defeat the purpose of the regulations.

Regulation of fundraising

Contribution limits are designed to prevent wealthy individuals or groups from exercising undue influence over parties (although, of course, the meaning of 'undue' is often in the eye of the beholder). In various places, foreigners, corporations (sometimes only public corporations or only firms in heavily regulated industries; in other cases, all businesses), or trade unions are barred from making, and parties from accepting, political contributions. Anonymous contributions are also generally barred, perhaps from fear that the anonymity will be in name only.

Regardless of who is allowed to make contributions, there may also be limits on the size of contributions from an individual donor to an individual recipient, in aggregate, or both. However, both kinds of limits are relatively easy to evade: rather than making a corporate contribution, a corporation can 'bundle' (collect centrally and then deliver together) what appear to be individual donations from its officers or employees; an individual can give many times the individual legal limit by 'arranging' to have donations made in the name of his/her spouse, children, and other close relatives. Moreover, the definition of 'contribution' itself is problematic. Money is obvious, but should in-kind contributions be included (and how should they be valued)? What about the donation of services? And perhaps most vexing of all, if a person or group independently advocates the election of a party or candidate (what in the US are called 'independent expenditures'), does that count as a contribution subject to limitation, or free speech that must be protected? Finally, whether or not contributions are restricted, their subversive (of democracy) effect may be limited by requirements of public disclosure.

Public subventions

A growing number of countries provide support for parties through their tax systems, through the direct provision of goods and services, or through direct financial subventions. In some cases, these supports are specifically tied to election campaigns (or, alternatively, limited to non-campaign-related research institutes) while in others they are unrestricted grants for general party activities (see Chapter 7 'Legislatures').

The earliest and most common public subventions are the provision of staff to parliamentary parties or their members, ostensibly to support their official functions, but often convertible to more general political purposes. Particularly in countries in which broadcasting is a public monopoly, parties are generally given an allocation of free air time; other examples of free provision of services include the mailing of candidates' election addresses (e.g. UK), free space for billboards (e.g. Spain, Israel, and Germany), free use of halls in public buildings for rallies (e.g. UK, Spain, Japan), and reduced rates for office space (e.g. Italy). Although these raise some problems, the more contentious question is the direct provision of money, which is nonetheless becoming nearly universal.

Public support for parties raises two questions (beyond the somewhat specious question of whether people should be compelled through their taxes to subsidize causes with which they do not agree). First, is the primary effect of **state subventions** to allow parties to perform better their functions of **policy formulation**, public education, and linkage between

society and the government? Or is it to further the separation between parties and those they are supposed to represent by making parties less dependent on voluntary support? Second, do systems of public support (in which the levels of support are almost always tied to electoral support at the previous election),[7] as well as rules limiting individual contributions, further fairness and equality, or do they unfairly privilege those parties that already are dominant?

KEY POINTS

* Party organizational types have evolved over time as suffrage was expanded and societies changed.

* Rather than reaching an endpoint, organizations continue to evolve, and new types continue to develop.

* Party membership, and involvement of citizens in party politics more generally, appears to be declining virtually throughout the democratic world.

* Parties are increasingly the subject of legal regulation which, while justified in the name of fairness, may also contribute to the entrenchment of the parties that currently are strong.

Parties and the stabilization of democracy

Parties were central to the transition from traditional monarchy to liberal democracy in the first wave of democratization, but they have also been central actors in the third wave (see Chapter 5 'Democracies'). In the older democracies, where the liberal rights of contestation were established before suffrage was expanded to the majority of citizens, parties helped to integrate newly enfranchised citizens into the established patterns of competition. While enfranchisement generally led to the rapid growth of parties (most often socialist) appealing specifically to the new voters, even what are now identified as 'bourgeois parties' found it in their interest to appeal to the new voters—for example, as citizens, or Christians, or members of a peripheral culture, rather than as workers.

In immigrant societies, such as the US, Canada, Australia, or those in South America, the parties also contributed to the integration of arrivals into their new country. The degree to which parties (and other institutions) could perform this function successfully was strongly influenced by the magnitude of the load placed upon them by the rapidity of suffrage expansion. Where the franchise was broadened in several steps spaced over decades, as in the UK, the existing parties were generally able to adapt, with the result that would-be demagogues or revolutionaries found a very limited market. When franchise expansion was more abrupt, as in France in 1848 or Italy in 1913, the twin dangers that masses of new voters would be mobilized by radicals, and that this possibility would be perceived by others to be a threat requiring drastic measures, often led to the collapse of democracy.

This function of integration and stabilization is also potentially important in the new democracies of the late twentieth century. Particularly in the formerly communist bloc (but not only there), the process of democratization has differed from that in the earlier waves in that political mobilization of the citizenry preceded the development of public contestation (Enyedi 2006: 228). Moreover, the levels of literacy, general education, access to mass media, and international involvement far exceed those of earlier waves. Coupled with this has been a deep distrust of the whole idea of political parties, rooted in the unhappy experience of the communist party state. Among the results have been extremely low rates of party membership (giving rise to the idea of a 'couch party'—one whose membership is so small that they could all sit on a single couch) and quite high electoral volatility. Not only has the attachment of voters to particular parties been problematic, but so too has the attachment of elected politicians, with parliamentary party groups showing such low levels of stability that in some cases parliamentary rules have been changed specifically to discourage party splits or defections.

A second major area in which the role of parties in stabilizing democracy is in doubt is the Islamic world, where the question is whether the electoral success of Islamist parties helps to integrate their followers into democratic politics, or, alternatively, threatens to undermine democracy altogether (Tepe 2006). The underlying conflict of values—the will of God as articulated by clerics versus the will of the people as articulated at the ballot box—is hardly unique to the Islamic world (and, indeed, was important throughout the nineteenth century in Europe), but now appears particularly pressing there.

KEY POINTS

- Parties have played, and continue to play, a vital role in stabilizing democracy by integrating new citizens (whether new because they have come of age, immigrated, or benefitted from expansion of the rights of citizenship) into the existing political system.

- Whether the electoral success of anti-democratic parties helps to moderate them and to integrate their followers into democracy, or instead serves to undermine democracy, is an unresolved but pressing issue.

Conclusion

Political parties remain central to democratic government in the twenty-first century. Nonetheless, parties face a number of potentially serious challenges.

Party membership is declining almost everywhere (Biezen et al. 2012). One result has been to force parties to become more dependent on financial contributions and other forms of support from corporations and organizations of special interests, and more recently to 'feed at the public trough' through direct public subventions. This decline in party involvement has not been limited to formal members, but is also reflected in declining party identification, and perhaps most significantly in the growth of hostility not just to the particular parties in a given country at a given time, but to the whole idea of parties and of partisanship.

The growing popularity of such ideas as 'consensus democracy' (Lijphart 1999) and 'deliberative democracy' (e.g. Budge 2000; Guttmann and Thompson 2004), like the complaint of former President Carter that the 2004 US presidential election campaign was 'too partisan', are reflective of a desire for amicable agreement that denies the existence of real conflicts of interest. But if one accepts Finer's (1970: 8) definition of politics as what happens when 'a given set of persons ... require a *common* policy; and ... its members advocate, for this common status, policies that are *mutually exclusive*', this is in effect to want to take the politics out of democracy.

Although rarely put overtly in these terms, the alternative to contentious and partisan politics is generally some form of government by experts or technocrats. Often these 'reforms' have been enacted by parties themselves as a way of avoiding responsibility for unpopular but unavoidable decisions or for outcomes that are beyond their control. Even when the parties remain centrally involved in policy, increasingly their role (and the basis upon which they compete) is defined in terms of management rather than direction. However, by reducing the policy stakes of elections, parties have also decreased the incentives for citizens to become active in them (Katz 2003) and given ammunition to those who ask why the state should provide subsidies and other special privileges (Mair 1995).

The role of parties as representatives of the people, or as links between the people and the state, has also been challenged by the increasing range of organizations that compete with them as 'articulators of interest'. Rather than being forced to choose among a limited number of packages of policy stances across a range of issues—some of which may be of little interest, and others which he/she may actually oppose—the modern citizen can mix and match among any number of groups, each of which will reflect his/her preferences more accurately on a single issue than any party could hope to do. With improved communications skills, and especially with the rise of the internet, citizens may feel less need for intermediaries—they can communicate directly with those in power themselves.

Many parties have themselves tried to adapt to more sophisticated electorates and new technologies, giving rise to the possibility of 'cyber parties' (Margetts 2006; see also Chapter 19 'Political communication'). In its initial stages, this may be little more than the use of mass e-mailings to 'members' (now of mailing lists rather than of real organizations) and the use of the mechanisms of e-commerce to facilitate fundraising from individuals. In a more developed form, it is likely to include chat rooms, discussion list-servers, and extensive fundraising facilities. In theory, the technology might allow what would amount to a party meeting that is always in session. To date, however, there has been more evidence of people at the grass roots using the internet to send messages to those in positions of authority, rather than evidence of those in authority actually listening. And as with the party congresses of the twentieth century, even if the internet (or simply the normal mail) is used to allow party members or supporters to make decisions, real power will continue to rest with those who frame the questions. It remains unlikely that the internet will somehow lead to the repeal of the iron law of oligarchy.

Overall, then, there are two challenges facing parties at the beginning of the twenty-first century. One is the increasing complexity of problems, the increasing speed of social and economic developments, and increasing globalization—all making the problems facing parties as governors less tractable. The other is the increasing political capacity of citizens (cognitive mobilization) running into the ineluctable limitations of individual influence in societies of the size of modern states—expectations of effective individual involvement, even if restricted to the minority who are politically interested, are often unrealistic. Both challenge widely held views of how democratic party government should work. How parties adapt to these changing circumstances, whether by redefining their roles or by altering public expectations, will shape the future of democracy.

? QUESTIONS

Knowledge-based

1. What is the 'iron law of oligarchy'?

2. How do cartel parties differ from catch-all parties?

3. What is the meaning of 'left' in political terms?

4. Do political parties play the same role in new democracies as in the established democracies?

5. Must a democratic political party be internally democratic?

Critical thinking

1. Is a group that nominates candidates in order to put pressure on other parties, but with no real hope of winning an election itself, properly called a political party?

2. Is 'political party' better understood as a category, into which each case either does or does not fit, or as an ideal type, which each case can more or less closely approximate?

3. Is democracy conceivable without political parties?

4. Does the US have 'real' political parties?

5. Is the regulation of political parties' finance compatible with political freedom?

≋ FURTHER READING

Katz, R. S. and Crotty, W. (eds) (2006) *Handbook of Party Politics* (London: Sage). Extensive discussions of many of the topics raised.

Katz, R. S. and Mair, P. (eds) (1992) *Party Organizations: A Data Handbook on Party Organizations in Western Democracies, 1960–90* (London: Sage). Extensive, but somewhat dated, data concerning party organizations.

Scarrow, S., Webb, P. D., and Poguntke, T. (eds) (2017) *Organizing Political Parties: Representation, Participation, and*

Power (Oxford: Oxford University Press). An updating, refinement, and expansion of the Katz and Mair project.

Classics on political parties

Duverger, M. (1954) *Political Parties* (New York: John Wiley).

Hershey, M. R. (2006) *Party Politics in America* (12th edn) (New York: Longman).

LaPalombara, J. and Weiner, M. (eds) (1966) *Political Parties and Political Development* (Princeton, NJ: Princeton University Press).

Panebianco, A. (1988) *Political Parties: Organization and Power* (Cambridge: Cambridge University Press).

Sartori, G. (1976) *Parties and Party Systems: A Framework for Analysis* (Cambridge: Cambridge University Press).

Annual reports (from 1991) on party politics in most established democracies are available in the *Political Data Yearbook*, published in conjunction with the *European Journal of Political Research*. In addition, the *European Journal of Political Research*, *West European Politics*, and *Party Politics* focus heavily on issues concerning political parties.

ENDNOTES

1. The importance of the referendum is one of the factors underlying the Swiss practice of entrusting executive power to an apparently permanent coalition of all the major parties. As Lehner and Homann (1987) explain, given the threat that any parliamentary decision can be overturned by referendum, the ruling parties are at pains to assemble overwhelming majorities in the hope of deterring any referendum in the first place (see also Chapter 10 'Elections and referendums').

2. To date, the only women's party that has had any lasting success was the Icelandic Kvinnalistinn (Women's List), which existed from 1983 to 1999, and at the height of its success (1987) won more than 10 per cent of the national vote, and six of sixty-three seats in parliament. In 1999, the Women's List merged into a more general left-wing alliance.

3. The term 'genetic myth' is used here in the same sense that the term 'stylized' is often used in rational choice theory to suggest the essence of a story without claiming that it fits the details of any particular case.

4. Or with different terms, but equivalent meaning, they might define the interest of their particular class to be the national interest.

5. There is no inherent reason why a cadre party must be on the right, but as history developed, they were generally parties of the propertied classes, who were the only ones who could vote under the *régimes censitaires*.

6. It should be noted that these regulations apply only to federal parties, which are organizationally distinct from provincial parties, even when they apparently have the same name. For example, the Liberal Party of Quebec has not been affiliated with the Liberal Party of Canada since 1955, and indeed when Jean Charest resigned the leadership of the federal Progressive Conservative Party in 1998, it was to become leader of the Quebec Liberal Party.

7. Exceptions include some schemes for media access (as well as the British free mailing of electoral addresses) that allocate resources equally among parties or candidates without regard to prior electoral success, schemes that base support at least in part on numbers of members rather than voters, and schemes of (partial) public matching of privately raised contributions.

Visit the Online Resources that accompany this book for additional material, including country profiles, comparative data sets, flashcard glossaries, and web directory.

www.oup.com/he/caramani5e

13

Party systems

Daniele Caramani

Reader's guide

This chapter looks at the competition between parties and how it leads to different party systems. First, the chapter looks at the *origins* of party systems. Historical cleavages between left and right, the liberal state and religious values or ethno-regional identities, agrarian and industrial sectors of the economy, led to socialist, liberal, religious, regionalist, and other party families. Why are they challenged as the main actors today? Second, the chapter looks at the *format* of party systems, some of which include two large parties (two-party systems), while others are more fragmented (multiparty systems). What is the influence of the electoral system, and what are the consequences for governmental stability of the recent fragmentation of party systems? Third, the chapter analyses the *dynamics* of party systems. To maximize votes, parties tailor their programmes to voters' preferences and converge towards the centre of the left–right axis. Is this why today new populist parties emerge at the extremes?

Introduction

This chapter views parties in their connections within a system. As in planet systems, the focus is not on single planets but on the constellations they form: their number, the balance of size between them, and the distance that separates them. Parties can be ideologically near or distant, there are systems with many small parties or few large ones or even—to pursue the analogy further—one large party with 'satellites' (as in some authoritarian systems). Over time, some systems change while others remain stable. Thus, the variety of party 'constellations' is very large. Furthermore, the 'space' itself can change—either by expanding or shrinking (the extremes of left and right), or by acquiring more than one dimension (as for economic and cultural positions).

Whereas the dynamic principle of planets is gravity, the motor of political interactions is competition for power. In liberal democracies, this competition is based on popular votes. The shape and dynamics of **party systems** are determined by the electoral game in which parties are the main actors. Therefore, a party system is the result of *competitive interactions* between parties. As in all 'games', there is a goal: the maximization of votes to control government. However, the set of interactions between parties is not exclusively composed of competition, but also of *cooperation* (for instance, when they build a coalition).

Three main elements of party systems are important.

1. *Which parties exist?* Why do some parties exist in all party systems (e.g. socialists), whereas others only in some (e.g. regionalists or religious parties)? This relates to the origin, or genealogy, of party systems.

2. *How many parties exist and how big are they?* Why are some systems composed of two large parties and others of many small ones? This relates to the format, or morphology, of party systems.

3. *How do parties behave?* Why in some systems do parties converge towards the centre, whereas in others they diverge to the extremes of the ideological 'space'? This relates to the dynamics of party systems.

An obvious but important point is that party systems must be composed of several parties. There is no 'system' with one unit only. The competitive interaction between parties requires **pluralism**. If the goal is to get the most votes, there must be free elections and pluralism, without which competition cannot exist. Therefore, this chapter focuses on democratic systems.

KEY POINTS

• Party systems are sets of parties that compete and cooperate with the aim of increasing their power in controlling government.

• Interactions are determined by (i) which parties exist; (ii) how many parties compose a system and how large they are; and (iii) the way in which they maximize votes.

• It is appropriate to speak of a party system only in democratic contexts in which several parties compete for votes in open and plural elections.

The genealogy of party systems

The 'national' and 'industrial' revolutions

Until recently, most contemporary parties and party families originated from the socio-economic and political changes between the mid-nineteenth century and the first two decades of the twentieth. Lipset and Rokkan (1967) distinguish two aspects of this transformation: (i) the *Industrial Revolution* refers to changes produced by industrialization and urbanization; (ii) the *National Revolution* refers to the formation of **nation-states** (homogeneous and centralized political units) and liberal democracy (parliamentarism, individual civil and voting rights, rule of law, and secular institutions).

The Industrial and National Revolutions created divisions opposing different social groups. Lipset and Rokkan called these conflicts **cleavages** (see Box: What is a cleavage?, in the Online Resources). With the birth of modern parliaments and free elections, and with the extension of franchise, political parties developed and mirrored the socio-economic and cultural divisions created by the two 'revolutions'.

Cleavages and their political translation

Lipset and Rokkan (1967) distinguish four main cleavages (see Table 13.1). The two revolutions have each produced two main cleavages. Subsequent transformations have produced additional cleavages, namely the 'International Revolution', triggered by the Soviet Revolution of 1917, and the 'Post-Industrial Revolution' in the 1960s–70s, which led to a value cleavage between generations, and **globalization** since the late 1990s.

In the nineteenth century, socio-economic and cultural conflicts emerged simultaneously with democratic reforms. The fundamental features of today's party systems were set during the early phases of **mobilization** of, at first, restricted electorates (only very few people had the right to vote when liberals and conservatives dominated in the nineteenth century) and, later, of 'massifying' electorates when socialist parties mobilized the vast working class that emerged from the Industrial Revolution.

The National Revolution produced two cleavages.

Centre–periphery cleavage

This conflict emerged when nation-states formed in the nineteenth century, and political power, administrative structures, and taxation systems were centralized. This process also brought about national languages and sometimes religions. Most national

Table 13.1 Stein Rokkan's cleavages and their partisan expression

Revolution	Timing	Cleavage	Divisive issue(s)	Party families	Examples
National	Early nineteenth century (restricted electorates)	Centre–periphery	Liberals face resistance to state centralization and cultural standardization (language/religion)	Regionalists, ethnic parties, linguistic parties, minorities	Scottish National Party, Bloc Québéquois, Partido Nacionalista Vasco
		State–church	Conflict between liberal and secularized state against clerical and aristocratic privilege, and over religious education, influence of church in politics	Conservative and religious parties (Catholic mainly), Christian democracy	Austrian People's Party, Christian-Democratic Union, Swiss Catholic Party, Partido Popular
Industrial	Late nineteenth century (suffrage extension)	Rural–urban	Conflict between industrial and agricultural sectors on trade policies: agrarian protectionism vs industrial liberalism (free trade vs tariffs)	Agrarian and peasant parties	Finnish Centre Party, Australian Country Party, Polish Peasant People's Party
		Workers–employers	Employers vs the working class on job security, pensions, social protection, degree of state intervention in economy	Workers' parties, socialists and social democrats, labour parties	British Labour Party, Argentinian Socialist Party, Swedish Social-Democratic Workers' Party, Spanish PSOE (Socialist Workers' Party)
International	Early twentieth century (mass electorates)	Communists–socialists	Division within the 'left' (workers' movement) over centrality of the Soviet Union Communist Party and its international leadership, and over reformism vs revolution	Communists	Partito Comunista Italiano, Izquierda Unida, Parti Communiste Français, Japan's Communist Party
Post-industrial	Late twentieth and early twenty-first centuries (demobilized electorates)	Materialist–post-materialist values	Generational cleavage over policy priorities: new values of civic rights, pacifism, feminism, environment	Green parties, libertarians	Die Grünen, Pirates Party, Austrian Grünen/Grüne Alternative, Democrats '66, Women's Party
		Open–closed societies	Globalization of the economy, opening up of labour markets, perceived threats of immigration to jobs and identity, and supranational integration	Populist parties of left and, above all, right	FPÖ, Rassemblement National, Danish People's Party, Fifth Republic Movement (Hugo Chávez), Movement for Socialism (Evo Morales), Tea Party (US), Syriza (Greece), Podemos (Spain), Five-Star Movement (Italy), Brexit Party, Alternative for Germany, Democratic Party (Rodrigo Duterte)

territories were heterogeneous, with different ethnicities and languages, and administration was fragmented. Nationalist and liberal elites carried out state formation and nation-building, facing resistance from subject populations in peripheral territories in two aspects.

1. *Administrative*: peripheries were incorporated in the bureaucratic and fiscal system of the new state (the central state controlled the territory of and extracted taxes), implying a loss of autonomy for regions.

2. *Cultural*: religious, ethnic, and linguistic identities in peripheral regions were replaced by the allegiance to the new nation-state fostered through compulsory schooling, military conscription, and other means of national socialization. As the first Italian prime minister said in 1870, after Italy unified, 'We have made Italy, let us make Italians.' Nation-building also took place in old-established states. In France in 1863, only 22 per cent of the communes spoke French, all located around Paris (Weber 1976: 67).

Resistance to administrative **centralization** and cultural standardization was, and still is, expressed in regionalist parties, such as the Scottish National Party, the various Basque and Catalan parties in Spain, the Bloc Québéquois in Canada, and so on. After **democratization**, one finds many such ethnic parties in Africa.

State–church cleavage

Nation-states in the nineteenth century were not only centralized and homogeneous, but also based on liberal ideology and secular institutions (no church influence), individualism, and sometimes republicanism. Liberal reforms and the abolition of the estates (clergy, aristocracy, bourgeoisie, peasantry) of pre-modern parliaments, as well as the individual vote and free elections, put an end to clerical and aristocratic privilege. In this, liberals were opposed by conservatives in a conflict between the rising industrial bourgeoisie and the privilege of clergy and aristocracy.

The new liberal secular state fought against the long-established role of the church in education. Compulsory education by the state was used to 'forge' new *citizens*. Especially in Catholic countries, this led to conflicts. The church was also expropriated of real estate and, in Italy, it lost its temporal power and state (about one-quarter of the Italian peninsula) when Italy unified as a nation-state in 1860–70.

Conservatives wanted the return to the old pre-democratic regime. In some countries, Catholics took the place of conservatives, as in Belgium, Switzerland, and Germany. In other countries, Catholics were banned from being candidates and voting by papal decree (for this reason, Catholic parties did not appear in Italy and France until the 1910s). In fact, it was not until after the breakdown of democracy and the inter-war fascist period that the Catholic Church fully accepted democracy. '**Christian democracy**' appears from this evolution after World War II. Today, some Islamic countries face a similar conflict, as in Turkey, Egypt, and Bangladesh.

An interesting case is that of countries with mixed religious structures. In the Netherlands, there was one unified Catholic party and a number of Reformed parties. In 1972, the religious parties merged into the Christian Democratic Appeal. An inter-confessional party also developed in Germany (the Christian Democratic Union). In Switzerland, a major Catholic party emerged from the opposition to the Protestant Radicals/Liberals.

The Industrial Revolution produced two additional cleavages.

Rural–urban cleavage

The first was the contrast between landed interests (agriculture) and the rising class of industrial and trading entrepreneurs. This cleavage focused on trade policies, with agrarians favouring trade barriers (protectionism) and urban industrialists favouring free market with low tariffs (**liberalism**).

Weak sectors of the economy tend to be protectionist because of the threat of imports, whereas strong sectors favour the opening up of economic borders to increase exports (Rogowski 1989). Agriculture was threatened by technological progress and growth of productivity. The defence of agrarian interests—when peasant populations received the right to vote—was expressed through agrarian parties (also called peasants' or farmers' parties). Large or small agrarian parties existed everywhere in Europe, but were particularly strong in Eastern Europe and in Scandinavia. They also existed in Latin America and in the US, with the Populist Party.

The period after World War II witnessed both the decline and the transformation of these parties. In most countries, peasants' parties disappeared. The large agrarian parties of the north and east abandoned the agrarian platform and changed into centre parties. The recent reawakening of this cleavage is most notable in Latin America, where opposition to multinational companies, defence of raw materials and resources, and the threat of globalization has led to protectionist policies (e.g. gas and oil nationalization in Bolivia and Venezuela). In the 1990s, a number of peasant upheavals took place in the Chapas region in Mexico. This cleavage is also present in the European Union, where farmers' pressure groups lobby for protectionist trade agreements and state subsidies.

Workers–employers cleavage

This is the cleavage between the industrial entrepreneurial bourgeoisie who started the Industrial Revolution and the working class that resulted from it. It is the opposition between 'capital' and 'labour' which, up to recently, characterized the left–right alignment. Left–right is the most common ideological dimension along which parties are placed, even in the US, where a socialist party never developed (see Box 13.1).

Industrialization had a very deep impact on Western societies. It radically changed the production mode, caused unprecedented geographical mobility through urbanization (from countryside to urban industrial centres), and transformed family structures. Living conditions in industrial centres were extremely poor. Therefore, workers were easy to mobilize through trade unions, with socialism providing a unifying ideology. With the extension of voting rights, social democratic and labour parties gained parliamentary representation.

Socialist parties campaigned for labour protection against the capitalist economy. They promoted social rights and **welfare state** provisions on top of civil and political rights, and a substantial equalization of living conditions in addition to formal legal equality

(Marshall 1950; Kitschelt 1994). These claims concerned under-age and female labour, wages, working hours, contract security, protection in the workplace and during unemployment or illness, progressive taxation, accident insurance, and pension schemes. Socialists favoured economic policies with a strong intervention of the state in steering the economy and public investments (later Keynesianism) against the liberal free-market ideology. They looked for state ownership of infrastructure (transportation, energy), industries, and sometimes finance.

Many socialist and labour parties originate from previously existing trade unions, the main organizations of the working class before universal suffrage, when workers did not have the right to vote. Unions responded to a number of needs of the working class, increased solidarity and cooperation within it, and provided a wide range of services.

The Soviet Revolution of 1917 produced a cleavage within the workers' movement.

Communism–socialism cleavage

In the aftermath of the Russian Revolution that led to the Soviet Union and the single-party regime controlled by the Communist Party, communist parties in all countries formed as splinters from the socialists. The main issue was the lead of the Soviet Communist Party in the international revolutionary movement and also ideological differences, namely whether a revolution would be necessary to take the

---

⬊ ZOOM-IN 13.1

Why is there no socialism in the US?

Factors explaining the absence of a socialist ideology and workers' party in the most advanced capitalist country are:

- *Open frontier* Geographical and social mobility gave US workers the possibility of moving on in search of better conditions.

- *Party machines* Dominance of Democrats and Republicans since the nineteenth century made the rise of third parties difficult.

- *The free gift of the vote* Working-class white men all had the right to vote, were integrated in the political system, and had a say in government's actions.

- *Roast beef and apple pie* The American working class was more affluent than the European and all socialist utopias come to grief with a satisfied working class.

- *No feudalism* The absence of aristocracy in the US made the working class very similar to the European bourgeoisie.

Ask yourself: Do these conditions still apply in today's America? Can the popularity of Senator Bernie Sanders or Representative Alexandria Ocasio-Cortez be seen as a proof of change, making socialism in the US possible?

Read:

- Lipset, S. M. (1977) 'Why No Socialism in the United States?', in S. Bialer and S. Sluzar (eds), *Sources of Contemporary Radicalism* (Boulder, CO: Westview Press), 131–49.

- Lipset, S. A. and Marks, G. (2000) *It Didn't Happen Here: Why Socialism Failed in the United States* (New York: Norton).

- Sombart, W. (1976) *Why is there No Socialism in the United States?* (London: Macmillan), translated from the German 1906 text.

proletariat to power, or if this goal could be achieved through elections.

As a reaction against the radicalization of the working class and its powerful action through a new type of **mass party** organization, fascist parties emerged in a number of European countries and, more or less directly, dominated government during the 1930s. These parties favoured the nation over class and 'internationalism', and private property over communism. Fascist parties were the product of the radicalization of the industrial bourgeoisie threatened by socialist policies, and of the aristocracy threatened by **redistribution** through land reforms.

Finally, the 'Post-Industrial Revolution' (Bell 1973) created two more recent cleavages.

Materialism–post-materialism cleavage

A cleavage between generations over sets of values emerged in the 1960s and 1970s as a consequence of the protracted period of international peace, economic wealth, and domestic security post World War II (Inglehart 1977). The younger cohort developed 'post-materialist values' focused on tolerance, equality, participation, expression, emancipation, respect for the environment, fair trade, peace, and Third World solidarity, as opposed to the 'materialist' values of the war generation centred around themes of national security, law and order, full employment, protection of private property, tradition, and authority (within the family and the state).

These new values were primarily expressed in a number of new **social movements** (see Chapter 16 'Social movements'): the civil rights movement in the US in the 1950s, pacifism from the Vietnam War in the 1960s, feminism in the 1970s, and environmentalism in the 1980s. In the 1990s, new anti-globalization movements developed against the globalization of the economy and the Americanization of culture (Della Porta 1999). From a party politics perspective, however, there are only a few examples of a significant impact of these 'new left' movements, the main one being green parties (Müller-Rommel and Poguntke 2002). A more pervasive impact of the Post-Industrial Revolution is on the 'new right'.

The globalization cleavage

Economic globalization has created a cleavage between sectors of the economy that profit from the blurring of national boundaries, and sectors that suffer from the competition from new markets and cheap labour from the East and Asia. 'Losers' of globalization and integration (Betz 1994) have reinforced support for populist protest parties who favour trade barriers to protect local manufacture and 'locals first' policies in the labour market. These groups are the small and medium enterprises, unskilled workers, craftsmen, and agricultural producers.

The economic defensive attitude of these groups is reinforced by cultural, anti-immigration, and xenophobic prejudice, stressing religious and national values against multi-ethnic society and cosmopolitanism. Increasingly, such a 'cultural backlash' (Ignazi 1992; Inglehart and Norris 2018) finds expression in referenda, as in Switzerland or in the case of the Brexit referendum in Britain in 2016. The effect on parties' systems is a vote for populist parties. Many of these parties rely upon an extreme-right heritage, such as the Austrian Liberal Party and the French National Rally (Kitschelt 1995). New parties include the UK Brexit Party, Alternative for Germany, Fidesz in Hungary, Vox in Spain, the Tea Party in the US, among many others. Others are sporadic parties, such as the One-Nation Party in Australia. In Southern Europe and Latin America, populist tendencies have a left-wing (inclusive) character, as in Bolivia, Ecuador, and Venezuela (Burgess and Levitsky 2003; Mudde and Kaltwasser 2013), and in Spain with Podemos or Greece with Syriza. Populism is also a reaction to changing security conditions which, with terrorist attacks and the refugee crisis in Europe, have created a resurgence of law-and-order values.

Variations in cleavage constellations

Cleavage constellations change across space and over time.

Space

Not all cleavages exist in all countries. There are a variety of constellations, and thus of party systems. Why do some cleavages exist in specific countries while not in others? Whereas the left–right cleavage exists everywhere and is a source of similarity, the state–church, rural–urban, and centre–periphery cleavages vary across countries and are a source of difference (Caramani 2015).

Country-specific cleavage constellations are determined by:

- differences in objective factors such as diverse social structures: multiple ethnicities or religious groups, structure of the peasantry, class relations;
- the extent to which socio-economic and cultural divisions have been politicized by parties, i.e. by the action of elites (Rose 1976; Lijphart 1968b);
- the relationship between cleavages: their existence and strength can prevent the development of new ones (e.g. agrarian claims have been incorporated by Catholic or conservative parties).

There are *homogeneous constellations* where there is one predominant cleavage, namely the left–right cleavage (e.g. the US), and *heterogeneous constellations*, in which various cleavages overlap or cut across one another in plural democracies, such as Belgium, Canada, India, the Netherlands, and Switzerland (Lijphart 1984).

Time

Until recently, party systems have remained extraordinarily stable since the 1920s. Even party labels have not changed (liberal, socialist, conservative), as a sort of political *imprint* (see Box: Party families, in the Online Resources) despite a decline in cleavage politics with the blurring of social divisions (Franklin et al. 1992). Lipset and Rokkan have formulated the so-called **freezing hypothesis**:

[T]he party systems of the 1960s reflect, with few but significant exceptions, the cleavage structures of the 1920s . . . [T]he party alternatives, and in remarkably many cases, the party organizations, are older than the majorities of the national electorates.

Lipset and Rokkan (1967: 50; italics omitted)

In the 1920s, the full mobilization of the **electoral market** through universal suffrage and PR caused its saturation. As in all markets, there are entry barriers. Little room was left for new parties. Thus, existing parties were able to maintain their control over electorates over generations.

Empirical research debates the basic stability of electorates over time, with theses of *dealignment and realignment* (Dalton et al. 1985) based on survey data, or *stabilization* in a long-term perspective (Bartolini and Mair 1990) based on electoral volatility data (the change of votes from one election to the next). Over the past ten years, however, dramatic change has occurred in Western party systems with the rise of populist parties in many countries and the decline of established parties. Current levels are as high as those around the two world wars (see bars in Figure 13.1), pointing to the 'de-institutionalisation' of party systems (Casal Bértoa 2017).

The morphology of party systems

The competitive interaction between parties depends on the shape of party systems. The two main elements

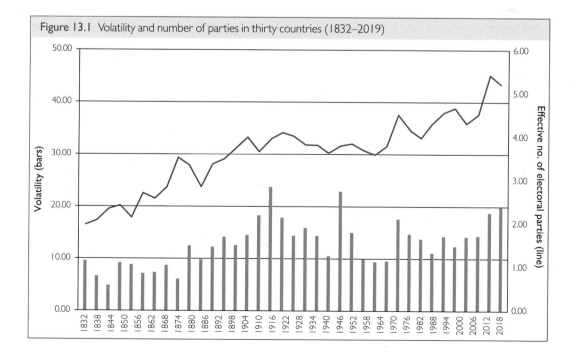

Figure 13.1 Volatility and number of parties in thirty countries (1832–2019)

of their morphology are: (i) the *number* of competing parties; and (ii) their *size*. How many players are there and how strong are they? The number and strength of actors can be observed at two levels: the *votes* parties get in elections and the *seats* in parliament. Therefore a 'variable' that must be considered is the **electoral system** through which votes are translated into parliamentary seats.

Two types of party systems are not considered in this section because they do not fulfil the democratic conditions that allow competition.

1. Single-party systems with only one legal party: the authoritarian experiences of the Communist Party in the Soviet Union and today in China, the National Socialist Party in Germany in the 1930s, and the Ba'athist Party in Iraq until 1993 and in Syria until 2011.

2. Hegemonic party systems in which other parties are legal but as 'satellites', under the control of the hegemonic party: these are also totalitarian or authoritarian systems which existed in Egypt and Tunisia until the Arab Spring, and in many communist regimes in Central and Eastern Europe before 1989.

There are four types of party systems.

Dominant-party systems

Dominant-party systems are characterized by one large party with a majority *above the absolute majority* of 50 per cent of seats for *protracted periods of time* (several decades). In these systems, all parties are allowed to compete in free elections to challenge the dominant party. However, no other party receives enough votes to come close to 50 per cent. Therefore, there is no alternation in power and the dominant party does not need to enter coalitions to form a government.

An example is India between 1947 and 1975. After Independence, the Congress Party received over 50 per cent of votes and was able to rule unchallenged until 1975–77 when the 'state of emergency' was declared. A more recent example of a dominant-party system is South Africa since the end of apartheid in the early 1990s. The African National Congress, initially led by Nelson Mandela, has been able to secure an absolute majority of votes because of the role it had in enfranchising the black population. In Europe, a case of a dominant-party system is Sweden. The Social Democratic Workers' Party formed almost all governments from 1945 until 1998, with around 45 per cent of the votes on average. In Mexico, the Institutional Revolutionary Party was in power from the revolution of 1917 until 2000. The AKP in Turkey since 2017 is also such a case.

Two-party systems

A two-party system is one in which two equally balanced large parties dominate the party system and alternate in power. The two parties have comparable sizes and equal chances of winning elections. Even a small number of votes changing from one party to the other (electoral swing) can cause a change of majority. Therefore, alternation in power is frequent. These are very competitive systems. Because both parties are large, the winning party is likely to receive an absolute majority of seats and form single-party governments without the need for partners.

The features of two-party systems are listed in Table 13.2. The two large parties have similar sizes (around 35–45 per cent of the votes each), which plurality electoral systems transform into absolute majorities of seats for the largest party. A number of other smaller parties compete in the elections. However, they are marginal, as they are usually not necessary to form a government.

In two-party systems, single-party governments tend to alternate from one legislature to the next. This is, to a large extent, an effect of plurality electoral systems. Because the **threshold** in first-past-the-post (FPTP) systems is very high, the two main parties propose policies and programmes that are acceptable to a large part of the electorate. Plurality leads to ideological moderation and similarity of programmes. In turn, this similarity makes it easier for voters to switch from one party to the other, creating alternation.

These systems are typical of the Anglo-Saxon world, where plurality in single-member districts has been maintained, unlike continental Europe, where around World War I countries changed to proportional representation (PR) systems. Today, only the US provides a 'perfect' example of a two-party system where Republicans and Democrats have dominated since 1860.[1] Australia maintains a strong two-party system with the Labour Party and the Liberals. Other examples include Costa Rica and Malta (where Labour and the Nationalist Party receive together close to 100 per cent of the votes). In Canada, Conservatives and Liberals dominated until 1993 (with a strong New Democratic Party), when the Bloc Québécois and the Reform Party increased their support.

Two-party systems can also be found in countries with PR electoral systems. Until the 2000s, Austria and Israel were dominated by two parties. After the end of Franco's regime in 1977, Spain moved towards a two-party system, which lasted until 2015 in spite of many (but small) regionalist parties. Germany was named a 'two-and-a-half system', with two large parties

Table 13.2 Types of party system in democracies

Type of party system	Features	Cases
Dominant party	One large party with an absolute majority of votes and seats No other party approaching 50% No alternation One-party government	India until 1975, Japan between 1955 and 1993, Mexico until 2000, South Africa since 1994
Two-party	Two large parties sharing together around 80% of votes and seats Balanced (35–45% each) with one of the two reaching 50% of seats Alternation between parties One-party government	Austria and Israel until roughly 2000, Canada, Costa Rica, Malta, and New Zealand until the 1990s, Spain until 2015, South Africa until 1989, Turkey, UK, US
Multiparty	Several or many parties, none approaching 50% of votes and seats Parties of different sizes Parties run for elections individually and form coalitions after elections Alternation through coalition changes Coalition government	Belgium, Canada, Colombia, Czech Republic, Denmark, Finland, Germany until 1989, Hungary, Italy, Netherlands, Poland, Russia, Switzerland
Bipolar	Two large coalitions composed of several parties sharing together around 80% of votes and seats Coalitions are balanced (40–50% each) Coalitions are stable over time and run elections as electoral alliances Alternation between coalitions Coalition government	France in the Fifth Republic, Germany since 1990, Italy between 1994 and 2013, Portugal

together (the Christian-Democratic Union and the Social Democratic Party) collecting more than 80 per cent of the votes and a smaller Liberal Party (around 5 per cent) with a pivotal position, which enabled it to decide—through alliance—which of the larger parties would be in charge of government. With the rise of populist parties and the decline of established parties these systems are changing, in particular in Austria, Germany, and Spain.

Multiparty systems

Multiparty systems are the most frequent and the most complex type of party system. The number of parties ranges from three to double-digit figures. None of the parties in a multiparty system is majoritarian (with 50 per cent of the votes or seats). Furthermore, parties that compose a multiparty system are of different sizes: some are large (say, 30 per cent of the votes) and some are small (less than 5 per cent).

Because no single party has an overall majority, parties form coalitions to support a government. In **parliamentary systems** (see Chapters 5 'Democracies' and 7 'Legislatures') the vote of confidence requires a 50 per cent majority of seats. Parties run individually in elections (contrary to bipolar systems) and governmental coalitions are negotiated after elections.

PR does not hinder niche parties from addressing small segments of the electorate and does not lead to ideological moderation, which, in turn, makes it more difficult for voters to switch from one party to the other and cause a government change. As a consequence, government change rarely takes place through electoral change, but rather by swaps of coalition partners.

While multiparty systems are considered to represent better pluralism in countries with religious, territorial, and ethno-linguistic cleavages, they are considered less stable, subject to frequent coalition 'crises', with no single party clearly accountable

(Powell 2000). Positive aspects of multiparty systems have been stressed since analyses in the 1960s and 1970s included small countries such as Belgium, the Netherlands, Switzerland, and the Scandinavian countries. In plural societies, PR and multiparty systems are a viable way to involve minorities in decision-making processes and reach consensus.[2] As Chapter 5 'Democracies' shows, consociational or consensus democracies represent a different model of democracy from the majoritarian or 'Westminster' model. Both have advantages and disadvantages (see Box 13.2).

The way in which multiparty systems function largely depends on the degree to which parties are ideologically polarized. Sartori (1976) has distinguished two main types of multiparty systems.

Moderate multiparty systems

The dynamic is similar to that of two-party systems. The number of parties is small and the direction of the competition is **centripetal**, i.e. the main parties tend to converge towards the centre of the left–right scale to attract the support of the moderate electorate. At the centre are small parties with whom the two large ones on either side may form a coalition. The ideological distance between parties is limited, so that all coalitions are possible.

Polarized multiparty systems

These have three main features. First, there is a large ideological distance between parties with a strong dose of radicalism. *Anti-system parties* aim to change

---

📣 FOR AND AGAINST 13.2

A normative debate: advantages and disadvantages of party systems

Two-party systems	Multiparty systems
Historically positive connotation	Historically negative connotation
Two-party systems resisted the breakdown of democracy between the First and Second World Wars: UK and US.	After the First World War in Italy, Weimar Germany, the Spanish Second Republic, and the French Fourth Republic (1946–56), instability led to a crisis of democracy.
Effective	Ineffective
Produces governments immediately after elections. Governments are stable because they are formed by a single party.	Governments take a long time to form after elections because of negotiations between parties. Coalitions lead to unstable governments.
Accountable	Non-accountable
Because there is only one party in government, responsibility is clearly identifiable by the electorate.	Because governments are formed by many parties, responsibility is obfuscated.
Alternation	No alternation
Two main parties alternate in power. Voters directly influence the formation of government, and a small shift can cause government change.	Coalition negotiations are out of the reach of voters' influence and shifts of votes are not necessarily followed by changes of government.
Distortive	Representative
FPTP under-represents minorities and over-represents large mainstream parties of left–right.	PR fairly represents minorities in societies with ethno-linguistic and religious parties.
Moderation	Radicalization
Main parties have a chance to govern and thus avoid extreme claims. Need to gather votes from large moderate segments of the electorate.	Multiparty systems allow representation of extreme parties. Some do not have any government prospect and do not hesitate to radicalize their claims.
Discontinuity	Continuity
Decisions are made by majority and subsequent cabinets often reverse legislation.	Decisions are made by consensus through consultation. More continuity in legislation.

not only government but also the *system of* government (Capoccia 2002). Thus, not all coalitions are viable, with some parties continuously excluded and in constant opposition. They become irresponsible and radicalize with promises they will never be called to put into practice. Second, there is one main party placed at the *centre of the left–right axis* which represents the 'system' against which extreme anti-system parties are opposed. Being always in power, it also becomes irresponsible and unaccountable. This party is not punished electorally because of the absence of viable alternatives. Third, the occupied centre discourages a centripetal move on the part of other parties. As a consequence, divergence and competition is **centrifugal**. Examples of polarized systems are the Weimar Republic in Germany from 1919 until 1933, and Italy between 1946 and 1992.

Bipolar systems

Bipolar party systems combine elements of multi- and two-party systems. As in multiparty systems, there are many parties, none of which has a majority. Again, coalition governments are the rule. These, however, form before elections and run as electoral alliances. They remain stable over time. There are usually two large coalitions of evenly balanced size alternating in power. Therefore, competition resembles that of two-party systems.

In France, left and right have alternated in power from 1958 to 2017, when the success of President Macron's 'En Marche' disrupted the party system.[3] The left included Socialists, Radicals, Communists, and Greens, whereas the right included Gaullists and Liberals (they merged in 2003 as the Union for a Popular Movement). In Italy after 1994, the centre-left coalition was composed of Social Democrats, Communists, Greens, and Catholics, whereas the centre-right coalition included Silvio Berlusconi's party (which merged with the post-fascist party) and the Northern League. The coalitions have alternated in power in 1996, 2001, 2006, 2008, and partly in 2013. In 2018, the Five-Star Movement became the largest party and interrupted the bipolar system.

The number of parties

As we have seen, the number of parties is important. But how, exactly, should parties be *counted*? If all parties that run in an election are counted (or even only those that get some votes), the number would be extremely large and useless for building a typology. In every election, there are dozens of parties and candidates that get no votes, or very few. Therefore, it is necessary to have reasonable rules to decide how to count. There are two ways to count parties: (i) *numerical*, with indices based on the *size* of parties; (ii) **qualitative**, with rules based on the *role* of parties in the system.

Numerical rules

These rules represent **quantitative** attempts to classify party systems on the basis of the number and size of parties that compose them. Various indices have been devised to summarize this basic information: are there many small parties (a *fragmented* party system) or a few large parties (a *concentrated* party system)?

The most frequently used indices are Rae's *fractionalization index* (Rae 1971) and the *effective number of parties* (Laakso and Taagepera 1979). The fractionalization index (F) varies from zero (full concentration of seats or votes in one party) to one (total fragmentation with each seat going to a different party). The effective number of parties (E) indicates the number of parties in a system and does not have an upper limit.

The two formulas are as follows:

$$F = 1 - \Sigma p_i^2 \quad E = 1 / \Sigma p_i^2$$

where p is the percentage of votes or seats for party i and Σ represents the sum for all parties. The percentages for all parties are squared to weight parties by their size. If there are two parties, A and B, each receiving 50 per cent of the seats, first calculate the squares for party A ($0.50 \times 0.50 = 0.25$) and party B ($0.50 \times 0.50 = 0.25$), and then add them together ($0.25 + 0.25 = 0.50$). Thus:

$$F = 1 - 0.50 = 0.50 \qquad E = 1 / 0.50 = 2.$$

In this example, F is exactly midway between zero and one (0.50) and E counts that there are two parties.

Table 13.3 lists the effective number of parties (based on seats) contesting recent elections in a number of countries.[4] As can be seen, there is a wide variation between countries. The less fragmented countries are those using plurality / majoritarian or transferable vote systems in single-member districts (Australia, France, UK, Hungary, Malta, the US), whereas the most fragmented countries are those with PR and many religious and ethno-linguistic parties (Belgium, Finland, the Netherlands, New Zealand, Norway, Switzerland). In general, there is a dramatic increase of party systems' fragmentation (Figure 13.1 above).

Qualitative rules

In many cases, it is not appropriate to consider numerical criteria only to decide whether or not a party is relevant. Often small parties—which quantitative rules would weight lightly—have far-reaching

Table 13.3 Rae's parliamentary fractionalization index (F), effective number of parliamentary parties (E), and Gallagher's index of disproportionality (LSq)

Country	Election	F	E	LSq
Argentina	2017	0.70	3.3	6.5
Australia	2019	0.54	2.2	13.4
Belgium	2019	0.91	10.9	4.4
Brazil	2018	0.94	16.4	3.3
Canada	2015	0.60	2.5	12.0
Chile	2017	0.68	3.1	7.5
France	2017	0.66	3.0	21.2
Germany	2017	0.82	5.6	2.5
Greece	2019	0.63	2.7	9.8
Hungary	2018	0.52	2.1	13.6
India	2019	0.67	3.0	18.6
Israel	2019	0.81	5.1	4.7
Italy	2018	0.77	4.3	4.4
Japan	2017	0.59	2.5	22.1
Malta	2017	0.49	2.0	1.2
Mexico	2018	0.79	4.7	10.6
Netherlands	2017	0.88	8.1	1.4
New Zealand	2017	0.63	2.7	2.8
Portugal	2015	0.65	2.9	6.1
Russia	2016	0.40	1.7	15.9
Spain	2019	0.79	4.8	6.0
Sweden	2018	0.82	5.6	1.2
Switzerland	2015	0.80	4.9	4.4
Turkey	2018	0.67	3.1	5.7
UK	2017	0.59	2.5	6.5
US	2018	0.50	2.0	1.3

Notes: For calculations, alliances have been considered (Australia, Chile, Hungary, India). In mixed electoral systems, PR votes have been used (Hungary, Japan, Mexico, New Zealand, and Russia). For Germany, *Zweitstimmen* have been used and in France first-ballot votes. For the US, 2018 are mid-term elections. Argentina renews only half of the Chamber. As a general rule, for including parties in the calculation, all parties/alliances polling at least 1% have been taken into account.

Source: See sources in Appendix 1 'Country Profiles' (see also the Online Resources).

consequences for coalitions, influencing important decisions, mobilizing people, and so on. Sometimes small parties are much more important than their sheer size would suggest. Sartori (1976) has developed two criteria to decide which parties really 'count' and should be 'counted'.

1. *Coalition potential*: a small party is irrelevant if over a period of time it is not necessary for any type of governmental coalition. On the contrary, a party must be counted if, disregarding its size, it is pivotal and determines whether or not a coalition is going to exist.

2. *Blackmail potential*: a small party must be considered relevant when it is able to exercise pressure on governmental decisions through threats or veto power.

The influence of electoral laws

Given the impact of party system fragmentation on stability, accountability, and representation, research in comparative politics has been concerned with the causes for varying numbers and size of parties. With the number of cleavages, the main cause is the electoral system.

Electoral systems are mechanisms for the translation of preferences into votes, and votes into parliamentary seats. Chapter 10 'Elections and referendums' shows that there are two main 'families' of electoral systems: (i) majoritarian systems in single-member constituencies; and (ii) PR systems in multi-member constituencies. The first and best-known formulation of the causal relationship between electoral and party systems is Duverger's laws from his classic book *Political Parties* (1954). As can be seen in Box 13.3, the two laws are simple: plurality or majoritarian electoral systems favour two-party systems, whereas PR leads to multiparty systems. This relationship between electoral and party systems is due to two effects.

Mechanical effects refer to the formula used to translate votes into seats. In single-member constituencies, winning the seat is difficult. Only the party with the most votes gets the single seat. The second, third, fourth, etc. do not get any seat (first-past-the-post). This means that the threshold is high, and all parties but the first one are eliminated. With PR, on the contrary, in each multi-member **constituency** many seats are allocated in proportion to the votes. Small parties are not excluded (a party with 5 per cent of votes gets roughly 5 per cent of seats) and therefore the overall number of parties making it into parliament is high.

Psychological effects refer to the behaviour of voters and parties.

1. On the *demand side* (voters), in electoral systems in which only large parties have a chance to win seats, voters tend to vote *strategically* (not necessarily their first party preference) to avoid wasting votes on small parties with no chance of getting seats. Converging votes on large parties reduces their overall number. On the contrary, with PR in which small parties can win seats, voters vote *sincerely* (their first preference) because their vote is not wasted. This increases the vote for small parties, and thus their overall number.

2. On the *supply* side (parties), with plurality small parties have an incentive to merge with others to increase their chances of passing the threshold, thus reducing the number of parties. On the contrary, with PR parties have no incentive to merge: they can survive on their own and small, splinter parties are not penalized. This increases the overall number of parties.

Rae (1971), Riker (1982), and Sartori (1986) have questioned these laws by asking whether the reductive effect of majoritarian electoral systems works at *the constituency level or at the national level*. At the constituency level, the high threshold reduces the number of parties. But does this always translate into a reduction at the national level?

Suppose that a parliament has 100 seats from 100 single-member constituencies. If in each constituency a different party wins the seat, we would end up with a fragmented parliament. Thus, the question is: under what conditions does the reductive effect of FPTP at the constituency level also reduce the number of parties at the national level? The answer is: majoritarian systems produce two-party systems at the national level only if parties are 'nationalized', i.e. receive homogeneous support in all constituencies (see Rae/Riker's propositions and Sartori's argument in Box 13.3). If there are parties with regionally concentrated support, this leads to fragmentation in the national party system, even if small nationwide.

In most countries, party systems nationalized at the beginning of competitive elections in the mid-nineteenth century, so the support parties receive is increasingly homogeneous across regions and territorialized support has declined. This can be observed not only in Europe and North America, but also in India and Latin America (Caramani 2004; Chhibber and Kollman 2004; Morgenstern 2017) due to the development of national party organizations and increasing candidate coordination (Cox 1997).

Therefore, where plurality systems exist, reduction of the number of parties has taken place. Plurality systems *distort* party votes when they translate them into seats.

Q   DEFINITION 13.3

The influence of electoral systems on party systems

Duverger's 'laws' (1954)

First Law
'The majority [plurality] single-ballot system tends to party dualism.'

Second Law
'The second ballot [majority] system or proportional representation tends to multipartyism.'

Rae/Riker's 'proposition' (1971, 1982)

'Plurality formulae are always associated with two-party competition except where strong local minority parties exist.'

Sartori's 'tendency laws' (1986)

Law 1
'Given systemic structuring and cross-constituency dispersion (as joint necessary conditions), plurality systems cause (are a sufficient condition of) a two-party format.'

Law 2
'PR formulas facilitate multipartyism and are, conversely, hardly conducive to two-partyism.'

Cox's 'coordination argument' (1997)

'Why . . . would the same two parties necessarily compete in all districts [cross-constituency coordination or nationalization]?' Local candidates link together to compete more effectively.'

'If a system (1) elects legislators by plurality rule in single-member districts; (2) elects its chief executive by something like nationwide plurality rule; and (3) holds executive and legislative elections concurrently, then it will tend to . . . have a national two-party or one-party-dominant system.'

- They *over*-represent large parties (the share of seats for big parties is larger than their share of votes).
- They *under*-represent small parties.

How can we measure the (dis)proportionality between votes and seats? The most frequently used measure is the least squares index of disproportionality (LSq) (Gallagher 1991; Gallagher and Mitchell 2008: appendix B):

$$LSq = \sqrt{1/2 \, \Sigma (v_i - s_i)^2}$$

where *v* is the percentage of votes for party *i*, *s* is the percentage of seats for party *i*, and Σ represents the sum for all parties. This index varies between zero (full proportionality) and 100 (total disproportionality). Take, as an example, the results of the 2015 UK election in Table 13.4. If the total of the squared differences is halved (450.4/2 = 225.2) and then the square root is taken, the result is 15.0, i.e. a high level of disproportionality between vote and seat distributions compared to other countries.

The values of the LSq index are given in the last column of Table 13.3. In countries with plurality systems (Canada, the UK, India), there is a stronger distortion of the popular vote. The same applies for other systems based on single-member constituencies, such as France with a two-ballot majoritarian system. On the contrary, disproportionality is lower for countries with PR systems.

However, PR systems also have a reductive effect on the number of parties if the *magnitude of constituencies* is small, as in Spain. The magnitude refers to the number of seats allocated in a given constituency. The larger the magnitude, the higher the proportionality between votes and seats. If the magnitude is small, the few seats go to the few largest parties.[5]

The dynamics of party systems

In the wake of Joseph Schumpeter's (1943) definition of democracy (a set of rules for selecting political leaders and making decisions by means of competition for votes), authors have developed analogies between *electoral competition* and *market competition*. In the electoral market, parties and candidates compete for 'shares' of the electorate, as happens in the economic world, where firms compete for shares of the market. Parties are organizations whose main motive is the *maximization of votes*, and the exchange between represented and representatives is similar to that between demand and supply in the economy (see Table 13.5).

Table 13.4 Results of the 2015 UK election and Gallagher's LSq index of disproportionality				
Party	Votes (%)	Seats (N)	Seats (%)	Difference (% seats−% votes)	Squared
Conservatives	36.9	331	50.9	14.0	196.0
Labour	30.5	232	35.7	5.2	27.0
Liberal Democrats	7.9	8	1.2	−6.6	43.6
Greens	3.8	1	0.2	−3.6	13.0
Scottish National Party	4.7	56	8.6	3.8	14.4
UK Independence Party	12.6	1	0.2	−12.5	156.3
Others	3.6	21	3.2	−0.4	0.2
Total	100.0	650	100.0		450.5

Table 13.5 The analogy between economic and electoral competition		
Dimensions	Economy	Elections
Market	Economic	Electoral
Actors	Firms	Parties
	Consumers	Voters
Profit	Money	Votes
Supply	Goods, services	Programmes, policies
Demand	Product preferences	Policy preferences
Communication	Advertising	Campaigns

The market analogy

Anthony Downs's *An Economic Theory of Democracy* (1957) is a pioneering book in which the basic elements of these models are spelled out for the first time. In this model, actors (parties and voters) are *rational*.

Parties calculate their strategies by formulating platforms with the goal of maximizing votes and being elected or re-elected. Parties are coalitions of individuals seeking to control institutions and act to gain office. To maximize votes, parties offer programmes that appeal to many voters. Voters face alternatives, which they order from most to least preferred and choose the alternative that ranks highest. Voters make a rational choice by voting for parties whose programmes are closest to their policy preferences, their interests, or their values and moral orientations. Voters vote on the basis of the *proximity* between parties' positions and their preferences. For that, they must know what the alternative proposals by different parties are, i.e. they are *informed* about their choices.

Once elected, parties seek re-election through policies appealing to large segments of the electorate. The goal of parties is to *maximize utility* in terms of votes; the voters' goal is to maximize utility through policies satisfying their interests and values. As in economic theory, the search for individual advantages produces *common goods*, namely responsiveness and accountability.

Competition models were first devised for two-party systems—mainly the US. However, maximization of votes is also the main motive in systems in which governments are coalitions. The more votes, the better the chances to enter a coalition, control governmental institutions, and place individuals in key positions.

The spatial analogy

The proximity/distance between individual preferences and parties' policies indicates that players move within a space. The second element that Downs 'imported' from economic models of competition is their spatial representation. In particular, Downs adapted models of the dynamics of competition between firms, i.e. where firms locate premises according to the physical distribution of the population.

Let us take the simple case of a village in which there is only one street (the example is from Hotelling (1929)). On each side of the street, there are evenly spaced houses (the square dots in Figure 13.2). What are the dynamics between two competitors, say two bakeries A and B? Assuming that both bakers offer the same quality of bread for the same price and that consumers will rationally try to reduce their 'costs' by buying bread in the nearest shop (proximity), if A and B are located as they are in Figure 13.2, B will have a larger share of the market. The share of B's market goes from the right-side end of the street to the M-point, which is the mid-point between the locations of A and B. Residents on the right of the M-point will buy bread in bakery B, and residents on the left of the M-point will buy bread in bakery A. The dynamic element in this model consists of A's move to increase its share of the market. By relocating the bakery at AA, the baker is able to gain the share of the market indicated by the dashed area. Obviously, B can also move towards the centre (BB) and win back part of the lost share of the market. Both bakers seek to *optimize their location*.

An additional element introduced by Smithies (1941) concerns the elasticity of demand. The further away they are from the edges, the higher the incentives for a new bakery at the edges of the village as people feel that AA and BB are too distant. The risk of strategies of relocation towards the centre

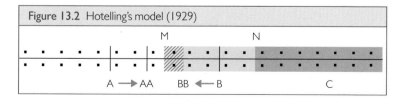

Figure 13.2 Hotelling's model (1929)

is that a new bakery C appears, taking away part of B's share of the market (the dark-shaded area). Therefore, there are two dynamic elements in these models: (i) the movement caused by the search for the optimal location; and (ii) the appearance of new competitors.

Downs's model

Through the analogy between physical and ideological space, Downs imports these elements into the analysis of the dynamics of party systems. Most elements are maintained: (i) the one-dimensionality of the space; (ii) the principle according to which costs are reduced by choosing the closest option (proximity); and (iii) competitors' search for the optimal location.

Downs represented the ideological space by a zero to 100 scale, ranging from left to right. As will be seen, one-dimensionality is maintained, even if it is not always a realistic assumption, because it summarizes other dimensions and is the most important one (in terms of size of parties that define themselves according to this dimension), and because it is present in all party systems.

Both Hotelling and Smithies had previously applied spatial models to politics and were able to predict that parties tend to converge towards one another in the effort to win the middle-of-the-road voters, and to present increasingly similar programmes. Downs adds one crucial element to the models: the *variable distribution of voters* along the left–right continuum. Voters are not distributed regularly along the scale, but concentrate in particular ideological positions, namely around the centre. For Downs, this is the crucial explanatory and predictive element of the dynamics of party systems: 'if we know something about the distribution of voters' preferences, we can make specific predictions about how ideologies change in content as parties maneuver to gain power' (Downs 1957: 114). If one assumes a normal (or 'bell-shaped') distribution of the electorate, with many voters at the centre of the scale and fewer at the extremes (see type

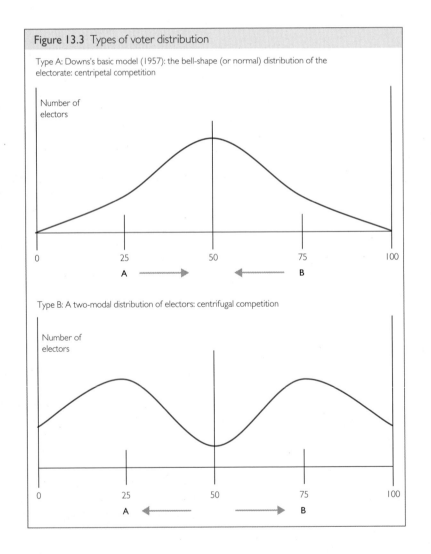

Figure 13.3 Types of voter distribution

Type A: Downs's basic model (1957): the bell-shape (or normal) distribution of the electorate: centripetal competition

Type B: A two-modal distribution of electors: centrifugal competition

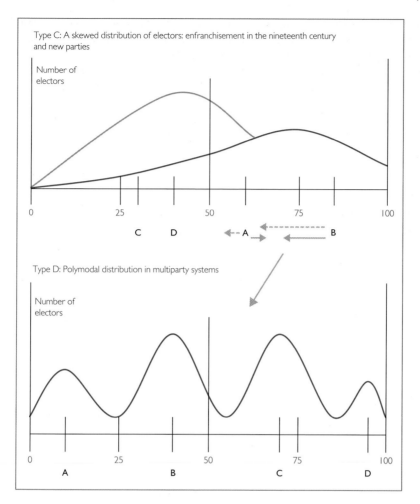

Type C: A skewed distribution of electors: enfranchisement in the nineteenth century and new parties

Type D: Polymodal distribution in multiparty systems

The median voter

The median voter is the voter who divides a distribution of voters placed on a left–right scale into two equal halves. In a distribution from zero to 100 in which for each point there is a voter (including position zero), the median voter is on position 50 (with fifty voters on each side). Suppose, however, that there are fifty voters on position 100, and the remaining voters are distributed regularly between positions 49 and 99 (one voter on each position). In this case, the median voter is on position 99.

A in Figure 13.3), the prediction of the model is that parties will converge towards the centre.[6]

First, these models predict the convergence towards the centre and the increasing similarity of platforms and policy actions. The centripetal competition is determined by the parties' aim to win the *median voter* (see Box 13.4).

Second, centripetal competition arises also because there are more voters in the centre. Party strategy does not depend only on the logic of the model (the assumption of proximity voting), but also on the *empirical distribution of the electorate*. The potential loss of voters at the extremes does not deter parties from converging because there are few voters at the extremes. This is not the case if the distribution of the electorate is different, for example a two-modal distribution as depicted in type B in Figure 13.3. This is a case of ideological polarization within a political system. Therefore, the distribution of the electorate determines the *direction* of competition (centrifugal or centripetal).

Third, voters in the middle of the left–right axis are more *flexible* than at the extremes, where they are firmly encapsulated in strict ideologies and/or party organizations. 'Available' voters (Bartolini and Mair 1990), located in the middle, are less ideologized and have weak party identifications. These voters are ready to change their minds and therefore are very appealing to parties seeking to 'seduce' them.

The broader application of rational choice models

What are the links of these models with other aspects of parties and party systems?

First, rational choice models help to interpret the transformation of *party organizations* from mass parties to **catch-all parties** (see Chapter 12 'Political parties'). This transformation can be seen as organizational and ideological adaptation to competition.

Second, they also help to interpret patterns of *dealignment*, i.e. the loosening of the relationship between parties and specific segments of society (workers for social democrats, for example). Centripetal competition and the maximization of votes lead parties to make their programmes and ideologies vaguer, to attract support from other groups. This blurs the connection between groups and parties, and causes a higher propensity to change vote from one election to the next (volatility).

Third, these models can be applied historically to processes of enfranchisement. In both type A and type B, the distributions are symmetrical. In type C, on the contrary, we have a *skewed distribution* towards the right of the axis. Here, the median voter is around position 65 rather than 50, and accordingly parties A and B (liberals and conservatives of 'internal origin') would converge towards this point. This is typical of restricted electorates in the nineteenth century, when lower classes were excluded from the franchise. Enfranchisement changed the shape of voters' distribution as represented by the dashed curve. This explains the emergence of new parties C and D of 'external origin' (social democrats and agrarians).

The dream of reformists (as opposed to revolutionary socialists) was that socialism and the proletariat could come to power through votes ('paper stones') and the extension of the franchise, rather than through revolution (real stones!). The development of the industrial society would lead workers to power through sheer numbers. Yet the numbers of industrial workers did not grow—in fact, they declined—and socialist parties faced a dilemma between moving towards the centre to maximize their appeal to the middle classes— thus relaxing their programme—and losing votes from workers (Przeworski and Sprague 1986).

Fourth, one needs to consider these models under *PR and multiparty systems*. Convergence is likely under FPTP because the threat of other parties appearing at the extremes is low, given the high threshold required to win a seat. Rather than new parties, under these systems the model predicts *high abstention levels*, as is the case in the US (Aldrich 1993).

Multiparty systems, on the other hand, develop when the distribution of the electorate is polymodal, with more than one or two peaks (type D). The dynamics of the competition is not centripetal. Existing parties have no incentive to converge towards the centre, as PR is no hindrance to new parties on the extremes. On the contrary, *ideological spaces are elastic*, with extremes widening and increasing ideological distance between parties. Parties may adopt such strategies to distinguish themselves from moderate parties. This leads to radicalization to maintain a distinctive character.

Despite critiques (see Box 13.5), spatial models are extremely useful. In all countries, a number of voters are ready to change their vote. This is an available electorate around which competition turns and on which these models focus. Rational choice models apply less to segments that are encapsulated through identification (ethno-linguistic and religious dimensions with

---

📢 **FOR AND AGAINST 13.5**

Critiques of rational choice models

Assumption	Critique
Rationality	As social psychology, experimental politics, and behavioural economics show, voters' motivations are not always rational.
Full information	Voters are not fully informed about programmes and are unable to evaluate the extent to which they correspond to their own interests. With technical issues, this often proves unlikely.
Vote maximization	Parties are not only 'vote-seeking' (Müller and Strøm 2000). As 'office-seeking', parties do not require to maximize votes but to get just enough (Riker 1962). As 'policy-seeking', parties seek to influence public policy rather than aiming for office (De Swaan 1973).
One-dimensionality	Not all parties compete along the left–right dimension. In most cases, the space of competition is multidimensional.

strong identities and non-available voters) and primarily to the left–right dimension. Even if applicable to parts of the electorate only, they are crucial, as they determine the direction of competition.[7]

Empirical spatial analysis

Recent empirical spatial research moved in different directions. First, to maximize electoral support parties shift positions as responsive adaptations to shifting voter preferences (Budge 1994; Adams et al. 2008). Second, parties shift learning from past electoral results (Adams et al. 2004). Third, parties' shifts are responsive to moves by competitor parties (Adams and Somer-Topcu 2009). Whatever the aim, knowing voters' distribution and where parties are located is a matter of empirical research. How can one measure the ideological space?

First, the *distribution of voters* can be measured empirically through surveys in which, through questions and scales, respondents are asked to position themselves, for example, along the left–right axis. Examples are the World Value Survey, Eurobarometers, European Social Survey, Latinobarometers, etc.

Second, the *position of parties* can be measured empirically through two main instruments. The most important one is based on *text data*, whereby party manifestos are analysed using special software able to identify the salience and favourable (or unfavourable) mentions of a large number of issues, from taxation and the free market to development aid and the environment. Such items are combined to build scales such as the left–right scale. The most important data are those of the Comparative Manifesto Project (Budge et al. 2001; Klingemann et al. 2006; Volkens et al. 2013). Others analyse the position of parties based on press

releases, newspaper articles, social media, websites, or parliamentary debates (see, for an important study based on the coding of newspapers, Kriesi et al. 2012).

The alternative possibility is *expert surveys*, whereby the position of parties on various issues is established by asking a sample of scholars. The problem with these data is that they rarely allow an estimation of parties' past positioning. Two main projects exist: the Benoit, Hunt, and Laver project (Benoit and Laver 2006) and the Chapel Hill project (Steenbergen and Marks 2007).

A number of empirical spatial analyses were able to establish that the space of competition is in fact composed of two dimensions. The first is the traditional left–right economic/instrumental dimension on the degree of redistribution between rich and poor, planning of the economy vs free market, which Kitschelt (1994) summarized as the socialism–capitalism axis (Figure 13.4). The second dimension has acquired salience more recently in the wake of the post-materialist and globalization transformations. Sometimes this axis is considered a cultural axis (Kriesi et al. 2012) insofar as it includes, at one extreme, post-materialist values (Green–Alternative–Libertarian) and, at the other extreme, materialist values (Traditional–Authoritarian–Nationalist). This has been labelled the GAL–TAN dimension (Hooghe et al. 2002).

This dimension, however, has also a class base insofar as the former is supported by the highly qualified 'winners' of globalization and economic openness (as well as by those in 'sheltered' state employment), while the latter is supported by the 'losers' of the globalized society, who favour protectionism and controlled borders (the less-qualified blue-collar workers working in economic sectors 'exposed' to the threat of open borders). Therefore, it includes more

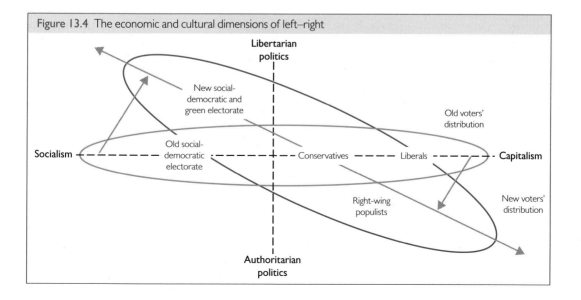

Figure 13.4 The economic and cultural dimensions of left–right

versus less favourable attitudes towards supranational integration. The integration–demarcation cleavage comprises also the willingness to integrate immigrants or, conversely, to demarcate more strongly cultural and national identities. This dimension affects party systems but also direct votes, as in the case of the Brexit referendum in Britain in 2016, as well as presidential elections, as in the US with Donald Trump's victory in 2016.

With the decline of industry and the working class, the strategy of established parties had been to mobilize voters on the cultural axis rather than on the economic one. This has tilted the left–right axis diagonally, creating the opportunity for new competitors (populists in particular) to mobilize precisely the 'losers' who would have traditionally voted for the left. This tendency has increased with the economic and financial crisis since 2008. In terms of spatial analysis, the emergence of populist challengers can be seen as a direct consequence of the convergence

(often also as great coalitions) between established parties on issues like immigration and supranational integration, which left uncovered vast sectors of the electorate. Long-term data show clearly how social democrats and centre-right parties have given radical-right populists the chance to emerge on issues such as economic and cultural threat (Caramani 2015).

Conclusion

Understanding party systems requires the combination of the various perspectives presented in this chapter.

The *macro-sociological* approach must be combined with *institutional* and *actor-oriented* models. They complement each other and are not mutually exclusive. We cannot understand party systems without reference to the social cleavages from which parties emerge. However, we must also take into account parties' capacity to act independently from social conditions—in fact, to shape them through ideology and policy. The motivations of parties are not entirely determined by their origins. Parties' strategies, in turn, must take into account the rules of the game—electoral laws being the most important ones—influencing the number and size of players.

Both *descriptive* and *explanatory research* is needed. The ultimate goal is to account for the shape and dynamics of party systems. However, before searching for causes, party systems should be described carefully. As seen with counting parties, this is often more complicated than it appears at first sight.

Finally, we cannot understand party systems in isolation. We need *comparison* to assess whether or not they are fragmented or unstable, as well as a *long-term* perspective rather than a myopic focus on just the most recent elections. This is the only way of assessing how exceptional a given party system or a given change really is.

KEY POINTS

- In the electoral market, parties (the supply side) present platforms to appeal to many voters whose vote is determined by the proximity of their preferences (the demand side) to the parties' offer. Voters are assumed to be rational, informed about alternative proposals, and able to choose the alternative closest to their top preferences.

- The dynamics of party systems is determined by parties' search for the optimal location on the left–right axis. Depending on the distribution of the electorate along the scale, parties move to a position where the support is largest.

- The prediction of competition models is that parties converge towards the centre of the left–right axis, as the point where most votes concentrate, and as the point where voters are less rigidly ideologized.

? QUESTIONS

Knowledge-based

1. What are the National and Industrial Revolutions?

2. What are Stein Rokkan's four main social cleavages and which party families emerged from them?

3. How should the number of parties in a system be counted?

4. What are the characteristic features of a two-party system?

5. What does 'effective number of parties' mean?

Critical thinking

1. What is the effect of electoral systems on the shape of party systems?

2. What does it mean when we say that parties are 'vote-maximizers'?

3. Describe centripetal and centrifugal party competition in Downs's model.

4. Are voters really rational?

5. Can the space of competition be reduced to one left–right dimension?

FURTHER READING

Classical texts on party systems

Cox, G. W. (1997) *Making Votes Count: Strategic Coordination in the World's Electoral Systems* (Cambridge: Cambridge University Press).

Downs, A. (1957) *An Economic Theory of Democracy* (New York: Harper Collins).

Duverger, M. (1954) *Political Parties* (New York: John Wiley).

Kitschelt, H. (1994) *The Transformation of European Social Democracy* (Cambridge: Cambridge University Press).

Lipset, S. M. and Rokkan, S. (1967) 'Cleavage Structures, Party Systems, and Voter Alignments: An Introduction', in

S. M. Lipset and S. Rokkan (eds), *Party Systems and Voter Alignments* (New York: Free Press), 1–64.

Sartori, G. (1976) *Parties and Party Systems: A Framework for Analysis* (Cambridge: Cambridge University Press).

For a more recent bibliography, see the works cited throughout in this chapter.

Up-to-date reports on party systems can be found in journals. Detailed country-by-country developments from 1991 onwards are reported in the *Political Data Yearbook*. Students may also find useful material in journals such as the *American Political Science Review, Comparative Politics, Comparative Political Studies, Electoral Studies, Party Politics,* and *West European Politics.*

ENDNOTES

1. In the US, two-party systems exist largely because of the rules for forming a party, which make it difficult for third parties to present candidates. For this reason, there is not a high disproportionality between votes and seats in Table 13.3 (LSq index).

2. The literature on the positive sides of multiparty systems insists on a different decision-making mode based on consensus. This literature includes Rustow (1955), Daalder (1966), Lorwin (1966a,b), Lijphart (1968a,b), McRae (1974), and Steiner (1974), all stressing accommodation, agreement, and compromise.

3. 1958 marks the beginning of the Fifth Republic in France with the new 'Gaullist' constitution and a two-ballot majority system in single-member constituencies.

4. If the effective number of parties is calculated on votes, this is usually referred to as 'effective number of elective parties' (ENEP), whereas if it is calculated

on seats it is called 'effective number of parliamentary parties' (ENPP).

5. Additional causes of distortion between votes and seats are the rules to form a party and present candidates, the size of parliamentary groups, the barrier clauses, the type of quota (Hare, Droop, Imperiali, etc.), and the number of tiers (i.e. various levels of constituencies for the allocation of seats).

6. A further assumption is that if a voter prefers ideological position 60 over 70, then the voter will also prefer 60 over 80, 90, etc. (transitivity). This is an assumption of single-peakedness of voter preferences, i.e. if a voter prefers 60, then the further away the position is from 60, the less it is liked.

7. As a response to the criticism about full information, rational choice theorists argue that it is not rational to spend a lot of time gathering political information (the costs outweigh benefits). This is a free-rider attitude.

Visit the Online Resources that accompany this book for additional material, including country profiles, comparative data sets, flashcard glossaries, and web directory.

www.oup.com/he/caramani5e

14

Interest groups

Roland Erne

Chapter contents

Reader's guide

Political scientists should not just compare political institutions, but also assess the role of associations that seek to advance particular socio-economic and political interests. Interest groups play a crucial role in all political systems. But the forms in which interests are articulated depend on the particular context. Accordingly, this chapter begins with a review of different definitions of interest groups that have been used across time and space. Scholars of interest politics have also been inspired by different theoretical paradigms. Hence, the chapter discusses the legacies of competing theoretical traditions in the field, namely republicanism, pluralism, and neocorporatism. The final sections of the chapter assess the role of interest associations in practice, distinguishing different types of action that are available to different interest associations, namely direct lobbying, political exchange, contentious politics, and private interest government.

Introduction

Arthur Bentley captured the focus of interest politics when he argued that it is necessary 'in considering representative government, or democracy, not only past or present, but future as well, to consider it in terms of the various group pressures that form its substance' (Bentley 1908: 452). Therefore, we should not just compare political institutions, but also assess the role of associations that seek to advance particular interests in the political process. The term 'interest group' is often used interchangeably with 'interest association' or 'pressure group'; but before reviewing different definitions of the term, I will go back to its origins.

It is no coincidence that the study of interest politics can be traced back to the US of the early twentieth century. The establishment of this academic field is closely related to the socio-economic and political conjunctures of the time. When Bentley published his pioneering *The Process of Government* in 1908, the interventions of ever larger corporations in US politics caused widespread popular alarm. At the same time, the rise of large-scale industrial capitalism triggered counter-reactions, namely industrial conflict and movements that sought to eliminate corruption, improve working conditions, and give citizens more control over the political process. Yet, it would be wrong to associate the origins of comparative interest politics exclusively with the rise of big business. The **behavioural revolution** in the social sciences, which changed the analytical focus from formal institutions to social processes, was equally important (see the Introduction to this volume by Daniele Caramani). The consequent broadening of perspectives made it possible to analyse tensions between pluralistic democratic theory and practice.

In post-1945 America, the steady rise of professional lobbyists provided political scientists not only with a new subject area and a new occupational domain for their graduate students, but also with a topic for heated debate (Dahl 1982): can a pluralistic democratic state regulate interest groups without questioning the right of association? The broader analytical focus also enabled scholars to capture alternative types of association–state relations, such as neocorporatism, which did not follow the Anglo-American model.

KEY POINTS

- Comparativists should not only analyse formal political institutions, but should also assess interest group pressures that shape the substance of politics.

- Interest groups play important, but also different, roles in political systems across time and space, even if the rise of interest politics is closely related to the rise of capitalist modes of production.

What are interest groups?

Interest groups are not easy to define. The US pioneers in the field proposed very encompassing definitions: Bentley (1908) and Truman (1971 [1951]) defined interest groups as associations that make claims to other groups in society. But is this definition still useful today? Many contemporary scholars disagree, because such a broad definition makes it impossible to distinguish interest associations from political parties (see Chapter 12 'Political parties'). Instead, interest groups are usually defined as membership organizations that appeal to government but do not participate in elections (Wilson 1990). However, this definition also raises questions. Whereas parties and interest groups are sharply differentiated in North America, this differentiation is much less evident in other parts of the world, where cross-organizational interactions blur the lines between interest groups and political parties. Therefore, Gabriel Almond (1958) did not use formal definitions when he was studying interest groups comparatively. Instead, he focused on the *function of interest representation* because the institutions by means of which interests are articulated would depend on the political and socio-economic context of the particular political system.

Functionalist approaches

Students of interest politics should indeed be cautious of comparisons based on context-free measures. Identical measures, such as the union density rate (i.e. the number of trade union members as a proportion of all workers in employment), mean different things in different countries. Given the high number of workers covered by collective agreements and the capacity of the French unions to instigate strike action, French unions are hardly the least influential labour organizations in the industrialized world (Laroche 2016). However, there is almost no industrialized country in the world where fewer people are union members as a percentage of the entire labour force (see Table 14.1). In turn, China displays one of the highest union densities in Table 14.1, but China's official unions function rather as a transmission belt of the ruling party than as an effective tool of labour representation (Cooke 2011; Kuruvilla et al. 2011). Obviously, unions play different roles in different political systems. In most countries, union influence is related to membership levels. However, in some parts of the world other factors are as important, such as close political party–trade union connections (Allern and Bale 2017), co-determination rights of worker representatives enshrined in corporate **governance** (Waddington and Conchon 2015), institutionalized access to policy-making, collective bargaining and trade union laws, and the ability of union activists to inspire **social movements** (Frege and Kelly 2013; Gumbrell-McCormick and Hyman 2013; Stan et al. 2015). The same observation also applies to employers' organizations.

For this reason, functionalists argue that studying interest associations comparatively may require using different measures for the same function (e.g. interest

Table 14.1 Trade union and employer organization density, and collective bargaining coverage

Country	Union density[a] (%)	Employer organization density[b] (%)	Collective bargaining coverage[c] (%)
Brazil	21[h]	–	44[e]
Canada	28	–	28
China	43[e]	–	39[d]
Denmark	67[h]	62[d]	82[h]
France	8[h]	75[d]	98[f]
Germany	17	60[f]	56[h]
Italy	34	65[d]	80[h]
Japan	17	–	17
South Africa	27[g]	–	29[g]
Sweden	62	88	90[h]
UK	23	33	26
US	11	–	12

[a] 2017, except where indicated otherwise. Here we used the UD variable in the ICTWSS database (UD_S where not available).

[b] 2016, except where indicated otherwise. Here we used the ED variable in the ICTWSS database.

[c] 2017, except where indicated otherwise. Here we used the AdjCov variable in the ICTWSS database (UnadjCov where not available).

[d] 2012; [e] 2013; [f] 2014; [g] 2015; [h] 2016.

Source: Amsterdam Institute for Advanced Labour Studies (2019).

representation) in different cases to reflect differences in context across political systems. This approach allows us to broaden the comparative analysis of interest politics beyond the boundaries of Anglo-American systems. However, functionalists also face a tricky analytical problem. Is it accurate to assume a universal interest representation function, as suggested by Almond? Or should we distinguish between different types of interest representation, as suggested by scholars who differentiate between private and public interest associations?

Private versus public interests

Most scholars use all-embracing definitions of interest groups (Cigler et al. 2015). These definitions are typically based on formal properties, namely 'voluntary membership, a more or less bureaucratic structure of decision-making, dependence upon material and motivational resources, efforts to change the respective environments into more favourable ones, and so

forth' (Offe and Wiesenthal 1985: 175). However, this view has not precluded some scholars from introducing different subcategories. For instance, Jeffrey Berry (1977) proposed distinguishing *public* and *private* interest groups on the basis of whether an association pursues public interests or only sectional interests of its members. Similar distinctions have been used by scholars around the world (Young and Wallace 2000; della Porta and Caiani 2009). But does it make sense to use the same label for associations that seek private profit and associations that advance public good? This question is not only of academic interest. The scope of the definition also predetermines the scope of laws that regulate the rights and obligations of associations.

Yet, however popular this distinction is, it is also analytically problematic, as all interest associations usually present their claims as measures that enhance the public good. For instance, business organizations frequently argue, invoking the theories of neoclassical economists, that the pursuit of private profit serves the public good. Claims that an action is consistent, or not within the public interest, are certainly influential in political debates. Analytically, however, the phrase 'public interest' is 'meaningless if it is taken to refer to an interest so persuasive that everyone in the system is agreed upon it' (Truman 1971: xiv). Does this mean that there is no way of distinguishing between types of interest associations in an analytically meaningful manner? Not necessarily, as we shall see in the section on 'Interest associations in practice'.

KEY POINTS

- Many scholars define interest groups as voluntary organizations that appeal to government but do not participate in elections. In a comparative context, however, this formal definition is problematic as the form of interest representation varies across countries.

- It has also been proposed to distinguish 'public' and 'private interest groups'. Claims that a group's action is in the 'public interest' are politically influential. Analytically, however, the term 'public interest' is problematic because of its contentious nature. Indeed, there is hardly a claim that is so persuasive that everyone can agree upon it.

Interest associations in theory

Republican (unitarist) traditions

Although the radical-democratic Swiss–French philosopher Jean-Jacques Rousseau (1712–78) recognized that every political body includes interest associations, he perceived them as a threat to the rule of the people. He feared that:

> there are no longer as many votes as there are men, but only as many as there are associations . . . Lastly, when one of these associations is so great as to prevail over all the rest . . . there is no longer a general will, and the opinion which prevails is purely particular.
>
> Rousseau 1973 [1762]

Therefore, Rousseau argued, 'there should be no partial society in a state and each citizen should express only his own opinion'. Yet, he also proposed a pragmatic solution to the interest group problem: 'But if there are partial societies, it is best to have as many as possible and to prevent them from being unequal' (Rousseau 1973 [1762] Book 2: 204).

Nonetheless, the leaders of the French Revolution clearly adopted a *unitarist* view of democracy, according to which interest associations would undermine the general will of the people. Accordingly, the French constitution of 24 June 1793 succinctly stated in its first sentence: 'The French Republic is one and indivisible'. This sentence still delineates the republican approach to interest groups today, despite the suspension of the constitution on 10 October 1793 because of the state of war.

Whereas the French Revolution established the right to hold popular assemblies and even a constitutional duty to rebel when the government violates the right of the people, the notion of a one and indivisible republic also justified banning associations that were assumed to interfere with the general will of the people. Incidentally, the French revolutionaries not only dissolved the guilds and congregations of the *Ancien Régime,* but also adopted a law that outlawed workers' associations. In 1791, the French constituent assembly adopted the *loi Le Chapelier,* which prohibited trade unions until the law's abrogation in 1884. With this law, the assembly responded to reports of alarmed employers:

> The workers, by an absurd parody of the government, regard their work as their property, the building site as a Republic of which they are jointly the citizens, and believe, as a consequence, that it is for them to name their own bosses, their inspectors and at their discretion to share out work amongst themselves.
>
> Magraw 1992: 24ff.

Thus, the *Le Chapelier* law was designed to 'put an end to such potential industrial anarchy' (Magraw 1992: 24ff).

The fact that employers convinced the constituent assembly to suspend the freedom of association of French workers highlights a contradiction within the unitarist republican tradition of thought. If particular interests aim to become dominant in order to prevail over the rest, as argued by Rousseau, how can one be sure that any restriction of freedom of association 'in the name of the general will of the people' does not simply serve the particular interests of a group that has acquired a dominant position in the political process?

As noted by Robert Dahl (1982), democratic republics face a major dilemma when dealing with interest associations. On the one hand, the larger a democratic political system becomes, the more likely interest associations are to play an important role in the political process. On the other hand, as with individuals, so with organizations: the ability to act autonomously also includes the ability to do harm. Whereas republicans try to solve the classical dilemma between control and autonomy in political life through the introduction of the democratic principle of popular **sovereignty**, liberals typically fear a tyranny of the majority and emphasize instead the liberty of individuals to act and to associate freely.

Liberal (pluralist) traditions

Liberal scholars do not perceive interest associations as a potential threat to the sovereignty of the democratic state, but as an essential source of liberty. This view is pertinently outlined by the French political thinker Alexis de Tocqueville (1805–59). In 1831, Tocqueville was charged by the French monarchy under King Louis-Philippe to examine the penitentiary system in America. Ironically, however, Tocqueville's travels in America also inspired him to write *Democracy in America* (Tocqueville 2006a [1835], 2006b [1840]), which became a crucial study within the pluralist tradition of interest politics.

Tocqueville, as an offspring of an ancient aristocratic dynasty which narrowly escaped the guillotine during the French Revolution, had very good reasons to be wary of the general will of the people. However, in contrast with many of his aristocratic contemporaries, he was also convinced that democracy was unavoidable. Whereas politics was a privilege of the few in pre-modern times, the changing social conditions caused by the modernization of the economy and society would affect more and more people. The scope of politics would increase, which in turn would also require a new source of legitimacy for politics—namely democracy. For this reason, Tocqueville studied democracy in America in search of social factors that would prevent it from turning into a tyranny of the majority.

Two strands of Tocqueville's analysis relate to this chapter, namely his observations regarding the role of interests and the role of associations in American politics. In relation to the former, Tocqueville found that Americans were fond of explaining almost all their actions by the 'principle of interest rightly understood'. In Europe, however, claims were justified in absolute moral terms, even if the principle of interest played a 'much grosser' role in Europe than in America (Tocqueville 2006b [1840]: Chapter VIII). For Tocqueville, the consequences of this distinction were obvious. On the one hand, absolute moral claims represented a danger to liberty, even if they were meant to advance the general will of the people. On the other hand, the mutual acknowledgement of conflicting interests, as observed in the US of the early nineteenth century, enabled the accommodation of conflict within democratic procedures.

With regard to the role of associations in democratic societies, Tocqueville made the following argument: as the rise of the modern state would make individual citizens weaker, they would need to learn to unite with fellow citizens to defend themselves against the despotic influence of the majority or the aggressions of regal power. Therefore, all kinds of associations, even those formed in civil life without reference to political objects, are important because they cultivate the habits and virtues that are necessary for self-rule.

Nothing, in my opinion, is more deserving of our attention than the intellectual and moral associations of America. . . . In democratic countries the science of association is the mother of science; the progress of all the rest depends upon the progress it has made. Amongst the laws which rule human societies there is one which seems to be more precise and clear than all others. If men are to remain civilized, or to become so, the art of associating together must grow and improve in the same ratio in which the equality of conditions is increased. Tocqueville (2006b [1840]: Chapter V)

This quotation highlights Tocqueville's views. Associations represent the lifeblood of civic life. Therefore, the state should guarantee its citizens' right of association. At the same time, however, it should not interfere with the associative life of its citizens. Nevertheless, contemporary pluralists are not against political regulation of associations. State involvement is especially warranted to guarantee the freedom of association of its citizens (Dahl 1982). This qualification is of particular importance in relation to workers' rights to organize. Until 2015, more than 150 nation states had ratified the two core *International Labour Organization* conventions regarding workers' freedom of association. However, important states, including China, India, South Korea, the US, and (partially)

Brasil, failed to do so (see Table 14.2), reflecting the rise of a new truncated view of **liberalism** called **neoliberalism**. Following the world economic crisis of 1973, General Pinochet in Chile, UK Prime Minister Margaret Thatcher, US President Ronald Reagan, and others across the world initiated a radical 'neoliberal' policy shift that curtailed workers' freedom of association in order to increase the profitability of enterprises (Harvey 2005; Nowak 2019).

Nevertheless, Tocqueville's classical liberal views on interests and associations still influence contemporary beliefs about the role of interest associations in democratic societies, as highlighted by the vast literature that treats interest associations as 'schools of democracy' (Sinyai 2006). Certainly, several contemporary

Table 14.2 Ratification of the core ILO conventions on workers' 'freedom of association'

Country	Freedom of Association and Protection of Right to Organise Convention (no. 87)	Right to Organise and Collective Bargaining Convention (no. 98)
Argentina	1960	1956
Australia	1973	1973
Brazil	Not ratified	1952
Canada	1972	2017
Chile	1999	1999
China	Not ratified	Not ratified
France	1951	1951
Germany	1957	1956
India	Not ratified	Not ratified
Indonesia	1998	1957
Italy	1958	1958
Japan	1965	1953
Nigeria	1960	1960
South Africa	1996	1996
South Korea	Not ratified	Not ratified
Spain	1977	1977
Sweden	1949	1950
Turkey	1993	1952
UK	1949	1950
US	Not ratified	Not ratified

Source: ILO (2019). © International Labour Organization 2019.

studies also deplore a decline in associative practices in the US, such as Robert Putnam's *Bowling Alone* (2000) or Theda Skocpol's *Diminishing Democracy* (2003), but it is equally noteworthy that these critical accounts of American civic and political life did not trigger a fundamental break with the pluralist **paradigm**. Whereas the classical pluralist approach to interest politics has repeatedly been criticized for its implicit assumptions—notably the assumption that all people enjoy the same capacity to associate and the resulting claim that interest associations are equally distributed across the entire political spectrum (Barach and Baratz 1969; Connolly 1969; Lowi 1969a, 1969b; Lukes 1974; Lindblom 1977; Offe and Wiesenthal 1985)—most students of democracy, explicitly or tacitly, continued to use the pluralist paradigm as a normative yardstick. However, there were exceptions, as shown by the growing interest in neocorporatism that emerged in the late 1970s.

Corporatist traditions

In the 1970s, European social scientists and US scholars of Latin America and Western Europe became increasingly aware of political systems that did not fit into the pluralist Anglo-American model. Some scholars established the concept of neocorporatism as an alternative to pluralist theory in the area of interest politics (Schmitter 1974; Katzenstein 1984). Others used concepts like **consensus democracy** or *consociational democracy* for political systems in which parties that represent different sections of society share power (Lijphart 2008; Armingeon 2002). Although the finding of a second tier of government composed of a complex system of intermediary associations was nothing new (Gruner 1956; Rokkan 1966), Schmitter's (1974) article 'Still the century of corporatism?' inspired a generation of comparativists. 'All of a sudden, a research field that to many had seemed hopelessly empiricist and American-centred, began to open up exciting perspectives on vast landscapes of democratic theory, political sociology and social theory in general' (Streeck 2006: 10).

Schmitter's concept of neocorporatism not only enabled comparativists to capture the particular role that the organizations of capital and labour play in many countries, but also challenged republican and pluralist notions of interest politics. Like republicans, neocorporatists perceive the political system as a *body politic* (Rousseau 1973 [1762] Book 2: 260) and not as an aggregation of particular interests, as pluralists would argue. Fittingly, the term **corporatism** had been derived from *corpus* (body). However, unlike republicans, neocorporatists argue that the body politic is

constituted not only by individual cells, but also by organs that perform different, but complementary, functions. Hence, the life and death of the body politic depends on the *organic solidarity* (Durkheim 1964 [1893]) between its organs as much as on the vitality of its individual cells. As with human bodies, so with the body politic—the uncontrolled growth of individual cells or organs could threaten the functioning of the entire system.

Unlike republicans, neocorporatists argue that interests and interest associations cannot be excluded from the political process. Contrary to pluralists, however, neocorporatists question the notion of free competition between different interests. Free competition would simply lead to the strongest interests prevailing over weaker interests. This would challenge governability, undermine social justice, and hamper the economic performance of modern mass democracies. Therefore, the state should not only guarantee freedom of association. **Public policies** should also include measures that guarantee a balance of power between the opposing social interests, notably between the organizations of capital and labour. Only in this case can the outcome of the policy-making process reflect the best arguments, rather than mere power relations between social interests.

The last point is of particular interest in relation to Western Europe, where both the political left and right agreed on the desirability of institutionalizing social interests. On the left, Social Democrats were the direct offspring of the organized **labour movement**. Moreover, labour parties favoured shifting the conflict between employers and employees from the marketplace to the political arena, where the number of workers tends to be higher than the number of capitalists. This explains why the labour movement fought for centuries for the extension of the franchise. On the right, Christian Democrats were closely related to the Catholic Church, which also doubted the ability of liberal individualism to provide social integration (Pope Leo XIII 2010 [1891]). Similarly, European and Latin American fascist and peronist movements were intrigued by an authoritarian variant of corporatism, namely the pre-modern *Ständestaat* or 'corporative state' (Pitigliani 1933; Manoïlesco 1936 [1934]) where power relied, at least on paper, on functional constituencies (*estates*). Incidentally, Schmitter introduced the term *neocorporatism* in order to distinguish it from the fascist corporative state. Arguably, the post-1945 neocorporatist class compromises have little in common with the authoritarian corporatism of the past. But despite the elective affinity between state traditions, Social Democrats, and Christian Democrats, neocorporatist arrangements have always remained controversial. Whereas Marxists criticized neocorporatist pacts as attempts to contain socialist labour activism (Panitch 1980), capitalists were never enthusiastic about sharing power with trade unions. Therefore, it is not surprising that business elites actively supported the shift towards **neoliberalism** from the 1970s onwards (Harvey 2005), which strengthened their power in politics and labour relations.

However, neocorporatism is not only a politically contentious subject; it has also been questioned methodologically. Whereas it is easy to define neocorporatism in theory, neocorporatist scholars have not been able to agree on a set of unambiguous measures of corporatism in practice (Schmitter 1981; Traxler et al. 2001). In Germany, for example, effective corporatist arrangements, both formal and informal, have been reached between the employers' associations and unions of a particular sector, whereas the national peak organizations of capital and labour have not signed national social pacts. In contrast, the Maastricht Treaty established the *European Social Dialogue* between the peak organizations of capital and labour as far back as 1993, but the fact that the European social partners can negotiate legally binding agreements has not led to a neocorporatist European Union (Erne 2008, 2015). Likewise, Hong Kong can hardly be described as a neocorporatist political system, even if half of its Legislative Council is composed of interest group representatives selected by functional constituencies, representing, however, predominately business interests (Goodstadt 2005). For this reason, any comparative analysis of interest politics systems, it has to be reiterated, must be very aware of the particular context of the different interest politics systems in place in different regions of the world.

Nevertheless, the theoretical divide between pluralist and neocorporatist systems of interest articulation has been very productive for **empirical research**, especially in comparisons of Anglo-American and European socio-economic and political systems. During the past two decades, the distinction between different coordinated and liberal **varieties of capitalisms** and industrial relations systems has inspired many studies (Crouch 1999; Hall and Soskice 2001*b*; Traxler et al. 2001; Pontusson 2005; Block 2007).

As outlined in Table 14.3, economic **globalization** and Europeanization processes did not lead to the demise of the coordinated industrial relations systems of Scandinavia, the Low Countries, and Germany. Cross-national differences persist (Meardi 2018). However, there has also been a shared liberalizing trend that led to much leaner forms of **corporatism**

Table 14.3 Evolution of industrial relations systems (1973–2014)

	The varieties of industrial relations systems			
	1973[a]	1996[a]	2008[b]	2014[b]
Norway	Neocorporatism	Lean corporatism	Lean corporatism	Lean corporatism
Denmark	Neocorporatism	Lean corporatism	Lean corporatism	(Lean corporatism)[c]
Germany	Neocorporatism	Lean corporatism	(Lean corporatism)	(Lean corporatism)[c]
Netherlands	Other corporatism	Lean corporatism	Lean corporatism	(Lean corporatism)[c]
Italy	(Other corporatism)	Lean corporatism	Lean corporatism	(Neoliberalism)[c]
Ireland	(Other corporatism)	Lean corporatism	Lean corporatism	(Neoliberalism)[c]
Spain	Authoritarian corporatism	(Lean corporatism)	(Lean corporatism)	(Neoliberalism)[c]
Canada	Pluralism	Neoliberalism	Neoliberalism	Neoliberalism
UK	(Pluralism)	Neoliberalism	Neoliberalism	Neoliberalism
US	Pluralism	Neoliberalism	Neoliberalism	Neoliberalism

[a] Traxler et al. (2001). Borderline cases in parenthesis.

[b] My categorization based on Traxler et al. (2001) and data on collective bargaining levels and types from the ICTWSS database (Amsterdam Institute for Advanced Labour Studies, 2019), Eurofound (2014), and Marginson and Welz (2015).

[c] Since 2011, EU member states have been subject to mutilatural surveillance procedures that are limiting the autonomy of national industrial relations systems, albeit to different degrees (Erne 2015; Jordan et al 2019).

(Baccaro and Howell 2017). This trend reflects the decentralization of collective bargaining levels, the decline of union density and collective bargaining coverage, and the flexibilization of labour market and social policies (Thelen 2014). In addition, many unions engaged in competitive beggar-thy-neighbour bargaining strategies to sustain and attract investment from multinational capital (Erne 2008; Bieler and Erne 2015). Hence, social inequality increased not only in the US and the UK, in response to the rise of neoliberalism, but also in the former heartlands of neocorporatism (Piketty 2014).

The dominant comparative approaches to interest politics in terms of varieties of capitalism, unionism, and social policy are also questioned by the EU's new economic governance regime (Eurofound 2014, 2016; Erne 2015; Marginson 2015). The more national (labour) politics is shaped by constraining EU interventions, the more the 'methodological nationalism' of classical country-by-country comparisons is producing biased results (Erne 2019). The recent shift to neoliberalism in Italian, Spanish, and Irish industrial relations, for example, must therefore be analysed from a perspective that conceptualizes European integration as a process 'among distinct units indeed but, at the same time, units belonging to one single system' (Caramani 2015: 283; Erne 2018). Finally, students of interest politics should also be aware that liberal and corporatist arrangements might also coexist within the very same country, reflecting different constellations of interest politics across different sectors and policy fields (Erne and Imboden 2015).

KEY POINTS

- Republican theorists, such as Rousseau, see in interest associations a danger for democracy, because the more particular interests prevail, the less politics would represent the general will of the people.

- In contrast, pluralist scholars, such as Tocqueville, perceive interest associations as an essential source of liberty. However, this view relies on two debatable assumptions: (i) all people enjoy the same capacity to associate; and (ii) interest associations are equally distributed across the political spectrum.

- Unlike republicans, neocorporatists claim that interest associations cannot be excluded from the political process. Contrary to pluralists, neocorporatists fear that free competition between interest groups would lead to stronger prevailing over weaker interests. Therefore, neocorporatists favour regulations that ensure a balance of power between opposing social interests, notably between the organizations of capital and labour.

Interest associations in practice

Interest group formation

In 1965, US economist Mancur Olson challenged the pluralist assumption that group formation was equally available to everybody. Assuming that individual action is determined by individual cost–benefit calculations, his book *The Logic of Collective Action* concluded that **selective incentives** motivate rational individuals to join interest groups (Olson 1965). According to the *logic of rational choice*, only associations that provide private benefits will prosper, whereas associations that provide public goods, i.e. general benefits without regard to a person's membership status, will find it almost impossible to attract members.

Why should rational individuals pay union subscriptions when collectively agreed wage increases or improvements in social benefits will be applied to everybody whether they are union members or not? Union organizers might respond by saying that the strength of a union, and therefore its capacity to improve working and living conditions, is directly related to the number of its adherents. But how decisive is this argument? The power of a union does not increase noticeably if its membership increases by one individual. Therefore, from Olson's perspective, it would be more rational for a potential union member to take a free ride, relying on the contributions of the existing union members, than to bear the cost of union membership. Consequently, Olson concluded that the formation of interest associations is biased in favour of those associations that are able to offer special advantages, such as automobile clubs that offer insurance cover to their members.

At first sight, a comparative assessment of trade union membership figures across countries seems to confirm Olson's arguments; in almost all countries, union membership density figures are considerably lower than in Denmark, Finland, Sweden, and Belgium (the so-called **Ghent system** countries), where union membership includes unemployment insurance cover (see Table 14.1 and Scruggs (2002); see also Chapters 21 'The welfare state' and 22 'The impact of public policies'). In turn, however, Olson cannot explain why rational people voluntarily join unions in countries where union membership does not include selective benefits. Olson's (1965) claim to have indentified *the* logic of **collective action** has also been proved wrong by the events of 1968, which triggered an unexpected resurgence of civic activism and social movements across the world (see Chapter 16 'Social movements'). Whereas Olson's model can explain why some groups have more members than others, it cannot explain the formation of interest associations generally.

Olson's individualistic logic of the *homo economicus* is not the only logic at play when people decide to join interest associations. Collective experiences and moral concerns can also trigger a feeling of an identity of interests between people, as shown in E. P. Thomson's seminal history *The Making of the English Working Class* (1963). Olson's logic has also been qualified by European social scientists who studied *The Resurgence of Class Conflict in Western Europe since 1968* (Crouch and Pizzorno 1978) and by scholars who emphasized the role of external sponsors or organizers (Salisbury 1969) in the formation of interest groups. For instance, Jeffrey Berry emphasized that at least one-third of the eighty-three US public interest organizations received at least 50 per cent of their funding from private foundations (Berry 1977: 72). Similarly, Greenwood quoted the 2010 records of the *European Transparency Register*, which indicate that EU grants represented on average 64 per cent of the total income of the EU's major 'citizen interest groups', such as the *European Environmental Bureau* or the *European Anti-Poverty Network* (Greenwood 2011: 139). But even if external support somewhat mitigates the disadvantages of **public interest groups**, a review of Olson's legacy suggested that groups that offer selective incentives to their members still have an advantage. However, the advantage may be declining, as insurance companies have started to undercut groups, such as the British *Automobile Association*, by offering insurance cover at a lower cost (McLean 2000).

The pluralist notion of equality between interest associations has also been losing ground among scholars of interest politics who did not follow Olson's rational choice paradigm. In the 1970s, several studies appeared which suggested that group formation and membership were biased in favour of particular social categories with particular resources, notably wealth and time. And in 1985, Offe and Wiesenthal (1985: 175) even challenged the entire 'interest group stereotype', arguing that it would make little sense to use the same label for business associations and trade unions, given the distinct logics of collective action used in the two cases.

Offe and Wiesenthal's two logics of collective action

In their influential work, Offe and Wiesenthal (1985) assessed the associational practices of labour and capital. They proposed distinguishing between *two logics of collective action* in terms of the individual *or* collective ability of an interest to affect the policy-making capacity of the political system. Offe and Wiesenthal did not argue that business organizations have an advantage because they tend to spend more money on lobbying than other organizations. Instead, they highlighted the structural dependence of politicians in capitalist

societies on the holders of capital. As any *individual* investment decision has an impact on the economic performance of a territory, politicians must consider the views of capitalists whether they are well organized or not. This simplifies the task of business interest representation enormously. Business interests do not face the difficult collective action problems that labour unions and other organizations face. Whereas investment strikes by capital holders do not require collective organization, the withdrawal of labour requires *collective organization* and the willingness of workers to act together despite the availability of individual exit options.

Certainly, at times, business associations also fail, for instance due to competition between different firms for government support, such as government contracts, government bailouts, or privatization bids. Accordingly, Traxler and colleagues have argued that 'it is problematic to translate the pre-associational power asymmetry between businesses and labour into corresponding differentials in terms of associational capacities' (Traxler et al. 2001: 37). Even so, the collective action problem facing workers is much more difficult to solve than that facing corporations. Trade unions rely on their members' willingness to act collectively. In contrast, business associations only have to tell policy-makers that individual firms will act in an undesirable way if politicians fail to accommodate their interests. In this vein, even the imminent ruin of an organization can turn out to be an effective political tool, as demonstrated in 2008 when business interests successfully lobbied governments around the world to bail out failing banks (Stiglitz 2010).

A new typology of interest associations

Offe and Wiesenthal's analysis allows us to introduce a new typology of interest associations in action which does not distinguish groups on the basis of their subject matter or the private or public nature of the interests represented. Instead, I propose a two-by-two table based on two analytical distinctions that relate to two dimensions of collective action. First, I distinguish interest groups on the basis of the nature of their members' ability to act: to what degree does the representation of an interest rely on collective action by the members of an interest group beyond the simple payment of membership fees? Second, I distinguish interest groups on the basis of their relation to the political system: to what degree can they shape public policy-making through autonomous action outside the formal democratic policy-making process? In other words, to what degree are interest groups capable of creating facts outside the formal parliamentary system that governments and parliaments cannot ignore? At the outset, this leads us to a typology that enables us to distinguish business interests (which are not obliged to act collectively) from other interest groups, such as trade unions and other organizations which must act collectively in order to have a political impact (Figure 14.1). In addition, our typology also enables us to distinguish both business groups and trade unions from other non-governmental organizations that do not have the power to affect policy-making through autonomous action in the economic sphere. In contrast with these organizations, business interests—especially global firms—are able to determine rules and regulations without having to go through government (Crouch 2010, 2011; Graz and Nölke 2008). In turn, globalization seems to be curbing workers' capacity to exercise political power through industrial action. Nevertheless, even transnational supply and production chains contain weak links which can be exploited by union action (Erne 2008: 36). Therefore, unions retain more power compared to other non-governmental organizations that play no role in the economic production process.

Figure 14.1 enables us not only to distinguish business associations, trade unions, and other non-governmental organizations analytically, but also to distinguish different repertoires of action that go beyond the *lobbying* activities that are available to all interest groups. Reflecting contributions to the study of interest politics from cognate disciplines, such as industrial and labour relations and political sociology, our typology also captures alternative action repertoires that are available only to specific types of interest associations:

- the capacity to conclude *political exchanges* with the government (Pizzorno 1978), available to organizations with a high degree of autonomy vis-à-vis the political system (e.g. business associations and trade unions);
- the capacity to engage in *contentious politics* (Tilly and Tarrow 2015), available to organizations with a high capacity to engage in collective action (e.g. trade unions and other social movement organizations);
- the capacity to set up *private interest government* structures (Streeck and Schmitter 1985), available to organizations with a high degree of autonomy vis-à-vis the political system (e.g. business associations).

Direct lobbying

Although the term 'lobbying' was originally used to describe attempts to influence lawmakers in the lobbies of the British Houses of Parliament, the lobbying literature usually refers to all activities that aim to influence any branch of government at any level of decision-making. However, in order to distinguish lobbying from other repertoires of action of interest associations, I am reserving this term for activities that are based on personal access to decision-makers in line with the concept of *direct* or *inside lobbying*.

The US lobbying literature, which still influences the agenda of lobbying researchers across the world, has been particularly concerned with practical questions. What factors explain the success of lobbyists? Whom to lobby to be effective? Truman (1971 [1951]) and numerous scholars who came after him described and compared the lobbying strategies of interest groups vis-à-vis the

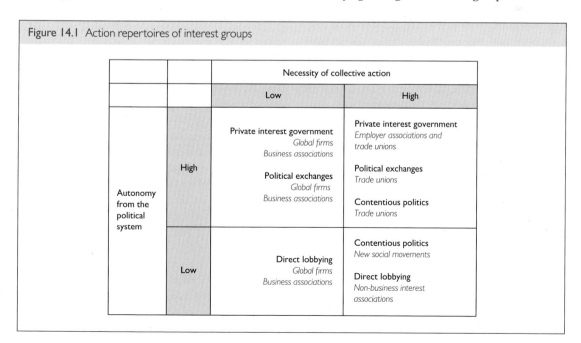

Figure 14.1 Action repertoires of interest groups

		Necessity of collective action	
		Low	High
Autonomy from the political system	High	Private interest government *Global firms* *Business associations* Political exchanges *Global firms* *Business associations*	Private interest government *Employer associations and trade unions* Political exchanges *Trade unions* Contentious politics *Trade unions*
	Low	Direct lobbying *Global firms* *Business associations*	Contentious politics *New social movements* Direct lobbying *Non-business interest associations*

branches of government: the executive, the state bureaucracy, the legislature, and even the courts. Predictably, most scholars concluded that the more an interest group is endowed with resources, such as money, legitimacy, and expertise, the higher is its capacity to influence decision-makers and policy outcomes. Lobbying specialists also came to the conclusion that the accessibility of institutions affects the degree of interest group influence on policy outputs. And, finally, there also seems to be a consensus among lobbying specialists that the nature of an issue influences the efficacy of lobbying.

In addition, growing popular concerns about the impact of interest group money in US elections triggered not only several studies (Rozell et al. 2006; Currinder et al. 2007) but also political reform. However, these reforms did not aim to balance power inequalities within the interest group system, in line with neocorporatist thought, but rather mirrored a shift from a pluralist to a republican understanding of interest group politics. Fittingly, in 2002 the US Congress passed the bipartisan McCain–Feingold Act which restricted the ability of corporations—but also trade unions—to advertise on behalf of, or in opposition to, a political candidate. However, on 21 January 2010, the Supreme Court of the United States ruled that the McCain–Feingold Act violated the Constitution, stating that its free-speech provisions should apply to corporations and unions as well as to individuals. It goes without saying that the ruling, which was determined by the Supreme Court's conservative majority, caused widespread dismay among commentators, who argued that elections should be won—not bought (Streisand 2010).

Be that as it may, a comparative assessment of European state traditions suggests that there are alternative ways to contain the influence of corporate money in the political process. European states do not limit the free-speech rights of interest groups; however, they do balance the power of competing interest associations through public policy measures that strengthen weaker interest associations, namely through financial assistance as well as institutionalized consultation, co-determination, and veto rights. Consequently, it seems implausible to suggest converging perspectives on interest group research in Europe and the US, as has been argued by Mahoney and Baumgartner (2008) and Dür (2008).

Perhaps the application of US questions and paradigms in European interest politics research can be justified by the presence of a plethora of professional lobbyists in Brussels (Greenwood 2017; Dialer and Richter 2018) or the EU's mode of multilevel governance, which resembles the federal US system at least to some extent (see Chapter 23 'The EU as a new political system'). However, interest groups must play a particular lobbying game in Brussels. For example, European business lobbyists do not set up US-style **political action committees** in order to campaign for or against political candidates or legislation (Coen 2010). Given the much more technocratic and consensual nature of the EU policy-making process, they try instead to establish themselves as trusted actors in EU-level policy networks that 'seek some kind of "negotiated order" out of conflict and uncertainty' (Coen and Richardson 2009: 348). This is leading to a system of interest intermediation called 'elite pluralism' (Coen 1997) in which only those players whose presence is politically welcome gain access to a particular EU policy network. In social policy, however, the automatic participation of employer associations and unions still reflects corporatist rather than pluralist patterns of interest intermediations (Léonard et al. 2007), although the unilateral EU labour market and social policy reforms that have been imposed in the EU after 2010 may also suggest a different conclusion (Erne 2015; Marginson 2015). Nevertheless, policy-making processes and the regulatory regimes that govern interest group–government relations vary across countries and different varieties of capitalism to such a degree (Grant 2005; McMenamin 2013) that any analysis that fails to go beyond US paradigms of lobbying must lead to flawed results.

Political exchange

As shown in Figure 14.1, direct lobbying is not the only mechanism through which interest associations influence political power. Associations that operate in the economic sphere, namely business associations and trade unions, are also able to conclude *political exchanges* with political leaders (Pizzorno 1978). Governments have frequently traded goods with unions or employers in exchange for social consent. In such cases, political exchange power is paradoxically linked to the (partial) renunciation of economic power, namely the capacity to withdraw capital or labour from the production process. In addition, political institutions are dependent on expert knowledge which might not be available within an increasingly restricted and residual public service (Crouch 2004: 89). Accordingly, even corporate lobbying can be conceptualized as political exchange, namely as an exchange of information that is crucial in the policy-making process as against access to the policy-making process (Bouwen 2002).

Sometimes, exchange power even takes on a symbolic form, in which neither politicians nor interest groups exchange any material goods, but only legitimacy (Crouch 2000). For example, trade unions have shared the burden of legitimizing contested *political* decisions in exchange for more or less favourable public policies, as in the case of past EU referendums (Hyman 2010). Unions have also offered employers their collaboration to persuade workers to use controversial technologies, to respect safety regulations, or to retrain. In addition, unions and employers have made joint submissions in favour of their industries, which political decision-makers usually find very hard to deny.

As capital depends on labour in the production process, and vice versa, the organizations of capital and labour may also decide to enter into tripartite agreements with the government in exchange for economic performance and social peace. In such agreements during the 1970s, unions often accepted wage moderation in exchange for legislation that strengthened workplace co-determination rights, and more recently simply to make a country more competitive (Erne 2008). In this context, interest associations can no longer be perceived as a counter-power to the state. Instead, they become actors within a policy network that also assumes governmental functions. However, given the increasing exit options introduced by neoliberal politics and the **internationalization** of capital, even the proponents of neocorporatism had doubts about whether the political exchanges that characterized neocorporatism could be sustained (Streeck and Schmitter 1991).

But, surprisingly, in the 1990s social pacts were concluded even in countries, such as Ireland, Italy, and Spain (Molina and Rhodes 2002), where the structural preconditions of neocorporatism—namely a strong policy coordination and enforcement capacity on the part of the participating 'social partners' and a balance of class forces between capital and labour—were missing (Schmitter and Lehmbruch 1979). Accordingly, Traxler et al. (2001) used the term 'lean corporatism' with reference to the unexpected reappearance of the 'corporatist Sisyphus' in the 1990s (Schmitter and Grote 1997). But after 2008, social partnership collapsed again in Ireland, Italy, and Spain, whereas the peak associations of capital and labour continue to play a major role in the face of the economic crisis in established neocorporatist countries (see Table 14.3).

The collapse of social pacting in Ireland highlights a particular problem related to 'competitive corporatism' (Rhodes 1998). Workers accepted wage moderation, i.e. a smaller share of the national income, in exchange for an overall higher growth rate that would follow from higher profits of Irish businesses. During the booming Celtic Tiger years, it seemed that capital, labour, and the state had found an arrangement that triggered a spectacular period of economic and employment growth. But when growth rates collapsed, the Irish government and employers' associations abandoned partnership and imposed unilateral wage cuts. Whereas Irish workers accepted a smaller share of the national income when it was growing, they found it very difficult to accept getting a 'smaller slice of a shrinking cake' (Erne 2013). It follows that corporatist

deals can be very risky, especially for labour. How can unions be sure that employers do not take advantage of unions' concessions within social pacts in boom years when unions are strong, and then abandon corporatist arrangements in crisis years when unions are weak?

The major difficulty with the exchange power of a union, however, is its dependence on the capacity to threaten social stability (Offe and Wiesenthal 1985). In contrast to the exchange power of capitalists, labour's exchange power depends entirely on its collective mobilization power. Hence, exchange power uses— but does not reproduce—mobilization power (Erne 2008). The use of exchange power might even cause a decline in union membership that would finally undermine the very capacity to conclude exchanges. This explains why unions that univocally support social partnership need to demonstrate occasionally that their consent cannot be taken for granted, as shown by Hyman (2001) with regard to the German case.

Contentious politics

Interest associations also engage at times in *contentious politics* (Tilly and Tarrow 2015; see Chapter 16 'Social movements')—or **outside lobbying** (Schattschneider 1975 [1960]), in the language of the US lobbying literature. Whereas business associations very rarely see the need to engage in contentious collective action (e.g. public demonstrations or lockouts), strike action is often seen as the constitutive power of labour. In contrast with other social movements, unions engage in contentious politics mainly to compel institutions to compromise. In contrast with Rosa Luxemburg (2008 [1906]), most unions understand contentious politics not as a tool to achieve a different society, but rather as an action of last resort to remind corporations and governments of labour's price for cooperation. However, the more the unions' capacity to wage collective action declined, the more difficult it became to defend the achievements of the mid-twentieth-century class compromise that led to the formation of the modern **welfare state** (see Chapter 21 'The welfare state').

The growing cross-border mobility of capital provides employers with a wider range of possibilities to counter collective action on the part of labour. Ongoing restructuring processes and threats to delocalize enterprises have considerably weakened union power in industrialized countries, even if capital is not as footloose as is often alleged. Nevertheless, it would be wrong to say that industrial conflict has disappeared in the new world of global capitalism (Silver 2003; van der Velden et al. 2007; Bieler et al. 2015; Stan et al. 2015). Yet, strikes often involve relatively small groups of core workers, especially in the public sector, and fail to include the marginalized peripheral workforce. Although the European peak organizations of employers and workers signed a legally binding *European Social Dialogue* agreement that stated that employees on fixed-term contracts cannot be treated less favourably than permanent staff (European Industrial Relations Dictionary 2010), Hyman (1999) observed a growing polarization between different sections of the working class. This obviously undermines working class solidarity, and thus the capacity of unions to conclude general political exchanges.

Although the contemporary orthodoxy that social class no longer exists can be contested with sociological analysis, the increasing difficulty of subordinate groups to unite as a class entails major consequences for interest politics and democracy alike (Crouch 2004: 53): how is it possible to reconcile democracy and interest politics, if the latter seem to be increasingly dominated by a self-confident global shareholding and business executive class? In the wake of the financial crisis of 2008, Crouch gave a pessimistic answer to this question: whereas democratic politics would continue to play a role in some areas, the democratic state would be vacating its 'former heartland of basic economic strategy'. Instead, economic policy would be shaped by 'the great corporations, particularly those in the financial sector' (Crouch 2009: 398), because of the decline of the manual working class and the failure of new social movements to constitute a new class that stands for a general social interest. Consequently, economic policy would become a private matter of business interests, even if corporations might, at times, be held accountable by public appeals to *corporate social responsibility* (Crouch 2011).

Private interest government

In neocorporatist systems, the state integrates associations into policy networks. In the case of *private interest government*, however, the state goes even further and delegates its authority to make binding decisions to interest groups (Streeck and Schmitter 1985). As far back as the Middle Ages, producer associations established private interest government structures, namely the guilds, in order to police the markets. However, after the French Revolution the regulation of markets became a domain of the nation-state, mainly to suit the needs of modern industry. When the working class entered as a compelling social force in politics, it seemed that the days of self-regulation of economic affairs by business would definitely be numbered. Yet, in a particular economic sector, guild-like patterns of private interest government remained crucially important.

In the agriculture sector, self-governing producer associations continued to police the production and distribution of goods throughout the twentieth century (Farago 1985; Streeck and Schmitter 1985; Traxler and Unger 1994; Stan 2005). Although agriculture policy became an important pillar of the European common market project, states continued to support the self-governing bodies of the sector by public policy and laws. Even in countries with no corporatist traditions, farmers' associations were co-opted into public policy networks that governed agricultural policy (Muller 1984; Smith 1993). However, the more the agricultural sector internationalized, the more evident conflicts between local farmers and international agribusiness corporations became. In several countries, small farmers left the once all-encompassing farmers' associations and founded autonomous farmers' groups (della Porta and Caiani 2009). In this context, it became increasingly difficult, but not impossible, to sustain private interest governing structures in this sector. Traditional private interest governments such as the *Swiss Cheese Union* collapsed. However, in some cases new self-governing private interest government systems also emerged, for instance around *Appellations d'Origine Contrôlée* (AOC) food certification, production control, and marketing regimes (Wagemann 2012). In other sectors, however, powerful interest groups were even able to establish *transnational private governance* structures to regulate, for example, the internet, international accountancy standards, and banking regulation in a way that suited their interests (Graz and Nölke 2008).

The shift in policy-making from partisan politics to autonomous agencies has also been the focus of scholars who studied the rise of *regulatory governance* (Majone 1994). According to Majone, regulatory governance is meant to keep interest groups out of policy-making process by relieving the process of the 'negative consequences' of electoral pressures on the quality of regulation. In other words, advocates of regulatory governance aim to reduce interest group influence by the exclusion of elected politicians from the policy-making process. Policy-making would be better if it was left to independent agencies—for example, to independent central banks in relation to monetary policy, or independent competition authorities in relation to competition policy. However, the exclusion of interests and interest intermediation from the policy-making process is at variance with both pluralist and neocorporatist paradigms of interest politics. To some extent, the theory of regulatory governance comes closest to the unitarist republican paradigm, but without its democratic rhetoric. Like republican theory, however, regulatory governance faces a major problem: how can one be sure that regulatory agencies do not serve the interest that was able to capture a dominant position in the agency's decision-making process? Regulative agencies tend to be shaped by powerful political actors and ideologies, as confirmed by the exclusion of social and labour interests from the frames of references that govern the monetary policy of the European Central Bank and the competition policy of the Directorate General for Competition of the European Commission (Erne 2008). For that reason, regulatory governance structure 'often masks ideological choices which are not debated and subject to public scrutiny beyond the immediate interests related to the regulatory management area' (Weiler wet al. 1995: 33). In this vein, regulatory governance might be more properly understood if it were conceptualized as disguised private interest government.

KEY POINTS

- Selective incentives motivate individuals to join interest groups. But collective experiences and moral concerns can also trigger collective action. Finally, organizers or external sponsors may also play a role in the formation of interest groups.

- Whereas business groups do not need to engage in collective action, as each individual investment decision has a political impact, trade unions and other citizens' organizations must organize collective action to have an impact.

- The power of interest groups depends on their ability to affect the policy-making capacity of a political system. Hence, powerful interest groups not only engage in direct lobbying, but also pressurize the government by other means, notably through actions in the economic sphere (business relocation threats, workers' industrial action, etc.).

- The different action repertoires (direct lobbying, political exchange, contentious politics, and private interest government) are not available to all interest groups to the same extent.

- Government–interest group relations reflect not only the power resources of interest groups, but also the institutional context of the particular political and socio-economic system.

porary scholars. Some analysts note that corporate interests are increasingly determining socio-economic policy (Crouch 2004, 2011), whereas others detect twin processes of popular and elite withdrawal from politics (Mair 2006c). To this, Tocqueville might have responded: the weaker individual citizens become, the more they need to learn to combine with fellow citizens to defend themselves against the despotic influence of corporate power. Accordingly, many studies ask what contribution interest associations make to the democratic involvement of citizens in the current era (Cohen and Rogers 1995; Jordan and Maloney 2007). This democracy–interest association nexus is also of particular importance in studies that assess EU politics (Smismans 2006; Balme and Chabanet 2008; Kohler-Koch et al. 2008Kohler-Koch and Quittkat 2011; Horn 2012; Georgakakis and Rowel 2013; Erne 2015).

Comparative studies of interest politics are also crucial in order to explain variations in capitalisms and welfare states across the developed world (Hancké 2009). Why did companies in Germany lay off fewer workers in 2009 than corporations in the US, although the global economic crisis hit both countries equally? Arguably, the difference can be explained by the different systems of interest intermediation that are in place in the two countries.

Given the impact of interest group politics on both democracy and the social and economic well-being of people, it is no exaggeration to claim that the study of politics and society cannot forego the contributions of comparativists in this field. However, there remains one caveat. Students of interest politics should remain sceptical of studies that seek to increase the field's coherence by reducing its scope to the narrowness and parochialism that dominated some sections of the lobbying and pressure group literature in the past.

Conclusion

Contemporary political conflicts have increasingly been interpreted as cultural rather than socioeconomic conflicts (see Chapter 17 'Political culture'; Inglehart and Norris 2016; Hooghe and Marks 2004). But whereas the current backslash against the globalization and European integration processes is indeed often framed in culturalist terms, we have argued that socioeconomic interest and interest associations continue to play a crucial role in the political process (Béthoux et al. 2018).

Furthermore, this chapter has also shown that there is no agreement on whether interest groups represent a danger or a 'school for democracy' (Sinyai 2006). Therefore, it is not surprising that government–interest group relations, which preoccupied Rousseau and Tocqueville centuries ago, still engage contem-

KEY POINTS

- Interest associations play a crucial role in the political process. But there is no agreement on whether interest associations sustain or undermine democracy, especially in the current context of a growing internationalization of interest politics. For this reason, the relationship between democracy and interest politics is of particular importance in studies that assess the democratic legitimacy of supranational organizations, such as the European Union.

- Interest associations—and the particular rules and regulations that govern them—also affect the socio-economic and political outcomes of a particular country. Therefore, comparative studies of interest politics have been crucial in order to explain variations in capitalisms and welfare states across the world.

QUESTIONS

Knowledge-based

1.   What is an interest group?

2.   Why are interest groups so difficult to define in a comparative context?

3.   On which assumptions are republican and pluralist paradigms of interest politics based?

4.   To what extent do US and EU lobbying activities differ from each other, and why?

5.   What repertoires of interest group action are available to trade unions?

Critical thinking

1.   To what extent do socioeconomic interests and interest associations continue to play a dominant role in politics.

2.   Does it make sense to distinguish 'public' and 'private' interest groups?

3.   What advantages do neocorporatist systems of interest intermediation offer governments?

4.   Why do business interest groups retain a privileged position in capitalist democracies?

5.   'The more national interest politics regimes are shaped by supranational developments, the more the "methodological nationalism" of classical country-by-country comparisons is producing biased results.' Discuss.

FURTHER READING

Béthoux, E., R. Erne, and D. Golden (2018) 'A primordial attachment to the nation? French and Irish workers and trade unions in past EU referendum debates', *British Journal of Industrial Relations*, 56 (3): 656–78. A contribution to a better understanding of the dynamics that are driving the politicization of the European integration process, which questions the dominant culturalists explanations for the rising Euroscepticism of workers and trade unions.

Cigler, A. J., Loomis, B. A., and Nownes, A.J. (eds) (2015) *Interest Group Politics* (9th edn) (Washington, DC: CQ Press). A contemporary review of US interest politics.

Coen, D., Grant, W., and Wilson, G. (2010) *The Oxford Handbook of Business and Government* (Oxford: Oxford University Press). A fine collection on business–government relations.

Crouch, C. and Streeck, W. (eds) (2006) *The Diversity of Democracy: Corporatism, Social Order and Political Conflict* (Cheltenham: Edward Elgar). A lucid reassessment of the neocorporatist argument by major protagonists in the field.

Erne, R. (2008) *European Unions: Labor's Quest for a Transnational Democracy* (Ithaca, NY: Cornell University Press). The book's discussion and analytic considerations relating to transnational democracy, collective action, and EU governance remain topical, notably considering the trade union and labour resistance to austerity measures being implemented throughout Europe today.

Greenwood, J. (2017) *Interest Representation in the European Union* (4th edn) (Cham: Springer). A comprehensive textbook on the role of interest associations in the EU.

Harvey, D. (2005) *A Brief History of Neoliberalism* (Oxford: Oxford University Press). A very readable book on the rise of business interests in politics since the 1970s.

McMenamin, I. (2013) *If Money Talks, What Does it Say? Corruption and Business Financing of Political Parties* (Oxford: Oxford University Press). An intelligent study of the role of business money across a variety of countries and capitalisms.

Offe, C. (1980) *Disorganized Capitalism: Contemporary Transformations of Work and Politics* (Cambridge: Polity Press). This book includes Offe and Wiesenthal's seminal chapter on 'Two Logics of Collective Action'.

Visit the Online Resources that accompany this book for additional material, including country profiles, comparative data sets, flashcard glossaries, and web directory.

www.oup.com/he/caramani5e

15

Regions

James Bickerton and Alain-G. Gagnon

Reader's guide

This chapter examines the concept of region and starts by reviewing the main theories and approaches that are used to understand the political role and importance of regions. It then discusses the various dimensions and aspects of regions and regionalism. Regionalism from below concerns the political mobilization of regional identities, whether by movements or political parties. Looking at regional institutions involves an examination of how regions have been politically constituted, recognized, and accommodated. Sometimes regions have been created by states through a process of regionalization 'from above', undertaken by central governments with administrative and governance purposes in mind; at other times it happens through a process of institution-building from within, initiated and pursued primarily by regional actors. Finally, the chapter focuses on the political economy of regions, tracing the changing economic role and place of regions within the national and global economy.

Introduction

What is a region? It is a geographical space. But beyond that, many meanings are attached to it, and many approaches are used to understand it. According to Michael Keating, it may relate to an identity; it often has a cultural element; it may sustain a distinct society and a range of social institutions. It can be an economic unit or a unit of government and administration. And all these meanings may coincide, to a greater or lesser degree (Keating 2004: xi).

The idea of region is both simple and highly ambiguous.

In most states, the region is a contested area, both territorially and functionally. Spatially, it exists between the national and the local and is the scene of intervention by actors from all levels, national, local, regional and now supranational. Functionally, it is a space in which different types of agency interact and, since it is often weakly institutionalized itself, a terrain of competition among them.

Keating (1997: 17)

Sometimes used when referring to intermediate levels of political representation or governance (provinces, states, *Länder,* counties, supra-urban areas), region also has been employed to refer to a spatial area within a state encompassing more than one political unit (New England), or a **supranational** area stretching across state boundaries (e.g. the Great Lakes or Cascadia regions of North America). It may not be demarcated by political boundaries at all but by particular cultural or economic characteristics (such as the Acadian region in Eastern Canada or Silicon Valley in California). The latter use of the term denotes 'a territorial entity having some natural and organic unity or community of interest that is independent of political and administrative boundaries' (Stevenson 1980: 17).

Not surprisingly, then, geographers, economists, sociologists, and political scientists all define region using different criteria, leading Richard Simeon to argue that 'regions are simply containers . . . and how we draw the boundaries around them depends entirely on what our purposes are: it is an a priori question, determined by theoretical needs or political purposes' (Simeon 1977: 293). In other words, the constitution of the regional demos or economic space is itself a political act that necessarily precedes questions about determining regional justice or fairness, not to mention the mobilization of regional political identities or resistance. Given this malleable nature, 'political entrepreneurs themselves seek to shape the definition of region to reflect their values and interests' (Keating 1997: 17). So, while the concept of region is clearly associated with territorial space, it needs to be understood as a social, economic, and political construction, which is the historical work of human actors and actions. Regions do have geographical, cultural, institutional, and economic underpinnings that persist over time, but they are not static and unchanging, or determined only by geography. As the continuous creation of human history, they are the product of complex interactions. The number, shape, character, meaning, and identities associated with regions is therefore dependent upon a host of factors.

From this standpoint, we can define region as follows: a territorial entity distinct from both locality and **nation-state** that constitutes an economic, political, administrative, and/or cultural space within which different types of human agency interact, and towards which individuals and communities may develop attachments and identities. **Regionalism** is the political manifestation of the values, attitudes, opinions, preferences, and behaviours, as well as the interests, attachments, and identities associated with a region.

As we intuitively know, not all the territorial spaces that we describe as regions should be considered as equally 'regional' in political terms. Following Michael Burgess, who introduced the concept of 'federality' to discuss the federal quality (or essential 'federalness') of diverse federations (2011: 200), as well as Hettne, Soderbaum and Rosamund's concept of 'regionness' to capture the same distinction with regard to regions (2002), we propose the concept of 'regionality' to suggest a continuum of regions based on the interaction of three factors. First, the extent of a region's *organic unity* is significant. This is a compound factor with territorial, historical, sociocultural, and economic dimensions. Second, *institutionalization* refers to both the quantity and quality of regional institutions, and how congruent they are with the 'organic regions' mentioned above. Institutions exert their own independent effect; they will shape, reinforce, and legitimize particular conceptions and representations of the region and the constellation of interests associated with it. Finally, there is regional *identity*. Like institutions, an identity can be harnessed and mobilized for political purposes, giving it the potential to reinforce and transform the region in important ways.

Whether exhibiting a strong or weak degree of regionality, all regions exist as *nested* entities: within more encompassing regions, nations, and various kinds of supranational collectivity. While this variety of territorial affiliation and identity is often benignly complementary or mutually reinforcing, it may also produce competitive or antagonistic relationships. This depends on the region's specific context: its historical legacy, cultural factors, institutional and fiscal arrangements, economic constraints and opportunities, and so on.

The examples and references employed here are drawn predominantly from Europe and Canada. However, regions and regionalism are an irrefutable fact of political life in almost all states, making their study an important part of the effort to understand politics in all its complexity. The impact of regions on both government and political processes has been significant. They shape constitutions, contribute to the composition and practices of political **party systems**, shape **constitutions**, legislatures, and administrative structures, and influence political agendas and public policies. Yet despite their pervasive character and evident political importance, their sometimes elusive and intangible quality can make their study a challenging and imprecise exercise. Still, the complicated dynamics of regions and regionalism have perhaps never been as important an aspect of politics as they are today.

KEY POINTS

- 'Region' is a concept with multiple meanings, though always referring to a territorial space. Its exact meaning in any particular instance is determined by the theoretical needs or political purposes for which it is being used, making the act of defining the region an 'a priori' political consideration.

- Regions are territorial entities spatially distinct from the national state and the local level (locality). They constitute political, economic, cultural, and/or administrative spaces within which different types of human agency interact. Regionalism is the expression of sentiments, opinions, attitudes, and behaviours, as well as interests, attachments and identities that are linked to a particular region.

- The strength and cohesiveness (or regionality) of a region will depend on three factors: (i) its 'organic unity'; (ii) degree of institutionalization; and (iii) salience of regional identity.

- Regions are always nested within other regions, nation-states, and supranational collectivities, and can interact with all the various structures and processes that define and shape the political system.

Theories and approaches

The modernization paradigm

Until the 1960s, the study of regions in social science was dominated by the modernization **paradigm** and development theory. Regions and regionalism were seen as remnants of pre-industrial, pre-modern societies, fated to be eclipsed by the inexorable march of progress in the form of the homogeneous, functionally organized, nationally integrated nation-state (Caramani 2004). For modernization theorists, cultural homogenization is a key process in the long-term and inevitable decline of territorial regionalism. Given this pre-determined outcome, the challenge for elites is to diffuse their 'modern' values to the peripheries, thereby universalizing within society the values and rules inherent in the ordering of modern societies (Tarrow 1977: 20). (For data on national communica-

tion networks, see Comparative Table 1 in Appendix 2 of this volume.)

In conjunction with this approach, a behaviouralist regional science emerged that emptied 'region' of its historical and social content, substituting abstract economic indicators of region such as population density or income. This made it possible to apply micro-economic models and technocratic forms of planning to these spatial units. Out of this grew such notions as 'stepping down' the economic dynamism of the core to peripheral regions, first elaborated by François Perroux (1950) and Gunnar Myrdal (1957), leading to the spread of growth-centre strategies as the leitmotiv of regional planning.

With the critique of the modernization perspective, scholarly interest in regions and regionalism was reinvigorated. In the 1960s, Stein Rokkan and others began to challenge the idea that territorial **cleavages** were of declining significance by demonstrating the persistence of territorial cleavages into modern times. Indeed, since the 1970s these cleavages have spawned protest movements and the political mobilization of regional opposition to ruling elites in many societies. Seeking more autonomy, recognition, and accommodation of their distinctive interests and identities, these movements, parties, and local/regional authorities have sometimes been successful in stimulating central governments to adopt decentralist, devolutionist, or *federalizing* strategies in response (Rokkan 1980).

Regional cultures and minority nations

One way that scholars have understood the persistence of regionalism is to view it from a cultural perspective. Regional cultures can sustain a sense of political community and provide the basis for values, attitudes, and policy preferences. This cultural approach has long informed the historical treatment of regions and the phenomenon of regionalism.

Hartz (1955, 1964), Almond and Verba (1963), Lipset (1990), and others have used culture to explain cross-national variations in political life based on differences in national values (see Chapter 17 'Political culture'). This general approach has also been used to explain regionalism *within* countries, for instance through settlement patterns (in Hartzian terms, regional 'founding fragments') that have produced spatially distinct value systems capable of supporting different regional outlooks and preferences (for Canada, see McRae 1964; Wiseman 1981).

However, regions as cultural spaces are difficult to pin down to a single spatial context. Cultural sensibilities, outlooks, or identities can be nested within particular geographies, economies, and institutions, and related to social characteristics such as class, religion, language, ethnicity, and community heritage (Soja 1989). To the extent that regional identities do exist, they can be mobilized politically, giving voice to a particular territorial identity and interests. A region's history, mythologies, and cultural symbols can become a discursive and ideological resource used to advance a particular conception of the region and any political strategies or development projects that may be associated with it.

When ethnolinguistic minorities with claims to historic nation status are present, the role of culture in shaping the distinctiveness, if not the singularity, of the regional experience is magnified. The political claims of these regions tend to be greater (Requejo and Nagel 2011). At the same time, given appropriate political and institutional arrangements, cultural convergence over time can expand the basis for people with distinct national identities to share a common **citizenship**; it can increase their potential for living together and living apart at the same time.

Marxism

Marxism has provided yet another theoretical jumping-off point for the study of regions, one critical of both the modernization paradigm and cultural approaches. A variety of class and dependency theorists share in common the premise that the unfettered market does not operate in a spatially impartial way, and that political power has been a key factor in structuring regional inequalities. Initially developed to explain continuing conditions of underdevelopment in the Third World, Marxist-inspired regional theories have also been applied to explain the situation of less-developed regions within industrialized countries. Generally, Marxist theorists have argued that regions can only be understood first and foremost in terms of the dynamics inherent in the process of capitalist development and linked to this their relationship with both the national and the global political economy.

However, within Marxism there are contending approaches to regions. What might be termed a 'logic of accumulation' approach sees regional underdevelopment as a necessary condition of accelerated **capital accumulation**. Regional disparities and inequalities are a structural (therefore inevitable) consequence of the internal development logic of capitalism (Carney 1980; Clark 1980). Others have contested this approach as too ahistorical and mechanistic, and instead advocate detailed analysis on a case-by-case basis, stressing the historical specificity of each region's experience (Vilar 1977). Yet another Marxist-inspired approach

to regions—the world systems approach—argues that areas of the world that are lagging economically and socially are locked into their underdeveloped condition through a process of imperialist exploitation by advanced capitalist countries (Wallerstein 1979). This is contested by classical Marxists, who claim that the problem of underdevelopment is an internal one, related to the persistence of traditional, pre-capitalist modes of production and class relations (Brenner 1977).

Disagreements over how to interpret regional inequalities parallel other disagreements within Marxism regarding the historical significance of regionalist and nationalist movements. The Hobsbawm–Nairn debate over the meaning of such movements is instructive here. Hobsbawm links them to the gradual disintegration of national economies due to changes within global capitalism. This creates a situation of vulnerability and exploitability for the smaller and more economically dependent states that are the outcome of separatist agendas (Hobsbawm 1977). Nairn agrees that the political fragmentation occasioned by secessionist movements is a response to changes in global capitalism, but he views the prospect of Britain's break-up as both a positive as well as an inevitable change (Nairn 1977).

These debates among Marxian thinkers over how to understand regional inequalities and regionalist movements illustrate the benefits of historical specificity for students of regionalism, as well as how an understanding of the dynamics of global capitalism can inform the study of territorial movements (Markusen 1987).

Institutionalism

Within Western liberal democratic states, regionalist and ethno-national movements pursuing secessionist agendas have had very little success. Certainly, there are instances where greater **regional autonomy** has been won, such as Belgium, Spain, and the UK, and the nationalist movement within Quebec has clearly altered both the structure and processes of Canadian federalism. But, as yet, no Western liberal democratic state has broken apart due to such movements; indeed, over time some have actually become less threatening to the stability of these states (Urwin 1998). They have successfully contained regionalist and minority nationalist sentiment, their resilience borne of institutional inertia and a willingness to bend if necessary, 'prepared to accommodate either symbolically or in limited ways the demands of minorities' (Urwin 1998: 226). Urwin claims that this experience shows that the interplay of state, territory, and ethno-national identity is constrained by some basic facts: 'powerful and influential structures and institutions; broad and positive acceptance of **pluralism** and difference; tolerance as an integral element of democratic practice; and the ability of many people to live reasonably comfortably with dual identities' (Urwin 1998: 240).

These empirical observations suggest the need for a corrective to cultural and economic approaches to the study of regions. This is supplied in the form of neo-institutional or new institutional theorists who argue that political analysis is best conducted through a focus on the design and workings of state institutions. In terms of the study of regions, institutionalists proclaim the central importance of constitutions, bureaucratic and governance structures, courts, and party and **electoral systems**, not only for providing the basic framework for regions, but for explaining the extent and form of regionalism in a society. Institutions can entrench and strengthen ethno-territorial politics and regional identities, or undermine and weaken this base of identity.

In the 1990s, an institutionalist perspective on regional economic development was developed to explain the 'new regionalism' then emerging, particularly in Europe. Building on the insights of institutional economics, this perspective uncovers the key role within regions of local networks of association and stresses the importance to the success of regions in the global economy of 'intermediate forms of governance [regions] to build up broad-based, local "institutional thickness" that could include political institutions and social citizenship' (Amin 1999: 313).

KEY POINTS

- The modernization paradigm defined regions as spatial units to be integrated into the nation-state and modern economy, but regions have resisted cultural homogenization, political centralization, and economic marginalization.

- Regions are, to varying degrees, cultural spaces, with distinct, meaningful systems and identities.

- Regions have been shaped and reshaped by capitalist development and global capitalism. Attention to the political economy of regions can inform the study of regionalism.

- Western liberal democratic states have proved highly resilient in the face of demands for greater political autonomy (or even secession) by regionalist and nationalist movements.

- Institutions exercise an independent influence on political processes and behaviour. Institutional design has an impact on territorial politics and regional identities.

Regionalism from below: cultures, identities, and parties

Regional identities and political parties constitute the main focus of this section. First, we discuss the notion of regional **political cultures** and examine a variety of examples drawn from different national contexts and political systems. While feeling some attachment to a particular place or territory is a universal phenomenon, this takes different forms and is embedded in different social, cultural, and historical experiences. We next study the political mobilization of these identities through movements and political parties, and examine how and why these identities become politicized.

Cultures and identities

Regional political cultures were initially studied in terms of their differential intensity with respect to political behaviour as it pertains to trust, efficacy, and modes of political participation, an approach formulated by Almond and Verba in their classic '**civic culture**' studies (Almond and Verba 1963) and replicated by others investigating regional cultures in various national contexts (Elkins and Simeon 1980; Henderson 2007). The civic culture approach has been extensively critiqued, and subsequent studies of national and regional cultures have both broadened and deepened their focus, providing evidence of a long-term trend towards cultural convergence both within and across the Western industrialized countries (Ornstein 1986; Nevitte 1996; Adams 2003). Also, some scholars have differentiated between various kinds of cultural and identity difference which may not only distinguish but also 'encode' (Bannerji 2000: 131–3), in other words become an expression of 'deep diversity' within countries (Taylor 1993). Where such 'distinct societies' have been constructed, the political repercussions will tend to be far-reaching.

In multinational countries, such as Belgium, Canada, Spain, and the UK, political and institutional actors in both the **majority** and **minority nations** are involved in the processes of socialization, cultural differentiation, and political education. When there are competing nation-building projects like this, citizens can acquire dual, or even multiple political identities. In such cases, we see some overlap between sub-nation (ethno-territorial) and state-nation identities. Maintaining some semblance of a balance between these two allegiances—which are often asymmetrically held by majority and minority (with the former identifying with one and the latter with two national communities)—is a key factor in determining the stability of multinational states. Table 15.1 conveys the potential tensions that exist between ethno-territorial and state identities in three regions: Catalonia, Quebec, and Scotland.

There is a presumed as well as demonstrated association between political identity and level of support for more regional autonomy or independence. In Quebec, where dual political identities continue to be common within the polity, most respondents to a 2015 survey had an asymmetrical sense of national attachment, with home language being a primary factor. Thus, whereas 58 per cent identified as 'Québécois above all', the proportion for francophones was 67 per cent; moreover, amongst those survey respondents who said they voted 'yes' in the 1995 Quebec **referendum** on independence, 94 per cent identified as 'Québécois above all'. For those identifying as 'Canadian above all', the corresponding 'voted yes' figure was a mere 6 per cent (CROP 2015).

Explaining the rise of regional parties

A general trend concerning regionalist parties can be identified all over Europe. They have been gaining prominence due to three processes: (i) the **democratization** of state structures and political practices; (ii) the resurgence of regional interests in the wake of the retrenchment of the welfare state; and (iii) the politicization of minority nations (see previous section, 'Theories and approaches').

Democratization

Let us first address the process of democratization as an explanatory variable. In the case of Spain, the emergence of regionalist parties is the result of the claims for regional autonomy that accompanied the democratization process in the post-Franco era and the adoption of the 1978 constitution (Gunther et al. 1986). This is especially so within the historic nations of Catalonia, Galicia, and the Basque Country, where demands for autonomy have been fed by a strong sentiment of shared identity and culture. In the Canadian case, it is worth noting that, although the Bloc Québécois (BQ) has as its principal goal the secession of Quebec from Canada, other federal parties have not contested the legitimacy of their elected representatives within the House of Commons. In turn, the BQ, though promoting an independentist stance, has made a valuable contribution to the overall performance of the parliament in its day-to-day work (Gagnon and Hérivault 2007).

Neoliberalism

Second, countrywide parties of national integration have been challenged by regional forces with renewed vigour since the early 1980s (Wilson 1983; Smith 1985: 1–68; Bickerton 2007: 412). During the heyday of the welfare state, stretching from 1945 to 1975, political parties pursuing national objectives tended to be more successful with voters (see Chapter 11 'Multilevel governance'). With the advance of globalization and the widespread implementation of a neoliberal agenda, regionalist political parties have gained in popularity, especially in countries characterized by deep divisions along ethnic, religious, cultural, or economic lines. A case in point is the Lega Nord, which advocates the establishment of an autonomous region, known as Padania, in Northern Italy (Brouillaud 2005: 119–46).

Table 15.1 Dual identity in Catalonia, Quebec, and Scotland (1997–2015) (%)

	Catalonia				Quebec				Scotland			
	1998	2010	2015	2019	1998	2010	2017	2019	1997	2010	2014	2018
Only (1)	12	14	24	27	12	11	14	18	23	30	23	24
More (1) than (2)	23	26	23	23	31	42	35	44	38	33	26	33
As (1) as (2)	43	41	38	36	32	19	25	18	27	28	32	23
More (2) than (1)	8	9	5	4	17	17	17	13	4	4	5	9
Only (2)	13	8	6	5	5	7	7	6	4	5	6	4
Do not know or refuse to answer	1	2	4	5	3	1	2	1	4	0	8	2

(1) = Catalan, Québécois, Scots.
(2) = Spanish, Canadian, British.

Sources: Wells (1998); National Centre for Social Research (2018), 8; You GOV (2018); Environics Research Institute for Survey, in partnership with the Mowat Centre, the Canada West Foundation, the Centre d'analyse politique: Constitution et fédéralisme, the Institute for Research on Public Policy, and the Brian Mulroney Institute of Government (2019); Moreno et al. (2019).

Scots, who were generally very critical of Westminster's neoconservative policies during the Thatcher years, became more receptive to nationalist arguments for secession as a means to establish a more progressive regime. The same arguments were used by Quebec independentists during the 1995 referendum in Quebec (Gagnon and Lachapelle 1996). The situation in Belgium—where there are no longer any countrywide parties—is unique, leaving the national parliament in the hands of regionalist parties (Peeters 2007: 38; Deschouwer 2012).

Minority nations

Third, we have witnessed the politicization of minority nations that have used various democratic instruments to advance their cause. Election campaigns and referendums (discussed later in this chapter in 'Managing and building regionalism') have been key means by which regional party leaders have given democratic legitimacy to their claims. In Spain, setting up of autonomous communities has led to the development of nationalist parties at the regional level in Catalonia and the Basque country. Other autonomous regions, with the notable exception of Galicia, have generally adhered to the national party system.

The role of regionalist parties in national party systems

Beyond the minority nationalism that so marks politics in Catalonia, Quebec, and Scotland, regionalism has played a key role as a marker of political identity in Canada, the UK, and Spain. Canada has long experienced distinct regional patterns of voting behaviour (Bickerton et al. 1999; Bickerton 2017). The classic works of Macpherson (1953) and Lipset (1968) on the emergence of regional parties in the Canadian West during the first half of the twentieth century were influential in accounting for the sources and impact of regionalism on Canadian politics. Their conclusions were that class structure and economic conditions were central to the emergence and persistence of right-wing and left-wing agrarian parties on the Canadian prairies. These initial studies were later joined by many others (Simeon 1977; Forbes 1979; Brym 1986; Bickerton 1990; Young and Archer 2002), highlighting the continuing importance of regionalism in Canadian politics.

Political parties are known to exercise a variety of functions, including aggregation of interests, elaboration and dissemination of political ideas, electoral campaigning, and ultimately assuming power (see Chapter 12 'Political parties'). In federal or federalizing countries such as Belgium, Canada, Spain, and the UK, political parties are involved at multiple levels of governance, and electoral success at one level is not necessarily replicated at other levels; indeed, parties may compete exclusively at one or the other level.

The tension between centralist parties and regionalist parties has too often been neglected by students of party politics. Canadian prime ministers have clashed repeatedly with Quebec-centred parties in the federal Parliament (Ralliement créditiste and Bloc Québécois), as well as the exclusively provincial parties that have governed Quebec since 1944 (Union Nationale, Parti Libéral, Parti Québécois, and Coalition Avenir Québec) (Bickerton et al. 1999: 164–92). During the past two decades, the Bloc Québécois and the Reform (later Canadian Alliance) Party are two regionalist parties that have championed regional issues and interests within the federal parliament, whereas the previous period had been marked by the domination of political parties with an almost exclusively national focus (Bickerton 2007: 412).

Similar behaviour has been witnessed in Spain, where both the Partido Socialista Obrero de España (PSOE) and the Partido Popular (PP) have taken a centralist stand, as a result alienating large segments of voters in the Basque Country, Catalonia, and Galicia. Concomitant with the democratization process, numerous regionally based political parties emerged, but most studies of political parties in Spain have explored the 'national' party system per se, rather than investigating regional parties. As a result, issues at the regional level tend to be neglected, although 'regional parties are part of the Spanish party system and yet are also distinct, competitively pitting themselves against the national parties' (Lancaster and Lewis-Beck 1989: 30).

In fact, regional parties can play a key role in the political stability of their host countries. During several years of minority governments in Canada, the Bloc Québécois often sided with the governing party in order to avoid triggering a snap election. In Spain, Convergencia i Unió (CiU) was doing the same, while negotiating more accommodating measures from Madrid. And regional parties have demonstrated their relevance and usefulness in other ways over time. They have addressed issues of regional representation in the case of fragmented societies. They have influenced the policy process, making governing parties accountable to a larger population by forcing them to pay greater attention to issues of redistribution, social security, political rights, and environmentalism. As Melissa Williams has argued with regard to historically marginalized groups, the more effectively representatives can give *voice* to the concerns of the group (or in this case, the region), the more *trust* this is likely to generate in the political process, which is a key factor in the legitimacy and stability of political systems (Williams 1998).

Pascal Delwitt, in a thorough account of regional parties within eight European countries, found that of the thirty-two regional parties that have obtained at least 4 per cent of the vote at a national election, twenty-two have assumed responsibilities within the executive branch of government, either at the regional or the national level. Four of those parties have assumed political leadership at both the regional and the national levels, while three others have been part of the executive at the national level only. The remaining sixteen were involved at the executive level within the regions (Delwitt 2005: 51–84).

The emergence and strengthening of regional parties can be connected to the mobilization of ethnic and nationalist movements; it can be attributed to political alienation within regional electorates in countries as varied as Belgium, Canada, the UK, India, Italy, Malaysia, and Spain. This suggests the utility of analyses of party dynamics that can account for the emergence and continuing salience of this regionalist pattern (Johnston 2005).

KEY POINTS

- 'Regionalism from below' has its roots in distinctive cultures and identities, which can be described in terms of differences in values, beliefs, attitudes, preferences, and patterns of participation. Ethno-territorial minorities often have dual national identities which coexist.

- The rise of regionalist parties can be explained by three general factors: democratization; the crisis of the welfare state and the turn towards neoliberalism; and the political mobilization of minority nations.

- Regional parties in multinational democracies tend over time to become integral parts of their respective national party systems; as such, they may no longer pose an existential threat, but instead constitute a potential partner in governing coalitions and an element of political stability.

Managing and building regionalism

Corresponding to the great variety of regionalisms that exist are different modes of regional government and governance, with the institutionalization of regions varying widely from country to country. The relations between regional and central institutions within any given political system (unitary, federalizing, or federal) can be seen as a complex interplay of **centrifugal** and **centripetal** pressures. Particu-

lar governmental and societal arrangements can be understood as different strategies of regional representation and the management of territorially based conflicts and tensions.

Regionalism and federalism

Regional government, meaning regionally autonomous legislative and executive institutions, is most advanced in federal countries like Canada, the United States, Germany, Switzerland, Australia, Austria, Belgium, India, and Malaysia, as well as in 'federalizing' countries like Spain and 'devolved unions' like the UK. In federal countries, regions are constituted as autonomous political entities with constitutionally protected powers and the right to participate in national politics through a second legislative chamber at the national level and through state-to-state mechanisms of institutionalized cooperation between governments (intergovernmental relations). In contrast, unitary systems that feature regional administrative institutions are simply decentralized arms of the central state. In France and Italy, there are regions with limited powers and without significant autonomy, created through processes of *de-concentration* and existing alongside traditional administrative units like cities, departments, communes, and provinces. However, some of these regions (for instance, Sicily, Sardinia, Valle d'Aosta, Trentino-Alto Adige, and Friuli-Venezia-Giulia in Italy; Corsica in France) can be granted a special status and various forms of asymmetric regionalization in response to their specific territorial claims (see Chapter 11 'Multilevel governance').

Clearly, regions take on a multiplicity of forms in different historical contexts. Quebec has seen its frontiers evolve over the centuries, as have other historic regions such as the Basque Country or Catalonia. Nor is there universal agreement on the meaning and status of these ethno-territorial regions. For instance, Quebec has been portrayed by some as an autonomous political entity best understood as a region-state or nation-state in waiting, while others see it as the *foyer* of the French–Canadian culture in a bilingual Canada. The same pattern of contestation applies to Catalonia. While in some cases what matters are the political institutions through which an ethno-territorial community can mobilize and assert demands for increased autonomy, in other cases it is a region's cultural role and influence within the overarching nation-state that matters most. These differences in regionalist strategies are ultimately linked to differences in regional political identities.

Federalizing processes

Devolutionist and federalizing strategies in some states have made it more difficult to clearly distinguish the patterns of territorial management and power-sharing arrangements that exist within **unitary states** versus federal systems. Spain is probably the best example of this, considering that it remains a unitary system that has acquired many of the features of a multinational federation (Moreno 2001). The Spanish case is one in which a variety of federalizing measures were implemented after a transition to democracy in the late 1970s. In the process, the central state has recognized the existence within Spain of several historical nations (Catalonia, Galicia, Basque Country; more recently, Andalusia, Aragon, Valencia, and the Balearic Islands). The main objective pursued by the central government in Madrid has been to provide each autonomous community with identical powers ('coffee for everyone' or *café para todos*) so as to avoid granting distinct status to the original group of historical nations. This has led to major conflicts between central and regional authorities over the years and has encouraged historical nations to demand an asymmetrical **devolution** of powers to their respective regions (Maiz and Losada 2011).

Varying self-definitions stimulate regions to make distinct political claims. Catalonia, the Basque Country, and Galicia make regional claims as historical nations, and on this basis call for the further devolution of powers from the central government, prompting other regions to seek similar status. Central government attempts to avoid or water down special recognition is an example of a territorial management strategy, which not surprisingly increases tensions with autonomy-seeking historical nations.

More recent developments suggest that further reforms to the Spanish State of Autonomies will be difficult to achieve. More than thirty years after its return to democracy, the Spanish state entered into a political impasse with Catalonia following the 2010 rejection by its Constitutional Court of key clauses of the 2006 Statute of Autonomy for Catalonia. Among these provisions was the recognition of Catalonia as a nation, preferential status for the Catalan language, and the power to levy its own taxes. Political reaction in Catalonia included the election to the Catalan Parliament of an independentist majority and a referendum on independence (Guibernau 2012; Muñoz and Guinjoan 2013). In the end, citizens were invited to cast a vote on a non-binding consultation, which initiated a major tug of war between Madrid and Barcelona. Since then, political tensions have remained very high, since no political party (central or regional) has been able to obtain a clear political mandate from their respective polity.

It is noteworthy that these developments in Spain coincided with an agreement between the Scottish and Westminster governments to hold a referendum on Scotland's secession from the UK in 2014. The historical context for this referendum is far removed from either the Quebec or Catalonia situations. In the UK, Scottish, English, Welsh, and Irish national identities have always coexisted, with each acknowledging the legitimacy of the others (Forsyth 1981). Over the years, tensions have appeared at different times, based on the political attitudes of Westminster towards regional claims emanating from the periphery nations.

To attenuate these tensions, a major devolution project was launched by the British government in 1997 with a view to providing varying forms of power to different regional assemblies. After a Scottish Referendum which approved this devolution plan, Prime Minister Tony Blair declared: 'This is a good day for Scotland, and a good day for Britain and the United Kingdom; the era of big centralized government is over!' (Leeke et al. 2003: 18). The process of devolution has continued ever since, though without any grand design about the final outcome (Jeffery 2011). During the past decade, the Scottish Nationalist Party (SNP) has enjoyed increased levels of popular support, leading to a 2014 referendum on independence, the outcome of which was a narrow majority decision to remain within the UK. As a consequence of the 2016 referendum on the UK leaving the European Union (Brexit), and the failed negotiations and political stalemate that followed, a second referendum on independence to secure Scotland's place in Europe (as well as gaining independence) seems more likely.

This brief survey suggests a competition for ascendancy between two approaches to defining the political community. On the one side, there are majority nations who envisage one national *demos*, despite the presence of minority nations (Canada and Spain). These majorities tend to cling to political arrangements based on modified unitary arrangements or territorial (symmetrical) federalism. In contrast, political leaders of minority nations wish to move towards different arrangements based on the idea of multiple nations (*demoi*) who self-govern within a multinational and asymmetrical model of federalism (Kymlicka 1998; Paquin 2003), or, failing that, political independence for the minority nation.

Finally, to explain the presence of region-states (such as Bavaria, Catalonia, Scotland, Flanders, and Quebec) in various international forums, what seems to matter most is 'the importance of nationalism in explaining the breadth, scope and intensity of a region's international activity in [multinational states] and its absence, or lesser prominence, in [nation-states]' (Lecours and Moreno 2003: 268).

KEY POINTS

- In general, regions have attained the greatest degree of autonomy where they are constitutionally protected through federal institutions.

- Asymmetric regionalization has occurred in some unitary states, and an institutional 'blending' is under way that blurs the difference between multinational unitary states and federal systems in terms of the power-sharing arrangements for regions.

- Regional autonomy and asymmetry have proceeded furthest where minority nations are territorially concentrated, whether or not the countries involved are federations.

Political economy of regions

A central theme in the study of the political economy of regions is the degree to which regional inequality and dependence have been internally determined—related to some indigenous characteristic of the region or its people—or alternatively ordained by structures and conditions that have been externally imposed on those regions that are less economically advantaged. This section introduces the reader to this theme and surveys the range of research and opinion to which it has given rise.

Regional inequalities: causes and consequences

From the mid-nineteenth to the mid-twentieth centuries, the industrializing states of the Western world were transformed by processes of political, social, and economic integration associated with the consolidation of nation-states, bureaucratic modernization, and capitalist development focused for the most part on protected national economies (with or without attached colonial empires). Diverse regions at uneven levels of development were incorporated into these national political economies, though not on equal terms. Location, initial resource endowments, transportation links, population base, previous rounds of investment in productive capacity, and various forms of infrastructure were all relevant factors in determining the advantages accruing to some regions versus others in subsequent phases of economic growth and development. The migration of labour from peripheral locales to expanding urban and industrial centres, and the stimulus this gave to new rounds of investment, produced what regional economists refer to as agglomeration effects. This reinforced the initial advantages of some regions, while draining capital and human resources from others, leading to their further differentiation (Massey 1978).

The role that politics and state policy played in this was not negligible. Politicians initiated, planned, and supervised the incorporation of lands and peoples into consolidated nation-states. It was through politics that the policy frameworks that supported and directed national development were developed and maintained. These multi-generational state and nation-building projects were legitimized with nationalist visions, symbols, and rhetoric that promised security and economic prosperity for all. Regionalist resistance was sometimes violent and dramatic (as with the wars of national unification in Europe, the American Civil War and Indian Wars, the Métis rebellion in Canada, or the Spanish Civil War), but more often was limited to periodic episodes of protest through **social movements** or regional political parties.

In the post-war era of economic expansion and relatively full employment (1945–75), regional concerns about inequality and fair representation tended to be subsumed under class politics and the social policy agenda associated with the construction of welfare states. The problem of regional inequalities was dealt with primarily as a residual matter for state managers focused on the 'main game' of full employment and price stability, which they pursued through fiscal policy (centralized taxation and spending). Like other citizens, the residents of less-developed regions generally benefited from the redistribution of income through progressive tax systems and the public provision of pensions, health care, and social services. In this fashion, welfare states relied on strong national economic growth and social spending to alleviate poverty and unemployment, though the extent to which this was accomplished through transfers to regional authorities varied from state to state. Both intergovernmental social transfers and regional equalization schemes went furthest in federal states, thereby contributing to the standardization of public services across regions in these countries. While this constituted an important historical phase of regional policy, it did not eliminate regional disparities in terms of economic growth, per capita income, and unemployment rates.

The rise and decline of regional development policy

In the 1950s and 1960s, various forms of regional planning arose in most western industrialized countries. Friedmann described these policies as 'the process of formulating and clarifying social objectives in the ordering of activities in supra-urban space—that is, in any area larger than a single city' (Wannop 1997: 154). Often initiated in connection with the development of satellite communities to relieve urban conges- tion, in the 1960s priorities began to shift towards the development of growth centres in peripheral regions. This second phase of regional policy was supported by emerging economic theories such as Perroux's strategy of 'growth poles'. It was meant to foster decentralized industrial growth to redress continu- ing regional disparities that persisted despite national economic growth and welfare state expansion. This new form of government intervention was made palatable by the growing diseconomies of metropoli- tan locations for industry, and the benefits of diverting new investment from the already overheated econo- mies of industrial core areas. Throughout Europe—in France, Italy, Germany, the UK—regions were viewed primarily as spatial economic units that could be managed by central states (Keating 2004: xii). In the US, sub-state regional councils became eligible for federal development funds, with regional planning organizations covering almost the entire US by 1980 (Wannop 1997). In Canada, a spate of regional devel- opment agencies and programmes was consolidated in 1969 in a new Department of Regional Economic Expansion, focused on reducing economic disparities between the country's poorest region (the Atlantic region, inclusive of eastern Quebec) and the rest of Canada (Savoie 1986).

The economic logic of regional development policies was to make regions self-sustaining, where- upon regional policies would no longer be necessary and regions could positively contribute to national economic growth. However, there were also politi- cal and social logics at work in the creation of these policies. The *political* weight of poorer regions could be used to counter their *economic* weakness, and their demands to bring work to the region rather than rely on migration to urban centres could not always or easily be ignored, especially during periods when their political importance to national governing coalitions was significant, or when they harboured the poten- tial for political disruption. Also, social citizenship in advanced industrial countries was undergoing a 'thickening' process, with the state expected to assume responsibility for the social integration of all its citi- zens by seeking to equalize opportunities and living standards, thereby preventing or reversing the margin- alization of groups or regions (Keating 1997: 18–20).

In its early phases, this form of **regional policy** being pursued by central states was largely a depo- liticized and technocratic affair, left in the hands of

central state bureaucrats. However, as state interven- tion became more far-reaching, local political and economic elites were inevitably drawn into the policy- making and implementation process, whereupon it quickly became apparent 'that regional preferences and priorities were not always consistent with those of central governments' (Keating 1997: 22–3).

Regional policy began to go into decline in the 1980s. The economic and political context for this decline was the widespread onset of stagflation (low growth, high unemployment, and rising inflation) in western indus- trialized economies, growing international competi- tive pressures, and eventually the widespread adoption of neoliberal policies. Gradually, the national systems of mass production and welfarist politics of the post- war era were constrained or reversed. The post-war model of territorial management through welfarist and regional development policies broke down as the governments increasingly shifted their attention to shoring up their national competitiveness. Reducing regional disparities suddenly became less of a prior- ity; in any event, such policies had met with limited success at best.

The political vacuum left by this retreat from terri- torial management was filled by three types of region- alist politics: *defensive regionalism*, tied to traditional economic sectors and the threatened communities that depended on them; *modernizing regionalism*, aimed at adapting to change and reinserting lagging regions into their national economies; and *autonomist region- alism*, where regions have historical claims to nation status. The latter have tended to seek their own path to modernization by combining greater political auton- omy, cultural promotion, and strategies of economic modernization (Keating 1997: 24). These three modes of regionalism are not mutually exclusive; they coexist within many countries, though sometimes disharmo- niously because of the basic contradictions between them at the level of public policies.

The new regionalism and the revival of regional policy

There is now a new international context for regions, creating for them opportunities but also dangers, and providing the conditions for the incubation of a new regionalism. A number of interrelated changes have contributed to this altered context: falling international trade barriers; the adoption of neoliberalism with its agenda of tax-cutting, deregulation, and free markets; the creation of free trade and economic union agree- ments (e.g. the North American Free Trade Agreement and the EU); and in general the economic, techno- logical, political, and cultural changes associated with globalization. In many ways, these changes have undermined or threatened to destroy the traditional employment base of peripheral regions, as well as the established programmes on which they rely. As a result, inter-regional income disparities have widened, while regional disparities in access to jobs remains one of the biggest development challenges (OECD 2014b).

The Janus-faced nature of globalization for regions, however, is that it has opened up new vistas that, practically speaking, were not previously available. This has occurred because of the changing character of international economic competition, itself a function of changes in technology, production methods, corporate organizations, and the removal of restrictions on international trade and investment. This has given regions access to global markets that absorb a growing volume and range of products and services. Traditional factors of comparative advantage—such as economies of scale, plentiful supplies of labour, access to cheap raw materials, and proximity to markets—still matter, but these are now joined and sometimes superseded by the entrepreneurial, technological, social, and cultural strengths of a region (Piore and Sabel 1984; Porter 1990).

In response to these changes, regional policies have been revamped, marking the onset of a third phase of regional policy. Governments have recognized that the competitive imperative is not only greater and more immediate for all economies, but also different in terms of the constraints and opportunities which it presents for regions, as well as the factors that are directly relevant to regional competitiveness. Governments have found it expedient, if not necessary, to support new forms of regionalization of policy-making and implementation. This usually involves new forms of regional governance in the form of partnerships between various levels of government, as well as the private sector and key actors in civil society. The goal is to create regional policy frameworks that are both flexible and collaborative. This often involves institutional reforms that modify the size and responsibilities of different levels of subnational government, usually consolidating local government bodies and increasing their areas of responsibility (OECD 2014b).

The phenomenon of 'devolved governance' and 'regionalization' varies greatly in practice. Certainly, the EU has been very active in this area, insisting on the creation of regional partnerships in the management of EU funds made available for regional development purposes. As a result, regionalization has become a contentious issue in many EU states, especially in the accession countries admitted to the EU since 1990 (Trigilia 1991; Sharpe 1993; Keating 1998a; Brusis 2002).

The regionalization trend has been accompanied by a re-evaluation of the key factors in regional development. Much greater significance is accorded to *endogenous* factors based on the region's human, social, and cultural capital—what some have called a **socially embedded growth model** (Amin 1999). This recognizes the development significance of high-quality health and education services, cultural amenities, entrepreneurial and managerial training, information and innovation networks, supports for marketing and technology transfer, as well as measures to nurture the local business environment. While financial incentives and infrastructure upgrades are still an important part of the regional development 'toolbox', the policy focus of governments is on improving regional competitiveness by building on regional potential and capabilities. In general, this approach seems to have the support of regional development researchers in Europe and beyond (Stohr 1990; Putnam 1993; Storper 1995; Amin 1999; Florida 2003; OECD 2014b).

The contemporary understanding of regional development has four aspects: economic development, social integration and redistribution, cultural development and identity, and environmental considerations (Keating 1997: 31). This approach involves a broader range of actors and policies in order to create more place-sensitive policies and region-specific strategies tailored to local needs, circumstances, and potentials. This also requires some degree of regionalization, involving cooperation between various levels of government, the private sector, and civil society actors. It also requires institutions capable of facilitating vertical and horizontal coordination at different scales, as the appropriate scale for policy intervention depends on the issues and challenges that need to be addressed.

Regional policy today requires all levels of government to acknowledge that the policies and decisions most likely to nurture sustainable regions will emerge from a strong network of regional actors brought together on the basis of a shared territorial and cultural identity, and a direct interest in the economic fate of the community and its residents. If regions can cohere socially and culturally, and if they are actively supported by government, they will be more capable of adapting to new economic challenges and opportunities, including, if necessary, a managed process of downsizing and transformation necessitated by long-term economic trends. Prominent amongst these is the emergence of looser regional formations anchored by great cities or metropolitan clusters, a trend stimulated by deepening global integration and the productivity gains linked to increased city size (OECD 2014b). More than ever, state authorities will need to cooperate across jurisdictional lines in order to respond to the public infrastructure, connectivity, and coordination needs of these 'super-regions' that drive national economic growth, while engaging in competition over global trade, investment flows, and supply chains (Khanna 2016). The prosperity of other regions comprised of smaller cities, towns, and rural areas may well depend upon the extent to which they can be 'tied in' or connect themselves to this new urban political economy.

KEY POINTS

- The differentiation of regions within nation-states occurred over an extended period of time. Ongoing state and nation-building projects were met by regional resistance in the form of military conflict, minority/majority nationalism, territorial movements, and party-based politics.

- The construction of welfare states in the post-war era included a regional dimension. At first largely submerged by class-based and redistributive politics, persistent regional economic disparities led to the introduction of regional development policies as a complement to national social programmes. Changes in the international political economy in the 1970s and 1980s led to the decline of regional development policy, giving rise to defensive, modernizing, and autonomist modes of regionalism.

- A new regionalism has emerged in the 1990s in the context of globalization. The traditional determinants of regional economic competitiveness are now supplemented by an endogenous growth model that benefits from new forms of regionalized governance to nurture collaborative policy frameworks.

Conclusion

Region as a social science concept is both pliable and abstract, due primarily to its multiple potential meanings. Political, economic, social, and cultural actors will define the region to reflect their values and identities, as well as their particular interests and needs. In this sense, though region is always associated with geographic space, it is very much a socially constructed entity or outcome.

A number of different theories and approaches have attempted to explain regions as economic, social, cultural, and political phenomena. Mainstream modernization and development theory ascribed diminishing significance to regions, since they were fated to fade as the economic and cultural integration processes linked to modernity and capitalism proceeded apace. Other approaches and perspectives remained sceptical of this outcome. Culturalists described the persistence of spatially distinct meaning systems that continued to define regions as cultural spaces, a persistence that was especially notable for regions populated by minority nations. In these cases, individuals frequently espouse multiple political identities, which continue to be available to political elites for mobilization purposes. Marxists are less sanguine than modernization theorists about the economic and cultural convergence of regions undergoing development within a global capitalist system. What is shared within this approach is certainty about the necessity to understand the past, present, and future of regions within the broader national and international contexts, particularly as this pertains to the economic forces acting on regions. Institutional theorists bring to the study of regions their insights into the independent shaping effect on regions and regionalism exerted by the design and workings of political and social institutions.

'Regionalism from below' refers to the societal forces that have given cultural and identity content to regions. This manifests itself through regional political cultures, the political alienation of regionally identifying electorates, or the multiple identities nurtured within individuals who are members of minority nations. It is central to the rise and role of regionalist parties in Western liberal democratic states, especially those that feature ethno-territorial minorities, or regions with claims to historical nation status.

The degree of institutionalization of regions, and the extent of their autonomy from central governments, is directly related to two broad factors:

- whether the country in question is a federal state with a constitutionally protected division of powers between central and regional governments and autonomous, democratically elected representative assemblies;
- whether the state in question is multinational, in the sense of having one or more clearly defined ethno-territorial minorities with claims to historic nation status.

Either or both of these conditions within liberal democratic states virtually ensures the gradual development over time of power-sharing arrangements between central and regional authorities, as democratically supported elites seek to accommodate regionalist sentiment. In those states with minority nationalist movements or parties, the tendency will be for this accommodation to take the form of asymmetrical power-sharing arrangements.

Finally, the economic differentiation of space conjointly produced by the processes of capitalist development and the state policies put in place to provide a national framework for this development have had a determinant effect not only on the formation of regions, but also on the timing and forms of regionalism which subsequently emerged. The rise, decline, and revival of regional policy can be related to changes in the macro-political economy of states and regions, most recently the economic, political, cultural, and technological changes associated with globalization. While this has generated a more complex understanding of regional development, one which has initiated movement towards more regionalized forms of governance, it has neither 'resolved' the challenge of region from the perspective of territorial management, nor ensured the success of complex projects of regional economic development.

? QUESTIONS

Knowledge-based

1. What is the relationship between regional political identities and distinct regional cultures?

2. Unitary and federal states have more in common than it seems at first glance. What accounts for this?

3. How are territorially concentrated national minorities influencing the prospects for democracy in the Western world and beyond?

4. What have been the contributions of minority nations in Canada, the UK, and Spain to the development of federal and regional practices in their respective countries?

5. How has the process of capitalist development affected the formation and uneven development of regions?

Critical thinking

1. Can it be argued that regions are on the rise, while the nation-state is becoming a thing of the past?

2. Do strong regions naturally produce federalism, or is it federalism that creates strong regions?

3. Why is the concept of region so difficult to define? What are the factors giving rise to a 'regionality' continuum?

4. What are some of the different theoretical approaches that can be used to understand the meaning and significance of regions?

5. What is the 'new regionalism' and how does it reflect the changing role of regions in the context of globalization? What are some of the economic challenges they face?

≋ FURTHER READING

Deschouwer, K. (2012) *The Politics of Belgium. Governing a Divided Society* (Basingstoke: Palgrave Macmillan).

Gagnon, A.-G. and Keating, M. (2012) *Political Autonomy and Divided Societies* (Basingstoke: Palgrave Macmillan).

Keating, M. (ed.) (2004) *Regions and Regionalism in Europe* (Cheltenham: Edward Elgar).

Loughlin, J., Kincaid, J., and Swenden, W. (eds) (2013) *Routledge Handbook of Regionalism and Federalism* (London: Routledge).

Markusen, A. (1987) *Regions: The Economics and Politics of Territory* (Totowa, NJ: Rowman & Littlefield).

OECD (2014b) *Regional Outlook 2014: Regions and Cities: Where Policies and People Meet* (Paris: OECD).

Requejo, F. and Nagel, K.-J. (2011) *Federalism beyond Federations: Asymmetry and Processes of Resymmetrisation in Europe* (Farnham: Ashgate).

Scott, A. J. (2001) *Global City-Regions: Trends, Theory, Policy* (Oxford: Oxford University Press).

Visit the Online Resources that accompany this book for additional material, including country profiles, comparative data sets, flashcard glossaries, and web directory.

www.oup.com/he/caramani5e

16

Social movements

Dieter Rucht

Chapter contents

Reader's guide

Unlike political campaigns that are relatively limited in their thematic range and duration, social movements aim at, or resist, fundamental changes of society. Inevitably, such changes would also affect the given power structures. Consequently, social movements are engaged not only in social, but also in political struggles. Based on a clarification of the concept of social movements that highlights four constitutive elements, the second part of this chapter presents the major theories and approaches in social movement research. Next, in a more descriptive approach, it outlines some general patterns and profiles of contemporary social movements, stressing the need to interpret social movements in relation to their key reference groups, of which, besides movements' opponents, also allies, third parties, and bystanders play a crucial role. A further section is devoted to comparative aspects and findings in social movement studies, including the more recent trend towards the transnationalization of some movements. Finally, a typology of the basic functions and effects of social movements is presented. The general thrust of this chapter is that the structural context, the shared perceptions and experiences, as well as the dynamic interactions between social movements and their reference groups are crucial for a better understanding of the functions and effects of social movements as potential creators of social change.

Introduction

People who suffer from hunger, mistreatment, marginalization, repression, and other serious burdens do not always resort to collective protest and engagement in social movements. So, there must be reasons why people remain apathetic and hopeless in some cases but energetic and hopeful in other cases. Even in democratically organized welfare states, some groups engage in various forms of political and social protest though, compared to authoritarian and/or poor countries, they live in favourable conditions. Yet most people do not tend to compare with those who are in a deplorable situation. Instead, they refer to a presence or future that, when compared to past times, looks grim. Or they compare with other groups that, in the eyes of their critics, are enjoying undeserved advantages and privileges. But even when people do feel relatively deprived in very similar ways (Walker and Smith 2001), only some of them engage in movements, whereas others remain silent. Moreover, some people, even when not directly concerned by a grievance, act as advocates for those who are weak or cannot speak out. So, there must be other motivational, structural, and contingent factors that account for these different reactions. In order to better understand such differences in the occurrence, scope, and form of social movement activity, comparative analyses, ideally across issues, time and place, are extremely useful. While a single-case study may provide valuable and detailed insights into a specific campaign or a specific social movement, only by comparison are we able to identify typical patterns and regularities as well as specificities and outliers. In order to explain the patterns, variations, and atypical cases to be found in the empirical world, we have to develop, test, and refine theoretical, conceptual, and definitional tools.

KEY POINTS

- People, even when confronted with the same kind of deprivation, react very differently.
- Not absolute but relative deprivation is the main source for people to resort to collective protest.

The concept of social movement

Around the mid-nineteenth century, the term 'social movement' was used in two ways. First, it referred to fundamental changes *of* society, for example the passage from feudalism to capitalism. Second, a social movement was understood as a collective actor, and especially a class actor *in* society.

In the following decades, the second meaning became dominant, though it was no longer bound to a specific collective actor, notably the socialist/communist movement. Rather, it referred to a variety of groupings engaged, for example, in abolishing slavery, enhancing women's rights, securing peace, or promoting nationalism and xenophobia.

Only in the second half of the twentieth century was the term 'social movement' more clearly delineated and thereby separated from diffuse public moods and discourses on the one hand and, on the other hand, more specific collective phenomena such as non-governmental organizations (NGOs) or political campaigns limited in scope and time. According to a gradually emerging scholarly consensus (see Diani 1992; Rucht 1994; Johnston 2014), a social movement can be defined by four constitutive elements. It is (i) a mobilized network of groups and organizations; (ii) resting on a sense of collective identity; that (iii) aims to bring about or resist fundamental changes of society; (iv) by using primarily techniques of public and collective protest. Each of these constituents would require further explanation. Referring only to the first constituent, obviously a social movement may incorporate large and formal organizations. However, as a whole, it is neither an organization with a clearly defined membership, nor does it have a centre that would be able to control and command the heterogeneous nodes of the movement's network.

In a historical perspective, one can argue that social movements are a modern phenomenon. In previous centuries back to ancient Greece and Rome, there were definite upheavals, such as the slavery rebellions. Further, in medieval times, we find many examples of peasant wars and riots and insurrections of city dwellers. These activities, however, were basically meant to re-install a natural or divine order that, in the eyes of the insurgents, was violated by power holders. In that sense, insurrection was a push back to a 'given' order. By contrast, the idea of 'making history' by creating a new social order according to human will and imagination is a modern concept closely related to the era of the Enlightenment. Against this backdrop, one should refrain from applying the concept of social movements to all kinds of contentious struggles in history. Instead, social movements are inherently bound to the idea of creating society—an idea that was only fully developed and radically put forward from the eighteenth century onwards.

While, according to this concept, social movements' ultimate reference point is society at large, there are also movements acting in a more specific terrain, which thus may be called political, cultural, or religious movements. In the real world, however, clear lines rarely exist between these kinds of movements. For example, a movement that strives for a fundamental change of society, including its power structures and economic base, can hardly avoid engaging in conflicts with political decision-makers. Taking this aspect into account, some scholars have promoted the term of 'socio-political movement' (Jenkins 1981), instead of separating political from social movements.

Related to, and partly overlapping with, the concept of social movement are a few other notions such as riots, rebellions, revolutions and, more recently, contentious politics. The latter term, broadly referring to collective political struggle, is more inclusive than social movements. It is defined as:

> episodic, public, collective interaction among makers of claims and their objects when (a) at least one government is a claimant, an object of claims, or a party to the claims and (b) the claim would, if realised, affect the interests of at least one of the claimants.
>
> McAdam et al. (2001: 5)

The problem with this concept is twofold: first, the unit of analysis is not an actor, but an interaction. So, it does not answer the question on how to name and conceptualize 'the makers of claims' who are challenging the government. Second, the definition of contentious politics is bound to the government as one of at least two conflict parties. While this applies to many empirical cases, it is not always so. Consider, for example, a labour conflict in which the government deliberately remains neutral. These reflections suggest not to abandon the concept of social movements, though it is obvious that such an actor can only be understood in relation to—and that is in series of interactions with—a number of reference groups, of which state actors may be one.

KEY POINTS

- Unlike rebellions and insurrections that can be traced back to the ancient world, social movements are a phenomenon of modernity.
- Social movements can be defined by four constitutive elements: network structure, collective identity, the aim to change society (or resist such a change), and collective and public protest.

Theories and approaches

Apart from historians who have described contentious acts occurring from the era of ancient Greece and Rome throughout medieval times to recent history, the study of social movements began with the rise of social sciences in the nineteenth century and, more specifically, the growth of the socialist labour movement that contemporary writers such as Lorenz von Stein and Karl Marx considered as *the* movement of their times. While Marx was fully aware of the structural and organizational underpinnings of social movements (e.g. by describing the difficulties of dispersed French farmers to act collectively; see Marx 1852), the mass of psychologists around the turn of the twentieth century focused on the seemingly irrational behaviour of crowds that are driven and orchestrated by agitators, who are evoking sentiments and instrumentalize the masses. The background of this crude version of mass psychology was clearly the bourgoisie's fear of a revolutionary overturn by the 'mob'.

Traces of simplistic mass psychology, though less explicitly prejudiced, also can be found in later decades in assumptions that scholars, in retrospect, called 'contagion theories' (Marx and Wood 1975). However, other more sophisticated and more empirically grounded theories of collective behaviour and, more specifically, social movements eventually gained ground. Geographically, the gravity centre of social movement studies shifted from Europe to the US, and there it was mainly hosted in sociology.

Important leaps towards genuine sociological approaches were made by representatives of the Chicago School in the early decades of the twentieth century. Another and somewhat later strand of theorizing about collective behaviour (including social movements) relied on the basic assumptions of symbolic interactionism, most prominently represented by Herbert Blumer (1939). A third strand, strongly influenced by the general sociology of Talcott Parsons, was Neil Smelser's structural-functionalist interpretation of social movements. He advanced a 'value-added model' based on several explanatory layers accounting for the emergence, rise, and persistence of collective behaviour and, most notably, social movements (Smelser 1962).

In the 1970s and 1980s, two additional approaches became prominent and persisted until the present. First, mainly based on the writings of Mayer Zald and John McCarthy, the resource mobilization approach took shape (McCarthy and Zald 1977). It was strongly influenced by studies in economic sociology. The central tenet of this approach is that deprivations are abundant, but do not necessarily produce social movements. The latter only come into existence when 'movement entrepreneurs' engage in collecting resources (such as money, time devoted by volunteers, expertise), building organizations and acting strategically in interplays with allies and opponents. Accordingly, 'social movement organizations' and 'social movement industries' became central units of analysis. In part, the success of this approach was its deliberate juxtaposition against what was perceived as old and outdated theories associated with mass psychology and the 'irrational' base of collective behaviour, thereby neglecting or bracketing not only symbolic interactionist and structural-functionalist approaches, but also analysts such as Rudolf Heberle, who immigrated from Nazi Germany to the US. With his deep knowledge of the German labour movement, he was fully aware of the structural and organizational underpinnings of social movements (Heberle 1951).

A second strand of theorizing gaining prominence parallel to resource mobilization was associated with the terms 'political process' and 'political opportunity structure'. These concepts are not identical, but overlap and complement each other. The political process approach as put forward mainly by Doug McAdam (1982) and Hanspeter Kriesi (2004) stresses the dynamics of interaction between social movements and their environment. This perspective also sheds light on what earlier theorists, though mainly in mechanistic ways, have coined (natural) social movement life cycles. In the more empirical grounded lens of the political process approach, the dynamics of social movement are not mainly driven by an internally anchored developmental sequence, but rather by external conditions including the position, resources, and strategies of movements' opponents.

Kriesi (2004: 70) was among those who conceptualized the impact of context factors on the strategies of collective political actors, as can be seen in Figure 16.1. His model is composed of two blocks of relatively stable structures (general structures and configuration of political actors) that, mediated by an interaction context, account for the strategies of different kinds of political actors, including social movements. However, an answer to the question which factors are likely to produce, for example, a moderate or a radical strategy of social movements is not provided; it would require a further specification of this general model, including the prevailing strategies of the movement's opponents.

The political opportunity structure approach, initially mainly conceptualized by Sidney Tarrow (1983) and later expanded and refined by others, including Herbert Kitschelt (1986), Hanspeter Kriesi (1991), and Dieter Rucht (1994), focuses on enabling and restricting structural political conditions for the emergence and further development of social movements. Among such factors are, for example, the degree of openness or closeness of the political system to challengers, the unity or division of political elites with regard to a movement's cause, the availability of allies that might support a movement, and the capacity of a political system to repress a social movement. With the emphasis on political opportunities that initially were studied by comparing mobilization and protest across US cities (Eisinger 1973), the comparative lens was soon widened to engage in cross-national comparison of specific movements

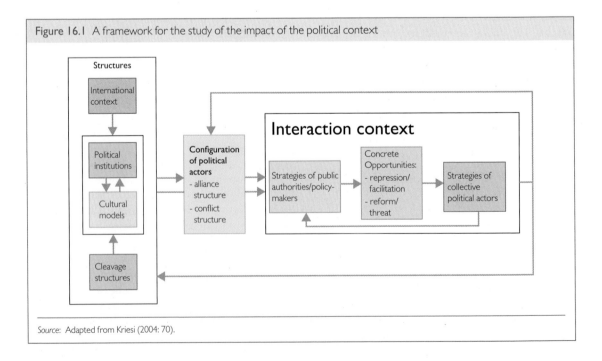

Figure 16.1 A framework for the study of the impact of the political context

Source: Adapted from Kriesi (2004: 70).

(such as anti-nuclear movements, peace movements, and women's movements) or of broader social movement families (such as the so-called new social movements surging in the 1970s and '80s).

A third prominent approach in social movement studies, again originating in the US, was centred around the category of framing. It was inspired by symbolic interactionism and social constructivism and gained prominence with the writings of David Snow and his collaborators (1986) and William A. Gamson (1992). Frames are communicative devices that give a specific meaning to a situation or process. In social movement research, framing denotes a discursive strategy that is geared to sensitize and activate followers and bystanders. According to Snow and Benford (1988), comprehensive framing serves three goals: first, it delivers an interpretation of a problem and its causes and culprits (diagnostic framing); second, it suggests how the problem might unfold in the future and what could be done to mitigate or solve the problem at stake (prognostic framing); third, it provides reasons and motives to engage and become committed (motivational framing). In a somewhat different take, Gamson (1992) has identified three kinds of frames, which he coined agency, injustice, and identity frames.

Frames may be condensed to short utterances or key words that evoke a specific sentiment or situation (e.g., 'abortion is Holocaust') but also can consist of a more elaborated ideological package (e.g. neo-colonialism or right-wing populism). Over time, the concept of framing has become fairly sophisticated by denoting, for example, broad master frames that encompass a variety of more specific frames, and identifying processes of frame bridging, frame extension, frame amplification, etc. (Benford and Snow 2000).

A fourth approach centres on the concept and role of collective identity. Though time and again the creation and maintenance of collective identity has been stressed as a constitutive element of social movement groups and broader social movements, it has remained a fuzzy and underspecified concept, often equated with the existence of a 'we-feeling'. Most proponents of this approach agree on the assumption that collective identity is neither necessarily a pre-existing condition for starting collective action, nor is it a stable property of an existing movement (Melucci 1995; Polletta 2001). Rather, it is a social construction that is constantly negotiated and re-shaped in sequences of interactions and the interplay of self-images and external perceptions and ascriptions. More recently, the concept of collective identity has been linked to the role of emotions, culture, symbols, storytelling, and narratives (Darnovsky et al. 1995; Jasper and Goodwin

1999; Polletta 2006; Jasper 2011, 2014) in reaction to a perceived overemphasis on structural dimensions and rationality in social movement activity.

Beyond those aforementioned approaches that stress the organizational and strategic rationality of social movements, rational choice theory anchored in methodological individualism is also holding its place in social movement studies. In this perspective, the focus is on the individual and his/her reasoning about the costs and benefits in participating in collective action. Representatives of this strand of research, among them Mancur Olson (1965), Edward Muller (1979), and Karl-Dieter Opp (1989), assume that what is considered as collective behaviour is just an aggregate of individuals' decisions and behaviours. According to this theory, only individuals, but not groups and organizations, can act. More recently, still maintaining the central premises of rational choice theory, Opp (2009) has made a synthetic effort by integrating aspects of resource mobilization, opportunity structure, framing, and identity into the framework of rational choice theory. However, thus far this approach has garnered little resonance in the wider community of social movement studies.

When overviewing the past few decades, it becomes clear that most approaches in social movement studies have concentrated on middle-range theories and shed light on specific aspects of movement activity at the neglect of more encompassing and comprehensive theories that (i) interlink more specific aspects such as ideology, organization, strategy, and tactics; and (ii) highlight the broader societal conditions and effects of social movements.

KEY POINTS

- In the nineteenth century, the term 'social movement' referred to both developments *of* society and collective actors *in* society.

- At the turn to the twentieth century, crude and prejudiced mass psychology became a dominant approach to explain collective behaviour.

- Social movement studies in the first half of the twentieth century were strongly influenced by the Chicago School sociologists, remnants of mass psychology, and symbolic interactionism.

- In the second half of the twentieth century, several middle-range approaches focusing on more specific aspects of social movements were proposed, among them resource mobilization, rational choice theories, political opportunity structures and political process, framing, collective identity, and the role of culture, emotions, and narratives.

Empirical patterns and profiles of social movements

As argued above in 'The concept of social movement', strictly defined social movements did not take shape before modern times, though probably during a longer period than Charles Tilly has assumed by pointing to the watershed from the eighteenth to the nineteenth centuries (Tilly 1986). Among the broader background processes spurring and shaping early social movements were the formation of nation-states and national parliaments, industrialization, urbanization, increasing spread and levels of education, and citizens' growing desire to partake in public discourses and matters of politics.

The visible side of social movements

The twentieth century and present times are marked by a great variety of social and political movements, ranging from the far left to the far right, mobilizing particular constituencies such as farmers, workers, students, and women, but also promoting causes such as disarmament, peace, human rights, and environmental protection, which are neither necessarily addressing a particular social group nor limited to national borders. Within the framework of broader movements, one can identify different cycles or waves (Tarrow 1989; Koopmans 2004). Also, broader and long-lasting movements typically engage in more specific campaigns, for instance focusing on the ban of nuclear weapons or land mines, the liberalization of abortion, the rescue of particular species, on debt relief for poor countries, taxation of financial transactions in stock markets, or the prevention of climate change.

Over time, the range of such issues has become wider and more variegated. Also, the kind of people active in social and political movements has broadened, so that not only deprived groups but also privileged groups become mobilized. In western democracies, generally people from the well-educated middle-class are most active in social movements (Dalton 2019). They tend to be better informed on political and other issues, are more articulate, and have more resources than lower classes, let alone the most deprived social groups including the poor, unemployed, and marginalized (Piven and Cloward 1979). Still, as in the past, absolute deprivation, for example exploding food prices in countries of the Southern globe, may also be a driving cause for collective protest (Gailus 2005; Walton and Seddon 2008). The case of contemporary Venezuela shows that dissatisfaction with mate-rial living conditions can also serve as a starting point for a popular movement that broadens its critique and eventually seeks to overcome the given political regime (see e.g. Corrales and Penfold 2011).

Parallel to the broadening of issues and groups involved in social movements, also the forms of action have become more variegated. These range from institutionalized forms of participation (e.g. referenda, litigation, voting for protest parties) to peaceful rallies and gatherings, to disruptive actions of civil disobedience, to physical destruction, rioting, and killing. Some elementary forms of collective protest (e.g. collection of signatures, rallies, marches and strikes) have remained basically unchanged, though their very specific designs vary over time. Other forms, for example sit-ins, theoretically backed acts of civil disobedience, or human chains spanning across large distances, were introduced in the twentieth century. Further, new technologies allow for variations of old forms of collective protest or stimulate new forms of action. Consider, for example, politically motivated cyber activism, the beaming of slogans on facades of buildings, and theatre-like performances orchestrated by directives transmitted to the earphones of the activists.

Whereas in earlier times large segments of collective protest were more spontaneous and localized, the mediation of protest via modern mass media, especially television (Gitlin 1980) and most lately internet-based means of communication (Bennett and Segerberg 2013), have spurred more professional and more sophisticated ways of protest geared to reach and attract large, if not potentially global, audiences (Karpf 2012; Cammaerts et al. 2013; Fahlenbrach et al. 2014). Apparently, issue cycles have become shorter; both mobilization and demobilization processes have accelerated. Accordingly, we witness processes of issue-related and tactical diffusion and mobilization that rapidly spread from one place to another, thereby often transcending national and cultural borders, as could be observed in the student rebellions of the 1960s, the Arab Spring, the Occupy movement in western countries and, most recently, in the Fridays of Future movement initiated by pupils and students.

Especially in these more recent mobilizations, net-based means of communication played a crucial role so that some observers claimed the existence of Facebook revolutions, usually without also investigating the role of 'real' networks formed by neighbourhoods, trade unions, religious congregations, etc. in protest mobilization. Doubtless, the use of digital media is on the rise. This, however, does not imply a decline of street protest. To the contrary, it seems that, on average, the frequency of protest acts and the number of mobilized people, though undergoing significant ups and downs in shorter periods, has generally increased. This is at least indicated by the official data on permitting protest by police and other authorities in a number of countries, including Germany. Protest event data based on newspaper reports may not adequately capture the actual increase of protest because the carrying capacity of newspapers basically remains unchanged. As a consequence, newspapers, radio, and television may become more selective in covering protest. To this also contributes the fact that protests, unless they are spectacular in terms of size and/or form, are more and more perceived as a 'normal' and 'rational' way of conducting interest politics. This latter aspect also has implications for the interaction between protesters and police, at least in liberal-representative democracies (della Porta and Reiter 1998). While in previous times, protest was often perceived as mob activity, disturbing the public order and accordingly repressed by police, today the police, though occasionally running out of control and stretching or violating legal boundaries, may also act as a neutral force, or even a force engaged in protection instead of repression of protesters. Such patterns,

however, are mainly to be found in contemporary representative-liberal countries. In many other cases, the police are a conflict party that does not shy away from killing even peaceful protesters in the name of 'internal security' and 'law and order', as occurred, for example, in Egypt in 2013, Burma in 2015, and Sudan in 2019.

To the extent that social movements engage in conflicts with opponents, try to win allies, and seek attention and possibly support from bystanders and large audiences, they can only be understood in their interplay with such reference groups. Apart from relatively few cases of spontaneous outbursts, social movements are engaged in a game that, depending on the issue and the circumstances, is sometimes more of a discursive struggle, but at other times more of a power struggle relying on the 'power of numbers' (DeNardo 1985), physical attack, and/or subversive tactics. Therefore, the strengths and weaknesses of social movements have to be evaluated not only in relation to enabling or restricting structural opportunities but also in relation to the capacities and strategies of movements' opponents, be they state authorities, economic and other interest groups, or fully fledged counter-movements (see Figure 16.2).

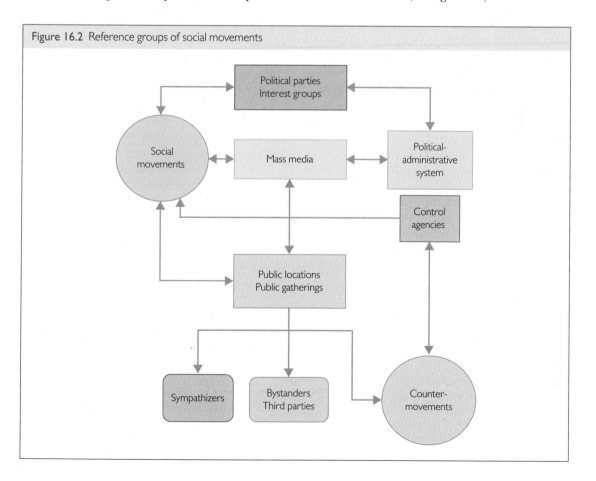

Figure 16.2 Reference groups of social movements

Unfortunately, this complex interplay is often and wrongly reduced to bipolar conflict, in which the state is the key reference point. While this is true for many conflicts, and especially so in authoritarian states, in many other cases it is crucial to take into account the role of third parties, e.g. mass media, courts, brokers and mediators (Rucht 2004). On the rhetorical level, the attack against the opponent is clearly to the fore in movement struggles. However, a closer look shows that social movements spend much energy in winning public attention and support which, in the long run may be decisive for the final outcome of a conflict. After all, in democratic systems political parties, and especially incumbent and potential office-holders, tend to respond in sensitive ways to social movements when reckoning that the latters' activities will have an impact on voting behaviour that, in turn, is decisive for the political fate of established political forces. Accordingly, while starting or remaining in a challenger position, social movements may also complement their activities by creating links and allying with interest groups and/or political parties. Indeed, quite a number of both traditional and more recent political parties are offspring of social movements, as the cases of labour parties, populist parties, and green parties show (Kitschelt 2006). As a rule, however, movement parties are transitionary phenomena, though they seek to keep their movement image associated with energy, dynamics, and progress. In the long run, however, the logics and imperatives of movement politics are quite different from those of party politics. The latter, to mention just one aspect, are embedded in a highly institutionalized game in which direct competition with other parties is key. When it comes to elections, the win of one side is a loss for the others. By contrast, social movements that are thematically or ideologically akin can mutually strengthen each other and easily carry out joint campaigns. Also, social movements are more flexible in their organizational structure and do not depend on formal rules of delegation and decision-making as prescribed by both national laws and party-specific statutes.

The internal life of social movements

Most mass media, and therefore the wider public, focus on social movements' public appearances and devices, including protest activities, speeches, brochures, and flyers. However, the internal life of social movements remains in the dark (della Porta and Rucht 2013). This is why movements are often equated with their public performances, whereas the extent, patterns, and significance of their shadow life is neglected. For most social movement groups, public protest is a crucial, but relatively rare and short, activity. Nevertheless, protest tends to require considerably time and energy before, and sometimes even after the event: collecting information about the issue at stake; mobilizing financial resources; co-ordinating with other protest groups; drafting flyers; designing posters and banners; motivating potential participants; solving conflicts with training organisers and key activists; selecting speakers; informing journalists; giving interviews after the event; and evaluating the course of action and press coverage to improve further activities (Rucht 2018). In extraordinary cases, specific preparatory groups are created and, as in the case of protests against the International Monetary Fund (IMF) and the World Bank meeting in Berlin in 1988, began to work almost two years before the actual protest took place (Gerhards and Rucht 1992; Gerhards 1993). Beyond activities that are directly or indirectly related to protest, social movement groups also socialize outside public appearances. For example, they invite foreign visitors who are committed to the same cause; celebrate birthdays; sing at a campfire, commemorate a deceased founding member, etc.

Protest acts are important occasions for strengthening collective identity, but the same applies to the less spectacular and more mundane group activities. Scholars have shown that social movements can survive over lengthy periods without or with only low-profile public appearances. Spurred by a trigger event or a shift in public mood, such 'movements in abeyance' (Taylor 1989) may become quickly re-activated, sometimes leading to the false image of the birth of a 'new' movement.

There is never one and only one image of a movement. Different external reference groups have different perceptions, and so also do various tendencies and factions within the movement. These perceptions are constantly compared and negotiated. Moreover, movements sometimes change quickly over time. They expand or shrink, they may split into several parts but re-unite after a while, they may cease to exist because of a full success, or gradually fade away because of a lack of success. All this leads to the observation of movements as 'moving targets' (Tarrow 1991) that, when compared to established political parties or highly formalized interest groups, are more difficult to study and to understand. For example, external observers often mistake movements as compact entities and search or, via ongoing contacts, even create leaders and spokespeople whose salient role, in some cases, is not acknowledged and embraced by the rank-and-file.

Social movements in a comparative perspective

Systematic comparison of social movements across theme, time, and place only began in the twentieth century. Before, the comparative study of social movements, mostly focusing on few, if not just two cases, was mainly undertaken by historians. In the second half of the twentieth century, comparative work became more refined, with the expansion of empirically grounded social science research including the use of quantitative methods, most notably standardized questionnaires, protest event analysis, and claims analysis (Klandermans and Staggenborg 2002).

In a thematic perspective, students of social movements have compared various kinds of movements, for example movements of affluence versus movements of crisis (Kerbo 1982), movements of the extreme left versus movements of the extreme right; decentralized grassroots movements versus more formally structured movements, etc. As a rule, these comparisons were conducted in an illustrative manner, rather than in a theoretically informed and rigorous empirical investigation.

In a cross-time perspective, scholars usually focused on one kind of movement in different periods, for example discerning different types of historically relevant movements (Turner 1969; Touraine 1974; Raschke 1985: 82). Inspired by these typologies, one can discern major societal formations from the era of the Enlightenment to present times and attribute to each formation a dominant movement plus a set of secondary movements (see Table 16.1).

Obviously, this dichotomy of old and new social movements builds on ideal types that only partially reflect empirical reality. The world of the old movements, even when reduced to the prototypical branch of socialist/communist labour movement, is by far more complex and heterogeneous than sketched in this typology. The traditional labour movement reached well beyond the sphere of production (e.g. by including leisure time activities such as sports and music); it mobilized not only workers but also intellectuals and artists; it comprised non-Marxist ideological strands (e.g. varieties of anarchism); it incorporated informal networks (the left-wing branch of the Youth Movement in the early twentieth century) and reform-oriented political strategies (the so-called reformist tendency within the broader labour movement). Similar arguments about a more complex reality can be raised with regard to the new social movements. Moreover, scholars argued that contrasting the old and new movements is misleading because some of the stated differences may not be inherent to these types, but rather represent different stages. According to Calhoun (1993), the typified image of the old movements reflects a phase of maturity, while the image of the new movements reflects a phase of infancy. He argues that characteristics ascribed to the new movements can be found in the early days of the old movements.

Nevertheless, contrasting old and new movements almost intuitively made sense, especially in a number of West European countries. This contrast was stressed by many activists and observers in Europe. In the US, however, this distinction was met with more reservation (Pichardo 1997) because of more continuities in the long-term evolution of the movement sector, as the example of the women's movement shows. Movement scholars also disagreed about where to place the student movement of the 1960s. While some attribute the student movement to the new social movements, to me it represents rather a bridge between the old and the new movements. In some respects, for example in its appraisal of Marxist thoughts and its revolutionary zeal, the student movement can be seen as a continuation of the old movements. In other respects, for example its social composition and its provocative protest tactics, the student movement paved the way for the subsequent new social movements.

Apart from attributing different types of movements to different eras, scholars have also identified

Table 16.1 Societal formations and related kinds of movements

Societal formation	Dominant kind of movement	Exemplary secondary movements
Early liberal capitalism	Civic movement	Peasant movements
Liberal capitalism	Workers' movement	Anti-slavery movement
		National movements
		Agrarian populism
		Temperance movement
Organized capitalism	Workers' movement	Women's movements
		Peace movements
		Life reform movements
		Fascist movements
		Anti-colonial movements
		Civil rights movements
Neo-liberal capitalism	New social movements	Movements on issues of peace and disarmament, human rights, women, gay and lesbian issues, environmental protection, nuclear power, animal rights, taxation, neo-colonialism, poverty, etc.
		Global justice movements
		Occupy movement
		Right-populist movements
		Neo-fascist movements

> **ZOOM-IN 16.1**

Differences between so-called 'old' and 'new' social movements

Starting in the late 1970s, especially European social movement scholars identified 'new social movements' and set them apart from 'old' movements (e.g. Melucci 1980; see also Box 16.1). This distinction is probably inspired by, but not identical to, the earlier juxtaposition of the Old Left versus the New Left. 'Old' social movements were not understood as the ideologically diverse range of quite different leftist movements of the past, but as a simplified image of the traditional socialist/communist labour movement that was set in contrast to the 'new' social movements (in plural!). In a typological rather than an empirical perspective, differences between these kinds of movements can be identified along various dimensions.

The old movements' key concerns were related to the sphere of economic production (e.g. control of the means of production, wages, working hours, lay offs, unemployment). The new movements' core concerns were related to the sphere of reproduction and aspects of quality of life (e.g. citizen participation, education, social services, urban problems, environmental problems, health, etc.).

In terms of ideological sources, the old movements drew heavily on classical writers, of which Marx, Engels, Lenin, and Luxemburg were most important. For the new movements, these classics played only a marginal role. Their ideological base was less consistent, more variegated and heterogeneous, comprising a broad range of mainly contemporary theorists from various disciplines, among them, for example, Paolo Freire, Ivan Illich, and André Gorz.

With regard to the social carriers, the workers and more specifically blue collar workers were seen as the core of the old movement, while the well-educated middle class, and specifically those working in the human service sectors (teachers, medical doctors, social workers, journalists, lawyers, etc.) were identified as the core constituency of the new movements.

Considering the organizational structure, the backbone of the typical old movements consists of firmly and hierarchically structured organizations (labour unions, left-wing parties, consumer co-operatives, etc.) with a clear distinction between 'leaders' and 'followers'. By contrast, the infrastructural basis of the new movements was seen as more informal and decentralized, consisting of a loose network of autonomous and often locally based groups that form a grassroots structure. Organizational discipline in old movements was set in contrast to the free and contingent commitment of individuals in various new movements.

With regard to strategy and tactics, the old movements were characterized by a revolutionary zeal to overcome capitalism, while the new movements were associated with a strategy of moderate or radical reform. The typical tactical weapon of the old movements was the strike and, for their most radical tendencies, violent action. The new movements incorporated a broader action repertoire, including newly established institutional channels of influence (e.g. procedural complaints, litigation, referenda), new forms of protests (e.g. human chains, protest camps), fun elements in the context of protest (e.g. street theatre), and provocative and subversive forms of dissidence (e.g. faked letters, allegedly distributed by public authorities).

various waves of a distinct moment, for example three or four waves of the women's movement (Evans and Chamberlain 2015) in a given country or a set of countries. The cross-time perspective was also useful to trace the development of a given movement from its start, to prime time activities, to decay and disappearance. While in the first half of the twentieth century, 'natural life cycle' models were proposed, subsequent and more empirically based work showed more variegated developmental patterns, thereby relativizing, or even rejecting, the idea of a typical evolutionary pattern according to which movements start completely unstructured and cease to exist with their institutionalization. While some movements (e.g. labour movements in Scandinavian countries) largely fit such a pattern, others (e.g. the civil rights movement in the US) incorporated into their emerging framework a host of pre-existing organizations, of which religious congregations were most important (Morris 1986). It also occurs that movements having become quite structured, formalized, and immobile over time are re-vitalized and made more flexible due to the critical aspirations of a new generation of activists, as exemplified by some smaller trade unions in the US and in France.

Cross-national comparison of specific movement campaigns (e.g. against the deployment of cruise missiles), of distinct movements (e.g. women's movements, environmental movements, anti-nuclear movements, peace movements, populist movements) or broader movement families (e.g. new social movements; Kriesi et al. 1995) were more numerous than the aforementioned kinds of comparisons. Cross-national work is especially instructive when it comes to matters that are mostly or exclusively regulated by national bodies of decision-making so that cross-country comparison makes sense. This applies to laws on abortion, social security, and education, to mention just three examples. In these cases, movements tend to exhibit a country-specific profile and dynamics that is strongly influenced by the kind and timing of politi-

cal decision-making, as well as channels of access to decision-makers and other factors of the political and discursive opportunity structure. This has been shown, for example, in much detail for the debate over abortion (Ferree et al. 2002).

Also, nation-specific rules and styles of protest policing (della Porta and Reiter 1998) can impact on the protest repertoire and produce strikingly different general levels of conflict, as a comparison between, say, Turkey and Norway might show. Levels of conflict, confrontation, and violence are not a direct expression of objectively given degrees of injustice and deprivation. Rather, they are influenced by a broad set of intervening factors, of which protest policing and channels of expressing dissent (via protest parties, referenda, litigation, mass media) are telling examples.

In addition, cross-national comparison has shown that the degree of social movement mobilization and the average intensity of conflicts is influenced by the kind of political regime. On the one hand, by their very nature repressive regimes that manage to control public discourse and public performances tend to produce low numbers and often subtle forms of protest, with some remarkable exceptions such as China. Only when repressive systems are weakened for economic and/or political reasons do they tend to be shaken, and eventually overcome, by an eruption of peaceful or violent protests (Goodwin 2001), as shown by the examples of the bloody revolutions in the Czarist Russia in 1917 and the Czechoslovakian velvet revolution in 1989, respectively. On the other hand, democratic systems that are very open and responsive to critique by the citizenry are also likely to have both low numbers and low intensities of protest, as exemplified by Scandinavian countries. By contrast, countries whose regimes are semi-open to dissenters tend to have more protest events and more protest participants, as indicated by a number of West European countries. Nevertheless, comparative protest event analysis based on newspaper reports shows that levels of participation differ considerably,

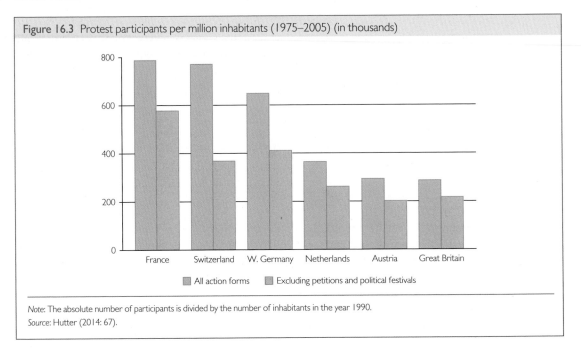

Figure 16.3 Protest participants per million inhabitants (1975–2005) (in thousands)

□ All action forms   □ Excluding petitions and political festivals

Note: The absolute number of participants is divided by the number of inhabitants in the year 1990.
Source: Hutter (2014: 67).

even within this group of countries, with France on top and Austria and the UK at the end (see Figure 16.3). Protest event data, though not available for more recent periods, also suggest that the degree of radicalness differs within the group of West European countries. Considering four countries in the period from 1975 to 1989, Kriesi et al. (1995: 50) found France to exhibit by far the greatest proportion of violent protests out of all protests (31.2 per cent), followed by Germany (15.2 per cent), Switzerland (12.2 per cent), and the Netherlands (11.1 per cent). Considering the past few years, including the activities of the French Yellow Vest Movement (starting in November 2018), which attacked the government's economic and social policies, there is little doubt that a considerable share of French protesters has maintained its propensity to violent action. One reason for this may be the greater acceptance of disruptive action against state authorities among the French population; another possible reason is the relative absence of institutionalized channels to express dissent. Accordingly, the situation in France resembles a steam boiler in which, up to a critical point, the heat and pressure increases without visible reaction, but then results in an explosion, rather than a channelled flow of energy. Explosions of violent protests, very likely fuelled by a lack of challengers' access to the system of decision-making and an absence of institutionalized settings for channelling and moderating conflict, can also be observed in a number of African countries that time and again are shaken by violent confrontations of rivalling political and ethnic groups.

Remarkable differences can also be found when comparing the performative style of public protest, including bodily movements, outfit, use of icons and language. South Korean worker protests typically provide the image of disciplined, serious, and semi-uniformed participants sitting on the ground, wearing identical headbands and being engaged in orchestrated moves, for example by raising their fists. In several ways, the bulk of South African protests look just the opposite. Protesters are wearing colourful clothes and are moving their extremities in more individual ways. When marching, they tend to wholeheartedly singing and even dance, thereby providing an image of joy, rather than threat. Of course, we also find in both countries other images and performances. Still, it is hard to imagine the kind of dancing protesters in the streets of Seoul.

With the ongoing and even accelerating processes of globalization and related negative side effects, a growing part of social movement activities is devoted to transnational, if not global problems, target groups and constituencies. 'Activists beyond borders', to cite the title of Keck and Sikkinks's (1998a) influential study, are by no means a new phenomenon, as the examples of the anti-slavery movement, the women's movement, and the peace movement show. However, their number and significance has grown in the past few decades. Political activists are protesting at the occasion of international conferences and summits of political and economic leaders; transnational groups such as amnesty international, Greenpeace, Friends of the Earth and Doctors without Borders have been formed and dispose on considerable amounts of financial resources, personnel, and expertise; broader and truly transnational social movements such as the global justice movements have emerged and continue to exist. At their prime time in the early 2000s, the annual global social forums brought together hundreds of thousands of participants (Smith et al. 2011).

While the global justice movements have experienced a gradual decline in the past few years, other transnational movement groups and campaigns have taken off, of which some (e.g. the Occupy movement), were only short-lived. Whether or not this also applies to the transnational Fridays for Future movement that began in late 2018 and experienced a spectacular rise in the first half of 2019 still remains to be seen.

The #Me Too movement fighting sexual harassment and sexual assault is another example of a genuine transnational movement. Though it is backed by the broader and internationally oriented feminist movement, it is an issue-driven activity of a new feminist generation. Supported by a number of celebrities, Me Too heavily relies on web-based communication, but also aptly deals with established mass media by scandalizing cases of sexual abuse committed by prominent figures, but also as a widespread male practice in daily life.

Interestingly, sometimes locally bound protests are of a much greater significance than their limited territorial scope would suggest. Consider, for example, the massive protest waves in Hong Kong. The wave in 2014, sometimes dubbed as the Umbrella Movement, was triggered by plans of the National People's Congress to pre-screen and preselect the candidates for the Chief Executive of Hong Kong. Faced with the government's intransigence, the movement soon faded away. The recent protest wave in 2019/2020 is broader and more enduring. Its initial focus was to fight the extradition bill proposed by Hong Kong's Security Council. Confronted with fierce opposition, including a series of mass protests, but also acts of violence, the local government first postponed and then withdrew the proposal. But protesters went on and broadened their claims by raising fundamental issues of democratic rights and political participation. Though these protests were challenging the local government, they first indirectly and then more explicitly addressed the leadership of the People's Republic of China. From the latter's perspective, loosening grip on Hong Kong and granting concessions may have the unintended consequence of encouraging protesters and dissidents also in mainland China.

From these scattered observations, we can conclude that context matters in many respects. The same kind of problem, say lay-offs because of the closure of a factory, are likely to produce strikingly different reactions, ranging from apathy to peaceful marches, to civil disobedience, to violent protest. As Charles Tilly has noted, the available repertoires of contention are:

a limited set of routines that are learned, shared and acted through a relatively deliberate process of choice. Repertoires are learned cultural creations, but they do not descend from abstract philosophy or take shape as a result of political propaganda; they emerge from struggle.

Tilly (1995: 26)

Accordingly, in order to understand why, when, and how social movements act and react, it is indispensable to have a look into the past as a source of collective experiences, memories, and narratives from which social movements as well as their opponents and adversaries draw their lessons.

KEY POINTS

- Systematic comparison across issues, time, and place is arguably the most promising way to identify patterns and regularities in social movements' origins, structures, dynamics, and outcomes.

- Comparative research has shown that there is no universal 'natural life cycle' of social movements.

- Numbers of protests and protesters tend to be higher in semi-open political systems when compared to both very closed and very open political systems.

- Accelerating processes of transnationalization and globalization are also reflected in social movement sectors. Nevertheless, national context factors still remain key in influencing the conditions and profile of social movements.

Functions and effects of social movements

Depending on their ambitions, capacities, and external conditions (including the power of counterforces), social movements may play different roles and have different functions and effects in a given historical constellation. Broadly speaking, one can identify five basic roles or functions.

First, movements can be rightly or wrongly perceived as troublemakers who create turmoil and disorder, spur anxieties, and polarize society so that they effectively play a destructive role. As a rule, movements' fiercest opponents eagerly draw such a picture in order to undermine the movement's unity, credibility, and public support. As mentioned above in 'Social movements in a comparative perspective', this was the prevailing attitude of the established classes when facing the socialist labour movement in many European countries. On the other hand, the perception of a social movement as a destructive force may be fully justified when, for example, a specific ethnic or religious group forcefully seizes power and suppresses other groups within the population so that deep divisions are created and aggravated. In the end, sharp cleavages may even result in civil war, as the bloody events in Rwanda in 1994 have shown.

Second, social movements can serve as indicators of, and even alarms for problems in society that thus far were denied or underestimated, and therefore unsolved. Though often dramatized by concerned groups, such problems can have an empirical base, and should be taken into account in order to avoid an aggravation of the problem and/or conflict escalation. Even in democratic states with actual freedom of press, some problems may remain under the radar of media's attention unless deprived groups or their attentive advocates raise their voices. One example is the practise of abortion that, when legally interdicted, was done in 'backyards', with considerable health risks for concerned women. Only when women and their allies collectively raised their voices did the scope and nature of the problem become visible. Another example of an initially neglected problem is the gradual decay of infrastructures in rural France that gave rise to the so-called yellow vest movement in Winter 2018/19. Triggered by the government's plan to increase taxes for fuel, a mass movement brought a plethora of grievances of the lower classes in rural France to the fore. This movement was met with sympathy by large parts of the French population and forced the government to make both symbolic and substantial concessions.

Third, social movements are not necessarily restricted to roles of refusers and rejecters. Instead, they may also serve as proponents of new and constructive ideas that help to overcome stalemate, initiate reforms thus far blocked by power holders, and/or mitigate, or even solve, evident problems. Consider, for example, the movement against nuclear energy production. In its initial phase, its common denominator was just saying no to nuclear power, often combined with a NIMBY (not in my backyard) position. In later periods, this movement became a strong advocate of renewable energy production. Individuals and small groups with technical expertise were among the first to develop and promote technologies based on wind, solar, and other non-fossil sources for electricity production. Also, this movement became a driver for various means and measures to reduce energy consumption.

Fourth, social movements are engaging in specific and often highly complex policy matters, but may also serve as more general critics and challengers of power holders and other privileged groups. Social movements can demand, and sometimes successfully initiate, structural reforms that affect the relationship between the rulers and the ruled, the division of power between the legislative and the executive branch, the party system as a whole, or the composition of the government. Consider, for example, social movements' efforts to introduce elements of direct democracy into a basically representative system, to get access to information hold by governmental agencies (e.g. freedom of information act), to bring a new movement party into parliaments, or push incapable or corrupt political leaders out of office. In that way, social movements may play an important role as watchdogs to signal misuses of power and as motors for deepening democracy.

Fifth, social movements can serve as agents of fundamental societal and political change. Such changes may occur gradually and slowly, so that the full range of their cumulative effects become only visibly from hindsight. Consider, for example, the relative slow transition from a feudal system to a capitalist and eventually democratic-representative system. Another example of gradual change is the move towards (more) gender equality, mainly resulting from numerous activities of women's movements over long periods. Moreover, these activities did not only stimulate legal regulations, but also more informal practices of daily life, such as the usage of a gender-sensitive language. On the other hand, fundamental changes may also occur relatively suddenly, as if they came out of the blue, as exemplified by many rebellions and some revolutions. Within a few days or weeks, a seemingly firmly established regime may tumble down due to masses of protesters taking the streets, as the fall of communist regimes in Eastern Europe has shown.

In short, social movements may have quite different functions and produce equally different results. Only rarely can single movements claim full success with regard to their declared goals. More often, they fail. But even then, their failure may pave the way for a wave of new movements that have learned lessons from their forerunners, or are meeting more favourable conditions. Also, the impact of social movements should not be only measured against the yardstick of declared goals. Social movements' effects can also consist in public agenda-setting; in influencing public moods, perceptions, and values; in changing daily behaviour of both parts of the wider population and movements' adherents. Beyond such more limited impacts, it is obvious that some social movements actually 'made history'. A great number of historical achievements—the abolition of serfdom and traditional slavery; the establishment of modern democracies, including universal suffrage and citizen rights; welfare provisions, to name just a few—would hardly exist without the struggles of progressive social movements. Yet the rise of historical fascist movements as well as contemporary right-populist movements also demonstrates that given achievements are by no means guaranteed. So, we should be careful in praising the very form of a social movement as a tool for making history.

KEY POINTS

- Social movements can fulfil strikingly different functions as destructive troublemakers, indicators of neglected or unsolved problems, promoters of new and valuable ideas, challengers of power elites and forces of regime change, and agents of broader and deeper societal changes.

- The outcomes of social movements should not only be measured in terms of their declared goals, but also by other dimensions, such as public agenda setting and impacts on people's perceptions, values, and behaviours.

Conclusion

Social movements are extremely variegated phenomena that can play both a constructive and destructive role in societies. Contrary to some observers, social movements should not be regarded as elements that, in principle, are remnants of earlier, pre-democratic times. Not only have they acted as drivers to put democracy in place, but they have also helped to improve the structures of modern democracies and

the living conditions of major parts of their populations. Next to NGOs, public interest groups, and political parties, social movements are a constitutive element of forming and representing a collective will, of challenging and controlling expansive political and economic powers, and bringing neglected or unsolved problems to the attention of policy-makers and the wider public. Unlike political parties that seek to occupy formal power positions based on elections, most social movements try to exert pressure on other groups, most notably political decision-makers. In extraordinary situations they act, as Jürgen Habermas has put it, in a 'mode of besiege' (Habermas 1992: 626), without necessarily seeking to acquire power.

Given the persistence and significance of social movements, we should welcome the fact that research on social movements has become an established field in the social sciences and produced a wide array of useful theories, concepts, and empirical findings. Among the various basic approaches to studying and understanding the origins, structures, dynamics, and outcomes of social movements, systematic comparison appears to be most promising. Thus far, however, comparative work has been mainly focusing on North America and Europe. Regrettably, Latin America, Africa, Asia, and Australasia have been neglected, although these regions are populated with a wide array of social movements. And to the extent that these regions have been covered at all, most of the work, at least when published in English, has been undertaken by 'Westerners' (see e.g. Escobar and Alvarez 1992; Eckstein 2001; Boudreau 2004; Piper and Uhlin 2004; Beinin and Vairel 2011). Time is ripe for a closer co-operation between scholars from the global North and the global South.

 QUESTIONS

Knowledge-based

1. How can you define a social movement?

2. Describe three theoretical approaches to study (aspects of) social movements.

3. What were the major trends of social movements in liberal-representative democracies in the past few decades?

4. Describe aspects of the internal life of social movements.

5. List three basic functions of social movements.

Critical thinking

1. Can social movements be found throughout human history?

2. Why do people experiencing basically the same kind and level of deprivation react differently?

3. In which sense are social movements rational actors?

4. Who are the major reference groups of social movements?

5. Are there impacts of social movements even when they fail to reach their declared goals?

FURTHER READING

Classical texts on social movements

Gamson, W. (1990) *The Strategy of Social Protest* (2nd rev. edn) (Belmont, CA: Wadsworth Press).

Oberschall, A. (1973) *Social Conflict and Social Movements* (Englewood Cliffs, NJ: Prentice Hall).

Smelser, N. (1962) *Theory of Collective Behavior* (Glencoe, ILL: Free Press).

Tarrow, S. (1994) *Power in Movement: Social Movements, Collective Action and Politics* (New York: Cambridge University Press).

Tilly, C. (1978) *From Mobilization to Revolution* (Reading: Addison-Wesley).

Turner, R. H. and Killian, L. M. (eds) (1987) *Collective Behavior* (3rd edn) (Englewood Cliffs, NJ: Prentice-Hall).

Useful collections of articles

della Porta, D. and Diani, M. (eds) (2015) *The Oxford Handbook of Social Movements* (Oxford: Oxford University Press).

Fahlenbrach, K., Klimke, M., and Scharloth, J. (eds) (2014) *Protest Cultures. A Companion.* (New York and Oxford: Berghahn).

Fillieule, O. and Accornero, G. (eds) (2016) *Social Movement Studies in Europe: The State of the Art* (New York and Oxford: Berghahn).

McAdam, D., McCarthy, J., and Zald, M. (eds) (1996) *Comparative Perspectives on Social Movements: Political Opportunities, Mobilization Structures, and Cultural Framings* (Cambridge: Cambridge University Press).

Snow, D. A., Soule, S. A., and Kriesi, H. (eds) (2004) *The Blackwell Companion to Social Movement Research* (Oxford: Blackwell).

Stekelenburg, J. van, Roggeband, C., and Klandermans, B. (eds) (2013) *The Future of Social Movement Research: Dynamics, Mechanisms, and Processes* (Minneapolis, MN and London: University of Minnesota Press).

Visit the Online Resources that accompany this book for additional material, including country profiles, comparative data sets, flashcard glossaries, and web directory.

www.oup.com/he/caramani5e

17
Political culture

Christian Welzel and Ronald Inglehart

Chapter contents

> A stable and effective democratic government . . . depends upon the orientations that people have to the political process . . . upon the political culture.
>
> (Almond and Verba 1963: 498)

Reader's guide

This chapter describes what role the concept of political culture plays in comparative politics. We outline the concept's premises, insights, and recent progress. Our chapter places special emphasis on what we see as the major contribution of the political culture field: increasing our understanding of the social roots of democracy and how these roots are transforming through cultural change. In examining the inspirational drivers of democracy, we compare key propositions of the political culture approach with the political economy approach. The chapter concludes with some suggestions regarding the rise of democratic values in non-Western cultures.

Introduction

The term 'culture' covers a broad set of phenomena. It includes traditions, habits, and patterns of behaviour shaped by a society's prevailing beliefs, norms, and values (Nolan and Lenski 1999). 'Political culture', then, denotes the subset of these phenomena that is shaped specifically by *political* beliefs, norms, and values (see Box 17.1).

A society's dominant beliefs, norms, and values are often described as if they constitute an inherited 'national character'. Such descriptions are at times unscientific. In the *Clash of Civilizations*, for example, Huntington (1996) provides anecdotal descriptions of the typical beliefs, norms, and values of entire 'families of nations' without any reference to systematic data.

To avoid confusing impressionistic narrations with factual evidence, sincere political culture research derives its descriptions and conclusions from systematically collected data. By far the most important type of data in this context comprises comparative public opinion data collected from nationally representative population samples. For this reason, this chapter focuses on works that gain their insights from representative mass surveys of this kind. Table 17.1 compiles a selection of milestone studies in this tradition of empirical, cross-nationally comparative studies of political culture.

The founding piece of the **quantitative** strand of cross-national political culture research is Almond and Verba's (1963) classic *The Civic Culture*. The authors define the term 'political culture' 'as the particular distribution of patterns of orientation towards political objects among the members of a nation' (Almond and Verba 1963: 13). This is to this day a widely accepted definition of the term 'political culture'. According to this definition, political culture concerns the psychological dimension of political systems; it includes all politically relevant beliefs, values, and attitudes. Focusing on different reference populations, one can examine elite cultures and mass cultures, as well as local, regional, and national cultures, or the subcultures of specific groups. Yet, in every case the concept refers to some *collective* unit of which people are aware and to which they have some feeling of belonging. If so, the collectivity in question is an imagined community that shapes people's social identity.

To what extent actual political behaviour is included in the notion of political culture is not always clear, but insofar as certain patterns of political behaviour are habitualized among significant population segments,

---

Q   DEFINITION 17.1

Norms, values, and beliefs

Beliefs comprise the things that people think are *factually* right or wrong. Values, by contrast, mean what people think is *morally* good or bad. Values are internalized and hence guide people's behaviour, even in the absence of social sanctions to enforce them. In contrast with values, norms are behavioural guidelines that are socially sanctioned, either informally or formally, no matter whether or not people have internalized these guidelines.

---

they can be considered as behavioural manifestations of political culture.

Because political orientations exist in individuals, political culture research collects data through mass surveys among randomly selected individuals. But the unit of interest is always some population, so individual-level data are aggregated to describe the *prevalence* pattern in orientations that characterize the population of interest.

The comparative study of political culture covers manifold themes. Since it is impossible to describe each of them in this chapter, we have limited ourselves to those themes that loom largest in the discussion of democracy's cultural foundations—arguably the normative lead concept in comparative politics. This limitation implies, for instance, that in this chapter we ignore, among others, the themes of national pride, ethnic identities, and left–right orientations. Furthermore, we elaborate more on the political culture in democracies than in authoritarian states. The reason is not that political culture is absent in authoritarian states. But, for obvious reasons, collecting reliable public opinion data in authoritarian states is difficult, and often not even possible. Consequently, there is much less solid knowledge about political culture in authoritarian states than in democracies.

KEY POINTS

- A scientific approach to studying political culture requires the reliance on systematic evidence based on representative data.

- Although political culture is anchored in the mindsets of individuals, it is an aggregate phenomenon referring to individual-level orientations insofar as they prevail in a given population.

Table 17.1 An overview of some milestone studies in the cross-national comparative tradition of political culture studies

Recent		Inglehart and Norris (2003): traditional–secular/rational values	Inglehart and Welzel (2005): human empowerment		Dalton (2008): engaged citizenship
2000s			Bratton and Mattes (2000): intrinsic and instrumental support for democracy	Rose and Shin (2000): idealistic and realistic support for democracy	Putnam (2000): social capital decline
Late 1990s	Huntington (1996): clash of civilizations	Inglehart (1997): world cultural map	Verba et al. (1995): civic voluntarism	Klingemann (1999): dissatisfied democrats	Norris (1999): critical citizens
Late 1980s/ early 1990s		Flanagan (1987): authoritarian–libertarian values	Dalton et al. (1987): old and new politics	Inglehart (1990): elite-challenging publics	Putnam (1993): civic community, civic trust, social capital
1970s			Sniderman (1975): personality and democracy	Inglehart (1977): materialist–post-materialist values	Barnes and Kaase (1979): unconventional political participation
1960s		Almond and Verba (1963): the civic culture	Easton (1965a,b): specific and diffuse support	Inkeles (1969a, b): individual modernity	Eckstein (1966): authority orientations, congruence theory
Modern classics		Adorno et al. (1950): authoritarian personality	Lasswell (1951): democratic character	Stouffer (1955): political (in)tolerance	Rokeach (1960): the open and closed mind
					Weber (1920): legitimacy beliefs
Classical classics					Tocqueville (1961 [1835]): *De la Démocratie en Amérique*
					Montesquieu (1748): *De l'Esprit des Lois*
					Aristotle (350 BC): *The Politics*, Book IV

Cultural differences around the world

Over several decades, comparative researchers have identified various sets of questions that can be used in standardized surveys to measure cultural differences between societies in valid ways. Arguably, the largest of these surveys, in both spatial and temporal scope, are the World Values Survey (WVS) and the European Values Study (EVS). Since the early 1980s, the WVS and EVS have been conducted at least once in more than 100 societies worldwide, including countries from all inhabited continents.

Repeated analyses of WVS/EVS data over more than two decades have found a robust pattern of cross-national cultural differences (Inglehart 1990, 1997). On a global scale, many of the cultural differences between nations boil down to just two major dimensions: *'sacred versus secular values'* and *'patriarchal versus emancipative values'* (for simplicity, henceforth secular values and emancipative values). *Between*-societal differences on these two-value dimensions are usually larger, and often much larger, than *within*-societal differences over such conflict lines as gender, age, race, and social class, for nations are still by far the most powerful imagined communities in shaping people's collective identity (Inglehart and Welzel 2010).

Mean national positions in secular values and emancipative values indicate a typical mindset that comes to dominance in a population at certain stages of its socio-economic and socio-political modernization. These values are mental representations of the development of given populations. For this reason, the nations' prevalent values cluster in relatively coherent culture zones, reflecting similar paths of historical development (Inglehart and Baker 2000).

In Figure 17.1, each national population's mean position on these two sets of values is plotted, including evidence from the WVS/EVS and using the most up-to-date measures of secular values[1] and emancipative values.[2] The theoretical range on both dimensions is from zero to 1.0.

The national mean positions in secular values and emancipative values in Figure 17.1 hide inner-national differences along the lines of social class, religion, and ethnicity. In fact, in almost any sample one can find at least some individuals at each corner of the cultural

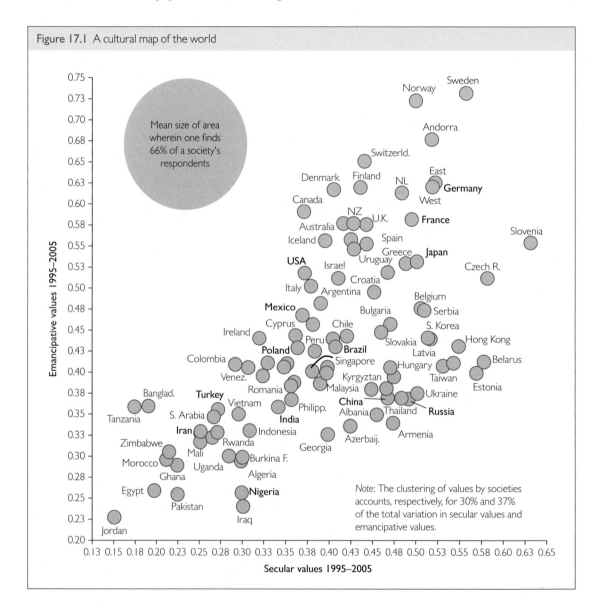

Figure 17.1 A cultural map of the world

Note: The clustering of values by societies accounts, respectively, for 30% and 37% of the total variation in secular values and emancipative values.

map. And the rule is that people from groups whose members are more prosperous, educated, and more widely connected tend to be more secular and emancipative in their values. Still, it is also true for each national sample that individual respondents cluster in increasing density the closer one comes to the national mean position. These mean positions represent a nation's cultural gravity centre.

Inglehart and Welzel's (2005) 'revised theory of modernization' explains why national populations are positioned at their given place on the secular/emancipative values map. In a nutshell, the placement results from an interplay between distinct historic traditions and consecutive phases of modernization. Specifically, communist, Confucian and Protestant traditions have placed nations in a more secular base position. A Protestant tradition also anchored nations in a more emancipatory base position. These base positions then shifted further, depending on how thoroughly societies have been transformed by the two main phases of modernization. Specifically, the industrial phase of modernization has shifted nations further towards secular values. The post-industrial phase of modernization, by contrast, has shifted them further towards emancipative values, and continues to do so. Because modernization is a reversible process, societies can also move in the opposite direction—towards sacred and patriarchal (i.e. more traditional) values. In fact, such reverse moves are likely to happen, especially under the imprint of economic breakdowns, state failure, and other societal crises.

KEY POINTS

- National populations differ systematically in how much emphasis they place on secular values and emancipative values.

- These differences reflect an interplay between distinct historic traditions and consecutive phases of modernization.

- Communist, Confucian and Protestant traditions have anchored societies in a more secular base position. The industrial phase of modernization then has shifted societies further towards secular values.

- The Protestant tradition in particular has also anchored societies in a more emancipative base position. The post-industrial phase of modernization then has shifted societies further towards emancipative values.

- A society's scoring, especially in emancipative values, influences its regime's position on the autocracy-vs-democracy continuum.

Historical roots of the political culture concept

A basic assumption of the political culture **paradigm** is that a population's prevailing orientations, beliefs, and values determine the type of political system by which this population is governed. This assumption was formulated more than 2,300 years ago by Aristotle (c. 350 BC) in Book IV of *The Politics*. In this work, Aristotle argued that democracies emerge from middle-class societies where an egalitarian ethos is predominant among the citizens.

Here we find the classical formulation of a threefold causal process in which (i) the social structures of a population make (ii) certain beliefs predominant among its members, which then make (iii) specific types of political systems more widely accepted. Thus, there is a sequence from social structures to subjective beliefs to the legitimacy of political institutions. This sequence provides an early theory explaining the origins of dictatorship and democracy: hierarchical social structures lead to authoritarian beliefs under which dictatorship becomes the legitimate form of government; horizontal social structures lead to egalitarian beliefs under which democracy becomes the legitimate form of government.

Aristotle's idea that the citizens' beliefs shape political systems seemed realistic in the world of the Greek city-states. In the history of the Greek *polis*, the citizenry itself appeared several times as an 'agent' of political change, for instance when popular movements expelled rulers who were considered tyrants (Finer 1999: Vol. II). But the idea of 'people power' fell into oblivion for centuries in the subsequent eras of Roman imperialism and medieval feudalism. In the agrarian empires outside of Europe, which were described as 'Oriental despotism' (Wittfogel 1957), the notion of people power never even surfaced.

Awareness of the fact that the 'masses' can direct political transformations re-emerged only when the liberal revolutions of early modern times brought the people back in as agents of change. Thus, some 2000 years after Aristotle, Montesquieu (1748) argued in *De l'Esprit des Lois* that whether a nation is constituted as a tyranny, a monarchy, or a republic depends on the prevalence of servile, honest, or egalitarian orientations among the people. Likewise, Tocqueville (1835) reasoned in *De la Démocratie en Amérique* that the flourishing of democracy in the US reflects the prevalence of liberal, egalitarian, and participatory orientations among the American people.

In modern times, a disastrous illustration of the fact that people's orientations influence a regime's chances of survival was the failure of democracy in Weimar Germany. Although the Weimar Republic had adopted what was considered a model **constitution** at the time, the constitutional order lacked legitimacy among much of the public as well as among the conservative elites, who viewed the authoritarian era of the Kaiser as 'the good old days'. In the wake of the Great Depression, the Nazi Party, supported by a plurality of the German electorate, came to power, with catastrophic consequences for the world. For decades, social scientists and intellectuals sought to understand the causes of the Holocaust and the Second World War, and many of them came to the conclusion that a 'democracy without democrats' is unlikely to survive.

In this vein, Lasswell (1951) claimed that democratic regimes emerge and survive where a majority of the people share orientations that are compatible with the operation of democracy. In Lasswell's eyes, these orientations are rooted in 'freedom from anxiety', which he saw nurturing a general 'belief in human potentialities' and a sense of 'self-esteem', as well as a sense of 'respect for others'. Similarly, when Lipset (1959: 85–9) asked why modernization is conducive to democracy, he concluded that modernization changes mass orientations in ways that make them more compatible with the operation of democracy, most notably by increasing people's tolerance for opposition, criticism, and political **pluralism**. In philosophical terms, Popper (1971 [1962]) described these characteristics as the prevailing mindset of *The Open Society*.

In **empirical research**, Almond and Verba (1963) and Eckstein (1966) introduced the term 'congruence', arguing that in order to be stable political institutions must accord with people's legitimacy beliefs. This is particularly true of democratic institutions, which cannot survive by repressing mass preferences without corrupting their own principles. The congruence theorem has become the most axiomatic assumption of the political culture school.

KEY POINTS

- There is a historical model of the society–regime link running from social structures to legitimacy beliefs to prevailing regimes.
- In the dictatorial version, vertical social structures nurture authoritarian beliefs that legitimize dictatorship.
- In the democratic version, horizontal social structures nurture egalitarian beliefs that in turn legitimize democracy.

The question of citizens' democratic maturity

Almond and Verba's *Civic Culture* study (1963) had an immense influence on subsequent political culture research. Comparing two old democracies (the UK and the US), two then-young democracies (Italy and Germany), and a developing nation (Mexico), this study aimed to identify the psychological attributes of a culture that sustain democracy. In identifying these attributes, the authors emphasized two concepts: civic competence and civic allegiance.

Like most scholars, Almond and Verba assumed that democracies put higher demands on the citizens than authoritarian forms of government. For democracy requires voluntary participation in the political process, at least in elections, to fill positions of power. Even in a limited democracy that restricts mass participation to elections, citizens must understand the electoral process. They must be capable of evaluating what the governing parties have done, and what the alternatives are, in order to make reasonable choices in an election. If these conditions are not met, the electoral process will be irrational and democracy itself is a flawed idea. Thus, civic competence is a fundamental precondition for democracy to be meaningful.

Since then, the field has explored citizens' political competence. To examine cognitive competence, researchers have developed survey questions asking people about their political knowledge (Zaller 1992; Delli Carpini and Keeter 1996). Inspired by an influential study by Converse (1964), scores of researchers demonstrated low levels of political knowledge, even among the electorates of the most mature democracies (McClosky and Brill 1983). Quite often, it was concluded from such studies that one should not burden democracy with too high expectations because the democratic process easily overwhelms most people's capacities. These conclusions then served as a justification for elite-guided, strictly representative versions of democracy. This position rejected any attempt at extending democracy into a more mass-participative version. Indeed, mass apathy was considered a stabilizing feature of democracy (Dye et al. 1970; Crozier et al. 1975).

The description of modern mass publics as insufficiently competent has not remained unquestioned (Lupia and McCubbins 1998). Invoking the theory of informational shortcuts, scholars argue that the demands for voter competence are more modest than the critics of voter sophistication suggest. Politics is a remote area that ranks low in most people's daily priorities, so people economize the time they invest to obtain the information needed to make reasonable judgements. Instead of studying given policy proposals in detail, most people pay attention to how the representatives of various groups position themselves. From this positioning, they draw conclusions about whether or not the proposal is in their own interest. What is important for people to make reasonable choices, then, is to have ready access to reliable clues.

The theory of informational shortcuts shifts the burden of democratic rationality from the expertise of the citizens to the quality of the intermediary system. To be capable of making reasonable choices, the citizens do not themselves need to become political experts. All that is needed is political pluralism on a fairly even playing field (Dalton 2006: 20–31).

Another phenomenon that weakens the criticism of incompetent citizens in post-industrial societies is what came to be known as 'cognitive mobilization' (Inglehart 1977; Dalton 2004: 20–31). Scholars argue that rising levels of education, the expansion of intellectual tasks in the growing knowledge sector, and the increasing exposure to informational diversity all have contributed to expand people's ability to arrive at independent judgements of given matters. People's factual political knowledge might not have significantly increased in post-industrial societies (Wattenberg 2006), but their skills in acquiring information and processing it have probably grown through cognitive mobilization. Thus, ordinary people have become more capable of thinking for themselves. A piece of evidence that supports this interpretation is the so-called 'Flynn effect': in all populations among whom IQ tests have been carried out repeatedly for many years, one finds a significant, continuous, and in many cases remarkable increase in test scores over recent decades (Flynn 2012; Trahan et al. 2014).

Civic competence has not only an objective cognitive component; it also involves a subjective perceptual component. Almond and Verba (1963: Chapter 8) defined subjective political competence as the feeling that one understands the political process and the belief that one can participate in meaningful ways, and—when one does so—that it helps to change things for the better. Certainly, citizens can misperceive their political competence. But, whether misperceived or not, subjective competence is consequential: people

who feel competent and efficacious about what they can contribute are more likely to participate in politics. They have a stronger sense of agency, which generally motivates action (Verba et al. 1995).

The allegiance model of the democratic citizen

As much as Almond and Verba's (1963) *The Civic Culture* emphasized civic competence, it also stressed the importance of civic allegiance. In contrast with competence, allegiance is an affective mode of orientation. A minimum of civic competence is thought to be necessary to make the democratic process rational. But the democratic process not only needs to be rational; in order to survive, democracy also needs to be widely accepted and to be seen as the most desirable way to organize politics. Accordingly, Almond and Verba considered a basic sense of allegiance to the norms, institutions, and actors of democracy as an attribute of the ideal democratic citizen.

From this point of view, the ideal democratic citizen is a person who takes part in elections and other forms of *elite-entrusting* participation—forms of participation necessary to make representation work. But the ideal citizen is not supposed to become active in non-institutionalized ways that challenge representatives. This is because representation is the constitutive principle of modern democracies. To retain legitimacy, this principle needs reliable party–voter alignments. Accordingly, voters must stay loyal to their representatives once they have been voted into office. Allegiant democratic citizens do not disobey or oppose decisions made by democratically elected representatives. They accept the leadership role of their representatives and when they are not in line with their policies, they respond by changing their political alignment. The allegiance model holds that democratic citizens operate within party–voter alignments. They might change their alignment, but cannot operate in a free-floating space beyond alignments. In the allegiant model, specific support for particular actors and parties is allowed to erode, but it must be compensated by realignments to new actors and parties, if the principle of representation is to continue to work.

As a consequence, the allegiance model holds that democracy is in danger when party–voter alignments decrease in general. Three decades of growing evidence from cross-national survey data seem to suggest that exactly this has been happening throughout post-industrial societies and beyond (Dalton and Wattenberg 2000).

KEY POINTS

- Democracies put a higher burden on citizens' information-processing capacities than other regimes.

- Cognitive mobilization and other processes related to the rise of knowledge societies seem to have improved citizens' information-processing abilities.

Party–voter dealignment

The allegiance model of **citizenship** came under strain with the emergence of protest politics and new **social movements** in the late 1960s. Scholars who believed that democracy suffers from mass mobilization outside institutionalized channels viewed this development with alarm, fearing that government would be overloaded with excessive demands by publics who were too highly mobilized. It was argued that civic mobilization outside the channels of representative institutions will render governments unable to fulfil increasingly inflated mass demands. This will disappoint the citizens, and democratic institutions will fall into disfavour. Thus, the emergence of a legitimacy crisis and a governability crisis were predicted as the consequence of increasingly elite-challenging masses (Crozier et al. 1975).

However, the first comparative empirical study of protest politics reached different conclusions (Barnes and Kaase et al. 1979). Based on surveys of representative samples in the US, Great Britain, Germany, the Netherlands, Austria, and other countries, the study found that:

1. protest participants had higher levels of formal education and greater political skills, and felt more efficacious than non-participants;

2. protest participants emphasized democratic norms *more* strongly, not less strongly, than non-participants;

3. protest participants were in general more engaged and active than non-participants.

Parallel studies on new social movements in the fields of environmental protection, gender equality, human rights, fair trade, and equal opportunities produced similar findings (Tarrow 1994; McAdam et al. 2001; Dalton et al. 2010). This line of research has helped reshape our understanding of protest behaviour and its role in democratic politics.

For a long time, the predominant explanation of elite-challenging mass activities was influenced by deprivation theories intended to explain violent mass upheavals (Gurr 1970). But collective violence is a way of expressing dissent that differs fundamentally from the peaceful forms of mass protest observed in post-industrial societies since the late 1960s. Still, the assumption of deprivation theories that some sense of grievance and frustration motivates protest behaviour strongly influenced the initial views on the rising protest movements in post-industrial societies. But what is true for the supporters of violent activities—that frustration about social marginalization is a prime motivation—is not true for most forms of peaceful dissent in advanced post-industrial societies. It is not marginalized parts of the population and the people who are most deprived of basic resources who constitute the mass base for elite-challenging activities. Rather, it is those who have relatively high levels of participatory resources, including the skills, education, and networks that enable them to launch or join in various campaign activities (Dalton and Kuechler 1990; Verba et al. 1995; Dalton et al. 2010).

Post-industrial society (Bell 1973) has been linked with rising levels of formal education, more easily accessible information, improved means of communication and mobility, and wider opportunities to connect people across the boundaries of locality, ethnicity, religion, or class (Inkeles and Smith 1974). These processes have increased the part of the population in possession of the participatory resources needed to sustain social movements and mass pressures on elites. Surprising as it may seem, societies that are most advanced in providing their populations with long, secure, prosperous, and entertaining lives show the highest rates of protest activity. In other words, people are more likely to initiate and sustain civic forms of protest when their objective living conditions are more enabling, not more miserable (Welzel et al. 2005).

This is surprising only if one believes that raising one's voice results from suffering. This can and does happen, of course, but then it is often an eruptive and violent outbreak of collective frustration that implodes as quickly as it surfaced. Suburban *gilets jaunes* riots, which emerged in 2019 among the populist protests in France, illustrate this pattern. Misery-induced types of protest are more radical in form but usually not sustainable over time because the most deprived lack in many ways the resources needed to express dissent repeatedly and continuously. Moderate, yet continuous, forms of protest are more prevalent where people have the capability to mount and sustain pressures and where they have adopted the critical spirit that motivates the expression of dissent. As Inglehart (1977, 1990, 1997) has argued, the transition from industrial to post-industrial societies increases both factors, enabling as well as motivating citizens to put elites under increasingly effective mass pressures.

The assertive model of the democratic citizen

Rising emancipative values

The rise of post-industrial societies nurtures elite-challenging mass activities in two ways. On one hand, it increases the participatory resources that *enable* people to initiate and sustain such activities. On the other hand, it is conducive to value changes bringing increasing emphasis on emancipatory attitudes that *motivate* people to engage in such activities.

The most refined and updated measurement of emancipative values has been presented by Welzel (2013). These values focus on the four emancipatory goals outlined in endnote 2:

1. an emphasis on democratic *voice* reflected in post-materialist priorities that give people more say in important government decisions and how things are done at their jobs and in their communities, and for protecting freedom of speech;

2. an emphasis on sexual *choice* reflected in the acceptance of divorce, abortion, and homosexuality;

3. an emphasis on gender *equality* reflected in support for women having equal access to education, work, and power;

4. an emphasis on child *autonomy* reflected in support for independence and imagination, but not obedience, as important qualities for children to learn.

The average position of national populations on the index of emancipative values varies between a score of 0.22 for Iraq and 0.75 for Sweden. All populations included in the WVS show single-peaked and mean-centred distributions on this index of emancipative values.

Emancipative values tend to be more firmly encultured in societies in which more enabling living conditions increase people's capacities to exercise freedoms. With growing emancipative values, entitlements that allow people to exercise freedoms become increas-ingly important to people's life satisfaction (Inglehart et al. 2008; Welzel and Inglehart 2010).

Welzel (2013) argues that the close connection tying emancipative values to socio-economic development, on the one hand, and to effective democracy, on the other, reflects a broader process of 'human empowerment'. In this framework (see Figure 17.2), socio-economic development empowers people on the level of *abilities* by widening the means, skills, and opportunities that enable them to exercise democratic freedoms. Emancipative values empower people on the level of *motivations* by increasing the priority they give to exercising democratic freedoms. Finally, effective democracy empowers people on the level of *entitlements* by giving them the rights to exercise democratic freedoms. Emerging from a broad process of human empowerment, democracy becomes increasingly effective in response to people's growing motivation to exercise freedoms, which in turn reflects their growing ability to do so.

In line with the human empowerment model, emancipative values have been on the rise throughout the post-industrial world and beyond, as Figure 17.3 illustrates. Indeed, the distribution of countries shows that emancipative values are in many more places increasing than decreasing and that the amount of increase often is simply a matter of how much time has elapsed between measurements. Most of the exceptions from this rule concentrate in the ex-communist world and among countries with a resurgence of religion and authoritarianism (most notably Russia, Turkey, and Nigeria). Apart from these noteworthy exceptions, rising emancipative values turn allegiant citizens into assertive citizens for whom the role of a loyal and obedient follower of elected elites loses

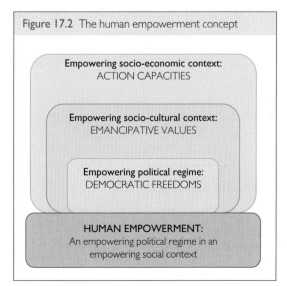

Figure 17.2 The human empowerment concept

Empowering socio-economic context:
ACTION CAPACITIES

Empowering socio-cultural context:
EMANCIPATIVE VALUES

Empowering political regime:
DEMOCRATIC FREEDOMS

HUMAN EMPOWERMENT:
An empowering political regime in an empowering social context

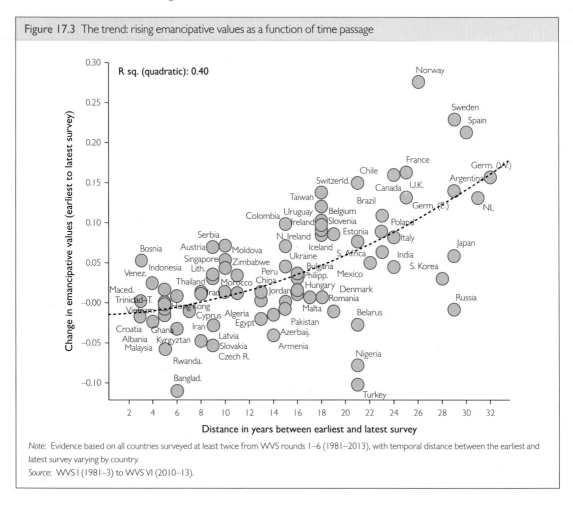

Figure 17.3 The trend: rising emancipative values as a function of time passage

Note: Evidence based on all countries surveyed at least twice from WVS rounds 1–6 (1981–2013), with temporal distance between the earliest and latest survey varying by country.

Source: WVS I (1981–3) to WVS VI (2010–13).

appeal (Dalton and Welzel 2014). Citizens become less attracted by those parts of the democratic process that are designed to entrust elites. They are more attracted to activities in which they express themselves and challenge elites (Norris 2002).

KEY POINTS

- As part of a broader process of human empowerment, emancipative values have been on the rise throughout post-industrial societies and beyond during the past decades, albeit with noteworthy exceptions.

Criticality and disaffection

As outlined by Nevitte (1996) in *Decline of Deference* and by Norris (1999) in *Critical Citizens*, value change in the wake of the post-industrial transformation of modern societies makes people increasingly critical of institutionalized authority. Indeed, all societies for which

survey data are available over a considerable time series show a decline of people's confidence in hierarchically structured mass organizations and in institutions that exert authority over people, as Dalton (2004) demonstrates in *Democratic Choices, Democratic Challenges*.

This tendency affects representative institutions directly, because the principle of representation is designed to transfer authority from the people to institutions. Accordingly, rates of confidence in parliaments and identification with political parties have shown a long-term decline (Dalton and Wattenberg 2000). These tendencies seem to be most pronounced in societies where emancipative values have become strongest.

In keeping with these findings, the evidence in Figure 17.4 shows that individuals with stronger emancipative values exhibit lower 'vertical' trust in institutions of order (i.e. the police and the military) but higher 'horizontal' trust in their fellow citizens. This tendency is most pronounced in 'strongly emancipative' societies, in which emancipative values are most widespread: individuals with the same scores on these values show lower levels of vertical trust and higher

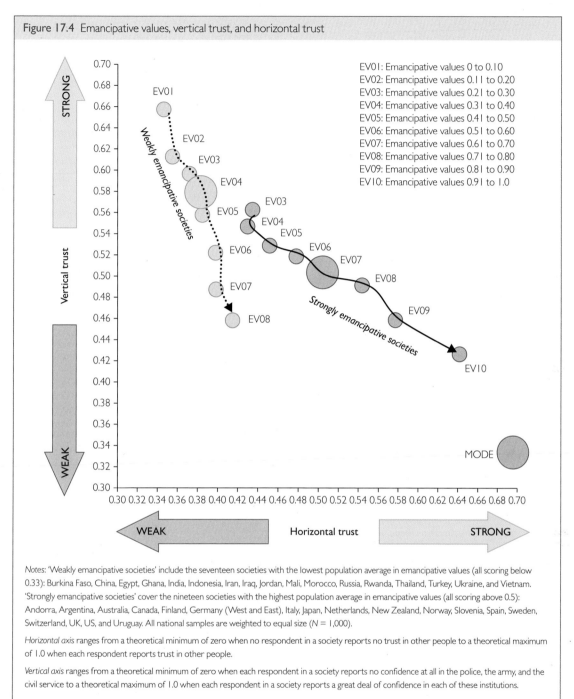

Figure 17.4 Emancipative values, vertical trust, and horizontal trust

EV01: Emancipative values 0 to 0.10
EV02: Emancipative values 0.11 to 0.20
EV03: Emancipative values 0.21 to 0.30
EV04: Emancipative values 0.31 to 0.40
EV05: Emancipative values 0.41 to 0.50
EV06: Emancipative values 0.51 to 0.60
EV07: Emancipative values 0.61 to 0.70
EV08: Emancipative values 0.71 to 0.80
EV09: Emancipative values 0.81 to 0.90
EV10: Emancipative values 0.91 to 1.0

Notes: 'Weakly emancipative societies' include the seventeen societies with the lowest population average in emancipative values (all scoring below 0.33): Burkina Faso, China, Egypt, Ghana, India, Indonesia, Iran, Iraq, Jordan, Mali, Morocco, Russia, Rwanda, Thailand, Turkey, Ukraine, and Vietnam. 'Strongly emancipative societies' cover the nineteen societies with the highest population average in emancipative values (all scoring above 0.5): Andorra, Argentina, Australia, Canada, Finland, Germany (West and East), Italy, Japan, Netherlands, New Zealand, Norway, Slovenia, Spain, Sweden, Switzerland, UK, US, and Uruguay. All national samples are weighted to equal size ($N = 1,000$).

Horizontal axis ranges from a theoretical minimum of zero when no respondent in a society reports no trust in other people to a theoretical maximum of 1.0 when each respondent reports trust in other people.

Vertical axis ranges from a theoretical minimum of zero when each respondent in a society reports no confidence at all in the police, the army, and the civil service to a theoretical maximum of 1.0 when each respondent in a society reports a great deal of confidence in each of these institutions.

levels of horizontal trust when they live in societies where emancipative values are more widespread.

Wider circles of solidarity and trust

One of the most surprising findings from this body of research is that rising emphasis on emancipative values is not linked with greater selfishness, as Flanagan and Lee (2003) assume. On the contrary, the evidence is clear that stronger emphasis on emancipative values widens the circle of others with whom people build up a sense of solidarity (Welzel 2010). Thus, emancipative values transcend self- and ingroup-centered parochialisms and oppose nativist populism.

The potential to embrace emancipative values is universally human, yet this potential remains dormant when existential fears—such as anxiety of physical harm, material deprivation, and cultural marginalization—push people into bonding behaviour. In so doing, people give up their individuality for the sake of maximal identification with a homogenously idealized in-group. Absorbed by group-identity within imagined ethnic, religious, or nationalist communities, people treat dissimilar others discriminantly as out-group members, which usually cements inter-group hostility.[3] But when more enabling living conditions eliminate people's group-related fears, the emancipatory drive for freedom from domination awakens and gives rise to emancipative values. As this happens, group boundaries become more variegated, porous, and permeable (Simmel 1984 [1908]). This reduces both the forcefulness of intra-group harmony and the fierceness of inter-group conflict, allowing people to overcome bonding behaviour and to engage in bridging behaviour. This process places human solidarity on a different basis. Familiarity, belongingness, and alikeness with others become less important, while mutually agreed interests and empathy with the situation of others become more important factors in creating a sense of solidarity. Group affinity becomes more intrinsically chosen and detaches from pre-fixed sameness criteria, most notably sameness in origin and lineage.

Evidence supporting these claims is provided by the WVS, which uses a battery of items to distinguish between 'bonding' trust in in-groups (i.e., related and familiar others) and 'bridging' trust in out-groups (i.e., unrelated and dissimilar others). Another set of questions can be used to measure nativist-versus-cosmopolitan solidarity orientations based on the extent to which people (i) reject a xenophobic notion of citizenship; (ii) tolerate ethnic diversity; and (iii) define themselves by identity categories that transcend rather than establish group boundaries. Analysing the responses to these questions, Figure 17.5 demonstrates that people with strong emancipative values have stronger bridging trust and a more cosmopolitan solidarity orientation. Once again, these tendencies are most pronounced in societies with a strong emphasis on emancipative values.

KEY POINTS

Emancipative values make citizens:

- more liberal in their understanding of democracy and more critical in the assessment of its operation;
- more open and tolerant in their attitude towards out-groups.

Similarly, Welzel (2013) finds that stronger emancipative values not only go together with stronger individualistic values (which is not surprising), but also with stronger altruistic values. Apparently, eman-cipative values merge individualism and altruism into what one might call humanism.

A cultural theory of autocracy versus democracy

Over the past 120 years, the world as a whole has become more democratic because of two tendencies: (i) continuous improvements of democracy's liberal qualities among Western countries; and (ii) consecutive waves of democratization by which countries in region after region outside the West adopted liberal democracy (Brunkert et al. 2018). Only China, the Islamic world and a handful of exceptional cases, like Cuba, Singapore and North Korea, withstood the democratic trend and it seemed only to be a matter of time before these islands of autocracy would also turn democratic. The long-term ascension of democracy and its spatial diffusion into various culture zones inspired an era of democratic euphoria in which scholars began to believe that democracy is not culture-bound but reflects a universal human aspiration (Fukuyama 1992; Huntington 1991).

The fact that international polls exhibit widespread support for democracy in literally every country that has been surveyed (autocracies included) seemingly confirms the view that the desire for democracy is a culturally unconditioned and, thus, natural human preference (Klingemann 1999; Dalton et al. 2007; Maseland and van Hoorn 2012).

The political economy literature lends additional support to this view, arguing that it is always in the *median voter*'s economic interest to prefer democracy over autocracy (Boix 2003; Acemoglu and Robinson 2006; Ansell and Samuels 2014). For democracy allows the median voter to use her/his majority position to elect governments into office that execute the median voter's interest in redistributing income from the elites to the masses. Clearly, this interpretation presumes that ordinary people understand democracy primarily as a tool to provide economic equality.

These premises imply a particular understanding of the foundations of autocratic rule. Most obviously, if the desire for democracy is universally human, autocracies can only emerge and endure by repressing this desire. Consequently, autocratic rule is never legitimate in the eyes of the people. Thus, when majorities of people in autocracies say to support democracy, they understand democracy perfectly well as the liberal alternative to their authoritarian form of government and express with this support their wish for a regime change. If so, for any given autocracy, one only needs to remove the tyrants to pave the respective country's way to democracy, in fulfilment of people's

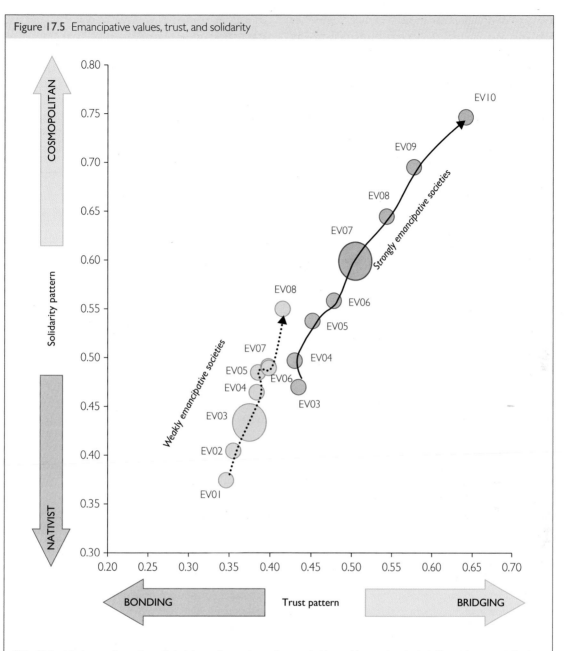

Figure 17.5 Emancipative values, trust, and solidarity

Notes: Horizontal axis ranges from a theoretical minimum of zero, when each respondent in a society reports no trust at all in people one meets for the first time, people of a different nationality, and people of a different religion, to a theoretical maximum of 1.0, when each respondent in a society reports complete trust in each of these three groups of people.

Vertical axis has a theoretical minimum of zero, when each respondent in a society supports an ethnocentric form of citizenship ('having ancestors from my country'), rejects ethnic diversity, and emphasizes identity categories that establish group boundaries (locality, nation) at the expense of categories that defy such boundaries (individual, world). The theoretical maximum is 1.0 when each respondent in a society holds opposite attitudes on each of these three accounts.

ubiquitous longing for it. This *a*-cultural view of the foundations of democracy has informed foreign policy when the US and its Western allies acted as if removing the Taliban, Saddam, and Ghaddafi from power would automatically turn Afghanistan, Iraq, and Libya into democracies.

The shortcomings of the *a*-cultural view of democracy

Recent evidence calls for a thorough revision of the *a*-cultural view of democracy (Kirsch and Welzel 2018; Kruse et al. 2018). To begin with, there is not a single country in the world ever surveyed where a sizeable segment of the population understands democracy primarily as a tool to provide economic equality—not even in highly unequal countries, like Brazil, or in poor countries, like Zimbabwe, where such an understanding would be in people's economic interest (Welzel 2013). Hence, the quintessential assumption in political economy about the motivation of democratic preferences has little empirical backing, if any.

Even more importantly, support for democracy itself is an altogether inconclusive indicator because it hides firmly encultured differences in how people around the world understand democracy. In many places, people understand democracy in outright authoritarian ways that revert the meaning of support for democracy into its own contradiction: support for autocracy, that is (Kirsch and Welzel 2018). In these instances, people systematically mistake autocratic regime features as democratic ones (Kruse et al. 2018). Accordingly, seemingly widespread support for democracy disguises the legitimacy of autocratic rule where people misunderstand democracy in authoritarian terms and where they confuse autocracy with democracy.

Autocrats cultivate authoritarian notions of democracy. They highjack the term 'democracy' and redefine it for their own purposes. The typical propaganda denounces Western-style democracy as an overly liberal perversion of 'true' democracy, which is then described as some form of 'guardianship' through which the 'wise' ruler governs in the best of people's interest, who are taught to be obedient for this reason. The autocratic narratives are usually couched in collectivist belongingness cults, fostered by religiosity and nationalism, that depict a country's cultural identity and geo-political interest in an explicitly anti-Western manner. Among the publics of major powers whose leaders advocate national missions for regional or global dominance, autocratic narratives of this kind usually find a welcoming audience, which helps the autocrats to silence opposition. China, Iran, Turkey, and Russia are cases in point. By emphasizing their countries' non-Western identity, autocrats in these and other places hope to erect a psychological shield against the intrusion of emancipative values whose anti-authoritarian thrust is in no dictator's interest. As Figure 17.6 illustrates, in the absence of emancipative values, people lack the moral resources to resist authoritarian propaganda.

Supporting this interpretation, evidence from the WVS shows that, where the elites are successful in breeding religious and nationalistic versions of collective identity, emancipative values remain weaker than one would expect in the face of a country's level of development. This also means that religiosity and

nationalism weaken the otherwise powerful emancipatory effect of enabling living conditions embedded in more widespread action resources. Yet, religiosity and nationalism do by no means eradicate this effect entirely, which is obvious from comparing the lower with the upper diagram in Figure 17.7. Instead, enabling living conditions remain a significant force in giving rise to emancipative values, even taking the negative impact of religiosity and nationalism into account.

The myth of democratic deconsolidation

Most people in most countries say in surveys that they support democracy. But such overt democratic support does not always mean support for truly liberal democracy. It only does when the seeming support exists in conjunction with emancipative values, but not in dissociation from them. Therefore, as Figure 17.6 illustrates, emancipative values provide a powerful antidote against illiberal misunderstandings and misperceptions of democracy.

The Deconsolidation Thesis by Foa and Mounk (2016) claims that support for democracy is in a generational decline around the world, including even the most long-standing Western democracies. The authors also imply that the rise of illiberal populism is a result of the young generations' evaporating passion for democracy, which suggests that younger cohorts have turned less liberal in their values. None of this is true, however. From the earliest to the latest WVS rounds, support for democracy has been increasing in just as many countries as it has been decreasing, with no net change overall. Most of these changes remain below five percentage points. And there is no generational decrease in support for democracy within mature democracies. The age differentiation in support for democracy is negligible to begin with and accounts for less than 0.1 per cent of the total individual-level variation in support for democracy. What is more, the negligibly lower support rates among younger people today have nothing generational about them, but reflect a lifecycle effect: younger people have been somewhat less supportive also in previous surveys but turned more supportive as they aged. Most importantly, support of democracy is an altogether inconclusive indicator because it hides substantial differences in how people understand democracy. Support for truly liberal democracy is limited to only those outspoken supporters of democracy who adhere to emancipative values. And this group has grown massively over the generations in mature democracies. The real generational change is, hence, a remarkable reshuffling in

Figure 17.6 Emancipative values, notions of democracy, and democracy ratings

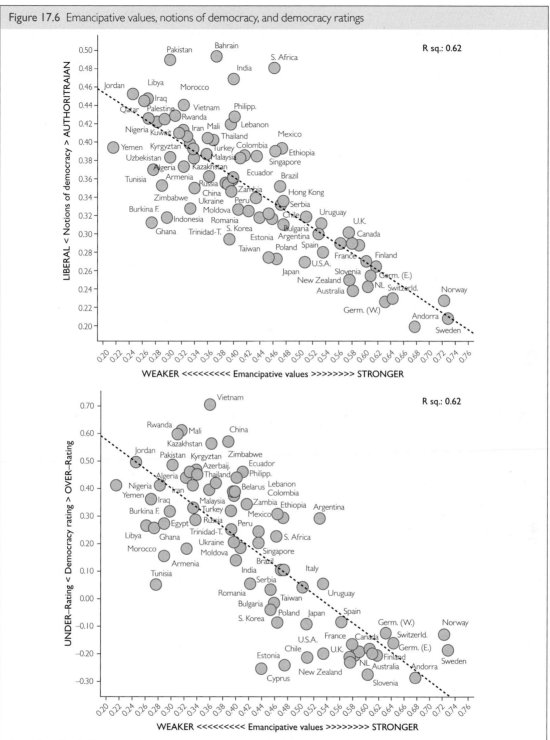

Source: Reproduced with permission by the authors—Kirsch and Welzel (2018: 59–92) for the left-hand diagram (https://doi.org/10.1093/sf/soy114); Kruse et al. (2018: 315–35) for the right-hand diagram (https://doi.org/10.1177/0022022118821437).

Notes: **Emancipative values** on the *horizontal axes in both diagrams* are measured as explained in Fig. 17.6. **Notions of democracy** on the *vertical axis in the left-hand diagram* measure the extent to which respondents approve three authoritarian meanings of democracy (i.e. military government, theocracy, people's obedience to rulers) and at the same time disapprove three liberal meanings of democracy (i.e. free elections, civil liberties, equal rights). The index has a theoretical minimum of 0, for the case that someone fully approves the three liberal meanings and at the same time fully disapproves the authoritarian meanings. The index has a theoretical maximum of 1.0 for the exact opposite constellation. For details of index construction, see Welzel and Kirsch (2018). **Democracy ratings** on the *vertical axis in the right-hand diagram* measure to what extent respondents over- or under-estimate their country's level of democracy relative to the country's score on Alexander et al.'s (2012) effective democracy for the same year. Over-estimations show up in positive scores up to a theoretical maximum of 1.0, for the case that a respondent perceives her country as fully democratic when in fact it is entirely undemocratic. Under-estimations show up in negative scores down to a theoretical minimum of -1.0, for the case that a respondent sees her country as entirely undemocratic when in fact it is fully democratic. Scores close to 0 indicate accurate estimations. For details of index construction, see Kruse et al. (2018).

Figure 17.7 Enabling living conditions' emancipatory consequences, before and after controlling national and religious sentiment

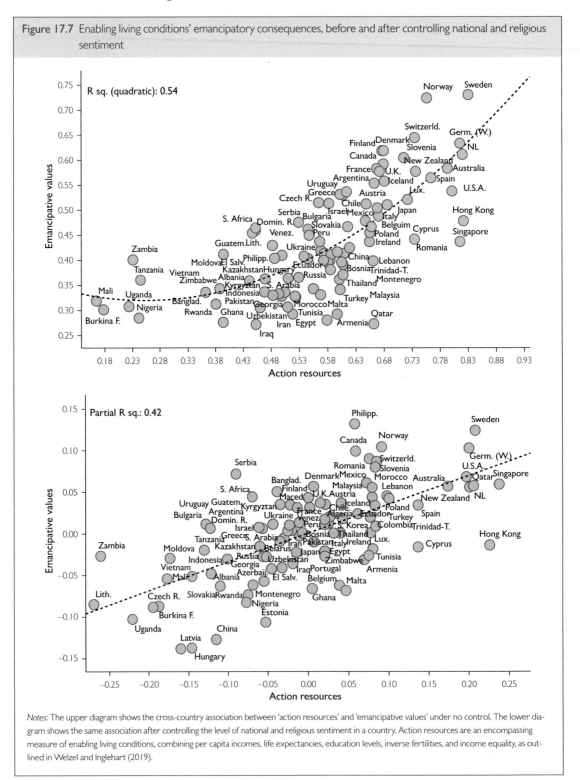

Notes: The upper diagram shows the cross-country association between 'action resources' and 'emancipative values' under no control. The lower diagram shows the same association after controlling the level of national and religious sentiment in a country. Action resources are an encompassing measure of enabling living conditions, combining per capita incomes, life expectancies, education levels, inverse fertilities, and income equality, as outlined in Welzel and Inglehart (2019).

the moral type of democracy supporter: indeed, as Figure 17.8 documents, the dominance of illiberal democracy supporters in the older generations has been replaced by a dominance of liberal democracy supporters in the younger generations.

Understanding the populist challenge

In light of our preceding discussion, the recent electoral successes of illiberal populism in some Western democracies are not the consequence of an erosion

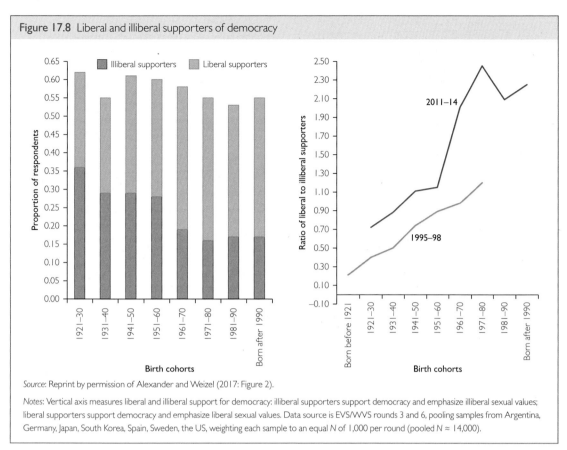

Figure 17.8 Liberal and illiberal supporters of democracy

Source: Reprint by permission of Alexander and Weizel (2017: Figure 2).

Notes: Vertical axis measures liberal and illiberal support for democracy: illiberal supporters support democracy and emphasize illiberal sexual values; liberal supporters support democracy and emphasize liberal sexual values. Data source is EVS/WVS rounds 3 and 6, pooling samples from Argentina, Germany, Japan, South Korea, Spain, Sweden, the US, weighting each sample to an equal *N* of 1,000 per round (pooled *N* ≈ 14,000).

of liberal values among younger generations. On the contrary, it is a reaction of illiberal older generations to the increasing liberalness of the younger generations. This reaction has picked up vigour because the generational rise of emancipative values has also increased polarization over these values, dropping those at the illiberal end of the polarization into an identity crisis that became even more virulent through the suddenly swelling influx of immigrants from non-Western cultures (Alexander and Welzel 2017). If anything, the generational differentiation in emancipative values does not forebode a forthcoming deconsolidation but, on the contrary, a revitalization of liberal democracy— as counter-intuitive as this may sound in light of the overly pessimistic tone of the current discourse.

For decades, discourses about the causes of autocracy and democracy have emphasized the economic interests of elites, the median voter and foreign powers (cf. Rueschemeyer et al. 1992; Acemoglu and Robinson 2006; Munck forthcoming). These discourses have neglected that democracy is a quintessentially normative concept that requires a moral commitment among the populations within which it is practiced. Thus, the question of democracy is a question of the given population's encultured mentality structures.

For this reason, democracy is and always has been a firmly culture-bound phenomenon, conditioned first and foremost by the spread of emancipative values.

In spite of these insights, scholars continue to advocate an *a*-cultural view of democracy, such as a recent article by Waldner and Lust (2018). The authors refer to critics of the cultural interpretation of democracy, such as for instance Dahlum and Knutsen (2015), who use panel regressions to show that emancipative values in a given year do not contribute to higher levels of democracy in the following year. Welzel et al. (2015) question this evidence, arguing that the elevating effect of emancipative values on democracy is not released in annually repeated, homeopathic doses of equally small volumes. Instead, emancipative values change incrementally, thus slowly building up a tension with inert regime structures, until a sudden disruptive regime change releases the tension in a manner that brings the regime structures back into equilibrium with the population's values. Because major regime changes happen infrequently and over only a short period, whose timing varies from country to country, the standard type of serial panel regressions easily misses these regime changes and how they surface in response to cultural conditions (but see the appendix in Brunkert et al. 2018).

To capture major regime changes and to visualize how they surface in response to cultural conditions, one needs to estimate in which direction and to what extent a country's regime 'misfits' the respective population's values at a fixed point in time and then use this structure–culture misfit as a predictor of regime changes over the years to follow, measuring these changes in both direction and degree. The time window within which one measures regime change must be rather wide to include the variable time points at which such changes occur in different countries. Thus, the wider the time window, the more regime changes one captures.

Congruence theory reloaded

Following this logic, Welzel et al. (2016) formulate a cultural theory of regime stability and change that they label the 'tectonic tension-release model'. The model conceptualizes the relationship between emancipative values and democracy levels as a supply–demand link with respect to freedoms. In this relationship, democracy levels constitute the elite-side supply of freedoms, while emancipative values constitute the mass-side demand for them. In analysing the relationship between freedom-demands and -supplies, it is important to recognize that values change continuously but slowly through generational replacement, whereas regime change is a rare and disruptive event. Therefore, the co-evolutionary dynamic between these differently paced processes can only follow a tectonic tension–release logic: incrementally changing emancipative values (i.e. demands for freedoms) build up an accruing tension with inert autocracy–democracy levels (i.e. supplies of freedoms), until this tension releases through a sudden disruptive shift that brings the supplies (i.e. democracy levels) back into equilibrium with the demands (i.e. emancipative values). Accordingly, the direction and scope of regime change operates as a correction of the supply's once accrued misfit to the demand. To confirm these propositions, three distinct regularities must be observed:

1. Where the elite-side supply of freedoms falls short of the mass-side demand, an occurring regime change shifts the supply *upward*—to the extent to which the supply previously fell short of the demand. In this case, we observe transitions towards democracy or, in short, democratization.

2. Where the elite-side supply of freedoms exceeds the mass-side demand, an occurring regime change shifts the supply *downward*—to the extent to which the supply previously exceeded

the demand. In this scenario, we witness backslides away from democracy or, in short, autocratization.

3. Where the elite-side supply of freedoms roughly fits the mass-side demand for them, no regime change occurs, and the supply stays where it was. This is the case for regime stability, which can be either democratic or autocratic stability.

The evidence in Figure 17.9 confirms all three propositions. On the horizontal axis, one sees to what extent a country's institutional supply of freedoms[4] in the first observation year of the WVS underbid or overbid the masses' demand for freedoms[5] in the same year.[6] On the vertical axis, we see to what extent and in which direction countries experienced a change in the supply of freedoms from the year of the first WVS observation in a given country (T_1) to the year of the last observation (T_2). The T_1–T_2 time distances cover on average sixteen years, but vary between three and thirty-six years, depending on the surveyed country, which Figure 17.9 controls for. Thus, the scores on the two axes display variation under temporal distances held constant.

The country distribution in Figure 17.9 exhibits three regularities: (i) countries autocratized from year T_1 to year T_2 to the extent to which freedom supplies in year T_1 overbid demands in that year; (ii) countries democratized from year T_1 to year T_2 to the extent to which freedom supplies in year T_1 underbid demands in that year; (iii) countries remained stable from year T_1 to year T_2 to the extent to which freedom supplies in year T_1 matched demands in that year. These three tendencies confirm exactly the three propositions of the 'tectonic tension-release model' and account for 65 per cent of the variation in both the direction and extent of the countries' regime change versus stability over a sixteen-year timespan on average. The evidence covers all ninety-eight nations that have been surveyed at least twice by the WVS, which represent more than 90 per cent of the world population.

The most important take-away message of these findings can be phrased like this: democracies are culturally stable and safe from backsliding down to lower levels of democracy to the extent to which they correspond with the population's overall emancipative values. In a nutshell, backsliding is more likely where emancipative values remain weak or recede.

Political science provides separate explanations of (i) the emergence of democracies; (ii) the breakdown of democracies and their backsliding into autocracies; (iii) the survival of democracies; and (iv) the stability of autocracies. Yet, these separate explanations co-exist in isolation from each other.

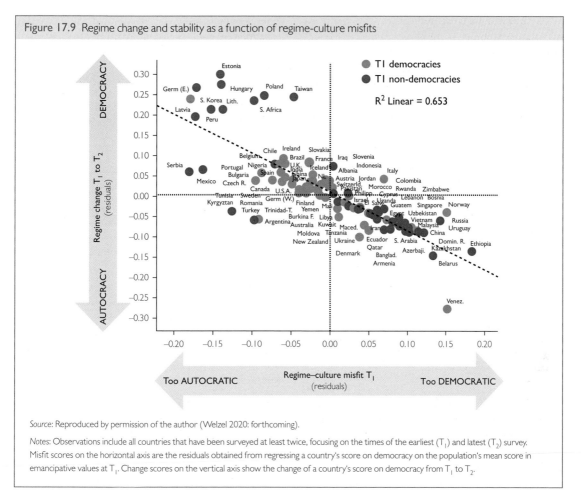

Figure 17.9 Regime change and stability as a function of regime-culture misfits

Source: Reproduced by permission of the author (Welzel 2020: forthcoming).

Notes: Observations include all countries that have been surveyed at least twice, focusing on the times of the earliest (T$_1$) and latest (T$_2$) survey. Misfit scores on the horizontal axis are the residuals obtained from regressing a country's score on democracy on the population's mean score in emancipative values at T$_1$. Change scores on the vertical axis show the change of a country's score on democracy from T$_1$ to T$_2$.

This is a drawback from the viewpoint of a general theory of regime evolution because such a theory needs to capture the selective forces that drive the world's long-term democratic trend and its intermittent reversals. Such a theory requires a simultaneous understanding of the factors that give rise to democracy or prevent their rise, as well as the factors that stabilize democracies or make them slide back into autocracy.

It is a significant feature of the 'tectonic tension-release model' that it integrates explanations of the two opposite versions of regime change (i.e. democratization and autocratization), as well as the two opposite forms of regime stability (i.e. democratic and autocratic stability) in a single theory. This single theory provides a unified framework to understand regime stability and regime change, based on a unitary principle: the direction and degree of incongruence between regime institutions and cultural values. Hence, the tectonic model provides a confirmation of the classic idea of congruence underlying the political culture paradigm.

Conclusion

Against the backdrop of our portrayal, sweepingly dismissive statements by Munck (forthcoming) as well as Waldner and Lust (2018) claiming that cultural theories have nothing on offer to understand the underpinnings of stable democracy appear misplaced. In light of the evidence in Figure 17.9, a theory that explains 65 per cent of the cross-national variance in regime stability versus change is certainly not everything; but it is at least something.

The cultural view of democracy informs a less euphoric account of the centennial democratic trend because democracy has established itself at high levels and persistently so only in societies at the forefront of emancipative values at their time. Likewise, the various waves of democratization have driven countries towards democracy only in as far as they developed emancipative values. Thus, the desire for democratic freedoms is not universally human, but culturally conditioned by the development of emancipative values.

The cultural view of democracy also informs a less gloomy account of the recent democratic recession around the globe. This is true for several reasons. First, the backsliding of liberal democracies into illiberal, more authoritarian forms of government is largely limited to societies in which emancipative values remain under-developed. Second, emancipative values are on a generational rise almost everywhere in the world, including such strongholds of autocracy as China and Russia, which suggests that generational replacement operates in favour of a continuation of the centennial democratic trend in the future. Third, the firmer enculturation of emancipative values among younger generations is likely to render temporary the recent electoral successes of illiberal populism. At the elections to the European Parliament in 2019, the mobilization of emancipation-oriented younger voters prevented populists from winning elections.

KEY POINTS

- The political economy approach argues that modernization favours democracy because it makes democracy more acceptable in the eyes of the elites.

- The political culture approach argues that modernization favours democracy because it confronts elites with more capable and ambitious mass publics.

? QUESTIONS

Knowledge-based

1. What is the difference between norms, values, and beliefs?

2. What is the difference between secular and emancipative values?

3. Do civilizations matter for politics? How compact are world religions and major cultures?

4. What is stated by the allegiance model of the democratic citizen?

5. How can one define social capital and trust?

Critical thinking

1. Is culture or the economy more important for understanding political modernization?

2. Can one say that there are distinct national cultures?

3. How important are secular values in the modern world?

4. Does political culture affect the functioning of political institutions and how?

5. Are all cultures compatible with or conducive to democracy?

 ## FURTHER READING

Almond, G. A. and Verba, S. (1963) *The Civic Culture: Political Attitudes and Democracy in Five Nations* (Princeton, NJ: Princeton University Press).

Dalton, R. J. and Welzel, C. (2013) *The Civic Culture Transformed: From Allegiant to Assertive Citizenship* (New York: Cambridge University Press).

Huntington, S. P. (1995) *The Clash of Civilizations and the Remaking of World Order* (New York: Simon & Schuster).

Inglehart, R. (1977) *The Silent Revolution: Changing Values and Political Styles Among Western Publics* (Princeton, NJ: Princeton University Press).

Inglehart, R. (1997) *Modernization and Postmodernization: Cultural, Economic and Political Change in 43 Societies* (Princeton, NJ: Princeton University Press).

Inglehart, R. and Norris, P. (2003) *Rising Tide: Gender Equality and Cultural Change Around the World* (Cambridge: Cambridge University Press).

Putnam, R. D. (1993) *Making Democracy Work: Civic Traditions in Modern Italy* (Princeton, NJ: Princeton University Press).

Putnam, R. D. (2000) *Bowling Alone: The Collapse and Revival of American Community* (New York: Simon & Schuster).

Welzel, C. (2013) *Freedom Rising: Human Empowerment and the Quest for Emancipation* (New York: Cambridge University Press).

ENDNOTES

1. Secular values are measured on the basis of twelve items, indicating a secular distance from the sacred authorities of religion, the nation, the state, and group norms. Each of these items is recoded in such a way that the least secular position is coded 0 and the most secular position 1.0. Distance from the authority of religion is measured by three items asking if the respondent considers religion important, defines him/herself as religious, and how frequently he/she practises religion. Distance from state authority is measured by three items asking how much confidence the respondent has in the army, the police, and the courts. Distance from national authority is measured by three items asking how much national pride the respondent has, if he/she is willing to fight for their country in case of war, and whether more respect of authority is needed. Distance from the authority of group norms is measured by three items asking the respondent how justifiable he/she finds taking a bribe, evading taxes, and claiming benefits for which one is not entitled. A respondent's final score on secular values is the average score over all twelve items. As shown in detail by Welzel (2013), dimensional analyses across individuals and nations justify this summary of items.

2. Emancipative values are measured on the basis of twelve items. Each of these items is recoded in such a way that the least emancipative position is coded 0 and the most emancipative position 1.0. Three of the twelve items refer to important child qualities and can be used to measure how much emphasis respondents place on 'autonomy', depending on whether they indicate 'independence' and 'imagination' as important child qualities but do not indicate 'obedience' as such a quality. Another three items address goals that a country's government should pursue. These items are used to measure how much emphasis respondents place on 'voice', depending on whether they assign first, second, or no priority to the goals of 'protecting freedom of speech', 'giving people more say in important government decisions', and 'giving people more say about how things are done at their jobs and in their communities'. The next three items refer to the status of women relative to men and are used to measure how much emphasis respondents place on 'equality', depending on how strongly they disagree

with the statements that 'Education is more important for a boy than a girl', 'When jobs are scarce, men should have priority over women to get a job', and 'Men make better political leaders than women'. The last set of three items addresses life choices and is used to measure how much emphasis respondents place on 'choice', depending on how acceptable they find 'divorce', 'abortion', and 'homosexuality'. A respondent's final score on emancipative values is the average score over all twelve items. As shown in detail by Welzel (2013), dimensional analyses across individuals and nations justify this summary of items.

3. Not all existential threats lead necessarily to in-group closure and inter-group hostility. That happens only when threats are perceived as group specific. Threats, by contrast, that are perceived as non-divisive—such as climate change—can trigger solidary mobilization across group boundaries.

4. To measure supply, we use Brunkert et al.'s (2018) index of 'comprehensive democracy', which combines the indicators of the 'electoral', 'liberal', and 'participatory' democracy components provided by V-Dem (Coppedge et al. 2017). Scale range is from minimum 0 for the lowest to 1 for the highest democracy level.

5. We measure demands using Welzel's (2013) index of emancipative values.

6. To obtain these misfit scores, one saves the residuals provided by regressing democracy levels in the earliest year of observation on emancipative values in the same year of observation. Note that we 'condition' these regime-culture misfit scores, multiplying them by 1 if a subsequent regime change occurred and 0 if no such change occurred. This procedure is informed by the idea that regime-culture misfits provide an opportunity for regime change but do not fully determine such a regime change because it always needs concrete actors who perceive and decide to utilize the opportunity. If no change occurred, obviously no actor utilized the opportunity. Hence, Figure 17.9 shows in what direction and to what extent regimes changed depending on the direction and extent of the regime-culture misfit, provided actors decided to utilize the opportunity embodied in the given misfit.

Visit the Online Resources that accompany this book for additional material, including country profiles, comparative data sets, flashcard glossaries, and web directory.

www.oup.com/he/caramani5e

18

Political participation

Herbert Kitschelt and Philipp Rehm

Reader's guide

This chapter tackles one of the most ubiquitous, yet also least understood phenomena in political science. Political participation covers a wide range of activities, from turning out to vote, to giving money to a campaign, to outright violence in the streets. This chapter addresses four fundamental questions. First, it explores different modes of political participation. How does it happen? How intense and how risky is political participation? Second, the chapter sheds some light on the motivation for political participation. Why do people engage in participation? If they do, why are they choosing one way of participation over another? Third, in which contextual conditions is participation more likely? What is the role of economic affluence? Are there systematic differences between democracies and autocracies? Finally, the chapter turns to the motivations of individuals to engage in participation. Who participates, and why are some people more likely to become involved in politics than others?

Introduction

Political participation establishes links from the mass public to the political elites. The term refers to a wide range of activities, including voting in elections, donating time or money to political campaigns, running for office, writing petitions, boycotting, organizing in unions, demonstrating, carrying out illegal sit-ins or occupations, blockades, and even physical assault on the forces of order.

Democracy does not work without the (voluntary and legal) political participation of its citizens. Consider, for example, the following famous definition of democracy as 'a system in which parties lose elections' (Przeworski 1991: 10; see also Chapter 5 'Democracies'). Parties have to be founded, financed, and run. People need to run for office, organize campaigns, collect money, and manage staff. Elections need the involvement of citizens, most obviously by the act of voting. But participation of citizens also occurs in non-democratic regimes. For example, many authoritarian regimes tolerate some modes of political participation in order to gather information about grievances among their subjects to quell pent-up frustration. Totalitarian regimes also institute compulsory participation to maintain the existing political order, while repressing autonomous, bottom-up participation of subjects. While these types of involuntary acts of political polarization may be included in a definition (see Box: Definitions of political participation, in the Online Resources), this chapter restricts its focus to *voluntary participation*, and puts an emphasis on *democracies*.

Voluntary political participation has attracted the attention of many scholars, and it raises fascinating puzzles. First, scholars are still trying to find out why people engage in political participation at all. After all, most of the acts of political participation are somewhat costly (in terms of time or money), and many of them are not effective. For example, the chance of a voter's vote being decisive in a mass democracy is (almost) zero, while casting the vote is costly. Yet millions of people go to the voting booths. Second, scholars also try to understand why some people engage in political participation, while others do not. Finally, why do people choose certain types of political participation over others?

As these examples suggest, political participation addressed to a central authority is costly and difficult to achieve. Thus, political participation is an activity that occurs *despite all kinds of obstacles and preferences for more spontaneous self-reliant action*. In a sense, it is a 'miracle' that political participation, as a voluntary and deliberate engagement with collective decision-making and authoritative decision-makers, occurs at all.

How? Modes of political participation

There is no unanimously agreed-upon typology of participatory practices, but the political science literature has established some rather widely accepted conventions that we try to capture in Tables 18.1 and 18.2. First, political participation may take place in *different arenas or political contexts*. Second, the *intensity* of participation (time and resources) varies greatly. Third, participatory activities can be distinguished in terms of their *riskiness* to the freedom, life, and limb of the participants.

Sites of participation

Table 18.1 distinguishes sites and intensities of participation. As in the online box already mentioned in the Introduction, (i) people can become involved in a public arena to advertise and communicate demands to anyone willing to listen; (ii) they may target policy-makers in legislatures or the executive branch as recipients of their communications; or (iii) they may get involved in the selection process of those who aspire to legislative or executive office. Each of these sites involves its own ladder of personal effort and commitment, as people move from intermittent to continuous participation and leadership in organized efforts. Unless actors are independently wealthy, high involvement is ultimately associated with monetary compensation once they allocate so much time to their political involvement that they cannot pursue regular jobs or professions as well.

The **riskiness of participation** depends on the legal and political regime in which it occurs. The less tolerant a regime is regarding the free expression and organization of citizens' political opinions, the more risky and costly are even restrained forms of political interest articulation. In democracies, activities expressed in two sites of participation—communication with governmental personnel and participation in the nomination and choice of elected politicians—are low risk. In contrast, in democracies, 'unconventional' participation in the public forum tends to run from low-risk activities to those that are legally prohibited because they inflict physical harm on human beings and property (Table 18.2).

Because our entries in Table 18.2 focus on the personal riskiness of political participation in different regimes, the division of categories is slightly at odds with common distinctions between 'conventional' and 'unconventional' participation or participation through institutionalized channels and extra-institutional protest politics. In democracies at least, some unconventional

KEY POINTS

- The object of analysis is voluntary, not coerced, political participation.

- Participation manifests itself in a wide variety of forms that need to be explained.

- Political participation is a costly undertaking and rarely occurs spontaneously.

Table 18.1 Sites of political participation and intensity of involvement

Intensity of involvement	Sites of participation		
	Community, street, and media politics: public expression of demands ('forum politics')	Communicating preferences to policy-makers in legislature and executive branch	Choosing legislative and executive policy-makers
Lowest	Persuasive rhetoric: public advocacy	Persuasive rhetoric: contacting elected or administrative officials	Voting for candidates/parties
	Participation in collective events	Contributions to sustain communication with political officials/associational membership	Contributions to sustain contenders for political office and coalitions of such contenders (parties)
	Activist/mobilizer for collective events	Volunteer activism, unpaid functionary	Volunteer activism, unpaid party functionary, or unpaid electoral office holder
Highest	Spokesperson, public leader	Paid officer, associational executive	Party executive leader or elected career politician

Table 18.2 Riskiness of political participation

Riskiness of participation	Democratic civic and political liberties	Mildly repressive authoritarianism (A) and severely repressive despotism (D)
Legally codified and permitted venues	Voting; contacting policy-makers (lobbying/petitioning); associational memberships; lawful industrial action (strikes, walkouts); lawful street politics (demonstrations)	Voting/often compulsory (D, some A); some state-directed associational memberships/often compulsory (D); some state-directed public manifestations/often compulsory (D)
Not legally codified, but tolerated forms	Boycotts; some unlicensed public manifestations; unofficial strikes	Lobbying/petitioning public officials (A); some voluntary associational memberships (A); some voluntary public manifestations (A)
Legally prohibited activities: breaking political–institutional and property laws (mild punishment)	Legally unregistered demonstrations; site occupations; sit-ins	Petitions (most D); strikes (some A); spontaneous public manifestations (some A; all D)
Legally prohibited activities: breaking laws, severe punishment (detention or capital punishment)	Destruction of property, political vandalism, sabotage; physical assault on the forces of order; assassinations, bombings, hijackings, kidnappings (terrorism)	Strikes (most A, all D); boycotts (all A and D); site occupations, sit-ins (all A and D); destruction of property, political vandalism, sabotage (all A and D); physical assault on the forces of order (all A and D); assassinations, bombings, hijackings, kidnappings

activities are low risk (e.g. lobbying or licensed street demonstrations). In all political regimes, protest politics that harms people or property rights is subject to criminal sanctions. In non-democratic regimes, more activities are 'unconventional' and punished.

Modes of participation

Most popular participation is organized and regular. While in some instances people may decide to become involved in a particular participatory event on a single-shot basis, most of the time actors contribute to a specific site of political interest articulation, where claims are advanced and specific organizational practices evolve over some extended period of time.

Social movements

Streams of activities that target demands at policy-makers through community, street, and media events as their primary sites of articulation are **social movements** (see Chapter 16 'Social movements'). Social movements may involve large numbers of people, but they have generally *small* formal organizational cores. Typically, there is no formal membership, and many participants are not interested in that. Likewise, movement leaders do not make major investments in the construction of an organizational infrastructure of coordination among activists.

Interest groups

Activities where participants mainly rely on communicating preferences, demands, and threats to policy-makers situated in legislative and executive arenas tend to create durable interest groups (see Chapter 14 'Interest groups'). They are typically formally organized, with explicit membership roles and internal statutes. This is one source of their influence (*encompassingness* of interest organization).

Membership is one indicator of an interest group's threat capacity vis-à-vis policy-makers, but it may be insufficient as such. In part, the power of an interest group derives from the **centralization** of its internal organization (the capacity of the association to make decisions that bind all members). Centralized interest groups can make *credible commitments* to holding their end of a bargain and therefore are attractive for policy-makers willing to craft compromises among contending interests.

Political parties

Activities in which participants cooperate in order to nominate legislative candidates, help them attract voters, and organize voter **turnout** in favour of such candidates amount to the formation of political parties (see Chapters 12 'Political parties' and 13 'Party systems'). In mass democracy, most candidates face obstacles to getting their message out, and parties help in overcoming these. From the voter's perspective, the decision to participate in an election is made easier if there are only a few alternative candidates under identifiable labels. Parties' reputations and promises play a crucial role in the competition for votes. Parties develop reputations and can credibly make promises only if they rally a large number of politicians for a long time period and make them agree on roughly similar policies.

Obviously, political activists using the same organizational label may at one point in time act more like a social movement, while at another more like a party. Nevertheless, almost all political associations focus on one 'core competence' and site of participatory **mobilization** at any given time.

KEY POINTS

- Participation occurs at different sites: in public places, in communication with political decision-makers, and by involvement in the electoral process.

- At each site of participation, actors decide about the depth and extent of their involvement.

- Participants face greater or lesser risks to their personal welfare as a consequence of their choice of political involvements. Political regimes shape the riskiness of different participatory acts.

- Participatory acts typically are not disjointed events, but happen around social movements, interest groups, or political parties.

Why? Determinants of political participation

Why do people engage in political participation? What types of actors become involved in certain types of political activity, but not others? And how do citizens and politicians choose their mix of political involvements between social movements, interest groups, and political parties?

Political versus other types of participation

Political participation is only one of several ways for members of a society to further their life chances. Alternatively, they may rely on *markets* or *families and communal associations*. This gives a first answer to the question of why people participate in politics. It is a *choice of last resort*. When existing problem-solving techniques fail to deliver, people participate.

The paradox of collective action

People participate in politics to bring about authoritative decisions which allocate goods and bads to large groups. These often are *collective goods*: once produced, no individual belonging to a polity can be excluded from enjoying (or suffering) the consequences of having such goods, regardless of whether or not that individual has contributed to their production. This generates a seeming **collective action paradox** (Olson 1965). If individuals are self-regarding and try to minimize the costs of benefits, they may not contribute to produce collective goods. Instead, people behave as freeriders. We would expect this in most large group situations where the personal costs of fighting for the political provision of the good ('participation') far outweigh the personal benefits of enjoying the good. Therefore, if *each* individual reasons that *others* should bear the costs of producing the collective good, no good will ever be produced at all.

Olson submits that, nevertheless, political participation occurs because **selective incentives** overcome the **free-rider problem**. Participants in a mobilizational effort to produce collective goods receive additional 'private' benefits that only accrue to participants. If such selective incentives are sufficiently valuable to *outweigh the costs* of participation, then political mobilization will occur.

But Olson's theory runs into an empirical challenge: political participation appears to happen much more frequently than the theory would permit. A particularly prominent example is the so-called 'paradox of voting' (Aldrich 1993). Millions of citizens regularly show up at the voting booth without obvious selective incentives. Much research since the appearance of Olson's book has focused on reasons why Olson's paradox of political participation may be less stark in practice than in theory (see Box: Internal solutions to the problem of collective action, in the Online Resources). One line of research suggests external solutions to the collective action problem. Solutions are 'external' if they deviate from Olson's original assumptions when setting up the paradox of collective action (see Box: Assumptions of the free-rider problem, in the Online Resources). An extensive review of such solutions can be found in Hardin (1982) and Lichbach (1995). Some solutions to the 'paradox of collective action' are as follows.

- There may be some **political entrepreneurs** who do not consider political involvement costly. They may disregard the costs of political action for reasons of moral passion or a striving for glory and be willing to supply the bread-and-butter selective incentives that make more economically rational self-regarding people join in.

- The premise of Olson's set-up is that people treat political participation as a cost. But what if it is a benefit or the benefit itself? Some may value the experience of enjoying solidarity with a large number of other human beings in collective action, all the way to building barricades and throwing Molotov cocktails at the forces of order, as an intrinsically gratifying experience. On a more mundane level, many people may derive satisfaction from the experience of communal deliberation over

the value of collective pursuits and over the strategies to obtain them. In all these instances, the process of participation itself is a most powerful benefit.

- Actors may be motivated to underrate the costs of participation. This may be a simple matter of misperception, or political entrepreneurs may have persuaded them to discount the costs of action, or such leaders may have made them believe that a major pay-off resulting from collective action is within reach with only a little more involvement, turning the cost–benefit balance of involvement positive.

- **Social networks** may serve as a monitoring device. This may motivate some individuals to join in the collective effort. Such mechanisms may amount to a dynamic of information cascades and tipping points in collective action (Kuran 1991; Chwe 2001). As more individuals signal willingness to participate, effective repression becomes harder to achieve and more costly for the forces of order. A spiral may unfold in which people observe a given level of collective action at a time t that, contrary to their prior expectations, triggers little repression. This signal, in turn, boosts greater participation in the next round at time $t + 1$, which makes it even more costly for the forces of order to deploy repressive measures. The catalyst of expanding participation and faltering repression emboldens even more participants to join in collective actions in subsequent rounds (Lohmann 1994).

Olson's work has stimulated a tremendous amount of research on political participation. But starting from an elegant simple theorem (freeriding and selective incentives), it has ultimately added a level of complexity that makes straightforward predictions of collective action impossible.

KEY POINTS

- Political participation as an appeal to a public authority to make a binding decision is a last-resort strategy to resolve social conflicts when other, more direct approaches fail.

- Much political participation aims at the provision of collective goods, from whose benefits those who did not contribute to their production cannot be excluded. This poses a free-rider problem.

- Selective incentives that provide benefits targeted only at those who contribute to the production of a collective good provide a partial, incomplete solution to the free-rider problem.

- Sometimes actors may contribute to collective action because participation itself is experienced as a reward, or the costs of participation are deemed to be minimal.

When and where? Explaining political participation at the macro-level

Political demands are a necessary, but not a sufficient, condition for political mobilization (see also Chapter 16 'Social movements' on this point). The answer to why people engage in political participation comes in two parts: (i) because they are in a certain place at a certain time (the role of context and opportunity) and because political entrepreneurs devise appropriate organizations of political action (this section); and (ii) because they have resources and dispositions that facilitate participation (individual or micro-level factors, which are dealt with in the next section, 'Who? Explaining political participation at the micro-level').

Differences in participation across regime types

The range of organizational vehicles that citizens and political leaders can employ to pursue political objectives varies by systemic context (see Table 18.3).

1. In *democracies* with elections for legislative and executive office through universal suffrage and institutions to protect civil and political rights of citizens, there exists a very wide range of participatory acts that crystallize in time and space around movements with small core organizations, large interest associations, and political parties.

2. In *authoritarian regimes*, such as nineteenth-century constitutional monarchies or many twentieth-century military and civilian dictatorships, the executive is beyond democratic accountability, but tolerates some activities of spontaneously emerging social movements, interest groups, and even political parties that may compete for legislative seats.

3. In *harshly repressive despotic regimes*, opportunities are substantially more restricted, particularly those with far-flung organizations to control and mobilize subjects from above. They do not simply thwart and repress any sort of organized sustained participatory coordination among actors from below, but also impose compulsory political participation through state-run mass organizations from above (see Chapter 6 'Authoritarian regimes').

Differences in participation within democracies

Participation varies not only across, but also within regime types. When we analyse participation and its organizational modes comparing democracies, there is considerable diversity in time and space. It appears that *levels of economic development* are somewhat related to participation. Figure 18.1 reports the percentage of respondents in several dozen countries indicating participation in at least one of three low-risk modes of political participation (signing a petition; joining a boycott; attending a lawful demonstration), as well as at least one of two high-risk modes (joining unofficial

Table 18.3 Political regimes and venues of political participation

Voluntary action	Liberal democracy	Authoritarian polity	Despotic polity
Repertoire of collective action	Wide range of legally permitted and tolerated modes of participation; severe sanctions against violence	Narrow range of legally licensed, but broader range of tolerated modes of participation; severe sanctions against participation using violence and some non-violent acts	Some legally compulsory participation; no tolerated spontaneous participation; severe sanctions against most forms of political participation, whether violent or non-violent
Social movements	Yes	Yes	No
Interest groups	Yes	Yes	No
Political parties	Yes	(Yes/no)(Semi-competitive elections to legislatures, but no legislative choice of the executive or direct democratic election of the executive)	(No)(Parties from above: single-party or single-list united front party ballots; no strategic deliberation in parties)

Figure 18.1 Low- and high-risk participation in selected countries

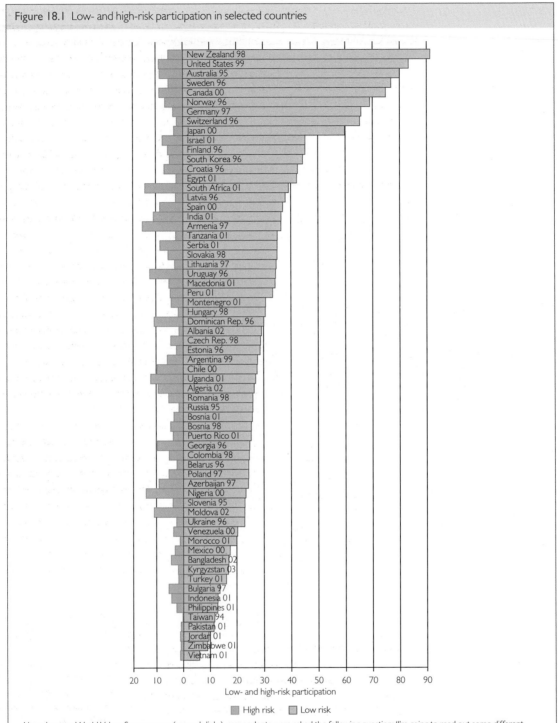

Notes: In some World Values Survey waves (see web links), respondents were asked the following question: 'I'm going to read out some different forms of political action that people can take, and I'd like you to tell me, for each one, whether you have actually done any of these things, whether you might do it or would never, under any circumstances, do it.' 'Low-risk political participation' refers to the following three items covered by this survey question: signing a petition (E025), joining in boycotts (E026), and attending lawful demonstrations (E027). 'High-risk political participation' refers to the following two items: joining unofficial strikes (E028), or occupying buildings or factories (E029)

.*Source:* World Value Surveys (www.worldvaluessurvey.org), WVS Longitudinal file, 1981-2014. Most recent year only (1994-2003; varies by country).

strikes; occupying buildings or factories).[1] A simple conclusion that can be drawn from the figure is that, clearly, the most affluent tier of countries shows much greater participatory experience than post-communist or other developing countries.

These differences may have to do with the political opportunity structure potential that entrepreneurs of a new political cause are facing.[2] If existing parties and interest groups are willing and able to incorporate new demands without alienating elements of their existing support coalitions, a new salient cause may have little impact on a polity's profile of participation. However, if existing vehicles of interest aggregation resist incorporation of new and salient demands in the polity, outside political entrepreneurs might decide to begin independent political mobilization.

Fragmented **multiparty systems** with a differentiated menu of party labels tend to make it more likely that established vehicles of interest aggregation pick up new demands. Counterbalancing this, however, is the easier entry in **electoral systems** with **proportional representation** (PR) that prevail among fragmented multiparty systems (see Chapter 13 'Party systems'). Such rules make it possible for political entrepreneurs to organize an effective independent electoral partisan challenge around a newly salient demand. However, in **two-party systems** a lack of internal party cohesion (such as within the two US parties) may create access points for new demands within established politics which make it unnecessary for such interests to

follow the route of sustained protest and construction of new rival political associations. Let us look at two examples where contextual effects in democracies can be reasonably expected to affect political participation. The first relates to the 'paradox of voting' mentioned earlier in 'Why? Determinants of political participation' (see Box: The paradox of voting, in the Online Resources), and connects a country's context to its level of turnout. The second example relates to different levels of union membership.

Voter turnout

Figure 18.2 shows average turnout rates for countries with and without compulsory voting laws. While, on average, turnout has declined everywhere, turnout rates in countries with compulsory voting are substantially higher compared to countries without compulsory voting, and the gap between those countries has somewhat widened over the past few decades. Figure 18.3 shows voter turnout rates in recent parliamentary elections in several dozen countries. Once again, the figure shows that countries with compulsory voting laws tend to have much higher turnouts. Beyond that, the figure does not reveal strong cross-national patterns. However, there is a sophisticated cross-national comparative literature on voting turnout.[3] Beyond such broad forces as development, political regime, and the timing of the enfranchisement of new voters (women, youths) who reach turnout levels of established voter groups only with a delay of a genera-

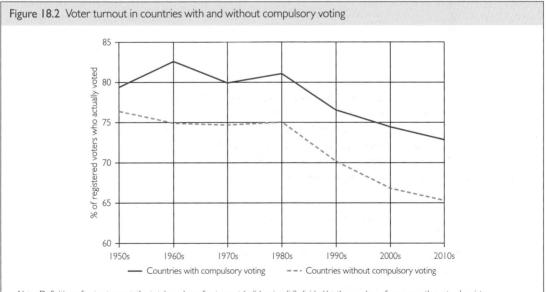

Figure 18.2 Voter turnout in countries with and without compulsory voting

Note: Definition of voter turnout: the total number of votes cast (valid or invalid) divided by the number of names on the voters' register, expressed as a percentage.

Source: Turnout data (parliamentary elections only) are from the International IDEA Voter Turnout database (https://www.idea.int/data-tools/data/voter-turnout). Information on compulsory voting comes from the same source (https://www.idea.int/data-tools/data/voter-turnout/compulsory-voting).

tion, there are several important institutional mechanisms that influence aggregate electoral turnout. In the following, we focus on four of them.

- *Compulsory voting* is linked to turnout. It is critical to know whether and how non-voting is punished. However, regardless of enforcement, it can be observed that, across Western democracies, countries with compulsory voting systems tend to have higher turnout rates (see Blais 2006: 112–13; see also box in the Online Resources).

- *Electoral rules* are linked to turnout. One usually distinguishes between proportional representation (PR) systems (every vote counts) and **majoritarian** or single-member districts (winner takes all). Under conditions of PR and low **thresholds** of representation, most voters can choose their preferred party and expect it to gain seats in the legislature. This is different in systems with single-member or a small number of member districts or other stipulations generating high electoral thresholds of representation. In all of these systems, rational voters who find that their favourite party or candidate has no chance of winning a seat and who dislike all second-best options intensely tend to stay home. Inspecting Figure 18.3, it can be seen that, among affluent Organisation for Economic Co-operation and Development (OECD) countries, PR electoral systems tend to go hand in hand with higher turnout rates (see also Chapters 10 'Elections and referendums' and 13 'Party systems').

- **Registration requirements** are linked to turnout. In many democracies, registration is automatic and therefore is not a constraint on voting. In the US, however, citizens have to seek out registration actively and many, particularly the young and mobile and the very old and infirm, as well as poorer citizens, are seriously under-represented in the registered electorate. Not surprisingly, turnout levels among registered voters in the US are low. In fact, Powell (1986) calculates that if European democracies were operating under the same institutional rules as the US (single-member districts, registration requirements, work-day voting, frequency of elections, and the number of offices on which people vote), voter turnout in Europe would be even lower than in the US.

- The *timing of elections* is linked to turnout outside parliamentary democracies. Turnout tends to be greater if *legislative and presidential elections take place on the same day*. In these so-called 'concurrent'

elections, voters award the big prizes for the executive and the legislature in one single go, rather than in staggered contests.

Beyond these and other more minor institutional rules, there are important strategic and political–economic conditions that affect turnout, such as the closeness of an election (Aldrich 1993; Franklin 2004) or income and educational inequality (Anderson and Beramendi 2008).

Labour union membership

In democracies, labour unions tend to have more members than other organized interest groups. Yet, membership varies dramatically in time and space. Four points can be made about the cross-national variance of labour union membership.

1. The transition from agriculture to urban manufacturing and service industries, particularly if they concentrate labour in large factories or offices, enables wage earners to overcome collective action problems and organize interest associations. This is one important reason why labour union membership tends to be higher in affluent polities than in developing countries.

2. Political regime also matters. Voluntary interest associations, such as unions, thrive in democratic polities. In the early European democratic transitions, unions promoted **democratization** (Collier 1999), but in highly repressive regimes government-sponsored labour unions may serve as organizational techniques to mobilize actors into the established order. An example is communist China. Also, in Latin America authoritarian regimes set up unions and business associations and deployed them as transmission belts of corporatist authoritarian **governance**, such as under Getulio Vargas in Brazil from the mid-1930s.

3. In both communist and corporatist authoritarian regimes, economic development policy comes into play as a catalyst of interest group participation. Both types of regime pursued strategies of nurturing domestic industries by protecting them from foreign competitors behind high tariff walls and by cheapening the factor inputs that could not be supplied domestically by overvalued currencies combined with discretionary import licences. This development strategy was promoted by the political mobilization of relatively scarce and expensive domestic industrial capital and labour seeking protection from foreign competitive

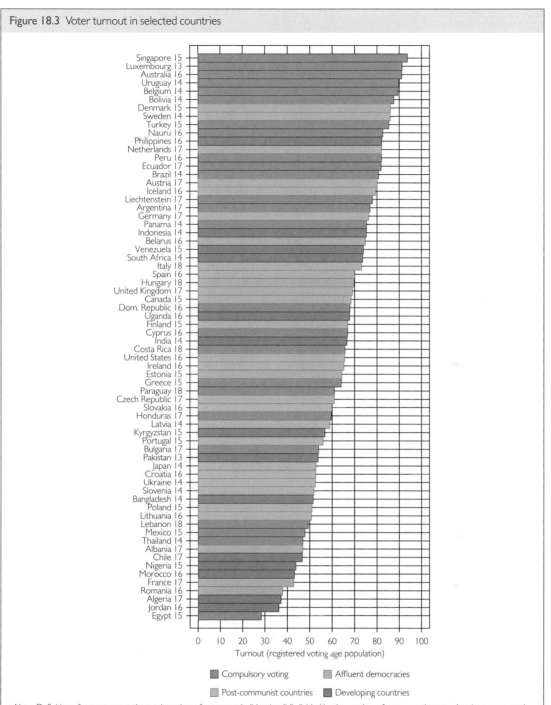

Figure 18.3 Voter turnout in selected countries

Note: Definition of voter turnout: the total number of votes cast (valid or invalid) divided by the number of names on the voters' register, expressed as a percentage.

Source: Turnout data are from https://www.idea.int/data-tools/data/voter-turnout; only selected countries and most recent parliamentary elections are displayed. Information on compulsory voting comes from the same source (https://www.idea.int/data-tools/data/voter-turnout/compulsory-voting).

pressure. But, conversely, it also reinforced such interest organization: as domestic industries grew, but remained relatively inefficient behind the protective walls of regulated international trade and capital flows, the mobilization of political influence became vital for its survival.

4. Beyond economic development and regime, however, there are also dramatic differences even within a set of seventeen relatively similar democracies, as can be seen from Figure 18.4. Not only are there huge differences in terms of levels (compare France and Sweden), but

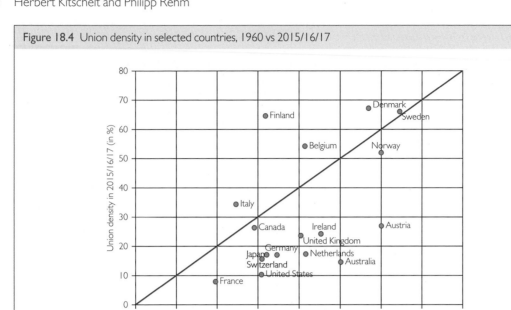

Figure 18.4 Union density in selected countries, 1960 vs 2015/16/17

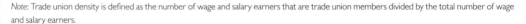

Note: Trade union density is defined as the number of wage and salary earners that are trade union members divided by the total number of wage and salary earners.

Source: OECD (https://stats.oecd.org/Index.aspx?DataSetCode=TUD).

there are also interesting differences in terms of trends: unionization remained high or *increased* in countries where it was strong to begin with, but it almost invariably *decreased* in countries where unions had only median strength or were already weak. Structural change away from large offices and workshops and towards post-industrial jobs and professions is fairly similar across all affluent OECD countries, but unionization clearly diverges. How can we make sense of this pattern?

We want to highlight just one factor that provides a powerful institutional explanation of the observed variance: the **Ghent system** (named after the Belgian city where it was first introduced). Under the Ghent system, initiated in countries where socialists had become a highly competitive party to win executive control, governments delegated the task of organizing and administering unemployment insurance to labour unions, thus providing a very powerful selective incentive, in Olson's sense, for wage earners to join unions and pay their dues in order to gain the private benefit of prompt unemployment pay compensation in case of job loss in the market economy. In Belgium, Denmark, Finland, and Sweden the Ghent system prevailed, and these countries are among the most unionized countries in the world.

The presence of the Ghent system also makes itself felt in change over time. Technological change,

de-industrialization, and other shocks that increased the risk of unemployment for typical union members led to different reactions in countries with and without the Ghent system (see Figure 18.5). In countries with the Ghent system, the increasing risk of unemployment prompted wage earners to rally to labour unions even more vigorously than in the past (see Chapter 22 'The impact of public policies'). In contrast, in countries without the Ghent system the value of unions in maintaining wages and job security appeared ever more marginal, a perception further reinforced where socialist parties were weak and in opposition. In most of these countries, we see a contraction of union density since the 1980s.

Political organizations and mobilization

Why is it that some forms of participation lead to the mobilization of social movements, while others gravitate towards interest group association or the rise of political parties? And why are political entrepreneurs across polities more successful in organizing parties and interest groups around some causes—such as social class or religion—whereas other demands routinely fail at the level of party mobilization—such as demands of women, retirees, taxpayers, or consumers—all of which have generated considerable efforts to build parties over the past fifty years?

To sketch an answer to these questions, let us assume that actors will invest in collective action only

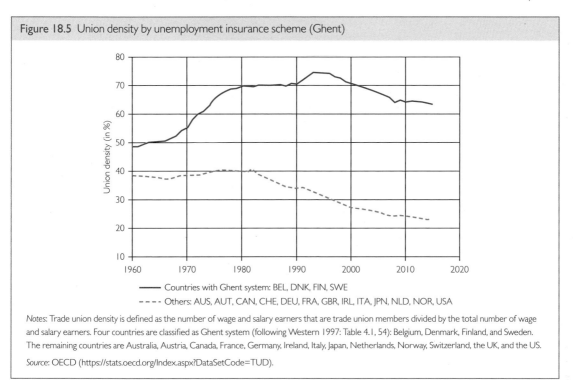

Figure 18.5 Union density by unemployment insurance scheme (Ghent)

——— Countries with Ghent system: BEL, DNK, FIN, SWE

- - - - Others: AUS, AUT, CAN, CHE, DEU, FRA, GBR, IRL, ITA, JPN, NLD, NOR, USA

Notes: Trade union density is defined as the number of wage and salary earners that are trade union members divided by the total number of wage and salary earners. Four countries are classified as Ghent system (following Western 1997: Table 4.1, 54): Belgium, Denmark, Finland, and Sweden. The remaining countries are Australia, Austria, Canada, France, Germany, Ireland, Italy, Japan, Netherlands, Norway, Switzerland, the UK, and the US.

Source: OECD (https://stats.oecd.org/Index.aspx?DataSetCode=TUD).

if future benefits justify current expenses. Two types of investment at the meso-level of participatory mobilization are particularly prevalent.

1. Mobilization may build on an *organizational infrastructure that facilitates coordination* among large numbers of people and disseminates political messages. This may require office space, communication equipment, and a full-time staff of specialists continuously processing information about 'who does what' and 'where' and attending to the maintenance of the organizational structure.

2. The goals of the mobilizational effort are not given exogenously, but undergo constant review and re-interpretation by leaders and followers. Leaders and participants might invest in the *process of redefining or expanding the objectives driving the mobilizational effort* in order to attract new allies and supporters.

The broader the range of political objectives over which participants try to coordinate collective action, the more they will have to invest time and procedural energies in either associational techniques of conflict deliberation and resolution or capabilities to punish deviators and enforce collective compliance.

What are the conditions under which incipient political entrepreneurs make investments in organizational

infrastructure and modes of interest aggregation to establish the domain of objectives over which a collective mobilization claims jurisdiction? The answer is that this depends on a *learning process* among participants in a mobilizational effort to establish how durable and how broadly interdependent their original demands are with other causes pursued in the polity.

At one extreme, political objectives are *temporally discrete*, single-shot demands that some authoritative policy should be granted, denied, or reversed. If political goals can be reached one-off and participants discover that they are pretty disconnected from other salient struggles in the polity, participants and their entrepreneurs may not find it worthwhile to invest in an elaborate associational structure and confine themselves to protest events.

At the other extreme, actors envision open-ended and permanent struggles around certain objectives. This encourages activists to invest in organizational structures that increase capabilities for operational coordination through associational statutes detailing internal governance and material resource acquisition. They scale up from social movement organizations to interest associations that incorporate a considerable share of their constituencies as members who pay dues, and many of whom are ready to participate in internal and external organizational activities when called upon by the associational functionaries.

Political interest associations, however, confine themselves to a *limited issue domain* and therefore are not compelled to make large investments in procedures of goal-finding, refinement, and generalization. In fact, in order to minimize internal disagreements and to maximize the external strategic capabilities of their association, political entrepreneurs may vigilantly police the boundaries of the issue domain over which they claim jurisdiction. Extending the claims of the organization to new issues may only inject dissent and create paralysis in the organization.[4]

Political interest groups, however, are not making authoritative political decisions in democracies, even if they may have the ear of political decision-makers and may participate in procedures of deliberation. The formal authoritative decisions lie with legislatures, parties in legislatures, and political executives. Can interest groups challenge unresponsive legislatures and executives by forming their own parties and joining the competitive fray? There is a large literature on party formation which typically emphasizes as preconditions for entry that (i) institutional thresholds of entry are low; and (ii) the party appeals to a salient issue demand that is not represented by existing parties. We would like to add a third stipulation that leads to a consideration of investments into procedures of strategic deliberation and generalization of political objectives.

Parties that strive to win representative legislative offices can never succeed and sustain themselves over many rounds of electoral contest if they appeal to a single issue, no matter how salient it may be.[5] Parties cannot restrict the agenda of legislatures to their favourite issues. As representatives of territorial constituencies, legislators participate in decisions over an uncertain and potentially infinite range of policies. Even if a party's constituencies rally around a single issue, the daily need for its legislators to make decisions on many other issues may generate internal divisions. Voters cannot perceive what parties stand for. Even on core issues, divided parties may become incapable of advancing their agenda. Therefore, political entrepreneurs have to find ways of overcoming the confines of single-issue appeals (see Box: Ways to overcome single issue appeals, in the Online Resources).

At the meso-level of mobilization, then, political entrepreneurs are not entirely free to choose their mode of action. Their differential capabilities to sustain the struggle over political objectives through time and generalize it across an encompassing issue space leads them to opt for different modes of mobilization, even if they face rather similar institutional and strategic contexts within a framework of liberal democracy.

KEY POINTS

- Actors participate only if they are motivated, and if they have the capacities and opportunities to act on their aspirations.
- More affluent societies provide more resources to stimulate political participation.
- Political regime—democracy and dictatorship—regulates the opportunities actors encounter to participate in politics.
- The nature of political stakes shapes the organization of political participation. Single-issue causes that aim for a one-off discrete decision typically result in *social movements* with little organizational structure. Efforts mobilizing around a narrowly specialized range of issues that persist over time facilitate the construction of *interest groups*. Where political causes pursue complex agendas of interdependent issues, they are likely to form *political parties* and enter the arena of electoral competition.

Who? Explaining political participation at the micro-level

As a last step, we explore why different individuals engage in different types of participatory activity. The choice of participatory practices may be governed by both *individual traits* (resources, capabilities, attitudes, dispositions) and *contextual cues* that actors glean from the strategic political situation and basic regime conditions, as discussed in the previous section, 'When and where? Explaining political participation at the macrolevel'. However, in what follows we will only consider individual traits.

Individual traits

We have already mentioned that people engage in political participation if they have resources and dispositions that facilitate participation. The most important individual-level factors can be further distinguished into five different sets (following Schlozman 2002: 439; Verba et al. 1995): (i) resources; (ii) recruitment; (iii) social networks; (iv) orientations towards politics; and (v) contextual cues. In other words, '[i]ndividuals are more likely to take part when they can, when they want to [, . . .] when they are asked to' (Schlozman 2002: 439), and when they are in certain contexts.

Resources

Probably the most generally and consistently confirmed influence on participation comes from socio-economic skills and endowments.[6] A simple baseline condition for political participation, especially more involved modes of participation, is the *availability of time*. People who do not work, or do not work full-time, tend to display higher levels of political participation. Young retirees or high school and university students, for example, provide great reservoirs for intensive political participation.

Once we move beyond this simple endowment, *schooling/education* is clearly a key variable. Better education enables citizens to process more information about ongoing political decisions and sort out what does or does not affect one's life chances in ways that might prompt political action. Better education also fosters a stronger self-confidence and sense of individual capacity to govern one's own life, rather than to let external authorities make decisions on one's behalf. Thus, education cuts down on paternalist deference. Furthermore, the capacity to process information enables actors to identify more efficient strategies to pursue their objectives through political action. Finally, better education enables people to participate in deliberative processes to determine desirable objectives of political action and to discover ways to pursue them.

Beyond these direct effects, education indirectly enhances participation through its impact on *income* and *occupational time* sovereignty. Better educated people tend to earn higher incomes, which enable them to divert part of their finances to discretionary activities, such as politics. Better educated people also tend to have jobs in which they enjoy more time sovereignty (but not more free time), which makes them available for complex time-consuming political activities.[7]

Education, income, and professional or occupational life also promote involvement in a variety of *civic activities*, such as professional and cultural associations. These, in turn, serve as intermediate relays that facilitate interpersonal communication of beliefs and political preferences (i.e. *orientations*). Enhanced communication among like-minded actors thus fosters a readiness for political participation, and even the coordination of collective action through mutual monitoring, if not sanctioning, of those individuals in the network who become freeriders.

Recruitment

This brings us to recruitment as an important explanation for participation. *Associational involvement* is a proximate mechanism that explains political participation not only for those who have favourable personal endowments to become involved in politics (education, time, money). Associational involvement may be an even greater and more important enhancer of participation precisely for individuals who lack such resources, but nevertheless reach levels of politi-

cal activism not foreseen by a naive socio-economic resource model of political participation. Under which conditions does exposure to civic associations and networks of communication lead to increased participation? Parameters of both occupational and residential life might be influential in this regard.

Occupations that do not require high human capital and that do not grant their practitioners great time sovereignty may stimulate political participation, if the *organization of the work process* affords actors plenty of exposure to others living under very similar social conditions. This tends to be particularly the case where people converge on large workplaces with many hundreds or even thousands of employees operating under exactly the same work conditions. Examples are manufacturing plants or mines, dockyards before the advent of containerized shipping, or newspaper printing factories before electronic text-editing. In the great factory, interpersonal communication can easily reach large numbers of people. Moreover, people can observe and monitor each other's behaviour to sanction freeriders. The resulting high capacity for collective action is further enhanced by the residential family life of employees being concentrated in neighbourhoods close to the work facilities. The chances are that occasional interactions, but also cultural, regional, or social civic associations, spring up that organize social communications.

The resulting *class and group milieux* foster and sustain a high capacity for collective action. Historically, the peak of milieu-based social organization and political participation was probably reached in the first half of the twentieth century when factory size reached its zenith and urbanization was far advanced, but had not yet given way to sprawling suburbanization. Going back to the late nineteenth and early twentieth centuries in Europe or the US up to the 1940s or 1950s, civic associations such as occupational and cultural organizations (e.g. churches or trade unions) served as 'quasi-schools', creating readiness for political participation among those who had acquired few educational skills and had low incomes.

Thus, the presence of encompassing associations draws into political life people who would otherwise linger at the margins of the polity. The shrinking size of workplaces, the increasing separation of work and residential life, and the dispersal of residential patterns that has come with the advent of the automobile as a relatively cheap mode of transportation since World War II have progressively undercut the capacity of the workplace and surrounding neighbourhoods to organize political participation. Thus, this process has reduced some of the social capital of civil society ties built up independently of—or even in compensation for—the lack of high personal socio-economic endowments that enable individuals to engage in political participation.

Social networks

Somewhere at the intersection between socio-economic resources (education, income, occupational time sovereignty) and civic associational memberships, we can consider the role of social networks, including the *role of the family* in political participation. The family unit bundles the experiences of work and residential life for members of the next generation. The family is the critical site at which youngsters acquire a taste for, or a dislike of, political participation. Parents introduce their children to political practices that shape their future dispositions towards politics and transmit essential skills of participation in collective action. An early exposure to political involvement often spawns lifelong political activism. The personalistic nature of political competition may create 'family dynasties' of political involvement at all levels of politics, particularly in countries with weak formal party structures. The US and Japan are good examples.

But networks beyond the family matter for political participation. In fact, the impact of various individual-level socio-economic resources on political participation may be mostly through networks that are built around income, education, occupations, churches, and other factors known to predict participation (Campbell 2013). Rather than being driven by individual cost–benefit calculation, political participation could be interpreted as a socially defined practice (Rolfe 2012) that entices individuals in certain networks to engage in political action. For example, if an individual's personal or virtual network (Facebook, Twitter, etc.) attaches much importance to voting, s/he may vote simply for social approval (Abrams et al. 2011; Bond et al. 2012: 295–8).

Resources and networks are often structured by *age and gender*, which in turn correlate with political participation. Nevertheless, they may have a net effect on political participation, once all these other factors are held constant. Young people and women tend to be less active in politics than older people and men, for reasons that have to do with political experience and cultural upbringing. And if they are active, their profile of activities tends to differ between age and gender groups, contingent upon the nature of participatory activities at stake.

Orientations

As another proximate determinant of political participation that is at least in part conditioned by all the elements we have already discussed, let us add *political interest and ideology*. Political participation results from, and stimulates, political knowledge formation. Individuals may organize their political knowledge in complex ideologies that combine descriptive and analytical propositions of how politics and social organizations work with normative images of desirable end states of a reformed or rebuilt social and political order and strategic prescriptions about how to move from the status quo to the desirable end state. While political ideologies may display some empirical association with individuals' socio-economic and occupational background and networks, more immediate causal mechanisms that shape ideology are civic involvement and engagement in political participation itself. The level of ideological organization in actors' belief systems, in turn, is a good predictor of political participation (Marsh 1990).

Contextual cues

Comparing levels of participation among countries—voting, campaigning, membership in unions or parties, protest activities—reveals that the distribution of citizens' resources and dispositions—education, income, interest in politics—explains only a small share of the cross-national differences: Swedes are not that much more likely to vote in national elections because they are, on average, so much more educated than Americans. Belgians, on average, are not that much more interested in politics to explain why they are so much more likely to be affiliated with unions than French citizens.

Large differences in citizens' average propensities to participate in politics, such as joining interest groups, result from contextual factors. We have already indicated some of them, such as the impact of electoral rules on voter turnout or the role of the Ghent system for differential levels and change rates of labour unionization. More generally, we can distinguish at least four different levels of contextual effects that leave their imprint on individual and aggregate profiles of political participation (see Morales 2009).

- At the micro-level, networks of family and friends influence participation. Where one's personal social networks are heavily politicized, the chances are high that one also will become politically active (see above, in 'Social networks').

- At the meso-level, the existence of large encompassing associations and densely organized parties makes a difference. The presence of such groups is likely to render it less costly and more attractive for citizens to join and get involved. As a legacy effect, where associational affiliations were always a widespread phenomenon in the past, say as early as the post-World War II decades, the chances are that later generations of citizens will also join political associations in great numbers, even as mobilization spreads from one type of political cause to another.

- At the macro-level, not only democratic institutions (such as electoral laws), but also strategic alignments among political forces may encourage or discourage involvement. Thus, where large hierarchically organized encompassing national interest groups, such as unions and employers' associations, dominate wage bargaining and have great clout in policy-making ('**corporatism**'), more people may join such interest groups, but also more activists might become involved in spontaneous disruptive grassroots movements when their voices on salient issues are simply not listened to by the leaders of large centralized associations.
- The nature of the party system also shapes participation. Where people choose from a wide variety of political parties rather than only two major parties, the chances are greater that one of them has a political programme very close to exactly what the individual citizen would like to see realized in policy-making. This may encourage him/her to contribute to that party by becoming a member. Hence, greater party system fragmentation may translate into greater partisan membership (Morales 2009: Chapter 6).

Political involvement may even be shaped by inter-action effects between citizens' individual resources and the broader context in which they operate. Thus, where labour unions involved in corporatist interest intermediation make the voice of less educated and less well-off citizens heard, they are likely to attract the affiliation of constituencies that would stay unor-ganized elsewhere. Conversely, highly educated and affluent citizens may seek out other ways to protect their interest than through political involvement.

Finally, contextual conditions can bring about complex causal chains that reinforce differentials of participation. In highly inegalitarian polities in which a large portion of citizens has poor general educa-tion and little political information, even the politi-cally interested members of this constituency may refrain from politics. They expect that low turnout among their own constituency will lead to **under-representation** of constituency interests in legislatures and executives. This expectation itself may generate cynicism and alienation from politics and reinforce the low turnout among poor, uneducated people. Then the effective median voter who elects legislatures and

parties that govern shifts further towards the affluent and educated who have little inclination to redistribute life chances to the worse off. Their political represent-atives choose policies that reinforce educational and income inequality, further reducing political participa-tion of the ill-endowed, thus once again exacerbating the under-representation of interests of disadvantaged groups in legislatures and political executives.

KEY POINTS

- At the individual level, more resourceful individuals, par-ticularly in terms of cognitive capabilities and disposable time, but also income and social ties, tend to participate more in politics than less resourceful individuals.
- Both formal associations and informal social networks, configured around family and friendship ties, supplement individual capacities to engage in political participation or compensate for weak capacities, so as to boost an individual's probability to become politically active.

Conclusion

Democracy without political participation simply does not work. Political participation covers such a broad set of phenomena—inside and outside democ-racies—that it is difficult to offer a concise definition, let alone detailed explanations for particular types of participation.

This chapter has illustrated that scholars have amassed a great deal of knowledge about political participation over the past half-century. But large open questions remain.

1. We need to better understand the interaction between the capacities and motivations of individuals to engage in political participation and the socio-economic, institutional, and political–strategic context in which such actors are embedded. Political behaviour cannot be explained merely in terms of individual-level traits or macro-level conditions and rules. We also need to consider contextual factors. For example, the correlation between education and turnout seems to be systematically higher in more unequal societies. Rather, we have to understand the contingent interaction between the micro- and macro-levels.

2. We need to understand more clearly why everyday political actors and political entrepreneurs who produce selective incentives for others to

participate in politics opt for different modes of political participation in different circumstances and in light of different demands. To be sure, there are grey zones between social movements, interest groups, and political parties that make it hard to discern distinctive modes of political participation. Nevertheless, it is a fascinating and by and large under-studied question why political actors sometimes invest in trajectories of political involvement that crystallize more around volatile social movements, or durable interest groups, or programmatically complex parties.

3. The differentiation between modes of political action appears to grow in post-industrial democratic polities. Consider the contrast with **labour movements** in the early twentieth century. The same actors who were activists in socialist parties also tended to lead labour unions—regardless of whether these were the 'transmission belt' of parties or whether parties were the electoral mouthpieces of labour unions. Furthermore, these core cadres also organized disruptive extra-institutional street politics that sustained labour mobilization as a social movement. However, by the late twentieth century socialist parties and unions rarely ever engaged in protest events. And even the relationship between labour mobilization as a functional interest group and as an electoral undertaking has become an arm's-length affair, where all sides struggle to preserve their mutual autonomy.

Not only the causes, but also the consequences, of increasing differentiation between modes of political action deserve more attention. What is taking place is a 'decentring' of democratic politics across diverse sites and modes of action—a pluralization of political democracy and political involvement. Why is there so much and such diverse political activism? This is a real and unresolved puzzle when thinking about political participation.

? QUESTIONS

Knowledge-based

1. What are the three principal sites of participation and what are the three principal modes of participation?

2. What is the 'paradox of collective action'?

3. What are the solutions to the paradox of collective action?

4. Why is union membership higher in Ghent systems?

5. What are the five different types of micro-level factors for participation? Give examples for each.

Critical thinking

1. Why do people participate in politics?

2. Which factors are known to increase levels of turnout?

3. Do you think that low turnout rates are a threat to democracy?

4. Why do political entrepreneurs sometimes initiate social movements, sometimes build interest organizations, and sometimes found parties?

5. Should theories of collective action start from the premise that participation is a 'cost' or should theories reverse the premise and treat participation as a 'benefit'?

≋ FURTHER READING

Barnes, S. H. and Kaase, M. (1979) *Political Action: Mass Participation in Five Western Democracies* (Newbury Park, CA: Sage).

Dalton, R. J. (2013) *Citizen Politics: Public Opinion and Political Parties in Advanced Industrial Democracies* (6th edn) (Chatham, NJ: Chatham House Publishers/Seven Bridges Press).

Franklin, M. N. (2004) *Voter Turnout and the Dynamics of Electoral Competition in Established Democracies since 1945* (Cambridge: Cambridge University Press).

Hardin, R. (1982) *Collective Action* (Baltimore, MD: Johns Hopkins University Press).

Lichbach, M. I. (1995) *The Rebel's Dilemma: Economics, Cognition, and Society* (Ann Arbor, MI: University of Michigan Press).

Lijphart, A. (1997) 'Unequal Participation: Democracy's Unresolved Dilemma', *American Political Science Review*, 91(1): 1–14.

Olson, M. (1965) *The Logic of Collective Action: Public Goods and the Theory of Groups* (Cambridge, MA: Harvard University Press).

Verba, S., Nie, N. H., and Kim, J. (1978) *Participation and Political Equality: A Seven-Nation Comparison* (Cambridge, MA: Cambridge University Press).

ENDNOTES

1. These data are from the World Value Survey, waves 3 and 4. They refer to years 1994–2003 (depending on the country). Unfortunately, data for more recent years are not available.

2. For a summary evaluation of research on political opportunity structures in democracies and political participation, see McAdam (1996), Tarrow (1996), and Goodwin (2001). See also Chapter 16.

3. Trail-blazing contributions were those of Powell (1986) and Jackman (1987), as well as the meticulous study by Franklin (2004). For a comprehensive meta-analysis, on which we rely here, see Geys (2006).

4. On the difference between the organizational requisites and strategic dilemmas of monological and dialogical interest association, see Offe and Wiesenthal (1980).

5. Examples are the French ecologistes of the 1970s or 1980s or the Swedish miljopartiet in the early 1990s. Both efforts failed, but not because of electoral system (institutions) or strategic configuration (no established party had fully occupied the potential 'place' of Greens). In the case of the unsuccessful British Green Party, its failure may be overdetermined by the single-member-district electoral system.

6. For this section, see especially Brady et al. (1995) and Verba et al. (1995). For an overview, see Schlozman (2002).

7. Time sovereignty refers to the capacity to determine when and where to work, not the absolute amount of free time beyond one's professional life. Highly educated people may have more time sovereignty, but less free time, than people with less education.

Visit the Online Resources that accompany this book for additional material, including country profiles, comparative data sets, flashcard glossaries, and web directory.

www.oup.com/he/caramani5e

19

Political communication

Frank Esser and Barbara Pfetsch

Chapter contents

Reader's guide

Political communication involves creating, shaping, disseminating, and processing information among actors from the political system, the media, and the public, as well as the effects of such communication. It ultimately refers to making sense of the exercise of discursive power and its potential consequences for citizens in terms of knowledge and participation. Political communication today is initiated by a multitude of actors who use a variety of different channels to spread their messages. The influences of the internet and globalization have led to the emergence of hybrid ecosystems of political communication. We describe these ecosystems in model form and propose them as macro-units for comparative research. On the basis of this model, the chapter shows that the literature on comparative political communication research to date has focused in particular on relationships between media institutions and political institutions, role relationships between politicians and journalists, messages produced and disseminated by political actors, messages produced and disseminated by media actors, and national audiences and their news consumption patterns, as well as effects of political communication on citizens and societies. We conclude the chapter with a critical assessment of the political communication conditions in the countries discussed here.

Introduction

Political communication refers to the flow of information and the exchange of messages among political actors, citizens, and the media. All three participants contribute to the creation of political **public spheres**.

In the past, political communication scholarship focused attention somewhat narrowly on *publicly* visible forms of *mass* communication featuring *organized* actors who addressed *core political* issues in the setting of *liberal democratic* **nation-states**. These conditions are no longer tenable. Today, political communication is, in many ways, characterized by a mix of public and personalized communication, mass media and social media, and established and non-established communicators. Its contents are affected by increasing **globalization**, and its frontiers extend to non-Western countries. These factors, individually and collectively, affect the status of the nation-state as a default unit of analysis in comparative research.

Although the days of clear-cut boundaries and narrow conceptualizations are clearly over, previous political communication theories have not become obsolete. Rather, the current conditions of political communication offer opportunities to update existing approaches in innovative ways (Vowe and Henn 2016). Political communication arrangements in various countries are exposed to simultaneous forces of stability and change. What has remained consistent is that political communication always encompasses the same factors: creating, shaping, disseminating, and processing information among actors from the political system, the media, and the public, as well as the effects of such communication. The *Oxford Handbook of Political Communication* defines it as 'making sense of symbolic exchanges about the shared exercise of power' and 'the presentation and interpretation of information . . . with potential consequences for the exercise of shared power' (Jamieson and Kenski 2017: 4). From the perspective of political communication, the power aspect emphasized in this definition manifests itself primarily as *discursive power*, which is 'the proven ability of contributors to the political communication space to introduce, amplify, and maintain topics, frames, and speakers that come to dominate attention in ongoing political discourse' (Jungherr et al. 2019: 17). Other aspects of politics that have nothing directly to do with acquiring and retaining power, such as the transmission of interests and demands of citizens, the symbolic legitimation of authority, and the clarification of alternative options in policymaking, also depend on communication (Blumler 2017).

It is self-evident that varying political communication settings affect political behaviours and the workings of democracy differently. National arrangements of political communication are highly differentiated and are conditional on contextual influences. Thus, the more we compare the various aspects of political communication, the more complex our understanding of political life becomes. Findings from comparative political communication research often reflect this complexity, and they can rarely be reduced to a simple formula. While we seek generalizable knowledge and systematic patterns in the communication of politics through comparisons, we often unveil contradictions, dilemmas, and idiosyncratic cases. These circumstances make the review of comparative political communication research an intricate task.

In this chapter, we first discuss the meaning and relevance of political communication to demonstrate the usefulness of comparative research in this field. Second, we introduce a heuristic model of the *political communication ecosystem* that allows us to identify and contextualize the relevant actors, relationships, and information flows. This model will help us to delineate some of the important trajectories of comparative research and lines of scholarly debate. In particular, we scrutinize structures, cultures, messages, and the consumption and effects of political information from a comparative perspective. We close the chapter with a reflection on achievements and normative implications.

KEY POINTS

- Political communication involves creating, shaping, disseminating, and processing information among actors from the political system, the media, and the public, as well as the effects of such communication. Discursive power refers to controlling this flow of information.

- Political communication conditions differ from one place to another. In order to understand them, the conditions must be closely examined as part of the media system and its relations to the political system.

Studying political communication comparatively

The rationale

Although the comparative study of political communication has become fairly commonplace, many observers agree that it is still growing and maturing (Gurevitch and Blumler 2004; Mancini and Hallin 2012). It is a relatively young research field, and scholars still display some uncertainty about its conceptual and methodological foundations and its level of achievement. Benson (2010: 614), for example, celebrated the increase in comparative studies for successfully challenging the 'American-centric narrative' found in much of the political communication literature. A more pessimistic outlook comes from Norris (2009: 322–323), who claims that 'it still remains difficult, if not impossible, to compare political communications systematically across national borders' because the field 'has not yet developed an extensive body of literature establishing a range of theoretically sophisticated analytical frameworks, buttressed by rigorously tested scientific **generalizations**, common concepts, standardized instruments, and shared archival datasets, with the capacity to identify common regularities which prove robust across widely varied contexts.' However, as a result of substantial progress in research since Norris made that statement, we now see the glass as half full, rather than half empty.

The comparative approach to examining political communication pays special attention to the fact that democratic political communication arrangements evolve differently under the influence of divergent contextual factors. The approach is occupied with comparing political communication arrangements in two or more places, regardless of whether they are defined as systems, cultures, ecologies, environments, spaces, spheres, or fields. A spatial comparison should be supplemented wherever possible by a longitudinal (cross-temporal) dimension to account for the fact that neither politics nor the media are frozen in time. Rather, they are constantly changing under the influence of globalization, neoliberalism/commercialism, and information communication technologies.

Comparative research guides our attention to the explanatory relevance of the contextual environment for communication outcomes and aims to demonstrate how the macro-level context shapes communication phenomena differently in different settings. The research is based on the assumption that different parameters of political and **media systems** differentially promote or constrain communication roles and behaviours of organizations and actors within those systems. Esser and Vliegenthart (2017) provided an overview of methodological approaches often taken in comparative political communication research.

The political communication ecosystem

The interplay between politics and the media is undergoing fundamental change, which has been described as the transition to a fourth age of political communication (Blumler 2016; Bennett and Pfetsch 2018; Davis 2019). This new age is characterized by the broad influence of the internet and associated technologies on commerce, culture, social relations, movements, politics, and media. Core representative organizations of democracy (including established parties and legacy news media) are losing their importance vis-à-vis new players who operate according to different rules. Although these new players (including Facebook and Twitter) contribute to greater diversity, they have also encouraged a disintegration of what was left of a national public sphere. The increased fragmentation of the media system has led to a rugged landscape of partly networked, partly isolated micro-publics, whereby life in demarcated micro-publics favours a radicalization and polarization of political discourse. The information that is disseminated in such a climate is not always rational or well founded, and sometimes it is even deliberately manipulative, aspects that can undermine citizens' trust in news and political information as a whole. A final characteristic of this new age of political communication lies in the growing gap between two spheres of politics: on one hand, the 'show politics' that politicians (must) offer as celebrities acting on a stage to entertain a fickle audience; on the other hand, the real 'decision-making politics' that takes place on the backstage, largely invisible to the public and under the influence of questionable lobbyists and technocrats, who are not accountable to anyone (Davis 2019: 5–9, 207–11).

In view of these transformations, we can adequately understand contemporary media systems only if we account for the complexity of the system in the development and revision of our theories. Recent approaches have pointed out that while media systems are flexible and adaptive, they are subject to longer periods of seemingly chaotic change (Neuberger 2019), which involves the simultaneity of fixity and fluidity (Hallin 2015; Chadwick et al. 2016). Thus, the functioning of today's political communication is characterized by two parallel modes of operation: the logic of traditional, top-down oriented mass communication, and the decentralized, participative interactive logic of Internet communication. This concurrence and its dynamics have turned contemporary media systems into 'hybrid media systems' (Chadwick et al. 2016), which means we can no longer reduce media systems to a single, one-dimensional communication logic, and we can no longer define dynamically changing media systems, such as that of the US, using static **classification** schemes (Nechushtai 2018).

Due to the logic of hybrid media systems (Chadwick et al. 2016), the exchange relations between media, politics, and citizens have also become more complex. While in the past we described their interrelations as an *ordered political communication system*, conditions have changed so much that we now prefer the term 'political communication ecosystem'. The concept of the ecosystem, borrowed from biology, better reflects the increased degree of complexity, flexibility, and mutual adaptation involved. Drawing on Anderson's (2016: 412) pioneering work, a communication ecosystem can be understood as the 'entire ensemble of individuals, organizations, and technologies within a particular geographic community or around a particular issue' engaged in the 'production' and 'consumption' of news and information.

Applied to the interplay of media, politics, and citizenship, this definition suggests that the boundaries of political communication ecosystems can be drawn in two ways. Either the system's boundaries are determined *geographically,* if the analytical focus is on the information exchange relations in a *particular territory,* or the boundaries can be drawn *thematically,* if the focus is on all political, media, and civic actors—regardless of their locality—involved in the creation, framing, dissemination, reception, and effect mechanisms of a *particular issue* (Wiard 2019).

The idea of political communication ecosystems is well suited for comparative international research (Wiard 2019). An advantage of this approach to viewing political communication is that the information exchange relationships in the ecosystem are assumed to be 'coopetitive', in other words, equally influenced by 'cooperation and competition' (Wiard 2019: 7). Competition influences political actors, media actors, and civic actors when they vie for attention and strive to control political communication through discursive power (Jungherr et al. 2019). Cooperation refers to the high degree of connectivity, mutual observation, mutual adaptation, and imitative behaviour that can explain issue attention cycles, hypes, news waves, and scandalizations (Neuberger 2019). Interactive group phenomena on the internet, including media storms, viral hits, or public furies, often occur spontaneously, and with unforeseeable consequences. Many politicians perceive such situations as loss of control and a cause of stress (Neuberger 2019).

A simple graphic representation of a geographically delimited political communication ecosystem is depicted in Figure 19.1. At the centre is a mixed ensemble of different communication channels that are relevant for political communication, and each has different conditions for realizing discursive power. Figure 19.1 shows only partial aspects of the hybrid media system (centre), society (boxes left and right), and the political system and the civic public (boxes above and below). Marked in blue are the essential elements of political communication ecosystems; their interplay is significant in five ways:

- From a cross-territorial perspective, the model refers to the significance of the structural, cultural, and situational *context* for explaining the communication behaviour of political actors, media actors, and public actors.

- From a cross-temporal perspective, the model refers to the *effects* of political communication. In the long term, changes in political communication can lead to changes in the structural, cultural, and situational conditions of a society (black arrows from 'time 1' to 'time 2'). In the short term, the political communication partners influence each other by means of messages sent, communicative reactions, and anticipated adaptations (grey arrows).

- From a cross-media perspective, the model refers to the different functions of the three key channels, each of which is characterized by different logics. Communication is possible through channels that are under the complete control of political actors, for instance, via email and direct messaging, newspaper ads, TV commercials, internet videos, billboards, or personal websites. News media organizations are under the communication control of journalists (e.g. Fox News, Washington Post, Politico); they follow organized decision-making processes according to the norms of the media profession and the editorial mission set by the publisher or management. Social media services focus on the distribution of content that comes from a wide range of contributors, including citizens, politicians, and journalists; this content is disseminated according to dynamics influenced by human interaction and algorithmically programmed connectivity (e.g. at Facebook, Twitter, Instagram, YouTube).

- From a communication flow perspective, the model refers to the fact that, in principle, any content that appears in or on one channel can be picked up, amplified, or challenged by another. The flow of political communication consists of action, reaction, and counter-reaction (grey arrows). In order to optimize the attention one's own content receives, communicators associated with one channel observe all other channels and adapt their strategies in anticipation of the other channels' operating logics.

- From an impact perspective, the pursuit of discursive power has become challenging for political actors. On one hand, many leading news organizations have long since ceased to see themselves merely as intermediaries; rather, they see themselves as active co-shapers of public opinion. On the other hand, social media services

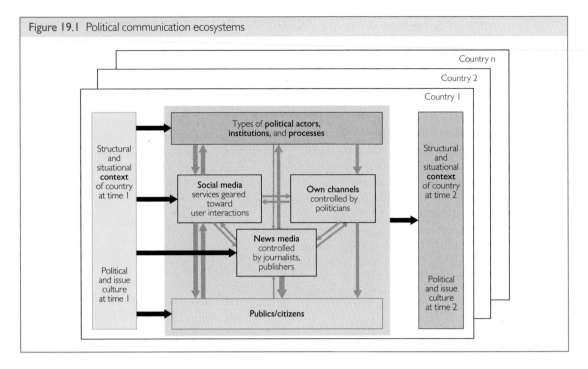

Figure 19.1 Political communication ecosystems

have also gained considerable power because politicians, journalists, and citizens have become extremely dependent on them as information sources and distribution mechanisms. In order to expand their dominant position, platforms like Facebook have continuously adjusted their operating modes in a controversial and intransparent manner.

Keeping the heuristic model of the political communication ecosystem in mind, we will review recent comparative studies that have made significant contributions to understanding specific aspects of political communication: (i) institutional interactions between news media and politics; (ii) professional interaction cultures between news journalists and political actors; (iii) patterns of message construction by political actors; (iv) patterns of message construction by media actors; (v) citizens' consumption of political information; and (vi) effects of political communication on national audiences. We will divide our overview of the literature according to these six topics.

KEY POINTS

- Comparative political communication research contrasts a minimum of two political communication ecosystems at one or more points in time. Political communication ecosystems are characterized by competitive

and cooperative information flows between political actors, own means of communication, news media organizations, social media platforms, and members of the public.

- The object of comparative analysis may refer to any component of the political communication ecosystem, for instance, the institutional relationships between media and politics, the attitudes of news journalists and politicians involved and their culture-specific interactions, the contents and dissemination dynamics of messages circulating among these actors, the patterns of consuming political information by the general public, and finally, the effects of political information on audiences and society at large.

Media–politics relations

Comparing institutional relationships between media and politics

An important body of the comparative political communication literature explores the macro-level relationships between media institutions and political institutions and how they differ across countries. Hallin and Mancini's (2004) study, *Comparing Media Systems—Three Models of Media and Politics*, has become a central reference point on this topic.

Drawing on Lijphart (1999), it assumes that a political system's influence on the news media depends on five factors: the role of the state and regulation in media policy; the presence of either a majoritarian or a consensus **government**; the pattern of interest mediation with respect to the form of **pluralism**; the type of political authority; and the political history regarding democratization. Hallin and Mancini (2004) argued that these political factors had a defining historical impact on how the media have been differently institutionalized across Western democracies. Based on research in sixteen European and two North American countries, their study offers a typology of three media system types—a North Atlantic liberal model, a North-West European democratic corporatist model, and a Southern European polarized pluralist model.

Hallin and Mancini's accomplishment was demonstrating how these three types of media systems differ regarding their relations with four key forces: the market, the **party system**, the state, and the autonomy of journalism. The first factor, the market, refers to the degree of commercialization and market success of news media in a given country. The second factor, the influence of the party and interest group system on the media, refers to press/party parallelism, namely, the degree to which news content reflects political orientations that represent party lines or ideological camps. Third, state relations refer to the degree and form of political/government intervention in the media by way of formal regulation or informal control. Finally, the nature of a national media system also depends on the autonomy of journalists, which is determined by the **professionalization** and independence of journalistic norms and practices. Table 19.1 shows how Western media systems can be classified into Hallin and Mancini's three models with the help of these comparative dimensions.

Much of Hallin and Mancini's (2004) original analysis focused on how the historical contexts and political structures analysed in political science and sociology relate to the development of media systems. It stimulated a new generation of media systems research that has since made remarkable progress in three areas:

1. the inclusion of measurable quantitative indicators for the purpose of verifying the framework empirically;

2. the inclusion of non-Western systems for the purpose of examining the framework's geographical scope;

3. the inclusion of modern information technologies for the purpose of enhancing the framework's relevance in the digital age.

A good example of the *first advancement* point is the study by Brüggemann and colleagues (2014), who tried to validate and refine Hallin and Mancini's (2004) theoretical assumptions using cluster analysis based on secondary data sources and new quantitative indicators. Their study produced four clusters of Western media systems, rather than Hallin and Mancini's three, because, in short, the democratic corporatist model is broken into two clusters. Hallin and Mancini (2017) did not consider this finding a refutation of their framework, but rather a reflection of the different approaches taken, namely more data-centred versus more theory-centred.

With regard to the *second advancement*, the inclusion of non-Western media systems, Hallin and Mancini (2012) edited a follow-up volume that contains qualitative case studies of Poland, Israel, Brazil, South Africa, Russia, and China, as well as the Baltic, Arab, and South Asian regions. Further follow-up studies have found, for example, that there is not one media system model in Eastern Europe, but several different models. Based on revised comparative dimensions and new quantitative indicators, a cluster analysis by Castro and colleagues (2017) identified one Eastern European model with a high degree of politicization and instrumentalization and a contrasting model with high journalistic independence and market competition. The first model may be designated as 'captured by political and economic elites' and the second as 'liberalized' (Mungiu-Pippidi 2013). A recent study by Dobek-Ostrowska (2019) added defective and non-democratic Eastern European systems and, as a consequence, identified a 'transitionary' and an 'authoritarian' model (by which to use labels). Thus, we are left with four Central and Eastern European media system models.

With regard to other non-Western regions, three types of media systems can be distinguished in Latin America and four in Africa (see overview in Hallin 2016). Regarding Asia, three subnational media systems can be identified in India. The national media system of China, however, does not fit into the categories and requires a different conceptual scheme. To understand the development of media systems in Eastern Europe, Latin America, Africa, and East Asia *as a whole*, the theory of path dependency states that we must consider the transformation processes of their political systems first. The media systems differ systematically based on

Table 19.1 Three models of media–politics relations

	Polarized pluralized model	Democratic corporatist model	Liberal model
	(France, Italy, Spain, Portugal, Greece)	(Nor, Swe, Fin, Den, Bel, Ger, Ned, Aut, Swi)	(United States, Canada, Great Britain, Ireland)
Political system			
Political history	Late democratization: polarized pluralism	Early democratization: moderate pluralism	Early democratization: moderate pluralism
Consensus or majoritarian govt	Both	Primarily consensus	Primarily majoritarian
Individual vs organized pluralism	Organized pluralism, powerful parties	Organized pluralism, democratic corporatism	Individualized representation
Role of state	Dirigism	Strong welfare state	Liberalism
Rational legal authority	Weak (clientelism)	Strong	Strong
Media system			
Newspaper industry	Low circulation, small news audiences	High circulation, mass news audiences	Medium circulation, mass news audiences
Parallelism b/w media and political camps	High, opinionated journalism	High, but declining	Low, informational journalism
Professional independence of journalists	Low	High	High
State intervention in media (policy)	High	High, but with freedom of media protected	Low, market-dominated

Source: Hallin and Mancini (2004: 67–68).

whether a new democracy has emerged from a military dictatorship (dominant in Latin America), communist one-party rule (Eastern Europe), one party rule in the context of substantial centralized state control (East Asia), or personalized one-party rule in the context of weak state institutions (sub-Saharan Africa). These different conditions determine, as Voltmer (2013) argued, whether and how the media can support the process of democratization. In these parts of the world, the media can only fulfil their democratic role if post-authoritarian governments provide the necessary freedom and protection, if markets are effective in providing the resources for quality journalism, and if citizens/audiences are willing to engage in an open and tolerant debate (Voltmer 2013: 217–27).

The *third advancement* of recent media systems research has been the inclusion of modern information technologies. Mattoni and Ceccobelli (2018) proposed a number of updates to Hallin and Mancini's (2004) framework to adequately take into account the influence of social media, digital forms of citizen participation, and non-journalistic forms of news distribution. They suggested a new comparative dimension called grassroot participation, together with several new indicators, to capture the contribution of all those alternative voices that are available on the internet that either complement or oppose traditional mainstream media. An empirical test of Mattoni and Ceccobelli's (2018) revised comparative framework is still missing. In addition, Jungherr and colleagues (2019) made various suggestions on how to combine the comparison of today's hybrid media systems with Hallin and Mancini's (2004) original comparative dimensions, but they also found several dimensions still useful. Their proposed additions refer to considering what types of novel news organizations and distribution channels are available in a given media system, and how the complex information flows can be used to exercise discursive power. Here, too, an empirical examination of the proposed instrument is still outstanding.

Comparing role relationships between politicians and journalists

The role perceptions held by journalists and politicians, their views of professional practices, and eventually, the degree of media–political elite integration are important because they influence the flow of information in a given country. To compare role relationships between politicians and journalists, we will discuss three strands of comparative research on values and attitudes. First, studies of *journalism culture* examine the professional orientations of news workers and explore whether the attitudes of journalists converge across cultures and countries. Second, studies in comparative politics focus specifically on political elites' and journalists' *perceptions of media and political power*. Third, studies on *political communication culture* investigate the interaction norms of politicians and journalists and link them to national political and media systems.

Comparative research on journalism cultures includes analysis of role perceptions and professional identities of news workers (Donsbach and Patterson 2004; Weaver and Willnat 2012) and reveal the predispositions that influence their professional conduct in reporting politics. For a long time, this work was limited to single-country studies that applied the Western model as a yardstick. Progress was made only when the debate about global journalism raised awareness of the implicit Western bias of journalism culture and when a theoretical framework for comparative research was proposed. Specifically, Hanitzsch (2007) suggested categories for assessing journalism cultures and identifying the commonalities and differences in journalistic norms across different national and cultural settings. The five dimensions for measuring journalistic cultures proposed by Hanitzsch (2007) and Hanitzsch et al. (2019) are journalists' perceived influences and constraints on their work, editorial autonomy, attitudes about professional roles, ethics of reporting, and trust in public institutions. A global survey of 27,500 journalists from sixty-seven countries showed that, with regard to ethics and roles, journalists generally share a strong belief in codes of conduct and professional norms, such as detachment, factuality, and reliability of information (Hanitzsch et al. 2019). With regard to trust, it is noteworthy that as a consistent pattern, journalists have low confidence in political institutions. While they have particularly little confidence in politicians and political parties, their trust in regulatory institutions and the courts is markedly higher (Hanusch and Hanitzsch 2019; see also Box 19.1). Among Western countries, journalists from the US stand out as the most distrusting of political institutions.

Journalists' cultural orientations relevant for their relationships with political actors are not universal, but instead are shaped by country-specific influences. The global Worlds of Journalism Study (Hanusch and Hanitzsch 2019) found four types of journalism cultures that differ according to political, socioeconomic, and cultural contexts:

- In the liberal democracies of Western Europe, Australia, the US, Japan, and Hong Kong, a *monitorial journalism culture* persists, in which distance between news workers and politicians guide reporting. In these countries, which usually enjoy high levels of freedom of the press, journalism is not threatened by political pressures but by technology-related changes and competition from social media as information suppliers.

- In transitional democracies, such as in Eastern Europe and Latin America, an *advocative journalism* culture is predominant. Here journalists display a strong interventionist ethos in an environment where democracy has not been consolidated and political trust is particularly low.

- A third type, a *developmental* journalistic culture, is found in Bangladesh, Bhutan, Indonesia, India, and sub-Saharan Africa. Many of these countries suffer from rather low levels of media freedom and low socioeconomic development. The defining element here is that journalists see themselves as agents of social change and, in this vein, prefer interventionist approaches to news making.

- Finally, in countries of the Middle East, such as Oman, Qatar, and the United Arab Emirates, and in countries in Southeast Asia, such as Thailand, Singapore, and Malaysia, as well as in China, a *collaborative journalism culture* is predominant. The collaborative aspect refers to the expectation that journalists will be instrumental for state authorities. In authoritarian political contexts with low press freedom, journalists are subject to government directives and expected to praise politicians, and non-cooperation is punished.

The four journalism culture types display significant variations with respect to the degree to which political pressures work and are perceived by the actors. Political constraints are particularly high in countries with weak democratic performance, low levels of press freedom, and a high degree of political parallelism (Hamada et al. 2019; Hanitzsch et al. 2019).

A second major line of research for comparing role relationships between politicians and journalists in the tradition of comparative politics involves the exploration of interactions between journalists and politicians with respect to perceptions of mutual power. Several studies showed that politicians in many countries attrib-

How is trust in political institutions distributed across different types of journalism culture?

A survey of 27,500 journalists in sixty-seven countries fielded in 2012–2016 by Hanitzsch et al. (2019) demonstrated that journalists' attitudes can be classified into four models of journalism cultures: monitorial, advocative, developmental, and collaborative. The types of journalism cultures vary according to three context-specific spheres of influence: politics and governance, socioeconomic development, and cultural value systems. Of the five dimensions used to determine journalistic cultures, one is the trust that journalists have in public and political institutions. In Figure 19.2, the distribution of trust measures in different public and political institutions is depicted. Please assign the trust level of different countries to the type of journalism culture (scale: 5 = complete trust; 1 = no trust at all). Why is the US an outlier?

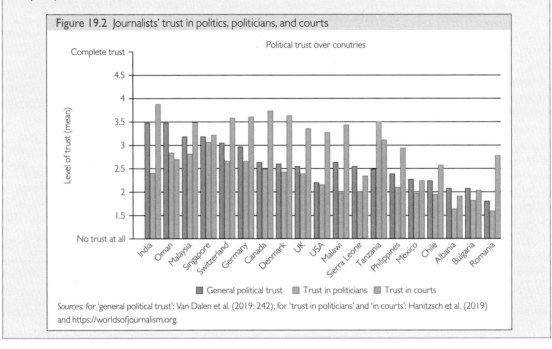

Figure 19.2 Journalists' trust in politics, politicians, and courts

Sources: for 'general political trust': Van Dalen et al. (2019: 242); for 'trust in politicians' and 'in courts': Hanitzsch et al. (2019) and https://worldsofjournalism.org.

ute much greater power to the media than journalists themselves (want to) recognize they have (Lengauer et al. 2014). The reason for this discrepancy is that politicians, unlike journalists, view various media behaviours, such as proactive forms of reporting, a broad understanding of objectivity, and the imposition of news logic on politics, as expressions of power (van Aelst et al. 2010; Vliegenthart and Skovsgaard 2017). While politicians across Europe believe that journalists are powerful in setting the political agenda and controlling the careers of politicians, media actors are reluctant to acknowledge their influential position in these respects (for details, see Box 19.2). Other comparative studies emphasized the mutual dependencies between the two groups and characterized their relationship as a back and forth between love and hatred and between friendly informality and deep-rooted suspicion (Van Aelst and Aalberg 2011). This suspicion points to the cynicism of political reporters towards politicians. Several studies of Western Europe highlighted the interactions between journalists' cyni-

cism about politicians and negative views of spin doctors and media salacity (van Aelst et al. 2008; van Dalen et al. 2011). However, politicians are also ambivalent towards media reporters and act out this ambivalence in two ways (Pfetsch et al. 2014b). In public, politicians describe their relationships with journalists as rather harmonic; internally, however, the relationships are clearly marked by diverging interests and conflicts. Therefore, the self-images of politicians and journalists have been characterized by tensions resulting from the conflicting objectives of their institutions of origin.

The intensity of this pattern varies between those countries with a high level of politicization of the media–politics relationship and those countries with less politicization (Esmark and Blach-Orsten 2014; Pfetsch et al. 2014b; Schwab Cammarano and Diez Medrano 2014). Comparative studies also revealed that the relationship between journalists and political actors is overshadowed by mistrust, particularly in transitional democracies and countries with a history of sudden

ZOOM-IN 19.2

How journalists and politicians perceive the power of the media in politics differently (percentage of those who 'agree' and 'strongly agree')

A survey of 2,652 news journalists, politicians, and political spokespersons from nine countries (Table 19.2) showed that there is a clear *perceptual divide* among political communication elites in evaluating media power: journalists perceive significantly lower levels of media power than politicians perceive (Lengauer et al. 2014).

Table 19.2 Role-specific perceptions of media's power in politics by country (percentage of agree/strongly agree with statement)

	Agenda-setting power of the media[1]			Career-controlling power of the media[2]		
	Journalists	Politicians	Spokespersons	Journalists	Politicians	Spokespersons
Finland (n^3 = 295)	29	54	51	71	91	89
Sweden (n =345)	24	41	35	32	44	54
Denmark (n = 187)	46	48	37	46	54	43
Germany (n= 357)	18	39	30	39	41	67
Austria (n =295)	27	45	32	39	48	40
Switzerland (n = 319)	23	50	30	40	57	53
France (n = 198)	27	53	49	78	82	78
Spain (n =167)	44	59	25	42	48	50
Slovenia (n = 296)	26	58	40	47	75	60
Total (n =2652)	29	50	37	48	60	59
	Cramer's V 0.147			Cramer's V 0.099		

Note: All chi square test results are significant at the .001 level. [1] "Media decide which issues are important in politics while politicians have little impact on this matter" (1 strongly disagree, 5 strongly agree). [2] "Mass media make and break politicians" (1 strongly disagree, 5 strongly agree). Data are weighted to reach equal distributions of journalists (n = 150), politicians (n = 100) and spokespersons (n = 50) in all countries. [3]n refers to the number of actual valid cases in each country (before weighting).

regime change. In new democracies, such as Chile, South Africa, Poland, Turkey, and South Korea, journalists are more mistrusting of political elites and dissatisfied with democratic institutions than in established democracies, such as Sweden and Germany (Beek 2010; Pfetsch and Voltmer 2012; Van Dalen et al. 2019).

A third major line of research for comparing role relationships between politicians and journalists follows in the tradition of political communication cultures (Gurevitch and Blumler 2004). Here, comparative studies aim to assess the cultures of interactions between media and political actors and link them to the conditions of the media and political systems. Regarding these milieus of exchange, there is a clear division between southern European countries (Spain, France, and Slovenia) and Northern European countries (Denmark, Sweden, and Finland) (Pfetsch et al. 2014a; Mayerhöffer 2018). In the southern European group, the exchange is subject to high politicization, and therefore, the culture is under some political and economic stress. In Northern Europe, the relationship has been more distant and the communication culture more civilized and professional.

A follow-up study on Sweden, Finland, Poland, and Lithuania maintained that political actors integrate the media logic into their political strategies in two ways (Johansson and Nygren 2019): as one strategy, they use news management, spin doctors, centralized communication, and informal personal networks to deal with journalists; as another strategy, they use social media to bypass the traditional media.

We may conclude from these comparative studies that political communication cultures in Western democracies are under stress, as journalism cultures suffer from political and economic pressures, and journalists and politicians perceive each other in the light of media salacity and suspicion. Mistrust seems to be a prevalent feature everywhere but is particularly strong in transformation democracies, as well as in the US. Within Western Europe, political communication cultures vary depending on whether autonomy, professionalism, and pluralism of the media are high or rather restricted or politicized. While research has made remarkable progress, comparative studies

---

KEY POINTS

- Based on characteristic constellations of political and media variables, Hallin and Mancini (2004) deduced and conceptualized three ideal models of media–politics relations for Western countries.

- Since then, research has concentrated on making the theoretical framework empirically measurable by means of quantitative indicators, by extending the typology to non-Western systems, and by integrating the significance of new modern information technologies.

- Based on elite surveys, several studies compared the professional attitudes, role self-perceptions, and interaction cultures of journalists and politicians. Most focused on European countries and found clear differences and divisions between North and South and between East and West.

- Future research should devote more attention to unveiling media–politics interactions in non-Western countries and in frail democracies. The role of political communication cultures is considered critical for understanding political transitions and system change.

---

of media–politics relations still suffer from shortcomings. The country samples are often small and skewed towards continental and northern European contexts, while the larger part of the world remains absent from comparative projects. Therefore, it is hardly possible to generalize from these findings to other systems outside of Europe. Additionally, the categories developed for Western European contexts capture only one segment of a much larger picture that remains in the dark.

Political information flows

Comparing messages produced and disseminated by political actors

Politicians, parties, and governments can assume powerful roles in political communications. Comparative social scientists have paid particular attention to three areas in which political actors engage in message production: government communication, parliamentary communication, and election communication.

In the area of government communication, early work based on the US, the UK, and Germany emphasized the strong connection between institutional structures of **governance** and communication strategies (Pfetsch 2007). In this vein, a multi-country study by Sanders and Canel (2013) found considerable differences between countries, depending on whether their governments had taken a party-centered or citizen-centered approach to communication. A party-centered approach refers to a partisan style that is primarily oriented towards the interests of the ruling party; it is found in countries like Zimbabwe, Singapore, and China, which all grant only limited political and media freedom. A more citizen-oriented and participatory approach is found in the US and the UK, where institutional resources and policy guidelines demand a non-partisan and civic minded style of addressing the public. Sanders and Canel (2013) further noted considerable differences in the level of professionalism in government communication. Strategically operating units of government recruit professionally trained specialists and afford them an autonomous organizational status at a senior level to manage communication, whereas a purely tactical approach goes hand in hand with low specialization and autonomy, weak coordination of tasks, an underdeveloped legal basis, and less advanced technical equipment. The Anglo-Saxon countries were classified as the most strategic, whereas Zimbabwe, Mexico, and Singapore were mainly tactical. In the middle ground between these two dimensions (party versus citizen-centred, strategic versus tactical), the researchers placed a diverse set of countries from Europe and Latin America, supplemented by South Africa and India. This middle group of countries combined various elements of both dimensions because of context-specific path-dependencies (see also Canel and Sanders 2014). A follow-up study among European countries revealed that the general trend towards more centralized, coordinated government communication, made necessary by growing pressure from a fragmented media environment and a polarized party landscape, was more pronounced in strategically operating countries than in tactically operating ones (Johansson and Raunio 2019).

In the field of parliamentary communication, comparative agenda-setting research has demonstrated that the news media in most political systems has a powerful impact on setting the parliamentary agenda. A seven-country study by Vliegenthart et al. (2016) demonstrated that opposition parties in their parliamentary activities are generally much more sensitive to media coverage than government parties are. More specifically, a three-country study by van Santen et al. (2015) illustrated that voicing criticism towards a member of government on a parliamentary question increases a politician's chances of getting covered by the press, explainable by the news value of conflict (see also Sevenans and Vliegenthart 2016). Those politicians with the highest motivation to use the news media as a political resource also use a simplified communication style in their parliamentary speeches, adapting to news logic, but only in countries where the electoral rules allow for a more central role of the news media (Amsalem et al. 2017).

In the field of election communication, the current 'fourth era of political communication' involves new campaigning tools, techniques, and capabilities opened up by the rise of big data technology (see Box 19.3). Semetko and Tworzecki (2018) argued that two further characteristics—in addition to advances in data mining, data analytics, microtargeting, automated bots, and algorithms—warrant the claim of a new era: first, the rising importance of social media platforms (Facebook, Twitter, and their counterparts in other countries) as content delivery mechanisms for political news and information; and second, the border-transgressing diffusion of campaign technologies and strategies, thanks to a global network of media, consultants, and other hidden channels that span democratic and authoritarian regimes alike. While many single country studies have already addressed these trends, there are only a few *comparative* international analyses that have focused on the role of digital campaign communication. However, two recent Facebook and two recent Twitter studies deserve our attention. We start with the Facebook studies because, according to international campaign managers, Facebook had developed into a catch-all campaign medium of transnational importance early on (Lilleker et al. 2015). Facebook gained in importance faster than Twitter and YouTube, but still lags behind television and face-to-face communication, both as information sources and strategic means for winning elections, a survey of European campaign managers found (Lilleker et al. 2015).

In the first Facebook study, Ceccobelli (2018) content-analysed how fifty-one political leaders from eighteen countries used 16,000 Facebook posts during national elections and compared them to non-election periods. He found that during election campaigns, politicians were motivated to increase their number of posts and increase the personalization of their posts, but also to reduce the share of policy discussions and reduce the level of negativity. The multinational

approach finds few differences among countries, and instead a general trend of cross-national homogenization with regard to campaigning on social media. The second Facebook study by Magin et al. (2017) content-analysed how five German and six Austrian parties used their Facebook pages 'to inform, interact with, and mobilize voters' during national elections. They found that the parties of both countries did not make use of Facebook's interactive and mobilizing potential (as Obama did so famously in 2008) and instead primarily relied on broadcasting mass-centred information. The authors attributed this conventional campaign approach to regulatory framework conditions that are tighter in Germany and Austria than they are in the US.

Turning to the Twitter studies, Graham et al. (2016) content-analysed how 454 British candidates and 221 Dutch candidates used 55,000 tweets during national elections, particularly with regard to the function and topic of the tweets. The authors found that Dutch politicians tweeted more often and in a more interactive way. The authors attributed the more conservative 'old habits' model of the British candidates to a more *party*-dominated campaign style, whereas the Dutch candidates pursued with their 'innovator' model a more *grassroots*-oriented approach. In a multinational Twitter study, Nulty et al. (2016) content-analysed the 900 most popular Twitter hashtags circulating between 3,200 members of the European Parliament (EP) and their followers during the 2014 EP election. The authors found that while the politicians used anti-EU and pro-EU hashtags fairly equally, the anti-EU hashtags did a better job in capturing citizens' attention. A high use of negative emotions in Twitter messages also seemed to correlate with anti-EU policy preferences (but not as much with left–right positioning in the national issue spectrum).

These international comparative analyses of the content of politicians' social media messages are commendable. However, they do not do justice to the hybrid character of modern election campaign dynamics, since they refrain from connecting the role of social media to traditional forms of media and election communication. Fortunately, we know a lot about the different ways in which traditional forms of communication are used in international election campaigns from the Global Political Consultants Survey by Plasser and Plasser (2002). Based on a survey of campaign managers in forty-three countries about their professional views and work practices, the authors distinguished between US-American, Australian, Western European, Latin American, East Asian, Russian, and post-communist styles of campaign communication (a follow-up publication with newer data confirmed the initial picture; see Plasser 2008).

The role of the internet in international election campaigns is influenced by contextual factors that define a country's electoral environment. Contex-

➤ **ZOOM-IN 19.3**

Welcome to the fourth age of political communication

The political communication literature distinguishes four ideal-typical ages of political communication (Table 19.3), each driven by particular technological developments. In the fourth age, features of the third age have further evolved and differentiated. Audiences have become more disperse, the number of non-voters and swing voters has further increased, and communication abundance has become exponentially high. The internet offers manifold new communication channels, including social networking sites. Consultants are being replaced by data analysts and traditional news organizations are flushed by influences of digital media. Highly fragmented and increasingly polarized public spheres require new techniques for effectively addressing and persuading voters.

Table 19.3 Four types of election campaigning

	Partisan-centred campaigns	Mass-centred campaigns	Target group-centred campaigns	Individual-centred campaigns
First possible in the . . .	First age (*ca.* 1850 –1960)	Second age (*ca.* 1960–1990)	Third age (*ca.* 1990 –2008)	Fourth age (since 2008)
Dominant state form	Nation-state	Welfare state	Competition state	Digital state
Public sphere	Centralized, party press	Two-step flows of communication	Growing fragmentation and mediatization	Interconnected niches and agendas; public awareness shaped by algorithms
Prime communication channel in campaigns	Printed press, face-to-face interactions	Limited-channel television	Multi-channel television and internet	Internet (esp. social network services), multi-channel TV
Key target audiences in campaigns	Partisans, party members (passive)	Masses (passive)	Targeted groups (passive)	Micro-targeted individuals (increasingly active)
Newly added campaigning tools	Print media, public spectacles, meet the candidate, foot soldiers	Scripted messages, broadcast news, polls, newspaper adverts	Internet, direct mail	Web 2.0 platforms, strategic data mining
Dominant campaign paradigm	Party logic (organize)	Media logic (advertise)	Marketing logic (customize)	Datafication logic (micro-analyse + mobilize)
Dominant reporting paradigm	Issue- and viewpoint-oriented journalism	Strategic and interpretive journalism	Critical and reflexive reporting	Networked, hybrid journalism
Causes of recent campaign controversies			Low regulation on campaign spending and attack-style political ads	Low regulation on social media advertising and data privacy

Sources: Based on Plasser (2003); Bimber (2014); Aagaard (2016); Magin et al. (2017); Gibson and Römmele (2019); own additions.

tual factors, especially the regulatory environment for technology and campaign finance, substantially influence electoral processes around the world. This explains, for example, why there are limits for an *Americanization of elections* in Asian countries. In Japan, campaign regulations are still draconian, the campaign period is short, and individual candidate advertisements are virtually banned. Candidates can put posters on boards along streets, although the size and number of the posters are strictly limited. They can distribute postcards as part of election campaigning, although the number of postcards is limited.

Facebook penetration is at 20 per cent, compared to over 60 per cent in the US (Kiyohara et al. 2018: 194–5). Taiwan, on the other hand, is moving more rapidly toward the Americanization of elections due to greater similarities with the US campaign environment. An extensive four-country comparison of Japan, South Korea, Taiwan, and the US clearly showed that the continued evolution of internet election campaigns is strongly related to the electoral and media environment (Kiyohara et al. 2018).

While important and insightful studies are conducted in the US, it is imperative to move beyond US-centric questions and study election campaigns in a comparative manner. Particularly for the role of social media, national contexts make a difference (see also Boulianne 2015). The major role of contextual factors can also be seen in the young field of comparative populism research. A content analysis of statements made by 103 politicians from six Western countries on Facebook, Twitter, TV talk shows, and in newspapers showed that the tendency to use populist ideas and styles is not evenly distributed. The highest probability of populist communication comes from (i) members of populist parties; and (ii) backbenchers in parliament; who address (iii) a specific set of mobilizable issues; in (iv) social media posts or newspaper articles (for details, see Ernst et al. 2019).

Comparing messages produced and disseminated by media actors

Political information is the key to many democratic functions of communication. Therefore, most comparative research on political media content focuses on news. In addition to its surveillance function, political news is expected to reflect public opinion, expose political misbehaviour, facilitate public discourse, and foster citizens' political participation (Schulz 2008). For comparative scholars, these functions provide a yardstick by which to assess cross-national differences in the selection, evaluation, and framing of news issues. Studies in the area of political news follow several trajectories, of which two will be discussed here in more detail. First, studies that focus on international and foreign news seek to establish how prevalent the allegedly outdated national perspective remains in globalized news arenas. Second, comparative research on domestic news aims to demonstrate relevant trends in political affairs coverage; these trends can be related to existing typologies of media systems and to standards of democratic news performance.

The key finding of comparative studies on international news is that mass media tend to domesticate transnational events by evaluating and framing them using national ideologies and national reception prisms (Lee et al. 2002; Clausen 2003). The same process of domestication was observed in the construction of news about the European Union, where evaluation and framing also follow an adaptation process at the national level within each EU member state (de Vreese et al. 2006; Pfetsch et al. 2008). Further, nation-specific framing mechanisms were explored in studies comparing how the same global event (such as the Iraq war) or a transnational issue (such as genetic engineering or climate change) is covered differently across political communication systems (Kohring and Goerke 2000; de Vreese et al. 2001; Brossard et al. 2004; Dardis 2006). The recurring evidence of dominant national angles has prompted the largest-scale comparative study on the topic to ask with exasperation, 'Where in the world is the global village?' (Cohen 2013). Whether there will be more cases of national media generating an encompassing global public sphere, or at least international convergence in national news reporting (Curran et al. 2017), in the future is an interesting empirical question. Until a few years ago, some researchers saw a European public sphere emerging; at least there were common European public debates related to a shared political identity of the European Union (Pfetsch and Heft 2015). Careful recent analyses showed, however, that even with prototypical global issues such as climate change, media coverage in various countries, despite indisputable indications of convergence, also reflected national political interests and national journalistic cultures (Lück et al. 2018).

The second line of comparative news research takes up the historical institutionalist approach of Hallin and Mancini (2004) and argues that each type of media system features a specific type of news journalism. Esser and Umbricht (2013) examined the empirical relevance of these theoretical models and were able—in a content analysis of eighteen news outlets from six countries from the 1960s to the 2000s—to largely confirm and further specify the news cultures in Western political communication systems. In US newspapers, they focused on the coexistence of objective and interpretative journalism (allowing for rational news analyses); in Italian newspapers, they found a coexistence of opinionated and negative news (promoting the provision of polarized information); and German and Swiss newspapers revealed a coexistence of news and views (although with an emphasis on rational, factual, and consensual reporting). French and British newspapers occupied intermediate positions because they combined elements from various traditions. Over the past decades, British newspapers have in many ways aligned more with continental European newspapers than with US papers, and are even absorbing some elements of polarized Mediterranean journalism in their day-to-day coverage of politics. French journalism differs from Italian journalism in its greater appreciation of rationality and empiricism (Esser and Umbricht 2013; Umbricht and Esser 2014; see Box 19.4).

These cross-national reporting styles are not set in stone, but have all drifted towards interpretative journalism as the decades have passed. Since the 1960s, the newspapers of all six countries have increased their interpretive news analyses and opinion-based stories (Esser and Umbricht 2014). Searching for an explanation of the high degree of interpretative news, a comparative study of sixteen countries by Salgado et al. (2016) showed that interpretive journalism *on television* is a function of commercialism and channel competition, whereas *in newspapers*, it is a function of an increasingly critical attitude of journalists towards politics. In

---

ZOOM-IN 19.4

Three approaches to political affairs coverage in Western newspapers

Esser and Umbricht (2013) conducted a correspondence analysis that cross-classified six newspaper systems with a set of story features commonly found in political affairs coverage. As indicated by the triangle in Figure 19.3, three prototypical reporting styles emerged. Although US newspapers prefer more interpretative story types, such as news analyses and background reports, they remain committed to a fact-based reporting style that relies on expert statements and presentation of both sides of a story, except when a scandal breaks. This US approach is very different from the prototypical Italian approach, where a fundamentally negative, conflict-oriented, and opinionated reporting style prevails. A third prototypical style is found in German and Swiss newspapers, where a strong emphasis on news concurs with a continuing interest in opinion, with both story types usually separated on a news page.

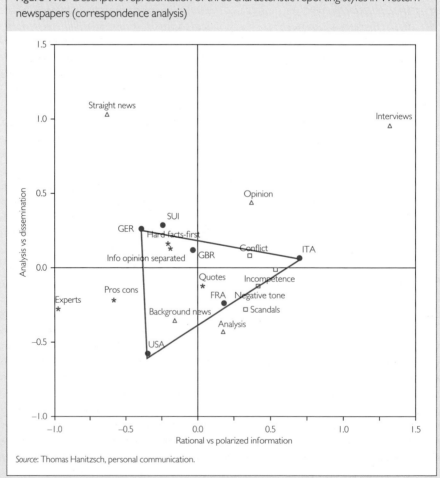

Figure 19.3 Descriptive representation of three characteristic reporting styles in Western newspapers (correspondence analysis)

Source: Thomas Hanitzsch, personal communication.

order to measure and evaluate the democratic performance of national news systems, comparativists have investigated not only the extent of interpretive journalism, but also how widespread strategic and game framing, negative news, imbalance, personalization, and soft news are in political reporting. Based on these six indicators, de Vreese and colleagues (2017) examined 160 online and offline news outlets from sixteen countries in an unusually elaborate content analysis. They found that influences related to the political economy primarily explained most of the variance in national news performance, and that news performance in Northern European, Southern European, and North American countries differed considerably (de Vreese et al. 2017: 164, 173, 177).

Another characteristic of current news formats is the intensive use of popularization techniques to make political news more appealing, leading to growing shares of sensationalism, scandalization, emotionalization, common people's perspectives, and private revelations of public figures. Indeed, these trends are increasing in both Anglo-American and polarized Mediterranean news systems, albeit for different reasons (for details, see Umbricht and Esser 2016). A careful operationalization of *populist* communication allowed researchers also to answer the question of whether international news media tend to provide an uncritical stage for populist politicians. A comprehensive content analysis of sixty news media outlets from ten European countries led Wettstein and colleagues (2018) largely to negate this question. The most pronounced critical attitude of European journalists towards populists was in those countries where, out of principle, established parties agreed not to cooperate with populist parties and erect a 'cordon sanitaire' around them (e.g. Germany, France, and Sweden). Media criticism of populist parties was considerably weaker in those countries where they were part of the government (e.g. Bulgaria or Austria).

While many studies are interested in delineating cross-national differences in long-term reporting styles, others are interested in discussing the causes and consequences of these reporting styles. Albaek et al. (2014) found close relationships between journalists' attitudes and role self-conceptions and the kind of political news they produced. For instance, Spanish journalists are fairly partisan and so is their news, whereas British journalists are more infotainment-oriented, and their coverage frequently focuses on scandals and politicians' private lives. In terms of audience effects, the authors found that the public tends to be more content with journalists if they are performing a good watchdog function. In Spain, where watchdog journalism is perceived to be less prevalent, citizen

satisfaction with media coverage is lower than in Great Britain, where reporters are seen to be more vigilant towards the government. The authors concluded their four-country study by arguing that the most favourable contextual conditions for political journalism include 'a high degree of professionalism in journalism, a low degree of political parallelism, a strong public broadcasting system, and moderate degrees of commercialism and competition' (Albaek et al. 2014: 170), a verdict that is difficult to disagree with.

However, not all media systems offer favourable conditions for exemplary journalism. Box 19.5 identifies those conditions under which 'junk news' and 'fake news' can thrive.

Comparing national audiences in their news consumption

Changes in the use of political information deserve special attention because news is the essential channel for disseminating political knowledge and motivating citizens to participate and make informed choices. For most countries, the Digital News Report (2019) states that television news and online news remain the most frequently used sources of political information, while readership of printed newspapers has been declining significantly.

As Table 19.4 in Box 19.6 illustrates, the biggest change in previous years has been the growth of news accessed via social media sites like Facebook and Twitter. About half of the internet users in the US, Hong Kong, Brazil, and Norway get their news via social media nowadays. Until a few years ago, this share was mostly attributable to Facebook, but controversies about 'fake news' and the preferences of younger users for alternative platforms have lessened Facebook's dominance (see Table 19.4, column 1). It should be noted that most news content on Facebook comes from traditional news organizations, and that most social media users also watch television news and visit mainstream news websites or apps directly (Digital News Report 2016). This illustrates that most people access news through a *combination* of sources and platforms.

Significant generational splits in the sources used for news are commonly found in most countries: senior citizens rely more on traditional news sources and use them frequently; younger groups rely more on digital and social media and use them less frequently for news (Nielsen and Schrøder 2014). It remains to be seen whether today's young consumers will increase their news usage over the course of their lives, or whether they will never reach the same level of interest of today's older cohort. One hope for

> ↘ **ZOOM-IN 19.5**

The debate on fake news from a cross-national perspective

The term 'fake news' is insufficient and dangerous to use because it has been appropriated by politicians around the world to describe news organizations whose coverage they find to be problematic. The Computational Propaganda Research Project at the University of Oxford speaks of 'junk news' instead, defined as ideologically extreme, hyper-partisan, or conspiratorial news and information, as well as various forms of propaganda. A study of tweets and Facebook posts related to the European parliamentary elections 2019 found that junk news circulated more easily on Facebook than on Twitter. The largest amounts of junk news on Twitter circulated in Poland and Italy, while junk news stories on Facebook had the highest probability of being shared in the UK, Germany, and Sweden. In the US, the share of junk news stories disseminated on Facebook increased steadily between the 2016 presidential election and the 2018 midterm elections (Marchal et al. 2018, 2019).

Depending on how one defines junk news or whether one prefers to work with more precise concepts such as 'misinformation' or 'disinformation', the results can vary greatly between countries (Burger et al. 2019; Quandt et al. 2019). From a comparative perspective, it is important to determine which contextual conditions are responsible for some countries being more vulnerable to widespread dissemination and use of online disinformation, while others appear to be more resilient. Focusing on 'disinformation,' Humprecht et al. (2020)

found the following country factors to be of particular relevance.

In countries where both the number of users of news media with public service ethos and the level trust in established news media are comparatively high, and where both the fragmentation and polarization of media and their users are comparatively low, one can expect fewer people be confronted with online disinformation. These contextual conditions apply, for instance, to Northern European media systems.

Countries marked by a history of polarized conflict, politicized, and partisan media, and opinionated and less professional journalism may be more susceptible to disinformation. This should apply above all when social media use, social polarization, and populist communication are comparatively high and trust in media and politics is comparatively low. These contextual conditions apply, for instance, to Eastern and Southern European countries.

The US context presents itself as most vulnerable to online disinformation. Not only because many conditions of the previous country category now apply to the US media system, but also because—in addition to weak public service broadcasting, low trust, high polarization and high populist communication—there is the sheer size of the media market, which makes the US extremely attractive to commercially minded protagonists of online disinformation (Humprecht et al. 2020).

---

young, politically disinterested users of social media is the so-called *incidental exposure to news*. Comparative research found that Twitter, YouTube, and Facebook can bring users 'accidentally' into contact with news while they are looking for non-political content. As a result, heavy users of social media report being in contact with more news sources than people who do not use these platforms (Fletcher and Nielsen 2018), and some of these 'inadvertent' encounters may even stimulate political participation online (Valeriani and Vaccari 2016).

The current multi-channel media landscape has made it much more difficult to analyse news consumption patterns cross-nationally. Digital technologies have prompted a transition from the days when entire nations gathered around the same televized broadcast to a more fragmented public that has access to a high number of alternative sources to news. Metaphors like *echo-chambers* and *filter bubbles* have flourished in many countries to describe a new scenario in which like-minded individuals only consume news from the set of outlets that match their interests and

beliefs. Fletcher and Nielsen (2017) examined this trend comparatively in four countries and found to their surprise that despite the abundance of media outlets that could lead to potential fragmentation, most people still consumed news sources used by many other citizens, rather than sorting themselves into separate echo chambers. The second surprising finding was that viewer fragmentation was not, as hypothesized, higher in the US and Germany, but in Denmark and Great Britain. However, this was only because Danish and British users, in addition to the news sources they otherwise used, still utilized the online and offline public service offerings of DR and BBC. This cross-over watching of several channels is rarer in the US, also because there is not one media 'lighthouse' that broadcasts news that should not be missed (Fletcher and Nielsen 2017).

This latter finding underlines the great importance that a strong public broadcasting system still has today for individual access to news. A study of twenty-seven countries by Castro and colleagues (2018) found that individuals in information environments with strong public service broadcasting are more willing to expose themselves to attitude-inconsistent, non-like-minded political news, thereby minimizing the risk of echo chambers (Castro et al. 2018). This fits well with the finding that Americans have a much greater tendency to favour attitude-consistent political news than, for instance, Japanese viewers—attributable to greater media trust and regulated news standards on public and commercial channels in Japan (Knobloch-Westerwick et al. 2019).

We see also clear country patterns in people's propensity to avoid news. According to the Digital News Report (2019), this tendency is least pronounced in Asian and Scandinavian countries (JP, FI), slightly stronger in West European corporatist systems and Canada, and somewhat stronger in Anglo-American (US, UK) and Latin-American (BR, MX) countries. It is strongest in those East European (HU), South European (GR, TUR), and South American (ARG) countries that have recently experienced a crisis (see Table 19.4 for details).

Comparing effects of political communication

From the perspective of citizens, exposure to political messages impacts their capacity to perform their political roles. This leads to the need to identify under which contextual conditions the use of certain media messages leads to democratically desirable effects, such as increased political knowledge or participation. These context conditions are theorized as opportunity structures in comparative effect research. The combined consideration of information opportunity structures at the media system level (such as degree of commercialization) and individual-level characteristics (such as news media exposure) allows comparatists to bring together micro-level theories of learning and participation through media with macro-level theories related to media system types, information environments, knowledge gaps, and democratic engagement. We will focus here on knowledge and participation, the key argument being that not all political communication ecosystems produce equally favourable opportunity structures for them. Dimock and Popkin (1997: 223) argued some time ago that Europeans were much better informed about world events than Americans, and suggested that this was due to 'substantial differences between countries in the communication of knowledge by TV'.

Several attempts to investigate this claim systematically followed, starting with a four-country study by Curran et al. (2009) and a six-country study by Aalberg and Curran (2012), followed by an eleven-country study by Soroka et al. (2013). The samples always included the US and varying compositions of European countries. The last study expanded its scope and

---

⤡ ZOOM-IN 19.6

How people use the news around the world

Social media has become a crucial source of news (see column 1 of Table 19.4), although Facebook's growth has declined recently in many countries, particularly among younger people. While news consumption via Facebook remains very popular in Latin America and Eastern Europe, people in Northern and Western Europe prefer to go directly to a news website or app; in Japan and South Korea, news aggregators like Yahoo are more dominant than Facebook (column 1). More than half of today's internet users are concerned about 'what is real and what is fake' when thinking about online news; the problem seems most severe in countries that have experienced increased polarization lately (column 2). Although trust in news is declining overall in most countries, there are stark cross-national differences: while the news media remain broadly trusted in Finland, Denmark, and Canada, people in Hungary, Greece, and Korea do not think they can 'trust most of the news most of the time' (column 3). In an environment of increasing polarization, misinformation, and distrust, substantial numbers of people find themselves 'actively trying to avoid the news these days'. News avoidance is highest in Turkey and Greece, and it is lowest in Japan and the Scandinavian countries, where following the news is still considered a civic duty (column 4). Countries with a low news avoidance rate are also among the countries with the highest news usage (Meulemann 2012; Aalberg et al. 2013a; Papathanassopoulos et al. 2013). In Greece, but also in Latin American and Anglo-Saxon countries, people are concerned about the media's tone in political news coverage and say that 'the news media often takes too negative views on events' (column 5). There is also large cross-national variation in people's attitudes towards the media's watchdog role. It is lowest in Japan, where the press is seen as being too close to government. Also, in Hungary and South Korea, few people agree that, 'the news media monitor and scrutinize powerful people and businesses' (column 6).

Table 19.4   What representative samples of online news users say

	1	2	3	4	5	6
	Used Facebook as source of news last week (%)	Concerned about mis-information on internet (%)	Trust the news and news media overall (%)	Actively avoid the news often or sometimes (%)	Think the news media is often too negative (%)	Agree that the news media monitor and scrutinize the powerful (%)
USA	39	67	32	41	43	45
UK	27	70	40	35	47	42
Ireland	38	61	48	32	36	40
Canada	38	61	52	29	36	49
Australia	41	62	44	29	44	45
Norway	40	39	46	21	36	51
Sweden	36	47	39	22	27	49
Finland	33	52	59	17	23	51
Denmark	34	39	57	15	29	45
Germany	24	38	47	25	32	37
Netherlands	29	41	53	29	23	36
Austria	30	40	44	29	42	39
Greece	60	61	27	54	59	39
Portugal	53	75	58	31	49	51
Czech Republic	57	41	33	25	34	42
Poland	54	43	48	41	43	52
Hungary	60	49	28	35	38	20
Turkey	51	63	46	55	39	45
Japan	9	51	39	11	29	17
South Korea	25	59	22	24	42	21
Hong Kong	56	45	46	20	25	38
Malaysia	64	64	31	29	32	42
Brazil	52	85	48	34	47	56
Mexico	61	68	50	37	48	45
Argentina	60	62	39	45	49	41

Source: Digital News Report (2018) (for column 1) and (2019) (for columns 2–6).

also included Australia, Canada, Colombia, Greece, India, Japan, and South Korea. Generally, the findings of these studies suggest that there is a negative relationship between the level of commercial media and general news knowledge.

In public service systems—countries that support public broadcasting and actively regulate commercial broadcasters—TV newscasts convey more hard news and more international news, and their domestic political news coverage is less game-centred and less tabloidized. Additionally, newscasts tend to air more frequently during prime-time viewing hours, when television audiences spike. In market-based systems, on the contrary, unregulated commercial networks respond to market forces and offer news programming that is sporadic and less substantial. The three largest US channels—ABC, CBS, and NBC—allocate considerably less airtime to their news and current affairs programming and attract considerably smaller audiences than generalist channels in Norway, Sweden, Belgium, or the Netherlands (Aalberg et al. 2010). As a result, there are significant cross-national differences in citizens' 'costs' of acquiring hard news and international news knowledge. The costs are higher in the US, and political knowledge among Americans is heavily dependent upon the individual's interest in politics. The costs are lower in the Northern European public service model because of the greater availability of news programming; this enables less-motivated citizens to acquire political information more easily than their counterparts in the US can (Iyengar et al. 2010).

Inadvertent or incidental exposure to political information during prime-time news programmes occurs more frequently in countries where public broadcasting is a strong component of the national media system. Using varying measures of knowledge testing, the consistent finding is that Americans are especially uninformed about international affairs, and compared to citizens in Northern Europe, they are also less knowledgeable about domestic politics (Curran et al. 2009, 2012). This is also largely true for international politics (see Box 19.7).

The challenge for research on the relationship between the content of news and citizens' knowledge patterns is to establish a causal relationship. For this reason, two of the available cross-national studies use propensity score matching (Soroka et al. 2013; Fraile and Iyengar 2014) and demonstrate the positive contribution of public service broadcasters to an informed citizenship. However, this can only be generalized to other countries if three conditions are met. First, public broadcasters ought to be funded largely by public money to keep dependence on additional advertising revenue low, as is the case for the BBC. Second,

public broadcasters need the backing of a substantial audience—something that PBS in the US fails to achieve. Third, public broadcasters require independence from government, meaning no undue political interference. The implication of these comparative studies is that in-depth political journalism from public broadcasters and quality newspapers plays an important role in public affairs knowledge and, ultimately, the functioning of democracy. It is simply not true that all news sources are equally informative (Soroka et al. 2013; Fraile and Iyengar 2014).

A second line of comparative effects research focuses on media and participation, particularly in the European Union. Many studies explored the consequences of EU citizens receiving very different kinds of news about the EU from the media in their respective home countries. Regarding the nature of coverage, it was found that the salience of EU politics in news depended on the controversy surrounding the issue in national public spheres. Thus, the more national parties were divided about the EU and took negative positions towards it, the greater the increase in EU news media coverage (Boomgaarden et al. 2013). The conflict framing of EU politics was also evident in the 2009 European election campaign news (Schuck et al. 2013) but was contingent upon the type of medium (quality or mass-oriented), the electoral system (proportional or not), and public opinion towards the EU (based on Eurobarometer data). The question of whether exposure to conflict-ridden EU-coverage affects political **mobilization** was explored with a multilevel analysis of twenty-one member-states (Schuck et al. 2016). The study confirmed that the overall evaluation of the EU in the news impacts political mobilization in European elections insofar as the more controversial and politicized the debate in the media, the more salient EU politics becomes, and the more the voters are motivated to go to the polls.

This positive effect of conflict coverage, however, only applies up to a certain point. This can be seen in the finding that persistent negative coverage of the EU leads to higher support for Eurosceptic parties (van Spanje and de Vreese 2014). This led researchers to examine also the effects of populist communication on political participation. Using identical parallel experiments in sixteen EU member countries, Hameleers and colleagues (2018) found that 'anti-elitist cues' in a news report increase people's willingness to share the news report on social network sites or to talk to a friend about it. This was true particularly in those countries where unemployment and electoral chances of populist parties were high.

What about the effects of various forms of social media use on political participation? In democratic systems with a free and independent press, political expression on social media (in tweets, posts, blogs) is the best predictor for political participation offline. In non-democratic systems without a free press, informational uses of social media (for searching and gathering) have the strongest effects on offline political engagement (Boulianne 2019). Cross-national effect studies outside Europe are generally rare. Some offer comparisons of Asian countries (Skoric et al. 2016; Chan et al. 2019), but very few studies look at Africa. Focusing on sub-Saharan Africa and Asia, Nisbet et al. (2012) examined the impact of internet use on citizen attitudes about democracy. They found that, while individual-level internet use increases citizens' demand for democracy, this relationship is stronger in countries with higher democratization and with higher internet penetration rates at the contextual level.

In short, comparative effects research has established strong relationships between macro-structural variables of the political communication system and individual-level variables like political knowledge and political participation. Further efforts to advance media effects research should concentrate, in particular, on the explanatory mechanisms connecting the broader media environment and individual effects.

Conclusion

While most studies on political communication focus on phenomena and problems in one country, for this chapter we have discussed comparative studies only. We find that the conditions of political communication in different countries are both homogenizing

---

ZOOM-IN 19.7

If the media do not report much about politics, citizens do not know much about politics

Aalberg et al. (2013b) found a clear relationship between TV broadcasters' supply of international hard news and audiences' knowledge of international hard news. They calculated political knowledge scores of respondents in eleven countries and matched them with the shares of international hard news that were supplied to them on leading national television channels prior to the survey in spring 2010. The scatterplot indicates a strong positive correlation, suggesting that when mainstream news media marginalize foreign affairs, citizens' understanding of the world seems to suffer.

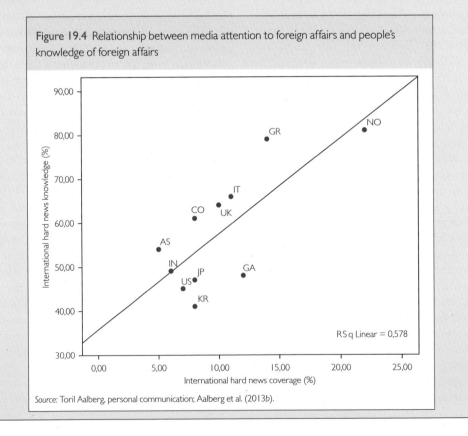

Figure 19.4 Relationship between media attention to foreign affairs and people's knowledge of foreign affairs

Source: Toril Aalberg, personal communication; Aalberg et al. (2013b).

- Political actors professionalize their approach to government communication, parliamentary communication, and election communication at the same time as they perceive the mass media as increasingly important. In the area of election communication, there is a strong trend towards social-based campaigning. However, the responses of campaign specialists to the demands of the fourth era of political communication are tailored to the specific conditions of their countries.

- The news media in many Western countries have become increasingly objective in their political affairs coverage since the 1960s, but they have also become more interpretive. To what extent they also rely on strategic game framing, negative news, bias, personalization, soft news, and populism in their reporting depends on specific country factors.

- News consumption via online and social media sources is becoming the norm, but the desire of citizens to be well informed and take advantage of multiple news sources is not distributed equally across societies. Young people follow the news in a very fickle manner. Countries differ in the degree to which their audiences are fragmented, polarized, or turn away from the news completely.

- Comparative effects research has concentrated on determining those opportunity structures of media systems that have a favourable impact on political knowledge and participation. A high degree of journalistic professionalism and effective regulation combined with a large supply and a low degree of commercialization facilitate an informed public. Political engagement, on the other hand, is fostered by news that is mobilizing without being populist, and by social media platforms that promote informational intentions and political expressions.

and heterogenizing. In some areas, the similarities are growing, while in others, the diversity and complexity are increasing. In many countries, we find hybrid conditions because the characteristics of different political systems, media systems, and media logics intersect as complex ecosystems of political communication emerge. In this chapter, we have presented theoretical models and specific aspects of media and communication ecosystems in order to provide some order and a certain baseline from which developments can be interpreted. Also, we have argued that there is not one Western model of political communication, but a broad variety of settings, structures, and roles of communication in a globalized world.

We also emphasized that the orientation towards Western models is always a mixed blessing. Why? Because there are some blatant disparities between high-minded ideals and disillusioning reality. The ideal textbook democracy would expect citizens to live in information-rich environments where media enjoy independence from political and business pressures and where people receive multiple opportunities to encounter high-quality political journalism. These ideals would further expect individuals to be highly interested in news and motivated to stay informed and acquire vast knowledge about domestic and international affairs. Also, they suggest that political actors provide citizen-oriented information and entertain cooperative relations with journalists. These ideals would expect reporters to provide objective stories that are fact-based and not sensationalized. In reality, we see, at least in some countries, indications of deteriorating media–politics relations, downgraded roles for established parties and news organizations, fragmented and polarized public spheres, declining substance of political information, strategically managed communication by candidates and governments, decreasing news consumption, waning knowledge, and ultimately, declining participation.

With regard to the future, there are no easy solutions at hand. Davis (2019: 212) recommends following the Scandinavian template, since he believes that the Nordic countries, together with Switzerland, the Netherlands, Canada, Australia, and New Zealand, offer the best conditions for democratic political communication in times of crisis. Some countries, however, seem to be going in a completely different direction due to the discrepancies and pathologies mentioned. Some political leaders have denounced the Western model of media and democracy and proclaimed the regimes of Russia, China, Turkey, and Singapore as templates to follow. For instance, Hungarian Prime Minister Viktor Orbán declared in 2014 that he was 'parting ways with Western dogmas, building an illiberal state, a non-liberal state' (Orbán 2014: 1). Keane (2015) saw a great danger in 'mediated despotism' in transitional states in some Eurasian, Arab, and Asia-Pacific regions, in particular. Protagonists of the model of mediated despotism use a mix of threats and rewards toward media firms to capture and colonize them. These states use sophisticated methods of controlling journalists and flows of information, in both traditional media and social networks, in an effort to misinform people and legitimize their powers (Keane 2015).

Thus, the coincidence of changing democracies and hybrid media and political communication ecosystems produces ambivalent outcomes. Under favourable circumstances, information, transparency, voice, mobilization, connective action, and effective participation are possible. Under unfavourable circumstances, the conditions play into the hands of authoritarian parties and leaders. Many countries are currently experiencing this ambivalence in the upsurge of populism, even when media and democracy are still working well.

? QUESTIONS

Knowledge-based

1. What is the rationale of comparative political communication?

2. What are core components of the political communication ecosystem, and how does it help to conceptualize the information flows between political actors and citizens?

3. What are relevant categories for comparing Western media systems, and how may these categories be modified to allow for meaningful comparisons of non-Western systems?

4. What are the main features in the use of political communication on different media and social media channels in election campaigns?

5. What are key characteristics of Western political affairs news coverage?

Critical thinking

1. How does the internet affect election campaigns?

2. Discuss the nature of the relationship between journalists and politicians. How does it vary across Europe, and what are the reasons for conflicts between the two actor groups?

3. What are the main types of Western news cultures, and what are the key characteristics for each type?

4. How do the usage patterns of social media vary across different groups of people and countries?

5. Discuss the contribution of quality media for informed citizenship.

≈ FURTHER READING

Aalberg, T. and Curran, J. (2012) *How the Media Inform Democracy. A Comparative Approach* (London: Routledge).

Bruns, A., Enli, G., Skogerbo, E., Larsson, A. O., and Christensen, C. (eds) (2016) *The Routledge Companion to Social Media and Politics* (New York: Routledge).

Esser, F. and Hanitzsch, T. (2012) *The Handbook of Comparative Communication Research* (London: Routledge).

Hallin, D. C. and Mancini, P. (2004) *Comparing Media Systems. Three Models of Media and Politics* (New York: Cambridge).

Mazzoleni, G., Barnhurst, K., Ikeda, K., Maia, R., and Wessler, H. (eds) (2016) *The International Encyclopedia of Political Communication* (London: Wiley-Blackwell).

 Visit the Online Resources that accompany this book for additional material, including country profiles, comparative data sets, flashcard glossaries, and web directory.

www.oup.com/he/caramani5e

Section 5
Public policies

20
Policy-making

Christoph Knill and Jale Tosun

Reader's guide

The process related to policy-making touches the core function of democratic politics, namely the elaboration and discussion of policy solutions to societal problems. This chapter provides a theoretical entrée to the analysis of policy-making and identifies potential determinants and consequences of policy choices. It pursues two core objectives. First, it intends to familiarize the reader with the general concept of the policy cycle, which helps to focus more specifically on the relevant actors and institutions. Second, it outlines the most crucial domestic and international factors shaping the design of policies. To demonstrate the relevance of the introduced theoretical arguments and analytical concepts, the chapter further presents some empirical findings.

Introduction

Policies follow a particular purpose: they are designed to achieve defined goals and present solutions to societal problems. More precisely, policies are government statements of what it intends to do or not to do, including laws, regulations, decisions, or orders. Public policy, on the other hand, is a more specific term, which refers to a long series of actions carried out to solve societal problems (Newton and van Deth 2010: 282). Hence, (public) policies can be conceived of as the main output of political systems (see Figure I.1 in the Introduction to this volume). But how are **public policies** actually made? Which factors determine their shape?

The classic policy analysis literature approaches these questions by using policy typologies as 'analytical shortcuts' for the underlying process (cf. Anderson 2003; Howlett et al. 2009; Knill and Tosun 2012). The most influential typology has been developed by Theodor J. Lowi (1964), who distinguishes between (i) *distributive policies* relating to measures which affect the distribution of resources from the government to particular recipients; (ii) *redistributive policies*, which are based on the transfer of resources from one societal group to another; (iii) *regulatory policies*, which specify conditions and constraints for individual or collective behaviour; and (iv) *constituent policies*, which create or modify the states' institutions (see Box 20.1). The typology's main objective is to offer scholars support in building more specific theories, since each of these four policy types is related to a varying degree of costs and potential opposition when the governments seek to modify the *status quo*—an idea taken up by the literature on comparative politics such as that on 'veto players' (Tsebelis 1995, 2000).

These considerations about costs and benefits are even more systematically addressed by James Q. Wilson's (1973, 1989, 1995) typology. The author distinguishes between policies on the basis of whether the related costs and benefits are either widely distributed or narrowly concentrated. Each of the four possible combinations yields different implications for policy-making. When both costs and benefits of a certain policy are widely distributed, a government may encounter no or only minor opposition, indicating **majoritarian politics** as the likely outcome. When, by contrast, both costs and benefits of a certain policy are concentrated, a government may be confronted with opposition of rivalling interest groups, which signals interest group politics. However, if costs are concentrated and benefits diffused, a government may encounter opposition from dominant interest groups. In this case, entrepreneurial politics are the probable outcome. This implies that policy change requires the presence of 'political entrepreneurs' who are willing to develop and put through political proposals despite strong societal resistance. The fourth and final scenario consists of a situation in which costs are diffuse and benefits concentrated. In such a case, governments are likely to be confronted with a relevant interest group that is favourable to its reform endeavour, indicating that clientelistic politics are the likely outcome.

The addressees' opposition or consent to policy options surely represents a central aspect in the analysis of policy-making, especially for understanding when policy reforms become initiated, and if and

---

Q DEFINITION 20.1

Types of policies

Lowi's typology (1964)		
Type of policy	**Definition**	**Examples**
Regulatory policies	Policies specifying conditions and constraints for individual or collective behaviour	Environmental protection; migration policy; consumer protection
Distributive policies	Policies distributing new resources	Agriculture; social issues; public works; subsidies; taxes
Redistributive policies	Policies modifying the distribution of existing resources	Land reform; progressive taxation; welfare policy
Constituent policies	Policies creating or modifying the states' institutions	Changes of procedural rules of parliaments

Wilson's typology (1973, 1989, 1995)		
Costs	**Benefits**	
	Concentrated	**Diffuse**
Concentrated	Interest group politics	Entrepreneurial politics
Diffuse	Clientelistic politics	Majoritarian politics

when they are successful. Furthermore, both typologies deserve credit for having introduced the notions of costs and benefits related to policy alternatives. Yet, we argue that we can raise the analytical leverage of policy analysis by focusing more explicitly on the political processes. This *politics* perspective involves scrutinizing the roles of the executive and legislative branches of government. Moreover, it implies the employment of theories of decision-making and the exploration of policy-making structures for understanding how besides political and institutional forces, social and economic interests shape the content of policies. From this, it follows that the politics perspective enables a more refined definition of the costs and benefits related to a given policy option. Consequently, studying policy-making in terms of comparative politics can significantly enhance our scientific understanding (see Chapter 22 'The impact of public policies').

KEY POINTS

- Policies are the main outputs of political systems; they come along in different forms, including laws, regulations, or rules.

- The 'classic' policy analysis literature relies on policy typologies as 'analytical shortcuts' for grasping the costs and benefits related to a certain policy option. Based on the respective magnitude of these two parameters, expectations about the likelihood of promulgating new policies and changing existing policies are formulated.

- By studying the policy-making process from a comparative politics perspective, we gain a fuller understanding of the causes and consequences of policy decisions.

Conceptual models of policy-making

What would an ideal policy look like? What is the best policy design that can be achieved? Both questions are crucial to policy-making. The first one refers to the functionality of a policy to be formulated, i.e. which design a particular policy should have in order to meet an *ex ante* defined goal. The second one touches upon the constraints that appear when policies are actually made. These are principally given by politics, i.e. the process by which the actors involved make decisions. Therefore, it is essential for our purpose to examine how politics shapes policies.

A number of conceptual models help to clarify our understanding of the relationship between politics and policies. The major models that can be found in the literature are (i) the institutional model; (ii) the rational model; (iii) the incremental model; (iv) the group model; (v) the elite model; and (vi) the process model. These models are not competitive, but rather complementary, as they focus on different aspects of political life, and hence concentrate on separate characteristics of policies (Dye 2005: 12).

The main implication of these models is that they make different assumptions about the importance of the actors involved—institutions, politicians, bureaucrats, interest groups, and the public—and their rationality. We now shortly explain these models—except the process model, which we address in the next section, 'Analysing policy-making as a process: the policy cycle'—to provide an initial theoretical access to policy-making.

Institutional model

For a long time, the central interest of political science was on how institutional arrangements influence the content of policies (cf. March and Olsen 1984, 2008; Weaver and Rockman 1993). The analytical focus of the institutional model is hence primarily on the extent to which formal and informal political institutions pre-structure policy decisions by defining strategic opportunities and constraints in which policy-makers operate (cf. Lijphart 2012 [1999]). This perspective might be accurate for democracies, but the more recent literature concentrating on autocracies shows that policy-making in these systems is to a lesser extent pre-structured by institutional arrangements that constrain, and hence predefine, political decision-making (cf. Miller 2014). If the analytical focus lies on such political systems, additional factors need to be taken into account to explain the design of policies, such as the size of the existing 'winning coalitions' (Bueno de Mesquita et al. 2003; Cao and Ward 2015).

Rational model

First developed in the field of economic analysis, the rational model of decision-making formulates guidance on how to secure 'optimal' policy decisions, implying that no other alternative is better according to the decision-makers' preferences (Shepsle and Bonchek 1997: 25). The rational model is also associated with a particular mode of learning, namely the concept of Bayesian learning. According to this perspective, governments update their beliefs on the consequences of policies with all available information about policy outcomes in the past and elsewhere and choose the policy that is expected to yield the best results (Meseguer Yebra 2009).

Rational policy-making involves a number of demanding assumptions. For example, policy-makers are expected to have perfect information, which has provoked strong criticism (Simon 1955, 1957). Despite this central point of criticism, the rational model remains important for analytical purposes as it helps to contrast ideal policy decisions with actual ones. By assuming that all political actors behave rationally, i.e. reduce costs and maximize benefits, it also provides the starting point for public choice approaches to policy-making. Public choice theory examines the logic and foundation of actions of individuals and groups that are involved in the policy-making process. In this regard, the main objects of analysis are voting behaviour and party competition, coalition and government formation, the involvement of interest groups, and bureaucracy in policy-making (cf. Mueller 2003 for an overview). Along the same lines, the rational model is related to game theory, which serves for analysing decisions in situations in which two or more rational players interact, and where the outcome depends on the choices made by each (cf. McCarthy and Meirowitz 2007).

Incremental model

Incrementalism emerged as a response to the rational model. Rather than an ideal, it purports to be a realistic description of how policy-makers arrive at their decisions (Lindblom 1959, 1977; Wildavsky 1964). This is related to its foundation on 'bounded rationality', i.e. an alternative concept to rational choice that takes into account the limitations of both knowledge and cognitive capacities of decision-makers. Generally, incremental decisions involve limited changes to existing policies (Anderson 2003: 123).

Similar to rational learning, there is also a concept of bounded learning. In that case, governments likewise engage in information-gathering activity but do not scan all available experience. Instead, they use analytical shortcuts and cognitive heuristics to process the information (cf. Weyland 2006). An example of such heuristics is the adoption of policies from countries that are considered to be particularly successful (cf. Braun and Gilardi 2006).

The Achilles heel of the incremental model is that it does not explain how decision-makers arrive at these incremental adjustments. In response to this central shortcoming, Jones and Baumgartner (2005) propose a model of choice that combines incrementalism and punctuated equilibrium theory. This approach states that political processes are generally characterized by stability and incrementalism, but occasionally produce large-scale departures from the past. By employing data on governmental processes in the US, Belgium, and Denmark, Baumgartner et al. (2009) show that incrementalism is an empirical reality. Incremental policy responses can even be observed subsequent to exogenous shocks, as shown by the case study of Baker (2013) on the incremental adoption of macro-prudential policy measures following the financial crash of 2008. More generally, to increase the analytical value of incrementalism, it appears useful to combine it with different types of policy learning (cf. Dunlop and Radaelli 2017).

Group model

Group theory hypothesizes that policies are the result of an equilibrium reached in group struggle, which is determined by the relative strength of each interest group (Truman 1971 [1951]; Latham 1965). Groups can be distinguished concerning several aspects, such as income, membership size, membership density and recruitment, organizational aspects, sanctioning mechanisms, and aspects of leadership (Newton and van Deth 2010: 170). Consequently, changes in the relative strength of the individual interest groups involved may trigger policy change.

More generally, group theory presupposes that policy-makers are constantly responding to group pressures, which motivates politicians to form majority coalitions for which they have the competence to define what groups are to be included (Dye 2005: 21).

The potential effect of groups for policy-making depends on the particular political structures. In (neo-)corporatist systems, for instance, economic interests are strongly integrated in policy-making (Schmitter and Lehmbruch 1979). Pluralist systems, by contrast, are a marketplace in which individuals, political parties, and interest groups compete for influence over policy domains. Despite its rather open nature, **empirical research** has shown that in the pluralist system of the US economic elites and business groups yield a greater impact on policy decisions than average citizens and mass-based interest groups (Gilens and Page 2014). Using data for Switzerland, Fischer et al. (2019) show that linkages between members of parliament and interest groups influence members of parliament's activities as concerns the co-sponsoring legislative proposals.

Elite model

Related to group theory is the view that policy-making is determined by the preferences of governing elites (Mills 1956). The elite model is more specific in a sense, as it claims that the electorate is generally poorly informed about policies and that the elites shape the public opinion on policy questions. In this way, the elite model mainly highlights the potential source of bias in policy-making in terms of the adoption of policy alternatives that correspond to the preferences of the elite, rather than of the general public. Research, however, also points to the importance of elites for the strategic management of policy reforms because elites possess the ability to influence the public discourse on the respective projects (Reed and Wallace 2015). From this, it follows that elites are crucial for policy-making in two ways: first, by demanding (specific types of) policy reforms; second, by moderating the reform process and helping to make it a success. A policy area in which the literature finds elites to hold a dominant position is foreign policy and therein more specifically aspects related to security (cf. Mulherin and Isakhan 2019).

KEY POINTS

- The institutional model, the rational model, the incremental model, the group model, and the elite model represent starting points for the analysis of policy-making.

- The models vary regarding their perception of policy actors as either fully or partly rational.

- The models also differ concerning their focus on either political institutions, actors, or both.

Analysing policy-making as a process: the policy cycle

What are the main characteristics of policy-making? Basically, three features can be identified. First, policy-making occurs in the presence of *multiple constraints*, for example shortage of time and resources, public opinion and, of course, the **constitution**. Second, policy-making involves the existence of *various policy*

processes. Governments are not unitary actors, but consist of different actors and institutions that overlap and compete with each other. Third, these policy processes form an *infinite cycle of decisions and policies*. Current policy decisions are not independent of decisions taken before, and policies under discussion today may have 'knock-on effects' leading to further policies tomorrow (Pierson 2003; Newton and van Deth 2010: 266).

Given these characteristics, it is convenient to conceive of policy-making as a process model, which is also often labelled *policy cycle* (Lasswell 1956), and which represents the sixth model mentioned in the previous section, 'Conceptual models of policy-making'. The policy cycle is a useful heuristic that breaks policy-making into different units to illustrate how policies are actually made and implemented. It models the policy process as a series of political activities, consisting of (i) **agenda setting**; (ii) **policy formulation**; (iii) **policy adoption**; (iv) **implementation**; and (v) **evaluation**. Each policy cycle begins with the identification of a societal problem and its placement on the policy agenda. Subsequently, policy proposals are formulated, from which one will be adopted. In the next stage, the adopted policy is taken to action. Finally, the impacts of the policy are evaluated. This last stage leads straight back to the first, indicating that the policy cycle is continuous and unending (see Figure 20.1).

Agenda setting

The first stage in policy-making refers to the identification of a societal problem requiring the state to intervene. There are many societal problems, but only a small number will be given official attention by legislators and executives (cf. Green-Pedersen and Walgrave 2014). Those that are chosen by the decision-makers constitute the political agenda. Setting the agenda is therefore an important source of power, as it is policy consequential. The factors determining

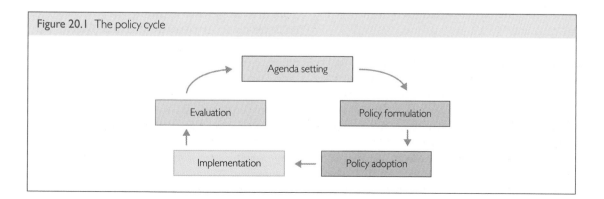

Figure 20.1 The policy cycle

whether an issue reaches the agenda may be cultural, political, social, economic, or ideological (cf. King 1973; Schattschneider 1975 [1960]; Howlett et al. 2009). Further, the ability to exclude societal problems from the policy agenda and to realize the occurrence of 'non-decisions' is an important source of policy-shaping power (Bachrach and Baratz 1962).

Cobb et al. (1976) distinguish between three basic policy initiation models:

1. The *outside-initiative model* refers to a situation where citizen groups gain broad public support and get an issue onto the formal agenda.

2. The *mobilization model* describes a situation in which initiatives of governments need to be placed on the public agenda for successful implementation.

3. In the *inside-initiation model*, influential groups with access to decision-makers present policy proposals, which are broadly supported by particular interest groups but only marginally by the public.

On the basis of these considerations, Kingdon (2003: 19) defines agenda setting as:

three process streams flowing through the system— streams of problems, policies, and politics. They are largely independent of one another, and each develops according to its own dynamics and rules. But at some critical junctures the three streams are joined, and the greatest policy changes grow out of that coupling of problems, policies, and solutions.

The result of the convergence of the three streams is the opening of a 'policy window', which allows advocates of a certain issue to put it on the policy agenda. Similar to the *garbage can model* (Cohen et al. 1972), Kingdon's conception of agenda setting emphasizes the relevance of chance, and therefore qualifies the view that agenda setting represents rational behaviour. Furthermore, it introduces the notion of the policy entrepreneur as a crucial actor for attaining convergence and therefore successful agenda setting (cf. Zohlnhöfer et al. 2015).

Baumgartner and Jones (1993/2010) modified Kingdon's model by extending it to the notion of 'policy monopolies', in which particular subsystems control the interpretation of a problem. These subsystems comprise both governmental and societal actors. The members of specific subsystems seek to change policy images in order to weaken the stability of existing policy arrangements. In doing so, the subsystem members can either publicize a problem and encourage the public to demand its resolution by govern- ment ('Downsian strategy'), or they can modify the institutional arrangements within which the subsystem operates ('Schattschneider strategy').

In most cases, the policy agenda is set by four types of *actors*: (i) public officials; (ii) bureaucracy; (iii) mass media; and (iv) interest groups (Gerston 2004: 52). Elected public officials—for example the president, the parliament, the ministries, and courts—are the most obvious agenda setters. However, actual agenda setting is related to the larger political game in terms of power and the intensity of ideological conflict both within and between the (coalition) government and parliament. Consequently, there exists a considerable variation in the rules and practices of agenda setting—even in the relatively similar Western European polities (Döring 1995: 224). Nonetheless, Bevan and Jennings (2014) observe the general pattern that the responsiveness of policy agendas to public priorities is greater when institutions are subject to less friction, and declines as a greater number of veto points and political interests or coalitions become involved.

Originally, the potential impact of the bureaucracy on agenda setting was proposed by William A. Niskanen (1971). His economic model of bureaucratic behaviour assumes that bureaucrats impose upon a passive legislature their most preferred policy alternative from among the set of alternatives that dominate the status quo. While theoretically plausible, empirical studies (cf. Hammond 1986) reveal that bureaucrats can influence the policy agenda, but certainly not impose their most preferred alternative on the voting bodies.

Mass media can influence agenda setting through priming and framing. Priming is about modifying the standards people use to evaluate policy-making through news coverage. Framing concerns the characterization of an issue by the mass media and how this influences people's feelings about it (Scheufele and Tewksbury 2006: 11).

The fourth source of agenda-setting power is interest groups (cf. Cobb and Elder 1972; Jones and Baumgartner 2005). Interest groups exchange policy-relevant information for bringing issues onto the policy agenda. In so doing, interest groups compete against each other over influence on policy decisions. Empirical findings indicate that informational tactics matter for the success of interest groups (cf. Chalmers 2013), which can include 'inside tactics' (i.e. interacting with policy-makers only) and 'outside tactics' (i.e. reaching out to the public). Over the years, research on agenda setting has become increasingly sophisticated, and now addresses a wide range of questions. Various scholars ask, for instance, how political representation affects agenda setting (cf. Jones and Baumgartner 2005; Penner et al. 2006). Another aspect is the role of political parties for agenda setting (cf. Walgrave et al. 2006; Green-Pedersen 2007). A further fashionable perspective on agenda setting scrutinizes the effects of experts and the scientific community (Scholten and Timmermans 2010).

Policy formulation

The second stage in the policy cycle—policy formulation—involves the definition, discussion, acceptance, or rejection of feasible courses of action for coping with policy problems. Policy formulation is strongly related to policy adoption—the subsequent stage here. Generally speaking, policy formulation deals with the *elaboration of alternatives of action,* whereas policy adoption refers to the *formal acceptance* of a policy.

Policy formulation takes place within the broader context of technical and political constraints of state action (see Box 20.2). The political constraints can be either substantive (i.e. related to the nature of the societal problem to be solved) or procedural (i.e. related to institutional and tactical issues) (cf. Howlett et al. 2009).

This phase brings the relationship between executives and legislatures to the forefront. The literature generally argues that executives dominate over legislatures, since they can rely on more resources. Also, the ministerial bureaucracy plays a role in policy formulation. Jann and Wegrich (2006), for instance, argue that policy formulation is a rather informal process of negotiations between ministerial departments and interest groups. Interest groups may especially play a big part in formulating legislation about complex and technical issues, and when elected officials and bureaucrats lack time, staff, and expertise to cope with such matters (Anderson 2003: 105–7). In this context, Varone et al. (2019) argue that the ministerial bureaucracy can influence policy formulation as policy broker and mediator in political conflicts; to seize this power, bureaucrats have to position themselves in the relevant policy networks.

Furthermore, scientific experts and policy advisors can inform the design of policies (cf. Stone 2005), which is discussed under the heading of evidence-based policy-making (Cairney 2016) According to Cairney et al. (2016), policy-makers use two shortcuts for making use of scientific advice: one is to related to emotions and beliefs in order to understand problems and the other to rational ways of exploring potential solutions to problems.

Policy adoption

In contrast to preliminary stages of decision-making, the final adoption of a particular policy alternative is determined by government institutions, and predominantly depends on two sets of factors. First, the set

---

🔍 DEFINITION 20.2

Formulating policy

Thomas R. Dye (2005: 42)

Policy formulation occurs in government bureaucracies; interest group offices; legislative committee rooms, meetings of special commissions; and policy-planning organizations otherwise known as 'think tanks'. The details of policy proposals are usually formulated by staff members rather than their bosses, but staff are guided by what they know their leaders want.

---

of feasible policies can be reduced by the necessity to build majorities for their approval, implying considerations about values, party affiliation, **constituency** interests, public opinion, deference, and decision rules (Anderson 2003: 126).

In this context, party loyalty is an important decision-making criterion for most members of parliament (cf. Benedetto and Hix 2007 for qualifications). Therefore, party affiliation is a central predictor for the likelihood of a member of parliament to approve a policy draft. Another important decision criterion is given by the expected costs and benefits of a policy proposal for the constituency. As a rule, a member of parliament is expected to adopt a policy option if the benefits for the constituency prevail, although considerations about re-election might lead to suboptimal policy projects (Weingast et al. 1981). Further, considerations about the public opinion also affect policy choices as well as decision rules, values, and perception of deference.

The second set of factors refers to the allocation of competencies between the actors involved in policy-making. Cross-national research concludes that the type of state organization, whether federal or unitary, affects the success, speed, and nature of governmental policy-making (cf. Lijphart 1999, 2012). An adequate theoretical underpinning for this aspect offers the concept of veto players (Tsebelis 1995, 2000, 2002; König et al. 2010). For example, in the French semi-presidential system, '**divided government**' (when the offices of president and prime minister are held by members of different political parties) can impede policy adoption as there are generally insufficient incentives for political parties to cooperate and build policy-making coalitions (cf. Lazardeux 2015).

Implementation

Implementation represents the conversion of new laws and programmes into practice. At first glance, implementation appears as an automatic continuation of the policy-making process. Yet there often exists a substantial gap between the passage of new legislation and its application (Pressman and Wildavsky 1973). It is the explicit objective of implementation research to open the 'black box' between policy formation and policy outcomes. To this end, various theoretical approaches were elaborated which Pülzl and Treib (2006) divide into three generic categories:

- Top-down models (cf. Pressman and Wildavsky 1973; Bardach 1977; Mazmanian and Sabatier 1983) primarily emphasize the ability of policy-makers to produce unequivocal policy objectives and control the implementation process.

- Bottom-up models (cf. Lipsky 1971, 1980) regard local bureaucrats as the central actors in policy delivery and view implementation as negotiation processes within networks.

- Hybrid models (cf. Mayntz 1979; Windhoff-Héritier 1980) integrate elements of both previously mentioned models and other theoretical models.

For successful implementation, there must be an entity that is able to translate the policy objectives into an operational framework and that is accountable for its actions (Gerston 2004: 98). Often bureaucracies emerge as principal actors during implementation, although it should be noted that private actors have been assigned a growing importance as implementation agents (Sager et al. 2014), which raises issues concern the accountability of these agents (Thomann et al. 2018). In his study of the US bureaucracy, Meier (2000) finds that implementation depends on the policy types proposed by Lowi (1964). When implementing regulatory policies, most agencies are responsive to the communities over which they preside, while distributive policies are implemented with some bureaucratic discretion, with congressional subcommittees and organized interest groups exercising continuous oversight. With redistributive policy, by contrast, little discretion is left to bureaucracy since US Congress puts in a lot of effort when designing these policies.

Related to this perspective is the choice of policy instruments, which are perceived to be vulnerable to specific kinds of implementation problems (Mayntz 1979). Yet it is not only the policy type and the instrument choice that determines the likelihood of proper implementation. In federal systems, for instance, implementation efforts may move between and within levels of government (Gerston 2004: 103). If implementation is a matter of horizontal implementation, in which a national legal act must be applied solely by an agency in the executive branch, the number of actors remains low and implementation can be attained smoothly. The opposite scenario is likely if vertical implementation is concerned, implying that various segments of the national government must interact with different sub-national levels (cf. Peters 2015). Furthermore, the involvement of both public and private actors in implementation can lead to conflicts and hamper service delivery (Sager et al. 2014; Tosun et al. 2016; Thomann et al. 2018).

The relevance of bureaucracies during implementation reveals a contradictory picture of great interest. On the one hand, bureaucracies are essential for making policies work. On the other hand, senior bureaucrats are often more experienced and better trained than their political masters, which paves the way for 'bureaucratic drift' (cf. Grossman and Hart 1983). Hence, a policy might drift towards the liking of bureaucracy and away from what was originally intended by legislation (cf. Hammond and Knott 1996).

Evaluation

After a policy is passed by the legislature and implemented by the bureaucracy, it becomes a subject of evaluation. The main question at this stage is whether the output of the decision-making process—a given public policy—has attained the intended goals. Evaluation is often a formal component of policy-making and is commonly carried out by experts who have some knowledge about the processes and objectives pertaining to the issue undergoing review. International organizations such as the Organization for Economic Cooperation and Development (OECD), too, are involved in evaluation activities, mostly by means of preparing and examining composite indices that seek to captures the progress made with regard to certain reform goals such as market liberalization or improving regulatory quality (cf. De Francesco 2016).

Evaluation can be carried out in different ways. In this context, Munger (2000: 20) differentiates between (i) purely *formal* evaluations (monitoring routine tasks); (ii) *client satisfaction* evaluation (performance of primary functions); (iii) *outcome* evaluation (satisfaction of a list of measurable intended outcomes); (iv) *cost–benefit* evaluation (comparison of costs and impacts of a policy); and (v) evaluation of *long-term consequences* (impact on the core societal problem, rather than symptoms alone).

Policy evaluation provides a feedback loop, which enables decision-makers to draw lessons from each particular policy in operation. This feedback loop identifies new problems and sets in motion the policy-making process once again, creating an endless policy cycle. This turns policy evaluation into a powerful tool of the policy-making process: it possesses the potential to reframe an issue once thought to be resolved by policy-makers.

In practice, policy evaluation presents numerous challenges to the evaluators (cf. Knill and Tosun 2012). Citizens and governments alike tend to interpret the actual effects of a policy so as to serve their own intentions. Often governments avoid the precise definition of policy objectives because otherwise politicians would risk taking the blame for obvious failure (Jann and Wegrich 2006). Further, policy decisions cannot be limited to intended effects only. An additional problem stems from the time horizon:

> Program circumstances and activities may change during the course of an evaluation, an appropriate balance must be found between scientific and pragmatic considerations in the evaluation design, and the wide diversity of perspectives and approaches in the evaluation field provide little firm guidance about how best to proceed with an evaluation
>
> Rossi et al. (2004: 29)

The results of the evaluation procedure can also lead to the termination of a certain policy. In theoretical terms, policy termination should be likely when a policy problem has been solved, or if evaluation studies reveal the dysfunctionality of a policy. Nonetheless, the empirical findings show that, once a policy is institutionalized within a government, it is hard to terminate it (Bardach 1976; Jann and Wegrich 2006). This immortality of policies stems from various sources. The most rampant view is that inefficient programmes continue because their benefits are concentrated in a small, well-organized constituency, while their greater costs are dispersed over a large, unorganized group. Additionally, legislative and bureaucratic interests may impede termination. This is related to the concept of incrementalism, which implies that attention to proposed changes focuses on parts of existing policies and not on their entirety (Dye 2005: 344–5). From this, it follows that termination should become more likely if a government experiences some kind of 'external shock', justifying drastic measures, such as economic crises (cf. Geva-May 2004; Knill et al. 2009; Peters et al. 2011; Jensen et al. 2014).

KEY POINTS

- In analytical terms, it is helpful to view policy-making as a series of political activities encompassing agenda setting, policy formulation, policy adoption, implementation, and evaluation.

- The number of actors involved decreases when we move from agenda setting to implementation and evaluation.

- The evaluation findings may lead to the modification of existing policies, which may entail adjustments of varying degrees (policy change), as well as complete policy termination.

Institutions, frames, and policy styles

While we scrutinized the different stages of policy-making rather generally in the first section, we now refine our analytical focus and examine how certain structures in different countries can impact policy decisions. In doing so, we concentrate on institutions, cognitive and normative determinants, and national policy styles.

The role of institutions

In a broader sense, we can interpret policy-making as a strategy for resolving societal problems given specific institutional contexts as well as by using institutions. From a rationalist perspective, institutions can structure the interaction of actors and avoid the suboptimal solutions they are given by the prisoner's dilemma. From a sociological point of view, institutions can support cooperation through the provision of moral or cognitive templates (Hall and Taylor 1996).

As policy interventions in democratic systems originate in **electoral systems**, it is the most essential formal institution when scrutinizing policy-making. Electoral competition is largely party competition, turning political parties into important actors (see Chapter 13 'Party systems'). One of their main functions is to structure and articulate public opinion. Most frequently, political parties are described by a left–right dichotomy, implying that they have diametrically opposed policy preferences. In fact various studies—based on expert judgements as well as content analysis of party manifestoes—found a level of consistency with this dichotomy (Budge and Klingemann 2001; Laver et al. 2003; Debus 2007).

Strongly related to this is the relevance of the voting systems, of which we can distinguish between three main types:

- **Plurality–majority systems**, in which the elected candidates get more votes than any other (e.g. UK).
- **Proportional representation**, in which seats are allocated according to a formula that seeks to ensure **proportionality** (e.g. Germany).
- **Mixed systems** that combine plurality–majority with proportional representation aspects (e.g. Japan).

Each system has strengths and weaknesses (see Chapters 5 'Democracies', 10 'Elections and referendums', and 13 'Party systems' for further discussions of these models). While the proportional system ensures the representation of all societal groups, including small parties, plurality–majority systems are usually associated with stable and effective governments. These aspects have strong repercussions on the quality of policy-making.

The relationship between legislative and executive is also of crucial importance. In parliamentary models, the executive is a group of ministers elected from the very parliament, while in pure presidential systems the two branches of government are separate. In this context, Lijphart (1999, 2012) claims that, despite strong variations among countries, democratic systems tend to fall into two categories: majoritarian and consensus democracies. The majoritarian system—which is generally associated with the UK, and hence is also known as the 'Westminster model'—concentrates power and fuses executive and legislative powers in the classic parliamentary manner (e.g. Colombia, Costa Rica, France, and Greece). By contrast, the consensus model focuses on sharing power by separating and balancing executive and legislative power (e.g. Austria, Germany, India, Japan, the Netherlands, and Switzerland). Remarkably, consensus democracies score higher in terms of democratic quality as well as the state's generosity in social welfare, environmental policy, criminal justice, and foreign aid than majoritarian democracies. One of the reasons Lijphart gives for the better performance of consensus democracies is that the search for consensus among different societal and political groups increases the acceptance of the policies adopted, which, in turn, facilitates their implementation.

The role of cognitive and normative frames

The concepts of normative and cognitive frames are crucial for explaining how actors understand and interpret policy-making situations. Cognitive frames refer to the schemes through which actors view and interpret the world (Campbell 1998: 382). Normative frames are about values and attitudes that shape the actors' view of the world (Fischer 2003). Both cognitive and normative frames can enable but also constrain policy action, as they can either emphasize or de-emphasize certain aspects of policy problems Thus, to gain a more comprehensive understanding of policy-making, we need to supplement our analytical framework by normative and cognitive determinants (cf. Surel 2000). Although rational motivation may explain the adoption of new policies, cognitive and normative factors may be essential for understanding better the decision-making at each stage of the policy process (Miller and Banaszak-Holl 2005: 214). Furthermore, the concepts of cognitive and normative frames can be combined with rationalist explanations since the number and types of frames can be be regarded as being dependent on the strategic choices of actors (Eising et al. 2016: 521).

In this context, Surel (2000) discusses three concepts: *policy paradigms* (Hall 1993), *advocacy coalitions* (Sabatier and Jenkins-Smith 1993; Sabatier 1998; Jenkins-Smith et al. 2014), and *référentiel*. According to Hall (1993), there are certain **paradigms** present in the real world that imply distinct policy goals. These goals—that are intertwined with the paradigm—then define the choice and specification of instruments. The advocacy coalition framework, by contrast, assumes a similar construct to affect the entire society, which is the 'deep core'. Subordinated to it is the 'policy core', which refers to the belief systems within a subsystem of public policy. From this perspective, 'secondary aspects' are the instrumental decisions that are necessary to implement the policy core. Finally, the référentiel equals a paradigm, as it comprises values and norms (Surel 2000: 496).

Cognitive and normative frames produce a sense of specific identity. Yet certain actors have a privileged role in policy-making as they generate and diffuse cognitive frames. Since elites and other privileged actors frame policy ideas to convince each other as well as the public, they are important for the adoption of policies (Campbell 1998: 380). This category of actors refers to policy-brokers (Sabatier 1998) or policy entrepreneurs (Zohlnhöfer et al. 2015). Furthermore, frames help to reduce tension and conflict by marking out 'the terrain for social exchanges and disagreements, rather than simply supporting an unlikely consensus' (Surel 2000: 502). The role of cognitive and normative frames has recently been taken up and associated with the notion of emotions and emotional entrepreneurs, which points to the direction of future work (cf. Maor and Gross 2015).

National policy styles

The concept of policy styles—or also regulatory styles—is another heuristic tool and refers to the routines and choices of actors involved in policy-making and implementation. To a certain extent, this concept takes up the discussion about institutional characteristics (Lijphart 1999, 2012) as well as Dyson's (1980) elaboration on 'strong' and 'weak' states. Further, it is related to the ideas of 'policy communities' and 'administrative culture' (van Thiel 2006: 118). The objective of this section is therefore to elucidate that for the analysis of policy-making nations matter.

The influential volume by Richardson (1982) distinguishes policy styles along two dimensions (see Figure 20.2). The first dimension is about how policy-makers respond to the issues on the policy agenda. Do decision-makers anticipate societal problems (technocratic approach), or do they merely react to them (diplomatic approach)? The first notion presupposes that the government is perfectly informed and able to foresee and forestall policy problems before they become critical. By contrast, the second notion about the government's approach is built around the concept of imperfect information and hence seems to be more realistic. The second dimension is about the relative autonomy of the state vis-à-vis other actors involved in policy-making and implementation. Here, the question is whether decision-makers seek to ensure consensus among the parties involved, or whether they simply impose their decisions on the executing actors. Recently, Richardson (2018) put forth a discussion of the degree to which the British policy style changed in the course of four decades, and other scholars have attempted to develop further the concept of policy styles (cf. Jordan and Cairney 2013; Adam et al. 2017; Howlett and Tosun 2018).

The above-mentioned dimensions correspond to Van Waarden's (1995) typology of regulatory styles, which comprises six sub-dimensions that refer to the 'what', 'how', and 'who' questions of policy-making:

1. Liberal-pluralist versus étatist versus corporatist style: the first style prefers 'market' solutions to policy problems, while étatism implies a preference for 'state solutions'. **Corporatism**, by contrast, favours 'associational' solutions to policy problems.

2. Active versus reactive styles: active styles are higher in their degree of intensity, radicalism, and innovation as compared to reactive ones.

3. Comprehensive versus fragmented or incremental styles: comprehensive policies are integrated into larger plans, while the latter are not.

4. Adversarial versus consensual paternalistic styles: the first type strongly relies on coercion and imposition, while the latter is based on consultation.

5. Legalistic versus pragmatic styles: legalistic styles are characterized by formalism, detailed regulation, and rigid rule application. The pragmatic style, on the other hand, is informal and flexible in both policy formulation and implementation.

6. Formal versus informal network relations between state agencies and organizations of state agencies.

Altogether, policy styles provide an analytically useful concept for determining the design of policies (Howlett 1991; Arentsen 2003) and the mode of implementation (Freeman 1985). Yet, assessing the extent of impact of national policy styles augers for systematic comparative analysis. Richardson's (1982) volume itself, however, could not deliver empirical evidence for existence of national policy styles. Howlett and Tosun (2018) also show that there is variation within the country groups expected to have similar policy styles in place.

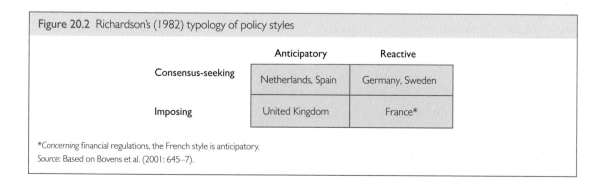

Figure 20.2 Richardson's (1982) typology of policy styles

	Anticipatory	Reactive
Consensus-seeking	Netherlands, Spain	Germany, Sweden
Imposing	United Kingdom	France*

*Concerning financial regulations, the French style is anticipatory.
Source: Based on Bovens et al. (2001: 645–7).

International factors for domestic policy-making

In this section, we concentrate on the impact of international factors on domestic policy-making. The notion that countries do not constitute independent observations has been known for a long time in comparative politics, and became discussed as 'Galton's problem' (Braun and Gilardi 2006; Jahn 2006; Chapter 3 'Comparative research methods', this volume). This recognition has led researchers to scrutinize more carefully the link between domestic processes and the international arena (Risse-Kappen 1995). The concepts of policy diffusion and transfer and the analysis of cross-national policy convergence provide an ideal basis for shedding light on the role of international factors (see also Chapter 22 'The impact of public policies' on these concepts).

Theories of policy diffusion, policy transfer, and cross-national policy convergence

Diffusion is generally defined as the socially mediated spread of policies across and within political systems, including communication and influence processes, which operate both on and within populations of adopters (Rogers 1995: 13). Diffusion studies typically start out from the description of adoption patterns for certain policy innovations over time. Subsequently, they analyse the factors that account for the empirically observed spreading process (cf. Gilardi 2008; Maggetti and Gilardi 2016).

Regarding domestic politics, diffusion mainly affects the stages of agenda setting and, to a lesser degree, policy formulation, since the policy innovations have already been developed elsewhere and the main decision is about whether or not to adopt them. The likelihood of adopting a diffusion policy increases if the proposal originates from a country that is culturally similar to the receiving country (Strang and Soule 1998) such as, for example, former members of the Soviet Union that share a common historical legacy and linguistic similarities (Weyland 2017: 1242). This, however, does not reduce the relevance of domestic factors, such as considerations about values, party affiliation, constituency interests, public opinion, and decision rules. Along these lines, Lenschow et al. (2005), for instance, argue that the extent to which a policy innovation is accommodated by a given country can be explained by three aspects: institutional, cultural, and socio-economic factors. Moreover, Tosun and Croissant (2016) point to the importance of the political regime type for the adoption and accommodation of policy innovations.

Transfer can best be described as 'processes by which knowledge about policies, administrative arrangements, institutions and ideas in one political system (past or present) is used in the development of policies, administrative arrangements, institutions and ideas in another political system' (Dolowitz and Marsh 2000: 5). It is not restricted to merely imitating policies of other countries, but can also include profound changes in the content of the exchanged policies, leading to four forms (Rose 1991, 1993; Dolowitz 1997; Dolowitz and Marsh 2000: 13):

- copying (direct and complete transfer);
- emulation (transfer of the ideas behind the programme);
- combinations (mixture of different policies);
- inspiration (final policy does not draw upon the original).

The focus of transfer studies is on the analysis of the specific processes and factors that influence the way and degree to which one country learns from other countries with regard to policy-making in a certain area. Here again, domestic factors come into play—it is important which actors engage in transfer, which negotiation power they possess, and whether they can build a supportive coalition. Another aspect for the success of a policy import might be its regulatory legitimacy (Majone 1996: ch. 13). It is indeed reasonable to hypothesize that some countries have more problems in regarding external policy proposals as legitimate than others.

Diffusion and transfer share a number of assumptions, for example, that governments do not learn about policy practices randomly, but rather through common affiliations, negotiations, and institutional membership (Simmons and Elkins 2004). They hence require that actors are informed about the policy choices of others (Strang and Meyer 1993: 488). Furthermore, transfer and diffusion might result in policy convergence, which can be defined as 'any increase in the similarity between one or more characteristics of a certain policy (e.g. policy objectives, policy instruments, policy settings) across a given set of political jurisdictions (supranational institutions, states, regions, local authorities) over a given period of time' (Knill 2005: 768). It has close proximity to the concept of isomorphism, which has been developed in organization sociology and is defined as a process of homogenization that 'forces one unit in a population to resemble other units that face the same set of environmental conditions' (DiMaggio and Powell 1991: 66).

International sources that affect domestic policy-making

Internationalization does not only affect policy sectors that are generally associated with externalities, e.g. environmental policy (cf. Holzinger et al. 2008; Tosun 2013; Daugbjerg and Swinbank 2015) or tax policy (cf. Genschel and Schwarz 2011), but also policy fields with no immediate international connection, for example social policy (cf. Brooks 2005; Jahn 2006; Starke et al. 2008; Jensen 2011; Schmitt et al. 2015). Yet, internationalization is a highly complex phenomenon with varying effects on different policy sectors and states. To disentangle the mechanisms behind internationalization, we rely on the concepts introduced by Holzinger and Knill (2005), who distinguish between (i) imposition; (ii) international harmonization; (iii) regulatory competition; and (iv) transnational communication.

Imposition—sometimes also labelled 'coercive isomorphism' (DiMaggio and Powell 1991) or 'penetration' (Bennett 1991)—occurs whenever an external political actor forces a government to adopt a certain policy. This presupposes asymmetry of power, and often policy adoption is accompanied by an exchange of economic resources. Policies can either be unilaterally imposed on a country by another, or imposition can occur as a condition of being part of an international institution (Dolowitz and Marsh 2000: 9). Unilateral imposition happens rarely and only in extreme situations, such as wars. Conditionality, on the other hand, can be observed more frequently, as where applicant countries for membership in the European Union have to adopt the entire *acquis communautaire*, i.e. the total body of European law accumulated thus far (cf. Lavenex 2002). Imposition implies that the country forced to adopt a certain model has not much choice in modifying the policy. In such cases, domestic politics are mainly bypassed.

International harmonization refers to a situation in which member states voluntarily engage in international cooperation, and hence corresponds to 'negotiated transfer' (Dolowitz and Marsh 2000: 15). This mechanism implies that countries comply with uniform legal obligations defined in international or supranational law. International harmonization presupposes the existence of interdependencies or externalities which push governments to resolve common problems through cooperation within international institutions, thus sacrificing some independence for the good of the community (Drezner 2001: 60). Once established, institutional arrangements will constrain and shape domestic policy choices (Martin and Simmons 1998: 743).

The mechanism of regulatory competition is closely related to the notion of internationalization as economic **globalization**. It is expected to homogenize the countries' policies when these are mutually faced with competitive pressures. The competitive pressure arises from (potential) threats of economic actors to shift their activities elsewhere, inducing governments to lower their regulatory standards. In this way, regulatory competition among governments may lead to a race to the bottom in policies (Drezner 2001: 57–9; Simmons and Elkins 2004).

Theoretical work, however, suggests that there are a number of conditions that may drive policy in both directions (Vogel 1995; Scharpf 1997d; Holzinger 2002, 2003). In this context, often a distinction is made between product and production process standards (Vogel 1995; Scharpf 1997d; Holzinger 2008). In the case of production standards, we find a widely shared expectation that states will gravitate towards the policies of the most laissez-faire country (Drezner 2001). If the regulation of production processes implies an increase in the costs of production, potentially endangering the international competitiveness of an industry, regulatory competition will generally exert downward pressures on economic regulations (Hahn 1990; Scharpf 1997d: 524).

Expectations are yet less homogeneous for product standards. While industries in both low-regulating and high-regulating countries have a common interest in harmonization of product standards to avoid market segmentation, the level of harmonization can hardly be predicted without the examination of additional factors. Most important in this context is the extent to which high-regulating countries are able to factually enforce stricter standards, for example through the erection of exceptional trade barriers (Vogel 1995; Scharpf 1997d; Tosun and de Moraes Marcondes 2016).

So far, most empirical findings for different policy sectors, such as environmental and social policy, do not support the race-to-the-bottom scenario, but, rather, give hints for the occurrence of a race to the top, i.e. upward ratcheting of regulatory standards (cf. Holzinger et al. 2008; Starke et al. 2008; Tosun 2013; Schmitt et al. 2015; Tosun and de Moraes Marcondes 2016; see also Chapter 21 'The welfare state' and Chapter 22 'The impact of public policies').

Transnational communication consists of a number of mechanisms, which are purely based on communication among countries, namely lesson-drawing, transnational problem-solving, emulation, and the transnational promotion of policy models. Lesson-drawing refers to constellations of policy transfer in which governments rationally utilize available experience from elsewhere in order to solve domestic problems (Rose 1991, 1993). Transnational problem-solving is also based on rational learning. It is driven by the joint development of common problem perceptions and solutions to similar domestic problems, as well as their subsequent adoption at the domestic level. In doing so, transnational elite networks or epistemic communities, international institutions, and common educational and normative backgrounds play an important role in forging and promulgating transnational problem-solving (DiMaggio and Powell 1991; Haas 1992; Elkins and Simmons 2005).

Emulation, on the other hand, is motivated by the desire for conformity with other countries rather than the search for effective solutions to given problems. States might sometimes copy the policies of other states simply to legitimate conclusions already reached (Bennett 1991; Powell and DiMaggio 1991). Finally, policy adoption can be driven by the active role of international institutions—for example, the EU—that are promoting the spread of distinctive policy approaches they consider particularly promising (Keck and Sikkink 1998a).

Similar to all the other mechanisms, the effects of transnational communication strongly depend on mediation by domestic politics (Radaelli 2005; see Box 20.3). Thus, as concerns the national effect of these mechanisms of internationalization, we must conclude that the political context matters (Steinmo et al. 1992). As already argued for policy diffusion, it can be expected that if the cultural, institutional, or socio-economic similarity between communicating countries and international institutions is high, the adoption of the corresponding policy proposals should become more likely.

KEY POINTS

- As internationalization is a complex phenomenon, it is useful to approach its underlying mechanisms via the concepts of policy diffusion, policy transfer, and cross-national policy convergence.
- There are four main mechanisms: imposition, harmonization, regulatory competition, and transnational communication.

Conclusion

Policy-making is complex. Therefore, the first approaches to understanding how policies come about were the so-called conceptual models. They focus on differential aspects of the policy-making process and primarily deal with issues about the actors' power resources and rationality. While these models certainly draw attention to crucial aspects of policy-making, they fall short of providing complete explanations.

More promising is the analysis of policy-making by focusing on the process. Since the number, nature, and interactions of actors change across the single stages, this theoretical disaggregation allows for deriving more clear-cut theoretical expectations. Agenda setting ensures important strategic advantages, turning this stage into a highly competitive one. Many actors participate in the selection of suitable items from an undefined universe of societal problems. Power fragmentation also affects policy formulation and adoption. If the political system is a rather

FOR AND AGAINST 20.3

International harmonization and domestic politics

Bernstein and Cashore (2000: 79–80)

The importance of domestic politics is largely limited along this path to the stage of rule creation/ratification and to the decision of whether to comply or not in specific circumstances. In the two-level game of international negotiations, governments balance, and sometimes play off, the interests of their negotiating partners and domestic constituencies. Domestic policy-making structures are also important when states require domestic ratification of international agreements or implementing legislation.

However, once rules are in place, assuming states view them as legitimate, they create a 'pull toward compliance', regardless of domestic political factors. Contravening the rule could result in costly disputes in international adjudication bodies or domestic courts or sanctions of various sorts. It could also erode the legitimacy of other related rules that a state may want others to obey or, in utilitarian terms, erode general reciprocity that creates a broad incentive to obey international rules in the long run. The rule also becomes a resource on which transnational and/or coalitions of domestic actors can draw when governments do not comply. For example, they can publicize non-compliance, pressurize governments to live up to their commitments, or press governments to launch disputes against other countries which do not fulfil their obligations.

cooperative one, decision-making in the political process remains unchallenging. Otherwise, there can be harmful delays in policy-making.

Once we move to implementation, the number of involved actors notably decreases. This stage is associated with the dominance of bureaucratic actors over political ones. In the subsequent evaluation stage, the floor is opened to experts and their appraisal of whether a policy performs well or poorly. In some (rare) instances, an evaluation can entail policy termination.

There are, however, also structures present in the political sphere that help to reduce the complexity of policy-making. Institutions, for instance, possess such a function. In a similar vein, cognitive and normative framing mechanisms serve to structure politics. Finally, the development of routines and particular national policy styles help to establish a stable negotiation framework and therewith ensure the continuity of the policy-making process.

In the final section, on 'International factors for domestic policy-making', we learnt that a policy is not exclusively the outcome of domestic bargaining processes. Policy-making is also affected by internationalization, implying a variety of stimuli and corresponding reaction patterns. Generally speaking, internationalization can either enable or constrain policy-making. How these effects are translated into policy outcomes depends on domestic policy-making processes.

? QUESTIONS

Knowledge-based

1. What are the main stages of the policy cycle, and how does this concept enhance our understanding of policy-making?

2. Which actors—societal and political—participate in the single stages?

3. What is the role of political institutions in policy-making?

4. How can we define normative and cognitive frames?

5. What are national policy styles?

Critical thinking

1. How can we think of policy-making in terms of theory?

2. In which ways are policy typologies related to the policy-making process?

3. Which theoretical concepts cope with the effects of internationalization on domestic policy-making?

4. What are the mechanisms behind these concepts? And how do they interact with domestic policy-making?

5. Does internationalization matter empirically?

≋ FURTHER READING

Birkland, T. A. (2015) *An Introduction to the Policy Process: Theories, Concepts, and Models of Public Policy Making* (London: Routledge). An accessible and comprehensive introduction to public policy, which is particularly useful for learning about different theories.

Howlett, M. and Mukherjee, I. (eds) (2017) *Handbook of Policy Formulation* (Cheltenham: Edward Elgar). This edited volume concentrates on the phase of policy formulation, but connects it with other stages of the policy process.

John, P. (2018) *How Far to Nudge?: Assessing Behavioural Public Policy* (Cheltenham: Edward Elgar). This book covers a recent development in public policy about using concepts from behavioural sciences to inform policy design and to explain policy outcomes.

Knill, C. and Tosun, J. (2020) *Public Policy—A New Introduction* (London: Palgrave Macmillan). The second edition of this book first published in 2012 covers the topics presented in this chapter in greater length.

Weible, C. and Sabatier, P. (eds) (2017) *Theories of the Policy Process* (Boulder, CO: Westview Press). An authoritative introduction to the most influential theoretical perspectives on public policy.

Visit the Online Resources that accompany this book for additional material, including country profiles, comparative data sets, flashcard glossaries, and web directory.

www.oup.com/he/caramani5e

21

The welfare state

Kees van Kersbergen and Philip Manow

Reader's guide

The welfare state is important for comprehending democratic politics in modern societies, just as knowing about modern politics is crucial for understanding the causes, sources of variation, and consequences of the state's social interventions. The chapter focuses on the key issues of the emergence, expansion, variation, and transformation of the welfare state. It explains that studying the welfare state necessarily means engaging in debates about some of the most fundamental and enduring questions of comparative political science and political economy.

Introduction

Why is the welfare state of interest for comparative political science? Because it represents the single most important transformation of **advanced capitalist democracies** in the post-World War II period. Understanding the welfare state is key to understanding modern politics, just as an understanding of modern politics is key to understanding the causes of welfare state formation and growth, as well as its various social and economic effects. Moreover, studying the welfare state confronts us with some of the most fundamental and enduring questions of political science.

From different normative perspectives, classical political economy (e.g. John Stuart Mill and Karl

Marx) was convinced that capitalism and democracy were incompatible. But the welfare states of the West prove that capitalism and democracy can indeed go together—even with beneficial consequences for both (Iversen and Soskice 2019). High social spending does not need to have detrimental effects on economic competitiveness, as the combination of a generous welfare state and a competitive market economy in a country like Sweden demonstrates. Apparently, the 'democratic class struggle' (see Lipset 1960: 220; Korpi 1983) can allow for a beneficial, economically viable class compromise (see Przeworski and Wallerstein 1982), and the welfare state seems to be its most prominent embodiment.

Comparative politics has studied the origins, growth, and crises of the welfare state, testing various theories of political **mobilization** and development. What and who were pivotal in this process—social classes, the workers' movement, historical legacies of state structures, wars, economic development, demographic pressures, employers' interests? How do the various political structures, actors, and struggles explain the differences in size, type, and quality among welfare states? Comparative political scientists have also looked at the impact of the welfare state (its performance) to see to what extent politics matters for society and economy. How does politics (e.g. the strength of political movements and parties or the composition of a government) matter for the type of social and economic policies (output) carried out in a country? And how do these policies influence social and economic **variables** (outcome) such as economic growth, unemployment, inequality, and poverty (see Chapter 22 'The impact of public policies')?

Finally, there is also a practical interest in the study of the welfare state. Many people care whether they live in a society in which the ratio between the highest and the lowest income decile is around 5.7 (US) or around 2.5 (Germany; see Smeeding and Gottschalk 1999). Also, many people care whether they live in a society in which taxation and welfare state transfers reduce poverty by 13 per cent (US) or by 82 per cent (Sweden; see Iversen 2006; see also Comparative tables 5 and 6 in Appendix 2). The study of the welfare state addresses fundamental questions of social fairness and basic notions of a good society. This also has its technical side: given certain political aims (like full employment), we would like to know how best to achieve them. Comparative studies of the working of social protection programmes promise to provide us with this kind of knowledge.

KEY POINTS

- The welfare state is the product of the interplay between political equality (democracy) and economic inequality (capitalism).
- The welfare state represents the most fundamental transformation of advanced capitalist democracies in the post-1945 period.
- Comparative politics tries to explain the emergence, growth, and consequences of welfare states, and addresses fundamental issues of social justice and the good society.

What is the welfare state?

What do we mean when we talk about the welfare state? Harold L. Wilensky described 'the essence of the welfare state' as 'government-protected minimum standards of income, nutrition, health, housing and education, assured to every citizen as a political right, not charity' (Wilensky 1975: 1). Here, the welfare state is first and foremost a democratic state that—in addition to civil and political rights (see Marshall 1950 and Box 21.1)—guarantees social protection as a right attached to **citizenship**. Most political scientists tend to think along the state-centric lines that Wilensky advocated and agree that social policy must be seen as 'lines of state action to reduce income insecurity and to provide minimum standards of income and services and thus to reduce inequalities' (Amenta 2003: 92). Other definitions of the welfare state stress protection against social risks and distribution of life chances, rather than income security and equality.

The advantage of state-centred definitions is that they are clear-cut and provide straightforward operationalizations for **empirical research**: the welfare state, its growth and expansion, are measured in terms of public social spending expressed as a proportion of total state spending or of the gross domestic product (GDP), and the social protection profile of a country can then be explained by its national politics and policies. However, there are drawbacks to this approach. An exclusive focus on social policy tends to overlook the fact that although the state is an important institution providing welfare, it is not the only one. Moreover, it is not easy to draw a clear line between social policies and other types of policies promoting welfare. Finally, not all social policies actually promote welfare, even though their intention may be to do so (M. Hill 2006: Chapter 1). An exclusive focus on the state might also underestimate the importance of

Marshall's three elements of citizenship

I propose to divide citizenship into three parts. I shall call these three parts, or elements, civil, political and social.

The civil element is composed of the rights necessary for individual freedom—liberty of the person, freedom of speech, thought and faith, the right to own property and to conclude valid contracts, and the right to justice …

By the political element I mean the right to participate in the exercise of political power, as a member of a body invested with political authority or as an elector of the members of such a body …

By the social element I mean the whole range from the right to a modicum of economic welfare and security to the right to share to the full in the social heritage and to live the life of a civilized being according to the standards prevailing in a society …

It is possible, without doing too much violence to historical accuracy, to assign the formative period in the life of each to a different century—civil rights to the eighteenth, political to the nineteenth and social to the twentieth.

Source: Marshall (1965: 78, 81)

the international dimension, when organizations like the International Labour Organization (ILO) define worldwide labour rights or when economic integration increases inequality and constrains the redistributive potential of national policies (see the section 'Globalization: efficiency versus compensation').

Esping-Andersen (1990) has criticized the exclusive focus on the state and public social spending, arguing that the welfare state 'cannot be understood just in terms of the rights it grants' and the amount of money it spends. It is hardly conceivable that 'anybody fought for spending per se'. What we need to know instead is for which purpose the money is used. Moreover, we have to avoid studying welfare state activity in isolation, because 'we must also take into account how state activities are interlocked with the market's and the family's role in social provision' (Esping-Andersen 1990: 21). It is the specific institutional mixture of market, state, and family that characterizes how a nation provides work and welfare to its citizens, and various nations do this in very different ways. The question of how much a state spends (welfare effort) is much less relevant than the questions that ask (i) *on what* it spends its public resources; (ii) *how it influences the distribution of resources and life chances* in other ways than through spending

(e.g. through regulations, but also through the 'hidden welfare' state, for instance tax expenditures) (Howard 1993; Hacker 2002)); and (iii) *what other social institutions* play a role in social provision.

Scharpf and Schmidt have argued that all welfare states:

provide free primary and secondary education, and all provide social assistance to avoid extreme poverty. Beyond that, the … models differ fundamentally from one another along two dimensions: the extent to which welfare goals are pursued through the regulation of labour markets and employment relations or through the 'formal welfare state' of publicly financed transfers and services, and the extent to which 'caring' services are expected to be provided informally in the family or through professional services.

Scharpf and Schmidt (2000: 7)

The market, the state, and the family can all be the main welfare providers (Esping-Andersen 1990, 1999, 2002). The interaction between these institutions in the provision of work and welfare is called a **welfare regime**. It is a *complex system of (producing and) managing social risks*, where each institution represents a radically different principle of doing this: 'Within the family, the dominant method of allocation is, presumably, one of reciprocity … Markets are governed by distribution via the cash-nexus, and the dominant principle of allocation in the state takes the form of authoritative redistribution' (Esping-Andersen 1999: 35–6). What one institution does affects what the others can, will, or must do. Esping-Andersen gives a succinct example:

[A] traditional male bread-winner's family will have less demand for private or public social services than a two-career household. But when families service themselves, the market is directly affected because there will be less labour supply and fewer service outlets [for data on labour markets see Comparative table 11 in Appendix at the end of this volume]. In turn, if the state provides cheap day care, both families and the market will change: there will be fewer housewives, more labour force participation, and a new demand multiplier caused by double-earner households' greater propensity to purchase services.

Esping-Andersen (1999: 36)

Certain risks of life potentially become **social risks** and subject to political struggles, (i) because they are shared by many people and therefore affect the welfare of society as a whole (say loss of income because of disability and/or old age); (ii) because they are interpreted as potentially turning into a political threat (say poverty and gross inequality destabilizing a political regime); (iii) because the risks are beyond the control of any individual (say mass unemployment in a market society); or (iv) because shared values of fairness and social justice seem to be violated. Why and how risks become social risks has been the topic of several decades of research. Furthermore, the character of social risks may change—so that the literature speaks of 'new social risks', for instance generated by the erosion of the standard employment relationship or the 'risk' of motherhood when female labour participation reaches high levels.

> **ZOOM-IN 21.2**
>
> ### The emergence of the welfare state
>
> The modern welfare state is a European invention—in the same way as the nation state, mass democracy, and industrial capitalism. It was born as an answer to problems created by capitalist industrialization; it was driven by the democratic class struggle; and it followed in the footsteps of the nation state.
>
> *Source:* Flora (1986: xii)

KEY POINTS

- Welfare states provide citizens with free education and protect them against extreme poverty. Beyond this minimum social protection, welfare states differ with respect to the generosity and the scope of social protection against the risks of sickness, invalidity, unemployment, and old age, or other 'new' social risks.

- The state is not the only institution providing welfare.

- Market, state, and family influence each other in how much of the task of providing work and welfare they assume. They form a welfare regime, which is a complex system of (producing and) managing social risks.

The emergence of the welfare state

What drives the emergence and development of the welfare state? Three theoretical perspectives can be identified: (i) a functionalist approach; (ii) a class-mobilization explanation; and (iii) an institutionalist account, emphasizing the impact of state institutions and the relative autonomy of bureaucratic elites.

Functionalist approach

'The welfare state is an answer to problems created by capitalist industrialization': functionalist theories see the welfare state as an answer to new citizen needs that emerge with the disappearance of traditional means of subsistence and traditional bonds of mutual assistance (in families, through guilds, or charities) and with the new risks of modern, urbanized, and industrialized society: industrial accidents, cyclical unemployment, the inability to gain one's own living due to sickness or old age, the health risks in the new urban agglomerations. With pressing demands for protection against these modern risks, the scope of state intervention increased tremendously and the nature of the state was transformed (Flora and Alber 1981; Flora and Heidenheimer 1981: 23) (see Box 21.2).

This theory expected policy *convergence*—different nations adopting similar social and economic policies. If welfare states differed with respect to the coverage they provided and the benefits they granted, the causes of variation were assumed to be 'chronological'— namely, explained by the *different timing of industrialization and modernization* in the various countries. These differences would disappear in the long run.

Class mobilization

'Welfare state growth was driven by the democratic class struggle': class mobilization and interest group theories emphasized that collective political actors, such as labour movements, special interest groups, and political parties, demand and fight for social policies in the interest of their clientele. The welfare state is then seen as the outcome of a struggle between social classes and their political organizations, each with their own power base.

In a market economy, in which income stems from selling one's labour power, anything which hinders labour from being 'marketable' turns into an existential threat for the worker: unemployment, sickness, invalidity due to accidents or old age, etc. The market could neither cope with this new type of social risk directly (e.g. through private insurance), nor provide the collective goods needed to solve these problems. If many of the new risks stemmed from treating *labour as a commodity*, the main task of the welfare state seemed to lie in partially *decommodifying labour*, i.e. in granting labour temporal relief from the pressure to sell itself in the labour market (Esping-Andersen 1990). Such a decommodifying effect of welfare state intervention lay in the interest of workers, and so it seems straightforward to identify the labour movement as the main political driving force behind welfare state formation and growth (Stephens 1979; Korpi 1983, 2006).

Not convergence, but *variation* among welfare states was emphasized by these approaches: the more powerful labour was, the more elaborate the welfare state tended to be. Variation is expected to persist in the longer run—or at least as long as the power differentials persist. And they are usually persistent, not least because the welfare state itself is, in turn, also an important power resource for the labour movement, easing collective action and providing unions and social democratic parties with important organizational resources (Huber and Stephens 2001).

However, the feminist critique of the class-mobilization literature has stressed that in order to be decommodified, you have to be commodified first (Pedersen 1990; Lewis 1992; Orloff 1993; Sainsbury 1994, 1996; O'Connor et al. 1999; Morgan 2002, 2003, 2006). Decommodification as an analytical concept ignored the fact that many women remained excluded from the labour market in the first place. It is in this context that concepts like 'de-familialization' were introduced, which discussed how and to what extent state provision of welfare could substitute those social services traditionally provided in the family, i.e. almost exclusively by women (Esping-Andersen 1999). As this debate demonstrates, its close link to the labour market renders the welfare state also important in employers' calculus, and they may perceive social protection not always exclusively as a cost factor, for instance if it underpins long-term economic coordination between management and workers (see the section on 'Globalization: efficiency versus compensation').

State institutions and bureaucracy

'The welfare state followed in the footsteps of the nation state': finally, institutionalist theories point to those rules and regulations of policy-making and state structures, such as federalism (cf. Obinger et al. 2005), that operate relatively autonomously from social and political pressures as the determinants of the emergence and growth of the welfare state.

This approach emphasized the 'state building' aspect in welfare states (Skocpol 1985, 1992; Skocpol and Orloff 1986). When countries were confronted with the social problems generated by modern society for the first time, it mattered whether their bureaucratic elite was relatively autonomous, as in Japan (Garon 1987) or Sweden (Heclo 1974), or whether the lack of bureaucratic autonomy led to a 'politicization' of early welfare state formation and subsequently to welfare clientelism. For instance, the harsh critique that the US progressive movement voiced against political clientelism in US veteran pensions delegiti-

mized and delayed state social protection in the US for a long time (Skocpol 1992). If one focuses on how the state took over social responsibility for its citizens, it is easier to recognize that early welfare state programmes were not always exclusively targeted at workers, but often at other social categories whose risks did not coincide with class—such as soldiers or mothers (Skocpol 1992; see also Pedersen 1990, 1993). A perspective on how the state responded to the perils of modern society also helps us to understand the diffusion of policies, international policy learning, and the travel of concepts across the Atlantic or Pacific (cf. Rodgers 2000) and to account for the important role that war (both hot and cold) played in modern welfare state development (Obinger et al. 2018). Finally, it points to the emergence of an international social policy, with international organizations like the World Health Organization or the International Labour Organization Office and declarations such as the Universal Declaration of Human Rights (UDHR) (Paris 1948) or the International Covenant on Economic, Social and Cultural Rights (adopted by the United Nations in 1966), in which labour rights, the right to health and education, and the right to an adequate standard of living were declared.

The insights of the institutionalist school nicely squared with earlier observations in the modernization literature, namely that often it was the *least* democratic countries where suffrage was *not* yet extended which had actually pioneered building the modern welfare state. Also, it was not always the most economically advanced countries which took the lead in the introduction of state social protection programmes. Rather, it is the early pre-emptive strategy of state elites who anticipate workers' unrest that explains much of the pioneering role of not yet fully democratic and economically less advanced nations like Germany and Austria in the late nineteenth century. Here, social rights were not granted because of the extended political participatory rights of workers, but as a kind of *compensation* for the lack of such participatory rights (Flora and Alber 1981; Alber 1982).

The power resources approach and the institutionalist literature reacted to the fact that the causal link between industrialization (or modernization more generally) and welfare state development was not always elaborated well theoretically and not often confirmed empirically (see Wilensky and Lebeaux 1965; Kerr et al. 1973; Cutright 1965; Pryor 1968; Rimlinger 1971; Jackman 1975; Wilensky 1975). In order to demonstrate the great variety among (mostly Western) welfare states, Figure 21.1 locates countries in two dimensions: first, according to the *chronological* point in time when they have introduced the first major social insurance programme and, second, according to the *economic* point in time, i.e. according to the level of economic development and prosperity when they introduced such a programme.

As Figure 21.1 shows, there is no clear relationship between the level of modernity, industrialization, or GDP per capita, and the relative 'earliness' or 'lateness' of welfare state formation. The Anglo-Saxon countries (UK, US, Canada) introduced social protection programmes relatively late and at a relatively high level of economic development. They are joined by Protestant liberal countries like the Netherlands or Switzerland, which also qualify as welfare latecomers (Manow 2004). Countries like Germany or Austria were welfare pioneers in a chronological sense, but several countries (e.g. Japan, Portugal, Finland, Italy) introduced their first social insurance programmes at much lower levels of economic development than those two countries. While the Latin American welfare states are chronologically late, the introduction of the first major social insurance programme spread over almost the entire range of possible economic levels of development (see Figure 21.1). But do the political and social forces which can be held responsible for early or late welfare state building also explain the different paths of further welfare state development? This is the question for the following section, 'The expansion of the welfare state'.

KEY POINTS

- The welfare state has been understood as the (functional) response to the social problems generated by modernization, as the result of the political conflicts between capital and labour in modern capitalist societies, and as a central element in modern **nation-state** building.

- There is no obvious connection between the level of economic development or **democratization** of a society and the development of its welfare state.

- Different approaches have different explanatory goals or problems: the functionalist approach tries to explain the convergence of modern welfare states; the power resources and institutionalist approaches attempt to account for the enduring variation among welfare states.

The expansion of the welfare state

The impact of social democracy

In the 1980s and 1990s, a new approach criticized the logic of industrialism thesis and the median voter view that democratic politics as such can explain the expansion of the welfare state (Jackman 1975, 1986). The theoretical goal was to demonstrate how differences in party political government composition explain differences in welfare state expansion (Hewitt 1977).

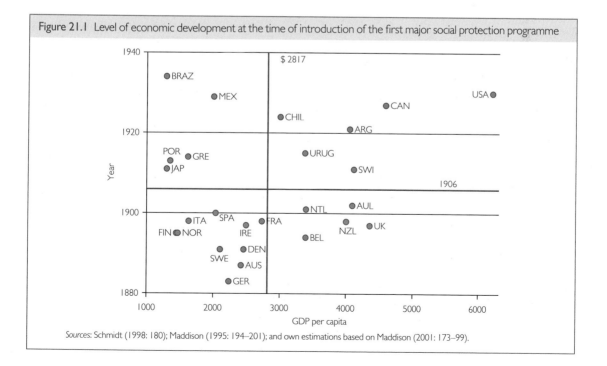

Figure 21.1 Level of economic development at the time of introduction of the first major social protection programme

Sources: Schmidt (1998: 180); Maddison (1995: 194–201); and own estimations based on Maddison (2001: 173–99).

The explanatory importance of party politics was also underlined by the failure of economic models, which predicted that welfare state **redistribution** should increase with increases in income inequality (Meltzer and Richard 1981). But to the contrary, countries like Norway and Finland have both a highly compressed wage and income structure *and* a generous welfare state, and countries like the US combine an unequal pre-tax income distribution with a regressive tax-benefit system that actually reinforces inequality (Congressional Budget Office (2013).

A large number of studies corroborated how and under which conditions social democratic power stimulates welfare state performance. Decommodification was found to be strongest if the *left was strong* (Stephens 1979) and the *right was divided* (Castles 1978). Moreover, social democratic attempts to expand the welfare state were most effective if the party was supported by a strong and coherent union movement (Stephens 1979; Higgins and Apple 1981).

Cross-national **quantitative** studies extensively tested the thesis that politically organized labour (**social democracy**) was primarily responsible for the social transformation of capitalism (Hewitt 1977; Stephens 1979; Korpi 1983, 1989; Hicks and Swank 1984; Esping-Andersen 1985a; Griffin et al. 1989; Alvarez et al. 1991; Hicks 1999; see also Huber and Stephens 2001). The main finding of this literature was that the more the mass of the population is organized as wage-earners within the social democratic movement, the higher the quality (universalism, solidarity, redistribution) of the welfare arrangements tended to be and, as a result, the higher the extent of equality. Therefore, a developed welfare state was interpreted as evidence for a decisive *shift in the balance of power in favour of the working class* and social democracy (see Shalev 1983).

Indeed, there was considerable evidence in favour of a social democratic effect on income distribution (Hewitt 1977; Björn 1979; Stephens 1979; Hicks and Swank 1984; Swank and Hicks 1985; Hage et al. 1989; Muller 1989). However, for several reasons, income distribution was still a problematic variable. On technical grounds, aggregate data available until the publication of the Luxembourg Income Study (Mitchell 1990; Smeeding et al. 1990) were not truly comparable. On theoretical grounds, income distribution was problematic to the extent that the kinds of universalistic and generous welfare programmes associated with successful social democratic politics tended to lose some of their redistributive effect because they increasingly favoured the middle classes (LeGrand 1982; Goodin and LeGrand 1987; Esping-Andersen 1990; Korpi and Palme 1998). There was some evidence to suggest that the social democratic

effect was more evident when measured against institutional characteristics of welfare states (Korpi 1989; Myles 1989; Esping-Andersen 1990; Kangas 1991).

Neocorporatism and the international economy

Others argued that the political efficacy of left-wing parties to decommodify labour and promote welfare state expansion depended structurally on centralized neocorporatist industrial relations systems, i.e. on the continuous cooperation between central representative organizations of both capital and labour under state tutelage (Cameron 1978, 1984; Schmidt 1983; Scharpf 1984, 1987; Hicks et al. 1989).

Cameron (1978, 1984) suggested that the association between strong social democracy and welfare states was linked to a country's position in the international economy. The vulnerability that small open economies faced vis-à-vis the international market favoured the expansion of the public economy so as to reduce uncertainty via social guarantees, full employment, and more active government management of the economy. Katzenstein (1985) argued that *small, open nations developed democratic corporatist structures as a way to enhance domestic consensus, facilitate economic adjustments, and maintain international competitiveness.* While democratic **corporatism** was promoted by the presence of strong social democratic **labour movements**, Katzenstein pointed to Switzerland and the Netherlands to suggest that they did not constitute a necessary condition (see Keman 1990; Garrett 1998). In the Latin American context, however, Segura-Ubiergo (2007) argues that these countries' export dependence on natural resources and agricultural products, with their price volatility and often unfavourable terms of trade, made economic openness rather a detriment than a catalyst of social programmes.

Social democracy was most likely to promote the expansion of the welfare state if its parliamentary power was matched by *strong consensus-building mechanisms* in both the polity and economy (Schmidt 1983; Keman 1988; Hicks et al. 1989). Neocorporatist intermediation came to play an important role in maintaining welfare policies during economic crisis periods; the distributive battles that erupt when growth declines were better managed with 'all-encompassing' interest organizations (Hicks and Swank 1984; Muller 1989).

By the end of the 1980s the literature came to agree that parties or unions alone had little effect and that successful social democratization required a configuration of strong left-wing parties in government supported by an encompassing and centralized trade union movement (Alvarez et al. 1991; Garrett 1998).

Only in the 'coherently' liberal political economies, in which a weak labour movement met with a political dominance of conservative parties, or in the coherently social democratic political economies, where a strong labour movement went hand in hand with left-wing governments, were macro-economic policies, wage bargaining, and welfare expenditures expected to complement each other. 'Incoherent political economies', on the other hand, were expected to perform much less well, when right-wing governments that pursued neoliberal economic policies met with strong union resistance, causing industrial strife, or when the attempt at macro-economic management by left-wing governments was counteracted by fragmented and particularistic unions that proved unable to engage in concerted wage restraint. The debate about the impact of **globalization** on the sustainability of generous welfare state programmes in many respects reflects this earlier corporatist debate about economic vulnerabilities in open economies and the concomitant need for welfare compensation (see later in this chapter, 'The challenges and dynamics of contemporary welfare states' and Chapter 24 'Globalization and the nation-state').

Risk redistribution

In one of the more fundamental challenges to the literature, Baldwin (1990) rejected the causal link between social democracy and solidaristic social policies altogether. While growing equality may have been a characteristic feature of modern welfare states, it has not been its goal. The welfare state was more about reapportioning risks than about the redistribution of wealth (Rehm 2016). Baldwin rejected what he called the labourist (i.e. class-mobilization) account for its narrow focus on the working class as the only risk category. The critical insight was that class is neither the only risk category, nor always a risk category. The labourist view mistakenly assumed that welfare policies were explained in terms of a victory of the working class over the bourgeoisie. What had historically determined the solidarity of social policy was not working-class strength but, in contrast, the fact that 'otherwise privileged groups discovered that they shared a common interest in reallocating risk with the disadvantaged' (Baldwin 1990: 292; see Heclo and Madsen 1986; Milner 1989; Therborn 1989).

Christian democracy and Catholic social doctrine

One of the major problems of the social democratic model was that several countries (e.g. the Netherlands or France) pursued equality and had a large welfare state without the advocacy of a strong social democratic labour movement (Castles 1978, 1985; Stephens 1979; Wilensky 1981; Skocpol and Amenta 1986). Both the incapacity to explain early reforms of capitalism by liberal and conservative state elites and the fact that other political parties also behaved as pro-welfare actors made it clear that the political process of welfare state construction and expansion needed to be reconsidered. One answer came from those who showed that **Christian democracy** (or political Catholicism) constituted a functional equivalent or alternative to social democracy for expanding the welfare state (Wilensky 1981; Schmidt 1982). Consequently, the power of labour could not be equalled with the power of social democracy. Christian democratic parties operating in the centre enjoyed considerable working-class support and were commonly backed by powerful Catholic unions (see van Kersbergen 1995). This political constellation was highly favourable to welfare state development.

Secular trends

Emphasizing political agency against the functionalist approaches has the danger of falling into the other extreme of neglecting how much the growth of the welfare state is influenced by secular processes beyond the control of single political actors. Some of them are as follows.

1. Demographic ageing: longer life expectancy and lower birth rates lead to demographic ageing and increase the demand for social spending on health, pensions, and care. Medical progress is costly and puts an increasing strain on health-care spending.

2. Baumol's cost disease: productivity increases more slowly in services than in manufacturing, which means that (social) services will increase in economic importance. But economies with a larger service sector will grow at a slower pace (Pierson 2001*a*).

3. Structural change: job losses in agriculture and industry increase the demand for welfare state compensation (job protection, retraining; active labour market policies) (Iversen and Cusack 2000; Wren 2013).

4. Wagner's law predicts an ever-increasing share of public expenditures in developed industrial economies, causing a secular trend towards higher public spending in all developed economies.

5. 'Politics for profit' (e.g. Buchanan 1977): politicians aim to expand public spending to

maximize their 'political income' and to increase their re-election prospects.

6. Programme maturity, 'positive feedback', and ratchet effects—each welfare programme breeds its own supporters. Once introduced, it proves very hard to abandon a welfare scheme later (Pierson 1994, 1998; Huber and Stephens 2001).

While all advanced welfare states have to cope with these secular challenges, their vulnerabilities and opportunities in coping with them vary according to their institutional set-up.

KEY POINTS

- The political impact of left-wing parties on the welfare state depended on a centralized neocorporatist industrial relations system that helped to enhance domestic consensus, facilitate economic adjustments, and maintain international competitiveness.

- Important criticisms of the social democratic or labourist model are: (i) the welfare state is about reapportioning social risks and the working class is only one risk category; (ii) there are countries that pursued equality and a developed welfare state, but did not have a strong social democratic labour movement.

- There are other pro-welfare state actors (e.g. Christian democracy) and important non-political processes (e.g. demographic ageing) that promote expansion and development.

Variations among developed welfare states

Each welfare state is a 'unique' combination of regulations and institutions. However, in comparative politics we are not interested in uniqueness, but in comparability and systematic variation. In order to compare welfare states, some simple dimensions of variation can be distinguished. They comprise the following.

1. Is the welfare state tax-financed or contribution-financed?

2. Is every *citizen* protected or is every *worker* (and his or her dependents) insured?

3. Are benefits a right, gained either through previous contributions to social insurance programmes or attached to the status of citizenship, or do benefits depend on proven need, i.e. are they conditional on means testing?

4. Are benefits uniform (flat rate) or do they reflect prior income, i.e. are pension or unemployment payments temporary substitutes for wages or do they aim to secure some 'minimum' standard of living?

That welfare states come in a limited variety can be partly explained by the fact that choosing a particular institutional solution in one dimension simultaneously narrows the choice set in others. The advanced welfare states represent packages or bundles of institutional and regulatory answers to the social problems of modern society.

Take welfare state financing, for example: if the welfare state is tax-financed, eligibility should be linked to the citizen status (with or without means testing), but not to the employment relation. But this would also mean that benefits are unlikely to reflect prior income but rather a social notion of a socially fair and accepted (minimum) standard of living. In a contribution-financed welfare state, in contrast, proportional deductions from the payroll justify differentiated benefits that reflect the length of the previous contribution period and the level of the contributions paid. If social protection is primarily linked to the employment relation, it seems to be a 'natural' solution to insure those who are not in dependent employment (e.g. spouse, children) via the family member who is dependently employed.

To select which institutional and regulatory solutions respond best to social problems is a deeply political decision, which sets the path for further developments and has vast ramifications for social outcomes, for instance for inequality. The tax-financed and universal welfare state, where social rights are based on citizenship, are more redistributive than contribution-financed welfare state, where social rights depend on labour market performance, even if the tax system is not progressive (Rothstein 1998: 147). As a result, the universal welfare states of Scandinavia have much lower levels of disposable income inequality than all other welfare states. A telling example is Sweden. In this country (in 2016) market inequality (before taxation and redistribution) was higher than in the UK. However, the tax-benefit system of the Swedish welfare state reduces income inequality by 52 per cent, making this country's income distribution much more equal than that of the UK (Eurostat 2019). Welfare states as bundles of institutional or regulatory solutions to social problems can be analysed as *models or regimes*. In the late 1950s, Richard M. Titmuss (1958) suggested distinguishing the following.

- the *residual welfare model*, in which social protection 'comes into play only after the breakdown of the private market and the family as the "natural" channels for the fulfilment of social needs' (Flora 1986: xxi);

- the *industrial achievement performance model*, in which welfare rights and benefits are linked to the employment relation and reflect 'merit, work performance and productivity' (Flora 1986: xxi);
- an *institutional redistributive model*, in which social welfare institutions are an integral part of society, providing 'universalist services outside the market' (Flora 1986: xxi) based on citizenship.

There is obviously considerable overlap between Titmuss's welfare state typology and Esping-Andersen's *Three Worlds of Welfare Capitalism* (1990). In his book, Esping-Andersen distinguished three regimes (see Box 21.3).

Anglo-Saxon liberal regime

In a liberal regime, benefits tend to be low and flat rate. They are means-tested or targeted at clearly delineated groups in society. The welfare state is predominantly tax-financed. More encompassing social protection has to be purchased individually on the market (e.g. life insurance or private pension plans), because the welfare state only protects those most in need. Public spending on social protection is comparatively low. This welfare regime is often to be found where conservative parties are in government, in the US and the UK, and to some extent also in Australia and New Zealand (see the section on 'Australia and New Zealand').

Scandinavian social democratic regime

The social democratic regime is also predominantly tax-financed, but in contrast with the liberal model, benefits are granted without means testing. They are a citizen's right and benefits tend to be much more generous. Subsequently, levels of public spending tend to be much higher. Social democratic regimes also provide many welfare services in care, health, and education, and the welfare state itself becomes a major employer, especially of women (Huber and Stephens 2000). This regime is found mainly in Scandinavian countries, in which social democratic parties are strong and often participate in government, where levels of unionization are high, and where the political right is divided.

Continental conservative regime

The continental conservative regime comes close to Titmuss's 'performance achievement' model. Here,

> ### DEFINITION 21.3
>
> ### Esping-Andersen's three welfare state regimes
>
> [In the liberal welfare state,] means-tested assistance, modest universalist transfers, or modest social insurance plans predominate. Benefits cater mainly to a clientele of low-income, usually working-class, state dependents ... In turn, the state encourages the market, either passively—by guaranteeing only a minimum—or actively—by subsidizing private welfare schemes. In conservative and strongly 'corporatist' welfare states, the liberal obsession with market efficiency and commodification was never pre-eminent and, as such, the granting of social rights was hardly ever a contested issue. What predominated was the preservation of status differentials; rights, therefore, were attached to class and status. This corporatism was subsumed under a state edifice perfectly ready to displace the market as a provider of welfare; hence, private insurance and occupational fringe benefits play a truly marginal role ... The third ... regime-cluster is composed of those countries in which the principles of universalism and decommodification of social rights were extended also to the new middle classes. We may call it the 'social democratic' regime-type since, in these nations, social democracy was clearly the dominant force behind social reform ... [and] pursued a welfare state that would promote an equality of the highest standards ... This model crowds out the market, and consequently constructs an essentially universal solidarity in favour of the welfare state. All benefit, all are dependent; and all will presumably feel obliged to pay.
>
> Esping-Andersen (1990: 26–8)

social rights are not based on citizen status, but on the employment relation. The welfare state is contribution-financed rather than tax-financed. Those not employed are covered via their employed spouse or relatives. Welfare benefits are differentiated according to income and to the record of contributions to the social insurance fund. The conservative welfare state is transfer heavy and service lean. Based on occupational principles, conservative welfare states display a high degree of programme fragmentation. The major occupational groups (white-collar and blue-collar workers, civil servants, free professions, self-employed, etc.) all have their own social insurance schemes (see Table 21.1). This welfare state is mainly to be found in continental European countries in which Christian democratic parties occupy a central position in the party system.

Esping-Andersen's welfare state typology has become extremely influential (Emmenegger et al. 2015). Whether studying employment growth in the

Table 21.1 Esping-Andersen's three worlds of welfare capitalism

Esping-Andersen's welfare regimes (Titmuss's welfare models)	'Liberal' (residual model)	'Conservative' (achievement performance model)	'Social democratic' (institutional redistributive model)
Prime example	US, UK	Germany	Sweden
Decommodification	Low	Medium	High
Social rights	Needs-based	Employment-related	Universal
Welfare provision	Mixed services	Transfer payments	Public services
Benefits	Flat benefits	Contribution-related	Redistributive

Source: Ebbinghaus and Manow (2001: 9).

service economy (Scharpf 1997*b*), or different political choices between full employment, balanced budgets, and income equality (Iversen and Wren 1998), or patterns of income inequality among the Organisation for Economic Co-operation and Development (OECD) countries (Korpi and Palme 1998), or the different degrees to which European political economies were affected by the Great Recession and the refugee crisis (Manow et al. 2018), the fruitfulness of the 'three worlds' heuristic has been confirmed time and again.

At the same time, the voluminous literature on Esping-Andersen's welfare state typology (see Arts and Gelissen 2010) has debated whether additional regime types should be added. Some add a distinct *Southern European welfare regime* (Italy, Spain, Portugal, Greece, sometimes including France), and some treat the two antipodean welfare states (Australia and New Zealand) as special cases (Castles 1989; Castles and Mitchell 1992; Ferrera 1996, 1997).

Southern Europe

The Southern European welfare regime distinguishes itself from the rest of continental conservative welfare states due to the following factors (Ferrera 2010; Manow 2015):

- the long-time absence of a nationwide uniform social assistance scheme;
- the dominance of pension spending among total social spending;
- a highly segmented labour market with the highest protection standards for the 'happy few' in the state sector and in state enterprises, combined with large segments of low protection in the private sector, plus unregulated employment in

the large shadow economy (leading to low female employment and high youth unemployment);
- national health systems which are rather untypical of the conservative welfare regimes on Europe's continent.

Australia and New Zealand

The welfare states of New Zealand and Australia represent a type of their own (Castles 1989, 1996; Castles and Mitchell 1992). While targeting plays a prominent role, eligibility rules are not particularly restrictive. Moreover, state social protection in both countries often works 'through the market', especially via state arbitration of industrial conflicts, high employment protection, and compressed wages, which makes post hoc welfare intervention and redistribution often unnecessary.

KEY POINTS

- The advanced welfare states represent packages or bundles of institutional and regulatory answers to the social problems and risks of modern society, such as unemployment, sickness, and inability to work due to old age or invalidity.

- The literature distinguishes three to five different welfare regimes: (i) an Anglo-Saxon liberal regime; (ii) a social democratic regime found in Scandinavia; (iii) a conservative model that is typical for continental Europe; (iv) a Southern European regime; (v) a 'radical' type found in Australia and New Zealand.

There is also increasing scholarly attention for the development of welfare states in Latin America (Segura-Ubiergo 2007; Huber and Bogliaccini 2010; Huber and

Table 21.2 Decommodification scores in the three worlds of welfare capitalism

	UE	Sick	Pension	Total decom		UE	Sick	Pension	Total decom
				Benefit generosity index results					
Australia	4.0	4.0	5.0	13.0	US	7.4	0	11.3	18.7
US[a]	7.2	0	7.0	13.8	Japan	4.5	6.2	9.4	20.0
New Zealand	4	4.0	9.1	17.1	Australia	5.0	5.0	10.1	20.1
Canada	8	6.3	7.7	22.0	Italy	3.2	7.3	10.0	20.5
Ireland	8.3	8.3	6.7	23.3	Ireland	6.9	6.2	8.3	21.4
UK	7.2	7.7	8.5	23.4	UK	7.2	7.2	8.5	22.9
Italy	5.1	9.4	9.6	24.1	New Zealand	5.0	5.0	13.3	23.3
Japan[a]	5.0	6.8	10.5	22.3	Canada	7.2	6.4	11.4	25.0
France	6.3	9.2	12.0	27.5	Austria	6.9	9.7	11.2	27.8
Germany	7.9	11.3	8.5	27.7	France	6.3	9.5	12.0	27.8
Finland	5.2	10.0	14.0	29.2	Finland	4.9	10.0	13.0	27.9
Switzerland	8.8	12.0	9.0	29.8	Germany	7.5	12.6	8.7	28.8
Austria	6.7	12.5	11.9	31.1	Netherlands	10.6	9.7	11.5	31.8
Belgium	8.6	8.8	15.0	32.4	Switzerland	9.2	11.0	12.0	32.2
Netherlands	11.1	10.5	10.8	32.4	Belgium	10.2	8.6	14.0	32.9
Denmark	8.1	15.0	15.0	38.1	Denmark	8.6	12.6	11.8	32.9
Norway	9.4	14.0	14.9	38.3	Norway	8.5	13.0	11.9	33.4
Sweden	7.1	15.0	17.0	39.1	Sweden	9.4	14.0	15.0	38.4
Mean	7.1	9.2	10.7	27.2		7.1	8.6	11.3	27.0
Standard deviation	1.9	4.0	3.4	7.7		2.1	3.5	1.9	5.8
Coefficient of variation	0.27	0.44	0.32	0.28		0.29	0.41	0.17	0.21
					Correlation with original scores	0.87	0.95	0.70	0.87

Correlation between programmes	Correlation between programmes
UE–Sickr = 0.44	UK–Sickr = 0.45
UE–Pensionr = 0.23	UE–Pensionr = 0.36
Sick–Pensionr = 0.72	Sick–Pensionr = 0.30
Cronbach's α = 0.72	Cronbach's α = 0.59

[a] 'Total decom' score is amount in Table 2.2 of Esping-Andersen (1990), not the sum of programme scores.

Source: Adapted from Scruggs and Allan (2006b: 68).

Stephens 2012; Cruz-Martínez 2014) and other world regions (Cook 2010; Peng and Wong 2010). Yet, country differences are such that it does not seem to make sense to try to identify regional welfare regimes that could be added to the three worlds typology.

Esping-Andersen's typology was based on his *index of decommodification* and used 1980 data. From the beginning, controversy arose over the categorization of single countries and over the clusters per se: for an overview, see Arts and Gelissen (2010), for a replication see Scruggs and Allan (2006a), and see Table 21.2 and the web links at the end of the chapter. Despite all criticism (see Van Kersbergen and Vis 2015), Esping-Andersen's typology has remained the single most important contribution to the comparative welfare state literature of the past three decades (see Emmenegger et al. 2015).

The effects of the welfare state

Comparative political science research has tended to take a broad approach to the study of the effects of social policies. Theoretically, they have been inspired by T. H. Marshall (1950) (see Box 21.1). His concept of social citizenship not only stresses social *rights,* but also how the granting of such rights structures and restructures *status* relations in society. The main questions were whether the welfare state (i) modifies social inequality; (ii) alleviates poverty; (iii) reduces social risks; and whether different welfare states have varying consequences for social stratification.

(In)equality and redistribution

The relevant social stratification in our societies concerns status or occupational groups, social classes, gender, and ethnicity. Social policies, their design and content, are likely to be affected by the prevailing differentiation in society and may or may not influence the unequal distribution of social risks. Research deals with the question of whether social policies structure, cause, reproduce, reinforce, or moderate social inequality.

Class, gender, and ethnicity as concepts are supposed to capture systematically how society is structured in such a way that certain groups of people are privileged or disadvantaged in terms of their occupational position, income, wealth, status, skills, education, and, above all, power. These structural characteristics are expected to determine to a large extent the life chances of the individuals within these groups and they are affiliated with many other things, including health, happiness, death rates, lifestyle, culture, political preference, etc.

With respect to class, the debate is whether and to what extent it is possible to 'escape' one's own class. Is social mobility, both within a generation and between generations, rare? Are social policies capable of decreasing class closure? Do social policies reduce or reproduce social inequalities? And do different welfare regimes (re)structure social divisions differently?

Universalism versus targeting

It is important to realize that redistribution does not always imply more equality. For instance, saving money during periods of relative prosperity (e.g. when in a job) for periods of need (e.g. when old and retired) is a form of redistribution, but does not lead to more equality. Redistribution is not necessarily from the rich to the poor. With respect to equality, the issue is whether social policies *targeted at specific groups* (e.g. the working class, women, migrants) reduce inequalities or whether *universalism* in social policy, i.e. 'the provision of a single, relatively uniform service or benefit for all citizens regardless of income or class' (M. Hill 2006: 192), actually does a better job.

Different welfare regimes vary precisely in this respect, with the *social democratic model being a universal system and the liberal regimes the most strongly targeting.* Moreover, in the conservative regime, social inequalities and status differentials are intentionally reproduced in the welfare system through occupational and earnings-related social insurance schemes. Inequalities are also reproduced, but to a lesser extent in the universalist schemes because the better-off and highly educated people with higher skills and competences are much more capable of taking advantage of universal services (health care, education) and tax deductions than poorer and less educated people.

At face value, it seems that targeting is ultimately better for the poor or the less well-off, primarily because social policies are designed exclusively for those who need it most. Moreover, redistribution via targeting is fair and efficient because it does not waste resources by transferring money to people who do not need aid. However, targeting is a kind of 'Robin Hood strategy' ('stealing' from the rich, giving to the poor) that antagonizes the rich and provokes them to defect from the system. As Korpi and Palme (1998: 672) explain: 'By discriminating in favour of the poor, the targeted model creates a zero-sum conflict of interests between the poor and the better-off workers and the middle classes who must pay for the benefits of the poor without receiving any benefits.' In other words, targeting may undermine broader cross-class coalitions in support of the welfare state.

An alternative is a *simple egalitarian system* with flat-rate benefits for all, giving relatively more to the poor than to the better off. However, this system (known as the Beveridge system) also has incentives for the middle classes to opt out and look for private insurance. Finally, there is the evangelical *Matthew strategy* ('For unto every one that hath shall be given, and he shall have abundance: but from him that hath not shall be taken away even that which he hath') of earnings-related provision that gives relatively more to the rich than to the poor. The Matthew effect is most pronounced in services, for instance in (higher) education, from which the rich profit much more than the poor, not only because they receive the service, but also because education greatly advances earning capacity (Bonoli et al. 2017).

When empirically comparing welfare state regimes, we find the *paradox of distribution*: 'The more we target benefits at the poor only and the more concerned we are with creating equality via equal public transfers to all, the less likely we are to reduce poverty and inequality' (Korpi and Palme 1998: 681–2). Encompassing models that combine a simple egalitarian system with the Matthew strategy are the most redistributive systems, which also have a high level of political support and legitimacy. How is this to be explained? Korpi and Palme provide an answer:

By giving basic security to everybody and by offering clearly earnings-related benefits to all economically active individuals . . . the encompassing model brings low-income groups and the better-off citizens into the same institutional structures. Because of its earnings-related benefits, it is likely to reduce the demand for private insurance. Thus the encompassing model can be expected to have the most favourable outcomes in terms of the formation of cross-class coalitions that include manual workers as well as the middle classes. By providing sufficiently high benefits for high-income groups so as not to push them to exit, in encompassing institutions the voice of the better-off citizens helps not only themselves but low-income income groups as well.

Korpi and Palme (1998: 672)

Similarly, Smeeding (2005) shows that the targeting welfare state regimes, especially the US, have the highest levels of poverty and inequality. Smeeding also argues that when the distance between the rich and the less well off becomes too great, the rich opt out and cater for themselves: they get private insurance, receive the best health care, and make sure that their children have the best education available. Similarly. Lupu and Pontusson argue that when the distance between the average income

of the middle class and the lower class is large relatively to the distance between the middle class and the rich, the middle class will not ally with the poor in a pro-redistribution coalition (see also Lupu and Pontusson 2011). This reproduces and even reinforces social divisions. Therefore, in a comparative politics perspective, we must look not only at the economic consequences, but also at the political preconditions of social protection.

Empirical research (e.g. Kenworthy 1999; Korpi and Palme 2003; Brady 2005; Scruggs and Allen 2006*a*) underscores the differential impact of various welfare state regimes on equality and poverty. Although some (e.g. Brady 2005: 1354) find that the welfare state, regardless of the period or the type one studies, strongly reduces poverty, there seems to be a consensus that *universalism in particular produces the most pronounced effects*. However, although Norway, for example, outperforms most other European countries, in 2017 it still had about 15 per cent of its population at risk of poverty and social exclusion (Eurostat 2019). We have to bear in mind, though, that poverty is usually measured as a relative concept (regularly as 60 per cent of the median household income), and that, thus, a country can also report more poverty if the middle-class gets richer, without anybody in the lower class having become poorer (cf. Atkinson 2015).

The issue of inequality is predominantly phrased in terms of income and market position, and especially addresses the class issue. Feminist critiques pointed out that this perspective had great difficulty in dealing with the class position of women, particularly those not active in the labour market. In order to understand the working of the regimes in terms of market, state, *and* family, one also needs to develop theoretical tools that can make sense of the gender dimension of social stratification and how social policies presuppose and affect the relations between men and women (see Bussemaker and van Kersbergen 1994).

Social policies often took the distribution of labour between men and women for granted and tended to reinforce it. For the position of women, it is crucial whether they are entitled to benefits as individuals or whether rights are tied to families, in which men are often the sole income earner. Also, women have different types of risks and needs (e.g. think of single parenthood). As a result, the outcomes of welfare state interventions in terms of equality and poverty and in terms of labour market behaviour are markedly different for men and women. For instance, in most member states of the European Union the poverty risk for women is considerably larger than for men, although the welfare state reduces the risk of poverty everywhere (Eurostat 2019).

In the golden age of the welfare state (the 1960s and 1970s), income security and redistribution were considered to be a matter not simply of social justice, but also of macro-economic efficiency. Welfare state expenditures could be viewed as part of Keynesian demand management that helped maximize economic performance, particularly economic growth and the prevention of mass unemployment. Also, a neocorporatist exchange between the expansion of social programmes and wage moderation was often part of the management of the macro-economy. Moreover, many of the welfare state's programmes contribute to the supply of labour. The welfare state's jobs and programmes (such as child care, parental leave, sickness benefits) have played a crucial role in increasing the supply of female labour. Or, to put it differently, the welfare state has helped women to enter the labour market on a scale that would have been impossible without it. The welfare state also facilitated economic reconstruction and adaptation by offering 'easy' exit routes for redundant workers in non-competitive industries via disability schemes and early retirement.

KEY POINTS

- The welfare state is itself a system of social stratification: it can counter, reproduce, or reinforce social (class, gender, ethnic) inequalities.

- The impact of social policies on poverty and inequality varies enormously among regimes, with the universalist social democratic regime the most and the liberal targeting regime the least redistributive.

- Paradoxically, the more benefits are targeted exclusively at the poor and the more public policies are devised to create equality via equal transfers to all, the less likely it is that poverty and equality are reduced.

- Men profit more than women from welfare state interventions to reduce equality and poverty and to improve their chances in the labour market.

The challenges and dynamics of contemporary welfare states

Today, the welfare state is under pressure from many sides: population ageing, sluggish economic growth, mass unemployment, changing family structures and life-cycle patterns, post-industrial labour markets that generate new risks and needs, the erosion of systems of interest intermediation and collective bargaining, disruptive technologies, and international pressures

from globalization and global financial crises (see Bermeo and Pontusson 2012; Beramendi et al. 2015; Dølvik and Martin 2015). In particular, the globalization literature started from the assumption that an increasingly internationalized market would force the generous welfare states of the Western world into a common downward movement (see Chapter 24 'Globalization and the nation-state').

Globalization: efficiency versus compensation

However, it seems that the advanced OECD economies have maintained their ability to 'tax and spend' to a surprising degree, even under conditions of crisis. What is most remarkable from the viewpoint of the early pessimistic predictions is that the welfare state basically survived (Kuhnle 2000). This has led to an as yet unresolved debate between, on the one hand, those researchers who think that globalization is indeed a major challenge that is potentially undermining the economic foundations of social policies and, on the other hand, those scholars who argue that the challenges and threats to the welfare state, such as ageing, are essentially endogenous and have little to do with globalization.

In the debate, one side holds that the internationalized market and its intensified economic competition have rendered high levels of welfare spending unsustainable (the *efficiency hypothesis*); others argue that welfare state compensation of those who lose from economic openness has historically been a social and political precondition for the liberal post-war trade regime (the *compensation hypothesis*) (Rodrik 1996; Rieger and Leibfried 1998, 2001; Glatzer and Rueschemeyer 2005; Van Kersbergen and Vis 2014: chapter 7; Busemeyer and Garritzmann 2018).

Adherents of the compensation hypothesis argue that economic openness and a liberal trade regime rested on the domestic political promise to compensate the losers of economic integration. With downward pressures on the advanced welfare states, economic openness is endangering the very social and political preconditions on which it rests. As of yet, the 'race to the bottom', commonly attributed to globalization, has failed to materialize. The link between economic openness and domestic social protection has not yet been convincingly established, either theoretically or empirically (Iversen and Cusack 2000), although recent research shows that, faced with the skill demands of the knowledge economy, citizens expect their governments to increase compensation in the form of public investment in education (Busemeyer and Garritzmann 2018). It is also evident that a successful transition to the service economy would particularly have to rely on the proliferation of high-productivity service jobs, which critically depends on whether a country's higher education system is able to provide the necessary qualifications (Ansell and Gingrich 2013, 2018). In the more recent debate on populism, some have held the absence of a European-style compensatory welfare state in the US or UK partly responsible for the protectionism under President Trump or as becoming manifest in the Brexit-vote in June 2016. The fact that regions that suffered from industrial decline mainly due to intensified import competition from China have displayed stronger support for right-wing populism is seen as evidence in support of an argument that emphasizes the critical role that welfare compensation plays for the political acceptance of a liberal trade regime (Autor et al. 2016; Colantone and Stanig 2018, Eichengreen 2018; Rodrik 2018).

Policies that redistribute wealth and risk in such a manner that the potential or actual victims of the global market are protected can be beneficial to economic growth, because they yield collective goods that the market cannot produce. These especially concern investments in human capital and the infrastructure. Recently, social investment policies (e.g. active labour market policy, early child care and education, etc.) have gained importance and can help people adjust to the new (skills) demands of the open knowledge economy (Hemerijck 2017).. The 'varieties of capitalism' literature already early on highlighted the important contribution of the welfare state to skill-intensive production regimes (Hall and Soskice 2001*a*; Iversen and Soskice 2001). Workers invest in those special skills on which skill-intensive production regimes in coordinated market economies depend only when they have a guarantee that their investment will pay off in the long run. Generous unemployment payments that take into account the previous wage level and that can be drawn for relatively long periods of time, as well as generous early retirement rules, make sure that investments in special skills will not be lost, even in the case of unemployment (Estevez-Abe et al. 2001). Employers may also value the welfare state's contribution to the stability of centralized wage bargaining and to the prevention of cut-throat price competition (Swenson 2004) by clearing the market of firms that underbid wages and working conditions. It also turns out that a nation's economic, political, and social stability is increasingly important for investment decisions, particularly for those investors who are forced to take their decisions under conditions of uncertainty and high risk. Certainty and predictability are highly valued in an increasingly uncertain and volatile global economy (but see Huber and Stephens 2001; Stephens 2005: 63).

After many years of debate on the effects of globalization on the generous welfare states of the West, the competing hypotheses can clearly be distinguished (Glatzer and Rueschemeyer 2005).

1. The *compensation hypothesis* holds that open markets create a need for new compensatory policies that (democratic) governments may supply. Moreover, social policies can also be productive assets as they foster a better educated, better trained, and healthier workforce, provide coordinated market economies with specific skill profiles, and contribute to the development of a more equal and less conflictual society. Where such compensatory schemes are absent, preferences for protectionism may intensify.

2. The *efficiency hypothesis* states that globalization hampers social policy. International competition forces national governments to reduce costs by scaling down taxes and social policies. At the same time, open capital markets critically reduce the nation state's taxing capacity, thereby undermining the welfare state's fiscal basis.

The literature reached a 'politics matters' conclusion (see Garrett and Nickerson 2005: 48; Huber and Stephens 2001; Stephens 2005). Trade openness leads to the expansion of the welfare state only under social democratic or Christian democratic leadership, but not when secular right parties are in power. Generous welfare states were not only compatible with competition on the world market, but 'to the extent that they enabled wage restraint and provided collective goods valued by employers, such as labor training, the generous social policies actually contributed to competitiveness' (Stephens 2005: 70). It is soaring unemployment and budget deficits that cause public spending cuts. Welfare state retrenchment is caused by globalization only to the extent that rising unemployment is an effect of globalization. But these effects are mediated by politics.

Most recent studies indicate that domestic politics and institutions are of great consequence for how the pressures of globalization make themselves felt in social policy and the welfare state. Globalization does not *always* undermine the welfare state. Under favourable political conditions, increasing openness can imply welfare state development, but if such conditions are absent, the compensation hypothesis also fails to convince (Busemeyer 2009; Marshall and Fisher 2015). This makes social policy outcomes more dependent on raw political struggles. Welfare state outcomes are predominantly the result of the complex *interplay* of international economic forces and domestic politics and institutions (Glatzer and Rueschemeyer 2005: 215).

Economic transformations and political responses

The post-1945 welfare state has produced an entirely novel *institutional context*. Once welfare programmes, like social housing and health care, were solidly established, they created their own programme-specific constituencies of clients and professional interests. This may have made the welfare state 'less dependent on the political parties, social movements, and labour organizations that expanded social programs in the first place' (Pierson 1996: 147). Therefore, a general weakening of social democratic and Christian democratic parties and the trade union movement—the main political supporters of welfare state expansion—need not translate into a commensurate weakening of social policy. The programme-specific constituencies of clients and professional interests have developed into powerful defenders of the status quo. Still, the dramatic decline of social and Christian democracy as the once most important political parties behind the expansion of social protection in the post-war period will not leave responses to future welfare state challenges unaffected (Manow et al. 2018).

Among these, we also need to count the transition to the service economy (see Wren 2013), which—to the extent that globalization contributes to the relocation of manufacturing from high-wage into low-wage countries—is connected to increased economic internationalization. In Esping-Andersen's (1999) analyses, post-industrialism leads to serious trade-offs, particularly between protecting labour market insiders and creating opportunities for outsiders (Rueda 2005) and, more generally, between employment and equality. Iversen and Wren (1998) even identify a post-industrial *trilemma* between (i) budgetary restraint; (ii) wage equality; and (iii) employment growth, where only two of these three policy goals can be successfully pursued simultaneously.

> Because budgetary restraint precludes any rapid expansion of public sector employment, governments wedded to such discipline must either accept low earnings equality in order to spur growth in private service employment or face low growth in overall employment. Alternatively, governments may pursue earnings equality and high employment, but they can do so only at the expense of budgetary restraint.
>
> Iversen and Wren (1998: 513)

It is also clear that with lower growth rates in services as compared to manufacturing, the times in which high growth allowed for the simultaneity of real wage increases, full employment, and low inflation are long gone, and, consequently, the redistributive leeway of national governments has shrunk substantially. A further intensification of this economic transformation with potentially dramatic consequences for labour market commodifaction and welfare state de-commodification is digitalization, which has made, or is going to make, many services 'tradable', i.e. for the first time exposing them to international wage competition, or simply substituting humans with machines (Baldwin 2016, 2019). Those affected, or those anticipating being affected sometime soon, have started to voice their concerns politically, often in support for a protectionist, neo-nationalist agenda (Kurer and Palier 2019). How to regulate this economic transformation will be one of the major future challenges for the tax-and-spend-capacity of the welfare state. As the recent global recession, and in its aftermath the Euro-crisis has made clear, further increases in public debt will not be a viable option for covering any revenue/expenditure-gaps (Alesina 2019). After seventy years of welfare state growth, the level of public debt in many European countries is again at levels prevalent in the immediate post-war years.

Finally, the refugee crisis has again put the question on the agenda as to what extent generous welfare states are compatible with open borders (cf. Boräng 2018). The economically skeptic 'welfare magnets' thesis (Alesina and Glaeser 2004) is now complemented with increasing evidence not only that preferences for redistribution are low in heterogeneous societies (Mau and Burkhardt 2009; Eger 2010; Alesina et al. 2018), but also that the lower the acceptance of migration, the more generous and universalist the welfare state is. Welfare chauvinism or nativism as the new winning formula of the populist right, i.e. a new combination of a left position on questions of redistribution and a right position on questions of immigration, seems to be particularly attractive to voters in Europe's continental and Scandinavian countries, but effects on social policy reform as of yet seem to be limited (Spies 2018).

The changing welfare state

How best can we conceptualize and operationalize welfare state change, reform, and retrenchment? This 'dependent variable problem' (see Green-Pedersen 2004; Kühner 2007) needs to be clarified before we can answer the question of how much welfare states have actually changed since the 1980s and what the political reverberations were (Armingeon and Giger 2008; Giger and Nelson 2011).

Pierson (2001a) argued that welfare state change should not be measured along a single scale, for example expenditures. This would reduce the problem of welfare state retrenchment and reform to a dichotomy of 'less' versus 'more' and 'intact' versus 'dismantled', which is an unwarranted theoretical simplification. He proposed looking at three dimensions of welfare state change.

- Recommodification: the attempt 'to restrict the alternatives to participation in the labour market by either tightening eligibility or cutting benefits' (Pierson 2001a: 422), i.e. strengthening the whip of the labour market. 'Welfare to work' or 'make work pay' reforms in Scandinavia and continental countries such as Germany have tried to bring the (long-term) unemployed back to work. Persisting 'structural' unemployment is a particular problem in countries in which wages are high and social benefits generous. Part of the measures were to allow for state-subsidized job growth in low productivity services and to tighten eligibility criteria and drawing periods for social benefits to avoid welfare dependency traps.

- Cost containment: the attempt to keep balanced budgets through austerity policies, including deficit reduction and tax moderation (Alesina 2019).

- Recalibration: 'reforms which seek to make contemporary welfare states more consistent with contemporary goals and demands for social provision' (Pierson 2001a: 425), in particular social investment reforms, emphasizing retraining and upskilling (Hemerijk 2017).

Conclusion

Institutional and electoral analyses have come a long way in explaining why welfare states have been capable of resisting (radical) change or reform. However, there are many empirical examples of substantial changes that seem momentous in the light of mainstream institutional theory. So, how and under what conditions is it possible to override the mechanisms of sclerosis and resilience? Some have offered answers by describing specific institutional mechanisms or political conditions under which substantial reform is possible (e.g. Kitschelt et al. 1999; Levy 1999; Bonoli 2000, 2001; Ross 2000; Green-Pedersen 2001; Kitschelt 2001; Swank 2001; see van Kersbergen and Vis 2014), and others suggest that ideational factors, discourse (e.g. framing), and **policy learning** can prevail over electoral and institutional resistance against major policy reform (Cox 2001; Schmidt 2002; see also Green-Pedersen and Haverland 2002; van Kersbergen 2002; Starke 2006). Most recently, researchers have documented how welfare states change in various dimensions, what their causes are, and what effects or consequences follow from such changes (e.g. Palier 2010; Emmenegger et al. 2012; Hemerijck 2013). In the coming years, research will certainly focus on the impact of the financial and economic crises (see e.g. the special issue on the crisis and the welfare state of *Social Policy & Administration* (2011: Vol. 45, Issue 4).

The welfare state will remain interesting for comparative political science, because it continues to have a profound influence on the quality of life of citizens. Welfare state reform is a political process in which power struggles are crucial, not only for understanding why and how reform occurs, but also for grasping what politics is all about: who gets what, when, and how. In this sense, the study of the welfare state will continue to offer us essential and never-ending questions in comparative political science and political economy.

KEY POINTS

- All welfare state regimes face various internal and external challenges and threats, but they have shown a remarkable capacity to survive.

- The argument that globalization forces welfare states to scale down seems compelling, but empirical evidence is not conclusive.

- Domestic politics and institutions still matter in how the pressures on the welfare state are translated and refracted; unemployment is a major threat, while ageing puts the greatest pressure on financial viability.

? QUESTIONS

Knowledge-based

1. Why is the welfare state an important topic for comparative political science?

2. What makes a risk a social risk?

3. Are left-wing parties that promoted the expansion of the welfare state also the main defenders of the welfare state?

4. What non-political processes have stimulated the growth of the welfare state?

5. Which are the three worlds of welfare capitalism?

Critical thinking

1. Why is an exclusive focus on the welfare *state* misleading if one tries to understand how a nation provides work and welfare?

2. Why is it that the more we target benefits at the poor only and the more concerned we are with creating equality via equal public transfers to all, the less likely we are to reduce poverty and equality?

3. Does the welfare state reduce poverty and inequality?

4. Why does globalization not necessarily lead to the downsizing of the welfare state?

5. Why are welfare states so resilient?

≋ FURTHER READING

Baldwin, P. (1990) *The Politics of Social Solidarity: Class Bases of the European Welfare State 1875–1975* (Cambridge: Cambridge University Press). A beautifully written historical analysis of how solidarity was produced 'through the back door' and the major challenger of the social democratic model of welfare state development.

Esping-Andersen, G. (1990) *The Three Worlds of Welfare Capitalism* (Oxford: Polity Press). The classic work that introduced the welfare regime typology and a central work of reference.

Flora, P. and Heidenheimer, A. J. (eds) (1981) *The Development of Welfare States in Europe and America* (Piscataway, NJ: Transaction Books). An early but still highly relevant work in the tradition of modernization theory that is very rich in historical data.

Hacker, J. S. (2002) *The Divided Welfare State: The Battle over Public and Private Social Benefits in the United States* (New York: Cambridge University Press). A highly informative analysis of US social policy.

Huber, E. and Stephens, J. D. (2001) *Development and Crisis of the Welfare State: Parties and Politics in Global Markets* (Chicago, IL: University of Chicago Press). An encompassing book that combines quantitative comparisons and detailed case analyses and gives the best overview of welfare state development currently available.

Korpi, W. (1983) *The Democratic Class Struggle* (London: Routledge & Kegan Paul). The study that firmly founded the social democratic/power resources approach to welfare state development.

O'Connor, J., Orloff, A., and Shaver, S. (1999) *States, Markets, and Families: Gender, Liberalism and Social Policy in Australia, Canada, Great Britain and the United States* (New York: Cambridge University Press). An analysis of the liberal regime from a gender perspective.

Pierson, P. (1994) *Dismantling the Welfare State? Reagan, Thatcher, and the Politics of Retrenchment* (Cambridge: Cambridge University Press). Why was it impossible, even for those who really tried, to dismantle the welfare state? The classic statement on the new politics of the welfare state.

Rehm, Philipp (2016) *Risk Inequality and Welfare States: Social Policy Preferences, Development, and Dynamics* (New York: Cambridge University Press). An important and insightful attempt to analytically base welfare state theory on preferences about insurance against risks.

Scharpf, F. W. and Schmidt, V. A. (eds) (2000) *Welfare and Work in the Open Economy*: (i) *From Vulnerability to Competitiveness*, (ii) *Diverse Responses to Common Challenges* (Oxford: Oxford University Press). An impressive book that collects theoretically sophisticated essays and valuable country studies of how welfare states adjust to their changing economic and social environments.

Van Kersbergen, K. and Vis, B. (2014) *Comparative Welfare State Politics. Development, Opportunities, and Reform* (Cambridge: Cambridge University Press). A comprehensive overview and analysis of the politics of welfare state reform, organized around 'big questions'. Why do we need to reform the welfare state? Why is reform difficult? Will the welfare state survive?

Visit the Online Resources that accompany this book for additional material, including country profiles, comparative data sets, flashcard glossaries, and web directory.

www.oup.com/he/caramani5e

22
The impact of public policies

Jørgen Goul Andersen

Reader's guide

This chapter looks at the effects of public policies. It analyses different policies of regulation of the economy and the welfare system, and their impact on economic performance and social equality. The chapter discusses not only the impact of concrete policies, but also the impact of broader patterns and principles of policies. First, the chapter describes the overriding historical changes in approaches to the economy, from Keynesian ideas of macro-economic steering to more market-oriented economic perspectives, and recent modifications to these. Second, the chapter presents the idea of institutional complementarity as expressed in the typologies of welfare regimes, varieties of capitalism, and flexicurity. Third, the chapter addresses some of the empirical analyses of the effects of welfare policies and the tension between welfare and economic efficiency. Finally, the chapter discusses the feedback mechanisms from policy effects to new demands for policy change.

Introduction

Whereas political decisions (also called policy or output) were traditionally taken as the final result of the political process, comparative political science has increasingly turned attention towards 'outcomes' or the impact of policies (see Chapter 1 'The relevance of comparative politics'). This change in focus has entailed a great interest in the **implementation** of political decisions, on the one hand, and in the relationship between **politics** and the economy—the economic and social effects of public policies—on the other. This chapter deals with the latter question (on implementation see Chapter 20 'Policy-making').

Many of these issues are on the borderline between politics and economics. The so-called 'new political economy' approach seeks to combine insights from both disciplines. To some extent, this also holds for comparative **welfare state** research (see Chapter 21 'The welfare state'). Many of these discussions revolve around the theme of reconciliation between welfare and economic efficiency in the broadest sense. In the so-called 'golden age' of the welfare state, governments applied Keynesian macro-economic steering to secure economic growth, full employment, and social welfare (see Chapter 21 'The welfare state'). However, after the widespread failure to combat unemployment by such measures in the 1970s, economists began searching for alternative diagnoses and solutions. In the fields of welfare, labour market, and tax policies, economists became increasingly concerned with the impact on economic incentives. The 1980s saw a revival of neoclassical thinking, with a focus on distortions of the smooth functioning of the market and the corresponding loss of economic efficiency. When Ronald Reagan was elected president of the US, and Margaret Thatcher became prime minister of the UK, this sort of criticism of the welfare state moved from the margins to the mainstream of politics.

The 'great recession' from 2008 onwards brought an end to the idea of ever further deregulation of financial markets, and for nearly a year, governments all over the world even turned to Keynesian instruments to protect the economy from a worldwide depression. Later followed unorthodox initiatives by the central banks with zero or negative interest rates, and with 'quantitative easing'—roughly speaking, printing money to buy bonds. However, the most important change was perhaps an increased focus on rising inequality and its potentially negative impacts (OECD 2008*b*; 2011*a*; Wilkinson and Pickett 2010; Piketty 2014; Putnam 2015). Even though policies have hardly become more egalitarian, at least until 2019, policy recommendations by such institutions as the OECD (2015*a*; 2018; 2019*a*) and many others have moved away from the neoclassical thinking of the past decades.

These turns in policies set the stage for many subsequent debates about the impact of public policy. What is the *impact of various public policies?* How should it be measured? Is there a trade-off between equality and efficiency, are they compatible, or is equality in fact beneficial for economic growth ? Some researchers have claimed that **globalization** enforces a harmonization towards more market conformity. Others have emphasized the need for policy intervention, including investment in human capital, to prevent and protect against negative social side effects of globalization—and against the new economic nationalism it may provoke.

Addressing such questions, researchers have constructed various conceptualizations of clusters of policies that tend to go together because they are mutually connected. Such configurations of policies that are *complementary* can also be labelled *regimes*. In one branch of research, scholars have formulated conceptions of **welfare regimes**, emphasizing (re) distribution and (initially) taking their point of departure in a 'politics against markets' way of thinking. Others have focused on the positive interplay between the state and different types of market economies, arguing that there are different types of regulation or coordination that work equally well—but differently. Still others have discussed various conceptualizations of flexicurity, i.e. combinations of economic flexibility and social security, in labour market policies. The common headline is *institutional complementarity*—institutions here meaning 'programmatic structures' of policy (Pierson 1994: 171–5; Green-Pedersen, 2002: 24). Institutions in different fields tend to cluster as they go together well.

Policies also impact on politics, and on future policies. In the final section 'Policy feedback and path dependence', we discuss such feedback effects on policy actors, and on the paths of public policy development. In addition, we briefly discuss policy transfer and policy diffusion from one national context (or policy field) to another, and finally we return to the issue of convergence between welfare states amid common exogenous pressures such as ageing and globalization.

KEY POINTS

- The impact of welfare policies on the economy is one of the most important—and one of the most controversial—issues in modern social science.
- Policies/institutions tend to cluster in characteristic configurations because they are complementary. This means that they can be viewed as policy regimes.
- Political decisions also have political effects. Past decisions are a major determinant of future decisions, sometimes also extending across policy areas or across countries.

Economic paradigms and approaches to welfare

The long-term expansion of the public sector after 1945, in particular social protection and services, took place in a climate of rapid economic growth. After the protectionist policies during the crisis of the 1930s which dramatically lowered international trade and economic growth, in 1944 the Western capitalist countries decided on the Bretton Woods system, which linked the American dollar to gold at a fixed price, and other currencies to the dollar at (in principle) fixed exchange rates.

This system, alongside a gradual lowering of tariffs, contributed to long-term uninterrupted economic growth, almost full employment, and relatively stable prices. For the twelve European countries for which statistics are available for the entire period, average annual growth in GDP between 1950 and 1973 was 4.6 per cent, compared with 1.6 per cent for 1890–1913 and 1.4 per cent for 1913–50. In the period 1973–92, growth rates slowed down—but only to 2.0 per cent (Table 22.1).

However, the financial crisis of 2008/09 also brought increasing attention to the 'emerging economies'—including the so-called BRIC-countries (Brazil, Russia, India, and China). China maintained very high growth rates, and since 2014—after correction for purchasing power—China has been the world's largest economy, followed by the US and India (http://data.worldbank.org/data-catalog/GDP-PPP-based-table). Until the 1970s, increasing public and social expenditure (see Table 22.2) was generally regarded as a 'natural' concomitant of industrialization and modernization, including population ageing (Wilensky 1975: 47). Political scientists, taking a more conflictual and less functionalist view, also emphasized the political **mobilization** of the lower social classes and the strength of socialist parties (Korpi 1983)—the 'power resources explanation'. Cameron (1978) described this as a sufficient but not necessary condition; economic openness and corporatist coordination were decisive. However, there was strong optimism about politics prevailing over markets

(Ringen 2006). Few questioned the impacts on welfare and employment, and few were concerned about negative side effects.

This changed after the breakdown of the Bretton Woods system in 1971, when the US suspended the convertibility of dollars to gold (which eventually made currencies free-floating), and after the first oil crisis in 1973–74 which resulted in mass unemployment in most countries. In the first place, the largely unsuccessful attempts to combat unemployment by traditional

Table 22.1 Economic growth in Europe (1890–1992)

Periods	Average annual growth in real GDP		
	Total	Per capita	Per person-hour
1890–1913	1.6	1.7	1.6
1913–1950	1.4	1.0	1.9
1950–1973	4.6	3.8	4.7
1973–1992	2.0	1.7	2.7[a]
1890–1992	2.5	1.9	2.6[a]

Notes: Countries: Germany, France, Italy, Austria, Belgium, Netherlands, Switzerland, UK, Sweden, Finland, Denmark, and Norway. For 1992–2007, real annual growth rate for the EU-15 was 2.3 per cent (as against 3.2 per cent in the US); per capita growth rate in the EU-15 was 1.9 per cent (as against 2.1 per cent in the US). It was mainly low growth in Germany and Italy that accounted for the lower per capita growth rate in EU-15 (http://stats.oecd.org). For the recession period 2008–2014 (OECD 2015b and http://stats.oecd.org) the US revealed a cumulative growth of 7.3 per cent, against –0.8 per cent for the Eurozone; in this period, however, economic growth in Germany stayed close to the US (5.3 per cent).

[a]Last year for the calculation of GDP per person-hour is 1987.
Source: Maddison (1991), quoted in Crafts and Toniolo (1996: 2).

Table 22.2 Median incomes grew more slowly than top incomes

	Bottom 10%	Bottom 20–40%	Median	Top 10%
2014–2016	3.4	2.6	2.9	4.0
2012–2014	2.7	1.9	1.9	3.3
2010–2012	−3.2	−1.8	−1.7	0.9
2008–2010	−3.6	−1.2	−0.7	−2.0
2008–2016	−1.0	1.5	2.3	6.3

Source: OECD (2019a) *Under Pressure. The Squeezed Middle Class* (Paris: OECD), 21.

Keynesian policies (stimulation of aggregate demand) and the anomaly of stagflation (stagnation combined with inflation)[1] paved the way for theories of rational expectations (Lucas 1972, 1973). These theories implied that economic actors would anticipate the inflationary effects of fiscal and monetary policies and adjust their behaviour accordingly. Thus, the negative effects of stimulating demand would, so to speak, come before the positive ones.

Further, economists began to question the assumption of the economic neutrality of redistribution (Sandmo 1991). Previously, economic redistribution via taxes and cash transfers to households had been described in textbooks as a matter of transferring a bucket of water from one person to another. This was challenged by Okun (1975), who argued that the 'bucket is leaking', i.e. there was an inevitable loss in economic efficiency associated with this **redistribution**, as it distorted the market mechanisms.

This was the beginning of a paradigmatic change in economic theory, away from macro-economic steering and towards a more 'neoclassical' focus on the micro-level. Economists and governments came to focus on the supply side of the economy, not least on the economic incentives that could stimulate labour supply and growth. Unemployment in Europe was increasingly seen as 'structural' or 'natural' unemployment, i.e. as unemployment that would *not* disappear even if demand for labour power increased. Only structural changes towards more market conformity in social policies, tax policies, labour market regulation, and wage formation could help.

The *OECD Jobs Study* report (OECD 1994) summarized the new approaches and underlined the constraints of globalization which would make it difficult for governments to avoid the necessary labour market reforms. However, this was disputed. Rather than seeing this policy change as an instance of social learning, Korpi (2002) maintained that it was more a matter of political choice, reflecting changing power balances between capital and labour.

At any rate, the policy impacts of the welfare state more frequently came to be seen as adverse: unintentionally, social protection could aggravate the very problems which it was supposed to solve. Owing to the phenomenon called 'hysteresis' (Blanchard and Summers 1986)—loss of skills during long-term unemployment—persistent unemployment could generate large-scale *unemployability* which, in turn, according to neoliberal scholars, might lead to the development of an underclass characterized by a dependency culture (Murray 1984). Even researchers known as proponents of the welfare state could sometimes question whether the price of equality might

sometimes be less wealth *plus* less equality if some groups were chronically marginalized from the labour market (Esping-Andersen 1996, 2002).

This diagnosis—or narrative—could be convincingly illustrated by the different employment/unemployment records of the EU and the US. In the 1960s and 1970s, the US seemed to suffer from a 'structural' unemployment problem which Europeans used to explain by poverty and the underdeveloped American welfare state (see Figure 22.1).

However, from the 1980s onwards it was the other way around: unemployment in Europe was chronically higher than in the US. Employment rates looked even worse, revealing a steady increase in the US, but equally steady decline in Europe. Europe had tried to combat unemployment by early retirement and other arrangements aimed at reducing labour supply, but the long-term dynamic effect seemed to be fewer jobs, rather than lower unemployment. Declining employment rates only aggravated the future ageing crisis, which for purely demographic reasons was also more threatening in Europe because of lower fertility rates (see Comparative tables 4 and 14 in Appendix 2 at the end of this volume).

In short, during the 1980s and 1990s the US was often praised for market conformity, whereas Europe was pictured as a victim of self-inflicted stagnation. The European welfare states were considered less sustainable (OECD 1994; Nickell 1997; Jackman 1998), or even described as 'virtual "time bombs" waiting to explode' (Ljungkvist and Sargent 1998: 546). The price for equality and security was persistent unemployment and long-term unsustainability of the welfare state. Under intensified global competition, it was argued, the effects were increasingly adverse.

However, even though wage differentials increased (Förster and d'Ercole 2005; OECD 2008b) and incentives were strengthened, European countries were reluctant to lower minimum wages or give up substantial elements of social protection. As can be seen from Table 22.2, the growth of social expenditure as a percentage of GDP slowed down, but there were few examples of genuine cuts in aggregated budgets. At the 2000 Lisbon summit, the European Union (EU) confirmed its devotion to pursuing a different employment strategy with more emphasis on education and training, (state-supported) innovation, and social cohesion.

The question of reconciliation between regulation, welfare, and equality on the one hand, and employment or economic growth on the other, has been a core theme of discussion in comparative research on the impact of public policies. However, modern economics has been accused of putting too much emphasis on theoretical arguments and modelling, and too little on

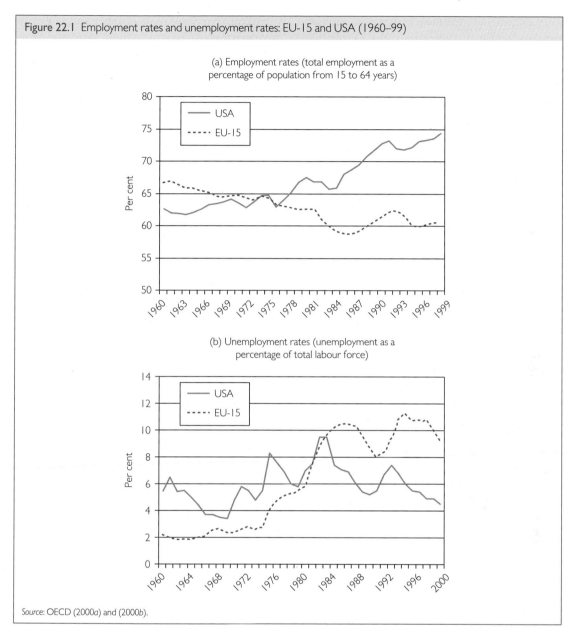

Figure 22.1 Employment rates and unemployment rates: EU-15 and USA (1960–99)

(a) Employment rates (total employment as a percentage of population from 15 to 64 years)

(b) Unemployment rates (unemployment as a percentage of total labour force)

Source: OECD (2000*a*) and (2000*b*).

empirical evidence. As argued by Lindert against key findings of neoclassical economics:

such findings … are not really findings. Contrary to the words offered … none of these authors actually 'found' or 'showed' their results. Rather, they *chose to imagine* the results … the crucial ingredient was a theoretical model laden with assumptions. It is educated, intelligent, plausible fiction—but fiction nonetheless.

Lindert (2004: 82)

It would be an exaggeration to claim that neoclassical ideas are withering away. Rather, they have been institutionalized in governments' economic models

that emphasize labour supply effects of changing incentives—but sometimes fail to incorporate fully the pay-offs from investment in education. Both effects are difficult to calculate, and even in policy-related analyses, assumptions with limited empirical evidence can play a crucial role. Besides, there is not really a new economic paradigm that is able to compete. However, there has been an accumulation of scepticism and of concern for negative side effects.

Not least, institutions like the International Monetary Fund (IMF), the World Bank, and in particular the Organisation for Economic Co-operation and Development (OECD) have been increasingly concerned with the impact of increasing inequality—not only the social and political impact (which is mostly outside the main focus of the OECD and IMF), but also the counterproductive *economic* impact.

Whereas the 1990s witnessed a long series of OECD publications on labour market problems and publications with the headline *Make Work Pay*, some of the most significant analyses since 2008 have been concerned with inequality. In the publication *Growing Unequal* (OECD 2008b), there was a thorough identification of the persistent trend towards increasing inequality in the rich countries over three decades. The subsequent publication *Divided We Stand* (OECD 2011a) identified some of the main mechanisms contributing to increasing inequality. *In it Together. Why Less Inequality Benefits All* (OECD 2015a) contained more explicit policy recommendations. Besides, it extended the perspective to a broader range of countries outside the OECD, not least the so-called emerging economies. Figure 22.2 presents the development in real household incomes for seventeen OECD countries since 1985. Not only the bottom 10 per cent is lagging behind; less dramatically, this also holds for the bottom 40 per cent. According to OECD (2011a; 2015a; 2018), adverse effects of inequality include, not least, insufficient investments in skills and education. From this perspective, the main concern is not the enormous accumulation of income and wealth among the most rich 1, 5, or 10 per cent, and not even the decline among the bottom 10 per cent, but rather the deteriorating capacity of the bottom 40 per cent

to improve their position and that of their children in the future (OECD 2015a: 22; 2018; 2019a). Equality of opportunity is a shared goal, but is difficult to ensure unless there is a quite substantial equality in outcomes (OECD 2015a: 27; Putnam 2015).

Some of the trends towards increasing inequality have their origin in technological and economic forces. Still, they could be considered an impact of governments (deliberately?) failing to act upon them—equivalent to *non-decisions* leading to so-called *drift* of welfare (Hacker 2004; Streeck and Thelen 2005). However, the trends also reflect adverse side effects of growth-promoting policies seeking to strengthen work incentives, for example through lower income taxes, less income tax progression, and lower compensation for the non-employed. In the 1990s and the 2000s, the dominant philosophy was that such growth-enhancing policies would 'lift all boats', but this has increasingly been questioned (e.g. Causa et al. 2014).

The increasing academic interest in the impact of inequality and of policies that promote inequality goes well beyond the impact on the economy, of course. In the best-selling book *The Spirit Level. Why Equality is Better for Everyone* Wilkinson and Pickett (2010) sought to demonstrate the negative impact of inequality on nearly any conceivable outcome in terms of well-being in the broadest sense. In *Our Kids. The American Dream Threatened*, Putnam (2015) pointed out the negative consequences for social trust and social cohesion.

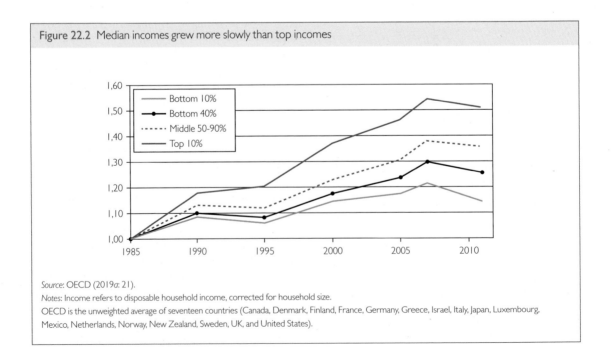

Figure 22.2 Median incomes grew more slowly than top incomes

Source: OECD (2019a: 21).

Notes: Income refers to disposable household income, corrected for household size.

OECD is the unweighted average of seventeen countries (Canada, Denmark, Finland, France, Germany, Greece, Israel, Italy, Japan, Luxembourg, Mexico, Netherlands, Norway, New Zealand, Sweden, UK, and United States).

Still others have pointed out the impact in terms of political alienation and populist reactions among those who feel insecure (Wroe 2016; Rodrik 2017).

Others have focused on the accumulation of wealth in the top. Piketty's (2014) *Capital in the Twenty-First Century* argued that with some exceptions (e.g. the Nordic welfare states), many countries were heading towards an accumulation of wealth among the few, possibly similar to the situation before the twentieth century. As regards the US, it has been calculated that 94 per cent of society's aggregate improvement in real income 1980–2008 was appropriated by the upper 10 per cent—as compared to 26 per cent in Denmark (Danish Economic Council 2011: 222). Hacker and Pierson (2010) have pointed out that in the US, the driving force is not globalization or technological change, but the *political power* that follows from the accumulation of wealth among the few. Summers (2014) has argued that, alongside ageing and other underlying long-term changes, increasing inequality may contribute to a 'secular stagnation' (further discussed, e.g., in Teulings and Baldwin 2015).

Needless to say, there is not a new consensus around this scepticism. For instance, against Piketty and others it is argued that it may be the case that the economic elite is not composed of the same people over time. Many of the richest people in the world did not inherit their wealth, but rather are successful entrepreneurs. Still, there is an accumulation of scepticism, at least among policy experts, against the almost hegemonic belief in the market in the 1990s and 2000s, and in the belief that rising top incomes would 'trickle down' and in the end 'lift all boats'.

KEY POINTS

- The failure of Keynesian policies to combat unemployment after 1973 paved the way for new economic perspectives focusing on the negative economic side effects of welfare/tax policies.

- European governments have been reluctant to reduce social expenditures; but they have managed to stop the growth in expenditures relative to the growth in GDP.

- Growing inequality over three decades has increased the attention to negative side effects of the post-Keynesian growth strategies.

- This concerns both the accumulation of income and wealth among the rich, the squeezed (lower) middle class, and the threat of poverty at the bottom. This is further spurred by disappointingly low growth rates, suggesting that the post-Keynesian economic growth strategies may even have counterproductive effects.

Institutional complementarity: welfare regimes, varieties of capitalism, and flexicurity

More than economists, political scientists often address analyses of the impact of policies or institutions from a 'regime' perspective. That is, they take their point of departure in ideal types of welfare states or political economies that build on a combination of variables that are seen as interdependent or complementary. The two best known are the concepts of **welfare regimes** (Esping-Andersen 1990, 1999) and **varieties of capitalism** (Hall and Soskice 2001b). In addition, there is a variety of concepts at a somewhat lower level of abstraction, among which the notion of **flexicurity** has been much debated. As far as causes are concerned, welfare regime theory has traditionally emphasized politics (interest conflicts), whereas varieties of capitalism theory is more 'functionalist' (with emphasis on what is beneficial for the economy). However, it is impact rather than causes that is our main concern here.

The concept of welfare regimes

The concept of welfare regimes builds on the observations that (i) welfare state characteristics tend to cluster; and (ii) there is a strong relationship between *labour markets, the family,* and *the welfare state.*[2] 'Welfare regimes' refers to the interaction, or the unison, between these three elements (Esping-Andersen 1999: 4). What differs between welfare states is not just the level of expenditure (Table 22.2), but even more the division of tasks and the ways entitlements and expenditures are structured. As in ' Varieties of capitalism' below, the propensity of institutional traits to cluster or reinforce each other because they work together well can be described as *institutional complementarities*.

Inspired by Titmuss (1974), Esping-Andersen (1990) distinguished between three ideal types of welfare regimes: Conservative, Liberal, and Social Democratic (described in detail in Chapter 21 'The welfare state').

According to the 'power resources model', the welfare model hinges on the political mobilization of the working class and its ability to forge alliances with the middle classes (Korpi 1983; Esping-Andersen 1990). However, scholars have increasingly objected to the idea of 'politics against markets' (Esping-Andersen 1985b). Instead, they have emphasized the possibilities of a positive interplay between state and market, for example through social investments (Morel et al. 2012) and through full incorporation of women on the labour market. As regards the family aspect, OECD and welfare researchers converge on the view that the 'Conservative' welfare regime is outdated. In Europe, there has been a substantial adaptation, if not transformation, of most 'Conservative' welfare states. However, as reflected in low fertility rates, the challenges are far from solved, and East Asian welfare states—probably including China—are even more threatened by the reliance on the family as welfare providers.

Varieties of capitalism

Varieties of capitalism theory imply that large welfare states, as well as being redistributive, can also have highly beneficial economic impacts. According to this theory, highly regulated economies with large welfare states develop competitive advantages of their own, which can make for equal or even superior economic performance (Hall and Soskice 2001b). One attraction of this approach is that it provides explicit theoretical arguments for this claim, which seems to be in accordance with real-world observations.

Rather than the 'decommodification' underlined in welfare regime theory (see Chapter 21 'The welfare state'), the point of departure for varieties of capitalism theory is companies' interests in using the market as the main instance of coordination, vis-à-vis using other forms of coordination (Hall and Soskice 2001b). These mechanisms tend to be self-reinforcing and create a permanent divide between liberal market economies (LMEs) and coordinated market economies (CMEs). This mutually reinforcing relationship between institutions that work together well is called *institutional complementarity*.

The *small state theory* proposed by Katzenstein (1985) argues that small, open economies, being vulnerable to international competition, are in extra need of coordination. Such states tend to develop consensual corporatist structures, which serve to stabilize the economy and enhance competitiveness. This argument is equivalent to the varieties of capitalism theory, only it spells out why some countries have been particularly inclined to develop those kinds of structure.

Trying to bridge the gap between varieties of capitalism and welfare regime theory, Iversen (2005) underlined the common insurance interests of workers and employers in different types of economies. According to this theory, a key variable is the nature of skills needed in production. Where companies demand specialized skills that are not transferable between branches, they are highly dependent on workers' willingness to invest in these skills. In turn,

the willingness among workers to do so depends on insurance against the risk of losing jobs. Therefore, employers are as dependent on protection as workers. In countries where companies demand general skills, employers are not interested in such protection, but prefer simple market regulation. Even workers may have less interest in social protection in this instance. In short, the level and composition of human capital is seen as a core determinant of welfare state characteristics (Iversen 2005: 13; Estevez-Abe et al. 2001). However, as a side effect, insurance almost inevitably involves redistribution.

Accordingly, theorists in this tradition have criticized power resources theories for their notion of 'politics against markets'. Social protection, according to Iversen (2005: 8), 'can improve the operation of markets as well as undermine them'. Some researchers claim that, historically, employers have been just as supportive of social protection as workers (Baldwin 1990; Swenson 2002).

Needless to say, protagonists of the power resources theory are critical. Korpi (2006) claims that historical accounts are flawed and points out that, even if the arguments were correct, they concern a much narrower range than the entire welfare state.

However, Korpi is far less critical of the arguments about *impact*. At this point, the varieties of capitalism theory has quite a lot to add, arguing that institutional differences constitute *comparative institutional advantages* (Hall and Soskice 2001a: 36–44). LMEs, where skills tend to be general, develop competitive advantages in 'radical innovation'. In contrast, CMEs, with emphasis on specific skills, including, not least, skilled work (like the German *Facharbeitertradition*), find themselves being particularly competitive in 'specialized quality production'—in what the Volkswagen car company has sometimes marketed as *Bessermachen*.

This theory also provides an explanation of why LMEs and CMEs have reacted differently to globalization—in fact, key indicators such as government outlays as a proportion of GDP reveal little convergence except for EU countries that are catching up (Table 22.3). Rather, data show an increasing *difference* between the US and Europe from the 1970s until the outbreak of the 2008 economic crisis. Apparently, LMEs had found one way of adapting to globalization, and CMEs another (Swank 2002).

Welfare regime theory could provide similar arguments, but is less developed at this point. However, the varieties of capitalism theory is silent on the relationship between family structure, the state, and the labour market. The approach also differs from the welfare regime approach by operating with only two worlds of capitalism—modelled on Germany and the

US, respectively—with Southern Europe typically described as a 'mixed' type. The conceptual scheme does not leave room for distinguishing between universal and corporatist/conservative welfare institutions.

Flexicurity

Theories of flexicurity are narrower in scope, but constitute another example of institutional complementarity. The concept of flexicurity simply refers to the combination of flexibility and security (Bredgaard et al. 2005). It was developed as political discourse after the 1995 Dutch labour market reform, as a kind of post hoc rationalization. In academic theory, it was introduced by Wilthagen (1998) and continued by Auer (2000) and Madsen (2002), for example.

Theories of flexicurity contain no grand theory of the origin of various arrangements—but they add the observation that welfare and labour market institutions are seldom deliberately designed. For example, until the concept of flexicurity emerged, few experts in Denmark had noticed the country's particular institutional complementarity of flexibility and security.

Rather, the country was considered a 'laggard' in the development from 'numerical' to 'functional' flexibility (Piore and Sabel 1984; Porter 1990).

Theories of flexicurity emphasize 'politics for markets' but may complement the varieties of capitalism approach by introducing new divisions among the CMEs. The theories have been formulated in both a narrow and a much broader version. The narrow concept of flexicurity refers to a specific combination of (i) liberal employment protection legislation ('flexibility'); (ii) generous employment protection, such as high compensation levels or long duration ('security'); and (iii) active labour market policies aimed at bringing people back to work (by solving matching problems between supply and demand of qualifications). This is sometimes described as a 'golden triangle'. Key countries are Denmark, and to some extent the Netherlands (Auer 2000; Madsen 2002). The notion of flexicurity acknowledges the economic need for flexibility. When employers are free to fire, they are less reluctant to hire. And when workers can rely on solid protection, they are more inclined to change jobs—and more willing to accept restructuring and change.

Table 22.3 Total outlays of general government as a percentage of GDP

	1960	1970	1980	1990	1995	2000	2005	2010	2015	2017
Germany	32.4[*]	38.6[*]	46.5[**]	46.2[***]	54.6x	44.7	46.3	47.4	43.8	43,9
Austria	36.3	39.6	49.5	51.2	55.9	50.9	51.2	52.9	51.1	49,1
France	34.6[*]	38.5[*]	46.4	50.1	54.8	51.6	53.4	56.9	56.8	56,4
Belgium	34.5[*]	43.3	56.9	52.6	52.4	49.0	51.6	53.3	53.7	52,1
Netherlands	33.7[*]	41.7	53.1	51.8	53.7	42.2	42.3	47.9	44.6	42,5
Sweden	32.9	41.8	57.7	56.5	63,5[a]	53.3	52.4	50.9	49.8	49,4
Finland	27.9	31.7	40.2	47.9	61.1[a]	48.0	49.3	54.8	57,0	54,2
Denmark	24.8[*]	42.6[****]	52.5	54.3	58.5	52.7	51.2	56.7	54.5	51,2
Norway	29.9[*]	41.0[*]	45.2	52.6	50.3	42.0	42.1	44.9	48.8	49,9
Italy	28.3	32.1	40.1	52.0	51.7	46.5	47.1	49.9	50.3	48,9
Greece	17.4[*]	22.4[*]	31.0[**]	47.5[**]	46.1	46.3	45.5	52.3	53.6	47,5
Spain	..	23.9	34.2	43.0	44.3	39.2	38.3	45.6	43.7	41,0
Portugal	17.0[*]	21.6[*]	33.1	39.4	42.6	42.6	46.7	51.8	48.2	45,7
Czech Republic	..	..	..	..	53.0[a]	40.9	42.3	43.6	41.7	38,9
Poland	..	..	..	..	48.8	42.2	44.4	45.8	41.7	41,2

(continued)

Table 22.3 Total outlays of general government as a percentage of GDP (continued)

	1960	1970	1980	1990	1995	2000	2005	2010	2015	2017
Switzerland	17.2*	21.3*	..	29.1	34.0	33.9	33.8	33.0	34.0	34,1
United Kingdom	32.2*	37.2	40.4	36.0	38.6	35.4	41.1	47.6	42.2	40,9
Ireland	28.0*	39.6*	47.3**	42.0	40.8	30.9	33.4	65.1[a]	29.0	26,3
Australia	21.2*	26.3*	32.2**	33.7	35.8	35.2	34.1	36.4	35.7	35,7
New Zealand	..	..	..	47.2	37.4	34.3	34.5	44.3	37.3	37,0
Canada	28.6*	36.0	40.7	48.1	47.7	40.6	38.5	43.1	40.0	40,3
United States	30.1	34.4	35.7	38.0	38.0	34.5	37.1	43.4	38.1	38,1
Japan	21.0	21.9	32.9	30.8	34.9	37.5	35.1	39.3	38.9	38,3

Source: OECD (2019d) 'OECD Economic Outlook No. 105 (May 2019)' (Total Disbursements of General Government)

* From OECD (2000a) *OECD Historical Statistics 1999* (1960 and 1970) (Paris: OECD) (Total Outlays of General Government. Old SNA).

** From OECD (2002) *OECD Economic Outlook No. 71. June 2002* (Paris: OECD)(Total Disbursements of General Government, old SNA).

*** 1991.

**** 1971.

[a] Outliers, e.g. because of extraordinary crisis, bailout of banks.

However, there is also a broader concept of flexicurity which is in the spirit of the varieties of capitalism approach by identifying varieties of flexicurity (e.g. numerical vs functional). Wilthagen et al. (2003) distinguish between four types of flexibility:

- external numerical flexibility (as described in the previous paragraph);
- internal numerical flexibility (working time, overtime, etc.);
- functional flexibility (workers move between tasks in the organization);
- wage flexibility (wage dispersion according to productivity).

They also add different aspects of security:

- job security (as described in the previous paragraph);
- employment security;
- income security (as described in the previous paragraph);
- combination security (combination of work, family, etc.).

According to this concept, there is a 4 × 4 matrix of various flexicurity arrangements, and countries which appear 'inflexible' on some combinations may be flexible on others. Whereas Denmark and,

to a lesser extent, the Netherlands have tended to substitute job security with employment security and income security, other countries have maintained job security but sought to enhance functional flexibility and / or internal numerical flexibility. As it recognizes the existence of some kind of flexicurity in most European countries and makes no a priori assumptions that any model is superior, Wilthagen's concept of flexicurity is complementary to the varieties of capitalism theory.

KEY POINTS

- Welfare regimes refer to particular combinations of the welfare state, the family, and the labour market.
- Varieties of capitalism refers to different methods of coordination in the economy—via the market, or via negotiations and regulation. A key variable is the types of skill (general vs specific) and, accordingly, the need for protection in order to secure willingness to invest in those skills.
- Welfare regime theory emphasizes conflict, whereas varieties of capitalism is more functionalist and emphasizes common interests between employers and workers and beneficial impacts on the economy.
- Flexicurity in the narrow sense refers to a particular hybrid between liberal and coordinated market economies.

Tensions between welfare and economic efficiency

Needless to say, studying the impact of public policies may involve a wide array of policy fields. When it comes to welfare policies, the most obvious question is how they impact on outcomes in terms of welfare and well-being. However, as mentioned, much research about the impact of policy—including the theories referred to in the preceding section, 'Institutional complementarity: welfare regimes, varieties of capitalism, and flexicurity'—is concerned with what can in broad terms be described as the tension between equality/welfare and economic growth/employment/efficiency. What is the impact of public welfare policies (taxation, cash benefit systems, and public services) and labour market policies/institutions on various aspects of economic performance? I first describe some findings from the literature, comparing welfare regimes or varieties of capitalism. Next, I address the issues of welfare/tax expenditure, equality, and economic growth. Finally, I discuss the impact of labour market policies.

Comparing social and economic impact of regimes

In an exploratory study that was consistent with a subsequent more detailed literature, Goodin et al. (1999) compared the social and economic accomplishments of three welfare states (US, Germany, and the Netherlands), representing three welfare regimes (liberal, conservative, and social democratic, respectively).[3] As regards equality and reduction of poverty, the authors found significant differences, confirming the predicted rank order, with the social democratic regime being the most redistributive and the liberal the least. Moreover, the US welfare state, despite being targeted at the poor, is extremely inefficient in redistributing income and alleviating poverty (Goodin et al. 1999: 152–86; see also Korpi and Palme 1998; Kenworthy 2004: 102–5; and Box: The distributional impact of welfare regimes, in the Online Resources). This corresponds to OECD studies showing an almost linear association between non-health social spending (towards working-age population) and poverty rates (Förster and d'Ercole 2005: 29).

Goodin et al. (1999) also found that the social democratic regime had the highest score on social integration, stability in life, and securing autonomy in life, whereas the liberal model failed in most of these respects as well. The economic performance of the liberal model was better as regards labour market integration (see also the section below on 'Impact

of labour market policies and institutions'), but they found little difference as regards economic growth and prosperity, confirming the classical statement that 'incentives are not behaviours' (Marmor et al. 1990: 219).

In their book about European unemployment regimes, Gallie and Paugam (2000a) examined the impact of welfare policies on the social conditions of the unemployed. The regime clustering was distinguished from Esping-Andersen's (1990) by singling out the 'sub-protective' Southern European model from the 'ordinary' conservative model (Gallie and Paugam 2000b: 17). Almost regardless of indicator—poverty, financial hardship, subjective well-being—they found the best conditions for the unemployed in social democratic regimes, followed by the conservative regimes. However, in several respects the long-term unemployed were worse off in the 'sub-protective' regimes than in the liberal ones. Similar country differences are found in a number of fields (e.g. Ferragina et al. 2015). Esping-Andersen (2015) demonstrates marked country differences in inter-generational mobility, but mainly for the generations growing up under the fully fledged Nordic welfare state—perhaps even more attributable to public child care than to school reform and low child poverty. Even for outcomes as 'remote' as obesity, welfare regimes seem to play a significant role (Offer et al, 2010).

Whereas the findings regarding the social impact of welfare regimes are robust, the reported impacts on economic performance are more sensitive to the delineation of time periods, data sources, and methods. This is also the case when we come to the distinction between LMEs and CMEs in the varieties of capitalism literature (Hall and Soskice 2001b). The prediction that CMEs are not economically inferior is largely confirmed by empirical analyses, for example, in Pontusson's (2005) study of 'Social Europe' versus 'Liberal America'. On average, the two regime types performed equally well as regards GDP growth rates or unemployment (Pontusson 2005: 5–9), but the LMEs were the most successful in reducing unemployment in the 1990s (Pontusson 2005: 71, 81–2). During the great recession since 2008/09, intra-regime differences have been significant because of variations in credit and housing bubbles and crisis strategies. The 'mixed' systems in Southern Europe have been especially negatively affected, not least because of the Euro crisis and the austerity strategy adopted by the EU (Blyth 2013a: 51–93; Hall 2014).

Both the welfare regime and the varieties of capitalism approach are basically modelled on Western Europe and the US. Countries outside the OECD, notably emerging economies like China, are difficult to fit into either (Peck and Zhang 2013). East Asian countries tend to share important characteristics with the conservative welfare model as regards family structures. The concept of the 'developmental (welfare) state' has been introduced to describe a model where the state plays a strategic role in economic development, and social policy is used mainly as an instrument of growth (Johnson 1999; Gough 2001). But conceptualizations remain somewhat biased to the 'old' world, and even the Eastern European OECD members diverge heavily on key measures (e.g. Hudson and Kühner 2012; Onaran and Boesch 2014).

A common challenge for emerging economies is to avoid the so-called 'middle income trap' (World Bank 2010; Griffith 2011). This is also a key question regarding China's future development after the impressive growth since the 1980s (Lewin et al. 2016). Korea managed to take the next leap, as Japan had done earlier. But the challenges are huge, for instance in terms of infrastructure, innovation capacity, governance structure, social security and—not least—raising the general level of education.

Tax/welfare system, equality, and economic efficiency

To what extent do taxes and transfers harm economic efficiency, as claimed by Okun (1975) and by many others since then? Theoretically, there are several arguments that welfare spending could have beneficial effects on economic performance. Everybody seems to agree that welfare expenditure has positive effects up to a certain limit, and that some welfare expenditure, for instance in child care and education, should be seen as social investment in human capital (Morel et al. 2012). Social security also helps to avoid child poverty and the transmission of poverty from one generation to the next. Further, unemployment insurance may boost 'good jobs' and make workers more willing to take risks (Andersen et al. 2007). Korpi (1985) protested against Okun's metaphor of a leaking bucket and stated that, rather, it should be seen as an irrigation system. At any rate, effects must be assessed empirically. I now address a sample of empirical studies.

Among the classic studies is Peter Lindert's two-volume book *Growing Public* (Lindert 2004), which treats the economic impact of welfare state growth over more than a century, and the book by Pontusson (2005) referred to in the previous section, 'Comparing social and economic impact of regimes'. An earlier overview of findings and arguments is provided in *The Economic Consequences of Rolling back the Welfare State* (Atkinson 1999). In *Egalitarian Capitalism*, Kenworthy

(2004) addressed the issue of compatibility of equality and economic efficiency.

As can be seen from the overview in Table 22.2, there is a large variation in social expenditure between countries. However, there are many pitfalls in such statistics, as benefits are paid as taxable incomes in some countries, but as net benefits in others. When these differences are corrected (Adema and Ladaique 2005, 2009; Adema et al. 2011, 2015) the ranking looks somewhat different. Further, if we include private welfare expenditure, the ranking changes completely (see Table 22.4). In particular, the US moves from the low-spending to the high-spending countries. Apparently, the demand for welfare is universal, but it is simply more privately financed in the US than in Europe. However, the impact on distribution is very different. In private insurance, people pay the same amount per head, or even according to risk (which is typically highest among the poor). Taxes, in contrast, are much higher on high incomes than on low incomes, and this holds even for regressive taxes such as taxes on consumption.

By avoiding disincentives and distortions of high taxes, countries with high private financing of welfare should theoretically be more efficient. However, no significant correlations are found between public expenditures on the one hand and level or growth of GDP on the other (see Table 22.5). In their survey of empirical findings, Atkinson (1999: 32–3) and Lindert (2004b: 86–8) conclude that most studies have found no significant associations. In his own test, Lindert (2004, vol.2: 172–93) found no significant associations either. As regards taxation, there has built a consensus among economists that tax *structure* matters for growth (consumption taxes and other regressive taxes being least harmful), whereas there is much less agreement regarding tax *levels* (Martin and Prasad 2014: 337)—at least when we speak of the advanced economies. For emerging economies, taxation may be an important element of state building.

The findings of Lindert and others cover the period until around 2000, and one may ask whether they are contradicted by the fact that US growth rates were significantly higher than those in Europe, at least from 1992 to 2005 (3.2 per cent, compared with 2.1 per cent). However, when population growth is discounted, the difference in per capita growth was small: 2.1 per cent compared with 1.7 per cent (Table 22.1). Moreover, as noted by Pontusson (2005), the US was more over-consuming than Europe in this period. Further, comparisons on productivity are sensitive to measurement. Pontusson (2005) has argued that measures should be discounted by the long working hours in the US; in contrast, Europeans have enjoyed reduction of weekly working hours as well as longer holidays. As can be seen from Table 22.1, measuring GDP per working hour also gives a more optimistic picture of economic growth after 1973 more generally. There are few signs in these data that pressures from globalization force welfare regimes to converge. It remains that the US has resumed growth much more convincingly than Europe after the great recession, but this is probably better explained by different economic strategies. The EU adopted strict austerity strategies, in part because the Euro crisis made it necessary to convince financial markets that Europe would act in a 'responsible' way that was anything but growth-promoting.

Why is the bumblebee flying? In line with findings regarding public expenditure, Kenworthy (2004) demonstrated that there is no obvious tension between equality and economic performance. Adjusting for catch-up effects, Kenworthy actually found the highest growth rate in the period 1980–2000 in countries with low inequality. The same association is found in comparisons between US states (Kenworthy 2004: 56). For extended comparisons of the impact of inequality across nations and across US states, see Wilkinson and Pickett (2010). As indicated above in the section 'Varieties of capitalism', one of the main efficiency gains of generous welfare is willingness and ability to invest in education among the less affluent (Headey and Muffels 2008). OECD (2015a, 2018) also highlights the impact of inequality on social mobility and efforts to promote labour market participation of women. OECD (2015a) recommends that considering growth-promoting reforms, potential negative economic side effects of inequality should be taken more into account.

Impact of labour market policies and institutions

The reinterpretation of unemployment was a core issue in the paradigmatic change from Keynesianism to what has been called supply-side economics. However, it should be added that many economists emphasize that their preoccupation with disincentives and distortions does not imply that all Keynesian insights are scrapped. It can be an add-on policy rather than a replacement (Nickell et al. 2004). In Europe, many mainstream economists have tended to be Keynesian in the short run, but focus on the supply side in long-term analyses.

In many countries, in accordance with *The OECD Jobs Study* (OECD 1994), the focus in economic policies and employment policies was shifted to the issue of structural unemployment. In economic terms, structural unemployment is defined as the non-accelerating inflation (or wage) rate of unemployment, i.e. the lowest level of unemployment compatible with stable price or wage increases (Elmeskov and MacFarland 1993). Structural unemployment will always be above zero because of 'frictional unemployment', i.e. the fact that people switch between jobs. Workers are involuntarily dismissed and cannot always find a new job immediately. Indeed, in a flexible labour market the absolute minimum level of structural unemployment is bound to be slightly higher than in an inflexible labour market because there is more job exchange. However, in most countries, structural unemployment is assumed to be far above that minimum level. In the mid-1990s structural unemployment estimates were usually very close to the actual level of unemployment (OECD 1997), indicating that only structural reforms could bring about significant improvement (see Table: Calculated structural unemployment in 1996 and subsequent development of unemployment (1996–2002), in the Online Resources).

Theoretically, there may be several causes of structural unemployment:

- high minimum wages, which mean that labourers with low productivity will not be hired;

- insufficient incentives—too generous levels and too long a duration of unemployment benefits, social assistance, etc.;

- employment protection legislation preventing employers from hiring when they cannot fire, and enabling the core labour force to demand high wage increases without meeting competition from those who are unemployed and would be willing to work for less (the 'insider–outsider' problem) (see Lindbeck and Snower 1988);

- (other) 'matching problems', such as insufficient mobility between geographical areas, or across trade borders, creating coexistence of unemployment and demand for labour power.

Economic recommendations from the OECD and others since the mid-1990s have focused on flexibility: more wage flexibility, more flexible employment protection legislation (i.e. less protection), more mobility across regions, trades, and occupations, and stronger work incentives or control/sanctions to make workers more flexible. This has also been the general trend of reforms in Europe, alongside disciplinary measures for the poor (Soss et al. 2011; Lødemel and Moreria 2014) and integrating the conditions of treatment for all groups of non-employed (Clasen and Clegg 2011).

Table 22.4 Net social expenditure as a percentage of GDP (2015)

	Gross public social expenditure	Gross private social expenditure	Net tax effect	Net total social expenditure
Germany	24.9	3.5	−3.6	24.8
Austria	27.7	2.2	−5.7	24.3
France	32.0	3.5	−3.8	31.7
Belgium	29.2	1.9	−4.4	26.7
Netherlands	17.7	13.4	−4.8	26.3
Luxembourg	22.1	1.3	−5.2	18.2
Sweden	26.3	3.6	−5.4	24.5
Finland	30.4	1.5	−6.7	25.3
Denmark	29.0	4.4	−8.1	25.4
Norway	24.7	2.5	−5.2	22.0
Iceland	15.5	6.5	−3.8	18.2
Italy	28.5	1.9	−5.0	25.4
Greece	25.4	1.1	−4.1	22.4
Spain	24.7	1.1	−2.9	22.9
Portugal	24.0	2.3	−3.4	23.0
Czech Rep.	19.4	0.8	−1.6	18.6
Hungary	20.9	0.3	−3.1	18.1
Poland	20.5	0.4	−3.4	17.4
Switzerland	15.9	11.5	−3.7	23.7
UK	21.6	6.2	−3.4	24.5
Ireland	15.5	2.2	−1.7	16.1
Australia	18.5	5.8	−0.9	23.5
NZ	19.2	0.7	−2.3	17.6
Canada	17.6	4.7	−1.4	20.9
United States	18.8	12.5	−1.3	30.0
Japan	21.9	3.1	−1.4	23.5
OECD	20.5	3.6	−3.6	20.5

Source: http://www.oecd.org/socialexpenditure.htm.

However, as regards the impact of labour market policy, empirical research has come up with rather nuanced answers.

In the first place, estimations of structural unemployment are quite uncertain. As can be seen from the table: Calculated structural unemployment in 1996 and subsequent development of unemployment (1996–2002), in the Online Resources, some countries believed to have high structural unemployment experienced sudden decline.

Next, systematic studies of the impact of the labour market and social policies give somewhat

Table 22.5 Correlations between social expenditure as a proportion of GDP and economic performance

Periods	Correlation between social expenditure and Growth of GDP per capita	Level of GDP per capita
1880s	0.10	−0.18
1890s	0.34	−0.05
1900s	−0.23	0.09
1910s	0.12	0.31
1920s	−0.24	0.49
1960s	−0.17	−0.07
1970s	0.14	0.00
1980s	−0.07	0.12
1990s	0.01	0.12
Simple average	0.00	0.09

Note: Social expenditure (1880–1930: welfare, employment, pensions, health, and housing subsidies) as percentage of GDP, initial year in decade.
Source: Lindert (2004, vol. 1: 17).

mixed results. As far as policy impact on unemployment is concerned, many studies have focused on the following effects (Nickell and Layard 1999; Nickell et al. 2004; OECD 2006).

Unemployment protection

There is consensus from most comparative studies that long duration of unemployment benefits tends to increase duration of unemployment spells and the proportion of long-term unemployed (OECD 2006: 61). Evidence regarding the effects of replacement rates is more mixed but overwhelmingly confirms the conventional wisdom (Blanchard and Katz 1996; Nickell 1997; Holmlund 1998; Nickell and Layard 1999; Nickell et al. 2004; OECD 2006: 61). However, as emphasized by the OECD (2006: 190–1), some countries have achieved low unemployment despite generous benefits, in particular if they are combined with a strict work test. In Scandinavia, long-term unemployment has for decades been very low, comparatively speaking (Dølvik et al. 2015). Lindert (2004, vol. 2: 119) adds that high replacement rates may boost productivity.

Minimum wages

Minimum wages were a main concern in *The OECD Jobs Study* (OECD 1994). However, no studies indicate that high minimum wages are associated with higher

unemployment rates (Holmlund 1998; Galbraith et al. 1999). For instance, the Nordic countries persistently reveal lower skill-based differences in unemployment and higher employment rates among the least skilled than most liberal and conservative welfare states. Eventually, the OECD became increasingly aware of dangers of entrapment in low-paid work (e.g. OECD 2006: 88, 174–9).

Employment protection

In actual practice, employment protection does not, on average, seem to have any impact on the *level* of unemployment (OECD 2006: 95–6), but it has a strong impact on the *structure* of unemployment. Long-term unemployment is most widespread in countries with strict employment protection (e.g. Bertola et al. 1999; Nickell and Layard 1999; Esping-Andersen 2000). This does not question theories of flexicurity, but it does mean that these systems should be analysed in relation to specific national contexts.

Taxation

Evidence indicates that targeted tax cuts may have effects on unemployment—and perhaps even more on employment—but this remains a contested issue (Blanchard and Katz 1996: 67; Jackman et al. 1996; Davieri and Tabellini 2000; Disney 2000). The OECD (2006: 95) has been reluctant to give strong advice on this issue, or on the appropriate balance between social contributions and income taxes. However, it has underlined that the negative effects of taxes may depend on corporatism and a feeling of responsibility among union leaders.

Activation

Activation was pointed out by the OECD (1994) as a good second-best solution and was advocated by the EU. However, both micro- and macro-level evaluations of the impact of activation have been disappointing (Martin 2000; OECD 2006: 68). It is far from being a panacea, and effects often seem small in relation to costs. However, some activation measures work in some contexts and, for whatever reason, countries that put emphasis on activation generally tend to perform better. Since 2000, and in particular after the Great Recession, 'activation' has increasingly come to mean obligations for the unemployed (Barbier 2015). And at least it is well documented that the test of availability in activation works (Kohnle-Seidl and Eichhorst 2008).

Corporatism

Probably the most robust finding in the literature is that corporatism and wage coordination have beneficial impacts on employment. The OECD (1994) used to be sceptical about corporatism because it tended to entail high minimum wages. But facing quite unambiguous empirical evidence, it modified its view (OECD 2006: 82). Some studies indicate that *unionization* as such has a negative impact on employment (OECD 2006). But it is the *coverage and centralization* of bargaining that count, probably because they inflict a sense of responsibility for the economy on union leaders. This leads to wage moderation in periods with a high demand for labour power. It is also important to note that unionization is not straightforwardly related to collective bargaining coverage. In Western European countries, collective bargaining results among organized workers are frequently extended to the unorganized by so-called *erga omnes* arrangements. Collective bargaining coverage may be 80 per cent, even if unionization is only 30 or 15 per cent.

It is often found that the relationship is U-shaped (OECD 2006: 84–5; Calmfors and Driffill 1988; Scarpetta 1996; Elmeskov et al. 1998; see also Hemerijck and Schludi 2000; Nickell and Layard 1999; Scharpf 2000). Both completely unorganized (market-determined) and centralized/coordinated bargaining have beneficial impact, whereas bargaining at the company or sectoral level is detrimental. The ability of trade unions to moderate wage demands even has a positive effect on the level of structural unemployment. This is basically in accordance with the varieties of capitalism predictions.

KEY POINTS

- Generous welfare policies have a very strong impact on the level of poverty.

- Universal or social democratic welfare regimes have lower poverty rates and more equality, whereas the opposite is typically found in liberal regimes.

- There are few indications that generous welfare policies have adverse effects on economic growth.

- The incentive effects of social protection on unemployment are generally quite uncertain, but duration of unemployment does seem to have negative effects and, on average, this also holds for compensation levels.

- Centralized and coordinated wage bargaining has a strong positive impact on employment.

- There is not one single equilibrium, but different combinations of policies that may have the same impact.

Policy feedback and path dependence

So far, we have only looked at policy feedback on welfare or on economic measures. However, policies also have impacts on future politics and policy. This is also labelled *policy feedback* (Pierson 1994: 39–50; see also Figure I.1 in the Introduction). This section briefly elucidates how policy change affects politics, how policy learning takes place, and how feedback mechanisms often mean that policy changes follow a particular course determined by pre-existing policy programmes. This is what has become known as *path dependence*. Finally, policies are *diffused* and *transferred* from one country to another, or from one policy field to another.

Policy feedback on politics

The most obvious feedback effect of policies is the impact on the constellation of interests in society and thereby on future inputs to the political process. This may happen in several ways.

- Policies generate 'vested interests' in maintaining particular programmes.

- Policies create entirely new interest groups (see Chapter 14 'Interest groups').

- Policies change distribution of power resources between interest groups.

- Policies create divisions of interests as well as unity of interests.

- Policies open or close access opportunities to influence future policies and shape actors' perceptions of interests.

These effects may be intentional or unintentional. All welfare programmes generate interest groups, many of which become organized. An example of unintentional generation of vested interests is found in early retirement policies in Europe in the 1980s. At that time, it became a popular strategy to combat youth unemployment by means of various programmes giving older workers an incentive to retire before pension age. Very soon, however, most such arrangements came to be seen as vested interests, so that it could involve substantial political costs to change them. This is one of the main reasons why policy change has been considered nearly irreversible (Pierson 1994), even though recent reforms have demonstrated this claim to be exaggerated (e.g. Ebbinghaus 2006, 2011; Palier 2010; Clasen and Clegg 2011; Bonoli and Natali 2012; Natali 2017).

Sometimes policy change involves the creation of entirely new interests which may contribute to new dynamics. A case in point is outsourcing of public services to private providers. Such policies instantly create a new interest group of private service providers who will lobby for further increases in outsourcing. If these service providers manage to capture a substantial proportion of the market, there may also be a division of interest between privately and publicly employed welfare service workers.

Power distribution between interest groups is also strongly related to policy. For instance, trade unions have remained much stronger in countries with voluntary state-subsidized unemployment insurance organized by trade unions—the **Ghent system** (see Chapter 18 'Political participation' and Figure 18.4.). Another key example is universal vs targeted welfare arrangements. Targeting is usually legitimized by the intention to improve conditions for those who are 'really in need'. But in the long run, those who are 'really in need' often find themselves worse off. In the first place, if welfare arrangements are universal, their numerical basis of support is broader. Further, they enjoy greater legitimacy as people find benefit recipients resembling themselves more 'deserving' (van Oorschot 2006). But perhaps most importantly, as noted by Titmuss (1974), when the middle classes are enrolled in a programme, they will not only make larger demands but will also have more resources to have such demands heard.

Policy learning, social learning

Another important instance of policy feedback is 'policy learning' or 'social learning'. The notion of learning is based on Hugh Heclo's classical remark that '[governments] not only "power" … they also puzzle' (Heclo 1974: 305). They try to find out how policies work and which policies can produce the intended effects. Sometimes the terms 'policy learning' and 'social learning' are used interchangeably, as describing 'the process by which civil servants, policy experts, and elected officials evaluate the performance of previously enacted policies' (Béland 2006: 361).

The broad definition may include learning that is relatively 'detached and technocratic in nature' (Béland 2006: 361) and is aimed at minor adjustments of policies after evaluation of their impact. This is linked to a classic idea of 'lesson drawing' which suffers from a rationalistic bias. However, comparative research has been more concerned with changes of the basic ideas and paradigms that define problems and possible solutions (Hall 1993), or with development of 'epistemic communities' of people coming to share the same general framework of ideas (Haas 1992). Bennett and Howlett (1992) distinguished between 'government learning', 'lesson drawing', and 'social learning' on the basis of a classification of who learns what. They reserved the label 'social learning' for a paradigm shift in an entire policy community.

A paradigm shift may have several sources. A standard source is some sort of crisis for the old paradigm, which includes its particular set of problem definitions and possible solutions, i.e. policy instruments. When these instruments successively fail, the old paradigm reaches a crisis. For instance, in Denmark, any imaginable Keynesian policy instrument was adopted between 1975 and 1986 to combat unemployment (Andersen 2002). When all these instruments had failed, this paved the way for a rapid paradigm shift which redefined unemployment not as a matter of insufficient demand for labour power, let alone excessive supply, but as a matter of 'structural' problems such as discrepancies between minimum wages and qualifications, insufficient mobility, work incentives, and so on. This interpretation gave meaning to unexpected phenomena such as wage inflation beginning at a high level of unemployment, indicating that the 'structural' level of unemployment had been reached. Over a couple of years, this paradigm shift was accepted by all major political actors. It was facilitated by the fact that a variety of policy options could be derived. This included options that were highly acceptable to social democrats, e.g. an 'active' labour market policy focused on enhancing qualifications and mobility for the unemployed.

Most contemporary scholars would emphasize that policy learning is not always rational. In the first place, people may often draw wrong lessons. Next, as pointed out by Weyland (2005) and Béland (2006), the search for alternative paradigms is often steered by a 'logic of availability', where political actors make cognitive shortcuts because they *need* new ideas that can give meaning to anomalies, 'reduce uncertainty [and] propose a particular solution to a moment of crisis' (Blyth 2002: 11). Following the crisis in 2008, Keynesianism had a short revival, simply because no governments could think of anything else to do.

Once accepted, a new policy paradigm also installs its own standards of evaluating policy impact. This is not just an 'objective' assessment. Crucial premises are seldom questioned. If the expected results appear, nobody asks whether they may have been caused by other factors. And even if a certain policy *does not* work, this rarely leads to a questioning of the underlying causal assumptions, but rather towards a focus on implementation problems, on problems of giving the medicine in sufficient doses, etc. In short, a paradigm carries its own learning and mislearning from observed policy impacts (Larsen 2002).

Path dependence

Policy learning in relation to paradigm shift is one among several mechanisms that tend to make policies path dependent. Path dependence in the very broadest sense means that policies at one point of time tend to impact on, or indeed determine, policies at a later point of time because of high switching costs. This also implies that initial policy choices at 'formative moments' are often crucial as they determine, or at least constrain, later policy choices (Powell 1991: 192–3). Thus, it is no accident that current variations in European welfare systems to a large extent reflect initial differences in choices that were made more than a hundred years ago.

The theory of path dependence is borrowed from institutional economics, where it was developed with the aim of explaining, for example, why inferior technologies survived in competition with superior ones. For instance, if a particular type of software obtains a dominant position in the market, compatibility with this software itself becomes a survival criterion for other products, and this in turn becomes an argument for adhering to this software. Or take the instance of a computer keyboard, where the position of letters is determined by their previous position on the QWERTY typewriter. Allegedly, the position of the letters on the typewriter was deliberately developed with the aim of *slowing down* the speed of typing because a mechanical typewriter cannot function beyond a certain speed—the keys will simply jam (Pierson 1994: 43). Today, it would seem rational to change the position of letters on the computer keyboard, as this could increase the speed of typing. But once everybody has learned this system, the switching costs are too high.

In politics too, there are switching costs. Many of these costs may be mainly practical/administrative, but the most important switching costs are political: switching policies involves losses and gains. Incumbent governments will almost certainly be punished by those voters who suffer significant losses, whereas they are far less likely to be rewarded by those who experience gains.

There are three main lines of interpretation of path dependence in comparative social research.

1. The first one emphasizes 'lock-in' effects and the 'stickiness' of policies—not least welfare policies—analogous with the example of the keyboard. Policies rarely change, except in extraordinary situations where external pressures and/or political conjunctures enable path-breaking reforms. In particular, vested interests tend to block major reforms. This version bears some resemblance to Baumgartner and Jones' (1993) punctuated equilibrium theory. In Pierson's terms, it is a theory of stasis—or negative feedback where equilibrium is reinstated. This has not only been criticized for being too static, but also for ignoring the possibility of incremental, but transformative change—'revolution in slow motion' (see below).

2. More in line with economic institutionalism, Pierson (2000) has attempted to develop path dependence into a *theory*. Here the concept refers to a model of 'positive feedback' which is basically analogous to the example of competing technologies. Unlike the first version, Pierson emphasizes path dependence as a *dynamic* theory, underlining the *mechanisms* which produce path dependence.

3. A broader version simply stresses that decisions at one point in time tend to impact strongly on decisions at a later point in time. This is why comparative policy analysis should be

extremely sensitive to history. This notion of path dependence is sometimes criticized for being too indiscriminate and too vague, and certainly, it does not run any risk of falsification. However, it should be assessed not as a theory but more as an *analytical perspective*.

Beyond the notion of *lock in*, all three perspectives also share the notion of *critical juncture*, that is, situations where feedback mechanisms are unusually strong, and where even small decisions may—sometimes unintentionally—have very significant long-term implications. Besides, regardless of perspective, it is always fruitful to look systematically for the *mechanisms* that produce path dependence in terms of positive feedback where each new policy step reinforces the current path.

To take a classic example, universal flat-rate pensions have the disadvantage that they do not cover the pension needs of the new middle classes sufficiently. As a consequence, a pension system of purely flat-rate pensions tends to 'crowd in' private pension arrangements if it is not supplemented by some kind of earnings-related scheme (Esping-Andersen 1990; Myles and Pierson 2001). The predictable consequence is that countries seeking to maintain universal flat-rate state pensions will eventually find themselves ending up with a 'multi-pillar' pensions system with a large private component. However, by the same token, countries introducing an earnings-related supplement will find themselves under pressure to switch to a contribution-defined system. In short, because of the mechanisms of path dependence, universal, taxfinanced, flat-rate pensions have tended to eliminate themselves.

Sometimes changes take place in sudden, path-breaking reforms. However, there is increasing awareness that small, incremental changes (that may even go unnoticed), may lead to large transformations in the long run (Hacker 2004; Thelen 2004; Streeck and Thelen 2005; Mahoney and Thelen 2010b). For instance, new layers may be inserted with faster growth rates ('*layering and differential growth*'); a classical case is insertion of pensions savings elements in the pensions system. Another example is policies that are not adjusted to deal with new problems—this is referred to as *drift*, an instance of (typically deliberate) *non-decisions*.

Often path dependence is more about changing interest constellations and power resources. In comparative welfare state research, an overly static notion of path dependence was previously widespread, resembling more a negative than a positive feedback model.

Alongside differences in interest constellations and in exposure to problem pressures, path dependence is the main explanation of continuing cross-national differences in policies, in particular welfare policies. However, there may also be instances of policy feedback that lead to convergence (alongside common problem pressure).

Policy transfer and policy diffusion

Policy transfer and policy diffusion are examples of such policy feedback mechanisms that may lead to convergence between policies in different countries. The two concepts are often used interchangeably (see Chapter 20 'Policy-making').

We should probably reserve *policy transfer* for the use of knowledge about policies and their impact in one system (or in one policy field) to deliberately change policies in another country (or in another policy field). Thus, policy transfer is about processes which do not always involve imitation or emulation, but may indeed occasionally involve substantial change while implanting policies from one institutional and cultural context to another (Knill 2005). It is a matter of deliberate cross-national or cross-sectoral policy learning.

Policy diffusion typically means that policy choices in one country affect those made in a second country. Studies of policy diffusion originated in international relations and international political economy, and some scholars have focused on structural determinants of diffusion (e.g. Simmons and Elkins 2004). Others use policy diffusion as a broader concept that refers to all conceivable channels of influence between countries (or between policy fields). This leads to an emphasis on studying various mechanisms of diffusion, from imposition to voluntary adoption of policy models that are communicated across borders or across policy fields (Rogers 1995; Knill 2005).

Since the 1990s, there have been waves of welfare and tax reforms across Europe, sometimes stimulated by the OECD or the EU, and sometimes just adopted by inspiration from neighbours, and implemented country by country (Barbier 2015). An interesting European framework is the open method of coordination (OMC) which is an instance of 'soft law' regulation based on recommendations rather than sanctioned rules. The OMC, which was given this label at the EU summit in Lisbon in 2000, is a deliberate attempt to encourage policy transfer by bringing actors together to formulate common goals on the basis of recognition of institutional differences. The OMC builds on policy learning and policy transfer (de la Porte et al. 2001).

Policy convergence

Policy transfer or policy diffusion constitute a sort of 'disturbance' in some cross-national research aiming to explain policy as an effect of structural, institutional, or political forces (Knill 2005). For instance, country variations in policy could be interpreted as an effect of variations in economic pressures, variations in institutions, or variations in strength of political parties. But then comes the problem that countries may simply have learned from each other. In purely quantitative analyses, this constitutes a serious 'disturbance' that is almost impossible to control.

However, there are some important problems relating to the issue of policy convergence itself. In the first place, should convergence be measured by policy or institutions on the one hand, or by the *impact* of policies—policy outcomes—on the other? What is the 'dependent variable' (Clasen and Siegel 2007; Andersen 2007)? Secondly, four different patterns are conceivable (Kautto and Kvist 2002):

- *convergence*: policies or policy outcomes become increasingly similar;
- *divergence*: policies or policy outcomes become increasingly different;
- *persistent difference*: policies or policy outcomes remain as they are;
- *parallel trends, persistent differences*: policies or policy outcomes change in the same direction, but differences are maintained.

The last of these patterns is often conflated with convergence. For instance, Gilbert (2002: 138) noted a common trend towards more targeting (means testing) of social benefits in nearly all welfare states. However, according to his indicators, this common trend is combined with persistent differences between Anglo-Saxon countries that generally target, and Scandinavian countries where targeting remains the exception.

Regarding outcomes in terms of equality, we also find a parallel trend towards higher inequality (OECD 2008a, 2011a), but regime differences remain. At a meta-level, however, we find stronger signs of convergence. As mentioned earlier in 'Tensions between welfare and economic efficiency', we find striking similarities across countries when we aggregate public and private social expenditures. Total expenditures seem to follow modernization, *public* expenditures much less so. Also, if we look at the profile of the entire pensions system, nearly all countries have developed some kind of earnings-related system, either within state arrangements or as a private proliferation of the welfare state. Moreover, by different means, the costs of ageing are increasingly imposed on future pensioners themselves. Such highly different policies may often be described as *functionally equivalent* in the sense that they produce similar outcomes.

> **KEY POINTS**
>
> - Policies shape politics and future policies.
> - Policies affect power resources and generate vested interests, or even new interest groups.
> - Policies are path-dependent, at least in the broad sense that past decisions structure and constrain new ones, and often also in the narrower sense that precise mechanisms can be identified.
> - Policy learning often takes place within a paradigm, but even paradigm shifts can be ascribed to learning.
> - Policy convergence may derive not only from 'functional necessity', but also from policy transfer.

Conclusion

The study of the impact of policy is a relatively novel branch of comparative politics. It is also a difficult one because it is complicated to disentangle effects of policies from all sorts of other effects. Furthermore, it is difficult in the sense that it often involves cross-disciplinary insights in both politics and economics. Nonetheless, it is also a very important field of research. To determine what the outcomes are of different types of policy and how policies should be designed to obtain desired outcomes is one of the most challenging fields of research in political science. It is also a field where economists begin to learn from comparative politics, not least from the insights in 'institutional complementarity'.

When it comes to the *political* impact of policies, this is also a rapidly expanding field of research that helps us to understand policy change in general, and not least policy change across nations. It helps to illuminate why countries exposed to the same external pressures often pursue quite different roads, as the theory of path dependence teaches us. It helps to understand some of the *political* forces behind policy convergence across programmes or across nations. And it helps to understand the *dynamics* of policy change.

QUESTIONS

Knowledge-based

1. What does institutional complementarity mean?

2. What is understood by flexicurity?

3. What is structural unemployment?

4. What generated a paradigm shift in the interpretation of unemployment?

5. What does path dependence mean, and are policies always path-dependent?

Critical thinking

1. How does corporatism impact on unemployment, and why?

2. How do different welfare models impact on equality, and why?

3. What is the difference between welfare regimes and the regimes of varieties of capitalism theory?

4. How can policy changes affect the mobilization of interests?

5. What contributes to policy transfer between countries, and between policy fields?

FURTHER READING

Classical texts on policy regimes

Esping-Andersen, G. (1990) *The Three Worlds of Welfare Capitalism* (Cambridge: Polity Press).

Hall, P. A. and Soskice, D. (eds) (2001) *Varieties of Capitalism: The Institutional Foundations of Comparative Advantage* (Oxford: Oxford University Press).

Titmuss, R. (1974) *Social Policy: An Introduction* (ed. by B. Abel-Smith and K. Titmuss) (New York: Pantheon).

Useful guides to impact of policies

Iversen, T. (2005) *Capitalism, Democracy, and Welfare* (Cambridge: Cambridge University Press).

Lindert, P. A. (2004) *Growing Public: Social Spending and Growth since the Eighteenth Century* (Cambridge: Cambridge University Press).

OECD (2006) *Employment Outlook 2006: Boosting Jobs and Incomes* (Paris: OECD).

OECD (2015a) *In it together. Why Less Inequality Benefits All* (Paris: OECD).

Classical texts on policy feedback

Heclo, H. (1974) *Modern Social Politics in Britain and Sweden: From Relief to Income Maintenance* (New Haven, CT: Yale University Press).

Pierson, P. (1993) 'When Effect Becomes Cause: "Policy Feedback" and Political Change', *World Politics*, 45(3): 595–628.

ENDNOTES

1. This was avoided in a few countries, where demand-stimulating policies were combined with tight incomes policies, for example Austria (see Scharpf 1987; Hemerijck et al. 2000).

2. Esping-Andersen (1990) initially spoke of 'welfare *state* regimes', but because of increasing emphasis on the relationship between the state and the family in provision of care this was substituted by welfare regimes (Esping-Andersen 1999).

3. The Netherlands is typically pictured as being closer to a conservative ideal type, but has been more of a hybrid in several respects. This is why it has sometimes served as representative of a social democratic regime.

 Visit the Online Resources that accompany this book for additional material, including country profiles, comparative data sets, flashcard glossaries, and web directory.

www.oup.com/he/caramani5e

Section 6
Beyond the nation-state

23

The EU as a new political system

Simon Hix

Chapter contents

Reader's guide

This chapter analyses the development and operation of the European Union (EU) from a comparative politics perspective. It starts by looking at the evolution of the EU and the process of European integration. The chapter then discusses what it means to think of the EU as a political system. There are two basic dimensions of the EU system: (i) the vertical dimension—the division of policy-making power between the EU and the member-states; and (ii) the horizontal dimension—the design and operation of EU decision-making. These two dimensions are considered separately, before we turn to the 'missing link' in the EU system—the lack of genuine democratic politics.

Introduction

In the twentieth century, Europe suffered the two most destructive wars in history as the pinnacle of bitter political and economic rivalries between the states of Europe. At the beginning of the twenty-first century the states of Eastern and Western Europe are united in a continental-scale political system, where certain executive, legislative, and judicial powers are collectively pooled. Despite its problems and the recent economic and migration challenges, the EU remains one of the most remarkable political achievements of modern times. The EU **single market** underpins the economic prosperity of half a billion people, and most EU citizens take for granted the investment, consumption, educational, travel, and lifestyle opportunities that exist because of the EU. Above all, for the first time in history, a war between the major states of Europe is almost unimaginable.

How did this happen? When six European states decided in the 1950s to place their coal and steel industries under collective **supranational** control, few would have expected that this would have led to a new continental-scale political system (see Box 23.1). In the 1960s, Western Europe became the first region in the world to establish a customs union, with an internal free-trade area and a common external tariff. Added to this 'common market' was the first genuinely supranational public expenditure programme: the Common Agricultural Policy (CAP). European integration then took a major step forwards in the 1980s. The so-far unique continental-scale 'single market' was created by the 1990s, with the removal of internal barriers to the cross-border flow of goods, services, capital, and labour, a single competition policy, and a single currency (the euro). Partly as a consequence of the single market, the EU began to coordinate national macro-economic, justice and policing, and foreign and security policies. But the EU also has its problems, and is now facing a profound crisis. In the wake of the financial crisis, discontent towards globalization, the sovereign debt crisis in the Eurozone, and the migration crisis, popular support for the EU declined significantly in many member-states. Most strikingly, in June 2016 the UK public voted in a **referendum** by 52 per cent to 48 per cent to leave the EU. When the UK will eventually leave is uncertain, but what is clear is that this vote will have a profound effect on the development of the EU going forward.

▶ ZOOM-IN 23.1

Key dates in the development of the European Union

18 February 1951	Belgium, France, Germany, Italy, Luxembourg, and the Netherlands sign the Treaty of Paris, launching the European Coal and Steel Community (ECSC)
23 July 1952	Treaty of Paris enters into force
1 January 1958	Treaties of Rome enter into force, establishing the EEC and Euratom
30 July 1962	Common Agricultural Policy starts
5 February 1963	Van Gend en Loos ruling of the European Court of Justice (ECJ) establishes the 'direct effect' of EEC law
15 July 1964	*Costa* v. *ENEL* ruling of the ECJ establishes the 'supremacy' of EEC law
29 January 1966	Luxembourg compromise, which effectively means that the Council must decide unanimously
1 July 1967	Merger Treaty, establishing a single set of institutions for the three communities
1–2 December 1969	Hague Summit: governments agree to push for further economic and political integration
27 October 1970	Governments start foreign policy cooperation (European Political Cooperation)
1 January 1973	Denmark, Ireland, and the UK join
10 February 1979	Cassis de Dijon ruling of the ECJ establishes 'mutual recognition' in the provision of goods and services in the common market
13 March 1979	European monetary system begins
7–10 June 1979	First 'direct' elections of the European Parliament
1 January 1981	Greece joins
26 June 1984	Margaret Thatcher negotiates the 'British rebate' from the annual budget
1 January 1985	First 'European Communities' passports are issued

1 January 1986	Portugal and Spain join
19 May 1986	European flag used for the first time
1 July 1987	Single European Act enters into force, launching the single-market programme
13 February 1988	First multi-annual framework for the EC budget agreed
9 November 1989	Berlin Wall falls
1 January 1993	European Single Market starts
1 November 1993	Maastricht Treaty enters into force, launching the EU and the plan for Economic and Monetary Union (EMU)
21 July 1994	European Parliament rejects a piece of EU legislation for the first time
1 January 1995	Austria, Finland, and Sweden join
1 January 1999	EMU starts
15 March 1999	Santer Commission resigns before a censure vote is held in the European Parliament
1 May 1999	Amsterdam Treaty enters into force, starting the 'area of freedom, security and justice'
24 March 2000	European Council agrees the 'Lisbon strategy' to promote growth and productivity
1 January 2002	Euro notes and coins replace national notes and coins for ten member-states
1 February 2003	Nice Treaty enters into force, launching defence cooperation and reforming the institutions in preparation for enlargement
1 May 2004	Cyprus, Czech Republic, Estonia, Hungary, Latvia, Lithuania, Malta, Poland, Slovakia, and Slovenia join
26 October 2004	European Parliament blocks the election of a new Commission
29 October 2004	Treaty establishing a Constitution for Europe signed
29 May/1 June 2005	'No' votes in referendums in France and the Netherlands on the Constitutional Treaty
1 January 2007	Bulgaria and Romania join
2009–2015	Eurozone sovereign debt crisis
1 December 2009	Lisbon Treaty enters into force
27 September 2012	European Stability Mechanism becomes effective
1 January 2013	'Fiscal Compact' Treaty between twenty-five member-states (EU27 minus UK and Czech Republic) enters into force
1 July 2013	Croatia joins
1 January 2015	Lithuania becomes nineteenth member of the Eurozone
Summer 2015	Migration crisis
23 June 2016	UK public votes in a referendum (52% to 48%) to leave the EU

Many aspects of the EU are unique. Yet, from the point of view of comparative politics, there are many things the EU shares with other multilevel polities. For example, the division of powers between the lower (national) and higher (European) levels of government determines how policy-making works. Moreover, at the European level, the design of **agenda setting** and veto powers in the decision-making process determines which actors are likely to secure the policies they most prefer and how easy or difficult it is to change existing policies. The field of comparative politics has developed analytical tools to understand aspects of multilevel political systems which are increasingly applicable to the EU.

Explanations of European integration

In the 1950s and 1960s, several scholars expected that 'regional integration' would happen in many parts of the world. However, by the mid-1960s, the extent of institution-building and the intensity of political and economic cooperation were far greater in Western Europe than in any other region. As a result, an explanatory framework developed for the sole purpose of understanding 'European integration'. Simplifying, explanations fall into two main camps: (i) *intergovernmental approaches*, which see preferences and decisions of national governments as primary; and (ii) *supranational approaches*, which see supranational political, social, and economic forces as primary.

Intergovernmental approaches

The basic assumption of these approaches is that the main actors in the EU are the governments of the member-states (e.g. Hoffmann 1966, 1982; Taylor 1982; Moravcsik 1991). National governments have a clear set of preferences about what policies they would like to see allocated to the European level. For example, British governments have traditionally preferred economic to political integration, while German governments have wanted both. British governments have wanted the EU to adopt a free-market approach to economic integration, while German governments have looked to adopt a 'social market' approach, with harmonized social and labour market regulations.

Governments usually 'bargain hard' with each other on the basis of these preferences, and only agree to outcomes at the European level if these outcomes promote their preferences.

One might expect that, if governments are self-interested and are determined not to lose any ground when bargaining at the European level, nothing will ever be done in the EU. Indeed, this was one of the conclusions of some of the early intergovernmental theorists, who assumed that European integration could not progress beyond a very minimal level (e.g. Hoffmann 1966). However, more recent intergovernmental approaches argue that there are good collective reasons for member-state governments to hand over significant powers to the EU institutions (Moravcsik 1993, 1998; Pollack 1997). For example, it is often in the governments' interests to have a common policy in the single market, yet agreement cannot be reached, as each government has their own particular policy preference which they are reluctant to give up. This 'coordination problem' can be resolved by delegating agenda-setting power to the European Commission, where the Commission works out which is the best policy option for the EU as a whole.

The intergovernmental approaches explain well why the process of integration stalled in the 1970s, as governments preferred national to European solutions to the economic problems in that period. These approaches also explain how a convergence of governments' preferences in favour of a continental-scale market, and the careful design of a set of new decision-making rules, enabled European integration to be relaunched in the 1980s and 1990s.

Nevertheless, there are several aspects of European integration that these approaches have not been able to explain so well. They cannot explain the increase in the powers of the European Parliament since the mid-1980s. In addition, if the governments are in control of European integration, it is hard to explain why there is declining support for the EU. Indeed, from an intergovernmental perspective, since the governments run the EU, and the governments are elected by the citizens, there is no '**democratic deficit**' in the EU (Moravcsik 2002). Finally, although intergovernmental approaches may be very useful for understanding the 'grand bargains' such as the Single European Act or the Maastricht Treaty, they seem less useful for understanding day-to-day decision-making, where there are multiple actors and interests and more complex sets of preferences.

To understand how the EU works on a day-to-day basis, it is more useful to think of it as a political system, and to apply approaches from comparative politics.

Supranational approaches

The basic assumption of these approaches is that European integration is a deterministic process driven by underlying political, economic, and social forces. In the early period of European integration, Ernst Haas proposed what he called a 'neo-functionalist' theory of economic and political integration (Haas 1958, 1961; cf. Lindberg 1963). At the heart of this theory was the concept of 'spillover', whereby 'a given action, related to a specific goal, creates a situation in which the original goal can be assured only by taking further actions, which in turn create a further condition and a need for more, and so forth' (Lindberg 1963: 9). For example, a common market in coal and steel would work more efficiently if there was a common market in other goods and services used in the production and distribution of coal and steel. Similarly, once the free movement of labour was established, there was pressure on the member-state governments to agree common justice and home affairs policies.

One variant of this approach was Béla Balassa's (1961) theory of economic integration. Balassa argued that once a customs union had been established, the potential economies of scale from such a union could not be met unless all barriers to the free movement of goods and services had been removed (in other words, a single market). Then, once a single market had been established, it would function more effectively if a single currency could be established, which would allow for greater price transparency and reduced transaction costs of doing business. Then, if a single currency were established, economic shocks to the currency union could no longer be addressed through monetary policies, so there would need to be fiscal transfers from high-growth regions to low-growth regions. These fiscal transfers would need to be legitimized somehow, which would require the establishment of genuine political union, with democratic elections for the central institutions. In other words, Balassa predicted a teleological development from a customs union to a political union.

Most scholars within the supranationalist approach were not as economically determinist as Balassa, in that they thought integration would not proceed without the input of actors. Economic forces are insufficient on their own to force states to take major integrationist steps. However, in contrast to the intergovernmental view, the supranational framework emphasizes the role of 'non-state' actors, such as interest groups and the institutions of the EU themselves (Marks et al. 1996; Pierson 1996; Sandholtz and Stone Sweet 1998 Pollack 2003). For example, transnational businesses in the early 1980s put pressure on the governments to create a single market in Europe (Sandholtz and Zysman 1989).

Meanwhile, the Commission, led by Jacques Delors, played an important role in shaping the single market, the reform of the EU budget in the late 1980s, and the plan for economic and monetary union (Pollack 2003). Similarly, by establishing the doctrines of the 'direct effect' and 'supremacy' of EC law in the early 1960s, the European Court of Justice (ECJ) has fashioned a quasi-federal legal framework, beyond the intentions of the signatories of the early treaties (Weiler 1991). And the European Parliament has interpreted the decision-making rules of the EU in a way that has maximized its influence (Hix 2002).

Overall, supranationalism does well in capturing the remarkable, and perhaps teleological, evolution of the EU from a customs union in the 1960s to a full-blown political system by the end of the twentieth century. Nevertheless, the inherent determinism of the supranationalist approaches means that they are less able to explain why the process of European integration slowed between the late 1960s and the mid-1980s, why some member-states decided to join the EU at different times, or indeed remain largely outside (such as Norway and Switzerland), and why when the EU faces major challenges—such as the Eurozone crisis in the late 2000s and the migration crisis in the mid-2010s—European integration seems to come to a standstill. These approaches are also less able to explain why the EU is more able to adopt common policies in some areas, such as environmental policy, than in other areas, such as social policy.

Again, thinking of the EU as a political system helps us to understand its internal workings in detail.

KEY POINTS

- For most of its history, the European Economic Community (EEC)/EU has been understood by social scientists as a unique case of political and economic 'integration' between sovereign nation-states.

- Intergovernmentalism focuses on how the policy preferences and actions of the governments, in particular Germany, France, and Britain, shape the design of the EU at the various stages of integration.

- Supranationalism focuses on how the underlying economic, political, and social factors and the behaviour of interest groups and EU institutions constrain the choices of governments and hence further integration.

Understanding the EU as a political system

A political system but not a state

In the 1950s, comparative political scientists tried to develop a common framework for analysing the complex array of political systems throughout the world (e.g. Almond 1956; Easton 1957; see also the Introduction to this volume). There are four essential characteristics of all democratic political systems.

1. There is a clearly defined set of institutions for collective decision-making and rules governing relations between these institutions.

2. Citizens seek to achieve their political desires through the political system, either directly or through intermediary organizations such as interest groups and political parties.

3. Collective decisions have an impact on the distribution of economic resources and the allocation of values across the whole system.

4. There is a continuous interaction between these political outputs, new demands on the system, new decisions, and so on.

The EU possesses all these characteristics. First, the level of institutional development in the EU is far greater than in any other international organization. Second, a large number of public and private groups, from multinational corporations and global environmental groups to individual citizens, are involved and influence the EU policy process. Third, EU policy outcomes are highly significant and are felt throughout the EU. Fourth, the EU political system is a permanent feature of political life in Europe. The quarterly meetings of the heads of government of the member-states in the European Council may be the only feature that many citizens and media outlets notice. Nevertheless, EU politics is a continuous process, within and between the EU institutions in Brussels, national governments and Brussels, national public administrations, private interests and governmental officials in Brussels and at the national level, and private groups involved in EU affairs at the national and European levels.

Conceptualizing the EU as a political system rather than a unique example of regional integration enabled social scientists in the late 1980s and early 1990s to start to apply tools and methods from the comparative study of political systems to the EU (Scharpf 1988; Streeck and Schmitter 1991; Sbragia 1992; Tsebelis 1994; van der Eijk and Franklin 1996; Majone 1996; McKay 1996; Hix 2005). These tools helped provide answers to a new set of generalizable questions, such as which actors are most influential in the EU legisla-

tive process, how independent from political control is the ECJ, why do some citizens support the EU while others oppose it, and why does the EU produce some policy outcomes but not others?

The constitutional architecture of the EU

The Treaty establishing a Constitution for Europe, which was signed by the member-states in 2004, was an effort to simplify and codify the rules of the EU. The proposed 'EU Constitution' was rejected by voters in France and the Netherlands in 2005. The resulting Lisbon Treaty, which entered into force in December 2009, stripped away many of the symbolic elements from the original 'Constitution' but kept almost all the provisions relating to the simplification of the competences of the EU relative to the member-states and the changes to the powers of the EU institutions. But even before the proposed EU Constitution and the resulting Lisbon Treaty, the EU had a basic 'constitutional architecture'. Indeed, one of the remarkable things about the new treaty is how little of the established policy and institutional architecture it actually changed.

As far as policies are concerned (Box 23.2), the EU level has exclusive responsibility for the regulation of the single market, and for managing the competition, customs, and trade policies that derive from this task. The EU level is also responsible for the monetary policies of the member-states whose currency is the euro, and for the common agricultural and fisheries policies. A wide array of policy competences is 'shared' between the EU and the member-states, in which EU policies aim to supplement existing national policies. This is the case, for example, in the areas of labour market regulation, regional spending, and immigration and asylum. The third area of policies can be described as 'coordinated competences'. Action remains primarily at the member-state level, but the governments accept that they need to coordinate their policies because there are effects on each other. For example, with the freedom of movement of persons inside the EU there is a need to coordinate some policing and criminal justice policies. Similarly, following the sovereign debt crisis that occurred after 2009, the states who share the single currency decided to undertake much deeper coordination of their macro-economic policies. Finally, all the major areas of public spending, such as education, health care, transport, housing, welfare provision, and pensions, remain formally the exclusive preserve of the member-states, although EU policies and agreements inevitably have an impact on how national governments deliver these policies.

Turning to the institutions, Box 23.3 describes the basic institutional architecture of the EU. Executive powers are shared between the Council and the

ZOOM-IN 23.2

The basic policy architecture of the EU

Exclusive EU competences

Regulation of the single market, including removing barriers and competition policy

Customs union and external trade policies

Monetary policy for the member-states whose currency is the euro

Price-setting and subsidy of production under the Common Agricultural Policy

Common fisheries policy

Shared competences (where action is taken at both national and European levels)

Social regulation, such as health and safety at work, gender equality, and non-discrimination

Environmental regulation

Consumer protection and common public health concerns, such as food safety

Economic, social, and territorial cohesion

Free movement of persons, including policies towards third-country nationals

Transport

Energy

Coordinated competences (where national actions are coordinated at the EU level)

Macro-economic policies

Foreign and defence policies

Policing and criminal justice policies

Health, cultural, education, tourism, youth, sport, and vocational training policies

Exclusive member-state competences

All other policies (e.g. most areas of public spending)

ZOOM-IN 23.3

The basic institutional architecture of the EU

Council of the European Union and the European Council (Brussels)

The Council of the European Union and the European Council bring together the governments of the EU member-states, and exercise by legislative and executive functions. On the legislative side, the Council adopts EU legislation and the budget. On the executive side, the Council coordinates the broad economic policies of the member-states, concludes international agreements of the EU, develops the common foreign and security policy, coordinates cooperation between national courts and police forces, and reforms EU treaties. The Council meets in ten configurations: general affairs; foreign affairs; economic and financial affairs; justice and home affairs; employment, social policy, health, and consumer affairs; competitiveness; transport, telecommunications and energy; agriculture and fisheries; environment; and education, youth, culture, and sport. The overall agenda of the Council, and the general direction of the EU, is set by a separate institution—the European Council—which brings together the twenty-eight heads of state and government of the EU member-states six or seven times a year. The current full-time president of the European Council is Charles Michel, the liberal former Prime Minister of Belgium (until the end of May 2022). The presidency of Council rotates between the member-states every six months. The Council is aided by the Committee of Permanent Representatives of the EU (COREPER), which is composed of the ambassadors of the member-states to the EU.

European Parliament (Brussels, Strasbourg, and Luxembourg)

There are 751 MEPs, who are elected every five years by the EU citizens, and organize together in transnational political groups. The Parliament is half of the EU's legislative authority (jointly with the Council). The Parliament amends and adopts EU legislation and the budget, and monitors the work of the other EU institutions. The Parliament formally 'elects' the Commission president and the team of commissioners and also has the right to censure the Commission as a whole (by a two-thirds majority vote).

European Commission (Brussels)

The Commission is composed of one member from each member-state and is the main executive body of the EU. The Commission is responsible for proposing EU legislation, managing and implementing EU policies and the budget, enforcing EU law (jointly with the ECJ), and representing the EU on the international stage (e.g. in the World Trade Organization). The Commission is divided into Directorates General (DGs), each of which is responsible for a different area of policy. Following each European Parliament election, the Commission president is nominated by a qualified majority vote in the European Council and elected or rejected by an absolute majority in the European Parliament. Ursula von der Leyen, the Christian democratic former cabinet minister of Germany, was elected Commission president in 2019 and her term expires in 2024.

European Court of Justice (Luxembourg)

The European Court of Justice (ECJ) is the judicial authority of the EU. The ECJ ensures that EU legislation is interpreted and applied in the same way in all member-states and undertakes judicial review of the Treaties, the secondary legislation, and the tertiary instruments of the EU. The ECJ is composed of one judge per member-state. The Court is assisted by eleven advocates general. Koen Lenaerts (from Belgium) was elected president of the ECJ in 2014. To help the ECJ

with the large number of cases, the ECJ is assisted by the Court of First Instance.

Other institutions

The *European Central Bank* (Frankfurt) is responsible for monetary policy, including setting interest rates for the European single currency (the euro).

The *European Court of Auditors* (Luxembourg) checks that EU funds are properly collected and spent legally, economically, and for their intended purpose.

The *Committee of the Regions* (Brussels) represents regions and local authorities in the member-states in the EU policy-making process.

The *European Investment Bank* (Luxembourg) finances EU investment projects.

There are over forty other EU agencies, such as the European Environment Agency (Copenhagen), European Food Safety Authority (Parma), European Agency for the Management of Operational Cooperation at the External Borders–FRONTEX (Warsaw), European Monitoring Centre on Racism and Xenophobia (Vienna), European Defence Agency (Brussels), and European Police Office–EUROPOL (the Hague).

Commission. Whereas the European Council sets the medium and long-term policy agendas and resolves the major political bargains in EU politics (such as the multi-annual budget or the appointment of the Commission president), the Commission has a formal monopoly on legislative initiative. The Commission and the member-states are also jointly responsible for the implementation of EU policies. Legislative

power is shared between two institutions: the legislative meetings of the Council and the European Parliament. The European Parliament has equal power with the Council under the main legislative procedure, the *co-decision procedure* (formally called the 'ordinary legislative procedure'). Finally, judicial power in the EU is shared between the ECJ and national courts, where national courts are primarily responsible for enforcing EU law and refer cases to the ECJ if a domestic case raises a significant point of EU law.

Vertical dimension: the EU as a 'regulatory state'

The dominant policy goal of the EU is the creation and regulation of a market on a continental scale. Other policies are in many respects 'flanking' policies of this goal. These policies make Europe's continental-scale market work more effectively (the single currency), or correct potential market failures (environmental and social policies), or compensate potential losers from market integration (budgetary policies), or address potential social and security externalities from market integration (justice and interior policies). Given the primacy of the single

KEY POINTS

- The EU is not a 'state' in that powers are shared between the EU and the member-states; the EU is based on voluntary cooperation between the member-states, there is no direct EU taxation, the EU budget is small, and the EU relies on the forces of coercion of its member-states.

- Nevertheless, the EU can be understood as a political system, in that it possesses a constitutional architecture which determines the balance between the EU and the member-states and between the institutions at the European level, and the policies of the EU have significant implications on the economy and society in Europe.

- Conceptualizing the EU as a political system allows application of tools and methods from the comparative study of political systems.

market and the centrality of EU market regulation policies, the EU is often described as a 'regulatory state' (Majone 1996). This concept nicely captures the contrast between the main policies of the EU and the main policies at the national level in Europe, via taxation and public spending.

Creation and regulation of the single market

The single market notionally started on 1 January 1993, after the passage of almost 300 pieces of legislation. However, in practice the single market is an ongoing project, as major areas of the economy (such as the provision of services and the professions) still operate in separate national markets.

The creation of the single market has both deregulatory and re-regulatory elements. On the *deregulatory* side, creating the single market involves the removal of barriers to the free movement of goods, services, capital, and labour between the EU member-states. Three types of barriers had to be removed:

1. *fiscal barriers*, such as the harmonization of value-added tax and excise duties (on goods like alcohol and tobacco);

2. *physical barriers* on the movement of goods and persons, such as the abolition of customs formalities. Removing border controls on the movement of persons was also an original aim of the single-market programme. However, several member-states (including the UK, Ireland, and Denmark) refused to accept that it was necessary to remove border controls in order for the free movement of persons to function effectively—all that was needed, they contended, was the right to move, reside, and work anywhere in the EU. In response, the other member-states agreed to remove their border controls as part of the Schengen Accord, which was initially outside the formal framework of the EU.

3. *technical barriers* to the free movement of goods and services, such as separate national product standards that could be used as 'non-tariff barriers'. The EU had tried to establish common standards via harmonized rules throughout the EU. However, in the landmark *Cassis de Dijon* judgment in 1979, the ECJ established the principle of 'mutual recognition', whereby any product meeting the standards of one member-state can be legally sold in all other member-states. Another key area of removal of technical barriers was in public procurement, where rules were established

preventing governments from favouring home companies in public contracts. A host of directives have also been passed to liberalize air, water, and road transport, and to open up national energy, telecoms, and television markets. Regarding the movement of capital, controls on the free flow of capital between the member-states were abolished, and the European Company Statute, which enables multinational companies to be registered as single European-wide entities, was adopted in 2001.

On the *re-regulatory* side, as part of the single-market programme, the EU replaced existing national regulations. The three clearest examples of this are EU competition policies, environmental policies, and social policies. On *competition policies*, the EU has antitrust regulations (which outlaw a variety of agreements between companies such as price-fixing or predatory pricing) and prohibits government subsidies to industry that threaten competition between the member-states, and the Commission is required to review mergers between companies of a certain size. On *environmental policy*, common EU regulations cover, among other things, air and noise pollution, waste disposal, water pollution, chemicals, biodiversity, environmental impact assessments, eco-labelling and eco-audits, and natural and technological hazards. On *social policy*, EU legislation covers the rights of workers to free movement, health and safety at work, working conditions, worker consultation, gender equality, anti-discrimination (race, ethnic origin, religion, disability, age, and sexual orientation), and rights of part-time and temporary workers.

Re-regulatory policies are usually regarded as benefiting all EU citizens, rather than particular groups by correcting certain 'market failures' that might arise in a continental-scale market. For example, harmonized consumer protection standards enable consumers to gain information about the quality of products that would otherwise not be publicly available. Health and safety standards and environmental standards reduce the adverse effects ('negative externalities') of market transactions on individuals not participating in the transactions. Competition policies prevent monopolistic markets from emerging, market distortions, and anticompetitive practices. Put this way, EU 'social regulations' are very different from national 'social policies', in that while the latter are usually geared towards providing benefits to particular social groups, the former aim to allow the labour market to function more efficiently.

Nevertheless, there are significant indirect redistributive consequences. The EU does not have the direct redistributive capacity of national **welfare states** (see Chapter 21 'The welfare state'), but the regulatory regime reflects a particular 'welfare compromise' at the European level that constrains existing welfare compromises and choices at the domestic level. For example, the single market places downward pressure on states with higher labour market standards (such as Germany and Scandinavia). In addition, the redistributive capacities of the national welfare states are further constrained by the restrictions on national fiscal policies as a result of economic and monetary union.

Economic and Monetary Union

The Maastricht Treaty (1993) established a three-point plan for Economic and Monetary Union (EMU).

1. It involved a timetable, with the launch of EMU on 1 January 1999 and the introduction of euro notes and coins on 1 January 2002.

2. It established four 'convergence criteria', which member-states have to meet to be able to join the single currency: (i) a stable currency; (ii) a convergent economic cycle with the EU average cycle; (iii) an annual government deficit of less than 3 per cent of GDP; and (iv) a gross public debt of less than 60 per cent of GDP.

3. It established an institutional design of EMU.

The European Central Bank (ECB) has the sole responsibility of defining and implementing monetary policy (including setting interest rates) for the member-states whose currency is the euro, with the sole aim of maintaining price stability. The ECB comprises a six-member executive board, appointed by the European Council, and a governing council, comprising the executive board members and the governors of the national central banks of the EMU member-states. However, the governments, meeting in the Council of Economic and Finance Ministers, have the final say over interventions in foreign exchange markets, adopt common economic policy guidelines for the EU as a whole, and monitor the national economic policies of the EU member-states.

Not all EU member-states are members of EMU. Eleven of the then fifteen EU states launched EMU in 1999—Austria, Belgium, Finland, France, Germany, Ireland, Italy, Luxembourg, the Netherlands, Portugal, and Spain. Greece became the twelfth EMU member in 2001. Of the 'old fifteen' states, the UK, Denmark, and Sweden chose to stay outside EMU, and none of the 'new ten' joined the EMU when they became members of the EU in 2004, but by 2015 seven of the new ten member-states had joined the euro (Cyprus, Estonia, Latvia, Lithuania, Malta, Slovakia, and Slovenia). Today, nineteen of the twenty-eight EU states are in the Eurozone, while nine remain outside.

A key element of the EMU is the Stability and Growth Pact (SGP). The German government, in particular, was concerned that once states had met the initial convergence criteria and entered EMU they might then be tempted to run large public deficits, which would undermine the stability of the euro and so negatively affect the more fiscally responsible states. Hence, the SGP was agreed in 1997 as a way to limit this problem by requiring that member-states must maintain an annual budget deficit of less than 3 per cent of GDP, or otherwise face a fine (established as a percentage of national GDP). However, one problem with the pact was that a fine could only be imposed by collective agreement. When France and Germany were the first major breakers of the SGP rules, no fine was imposed, which brought its credibility into question.

However, almost two decades after the launch of the euro it became clear that the convergence criteria and the SGP rules were insufficient to guarantee economic convergence among the Eurozone member-states. In 2009, the banking liquidity crisis spilled over into a sovereign debt crisis. The interest rates charged on Greek government bonds rose to unprecedented levels. Member-states feared that if the Greek government defaulted on its debts it would have to leave the euro. Hence, the other member-states—particularly those countries (such as Germany) whose banks were lending money to Greek, Irish, and Portuguese governments and banks—had to prevent the potential collapse of the Eurozone. The Eurozone member-states pieced together a plan to ensure stability in the Eurozone.

There are three main elements to the emerging new architecture of the Eurozone. First, the European Stability Mechanism (ESM), which entered into force in 2012, is a financial instrument backed by national taxpayers. Second, in return for this 'emergency bailout fund', the creditor states (such as Germany, the Netherlands, and Finland) insisted that measures should be taken by debtor states to ensure economic stability. These measures include 'austerity' agreements in return for loans, a new Fiscal Compact Treaty under which states must introduce a 'balanced budget' clause in their national constitutions, and more extensive oversight of national macro-economic policies (including pensions, unemployment benefits, labour market rules). Third, to reduce the likelihood of future banking crises, and to guarantee banking liquidity, a 'banking union' was set up, under which all banks would be governed by a single set of rules and regulated by the European Central Bank. Only time will tell whether these measures are sufficient to guarantee stability in the Eurozone.

The main theoretical framework for understanding economic and monetary integration is the 'optimal currency area' (OCA) theory, developed by Robert Mundell (1961). According to this theory, independent states will form a monetary union if the benefits of joining exceed the costs. The main cost of a monetary union is the loss of an independent exchange rate. With a 'one-size-fits-all' monetary policy, differential economic cycles between states have to be tackled by other policies, such as labour mobility (from states in recession to states growing more quickly), wage flexibility (where workers in the state where there is low demand reduce their wages), or fiscal transfers (from high-growth to low-growth states). If labour mobility is low, if there is limited wage flexibility, and if fiscal transfers are small, a group of states do not form an OCA. Put this way, the EU is clearly not an OCA.

However, for some states, the economic benefits of EMU might outweigh some of these potential costs. A single currency lowers transactions costs in the economy (by removing the need to change money), produces a more efficient market, leads to greater economic certainty, and in general creates lower interest rates and higher growth rates. In general, for states with high levels of trade integration with the Eurozone, the benefits of joining EMU outweigh the costs, since higher trade integration means higher economic convergence and the greater transaction costs benefits of a single currency (e.g. Krugman 1990). In contrast, for states with lower trade integration and less convergent economic cycles, the costs of joining EMU are likely to outweigh the benefits—which is, broadly speaking, the current situation of the UK.

EU expenditure policies

Compared with the powerful effects of the single market and EMU on the lives of EU citizens, and in contrast with the huge public spending programmes of the national governments, the spending power of the EU is small, since the EU budget represents only about 1 per cent of the total GDP of the EU member-states. Spread across all EU citizens, the costs of the EU budget are absolutely tiny. However, for those who receive money out of the EU budget—namely poorer states, farmers, backward economic regions, and scientists—the sums can be huge.

The EU adopts multi-annual budgets. The main EU spending policy is the Common Agricultural Policy (CAP), which is a system of price support for a wide range of agricultural products and other subsidies to farmers. The CAP represents more than 25 per cent of total EU spending. The second main area of EU spending is on regional policy, which is targeted at economically backward regions, regions with high levels of unemployment, and regions undergoing major industrial restructuring. EU regional funds are mainly spent on infrastructure projects, such as roads, schools, airports, and telecommunications systems. The third main area of EU spending is on scientific research. Most of the EU's research and development funds are distributed to networks of researchers working in the natural sciences, such as biotechnology and telecommunications.

EU spending policies are a combination of 'solidarity' and 'side payments'. On the *solidarity* side, transfers through the EU budget have generally passed from the richer states to the poorer states, on the grounds that the EU is more than simply an economic union, and so there should be some mechanism for redistributing wealth. On the *side-payments* side, however, most EU spending policies are the result of specific intergovernmental bargains, where member-states who expect to 'lose' from major policy changes in the EU demand some compensation. For example, in the Treaty of Rome negotiations, France proposed the CAP, as a subsidy regime mainly for French farmers, because the common market was expected to benefit Germany's manufacturing-based economy. Similarly, in return for agreeing to the single-market programme (which was expected to benefit the main exporting economies of central and northern Europe), Spain, Italy, Portugal, Ireland, and Greece requested a doubling of EU spending under the regional funds.

Figure 23.1 shows the relationship between a member-state's GDP per capita and their per capita net contributions to the EU budget in 2017 (excluding Luxembourg, and excluding EU administrative spending). Those member-states about 0 on the y axis are net contributors into the EU budget (with Germany and Sweden at the top, as measured by net contributions per capita), while those member-states below 0 are net beneficiaries. The figure also plots a linear regression 'best fit' line between GDP per capita and net contributions per capita. Those member-states above this line contribute more to the EU budget or do not receive enough from the EU budget given their per capita wealth, while those states below the line receive more from the EU budget than their per capita wealth predicts. Prior to the 2004 enlargement, there were four main net beneficiary states: Greece, Ireland, Portugal, and Spain. Nevertheless, after the 2004 enlargement, the benefits to these countries fell considerably, as the funds began to be targeted towards the poorer regions in many of the new member-states. Nevertheless, the three member-states that joined later—Bulgaria,

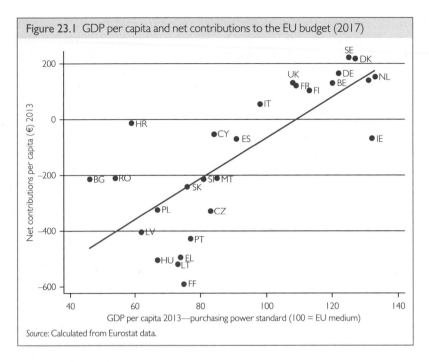

Figure 23.1 GDP per capita and net contributions to the EU budget (2017)

Source: Calculated from Eurostat data.

Romania, and Croatia—receive less money from the EU budget per capita than most of the Central and East European states who joined earlier.

Once spending policies have been set up, they are very difficult to change, even if the original policy aims are no longer justified. This is because any change to the multi-annual EU budget requires unanimous agreement among the governments.

Interior policies and external relations

Finally, there are two main areas of EU policy-making that are not strictly related to the EU's main economic policies:

- the array of justice and interior affairs policies, which include immigration, asylum, and other policies on the free movement of persons (both from third countries into the EU and between EU member-states), as well as police and judicial cooperation;
- the EU's external relations policies, which include trade policies, development and humanitarian aid, the Common Foreign and Security Policy (CFSP), and European Security and Defence Cooperation (ESDP).

While in economic terms the EU is more a 'regulatory state' than a 'welfare state', where the EU's interior and external relations policies are concerned, the EU is developing some elements of a 'security state' managing the *internal and external* political rights, responsibilities, and security of their citizens.

Justice and interior policies

On the internal side, the Maastricht Treaty established the Justice and Home Affairs pillar of the EU, which brought into the legal framework of the EU a number of existing intergovernmental cooperation arrangements between the interior ministries of the EU member-states. These provisions covered the removal of border controls between the member-states, immigration and asylum policies and common policies towards 'third-country nationals', and police and judicial cooperation to combat drug-trafficking, terrorist activities, cross-border crime, and illegal immigration.

The Amsterdam Treaty separated the policies covering the movement of persons (immigration, asylum, internal and external borders, etc.) from the police and judicial cooperation policies. The free-movement policies were set up in the main body of the EU treaty in the framework of a new 'area of freedom, security and justice'. Since the Amsterdam Treaty, the EU has adopted a large number of legislative acts in this area covering common rules for non-EU nationals working in the EU. The Amsterdam Treaty also incorporated the Schengen Agreement into the EU treaties—an agreement between twenty-two EU member-states (excluding Bulgaria, Croatia, Cyprus, Ireland, Romania, and the UK) plus Iceland, Liechtenstein, Norway, and Switzerland, to remove border controls and passport checks between them.

A key element of the EU's migration policies is the Dublin Regulation, of 2003 (revised in 2013), which sets out how the member-states should apply a common EU asylum policy, including the provision that the first member-state where an asylum claim is lodged is then responsible for a person's asylum claim. This was meant to prevent 'asylum shopping', where a refugee could apply for asylum in one member-state and then move to another one and apply again. However, this system came under huge strain following the migration crisis that developed in the summer and autumn of 2015, as a result of the transit of over 1 million refugees to Europe from the conflicts in Syria and Iraq in the space of a few months. Greece and Italy, who received most of the refugees, were simply unable to process all the new arrivals or prevent them from moving on to the other states they wanted to reach, such as Germany or Sweden. In practice, the Dublin system had collapsed.

Related to this, in 2004 the EU set up a new agency, FRONTEX, to manage the cooperation between national border guards securing its external borders. Then, following the 2015 refugee crisis, the European Commission proposed a new European Border and Coast Guard Agency to replace FRONTEX, which would have a stronger mandate, and a new European Border and Coast Guard, which would operate alongside national authorities for border control. Nevertheless, despite these new common policies and institutions for managing the EU's external borders, by the end of 2015 many member-states had re-established internal border checks in response to the growing volume of asylum seekers and refugees crossing the continent—against the principles of the Schengen Agreement.

Foreign and defence policies

On the external side, since the establishment of a common market, the EU has had a single external trade policy, where the Commission represents the EU in the World Trade Organization (WTO) and in bilateral and multilateral trade negotiations. The EU has also developed an array of external economic policy instruments that it uses to project 'soft power' on the world stage (see Chapter 25 'From supporting democracy to supporting autocracy'). These include direct humanitarian and economic assistance, as well as various preferential trade agreements, such as the European Economic Area (EEA), association agreements, free-trade agreements, partnership agreements (e.g. with the EU member-states' former colonies in Africa, the Caribbean, and the Pacific), inter-regional association agreements with other regional trade blocs, and mutual recognition agreements (mainly with the US).

External security and defence policies developed more slowly. However, the Maastricht Treaty formally established the CFSP pillar of the EU, to which the Nice Treaty added the ESDP—as the 'European pillar' of the North Atlantic Treaty Organization (NATO) transatlantic defence alliance. Under CFSP, the EU member-states adopt, by unanimity, 'common strategies' and 'common positions' which set out the EU's position on a key foreign policy issue. Then, the EU member-states only require a qualified majority vote to adopt a 'joint action' implementing a common position. This combination has allowed the EU to act in a wide variety of areas. For example, in 2003 the EU adopted a common European Security Strategy, which set out how and why EU security policies differed from the US administration's 'pre-emptive strike' doctrine. Since 2003, the EU has carried out many civilian missions and military operations, as well as several rapid-response operations by EU-led battle groups. In 2008, the EU helped broker a ceasefire between Georgia and Russia, and in 2013 the EU played a leading role in the international agreement on Iran's nuclear programme, which enabled US and EU sanctions on Iran to be relaxed.

Nevertheless, a genuinely 'common' EU foreign policy is inevitably hampered by the conflicting security and foreign policy preferences of the key EU member-states, as was so clearly demonstrated by the inability of the EU to have a clear and decisive strategy towards Russia's actions in the Ukraine and the conflict in Syria and Iraq.

KEY POINTS

- Regulation of the free movement of goods, services, capital, and labour is the main policy instrument, as part of the creation and organization of the single market.

- Economic and monetary union is a complement to the single market, in that a single market functions more effectively with a single currency, and a single currency governed by an interdependent central bank ensures economic stability.

- EU expenditure policies, in contrast, are a secondary policy instrument of the EU, and have mainly been used to enable major steps in the process of economic integration by consensus.

- The EU has begun to expand beyond economic policies, into justice and interior affairs policies and foreign and security policies, and policy-making in these areas has developed rapidly in recent years.

- The basic policy architecture of the EU, where a continental-scale market is created and regulated at the European level while spending and security policies remain largely at the national level, means that the EU is more a 'regulatory state' than a welfare state or security state.

Horizontal dimension: a hyper-consensus system of government

The main determinant of how policies are made by the central institutions in a political system is how far the power to set the agenda and the power to veto decisions are centralized in a single actor or dispersed between multiple actors. At one extreme, a political system can have a single 'agenda setter' and 'veto player'—for example, where there is single-party government. At the other extreme, multiple actors could potentially veto any change to existing policies—for example, where there is coalition government or where there is a separation of powers between the executive (the president) and the legislature (Tsebelis 2002). In the EU, multiple actors have the ability to block policy changes in its legislative process. As a result, the EU has an extremely consensual model of government.

Executive politics: competing agenda setters

First of all, agenda-setting power is split between the heads of government in the European Council and the Commission. The heads of government, meeting in the European Council, decide on treaty reforms, which determine the allocation of powers between the EU institutions, and set the medium-term policy agenda. The European Commission, meanwhile, has a formal monopoly on the initiative of most EU legislation.

In the European Council, political leadership is shared between the permanent president of the European Council (often mislabelled the 'EU president') and the government of the member-state who holds the six-monthly rotating presidency of the other meetings of the Council (Hayes-Renshaw and Wallace 2006; Tallberg 2006). Because the president of the European Council, who is appointed for a period of two-and-a-half years (renewable once), is a new position created by the Lisbon Treaty, it is not yet clear how powerful the person holding this position is. Regarding the rotating presidency of the Council, some member-states are clearly better at this role than others. For example, larger member-states generally have more administrative capacity. However, the largest member-states also tend to try to place their domestic political issues on the EU agenda, and are less concerned about coordinating the overall policy agenda with the Commission. Furthermore, the powers of the rotating Council presidency are actually quite limited. This is because the member-state holding the rotating Council presidency cannot initiate legislation, and must deal with legislation that has already been initiated by the Commission and may already have been through several stages of negotiations.

The Commission, on the other hand, has traditionally been regarded as being politically and institutionally committed to the process of European integration, and so is often assumed to have policy preferences that are more 'integrationist' than most member-states. For example, in the process of creating the single market, the Commission generally wants legislation that promotes further market integration or a high level of EU-wide regulation. Nevertheless, this view of the Commission as an 'integrationist preference outlier' may be unfounded. The commissioners are appointed by national governments, and most commissioners have strong ties to the political parties who chose them and seek to return to domestic politics after their careers in the Commission. Hence, commissioners are unlikely to be very much more pro-integrationist than the governments that appoint them. Also, below the level of the commissioners, research has shown that the senior officials in the Commission bureaucracy have policy preferences that are typical of politicians from the member-states from which they come and from the national political parties they support (Hooghe 2001).

In addition, since the college of commissioners formally decides by a majority vote, the Commission generally initiates policies that are close to the policy preferences of the median member of the Commission (Crombez 1997; Hug 2003). Nevertheless, the left–right policy location of the Commission has changed dramatically in recent years. Whereas the Prodi Commission was relatively evenly balanced between left and right, a clear majority of the members of both the first and second Barroso Commissions were on the centre-right, and the Juncker Commission is again more politically balanced. This change is partly explained by the shifting make-up of the governments who appoint the commissioners. The shift is also explained by a change introduced by the Nice Treaty, whereby the larger member-states no longer have two commissioners each. Now that each member-state has only one commissioner, the make-up of the Commission mirrors the political make-up of the Council at the time that the commissioners are appointed.

Bicameral legislative politics: rising power of the European Parliament

The most significant change over the past thirty years in the way that the EU institutions work has been the steady increase in the powers of the European Parliament. Originally, the European Parliament had a limited right to be consulted. However, with the programme to establish the single market, which required the adoption of over 300 pieces of legislation, the European Parliament was granted two readings of most major pieces of legislation and was able to have a significant impact on how the single market was designed (Tsebelis 1994). The Maastricht Treaty then established the **co-decision** procedure, which was extended by the Amsterdam and the Lisbon Treaties. As a result, today the European Parliament and the Council have equal power in almost all areas of EU legislation.

The co-decision procedure works as follows. The Commission is responsible for proposing legislation to the Parliament and Council. The Parliament then adopts an 'opinion', in the form of a series of amendments. These amendments are prepared in one of the Parliament's committees, where one of the members of the European Parliament (the 'rapporteur') is responsible for writing the Parliament's report on the bill and shepherding the legislation through the committee and the plenary. Once the plenary of the Parliament has adopted the report, the Council takes a 'common position' on the bill. If the texts adopted by the Council and Parliament are identical after the first readings, the legislation is adopted and becomes law. If the texts are not identical, the legislation passes back to the European Parliament for a second reading and back to the Council for a second reading. If the two institutions still cannot agree, a Conciliation Committee is convened. If the Conciliation Committee reaches an agreement on a 'joint text', this is put to the Parliament and the Council for a final reading. In addition, throughout the procedure, the key actors from the Commission (the Commissioner responsible), the Parliament (the rapporteur and committee chair), and the Council (the officials from the member-state holding the rotating presidency) meet in a series of informal 'trialogues' to try to reach agreement.

This may sound complicated; however, the procedure is remarkably efficient in that the EU adopts approximately 100 pieces of legislation a year through the procedure. Also, in recent years, over 80 per cent of the bills that pass through the co-decision procedure are adopted after just the first reading, although these 'early agreements' are more common in some policy areas than others—namely in justice and home affairs (where there is often high political pressure to reach agreement), and where existing legislation is amended (Reh et al. 2013).

Table 23.1 shows the system of representation in the Council and European Parliament. When voting on legislation the Council usually acts by 'qualified majority voting' (QMV). Unanimous voting is kept for some highly sensitive policy issues, such as tax harmonization. Before the Lisbon Treaty, QMV was based on a system of weighted voting, with bigger states having more votes than smaller states. Lisbon replaced this system with a 'double-majority', wherein to adopt a measure a qualified majority must be composed of 55 per cent of the member-states (sixteen out of the current twenty-eight) as well as 65 per cent of the total EU population. As the table shows, the largest states (particularly Germany) have significantly more 'power' under this system than the medium-sized and smaller states, but still less power than if the system were based purely on population size.

Nevertheless, this measure of the 'power' of the member-states in the Council is only one way of understanding how the Council works. Voting rarely takes place in the Council, as there are strong incentives for the governments to decide by 'consensus' (Naurin and Wallace 2008). And, when votes do take place, coalitions form between the governments in the Council along geopolitical, economic, and ideological lines—for example, north versus south, east versus west, net contributors versus net beneficiaries, and left governments versus right governments (e.g. Mattila 2004; Hagemann 2008).

Table 23.1 also shows the number of seats per member-state in the European Parliament. The size of the Parliament has increased tenfold since it was first established in the early 1950s, and has almost doubled in size since it was first elected in June 1979. The number of seats per member-state has also been changed with successive enlargements. In general, large member-states have more seats than smaller member-states, but there are still more citizens per Member of the European Parliament (MEP) in a larger member-state than in a smaller member-state.

However, again, these numbers are misleading, in that the MEPs do not sit or vote along national lines. Ever since the first session of the Parliament in September 1952, the MEPs have formed transnational political groups, and sat in the Parliament along left–right lines. The European People's Party (EPP), which brings together all the main Christian democratic and conservative parties, has been the largest group in the European Parliament since 2004, with the Alliance of Socialists and Democrats (S&D), which brings together all the socialist, social democratic, and labour parties, the second largest. Between these two groups is a coalition of centrist and liberal parties: the Alliance of Liberals and Democrats for Europe. There are two smaller parties who sit to the left of the socialists: a coalition of green and left-regionalist parties (the Greens/European Free Alliance), and a group of left-socialist and ex-communist

Table 23.1 Representation in the Council and European Parliament				
Member-state	Pop'n, 2018 (m)	Council voting 'power'	MEPs	Pop'n per MEP, 2018
Germany	81.1	10.22	96	844,681
France	66.4	8.47	74	896,655
UK	64.8	8.29	73	887,221
Italy	61.4	7.84	73	841,623
Spain	46.4	6.21	54	859,997
Poland	38.0	5.09	51	745,208
Romania	19.9	3.79	32	620,669
Netherlands	17.2	3.48	26	659,814
Belgium	11.3	2.90	21	536,116
Greece	10.8	2.85	21	516,523
Czech Republic	10.4	2.82	21	496,178
Portugal	10.4	2.81	21	494,039
Hungary	9.9	2.75	21	469,313
Sweden	9.8	2.74	20	489,500
Austria	8.6	2.63	18	476,750
Bulgaria	7.2	2.49	17	423,659
Denmark	5.7	2.33	13	434,874
Finland	5.5	2.31	13	420,904
Slovakia	5.4	2.30	13	415,626
Ireland	4.6	2.22	11	420,535
Croatia	4.2	2.18	11	384,120
Lithuania	2.9	2.05	11	265,569
Slovenia	2.1	1.96	8	257,859
Latvia	2.0	1.95	8	248,262
Estonia	1.3	1.88	6	218,879
Cyprus	0.8	1.83	6	141,168
Luxembourg	0.6	1.81	6	93,826
Malta	0.4	1.79	6	71,557
Total	**509.1**	**100.00**	**751**	**677,684**

Note: Council voting power is measured by the normalized Banzhaf power index.

parties (the European United Left/Nordic Green Left). Three groups sit to the right of the EPP: a group of more Eurosceptic conservative parties (the European Conservatives and Reformists Group), a group of anti-European parties (Europe of Freedom and Direct Democracy), and a group of radical right MEPs (Europe of Nations and Freedoms), which was formed after the 2014 elections. Finally, the remaining MEPs sit as 'non-attached' members, who are mostly from extreme right parties.

Judicial politics: a powerful and independent court

The ECJ, together with national courts, provides a powerful check on the EU's executive and legislative institutions. The ECJ played a significant role in the development of the legal basis of the EU political system, in particular by developing *the doctrines of the direct effect and supremacy of EU law*. On several occasions, the ECJ has struck down legislation adopted by the Council and Parliament on the grounds that the treaties did not give the EU the right to adopt legislation in a particular area. Like all supreme courts, the ECJ is not completely isolated from external pressures, since it knows that if it strays too far from the meaning of the treaties, the governments can act collectively to rein in its powers. The ECJ is also aware that national courts, particularly the German Constitutional Court, are protective of their right to interpret whether EU law is in breach of fundamental human rights as set out in national constitutions (see Chapter 9 'Constitutions, rights, and judicial power'). The EU's Charter of Fundamental Rights, which became part of EU law with the Lisbon Treaty, is an attempt to provide a set of basic rights for the ECJ to apply, but it is not yet clear whether the highest national courts will accept ECJ supremacy in this area.

KEY POINTS

- With multiple actors and checks and balances, the EU has a hyper-consensus system of government.

- On the positive side, the checks and balances mean that legislation cannot be adopted without overwhelming support in the Commission, amongst the governments in the Council, and the parties in the European Parliament, and with the approval of the ECJ.

- On the negative side, the checks and balances mean that the EU is prone to 'gridlock' and lowest common denominator policy outcomes, and these problems are likely to increase with the enlargement of the EU from fifteen to twenty-eight or more states.

Democratic politics: the missing link?

Procedurally, the EU is 'democratic', in that the governments in the Council and the MEPs are elected by EU citizens, the EU's decision-making procedures are fair and transparent, and the checks and balances in the EU system ensure that policy outcomes from the EU are inevitably close to some notional EU-wide median voter (Moravcsik 2002). In a substantive sense, however, the EU does not have real 'democratic politics', meaning that there is competition between political elites for political office and in the policy process, there are identifiable winners and losers of this competition, and there is participation and identification of the public with one side or another in the political process (Føllesdal and Hix 2006).

Low public support for the EU

One of the key problems facing the EU is the relatively low and declining support for the project. Since the early 1970s, Eurobarometer polls of public attitudes towards the EU have been conducted every six months in every member-state. Public support for the EU rose in the late 1980s, with the widespread enthusiasm for the single-market project, but then declined rapidly until the mid-1990s and has remained at a relatively low level ever since. These days, only about one in two EU citizens think that their country's membership of the EU is a good thing. There is a widespread belief that the EU is an elitist project and European citizens no longer trust their political leaders to 'go off to Brussels' and negotiate on their behalf, as was starkly shown by the rejection of the EU Constitution in the French and Dutch referendums and in the vote to leave the EU in the referendum in the UK.

Part of the pattern of support for the EU can be explained by economics: the EU is popular when the European economy is booming and is blamed when the EU economy is performing badly. However, the economy does not tell the whole story. At an individual level, research has shown that those with higher incomes and higher levels of education (who benefit most from the single market) are more likely to support the EU than those on lower incomes and with lower levels of education. Also, political extremists tend to be more anti-EU than political centrists. However, political parties and domestic institutions can influence which people like the EU. For example, the political party a person supports, and the position that party takes towards the EU, has a strong influence on whether that person is 'pro' or 'anti' EU. Also, concerns about a 'democratic deficit' in the EU have a significant impact on attitudes towards it in countries that have strong domestic democratic institutions (Rohrschneider 2002). Nevertheless, public support for the EU has declined in all EU member-states and across all groups in society since its peak in the early 1990s (de Vries 2018).

A competitive party system in the European Parliament

Democratic politics has begun to emerge inside the EU institutions. As discussed, the policy direction of the Commission is influenced by whether it is dominated by left-wing or right-wing politics. Also, votes in the Council split along ideological as well as national-interest lines. However, it is in the European Parliament that a genuine 'party system' has emerged. As discussed in the section 'Horizontal dimension: a hyper-consensus system of government', the MEPs have always sat in transnational, rather than national, political groups. Over the past twenty years, these groups have gradually become more powerful and more competitive. For example, votes in the Parliament increasingly split along left–right lines, and the two largest groups now vote against each other as often as they vote together, which places the Liberals in the centre of the Parliament in a powerful position, since they determine whether a centre-left or a centre-right majority wins in a particular vote (e.g. Hix et al. 2006, 2007).

As an illustration of this, Figure 23.2 shows the voting patterns in the 2009–14 parliament, where each dot is an MEP and the distances between any two dots indicates how frequently these MEPs voted the same way in all the recorded ('roll-call') votes in that period. As the figure shows, the groups are lined up on the main dimension of voting (on the x-axis) from left to right as you would expect. The other feature to note is the high level of voting cohesion in the European Parliament: where the MEPs are clustered into the political groups—in fact, the political groups in the European Parliament are more 'cohesive' in voting than the Democrats and Republicans in the US Congress.

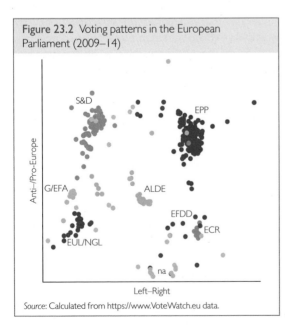

Figure 23.2 Voting patterns in the European Parliament (2009–14)

Left–Right

Source: Calculated from https://www.VoteWatch.eu data.

The 'failure' of European Parliament elections

Despite the growing levels of party competition and cohesion in the European Parliament, elections do not provide a very effective link between the citizens and the behaviour of the MEPs and the transnational political parties. This is because European Parliament elections are less important than national parliamentary elections and so are generally regarded by political parties, the media, and the voters as 'second-order' contests (see especially van der Eijk and Franklin 1996). Because they are second-order national contests, like regional or local elections, European Parliament elections are fought by national parties and on the performance of national party leaders and national governments, rather than by European parties and on the performance of the European Commission or the political groups in the European Parliament.

This has two significant implications:

1. Turnout in European Parliament elections is approximately 20 per cent lower than in national parliament elections and has fallen steadily, to just over 40 per cent of EU citizens in the 2009 and 2014 elections (although turnout rose to 51 per cent in 2019).

2. Voters use European Parliament elections to express their views on national rather than European political issues, and so vote to punish unpopular governments or to express their views on particular issues, thus voting for smaller, single-issue parties.

As a result, throughout the EU, governing parties tend to lose votes in European Parliament elections, while opposition parties tend to gain votes.

But, in an effort to add a 'European' element to the campaigns, and to link European Parliament elections to the choice of the Commission president, before the 2014 elections the main political groups choose 'lead candidates', which became known by their German word: *Spitzenkandidaten*. These lead candidates held live TV debates, and these debates and their campaigns were covered in some member-states. Jean-Claude Juncker, who was the candidate of the largest group in the European Parliament after the elections, the EPP group, was then nominated by the European Council to be the next Commission president. Although the 2014 *Spitzenkandidaten* process did not transform the elections into genuinely 'European' contests, many commentators see this process as the start of a new phase in EU democratic politics. If more people are to engage with the elections, then higher-profile leaders will need to be chosen as *Spitzenkandidaten*, and national parties and the national media will need to accept and support the process.

Interest groups in Brussels: an EU civil society

One aspect of democratic politics which is highly developed in the EU is interest group organization and **mobilization**. In terms of the number of interest groups trying to influence government and policy-making, Brussels is more like Washington, DC than any national capital in Europe (see Chapter 14 'Interest groups'). This is partly because many groups in society have stakes in how the single market is regulated, and so have an incentive to try to shape EU legislation in their preferred direction. It is also because there are multiple points of access in EU decision-making for interest groups, whereas policy-making at the national level in Europe tends to be dominated by governmental and party political elites, with only limited access for particular interest groups.

There are over 11,000 groups and individuals in the EU Commission's interest group register, and together these groups employ an estimated 30,000 people (Greenwood 2017). In other words, there are more people on the outside in Brussels trying to influence the EU institutions than there are on the inside involved in drafting and negotiating EU policies. These numbers might suggest that business interests dominate Brussels. However, this is misleading, as many groups representing 'public interests', such as the environmental lobby, the consumer lobby, and the trade unions, are part-funded directly from the EU budget and also have direct access to many governments and the party groups in the European Parliament. As a result, the EU has a very vibrant civil society, with more or less equal access for every major group in society.

Conclusion

The EU was established by sovereign **nation-states** primarily to create and govern a Europe-wide market and to tackle the policy questions that arise at both the European and national levels from the free movement of goods, services, capital, and persons on a continental scale. As such, the EU is a remarkable and unique achievement: the only genuinely supranational polity that is the result of voluntary choices of citizens and democratic governments. However, the EU possesses many of the features and processes of other democratic political systems. As in other multilevel polities, policy powers are divided between the European and national levels. Also, how policies are made by the EU institutions is similar to that in other political systems which have a separation of powers between the executive and the legislature and where large coalitions are required for legislation to pass. Multiple checks and balances guarantee broad consensus, but also make it difficult for policies to be changed. Nonetheless, compared with other democratic political systems, the connection between citizens' policy preferences and policy outcomes from the EU is extremely indirect. Citizens elect national governments and the European Parliament, but in no sense do citizens have a choice about who governs them at the European level and the direction of the EU policy agenda.

> **KEY POINTS**
>
> - There are growing concerns about a 'democratic deficit' in the EU, in that many citizens feel that they have little influence over the direction of EU policies.
>
> - Public support for the EU has declined since widespread enthusiasm for the single-market programme in the late 1980s, and the EU is widely perceived as an elitist project which benefits highly educated and highly skilled citizens.
>
> - Although European Parliament elections do not provide an effective link between EU citizens and EU policy-making, there is growing political contestation inside the EU institutions, particularly in the European Parliament, where the political groups compete and coalesce along left–right lines.
>
> - There is a vibrant and representative civil society in Brussels in terms of the number and extent of interest groups involved in the EU policy process.

 QUESTIONS

Knowledge-based

1. Is the EU a political system?

2. Why is regulation the main policy instrument of the EU?

3. Why have some member-states joined the euro, but not others?

4. Who is the main agenda setter in the EU—the Council or the Commission?

5. Is the European Court of Justice beyond political influence?

Critical thinking

1. How powerful is the European Parliament?

2. Who are the winners and losers from the EU budget, and why?

3. Why has public support for the EU declined since the early 1990s?

4. Why do European parties vote cohesively in the European Parliament?

5. Why are European elections 'second-order national elections'?

FURTHER READING

Classics in European integration and EU politics

Haas, E. B. (1958) [2004] *The Uniting of Europe: Political, Social, and Economic Forces, 1950–1957* (South Bend, IN: University of Notre Dame Press).

Majone, G. (1996) *Regulating Europe* (London: Routledge).

Milward, A. S. (2000) *European Rescue of the Nation-State* (2nd edn) (London: Routledge).

Moravcsik, A. (1998) *The Choice for Europe: Social Purpose and State Power from Messina to Maastricht* (Ithaca, NY: Cornell University Press).

Pollack, M. A. (2003) *The Engines of European Integration: Delegation, Agency, and Agenda Setting in the EU* (Oxford: Oxford University Press).

Weiler, J. H. H. (1999) *The Constitution of Europe: 'Do the New Clothes have an Emperor?' and Other Essays on European Integration* (Cambridge: Cambridge University Press).

General reference books

Corbett, R., Jacobs, F., and Shackleton, M. (2011) *The European Parliament* (8th edn) (London: John Harper).

Dinan, D. (2014) *Europe Recast: A History of European Union* (2nd edn) (Basingstoke: Palgrave).

Hix, S. and Høyland, B. (2011) *The Political System of the European Union* (3rd edn) (Houndsmill, Basingstoke: Palgrave Macmillan).

Rosamond, B. (2000) *Theories of European Integration* (Houndsmill, Basingstoke: Palgrave Macmillan).

Wallace, H., Pollack, M. A., and Young, A. R. (eds) (2014) *Policy-Making in the European Union* (7th edn) (Oxford: Oxford University Press).

Books on specific aspects of the EU system

Alter, K. J. (2001) *Establishing the Supremacy of EU Law: Making of an International Rule of Law in Europe* (Oxford: Oxford University Press).

De Grauwe, P. (2014) *Economics of Monetary Union* (10th edn) (Oxford: Oxford University Press).

de Vries, C. (2018) *Euroscepticism and the Future of European Integration* (Oxford: Oxford University Press).

van der Eijk, C. and Franklin, M. (eds) (1996) *Choosing Europe? The European Electorate and National Politics in the Face of Union* (Ann Arbor, MI: University of Michigan Press).

Franchino, F. (2007) *The Powers of the Union: Delegation in the EU* (Cambridge: Cambridge University Press).

Greenwood, J. (2017) *Interest Representation in the European Union* (4th edn) (Houndsmill, Basingstoke: Palgrave Macmillan).

Hix, S., Noury, A., and Roland, G. (2007) *Democratic Politics in the European Parliament* (Cambridge: Cambridge University Press).

Hobolt, S. B. (2009) *Europe in Question: Referendums on European Integration* (Oxford: Oxford University Press).

Hooghe, L. (2002) *The European Commission and the Integration of Europe* (Cambridge: Cambridge University Press).

Naurin, D. and Wallace, H. (eds) (2008) *Unveiling the Council of the European Union: Games Governments Play in Brussels* (London: Palgrave).

Thomson, R. (2011) *Resolving Controversy in the European Union* (Cambridge: Cambridge University Press).

Visit the Online Resources that accompany this book for additional material, including country profiles, comparative data sets, flashcard glossaries, and web directory.

www.oup.com/he/caramani5e

24

Globalization and the nation-state

Georg Sørensen

Reader's guide

Processes of globalization and other forces significantly increase connections and exchanges between nation-states at all levels: social, economic, political, and cultural. As a result, states become much more dependent on their surroundings. The old distinction between a First, a Second, and a Third World is being replaced by a new typology of states: the *advanced capitalist state* is today postmodern rather than modern, and a group of *weak post-colonial states* in the South are increasingly marginalized, fragile, and unable to stand on their own feet. Between these two groups are a number of *modernizing states* in Asia, Eastern Europe, Latin America, and elsewhere. These changes are critical to the study of comparative politics. First, the state units that comparativists compare have changed significantly. Second, 'international' and 'domestic' politics are now intimately related. This calls for an approach which emphasizes both; therefore, the disciplines of comparative politics and international relations need to work much more closely together or maybe even merge.

Introduction

The standard image of the sovereign **nation-state** is that of an entity within well-defined territorial borders: a national polity, a national economy, and a national community of citizens. The focus of comparative politics is on politics *within* countries; the focus of *international relations* is on politics *across* countries. Each discipline has developed a specific set of approaches and theories (see the Introduction to this volume). Many of these approaches and theories rest on the premise 'other things being equal' (Riggs

1994: 1); that is to say, comparative politics researchers can safely ignore what takes place outside the borders of the countries they are studying and international relations researchers can equally ignore what takes place inside countries. This in turn is predicated on the idea that domestic politics and international politics are two qualitatively different things. The former takes place in an environment where there is an ultimate locus of final authority (see Chapter 4 'The nation-state'), and the latter takes place in an environment where there is no such authority—'anarchy' is the label that international relations scholars use for that situation.

A number of questions related to comparative politics can possibly be studied without considering the international context (and vice versa for international relations) in the future. But many of the most interesting research questions, including the core issue of the fate of the state itself, can only be studied if the relationship between 'domestic' and 'international' is given serious consideration. That is because the standard image of a sovereign nation-state does not apply any more; the national polity, the national economy, and the national community are no longer neatly separated from the outside in the way that the traditional approaches and theories would have us believe. Even **sovereignty** is changing in ways that indicate the decreasing significance of borders.

The focus in this chapter is on **globalization** and the changes in sovereign statehood that it has helped to bring about. The next section, 'The debate about globalization and states' briefly introduces the debate that is taking place about the consequence for states of globalization; in that connection we must look more closely at the core concepts for analysis—globalization and the sovereign state. The following three sections trace the modalities of statehood as they have developed over the last several decades.

First, the **advanced capitalist** states are transforming from modern into post-modern states. This involves changes at the levels of economics, politics, and nationhood (i.e. the transformation of community). It also involves changes in the institution of sovereignty; a new 'sovereignty game' is in the making.

Second, the *weak post-colonial* states were created out of special circumstances—the globalization of the institution of sovereignty in the context of decolonization. The core features of weak statehood will be identified in the section on 'Weak post-colonial states'. Weak states also play a special sovereignty game which reflects their fragility; they remain highly dependent on the international community.

Third, the *modernizing states*, such as China, India, Russia, and Brazil, amalgamate features of modern, post-modern, and weak post-colonial statehood in different combinations. In economic terms, the international context is increasingly important for them, but in broader political terms their relationship to international society is more unstable. Finally, against the background of this new typology of states, the last section speculates about the pursuit of 'Comparative politics in a new setting'.

> **KEY POINTS**
>
> - Globalization has made a considerable contribution to the change in sovereign statehood.
> - The fate of the state can only be assessed if the relationship between 'domestic' and 'international' is taken into consideration.
> - As a result of state transformation due to globalization, a new typology of states is proposed: (i) post-modern; (ii) weak post-colonial; and (iii) modernizing states.

The debate about globalization and states

There are three major positions in the debate about globalization and states. First, there are scholars who think that states are losing power and influence as a result of globalization. There is a *retreat of the state* because 'globalization erodes the power of states' (Julius 1997: 454). Second, there are *state-centric* scholars who believe that states remain in charge of globalization and have even managed to expand their capacities for regulation and control (Weiss 1998; Hirst and Thompson 2000; Iversen and Soskice 2019). At the same time, very few 'retreat' scholars would claim that the state is 'losing out' to the extent that states are withering away or becoming entirely powerless. And very few 'state-centric' scholars would maintain that states are always 'winning' and are all-powerful (see Box 24.1).

Therefore, most scholars support some version of a third pragmatist middle position; instead of a zero-sum view of either 'winning' or 'losing', it is accepted that both can take place at the same time. As a result of globalization, states are becoming stronger in some respects and weaker in others. A process of state *transformation* is taking place and it plays out differently in different states (Held and McGrew 2002; Jessop 2002; Brenner et al. 2003). The 'transformationalist' position is more open than the 'retreat' and 'state-centric' views, but it is not very precise. If states are indeed changing, what exactly is going on and what are the

FOR AND AGAINST 24.1

'Retreat' vs 'state-centric' scholars

Three 'retreat' scholars	Three 'state-centric' scholars
The nation-state has become an unnatural, even dysfunctional unit for organizing human activity and managing economic endeavour in a borderless world. It represents no genuine, shared community of economic interest. It defines no meaningful flows of economic activity. (Ohmae 1993: 78)	There are now sufficient grounds to suggest that globalization tendencies have been exaggerated, and that we need to employ the language of internationalization to understand better the changes taking place in the world economy. In this kind of economy, the nation-state retains its importance as a political and economic actor. (Weiss 1998: 212)
The nation-state is dead. Not because states were subsumed by super-states, but because they are breaking up into smaller, more efficient parts—just like big companies … We are moving toward a world of 1,000 countries because many people of the new tribalism want self-rule and every day they see others getting self-rule, or moving toward it. (Naisbitt 1994: 43)	[M]ost of the social, economic, and other problems ascribed to globalization are actually due to technological and other developments that have little or nothing to do with globalization. Even though its role may have diminished somewhat, the nation-state remains prominent in both domestic and international economic affairs. To borrow a phrase from the American humorist Mark Twain, I would like to report that the rumours of the death of the state 'have been greatly exaggerated.' (Gilpin 2002: 350)
[T]he domain of state authority in society and economy is shrinking … what were once domains of authority exclusive to state authority are now being shared with other loci of sources of authority. (Strange 1996: 82)	Economic actors look to states in order to gain market access and to level the playing field of international competition. (Kapstein 1994: 6)
	[S]tates continue to adapt to ongoing changes in the world economy … and firms continue to value their national identity … (Kapstein 1993: 503)

larger implications? That is the central question in what follows.[1]

Globalization is a contested concept (see Box 24.2). There is general agreement about what it means in the broadest sense, namely the expansion and intensification of all kinds of social relations across borders—economic, political, cultural, and so on (Holm and Sørensen 1995: 1). Globalization is uneven in terms of cross-national intensity, geographical scope, and national and local depth. It is driven by various forces, including governments, corporations, popular groups, and many others; they help shape what globalization is and what it does. In other words, globalization is both a cause and a consequence. It is not an anonymous entity that has suddenly taken control of peoples and states. At the same time, globalization increasingly shapes the context for inter-state relations as well as for the everyday lives of ordinary citizens.

For some observers, globalization has become so taken for granted that it appears to be a juggernaut out of control (Lane 2008: 8). But this view is misleading because as we have just noted, economic globalization is shaped by a host of political and economic factors and when they change, globalization changes with them. For example, intensified regional cooperation, such as the EU, tends to promote regional

as opposed to truly global economic exchange; some European countries have actually 'de-globalized' in recent years in the sense that regional flows have replaced global flows (Ghemawat and Altman 2014). Further, the Trump presidency in the US and the British Brexit vote may invoke a phase where many politicians adopt a much more sceptical approach towards

DEFINITION 24.2

Definitions of globalization

Globalization refers to all those processes by which the peoples of the world are incorporated into a single world society, global society.

Albrow (1996: 9)

The world is becoming a global shopping mall in which ideas and products are available everywhere at the same time.

Kanter (1995: 13)

Globalization can be defined as the intensification of worldwide social relations which link distant localities in such a way that local happenings are shaped by events occurring many miles away and vice versa.

Giddens (1990: 64)

globalization. Finally, technological developments can change the economic calculation away from globalizing and in favour of 'staying home' or even 'reshoring' activities that were previously outsourced (*The Economist* 2013; for one way of measuring globalization, see Ghemawat and Altman 2014).

Here, I want to concentrate on the consequences of globalization for salient aspects of sovereign statehood. What is a state? It is a *sovereign territorial entity with a population and a government*. For the present purposes, it is relevant to focus on four aspects of statehood.

1. All states have *political–administrative* (including military) *institutions of government*, but there are huge differences between them in terms of efficiency, capacity, and legitimacy. It cannot be taken for granted, for example, that all states enjoy a monopoly on the legitimate use of force.

2. The *economic basis of the state* comprises the ability to design, construct, produce, finance, and distribute economic goods. Some states have well-defined national economies; others do not. Weak states are highly dependent on the world market and have extremely heterogeneous economies.

3. The content of *nationhood and identity* must be examined. Nationhood means that people within a territory make up a community. The community is based on nationality or 'sentiment' (meaning a common language and a common cultural and historical identity), as well as on citizenship (including political, social, and economic rights and obligations).

4. *Sovereignty* is an institution which defines the rules that, in turn, define the locus of political authority and set the context for relations between states. We must trace the major changes in sovereignty related to processes of globalization.

KEY POINTS

- Globalization is a contested concept. In the broadest sense, it means the expansion and intensification of all kinds of social relations across borders.

- As a result of globalization, a process of state transformation is taking place. States are becoming stronger in some respects and weaker in others.

- Four aspects of statehood are in focus when discussing the transformation of the state: (i) the political–administrative institutions of government; (ii) the economic basis of the state; (iii) nationhood and identity; (iv) the institution of sovereignty.

Advanced capitalist states
From modern to post-modern

Since the debate about globalization and state transformation has primarily concerned the advanced capitalist states, it is appropriate to begin with them. In order to be precise about how these states have been transformed, it is necessary to have an idea about how they looked in the past. It is common to focus on the Peace of Westphalia at the end of the Thirty Years War in 1648 as the birthplace of the modern sovereign state. That peace accord undermined the power of the church and strengthened secular power. The power and authority of kings was further strengthened in a context of fierce competition and violent conflict with rivals. The build-up of state power changed the relationship between the state and the people. A large group of individuals within a defined territory, subject to one supreme authority, became 'the people'. They are subjects and citizens of a particular state, and at the same time they have a shared idea of themselves as a cultural and historical entity; they are an 'imagined community' (Anderson 1991), or a nation. A modern state is a nation-state in the sense that the population shares the characteristics of **citizenship** and *nationhood*. A nation-state is not necessarily based on a homogeneous ethno-national group of people. Very few modern states are nation-states in this narrower sense.

The modern state is based on a national economy. The state rulers helped create a national space for economic development by removing local barriers to exchange and supporting both industry and infrastructure. The modern national economy is characterized by the combined presence within its territory of the major economic sectors, i.e. means of production and distribution as well as means of consumption. What particularly defines a national economy is the fact that the most important inter- and intra-sectoral links are domestic. There is external trade, of course, but the economic structure is introvert rather than extrovert (for data on trade, see Comparative table 15 in Appendix 2 at the end of this volume). The modern state emerged in tandem with the process of capitalist economic development, which first took hold in Britain.

The political–administrative institutions of government were considerably strengthened in the course of major wars, in particular the world wars of the twentieth century. State intervention in the economy was pushed by a need to mitigate social tensions via **redistribution** and to procure the necessary means for the war effort. That had to be combined with great increases in the level of taxation (Porter 1994; Zürn 1998).

The core characteristics of the modern West-phalian state, as it had developed mainly in Western Europe and North America around 1950, are summarized in Table 24.1. This ideal type provides an image of the previous shape of the state against which later changes can be assessed.

How do these characteristics transform in the context of intensified globalization? Let us begin with the economy. Capitalist economies are increasingly connected across borders. Technological changes in transport, communication, and production, together with a more liberalized world economy, mean that

Table 24.1 Four types of state				
State dimensions	Modern state	Post-modern state	Weak post-colonial state	Modernizing state
Government	A centralized system of democratic rule based on a set of administrative, policing, and military organizations, sanctioned by a legal order, claiming a monopoly of the legitimate use of force, all within a defined territory.	Multilevel governance in several interlocked arenas overlapping each other. Governance in the context of supranational, international, transgovernmental, and transnational relations.	Inefficient and corrupt administrative and institutional structures. Rule based on coercion rather than the rule of law. Monopoly on the legitimate use of violence not established.	The modernizing states combine features of the modern, the post-modern, and the weak post-colonial state.
Nationhood	A people within a territory making up a community of citizens (with political, social, and economic rights) and a community of sentiment based on cultural and historical bonds. Nationhood involves a high level of cohesion, binding nation and state together.	Identities less exclusively national. Collective identities 'above' and 'below' the nation reinforced. Transformation of citizenship. Less coherent 'community of citizens'.	Predominance of local/ethnic community. Weak bonds of loyalty to state and low level of state legitimacy. Local community more important than national community.	Brazil, China, India, and Russia are major examples of modernizing states.
Economy	A segregated national economy, self-sustained in the sense that it comprises the main sectors needed for its reproduction. The major part of economic activity takes place at home.	National economies much less self-sustained than earlier because of 'deep integration'. Major part of economic activity embedded in cross-border networks.	Heterogeneous combination of traditional agriculture, an informal petty urban sector, and some fragments of modern industry. Strong dependence on the global economy.	Additional examples include Argentina, Chile, and Mexico in Latin America, as well as Indonesia, Malaysia, and Thailand in Asia.
Sovereignty	National authority in the form of constitutional independence. The state has supreme political authority within the territory. Non-intervention: right to decide without outside interference.	From non-intervention towards mutual intervention. Regulation by supranational authority increasingly important.	Constitutional independence combined with 'negotiated intervention' (donor control of aid, supervision by international society). 'Non-reciprocity' (special treatment of weak states because they cannot reciprocate).	Each of these countries contains a unique mixture of different types of statehood.

'shallow integration', manifested as arm's length trade between independent firms, is being replaced by 'deep integration', where production chains (i.e. the various stages in the production of goods and services, from procurement of inputs to sales and service) are globally organized within the framework of a single transnational corporation (UNCTAD 1993: 113). As a result, trade increasingly takes place within the context of the same company or network of companies. Such intra-firm trade now accounts for roughly one-third of world trade.

The real world is probably a mixture of old and new in the terms described here, uneven across countries and economic sectors. On the one hand, a unified, homogeneous, and fully integrated **global economy** has not emerged. On the other hand, 'national' economies are less self-sustained than they used to be because of the processes of 'deep integration' which have been combined with more intense integration in other economic sectors, not least the financial sector (Dicken 2015).

A financial and economic crisis engulfed the postmodern states and much of the rest of the world by 2008. It began with a burst housing bubble in the US; opaque derivative markets, labelled 'financial weapons of mass destruction' by Warren Buffett, aggravated the crisis. The financial system is deeply integrated on a global scale, but regulation and control remains almost purely national. Thus, it was left to national governments to respond to the crisis with different national 'packages', only thinly coordinated. The crisis has not led to protectionism; markets remain open. But there is more emphasis on the downsides of economic globalization than earlier. At the same time, there are no indications of impending institutional reform that will prevent a new crisis. The international financial institutions continue to place their confidence in perfect markets; the task is to 'restore confidence' in those markets. That might not be sufficient in the longer term; in any case, the crisis has re-emphasized the role of states in the regulation of the globalized economy and in many countries, national economic interests are being re-emphasized.

We turn to the political level. What has happened to national government? Economic globalization tends to increase the demand for political cooperation across borders because states are increasingly dependent on activities outside their territory. More cooperation is a way of gaining influence outside the state's jurisdiction (Zürn 1998). At the same time, political initiatives, such as the creation of the **single market** in the European Union (EU), or liberalizations in context of the World Trade Organization (WTO), also significantly push economic globalization.

> ↘ **ZOOM-IN 24.3**
>
> ## Settlement system of the WTO
>
> By reinforcing the rule of law, the dispute settlement system makes the trading system more secure and predictable. Where non-compliance with a World Trade Organization (WTO) agreement has been alleged by a WTO member, the dispute settlement system provides for a relatively rapid resolution of the matter through an independent ruling that must be implemented promptly, or the non-implementing member will face trade sanctions.
>
> *Source:* http://www.wto.org.

Several observers point to the combined growth of transnational, transgovernmental, international, and **supranational** relations. Transnational relations are cross-border relations between individuals, groups, and organizations from civil society. Transgovernmental relations are relations between governments at different levels. External relations are no longer the prerogative of foreign ministries and heads of state. Sector ministries, regulatory agencies, officials responsible for corporate supervision, and so on are connected with their counterparts in other countries (Slaughter 1997). The growth of conventional inter-state relations is evidenced in the growth of international governmental organizations (IGOs) from 123 in 1951 to 262 by the 2012 (Table 24.2). The most far-reaching form of political cooperation across borders is supranational **governance**. Governance, in contrast with government, refers to activities everywhere (local, national, regional, global) involving regulation and control. 'Supranational' refers to the fact that some institutions, such as the EU, have the powers to write the rules for member-states in some areas. For example, rulings by the European Court of Justice (ECJ) take priority over rulings by national courts.

Table 24.2 Number of international governmental organizations (IGOs) and international non-governmental organizations (INGOs)

Year	IGOs	INGOs
1909	37	176
1951	123	832
2012	262	8,382

Source: Zacher (1992: 65); Held et al. (1999: 53); Kegley and Blanton (2014: 146).

The EU, then, is the clearest example of what could be called multilevel governance (see Chapter 23 'The EU as a new political system'), i.e. a situation where political power is diffused and decentralized. Instead of a purely national political regulation, a complex network of supranational, national, and subnational regulation has developed. The EU is in a class by itself in terms of the intensity and extensity of regional cooperation among member-states. Other regional initiatives are primarily based on conventional forms of inter-state cooperation. At the global level, supranational elements can be found in some places—for example, the dispute settlement system in the WTO (see Box 24.3) or in the International Criminal Court (jurisdiction over persons for the most serious crimes of international concern)—but the bulk of global governance continues to be of a more conventional kind.

In any case, there appears to be a general trend away from national government within a defined territory towards multilevel governance in several interlocked arenas overlapping each other. Some of that governance reflects a more intense conventional cooperation between independent states. Some of it reflects a more profound transformation towards supranational governance in a context of highly interconnected societies. There are also sceptical voices who want to preserve national autonomy, as can be seen currently among Conservatives in the UK; and President Trump's 'America First' policy is involving trade disputes with both China and the EU, as well as an attack on the WTO settlement system, so the continued development of supranational governance cannot be taken for granted.

National identity

As regards nationhood and identity, the modern state is based on two kinds of community: (i) a *community of citizenship*, concerning the relations between citizens and the state, including political, social, and economic rights and obligations; (ii) a *community of sentiment*, based on a common language and a common cultural and historical identity.

What happens to these two types of communities in the context of globalization? The community of citizens transforms in the sense that civil and other rights are no longer being granted solely by the sovereign state. At the global level, a set of universal human rights has been defined. In some regional contexts, common rights for citizens of different countries have emerged. The EU has established a common citizenship which grants a number of rights to EU citizens in all member-states (Soysal 1994: 148). The process is not confined to Europe. According to one scholar, the increasing adherence to universal human rights means that national citizenship is in the process of being replaced by 'post-national membership' based on these universal rights. This indicates a transformation of citizenship 'from a more particularistic one based on nationhood to a more universalistic one based on person-hood' (Soysal 1994: 137). It goes together with a much increased forging of transnational links among people that practice 'citizenship without moorings' (Rosenau 1993: 282) in order to address issues of common concern (e.g. environment, equality, or security problems). In short, there is no breakdown of national citizenship, but there are different forces at work to transform the coherent community of citizens as it existed in the context of the modern state.

What about the community of sentiment—the cultural and emotional attachment to the nation? According to Anthony Giddens (1990), the creation of identity is increasingly becoming an individual project. Religious and other beliefs, for example, are not simply taken over from previous generations. Rather, they are reflected upon, evaluated, and then actively accepted or rejected. When identity is something that has to be actively created and sustained by individuals, the result may be less commitment to the national community of sentiment. At the same time, new collective identities 'above' the nation could be in the process of emerging. One analysis speaks of a 'Western civic identity'; at its core is a 'consensus around a set of norms and principles, most importantly political democracy, constitutional government, individual rights, private property-based economic systems, and toleration of diversity' (Deudney and Ikenberry 1999: 193).

It is indicated in this analysis that the emergence of a Western civic identity is concentrated among the elite groups of Western societies because they are the ones who have engaged in circulation and educational exchange. Possibly the creation of self-identities analysed by Giddens, taking place in sophisticated processes of reflexive endeavour, is also primarily an elite phenomenon. If so, what happens with collective identities among those for whom economic globalization is more of a threat than an opportunity? According to Manuel Castells, such groups frequently develop a 'resistance identity' (Castells 1998: 60). They might be nationalistic groups turning against immigration and seeking to emphasize a narrow understanding of national identity, such as the Front National in France or the Alleanza Nazionale in Italy. They might also be regional community organizations, or religious or ethnic movements (see also Chapter 13 'Party systems' on neopopulist parties). The increased arrival of migrants to the European Union since 2014 has helped strengthen nationalist political voices in many member-states.

In short, globalization would appear to reinforce collective identities both 'above' and 'below' the nation. What were previously more coherent national identities are now undergoing a process of fragmentation in many countries. A major dividing line is between, on the one hand, nationalist sceptics that turn against globalization, migration, and open borders, and, on the other hand, supporters of globalization and more intensified transnational cooperation (Fukuyama 2018).

Sovereignty

Finally, there is the issue of sovereignty. The juridical core of sovereignty is constitutional independence. The sovereign state stands apart from all other sovereign entities. There is no final political authority outside or above the state (James 1999: 461). Even in the face of globalization, the international system continues to be organized in this manner: it consists of sovereign states that have final political authority within their territory.

However, this does not mean that the institution of sovereignty has remained completely unchanged (Sørensen 2001). Sovereignty can be seen as a special kind of game played by states that have it. Constitutional independence defines what the game is all about (i.e. political authority and its appropriate distribution among the players). The rules regulating the game stipulate how the players should behave towards each other in various situations. There are many such rules (Jackson 1990: 35), the most important one being *non-intervention*, i.e. the right for states to choose their own path and to conduct their affairs without outside interference. The rule of non-intervention has been changed, or at least strongly modified, because of the more intense political cooperation across borders that globalization has stimulated.

The EU is a good example in this respect. Instead of non-intervention, the EU member-states undertake comprehensive intervention in each other's affairs. During the past decade, institutions at the European level have gained considerable influence over areas that were traditionally thought to be prerogatives of national politics: currency, social policies, border controls, law and order. A key player in this development is the ECJ, which has helped push supranational governance by establishing the supremacy of European law in several important areas (Caldeira and Gibson 1995).

This does not mean that we approach the 'twilight of sovereignty' (Wriston 1992), as some 'retreat' scholars have implied. States can withdraw from this kind of cooperation if they want to—they do retain constitutional independence. But because of the demand for more cooperation spurred by globalization, it is unlikely that they would wish to do so. This is the dilemma faced by the UK in the context of Brexit.

Having gone through changes in salient aspects of changes of sovereign statehood among the advanced capitalist states, we can summarize the results and compare them with the characteristic features of modern statehood as they were presented above. The modern state was first and foremost a national entity, with national government, national community, national economy, and national sovereignty. The emerging entity is less 'national' on all counts. At the same time, it is not certain where the processes of change will eventually lead. Together with several others, I prefer to speak of 'post-modern' states (Holm and Sørensen 1995: 187) in order to indicate these processes of transformation. The 'post-' terminology indicates that the traditional picture of the modern state needs revision, but we remain unsure about what exactly is taking its place. Further integration among states is not assured; we may also see a process of de-integration and increased emphasis on national autonomy.

Some state-centric scholars will argue that the image of the post-modern state is merely applicable to the members of the EU. It is a regional phenomenon not very relevant for larger advanced states outside Europe, such as the US and Japan (Waltz 1999). The counter-argument is that these latter states are deeply involved in economic and other processes of globalization (*Foreign Policy* and Kearney 2006) and that even super-powers cannot 'go it alone' (Nye 2002) in an increasingly integrated world. These views reflect the ongoing debate about globalization and state transformation.

KEY POINTS

- In order to be precise about how the advanced capitalist states have been transformed, it is necessary to have an idea about how they looked in the past. By the mid-twentieth century, these states were *modern*.

- Modern states are based on: (i) a national economy, the major part of economic activity takes place at home; (ii) a national government, a centralized system of democratic rule within a defined territory; (iii) a nation, a people within a territory making up a community of sentiment and a community of citizens. Modern states are sovereign and emphasize non-intervention, i.e. the right to decide without outside interference.

- Modern states are transforming into *post-modern* states. That transformation is pushed by a variety of economic, political, and other forces.

- Post-modern states are less 'national' on all counts: (i) a major part of economic activity is embedded in cross-border networks; (ii) national government is being replaced by multilevel governance in several interlocked arenas; (iii) identities are less exclusively national. Post-modern states underline mutual intervention instead of non-intervention. At the same time, the processes towards 'less national' have provoked counter-reactions that re-emphasize the national features of modern states.

Weak post-colonial states

The lack of 'stateness'

The debate between 'state-centric' and 'retreat' scholars about the consequences of globalization for sovereign states is focused on the advanced states in Western Europe, North America, and Japan. As discussed in the previous section on 'Advanced capitalist states', that debate concentrates on the extent to which there has been a transformation away from the traditional modern state towards a type of state that is less 'national' in basic respects. This is not a relevant debate for weak post-colonial states in the Third World. They were never 'modern states' in the first place and they are not on the way to becoming 'post-modern'. The weak states display a different trajectory of state formation. Since most of these states are in Sub-Saharan Africa, I shall focus on that region. But the ideal type of the weak state defined here is relevant for other areas as well.

Before colonization, these areas were not states with distinct territories. They were tribal and other communities with no clearly defined jurisdictions. Therefore, borders were created from the outside and the surprisingly straight lines on the map were drawn by the colonizers. The colonial powers took no particular interest in the political and economic development of the areas they took into possession. They were more interested in maximizing profits, so the focus was on the extraction and export of natural resources, combined with an effort to keep down the cost of controlling the colonies. In some places, colonial rule involved building infrastructure, together with some political as well as social and economic institutions; in the worst cases, such as the Belgian King Leopold's rule in Congo, the colonizers left nothing behind in terms of development.

After World War II, the prevailing view on colonies changed dramatically. Before the war, colonial rule was considered legitimate and even necessary, given the backward condition of the colonized areas. After the war, colonialism came to be considered fundamentally wrong, even 'a crime' (UN General Assembly Resolution 3103, quoted in Jackson 1990: 107). That normative change led to decolonization, which in turn meant the globalization of the institution of sovereignty. For the first time, sovereign statehood became the only form of political authority worldwide.

The modern states introduced in the previous section, 'Advanced capitalist states' were, in a manner of speaking, *created from the inside*. The struggle between various state-seeking groups ended with victory for one group or coalition of groups that went on to achieve—in Max Weber's expression—a monopoly of the legitimate use of force within a defined territory. At the same time, states were constantly at each other's throats. War between states was an important aspect of **state-building**, as emphasized by Charles Tilly: 'war and the preparation for war strongly affected the entire process of state formation' (Tilly 1990: 14; see also Chapter 4 'The nation-state'). An important ingredient in war was the conquest of enemy territory: the stronger swallowed the weaker.

Fundamentally, this kind of competition was a basic driving force in European state-making and development. The preparation for war forced power holders into a series of compromises with their subject populations which constrained their power and paved the way for rights of citizenship. Citizenship, in turn, meant material benefits for the population. Combined with the creation of domestic order and the promotion of **capital accumulation**, these processes furthered the building of bonds of loyalty and legitimacy between kings and people.

By contrast, in the case of weak states in the Third World, decolonization gave independence (i.e. recognition as a sovereign state) to entities which had very little in terms of substantial statehood (Jackson 1990). In that sense, these states were *created from the outside* when the international society rejected colonialism. Power holders in weak states faced no serious external threat. Both states and regimes were protected from outside threat by the strong international norms created in the context of decolonization, and strengthened during the Cold War. Recolonization, annexation, or any other format of strong states in the North taking over weak states in the South is not on the agenda. For most post-colonial leaders, the situation at independence was one of no severe external threats against the state and the regime, combined with few domestic institutional constraints. It was under those circumstances that a large number of leaders chose the path that led to the formation of weak states. Why?

After the successful anti-colonial struggle, there was little left to create unity. It was a huge task to bring together diverse ethnic groups with different languages and traditions. The state elites quickly gave up trying. At the same time, institutional structures were generally weak, lacking capacity, competence, and resources. In this context, a system of 'personal rule' emerged (Jackson and Rosberg 1982) where key positions in the state apparatus are manned by loyal followers of the leader. State elites do not primarily seek to provide public or collective goods. The state apparatus is rather a source of income for those clever enough to control it. The spoils of office are shared by a group of followers making up a network of patron–client relationships.

The lack of 'nationness'

Ethnic identities connected to tribal, religious, and similar characteristics continue to dominate over the national identity in weak states. Because the state does not deliver on political, social, and legal rights, it creates no bonds of loyalty leading to state legitimacy. When the ethnic community becomes the primary focus for the satisfaction of people's needs, loyalties are projected in that direction, and ethnic identities are reinforced; the national 'community of citizens' fails to develop. Similarly, the national 'community of sentiment' is in trouble because local (ethnic, tribal, religious) communities are primary. They provide sources of identification via rituals and myths. Patron–client relationships serve to reinforce ethnic loyalties (Ndegwa 1997: 602).

The weakness of the economy

The economy in weak post-colonial states is a hetero-geneous amalgamation of traditional agriculture, an informal petty urban sector, and some elements of modern industry, frequently controlled by external interests. In both urban and rural areas large parts of the population are outside the formal sectors, living in localized subsistence economies. Exports consist of few primary products, and the economies are strongly dependent on imports of manufactured and technology-intensive products.

Weak states are not attractive sites for foreign investment. There is no dynamic domestic market, no adequate supply of skilled or semi-skilled labour, and no developed physical infrastructure, and they do not offer stable market-friendly conditions of operation. A little more than 5 per cent of total foreign direct investment (FDI) goes to Sub-Saharan Africa (OECD 2014a,b, shrinking to 2.9 per cent in

2017 (Brookings 2018)), In other words, the circuits of global capital—often thought to be the spearheads of globalization—do not include the weak states in any major way. In that sense, they are marginalized bystanders in the process of economic globalization. At the same time, they remain strongly dependent on the global economy. On the one hand, export earnings from primary products are of great importance for the economies. On the other hand, economic aid makes up an increasing share of the means they have at their disposal. Official development assistance (ODA) increased from 12 to 18.6 per cent of gross domestic product (GDP) in Sub-Saharan Africa between 1990 and 2003 (UNDP 2005). Even if the share fell to about 13 per cent in 2010 (Klingebiel 2012), more than half the state budget is financed by ODA in the most fragile countries.

The weakness of sovereignty

Weak states have formal sovereignty, understood as constitutional independence granted in the context of decolonization. Formal sovereignty is of great importance for weak states because sovereignty offers access to international institutions, including the UN system where states are legally equal (e.g. every country has one vote in the General Assembly). It also provides access to economic, military, and other forms of aid. In formal terms, sovereignty leaves supreme legitimate power in domestic affairs to the government. Therefore, rulers of weak states seek to emphasize and confirm the principles and rules of sovereignty (Ayoob 1995: 3). This emphasis amounts to a demand to be treated as *equals* in the international society of states—to have their sovereignty respected and counted on a par with every other country in the international system—irrespective of the fact that these states are terribly weak and able to do very little on their own.

But rulers of weak states also seek to be considered *unequal* as they are at the losing end of the international system. To compensate for that situation, weak states demand special treatment in terms of economic aid, market access, compensation for natural resources and colonialism, and so on—i.e. weak states want to be allowed to receive extra resources from the developed world. The demand is that economic aid, for example, should be a clear international obligation for the developed countries and not something that the weak states have to respectfully apply for.

So even if weak states have sovereignty in the form of constitutional independence, they cannot play the classical game of sovereignty based on non-intervention. Aid flows mean that donors will want to make sure that the resources they provide are used according to plan. This creates a pressure in the direction of 'negotiated intervention' for that kind of supervision to take place. Weak states can refuse, of course, but that might cut them off from significant funding. The most obvious cases of external intervention are the 'humanitarian interventions' in 'failed states' such as Somalia, Liberia, Rwanda, or Sierra Leone. International society steps in primarily for humanitarian reasons when domestic conflict has got out of hand.

There is another respect in which the fragility of weak states influences their sovereignty game. The classical sovereignty game is based on reciprocity: states are equals and deal with each other on an equal *quid pro quo* basis. Weak states cannot do that because they are not in a position to reciprocate. They want something (e.g. economic aid) but are unable to give anything in return. Sovereignty is built on the assumption that states that have it *can basically take care of themselves*. Weak states fail to meet that requirement; they cannot play a game of self-help. They play a different game of 'non-reciprocity' and 'negotiated intervention', and that is a source of tension in the international society of states.

It is the combined presence of the elements summarized in Table 24.1 that amounts to a 'lack of stateness'. Even if the ideal type is inspired mainly by the weak states in Sub-Saharan Africa, lack of stateness is also a problem elsewhere—for example, in such countries as Afghanistan, Burma, Haiti, Nepal, Kyrgyzstan, Uzbekistan, and Yemen.

The larger question is whether weak states are also developing countries, i.e. are they really on the road to development? The idea that every country can achieve development is an ideology created in the context of decolonization. We only have to go back to the 1930s to find an entirely different ideology, which was especially dominant in the colonial motherlands. On that view, only some, maybe even rather few, colonies would ever be able to stand on their own feet and thus achieve development. Most peoples in the colonies were seen to require 'an indefinite period of European tutelage' and some were likely to 'remain wards of the states-system for centuries, if not forever' (Jackson 1990: 73). That outlook was sustained by a Western belief in its own superiority which was rejected with decolonization. But the adoption of a new outlook does not alter the empirical conditions for development, which continue to be almost absent in the weakest states. These conditions are behind the processes of state breakdown or the emergence of 'failed states', a notion indicating the breakdown of states in various ways (Brock et al. 2011).

KEY POINTS

- Decolonization gave independence (i.e. recognition as a sovereign state) to entities which had very little in terms of substantial empirical statehood.

- Weak post-colonial states are plagued by political institutions that are inefficient and corrupt, and by weak bonds of loyalty to the state and a low level of state legitimacy.

- The economic basis is fragile and dependent on links to the outside.

- Weak states play a special sovereignty game focused on 'negotiated intervention' and 'non-reciprocity'.

- It is an open question whether the weak states are on the road towards development or to further breakdown and 'state failure'.

Modernizing states

Between post-colonialism and post-modernism

The previous sections argue that in the current international system there are two radically different modalities of sovereign statehood. On the one hand, the advanced capitalist states are transforming from modern to post-modern. On the other hand, the weak post-colonial states display a particular set of features that amount to a lack of 'stateness'. Between these ends of the spectrum is a large group of states that will be called 'modernizing' states. They combine features of the three ideal types of state presented so far: the modern, the post-modern, and the weak post-colonial state. The term 'modernizing' is meant to indicate that such states are in a general process of transition. It is not meant to indicate that they will certainly discard every aspect of weak statehood, and graduate to modern and then to post-modern. No such teleology is implied, as transitions can move in different directions and change may not mean change for the better.

Brazil, China, India, and Russia are major examples of modernizing states; additional examples include Argentina, Chile, and Mexico in Latin America, as well as Indonesia, Malaysia, and Thailand in Asia, and also South Africa. Each of them contains a unique mixture of different types of statehood. Many parts of India, for example, display the economic characteristics of weak statehood (i.e. a heterogeneous combination of traditional agriculture, an informal petty urban sector, and some fragments of modern industry), but the country also has larger elements of a modern industrial structure. It even has advanced economic sectors that are now seeking active integration in cross-border networks via direct investment and much more involvement in economic globalization. A similar mixture can be found in China, but this country is already a highly active participant in economic globalization. Russia may have modernized even more, but its relationship to the global economy remains more like that of a member of the Organization of Petroleum Exporting Countries (OPEC), in that it exports energy and raw materials and imports more sophisticated products.

The mixture of state types also applies to the political level. Massive corruption and weak state structures remain a serious problem in all four states, but in some areas, there is a higher degree of effective national government. The countries are all seeking closer integration into the global economy and also to some extent into the international organizations and networks of multilevel governance. The question, then, is what the consequences will be of this economic and political globalization for their trajectories of development.

New global competitors: India and China

Compared with the weak states discussed earlier, modernizing states are better positioned to benefit from economic globalization. They possess companies of their own that are able to participate in strategic alliances and economic networks, and that increases their prospects for gaining from economic globalization in terms of technology transfers, market access, product upgrading, and competence development. The host states possess sufficient regulatory capacity for establishing the necessary frameworks concerning relations to foreign operators.

The liberalizing measures that have widely opened the doors to comprehensive participation in economic globalization have certainly boosted economic growth in both India and China. India began liberalization in 1991. India's opening up to globalization represents a crucial breakthrough for its development (Singh and Srinivasan 2003). Yet serious problems remain. There have not been significantly positive effects on employment because the traditional sectors are being squeezed while the modern sector provides only a limited increase in the workforce. With 32.7 per cent of the population living on less than $1.25 a day (UNDP 2014), poverty continues to be widespread.

China began liberalizing much earlier and has been able to attract a much higher level of foreign investment. Economic growth has averaged more than 9 per cent annually over the past twenty-five years, an unparalleled achievement; and the number of extreme

poor (less than $1.25 a day) has dropped to 11.8 per cent of the population (UNDP 2014). But even in China, economic globalization is a mixed blessing. Inequality has risen sharply: 'by 2005, the top 10 per cent earned 45 per cent of the income, while the bottom 10 per cent earned only 1.4 per cent' (Wen 2005: 2). The Gini ratio rose from 0.20 in 1980 to 0.42 in 2012 (see Comparative tables 3 and 16 in Appendix 2 at the end of this volume).

Another aspect of globalization in both China and India are sweatshop factories with poor working conditions, low job security, low wages, and long hours of work. In the Pearl River and Yangtze River delta regions in China, for example, 'migrant workers routinely work twelve hours a day, seven days a week; during the busy season, a thirteen- to fifteen-hour day is not uncommon' (Wen 2005: 3). In other words, even in relatively successful modernizing states, a significant part of their participation in economic globalization has nothing to do with upgrading and sophisticated production. It might better be called 'downgrading', with deteriorating conditions for labour. Some will argue that there is improvement in the sense that previously unproductive work in stagnant and inefficient public enterprises is being replaced by more productive work in a competitive world market, but from the point of view of the labour force it is hardly a great leap forward.

Economic globalization in China has led to serious environmental problems because rapid economic growth has taken place with little or no attention to the environment. Some 60 per cent of China's major rivers are classified as being 'unsuitable for human contact'. China's Deputy Minister of the Environment recently stated that 'cities are growing, but desert areas are expanding at the same time; habitable and usable land has been halved over the past 50 years' (Wen 2005: 10). Seven of the ten most polluted cities in the world are in China. More than one-third of industrial wastewater enters waterways without any treatment.

The economic changes in China have pushed some political change. For example, private entrepreneurs, i.e. 'capitalists', have been allowed to become members of the Communist Party since 2002. There is less direct party control of people's daily lives. But independent trade unions are still not permitted, and freedom of assembly and association is highly restricted. The judiciary is not independent; it is controlled by the party. Human rights abuse remains widespread (Freedom House 2019). This might help explain why a strong increase in social unrest is combined with a new popularity of Maoism, especially in the poorest sections of society.

The international community, meanwhile, demands in principle that China should pay more respect to civil and political rights in order to become a fully legitimate member of international society. But because of China's economic importance, such demands are formulated in a low voice and are not backed by strong political or economic pressure. In sum, even if modernizing states are able to benefit from globalization, the process of participating in it is no panacea. It does not open a smooth course to economic and political change. Involvement in globalization increases several tensions in the process of development that present new challenges to both the modernizing states and the international community.

KEY POINTS

- Modernizing states combine features of the three ideal types of state: the modern, the post-modern, and the weak post-colonial state.

- The term 'modernizing' is meant to indicate that such states are in a general process of transition; transitions can move in different directions and change may not mean change for the better.

- Brazil, China, India, and Russia are examples of modernizing states.

- Modernizing states are in a better position than weak states to benefit from participation in globalization. But such participation is not a cure-all; it can also increase tensions in their process of development.

Comparative politics in a new setting

Methodological implications

The discipline of comparative politics is built on the idea that 'comparison is the methodological core of the scientific study of politics' (Almond et al. 2004: 31). Political systems exist within the framework of sovereign states; for this reason, comparison is understood to be comparison between countries (i.e. sovereign states). The principle that comparative politics compares countries is so entrenched that major introductions to the discipline (e.g. Landman 2003; Almond et al. 2004) do not find it necessary to explain why that is the case—it is considered self-evident. Similarly, a dominant view in the discipline of international relations is that the international system is a system of sovereign states—they are the basic components of the international system (e.g. Waltz 1999).

Both disciplines have a point. As Chapter 4 'The nation-state' shows, almost every individual on earth is the citizen or subject of a state. Whether or not people are provided with basic social values—security, wealth, welfare, freedom, order, justice—strongly depends on the ability of the state to ensure them. Furthermore, states have not withered away because of globalization and other forces. They continue to be overwhelmingly important for the lives of people. It is not attractive to live in a very weak or 'failed' state; it can even be mortally dangerous. Therefore, states continue to be extremely significant for any kind of political or social analysis.

At the same time, states are constantly in a process of change. Therefore, it is always relevant to ask questions about the current major modalities of statehood, not least because such modalities help explain how and why states are able or unable to provide basic social values. During the Cold War, the prevalent distinction was between the advanced capitalist states in the First World, the communist states in the Second World, and the post-colonial states in the Third World. With the collapse of most communist states, some use a distinction between the rich countries of the North and the poor countries of the South. This is not a very precise categorization. This chapter has suggested a different one: (i) the advanced capitalist states are in a process of transition from modern to post-modern statehood; (ii) the weak post-colonial states display a serious lack of 'stateness'—and they are by no means on a secure path to the development of more substance; (iii) the modernizing states are different combinations of these three ideal types. Of course, even this categorization can be further refined.

The typology suggested here is not meant to replace any other possible distinction. It will remain relevant—depending on the research question—to differentiate between large and small states, nation-states and non-nation-states, old and new states, states from various regions and sub-regions, and so on. However, the modalities put forward here help to explain how sovereign states have transformed in the context of globalization. It has also been emphasized that 'globalization' is itself a complex entity that must be explained; it is not an anonymous force that throws states around at will. To the extent that 'globalization' applies pressures on single states, that pressure often originates in actions undertaken by other states, as demonstrated by several examples given in this chapter. The major point is that the transformation of statehood over time is the result of an interplay between international and domestic forces. As a consequence, a (re-)marriage of 'international' and 'domestic' political theory is required. The result, hopefully, is a more comprehensive political theory which is dedicated to speculating about the state both in its 'international' and in its 'domestic' aspects (see Sørensen 2001).

Thus, the first recommendation to comparativists is to be aware of the larger context in which political, economic, and other processes play out. This is not a very dramatic proposition as awareness of context is nothing new in comparative politics. The second recommendation goes further: it is to accept that 'international' and 'domestic' are intimately connected and this requires that both elements are taken into the analysis of the development and change of sovereign statehood. The proposition can be translated into two practical guidelines for future study.

1. Proceed on the assumption that the core values pursued by states—i.e. security, wealth, welfare, freedom, order, and justice—each contain 'domestic' as well as 'international' aspects. None of these values can be reduced to a purely 'domestic' or a purely 'international' issue.

2. Therefore, avoid purely 'systemic' or purely 'domestic' analysis. Put the international–domestic interplay at the centre of inquiry and ask questions about 'outside–in' and 'inside–out' relationships.

Conclusion

What are the consequences of these guidelines if we focus, for example, on contemporary problems of democracy? Historically, democratic rule has always developed within the context of independent states. But the emergence of multilevel governance raises the question of whether and how that new context can be democratic. According to one view, 'the only forum within which genuine democracy occurs is within national boundaries' (Kymlicka 1999: 124). The reasoning is that outside that context there is no obvious *demos*, no well-defined political or moral community. An opposing view argues that such a community can be created, just as it had to be created within national boundaries in the early phases of sovereign statehood (Habermas 1999). In any case, the emergence of multilevel governance means that the previously well-defined national context for democracy is being replaced by a new context that integrates 'domestic' and 'international' elements in a different kind of polity.

Some optimistic liberal scholars argue that democratic problems in this new setting can be relatively easily confronted by designing international institutions in such a way as to 'preserve as much space as possible for domestic political processes to operate'

(Nye 2001: 3). For those who more strongly emphasize the changes invoked by globalization, however, a whole new structure of cosmopolitan democracy must be created, based on an ensemble of organizations at different levels, bound by a common framework of cosmopolitan democratic law with a charter of rights and obligations (Held 1995). In short, globalization poses new challenges to liberal democracy. It raises issues of community and identity: who belongs to the democratic community of what used to be a clearly identifiable nation-state but is now intermeshed in all kinds of cross-border interlinkages? The Brexit slogan of 'Take back control' has raised that question in a particularly sharp manner.

In weak states, institutions at the national level are fragile and ineffective. They are controlled by state elites who do not primarily seek to provide public or collective goods. At the global level, international institutions and stronger states increasingly attempt to constrain, influence, and direct policy measures in weak states. Their ticket to influence is the high level of external dependence, economically and otherwise, of weak states. Again, political developments including attempts at **democratization** are decided in an interplay between 'domestic' and 'international' elements.

The economic basis of sovereign statehood has also been transformed. In the modern state, there was a segregated national economy; the major part of economic activity took place at home. In the post-modern state, national economies are much less self-sustained than previously because of 'deep integration', and major parts of economic activity are embedded in cross-border networks. In other words, the economic basis of the post-modern state contains a 'domestic' as well as an 'international' component. That creates a new setting for the provision of wealth and welfare—a key feature of mass democracy (see Chapter 21 'The welfare state'). When 'national' economies are integrated to an extent where opting out of the world market is no longer a viable option, there must be substantially higher vulnerability. Such vulnerability has been a permanent characteristic of weak post-colonial states, because they were always highly dependent on the global economy. In post-modern states, the increase of economic inequality has turned many people against globalization; instead, they embrace a more national attitude of 'my country first'.

The changes discussed here are reflected in the transformation of the institution of sovereignty. In the context of the modern state, sovereignty is closely connected with the 'golden rule' of non-intervention (Jackson 1990). But multilevel governance is quite the opposite of non-intervention; it is systematic *intervention* in national affairs by supranational and international institutions. It means something else to be sovereign under conditions of multilevel governance than it did under traditional conditions of national government. Cooperation brings mutual advantages, because common problems such as climate change and economic crime require collaboration. At the same time, many people are sceptical about the influence of international institutions in 'their' countries.

In weak states, sovereignty has changed as well. Traditionally, sovereignty means international legal equality: equal rights and duties of member-states in the international system. But weak states are highly *unequal* so they need help from the developed world. A number of weak states are unable to take care of themselves, but formal sovereignty, which they have, assumes that they can. They possess sovereignty without being able to meet its requirements. That is what lies behind new practices of 'humanitarian intervention' and trusteeship. In short, the institution of sovereignty changes to make room for a situation where 'domestic' and 'international' affairs can no longer be easily separated.

In conclusion, the sovereign state is alive and doing well. By no means has it been obliterated by forces of globalization. But it has been transformed in ways which closely connect 'domestic' and 'international'. That insight must be taken on board when conducting comparative analysis of political systems.

KEY POINTS

- States continue to be extremely significant for any kind of political or social analysis. But states are constantly in a process of change. It is necessary to ask questions about the current modalities of statehood, not least because such modalities help explain how and why states are able or unable to provide basic social values.

- Changes in statehood place the discipline of comparative politics in a new setting. In particular, it is necessary to accept that 'international' and 'domestic' are intimately connected.

- The core values pursued by states—i.e. security, wealth, welfare, freedom, democracy, order, and justice—each contain 'domestic' as well as 'international' aspects. That insight must be taken on board when conducting comparative analysis of political systems.

? QUESTIONS

Knowledge-based

1. What is globalization? Why is there such an intense debate about globalization and its consequences?

2. What are the major aspects of statehood that are relevant in a debate about globalization and states?

3. Describe the changes involved in the transformation from modern to post-modern statehood. Identify three states that you would consider post-modern.

4. Identify the characteristics of weak post-colonial statehood. Where can we find such states?

5. Can multilevel governance be democratic? Why or why not?

Critical thinking

1. Set out the standard image of the modern state. Does that image apply to your own country?

2. Are identities changing so that we are increasingly becoming citizens of the world rather than nationals belonging to our countries?

3. Are weak post-colonial states on the road to development or are they on the road to further breakdown and 'state failure'? Discuss examples.

4. Will states gain from participating in economic globalization or will it further aggravate their problems? Discuss the cases of the UK and China.

5. Will the process of state transformation lead to a more peaceful and prosperous world?

≋ FURTHER READING

Brock, L., Holm, H.-H., Sørensen, G., and Stohl, M. (2011). *Fragile States. Violence and the Failure of Intervention* (Cambridge: Polity Press). Defines fragile states, examines their characteristics, and explains their development from pre-colonial times to the present day.

Dicken, P. (2015) *Global Shift: Mapping the Changing Contours of the World Economy* (London: Sage). Provides a detailed introduction to all major aspects of economic globalization.

Held, D. and McGrew, A. (2007) *Globalization/Anti-Globalization* (Cambridge: Polity Press). Presents the pro- and anti-views in the debate on globalization and state transformation.

Iversen, T. and Soskice, D. (2019) Democracy *and Prosperity* (Princeton, NJ: Princeton University Press). Discusses the effects of economic globalization on social welfare and democracy.

Scholte, J. A. (2005) *Globalization: A Critical Introduction* (2nd edn) (Houndsmill, Basingstoke: Palgrave Macmillan). Presents a sociological overview of all major dimensions of globalization.

Sørensen, G. (2001) *Changes in Statehood: The Transformation of International Relations* (Houndsmill, Basingstoke: Palgrave Macmillan). Explains the dynamics of state transformation and the emergence of post-modern and weak post-colonial states.

Zielonka, J. (2018) Counter-*Revolution. Liberal Europe in Retreat* (Oxford: Oxford University Press). Examines the new popular movements in Europe and argues that the liberal project needs to be reinvented and recreated.

ENDNOTE

1.   I have discussed the subject in two books (Sørensen 2001, 2004). Some formulations in this chapter draw on those works.

Visit the Online Resources that accompany this book for additional material, including country profiles, comparative data sets, flashcard glossaries, and web directory.

www.oup.com/he/caramani5e

25
From supporting democracy to supporting autocracy

Peter Burnell

Chapter contents

Reader's guide

The politics of nations are affected by relations with the international environment. International efforts to spread democracy lie at the juncture between the study of politics and the worlds of public policy and actors promoting democracy. This chapter explores the controversies surrounding democracy support and its significance for comparative politics. It compares policy drivers, institutions, actors, and methods, before inquiring whether democracy support is now fit for purpose in a world where economic performance in the West is faltering and the international presence of China and Russia continues to grow. It ends by comparing democracy support with the increasing attention now being given to the sustenance that authoritarian and semi-authoritarian regimes receive from powerful like-minded regimes.

Introduction: comparing definitions of democracy support

The increasing number of democracies is a distinctive feature of the world since the 1980s, although from around 2005 progress seemed to stop, and in some aspects even reverse. These developments have not come about entirely by chance. In an increasingly interdependent world, nowhere is political change completely isolated from external influences. From the late 1980s, the West has supported democratic change abroad to a degree and in ways that have no historical precedent (see Box 25.1). The term 'support for democracy' is superceding 'democracy promotion', in part owing to the latter's confusing association with the forcible removal of governments like Saddam Hussein's in Iraq. The switch also reflects an awareness of the limits to what can be achieved by international agency anywhere, and the importance of internal determinants of long-term political change. Growing attention to autocracy support now complements the apparent stalling of democracy's global progress. This captures how some authoritarian and semi-authoritarian regimes receive sustenance from their relations with the present-day governments of such countries as China, Russia, Saudi Arabia, and Iran. For example, Russia offers diplomatic and even military support to the beleaguered presidency of Nicolás Maduro in Venezuela, who faces mounting domestic political opposition, as well as hostility from the United States.

Basic vocabulary of democracy support

The idea of supporting democracy has an *active* and a *passive* sense. The *active* sense comprises deliberate actions undertaken with a view to achieving a democratic purpose. There is intentionality. This frames questions about which democracy support actors are doing what, how, and to what effect. The *passive* sense orients us more towards how far democratic trends are occurring in prospective, emerging, and new democracies; the kind of democracy that is emerging; and, crucially, how these developments are influenced by external actors and international events. Of course, democracy may be supported (or, conversely, challenged) by different kinds of external stimuli or force, including international structures and not just purposive foreign agency.

Intentionality is central to the active sense of supporting democracy. In the passive sense, however, democratic impulses could still emerge as a by-product of international exposure. Political developments inside one country can have 'spillover' effects elsewhere. Terms like 'demonstration effect', 'democratization by emulation', and 'contagion' appear in the literature, and all reflect this. A parallel debate to democracy promotion and the international diffusion of **democratization** is emerging on international support for autocracy (examined below in the section 'The rise of autocracy support').

> ↘ **ZOOM-IN 25.1**
>
> ### Democracy and democracy support in the twenty-first century
>
> The idea of democracy as a universal commitment is quite new, and it is quintessentially a product of the twentieth century … While democracy is not yet universally practiced, nor indeed uniformly accepted, in the general climate of world opinion, democratic **governance** has now achieved the status of being taken to be generally right.
>
> Sen (1999: 5)
>
> Democracy promotion as a foreign policy goal has become increasingly acceptable throughout most of the international community … an international norm embraced by other states [than the US], transnational organizations, and international networks … in the community of democratic states the normative burden has shifted to those not interested in advocating democracy promotion.
>
> McFaul (2004: 148, 158)

The intentional support of democracy employs various methods or approaches. An initial distinction is between direct and indirect support. **Direct support** targets some defining political characteristics of democracy, whether political values, norms, and principles or more concrete institutions. **Indirect support** addresses the conditions for democratization, such as any socio-economic requisites and need for social peace. Direct approaches must embody some idea about what democracy means and its manifestations. Although liberal democracy has been dominant, Hobson and Kurki (2012, see also Bridoux 2019) argue that democracy promotion should now embrace alternative conceptualizations adapted to the circumstances and aspirations specific to different societies. Indirect approaches demand an understanding of what makes democracy possible and how it comes about—a theory of democratization, where competing accounts exist. For example, disagreements exist over why economic development matters, although it seems less important to democratic transition than to democratic consolidation.

Democracy support

The political instruments or methods that are employed in supporting democracy directly can be placed along a continuum running from **soft power** to **hard power** (Nye 2005). If power means coercion, the continuum spans assistance, persuasion, influence, and incentives on the one side. On the other side, it includes pressure (e.g. 'diplomatic pressure'); political conditionalities, especially negative conditionalities that embody threats in the event of non-compliance (whereas positive conditionalities stress incentives or inducements); economic and other sanctions (threatened or actual); and, possibly (but more controversially), covert or overt military intervention. In practice, different methods or approaches are often in play simultaneously, or are employed in sequence, depending on the political circumstances and trajectory of the country on the receiving end. Thus, assistance may be offered for democracy-building projects after external pressure has helped replace autocracy, as in post-Gadhafi Libya—albeit without success there.

The democracy supporters comprise different kinds of organization—governmental, inter-governmental, semi-autonomous, and non-governmental—varying greatly in their mandates and access to diverse instruments for supporting democracy. United Nations (UN) initiatives can employ a form of international legitimacy which other actors lack. Governments in the West have more tools at their disposal than the private political foundations or institutes that specialize in democracy assistance projects.

Democracy assistance

Democracy assistance is usually consensual: it comprises grant-aided support that can take the form of technical, material, or financial assistance to pro-democracy initiatives. Assistance includes what Carothers (2004) calls 'institutional modelling'—attempts to transfer blueprints of democratic practice, procedure, and organizations that resemble working models borrowed from established democracies. For Carothers, assistance should also extend to helping pro-democracy activists challenge authoritarian and semi-authoritarian rulers. This approximates to direct involvement in domestic political struggles. It moves closer to harder forms of power when combined with the application of external pressure on rulers to open up political space.

The financial value of democracy assistance is hard to gauge; reporting practices vary, and lack precise or standardized definitions. There are disagreements over what should be included: reported sums can include spending on human rights and governance as well as democracy, or what the United Nations Development Programme's (UNDP) calls 'democratic governance'. A leading example is the European Commission's

European Instrument for Democracy and Human Rights (EIDHR), which was voted 1.3 billion Euros for 2014–20. All the sums are dwarfed by net official development assistance. But money is not everything: the timing, quality, and suitability of democracy support all matter too.

Political conditionality

The European Union (EU) has been a major exponent of **political conditionality** as a distinctive approach to supporting democracy. The EU's Copenhagen criteria (1993) lay down conditions referring to 'stability of institutions guaranteeing democracy, the rule of law, human rights, and respect for the protection of minorities' in exchange for eligibility for membership. The EU 'speaks softly and carries a big carrot' is one way of describing this approach. A broad consensus exists that this conditionality initially helped push the democratization of post-communist countries in Central and Eastern Europe, although illiberal trends have emerged in states like Hungary more recently. Although conditionality can be deployed on its own, some scholars attached considerable weight to what was called 'normative power Europe' (Manners 2002). This refers to the claim that the EU helps spread certain values which in turn translate into liberal democratic principles and processes, without necessarily exporting particular institutional models such as parliamentary democracy. Socialization or social learning can change attitudes and beliefs or, maybe, just behaviour. The result may lead newly adopted democratic practices to become deeply embedded, once the prize of EU membership has been secured. However, the EU's capacity for projecting normative power is increasingly being brought into question due to competition from other foreign objectives such as security. Major reservations remain about its ability to deploy political conditionalities (either incentives or deterrents) effectively towards countries that will never be offered (or seek) EU membership, such as those associated with the 'Arab Spring'.

The United States and the European Union

Historically, the US has enjoyed the larger profile in supporting democracy around the globe. It is the one country with both the capacity and political will to deploy the full range of methods or approaches, including harder forms of power such as force. From the time of President Reagan's interest in furthering democracy as a way of combating Soviet influence, to President G. W. Bush making freedom (in the

Middle East especially) central to his foreign policy rhetoric after 9/11, the US has set agendas in democracy support. This has not been wholly beneficial, as indicated by the widely held view that democracy promotion was tainted by its association with what came to be dubbed 'regime change' (the forcible overthrow of a government). Europeans struggled to keep their distance from this, although for a time President Obama's move in the direction of multilateralism and policies that shared European sensitivity to democracy's developmental needs offered a way forward.

KEY POINTS

- Political change inside countries has to be understood with reference to international influences.

- Supporting democracy abroad has developed over the past thirty five years, with the US and Europe in the forefront.

- Active democracy support employs soft and harder forms of power, but the use of military force is challenged on ideological and practical grounds.

- The EU prides itself on dialogue and partnership with governments, but its greatest successes stem from political conditionality in EU accession. The US is generally more willing to actively support the local political opposition to autocrats in places where vital US interests are not jeopardized (Carothers 2012).

Explaining democracy support

Since 1945, a strong sense of the value of democracy and a desire to see it spread far and wide have never been absent from the West. The dismantling of European empires in Africa and Asia saw attempts to implant formal democratic structures, many of them very transient. The end of the Cold War saw a dramatic new willingness to adopt democracy support as a foreign policy objective. The erosion of Soviet influence followed by the collapse of the Soviet Union made it safer for Western governments to demand democracy, human rights, and good governance in countries that previously were valued primarily as Western allies. These countries no longer had a strong alternative international partner to (threaten to) turn to if they felt uncomfortable with Western pressure to undertake political reform.

At the same time, sizeable mobilizations of support for political change began to take place inside many so-called Second and Third World countries. Often this was spurred by social and economic grievances. International support of democracy gained legitimacy

from this *pull-factor*—demands for political reform by people living in societies with non-democratic regimes—alongside the *push-factors* of foreign policy goals in the West.

Idealism

Idealism offers one possible reason for supporting democracy. The intrinsic value of freedom and democracy may be considered so great that societies which claim to enjoy these must help other societies share them too. It could be a disinterested act, even when not tinged with missionary zeal. Historians see a close association of the US with democratic idealism, dating to the presidency of Woodrow Wilson (1913–21). One view is that the US is 'born to lead'; advancing freedom and democracy is the 'manifest destiny' of the US. Other, more sceptical views link US policy to imperialism (explored in Cox et al. 2000).

Democracy support and US imperialism

A critical view maintains that the US defines its aims in such a way as to pursue global hegemony. And furthering democracy abroad can sometimes serve US imperialism. In the 1980s, efforts to support democratization were indeed part of a strategy to confront the Soviet Union. However, it is not obvious why all the countries that subsequently endorsed the idea of democracy would do so for the sake of US domination. Undoubtedly, governments shape their foreign policies in accord with their national interest. But public opinion studies have shown that many citizens in the West subscribed to the idea of spreading democracy, complicating simple notions that the endeavour is largely a power play by Western leaders. Just as pertinent, US foreign policy under President Trump appears to question the importance of democracy support to realizing US objectives of power and influence in the world. (see Carothers and Brown 2018).

Developmental arguments

Paradigms depicting the relationships between development in the developing world and democracy or democratization underwent a double shift from the 1980s. Previously, the dominant reasoning was economistic, arguing that developing countries must address economic needs before they could expect to sustain democracy. By trying to democratize prematurely they would place their development in peril. What made this 'cruel choice' seem inevitable was the belief that economics determines politics. Insofar as some particular kind of political rule is most favourable to development, authoritarian regimes have the edge. The economic 'miracle' of East Asia's 'dragons' lent support.

However, this chain of reasoning came under fire. Many non-democracies in Africa were not developing. Social science increasingly argued that politics can make a difference, connected to a recognition that institutions and agency do matter. Not everything is determined by structural 'causes'. Furthermore, development came to be understood not just as economic growth but as improved social conditions and human development. Attention turned to how better governance, democracy, and human rights could benefit development. Values like dignity and freedom were even incorporated within the very definition of development itself. The double-paradigm shift, endowing politics and democracy with potential causal powers, lent plausibility to democracy support.

Some major international development agencies like the World Bank steadfastly attached most importance to better governance, not democracy. This builds on arguments that the rule of law and secure property rights are fundamental for development. And although democracy and good governance are often thought to go together, this is not true everywhere. Furthering one of them does not necessarily advance the other straight away (Emmerson 2012). In some countries, rectifying state weakness and state fragility demands a higher priority. So, although the developmental case for spreading democracy was never accepted by everyone and may even have lost ground in recent years, the case for aiding development as a way to consolidate stable democracy has, if anything, gained new ground. Lipset's (1959) thesis that stable democracy is more difficult to maintain in the absence of social modernization and economic development still commands widespread overwhelming support.

Democracy support and international capitalism

Arguments originating in neo-Marxist and Gramscian perspectives explain democracy support as an instrument of global capitalism. And it is true that the vision of democracy offered by much democracy support resembles what Marxists criticize as bourgeois democracy. It lacks the full popular participatory content and truly egalitarian ideals that speak more about empowering the people than safeguarding individual (property) rights.

Therefore, democracy support has been seen as a handmaiden of capital, whether national, international, or transnational (Robinson 1996). It is likened to a Trojan horse for the kind of selective economic liberalization that serves corporate interests best. It has been portrayed as targeting the removal of regimes that claim to put social justice first, like President Hugo Chávez (and his successor, Nicolás Maduro) in Venezuela, and other oil-rich countries like Saddam's Iraq and Gadhafi's Libya. Yet, as China's economic success shows, capitalist forces can thrive even in a non-democracy. Capitalism might be essential to Western ideas of democracy, but democracy does not appear to be essential to capitalism. This challenges readings of democracy support as merely an instrument of capitalism.

Democratization, international peace, and national security

The **democratic peace thesis** has regularly featured in the policy rationales of most western actors. This long-standing thesis maintains that democracies do not go to war with one another. Thus, everyone gains as more states become democratic.

The democratic peace thesis has generated much controversy. One objection is that it holds only under limiting conditions, such as a restrictive definition of war, or during the Cold War era, or when most democracies were economically advanced. There is little agreement on why democracies only rarely go to war with democracies. And democracies occasionally initiate wars against non-democracies. Democratization can increase the likelihood of internal turmoil and then fracture external relations, as happened with the bloody transformation of former Yugoslavia. The devastating consequences the 'Arab Spring' had for Syria and the impact of Syria's civil war on it neighbours is another example, although a counter-argument states that if democratic opening had been allowed to proceed peacefully towards democratic transition and consolidation, then these consequences would have been avoided.

Nevertheless, views close to the democratic peace thesis probably still feature in justifications for supporting democratization as a long-term goal, notwithstanding significant short-to-medium-term risks. Furthermore, after the terrorist events of 9/11 and the US government's espousal of a freedom agenda in the Middle East, political leaders in the West, UK Prime Minister Tony Blair for instance, also came to present the spread of democracy as an antidote to international terrorism. Yet this reasoning was always suspect. Oppressive rule might provoke a violent response in society, but the primary 'causes' often lie elsewhere. Rival interpretations highlight xenophobia, the radicalizing effects of poverty and resentment at global social injustice, and the militant tendencies inherent in extremist religious views—the so-called Islamic State movement in Syria and Iraq, for example. In any case, Western governments undermine the credibility of their case when appearing content with electoral processes abroad only when comfortable with the electorate's actual choice of rulers, let alone when making large arms sales to autocratic regimes like Saudi Arabia's.

Fresh thinking about democracy support seems to be required as a result of failing to foresee the timing, nature, and spread of the 2011 'Arab Spring' (see Burnell 2013). A realization that their former stance of valuing the illusion of political stability in these countries over democratization was misguided is another spur. The descent into chaos (as in Libya), or rapid return to highly illiberal rule (as in Egypt), also demand revised thinking—even before the emerging need to come to terms with the growing ability of Russia and China to help frustrate or undermine democracy or democratic trends beyond their borders.

KEY POINTS

- No single theory captures well all the actors and/or covers all years.

- After 9/11, the contribution of democratization to securing peace within and between nations gained some prominence in the rhetoric of politicians, but their actions in support of democracy proved inconsistent.

- Even if a Western consensus on the desirability of democracy still exists, the grounds for supporting democratization now seem less self-evident at a time when geopolitical developments appear to render it more difficult

---

Suppliers of democracy support

The international complex of actors engaged in supporting democracy abroad grew from the late 1980s to include different kinds of organization: governmental, inter-governmental, autonomous but largely publicly funded, and genuinely non-governmental actors, some of them not-for-profit and others more commercially motivated. One useful distinction is between those for whom democracy support is only one of several activities, such as the UNDP, and those where it provides the sole rationale, like the UK's Westminster Foundation for Democracy (WFD). Another differentiates between the kinds of activities they engage in: giving grants, offering technical support, or being operational. Different again is the inter-governmental International Institute for Democracy and Electoral Assistance (IDEA), based in Sweden, whose aim is to assemble and share knowledge with democracy builders.

Inter-governmental actors

The UN is the one truly multilateral organization of great note that is prominent in democracy support. Its contribution ranges from broad statements of support for democratic values by the Office of the Secretary General and considerable experience in helping stage, monitor, and observe elections, especially in new states, to UNDP 'democratic governance' projects. A separate UN Democracy Fund, funded voluntarily by around forty governments (to the tune of $180 million in 2017), supports civil society initiatives.

Regional-level organizations expressing a commitment to democracy in member-states include the Organization of American States (OAS), and the African Union, through its New Partnership for Africa's Development (NEPAD) and African Peer Review Mechanism. The Commonwealth exchanges experiences in matters such as parliamentary training and legislative oversight of the executive among member-states. The Organization for Security and Co-operation in Europe (OSCE) Office for Democratic Institutions and Human Rights observes national elections, but obstruction by Russia and its allies are a brake (Fawn 2006). In the EU, a European Endowment for Democracy (EED) established in response to the 'Arab Spring' also depends on voluntary funding by member-states, but is supposed to have more political flexibility than the EIDHR. The European Partnership for Democracy is a Brussels-based umbrella for fifteen European democracy assistance organizations such as the UK's WFD.

Governmental and government-funded actors

Western governments support democracy through various channels, including foreign ministries and other ministries, embassies, and development aid agencies, and by funding formally autonomous democracy institutes or foundations.

The United States Agency for International Development (USAID) developed a Center of Excellence on Democracy, Human Rights and Governance with a view to integrating democracy programming throughout its core development work, but as of 2019 faces significant structural reorganization. The National Endowment for Democracy (NED), a private organization funded by the US Congress and its grantee organizations, including the National

Democratic Institute for International Affairs (NDI) and the International Republic Institute (IRI), has worked in around ninety countries, but is facing drastic cuts to its budget (reducing to $67.3 million in 2020). Democracy institutes and foundations in countries like the US, the Netherlands, and the UK, and Germany's political foundations or *Stiftungen*, usually have private non-profit status and formal autonomy alongside their public funding and other income. They possess considerable collective experience in practical support.

The European Union

Although the EU is not a state and and the lens of foreign policy does not illuminate all EU external behaviour, the EU formally aspires to a common foreign and security policy. One of the most established institutional expressions now of its commitment to the idea of supporting democracy is the EIDHR. This is authorized to cooperate directly with human rights defenders and local civil society actors without first gaining approval from the national authorities; and disburses grants in over thirty countries.

The EU's role in supporting democratic political reform in Central and East European countries in the 1990s, through the accession process, was noted in the section 'Political conditionality'. This was not disinterested. Just as many people in the post-communist societies believed democratization would help them recover freedom both from authoritarian rule and domination by the Soviet Union (Russia), so Western Europeans saw democratic reform in the 'near abroad' as advantageous to their own security. EU expansion appealed to many members, although not all for the same reasons. The EU in the past had a strong dynamic of its own: increase in membership could help the institution to become a more powerful actor in world affairs; democracy support itself could be presented as a symbol and tool of powerful actor status. And by expressing its support for democracy in ways that chime with liberal values and not coercion, the EU reaffirmed the kind of identify that Europeans have claimed for Europe.

The EU's European Neighbourhood Policy (ENP) offers about sixteen neighbours privileged bilateral ties that build on a supposedly mutual commitment to common values such as democracy, human rights, and rule of law. It seems to have been only marginally effective as a tool for furthering democratic progress. Reconsideration in light of the 'Arab Spring' produced a new initiative to offer EU partners 'more for more'—concessions like greater market access to the EU and investment in exchange for seeing democratic progress: positive conditionality was revitalized. The ability of the EU and its partners to deliver remains in doubt, with very few partners seeming able to maintain a democratizing trajectory. Europe's south Tunisia is a notable exception; in the east, Ukraine remains blighted by corruption fuelling growing rejection by society of the established political elites, combined with destabilizing pressure from Russia.

Finally, there has been a conviction that Europe since 1945 offers a model of political harmony both within and among states that speaks to the needs of other countries and regions suffering violent conflict. This model shows how to rise above long periods of inter-state violence—Europe having been at the heart of two 'world wars' and one 'cold war' in the twentieth century alone. The political values on which this stability in Europe has been constructed are for Europe to demonstrate and share by engaging in 'partnership' and ideological suasion. And yet the political strains opened up in Europe first by the Eurozone financial crisis and major disagreements among EU states over how to tackle sovereign indebtedness, and then over how to respond to the dramatic influx of refugees and economic migrants from the Middle East and Africa beginning 2015 onwards, put that model to the test. The advances made by Eurosceptic populist and right-wing nationalist forces in several countries, manifest in the European Parliamentary elections of May 2019, contributes additional strains on the union. The UK's decision to leave the EU altogether is both symptomatic and something that could cause leaders among the remaining twenty-seven member-states to hold together more firmly, as the UK's fractious departure demonstrates the negative domestic consequences of seeking to leave. The political energy consumed in Europe by coping with these and other challenges, both at the EU and individual country level, when transatlantic divisions with the Trump administration in the US grow wider, undermine democracy support's chances of commanding high-level political commitment. Attempts such as those of the British government to cultivate a so-called 'golden era' of enhanced financial and commercial relations with China, first launched in 2015, also prompt questions about whether even human rights abroad might increasingly be consigned to a back seat.

Democracy support by new democracies

If, as Schenkkan and Repucci (2019: 106) claim about the US especially, 'major democracies are now flagging in their support for democratic norms, or even working in the opposite direction', then it cannot be said that newer democracies or sizeable developing-world democracies are making adequate compensatory efforts of their own. Seasoned sympathetic observers of democracy support like Carothers and Youngs (2011) express their disappointment. The support of such countries for international human rights initiatives led by the US or EU countries in UN forums has been patchy too. The reasons range from the desire of former colonies such as India to declare their attachment to principles of **sovereignty** and non-interference, tact, emulating positions taken by China and (less convincingly) Russia on this issue, to suspicions about the policy inconsistencies and underlying agendas of the West. Turkey is an example of failed hopes (see Box 25.2).

KEY POINTS

- Institutional actors in the West involved in supporting democracy have proliferated, and comprise different kinds. International development agencies value 'democratic governance' but democracy institutes and foundations support democracy for its own sake.

- New sources of democracy support from outside the US and Western Europe have been slow to emerge.

- The EU finds it difficult to replicate its contribution to democratization outside the EU zone; competing ideas about the national interest that elevate security and commercial gains appear to have downgraded democracy support as a foreign policy goal in the US, especially in the Trump administration.

The demand for democracy support

The demand for democracy support is not the same as the demand for democracy. Both are difficult to gauge, especially wherever people cannot express themselves freely. Pressure for autocrats to retire is often bound up with popular economic discontents. Even strong popular demands for dignity and freedom as in the 'Arab Spring' do not necessarily mean much knowledge of, or indeed appetite for, Western-style liberal democracy (see Hobson and Kurki 2012), let alone for democracy support. Nevertheless, the West assumes a hunger for (liberal) democracy exists almost everywhere, and believes international support can be effective. Identifying countries that are not very democratic or where freedoms are absent is not difficult, but there is no strong fit between these countries and actual patterns of allocation of democracy support.

Over time, major changes in the market for democracy support have followed national political trends. Whereas in the early 1990s countries in the former Second World were at the forefront of demand, several European examples have now 'graduated'. Other countries, some in Central Asia for instance, have since become resistant to change. States in the Balkans became candidates for democracy support as they emerged from the violent break-up of Yugoslavia and hope to become members of the EU. But Russia since Putin became president has led a 'backlash' against democratization; and Russian sensitivity to Western (specifically American) influence in nearby countries like Ukraine and Georgia hinders their

---

↘ ZOOM-IN 25.2

Democracy support by 'rising democracies'

Case of India

India, a democracy since independence in 1947 and the world's largest democracy, is, along with Brazil, Russia, and China, one of the original BRIC states. But apart from being a notable funder of the UN Democracy Fund, India has shown little enthusiasm for supporting democracy in its bilateral foreign relations. This has been explained by its traditional non-aligned stance in world politics and a sensitivity towards colonialist and imperialist adventures; the strategic importance of maintaining stable relations with China and Pakistan, although critical of past US support for Pakistan's military rulers; and the commercial and economic benefits from prioritizing good relations with countries like Myanmar. India supported Nepal's

peaceful transition to democracy in 2005–08 to engender peace on its border and prevent China gaining influence (Destradi 2012).

Case of Turkey

Around the time of the 'Arab Spring' Turkey was discussed as a model of democracy-building for Islamic societies in the region. Turkey's ruling Justice and Development Party (AKP) historically has Islamist roots and is easily the most popular party. By keeping the military in the barracks and seeming to show allegiance to democratic principles, Turkey and the AKP could encourage, inform, and support pro-democracy forces in North Africa and the Middle East. Turkey began to respond to requests for assistance in undertaking political transition from some 'Arab Spring' countries. However, the relevance of Turkey's own experience was always in doubt.

First, Turkey has a strong state, unlike such countries as Libya and Yemen. Second, Turkey is a secular state, which is not true of every Arab country. Third, as a member of the North Atlantic Treaty Organization (NATO), Turkey has long-standing ties with the US and has long sought to join the EU, in contrast to Egypt, for example, which claims no European identity and has ambivalent relations with the US. Whereas the Turkish military's political interventions before 2002 seemed to prepare the way for democracy by promoting secularism and a largely unifying (but not anti-Western) **nationalism**, Egypt's armed forces have never relinquished a key political role and actually derailed the brief democratic transition following President Mubarak's fall from power. Fourth, global economic problems emerging since 2007 mean that Turkey's economic boom under AKP rule, which had served political stability during democratization, now looks a distant prospect for the wider region. Finally, although Turkey had made some progress in human rights, partly at the EU's behest, recent years have witnessed increasingly illiberal and authoritarian tendencies, as President Erdoğan now seems determined to further concentrate power in his own hands, indefinitely, and increase the state's conformity to stricter Islamic values. A failed coup by some military officers in 2016 accelerated these trends. Relations between the authorities and Kurdish separatists have deteriorated. With hindsight, Turkey's active democracy support in the region early during the 'Arab Spring' looks less like a principled attachment to democratic ideas and more a means to advance Turkey's own geostrategic political and commercial aims, just as its credentials now to be a role model for democratization in the Islamic world are completely devalued.

democratic progress, and seeks to counter Western democracy support there, too. In Africa, China's growing financial and commercial engagement frees a number of countries from the political, governance, and economic conditionalities that traditional Western partners tried to impose. Strong (and unexpected) domestic protests against the military or military-backed governments in Sudan and Algeria in 2019 will certainly bring changes among the governing elites there. But it is too soon to say whether there will be any significant democratic transition or an opening up to democracy support from outside. In Latin America, the Organization of American States (OAS) provides a regional inter-governmental forum that has intervened diplomatically to arrest or reverse military coups against elected rulers there. But it seems incapable of countering the threats to democracy posed by poor governance and violent crime. And although the Trump administration is targeting Venezuela with offers of 'democracy assistance', securing something

akin to 'regime change' more than responding to local calls for systemic political reform is how US policy is being received. A similar comment applies to growing US economic pressure on Iran. Meanwhile, in the world's most populous non-democracy, China, society's demand for anything like Western-style democracy is extremely hard to gauge even as the country's leadership moves further and further away from this.

Democracy support strategies

Democracy support faces questions of strategy—choices about what to do and how to go about it.

Constraints on intervention

Democracy support is not license to do anything in the name of advancing the cause. There are constraints in international law. The limited circumstances whereby the UN Security Council may authorize military intervention in the internal affairs of a country against its government's will were narrowly defined at a time when ideas of state sovereignty were paramount. In the first instance, they require that the country be regarded as a serious threat to others, such as exporting instability to neighbouring countries. The post-Cold War world saw academic discussions of the rights that all peoples have to democratic government. That the UN might have a responsibility to protect and enforce those rights is one possible corollary, but is hugely contentious. The UN and actors such as the North Atlantic Treaty Organization (NATO) have tended to intervene militarily only where there has been massive

KEY POINTS

- The true demand for democracy support is hard to fathom, but the importance of consulting the intended beneficiaries has gained in recognition (Barkan 2012).

- Democracy support has never corresponded very closely to patterns of greatest democratic deficit.

- Allocations of democracy support have changed over time in response to political developments on the ground. For example, Russia has become extremely hostile and Tunisia has become more receptive.

abuse of human rights, and even then, not in all cases. In 2011, the UN Security Council approved the use by UN states of 'all necessary measures' to protect Libya's civilians under threat of attack by Colonel Gadhafi's forces, but there was no mention of supporting transition to democracy. Russian and Chinese perceptions that NATO's intervention subsequently overstepped the UN resolution hardened their resolve to oppose UN-authorized interventions in Syria, where state violence against popular uprising accelerated in 2012.

Spreading democracy at gunpoint is an unpromising strategy, anyway. Pei and Kasper (2003) calculated that of sixteen US military interventions abroad since 1898, democracy was sustained ten years after the departure of US forces in only four cases. More recent experience in Afghanistan, Iraq, and Libya is no improvement. But military intervention to end internal war can contribute to peace-building and thereby offer a service to democracy-building. For example, UK military deployment in Sierra Leone from 1999 was critical to ending civil war and restoring elected civilian rule.

Types of democracy assistance

Governmental and inter-governmental actors share a comparative advantage in being able to mount a wide range of approaches to supporting democracy. Democracy assistance is the one method that is available to the greatest number and variety of actors, the foundations included. Assistance also tends to be much more visible than diplomatic dialogue or pressure. Carothers (2004) categorized democracy assistance as a 'democracy template' comprising three sectors: electoral process, state institutions, and civil society. For each sector there are sector goals and related forms of assistance. Boxes 25.3 and 25.4 present illustrative material for UNDP and USAID.

Broadly speaking, democracy assistance has evolved along a path from electoral support through an emphasis on civil society to an increased willingness in some circles to view political party strengthening as essential. For international development agencies who believe that better governance serves development, strengthening the capacity of legislatures to hold the executive to account (especially over public expenditure) is a prime candidate. These trends reflect progress in our understanding of democratization and its connections to development. A lesson grasped fairly early on was that elections alone do not make a democracy, even where international election observation furthers a largely free and fair process on election-day. Kelley (2012) contested the reliability of monitoring, after studying 1,324 national elections and

---

> **ZOOM-IN 25.3**
>
> ## United Nations Development Programme democratic governance
>
> Main services: responding to the requests and needs of developing countries, UNDP offers support in the following focus areas:
>
> - access to information and e-governance
> - access to justice and rule of law
> - anti-corruption
> - civic engagement
> - electoral systems and processes
> - human rights
> - local governance and local development
> - parliamentary development
> - public administration
> - women's empowerment
> - youth.
>
> *Source*: UNDP (2015).

> **ZOOM-IN 25.4**
>
> ## USAID's Democracy, Human Rights and Governance (DRG) Strategic Framework
>
> Promote participatory, representative and inclusive political processes and government institutions.
>
> Foster greater accountability of institutions and leaders to citizens and to the law.
>
> Protect and promote universally recognized human rights.
>
> Improve development outcomes through the integration of DRG principles and practices across USAID's development portfolio.
>
> *Source*: USAID (2013).

---

600 monitoring missions. Of course, fraudulent elections may spark unstoppable protest, as in Ukraine's 'Orange Revolution' in 2004–05, creating new openings for democracy support (then squandered, in Ukraine's case). Elections can be instrumental for democratic transition, but this is only one of several possible outcomes.

Partly because the electoralist fallacy gained wide recognition, civil society support became a growth area for democracy assistance. The attraction was that it seemed to avoid direct interference in a country's internal politics, and hence it should be more acceptable to governments. It seemed especially pertinent to consolidating democracy after initial transition. However, lengthy experience has now revealed many problems. For example, much evidence of donor dependency has come to light—civic groups that are unlikely to be sustained after foreign support ceased. Many such groups tend to comprise elites who are neither very representative nor committed to developing extensive roots in society. Increasingly, around the world from Russia and China to Cambodia and Uganda, there has been a government backlash against foreign support of civil society groups, closing the space for foreign funding and triggering wider crackdowns on civil society. This leaves leaving international supporters divided over how to react, and bereft of a strong collective response (Carothers 2015). That said, new forms of civic activism emerging in the last decade or so provide fresh impetus for political change, offering enhanced scope for outside actors to lend support (Youngs 2019).

Newer areas of interest for democracy assistance, propelled by the role played by social media in the 'Arab Spring', embrace new communications technology in ways that will help democracy activists, while also countering its self-serving use (and censorship) by authoritarian regimes.

Finally, there is the idea of a governance approach to democracy support (Freyburg et al. 2015), especially focusing on EU efforts to improve governance in partner countries through cooperating across a wide range of public policy initiatives. The claim is that democratic or pro-democracy norms and practices can come to be embedded in the ways the machinery of state administers public business, even where the political regime is not a liberal democracy. A limiting factor—acknowledged by exponents of this idea—is that such functional cooperation may do little to alter fundamental power structures such as a high concentration of executive power with weak accountability. Only by jettisoning or dismantling the prevailing power structure will real or meaningful democratic change become possible. Further investigation of the actual democratizing potential is required before confidence in this approach to supporting democracy is warranted (see Muhhina 2018).

Democracy support and state-building

Democracy support's greatest challenges include societies seeking to emerge from violent conflict, especially those where the state is fragile or ineffective, such as Afghanistan and the Democratic Republic of the Congo.

Sub-state violence—or, at minimum, weak governance—is placed under the spotlight that previously focused more on threats of large-scale inter-state war, East–West conflict in particular. Where multiple weaknesses exist, possible solutions tend to be interconnected, even though the relationships are often not well understood. The challenges may include not just **state-building** (or rebuilding) and improving the quality of governance, but also nation-building, economic reconstruction and development, and even tackling humanitarian crises. The correct order of priorities, the trade-offs, and the sequencing issues between meeting these several different requirements and installing stable democracy are complex issues for the societies themselves and for well-intentioned international actors too. The issues lie at the interstices of different discourses and international policy communities having different mandates, competencies, and expertise that are not well joined up. For all these reasons, Syria could become a severe test case of the West's commitment and ability to support political reform once order is restored there, but the opportunity will not become available at least until President Bashar al Assad departs the scene.

Democratization versus state-building

One of the larger theoretical questions is whether state-building should take precedence when public order is weak, especially if political instability also endangers (democracy in) neighbouring countries. Rapid moves towards participatory and competitive politics risk mobilizing uncivil elements; populist **political entrepreneurs** take advantage of ethnic, racial, regional, and religious or sectarian divides to widen societal cleavages and gain support, (re)igniting violence in consequence. Hallmarks of stateness—monopoly of the means of violence, for instance—can be difficult to achieve. External encouragement to diffuse power may end up bolstering regional warlords or local despots.

However, the alternative of pursuing a 'state first' approach—strengthening the powers of central government and trying to establish the rule of law before building democracy—is no perfect solution. It can create vested interests in power concentration; **path dependence** then takes over, making democratization and the deconcentration of power more difficult later. All international actors must be sensitive to these dilemmas. Failure to make sufficient resources available to address all the issues, especially where the country lacks strategic importance, has been usual. Yet the capacity of any country, especially one emerging from violence, to put international help, including democracy support, to good use is limited. Material aid essential to rebuilding the economic foundations may fuel corruption and bad governance, for example. In extreme cases which have resembled international trusteeship or administration, such as Kosovo and Bosnia Herzegovina, political self-determination (and hence democracy) may be significantly compromised (e.g. Nenadović 2012).

KEY POINTS

* Civil society support, which formerly seemed to offer politically safe opportunities for foreign assistance, now elicits a hostile response from many host governments that include some recognized democracies. But newer forms of civic activism could be changing the mould.

* Concentrating on elections and civil society limits what democracy assistance can achieve, but strengthening legislatures and political parties is no less problematic.

* Violent internal conflict due to oppression, discrimination, and human rights abuse makes the idea that support for establishing peace and building democracy go together seem obvious. But firmly establishing peace and democracy can be challenging even with substantial international assistance.

The record of supporting democracy

Supporting democracy has lasted long enough for us to ask, 'Does it work?' Although the short answer is that its performance has disappointed the democracy supporters, the question is actually far too simple.

Evaluating democracy assistance is fraught with methodological difficulties that are compounded when assessing democracy support *tout court*, whose methods are so diverse as to defy easy comparison—just note the differences between money, technical know-how, pressure, and expenditure of 'political capital', or between quiet diplomacy and conditionality-based threats of coercion. Attributing causal effectiveness to a democracy aid intervention is difficult; and impact assessments must take account of any unintended or negative effects while foreseeing long-term consequences. Naturally, the counterfactual—what would have been the outcome in the absence of intervention—cannot be known.

A sensitive comparison of interventions would also take account of differences in the obstacles encountered en route. Eroding an authoritarian regime, encouraging a process of political liberalization, supporting democratic transition, aiding democratic consolidation, helping secure a fragile democracy against subversion, and combating headlong democratic reversal, are all different scenarios. What might be judged a minor achievement in the context of one country could be a major breakthrough in different surroundings. And increasingly the net effect of international actors and influences opposing democratization or threatening democracy must be factored into the calculation.

Finally, there is a view that evaluations of democracy assistance must themselves be done democratically, which means a participatory approach that involves partners and 'stakeholders' in the receiving country. This is easier said than done. Findings from consulting the civic actors receiving support send conflicting messages: insistence on more generous, sustained funding but less financial dependence on donors; demands for less outside political interference but more international pressure on the regime to reform.

KEY POINTS

* Assessments of the effectiveness of democracy support must rest on what we mean by democracy and effectiveness, where different conceptions exist.

* Many analysts impute only modest credit for democracy assistance's record of achievement, noting the importance of domestic drivers of change and resistance to change.

* The interactions between external (foreign) and internal (domestic) influences—both actors and impersonal forces—are important determinants of the result (see Poppe et al. 2019).

Growing challenges

Of the numerous challenges facing democracy support, 'globalization' seems to encompass many. For some, globalization is reducible to global economic integration powered by the ascendancy of neoliberal economics and the increasing domination of social relations by market forces. This can have profoundly anti-democratic consequences, insofar as the disequalizing economic and social effects translate into substantial inequalities of political power and influence. Political self-determination may be made more difficult for whole societies or for specific groups, such as women in poverty.

The cultural side of globalization might be no less pernicious. For instance, there is the spread of individual consumerism which displaces the civic engagement and public service ethos on which the strength and depth of liberal democracies depend.

Some notions of globalization also claim that power is being redistributed away from national states to non-state institutions of multilevel governance, the European Union for example. Lacking adequate accountability, decisions made by these institutions have a major impact on lives and livelihoods. For many years, critical analysts drew attention to the power that international financial and economic institutions exercised over politics in developing countries. Now parallel situations seem to arise among some Western democracies too, promoting a nationalist backlash there. Anti-globalization sentiments fuel the rise of populist politicians, such as Donald Trump in the US. This in turn leads numerous commentators to question the health of democracy in these countries. And but a short step from this is needed to believing that the West's soft power to spread democracy abroad must inevitably suffer as a consequence. Added to this is the growing international influence of China, Russia, and a few other prominent states that reject liberal democracy, so adding to the other challenges now facing democracy support. Indeed, there is growing speculation about what is loosely termed 'autocracy promotion', or, more accurately, 'autocracy support'.

KEY POINTS

- Delivering what people want—better governance and improved material well-being—is now seen to be more vital to effective support for democracy compared to a former concentration on improving individual democratic procedures and practices.

- Globalization can provoke a nationalistic backlash, setting in train social and political forces inimical to liberal democracy and potentially harmful to democracy support.

The rise of autocracy support

Politics literature (e.g. Burnell 2011: chapters 11 and 12; Vanderhill 2013; Babayan and Risse 2015; *APSA Comparative Democratization* February 2015; von Soest 2015; Tansey 2016) is witnessing an emerging debate about the conceptual meaningfulness of autocracy promotion and the political relevance of its rise. The subject refers to international support given to and received by authoritarian and semi-authoritarian governments—also sometimes called illiberal regimes—in various regions, originating from a core group comprising China, Russia, Iran, Saudi Arabia, and Venezuela when Hugo Chávez was president (1999–2013). International collaboration or cooperation with these regimes and emulation and learning

from them attract a growing body of studies. Subversion of liberal or pro-democracy international institutions and standards, such as by manipulation of competing media narratives, is increasing (detailed in for example, http://www.resurgentdictatorship.org). All of this is taking place against a background of renewed scholarly interest in the idea that autocracy can be (perceived as) legitimate (see Dukalskis and Gerschewski 2018).

The terms of the debate on autocracy support echo the distinction between **active** and **passive democracy support** advanced earlier in the section 'Basic vocabulary of democracy support', passive support being more concerned with the actual effects on another regime than with the external actors' motives and intentions. The efforts by core autocracies to deliberately influence the type of regime in other countries must be kept distinct from any unsought or unintended effects that their international dealings might have. General collaboration among authoritarian regimes should also be distinguished from specific collaboration aimed at countering democratization pressures (von Soest 2015: 626). The deliberate support of autocracy as a value in itself is generally believed to be fairly modest, especially in comparison to the more extensive history of *active* democracy support. Indeed, Tansey (2016: 154) argues that much of what has been called autocracy promotion should really be called democracy prevention or resistance instead. More prevalent than intentions to support the growth of autocracy abroad, then, are attempts to undermine or erode an established democracy or a democratically elected government, including in some countries where (liberal) democracy is still fairly new and potentially fragile, as, for example, in Ukraine.

The motivation is open to interpretation, one view being that what autocracies value most in nearby countries is political stability if that suits their own interests, irrespective of the type of regime (Bader et al. 2012; Babayan and Risse 2015). This helps explain China's support for North Korea's dictatorship, for example. But destabilization will be pursued instead, especially if a neighbouring regime is believed to pose some kind of threat, again irrespective of the regime type. So, autocracy abroad is supported not for its own sake but mainly for self-serving reasons. Only in exceptional cases is the aim to advance a shared ideology, as with Venezuela's anti-capitalist agenda in Nicaragua and Bolivia (Vanderhill 2013). So, whereas democracy support aims to socialize other countries' elites into preferring democracy, much autocracy support does not seek to win converts to autocratic values (Vanderhill 2013: 14). In reality, the foreign policy agendas of core autocracies—whose regimes are politically diverse—show much greater variation compared to the single goal of supporting democracy associated with leading Western countries. But, naturally, Western countries also have instrumental self-regarding reasons for valuing democratic progress abroad (see the sections 'Explaining democracy support' and 'Suppliers of democracy support'). Two areas of activity that warrant much more research now into how autocracy support operates, and its similarities and dissimilarities with democracy support (Box 25.5), are efforts to influence political parties and electoral outcomes in foreign countries (see Burnell 2017), including giving attention to involvement in spreading what is commonly called 'fake news'.

Ukraine is a high-profile example of how careful we must be in characterizing autocracy support. Beginning with Ukraine's 'Orange revolution' in 2004–05, Russia's President Putin seemed alarmed that similar grass-roots protest and pressure for political reform could spread to Russia, thereby undermining his own rule. It also chimed with more widespread Russian fears that Western-orientated democracy in Ukraine could compromise Russia's security by removing a territorial buffer against NATO powers. These considerations help explain both Putin's increasing assault on freedoms in Russia and Russian efforts to weaken or fragment Ukraine, complementing Russia's illegal annexation of Crimea in 2014. A democratically elected government in Ukraine that abandoned claims to Crimea and proved pliant with Russian interests in the east of the country as well as Russia's larger geopolitical ambitions in the region would be treated very differently than the current hostile relationship. The fall-out from the election of a previously untested politician (President Zelenskyi) in Ukraine in April 2019 will offer a crucial test.

Apart from any *active* autocracy support by an authoritarian regime, the growing international dealings of core autocracies can still have a range of side effects on other governments and regimes, whether by serving to maintain or actually increase autocracy, or by undermining democracy and its progress, or infusing it with illiberal dimensions. Thus, authoritarian governments like those in Zimbabwe and Sudan have seen their exports to or aid and investment inflows and arms imports from China climb considerably, thereby emboldening them to resist the conditionalities (democratic, good governance, and economic) demanded by Western aid donors. No less important has been insistence by China (and, less convincingly, Russia) that the principle of individual state sovereignty should be respected. This message is well received by regimes that oppose (liberal) democracy

and ward off Western efforts to democratize their country. At the same time, China's outstanding record of economic progress in the absence of liberal democracy sends a powerful message that is often likened to a form of soft power, even though China shows no desire to export any particular political or economic model of its own.

The important point is that all these different international developments—and not just incontrovertible cases of *active* autocracy support—should be considered when making a comprehensive assessment of the comparative politics of affected countries. As Cooley (2015: 60) argues in respect of China's and Russia's growing provision of global media, there is now 'more contention over the normative foundations of the international order (with nonliberal voices having a bigger say than before), more authority for counter-norms such as noninterference in countries' internal affairs, and more influence for various authoritarian alternatives to liberal democracy'. The combined net effect of taking all this and democracy support into account is undoubtedly complex, and hard to predict—a judgement buttressing Börzel's (2015: 527) notion of 'crossed-over empowerment', where 'illiberal regional powers strengthen liberal domestic forces and Western democracy promoters stabilize non-democratic regimes', directly or indirectly, intentionally or unintentionally. How politicians inside a country on the receiving end of international influences use and manipulate conflicting and competing external forces to their own advantage will be constitutive of who finally prevails in domestic power struggles. This will impact the regime or any change of regime that ensues.

KEY POINTS

- Recent scholarship takes note of the influence exercised by some increasingly powerful core authoritarian and semi-authoritarian regimes on politics in other countries.

- How far core autocracies are committed to promoting authoritarian/semi-authoritarian or illiberal rule abroad for its own sake, rather than for other reasons, including purely instrumental self-regarding ones, is debatable.

- The rise of democracy support by western powers never banished a willingness to actively support authoritarian/semi-authoritarian governments in certain countries, when deemed necessary.

- Democracy support is struggling to devise adequate strategies to counter international autocracy support in all its forms, let alone erode authoritarian rule in core autocracies.

FOR AND AGAINST 25.5

Comparing autocracy support and democracy support

Similarities

Who: not all democracies and not all autocracies are fairly *active* supporters abroad, but in all cases there is minimal domestic opposition to policy—but for different reasons: in democracies voters give consent; in autocracies public dissent is discouraged or disallowed.

How: the regime type in all affected states may be influenced directly or indirectly, intentionally or unintentionally.

Means: international support can be economic; financial; commercial; technical cooperation, including sharing of governance models and techniques (e.g. for organizing intelligence services and internet surveillance, in autocracy support); diplomatic cooperation, including collaboration through membership of inter-governmental and regional organizations (e.g. China, Russia, and others in the Shanghai Cooperation Organisation); withdrawal/denial of support may also be used to pursue political ends (e.g. Western countries imposed economic sanctions against Myanmar's military rule; Russia manipulates gas supplies to Ukraine and Belarus).

Effects: the actual regime consequences in affected countries do not necessarily comport with—and may even contradict—the external actors' desires or intentions, including influence on regime type (e.g. see Delacour and Wolczuk 2015; Way 2015).

Explaining the result: exploring interactions between domestic actors and *all* external actors (including, where relevant, democracies and autocracies too) can be crucial to understanding the power balance among different domestic actors and, possibly, explaining the type of regime too.

Differences

Who: different sets of countries lie behind autocracy and democracy support (although Western democracies, especially the US, have long supported authoritarian and semi-authoritarian governments where judged necessary). The political differences among different core autocracies exceed those prevailing among Western democracy-support countries.

Why: whereas democracy support ostensibly aims to achieve a specific regime outcome (liberal democracy) as a value in its own right, autocracies usually support like-minded regimes for instrumental reasons pertaining to their own interest (e.g. Putin's rule) and/or national interests (e.g. Russia's security).

What: autocracy support neither purports to offer nor provides a (single) transferable model of a type of regime, unlike democracy support's main commitment to (liberal) democracy.

Where: active autocracy support's main focus is usually on its own backyard (e.g. Russia in post-Soviet countries; Iran in Syria; Saudi Arabia in the Arab world); but all non-democracies or weak/struggling democracies everywhere rate as (potential) candidates for democracy support. Even so, China's proliferating international (economic) ties may have unintended regime consequences far and wide, in Africa for instance.

Means: autocracy support has used coercion—for example, Saudi Arabia crushed Bahrain's popular uprising in 2011, to check Iranian influence (see Hassan 2015); but democracy assistance is noncoercive (although critics align US and allied military efforts to force 'regime change' in Iraq and Afghanistan with democracy promotion). And the employment of negative conditionalities may be coercive in its own way. Democracy support proceeds through a greater variety of organizations, including formally independent non-governmental organizations (although autocracies employ pseudo-nongovernmental organizations at home and abroad).

International legitimation: the UN endorses democracy, and provides support for democratic governance. It neither endorses autocracy nor actively promotes autocratic rule. However, it enshrines principles of national sovereignty and non-interference in international law.

Studying comparative politics: relations between autocracies can be opaque and reliable, independent evidence patchy, compared to studying democracies. Even so, diplomatic channels of democracy support and inner workings of democracy assistance are not wholly transparent.

Conclusion

International context impacts on politics at national and sub-national levels. The emergence of an increasingly multipolar world means that a fully comparative study of the politics of diverse countries must look beyond the international influence of the West alone.

Following the end of the Cold War and the collapse of Soviet power, democracy support began a seemingly inexorable rise. The US and European actors led the way. A large market for democracy support still exists in the sense that many people do not live in liberal democracies. But they do not necessarily endorse Western-style liberal democracy, let alone welcome all the methods of democracy support.

Different explanations have been offered for the increase in democracy support after the 1980s. Most link it to agendas of national interest of the democracy-supporting countries, but the way countries define their interests, especially national security, can still eclipse support for democratic change, just as it has in the past. US President Trump's foreign policy leanings look set to accentuate this in the future. Democracy assistance projects and programmes have attracted considerable attention, although much remains to be learned about their impact. The methodological challenges of comparing the effectiveness of different objectives—reconfiguring political institutions, changing political attitudes, and reforming behaviour—all with their own time horizons, is scientifically daunting.

Democracy support has worked best where the conditions were favourable or democratic momentum was already under way—that is, where least needed. The most receptive countries have now become democracies. But globally, democracy's progress is now stagnating: Freedom House's survey of freedom in the world for 2018 'recorded the thirteenth consecutive decline of freedom' (Schenkkan and Repucci 2019: 100): this is indicative. Several mid-sized countries that once were thought to be well on their way to sustainable democratization have fallen back, and show little or no willingness to host incoming democracy support initiatives. Turkey, Thailand, Egypt, and Venezuela are examples. And in countries like Pakistan, South Africa, and Ukraine, democracy's progression in the future is still not assured. So, the challenges facing democracy support look greater now than at any time since the 1980s. For while recent history reconfirms the enduring importance of domestic forces to explaining outcomes and events, sizeable geopolitical shifts leading China and Russia to become more powerful abroad are posing big issues too. While autocracy support is certainly no mirror image of democracy support, its relevance to explaining politics inside a growing number of countries cannot be ignored.

So in light of all the threats to liberal democracy and to democratic advance that are coming from within and from without many individual countries, what in its early years was known as democracy promotion could more appropriately be rebranded to include democracy protection, or democracy safeguarding, now. Although far from the upbeat vision espoused by writers like Sen and McFaul fifteen to twenty years ago (See Box 25.1), universal convergence on (liberal) democracy benefitting from international support looks a very distant prospect, for the forseeable future anyway.

?   QUESTIONS

Knowledge-based

1. Why have the US and EU been the main international sources of democracy support?

2. How do the different ways of supporting democracy compare with one another?

3. How do non-state actors compare with states as agents of democracy support?

4. How does autocracy support differ from democracy support?

5. Compare the different ways that different authoritarian regimes can influence democracy's prospects in other countries.

6. How does seeing democracy promotion as a process of negotiation affect our understanding of the process and outcomes of democracy promotion?

Critical thinking

1. Should the international community concentrate on helping to bolster state power rather than build democracy, in societies recently torn by civil war?

2. Could the democracies' best way of supporting democratic progress elsewhere be to improve their own democratic credentials?

3. Should Western democracies support ideas of democracy significantly different from Western liberal democracy—for example, ideas that accommodate political Islam?

4. What lessons must democracy support learn from its own performance if it is to be fit for purpose in the future?

5. Compare the significance of international influences versus domestic influences on the type of political regime inside countries undergoing political change.

FURTHER READING

APSA Comparative Democratization (official newsletter of APSA's Comparative Democratization section) (February 2015), 'The International Dimensions of Authoritarianism', 13(1): 1–22. Selected commentaries.

Babayan, N. and Risse, T. (eds) (2015) 'Democracy Promotion and the Challenges of Illiberal Regional Powers', special issue of *Democratization*, 22(3): 381–535.

Burnell, P. (2011) *Promoting Democracy Abroad. Policy and Performance* (New Brunswick, NJ: Transaction). Critically examines major issues.

Burnell, P. and Gerrits, A. (eds) (2012) *Promoting Party Politics in Emerging Democracies* (Abingdon: Routledge). Examines problems of party support.

Carothers, T. and Brown, F. (October 2018) 'Can U.S. Democracy Policy Survive Trump?' (Washington, DC: Carnegie Endowment for International Peace) (https://carnegieendowment.org/2018/10/01/can-u.s.-democracy-policy-survive-trump-pub-77381). Examines prospects for mitigating the Trump effect.

Diamond, L. (2019) *Ill Winds: Saving Democracy from Russian Rage, Chinese Ambition and American Complacency* (New York: Penguin).

Hobson, C. and Kurki, M. (eds) (2012) *The Conceptual Politics of Democracy Promotion* (Abingdon: Routledge). Argues non-liberal conceptions of democracy should be adopted by democracy promotion, for example social democracy.

Kelley, J. (2012) *Monitoring Democracy. When International Election Observation Works, and Why It Often Fails* (Princeton, NJ and Oxford: Princeton University Press). Shows international monitoring of elections is broken, but still worth fixing.

Magen, A., Risse, T., and McFaul, M. (eds) (2009) *Promoting Democracy and the Rule of Law* (Houndmills, Basingstoke: Palgrave Macmillan). Documents convergence between EU and US approaches at the time of writing.

Poppe, A. Leininer, J., and Wolff, J. (eds) (2019) 'The Negotiation of Democracy Promotion'. Special Issue of *Democratization*, 26(5). This special issue examines democracy promotion as an interactive process of negotiation between external and local actors, where democracy is a contested concept and the practice must be responsive to local priorities and initiatives.

Tansey, O. (2016) 'The Problem with Autocracy Promotion', *Democratization*, 23(1): 141–63. Incisive conceptual analysis.

von Soest, C. (2015) 'Democracy Prevention: The International Collaboration of Authoritarian Regimes', *European Journal of Political Research*, 54(4): 623–38. Reviews actual cases.

Youngs, R. (2019) *Civic Activism Unleashed: New Hope or False Dawn for Democracy?* (Oxford: Oxford University Press). Details the potential of newly emerging forms of civic activism to drive democratization and enhance the scope for democracy support.

Visit the Online Resources that accompany this book for additional material, including country profiles, comparative data sets, flashcard glossaries, and web directory.

www.oup.com/he/caramani5e

Appendix 1

Country profiles

Country Profile Argentina
Argentine Republic (*República Argentina*)

State formation

Argentina was first explored by Europeans in 1516, became a Spanish colony in 1580, and later a part of the Viceroyalty of the Rio de la Plata in 1776. After two unsuccessful invasions by the British Empire in 1806 and 1807, the first government junta was established in Buenos Aires when King Ferdinand VII was overthrown by Napoleon in 1810 (May Revolution). Formal independence was gained on 9 July 1816.

Constitution 1853; amended many times, last in 1994.

Form of government

Presidential republic.

Head of state President and vice-president; elected on the same ticket; term of four years; eligible for another term. After two terms, the president must sit out one term before being eligible to run again.

Head of government President.

Cabinet Ministers; appointed by the president.

Administrative subdivisions Twenty-three provinces and one autonomous city.

Legal system

Mixture of US and West European legal systems.

Legislature

Bicameral National Congress (*Congreso Nacional*).

Lower house Chamber of Deputies (*Cámara de Diputados*): 257 seats (staggered elections with half of the seats renewed every two years, see table); term of four years.

Upper house Senate (*Honorable Senado de la Nación Argentina*): seventy-two seats (three per district; staggered elections—one-third of the members elected every two years); term of six years.

Electoral system (lower house)

Proportional representation.

Formula D'Hondt. One-third of the candidates of each party must be women.

Constituencies Twenty-four multi-member constituencies corresponding to the provinces.

Electoral threshold Three per cent votes of the registered voters in the multi-member constituencies.

Suffrage Universal; compulsory for citizens between eighteen and seventy years of age; sixteen, seventeen years of age and above seventy optional.

Direct democracy

Optional, but binding legislative referendum can be called by parliament. Other non-binding referenda can be called by the president or the Congress. A non-binding legislative popular initiative is possible.

Election results 2017 legislative elections (Chamber of Deputies):

Electorate	33,454,411	100.0%
Voters:	25,699,629	76.8%

Party	Valid votes	%	Seats
Let's Change	10,261,343	41.8	61
Citizen's Unity	5,533,334	22.5	28
Justicialist Party	2,679,782	10.9	18
I Pais	1,441,332	5.9	4
Worker's Left Front	1,051,300	4.3	2
Union for Cordoba	626,887	2.6	3
Civic Front for Santiago	384,125	1.6	3
Progressive, Civic and Social Front	287,613	1.2	1
Front for the Renewal of Concord	268,646	1.1	2
Evolution	237,132	1.0	2
Intransigent Party	184,610	0.8	1
Chubut for All	101,613	0.4	1
Nequen People's Movement	81,077	0.3	1
Others	1,441,006	5.6	0
Total valid votes	**24,579,800**	**100.0**	**127**

Source: IFES Election Guide; Wikipedia.

Country Profile Australia
Commonwealth of Australia

State formation

Europeans began exploration of Australia in the seventeenth century. James Cook took possession of eastern Australia in the name of Great Britain in 1770. Beginning in 1788, six colonies were successively established that federated and became the Commonwealth of Australia in 1901.

Constitution Entered into force in 1901; amended many times, last in 1977.

Form of government

Federal state.

Head of state English monarch; represented by a Governor General; the monarchy is hereditary.

Head of government Prime minister; appointed by the Governor General.

Cabinet Ministers; nominated by the prime minister; appointed by the Governor General.

Administrative subdivisions Six states and two territories.

Legal system

English common law with a High Court (the chief justice and six other justices are appointed by the Governor General).

Legislature

Bicameral Parliament.

Lower house House of Representatives: 151 members; directly elected; term of three years.

Upper house Senate: seventy-six members (twelve from each of the six states and two from each of the two territories; staggered elections—one-half of state members are elected every three years by popular vote; territory members are elected every three years); term of six years.

Electoral system (lower house)

Alternative vote system.

Formula Absolute majority of first preferences or, if necessary, of first preferences plus preferences for eliminated candidates in subsequent counts.

Constituencies 151 single-member constituencies.

Electoral threshold Not applicable.

Suffrage Universal, eighteen years of age; compulsory.

Direct democracy

Constitutional referendum must be initiated through a parliamentary bill; requirement of double majority of states/territories and voters. In addition, non-binding 'plebiscites' are held on non-constitutional matters.

Election results 2019 legislative elections (House of Representatives):

Electorate	16,424,248	100.0%
Voters	12,981,005	78.7%

Party	Valid votes	%	Seats
Liberal National Coalition	5,088,444	41.6	78
Australian Labor Party	4,127,206	33.8	67
Australian Greens	1,215,284	3.4	1
Katter's Australian Party	62,380	0.5	1
Centre Alliance	41,921	0.3	1
Independents	425,783	3.5	3
Others	1,266,831	16.9	0
Total valid votes	12,277,849	100.0	151

Note: Others include parties with no seats.
Source: Wikipedia.

Country Profile Botswana
Republic of Botswana (*Lefatshe la Botswana*)

State formation

Between the twelfth and fourteenth centuries, several powerful dynasties of the Tswana people began to emerge in the territory. From the beginning of the nineteenth century, missionaries started to explore the region. During those times, many Boer settlers entered the country while escaping from the British. The oppressed local Tswana people appealed to the British Government for assistance in 1876. From 1885, the territory was made a British protectorate. On 30 September 1966, independence was declared.

Constitution Entered into force in 1966; amended several times, last in 2006.

Form of government

Parliamentary republic.

Head of state President; elected by the National Assembly; five-year term; eligible for another term.

Head of government President.

Cabinet President, vice-president and seventeen minsters; appointed by the president.

Administrative subdivisions Ten rural districts and seven urban districts.

Legal system

Based on Roman-Dutch law and local customary law.

Legislature

Unicameral parliament.

National Assembly: sixty-three seats (fifty-seven members directly elected, four nominated by the president and indirectly elected by the rest of the National Assembly, and the president and Attorney General); term of five years.

Note: There is an important advisory body to the National Assembly but it does not constitute a house of the parliament: House of Chiefs (*Ntlo ya Dikgosi*): fifteen seats (eight permanent members consisting of the chiefs of the principal tribes; seven non-permanent members serving five-year terms; consisting of four elected sub-chiefs and three members selected by the other twelve members).

Electoral system

Majoritarian system.

Formula Plurality.

Constituencies Fifty-seven single-member constituencies.

Electoral threshold Not applicable.

Suffrage Universal; eighteen years of age.

Direct democracy

Provisions for referenda on constitutional matters.

Election results 2014 legislative elections (National Assembly):

Electorate	824,073	100.0%
Voters	698,409	84.8%

Party	Valid votes	%	Seats
Botswana Congress Party	140,988	20.4	2
Botswana Democratic Party	320,647	46.5	37
Umbrella for Democratic Change	207,013	30.0	17
Others	21,584	3.1	1
Total valid votes	690,232	100.0	57

Note: The table includes information only about the directly elected parliamentarians.
Source: Adam Carr's website.

Country Profile Brazil
Federative Republic of Brazil (*República Federativa do Brasil*)

State formation

Brazil gained independence from Portugal in 1822. The Republic was established in 1889. An authoritarian regime prevailed from 1930 to 1945. Democratization took place after the Second World War, but in 1964 the military overthrew the president and Brazil was ruled by a succession of military governments that suspended constitutional guarantees. A civilian government was restored in 1985.

Constitution 1988; amended many times, last in 2015.

Form of government

Presidential federal republic.

Head of state President and vice-president elected on same ticket with two-ballot system (run-off between the two candidates with most votes in first ballot); term of four years; eligible for a second term.

Head of government President.

Cabinet Appointed by the President.

Administrative subdivisions Twenty-six states and one federal district.

Legal system

Civil law based on Roman and Germanic traditions.

Legislature

Bicameral National Congress (*Congresso Nacional*).

Lower house Chamber of Deputies (*Câmara dos Deputados*): 513 members; term of four years.

Upper house Federal Senate (*Senado Federal*): eighty-one members (three members from each constituency, majority vote; staggered elections—one-third elected after a four years, two-thirds elected after the next four years); term of eight years.

Electoral system (lower house)

Proportional representation.

Formula Hare quota and highest average, closed non-blocked lists, and preferential voting within lists.

Constituencies Twenty-six and one federal district.

Electoral threshold Five per cent nationwide.

Suffrage Universal, compulsory for citizens between eighteen and seventy years of age; sixteen, seventeen years of age and above seventy optional; military conscripts are not allowed to vote.

Direct democracy

The National Congress can call non-binding referenda and plebiscites. Legislative popular initiative is not binding either.

Election results 2018 legislative elections (Chamber of Deputies):

Electorate:	146,750,529	100.0%
Voters:	117,111,476	79.8%

Party	Valid votes	%	Seats
Social Liberal Party	11,757,878	11.7	52
Workers' Party	10,126,611	10.3	56
Brazilian Social Democratic Party	5,905,541	6.0	29
Social Democratic Party	5,749,008	5.8	34
Progressistas	5,480,067	5.6	37
Brazilian Democratic Movement	5,439,167	5.5	34
Brazilian Socialist Party	5,386,400	5.5	32
Republic Party	5,224,591	5.3	33
Brazilian Republican Party	4,992,016	5.1	30
Democrats	4,581,162	4.7	29
Democratic Labour Party	4,545,846	4.6	28
Socialism and Liberty Party	2,783,669	2.8	10
New Party	2,748,079	2.8	8
Podemos	2,243,320	2.3	11
Republican Party of the Social Order	2,042,610	2.1	8
Brazilian Labour Party	2,022,719	2.1	10
Solidariedade	1,953,067	2.0	13
Avante	1,844,048	1.9	7
Social Christian Party	1,765,226	1.8	8
Green Party	1,592,173	1.6	4
Popular Socialist Party	1,590,048	1.6	8
Patriota	1,432,304	1.5	5
Humanist Party of Solidarity	1,426,444	1.5	6
Communist Party of Brazil	1,329,575	1.4	9
Pogressive Republican Party	851,368	0.9	4
Sustainability Network	816,784	0.8	1
Party of National Mobilization	634,129	0.6	3
Christian Labour Party	601,814	0.6	2
Free Homeland Party	385,197	0.4	1
Christian Democracy	369,386	0.4	1
Others	1,018,710	1.0	0
Total valid votes	**98,638,957**	**100.0**	**513**

Note: Others include all parties with no seats.
Source: Wikipedia.

Country Profile Canada
Canada

State formation

After the first French and English settlements in the seventeenth century, several wars broke out. Britain finally seized New France in 1763. In 1867, British colonies in North America were united under the British North American Act to become the Dominion of Canada. Through the Statute of Westminster of 1931, Canada gained full legislative authority in both internal and external affairs. The Governor General became the official representative of the Crown.

Constitution Unwritten customs, judicial decisions, and written acts, including the Constitution Act of 1867 (establishing a federation of provinces), the Constitution Act of 1982 (transferring the formal control of the constitution from Britain to Canada), and the Canadian Charter of Rights and Freedoms.

Form of government

Parliamentary, federal commonwealth.

Head of state English monarch represented by Governor General; the monarchy is hereditary.

Head of government Prime minister; usually the leader of the majority party or coalition in the House of Commons; appointed by the Governor General.

Cabinet Federal Ministry; nominated by the prime minister and appointed by the Governor General.

Administrative subdivisions Ten provinces and three territories.

Legal system

Common law; in the province of Québec a civil law system based on traditional French law prevails.

Legislature

Bicameral parliament.

Lower house House of Commons (or Chambre des Communes): 338 members; term of four years.

Upper house Senate (or Sénat): 105 members appointed by the Governor General on the advice of the prime minister; they serve until reaching seventy-five years of age.

Electoral system (lower house)

Majoritarian representation.

Formula Plurality.

Constituencies 338 single-member constituencies.

Electoral threshold Not applicable.

Suffrage Universal; eighteen years of age.

Direct democracy

Referendum (also referred to as plebiscite) may be conducted on constitutional matters at a national level; some provinces have referendum legislation as well.

Election results 2015 legislative elections (House of Commons):

Electorate	25,638,379	100.0%
Voters	17,559,353	68.5%

Party	Valid votes	%	Seats
Liberal Party	6,930,136	39.5	184
Conservative Party	5,600,496	31.9	99
New Democratic Party	3,461,262	19.7	44
Bloc Québécois	818,652	4.7	10
Green	605,864	3.4	1
Others	142,943	0.8	0
Total valid votes	17,559,353	100.0	338

Source: Adam Carr's website; Elections Canada.

Country Profile Chile
Republic of Chile (*República de Chile*)

State formation

Spanish conquerors arrived in Chile in the sixteenth century and founded the city of Santiago in 1541. Chile became a part of the Spanish Viceroyalty of Peru. In 1810, when the Spanish throne had been toppled by Napoleon, a national junta was formed that proclaimed Chile as an autonomous republic within the Spanish monarchy. Warfare continued until the royalists were defeated in 1817. Independence was formally proclaimed in 1818.

Constitution Entered into force in 1981; amended many times, last in 2011.

Form of government

Presidential republic.

Head of state Directly elected president; term of four years; unlimited non-consecutive terms.

Head of government President.

Cabinet Cabinet of Ministers; appointed by the president.

Administrative subdivisions Sixteen regions.

Legal system

Derived from Spanish, French, and Austrian law; criminal justice system modelled on the US system.

Legislature

Bicameral National Congress (*Congreso Nacional*).

Lower house Chamber of Deputies (*Cámara de Diputados*): 155 seats; term of four years.

Upper house Senate (*Senado*): fifty seats (staggered elections; one-half renewed every four years); term of eight years.

Electoral system (lower house)

Proportional representation.

Formula D'Hondt.

Constituencies Sixty-four constituencies.

Electoral threshold Not applicable.

Suffrage Universal; eighteen years of age.

Direct democracy

Optional constitutional referendum can be called by the president if he/she has rejected a constitutional modification proposed by the Congress, but the Congress insists on that modification.

Election results 2017 legislative elections (Chamber of Deputies):

Electorate	14,347,288	100.0%
Voters	6,675,146	46.5%

Party	Valid votes	%	Seats
Renovacion Nacional	1,067,270	17.8	36
Union Democrata Independiente	957,245	16.0	30
Evolucion Politica	355,221	4.3	6
Partido Regionalista Independiente	39,692	0.7	0
Total Chile Vamos	**2,419,428**	**38.7**	**72**
Partido Socialista de Chile	585,128	9.8	19
Partido por la Democracia	365,988	6.1	8
Partido Comunista de Chile	275,096	4.6	8
Partido Radical Socialdemocrata	216,355	3.6	8
Total La Fuerza de la Mayoria	**1,442,567**	**24.1**	**43**
Revolucion Democratica	343,019	5.7	10
Partido Humanista	253,787	4.2	5
Partido Igualdad	129,232	2.2	1
Partido Ecologista Verde	128,629	2.1	1

(Continued)

Party	Valid votes	%	Seats
Poder	87,605	1.5	1
Partido Liberal de Chile	46,605	0.8	2
Total Frente Amplio	**988,877**	**16.5**	**20**
Partido Democrata Cristiano	616,550	10.3	14
Others	23,940	0.4	0
Total Convergencia Democatica	**640,490**	**10.7**	**14**
Partido Progresista	199,566	3.3	1
Paîs	35,468	0.6	0
Total Por Todo Chile	**235,034**	**3.9**	**1**
Federacion Regionalista Verde Social	94,666	1.6	4
Democracia Regional Patagonica	20,575	0.3	0
Total Coalición Regionalista Verde	**115,241**	**1.9**	**4**
Others	470,959	7.6	1
Total	6,212,596	100	155

Source: Adam Carr's website.

Country Profile China
People's Republic of China (*Zhōnghuá Rénmín Gònghéguó*)

State formation

The first unification under the Qin Dynasty dates back to the year 221 BC. The Republic of China was established in 1912 after the Qing Dynasty had been overthrown, but no political stability was achieved. Between 1927 and 1950 the Kuomindang (or Nationalist Party) opposed the Chinese Communist Party in a civil war. The People's Republic was established under the leader of the latter, Mao Zedong, in 1949.

Constitution Entered into force in 1982; amended several times, last in 2004.

Form of government

Communist state.

Head of state President and vice-president elected by the National People's Congress; term of five years; no term limit since 2018.

Head of government Prime minister; nominated by the president and confirmed by the National People's Congress.

Cabinet State Council; appointed by the National People's Congress.

Administrative subdivisions Twenty-three provinces, five autonomous regions, four municipalities, two special administrative regions (Hong Kong and Macau), and one claimed province (Taiwan).

Legal system

Derived from Soviet and continental European civil code.

Legislature

Unicameral parliament.
National People's Congress (*Quánguó Rénmín Dàibiao Dàhui*): 2,987 members elected by municipal, regional, and provincial people's congresses; term of five years. Additionally, there is the Chinese People's Political Consultative Conference, which is not anchored in the constitution but in some sense fulfils the functions of an advisory upper house.

Electoral system

A half-year-long series of layered indirect elections is conducted, beginning from local popularly elected people's congresses up to the National People's Congress. In practice, the selection of members for the higher people's congresses is controlled by the Communist Party. Approximately one-third of the seats of the National People's Congress are informally reserved for non-party members, such as technical experts and members of the smaller allied parties.

Constituencies The delegates from each of the thirty-four administrative subdivisions form a delegation.

Suffrage Universal; eighteen years of age.

Direct democracy

Not applicable.

Election results 2013 legislative elections (National People's Congress):

Electorate	n.a.	100.0%
Voters	n.a.	n.a.

Party	Valid votes	%	Seats
Communist Party of China	n.a.	n.a.	2,157
United front, Independents	n.a.	n.a.	830
Total valid votes	**n.a.**	**100.0**	**2,987**

Note: Besides the dominant Communist Party of China, registered minor parties exist which, however, do not form any political opposition.

Source: Wikipedia.

Country Profile Colombia
Republic of Colombia (*República de Colombia*)

State formation

In the middle of the sixteenth century, Spanish conquerors started to enslave the indigenous people of South America. In 1819, Colombia became independent under President Simon Bolivar and was called New Granada. This state was a part of Great Colombia, which encompassed today's Venezuela, Ecuador, Panama, and Colombia. After the breakdown of Great Colombia in 1831, the state was renamed Colombia in 1861.

Constitution Entered into force in 1991; amended many times, last in 2012.

Form of government

Presidential republic.

Head of state President; directly elected; restricted to a single term of four years.

Head of government President.

Cabinet Appointed by the president, approved by Congress.

Administrative subdivisions Thirty-two departments and one capital district.

Legal system

Based on Spanish law; judicial review of legislative and executive acts.

Legislature

Bicameral Congress (*Congress of Colombia*).

Lower house Chamber of Representatives (*Cámara de Representantes*): 166 seats; term of four years.

Upper house Senate of Colombia (*Senado de la República de Colombia*): 102 seats; term of four years.

Electoral system (lower house)

Proportional representation.

Formula Closed party list, with remaining seats allocated on the basis of greatest remainders.

Constituencies Thirty-three multi-member constituencies and three special constituencies (Afro-Colombians, Colombian citizens abroad, and Indigenous communities).

Electoral threshold Not applicable.

Suffrage Universal (except for members of the armed forces on active duty and police officers); eighteen years of age.

Direct democracy

Referenda on matters of national importance (called by the president); legislative matters (10 per cent of the citizenry required) and constitutional matters (5 per cent of the citizenry or the Congress). Legislative and constitutional popular initiative possible (5 per cent of the citizenry required).

Election results 2018 legislative elections (Chamber of Representatives):

Electorate	36,493,318	100.0%
Voters	17,774,413	48.7%

Party	Valid votes	%	Seats
Santander Alternative (AS)	71,953	0.5	1
Democratic Center (CD)	2,382,357	16.1	32
Colombia Fair Free (CGL)	114,174	0.8	1
List of Decency (LD)	262,282	1.8	2
Alternative Indigenous Mvt (MAIS)	44,034	0.3	1
Ind Mvt of Absolute Renovation (MIRA)	584,723	4.0	2
Citizens' Option (OC)	310,679	2.1	2
Green Alliance Party (PAV)	883,547	6.0	9
Colombian Conservative Party (PCC)	1,819,634	12.3	21
Party of Radical Change (PCR)	2,140,464	14.5	30
Democratic Alternative Pole (PDA)	444,746	3.0	2
Colombian Liberal Party (PLC)	2,471,400	16.7	35
Social Party of National Unity (PSUN)	1,840,253	15.5	25
Others	587,305	4.0	0
Blank votes	807,028	5.5	0
Total valid votes	**14,764,579**	**100.0**	**163**

Note: Not included are the two members elected by the Afro-Colombian community and the one by Colombian expatriates.
Source: Adam Carr's website.

Country Profile Denmark
Kingdom of Denmark (*Kongeriget Danmar*)

State formation

During the Viking Age, Danish people had great power. After the introduction to Christianity, several rivalries and the formation of a Union later, Denmark abolished absolutism in 1848 and became a modern state. It turned into a constitutional monarchy in 1849, maintaining its traditional policy of neutrality in the First World War. During the Second World War, Denmark surrendered after little resistance to the German invasion in 1940. In 1948, Denmark accepted the secession of its former colony Greenland and granted a high degree of self-governance to the Faroe Islands.

Constitution Entered into force in 1953; amended several times, last in 2009.

Form of government

Constitutional monarchy.

Head of state Monarch; the monarchy is hereditary.

Head of government Prime minister; usually leader of the majority party or majority coalition; appointed by the monarch; term of four years; no term limit.

Cabinet Cabinet of Denmark; appointed by the monarch.

Administrative subdivisions Five regions and ninety-eight municipalities.

Legal system

Civil law system, judicial review of legislative acts.

Legislature

Unicameral parliament.
National Assembly (*Folketing*): 179 seats (including two from the Faroe Islands, and two from Greenland); 135 elected from the multi-member constituencies and forty allocated to ensure proportionality; term of four years.

Electoral system

Proportional representation.

Formula D'Hondt and Sainte-Laguë method.

Constituencies Ten multi-member constituencies.

Electoral threshold Two per cent nationwide to get a share of supplementary seats.

Suffrage Universal; eighteen years of age.

Direct democracy

Referenda on constitutional matters and political issues of great importance.

Election results 2019 legislative elections (National Assembly)

Electorate	4,219,537	100.0%
Voters	3,569,520	84.6%

Party	Valid votes	%	Seats
Social Democratic Party	914,883	25.9	48
Left, Liberal Party of Denmark	826,161	23.4	43
Danish People's Party	308,512	8.7	16
Radical Left	304,714	8.6	16
Socialist People's Party	272,304	7.7	14
Unity List—Red Green Alliance	245,100	6.9	13
Conservative People's Party	233,865	6.6	12
The Alternative	104,278	3.0	5
New Civil	83,201	2.4	4
Liberal Alliance	82,270	2.3	4
Others	156,432	4.5	0
Total valid votes	**3,531,720**	**100.0**	**175**

Note: Election results without the two seats from Faroe Islands and Greenland. Category 'Others' includes parties with no seats.
Source: IFES Election Guide.

Country Profile France
French Republic (*République française*)

State formation

The fragmentation of the Carolingian empire in the tenth century led to the emergence of France. In the following centuries, France continued to expand territorially and, in the process, consolidated its power. There were numerous wars over territories against the English monarchs and the Habsburgs. During the seventeenth century, in the period that is known as absolutism, the power of the French royalty was at its peak. In 1789, the French Revolution began, which consequently led to the overthrow of the monarchical rule, and the transformation of France into a republic. The ideals behind the French Revolution, of nationhood and universal rights, continually served as an inspiration to many national movements across the globe. Napoleon managed to usurp the republic and then established France as a dominant military force through the Napoleonic Wars. After the defeat of Napoleon, monarchy was restored in France, but instability ensued constantly, which led to the formation of a second republic, second empire, and a third republic in the nineteenth century. After the two world wars in the twentieth century, France was established as a republic in 1946. As of now, France is in its fifth republic, which was established in 1959.

Constitution Entered into force in 1958; amended many times, last in 2008.

Form of government

Semi-presidential republic.

Head of state President; directly elected; term of five years; eligible for another term.

Head of government Prime minister appointed by the president.

Cabinet Council of Ministers suggested by the prime minister; appointed by the president.

Administrative subdivisions Thirteen regions.

Legal system

Civil law system.

Legislature

Bicameral parliament *(Parlement)*.

Lower house National Assembly *(Assemblée nationale)*: 577 members; directly elected; term of five years.

Upper house Senate *(Sénat)*: 348 members; staggered elections (one-half of the members renewed every three years); term of six years.

Electoral system (lower house)

Majoritarian representation.

Formula Two-round system. In the first round of the elections, absolute majority is required. In the second round, the formula is plurality between the candidates from the first round.

Constituencies 577 single-member constituencies.

Electoral threshold 12.5 per cent of the electorate in the first round.

Suffrage Universal; eighteen years of age.

Direct democracy

The constitution provides for national and local-level referenda.

Election results 2017 legislative elections (National Assembly):

Electorate	47,570,988	100.0%
Voters	23,167,508	48.7%

Party	Valid votes	%	Seats
Socialist Party (PS)	185,677	7.4	30
Europe Ecology—The Greens (EEV)	973,527	4.3	1
Radical Party of the Left (PRG)	106,311	0.5	3
Miscellaneous left	362,281	1.6	12
France Unbowed (FI)	2,497,622	11.0	17
French Communist Party (PCF)	615,487	2.7	10
The Republic on the March (REM)	6,391,269	28.2	308
Democratic Movement (MoDem)	932,227	4.1	42
The Republicans (LR)	3,573,427	15.8	112
France Arise (DLF)	265,420	1.2	1
Union of Democrats and Independents (UDI)	687,225	3.0	18
Miscellaneous right (DVD)	625,345	2.8	6
National Front (FN)	2,990,454	13.2	8
Extreme right (EXD)	68,320	0.3	1
Regionalists (REG)	204,049	0.9	5

Independents (DIV)	500,309	2.2	3
Total valid votes	**20,978,950**	**100.0**	**577**

Notes: The results present the valid votes cast in the first round of the elections, the total percentage gained by every party after this round, and the total number of seats obtained after the second round.

Source: Ministry of the Interior; Adam Carr's website, Wikipedia.

Country Profile Germany
Federal Republic of Germany (*Bundesrepublik Deutschland*)

State formation

The German Empire was officially unified in 1871 as a result of the Franco-Prussian war. After the Second World War, Germany was divided into four zones of occupation administered by the UK, the US, the USSR, and France, respectively. The Federal Republic of Germany (West Germany), which included the former UK, US, and French occupation zones, was proclaimed in 1949, whereas the USSR zone became the German Democratic Republic (East Germany). In 1990, the year following the fall of the Berlin wall, the two reunified.

Constitution Entered into force in 1949; amended many times, last in 2012.

Form of government

Federal republic.

Head of state President; elected by a federal convention, including all members of the Federal Assembly and an equal number of delegates elected by the state parliaments; term of five years; eligible for a second term.

Head of government Chancellor; elected by an absolute majority of the Federal Assembly, term of four years.

Cabinet Federal ministers; appointed by the president on the recommendation of the chancellor.

Administrative subdivisions Sixteen states (*Länder*).

Legal system

Civil law system; judicial review of legislative acts in the Federal Constitutional Court.

Legislature

Bicameral parliament.

Lower house Federal Assembly (*Bundestag*): 709 seats; term of four years.

Upper house Federal Council (*Bundesrat*): sixty-nine members (each state government delegates between three and six of the total sixty-nine seats, depending on the population size of the state).

Electoral system (lower house)

Mixed system.

Formula Elections are carried out on two ballots—on the first ballot, voters vote for candidates from their single-member constituency, whereas on the second ballot, for party lists in multi-member constituencies. The overall seats in the lower house (598) are allocated according to the Sainte-Laguë/Schepers formula. If the number of direct mandates for a party exceeds the overall share of seats the party is entitled to, it is allocated these 'excess' seats (*Überhangsmandate*).

Constituencies 299 single-member constituencies and sixteen multi-member constituencies corresponding to the states.

Electoral threshold Five per cent, unless at least three candidates of the party in question have been elected in single-member constituencies.

Suffrage Universal; eighteen years of age.

Direct democracy

There is an option for the conduct of referenda on both the national and the local levels. On the national level, there is only a mandatory binding referendum in cases of changes of boundaries.

Election results 2017 legislative elections (Federal Assembly):

Electorate	61,675,529	100.0%
Voters	46,973,799	76.2

Party	Valid votes	%	Seats
Christian Democratic Union (CDU)	12,445,832	26.8	200
Social Democratic Party (SDP)	9,538,367	20.5	94
Alternative for Germany (AFD)	5,877,094	12.6	91
Free Democratic Party (FDP)	4,997,178	10.7	80
The Left (DIE LINKE)	4,296,762	9.2	64
The Greens	4,157,564	8.9	66
Christian Social Union (CSU)	2,869,832	6.2	46
Others	2,324,316	5.0	0
Total valid votes	**46,506,945**	**100.0**	**641**

Note: The table shows the number of valid votes in the second voting tour, where the voters chose from party lists (proportional representation) and the total number of seats obtained by the parties. Seats do not include the 'excess' seats (*Überhangsmandate*). In the federal institutions, the Christian Social Union (from the state of Bavaria) forms a joint faction with the Christian Democratic Union (present in all of the other states).

Source: Adam Carr's website, Wikipedia.

Country Profile Greece
Hellenic Republic (*Elliniki Dimokratía*)

State formation

By the turn of the fifth century BC, the Classical Greeks had already organized themselves into multiple independent citizen states. During the second century BC, Greece became a part of the Roman Empire. As the Roman Empire split in the fourth century, Greece remained a part of the unified eastern part, better known was the Byzantine Empire. Over centuries of its existence, the empire was a force to be reckoned with, in terms of economics, culture, and military might. In 1453, the Ottoman Turks took over the Byzantine Empire, which led to four centuries of Ottoman control. The War of Independence ensued, which led to Greece proclaiming independence in 1832. During the Second World War, Greece came under the German occupation. After the war, there was a civil war between the communists and western-backed government forces, where the communists were defeated. A military junta overthrew the government in 1967, effectively bringing an end to the monarchy. The newly formed military regime imploded in 1974, and from 1975 onwards, Greece has been a democratic republic.

Constitution Entered into force in 1975; amended in 1986 and 2001, last in 2008.

Form of government

Parliamentary republic.

Head of state President; elected by the Hellenic Parliament; term of five years; eligible for another term.

Head of government Prime minister; the prime minister is usually the leader of the majority party in the parliament.

Cabinet Appointed by the president on the recommendation of the prime minister.

Administrative subdivisions Thirteen regions and one autonomous monastic state.

Legal system

Civil legal system based on Roman law.

Legislature

Unicameral parliament.
Hellenic Parliament *(Vouli ton Ellinon)*: 300 members; term of four years.

Electoral system

Proportional representation.

Formula 250 seats proportionally divided; fifty bonus seats to the first party (abolished in 2016, but will still be applied in the 2019 legislative elections).

Constituencies Fifty-nine constituencies account for 288 seats; twelve seats are elected on a national level.

Electoral threshold Three per cent nationwide.

Suffrage Universal; eighteen years of age; compulsory.

Direct democracy

The constitution provides for the conduct of referenda on matters of national importance and referenda concerning an already passed law.

Election results 2015 legislative elections (Hellenic Parliament):

Electorate	9,840,525	100.0%
Voters	5,566,295	56.6%

Party	Valid votes	%	Seats
Independent Greeks	200,423	3.7	10
Democratic Coalition	341,390	6.3	17
Union of the Centre	186,457	3.4	9
Golden Dawn	379,581	7.0	18
Communist Party	301,632	5.6	15
New Democracy	1,526,205	28.1	75
Coalition of Radical Left	1,925,904	35.5	145
The River	222,166	4.1	11
Others	348,092	6.4	0
Total valid votes	**5,431,850**	**100.0**	**300**

Source: Adam Carr's website.

Country Profile Hungary
Republic of Hungary (*Magyar Köztársaság*)

State formation

The original unification by King Stephen I dates back to the year 1001. From the sixteenth century onwards, the country struggled against occupation and dependence from the Ottoman Empire and the Habsburg dynasty, respectively. Hungary became an equal half of the Austro-Hungarian Empire in 1867 and an independent Hungarian Republic in 1918. Hungary was an ally of Nazi Germany, and later became a communist satellite state of the Soviet Union after the Second World War. In the late 1980s, Hungary led the movement to dissolve the Warsaw Pact and shifted towards democracy. The Third Hungarian Republic was declared in 1989.

Constitution Entered into force in 2012; amended several times, last in 2018.

Form of government

Parliamentary republic.

Head of state President elected by the National Assembly; term of five years; two-term limit.

Head of government Prime minister; nominated by the president and elected by the parliament; usually leader of the majority party; term of four years.

Cabinet Council of Ministers; proposed by the prime minister and appointed by the president.

Administrative subdivisions Nineteen countries and the capital city.

Legal system

Civil law system based on the German model.

Legislature

Unicameral parliament.
National Assembly (*Országgyulés*): 199 seats; term of four years.

Electoral system

Mixed system.

Formula Two-ballot system: 106 members directly elected in single-member constituencies by simple majority vote; ninety-three members directly elected in a single nationwide constituency by party-list, proportional representation vote.

Constituencies 106 single-member constituencies, one nationwide multi-member constituency.

Electoral threshold Five per cent threshold in case of party list; 10 per cent in case of two parties' joint list; 15 per cent in case of three or more parties' joint list.

Suffrage Universal; eighteen years of age, sixteen if married and marriage registered in Hungary.

Direct democracy

Extraordinary referendum can be called by the president or parliament or initiated by 200,000 eligible citizens.

Election results 2018 legislative elections (National Assembly):

Electorate	8,312,173	100.0%
Voters	5,562,245	66.9%

Party	Valid votes	%	Seats
Movement for a Better Hungary (Jobbik)	1,276,840	23.2	26
Fidesz—MPS—KDN	2,636,201	47.5	133
Democratic Coalition (DK)	348,176	6.3	9
Politics Can Be Different (LMP)	312,731	5.5	8
Socialist Party—Dialogue for Hungary	622,458	10.9	20
Together	58,591	1.1	1
National Self-Government of Germans in Hungary	n.a.	n.a.	1
Independents	55,612	1.0	1
Others	184,682	4.5	0
Total valid votes	**5,495,291**	**100.0**	**199**

Note: Results are from the single-member constituencies. Category 'Others' includes parties with less than 1 per cent nationwide and no seats.

Source: National Election Office of Hungary, Adam Carr's website, Wikipedia.

Country Profile India
Republic of India (*Bhārat Gaṇarājya*)

State formation

From the sixteenth century, several European countries established colonies in India. By 1856, most of the country was under the control of the British East India Company. It became a colony of the British Empire after a failed insurrection in 1857. In the twentieth century, the Indian National Congress and other political organizations engaged in a non-violent struggle for independence, which was finally won in 1947. However, India lost territories that became independent Pakistan and later Bangladesh. After the partition, over 7 million Indian Muslims moved to these countries and another 7 million Hindus and Sikhs moved the other way.

Constitution Entered into force in 1950; amended many times, last in 2019.

Form of government

Federal republic.

Head of state President; elected by an electoral college (elected members of both houses of parliament and the legislatures of the states); term of five years; two-term limit.

Head of government Prime minister; elected from majority party of parliament, appointed by the president.

Cabinet Union Council of Ministers; appointed by the president on the recommendation of the prime minister.

Administrative subdivisions Twenty-nine states and seven Union territories.

Legal system

Based on English common law; judicial review of legislative acts.

Legislature

Bicameral parliament (*Sansad*).

Lower house People's Assembly (*Lok Sabha*): 545 seats (543 elected by popular vote; two appointed by the president); term of five years.

Upper house Council of States *(Rajya Sabha)*: 245 members (up to twelve appointed by the president, the remaining chosen by the elected members of the state and territorial assemblies); staggered term of six years, one-third of the members retire every two years.

Electoral system (lower house)

Majoritarian representation.

Formula Hare quota.

Constituencies 543 single-member constituencies.

Electoral threshold Not applicable.

Suffrage Universal; eighteen years of age.

Direct democracy

None.

Election results 2019 legislative elections (People's Assembly):

Electorate	n.a.	100.0%
Voters	n.a.	67.1%

Party	Valid votes	%	Seats
Total 'National Democratic Alliance'	*n.a.*	43.9	353
Total 'United Progressive Alliance'	*n.a.*	24.6	91
Mahagathbandhan	*n.a.*	6.2	15
Left Front	*n.a.*	2.3	5
Non-aligned parties	*n.a.*	23.0	79
Total valid votes	*n.a.*	**100.0**	**543**

Note: Each of the top two alliances consists of a leading party i.e. the *Bharatiya Janata Party*, and the *Indian National Congress*, respectively.

Source: Official Election Commission of India.

Country Profile Indonesia
Republic of Indonesia *(Republik Indonesia)*

State formation

During the early seventeenth century, the Dutch had begun to colonize Indonesia. Later on, during the Second World War, it was under the occupation of Japan. In 1945, Indonesia declared independence, but was met with fierce resistance from the Netherlands, which led to a long guerrilla war. In 1949, the Netherlands agreed to grant sovereignty to Indonesia. A short period of parliamentary democracy ensued, which came to an abrupt end in 1957, when President Sukarno instituted 'guided democracy'. An abortive coup was instigated by alleged communist sympathizers, which led to Sukarno being removed from power. President Suharto ruled Indonesia from 1967 until 1998. Free and fair legislative elections were conducted in 1999.

Constitution Entered into force in 1945; replaced by the constitutions of 1949 and 1950; restored in 1959; amended many times.

Form of government

Presidential republic.

Head of state President; directly elected; term of five years; eligible for another term.

Head of government President.

Cabinet Appointed by the president.

Administrative subdivisions Thirty-one provinces, one autonomous province, one special region, one national capital district.

Legal system

Based on the Roman-Dutch model; civil law system.

Legislature

Bicameral parliament *(People's Consultative Assembly)*.

Lower house House of Representatives *(Dewan Perwakilan Rakyat)*: 575 members; term of five years.

Upper house Regional Representative Council *(Dewan Perwakilan Daerah)*: 136 members; four per province; term of five years.

Electoral system (lower house)

Proportional representation.

Formula Sainte-Laguë method.

Constituencies Eighty multi-member constituencies.

Electoral threshold Four per cent nationwide.

Suffrage Universal; seventeen years of age or less if already married.

Direct democracy

The constitution does not provide for the conduct of referenda.

Election results 2019 legislative elections (House of Representatives):

Electorate	n.a.	100.0%
Voters	n.a.	75.1%

Party	Valid votes	%	Seats
Indonesian Democratic Party of Struggle	27,053,691	19.3	128
Great Indonesia Movement Party	17,594,839	12.6	78
Golkar	17,229,789	12.3	85
National Awakening Party	13,570,097	9.7	58
Nasdem Party	12,661,792	9.1	59
Prosperous Justice Party	11,493,663	8.2	50
Democratic Party	10,876,507	7.8	54
National Mandate Party	9,572,623	6.8	44
United Development Party	6,323,147	4.5	19
Others	13,597,842	9.7	0
Total valid votes	**124,972,491**	**100.0**	**575**

Source: Wikipedia.

Country Profile Iran
Islamic Republic of Iran (*Jomhuri ye Eslāmi ye Irān*)

State formation

Known as Persia until the Iranian Revolution of 1979, when the Islamic Republic of Iran was formed after overthrowing the ruling monarchy and forcing the Shah into exile. Conservative clerical forces established a theocratic system of government. Following the bloody war against Iraq between 1980 and 1988, Iran became an important ally and financier for Shia minorities around the world, of whom many are considered terrorist groups. Furthermore, the possible military dimension of Iran's nuclear program led the US, the EU, and the UN to impose economic sanctions and export controls from early 2000. In 2016, prior ongoing negotiations resulted into sanctions relief.

Constitution Entered into force 1979; amended in 1989.

Form of government

Islamic republic.

Head of state Supreme Leader, elected by the Assembly of Experts.

Head of government President; approved by the Guardian Council; elected by popular vote; term of four years; two-term limit.

Cabinet Council of Ministers; selected by the president with legislative approval, although the Supreme Leader has some control over appointments to several ministries.

Administrative subdivisions Thirty-one provinces.

Legal system

Religious legal system based on secular and Islamic law.

Legislature

Unicameral parliament.

Islamic Consultative Assembly (*Majlies-e Shura-ye Eslami*): 290 seats (five seats are reserved for Zoroastrians, Jews, Assyrians and Chaldeans, and North and

South Armenians); all candidates must be approved by the Guardian Council (twelve-member group, of which six are appointed by the Supreme Leader and six are jurists, nominated and elected by the Assembly); term of four years.

Electoral system

Mixed system.

Formula Hare quota.

Constituencies 207 single- or multi-seat constituencies by two rounds (five single-seat constituencies are for religious minorities).

Electoral threshold Not applicable.

Suffrage Universal; eighteen years of age.

Direct democracy

Not applicable.

Election results 2016 legislative elections (Islamic Consultative Assembly):

Electorate	54,915,024	100.0%
Voters	n.a.	n.a.

Party	Valid votes	%	Seats
Pervasive Coalition of Reformists (List of Hope)	n.a.	n.a.	119
Principlists Grand Coalition	n.a.	n.a.	84
People's Voice Coalition	n.a.	n.a.	11
Independents	n.a.	n.a.	65
Religious Minority	n.a.	n.a.	5
Others	n.a.	n.a.	6
Total valid votes	**n.a.**	**n.a.**	**287**

Source: Wikipedia.

Country Profile Israel
State of Israel (*Medinat Yisra'el*)

State formation

In the late nineteenth century, the Austro-Hungarian Theodor Herzl founded the Zionist movement that strived for the establishment of a national Jewish state. By the end of the Second World War, some 800,000 Jewish people had immigrated to Palestine, mostly from Russia and Europe following pogroms and outbreaks of anti-Semitism. In 1948, two years after the resolution of the United Nations' General Assembly to form the State of Israel, Palestine and Israel were granted independence from the League of Nations mandate administered by Britain.

Constitution No formal constitution.

Form of government

Parliamentary republic.

Head of state President; elected by parliament; term of seven years; one-term limit.

Head of government Prime minister; assigned by the president; usually leader of the majority party in parliament; term of four years.

Cabinet Cabinet, selected by the prime minister and approved by parliament.

Administrative subdivisions Six districts.

Legal system

Mixture of English common law, British mandate regulations, and Jewish, Christian, and Muslim legal systems.

Legislature

Unicameral parliament.

National Assembly (*Knesset*): 120 seats; term of four years.

Electoral system

Proportional representation.

Formula D'Hondt.

Constituencies One multi-member constituency.

Electoral threshold 3.25 per cent nationwide.

Suffrage Universal; eighteen years of age.

Direct democracy

There can be a referendum in cases where territory is ceased.

Election results 2019 legislative elections (National Assembly):

Electorate	6,339,729	100.0%
Voters	4,261,683	67.2%

Party	Valid votes	%	Seats
Likud	1,140,370	26.5	35
Blue and White	1,125,881	26.1	35
Shas	258,275	6.0	8
United Torah Judaism	249,049	5.8	8
Hadash-Ta'al	193,442	4.5	6
Labor Party	190,870	4.4	6
Yisrael Beiteinu	173,004	4.0	5
Union of Right-Wing Parties	159,468	3.7	5
Meretz	156,473	3.6	4
Kulanu/All of us	152,756	3.5	4
Ra'am—Balad	143,666	3.3	4
Others	288,170	8.6	0
Total valid votes	**4,231,424**	**100.0**	**120**

Note: Others include parties with no seats.
Source: IFES Election Guide.

Country Profile Italy
Italian Republic (*Repubblica Italiana*)

State formation

Under the Roman Empire Italy flourished until 476 AD, with the death of the emperor Romulus Augustus. The modern nation-state of Italy was founded in 1861 following the unification of the regional states of the peninsula with Sardinia and Sicily in 1870. The parliamentary government was disrupted in early 1920 when Mussolini established a fascist dictatorship. His alliance with Germany led to its defeat in World War II. A democratic republic replaced the monarchy in 1946.

Constitution Entered into force in 1948; amended many times, last in 2012.

Form of government

Parliamentary republic.

Head of state President; elected by an electoral college consisting of the parliament and fifty-eight regional representatives; term of seven years; no term limit.

Head of government President of the Council of Ministers or prime minister; appointed by the president; confirmed by parliament.

Cabinet Council of Ministers; nominated by the prime minister; approved by the president.

Administrative subdivisions Fifteen regions and five autonomous regions.

Legal system

Civil law system, judicial review under certain conditions in Constitutional Court.

Legislature

Bicameral parliament.

Lower house Chamber of Deputies (*Camera dei Deputati*): 630 seats (the winning national coalition receiving 54 per cent); term of five years.

Upper house Senate (*Senato*): 315 seats (the winning coalition in each region receiving 55 per cent of that region's seats); term of five years.

Electoral system (lower house)

Mixed system (36.8 per cent of seats allocated using the plurality voting method and 63.2 per cent of the seats using a proportional method).

Formula Largest remainder method.

Constituencies 232 single-member constituencies, eight multi-member constituencies, and four multi-member abroad constituencies.

Electoral threshold Three per cent.

Suffrage Universal; eighteen years of age; twenty-five years of age for senatorial elections.

Direct democracy

A consultative referendum can be called by parliament. An abrogative referendum (with a quorum of participation of 50 per cent) can be called by 500,000 citizens or five regional councils. An optional constitutional referendum has been practiced in 2016.

Election results 2018 legislative elections (Chamber of Deputies):

| Electorate | 46,505,350 | 100.0% |
| Voters | 33,923,321 | 72.9% |

Party	Valid vote	%	Seats
Democratic Party	6,161,896	18.8	112
SVP—PATT	134,651	0.4	4
More Europe	841,468	2.6	3
Together	190,601	0.6	1
Popular Civic List	178,107	0.5	2
Total Centre-Left Coalition	7,506,723	22.9	122
League (Lega)	5,698,687	17.4	125
Forza Italia	4,596,956	14.0	104
Brothers of Italy	1,429,550	4.4	32
Us with Italy—UCD	427,152	1.3	4
Total Centre-Right Coalition	12,152,345	1	265
Five Star Movement	10,732,066	32.7	227
Free and Equal	1,114,799	3.4	14
Associate Movement Italians Abroad	n.a.	n.a.	1
South American Union Italian Emigrants	n.a.	n.a.	1
Total valid votes	31,505,933	100.0	630

Note: Votes and percentages are from the proportional vote.
Source: Ministero Dell'Interno—Ministry of the Interior Italy; Election Resources.

Country Profile Japan
Japan (*Nihon-koku/Nippon-koku*)

State formation

The foundation of Japan dates back to 660 BC. After more than 1,000 years of changing empires, Japan became a modern state in 1603. In 1854, Japan was forced to open up and sign a treaty with the US, and thus began modernization and industrialization. In the nineteenth and twentieth centuries, the country became a regional power that was able to defeat both China and Russia. It occupied Korea, Taiwan, and the southern Sakhalin Island. In the 1930s, Japan occupied Manchuria and launched a full-scale invasion of China. After the devastating defeat in World War II, Japan recovered and become an economic power in the region. The country still has some territorial disputes with China about the Paracel Islands in the East China Sea.

Constitution Entered into force in 1948.

Form of government

Constitutional monarchy.

Head of state Emperor; the monarchy is hereditary.

Head of government Prime minister; appointed by the emperor; usually leader of the majority party or coalition; term of four years; no term limit.

Cabinet Cabinet, appointed by the prime minister.

Administrative subdivisions Forty-seven prefectures.

Legal system

Modelled on the European civil law system, with some English and American influences, judicial review of legislative acts in the Supreme Court.

Legislature

Bicameral parliament (*Diet* or *Kokkai*).

Lower house House of Representatives (*Shugi-in*): 465 seats; term of four years.

Upper house House of Councillors (*Sangi-in*): 242 seats (146 members directly elected by majority vote and ninety-six by multi-seat proportional representation vote, one-half renewed every three years); term of six years.

Electoral system (lower house)

Mixed system.

Formula D'Hondt; 289 seats allocated by plurality. 176 seats allocated by proportional representation. Candidates may run in both the single-seat constituencies and the proportional representation poll. However, the single-seat constituency must be located within their proportional representation block. Candidates running in single-seat constituencies must obtain at least one-sixth of the number of valid votes.

Constituencies 300 single-member constituencies (plurality vote) and eleven multi-member or 'block' constituencies (proportional representation vote).

Electoral threshold Not applicable.

Suffrage Universal; eighteen years of age.

Direct democracy

The constitution contains a provision for an obligatory referendum in case of constitutional changes.

Election results 2017 legislative elections (House of Representatives):

Electorate	106,091,229	100.0%
Valid Votes	55,757,552	52.5%

Party	Valid votes	%	Seats
Liberal Democratic Party	18,555,717	33.3	281
Clean Government Party	6,977,712	12.5	29
Constitutional Democratic Party	11,084,890	19.9	54
Party of Hope	9,677,524	17.4	50
Japan Communist Party	4,404,081	7.9	12
Japan Restoration Party	3,387,097	6.1	11
Social Democratic Party	941,324	1.7	2
Others	729,207	1.326	26
Total valid votes	**55,757,552**	**100.0**	**465**

Source: Adam Carr's website, IFES Election Guide.

Country Profile Mexico
United Mexican States (*Estados Unidos Mexicanos*)

State formation

Spain occupied what is now known as Mexico in 1519 and conquered the Aztec capital in 1521. Mexican independence was declared in 1810, when Spain was occupied by Napoleon's army, but only recognized after a long war in 1821. The first republic was established in 1824. From 1920 to 2000 Mexico was ruled by reformists who emerged from the Revolution. The government started out with radical social policies and steadily got more conservative, corrupt, and repressive. In 2000, the opposition candidate from the revolutionary party won, but the economic and social struggles have not been resolved.

Constitution Entered into force in 1917; amended many times, last in 2019.

Form of government

Federal presidential republic.

Head of state President, elected by popular vote; term of six years; one-term limit.

Head of government President.

Cabinet Cabinet and Attorney General; appointed by the president; approved by the Senate.

Administrative subdivisions Thirty-one states; one federal district.

Legal system

Mixture of civil law system and US constitutional theory; judicial review of legislative acts.

Legislature

Bicameral National Congress (*Congreso de la Unión*).

Lower house Chamber of Deputies (*Cámara de Diputados*): 500 seats; term of three years.

Upper house Senate (*Cámara de Senadores*): 128 seats (ninety-six members are elected in thirty-two multi-member constituencies in the federal entities with the plurality vote; thirty-two members are elected by proportional representation in a single national constituency according to the Hare quota and highest remainder); term of six years.

Electoral system (lower house)

Mixed system.

Formula Simple quotient plus greatest remainder for the 200 seats allocated by proportional representation. The remaining seats are allocated by plurality.

Constituencies 300 single-member constituencies (plurality vote); five multi-member or 'block' constituencies (proportional representation vote).

Electoral threshold Two per cent of the votes in the multi-member constituencies.

Suffrage Universal; eighteen years of age; compulsory (but not enforced).

Direct democracy

Referendums on constitutional matters, administrative reforms, and political issues of great importance; last in 1867.

Election results 2018 legislative elections (Chamber of Deputies):

Electorate	89,994,039	100.0%
Voters	56,300,247	63.2

Party	Valid votes	%	Seats
National Regeneration Movement	20,972,573	38.63	189
National Action Party	10,096,588	18.5	83
Institutional Revolutionary Party	9,310,523	17.1	45
Party of the Democratic Revolution	2,967,969	5.4	21
Ecologist Green Party	2,695,405	4.9	16
Citizens' Movement	2,485,198	4.6	27
Labour Party	2,211,753	4.1	61
New Alliance Party	1,391,376	2.5	2
Social Encounter Party	1,353,941	2.4	56
Others	572,306	1.9	0
Total valid votes	**54,300,247**	**100.0**	**500**

Note: Category 'Others' includes parties and Independents with less than 1 per cent nationwide. Votes and vote-share are from the proportional vote. Seats are in total.
Source: Wikipedia.

The Netherlands
Kingdom of the Netherlands (*Koninkrijk der Nederlanden*)

State formation

In 1579, the Dutch United Provinces declared their independence from Spain. During the seventeenth century, the country became one of the leading sea and commercial powers, with colonies and settlements around the world. In 1815, after the French occupation, the Kingdom of the Netherlands was formed. During World Wars I and II, the country remained neutral, but suffered from the German occupation between 1940 and 1945.

Constitution Entered into force in 1815; substantially revised in 1848; amended many times, last in 2010.

Form of government

Constitutional monarchy.

Head of state King; the monarchy is hereditary.

Head of government Prime minister; usually leader of the majority party or coalition of the parliament; appointed by the monarch.

Cabinet Council of Ministers; appointed by the monarch.

Administrative subdivisions Twelve provinces.

Legal system

Civil law system based on the French system.

Legislature

Bicameral parliament.

Lower house Second Chamber (*Tweede Kamer*): 150 seats (members directly elected by popular vote); for a four-year term.

Upper House First Chamber (*Eerste Kamer*): seventy-five seats (members indirectly elected in each province by popular vote); four-year term.

Electoral system (lower house)

Proportional representation.

Formula D'Hondt.

Constituencies One nationwide, multi-seat constituency.

Electoral threshold 0.67 per cent nationwide.

Suffrage Universal; eighteen years of age.

Direct democracy

From 2015, a consultative referendum could be proposed by 300,000 citizens; exempted were revisions of the constitution, laws on monarchy system, and international treaties. A referendum was valid if the voter turnout was over 30 per cent. In 2018, the First and the Second Chamber repealed the referendum law.

Election results 2017 legislative elections (Second Chamber):

Electorate	12,893,466	100.0%
Voters	10,563,456	81.9%

Party	Valid votes	%	Seats
People's Party for Freedom and Democracy (VVD)	2,238,351	21.3	33
Party for Freedom (PVV)	1,372,941	13.1	20
Christian Democratic Appeal (CDA)	1,301,796	12.4	19
Democrats 66 (D66)	1,285,819	12.2	19
Green Left (GL)	959,600	9.1	14
Socialist Party (SP)	955,633	9.1	14
Labour Party (PvdA)	599,699	5.7	9
Christian Union (CU)	356,271	3.4	5
Party for the Animals (PvdD)	335,214	3.2	5
50PLUS (50+)	327,131	3.1	4
Reformed Political Party (SGP)	218,950	2.1	3
Equality (DENK)	216,147	2.1	3
Forum for Democracy (FvD)	181,162	1.8	2
Others	164,327	1.6	0
Total valid votes	**10,513,041**	**100.0**	**150**

Note: Category 'Others' includes parties with less than 1 per cent nationwide and no seats.

Source: Niederlandse Kiesraad, Adam Carr's website.

Country Profile Nigeria
Federal Republic of Nigeria

State formation

Nigeria was run by the British Royal Niger Company until 1900. The country was formally united in 1914 and became a colony under the rule of the British government. Following the Second World War, successive constitutions legislated by the British government increased the autonomy of Nigeria. Independence was finally gained in 1960. From 1966, Nigeria was ruled by military regimes (except the Second Republic from 1979 to 1983). It returned to democracy in 1999.

Constitution Entered into force in 1999; amendment several times, last in 2012.

Form of government

Federal republic.

Head of state President.

Head of government President; elected by popular vote; term of four years; two-term limit.

Cabinet Federal Ministers appointed by the President.

Administrative subdivisions Thirty-six states and one Federal Capital Territory.

Legal system

Based on English common law, Sharia law (in twelve northern states), and traditional law.

Legislature

Bicameral National Assembly.

Lower house House of Representatives: 360 seats; term of four years.

Upper house Senate: 109 seats (each state is divided into three districts, each electing one senator; the federal district elects one senator); term of four years.

Electoral system (lower house)

Majoritarian representation.

Formula Plurality.

Constituencies 360 single-member constituencies.

Electoral threshold Not applicable.

Suffrage Universal; eighteen years of age.

Direct democracy

Not applicable.

Election results 2019 legislative elections (House of Representatives):

Electorate	84,004,417.	100.0%
Voters	n.a.	n.a.

Party	Valid votes	%	Seats
All Progressives Congress (APC)	n.a.	n.a.	217
People's Democratic Party	n.a.	n.a.	115
All Progressives Grand Alliance (APGA)	n.a.	n.a.	9
African Democratic Congress (ADC)	n.a.	n.a.	3
People's Redemption Party (PRP)	n.a.	n.a.	2
Action Alliance (AA)	n.a.	n.a.	2
Social Democratic Party (SDP)	n.a.	n.a.	1
Labor Party (LP)	n.a.	n.a.	1
Allied People's Movement	n.a.	n.a.	1
To be determined	n.a.	n.a.	9
Total	**n.a.**	**n.a.**	**360**

Note: There were no elections in one of the states.
Source: IFES Election Guide.

Country Profile Poland
Republic of Poland (*Rzeczpospolita Polska*)

State formation

The political unit of Polska under the Piast dynasty was established in the tenth century, which was the advent of statehood for Poland. Over the next six centuries, the territories expanded and the Polish-Lithuanian Commonwealth was ruling vast tracts of land in central and eastern parts of Europe. The state, weakened by internal disorders in the eighteenth century, was partitioned amongst Russia, Prussia, and Austria. A short period of independence ensued in Poland after the First World War, which ended with the German and the Soviet occupations during the Second World War. Although, Poland acted as a satellite state of the USSR during the Cold War era, the government was relatively tolerant. The trade union 'Solidarity', which later became a powerful political force was formed in 1980 as a consequence of the ensuing labour turmoil. The communist era was brought to an end with the victory of 'Solidarity' in the free elections in 1989 and 1990.

Constitution Entered into force in 1997; amended in 2006, 2009, last in 2015.

Form of government

Semi-presidential republic.

Head of state President; directly elected; term of five years; eligible for another term.

Head of government Prime minister; nominated and appointed by the president; confirmed by the *Sejm* through a vote of confidence.

Cabinet Council of Ministers; proposed by the prime minister; appointed by the president.

Administrative subdivisions Sixteen provinces.

Legal system

Civil law system.

Legislature

Bicameral parliament.

Lower house Sejm: 460 members; term of four years.

Upper house Senate (*Senat*): 100 members; elected in single-member constituencies; term of four years.

Electoral system (lower house)

Proportional representation.

Formula D'Hondt.

Constituencies Forty-one multi-member constituencies with between seven and nineteen seats.

Electoral threshold five per cent of the total votes cast for individual parties; eight per cent for a coalition of parties; national minorities' parties are exempt from threshold requirements.

Suffrage Universal; eighteen years of age.

Direct democracy

The constitution provides for the conduct of a nationwide referendum on constitutional matters, electoral system amendments, and on matters of high importance to the state. There are provisions for referendums on the local level as well. Referendums require a 50 per cent voter turnout threshold to be legally binding.

Election results 2015 legislative elections (*Sejm*):

Electorate	30,762,931	100.0%
Voters	15,076,705	49.0%

Party	Valid votes	%	Seats
German Minority	28,014	0.2	1
Law and Justice	4,295,016	29.9	157
Citizens' Platform	5,629,773	39.2	207
Polish People's Party	1,201,628	8.4	28
Palikot Movement	1,439,490	10.0	40
Union of the Democratic Left	1,184,303	8.2	27
Others	591,279	4.1	0
Total valid votes	**14,369,503**	**100.0**	**460**

Source: Adam Carr's website.

Country Profile Russia
Russian Federation (*Rossiyskaya Federatsiya*)

State formation

The principality of Muscovy was established in the twelfth century. After more than two centuries of Mongol domination between the thriteenth and fifteenth centuries, it gradually conquered the surrounding principalities. The hegemony continued to expand through the nineteenth century, and finally the country was given the moniker of the Russian Empire. During World War I, the Russian army faced multiple defeats on many fronts, which led to widespread rioting across the major cities, and paved the way for the Revolution of 1917. This was the beginning of decades of communist rule, during which in 1922, the USSR was established. During the Second World War, the USSR fought on the side of the Allies and played a major hand in defeating Germany and hence expanded its territory and came to be reckoned as a global power. The US and the USSR were engaged in what is known as the Cold War until the dissolution of the USSR in 1991.

Constitution Entered into force in 1993; amended in 2008, last in 2014.

Form of government

Federal semi-presidential republic.

Head of state President; directly elected; six-year term with the option of one consecutive re-election; further re-election possible after a pause lasting at least one term.

Head of government Chairman of the Government of the Russian Federation; appointed by the president with the approval of the Duma.

Cabinet Appointed by the president.

Administrative subdivisions Forty-six oblasts, twenty-two republics, nine krays, four autonomous okrugs, three federal cities, and one autonomous oblast; one republic and one federal city are internationally recognized as part of the Ukraine.

Legal system

Based on civil law system; judicial review of legislative acts.

Legislature

Bicameral Federal Assembly (*Federalnoye Sobraniye*).

Lower house State Duma (*Gosudarstvennaya Duma*): 450 seats; term of five years.

Upper house Federation Council (*Soviet Federatsii*): 170 seats (members appointed by the top officials in each of the eighty-five federal administrative units); terms are determined according to the regional bodies they represent.

Electoral system (lower house)

Mixed system.

Formula Hare quota and largest remainder.

Constituencies One multi-member nationwide constituency and 225 single-member constituencies.

Electoral threshold Five per cent of the party-list vote.

Suffrage Universal; eighteen years of age.

Direct democracy

The constitution provides the possibility for the president to call an extraordinary referendum under procedures established by federal constitutional law.

Election results 2016 legislative elections (State Duma):

Electorate:	110,061,200	100.0%
Voters:	52,631,849	47.8%

Party	Valid votes	%	Seats
United Russia	28,527,828	55.2	343
Communist Party	7,019,752	13.6	42
Liberal Democratic Party	6,917,063	13.4	39
Fair Russia	3,275,063	6.3	23
Others	5,909,557	9.9	3
Total valid votes	**51,649,263**	**100.0**	**450**

Notes: Category 'Others' includes parties with less than 1 per cent nationwide or no seats.
Source: Adam Carr's website.

Country Profile South Africa
Republic of South Africa

State formation

Dutch settlement at the Cape of Good Hope started with the foundation of a station by the Dutch East India Company in 1652. The region was seized by Great Britain in 1797 and annexed in 1805, but the Boers (of Dutch origin) resisted British rule throughout the nineteenth century. The second Anglo-Boer War ended in 1902, with Great Britain assuming sovereignty over the South African republics. In 1910, the Union of South Africa was created. From 1948 to 1990, the country was ruled under a regime of segregationist legislation (apartheid); the first multi-racial elections were held in 1994.

Constitution Entered into force in 1997; amended several times, last in 2013.

Form of government

Parliamentary republic.

Head of state President; elected by the National Assembly; term of five years; two-term limit.

Head of government President.

Cabinet Cabinet, appointed by the president.

Administrative subdivisions Nine provinces.

Legal system

Based on Roman-Dutch law and English common law.

Legislature

Bicameral parliament.

Lower house National Assembly: 400 seats; term of five years.

Upper house National Council of Provinces: ninety seats (ten members elected by each of the nine provincial legislatures); term of five years.

Electoral system (lower house)

Proportional representation.

Formula Droop quota; 200 members chosen from national party lists, the other 200 members chosen from regional party lists.

Constituencies Ten multi-member constituencies; nine represent the provinces and one is a national constituency.

Electoral threshold Not applicable.

Suffrage Universal; eighteen years of age.

Direct democracy

Three referenda have been held on the constitution, i.e. to abolish apartheid.

Election results 2019 legislative elections (National Assembly):

Electorate:	26,779,025	100.0%
Voters:	17,671,616	66.0%

Party	Valid votes	%	Seats
African National Congress (ANC)	10,026,475	57.5	230
Democratic Alliance (DA)	3,621,188	20.8	84
Economic Freedom Fighters (EFF)	1,881,521	10.8	44
Inkatha Freedom Party (IFP)	588,839	3.4	14
Freedom Front Plus	414,864	2.4	10
African Christian Democratic Party	146,262	0.8	4
United Democratic Movement	78,030	0.5	2
African Transformation Movement	76,830	0.4	2
Good	70,408	0.4	2
National Freedom Party	61,220	0.4	2
African Independent Congress	48,107	0.3	2
Pan Africanist Congress of Azania	32,677	0.2	1
Al Jama-ah	31,468	0.2	1
Others	358,155	1.9	2
Total valid votes	17,436,044	100.0	400

Notes: Category 'Others' includes parties with less than 0.2 per cent nationwide and no seats.
Source: IFES Election Guide.

Country Profile Spain
Kingdom of Spain (*Reino de España*)

State formation

During the sixteenth and seventeenth centuries, Spain was a powerful world empire with main colonies in Central and South America. In the eighteenth century, the country failed to embrace the mercantile and industrial revolutions and, thus, fell behind Britain, France, and Germany in economic and political power. Spain remained neutral in World Wars I and II but suffered a devastating civil war in 1936–1939. After an authoritarian regime that lasted until 1975, the country transitioned peacefully to a democracy.

Constitution Entered into force in 1978; amended in 1992 and in 2011.

Form of government

Parliamentary monarchy.

Head of state King; the monarchy is hereditary.

Head of government Prime minister; appointed by the monarch; indirectly elected by the Congress of Deputies.

Cabinet Council of Ministers; appointed by the president.

Administrative subdivisions Seventeen semi-autonomous communities, two autonomous cities.

Legal system

Civil law system with regional variations.

Legislature

Bicameral General Courts (*Las Cortes Generales*).

Lower house Congress of Deputies (*Congreso de los Diputados*): 350 seats (directly elected by popular vote); term of four years.

Upper house Senate (*Senado*): 266 seats (directly elected by simple majority vote; fifty-eight members appointed by the regional legislatures); term of four years.

Electoral system (lower house)

Proportional representation.

Formula D'Hondt.

Constituencies Fifty multi-seat constituencies, two directly elected from the North African Ceuta and Melilla enclaves by simple majority vote.

Electoral threshold Three per cent nationwide.

Suffrage Universal; eighteen years of age.

Direct democracy

A mandatory referendum is needed for total or partial revision of the constitution, an optional referendum for smaller adjustments, if one-tenth of the General Courts demand it. Further a referendum is required for secession, and 500,000 citizens are needed for an initiative to change laws.

Election results 2019 legislative elections (Congress of Deputies):

Electorate	36,085,641	100.0%
Voters	26,361,051	75.8%

Party	Valid votes	%	Seats
Spanish Socialist Workers' Party (PSOE)	7,480,755	28.7	123
People's Party (PP)	4,356,023	16.7	66
Citizens—Party of the Citizenry (C's)	4,136,600	15.9	57
United We Can (Unidas Podemos)	3,732,929	14.3	42
Vox	2,677,173	10.3	24
Republican Left of Catalonia-Sovereigntists (ERC-Sobiranistes)	1,019,558	3.9	15
Together for Catalonia (JxCat-Junts)	497,638	1.9	7
Basque Nationalist Party (EAJ-PNV)	394,627	1.5	6
Basque Country United (EH Bildu)	258,840	1.0	4
Commitment: Bloc-Initiative-Greens Equo (Compromis 2019)	172,751	0.7	1
Sum Navare (NA+)	107,124	0.4	2
Regionalist Party of Cantabria (PRC)	52,810	0.2	1
Others	1,371,564	4.5	2
Total valid votes	**26,258,392**	**100.0**	**350**

Notes: Category 'Others' includes parties with no seats.
Source: Wikipedia.

Country Profile Switzerland
Swiss Confederation (*Schweizerische Eidgenossenschaft/Confédération Suisse/ Confederazione Svizzera/Confederaziun Svizra*)

State formation

The Swiss Confederation was founded as a defence alliance in 1291. Switzerland gained independence from the German Empire in 1499 and became a republic in 1848, turning from an alliance to a federal state.

Constitution Entered into force 2000; a revised version of the 1874 constitution; amended many times, last in 2015.

Form of government

Federal republic.

Head of state President and vice-president elected by the Federal Assembly from among the seven members of the cabinet; one-year term (no consecutive terms).

Head of government President.

Cabinet Federal Council (*Bundesrat/Conseil Fédéral/ Consiglio Federale/Cussegl federal*) elected by the Federal Assembly; term of four years.

Administrative   subdivisions Twenty-six   cantons, including six half-cantons.

Legal system

Civil law system influenced by customary law; judicial review of legislative acts, except with respect to federal decrees of general obligatory character.

Legislature

Bicameral Federal Assembly (*Bundesversammlung/Assemblee Fédérale/Assemblea Federale/Assamblea Federala*).

Lower house National Council (*Nationalrat/Conseil National/Consiglio Nazionale/Cussegl naziunal*): 200 seats; term of four years.

Upper house Council of States (*Ständerat/Conseil des Etats/Consiglio degli Stati/Cussegl dals Stadis*): forty-six seats (two representatives from each canton and one from each half-canton); term of four years.

Electoral system (lower house)

Proportional representation, but plurality system for five single-member constituencies (two cantons, three half-cantons).

Formula Hagenbach-Bischoff method, with remaining seats being distributed according to the rule of highest average, in multi-member constituencies. Each elector can vote for a list as it stands or modify by crossing out candidates and repeat (*kummulieren*) the vote for one candidate or vote for a candidate from a different list (*panachage*).

Constituencies Twenty-six multi- or single-member constituencies corresponding to the country's twenty cantons and six half-cantons.

Electoral threshold Not applicable.

Suffrage Universal, eighteen years of age; one canton (Glarus) sixteen years of age.

Direct democracy

Mandatory referendum on constitution and international treaties, optional referendum on laws. Popular initiatives for the total or partial revision of the constitution. The 'general popular initiative' allows 100,000 citizens to put not only constitutional changes, but also the implementation and modification of federal laws, on the political agenda.

Election results 2015 legislative elections (National Council):

Electorate	5,283,556	100.0%
Voters	2,563,052	48.5%

Party	Valid votes	%	Seats
Swiss People's Party (SVP)	740,967	29.4	65
Social Democratic Party (SP)	475,075	18.8	43
Free Democratic Party (FDP)	413,444	16.4	33
Christian Democrat People's Party (CVP)	293,653	11.6	27
Green Party (GPS)	177,944	7.1	11
Green Liberal Party (GLP)	116,641	4.6	7
Conservative Democratic Party (BDP)	103,476	4.1	7

Evangelical People's Party (EVP)	48,698	1.9	2
Ticino League (Lega)	25,631	1	2
Christian Social Party (CSP)	5,126	0.2	0
Federal Democratic Union (EDU)	30,757	1.2	0
Swiss Labour Party (PdA)	10,252	0.4	1
Geneva Citizens' Movment (MCG)	7,689	0.3	1
Solidarities (Sol)	12,815	0.5	0
Swiss Democrats (SD)	2,563	0.1	0
Others	61,513	2.4	1
Total valid votes	**2,526,244**	**100.0**	**200**

Source: Federal Assembly; Swiss Federal Statistical Office.

Country Profile Turkey
Republic of Turkey (*Türkiye Cumhuriyeti*)

State formation

After defeat in the First World War, the constitutional Republic of Turkey succeeded to the 600-year-old Ottoman Empire under the leadership of its founder and first president Mustafa Kemal (honorifically re-baptized Atatürk, Father of the Turks, in 1934). Since the establishment of a multi-party system in 1945, the country has suffered several military *coups d'état*; the current constitution was ratified by popular referendum during a military junta that lasted until 1983.

Constitution Entered into force in 1982; amended several times, last in 2017.

Form of government

Presidential republic.

Head of state President; elected by popular vote: term of five years; two-term limit.

Head of government President.

Cabinet Council of Ministers; appointed by the president.

Administrative subdivisions Eighty-one provinces.

Legal system

Civil law system derived from various European continental legal systems, notably the Swiss civil code.

Legislature

Unicameral parliament.
National Assembly (*Türkiye Büyük Millet Meclisi*): 600 seats; term of four years.

Electoral system

Proportional representation.

Formula D'Hondt.

Constituencies Eighty-seven multi-member constituencies.

Electoral threshold ten per cent nationwide for parties. For independent candidates, the threshold is reduced.

Suffrage Universal; eighteen years of age.

Direct democracy

Since the 1982 constitutional referendum, three more referenda have been held, most recently in 2017.

Election results 2018 legislative elections (National Assembly):

Electorate	56,322,632	100.0%
Voters	49,644,165	88.2%

Party	Valid votes	%	Seats
Justice and Development Party (AKP)	20,559,732	40.3	295
Republican People's Party (CHP)	11,086,897	22.8	146
Nationalist Movement Party (MHP)	5,444,728	11.2	49
Good Party (Iyi)	4,932,510	10.1	43
Peoples' Democratic Party (HDP)	5,606,622	11.5	67
Others	1,000,877	2.1	0
Total valid votes	48,631,366	100.0	600

Notes: Category 'Others' includes parties with no seats.
Source: Adam Carr's website.

Country Profile United Kingdom
United Kingdom of Great Britain and Northern Ireland

State formation

England has existed as a unified entity since the tenth century. The union with Wales was first formalized in 1536. In 1707, England and Scotland joined as Great Britain. The union of Great Britain and Ireland was implemented in 1801. After the partition of Ireland in 1921, six Northern Irish counties remained part of the United Kingdom.

Constitution Unwritten; partly statutes, common law, and practice.

Form of government

Constitutional monarchy.

Head of state Monarch; the monarchy is hereditary.

Head of government Prime minister; appointed by the monarch; usually leader of the majority party in the lower house.

Cabinet Cabinet, appointed by the prime minister.

Administrative subdivisions England: nine regions; Northern Ireland: eleven districts; Scotland: thirty-two council areas; Wales: twenty-two unitary authorities.

Legal system

Common law tradition with early Roman and modern continental influences; non-binding judicial review of acts of Parliament.

Legislature

Bicameral parliament.

Lower house House of Commons: 650 seats; term of five years.

Upper house House of Lords: approximately 600 life peers, ninety-two hereditary peers, and twenty-six clergy (no elections, but in 1999 elections were held to determine the ninety-two hereditary peers; elections are held only as vacancies in the hereditary peerage arise).

Electoral system (lower house)

Majoritarian representation.

Formula Plurality.

Constituencies 650 single-member constituencies.

Electoral threshold Not applicable.

Suffrage Universal; eighteen years of age.

Direct democracy

Every referendum needs a special ad hoc law.

Election results 2017 legislative elections (House of Commons):

Electorate	46,843,896	100.0%
Voters	32,278,373	68.8%

Party	Valid votes	%	Seats
Conservative Party (Con)	13,636,684	42.3	317
Labour Party (Lab)	12,877,918	40.0	262

Liberal Democratic Party (Lib Dem)	2,371,861	7.4	12
Scottish National Party (SNP)	977,568	3.0	35
Green Party	525,664	1.6	1
Sinn Féin	238,915	0.7	7
Democratic Unionist Party (DUP)	292,316	0.9	10
Plaid Cymru	164,466	0.5	4
Independent candidates	151,471	0.5	1
Speaker	34,299	0.1	1
Others	933,022	3.0	0
Total valid votes	**32,204,184**	**100.0**	**650**

Source: Official Parliament—the House of Commons UK.

Country Profile United States
United States of America

State formation

Spanish, French, and English settlers founded American colonies during the sixteebth century. The US was founded by thirteen colonies declaring their independence from Great Britain in 1776. It expanded to the western coast of the continent and has since received more immigrants than the rest of the world combined. Between 1861 and 1865, the northern Union of the states defeated the secessionist Confederacy of eleven southern states. During World Wars I and II, the US was victorious and became the world's most powerful nation-state.

Constitution Entered into force in 1789; amended many times, last in 1992.

Form of government

Federal republic.

Head of state President and vice-president elected on the same ticket by a college of representatives; elected directly from each state; term of four years; two-term limit.

Head of government President.

Cabinet Cabinet, appointed by the president with the approval of the Senate.

Administrative subdivisions Fifty states and one district.

Legal system

Based on English common law; each state has its own legal system; judicial review of legislative acts.

Legislature

Bicameral Congress.

Lower house House of Representatives: 435 seats; term of two years.

Upper house Senate: 100 seats (two members from each state; fifty multi-member constituencies); staggered elections (one-third renewed every two years); term of six years.

Electoral system (lower house)

Mixed system. Simple majority vote; absolute majority in the state of Georgia.

Formula Plurality in forty-five states; varieties in five states.

Constituencies 435 single-member constituencies. Each representative represents roughly the same number of citizens, provided that each state has at least one representative.

Electoral threshold Not applicable.

Suffrage Universal; eighteen years of age.

Direct democracy

Referendums at state level.

Election results 2018 legislative elections (House of Representatives):

Electorate:	235,714,420	100.0%
Voters:	118,531.932	50.3%

Party	Valid votes	%	Seats
Democratic Party	60,727,598	53.4	235
Republican Party	50,983,895	44.8	199
Others	1,967,161	1.8	1
Total valid votes	**113,678,654**	**100.0**	**435**

Notes: Category 'Others' includes parties without seats.
Sources: Wikipedia, IFES Election Guide.

Appendix 2

Comparative tables

Additional comparative tables with a range of important themes and issues including communication, economy, health, and more are available online:

www.oup.com/he/caramani5e.

Comparative table 1 Development and inequality

Country	Human development index (HDI)	General government gross debt as of GDP %	Income share held by lowest 10%	Income share held by highest 10%	Inequality measures highest 10%/lowest 10%
	2018	2017	2000–2017 (latest available)	2000–2017 (latest available)	2000–2017 (latest available)
Afghanistan	0.498	7.0	–	–	–
Albania	0.785	71.8	3.7	22.9	6.2
Algeria	0.754	27.5	4.0	22.9	5.7
Angola	0.581	65.0	2.1	32.3	15.4
Argentina	0.825	57.6	1.8	30.9	17.2
Azerbaijan	0.757	54.1	6.1	17.4	2.9
Belarus	0.808	53.4	4.1	22.9	5.6
Botswana	0.717	14.0	1.1	49.6	45.1
Brazil	0.759	84.0	1.2	40.4	33.7
Bulgaria	0.813	23.9	2.0	28.8	14.4
Cambodia	0.582	30.4	3.3	–	–
Canada	0.926	89.7	2.4	25.3	10.5
Chile	0.843	23.6	1.7	38	22.4
China	0.752	47.0	2.1	31.4	15.0
Colombia	0.747	49.4	1.3	40	30.8
Costa Rica	0.794	48.9	1.5	37.3	24.9
Croatia	0.818	77.8	2.7	23.2	8.6
Cuba	0.777	–	–	–	–
Cyprus	0.869	97.5	3.2	27.4	8.6
Denmark	0.929	35.3	3.7	23.8	6.4
Egypt, Arab Rep.	0.696	103.0	3.9	27.8	7.1
France	0.901	96.8	3.1	26.6	8.6
Germany	0.936	63.9	3.1	24.8	8.0
Greece	0.870	181.8	1.9	26.2	13.8
Hungary	0.838	73.6	3.0	23.8	7.9
India	0.640	71.2	3.6	29.8	8.3
Indonesia	0.694	28.8	3.1	31.9	10.3
Iran, Islamic Rep.	0.798	39.5	2.4	29.8	12.4

Comparative table 1 Development and inequality (*continued*)

Country	Human development index (HDI)	General government gross debt as of GDP %	Income share held by lowest 10%	Income share held by highest 10%	Inequality measures highest 10%/lowest 10%
	2018	2017	2000–2017 (latest available)	2000–2017 (latest available)	2000–2017 (latest available)
Israel	0.903	60.9	1.7	29.6	17.4
Italy	0.880	131.8	1.8	25.7	14.3
Japan	0.909	237.6	2.7	24.7	9.1
Kenya	0.590	54.2	2.4	31.6	13.2
Korea, Rep.	0.903	39.5	2.6	23.8	9.2
Latvia	0.847	36.3	2.5	26.1	10.4
Lebanon	0.757	146.8	3.1	24.8	8.0
Liechtenstein	0.916	–	–	–	–
Mexico	0.774	54.3	2.2	34.8	15.8
Moldova	0.700	31.5	4.3	22.7	5.3
Morocco	0.667	65.1	2.7	31.9	12.0
Netherlands	0.931	56.5	3.5	23	6.6
Nicaragua	0.658	33.3	2.0	37.2	18.6
Nigeria	0.532	21.8	2.0	32.7	16.4
Norway	0.953	36.5	3.5	22.3	6.4
Philippines	0.699	39.9	–	–	–
Poland	0.865	50.6	–	–	–
Russian Federation	0.816	15.5	2.8	29.7	10.8
Saudi Arabia	0.853	17.2	–	–	–
Slovak Republic	0.855	50.9	3.1	20.9	6.7
Slovenia	0.896	73.6	3.9	21	5.4
South Africa	0.699	53.0	0.9	50.5	56.1
Spain	0.891	98.4	1.9	26.2	13.8
Switzerland	0.944	41.8	3.2	25.2	7.9
Tajikistan	0.650	50.4	3.0	26.4	8.8
Turkey	0.791	28.3	2.2	32.1	14.6
Ukraine	0.751	71.0	4.3	21.2	4.9
United Kingdom	0.922	87.5	2.9	25.4	8.8
United States	0.924	105.2	1.7	30.6	18.0
Uruguay	0.804	65.7	2.2	29.7	13.5
Vietnam	0.694	58.5	2.6	27.1	10.4

Notes: The first Human Development Report introduced a new way of measuring development by combining indicators of life expectancy, educational attainment, and income into a composite human development.

Percentage share of income or consumption is the share that accrues to subgroups of population indicated by deciles or quintiles. Ratio of percentage share of income or consumption of richest 10 per cent to poorest 10 per cent.

Sources: United Nations Development Programme; International Monetary Fund (IMF) World Economic Outlook Database; World Bank Data.

Comparative table 2 Education

Country	Government expenditure on education as % of GDP	Gross enrolment ratio, primary, gender parity index (GPI)	Out-of-school children of primary school age, both sexes (number)	Primary completion rate, both sexes (%)	Gross enrolment ratio, primary and lower secondary, both sexes (%)
	2010–2017	2012–2017	2012–2017	2012–2017	2010–2017
Afghanistan	3.93	0.7	–	–	92.5
Albania	2.19	1.0	4,665	106.7	105.9
Algeria	–	1.0	21,362	105.6	123.5
Angola	3.47	0.9	–	–	93.7
Argentina	5.57	1.0	28,723	102.4	115.8
Azerbaijan	2.90	1.0	34,961	107.2	99.8
Belarus	4.82	1.0	16,598	100.9	99.5
Botswana	–	1.0	33,883	69.2	104.5
Brazil	6.24	1.0	395,798	–	111.8
Bulgaria	4.06	1.0	18,895	94.6	92.0
Cambodia	1.91	1.0	184,824	89.6	95.9
Canada	5.27	1.0	863	–	104.1
Chile	5.35	1.0	105,592	92.8	100.0
China	–	1.0	–	99.9	98.9
Colombia	4.40	1.0	243,808	105.0	109.7
Costa Rica	7.43	1.0	13,887	96.4	117.8
Croatia	4.56	1.0	4,007	97.7	101.0
Cuba	12.84	1.0	30,961	91.6	102.5
Cyprus	6.38	1.0	1,176	96.8	99.4
Denmark	7.63	1.0	4,537	103.9	106.9
Egypt, Arab Rep.	–	1.0	163,886	95.0	102.2
France	5.46	1.0	37,422	–	101.4
Germany	4.81	1.0	6,133	99.2	101.7
Greece	–	1.0	48,705	94.1	95.6
Hungary	4.58	1.0	12,152	98.6	100.9
India	3.84	1.2	2,897,747	96.3	104.6
Indonesia	3.58	1.0	2,359,548	99.2	100.7
Iran, Islamic Rep.	3.79	1.1	41,355	101.5	106.3
Israel	5.88	1.0	25,499	102.4	104.0
Italy	4.08	1.0	39,161	98.5	102.0
Japan	3.47	1.0	118,248	100.5	99.7
Kenya	5.24	1.0	1,214,199	102.0	102.9
Korea, Rep.	5.25	1.0	95,530	96.1	97.4
Latvia	5.34	1.0	3,890	98.1	100.6
Lebanon	2.48	0.9	61,661	74.1	85.3
Liechtenstein	2.56	1.0	13	100.3	103.1
Mexico	5.24	1.0	139,577	101.3	110.9
Moldova	6.66	1.0	15,706	89.9	88.7
Morocco	–	1.0	117,890	92.7	107.2

Comparative table 2 Education (*continued*)

Country	Government expenditure on education as % of GDP	Gross enrolment ratio, primary, gender parity index (GPI)	Out-of-school children of primary school age, both sexes (number)	Primary completion rate, both sexes (%)	Gross enrolment ratio, primary and lower secondary, both sexes (%)
	2010–2017	2012–2017	2012–2017	2012–2017	2010–2017
Netherlands	5.40	1.0	–	–	113.7
Nicaragua	4.35	–	–	–	100.3
Nigeria	–	0.9	–	–	72.8
Norway	7.55	1.0	848	100.9	101.2
Philippines	–	1.0	586,284	104.0	105.0
Poland	4.81	1.0	99,207	100.2	106.9
Russian Federation	3.82	1.0	146,591	97.9	101.5
Saudi Arabia	–	1.0	80,255	114.4	118.3
Slovak Republic	4.65	1.0	–	92.5	96.7
Slovenia	4.91	1.0	2,691	97.3	99.4
South Africa	6.13	1.0	620,845	81.7	100.9
Spain	4.28	1.0	42,849	97.2	109.2
Switzerland	5.10	1.0	1,146	96.6	104.8
Tajikistan	5.23	1.0	11,435	92.4	97.6
Turkey	4.29	1.0	294,314	92.5	99.6
Ukraine	5.01	1.0	122,010	103.4	99.0
United Kingdom	5.54	1.0	11,014	101.0	118.7
United States	4.99	1.0	1,013,950	–	101.6
Uruguay	4.36	1.0	4,858	102.2	111.1
Vietnam	5.65	1.0	127,071	104.8	104.0

Notes: General government expenditure on education (current, capital, and transfers) is expressed as a percentage of GDP. It includes expenditure funded by transfers from international sources to government. General government usually refers to local, regional, and central governments.

Gender parity index for gross enrolment ratio in primary education is the ratio of girls to boys enrolled at primary level in public and private schools.

Out-of-school children of primary school age, both sexes (number) refers to children in the official primary school age range who are not enrolled in either primary or secondary schools.

Primary completion rate or gross intake ratio to the last grade of primary education is the number of new entrants (enrolments minus repeaters) in the last grade of primary education, regardless of age, divided by the population at the entrance age for the last grade of primary education. Data limitations preclude adjusting for students who drop out during the final year of primary education.

Gross enrolment ratio, secondary, both sexes (%) refers to total enrolment in secondary education, regardless of age, expressed as a percentage of the population of official secondary education age. The gross enrolment ratio can exceed 100 per cent due to the inclusion of over-aged and under-aged students because of early or late school entrance and grade repetition.
Sources: UNESCO Institute for Statistics.

Comparative table 3 Environment

Country	CO$_2$ emissions (metric tons per capita)	Electric power consumption (kWh per capita)	GDP per unit of energy use (PPP $ per kg of oil equivalent)	Electricity production from renewable sources, excluding hydroelectric (kWh)
	2014	2014	2014	2015
Afghanistan	0.3	–	–	–
Albania	2.0	2,309.4	13.9	–
Algeria	3.7	1,356.3	10.8	77,000,000
Angola	1.3	312.5	13.2	–
Argentina	4.8	3,052.4	9.8	2,752,000,000
Azerbaijan	3.9	2,202.4	11.7	101,000,000
Belarus	6.7	3,680.0	6.5	171,000,000
Botswana	3.2	1,748.6	13.1	1,000,000
Brazil	2.6	2,601.4	10.9	70,487,000,000
Bulgaria	5.9	4,708.9	7.1	3,107,000,000
Cambodia	0.4	271.4	7.9	41,000,000
Canada	15.1	15,545.5	5.8	42,037,000,000
Chile	4.7	3,911.7	11.2	8,991,000,000
China	7.5	3,927.0	6.0	283,851,000,000
Colombia	1.8	1,289.6	18.8	2,262,000,000
Costa Rica	1.6	1,957.9	14.7	2,637,000,000
Croatia	4.0	3,714.4	11.6	1,119,000,000
Cuba	3.1	1,434.0	–	753,000,000
Cyprus	5.3	3,624.9	13.1	398,000,000
Denmark	5.9	5,858.8	16.7	18,944,000,000
Egypt, Arab Rep.	2.2	1,657.8	12.8	1,598,000,000
France	4.6	6,939.5	11.0	34,917,000,000
Germany	8.9	7,035.5	12.5	168,389,000,000
Greece	6.2	5,062.6	12.6	8,752,000,000
Hungary	4.3	3,966.0	11.0	2,977,000,000
India	1.7	805.6	8.9	74,143,000,000
Indonesia	1.8	811.9	11.9	11,181,000,000
Iran, Islamic Rep.	8.3	2,985.7	5.9	236,000,000
Israel	7.9	6,600.9	12.3	1,190,000,000
Italy	5.3	5,002.4	14.9	63,368,000,000
Japan	9.5	7,819.7	11.3	80,292,000,000
Kenya	0.3	166.7	5.7	4,659,000,000
Korea, Rep.	11.6	10,496.5	6.4	8,260,000,000
Latvia	3.5	3,507.4	10.9	916,000,000
Lebanon	4.3	2,892.8	10.9	–
Liechtenstein	1.2	–	–	–
Mexico	3.9	2,090.2	11.6	17,082,000,000
Moldova	1.4	1,386.2	5.4	19,000,000

Comparative table 3 Environment (*continued*)

Country	CO$_2$ emissions (metric tons per capita)	Electric power consumption (kWh per capita)	GDP per unit of energy use (PPP $ per kg of oil equivalent)	Electricity production from renewable sources, excluding hydroelectric (kWh)
	2014	2014	2014	2015
Morocco	1.7	901.1	13.7	2,525,000,000
Netherlands	9.9	6,712.8	11.2	13,602,000,000
Nicaragua	0.8	580.5	8.3	1,997,000,000
Nigeria	0.6	144.5	7.9	—
Norway	9.3	22,999.9	11.8	2,712,000,000
Philippines	1.1	699.2	14.6	12,279,000,000
Poland	7.5	3,971.8	10.4	20,851,000,000
Russian Federation	11.9	6,602.7	5.3	9,0,000,000
Saudi Arabia	19.5	9,444.2	7.6	10,00,000
Slovak Republic	5.7	5,137.1	9.8	2,174,000,000
Slovenia	6.2	6,728.0	9.5	547,000,000
South Africa	9.0	4,198.4	4.8	4,763,000,000
Spain	5.0	5,356.0	13.7	68,948,000,000
Switzerland	4.3	7,520.2	20.2	2,853,000,000
Tajikistan	0.6	1,479.8	8.0	—
Turkey	4.5	2,854.6	15.2	16,511,000,000
Ukraine	5.0	3,418.6	3.5	1,706,000,000
United Kingdom	6.5	5,129.5	14.7	77,262,000,000
United States	16.5	12,984.3	7.9	317,421,000,000
Uruguay	2.0	3,068.0	15.2	3,902,000,000
Vietnam	1.8	1,410.9	—	181,000,000

Notes: Carbon dioxide emissions are those stemming from the burning of fossil fuels and the manufacture of cement. They include carbon dioxide produced during consumption of solid, liquid, and gas fuels and gas flaring.

Sources: World Bank Data.

Comparative table 4 Gender

Country	Life expectancy at birth (years), 2016		Literacy rate (%, age 15 and above, 2000–2017)		Gross intake ratio in first grade of primary education (% of relevant age group, 2015–2017, latest available)		Labour force participation rate female (% of female population ages 15–64)	Seats in national parliament (% female)	Ratio female/ male Income
	Female	Male	Female	Male	Female	Male	2018	2018	2018
Afghanistan	65.0	61.4	17.6	45.4	87.6	119.9	20.3	27.7	–
Albania	80.5	76.4	96.1	98.4	110.2	114.5	55.7	27.9	0.7
Algeria	77.3	74.9	67.5	82.6	100.9	102.4	16.9	25.8	0.6
Angola	64.4	58.7	67.5	80.0	118.8	–	76.3	30.5	0.6
Argentina	80.3	72.8	99.1	99.1	105.2	106.1	55.3	38.9	0.7
Azerbaijan	75.1	69.0	99.7	99.9	102.3	101.2	68.7	16.8	0.7
Belarus	79.0	68.9	99.5	99.8	97.6	98.6	74.7	34.5	0.7
Botswana	69.5	64.0	88.7	86.7	94.7	–	68.9	9.5	0.7
Brazil	79.1	71.9	92.3	91.7	–	–	59.7	10.7	0.7
Bulgaria	78.2	71.2	98.0	98.7	94.4	95.2	65.4	23.8	0.8
Cambodia	71.0	66.8	75.0	86.5	102.7	108.5	83.8	20.0	0.7
Canada	84.3	80.4	–	–	100.5	131.5	74.8	27.0	0.8
Chile	81.9	76.9	96.7	97.0	98.7	98.6	57.9	22.6	0.7
China	77.8	74.8	92.7	97.5	105.3	103.7	68.6	24.9	0.7
Colombia	78.0	70.9	94.9	94.4	106.1	111.9	64.2	18.1	0.7
Costa Rica	82.3	77.5	97.5	97.3	101.7	102.4	51.7	45.6	0.7
Croatia	81.3	74.9	98.7	99.6	95.8	94.4	61.6	18.5	0.7
Cuba	81.8	77.8	99.8	99.7	103.1	102.1	50.6	53.2	0.7
Cyprus	82.7	78.3	98.1	99.3	96.0	97.0	69.8	17.9	0.7
Denmark	82.6	78.9	–	–	96.9	96.7	77.3	37.4	0.8
Egypt, Arab Rep.	73.8	69.3	75.0	86.5	105.1	104.8	24.3	14.9	0.6
France	85.5	79.2	–	–	–	–	67.8	39.6	0.8
Germany	83.1	78.3	–	–	102.9	103.6	74.0	30.7	0.8
Greece	83.7	78.5	96.5	98.3	95.3	94.5	60.6	18.7	0.7
Hungary	79.0	72.3	99.1	99.2	97.0	96.9	64.3	12.6	0.7
India	70.2	67.1	59.3	78.9	105.7	102.2	28.5	11.8	0.7
Indonesia	71.4	67.2	93.6	97.2	98.6	103.7	52.9	19.8	0.7
Iran, Islamic Rep.	77.1	74.9	80.8	90.4	98.0	101.3	17.7	5.9	0.6
Israel	84.2	80.7	–	–	106.5	102.6	69.2	27.5	0.7
Italy	84.9	80.3	98.6	99.1	98.9	99.0	55.0	35.7	0.7
Japan	87.1	81.0	–	–	98.5	98.0	68.7	10.1	0.7
Kenya	69.4	64.6	74.0	83.8	–	97.4	63.0	21.8	0.7
Korea, Rep.	85.2	79.0	–	–	96.4	96.7	58.8	17.0	0.7
Latvia	79.6	69.7	99.9	99.9	98.6	98.3	74.5	16.0	0.8
Lebanon	81.4	78.0	88.1	94.3	102.5	108.1	26.1	4.7	0.6
Liechtenstein	84.5	80.9	–	–	104.9	104.1	–	12.0	–
Mexico	79.5	74.7	94.0	95.8	103.6	102.8	47.6	48.2	0.7
Moldova	75.9	67.3	98.9	99.4	93.9	91.0	44.9	22.8	0.7

Comparative table 4 Gender (*continued*)

Country	Life expectancy at birth (years), 2016		Literacy rate (%, age 15 and above, 2000–2017)		Gross intake ratio in first grade of primary education (% of relevant age group, 2015–2017, latest available)		Labour force participation rate female (% of female population ages 15–64)	Seats in national parliament (% female)	Ratio female/ male Income
	Female	Male	Female	Male	Female	Male	2018	2018	2018
Morocco	77.0	74.6	59.1	80.4	108.5	110.3	26.7	20.5	0.6
Netherlands	83.2	79.9	–	–	–	–	75.5	36.0	0.7
Nicaragua	78.4	72.3	77.9	78.1	–	–	53.8	45.7	0.8
Nigeria	54.2	52.7	41.4	61.3	–	–	50.4	5.6	0.6
Norway	84.2	80.9	–	–	101.5	101.3	76.0	41.4	0.8
Philippines	72.7	65.8	96.8	96.0	101.7	105.8	51.7	29.5	0.8
Poland	81.6	73.5	98.3	99.3	132.6	130.9	62.8	28.0	0.7
Russian Federation	76.9	66.5	99.6	99.7	109.6	106.4	69.0	15.8	0.7
Saudi Arabia	76.3	73.3	91.4	96.5	115.8	109.1	23.5	19.9	0.6
Slovak Republic	80.2	73.1	–	–	95.3	97.2	66.0	20.0	0.7
Slovenia	83.9	77.8	99.6	99.7	99.4	100.0	68.8	24.4	0.8
South Africa	66.4	59.2	93.4	95.4	94.2	96.7	52.4	42.3	0.8
Spain	85.7	80.1	97.7	98.8	96.3	96.8	69.3	39.1	0.7
Switzerland	85.1	80.8	–	–	99.2	97.9	79.8	32.5	0.8
Tajikistan	74.2	68.3	99.7	99.8	103.4	105.6	48.0	19.0	0.6
Turkey	79.0	72.5	93.6	98.8	90.0	91.3	36.1	17.4	0.6
Ukraine	76.5	66.7	100.0	100.0	–	–	60.5	12.3	0.7
United Kingdom	82.8	79.2	–	–	97.5	97.5	72.4	32.2	0.8
United States	81.2	76.3	–	–	103.9	101.8	66.1	19.6	0.7
Uruguay	80.9	73.9	99.0	98.2	96.1	95.3	68.9	20.2	0.7
Vietnam	80.9	71.5	91.4	95.8	115.4	113.5	79.4	26.7	0.7

Notes: Labour force participation rate is the proportion of the population aged between fifteen and sixty-four and older that is economically active: all people who supply labour for the production of good and services during a specified period.

Sources: World Bank Data; World Economic Forum (WEF) Global Gender Gap Report.

Comparative table 5 Globalization and democratization

Country	Freedom House ranking 2019	Corruption perception index	Overall globalization index (KOF)
	2019	2018	2016
Afghanistan	5.5	16	38.6
Albania	3.0	36	66.1
Algeria	5.5	35	55.9
Angola	5.5	19	41.8
Argentina	2.0	40	65.9
Azerbaijan	6.5	25	63.9
Belarus	6.5	44	68.6
Botswana	2.5	61	56.2
Brazil	2.0	35	59.2
Bulgaria	2.0	42	80.2
Cambodia	5.5	20	57.9
Canada	1.0	81	84.4
Chile	1.0	67	77.1
China	6.5	39	64.5
Colombia	3.0	36	64.4
Costa Rica	1.0	56	71.8
Croatia	1.5	48	80.9
Cuba	6.5	47	58.8
Cyprus	1.0	59	78.3
Denmark	1.0	88	89.1
Egypt, Arab Rep.	6.0	35	63.1
France	1.5	72	87.2
Germany	1.0	80	88.2
Greece	1.5	45	80.8
Hungary	3.0	46	85.1
India	2.5	41	61.2
Indonesia	3.0	38	63.0
Iran, Islamic Rep.	6.0	28	54.2
Israel	2.5	61	77.2
Italy	1.0	52	82.6
Japan	1.0	73	78.4
Kenya	4.0	27	55.2
Korea, Rep.	2.0	57	79.2
Latvia	2.0	58	79.9
Lebanon	4.5	28	68.2
Liechtenstein	1.5	–	54.4
Mexico	3.0	28	71.5
Moldova	3.5	33	69.0
Morocco	5.0	43	69.4

Comparative table 5 Globalization and democratization (*continued*)

Country	Freedom House ranking 2019	Corruption perception index	Overall globalization index (KOF)
	2019	2018	2016
Netherlands	1.0	82	91.0
Nicaragua	5.5	25	61.2
Nigeria	4.0	27	54.4
Norway	1.0	84	86.4
Philippines	3.0	36	67.0
Poland	2.0	60	81.2
Russian Federation	6.5	28	72.3
Saudi Arabia	7.0	49	65.5
Slovak Republic	1.5	50	82.9
Slovenia	1.0	60	81.3
South Africa	2.0	43	69.9
Spain	1.0	58	85.3
Switzerland	1.0	85	91.2
Tajikistan	6.5	25	46.4
Turkey	5.5	41	70.5
Ukraine	3.5	32	74.3
United Kingdom	1.0	80	89.4
United States	1.5	71	82.1
Uruguay	1.0	70	72.5
Vietnam	6.0	33	64.3

Notes: *Freedom in the World*, Freedom House's flagship publication, is the standard-setting comparative assessment of global political rights and civil liberties. Published annually since 1972, the survey ratings and narrative reports on 195 countries and fifteen related and disputed territories are used by policy makers, the media, international corporations, civic activists, and human rights defenders to monitor trends in democracy and track improvements and setbacks in freedom worldwide. The Freedom in the World data and reports are available in their entirety on the Freedom House website. The corruption perception index ranks countries and territories based on how corrupt their public sector is perceived to be. A country or territory's score indicates the perceived level of public sector corruption on a scale from 0 to 100, where 0 means that a country is perceived as highly corrupt and 100 means it is perceived as very clean. A country's rank indicates its position relative to the other countries and territories included in the index. The 2014 index includes 176 countries and territories.

The KOF index on globalization measures the three main dimensions of globalization: economic, social, and political. In addition to the three indices measuring these dimensions, an overall index of globalization refers to actual economic flows, economic restrictions, data on information flows, data on personal contact, and data on cultural proximity. Data are available on a yearly basis for 208 countries over the period 1970–2012.

Sources: Freedom House; Transparency International; KOF.

Comparative table 6 Trade

Country	Imports of goods and services (% of GDP)	Exports of goods and services (% of GDP)	High-technology exports (% of manufactured exports)	Manufactures exports (% of merchandise exports)
	2017	2017	2017	2017
Afghanistan	45.3	5.9	–	–
Albania	46.6	31.5	0.1	51.9
Algeria	33.5	22.6	0.5	4.3
Angola	23.3	29.0	–	–
Argentina	13.8	11.2	9.0	28.8
Azerbaijan	42.0	48.7	2.0	3.4
Belarus	67.1	67.0	3.8	54.0
Botswana	33.9	39.8	0.9	95.4
Brazil	11.6	12.6	12.3	37.6
Bulgaria	63.7	67.4	7.4	57.1
Cambodia	64.2	60.7	–	–
Canada	33.2	30.9	12.9	50.6
Chile	27.0	28.7	6.1	14.1
China	18.1	19.8	23.8	93.6
Colombia	19.7	14.6	8.7	21.5
Costa Rica	32.9	33.3	–	–
Croatia	48.8	51.1	7.5	66.9
Cuba	11.7	14.5	–	–
Cyprus	68.6	65.0	14.6	29.5
Denmark	48.2	55.2	11.6	68.6
Egypt, Arab Rep.	29.3	15.8	0.6	53.6
France	32.0	30.9	23.6	80.3
Germany	39.7	47.2	13.7	84.9
Greece	34.3	33.2	10.4	35.9
Hungary	82.3	90.1	13.8	86.7
India	22.0	19.1	7.0	70.7
Indonesia	19.2	20.4	5.4	43.6
Iran, Islamic Rep.	23.8	24.9	–	–
Israel	–	–	13.0	92.4
Italy	28.2	31.3	6.8	83.5
Japan	–	–	13.8	88.1
Kenya	24.1	13.2	3.2	28.4
Korea, Rep.	37.7	43.1	14.2	89.5
Latvia	61.8	60.5	16.6	61.7
Lebanon	43.9	23.9	–	–
Liechtenstein	–	–	–	–
Mexico	39.7	37.9	15.2	82.1
Moldova	–	–	5.2	34.0
Morocco	46.6	37.1	–	–
Netherlands	74.8	86.5	18.6	67.8
Nicaragua	55.4	41.2	0.5	45.8

Comparative table 6 Trade (*continued*)

Country	Imports of goods and services (% of GDP)	Exports of goods and services (% of GDP)	High-technology exports (% of manufactured exports)	Manufactures exports (% of merchandise exports)
	2017	2017	2017	2017
Nigeria	13.2	13.2	1.9	2.2
Norway	33.1	35.5	18.4	19.1
Philippines	40.9	31.0	57.7	82.6
Poland	50.3	54.3	7.7	80.0
Russian Federation	20.7	26.0	11.5	22.3
Saudi Arabia	28.6	34.8	–	–
Slovak Republic	92.9	96.3	10.9	88.8
Slovenia	72.6	82.2	6.2	84.7
South Africa	28.4	29.8	4.6	47.2
Spain	31.4	34.1	7.1	69.4
Switzerland	53.9	65.0	11.4	91.7
Tajikistan	41.0	15.8	–	–
Turkey	29.3	24.8	2.5	80.2
Ukraine	55.6	48.0	5.0	46.7
United Kingdom	31.9	30.5	21.1	76.7
United States	–	–	13.8	61.9
Uruguay	18.4	21.6	7.4	20.2
Vietnam	98.8	101.6	–	–

Notes: Imports of goods and services represent the value of all goods and other market services received from the rest of the world. They include the value of merchandise, freight, insurance, transport, travel, royalties, license fees, and other services, such as communication, construction, financial, information, business, personal, and government services. They exclude compensation of employees and investment income (formerly called factor services) and transfer payments.

Exports of goods and services represent the value of all goods and other market services provided to the rest of the world. They include the value of merchandise, freight, insurance, transport, travel, royalties, license fees, and other services, such as communication, construction, financial, information, business, personal, and government services. They exclude compensation of employees and investment income (formerly called factor services) and transfer payments.

High-technology exports are products with high R&D intensity, such as in aerospace, computers, pharmaceuticals, scientific instruments, and electrical machinery.

Source: World Bank Data.

Comparative table 7 Migration

Country	Net migration rate (migrants per 1,000 population)	Refugees, country of asylum	Refugees, country of origin
	2017 (estimations)	2017	2017
Afghanistan	-0.9	75,927	2,624,225
Albania	-3.3	89	12,163
Algeria	-0.9	94,243	3,991
Angola	0.2	41,109	8,267
Argentina	-0.1	3,287	111
Azerbaijan	0.0	1,115	10,878
Belarus	0.7	2,145	3,635
Botswana	3.0	2,106	279
Brazil	-0.1	10,230	836
Bulgaria	-0.3	19,141	716
Cambodia	-0.3	61	12,213
Canada	5.7	104,748	75
Chile	0.3	1,841	483
China	-0.4	321,699	207,691
Colombia	-0.6	240	191,607
Costa Rica	0.8	4,464	190
Croatia	-1.7	448	24,859
Cuba	-4.9	338	5,316
Cyprus	8.7	9,745	–
Denmark	2.1	35,593	–
Egypt, Arab Rep.	-0.5	232,617	22,056
France	1.1	337,143	49
Germany	1.5	970,302	66
Greece	2.3	38,948	101
Hungary	1.3	5,641	3,331
India	0.0	197,122	7,891
Indonesia	-1.1	9,777	12,480
Iran, Islamic Rep.	-0.2	979,435	118,595
Israel	2.2	25,637	459
Italy	3.7	167,260	47
Japan	0.0	2,189	44
Kenya	-0.2	431,880	7,547
Korea, Rep.	2.5	2,203	234
Latvia	-6.1	638	157
Lebanon	-20.3	1,468,137	5,287
Liechtenstein	5.0	154	–
Mexico	-1.8	8,963	11,659
Moldova	-9.4	371	2,314
Morocco	-3.2	4,678	3,064

Comparative table 7 Migration (*continued*)

Country	Net migration rate (migrants per 1,000 population)	Refugees, country of asylum	Refugees, country of origin
	2017 (estimations)	2017	2017
Netherlands	1.9	103,818	34
Nicaragua	-2.7	322	1,467
Nigeria	-0.2	1,900	238,942
Norway	5.9	59,160	–
Philippines	-2.0	482	433
Poland	-0.4	12,190	1,108
Russian Federation	1.7	125,986	61,569
Saudi Arabia	-0.5	148	1,169
Slovak Republic	0.1	887	913
Slovenia	0.4	591	7
South Africa	-0.9	88,694	446
Spain	7.8	17,526	34
Switzerland	4.7	92,995	–
Tajikistan	-1.1	2,516	1,354
Turkey	-4.5	3,480,310	61,338
Ukraine	0.0	3,211	139,561
United Kingdom	2.5	121,766	85
United States	3.9	287,065	285
Uruguay	-0.9	304	7
Vietnam	-0.3	–	334,044

Notes: Net migration rate is the difference between the number of persons entering and leaving the country during the year per 1,000 persons (based on mid-year population). An excess of persons entering the country is referred to as net immigration (e.g. 3.56 migrants/ 1,000 population); an excess of persons leaving the country is referred to as net emigration (e.g. -9.26 migrants/1,000 population). The net migration rate indicates the contribution of migration to the overall level of population change. The net migration rate does not distinguish between economic migrants, refugees, and other types of migrants, nor does it distinguish between lawful migrants and undocumented migrants.

Sources: CIA *World Factbook*; World Bank Data.

Appendix 3

World trends

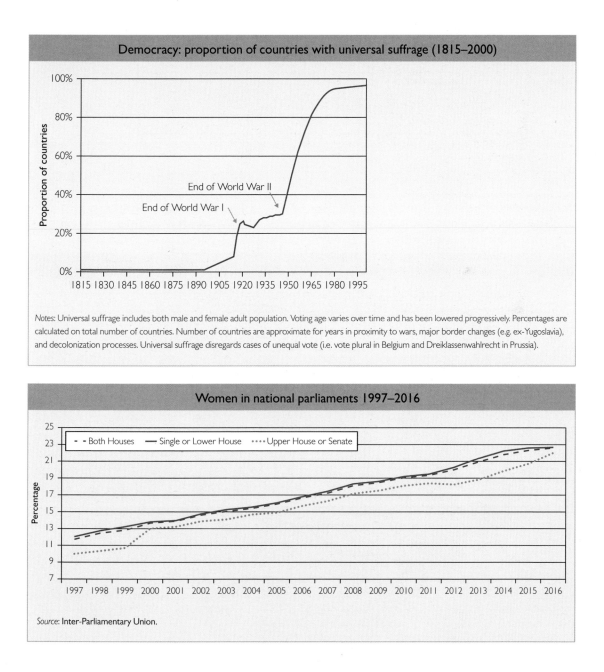

Democracy: proportion of countries with universal suffrage (1815–2000)

End of World War II

End of World War I

Notes: Universal suffrage includes both male and female adult population. Voting age varies over time and has been lowered progressively. Percentages are calculated on total number of countries. Number of countries are approximate for years in proximity to wars, major border changes (e.g. ex-Yugoslavia), and decolonization processes. Universal suffrage disregards cases of unequal vote (i.e. vote plural in Belgium and Dreiklassenwahlrecht in Prussia).

Women in national parliaments 1997–2016

- - - Both Houses ——— Single or Lower House ······ Upper House or Senate

Source: Inter-Parliamentary Union.

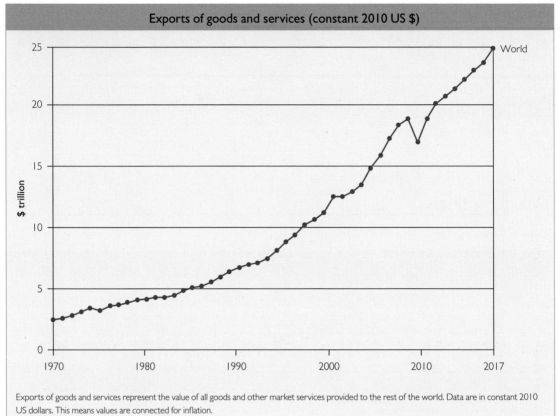

Exports of goods and services represent the value of all goods and other market services provided to the rest of the world. Data are in constant 2010 US dollars. This means values are connected for inflation.
Source: World Bank.

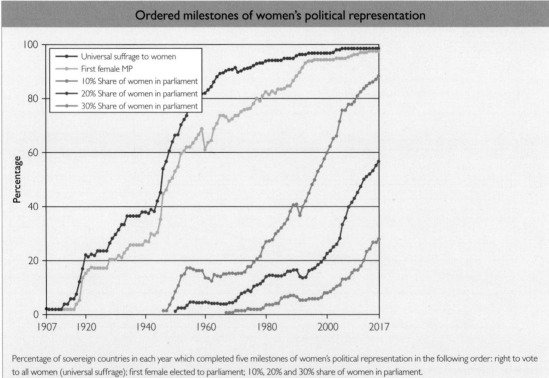

Percentage of sovereign countries in each year which completed five milestones of women's political representation in the following order: right to vote to all women (universal suffrage); first female elected to parliament; 10%, 20% and 30% share of women in parliament.
Source: OWID Women's Political Representation using Paxton et al. (2006), OPU & WDI (2017).
http://archive.ipu.org

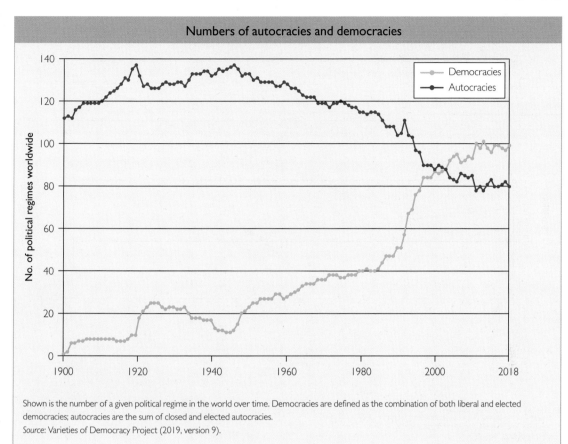

Numbers of autocracies and democracies

Shown is the number of a given political regime in the world over time. Democracies are defined as the combination of both liberal and elected democracies; autocracies are the sum of closed and elected autocracies.
Source: Varieties of Democracy Project (2019, version 9).

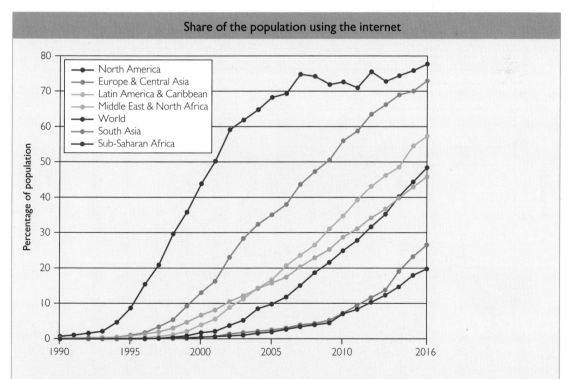

Share of the population using the internet

All individuals who have used the internet in the past three months are counted as internet users. The internet can be used via a computer, mobile phone, personal digital assistant, game machine, digital TV, etc.
Source: World Bank.

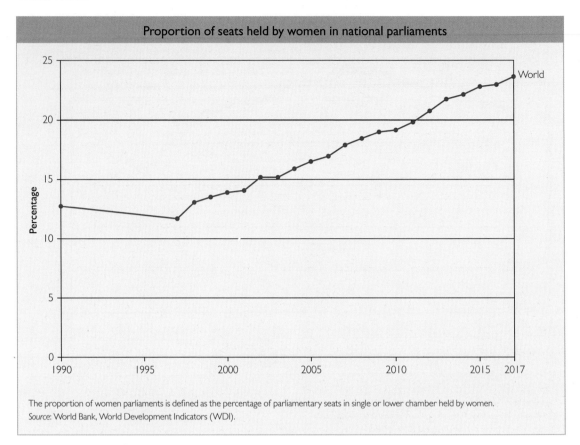

Proportion of seats held by women in national parliaments

The proportion of women parliaments is defined as the percentage of parliamentary seats in single or lower chamber held by women.
Source: World Bank, World Development Indicators (WDI).

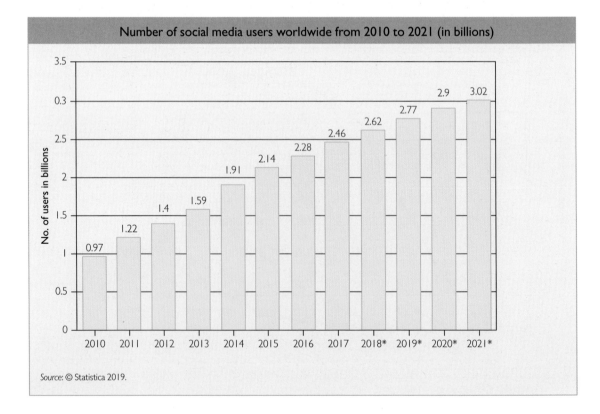

Number of social media users worldwide from 2010 to 2021 (in billions)

Source: © Statistica 2019.

Annual CO₂ emissions

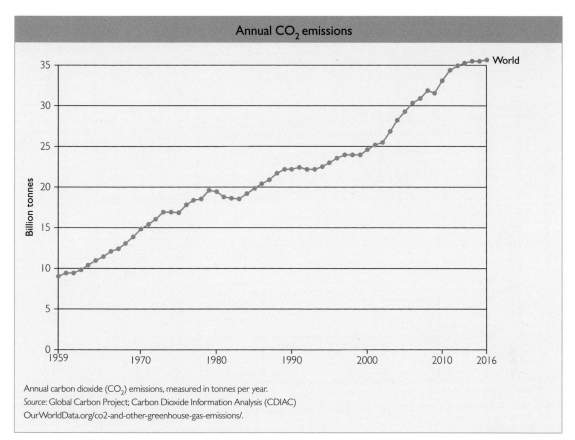

Annual carbon dioxide (CO₂) emissions, measured in tonnes per year.

Source: Global Carbon Project; Carbon Dioxide Information Analysis (CDIAC)

OurWorldData.org/co2-and-other-greenhouse-gas-emissions/.

Battle-related deaths in state-based conflicts since 1946

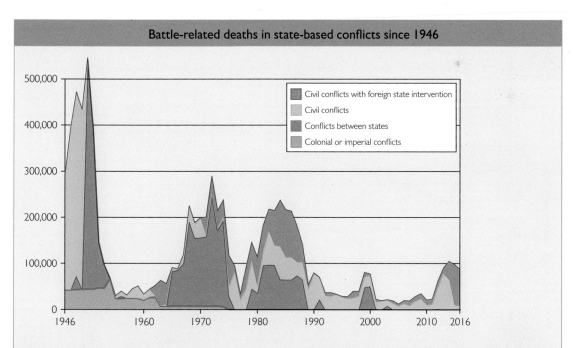

Only conflicts in which at lest one party was the government of a state and which generated more than twenty-five battle-related deaths are included. The data refer to direct violent deaths. Deaths due to disease or famine caused by conflict are excluded. Extra-judicial killings in custody are also excluded.

Note: The war categories paraphrase UCDP/PRIO'S technical definitions of 'Extrasystemic', 'Internal', 'Internationalised internal' and 'Interstate', respectively. In a small number of cases where wars were wars were ascribed more than one type, death have been apportioned evenly to each type.

Source: Uppsala Conflict Data Program/Peace Research Institute, Oslo (UCDP/PRIO).

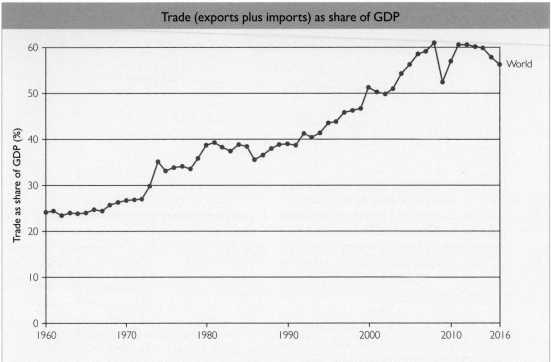

Trade (exports plus imports) as share of GDP

Figures correspond to the 'trade openness index': the sum of exports and imports of goods and services, divided by gross domestic product.
Source: World Bank.

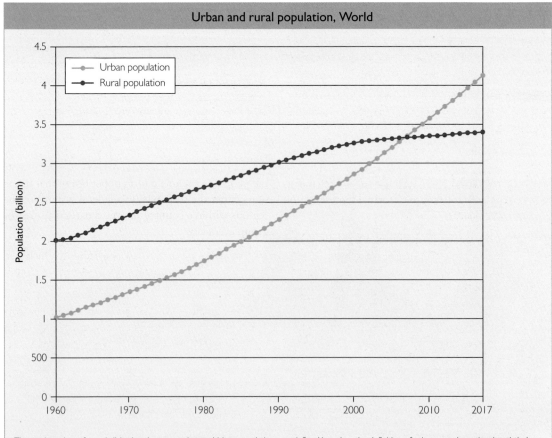

Urban and rural population, World

The total number of people living in urban or rural areas. Urban populations are defined based on the definition of urban areas by national statistical offices.
Source: World Bank, based on UN estimates.

Glossary

Abstract review Refers to a procedure of constitutional review in the absence of a concrete judicial case and before the law has been enforced. Also called 'preventive review', since it allows the system to filter out unconstitutional laws before they can harm people.

Active democracy support Support action resting on intentionality.

Advanced capitalist democracies Political and economic systems that combine a highly developed (industrial/post-industrial) economy with a democratic political system.

Agenda setting Processes through which attention is directed towards a particular public problem.

Agents In the context of political science, institutions, or persons to whom power is delegated. Trustees are a particular kind of agent possessing the power to govern those who have delegated in the first place.

American judicial review A model of judicial constitutional review carried out by all types of courts (decentralized) expected to be fundamentally concrete.

Ancillary organization An organization such as a trade union or women's club that is formally affiliated with a political party through such mechanisms as overlapping memberships or formal representation on governing boards.

Assembly Any group or gathering of people drawn together for a common purpose or reason. Assemblies can be of numerous types including religious, educational, social, or political, based on the character of their objectives and the subject of their activities.

Asymmetric chambers A bicameral system in which the two legislative chambers are not equal in power. In most cases in the modern era the lower chamber (representing the people as a whole) is the more powerful.

Asymmetric regionalism The uneven or imbalanced distribution of powers, responsibilities, and/or revenues between regional governments within that state. This often occurs in states with politicized ethno-territorial minorities or minority nations that consistently demand a range of powers and responsibilities which differs from those exercised by other regional governments populated by members of the ethno-linguistic majority.

Audience democracy Term coined by Bernard Manin (1997) to indicate a contemporary form of democracy in which citizens are not actively engaged in the process but view their political leaders as if they were performing on a distant stage.

Ballot access The requirements (such as support of electors as expressed through signatures, or a financial deposit) that must be met before a party or candidate is allowed to stand for election.

Behavioural revolution Important turn in the 1940s–50s, when empirical political theories replaced normative theories. Data were collected by means of surveys and analysed by statistical and computerized instruments. Linked to the structural–functional paradigm, with broad concepts applicable to a large number of diverse cases.

Bicameral legislature A legislature that consists of two chambers, with a lower chamber that represents the people as a whole and an upper house that represents either the sub-units (in a federal system) or the regions within a country, or even a particular class or group in society.

Bipolar party systems A party system in which two large and equally balanced stable coalitions of parties run for elections and alternate in government.

Cabinet government Collective and collegial government, with all important decisions to be made by the full cabinet and the prime minister acting as first among equals.

Cadre (elite) party A form of party with little formal organization that is primarily an alliance of politicians and their patrons (or clients) to coordinate activities within government.

Capital accumulation Dynamic process that underlies economic growth and the transformation of the production process within a capitalist economy. This occurs because the competitive business units within capitalism must 'accumulate' in order to survive, forcing them to reinvest a portion of the economic surplus produced by their workers to keep up with the new efficiencies and technological breakthroughs being made by other firms in the national and global economy.

Catch-all party A form of party characterized by appeals, for both votes and material support, that cross cleavage lines and by a shedding of the 'ideological baggage' associated with the mass party model.

Centralization The policy undertaken by a political entity in order to restrict and eliminate the extent to which other, peripheral, regional entities seek to preserve their traditional entitlements, and thus limit its own initiative and its own disposition over political practices and resources.

Central–local relations The way in which relations between central and local governments are organized. These differ in different types of state (federal/unitary) and in different state traditions (Anglo-Saxon, French, Scandinavian). Today, local authorities are less constrained by central governments and are given greater freedom over policy choices and forms of organization.

Centrifugal and centripetal competition Alternative dynamics of competition with parties either distancing themselves from the centre of the left–right axis towards the extremes or converging towards the centre and increasingly resembling each other.

Christian democracy Political movement that is inspired by the Christian faith and has as its main goal the provision of order in society by promoting a harmonious relationship between all classes and layers of society.

Citizenship Historically variable set of rights and obligations which, in the course of modernization, individuals come to possess vis-à-vis the state.

Civic culture Type of political culture that emphasizes social activism, participation in networks of free associations, democracy, and a vibrant civil society.

Clash of civilizations Theory stating that cultural, ethnic, and religious differences have replaced the ideological division of the Cold War as the primary source of international conflict.

Classification Process and result of grouping cases by minimizing differences within each class and maximizing differences between classes, according to a dimension or property. Classes are mutually exclusive and jointly exhaustive.

Cleavage A division of interest and values within a polity, opposing groups structurally, culturally, and organizationally.

Co-decision procedure The main legislative procedure of the EU under which the Commission makes legislative proposals, and legislation must be passed by a majority of MEPs and a qualified-majority vote in the Council.

Collective action Type of action in which more than one individual is required to contribute to an effort in order to pursue a goal or achieve an outcome.

Collective action paradox Mancur Olson's (1965) argument that under certain conditions it is not rational for individuals to join interest groups, as they can enjoy the benefits that stem from the group's existence without having to pay the cost to create or maintain the organization (i.e. they can free-ride).

Comparative method Method for testing against empirical evidence alternative hypotheses (and thereby either corroborate or reject them) about necessary and sufficient conditions for events to occur based on the association between configurations of values of different independent variables across cases, and the values of the dependent variable.

Comparison The inquiry of similarities and differences. It is a tool for building empirically falsifiable explanatory theories. In the course of scientific development, systematic and inductive comparison has replaced anecdotal and deductive approaches.

Competitive authoritarianism A term most notably used by Steven Levinsky and Lucan Way to describe a hybrid regime that holds elections but where the incumbent has an enormous advantage. Though the elections are free of massive fraud, the regime represses civil liberties and the executive does not face checks and balances from other branches of government.

Conceptual stretching Distortion occurring when a concept developed for one set of cases is extended to additional cases to which the features of the concept do not apply.

Concrete review When an ordinary judge refers, within a specific litigation, to a constitutional question.

Congress General term for a legislative assembly within a separation-of-powers political system.

Congresses can consist of one chamber or two; if bicameral, they may be symmetrical or asymmetrical.

Consensus democracy Form of democracy in which the emphasis is placed on the inclusion of all social groups at all stages in the decision-making process and in which the most widespread possible agreement is sought for public policies and programmes.

Consociationalism A mode of governing in which political elites representing different communities coalesce around the need to govern, even in the face of intense divisions across their communities.

Constituency The unit, usually defined territorially, into which the country is divided for electoral purposes and from which MPs are returned. Single-member constituencies return just one MP, whereas multimember constituencies return several MPs.

Constitution Statute in which the fundamental political institutions, procedures, and principles of a state are established and in which the basic rights are guaranteed.

Constitutionalism Refers on the one hand to the commitment of a political community to accept the legitimacy of constitutional rules and principles and, on the other hand, to an understanding of government that is derivable from a specific constitutional order. Typical examples are federalism and checks and balances.

Constructive vote of no confidence A constructive vote of no confidence requires that there be a majority in support of an alternative government (single party of coalition). This increases the difficulty of removing a government from office as there must be a majority support for an alternative, not just a majority opposed to current government.

Constructivism Basic assumption that social realities are not primordially given but constructed in the course of history.

Control Process through which the influence of some variables on the relationship between operational (independent and dependent) variables is reduced or entirely eliminated (*ceteris paribus* clause).

Conventional and unconventional participation Conventional participation is expressed within accepted institutional channels. Unconventional participation takes place through activities that range from public events to direct physical attacks on property or people.

Corporatism Institutionalized patterns of linkage between social interests and the state, focusing especially on the legitimate role of social interests in influencing policy.

Coup Literally, a blow by/of the state, but typically an attack by the military arm of the state against its own government and aimed at seizing power, whether as a 'corporate' coup by the military as a united corporate body or as a 'factional' coup by part of the military.

Decentralization A process whereby power is transferred from the central level of government and/or administration to other levels.

Democracy assistance Concessionary and largely consensual provision of support for democracy and democratization from a state or international organization by way of projects and programmes.

Democracy support Attempts to influence democratization by a variety of methods and approaches that can include linkage and leverage and various measures of soft and hard power.

Democratic deficit The notion that the EU institutions are not as democratically accountable as national institutions. Common allegations associated with the democratic deficit are that the European Commission is appointed rather than elected, that Council decision-making is not as transparent as it could be, and that national parliaments cannot control their governments when they do business in Brussels.

Democratic disguise The disguise that an authoritarian regime uses to hide the fact that it is a non-democratic regime—a disguise that now typically involves the use of semi-competitive multiparty elections.

Democratic peace thesis Statement that democracies tend not to go to war with one another.

Democratization The process by which non-democratic institutions or polities become democratic.

Descriptive analysis Type of analysis aimed at establishing empirical patterns: the degree to which phenomena occur, variations between cases, and changes over time.

Devolution Process by which political, administrative, and/or judicial powers are transferred from central state authorities to regional authorities. Whereas decentralization or deconcentration results in no diminution of central state authority, devolution does involve a reduction of power and authority for the centre and more political autonomy for the region.

Digital communication The transmission of digital data through independent new sources that rival mainstream media channels.

Direct support of democracy Action employing political methods and engaging with political institutions.

Disguised military rule The military's rule can be disguised either by civilizing the regime or by ruling indirectly through behind-the-scenes influence upon a puppet civilian government.

District magnitude The number of MPs returned per constituency.

Divided government Configuration of power in which at least one of the chambers of the legislature is controlled by a party that does not hold the presidency.

Economic development The process by which low-income economies transit into wealthy economies with high living standards. Traditionally seen as the transition between agriculture-based and industry-based economics, economic development was conventionally measured through national per capita income. In recent decades, broader definitions of development emphasize economic well-being, the improvement in the quality of life, and human capabilities.

Electoral authoritarianism A type of hybrid regime that holds elections, but where the outcomes largely favour the incumbent. With the exception of holding elections, the regime is otherwise authoritarian.

Electoral market Hypothetical space where political parties present programmes and policies (offer) and voters choose on the basis of their preferences (demand), with the former aiming at maximizing votes and the latter aiming at maximizing utility deriving from specific policies.

Electoral system The set of rules that structure how votes are cast at elections and how these votes are then converted into the allocation of offices/seats.

Empirical research Type of research based on evidence from the real world and disjoined from any type of moral, normative, or value judgement.

Equivalence Feature of concepts and properties whose connotation is similar for all the cases compared.

European model of constitutional review A model of judicial constitutional review carried out by constitutional courts (centralized 'Kelsenian' courts) which are allowed to be abstract.

Evaluation (of policy) Procedure asking whether the output of a given public policy has attained the intended goals.

Explanatory analysis Type of analysis that relates two or more variables (phenomena) with the aim of formulating general causal statements about their relationship. Also referred to as multivariate analysis.

Extension (or denotation) Set (or class) of cases to which a concept refers.

External (extra-parliamentary) origin (of parties) Parties of external origin founded outside government in order to contest elections and thereby first make demands on government and ultimately elect officials from among their own ranks.

Federal state State where sovereignty is shared across several levels of government and in which one level may not intervene in defined areas of competence of the other. There are different kinds of federal state (e.g. dual federalism in the US and cooperative federalism in Germany).

Flexicurity Combination of flexibility and social protection. In a narrow version, this refers to the combination of liberal employment protection, generous social protection, and active labour-market policies. In a broader version, it refers to a multitude of combinations between different modes of flexibility and security.

Fractionalization Degree of fragmentation in a party system. The higher the number of parties, the higher the fragmentation in a party system.

Free-rider problem A problem faced when public non-excludable goods are provided. Free-riders are individuals who consume a good, but let others pay for its production.

Freezing hypothesis Consolidation of party alternatives and electoral alignments from the 1920s until the 1970s due to the saturation of the electoral market caused by full franchise and proportional representation electoral systems.

Functionalism The functionalist approach aimed at identifying the necessary activities (functions) of all political systems and then comparing the manner in which these functions were performed. This theoretical paradigm, coupled with structuralism and systems theory, aimed to bridge diverse empirical contexts but it was built on assumptions that turned out to be closely related to the Western democratic model.

Fused-powers system Regime in which the executive is selected by the legislature, usually from those within the legislature, and is dependent upon the 'confidence' of the legislature to remain in power. In many cases, the executive may also dissolve the legislature by calling for new elections.

Generalizations Law-like statements about relationships between social and political phenomena independent of the specific spatial or temporal context.

Ghent system A system of voluntary unemployment insurance which is administered by trade unions. The name of the system comes from the Belgian town Ghent, where it was first introduced.

Global economy, globalization Terms that refer to the increasing interdependencies between national economies that challenge existing domestic social policy arrangements.

Good governance A commonly used term in the development discourse which, in its most expansive meaning, embraces inclusive and participatory democracy, and at a minimum is used to denote freedom from corruption.

Governance Approach in comparative politics interested in the roles that social actors may play in the process of making and implementing governmental decisions.

Hard power A country's military and economic might.

Human development index The United Nations Development Programme's human development index is a summary measure comprising life expectancy, adult literacy rate, and a decent standard of living measured in income per capita terms. It falls short of the definition provided.

Hybrid regimes Regimes that are somewhat authoritarian but have elements of democracy, such as relatively free elections. A number of categories can be referred to as hybrid regimes, such as competitive regimes and electoral authoritarian regimes.

Implementation The conversion of new laws and programmes into practice.

Incomplete contract Contract allowing for uncertainty as to the precise nature of commitments (e.g. the rights and obligations of the parties under the contract).

Indirect support of democracy Action focusing on conditions or preconditions for democratization that may be described as non-political (e.g. economic variables).

Initiative (popular) Referendum held at the behest of a prescribed number of ordinary citizens.

Institutional competitiveness The fact that different regimes develop different comparative advantages. There is not a single road to competitiveness (or to employment), but different strategies that fit into different institutional contexts.

Institutional complementarity Clusters or configurations of (policy) institutions that are mutually supportive (for instance, combinations of various welfare arrangements or combinations of regulation of the economy).

Institutionalism Set of approaches focusing on the central role of structures in shaping politics and individual behaviour. As well as formal institutional patterns, institutions may be defined in terms of their rules and their routines, and thus emphasize the normative structure of the institutions.

Institutions Formal rules of political decision-making and less formal standard operating procedures. These serve to reduce complexities inherent in the policy-making process, shaping the behaviour of actors and the use of policy instruments.

Intention (or connotation) Set of properties shared by cases to which a concept applies.

Inter-governmentalism One of the two main modes of EU decision-making. Key features of inter-governmentalism are that decisions are reached by unanimous agreement between the EU governments, the European Parliament plays a consultative rather than a legislative role, and the European Court of Justice does not have full judicial review power.

Internal (inter-parliamentary) origin (of parties) Parties of internal origin were originally organized within parliament to coordinate the activities of their members (MPs) in pursuing legislative goals and supporting or opposing cabinets.

International leverage Vulnerability of authoritarian governments to external democratizing pressure. Three important determinants are the state's raw size and military and economic strength, the existence of competing issues on Western foreign policy agendas, and access to support from an alternative regional power.

International linkage Concept composed of five dimensions: economic, geopolitical, social, communication, and transnational civil society. Linkage raises the cost of authoritarianism.

Internationalization (of policies) Describes the processes of policy diffusion, policy transfer, and cross-national policy convergence.

Iron law of oligarchy 'Who says organization, says oligarchy.' The fact of organization leads all parties, including those that proclaim themselves to be democratic, to be dominated by their leaders.

Iron triangle Depiction of the role of interest groups in policy-making. Within a given issue area, a subsystem consisting of a key bureaucrat, a key legislator, and a key interest group would form and set the contours of governmental policy, allowing for little input from outside this group of three.

Judicial review See **American judicial review**.

Judicialization of politics Process through which the influence of courts on legislative and administrative power develops over time.

Junta Spanish term for a council or committee which is used by political scientists to describe the political committee of military leaders that is formed during a coup to represent the military in its new role as a ruling organization.

Labour movement Social movement that began during the industrial revolution, fighting for better working conditions and higher living standards for industrial workers. For this purpose, it was organized in labour and trade unions.

Ladder of generality Representation of the relation between intension and extension obeying a law of inverse variation. The larger the extension (and the smaller the intension), the higher the level of abstraction of a concept.

Legislature A kind of assembly in which individuals and/or groups are gathered together for explicitly political purposes. At least one of the political goals of a legislature will entail policy-making or legislating.

Liberalism A complex of political values and principles which, through varied constitutional arrangements, seeks to lay relatively narrow boundaries on the activities of the state, committing them first and foremost to respecting and fostering the autonomy of private individuals in their capacity as economic actors.

List systems The most common method of implementing the principle of proportional representation; voters choose between lists of candidates presented by different parties.

Majoritarian democracy Form of democracy in which the emphasis is placed on one side winning an outright (if also temporary) victory over the other, and in which success at the polls offers political control over all the key institutions.

Majority (system) government The parties represented in government hold at least 50 per cent of the seats plus one in parliament.

Mass party (of integration) A party form characterized by the formal dominance of the extra-governmental membership organization, and a strategy of mobilization and encapsulation aimed at a well-defined social constituency (the *classe gardée*).

Media system The social and technological systems through which information is created, gathered, processed, and disseminated.

Merit system Access to the administration is not restricted to particular segments of society; selection and promotion aim at appointing the best-qualified individuals.

Method of Agreement Logic of comparison of cases with similar values on as many variables as possible in order to account for the variation in the dependent variable through the association with independent variables that also vary.

Method of Difference Logic of comparison with cases with different values on as many variables as possible in order to account for the invariance in the dependent variable through the association with invariant independent variables.

Ministerial government Type of government in which decision-making power is dispersed among the individual cabinet members ('fragmented government').

Minority government Type of government in which the parties represented in government hold less than 50 per cent of the seats plus one.

Minority nations Cultural minority groups deprived of their own state (or stateless nations) within a country in which another group is majoritarian and with whom they share the state institutions.

Misappropriation of power (by a party) Usurpation arising when (1) a democratic election victory gives a party access to the key public offices; and then (2) the party misappropriates its newly acquired public offices by misusing public powers to ensure that it cannot be defeated in any future elections.

Mixed system Electoral system in which some MPs are returned by plurality or majority from local (usually single-member) constituencies and others by proportional representation from national or regional lists (usually multimember).

Mobilization Attempts by political entrepreneurs (in parties, interest groups, and social movements) to encourage political participation of others.

Most Different Systems Design Research design in which the cases selected are characterized by different values on a large number of independent variables.

Most Similar Systems Design Research design in which the cases selected are characterized by similar values on a large number of independent variables.

Multinational state Type of country comprised of a populace that has two or more ethnically differentiated, culturally distinct, and territorially concentrated political communities that have historical claims to nationhood.

Multiparty systems A party system in which many parties exist, with at most only one party approaching the absolute majority of seats, and therefore they need to form coalitions to support a government that is negotiated after the elections.

Nation A political community may be considered a nation when it is unified not only by the shared subjection to a system of rule but also by a complex and historically variable set of social and cultural bonds of diverse nature (commonalities of ethnic origins, language, religion, customs, historical experience, political values) which generate among individuals a significant feeling of affinity and distinctiveness.

National and industrial 'revolutions' Concepts indicating broad political changes in the nineteenth century in politics (formation of nation-states and the democratization and secularization of political systems) and in economy (industrialization and urbanization, and the emergence of a working class).

Nationalism An ideology and political movement based on the nation-state principle in which those who consider themselves to be members of a nation seek to obtain an independent state. A distinction may be made between 'majoritarian nationalism', which refers to established nation-states such as France or Germany, and 'minority nationalism', which refers to stateless nations such as Scotland or Catalonia.

Nation-building Sometimes conflated with state-building, refers to attempts to bring a common sense of national belonging and solidarity to plural communities who reside in the same state.

Nation-state A form of political organization, first advocated during the French Revolution, which links together 'state' and 'nation', whereby each nation should have a single state and each state should correspond to a nation.

Neo-institutionalism Theory that puts forward the role of institutions and norms. Institutions are sets of rules and structures that shape individual behaviour. Other types of institutionalism stress the incentives that institutions set for individual behaviour. In a historical perspective, institutions persist over time and determine future choices (path dependence).

Neoliberalism School of thought that promotes private property rights and free-market capitalism through the deregulation of business activities, the limitation of workers' collective bargaining rights, the retrenchment of the welfare state, and the privatization of public utilities.

Networks Corporatist patterns of linkage between social interests and the state are being replaced by more loosely defined relationships such as networks.

New constitutionalism New model of democratic state legitimacy, based on the following three elements: a written constitution, a charter of rights, and a judicial review mechanism.

New Public Management The application of market mechanisms in the public sector: fixed-term contracts, 'internal markets' and competition, encouragement of managerialism and entrepreneurship, and performance-related contracts.

New social movements Social movements since the mid-1960s which departed from the 'old' labour movement. These movements include the ecology, peace, solidarity, women's rights, human rights, and squatters' movements, as well as various other movements mobilizing for the rights of discriminated minorities (such as the gay movement).

One-party rule This arises when a political party rules dictatorially as some form of open or disguised one-party state and operates a communist, fascist, or Third World type of one-party rule.

Open military rule The open form of military rule occurs when the military seizure of power leads to military officers openly taking over the governing of the country, such as by establishing a junta or appointing one of themselves as president or prime minister.

Operationalization The process by which researchers quantify variables into measurable factors.

Outside lobbying Refers to more recent techniques, such as grass-roots campaigns, in which elites attempt to use mass memberships or the public more broadly to influence key political players.

Over-determination Insufficient number of cases to test for all potentially relevant independent variables (low degree of freedom).

Over-representation The share of the seats that a party wins over and above its share of the votes.

Over/under-representation Distortion between the proportion of votes parties receive and the proportion of seats they are allocated, caused by different types of electoral systems. Through over-representation, large parties receive a share of seats that is larger than their share of votes, and through under-representation, small parties receive a share of seats that is smaller than their share of votes.

Paradigm Dominant mainstream approach, including a set of assumptions and possible research questions. Of the evolutionary stages of comparative politics, only the dominance of the 'behavioural revolution' came close to Kuhn's idea of a paradigm change.

Parliament A legislative assembly within a fused-powers system. Parliaments can consist of one chamber or two; if bicameral, they may be symmetrical or asymmetrical.

Parliamentary systems Regimes in which the executive is not directly elected by the citizens, but is placed in office and held accountable to parliament, which is directly elected.

Party government Regime in which the actions of office-holders are determined by values and policies derived from their party.

Party system Set of political parties within a democratic system competing with each other for the largest share of the electoral vote, with the aim of winning elections and controlling government.

Passive democracy support Type of democratization influenced by external and international forces which do not have democratic outcomes as their aim.

Path dependence Concept originally developed in institutional economics, referring to the large political, as well as practical, costs of changing policy. In addition to this strict notion of path dependence as a theory, with emphasis on mechanisms, one also finds 'softer' versions that apply path dependence as a perspective.

Patrimonialist Type of regime whose legitimacy is based on the distribution of goods by a leader or group to large segments of the population (typical of pre-modern societies or developing countries).

Personal dictatorship The leader of a military or party that has seized or misappropriated power, but instead of acting as its representative has established a personal dictatorship.

Pluralism A school of thought that argues that groups within society form to influence government through a process of competition. Individuals themselves are believed to belong to multiple and competing groups, thus further ensuring the stability of the system.

Plurality–majority system This is a voting system in which a candidate needs more votes than any other single opponent in order to win a constituency seat in parliament.

Policy adoption The formal acceptance of a policy.

Policy feedback Concept covering feedback effects from output and outcomes of policies to new input to policies. It includes path dependence, policy learning, policy diffusion, and changing power relations between political actors.

Policy formulation The definition, discussion, acceptance, or rejection of feasible courses of action for coping with policy problems.

Policy learning A 'change in thinking' about a specific policy issue.

Policy paradigms Overall worldview underlying policies. The notion of paradigm is borrowed from the study of revolutions in the worldview of natural sciences (e.g. from a geocentric to a heliocentric paradigm). Policy paradigms provide particular problem definitions and, to a large extent, solutions.

Political action committees (PACs) are vehicles formed by entities such as corporations and unions that bundle contributions from their employees or members and then distribute them to politicians running for office in the US. These PACs are necessary because corporations and unions are not legally allowed to contribute directly to candidates.

Political conditionality Attachment of democracy, human rights, and governance conditions to offers of assistance to development. Certain political conditions may also be applied to membership entitlement to inter-governmental organizations such as the European Union and the Organization of American States.

Political culture The orientation of the citizens of a nation towards politics, and their perceptions of political legitimacy and the traditions of political practice. Set of values, attitudes, and beliefs related to state authority and the political system.

Political entrepreneurs Individuals who instigate collective action without receiving selective benefits, but often induce others with such benefits to participate in the mobilization.

Political opportunity structures The degree to which social movements have access to the political system.

Political process approach Approach that interprets social movements as a form of mass politics. The chances of the movement achieving success are discussed in terms of the 'opportunities' that are available.

Politics, policy, polity Politics is the struggle for power within a system of rules, institutions, and norms (polity) to be exercised (policies) in order to achieve given outcomes.

Polyarchy Term developed primarily by Robert Dahl (1971) to indicate a system of government that is the closest that real existing polities come to democracy. Polyarchies offer inclusive participatory rights to citizens and also guarantee full and fair competition between alternative groups and leaders.

Population An ensemble of human individuals which reproduces itself biologically and which normally occupies the same territory over several generations.

Post-materialism Value orientation that emphasizes quality of life, social equality, protection of the environment, and participation in social and political life, and is expressed in a number of new social movements such as pacifism and feminism.

Prediction Scientific statements about the relationship between social and political phenomena should include elements of prediction, i.e. statements about outcomes if certain conditions are fulfilled.

Preferential voting Opportunity, under some list systems, for voters to cast a preference vote for an individual candidate on a list, rather than just for the list as a whole.

Presidential systems (democracies) Systems in which the chief executive, usually an individual political leader, is directly elected by the citizens and enjoys a fixed term of office.

Presidentialization of politics Strengthening of the chief executive in his/her party and executive functions and increasingly leadership-centred electoral processes.

Prime ministerial government Monocratic decision-making by the prime minister by taking up issues at will, or by deciding key issues with subsequent implications on government policy, or by defining a governing ethos which generates solutions to most policy problems.

Principal The 'principal' in principal agent theory is the actor who wishes to engage an 'agent' to perform a specific activity or service. The principal benefits from the agent performing the task, but must also consider what kind of oversight is necessary to ensure the agent's activities are in line with the preferences of the principal.

Procedural democracy Form of democracy in which the definition emphasizes the process by which political leaders are elected and held accountable, rather than the political or ideological goals that are set by the regime.

Professionalization The social process by which the communication occupation transforms itself into a true profession and by which the qualified are demarcated from unqualified amateurs.

Proportional representation The principle that the distribution of seats among parties brought about by an election should closely correspond to the distribution of votes among those parties. This principle can be effected by a wide range of different specific methods.

Proportionality Degree of correspondence between parties' vote shares and their shares of seats.

Protest events Means for social movements to draw attention to their cause. They range from petitions, festivals, and demonstrations to violent confrontations.

Public interest groups Groups that seek to achieve a non-self-interested collective goal (e.g. clean air) that will benefit society at large and not just the members of the interest groups.

Public policies A long series of actions carried out to solve societal problems. They are the main output of political systems.

Public sphere A large number of autonomous individuals find themselves enabled by the resources they possess, activated by their interests, and authorized by the existing constitutional arrangements to communicate to one another their opinions on political issues and policies, to articulate both their disagreements and their agreements, and to align themselves accordingly.

Purge The process of eliminating elites that may be politically or intellectually threatening to a regime. Purges either result in exile of these individuals or in their execution.

Qualified-majority voting System of weighted voting in the EU Council, where each member state government has a number of votes in proportion to its population.

Qualitative Type of research in which no quantification of the strength of the association between independent and dependent variables is possible due to the nature of the data. The focus is on understanding political phenomena (often in case studies), and the development over time in tracing the detailed process that leads to an outcome. Explanations are based on unquantifiable data such as in-depth interviews, the analysis of documents, or content and text analysis.

Quantitative Type of research based on coefficients able to capture numerically the strength of the effect of one or more factors (independent variables) on the phenomenon that the research aims to explain (dependent variable). This type of research is typically econometric and statistical. As it relies on a high number of observations, it is usually not intensive in describing cases.

Quasi-experimental research design The comparative method is called 'quasi-experimental' because conclusions are inferred from empirically informed comparisons and not from experiments.

Rational choice A set of (more or less formal) deductive models based on assumptions of rationality: ordering of preferences, maximization of utility, and full information.

Rationalization The tendency to engage in action, individual or collective, in a deliberate manner, so as to optimize its bearing on one's interests and preferences. In the case of political and administrative activity, the attempt to optimize the relationship between costs and benefits of public activity by rendering that activity as far as possible uniform, predictable, and economical.

Redistribution Reallocation of both social risks and material resources, either from one social group to another or over the life course.

Referendum Vote held not to elect a parliament but to decide on some specific issue.

Regional autonomy The location of state powers and responsibilities with authorities and institutions at the regional level. The extent of regional autonomy varies from state to state and constitutes a key element of power-sharing arrangements in both federal and non-federal countries.

Regional policy Range of policies, programmes, and fiscal arrangements with the objective of reducing economic and social disparities between regions within a nation-state, a sub-national state, or an affiliated group of nation-states.

Regionalism The social, cultural, economic, and political expression of a spatially distinct pattern of values, attitudes, orientations, opinions, behaviours, preferences, interests, and/or actions that reflect the sense of belonging or attachment to, and the personal and community interests that are vested in, a particular territorial space distinct from either local or nation-state level.

Registration requirements Obligations in order to receive the right to vote. They increase the cost of voting. The low turnout in the US can be partly explained by the time-consuming registration requirements compared with other rich democracies.

Rejective referendum Type of referendum in which the people vote on a proposal that some measure of government or parliament should be rejected.

Rentierism When resource-rich authoritarian regimes use rents to buy political support.

Repertories of contention The means groups choose to protest. Includes demonstrations, general strike actions, or civil disobedience.

Research design Basic organization of a research programme which formulates hypotheses concerning the relationship between variables, identifies the relevant indicators, selects cases and data, discusses measurement and comparability problems, and identifies suitable techniques for data analysis.

Resource mobilization The amount of people, money, and media coverage that a particular social movement can mobilize.

Riskiness of participation Attribute to classify political participation by the sanctions political authorities might impose on it, from monetary fines and minor harassments to incarceration and death.

Ruling monarchy A ruling monarch exercises the same sort of power as a personal dictator and, unlike a reigning monarch, is not a constitutional and largely ceremonial head of state.

Secularization The decline of religious values as well as the institutional separation of state and church.

Selection bias (1) Distortion affecting the inference from sample to population arising from the non-random inclusion in the analysis of a number of cases chosen from a larger pool that are not representative of the population (external validity); (2) over-representation of cases at one end or the other of the distribution of the dependent variable (internal validity).

Selective incentives 'Private' benefits that political entrepreneurs can direct to those who help to overcome the free-rider problem in the production of a collective good. These incentives can be material (e.g. a gift), expressive (e.g. a sense that one is doing the right thing), or solidarity (e.g. the comfort that comes from being part of the group).

Semi-competitive elections Low level of democratic competition between the official party and one or more other parties, but the dictatorship ensures by various subtle or not so subtle means that its official party will win the elections.

Semi-presidentialism Democratic system that combines a popularly elected president and a prime minister responsible to parliament. Depending on the system, power is allocated differently between the prime minister and the president. Some semi-presidential countries effectively operate as parliamentary (e.g. Ireland), others as presidential (e.g. South Korea), and others as hybrid systems (e.g. France).

Separation-of-powers system Regime in which the legislative and executive branches are selected independently from one another and neither can dismiss the other (with certain rare exceptions for criminal activity or incapacitation). Both branches are generally elected by citizens through distinct votes.

Single market A single market to replace the separate markets of the member states is the main aim and achievement of the EU. The creation of the single market involved the removal of technical, physical, and fiscal barriers to the free movement of goods, services, capital, and labour in Europe.

Social capital Positive outcomes generated by the networks that bind a community together. The more of these there are and the stronger they are, the greater the social and political benefits they generate and hence civil society and quality of life have a higher potential to flourish. Social capital is a key component for building and maintaining democracy.

Social democracy Political movement that has as its main goal the material and immaterial improvement of the position of workers and employees in capitalist society by stressing equality.

Social movement Streams of public collective unconventional participation that target demands at policy-makers primarily through community, street, and media events, often involving disruption of regular social life, e.g. through blockades and sit-ins.

Social movement organization (SMO) Conscious, collective, organized groups that attempt to bring about, or resist, large-scale change in the social order by non-institutionalized means.

Social networks Connection of several individuals tied by one or more types of relation, such as values, partisanship, or friendship. Social networks are thought of as enabling political participation in various ways (mobilization, group pressure, monitoring).

Social risks Risks that are shared by many people and affect the welfare of society as a whole that are interpreted as a threat to certain strata of society, and are beyond the control of any individual.

Socially embedded growth model Various institutional and political economy theories about the new regionalism. The emphasis within this model is on the internal or endogenous social and economic factors responsible for regional economic success, such as the character and quality of a region's human, social, and cultural capital.

Soft power Strategy based on attraction and persuasion rather than coercion. It arises from the attractiveness of a country's culture, political ideals, policies, and practices, both domestic and as displayed in how it conducts external relations.

Sovereignty A principle originally articulated by rulers involved in early state-making who (1) claimed that within their territories their political faculties and prerogatives overrode all those claimed by lesser powers; and (2) acknowledged no centre of rule operating outside those territories as having political faculties and prerogatives superior to their own.

Spoils system System through which the victorious party appoints large layers of the administration after each election, with the jobs going to party trustees.

Staatslehre Originally a subfield of legal studies, it was among the precursors of modern political science. However, its affirmative, somewhat metaphysical focus on the state was soon left behind.

State A polity which claims in law (and is able to assert in fact) that within a given portion of the Earth its properly constituted organs are exclusively entitled to practice legitimate violence in the pursuit of political interests, beginning with the maintenance of public order and defence of the territory from foreign encroachments.

State-building Activities intended to create the essential conditions for, and the substance of, a state, defined in terms of a monopoly of the means of violence and an ability to procure certain basic functions such as security throughout the territory.

State subventions Subsidies from the public treasury to support the activities of political parties.

Supranationalism One of the two main modes of EU decision-making involving a monopoly on legislative initiative by the European Commission, co-equal power in the adoption of legislation by the governments (in the Council) and the European Parliament (under the co-decision procedure), and judicial review of EU legislation by the European Court of Justice.

Symmetric chambers Bicameral legislatures in which both chambers have exactly the same powers, both in terms of investiture/censure of the government and as regards the policy-making process.

Synchronic Type of research based on data collected at only one time point (usually the most recent one) and not taking into account change over time. Usually this type of research is interested in differences between countries or other cases (such as parties or other organizations, regions within a country, institutions, etc.) rather than between time periods.

Systemic functionalism Theoretical paradigm based on the functions of structures within a social or political system.

Systems theory General empirical theory replacing the narrow concept of state and its institutions with the broader concept of the political system as a set of structures (institutions and agencies) whose decision-making function is to reach the collective and authoritative allocation of values (*output*, i.e. public policies) receiving support as well as demands (*inputs*) from the domestic as well as the international *environment*, which it shapes through outputs in the *feedback loop*.

Territoriality Each state rules over a clearly bounded portion of land (and the adjoining waters), and its commands and other practices of rule apply in principle to all individuals operating, at a given time, over that territory.

Third wave Term coined by Samuel Huntington (1991) to distinguish the wave of democratic transition that took place between 1974 and 1990 from earlier waves of democratic transition that took place between 1828 and 1926 and between 1942 and 1962.

Threshold Level of support (usually expressed as a percentage of the total vote) that a party must reach in order to achieve representation.

Traditions Cultural elements inherited from the past and maintained through recurrent rituals.

Transnational social movements Deal with issues that exceed the local and national level and that are transboundary or 'global' in their character. Typical examples are ecology or human rights movements.

Triangulation Research strategies aiming at exploring the same set of data with several alternative theories or to go into the field with alternative approaches in mind in order to become more open to unexpected findings.

Trust Type of social relationship based on reliance. The relationship can be horizontal (trust in fellow citizens) as well as vertical (trust in political, cultural, social, and economic elites and authorities).

Turnout The ratio of voters to the electorate. The electorate can be defined in different ways: all residents in a polity, all citizens, or all citizens who are also registered to vote.

Two-party system A party system with two equally balanced parties that receive almost all votes and alternate in power, forming single-party governments.

Under-representation The share of the seats that a party wins below its share of the votes.

Unicameral legislature A legislature that consists of only one chamber. Unicameral legislatures are never found in federal political systems and are often associated with smaller, more homogeneous societies.

Unified government All three branches of presidential government—the presidency and both houses of the legislature—are under the control of the same party.

Union state A pre-modern form of state organization constructed through 'acts of union' between political entities.

Unitary state A state in which sovereignty is concentrated at the level of a single central government. Unitary states may be centralized, decentralized, or regionalized.

Variables A property or attribute that has been made measurable.

Varieties of capitalism Different methods of coordination between economic actors. The concept is parallel to the welfare regime concept, but the cornerstone is the interest of firms in using the market vs negotiations and public regulation as the main instance of coordination.

Welfare regime Specific configuration of state, market, and family that nations adopt in their pursuit of work and welfare and the management of social risks. Three or more such clusters are usually identified: conservative, liberal, and social democratic.

Welfare state Type of democratic state, influenced by Keynesianism, which offers (some) protection to its citizens against the hardships of the (labour) market (e.g. unemployment) and life (e.g. sickness).

Welfare state reform Generic term to refer to political interventions that are meant to adjust existing welfare arrangements to changing social (e.g. ageing) and economic (e.g. globalization) conditions, ranging from the incremental fine-tuning and correction of policy instruments to radical measures such as the abolition of old social programmes and the introduction of new ones.

References

Aagaard, P. (2016) 'The Fourth Age of Political Commuication: Democratic Decay or the Rise of Phronetic Political Communication?', *Nordicum Mediterraneum*, 11(3): n.p.

Aalberg, T. and Curran, J. (2012) *How Media Inform Democracy: A Comparative Approach* (New York: Routledge).

Aalberg, T., Aelst, P. V., and Curran, J. (2010) 'Media Systems and the Political Information Environment. A Cross-National Comparison', *International Journal of Press/Politics*, 15(2): 255–71.

Aalberg, T., Blekesaune, A., and Elvestad, E. (2013a) 'Media Choice and Informed Democracy: Toward Increasing News Consumption Gaps in Europe?', *International Journal of Press/Politics*, 18(3): 281–303.

Aalberg, T., Papathanassopoulos, S., Soroka, S., Curran, J., Hayashi, K., Iyengar, S., Jones, P. K., Mazzoleni, G., Rojas, H., Rowe, D., and Tiffen, R. (2013b) 'International TV News, Foreign Affairs Interest and Public Knowledge', *Journalism Studies*, 14(3): 387–406.

Aboura, S. (2005) 'French Media Bias and the Vote on the European Constitution', *European Journal of Political Economy*, 21(4): 1093–8.

Abrams, S., Iversen, T., and Soskice, D. (2011) 'Informal Social Networks and Rational Voting', *British Journal of Political Science*, 41(2): 229–57.

Acemoglou, D. and Robinson, J. A. (2006) *Economic Origins of Dictatorship and Democracy* (Cambridge: Cambridge University Press).

Acemoglu, D. and Robinson, J. A. (2012) *Why Nations Fail: The Origins of Power, Prosperity and Poverty* (London: Profile).

Acemoglu, D., Johnson, S., Robinson, J. A., and Yared, P. (2008) 'Income and Democracy', *American Economic Review*, 98(3): 808–42. Doi: 10.1257/aer.98.3.808.

Adam, B. (1990) *Time and Social Theory* (Cambridge: Polity Press).

Adam, C., Hurka, S., and Knill, C. (2017) 'Four Styles of Regulation and their Implications for Comparative Policy Analysis', *Journal of Comparative Policy Analysis: Research and Practice*, 19(4): 327–44.

Adams, J. and Somer-Topcu, Z. (2009) 'Policy Adjustment by Parties in Response to Rival Parties' Policy Shifts: Spatial Theory and the Dynamics of Party Competition in Twenty-Five Post-War Democracies', *British Journal of Political Science*, 39(4): 825–46.

Adams, J., Clark, M., Ezrow, L. and Glasgow, G. (2004) 'Understanding Change and Stability in Party Ideologies: Do Parties Respond to Public Opinion or to Past Election Results?', *British Journal of Political Science*, 34(4): 589–610.

Adams, J., Haupt, A.B., and Stoll, H. (2008) 'What Moves Parties? The Role of Public Opinion and Global Economic Conditions in Western Europe', *Comparative Political Studies*, 42(5): 611–39.

Adams, M. (2003) *Fire and Ice: The Myth of Converging Values in the United States and Canada* (Toronto: Penguin).

Adcock, R. and Collier, D. (2001) 'Measurement Validity: A Common Standard for Quantitative and Qualitative Research', *American Political Science Review*, 95: 529–46.

Adema, W. and Ladaique, M. (2005) 'Net Social Expenditure', OECD Social, Employment and Migration Paper 29 (Paris: OECD).

Adema, W. and Ladaique, M. (2009) 'How Expensive is the Welfare State? Gross and Net Indicators in the OECD Social Expenditure Database (SOCX)', OECD Social, Employment and Migration Working Paper 92 (Paris: OECD).

Adema, W., Fron, P., and Ladaique, M. (2011) 'Is the European Welfare State Really More Expensive? Indicators on Social Spending, 1980–2012', OECD Social, Employment and Migration Working Papers 124 (Paris: OECD).

Adema, W., Fron, P. and Ladaique, M. (2015) 'How Much Do OECD Countries Spend on Social Protection and How Redistributive Are Their Tax/Benefit Systems?', *International Social Security Review*, 67(1): 1–25.

Adorno, T. W., Frenkel-Brunswik, E., Levinson, D. J., and Sanford, R. N. (1950) *The Authoritarian Personality* (New York: Norton).

Agresti, A. and Finley, B. (2009) *Statistical Methods for the Social Sciences* (Upper Saddle River, NJ: Prentice Hall).

Ahrend, R., Gamper, C., and Schumann, A.(2014) *The OECD Metropolitan Governance Survey: A Quantitative Description of Governance Structures in Large Urban Agglomerations* (Paris: OECD).

Albæk, E., Dalen, A. V., Jebril, N., and de Vreese, C. (2014) *Political Journalism in Comparative Perspective* (New York: Cambridge University Press).

Alber, J. (1982) *Vom Armenhaus zum Wohlfahrtsstaat. Analysen zur Entwicklung der Sozialversicherung in Westeuropa* (Frankfurt am Main: Campus).

Albrow, M. (1996) *The Global Age: State and Society beyond Modernity* (Cambridge: Polity Press).

Aldrich, J. H. (1993) 'Rational Choice and Turnout', *American Journal of Political Science*, 37(1): 246–78.

Aldrich, J. H. (1995) *Why Parties? The Origin and Transformation of Political Parties in America* (Chicago, IL: University of Chicago Press).

Alesina, A. and Glaeser, E. L. (2004) *Fighting Poverty in the US and Europe: A World of Difference* (Oxford, Oxford University Press).

Alesina, A., Miano, A., et al. (2018) 'Immigration and Redistribution', NBER Working Paper 24733 (National Bureau of Economic Research).

Alesina, A., Favero, C., and Giavazzi, F. (2019) *Austerity: When It Works and When It Doesn't* (Princeton, NJ, Princeton University Press).

Alexander, G. (2002) *The Sources of Democratic Consolidation* (Ithaca, NY: Cornell University Press).

Allain-Dupré, D. (2018) *Making Decentralisation Work: A Handbook for Policy-Makers* (Paris: OECD).

Allern, E. H. and Bale, T. (2016) *Centre-Left Parties and Trade Unions in the Twenty-First Century* (Oxford: Oxford University Press).

Allison, G. T. (1971) *Essence of Decision* (Boston, MA: Little, Brown).

Almond, G. A. (1956) 'Comparative Political Systems', *Journal of Politics*, 18(3): 391–409.

Almond, G. A. (1958) 'Research Note: A Comparative Study of Interest Groups and the Political Process', *American Political Science Review*, 52(1): 270–82.

Almond, G. A. (1978) *Comparative Politics: System, Process, and Policy* (Boston, MA: Little, Brown).

Almond, G. A. (1990) *A Discipline Divided: Schools and Sects in Political Science* (London: Sage).

Almond, G. A. (1996) 'Political Science: The History of the Discipline', in R. E. Goodin and H.-D. Klingemann (eds), *A New Handbook of Political Science* (Oxford: Oxford University Press), 50–96.

Almond, G. A. and Powell, G. B., Jr (1966) *Comparative Politics: A Developmental Approach* (Boston, MA: Little, Brown).

Almond, G. A. and Verba, S. (1963) *The Civic Culture: Political Attitudes and Democracy in Five Nations* (Princeton, NJ: Princeton University Press).

Almond, G. A. and Verba, S. (eds) (1980) *The Civic Culture Revisited* (Boston, MA: Little, Brown).

Almond, G. A., Powell, G. B., Jr, Strøm, K., and Dalton, R. J. (2004) *Comparative Politics Today: A World View* (8th edn) (New York: Pearson Longman).

Alter, K. (2014) *The New Terrain of International Law: Courts, Politics, Rights* (Princeton, NJ: Princeton University Press).

Alter, P. (1994) *Nationalism* (2nd edn) (London: Edward Arnold).

Altman, D. and Chasquetti, D. (2005) 'Re-Election and Political Career Paths in the Uruguayan Congress, 1985–99', *The Journal of Legislative Studies*, 11(2), 235–53. Doi: 10.1080/13572330500158656.

Alvarez, R. M., Garrett, G., and Lange, P. (1991) 'Government Partisanship, Labor Organization, and Macroeconomic Performance', *American Political Science Review*, 85(2): 539–56.

Amadae, S. M. and Bueno de Mesquita, B. (1999) 'The Rochester School: The Origins of Positive Political Economy', *Annual Review of Political Science*, 2: 269–95.

Amalrik, A. A. (1970) *Kann die Sowjetunion das Jahr 1984 erleben?* (Zurich: Diogenes).

Amenta, E. (2003) 'What We Know about the Development of Social Policy: Comparative and Historical Research in Comparative and Historical Perspective', in J. Mahoney and D. Rueschemeyer (eds), *Comparative Historical Analysis in the Social Sciences* (Cambridge: Cambridge University Press), 91–130.

Ames, B. (2002) *The Deadlock of Democracy in Brazil* (Ann Arbor, MI: Michigan University Press).

Amin, A. (1999) 'An Institutionalist Perspective on Regional Economic Development', *International Journal of Urban and Regional Research*, 23(2): 365–78.

Amoretti, U. and N. Bermeo (eds) (2004) *Federalism and Territorial Cleavages* (Baltimore, MD: Johns Hopkins University Press).

Amsalem, E., Sheafer, T., Walgrave, S., Loewen, P. J., and Soroka, S. N. (2017) 'Media Motivation and Elite Rhetoric in Comparative Perspective', *Political Communication* (34:3): 385–403.

Amsterdam Institute for Advanced Labour Studies (2019) ICTWSS: Database on Institutional Characteristics of Trade Unions, Wage Setting, State Intervention and Social Pacts in 55 countries between 1960 and 2017. Version 6.0. (http://uva-aias.net/en/ictwss).

Andersen, J. G. (2002) 'Work and Citizenship: Unemployment and Unemployment Policies in Denmark, 1980–2000', in J. G. Andersen and P. H. Jensen (eds), *Changing Labour Markets, Welfare Policies and Citizenship* (Bristol: Policy Press), 59–84.

Andersen, J. G. (2007) 'Conceptualizing Welfare State Change. The "Dependent Variable Problem" Writ Large', paper prepared for ECPR general conference, Pisa. CCWS Working Paper No. 51 (CCSW).

Andersen, J. G. and Christiansen, P. M. (1991) *Skatter uden velfærd* (Copenhagen: Jurist-og Økonomforbundets Forlag).

Andersen, T. M., Holmström, B., Honkapohja, S., Korkman, S., Söderström, H., and Vartiainen, J. (2007) *The Nordic Model. Embracing Globalization and Sharing Risk* (Helsinki: ETLA).

Anderson, B. (1983) *Imagined Communities: Reflections on the Origin and Spread of Nationalism* (London: Verso).

Anderson, B. (1991) *Imagined Communities: Reflections on the Origin and Spread of Nationalism* (rev. edn) (London: Verso).

Anderson, C. (1998) 'When in Doubt, Use Proxies: Attitudes towards Domestic Politics and Support for European Integration', *Comparative Political Studies*, 31(5): 569–601.

Anderson, C. J. (2009) 'Nested Citizenship: Macropolitics and Microbehavior in Comparative Politics', in M. I. Lichbach and A. S. Zuckerman (eds), *Comparative Politics: Rationality, Culture and Structure* (2nd edn) (Cambridge: Cambridge University Press).

Anderson, C. J. and Beramendi, P. (2008) 'Income Inequality and Electoral Participation', in P. Beramendi and C. J. Anderson (eds), *Democracy, Inequality and Representation* (New York: Russell Sage Foundation).

Anderson, C. W. (2016) 'News Ecosystems', in C. Anderson, T. Witschge, D. Domingo, and A. Hermida (eds), *The SAGE Handbook of Digital Journalism* (London: SAGE), 410–23.

Anderson, J. E. (2003) *Public Policymaking* (Boston, MA: Houghton Mifflin).

Anderson, L. (1991) 'Absolutism and the Resilience of Monarchy in the Middle East', *Political Science Quarterly*, 106(1): 1–15.

Anderson, P. (2007) 'Russia's Managed Democracy', *London Review of Books*, 29(2).

Andersson, S. and Ersson, S. (2012) 'The European Representative Democracy Data Archive', principal investigator T. Bergman (http://www.endda.se).

Andeweg, R. (1997) 'Collegiality and Collectivity: Cabinets, Cabinet Committees and Cabinet Ministers', in P. Weller, H. Bakevits, and R. A. W. Rhodes (eds), *The Hollow Crown: Countervailing Trends in Core Executives* (London: Macmillan).

Andeweg, R. (2008) 'The Netherlands: The Sanctity of Proportionality', in M. Gallagher and P. Mitchell (eds), *The Politics of Electoral Systems* (Oxford: Oxford University Press), 491–510.

Andrews, K. T. and Biggs, M. (2006) 'The Dynamics of Protest Diffusion: Movement Organizations, Social Networks and News Media in the 1960 Sit-Ins', *American Sociological Review*, 781: 752–77.

Andrews, M. (2013) *The Limits of Institutional Reform in Development: Changing Rules for Realistic Solutions* (New York: Cambridge University Press).

Anduiza, E., Cristancho, C., and Sabucedo, J. M. (2012) 'Mobilization through Online Social Networks: The Political Protest of the Indignados in Spain' (http://www.protestsurvey.eu/publications/ 1344588239.pdf).

Ansell, B. and Gingrich, J. (2013) 'A Tale of Two Dilemmas: Varieties of Higher Education and the Service Economy', in A. Wren (ed.), *The Political Economy of the Service Transition* (Oxford: Oxford University Press), 195–224.

Ansell, B. and Gingrich, J. (2018) 'Skills in Demand? Higher Education and European Social Investment in Europe', in P. Manow, B. Palier, and H. Schwander (eds), *Worlds of Welfare Capitalism and Electoral Politics* (Oxford: Oxford University Press), 225–53.

Ansell, B. W. and Samuels, D. J. (2014) *Inequality and Democratization: An Elite-Competition Approach* (Cambridge: Cambridge University Press).

APSA Comparative Democratization (official newsletter of APSA's Comparative Democratization section) (February 2015), 'The International Dimensions of Authoritarianism', 13(1): 1–22.

Apter, D. E. (1965) *The Politics of Modernization* (Chicago, IL: University of Chicago Press).

Ardanaz, M., Leiras, M., and Tommasi, M. (2014) 'The Politics of Federalism in Argentina and its Implications for Governance and Accountability', *World Development, 53*: 26–45.

Arendt, H. (1973) *The Origins of Totalitarianism* (Vol. 244) (Orlando, FL: Houghton Mifflin Harcourt).

Arentsen, M. J. (2003) 'The Invisible Problem and How to Deal with It: National Policy Styles in Radiation Protection Policy in the Netherlands, England and Belgium', in M.-L. Bemelmans-Videc, R. C. Rist, and E. Vedung (eds), *Carrots, Sticks and Sermons: Policy Instruments and their Evaluation* (Piscataway, NJ: Transaction Publishers), 211–30.

Armingeon. K. (2002) 'Interest Intermediation: The Cases of Consociational Democracy and Corporatism', in H. Keman (ed.), *Comparative Democratic Politics: A Guide to Contemporary Theory and Research* (London: Sage), 143–65.

Armingeon. K. and Giger, N. (2008) 'Conditional Punishment. A Comparative Analysis of the Electoral Consequences of Welfare State Retrenchment in OECD Nations, 1980–2003', *West European Politics*, 31(3): 558–80.

Arrow, K. J. (1991) 'Scale Returns in Communication and Elite Control of Oorganizations', *Journal of Law, Economics, & Organization, 7*: 1–6.

Arts, W. and Gelissen, J. (2002) 'Three Worlds of Welfare Capitalism or More? A State-of-the-Art Report', *Journal of European Social Policy*, 12(2): 137–58.

Arts, W. A. and Gelissen, J. (2010) 'Models of the Welfare State', in F. G. Castles, S. Leibfried, J. Lewis, H. Obinger, and C. Pierson (eds), *The Oxford Handbook of the Welfare State* (Oxford: Oxford University Press), 586–83.

Ashford, D. (1977) 'Political Science and Policy Studies: Toward a Structural Solution', *Policy Studies Journal*, 5: 570–83.

Atkinson, A. B. (1999) *The Economic Consequences of Rolling Back the Welfare State* (Cambridge, MA: MIT Press).

Atkinson, A. B. (2015) *Inequality—What Can Be Done?* (Cambridge, MA: Harvard University Press).

Auer, A. and Bützer, M., (eds) (2001) *Direct Democracy: The Eastern and Central European Experience* (Aldershot: Ashgate).

Auer, P. (2000) *Employment Revival in Europe: Labour Market Success in Austria, Denmark, Ireland and the Netherlands* (Geneva: International Labour Organization).

Autor, D. H., Dorn, D., et al. (2016) 'A Note on the Effect of Rising Trade Exposure on the 2016 Presidential Election', manuscript.

Ayoob, M. (1995) *The Third World Security Predicament* (Boulder, CO: Lynne Rienner).

Babayan, N. and Risse, T. (eds) (2015) 'Democracy Promotion and the Challenges of Illiberal Regional Powers', special issue of *Democratization*, 22(3).

Baccaro, L. and Heeb, S. (2012) 'Tripartite Responses to the Global Crisis: A Qualitative Comparative Analysis', *Swiss Journal of Sociology*, 38(3), 349–74.

Baccaro, L. and Howell, C. (2017) *Trajectories of Neoliberal Transformation: European Industrial Relations Since the 1970s* (Cambridge: Cambridge University Press).

Bache, I. and Flinders, M. (2004) *Multi-Level Governance* (Oxford: Oxford University Press).

Bachrach, P. and Baratz, M. S. (1962) 'Two Faces of Power', *American Political Science Review*, 56: 947–52.

Bader, J., Grävingholt, J., and Kästner, A. (2012) 'Would Autocracies Promote Autocracy? A Political Economy Perspective on Regime-Type Export in Regional Neighbourhoods', in P. Burnell and O. Schlumberger (eds) (2012) *International Politics and National Political Regimes. Promoting Democracy—Promoting Autocracy* (Abingdon: Routledge), 81–100.

Bagehot, W. (1889) *The Works of Walter Bagehot* (Hartford, CT: Travelers Insurance Companies).

Bågenholm, A. and Charron, N. (2015) 'Anti-Corruption Parties and Good Government', in C. Dahlström and L. Wängnerud (eds), *Elites, Institutions and the Quality of Government* (New York: Palgrave Macmillan), 263–82.

Bairoch, P. (1985) *De Jéricho à Mexico: Villes et économie dans l'histoire* (Paris: Gallimard).

Baker, A. (2013) 'The Gradual Transformation? The Incremental Dynamics of Macroprudential Regulation', *Regulation & Governance*, 7(4): 417–34.

Balassa, B. (1961) *The Theory of Economic Integration* (Homewood, IL: Richard D. Irwin).

Baldwin, P. (1990) *The Politics of Social Solidarity: Class Bases of the European Welfare State 1875–1975* (Cambridge: Cambridge University Press).

Baldwin, R. (2016) *The Great Convergence. Information Technology and the New Globalization* (Cambridge, MA: Harvard University Press).

Baldwin, R. (2019) *The Globotics Upheaval: Globalization, Robotics, and the Future of Work* (Oxford: Oxford University Press).

Balkin, J. (2005) 'Wrong the Day it was Decided: Lochner and Constitutional Historicism', *Boston University Law Review*, 85: 677–725.

Balme, R. and Chabanet, D. (2008) *European Governance and Democracy: Power and Protest in the EU* (Plymouth: Rowman & Littlefield).

Bamber, G. J., Landsbury, R. D., and Wailes, N. (2011) *International and Comparative Employment Relations: Globalisation and Change* (London: Sage).

Banfield, E. (1958) *The Moral Basis of a Backward Society* (New York: Free Press).

Banisar, D. (2006) 'Freedom of Information around the World 2006: A Global Survey of Access to Government Records Laws' (www.freedominfo.org).

Bannerji, H. (2000) *The Dark Side of Nation: Essays on Multiculturalism and Gender* (Toronto: Canadian Scholar's Press).

Banting, K. and W. Kymlicka (eds) (2017) *The Strains of Commitment. The Political Sources of Solidarity in Diverse Societies* (Oxford: Oxford University Press).

Barach, P. and Baratz, M. S. (1969) 'Two Faces of Power', in W.E. Connolly (ed.), *The Bias of Pluralism* (New York: Atheron Press), 51–64.

Barber, J. D. (1992) *Presidential Character: Predicting Performance in the White House* (4th edn) (Englewood Cliffs, NJ: Prentice-Hall).

Barbier, J. (2015) 'Aktivering, Flexicurity, the Surface Europeanization of Employment?', *Cuadernos de Relaciones Laborales*, 33(2): 357–95.

Bardach, E. (1976) 'Policy Termination as a Political Process', *Policy Sciences*, 7: 123–31.

Bardach, E. (1977) *The Implementation Game: What Happens after a Bill Becomes a Law* (Cambridge, MA: MIT Press).

Barkan, J. (2012) 'Democracy Assistance: What Recipients Think', *Journal of Democracy*, 23(1): 129–37.

Barnes, S. H. and Kaase, M. (1979) *Political Action: Mass Participation in Five Western Democracies* (London: Sage).

Barnett, G. A. (2001) 'A Longitudinal Analysis of the International Telecommunication Network, 1978–1996', *American Behavioral Scientist*, 44: 1638–55.

Barnett, G. A. and Choi, Y. (1995) 'Physical Distance and Language as Determinants of the International Telecommunications Network', *International Political Science Review*, 16: 249–65.

Barnett, G. A., Jacobson, T., Choi, Y., and Sun-Miller, S. (1996) 'An Examination of the International Telecommunications Network', *Journal of International Communication*, 32: 19–43.

Barnett, G. A., Salisbury, J., Kim, C., and Langhorne, A. (1999) 'Globalization and International Communication Networks: An Examination of Monetary, Telecommunications, and Trade Networks', *Journal of International Communication*, 62: 7–49.

Barros, R. (2002) *Constitutionalism and Dictatorship: Pinochet, the Junta, and the 1980 Constitution* (Cambridge: Cambridge University Press).

Bartolini, S. (1993) 'On Time and Comparative Research', *Journal of Theoretical Politics*, 5(2): 131–67.

Bartolini, S. (2000) *The Political Mobilization of the European Left, 1860–1980: The Class Cleavage* (Cambridge: Cambridge University Press).

Bartolini, S. and Mair, P. (1990) *Identity, Competition and Electoral Availability: The Stabilisation of European Electorates 1885–1985* (Cambridge: Cambridge University Press).

Bastian, S. and Luckham, R. (eds) (2003) *Can Democracy be Designed? The Politics of Institutional Choice in Conflict-Torn Societies* (London: Zed Books).

Bates, R. H. (1981) *Markets and States in Tropical Africa: The Political Basis of Agricultural Policies* (Berkeley, CA: University of California Press).

Bates, R., Greif, A., Levi, M., Rosenthal, J.-L., and Weingast, B. (2002) *Analytic Narratives* (Princeton, NJ: Princeton University Press).

Bauer, G. and Tremblay, M. (eds) (2011) *Women in Executive Power. A Global Overview* (Abingdon, Oxon: Routledge).

Bauer, R. A. and Jones, B. D. (1993) *Agendas and Instability in American Politics* (Chicago, IL: University of Chicago Press).

Bauer, R. A. and Jones, B. D. (2009) *Agendas and Instability in American Politics* (2nd edn) (Chicago, IL: University of Chicago Press).

Bauer, R. A., Breunig, C., Green-Pedersen, C., et al. (2009) 'Punctuated Equilibrium in Comparative Perspective', *American Journal of Political Science*, 53(3): 602–19.

Baumgartner, F. R. and Jones, B. D. (1993) *Agendas and Instability in American Politics* (Chicago, IL: University of Chicago Press).

Baumgartner, F. R. and Jones, B. D. (2015) *The Politics of Information: Problem Definition and the Course of Public Action in America* (Chicago, IL: University of Chicago Press).

Baumgartner, F. R., Breunig, C., Green-Pedersen, C., Jones, B. D., Mortensen, P. B., Nuytemans, M., and Walgrave, S. (2009) 'Punctuated Equilibrium in Comparative Perspective', *American Journal of Political Science*, 53(3): 603–20.

Beach, D. (2018) 'Combining QCA and Process Tracing in Practice', *Sociological Methods & Research*, 47(1): 64–99.

Beach, D. (2019) 'Multi-Method Research in the Social Sciences: A Review of Recent Frameworks and a Way Forward', *Government and Opposition*, Doi: 10.1017/gov.2018.53.

Beach, D. and Pedersen, R. B. (2012) *Process-Tracing Methods: Foundations and Guidelines* (Ann Arbor, MI: The University of Michigan Press).

Beach, D. and Pedersen, R. B. (2019) *Process-Tracing Methods: Foundations and Guidelines* (2nd edn) (Ann Arbor, MI: University of Michigan Press).

Beach, D. and Rohlfing, I. (2018) 'Integrating Cross-Case Analyses and Process Tracing in Set-Theoretic Research: Strategies and Parameters of Debate', *Sociological Methods & Research*, 47(1): 3–36.

Bechtel, M. and Tosun, J. (2009) 'Changing Economic Openness for Environmental Policy Convergence: When Can Bilateral Trade Agreements Induce Convergence of Environment Regulation?', *International Studies Quarterly*, 53(4): 931–53.

Beck, N. and Jonathan N. K. (1995) 'What to Do (and Not to Do) with Time-Series Cross-Section Data', *American Political Science Review*, 89(3): 634–47.

Beck, U. (2002) 'Losing the Traditional: Individualization and "Precarious Freedoms"', in U. Beck and E. Beck-Gernsheim (eds), *Individualization* (London: Sage), 1–21.

Beek, U. J. van (ed.) (2010) *Democracy under Scrutiny. Elites, Citizens, Cultures* (Leverkusen: Barbara Budrich).

Beer, S. H. and Ulam, A. B. (eds) (1958) *Patterns of Government: The Major Political Systems of Europe* (New York: Random House).

Begg, C. B. and Berlin, J. A. (1988) 'Publication Bias: A Problem in Interpreting Medical Data', *Journal of the Royal Statistical Society*, Series A: 419–63.

Beinin, J. and Vairel, F. (eds) (2011) *Social Movements, Mobilization, and Contestation in the Middle East and North Africa* (Stanford, CA: Stanford University Press).

Beissinger, M. (2002) *Nationalist Mobilization and the Collapse of the Soviet State* (Cambridge: Cambridge University Press).

Béland, D. (2006) 'The Politics of Social Learning: Finance, Institutions, and Pensions Reform in the United State and Canada', *Governance*, 19(4): 559–83.

Béland, D. and Cox, R. (2011) *Ideas and Politics in Social Science Research* (New York: Oxford University Press).

Bell, D. (1965) *The End of Ideology: On the Exhaustion of Political Ideas in the Fifties* (Glencoe, IL: Free Press).

Bell, D. (1973) *The Coming of Post-Industrial Society* (New York: Basic Books).

Bellin, E. (2004) 'The Robustness of Authoritarianism in the Middle East: Exceptionalism in Comparative Perspective', *Comparative Politics*, 36(2): 139–57.

Bendix, R. (1960) *Max Weber: An Intellectual Portrait* (Garden City, NY: Doubleday).

Benedetto, G. and Hix, S. (2007) 'The Rejected, the Dejected and the Ejected: Explaining Government Rebels in the 2001–05 British House of Commons', *Comparative Political Studies*, 40: 755–81.

Benford, R. D. and Snow, D. A. (2000) 'Framing Processes and Social Movements: An Overview and Assessment', *Annual Review of Sociology*, 26: 611–39.

Bennett, A. and Checkel, J. T. (eds) (2015) *Process Tracing. From Metaphor to Analytical Tool* (Cambridge: Cambridge University Press).

Bennett, C. (1991) 'What is Policy Convergence and What Causes It?', *British Journal of Political Science*, 21: 215–33.

Bennett, C. J. and Howlett, M. (1992) 'The Lessons of Learning: Reconciling Theories of Policy Learning and Policy Change', *Policy Sciences*, 25(3): 275–94.

Bennett, L. W. and Pfetsch, B. (2018) 'Rethinking Political Communication in a Time of Disrupted Public Spheres', *Journal of Communication*, 68(2): 243–53.

Bennett, L. W. and Segerberg, A. (2013) *The Logic of Connective Action: Digital Media and the Personalization of Contentious Politics* (New York: Cambridge University Press).

Benoit, K. and Laver, M. (2006) *Party Policy in Modern Democracies* (Abingdon: Routledge).

Benson, R. (2010) 'Comparative News Media Systems: New Directions in Research', in S. Allen (ed.), *Routledge Companion to News Media and Journalism Studies* (London: Routledge), 614–26.

Bentley, A. F. (1908) *The Process of Government: A Study of Social Pressures* (Chicago, IL: University of Chicago Press).

Bentley, A. F. (1949) *The Process of Government: A Study of Social Pressures* (Evanston, IL: Principia Press).

Beramendi, P., Häusermann, S., Kitschelt, H., and Kriesi, H. (eds) (2015) *The Politics of Advanced Capitalism* (New York: Cambridge University Press).

Berelson, B. R., Lazarsfeld, P. F., and McPhee, W. N. (1954) *Voting: A Study of Opinion Formation in a Presidential Campaign* (Chicago, IL: University of Chicago Press).

Berglund, S. and Thomsen, S. (eds) (1990) *Modern Political Ecological Analysis* (Åbo: Åbo Akademis Förlag).

Bergman, T., Ecker, A., and Müller, W. C. (2013) 'How Parties Govern—Political Parties and the Internal Organization of Government', in W. C. Müller and H. M. Narud (eds), *Party Governance and Party Democracy* (New York: Springer).

Bergman, T., Ilonszki, G., and Müller, W. C. (eds) (2019) *Coalition Governance in Central Eastern Europe* (Oxford: Oxford University Press).

Berg-Schlosser, D. (2008) *Democratization: The State of the Art* (Leverkusen: Budrich).

Berg-Schlosser, D. (2012) *Mixed Methods in Comparative Politics* (Houndmills, Basingstoke: Palgrave Macmillan).

Berg-Schlosser, D. and de Meur, G. (1996) 'Conditions of Authoritarianism, Fascism, and Democracy in Interwar Europe: Systematic Matching and Contrasting of Cases for "Small N" Analysis', *Comparative Political Studies*, 29(4): 423–68.

Berg-Schlosser, D. and Meur, G. De (2009) 'Comparative Research Designs', in B. Rihoux and C. C. Ragin (eds), *Configurational Comparative Methods* (Los Angeles, CA: Sage), 19–32.

Berman, L. (2006) *The Art of Political Leadership: Essays in Honor of Fred I. Greenstein* (Lanham, MD: Rowman & Littlefield).

Bermeo, N. (2003) *Ordinary People in Extraordinary Times. The Citizenry and the Breakdown of Democracy* (Princeton, NJ: Princeton University Press).

Bermeo, N. (2016) 'On Democratic Backsliding', *Journal of Democracy*, 27(1), 5–19.

Bermeo, N. and Pontusson, J. (eds) (2012) *Coping with the Crisis: Government Reactions to the Great Recession* (New York: Russell Sage).

Bernstein, S., and Cashore, B. (2000) 'Internationalization and Domestic Policy Change: The Case of Eco-forestry Policy Change in British Columbia, Canada', *Canadian Journal of Political Science*, 33(1): 67–99.

Berry, J. M. (1977) *Lobbying for the People: The Political Behavior of Public Interest Groups* (Princeton, NJ: Princeton University Press).

Bertola, G., Boeri, T., and Cazes, S. (1999) 'Employment Protection and Labour Market Adjustments in OECD Countries: Evolving Institutions and Variable Enforcement', Employment and Training Papers, 48 (Geneva: Employment and Training Department, International Labour Organization).

Bertrand, M., Duflo, E., and Mullainathan, S. (2004) 'How Much Should We Trust Differences-in-Differences Estimators?', *Review of Economic Studies*, 72(1): 1–19.

Besley, T. and Burgess, R. (2002) 'The Political Economy of Government Responsiveness: Theory and Evidence from India', *Quarterly Journal of Economics*, 117(4): 1415–51.

Besley, T. and Coate, S. (2003) 'Centralized versus Decentralized Provision of Local Public Goods: A Political Economy Approach', *Journal of Public Economics*, 87: 2611–37.

Best, R. E. (2012) 'The Long and the Short of It: Electoral Institutions and the Dynamics of Party System Size, 1950–2005', *European Journal of Political Research*, 51(2): 141–65.

Béthoux, E., Erne, R., and Golden, D. (2018) 'A Primordial Attachment to the Nation? French and Irish Workers and Trade Unions in Past EU Referendum Debates', *British Journal of Industrial Relations*, 56(3): 656–78.

Betz, H.-G. (1994) *Radical Right-Wing Populism in Western Europe* (New York: St Martin's Press).

Bevan, S. and Jennings, W. (2014) 'Representation, Agendas and Institutions', *European Journal of Political Research*, 53(1), 37–56.

Bevir, M. and Rhodes, R. A. W. (2010) *The State as Cultural Practice* (Oxford: Oxford University Press).

Beyme, K. von (1998) *The Legislator. German Parliament as a Centre of Political Decision-Making* (Aldershot: Ashgate).

Bickerton, J. (1990) *Nova Scotia, Ottawa, and the Politics of Regional Development* (Toronto: University of Toronto Press).

Bickerton, J. (2007) 'Between Integration and Fragmentation: Political Parties and the Representation of Regions', in A.-G. Gagnon and B. Tanguay (eds), *Canadian Parties in Transition* (3rd edn) (Peterborough, Ontario: Broadview Press), 411–35.

Bickerton, J. (2017) 'Parties and Regions: Representation and Resistance', in A. B. Tanguay and A.-G. Gagnon (eds), *Canadian Parties in Transition* (4th edn) (Toronto: University of Toronto Press), 44–63.

Bickerton, J. Gagnon, A.-G., and Smith, P. (1999) *Ties that Bind: Parties and Voters in Canada* (Toronto: Oxford University Press).

Bieler, A. and Erne, R. (2015) 'Transnational Solidarity? The European Working Class in the Eurozone Crisis', *Socialist Register*, 51(1): 157–77.

Bieler, A. and Lindberg, I. (eds) (2010) *Global Restructuring, Labour and the Challenges for Transnational Solidarity* (Abingdon: Routledge).

Bieler, A., Erne, R., Golden, D., Helle, I., Kjeldstadli, K., Matos T., and Stan, S. (eds) (2015) *Labour and Transnational Action in Times of Crisis* (Lanham, MD: Rowman & Littlefield International).

Biezen, I. van (2003) *Political Parties in New Democracies: Party Organization in Southern and East-Central Europe* (Houndmills, Basingstoke: Palgrave Macmillan).

Biezen, I. van and Caramani, D. (2006) '(Non)Comparative Politics in Britain', *Politics*, 26: 29–37.

Biezen, I. van, Mair, P. and Poguntke, T. (2012) 'Going, Going, … Gone? The Decline of Party Membership in Contemporary Europe', *European Journal of Political Research*, 51(1): 24–56.

Biggs, Michael (2003) 'Positive Feedback in Collective Mobilization: The American Strike Wave of 1886', *Theory and Society*, 32: 217–54.

Bimber, B. (2014) 'Digital Media in the Obama Campaigns of 2008 and 2012: Adaptation to the Personalized Political Communication Environment', *Journal of Information Technology and Politics*, 11(2): 130–50.

Binder, S. H. (2003) *Stalemate* (Washington, DC: Brookings Institution Press).

Binzer Hobolt, S. (2009) *Europe in Question: Referendums on European Integration* (Oxford: Oxford University Press).

Birch, A. H. (1967) *Representative and Responsible Government* (London: Allen & Unwin).

Björn, L. (1979) 'Labor Parties, Economic Growth, and Redistribution in Five Capitalist Countries', *Comparative Social Research*, 2: 93–128.

Bjørnskov, C. (2004) *Social Capital, Political Competition, and Corruption* (Aarhus: Aarhus School of Business, Aarhus University).

Blais, A. (2006) 'What Affects Voter Turnout?' *Annual Review of Political Science*, 9: 111–25.

Blais, A. and Dion, S. (eds) (1991) *The Budget-Maximizing Bureaucrat: Appraisals and Evidence* (Pittsburgh, PA: University of Pittsburgh Press).

Blais, A., Massicotte, L., and Dobrzynska, A. (1997) 'Direct Presidential Elections: A World Summary', *Electoral Studies*, 16(4): 441–55.

Blanchard, O. and Katz, L. F. (1996) 'What We Know and Do Not Know about the Natural Rate of Unemployment', *Journal of Economic Perspectives*, 11(1): 51–72.

Blanchard, O. and Summers, L. H. (1986) 'Hysteresis and the European Unemployment Problem', in S. Fischer (ed.), *NBER Macroeconomics Annual*, 1 (Fall): 15–78.

Blatter, J. and Blume, T. (2008) 'In Search of Co-Variance, Causal Mechanisms or Congruence? Towards a Plural Understanding of Case Studies', *Swiss Political Science Review*, 14(2): 315–56.

Blatter, J. and Haverland, M. (2012) *Designing Case Studies. Explanatory Approaches in Small-N Research* (Houndmills, Basingstoke: Palgrave Macmillan).

Block, F. (2007) 'Understanding the Diverging Trajectories of the United States and Western Europe: A Neo-Polanyian Analysis', *Politics and Society*, 35(1) 3–33.

Blondel, J. (1970) 'Legislative Behaviour: Some Steps toward a Cross-National Measurement', *Government and Opposition*, 5(1): 67–85.

Blondel, J. (1988) 'Introduction: Western European Cabinets in Comparative Perspective', in J. Blondel and F. Müller-Rommel (eds), *Cabinets in Western Europe* (London: Macmillan).

Blondel, J. and Cotta, M. (eds) (1996) *Party and Government* (London: Macmillan).

Blondel, J. and Cotta, M. (eds) (2000) *The Nature of Party Government* (Basingstoke: Palgrave).

Blumer, H. (1939) 'Elementary Collective Behavior', in Lee, A. M. (ed.), *Principles of Sociology* (New York: Barnes & Noble) (rev. 1951), 167–222.

Blumler, J. G. (2016). 'The Fourth Age of Political Communication', *Politiques de Communication*, 6(1): 19–30.

Blumler, J. G. (2017) 'The Shape of Political Communication', in K. Hall Jamieson and K. Kenski (eds), *The Oxford Handbook of Political Communication* (Oxford: Oxford University Press), 47–58.

Blumler, J. G. and Gurevich, M. (1975) 'Towards a Political Framework for Political Communication Research', in S. H. Chaffee (ed.), *Political Communication: Issues and Strategies for Research* (Beverly Hills, CA: Sage), 165–93.

Blyth, M. (2002) *Great Transformations: Economic and Institutional Change in the Twentieth Century* (Cambridge: Cambridge University Press).

Blyth, M. (2013a) *Austerity. The History of a Dangerous Idea* (Oxford: Oxford University Press).

Blyth, M. (2013b) 'Paradigms and Paradox: The Politics of Economic Ideas in Two Moments of Crisis', *Governance*, 26(2): 197–215.

Boccalini, T. (1614) *Ragguagli di Parnaso: Centuria Prima* (Milan: Battista Bidelli).

Bogaards, M. (2000) 'The Uneasy Relationship between Empirical and Normative Types in Consociational Theory', *European Journal of Political Research*, 12: 395–423.

Bogdani, M. and Loughlin, J. (2007) *Albania and the European Union: The Tumultuous Journey towards Integration and Accession* (London: Tauris).

Boix, C. (1999) 'Setting the Rules of the Game: The Choice of Electoral Systems in Advanced Democracies', *American Political Science Review*, 93(3): 609–24.

Boix, C. (2003) *Democracy and Redistribution* (Cambridge: Cambridge University Press).

Bollen, Kenneth A. (1990) 'Political Democracy: Conceptual and Measurement Traps', *Studies in Comparative International Development* 25, 1: 7–24.

Bolton, P. and Roland, G. (1997) 'The Breakup of Nations: A Political Economy Analysis', *Quarterly Journal of Economics*, 112: 1057–90.

Bond, R. M., Fariss, C. I., Jones, J. J., Kramer, A. D., Marlow, C., Settle, J. E., and Fowler, J. H. (2012) 'A 61-Million-Person Experiment in Social Influence and Political Mobilization', *Nature* 489(7415): 295–8. (https://doi.org/10.1038/nature11421).

Bonoli, G. (2000) *The Politics of Pension Reform* (Cambridge: Cambridge University Press).

Bonoli, G. (2001) 'Political Institutions, Veto Points, and the Process of Welfare State Adaptation', in P. Pierson (ed.), *The New Politics of the Welfare State* (Oxford: Oxford University Press), 238–64.

Bonoli, G. and Natali, D. (eds) (2012) *The Politics of the New Welfare State* (Oxford: Oxford University Press).

Bonoli, G., Cantillon, B. and Van Lancker, W. (2017) 'Social Investment and the Matthew Effect: Limits to a Strategy', in A. Hemerijck (ed.), *The Uses of Social Investment* (Oxford: Oxford University Press), 66–76.

Boomgaarden, H. G. and Song, H. (2019). 'Media Use and Its Effects in a Cross-National Perspective', *Kölner Zeitschrift für Soziologie und Sozialpsychologie*, 71(1): 545–71.

Boomgaarden, H. G., de Vreese, C. H., Schuck, A. R. T., Azrout R., Elenbaas, M., van Spanje, J. H. P., and Vliegenthart, R. (2013) 'Across Time and Space: Explaining Variation in News Coverage of the European Union', *European Journal of Political Research*, 52(5): 608–29.

Boräng, F. (2018) *National Institutions—International Migration. Labour Markets, Welfare States and Immigration Policy* (London, ECPR Press, Rowman & Littlefield).

Börzel, T. (2015) 'The Noble Rest and the Dirty Rest? Western Democracy Promoters and Illiberal Regional Powers', *Democratization*, 22(3): 519–35.

Bossetta, M. (2018). 'The Digital Architectures of Social Media: Comparing Political Campaigning on Facebook, Twitter, Instagram, and Snapchat in the 2016 U.S. Election', *Journalism & Mass Communication Quarterly*, 95(2): 471–96.

Botero, G. (1589) [1948] *Della Ragion di Stato* (Turin: UTET).

Boudreau, V. (2004) *Resisting Dictatorship: Repression and Protest in Southeast Asia* (Cambridge: Cambridge University Press).

Boulianne, S. (2015) 'Social Media Use and Participation: A Meta-Analysis of Current Research', *Information, Communication & Society*, 18(5): 524–38.

Boulianne, S. (2019). 'Revolution in the Making? Social Media Effects across the Globe', *Information, Communication & Society*, 22(1): 39–54.

Bouwen, P. (2002) 'Corporate Lobbying in the European Union: The Logic of Access', *Journal of European Public Policy*, 9(3): 365–90.

Bovens, M., Hart, P., and Peters, B. G. (eds) (2001) *Success and Failure in Public Governance* (Cheltenham: Edgar Elgar).

Bowler, S. and Donovan, T. (1998) *Demanding Choices: Opinion, Voting, and Direct Democracy* (Ann Arbor, MI: University of Michigan Press).

Bowler, S., Donovan, T., and Tolbert, C. (eds) (1998) *Citizens as Legislators: Direct Democracy in the United States* (Columbus, OH: Ohio State University Press).

Bowler, S., Farrell, D. M., and Pettit, R. T. (2005) 'Expert Opinion on Electoral Systems: So Which Electoral System is "Best"?', *Journal of Elections, Public Opinion, and Parties*, 15(1): 3–19.

Brady, D. (2005) 'The Welfare State and Relative Poverty in Rich Western Democracies, 1967–1997', *Social Forces*, 83(4): 1329–64.

Brady, D. and Lee, H. Y. (2014) 'The Rise and Fall of Government Spending in Affluent Democracies, 1971–2008', *Journal of European Social Policy*, 24(1): 56–79.

Brady, H. D. and Collier, D. (eds) (2004) *Rethinking Social Enquiry: Diverse Tools, Shared Standards* (Lanham, MD: Rowman & Littlefield).

Brady, H. E., Verba, K., and Schlozman, L. (1995) 'Beyond SES: A Resource Model of Political Participation', *American Political Science Review*, 89: 271–94.

Brancati, D. (2006) 'Decentralization: Fueling or Dampening the Flames of Ethnic Conflict and Secessionism', *International Organization*, 60(3): 651–85.

Bratton, M. and Mattes, R. (2000) 'Support for Democracy in Africa', *British Journal of Political Science*, 31: 447–74.

Braumoeller, B. F. (2015) 'Guarding against False Positives in Qualitative Comparative Analysis', *Political Analysis*, 23(4): 471–87.

Braun, D. (ed.) (2000) *Public Policy and Federalism* (Aldershot: Ashgate).

Braun, D. (2015) 'Between Parsimony and Complexity. System-Wide Typologies as a Challenge in Comparative Politics', in D. Braun and M. Maggetti (eds), *Comparative Politics: Theoretical and Methodological Challenges* (Cheltenham: Edward Elgar), 90–124.

Braun, D. and Busch, A. (1999) *Public Policy and Political Ideas* (Cheltenham: Edward Elgar).

Braun, D. and Gilardi, F. (2006) 'Taking Galton's Problem Seriously: Towards a Theory of Policy Diffusion', *Journal of Theoretical Politics*, 18(3): 298–322.

Braun, D and Maggetti, M. (eds) (2015) *Comparative Politics: Theoretical and Methodological Challenges* (Cheltenham: Edward Elgar).

Bräuninger, T. and Debus, M. (2009) 'Legislative Agenda-Setting in Parliamentary Democracies', *European Journal of Political Research*, 48(6): 804–39.

Bräuninger, T. and König, T. (1999) 'The Checks and Balances of Party Federalism: German Federal Government in a Divided Legislature', *European Journal of Political Research*, 36(6): 207–34.

Bredgaard, T., Larsen, F., and Madsen, P. K. (2005) 'The Flexible Danish Labour Market: A Review', *CARMA Research Papers*, 1 (Aalborg: Aalborg University).

Brehm, J. and Gates, S. (1997) *Working, Shirking, and Sabotage: Bureaucratic Response to a Democratic Public* (Ann Arbor, MI: University of Michigan Press).

Brenner, N., Jessop, B., Jones, M., and Macleod, G. (eds) (2003) *State/Space: A Reader* (Oxford: Basil Blackwell).

Brenner, R. (1977) 'The Origin of Capitalist Development: A Critique of Neo-Smithian Marxism', *New Left Review*, 104(July–August): 25–92.

Breslin, S. (2010) 'Democratizing One-Party Rule in China', in P. Burnell and R. Youngs (eds), *New Challenges to Democratization* (Abingdon: Routledge), 134–52.

Brewer-Carias, A. (2014) *Constitutional Protection of Human Rights in Latin America: A Comparative Study of Amparo Proceedings* (Cambridge: Cambridge University Press).

Bridoux, J. (2019) 'Shaking Off the Neoliberal Shackles', *Democratization*, 26(5): 796–814.

Brinks, D. and Coppedge, M. (2006) 'Diffusion is No Illusion–Neighbor Emulation in the Third Wave of Democracy', *Comparative Political Studies*, 39(4): 463–89.

Brock, L, Holm, H.-H., Sørensen, G., and Stohl M. (2011) *Fragile States. Violence and the Failure of Intervention* (Cambridge: Polity Press).

Brooker, P. (1997) *Defiant Dictatorships: Communist and Middle-Eastern Dictatorships in a Democratic Age* (Houndmills, Basingstoke: Palgrave Macmillan).

Brooker, P. (2009) *Non-Democratic Regimes* (rev. edn) (Houndmills, Basingstoke: Palgrave Macmillan).

Brooker, P. (2013) *Non-Democratic Regimes* (Houndmills, Basingstoke: Macmillan International Higher Education).

Brooker, P. (2014) *Non-Democratic Regimes* (3rd edn) (Houndmills, Basingstoke: Palgrave Macmillan).

Brookings (2018). 'Figures of the Week: African and Global FDI Inflows Weaken in 2017 (https://www.brookings.edu/blog/africa-in-focus/2018/06/14/figures-of-the-week-african-and-global-fdi-inflows-weaken-in-2017).

Brooks, S. M. (2005) 'Interdependent and Domestic Foundations of Policy Change: The Diffusion of Pension Privatization around the World', *International Studies Quarterly*, 49(2): 273–94.

Brossard, D., Shanahan, J., and McComas, K. (2004) 'Are Issue Cycles Culturally Constructed? A Comparison of French and American Coverage of Global Climate Change', *Mass Communication and Society*, 7(3): 359–77.

Brouillaud, C. (2005) 'La Ligue du Nord et les politiques publiques italiennes: Influence, instrumentalisation et échecs (1991–2004)', in *Les Partis Régionalistes en Europe: Des Acteurs en Développement?* (Brussels: Éditions de l'Université de Bruxelles), 119–46.

Brownlee, J., Masoud, T., and Reynolds, A. (2013) 'Why the Modest Harvest?', *Journal of Democracy*, 24(4): 29–44.

Brüggemann, M., Engesser, S., Büchel, F., Humprecht, E., and Castro, L. (2014), 'Hallin and Mancini Revisited: Four Empirical Types of Western Media Systems', *Journal of Communication*, 64(6): 1037–65.

Brusis, M. (2002) 'Between EU Requirements, Competitive Politics and National Traditions: Recreating Regions in the Accession Countries of Central and Eastern Europe', *Governance*, 15(4): 531–59.

Brym, R. (ed.) (1986) *Regionalism in Canada* (Richmond Hill, Ontario: Irwin).

Buchanan, J. M. (1977) 'Why Does Government Grow?', in T. Borcherding (ed.), *Budgets and Bureaucrats: The Sources of Government Growth* (Durham, NC: Duke University Press), 3–18.

Buchanan, J. M. and Faith, R. L. (1987) 'Secession and the Limits of Taxation: Toward a Theory of Internal Exit', *American Economic Review*, 77: 1023–31.

Budge, I. (1994) 'A New Spatial Theory of Party Competition: Uncertainty, Ideology and Policy Equilibria Viewed Comparatively and Temporally', *British Journal of Political Science*, 24(4): 443–67.

Budge, I. (2000) 'Deliberative Democracy versus Direct Democracy—Plus Political Parties!', in M. Saward (ed.) *Democratic Innovation* (London: Routledge).

Budge, I. and Keman, H. E. (1990) *Parties and Democracy: Coalition Formation and Government Functioning in 22 Democracies* (Oxford: Oxford University Press).

Budge, I. and Klingemann, H.-D. (2001) 'Finally! Comparative Over-Time Mapping of Party Policy Movement', in I. Budge, H.-D. Klingemann, A. Volkens, J. Bara, and E. Tanenbaum (eds), *Mapping Policy Preferences: Estimates for Parties, Electors and Governments 1945–1998* (Oxford: Oxford University Press), 75–90.

Budge, I., Klingemann, H.-D., Volkens, A., Bara, J., and Tanenbaum, E. (2001) *Mapping Policy Preferences: Estimates for Parties, Electors, and Governments, 1945–1998* (Oxford: Oxford University Press).

Buechler, S. M. (2004) 'The Strange Career of Strain and Breakdown Theories of Collective Action', in D.A. Snow, S. A. Soule, and H. Kriesi (eds), *The Blackwell Companion to Social Movements* (Malden, MA: Blackwell), 47–66.

Bueno de Mesquita, B., Smith, A., Siverson, R. M., and Morrow, J. D. (2003) *The Logic of Political Survival* (Cambridge, MA: MIT Press).

Bunte, J. B. and Kim A. A. (2017) 'Citizens' Preferences and the Portfolio of Public Goods: Evidence from Nigeria', *World Development*, 92: 28–39.

Burch, M. and Holliday, I. (1996) *The British Cabinet System* (London: Prentice-Hall/Harvester Wheatsheaf).

Burger, P., Kanhai, S., Pleijter, A., and Verbene, S. (2019) 'The Reach of Commercially Motivated Junk News on Facebook', PLoS ONE 14(8) (https://doi.org/10.1371/journal.pone.0220446).

Burgess, K. and Levitsky, S. (2003) 'Explaining Populist Party Adaptation in Latin America: Environmental and Organizational Determinants of Party Change in Argentina, Mexico, Peru, and Venezuela', *Comparative Political Studies*, 36(8): 881–911.

Burgess, M. (ed.) (1986) *Federalism and Federation in Western Europe* (London: Croom Helm).

Burgess, M. (2011) 'Success and Failure in Federation: Comparative Perspectives', in T. Courchene, J. Allan, C. Leuprecht, and N. Verelli (eds), *The Federal Idea: Essays in Honour of Ronald L. Watts* (Montreal/Kingston: McGill-Queen's University Press), 189–206.

Burgess, M. and Gagnon, A.-G. (eds) (1993) *Comparative Federalism and Federation: Competing Traditions and Future Directions* (Harlow: Harvester Wheatsheaf).

Burke, E. (1770) [1889] 'Thoughts on the Present Discontents', in *The Works of the Right Honourable Edmund Burke* (9th edn) (Boston, MA: Little, Brown), 433–551.

Burnell, P. (2011) *Promoting Democracy Abroad. Policy and Performance* (Piscataway, NJ: Transaction Publishers).

Burnell, P. (2013) 'Democratisation in the Middle East and North Africa: Perspectives from Democracy Support', *Third World Quarterly*, 34(5): 838–55.

Burnell, P. (2017) 'International Political Party Support by "Bad Guys"', CSGR Working Paper 283/17 (http://www.warwick.ac.uk/csgr/papers/283–17.pdf).

Burnell, P. and Gerrits, A. (eds) (2012) *Promoting Party Politics in Emerging Democracies* (Abingdon: Routledge).

Burnham, P., Gilland, K., Grant, W., and Layton-Henry, Z. (2004) *Research Methods in Politics* (Houndmills, Basingstoke: Palgrave Macmillan).

Busemeyer, M. R. (2009) 'From Myth to Reality: Globalisation and Public Spending in OECD Countries Revisited', *European Journal of Political Research*, 48(4): 455–82.

Busemeyer, M. R. and Garritzmann, J. L. (2018) 'Compensation or Social Investment? Revisiting the Link between Globalisation and Popular Demand for the Welfare State', *Journal of Social Policy*, https://doi.org/10.1017/S0047279418000569.

Bussemaker, J. and van Kersbergen, K. (1994) 'Gender and Welfare States: Some Theoretical Reflections', in D. Sainsbury (ed.), *Gendering Welfare States* (London: Sage), 8–25.

Büthe, T. (2002) 'Taking Temporality Seriously: Modeling History and the Use of Narratives as Evidence', *American Political Science Review*, 96(3): 481–93.

Butler, D. and Ranney, A. (1994a) 'Practice', in D. Butler and A. Ranney (eds), *Referendums around the World: The Growing Use of Direct Democracy* (Houndmills, Basingstoke: Palgrave Macmillan), 1–10.

Butler, D. and Ranney, A. (eds) (1994b) *Referendums around the World: The Growing Use of Direct Democracy* (Basingstoke: Macmillan).

Cairney, P. (2016) *The Politics of Evidence Based Policy* (Berlin: Springer).

Cairney, P., Oliver, K., and Wellstead, A. (2016) 'To Bridge the Divide between Evidence and Policy: Reduce Ambiguity as Much as Uncertainty', *Public Administrative Review*, 76(3): 339–402.

Cairns, A. (1968) 'The Electoral System and the Party System in Canada, 1921–1965', *Canadian Journal of Political Science*, 1(1): 55–80.

Caldeira, G. A. and Gibson, J. L. (1995) 'The Visibility of the Court of Justice in the European Union', *American Political Science Review*, 89(2): 356–76.

Calhoun, C. (1993) '"New Social Movements" of the Early Nineteenth Century', *Social Science History*, 17(3): 385–427.

Calmfors, L. and Driffill, J. (1988) 'Bargaining Structure, Corporatism and Macroeconomic Performance', *Economic Policy*, 6(1): 12–61.

Cameron, D. R. (1978) 'The Expansion of the Public Economy: A Comparative Analysis', *American Political Science Review*, 72(4): 1243–61.

Cameron, D. R. (1984) 'Social Democracy, Corporatism, Labor Quiescence and the Representation of Economic Interests in Advanced Capitalist Society', in J. H. Goldthorpe (ed.), *Order and Conflict in Contemporary Capitalism* (Oxford: Oxford University Press), 143–78.

Camia, V. and Caramani, D. (2011) 'Family Meetings: Ideological Convergence within Party Families across Europe, 1945–2009', *Comparative European Politics*, 10(1): 48–85.

Cammack, P. (1997) 'Globalisation and Liberal Democracy', *European Review*, 6(2): 249–63.

Cammaerts, B., Mattoni, A., and McCurdy, P. (eds) (2013) *Mediation and Protest Movements* (Bristol, UK and Chicago: Intellect).

Campbell, D. E. (2013) 'Social Networks and Political Participation', *Annual Review of Political Science*, 16(1): 33–48.

Campbell, J. L. (1998) 'Institutional Analysis and the Role of Ideas in Political Economy', *Theory and Society*, 27: 377–409.

Canel, M. J. and Sanders, K. (2014) 'Is It Enough to Be Strategic? Comparing and Defining Professional Government Communication across Disciplinary Fields and between Countries', in M. J. Canel and K. Voltmer (eds), *Comparing Political Communication across Time and Space: New Studies in an Emerging Field* (Basingstoke: Palgrave), 98–116.

Cantoni, D., Chen, Y., Yang, D., Yuchtman, N., and Zhang, Y. (2014) 'Curriculum and Ideology', National Bureau of Economic Research Working Paper No. w20112.

Cao, X. and Ward, H. (2015) 'Winning Coalition Size, State Capacity, and Time Horizons: An Application of Modified Selectorate Theory to Environmental Public Goods Provision', *International Studies Quarterly*, 59(2): 269–79.

Capoccia, G. (2002) 'Anti-System Parties: A Conceptual Reassessment', *Journal of Theoretical Politics*, 14(1): 9–35.

Capoccia, G. (2005) *Defending Democracy: Reactions to Extremism in Interwar Europe* (Baltimore, MD: Johns Hopkins University Press).

Capoccia, G. and D. Keleman (2007) 'The Study of Critical Junctures: Theory, Narratives and Counterfactuals in Historical Institutionalism', *World Politics* 69: 341–69.

Caramani, D. (2000) *Elections in Western Europe since 1815: Electoral Results by Constituencies* (supplemented with CDROM) (London: Palgrave).

Caramani, D. (2004) *The Nationalization of Politics: The Formation of National Electorates and Party Systems in Western Europe* (Cambridge: Cambridge University Press).

Caramani, D. (2009) *Introduction to the Comparative Method with Boolean Algebra* (Beverly Hills, CA: Sage).

Caramani, D. (2015) *The Europeanization of Politics: The Formation of a European Electorate and Party System in Historical Perspective* (Cambridge: Cambridge University Press).

Card, D. and Krueger, A. B. (1994) 'Minimum Wages and Employment: A Case Study of the Fast-Food Industry in New Jersey and Pennsylvania', *American Economic Review*, 84(4): 772–93.

Carey, J. M. and Shugart, M. S. (eds) (1998) *Executive Decree Authority* (Cambridge: Cambridge University Press).

Carney, J. (1980) 'Regions in Crisis: Accumulation, Regional Problems and Crisis Formation', in J. Carney, R. Hudson, and J. Lewis (eds), *Regions in Crisis: New Perspectives in European Regional Theory* (London: Croom Helm), 28–59.

Carothers, T. (2004) *Critical Mission: Essays on Democracy Promotion* (Washington, DC: Carnegie Endowment for International Peace).

Carothers, T. (2012) 'Democracy Policy under Obama: Revitalization or Retreat?', Carnegie Report (Washington, DC: Carnegie Endowment for International Peace).

Carothers, T. (2015) 'The Closing Space Challenge: How Are Funders Responding?', paper 2 November 2015 (Washington, DC: Carnegie Endowment for International Peace) (http://www.carnegieendowment.org/files/**closing_space**.pdf).

Carothers, T. and Brown, F. (October 2018) 'Can U.S. Democracy Policy Survive Trump?' (Washington, DC: Carnegie Endowment for International Peace) (https://carnegieendowment.org/2018/10/01/can-u.s.-democracy-policy-survive-trump-pub-77381).

Carothers, T. and Youngs, R. (2011) 'Looking for Help. Will Rising Democracies Become International Democracy Supporters?', Democracy and Rule of Law Paper (Washington, DC: Carnegie Endowment for International Peace).

Cartwright, N. (2002) 'The Limits of Causal Order, From Economics to Physics', in Uskali Mäki (ed.), *Fact and Fiction in Economics: Models, Realism, and Social Construction* (Cambridge: Cambridge University Press), 137–51.

Casal Bértoa, F. (2017) 'Political Parties or Party Systems? Assessing the "Myth" of Institutionalisation and Democracy', *West European Politics*, 40(2): 402–29.

Castells, M. (1998) *The Power of Identity* (Oxford: Blackwell).

Castles, F. G. (1978) *The Social Democratic Image of Society: A Study of the Achievements and Origins of Scandinavian Social Democracy in Comparative Perspective* (London: Routledge & Kegan Paul).

Castles, F. G. (1985) *The Working Class and Welfare: Reflections on the Political Development of the Welfare State in Australia and New Zealand, 1890–1980* (London: Allen & Unwin).

Castles, F. G. (1987) 'Comparative Public Policy Analysis: Problems, Progress and Prospects', in F. G. Castles, F. Lehner, and M. G. Schmidt (eds), *Managing Mixed Economies* (Berlin: de Gruyter), 197–224.

Castles, F. G. (1989) 'Social Protection by Other Means: Australia's Strategy of Coping with External Vulnerability', in F. G. Castles (ed.), *The Comparative History of Public Policy* (Cambridge: Polity Press), 16–55.

Castles, F. G. (1996) 'Needs-Based Strategies of Social Protection in Australia and New Zealand', in G. Esping-Andersen (ed.), *Welfare States in Transition: National Adaptations in Global Economies* (London: Sage) 88–115.

Castles, F. G. and Mitchell, D. (1992) 'Identifying Welfare State Regimes: The Links between Politics, Instruments and Outcomes', *Governance*, 5(1): 1–26.

Castles, F. G. and Wildenmann, R. (eds) (1986) *Visions and Realities of Party Government* (Berlin: de Gruyter).

Castro Herrero, L., Humprecht, E., Engesser, S., Brüggemann, M., and Büchel, F. (2017) 'Rethinking Hallin and Mancini beyond the West: An Analysis of Media Systems in Central and Eastern Europe', *International Journal of Communication*, 11: 4797–823.

Castro Herrero, L., Nir, L., and Skorsgaard, M. (2018) 'Bridging Gaps in Gross-Cutting Media Exposure: The Role of Public Service Broadcasting', *Political Communication*, 35(4): 542–65.

Caulfield, J. (2000) 'Local Government Finance in OECD Countries', paper presented at 'Local Government at the Millenium' International Seminar, University of New South Wales, 19 February 2000.

Causa, O., de Serres, A., and Ruiz, N. (2014) 'Can Pro-Growth Policies Lift All Boats? An Analysis Based on Household Disposable Income', OECD Economics Department Working Papers, No. 1180 (OECD).

Ceccobelli, D. (2018) 'Not Every Day is Election Day: A Comparative Analysis of Eighteen Election Campaigns on Facebook', Journal of Information Technology & Politics, 15(2): 122–41.

Chadwick, A., Dennis, J., and Smith, A. P. (2016). 'Politics in the Age of Hybrid Media: Power, Systems, and Media Logics', in A. Bruns, E. Gunn, E. Skogerbo, et al. (eds), The Routledge Companion to Social Media and Politics (New York: Routledge), 7–22.

Chalmers, A. W. (2013) 'Trading Information for Access: Informational Lobbying Strategies and Interest Group Access to the European Union', Journal of European Public Policy, 20(1): 39–58.

Chambers, W. N. (1967) The American Party Systems: Stages of Political Development (New York: Oxford University Press).

Chan, M., Chen, H. T., and Lee, F. L. F. (2019) 'Examining the Roles of Political Social Network and Internal Efficacy on Social Media News Engagement: A Comparative Study of Six Asian Countries', International Journal of Press/Politics, 24(2): 127–45.

Chang, E. C. C. and Golden, M. A. (2007) 'Electoral Systems, District Magnitude and Corruption', British Journal of Political Science, 37: 115–37.

Chang, E. and Golden, M. A. (2010) 'Sources of Corruption in Authoritarian Regimes', Social Science Quarterly, 91(1): 1–20.

Charron, N. (2016) 'Do Corruption Measures have a Perception Problem? Assessing the Relationship between Experiences and Perceptions of Corruption among Citizens and Experts', European Political Science Review, 8(1): 147–71.

Charron, N., Lapuente V., and Annoni, P. (2019) 'Measuring Quality of Government in EU Regions across Space and Time', Regional Science, https://doi.org/10.1111/pirs.12437.

Chehabi, H. E. and Linz, J. J. (1998) Sultanistic Regimes (Baltimore, MD: Johns Hopkins University Press), chs 1 and 2.

Cheibub, J. A. (2007) Presidentialism, Parliamentarism, and Democracy (Cambridge: Cambridge University Press).

Cheibub, J. A., Przeworski, A., and Saiegh, S. M. (2004) 'Government Coalitions and Legislative Success under Presidentialism and Parliamentarism', British Journal of Political Science, 34: 565–87.

Chen, X. (2012) Social Protest and Contentious Authoritarianism in China (Cambridge: Cambridge University Press).

Chenoweth, E. and Stephan, M. J. (2012) Why Civil Resistance Works: The Strategic Logic of Nonviolent Conflict (New York: Columbia University Press).

Chhibber, P. and Kollman, K. (2004) The Formation of National Party Systems: Federalism and Party Competition in Canada, Great Britain, India, and the United States (Princeton, NJ: Princeton University Press).

Chilcote, R. H. (1994) Theories of Comparative Politics: The Search for a Paradigm Reconsidered (2nd edn) (Boulder, CO: Westview Press).

Christensen, D. and Weinstein, J. (2013) 'Defunding Dissent: Restrictions on Aid to NGOs', Journal of Democracy, 24(2): 77–91.

Chua, A. (2003) World on Fire: How Exporting Free Market Democracy Breeds Ethnic Hatred and Global Instability (New York: Doubleday).

Chwe, M. S.-Y. (2001) Rational Ritual: Culture, Coordination, and Common Knowledge (Princeton, NJ: Princeton University Press).

Cigler, A. J. and Loomis, B. A. (eds) (2011) Interest Group Politics (8th edn) (Washington, DC: CQ Press).

Cigler, A. J., Loomis, B. A., and Nownes, A. J. (eds) (2015) Interest Group Politics (Washington, DC: CQ Press).

Clark, G. (1980) 'Capitalism and Regional Disparities', Annals of the American Association of Geographers, 70(2): 521–32.

Clasen, J. and Clegg, D. (eds) (2011) Regulating the Risk of Unemployment. National Adaptations to Post-Industrial Labour Markets in Europe (Oxford: Oxford University Press).

Clasen, J. and Clegg, D. (eds) (2011) Regulating the Risk of Unemployment. National Adaptations to Post-Industrial Labour Markets in Europe (Oxford: Oxford University Press).

Clasen, J. and Siegel, N. A. (2007) Investigating Welfare State Change. The 'Dependent Variable Problem' in Comparative Analysis (Cheltenham: Edward Elgar).

Clausen, L. (2003) Global News Production (Copenhagen: CBS Press).

Clayton, R. and Pontusson, J. (1998) 'Welfare-State Retrenchment Revisited: Entitlement Cuts, Public Sector Restructuring, and Inegalitarian Trends in Advanced Capitalist Societies', World Politics, 51(1): 67–98.

Clement, S. A. and Andersen, J. G. (2007) 'Unemployment and Incentives: What Do We Know? Micro-Level Evidence from Scandinavian Surveys', CCWS Working Papers (Baltimore, MD: Johns Hopkins University Press).

Cobb, R. W. and Elder, C. D. (1972) Participation in American Politics: The Dynamics of Agenda-Building (Baltimore, MD: Johns Hopkins University Press).

Cobb, R. W., Ross, J.-K., and Ross, M.-K. (1976) 'Agenda Building as a Comparative Political Process', American Political Science Review, 70: 26–138.

Coen, D. (1997) 'The Evolution of the Large Firm as a Political Actor in the European Union', Journal of European Public Policy 4(1): 91–108.

Coen, D. (2010) 'European Business–Government Relations', in D. Coen, W. Grant, and G. Wilson (eds), The Oxford Handbook of Business and Government (Oxford: Oxford University Press).

Coen, D. and Richardson, J. (2009) Lobbying in the European Union: Institutions, Actors, and Issues (Oxford: Oxford University Press).

Cohen, A. A. (ed.) (2013) Foreign News on Television: Where in the World is the Global Village? (New York: Peter Lang).

Cohen, J. (1994) 'The Earth Is Round (p. < .05)', American Psychologist, 49(12): 997–1003.

Cohen, J. and Rogers J. (eds) (1995) Associations and Democracy (London: Verso).

Cohen, M., March, J., and Olsen, J. (1972) 'A Garbage Can Model of Organizational Choice', Administrative Science Quarterly, 17(1): 1–25.

Colantone, I. and Stanig, P. (2018) 'Global Competition and Brexit', American Policial Science Review, 112(2): 201–18.

Coleman, J. S. (1988) 'Social Capital in the Creation of Human Capital', American Journal of Sociology, 94: 95–120.

Colley, L. (1992) Britons: Forging the Nation, 1707–1837 (New Haven, CT: Yale University Press).

Collier, D. (1991) 'New Perspectives on the Comparative Method', in D. A. Rustow and K. P. Ericksen (eds), Comparative Political Dynamics: Global Research Perspectives (New York: Harper & Collins), 7–31.

Collier, D. (1993) 'The Comparative Method', in A. W. Finifter (ed.), Political Science: The State of the Discipline II (Washington D.C.: American Political Science Association), 105–19.

Collier, D. (2011) 'Understanding Process Tracing', *Political Science and Politics*, 44(4): 823–30.

Collier, D. and Elman, C. (2008) 'Qualitative and Multi-Method Research: Organizations, Publication, and Reflections on Integration', in J. M. Box-Steffensmeier, H. E. Brady, and D. Collier (eds), *Oxford Handbook of Political Methodology* (Oxford: Oxford University Press), 780–95.

Collier, D. and Levitsky, S. (1997) 'Democracy with Adjectives: Conceptual Innovation in Comparative Research', *World Politics*, 49(3): 430–51.

Collier, D. and Mahon, J. E., Jr (1993) 'Conceptual Stretching Revisited: Adapting Categories in Comparative Analysis', *American Political Science Review*, 87(4): 845–55.

Collier, R. B. (1999) *Paths toward Democracy: The Working Class and Elites in Western Europe and South America* -(Cambridge: Cambridge University Press).

Collier, R. B. and Collier, D. (1991) *Shaping the Political Agenda: Critical Junctures, the Labor Movement and Regime Dynamics in Latin America* (Notre Dame, IN: University of Notre Dame Press).

Collins, K. (2006) *Clan Politics and Regime Transition in Central Asia* (Cambridge: Cambridge University Press).

Colomer, J. (ed.) (2004) *Handbook of Electoral System Choice* (Houndmills, Basingstoke: Palgrave Macmillan).

Colomer, J. and Negretto, G. L. (2005) 'Can Presidentialism Work like Parliamentarianism?', *Government and Opposition*, 40(1): 60–89.

Congressional Budget Office (2013) 'The Distribution of Major Tax Expenditures in the Individual Income Tax System' (Congress of the United States / Congressional Budget Office).

Connolly, W. E. (1969) 'Challenge to Pluralist Theory', in W. E. Connolly (ed.), *The Bias of Pluralism* (New York: Atheron Press), 3–34.

Conrad, C. R. and Golder, S. N. (2010) 'Measuring Government Duration and Stability in Central Eastern European Democracies', *European Journal of Political Research*, 49(1): 119–50.

Converse, P. E. (1964) 'The Nature of Belief Systems in Mass Publics', in D. Apter (ed.), *Ideology and Discontent* (Glencoe: Free Press).

Cook, L. (2010) 'Eastern Europe and Russia', in F. G. Castles, S. Leibfried, J. Lewis, H. Obinger, and C. Pierson (eds), *The Oxford Handbook of the Welfare State* (Oxford: Oxford University Press), 671–86.

Cooke, F. L. (2011) 'Employment Relations in China', in G. J. Bamber, R. D. Landsbury, and N. Wailes (eds) *International and Comparative Employment Relations. Globalisation and Change* (London: Sage), 307–29.

Cooley, A. (2015) 'Countering Democratic Norms', *Journal of Democracy*, 26(3): 49–63.

Coppedge, M. (2012) *Democratization and Research Methods* (Cambridge: Cambridge University Press).

Coppedge, M., and Reinicke, W. H. (1990) 'Measuring Polyarchy', *Studies in Comparative International Development*, 25: 51–72.

Coppedge, M., Gerring, J., Altman, D., Bernhard, M., Fish, S., Hicken, et al. (2011) 'Conceptualizing and Measuring Democracy: A New Approach', *Perspectives on Politics*, 9(2): 247–67.

Corrales, J. and Penfold, M. (2001) *Dragon in the Tropics: Hugo Chavez and the Political Economy of Revolution in Venezuela* (Washington, DC: Brookings Institution Press).

Council of Europe (1985) 'The European Charter of Local Self-Government' (http://conventions.coe.int/Treaty/EN/Reports/HTML/122.htm).

Council of Europe (2000) 'The Financial Resources of Local Authorities in Relation to Their Responsibilities: A Litmus Test for Subsidiarity', Fourth General Report on Political Monitoring of the Implementation of the European Charter of Local Self-Government, rapporteur Jean-Claude Frécon, Strasbourg, 20 April 2000.

Cox, G. (1997) *Making Votes Count: Strategic Coordination in the World's Electoral Systems* (Cambridge: Cambridge University Press).

Cox, G., and McCubbins, M. D. (2001) 'The Institutional Determinants of Economic Policy Outcomes', in S. Haggard and M. D. McCubbins (eds), *Presidents, Parliaments, and Policy* (Cambridge: Cambridge University Press), 21–63.

Cox, G. and Morgenstern, S. (2002) 'Epilogue: Latin America's Reactive Assemblies and Proactive Presidents', in S. Morgenstern and B. Nacif (eds), *Legislative Politics in Latin America* (Cambridge: Cambridge University Press), 446–68.

Cox, M., Ikenberry, J., and Inoguchi, T. (eds) (2000) *American Democracy Promotion: Impulses, Strategies, and Impacts* (Oxford: Oxford University Press).

Cox, R. H. (2001) 'The Social Construction of an Imperative: Why Welfare Reform Happened in Denmark and the Netherlands But Not in Germany', *World Politics*, 53(3): 463–98.

Crafts, N. and Toniolo, G. (1996) 'Postwar Growth: An Overview', in N. Crafts and G. Toniolo (eds), *Economic Growth in Europe since 1945* (Cambridge: Cambridge University Press), 1–37.

Creswell, J. W. (2015) *A Concise Introduction to Mixed Methods Research* (London: Sage).

Crombez, C. (1997) 'Policy Making and Commission Appointment in the European Union', *Aussenwirtschaft*, 52(1–2): 63–82.

Crossman, R. H. S. (1963) 'Introduction', in W. Bagehot, *The English Constitution* (Glasgow: Collins).

Crossman, R. H. S. (1972) *The Myths of Cabinet Government* (Cambridge, MA: Harvard University Press).

Crouch, C. (1999) *Social Change in Western Europe* (Oxford: Oxford University Press).

Crouch, C. (2000) 'The Snakes and Ladders of Twenty- First Century Trade Unionism', *Oxford Review of Economic Policy*, 16(1): 70–83.

Crouch, C. (2004) *Post-Democracy* (Cambridge: Polity Press).

Crouch, C. (2009) 'Privatised Keynesianism: An Unacknowledged Policy Regime', *British Journal of Politics & International Relations*, 11(3): 382–99.

Crouch, C. (2010) 'The Global Firm', in D. Coen, W. Grant, and G. Wilson (eds), *The Oxford Handbook of Business and Government* (Oxford: Oxford University Press).

Crouch, C. (2011) *The Strange Non-Death of Neo-Liberalism* (Cambridge: Polity Press).

Crouch, C. and Pizzorno A. (1978) *The Resurgence of Class Conflict in Western Europe since 1968, Vol. 2: Comparative Analysis* (New York: Holmes and Meier).

Crozier, M., Huntington, S. P., and Watanuki, J. (1975) *The Crisis of Democracy* (New York: New York University Press).

Cruz-Martínez, G. (2014) 'Welfare State Development in Latin America and the Caribbean (1970s–2000s): Multidimensional Welfare Index, Its Methodology and Results', *Social Indicators Research*, 119(3): 1295–317.

Curran, J., Iyengar, S., Lund, A. B., and Salovaara-Moring, I. (2009) 'Media System, Public Knowledge and Democracy: A Comparative Study', *European Journal of Communication*, 24(1): 5–26.

Curran, J., Coen S., Aalberg T., and S. Iyengar (2012) 'News Content, Media Consumption and Current Affairs Knowledge', in T. Aalberg and J. Curran (eds), *How Media Inform Democracy: A Comparative Approach* (New York: Routledge) 81–97.

Curran, J., Esser, F., Hallin, D. C., Hayashi, K.,and Lee, C. C. (2017) 'International News and Global Integration: A Five-Nation Reappraisal', *Journalism Studies*, 18(2): 118–34.

Currinder M., Green J. C., and Conway M. M. (2007) 'Interest Group Money in Elections', in A. J. Cigler and B. A. Loomis (eds), *Interest Group Politics* (Washington, DC: CQ Press), 182–211.

Cutright, P. (1963) 'National Political Development: Measurement and Analysis', *American Sociological Review*, 28(2): 253–64.

Cutright, P. (1965) 'Political Structure, Economic Development and National Social Security Programs', *American Journal of Sociology*, 70(5): 537–50.

Daalder, H. (1966) 'The Netherlands: Opposition in a Segmented Society', in R. Dahl (ed.), *Political Oppositions in Western Democracies* (New Haven, CT: Yale University Press), 188–236.

Daalder, H. (1991) 'Paths towards State Formation in Europe: Democratization, Bureaucratization and Politicization', Working Paper 1991/20 (Madrid: Madrid Instituto Juan March de Estudios e Investigaciones).

Daalder, H. (2002) 'The Development of the Study of Comparative Politics', in H. Keman (ed.), *Comparative Democratic Politics: A Guide to Contemporary Theory and Research* (London: Sage), 16–31.

Dahl, R. A. (1956) *A Preface to Democratic Theory* (Chicago, IL: University of Chicago Press).

Dahl, R. A. (ed.) (1966) *Political Oppositions in Western Democracies* (New Haven, CT: Yale University Press).

Dahl, R. A. (1971) *Polyarchy* (New Haven, CT: Yale University Press).

Dahl, R. A. (1982) *Dilemmas of Pluralist Democracy: Autonomy vs. Control* (New Haven, CT: Yale University Press).

Dahl, R. A. (1989) *Democracy and its Critics* (New Haven, CT: Yale University Press).

Dahl, R. A. (2000) 'A Democratic Paradox?', *Political Science Quarterly*, 115(1): 35–40.

Dahl, R. A. (2002) *How Democratic is the American Constitution?* (New Haven, CT: Yale University Press).

Dahlberg, S. and Holmberg, S. (2014) 'Democracy and Bureaucracy: How Their Quality Matters for Popular Satisfaction', *West European Politics*, 37(3): 515–17.

Dalacoura, K. (2012) 'The 2011 Uprisings in the Arab Middle East: Political Change and Geopolitical Implications', *International Affairs*, 88(1): 63–79.

Dalton, R. J. (1991) 'Comparative Politics of the Industrial Democracies: From the Golden Age to Island Hopping', in W. Crotty (ed.), *Political Science* (Evanston, IL: Northwestern University Press), 15–43.

Dalton, R. J. (ed.) (2004) *Democratic Challenges, Democratic Choices: The Erosion of Political Support in Advanced Industrial Democracies* (Oxford: Oxford University Press).

Dalton, R. J. (2006) *Citizen Politics* (New York: CQ Press).

Dalton, R. J. (2008) *The Good Citizen* (London: Sage).

Dalton, R. J. (2019) *Citizen Politics: Public Opinion and Political Parties in Advanced Industrial Democracies* (Thousand Oaks, CA: Sage).

Dalton, R. J. and Kuechler, M. (eds) (1990) *Challenging the Political Order* (Cambridge: Polity Press).

Dalton, R. J. and Wattenberg, M. (eds) (2000) *Comparing Democracies: Elections and Voting in Global Perspective* (Thousand Oaks, CA: Sage).

Dalton, R. J. and Weldon, S. A. (2005) 'Public Images of Political Parties: A Necessary Evil?', *West European Politics*, 28: 931–51.

Dalton, R. J. and Welzel, C. (2013) *The Civic Culture Transformed: From Allegiant to Assertive Citizenship* (New York: Cambridge University Press).

Dalton, R. J. and Welzel, C. (2014) 'Political Culture and Value Change', in R. J. Dalton and C. Welzel (eds), *The Civic Culture Transformed: From Allegiant to Assertive Citizens* (New York: Cambridge University Press), 1–16.

Dalton, R. J., Baker, K. L., and Hildebrandt, K. (1987) *Germany Transformed* (Boston, MA: Harvard University Press).

Dalton, R. J., Flanagan, S., and Beck, P. A. (1985) *Electoral Change in Advanced Industrial Democracies: Realignment or Dealignment?* (Princeton, NJ: Princeton University Press).

Dalton, R. J., van Sickle. A., and Weldon, S. (2010) 'The Individual-Institutional Nexus of Protest Behavior', *British Journal of Political Science*, 40: 51–73.

Dandoy, R. and Schakel, A. H. (eds) (2013) *Regional and National Elections in Western Europe. Territoriality of the Vote in Thirteen Countries* (Houndmills, Basingstoke: Palgrave Macmillan).

Danish Economic Council (2011) *Dansk Økonomi. Efteraaret 2011* (Copenhagen: The Economic Council).

Darcy, R. and Laver, M. (1990) 'Referendum Dynamics and the Irish Divorce Amendment', *Public Opinion Quarterly*, 54(1): 1–20.

Dardis, F. E. (2006) 'Military Accord, Media Accord. A Cross-National Comparison of UK versus US Press Coverage of Iraq War Protest', *International Communication Gazette*, 68(5–6): 409–26.

Darnovsky, M., Epstein, B., and Flacks, R. (1995) *Cultural Politics and Social Movements* (Philadelphia, PA: Temple University Press).

Däubler, T., Müller, J., and Stecker, C. (2018) 'Assessing Democratic Representation in Multi-Level Democracies', *West European Politics*, 41(3): 541–64.

Daugbjerg, C. and Swinback, A. (2015) 'Globalization and New Policy Concerns: the WTO and the EU's Sustainability Criteria for Biofuels', *Journal of European Public Policy*, 22(3): 429–46.

Davieri, F. and Tabellini, G. (2000) 'Unemployment, Growth and Taxation in Industrial Countries', *Economic Policy*, 30(1): 49–90.

Davis, A. (2019). *Political Communication. A New Introduction for Crisis Times* (Cambridge: Polity Press).

De Francesco, F. (2016) 'Transfer Agents, Knowledge Authority, and Indices of Regulatory Quality: A Comparative Analysis of the World Bank and the Organisation for Economic Co-operation and Development', *Journal of Comparative Policy Analysis: Research and Practice*, 18(4): 350–65.

de la Porte, C., Pochet, P., and Room, G. (2001) 'Social Benchmarking, Policy Making and the Instruments of New Governance', *Journal of European Social Policy*, 11(4): 291–307.

De Smaele, H. (1999) 'The Applicability of Western Media Models on the Russian Media System', *European Journal of Communication*, 14(2): 173–89.

De Swaan, A. (1973) *Coalition Theory and Cabinet Formation* (Amsterdam: Elsevier).

De Vreese, C. H., Peter, J., and Semetko, H. A. (2001) 'Framing Politics at the Launch of the Euro: A Cross-National Comparative Study of Frames in the News', *Political Communication*, 18(2): 107–22.

De Vreese, C. H., Banducci, S., Semetko, H. A., and Boomgaarden, H. G. (2006) 'The News Coverage of the 2004 European Parliamentary Election Campaign in 25 Countries', *European Union Politics*, 7(4): 477–504.

De Vreese, C., Esser, F., and Hopmann, D. (2017) *Comparing Political Journalism* (London: Routledge).

De Winter, L. (2008) 'Belgium: Empowering Voters or Party Elites?', in M. Gallagher and P. Mitchell (eds), *The Politics of Electoral Systems* (Oxford: Oxford University Press), 417–32.

Debus, M. (2007) *Pre-Electoral Alliances, Coalition Rejections, and Multiparty Governments* (Baden-Baden: Nomos).

Delacour, L. and Wolczuk, K. (2015) 'Spoiler or Facilitator of Democratization? Russia's Role in Georgia and Ukraine', *Democratization*, 22(3): 459–78.

Delhey, J. and Newton, K. (2005) 'Predicting Cross-National Levels of Social Trust: Global Pattern or Nordic Exceptionalism?', *European Sociological Review*, 21(4): 311–27.

della Porta, D. (1999) *Social Movements: An Introduction* (Oxford: Blackwell).

della Porta, D. and Caiani, M. (2009) *Social Movements and Europeanization* (Oxford: Oxford University Press).

della Porta, D. and Reiter, H. (1998) *Policing Protest: The Control of Mass Demonstrations in Western Democracies* (Minneapolis, MN: University of Minnesota Press).

della Porta, D. and Rucht, D. (eds) (2013) *Meeting Democracy: Power and Deliberation in Global Justice Movements* (Cambridge: Cambridge University Press).

della Porta, D. and Vannucci, A. (2007) 'Corruption and Anti-Corruption: The Political Defeat of "Clean Hands" in Italy', *West European Politics*, 30(4): 830–53.

della Porta, D., Kriesi, H., and Rucht, D. (eds) (1999) *Social Movements in a Globalizing World* (London: Macmillan).

Delli Carpini, M. X. and Keeter, S. (1996) *What Americans Know about Politics and Why It Matters* (Yale, CT: Yale University Press).

Delwitt, P. (2005) 'Les Partis régionalistes, des acteurs politico-électoraux en essor? Performances électorales et participations gouvernementales', in *Les Partis Régionalistes en Europe: Des Acteurs en Développement?* (Brussels: Éditions de l'Université de Bruxelles), 51–84.

DeNardo, J. (1995) *Power in Numbers: The Political Strategy of Protest and Rebellion* (Princeton, NJ: Princeton University Press).

Deng, Y. (1998) 'The Chinese Conception of National Interests in International Relations', *China Quarterly*, 154: 308–29.

Deschouwer, K. (2012) *The Politics of Belgium. Governing a Divided Society* (Houndmills, Basingstoke, Palgrave Macmillan).

Destradi, S. (2012) 'India as a Democracy Promoter? New Delhi's Involvement in Nepal's Return to Democracy', *Democratization*, 19(2): 286–311.

Deudney, D. and Ikenberry, G. J. (1999) 'The Nature and Sources of Liberal International Order', *Review of International Studies*, 25(2): 179–96.

Deutsch, K. (1966a) *Nationalism and Social Communication: An Inquiry into the Foundations of Nationality* (Cambridge, MA: MIT Press).

Deutsch, K. (1966b) *The Nerves of Government: Models of Political Communication and Control* (New York: Free Press).

Deutsch, K., Lasswell, H. D., Merritt, R. L., and Russett, B. M. (1966) 'The Yale Political Data Program', in R. Merritt and S. Rokkan, S. (eds), *Comparing Nations* (New Haven, CT: Yale University Press), 81–94.

Dialer, D and M. Richter (eds) (2018) *Lobbying in the European Union.* (Cham: Springer).

Diamond, L. (1999) *Developing Democracy* (Baltimore, MD: Johns Hopkins University Press).

Diamond, L. (2007) 'A Quarter-Century of Promoting Democracy', *Journal of Democracy*, 18(4): 118–20.

Diamond, L. and Morlino, L. (eds) (2005) *Assessing the Quality of Democracy* (Baltimore, MD: Johns Hopkins University Press).

Diani, M. (1992) 'The Concept of Social Movement', *The Sociological Review*, 40(1): 1–25.

Diani, M. and Bison, I. (2004) 'Organizations, Coalitions, and Movements', *Theory and Society*, 3: 281–309.

Dicken, P. (2015) *Global Shift: Mapping the Changing Contours of the World Economy* (New York: Guilford Press).

Digital News Report (2016, 2017, 2018, 2019). Oxford Reuters Institute for the Study of Journalism. Open Access.

DiMaggio, P. J. and Powell, W. W. (1991) 'The Iron Cage Revisited: Institutionalised Isomorphism and Collective Rationality in Organizational Fields', in P. J. DiMaggio and W. W. Powell (eds), *The New Institutionalism in Organizational Analysis* (Chicago, IL: Chicago University Press), 63–82.

Dimock, M. and S. Popkin (1997) 'Political Knowledge in Comparative Perspective', in S. Iyengar and R. Reeves (eds), *Do the Media Govern?* (Thousand Oaks, CA: Sage), 217–24.

Dippel, H. (2005) 'Modern Constitutionalism: A History in the Need of Writing', *Legal History Review*, 73(1–2): 153–70.

Disney, R. (2000) *Fiscal Policy and Employment. I: A Survey of Macroeconomic Models, Methods and Findings* (Washington, DC: International Monetary Fund).

Dobbin, F. (1994) *Forging Industrial Policy: The United States, Britain, and France in the Railway Age* (Cambridge: Cambridge University Press).

Dobek-Ostrowska, B. (2019) 'How the Media Systems Work in Central and Eastern Europe', in E. Potonska and C. Beckett (eds), *Public Service Broadcasting and Media Systems in Troubled European Democracies* (Cham: Palgrave Macmillan), 259–78.

Dogan, M. and Pelassy, D. (1990) *How to Compare Nations: Strategies in Comparative Politics* (2nd edn) (Chatham, NJ: Chatham House).

Dogan, M. and Rokkan, S. (eds) (1969) *Quantitative Ecological Analysis in the Social Sciences* (Cambridge, MA: MIT Press).

Dolowitz, D. (1997) 'British Employment Policy in the 1980s: Learning from the American Experience', *Governance*, 10(1): 23–42.

Dolowitz, D. and Marsh, D. (2000) 'Learning from Abroad: The Role of Policy Transfer in Contemporary Policy Making', *Governance*, 13: 5–24.

Dølvik, E. and Martin, A. (eds) (2015) *European Social Models from Crisis to Crisis: Employment and Inequality in the Era of Monetary Integration* (Oxford: Oxford University Press).

Dølvik, J. E., Goul Andersen, J., and Vartianen, J. (2015) 'The Nordic Social Models in Turbulent Times. Consolidation and Flexible Adaptation', in J. E. Dølvik and A. Martin (eds), *European Social Models from Crisis to Crisis. Employment and Inequality in the Era of Monetary Integration* (Oxford: Oxford University Press), 246–86.

Donovan, T. and Bowler, S. (1998) 'Responsive or Responsible Government?', in S. Bowler, T. Donovan, and C. Tolbert (eds),

Citizens as Legislators (Columbus, OH: Ohio State University Press), 249–73.

Donovan, T. and Karp, J. A. (2006) 'Popular Support for Direct Democracy', *Party Politics*, 12(5): 671–88.

Donsbach, W. and Patterson, T. E. (2004) 'Political News Journalists: Partisanship, Professionalism, and Political Roles in Five Countries', in F. Esser and B. Pfetsch (eds), *Comparing Political Communication: Theories, Cases, and Challenges* (New York: Cambridge University Press), 251–70.

Doorenspleet, R. (2000) 'Reassessing the Three Waves of Democratization', *World Politics*, 52(3): 384–406.

Doorenspleet, R. (2005) *Democratic Transitions: Exploring the Structural Sources of the Fourth Wave* (Boulder, CO: Lynne Rienner).

Döring, H. (ed.) (1995) *Parliaments and Majority Rule in Western Europe* (Frankfurt: Campus).

Döring, H. (2001) 'Parliamentary Agenda Control and Legislative Outcomes in Western Europe', *Legislative Studies Quarterly*, 26: 145–66.

Douglas, M. (1978) *Cultural Bias* (London: Royal Anthropological Institute).

Downs, A. (1957) *An Economic Theory of Democracy* (New York: Harper & Row).

Downs, A. (1967) *Inside Bureaucracy* (Boston, MA: Little, Brown).

Drezner, D. W. (2001) 'Globalization and Policy Convergence', *International Studies Review*, 3: 53–78.

Droysen, J. G. (1858) [1969] *Historik* (Darmstadt: Wissenschaftliche Buchgesellschaft).

Druckman, J., Green, D., Kuklinski, J., and Lupia, A. (2006) 'The Growth and Development of Experimental Research in Political Science', *American Political Science Review*, 100(4): 627–35.

Ducheyne, S. (2008) 'J. S. Mill's Canons of Induction: From True Causes to Provisional Ones', *History and Philosophy of Logic*, 29(4): 361–76.

Dukalskis, A. and Gerschewski, J. (eds) (2018) *Justifying Dictatorship. Studies in Autocratic Legitimation* (London and New York: Routledge).

Dunleavy, P. and Bastow, S. (2001) 'Modelling Coalitions that Cannot Coalesce: A Critique of the Laver-Shepsle Approach', *West European Politics*, 24: 1–26.

Dunleavy, P. and Rhodes, R. A. W. (1990) 'Core Executive Studies in Britain', *Public Administration*, 68: 3–28.

Dunning, T. (2012) *Natural Experiments in the Social Sciences* (Cambridge: Cambridge University Press).

Dür, A. (2008) 'Interest Groups in the EU: How Powerful Are They?', *West European Politics*, 32(1): 1212–30.

Durant, T. C. and M. Weintraub (2014) 'How to Make Democracy Self-Enforcing after Civil War: Enabling Conflict Management Yet Adaptable Elite Pacts', *Conflict Management and Peace Science* 1: 1–20.

Durkheim, É. (1950) *Les Règles de la Méthode Sociologique* (11th edn) (Paris: PUF).

Durkheim, É. (1964) [1893] *The Division of Labor in Society* (New York: Free Press).

Durkheim, É. (1988 [1893]) *Über soziale Arbeitsteilung* [*On Social Division of Labor*] (Frankfurt am Main: Suhrkamp).

Duverger, M. (1954) *Political Parties* (New York: Wiley).

Duverger, M. (1972) *Party Politics and Pressure Groups*. New York: Crowell.

Duverger, M. (ed.) (1988) *Les Régimes Sémi-Présidentiels* (Paris: PUF).

Dye, T. R. (1966) *Politics, Economics, and the Public: Policy Outcomes in the American States* (Chicago, IL: Rand McNally).

Dye, T. R. (2005) *Understanding Public Policy* (Upper Saddle River, NJ: Pearson/Prentice-Hall).

Dye, T. R., Schubert, L., and Zeigler, H. (1970) *The Irony of Democracy* (Boston, MA: Wadsworth).

Dyson, K. (1980) *The State Tradition in Western Europe: A Study of an Idea and Institution* (Oxford: Martin Robertson).

Earnest, D. C. (2006) 'Neither Citizen nor Stranger: Why States Enfranchise Resident Aliens', *World Politics*, 58(2): 242–75.

Easton, D. (1953) *The Political System: An Inquiry into the State of Political Science* (New York: Alfred A. Knopf).

Easton, D. (1957) 'An Approach to the Study of Political Systems', *World Politics*, 9(5): 383–400.

Easton, D. (1965a) *A Framework for Political Analysis* (Englewood Cliffs, NJ: Prentice-Hall).

Easton, D. (1965b) *A Systems Analysis of Political Life* (New York: Wiley).

Eaton, K. (2017) *Territory and Ideology in Latin America: Policy Conflicts between National and Subnational Governments* (Oxford: Oxford University Press).

Ebbinghaus, B. (2006) *Reforming Early Retirement in Europe, Japan and the USA* (Oxford: Oxford University Press).

Ebbinghaus, B. (ed.) (2011) *The Varieties of Pension Governance. Pension Privatization in Europe* (Oxford: Oxford University Press).

Ebbinghaus, B. and Manow, P. (eds) (2001) *Comparing Welfare Capitalism: Social Policy and Political Economy in Europe, Japan and the USA* (London: Routledge).

Eckstein, H. (1966) *A Theory of Stable Democracy* (Princeton, NJ: Princeton University Press).

Eckstein, H. (1975) 'Case Studies and Theory in Political Science', in F. Greenstein and N. W. Polsby (eds), *Handbook of Political Science 7* (Reading, MA: Addison-Wesley), 79–138.

Eckstein, S. (ed.) (2001) *Power and Popular Protest. Latin American Social Movements* (updated and expanded edn) (Berkeley, CA: University of California Press).

Eger, M. A. (2010) 'Even in Sweden: The Effect of Immigration on Support for Welfare State Spending', *European Sociological Review*, 26(2): 203–17.

Eichengreen, B. (2018) *The Populist Temptation. Economic Grievance and Political Reaction in the Modern Era* (Oxford: Oxford University Press).

Eising, R., Rasch, D., and Rozbicka, P. (2015) 'Institutions, Policies and Arguments: Contexts and Strategy in EU Policy Framing', *Journal of European Public Policy*, 22(4): 516–33.

Eisinger, P. K. (1973) 'The Conditions of Protest Behavior in American Cities', *American Political Science Review*, 67: 11–28.

Ekiert, G., Kubik, J., and Vachudova, M. A. (2007) 'Democracy in the Post-Communist World: An Unending Quest?', *East European Politics and Societies*, 21(1): 7–30.

Elazar, D. J. (1987) *Exploring Federalism* (Tuscaloosa: University of Alabama Press).

Elazar, D. J. (ed.) (1991) *Federal Systems of the World: A Handbook of Federal, Confederal and Autonomy Arrangements* (Harlow: Longman Current Affairs).

Elazar, D. J. (1995) *Federalism: An Overview* (Pretoria: HSR).

Elgie, R. (1998) 'The Classification of Democratic Regime Types: Conceptual Ambiguity and Contestable Assumptions', *European Journal of Political Research*, 33(2): 219–38.

Elgie, R. (ed.) (1999) *Semi-Presidentialism in Europe* (Oxford: Oxford University Press).

Elgie, R. (ed.) (2001) *Divided Government in Comparative Perspective* (Oxford: Oxford University Press).

Elgie, R. (2008a) 'France: Stacking the Deck', in M. Gallagher and P. Mitchell (eds), *The Politics of Electoral Systems* (Oxford: Oxford University Press), 119–36.

Elgie, R. (2008b) 'The Perils of Semi-Presidentialism. Are They Exaggerated?', *Democratization*, 15(1), 49–66.

Elkins, D. and Simeon, R. (1974) 'Regional Political Cultures in Canada', *Canadian Journal of Political Science*, 6(3): 397–437.

Elkins, D. and Simeon, R. (1979) 'A Cause in Search of an Effect: Or What Does Political Culture Explain?', *Comparative Politics*, 11: 127–45.

Elkins, D. and Simeon, R. (eds) (1980) *Small Worlds: Provinces and Parties in Canadian Political Life* (Agincourt, Ontario: Methuen).

Elkins, Z., and Simmons, B. (2005) 'On Waves, Clusters, and Diffusion: A Conceptual Framework', *The Annals of the American Academy of Political and Social Science*, 598(1): 33–51.

Ellis, A., Navarro, C., Morales, I., Gratschew, M., and Braun, N. (2007) *Voting from Abroad: The International IDEA Handbook* (Stockholm: International IDEA & IFE Mexico).

Elmeskov, J. and MacFarland, M. (1993) *Unemployment Persistence*, OECD Economic Studies 21 (Paris: OECD), 59–88.

Elmeskov, J., Martin, J., and Scarpetta, S. (1998) 'Key Lessons for Labour Market Reforms: Evidence from OECD Countries' Experiences', *Swedish Economic Policy Review*, 5(2): 205–52.

Emmenegger, P., Häusermann, S., Palier, S., and Seeleib-Kaiser, S. (eds) (2012) *The Age of Dualization. The Changing Face of Inequality in Deindustrializing Societies* (Oxford: Oxford University Press).

Emmenegger, P., Kvist, J., Marx, P., and Petersen, K. (2014) 'Three Worlds of Welfare Capitalism: The Making of a Classic', *Journal of European Social Policy*, 25(1): 3–13.

Emmenegger, P. Kvist, J., Marx, P., and Petersen, K. (2015) 'Three Worlds of Welfare Capitalism: The Making of a Classic', *Journal of European Social Policy*, 25(1): 3–13.

Emmerson, D. (2012) 'Minding the Gap between Democracy and Governance', *Journal of Democracy*, 23(2): 62–73.

Enyedi, Z. (2006) 'Party Politics in Post-Communist Transition', in R. S. Katz and W. Crotty (eds), *Handbook of Party Politics* (London: Sage), 228–38.

Epp, C. (1998) *The Rights Revolution: Lawyers, Activists, and Supreme Courts in Comparative Perspective* (Chicago, IL: University of Chicago Press).

Epstein, L. D. (1986) *Political Parties in the American Mold* (Madison, WI: University of Wisconsin Press).

Erne, R. (2008) *European Unions: Labor's Quest for a Transnational Democracy* (Ithaca, NY: Cornell University Press).

Erne, R. (2013) 'Let's Accept a Smaller Slice of a Shrinking Cake. The Irish Congress of Trade Unions and Irish Public Sector Unions in Crisis', *Transfer*, 19(3): 425–30.

Erne, R. (2015) 'Politicizing the New European Economic Governance Regime? Explaining Transnational Trade Union Action in Times of Crisis', *Labor History*, 56(3): 345–68.

Erne, R. (2018) 'Labour Politics and the EU's New Economic Governance Regime (European Unions): A New European Research Council Project', *Transfer*, 24(2): 237–47.

Erne, R. (2019) 'How to Analyse a Supranational Regime that Nationalises Social Conflict? The European Crisis, Labour Politics and Methodological Nationalism', in E. Nanopoulos, and F. Vergis (eds), *The Crisis behind the Eurocrisis: The Eurocrisis as a Multidimensional Systemic Crisis of the EU* (Cambridge: Cambridge University Press), 346–68.

Erne, R. and Imboden, N. (2015) 'Equal Pay by Gender and by Nationality: A Comparative Analysis of Switzerland's Unequal Equal Pay Policy Regimes across Time', *Cambridge Journal of Economics*, 39(2): 655–74.

Ernst, N., Esser, F., Blassnig, S., and Engesser, S. (2019) 'Favorable Opportunity Structures for Populist Communication: Comparing Different Types of Politicians and Issues in Social Media, Television and the Press', *International Journal of Press/Politics*, 24(2): 165–88.

Escobar, A. and Alvarez, S. E. (1992) *The Making of Social Movements in Latin America. Identity, Strategy, and Democracy* (New York: Routledge).

Escribà-Folch, A. (2013) 'Repression, Political Threats, and Survival under Autocracy', *International Political Science Review*, 34(5): 543–60.

Esmark A. and Blach-Orsten, M. (2014), 'Political Communication Roles Inside Out', in B. Pfetsch (ed.), *Political Communication Cultures in Europe: Attitudes of Political Actors and Journalists in Nine Countries* (Houndmills, Basingstoke: Palgrave Macmillan), 246–70.

Esping-Andersen, G. (1985a) *Politics against Markets: The Social Democratic Road to Power* (Princeton, NJ: Princeton University Press).

Esping-Andersen, G. (1985b) 'Power and Distributional Regimes', *Politics and Society*, 14: 223–56.

Esping-Andersen, G. (1990) *The Three Worlds of Welfare Capitalism* (Cambridge: Polity Press).

Esping-Andersen, G. (1996) 'After the Golden Age? Welfare State Dilemmas in a Global Economy', in G. Esping-Andersen (ed.), *Welfare States in Transition. National Adaptations in Global Economies* (London: Sage), 1–31.

Esping-Andersen, G. (1999) *Social Foundations of Post-Industrial Economies* (Oxford: Oxford University Press).

Esping-Andersen, G. (2000) 'Who is Harmed by Labour Market Regulations?', in G. Esping-Andersen and M. Regini (eds), *Why Deregulate Labour Markets?* (Oxford: Oxford University Press), 66–98.

Esping-Andersen, G. (ed.) (2002) *Why We Need a New Welfare State* (Oxford: Oxford University Press).

Esping-Andersen, G. (2015) 'Welfare Regimes and Social Stratification', *Journal of European Social Policy*, 25(1): 124–34.

Esser, F. and Pfetsch, B. (eds) (2004a) *Comparing Political Communication: Theories, Cases, and Challenges* (New York: Cambridge University Press).

Esser, F. and Pfetsch, B. (2004b) 'Meeting the Challenges of Global Communication and Political Integration: The Significance of Comparative Research in a Changing World', in F. Esser and B. Pfetsch (eds), *Comparing Political Communication: Theories, Cases, And Challenges* (New York: Cambridge University Press), 384–410.

Esser, F. and Vliegenthart, R. (2017) 'Comparative Research Methods', in J. Matthes, C. S. Davis, and R. Potter (eds), *The International*

Encyclopedia of Communication Research Methods (Oxford: Wiley-Blackwell), 248–69.

Esser, F. and Umbricht, A. (2013) 'Competing Models of Journalism? Political Affairs Coverage in U.S., British, German, Swiss, French and Italian Newspapers', *Journalism*, 15(8): 989–1007.

Esser, F. and Umbricht, A. (2014) 'The Evolution of Objective and Interpretative Journalism in the Western Press. Comparing Six News Systems since the 1960s', *Journalism and Mass Communication Quarterly*, 91(2): 229–49.

Estevez-Abe, M., Iversen T., and Soskice D. (2001) 'Social Protection and the Formation of Skills: A Reinterpretation of the Welfare State', in P. A. Hall and D. Soskice (eds), *Varieties of Capitalism: The Institutional Foundations of Comparative Advantage* (Oxford: Oxford University Press), 145–83.

Eurofound (2014) *Changes to Wage-Setting Mechanisms in the Context of the Crisis and the EU's New Economic Governance Regime* (Luxembourg: Publications Office of the European Union).

Eurofound (2016) *The Role of Social Partners in the European Semester* (Luxembourg: Publications Office of the European Union).

European Commission (2004) *The Social Situation in the European Union 2004* (Luxembourg: European Commission).

European Industrial Relations Dictionary (2010) 'Fixed-Term Work' (www.eurofound.europa.eu/areas/industrialrelations/dictionary/definitions/fixed-termwork.htm).

Evangelista, M. (2015) 'Explaining the Cold War's End: Process Tracing All the Way Down?', in A. Bennett and J. T. Checkel (eds), *Process Tracing. From Metaphor to Analytic Tool* (Cambridge: Cambridge University Press), 153–85.

Evans, E. and Chamberlain, P. (2015) 'Critical Waves: Exploring Feminist Identity, Discourse and Praxis in Western Feminism', *Social Movement Studies*, 14(4): 396–409.

Evans, P. B. (1995) *Embedded Autonomy: States and Industrial Transformation* (Princeton, NJ: Princeton University Press).

Ezrow, N. M. and Frantz, E. (2011) *Dictators and Dictatorships: Understanding Authoritarian Regimes and Their Leaders* (New York: Bloomsbury).

Faguet, J. (2014) 'Decentralization and Governance', *World Development*, 53: 2–13.

Faguet, J. (2019) 'Revolution from Below: Cleavage Displacement and the Collapse of Elite Politics in Bolivia', *Politics and Society*, https://doi.org/10.1177/0032329219845944.

Faguet, J. and Pöschl, C. (eds) (2015) *Is Decentralization Good for Development? Perspectives from Academics and Policy Makers* (Oxford: Oxford University Press).

Fahlenbrach, K., Sivertsen, E., and Werenskjold, R. (eds) (2014) *Media and Revolt: Strategies and Performances from the 1960s to the Present* (New York/Oxford: Berghahn).

Falleti, T. (2005) 'A Sequential Theory of Decentralization: Latin American Cases in Comparative Perspective', *American Political Science Review*, 99(3): 327–46.

Faletti, T. and Mahoney, J. (2015) 'The Comparative Sequential Method', in J. Mahoney and K. Thelen (eds), *Advances in Comparative-Historical Analysis* (Cambridge: Cambridge University Press), 211–39.

Falter, J. and Klingemann H.-D. (1998) 'Die deutsche Politikwissenschaft im Urteil der Fachvertreter', in M. T. Greven (ed.), *Demokratie eine Kultur des Westens?* (Wiesbaden: Westdeutscher Verlag), 306–41.

Farago, P. (1985) 'Regulating Milk Markets: Corporatist Arrangements in the Swiss Dairy Industry', in W. Streeck and P. C. Schmitter (eds), *Private Interest Government: Beyond Market and State* (London: Sage), 168–81.

Farrell, D. M. (2010) *Electoral Systems: A Comparative Introduction* (2nd edn) (Houndmills, Basingstoke: Palgrave Macmillan).

Farrell, D. M. and McAllister, I. (2008) 'Australia: The Alternative Vote in a Compliant Political Culture', in M. Gallagher and P. Mitchell (eds), *The Politics of Electoral Systems* (Oxford: Oxford University Press).

Farrell, D. M. and Sinnott, R. (2018) 'The electoral system', in J. Coakley and M. Gallagher (eds), *Politics in the Republic of Ireland*, 6th edn (London: Routledge and PSAI Press), 89–110.

Fawn, F. (2006) 'Battle Over the Box: International Election Observation Missions, Political Competition and Retrenchment in the Post-Soviet Space', *International Affairs*, 82(6): 1133–53.

Fearon, J. D. and Laitin, D. D. (1996) 'Explaining Interethnic Cooperation', *American Political Science Review*, 90(4): 715–35.

Ferragina, E., Seeleib-Kaiser, M., and Spreckelsen, T. (2015) 'The Four Worlds of "Welfare Reality"— Social Risks and Outcomes in Europe', *Social Policy & Society*, 14(2): 287–307.

Ferree, M. M., and McClurg Mueller, C. (2004) 'Feminism and the Women's Movement: A Global Perspective', in D. A. Snow, S. A. Soule, and H. Kriesi, H. (eds), *The Blackwell Companion to Social Movements, Blackwell Companions to Sociology* (Malden, MA: Blackwell), 576–607.

Ferree, M. M., Gamson, W. A., Gerhards J., and Rucht, D. (2002) *Shaping Abortion Discourse: Democracy and the Public Sphere in Germany and the United States* (Cambridge: Cambridge University Press).

Ferrera, M. (1996) 'The "Southern Model" of Welfare in Social Europe', *Journal of European Social Policy*, 6(1): 17–37.

Ferrera, M. (1997) 'Introduction Génerale', in *MIRE: Comparer les Systèmes de Protection Sociale en Europe du Sud* (Paris: Ministère Affaire Sociales), 15–26.

Ferrera, M. (2010) 'The South European Counties', in F. G. Castles, S. Leibfried, J. Lewis, H. Obinger, and C. Pierson (eds), *The Oxford Handbook of the Welfare State* (Oxford: Oxford University Press), 616–29.

Field, A. (2014) *Discovering Statistics Using IBM SPSS Statistics* (Los Angeles, CA: Sage).

Fieretos, O., Falleti, T., and Sheingate, A. (2016) 'Historical Institutionalism in Political Science', in O. Fieretos, T. Falleti, and A. Sheingate (eds), *Oxford Handbook of Historical Instttutionalism* (Oxford: Oxford University Press).

Finer, S. E. (1970) *Comparative Government* (London: Allen Lane).

Finer, S. E. (1976) [1962] *The Man on Horseback: The Role of the Military in Politics* (Harmondsworth: Penguin).

Finer, S. E. (1997) *The History of Government from the Earliest Times, Vol. III. Empires, Monarchies, and the Modern State* (Oxford: Oxford University Press).

Finer, S. E. (1999) *The History of Government* (Oxford: Oxford University Press).

Finkel, S., Pérez-Liñán, A., and Seligson, M. A. (2007) 'The Effects of U.S. Foreign Assistance on Democracy Building, 1990–2003', *World Politics*, 59(3): 404–39.

Finnemore, M. and Sikkink, K. (2001) 'Taking Stock: The Constructivist Research Program in International Relations and Comparative Politics', *Annual Review of Political Science*, 4: 391–416.

Fiorina, M. (1996) *Divided Government* (2nd edn) (Boston, MA: Allyn & Bacon).

Fischer, F. (2003) *Reframing Public Policy: Discursive Politics and Deliberative Practices* (Oxford: Oxford University Press).

Fischer, M., Vanone, F., Gava, R., and Sciarini, P. (2019) 'How MPs' Ties to Interest Groups Matter for Legislative Co-Sponsorship', *Social Networks*, 57: 34–42.

Fjelde, H. and De Soysa, I. (2009) 'Coercion, Co-optation, or Co-operation? State Capacity and the Risk of Civil War, 1961–2004', *Conflict Management and Peace Science*, 26(1): 5–25.

Flanagan, S. (1987) 'Value Change in Industrial Society', *American Political Science Review*, 81: 1303–19.

Flanagan, S. and Lee, A.-R. (2003) 'The New Politics, Culture Wars, and the Authoritarian-Libertarian Value Change in Advanced Industrial Democracies', *Comparative Political Studies*, 36: 235–70.

Fletcher, R. and Neilsen, R. K. (2017) 'Are News Audiences Increasingly Fragmented? A Cross-National Comparative Analysis of Cross-Platform News Audience Fragmentation and Duplication', *Journal of Communication*, 67(4): 476–98.

Fletcher, R. and Neilsen, R. K. (2018) 'Are People Incidentally Exposed to News on Social Media? A Comparative Analysis', *New Media and Society*, 20(7): 2450–68.

Flew, T. and Waisbord, S. (2015) 'The Ongoing Significance of National Media Systems in the Context of Media Globalization', *Media, Culture & Society*, 37(4): 620–36.

Flora, P. (1974) *Modernisierungsforschung: Zur empirischen Analyse der gesellschaftlichen Entwicklung* (Opladen: Westdeutscher Verlag).

Flora, P. (1977) *Quantitative Historical Sociology: A Trend Report and Bibliography* (The Hague: Mouton).

Flora, P. (ed.) (1986) *Growth to Limits: The Western European Welfare States since World War II* (Berlin: de Gruyter).

Flora, P. and Alber, J. (1981) 'Modernization, Democratization, and the Development of Welfare States in Western Europe', in P. Flora and A. J. Heidenheimer (eds), *The Development of Welfare States in Europe and America* (Piscataway, NJ: Transaction Publishers), 37–80.

Flora, P. and Heidenheimer, A. J. (1981) 'Introduction', in P. Flora and A. J. Heidenheimer (eds), *The Development of Welfare States in Europe and America* (Piscataway, NJ: Transaction Publishers), 17–34.

Florida, R. (2003) *The Rise of the Creative Class* (New York: Basic Books).

Flynn, J. R. (2009) *What Is Intelligence? Beyond the Flynn Effect* (New York: Cambridge University Press).

Flynn, R. (2012) *Are We Getting Smarter?* (New York: Cambridge University Press).

Foley, M. (1993) *The Rise of the British Presidency* (Manchester: Manchester University Press).

Foley, M. (2000) *The British Presidency: Tony Blair and the Politics of Public Leadership* (Manchester: Manchester University Press).

Føllesdal, A. and Hix, S. (2006) 'Why There is a Democratic Deficit in the EU: A Response to Majone and Moravcsik', *Journal of Common Market Studies*, 44(3): 533–62.

Forbes, E. (1979) *The Maritime Rights Movement, 1919–1927: A Study in Canadian Regionalism* (Montreal/Kingston: McGill-Queen's University Press).

Förster, M. and d'Ercole, M. M. (2005) 'Income Distribution and Poverty in OECD Countries in the Second Half of the 1990s', OECD Social, Employment and Migration Working Paper 22 (Paris: Organization for Economic Cooperation and Development).

Forsyth, M. (1981) *Union of States: The Theory and Practice of Confederation* (Leicester: Leicester University Press).

Foucault, M. (1969) *L'Archéologie du savoir* (Paris: Gallimard).

Fraile, M. and Iyengar, S. (2014) 'Not All News Sources Are Equally Informative. A Cross-National Analysis of Political Knowledge in Europe', *International Journal of Press Politics*, 19(3): 275–94.

Franklin, M. N. (1992) 'The Decline of Cleavage Politics', in M. N. Franklin, T. Mackie, and H. Valen (eds), *Electoral Change: Responses to Evolving Social and Attitudinal Structures in Western Countries* (Cambridge: Cambridge University Press), 383–405.

Franklin, M. N. (2004) *Voter Turnout and the Dynamics of Electoral Competition in Established Democracies since 1945* (Cambridge: Cambridge University Press).

Franklin, M. (2008) 'Quantitative Analysis', in D. della Porta and M. Keating (eds), *Approaches and Methodologies in the Social Sciences* (Cambridge: Cambridge University Press), 240–62.

Franklin, M. N., Mackie, T. T., and Valen, H. (1992) *Electoral Change: Responses to Evolving Social and Attitudinal Structures in Western Countries* (Cambridge: Cambridge University Press).

Frantz, E. and Ezrow, N.M. (2011) *The Politics of Dictatorship: Institutions and Outcomes in Authoritarian Regimes* (Boulder, CO: Lynne Rienner Publishers).

Fredman, S. (2008) *Human Rights Transformed: Positive Rights and Positive Duties* (Oxford: Oxford University Press).

Freeman, G. P. (1985) 'National Styles and Policy Sectors: Explaining Structured Variation', *Journal of Public Policy*, 5(4): 467–96.

Frege, C. and Kelly, J. (1999) *Comparative Employment Relations in the Global Economy* (London: Routledge).

Freitag, M. and Bühlmann M. (2005) 'Political Institutions and the Formation of Social Trust. An International Comparison', *Politische Vierteljahresschrift*, 46(4): 575–86.

Freud, S. and Bullitt, W. C. (1967) *Thomas Woodrow Wilson: A Psychological Portrait* (Boston, MA: Houghton Mifflin).

Freyburg, T., Lavenex, S., Schimmelfennig, F., Skripka, T., and Wetzel, A. (2015) *EU Democracy Promotion by Functional Cooperation: The European Union and Its Neighbourhood* (Houndmills, Basingstoke: Palgrave Macmillan).

Friedrich, C. J. (1950) *Constitutional Government and Democracy: Theory and Practice in Europe and America* (Boston, MA: Ginn).

Friedrich, C. J. (1963) *Man and His Government* (New York: McGraw-Hill).

Friedrich, C.J. and Brzezinski, Z. K. (1965) *Totalitarian Dictatorship* (Cambridge, MA: Harvard University Press).

Fukuyama, F. (1992) *The End of History and the Last Man* (New York: Free Press).

Fukuyama, F. (2011) *The Origins of Political Order* (New York: Farrar, Straus and Giroux).

Fukuyama, F. (2014) *Political Order and Political Decay* (New York: Farrar, Straus and Giroux).

Fukuyama, F. (2018) *Identity. Contemporary Identity Politics and the Struggle for Recognition* (London: Profile Books).

Gabel, M. J. (1998) *Interests and Integration: Market Liberalization, Public Opinion, and European Union* (Ann Arbor, MI: University of Michigan Press).

Gagnon, A.-G. and Hérivault, J. (2007) 'The Bloc Québécois: Charting New Territories?', in A.-G. Gagnon and A. B. Tanguay (eds), *Canadian Parties in Transition* (Peterborough, Ontario: Broadview Press), 111–36.

Gagnon, A.-G. and Lachapelle, G. (1996) 'Québec Confronts Canada: Two Competing Projects Searching for Legitimacy', *Publius*, 26(3): 177–91.

Gagnon, A.-G. and Tully, J. (eds) (2001) *Multinational Democracies* (Cambridge: Cambridge University Press).

Gailus, M. (2005) 'Contentious Food Politics. Sozialer Protest, Märkte und Zivilgesellschaft (18.–20. Jahrhundert)', Discussion Paper SP 2004–504 (Berlin: Wissenschaftszentrum Berlin für Sozialforschung).

Galbraith, J. K., Conceicao, P., and Ferreira, P. (1999) 'Inequality and Unemployment in Europe: The American Cure', *New Left Review*, 237(September–October): 28–51.

Gallagher, M. (1991) 'Proportionality, Disproportionality, and Electoral Systems', *Electoral Studies*, 10(1): 33–51.

Gallagher, M. (1996) 'Conclusion', in M. Gallagher and P. V. Uleri (eds), *The Referendum Experience in Europe* (Houndmills, Basingstoke: Palgrave Macmillan), 226–52.

Gallagher, M. (2008a) 'Conclusion', in M. Gallagher and P. Mitchell (eds), *The Politics of Electoral Systems* (Oxford: Oxford University Press), 535–78.

Gallagher, M. (2008b) 'Ireland: The Discreet Charm of PR-STV', in M. Gallagher and P. Mitchell (eds), *The Politics of Electoral Systems* (Oxford: Oxford University Press), 511–32.

Gallagher, M. and Mitchell, P. (eds) (2008) *The Politics of Electoral System* (Oxford: Oxford University Press).

Gallagher, M. and Uleri, P. V. (eds) (1996) *The Referendum Experience in Europe* (Basingstoke: Macmillan).

Gallagher, M., Laver, M., and Mair, P. (2005) *Representative Government in Modern Europe* (4th edn) (New York: McGraw-Hill).

Gallie, D. (1983) *Social Inequality and Class Radicalism in France and Britain* (Cambridge: Cambridge University Press).

Gallie, D. and Paugam, S. (eds) (2000a) *Welfare Regimes and the Experience of Unemployment in Europe* (Oxford: Oxford University Press).

Gallie, D. and Paugam, S. (eds) (2000b) 'The Experience of Unemployment in Europe: The Debate', in D. Gallie and S. Paugam (eds), *Welfare Regimes and the Experience of Unemployment in Europe* (Oxford: Oxford University Press), 1–24.

Gambetta, D. (1993) *The Sicilian Mafia: The Business of Private Protection* (Cambridge, MA: Harvard University Press).

Gambetta, D. (2005) *Making Sense of Suicide Missions* (Oxford: Oxford University Press).

Gamson, W. (1975) *The Strategy of Social Protest* (Homewood, IL: Dorsey).

Gamson, W. (1992) *Talking Politics* (Cambridge: University of Cambridge Press).

Gamson, W. and Meyer, D. S. (1996) 'Framing Political Opportunity', in D. McAdam, J. D. McCarthy, and M. N. Zald (eds), *Comparative Perspectives on Social Movements: Political Opportunities, Mobilizing Structures, and Cultural Framings* (Cambridge: Cambridge University Press), 275–90.

Gamson, W., Croteau, D., Hoynes, W., and Sasson, T. (1992) 'Media Images and the Social Construction of Reality', *Annual Review of Sociology*, 18: 373–93.

Gandhi, J. (2008) *Political Institutions under Dictatorship* (Cambridge: Cambridge University Press).

Gandhi, J. (2010) *Political Institutions under Dictatorship* (Cambridge: Cambridge University Press).

Gandhi, J. and Przeworski, A. (2007) 'Authoritarian Institutions and the Survival of Autocrats', *Comparative Political Studies*, 40(11): 1279–301.

Ganz, M. (2000) 'Resources and Resourcefulness: Strategic Capacity in the Unionization of California Agriculture, 1959–1966', *American Journal of Sociology*, 105(4): 1003–62.

Gardbaum, S. (2001) 'The New Commonwealth Model of Constitutionalism', *American Journal of Comparative Law*, 49(4): 707–61.

Gardbaum, S. (2013) *The New Commonwealth Model of Constitutionalism: Theory and Practice* (Cambridge: Cambridge University Press).

Garon, S. (1987) *The State and Labor in Modern Japan* (Berkeley, CA: University of California Press).

Garrett, G. (1998) *Partisan Politics in the Global Economy* (Cambridge: Cambridge University Press).

Garrett, G. and Nickerson, D. (2005) 'Globalization, Democratization, and Government Spending in Middle-Income Countries', in M. Glatzer and D. Rueschemeyer (eds), *Globalization and the Future of the Welfare State* (Pittsburgh, PA: University of Pittsburgh Press), 23–48.

Gat, A. (2006) *War in Human Civilization* (New York: Oxford University Press).

Geddes, B. (1999) 'What Do We Know about Democratization after Twenty Years?', *Annual review of Political Science*, 2(1): 115–44.

Geddes, B. (2003) *Paradigms and Sand Castles: Theory Building and Research Design in Comparative Politics* (Ann Arbor, MI: University of Michigan Press).

Geddes, B., Wright, J. and Frantz, E. (2014) 'Autocratic Breakdown and Regime Transitions: A New Data Set', *Perspectives on Politics*, 12(2): 313–31.

Genschel, P. and P. Schwarz (2011) 'Tax Competition: A Literature Review', *Socio-Economic Review*, 9(2): 339–70.

Georgakakis, D. and Rowel, J. (eds) (2013) *The Field of Eurocracy. Mapping EU Actors and Professionals* (London: Palgrave Macmillan).

George, A. and Bennett, A. (2005) *Case Studies and Theory Development in the Social Sciences* (Cambridge, MA, and London: MIT Press).

Gerhards, J. (1993) *Neue Konfliktlinien in der Mobilisierung öffentlicher Meinung. Eine Fallstudie.* (Opladen: Westdeutscher Verlag).

Gerhards, J. and Rucht, D. (1992) 'Mesomobilization: Organizing and Framing in Two Protest Campaigns in West Germany', *American Journal of Sociology*, 98(3): 555–95.

Gerring, J. (2007) *Case Study Research* (Cambridge: Cambridge University Press).

Gerring, J. (2008) 'The Mechanistic Worldview: Thinking Inside the Box', *British Journal of Political Science*, 38(1): 161–79.

Gerring, J. (2011) 'How Good is Good Enough? A Multidimensional, Best-Possible Standard for Research Design', *Political Research Quarterly*, 64(3): 625–36.

Gerring, J. (2012) *Social Science Methodology* (Cambridge: Cambridge University Press).

Gerring, J. (2014) 'Causal Mechanisms: Yes, But …', *Comparative Political Studies*, 43(11): 1499–526.

Gerring, J. (2015) 'The Relevance of Relevance', in G. Stoker, B. G. Peters, and J. Pierre (eds), *The Relevance of Political Science* (London: Palgrave Macmillan), 36–49.

Gerring, J., Thacker, S. C., and Moreno, C. (2005) 'Centripetal Democratic Governance: A Theory and Global Inquiry', *American Political Science Review*, 99(4): 567–81.

Gerring, J., Thacker, S. C., and Alfaro, R. (2012) 'Democracy and Human Development', *Journal of Politics*, 74(1): 1–17.

Gerschewski, J. (2013) 'The Three Pillars of Stability: Legitimation, Repression, and Co-Optation in Autocratic Regimes', *Democratization*, 20(1): 13–38.

Gerston, L. N. (2004) *Public Policy Making: Process and Principles* (Armonk, NY: M. E. Sharpe).

Gervasoni, C. (2010) 'A Rentier Theory of Subnational Regimes: Fiscal Federalism, Democracy, and Authoritarianism in the Argentine Provinces', *World Politics*, 62(2): 302–40.

Geva-May, I. (2004) 'Riding the Wave Opportunity: Termination in Public Policy', *Journal of Public Administration Research and Theory*, 14: 309–33.

Geys, B. (2006) 'Explaining Voter Turnout: A Review of Aggregate-Level Research', *Electoral Studies*, 25(4): 637–63.

Gheciu, A. (2005) 'Security Institutions as Agents of Socialization? NATO and the "New Europe"', *International Organization*, 59: 973–1012.

Ghemawat, P. and Altman, S. A. (2014) 'DHL Global Interconnectedness Index 2014' (http://www.dhl.com/content/dam/Campaigns/gci2014/downloads/dhl_gci_2014_study_high.pdf).

Gibbins, R. (2004) 'Regional Integration and National Contexts: Constraints and Opportunities', in S. Tomblin and C. Colgan (eds), *Regionalism in a Global Society: Persistence and Change in Atlantic Canada and New England* (Peterborough, Ontario: Broadview Press), 37–56.

Gibbins, R. (2005) 'Early Warning, No Response: Alan Cairns and Electoral Reform', in G. Kernerman and P. Resnick (eds), *Insiders and Outsiders: Alan Cairns and the Reshaping of Canadian Citizenship* (Vancouver: University of British Columbia Press), 39–50.

Gibson, R., and Römmele, A. (2019) *Populism and Subversive Campaigning: A Fourth Era of Political Communication?* Paper presented at the 115th American Political Science Association's Annual Meeting in Washington, 29 August–1 September.

Giddens, A. (1990) *The Consequences of Modernity* (Cambridge: Polity Press).

Giger, N. and Nelson, M. (2011) 'The Electoral Consequences of Welfare State Reform. Blame Avoidance or Credit Claiming in the Era of Permanent Austerity?', *European Journal of Political Research*, 50(1): 1–23.

Gilardi, F. (2008) *Delegation in the Regulatory State: Independent Regulatory Agencies in Western Europe* (Cheltenham: Edward Elgar).

Gilbert, N. (2002) *Transformation of the Welfare State: The Silent Surrender of Public Responsibility* (Oxford: Oxford University Press).

Gilens, M. and Page, B. I. (2014) 'Testing Theories of American Politics: Elites, Interest Groups, and Average Citizens', *Perspectives on Politics*, 12(3): 564–81.

Gilland Lutz, K. and Hug, S. (2010) *Financing Referendum Campaigns* (Houndmills, Basingstoke: Palgrave Macmillan).

Gilley, B. (2006) 'The Meaning and Measure of State Legitimacy: Results for 72 Countries', *European Journal of Political Research*, 45: 499–525.

Gilley, B. (2009) *The Right to Rule: How States Win and Lose Legitimacy* (New York: Columbia University Press).

Gilpin, R. (2002) 'The Nation-State in the Global Economy', in D. Held and A. McGrew (eds), *The Global Transformations Reader* (Cambridge: Polity Press), 349–58.

Ginsburg, T. (2003) *Judicial Review in New Democracies: Constitutional Courts in Asian Cases* (Cambridge: Cambridge University Press).

Ginsburg, T. and Simpser, A. (eds) (2013) *Constitutions in Authoritarian Regimes* (Cambridge, MA: Harvard University Press).

Giraud, O. and Maggetti, M. (2015) 'Methodological Pluralism', in D. Braun and M. Maggetti (eds), *Comparative Politics: Theoretical and Methodological Challenges* (Cheltenham: Edward Elgar), 90–124.

Giraudy, A., Moncada, E. and Snyder, R. (eds) (2019) *Inside Countries: Subnational Research in Comparative Politics* (Cambridge: Cambridge University Press).

Gitlin, T. (1980) *The Whole World is Watching: Mass Media and the Making and Unmaking of the New Left* (Berkeley, CA: University of California Press).

Giugni, M. G. (1998) 'Was It Worth the Effort? The Outcomes and Consequences of Social Movements', *Annual Review of Sociology*, 98: 171–93.

Giugni, M. G., McAdam, D., and Tilly, C. (eds) (1999) *How Social Movements Matter* (Minneapolis, MN: University of Minnesota Press).

Glatzer, M. and Rueschemeyer, D. (eds) (2005) *Globalization and the Future of the Welfare State* (Pittsburgh, PA: University of Pittsburgh Press).

Gleditsch, K. S. (2002) *All International Politics is Local—The Diffusion of Conflict, Integration, and Democratization* (Ann Arbor, MI: The University of Michigan Press).

Goertz, G. (2005) *Social Science Concepts* (Princeton, NJ: Princeton University Press).

Goertz, G. (2016) 'Multimethod Research', *Security Studies*, 25(1): 3–24.

Goertz, G. and Starr, H. (2003) *Necessary Conditions: Theory, Methodology, and Applications* (Lanham, MD and Boulder: Rowman & Littlefield).

Goldstone, J. (1997) 'Methodological Issues in Comparative Macrosociology' *Comparative Social Research*, 16: 107–20.

Goldthorpe, J. (2000) *On Sociology: Numbers, Narratives, and the Integration of Research and Theory* (Oxford: Oxford University Press).

Goldthorpe, J. (ed.) (1984) *Order and Conflict in Contemporary Capitalism: Studies in the Political Economy of Western European Nations* (Oxford: Oxford University Press).

Goodin, R. E. and LeGrand, J. (1987) *Not Only the Poor: The Middle Classes and the Welfare State* (London: Allen & Unwin).

Goodin, R. E., Headey, B., Muffels, R., and Dirven, H.-J. (1999) *The Real Worlds of Welfare Capitalism* (Cambridge: Cambridge University Press).

Goodstadt, L. F. (2005) *Uneasy Partners: The Conflict between Public Interest and Private Profit in Hong Kong* (Hong Kong: Hong Kong University Press).

Goodwin, J. (2001) *No Other Way Out: States and Revolutionary Movements, 1945–1991* (Cambridge, MA: Cambridge University Press).

Goodwin, J. and Jasper, J. M. (1999) 'Caught in a Winding, Snarling Vine: The Structural Bias of Political Process Theory', *Sociological Forum*, 14(1): 27–92.

Gough, I. (2001) 'Globalization and Regional Welfare Regimes: The East Asian Case', *Global Social Policy*, 1(2): 163–89.

Granovetter, M. (1978) 'Threshold Models of Collective Behavior', *American Journal of Sociology*, 83(6): 1420–43.

Graham, T., Jackson, D., and Broersma, M. (2016) 'New Platform, Old Habits? Candidates' Use of Twitter during the 2010 British and

Dutch General Election Campaigns', *New Media and Society,* 18(5): 765–83.

Grant, T. D. (2005) *Lobbying, Government Relations and Campaign Financing Worldwide. Navigating the Law, Regulations and Practices of National Regimes* (New York: Oxford University Press).

Graz, J.-C. and Nölke, A. (2008) *Transnational Private Governance and its Limits* (Abingdon: Routledge).

Green, D. and Shapiro, I. (1994) *Pathologies of Rational Choice: A Critique of Applications in Political Science* (New Haven, CT: Yale University Press).

Green-Pedersen, C. (2001) 'Welfare-State Retrenchment in Denmark and the Netherlands, 1982–1998: The Role of Party Competition and Party Consensus', *Comparative Political Studies,* 34(9): 963–85.

Green-Pedersen, C. (2002) *The Politics of Justification. Party Competition and Welfare State Retrenchment in Denmark and the Netherlands from 1982 to 1998* (Amsterdam: Amsterdam University Press).

Green-Pedersen, C. (2004) 'The Dependent Variable Problem within the Study of Welfare-State Retrenchment: Defining the Problem and Looking for Solutions', *Journal of Comparative Policy Analysis,* 6(1): 3–14.

Green-Pedersen, C. (2007) 'The Conflict of Conflicts in Comparative Perspective: Euthanasia as a Political Issue in Denmark, Belgium, and the Netherlands', *Comparative Politics,* 39(3): 273–91.

Green-Pedersen, C. and Haverland, M. (2002) 'The New Politics and Scholarship of the Welfare State', *Journal of European Social Policy,* 12(1): 43–51.

Green-Pedersen, C. and Walgrave, S. (eds) (2014) *Agenda Setting, Policies, and Political Systems: A Comparative Approach* (Chicago, IL and London: Chicago University Press).

Greenwood, J. (2011) *Interest Representation in the European Union* (3rd edn) (Houndmills, Basingstoke: Palgrave Macmillan).

Greenwood, J. (2017) *Interest Representation in the European Union* (4th edn) (Cham: Springer).

Griffin, L. J., O'Connell, P. J., and McCammon, H. J. (1989) 'National Variation in the Context of Struggle: Postwar Class Conflict and Market Distribution in the Capitalist Democracies', *Canadian Review of Sociology and Anthropology,* 26: 37–68.

Griffith, B. (2011) 'Middle-Income Trap', in R. Nallari, S. Yusuf, B. Griffith, and R. Bhattacharya (eds), *Frontiers in Development Policy: A Primer on Emerging Issues* (Washington, DC: The World Bank), 39–44.

Gros, J.-G. (1996) 'Towards a Taxonomy of Failed States in the New World Order', *Third World Quarterly,* 17(3): 455–71.

Gross, A. M. (1998) 'The Politics of Rights in Israeli Constitutional Law', *Israel Studies,* 3: 80–118.

Grossman, S. J. and Hart, O. D. (1983) 'An Analysis of the Principal-Agent Problem', *Econometrica,* 51(1): 7–46.

Gruner, E. (1956) *Die Wirtschaftsverbände in der Demokratie. Vom Wachstum der Wirtschaftsorganisationen im Schweizerischen Staat* (Erlenbach: E. Rentsch).

Grzymala-Busse, A. (2006) 'The Discreet Charm of Formal Institutions: Postcommunist Party Competition and State Oversight', *Comparative Political Studies,* 39(3): 271–300.

Grzymala-Busse, A. (2011) 'Time Will Tell? Temporality and the Analysis of Causal Mechanisms and Processes', *Comparative Political Studies,* 44(9): 1267–97.

Guéhenno, J.-M. (1995) *The End of the Nation-State* (Minneapolis, MN: University of Minnesota Press).

Guibernau, M. (1996) *Nationalisms: The Nation-State and -Nationalism in the Twentieth Century* (Cambridge: Polity Press).

Guibernau, M. (2012) 'Calls for Independence in Catalonia are Part of an Evolution of Spain's Democracy that the Country's Constitution may have to come to Accommodate' (http://blogs.lse.ac.uk/europpblog/2012/10/08/catalonia-independence-spain-constitution).

Gumbrell-McCormick, R. and Hyman, R. (2013) *Trade Unions in Western Europe* (Oxford: Oxford University Press).

Gunther, R. and Mughan, A. (eds) (2000) *Democracy and the Media: A Comparative Perspective* (New York: Cambridge University Press).

Gunther, R., Sani, G., and Shabad, G. (1986) 'Micronationalism and the Regional Party Systems of Euskadi, Catalunya, and Galicia', in R. Gunther, G. Sani, and G. Shabad (eds), *Spain after Franco: The Making of a Competitive Party System* (Berkeley, CA: University of California Press).

Gurevitch, M. and Blumler, J. G. (1977) 'Linkages between the Mass Media and Politics: A Model for the Analysis of Political Communication Systems', in Curran, J., Gurevitch, M. and Wollacott, J. (eds) *Mass Communication and Society* (London: Arnold), 270–90.

Gurevitch, M. and Blumler, J. G. (2004), 'State of the Art of Comparative Political Communication Research: Poised for Maturity?', in F. Esser and B. Pfetsch (eds), *Comparing Political Communcation. Theories, Cases, and Challenges* (New York: Cambridge University Press), 325–43.

Gurr, T. (1970) *Why Men Rebel* (Princeton, NJ: Princeton University Press).

Guttmann, A. and Thompson, D. (2004) *Why Deliberative Democracy?* (Princeton, NJ: Princeton University Press).

Haas, E. B. (1958) *The Uniting of Europe: Political, Social and Economic Forces 1950–1957* (London: Stevens).

Haas, E. B. (1961) 'International Integration: The European and the Universal Process', *International Organization,* 15(3): 366–92.

Haas, P. M. (1992) 'Introduction: Epistemic Communities and International Policy Coordination', *International Organization,* 46(1): 1–37.

Haas, T. (2005), 'From Public Journalism to the Public's Journalism? Rhetoric and Reality in the Discourse on Weblogs', *Journalism Studies,* 6(3): 387–96.

Habermas, J. (1992) *Faktizität und Geltung* (Frankfurt am Main: Suhrkamp).

Habermas, J. (1999) 'The European Nation-State and the Pressures of Globalization', *New Left Review,* 235: 46–59.

Hacker, J. S. (2002) *The Divided Welfare State: The Battle over Public and Private Social Benefits in the United States* (New York: Cambridge University Press).

Hacker, J. S. (2004) 'Privatizing Risk without Privatizing the Welfare State: The Hidden Politics of Social Policy Retrenchment in the United States', *American Political Science Review,* 98(2): 243–60.

Hacker, J. S. and Pierson, P. (2010) *Winner-Take-All Politics: How Washington Made the Rich Richer—and Turned Its Back on the Middle Class* (New York: Simon & Schuster).

Hadenius, A. and Teorell, J. (2005) 'Cultural and Economic Prerequisites of Democracy: Reassessing Recent Evidence', *Studies in Comparative International Development,* 39(4): 87–106.

Hadenius, A. and Teorell, J. (2007) 'Pathways from Authoritarianism', *Journal of Democracy,* 18(1): 143–57.

Hage, J., Hanneman, R., and Gargan, E. T. (1989) *State Responsiveness and State Activism: An Examination of the Social Forces and*

State Strategies that Explain the Rise in Social Expenditure in Britain, France, Germany and Italy 1870–1968 (London: Unwin Hyman).

Hagemann, S. (2008) 'Voting, Statements and Coalition-Building in the Council from 1999–2006', in D. Naurin and H. Wallace (eds), *Unveiling the Council of the European Union: Games Governments Play in Brussels* (London: Palgrave), 36–64.

Hahn, R. W. (1990) 'The Political Economy of Environmental Regulation: Towards a Unifying Framework', *Public Choice*, 65(1): 21–47.

Hainsworth, P. (2006) 'France Says No: The 29 May 2005 Referendum on the European Constitution', *Parliamentary Affairs*, 59 (1): 98–117.

Hall, P. A. (1989) *The Political Power of Economic Ideas* (Princeton, NJ: Princeton University Press).

Hall, P. A. (1993) 'Policy Paradigms, Social Learning and the State', *Comparative Politics*, 25(3): 275–96.

Hall, P. A. (1997) 'The Role of Interests, Institutions and Ideas in the Political Economy of Industrialized Nations', in M. I. Lichbach and A. S. Zuckerman (eds), *Comparative Politics: Rationality, Culture and Structure* (Cambridge: Cambridge University Press), 174–207.

Hall, P. A. (2004) 'Beyond the Comparative Method', *APSA Comparative Politics Newsletter*, 15(2): 1–4.

Hall, P. A. (2014) 'Varieties of Capitalism and the Euro Crisis', *West European Politics*, 37(6): 1223–43.

Hall, P. A. and Lamont, M. (eds) (2009) *Successful Societies: How Institutions and Culture Affect Health* (New York: Cambridge University Press).

Hall, P. A. and Soskice, D. (2001a) 'An Introduction to Varieties of Capitalism', in P. A. Hall and D. Soskice (eds), *Varieties of Capitalism: The Institutional Foundations of Comparative Advantage* (Oxford: Oxford University Press), 1–70.

Hall, P. A. and Soskice, D. (eds) (2001b) *Varieties of Capitalism: The Institutional Foundations of Comparative Advantage* (Oxford: Oxford University Press).

Hall, P. A. and Taylor, R. (1996) 'Political Science and the Three New Institutionalisms', *Political Studies*, 44(5): 936–57.

Halleröd, B., Rothstein, B., Daoud, A., and Nandy, S. (2013) 'Bad Governance and Poor Children: A Comparative Analysis of Government Efficiency and Severe Child Deprivation in 68 Low- and Middle-Income Countries', *World Development*, 48: 19–31.

Hallin, D. (2015). 'Media System', in G. Mazzoleni (ed.), *The International Encyclopedia of Political Communication* (Oxford: Wiley Blackwell), 801–12.

Hallin, D. (2016). 'Typology of Media Systems', in *Oxford Research Encyclopedia of Politics* (Oxford: Oxford University Press), DOI: 10.1093/acrefore/ 9780190228637.013.205.

Hallin, D. C. and Mancini, P. (2004) *Comparing Media Systems: Three Models of Media and Politics* (Cambridge: Cambridge University Press).

Hallin, D. C. and Mancini P. (2012) (eds) *Comparing Media Systems Beyond the Western World* (Cambridge: Cambridge University Press).

Hallin, D. C. and Mancini, P. (2017). 'Ten Years after Comparing Media Systems: What Have We Learned?', *Political Communication*, 34(2): 155–71.

Hamada, B., Huges, S., Hanitzsch, T., Hollings, J., Lauerer, C., Arroyave, J., Rupar, V., and Splendore, S.(2019) 'Editorial Autonomy: Journalists' Perceptions of Their Freedom', in T. Hanitzsch, F. Hanusch, J. Ramaprasad, and A. S. de Beer (eds), *Worlds of Journalism. Journalistic Cultures around the Globe* (New York: Columbia University Press), 133–60.

Hameleers, M., Bos, L., Fawzi, N., Reinemann, C., et al. (2018) 'Start Spreading the News: A Comparative Experiment on the Effects of Populist Communication on Political Engagement in Sixteen European Countries', *International Journal of Press/Politics* 23: 517–38.

Hammond, T. H. (1986) 'Agenda Control, Organizational Structure, and Bureaucratic Politics', *American Journal of Political Science*, 30: 379–420.

Hammond, T. H. and Knott, J. (1996) 'Who Controls the Bureaucracy? Presidential Power, Congressional Dominance, Legal Constraints, and Bureaucratic Autonomy in a Model of Multi-Institutional Policy-Making', *Journal of Law, Economics, and Organization*, 12: 119–66.

Hamrin, C. L. (1992) 'The Party Leadership System', in K. G. Lieberthal and D. M. Lampton (eds), *Bureaucracy, Politics, and Decision Making in Post-Mao China* (Berkeley, CA: University of California Press).

Hancké, B. (ed.) (2009) *Debating Varieties of Capitalism. A Reader* (Oxford: Oxford University Press).

Hanitzsch, T. (2007) 'Deconstructing Journalism Culture: Toward a Universal Theory', *Communication Theory*, 17(4): 367–85.

Hanitzsch, T., Hanusch, F., Ramaprasad, J., and de Beer, A. S. (2019). 'Exploring the Worlds of Journalism. An Introduction', in T. Hanitzsch, F. Hanusch, J. Ramaprasad, and A. S. de Beer (eds), *Worlds of Journalism. Journalistic Cultures around the Globe* (New York: Columbia University Press), 1–21.

Hanusch, F. and Hanitzsch, T. (2019) 'Modeling Journalistic Cultures: A Global Approach', in T. Hanitzsch, F. Hanusch, J. Ramaprasad, and A. S. de Beer (eds), *Worlds of Journalism. Journalistic Cultures around the Globe* (New York: Columbia University Press), 283–308.

Harbers, I. and Ingram, M. (2017) 'Incorporating Space in Multimethod Research: Combining Spatial Analysis with Case-Study Research', *PS: Political Science & Politics*, 50(4): 1032–37.

Hardin, R. (1982) *Collective Action* (Baltimore, MD: Johns Hopkins University Press).

Harper, D. (2001) *The Online Etymology Dictionary* (http://www.etymonline.com).

Hartz, L. (1955) *The Liberal Tradition in America* (New York: Harcourt, Brace & World).

Hartz, L. (ed.) (1964) *The Founding of New Societies* (New York: Harcourt, Brace & World).

Harvey, D. (2005) *A Brief History of Neoliberalism* (Oxford: Oxford University Press).

Hassan, O. (2015) 'Undermining the Transatlantic Democracy Agenda? The Arab Spring and Saudi Arabia's Counteracting Democracy Strategy', *Democratization*, 22(3): 479–95.

Hayes-Renshaw, F. and Wallace, H. (2006) *The Council of Ministers* (2nd edn) (Houndmills, Basingstoke: Palgrave Macmillan).

Hayward, J. E. S. (1983) *Governing France: The One and Indivisible Republic* (2nd edn) (London: Weidenfeld & Nicolson).

Haywood, T. (1995) *Info-Rich, Info-Poor: Access and Exchange in the Global Information Society* (New Providence, NJ: Bowker).

Heady, B. and Muffels, R. (2008) 'Do Generous Welfare States Generate Efficiency Gains Which Counterbalance Short Run Losses? Testing Downside Risk Theory with Economic Panel Data for the U.S., Germany and the Netherlands', *Social Indicators Research*, 86(2): 337–54.

Heath, A., Glouharova, S., and Heath, O. (2008) 'India: Two-Party Contests within a Multiparty System', in M. Gallagher and P. Mitchell (eds), *The Politics of Electoral Systems* (Oxford: Oxford University Press), 137–56.

Heberle, R. (1951) *Social Movements: An Introduction to Political Sociology* (New York: Appleton-Century-Crofts).

Hechter, M. (1975) *Internal Colonalism: The Celtic Fringe in British National Development, 1536–1966* (Berkeley, CA: University of California Press).

Heclo, H. (1974) *Modern Social Politics in Britain and Sweden: From Relief to Income Maintenance* (New Haven, CT: Yale University Press).

Heclo, H. (1977) *A Government of Strangers* (Washington, DC: Brookings Institution Press).

Heclo, H. and Madsen, H. J. (1986) *Policy and Politics in Sweden* (Philadelphia, PA: Temple University Press).

Hedström, P. and Ylikoski, P. (2010) 'Causal Mechanisms in the Social Sciences', *Annual Review of Sociology*, 36: 49–67.

Heidenheimer, A. J., Heclo, H., and Adams, C. T. (1975) *Comparative Public Policy: The Politics of Social Choice in Europe and America* (New York: St Martin's Press).

Held, D. (1995) *Democracy and the Global Order* (Cambridge: Polity Press).

Held, D. and McGrew, A. (2002) *Globalization/Anti-Globalization* (Cambridge: Polity Press).

Held, D., McGrew, A., Goldblatt, D., and Perraton, J. (1999) *Global Transformation: Politics, Economics and Culture* (Cambridge UK: Cambridge University Press).

Helms, L. (2013) *Oxford Handbook of Political Leadership* (Oxford: Oxford University Press).

Hemerijck, A. C. (2013) *Changing Welfare States* (Oxford: Oxford University Press).

Hemerijck, A. C. (ed.) (2017) *The Uses of Social Investment* (Oxford, Oxford University Press).

Hemerijck, A. C. and Schludi, M. (2000) 'Sequences of Policy Failures and Effective Policy Responses', in F. W. Scharpf and V. A. Schmidt (eds), *Welfare and Work in the Open Economy*, Vol. I (Oxford: Oxford University Press), 125–228.

Hemerijck, A. C., Unger, B., and Visser, J. (2000) 'How Small Countries Negotiate Change: Twenty-Five Years of Policy Adjustment in Austria, the Netherlands, and Belgium', in F. W. Scharpf and V. A. Schmidt (eds), *Welfare and Work in the Open Economy*, Vol. II (Oxford: Oxford University Press), 175–263.

Henderson, A. (2007) *Nunavut: Rethinking Political Culture* (Vancouver: University of British Columbia Press).

Henderson, A., Jeffery, C., Wincott, D., and Wyn Jones, R. (2013) 'Reflections on the "Devolution Paradox": A Comparative Examination of Multilevel Citizenship', *Regional Studies*, 47(3): 303–22.

Herb, M. (1999) *All in the Family: Absolutism, Revolution, and Democratic Prospects in the Middle Eastern Monarchies* (Albany, NY: State University of New York Press).

Herrmann-Pillath, C. (2006) 'Reciprocity and the Hidden Constitution of World Trade', *Constitutional Political Economy*, 17(3): 133–63.

Hetherington, M. J. and Huser, J. A. (2014) 'How Trust Matters: The Changing Political Relevance of Political Trust', *American Journal of Political Science*, 56: 312–25.

Hettne, B., Soderbaum, F., and Rosamond, B. (2002) 'Theorizing the Rise of Regionness', in S. Breslin, C. Hughes, and N. Philips (eds), *New Regionalisms in the Global Political Economy* (Milton Park: Routledge), 33–47.

Hewitt, C. (1977) 'The Effect of Political Democracy and Social Democracy on Equality in Industrial Societies: A Cross-National Comparison', *American Sociological Review*, 42(1): 450–64.

Hibbing, J. and Theiss-Morse, E. (2002) *Stealth Democracy: Americans' Beliefs about How Government Should Work* (Cambridge: Cambridge University Press).

Hicken, A. (2011) 'Clientelism', *Annual Review of Political Science*, 14(1): 289–310.

Hicks, A. M. (1999) *Social Democracy and Welfare Capitalism: A Century of Income Security Politics* (Ithaca, NY: Cornell University Press).

Hicks, A. M. and Swank, D. H. (1984) 'On the Political Economy of Welfare Expansion: A Comparative Analysis of 18 Advanced Capitalist Democracies, 1960–1971', *Comparative Political Studies*, 17 (1): 81–119.

Hicks, A. M., Swank, D. H., and Ambuhl, M. (1989) 'Welfare Expansion Revisited: Policy Routines and their Mediation by Party, Class and Crisis, 1957–1982', *European Journal of Political Research*, 17(4): 401–30.

Hiebert, Janet (2011) 'Governing Like Judges', in T. Campbell, K. D. Ewing, and A. Tomkins (eds), *The Legal Protection of Human Rights* (Oxford: Oxford University Press).

Higgins, W. and Apple, N. (1981) *Class Mobilization and Economic Policy: Struggles over Full Employment in Britain and Sweden* (Stockholm: Arbetslivcentrum).

Higley, J. and Gunther, R. (1992) *Elites and Democratic Consolidation in Latin America and Southern Europe* (Cambridge: Cambridge University Press).

Hill, L. (2006) 'Low Voter Turnout in the United States: Is Compulsory Voting a Viable Solution?', *Journal of Theoretical Politics*, 18 (2): 207–32.

Hill, M. (2006) *Social Policy in the Modern World* (Malden, MA: Blackwell).

Hinnebusch, R. (2006) 'Authoritarian Persistence, Democratic Theory and the Middle East', *Democratization*, 13: 373–95.

Hirschl, R. (2001) 'The Political Origins of Judicial Empowerment through Constitutionalization: Lessons from Israel's Constitutional Revolution', *Comparative Politics*, 33(3): 315–36.

Hirschl, R. (2011) 'The Nordic Counternarrative: Democracy, Human Development, and Judicial Review', *International Journal of Constitutional Law*, 9: 449–69.

Hirst, P. (1990) *Representative Democracy and its Limits* (Cambridge: Polity Press).

Hirst, P. and Thompson, G. (2000) *Globalization in Question* (2nd edn) (Cambridge: Polity Press).

Hix, S. (2002) 'Constitutional Agenda-Setting through Discretion in Rule Interpretation: Why the European Parliament Won at Amsterdam', *British Journal of Political Science*, 32(2): 259–80.

Hix, S. (2005) *The Political System of the European Union* (2nd edn) (Houndmills, Basingstoke: Palgrave Macmillan).

Hix, S., Noury, A., and Roland, G. (2006) 'Dimensions of Politics in the European Parliament', *American Journal of Political Science*, 50(2): 494–511.

Hix, S., Noury, A., and Roland, G. (2007) *Democratic Politics in the European Parliament* (Cambridge: Cambridge University Press).

Hoberg, G. (2001) 'Globalization and Policy Convergence: Symposium Overview', *Journal of Comparative Policy Analysis: Research and Practice*, 3: 127–32.

Hobsbawm, E. (1977) 'Some Reflections on "The Breakup of Britain"', *New Left Review*, 105: 3–23.

Hobson, C. and Kurki, M. (eds) (2012) *The Conceptual Politics of Democracy Promotion* (Abingdon: Routledge).

Hoffmann, S. (1966) 'Obstinate or Obsolete? The Fate of the Nation State and the Case of Western Europe', *Daedalus*, 95(4): 862–915.

Hoffmann, S. (1982) 'Reflections on the Nation-State in Western Europe Today', *Journal of Common Market Studies*, 21(1–2): 21–37.

Hofstede, G. (2001) *Culture's Consequences: Comparing Values, Behaviors Institutions and Organizations* (Thousand Oaks, CA: Sage).

Holm, H. H. and Sørensen, G. (eds) (1995) *Whose World Order? Uneven Globalization and the End of the Cold War* (Boulder, CO: Westview).

Holmberg, S. and Rothstein B. (2011) 'Dying of Corruption', *Health Economics, Policy and Law*, 6 (4): 529–47.

Holmberg, S., and Rothstein, B. (eds) (2012) *Good Government: The Relevance of Political Science* (Cheltenham, Edward Elgar).

Holmberg, S. and Rothstein B. (2014) 'Correlates of the Level of Democracy', QoG Working Paper (Gothenburg: The Quality of Government Institute, University of Gothenburg), 18.

Holmes, L. (1986) *Politics in the Communist World* (Oxford: Oxford University Press).

Holmlund, B. (1998) 'Unemployment Insurance in Theory and Practice', *Scandinavian Journal of Economics*, 100: 113–41.

Holzinger, K. (2002) 'The Provision of Transnational Common Goods: Regulatory Competition for Environmental Standards', in A. Héritier (ed.), *Common Goods: Reinventing European and International Governance* (Lanham, MD: Rowman & Littlefield), 59–82.

Holzinger, K. (2003) 'Common Goods, Matrix Games, and Institutional Solutions', *European Journal of International Relations*, 9: 173–212.

Holzinger, K. (2008) *Transnational Common Goods: Strategic Constellations, Collective Action Problems, and Multi-Level Provision* (New York: Palgrave Macmillan).

Holzinger, K. and Knill, C. (2005) 'Causes and Conditions of Cross-National Policy Convergence', *Journal of European Public Policy*, 12(5): 775–96.

Holzinger, K., Knill, C., and Arts, B. (eds) (2008) *Environmental Policy Convergence in Europe? The Impact of International Institutions and Trade* (Cambridge: Cambridge University Press).

Hood, C. (2000) *The Art of the State: Culture, Rhetoric and Public Management* (Oxford: Oxford University Press).

Hooghe, L. (ed.) (1996) *Cohesion Policy and European Integration: Building Multi-Level Governance* (Oxford: Oxford University Press).

Hooghe, L. (2001) *The European Commission and the Integration of Europe: Images of Governance* (Cambridge: Cambridge University Press).

Hooghe, L. and Marks, G. (2001) *Multi-Level Governance and European Integration* (Lanhan, MD: Rowman & Littlefield).

Hooghe, L. and Marks, G. (2003) 'Unraveling the Central State, But How? Types of Multi-Level Governance', *American Political Science Review*, 97(2): 233–43.

Hooghe, L. and Marks, G. (2004). 'Europe's Blues: Theoretical Soul-Searching after the Rejection of the European Constitution'. *PS: Political Science and Politics*, 39(2): 247–50.

Hooghe, L. and Marks, G. (2009) 'Efficiency and the Territorial Structure of Government', *Annual Review of Political Science*, 12: 225–41.

Hooghe, L. and Marks, G. (2013) 'Beyond Federalism: Estimating and Explaining the Territorial Structure of Government', *Publius*, 43(2): 179–204.

Hooghe, L. and Marks, G. (2016) *Community, Scale and Regional Governance: A Postfunctionalist Theory of Governance, Vol. II.* (Oxford: Oxford University Press).

Hooghe, L., Marks, G., and Wilson, C. J. (2002) 'Does Left/Right Structure Party Positions on European Integration?', *Comparative Political Studies*, 35: 965–89.

Hooghe, L., Marks, G., Schakel, A. H., Niedzwiecki, S., Chapman Osterkatz, S., and Shair-Rosenfield, S. (2016) *Measuring Regional Authority: A Postfunctionalist Theory of Governance, Vol. I.* (Oxford: Oxford University Press).

Hopkin, J. (2008) 'Spain: Proportional Representation with Majoritarian Outcomes', in M. Gallagher and P. Mitchell (eds), *The Politics of Electoral Systems* (Oxford: Oxford University Press), 375–94.

Hopkin, J. and Paolucci, C. (1999) 'New Parties and the Business Firm Model of Party Organization: Cases from Spain and Italy', *European Journal of Political Research*, 35(3): 307–39.

Hopkins, N. (2013) 'UK Approved £112m of Arms Exports to Saudi Arabia Last Year', *The Guardian*, 20 May 2013.

Horn, L. (2012) *Regulating Corporate Governance in the EU. Towards Marketization of Corporate Control* (Houndmills, Basingstoke: Palgrave Macmillan).

Hotelling, H. (1929) 'Stability in Competition', *Economic Journal*, 29(1): 41–57.

Howard, C. (1993) 'The Hidden Side of the American Welfare State', *Political Science Quarterly*, 108(3): 403–36.

Howlett, M. (1991) 'Policy Instruments, Policy Styles and Policy Implementation', *Policy Studies Journal*, 19(2): 1–21.

Howlett, M. and Tosun, J. (eds) (2018) *Policy Styles and Policy Making* (London: Routledge).

Howlett, M., Ramesh, M., and Pearl, A. (2009) *Studying Public Policy: Policy Cycles and Policy Subsystems* (Oxford: Oxford University Press).

Hox, J. J. (2002) *Multilevel Analysis: Techniques and Applications* (Mahwah, NJ: Lawrence Erlbaum Associates).

Huber, E. and Bogliaccini, J. (2010) 'Latin America', in F. G. Castles, S. Leibfried, J. Lewis, H. Obinger, and C. Pierson (eds), *The Oxford Handbook of the Welfare State* (Oxford: Oxford University Press), 645–55.

Huber, E. and Stephens, J. D. (2000) 'Partisan Governance, Women's Employment, and the Social Democratic Service State', *American Sociological Review*, 65(3): 323–42.

Huber, E. and Stephens, J. D. (2001) *Development and Crisis of the Welfare State: Parties and Policies in Global Markets* (Chicago, IL: University of Chicago Press).

Huber, E. and Stephens, J. D. (2012) *Democracy and the Left: Social Policy and Inequality in Latin America* (Chicago, IL: University of Chicago Press).

Huber, J. D. (1996) *Rationalizing Parliament* (Cambridge: Cambridge University Press).

Huckshorn, R. (1984) *Political Parties in America* (Monterey, CA: Brooks/Cole).

Hudson, J. and Kühner, S. (2012) 'Analyzing the Productive and Protective Dimensions of Welfare: Looking Beyond the OECD', *Social Policy & Administration*, 46(1): 35–60.

Hueglin, T. (1979) 'Johannes Althusius: Medieval Constitutionalist or Modern Federalist?', *Publius*, 9(4): 9–41.

Hueglin, T. (2003) 'Federalism at the Crossroads: Old Meanings, New Significance', *Canadian Journal of Political Science*, 36(2): 275–94.

Hueglin, T. and A. Fenna (2015) *Comparative Federalism: A Systematic Inquiry* (2nd edn) (Toronto: University of Toronto Press).

Hug, S. (2003) 'Endogenous Preferences and Delegation in the European Union', *Comparative Political Studies*, 36(1–2): 41–74.

Hug, S. (2013) 'Qualitative Comparative Analysis: How Inductive Use and Measurement Error Lead to Problematic Inference', *Political Analysis*, 21(2): 252–65.

Hume, D. (1741) *Essays, Literary, Moral, and Political* (Edinburgh: Kincaid).

Humprecht, E., Esser, F., and van Aelst, P. (2020) 'Resilience to Online Disinformation: A Framework for Cross-National Comparative Research', *International Journal of Press/Politics*: forthcoming.

Huntington, S. P. (1968) *Political Order in Changing Societies* (New Haven, CT: Yale University Press).

Huntington, S. P. (1991) *The Third Wave: Democratization in the Late Twentieth Century* (Norman, OK: University of Oklahoma Press).

Huntington, S. P. (1996) *The Clash of Civilizations and the Remaking of World Order* (New York: Simon & Schuster).

Husa, J. (2000) 'Guarding the Constitutionality of Laws in the Nordic Countries: A Comparative Perspective', *American Journal of Comparative Law*, 48(3): 345–81.

Hutter, S. (2014) *Protesting Culture and Economics in Western Europe* (Minneapolis, MN and London: University of Minnesota Press).

Hutter, S. and Kriesi, H. (2013) 'Movements of the Left, Movements of the Right Reconsidered', in J. van Stekelenburg, C. Roggeband, and B. Klandermans (eds), *The Future of Social Movement Research. Dynamics, Mechanisms, and Processes* (Minneapolis, MN: University of Minnesota Press), 281–298.

Hyden, G., Leslie, M., and Ogundimu, F. F. (eds) (2002) *Media and Democracy in Africa* (Uppsala: Nordiska Afrikainstitutet).

Hyman, R. (1975) *Industrial Relations: A Marxist Introduction* (London: Macmillan).

Hyman, R. (1999) 'Imagined Solidarities: Can Trade Unions Resist Globalisation?' in P. Leisink (ed.), *Globalisation and Labour Relations* (Cheltenham: Edward Elgar), 94–115.

Hyman, R. (2001) *Understanding European Trade Unionism: Between Market, Class and Society* (London: Sage).

Hyman, R. (2010) 'Trade Unions and "Europe": Are the Members Out of Step?', *Relations Industrielles/Industrial Relations* 65(1): 3–29.

Ignazi, P. (1992) 'The Silent Counter-Revolution: Hypotheses on the Emergence of Extreme Right-Wing Parties in Europe', *European Journal of Political Research*, 22(1): 3–34.

Inglehart, R. (1977) *The Silent Revolution: Changing Values and Political Styles among Western Publics* (Princeton, NJ: Princeton University Press).

Inglehart, R. (1990) *Culture Shift* (Princeton, NJ: Princeton University Press).

Inglehart, R. (1997) *Modernization and Postmodernization: Cultural, Economic and Political Change in 43 Societies* (Princeton, NJ: Princeton University Press).

Inglehart, R. (2003) 'How Solid is Mass Support for Democracy—And How Do We Measure It?', *PS: Political Science and Politics*, 36: 51–7.

Inglehart, R. and Baker, W. E. (2000) 'Modernization, Cultural Change, and the Persistence of Traditional Values', *American Sociological Review*, 65: 19–51.

Inglehart, R. and Norris, P. (2003) *Rising Tide: Gender Equality and Cultural Change around the World* (Cambridge: Cambridge University Press).

Inglehart, R. F. and Norris, P. (2016). 'Trump, Brexit, and the Rise of Populism', Working Paper, Harvard Kennedy School, RWP16-026 (https://research.hks.harvard.edu/publications/workingpapers).

Inglehart, R and Norris, P. (2018) *Cultural Backlash: Trump, Brexit and the Rise of Authoritarian Populism* (Cambridge: Cambridge University Press).

Inglehart, R. and Welzel, C. (2005) *Modernization, Cultural Change, and Democracy: The Human Development Sequence* (Cambridge: Cambridge University Press).

Inglehart, R. and Welzel, C. (2010) 'Changing Mass Priorities: The Link between Modernization and Democracy', *Perspectives on Politics*, 8(2): 551–67.

Inglehart, R., Foa, R., Peterson C., and Welzel, C. (2008) 'Development, Freedom and Rising Happiness: A Global Perspective 1981–2006', *Perspectives on Psychological Science*, 3(4): 264–85.

Inglehart, R., Haerpfer, C., Moreno, A., Welzel, C., Kizilova, K., Diez-Medrano, J., Lagos, M., Norris, P., Ponarin, E., Puranen, B. et al. (2016). World Values Survey: Round Four—Country-Pooled Datafile Version', Madrid, J. D. Systems Institute (https://www.worldvaluesurvey.org/WVSDocumentationWV4.jsp).

Inkeles, A. (1969a) 'Participant Citizenship in Six Developing Countries', *American Political Science Review*, 63: 112–41.

Inkeles, A. (1969b) 'Making Men Modern', *American Journal of Sociology*, 75: 208–25.

Inkeles, A. and Smith, D. (1974) *Becoming Modern* (Cambridge, MA: Harvard University Press).

Inman, R. P. and Rubinfeld, D. L. (1997) 'Rethinking Federalism', *Journal of Economic Perspectives*, 11: 43–64.

International Labour Organization (2019) 'NORMLEX Information System on International Labour Standards' (https://www.ilo.org/dyn/normlex/en).

International Monetary Fund (2018). 'Report for Selected Countries and Subjects', (https://www.imf.org/external/pubs/ft/weo/2019/01/weodata/weorept.aspx?sy=2018&ey=2018&scsm=1&ssd=1&sort=country&ds=.&br=1&c=512%2C668%).

Iversen, T. (2005) *Capitalism, Democracy and Welfare* (Cambridge: Cambridge University Press).

Iversen, T. (2006) 'Capitalism and Democracy', in D. Wittman and B. R. Weingast (eds), *Oxford Handbook of Political Economy* (New York: Oxford University Press), 601–23.

Iversen, T. and Cusack, T. R. (2000) 'The Causes of Welfare State Expansion: Deindustralization or Globalization?', *World Politics*, 52(3): 313–49.

Iversen, T. and Soskice, D. (2001) 'An Asset Theory of Social Policy Preferences', *American Political Science Review*, 95(4): 875–93.

Iversen, T. and Soskice, D. (2019) *Democracy and Prosperity. Reinventing Capitalism through a Turbulent Century* (Princeton, NJ: Princeton University Press).

Iversen, T. and Wren, A. (1998) 'Equality, Employment, and Budgetary Restraint: The Trilemma of the Service Economy', *World Politics*, 50(4): 507–46.

Iyengar, S., Curran, J., Lund, A. B., Salovaara-Moring, I., Hahn, K. S., and Coen S. (2010) 'Cross National versus Individual-Level Differences in Political Information: A Media Systems Perspective', *Journal of Elections, Public Opinion and Parties*, 20(3): 291–309.

Jackman, R. (1973) 'On the Relation of Economic Development to Democratic Performance', *American Journal of Political Science*, 17(3): 611–21.

Jackman, R. (1998) 'European Unemployment: Why Is It So High and What Should Be Done About It?', in G. Debelle and J. Borland (eds), *Unemployment and the Australian Labour Market* (Sydney: Reserve Bank of Australia), 39–63.

Jackman, R. W. (1975) *Politics and Social Equality: A Comparative Analysis* (New York: Wiley).

Jackman, R. W. (1986) 'Elections and the Democratic Class Struggle', *World Politics*, 39(1): 123–46.

Jackman, R. W. (1987) 'Political Institutions and Voter Turnout in the Industrial Democracies', *American Political Science Review*, 81(2): 405–24.

Jackman, R., Layard, R., and Nickell, S. (1996) 'Combating Unemployment: Is Flexibility Enough?', presented at OECD Conference on Interactions between Structural Reform, Macroeconomic Policies and Economic Performance (London: London School of Economics).

Jackson, R. (1990) *Quasi-States: Sovereignty, International Relations and the Third World* (Cambridge: Cambridge University Press).

Jackson, R. and Rosberg, C. G. (1982) *Personal Rule in Black Africa: Prince, Autocrat, Prophet, Tyrant* (Berkeley, CA: University of California Press).

Jahn, D. (2006) 'Globalization as Galton's Problem: The Missing Link in the Analysis of Diffusion Patterns in Welfare State Development', *International Organization*, 60(2): 401–31.

Jahn, D. and Stephan, S. (2015) 'The Problem of Interdependence', in D. Braun and M. Maggetti (eds), *Comparative Politics: Theoretical and Methodological Challenges* (Cheltenham: Edward Elgar), 14–54.

James, A. (1999) 'The Practice of Sovereign Statehood in Contemporary International Society', *Political Studies*, 47(3): 457–74.

James, B. (ed.) (2006) *Media Development and Poverty Eradication* (Paris: UNESCO).

James, J. (2008) 'Digital Divide Complacency: Misconceptions and Dangers', *Information Society*, 24(1): 54–61.

James, S. (1999) *British Cabinet Government* (2nd edn) (London: Routledge).

Jamieson, K. H. and Kenski, K. (2017) 'Political Communication: Then, Now, and Beyond', in K. H. Jamieson and K. Kenski (eds), *The Oxford Handbook of Political Communication* (Oxford: Oxford University Press), 3–12.

Janis, I. L. (1972) *Victims of Groupthink* (Boston, MA: Houghton Mifflin).

Jann, W. and Wegrich, K. (2006) 'Theories of the Policy Cycle', in F. Fischer, G. Miller, and M. Sidney (eds), *Handbook of Public Policy Analysis: Theory, Politics, and Methods* (Boca Raton, FL: CRC Press), 43–62.

Jasper, J. M. (2011) 'Emotions and Social Movements: Twenty Years of Theory and Research', *Annual Review of Sociology*, 37: 285–303.

Jasper, J. M. (2014) *Protest: A Cultural Introduction to Social Movements* (Cambridge: Polity Press).

Jasper, J. M. and Goodwin, J. (1999) 'Trouble in Paradigms', *Sociological Forum*, 14(1): 107–25.

Jeffery, C. (ed.) (1997) *The Regional Dimension of the European Union: Towards a Third Level in Europe?* (London: Frank Cass).

Jeffery, C. (ed.) (2011) 'Problems of Territorial Finance: UK Devolution in Perspective' in T. Courchene, J. Allan, C. Leuprecht, and N. Verelli (eds), *The Federal Idea: Essays in Honour of Ronald L. Watts* (Montreal/Kingston: McGill-Queen's University Press), 379–94.

Jeffery, C. (2013) 'Devolution in the United Kingdom', in J. Loughlin, J. Kincaid, and W. Swenden (eds), *The Routledge Handbook of Regionalism and Federalism* (London: Routledge), 317–31.

Jenkins, C. J. (1981) 'Sociopolitical Movements', in S. L. Long (ed.), *Handbook of Political Behavior, Vol. 4* (New York and London: Plenum Press), 81–153.

Jenkins-Smith, H., Nohrstedt, D., Weible, C., and Sabatier, P. A. (2014) 'The Advocacy Coalition Framework: Foundations, Evolution, and Ongoing Research', in P. Sabatier and C, Weible (eds), *Theories of the Policy Process* (Boulder, CO: Westview Press), 183–223.

Jensen, C. (2011) 'Conditional Contraction: Globalisation and Capitalist Systems', *European Journal of Political Research*, 50(2): 168–89.

Jensen, C., Knill, C., Schulze, K., and Tosun, J. (2014) 'Giving Less by Doing More? Dynamics of Social Policy Expansion and Dismantling in 18 OECD Countries', *Journal of European Public Policy*, 21(4): 528–48.

Jervis, R. (1997) *System Effects: Complexity in Political and Social Life* (Princeton, NJ: Princeton University Press).

Jessop, B. (2002) *The Future of the Capitalist State* (Cambridge: Polity Press).

Johansson, K. M. and Raunio, T. (2019) 'Government Communication in a Comparative Perspective', in K. M. Johansson and G. Nygren (eds), *Close and Distant: Political Executive–Media Relations in Four Countries* (Göteborg: Nordicom), 127–48.

Johansson, K. M. and Nygren, G. (2019) 'Locked in a Mutual Dependency; Media and the Political Executive in Close Interplay', in K. M. Johansson and G. Nygren (eds), *Close and Distant: Political Executive–Media Relations in Four Countries* (Göteborg: Nordicom), 247–60.

Johansson, K. M. and Raunio, T. (2019) 'Government Communication in a Comparative Perspective', in K. M. Johansson and G. Nygren (eds), *Close and Distant: Political Executive–Media Relations in Four Countries* (Göteborg: Nordicom), 127–48.

John, P. (2001) *Local Governance in Western Europe* (London: Sage).

Johnson, C. (1999) 'The Developmental State: Odyssey of a Concept', in Meredith Woo-Cumings (ed.), *The Developmental State* (Ithaca, NY: Cornell University Press).

Johnston, H. (2014) *What is a Social Movement?* (Oxford: Polity Press).

Johnston, R. (2005) 'The Electoral System and the Party System Revisited', in G. Kernerman and P. Resnick (eds), *Insiders and Outsiders: Alan Cairns and the Reshaping of Canadian Citizenship* (Vancouver: UBC Press), 51–64.

Jones, B. D. and Baumgartner, F. R. (2004) 'Representation and Agenda-Setting', *Policy Studies Journal*, 32(1): 1–24.

Jones, B. D. and Baumgartner, F. R. (2005) 'A Model of Choice for Public Policy', *Journal of Public Administration Research and Theory*, 15(3): 325–51.

Jones, E. L. (1981) *The European Miracle: Environments, Economies, and Geopolitics in the History of Europe and Asia* (Cambridge: Cambridge University Press).

Jones, M. and Mainwaring, S. (2003) 'The Nationalization of Parties and Party Systems: An Empirical Measure and an Application to the Americas', *Party Politics*, 9(2): 139–66.

Jordan, G. and Cairney, P. (2013) 'What is the "Dominant Model" of British Policymaking? Comparing Majoritarian and Policy Community Ideas', *British Politics*, 8(3): 233–59.

Jordan, G. and Maloney, W. A. (2007) *Democracy and Interest Groups: Enhancing Participation* (Houndmills, Basingstoke: Palgrave Macmillan).

Jordan, J., Maccarrone, V. and Erne, R. (2019) 'Towards a Socialisation of the EU's New Economic Governance Regime? EU Labour Policy Interventions in Germany, Italy, Ireland and Romania'

ERC European Unions Working Paper, 7 (https://www.erc-europeanunions.eu/working-papers).

Julius, D. (1997) 'Globalization and Stakeholder Conflicts: A Corporate Perspective', *International Affairs*, 73(3): 453–69.

Jungherr, A., Posegga, O., and An, J. (2019) 'Discursive Power in Contemporary Media Systems: A Comparative Framework', *International Journal of Press/Politics*, online first, Doi: https://doi.org/10.1177/1940161219841543.

Kalathil, S. and Boas, T. C. (2001) *The Internet and State Control in Authoritarian Regimes: China, Cuba and the Counterrevolution, Global Policy Program No. 21* (Washington, DC: Carnegie Endowment for International Peace).

Kanter, R. M. (1995) *World Class: Thriving Locally in the Global Economy* (New York: Simon & Schuster).

Kaplan, D. (2009) *Structural Equation Modeling* (Thousand Oaks, CA, and London: Sage).

Kapstein, E. B. (1993) 'Territoriality and Who is "US"', *International Organization*, 47: 501–3.

Kapstein, E. B. (1994) *Governing the Global Economy: International Finance and the State* (Cambridge, MA: Harvard University Press).

Karapin, Roger (2011) 'Opportunity/Threat Spirals in the U.S. Women's Suffrage and German Anti-Immigration Movements', *Mobilization*, 16(1): 65–80.

Karmis, D. and Norman, W. (2005) 'The Revival of Federalism', in D. Karmis and W. Norman (eds), *Theories of Federalism: A Reader* (Houndmills, Basingstoke: Palgrave Macmillan).

Karpf, D. (2012) *The MoveOn Effect* (Oxford: Oxford University Press).

Katz, R. S. (1986) 'Party Government: A Rationalistic Conception', in F. W. Scharpf and V. A. Schmidt (eds), *Welfare and Work in the Open Economy* (Oxford: Oxford University Press).

Katz, R. S. (1990) 'Party as Linkage: A Vestigial Function?', *European Journal of Political Research*, 18: 143–61.

Katz, R. S. (1997) *Democracy and Elections* (Oxford: Oxford University Press).

Katz, R. S. (2003) 'Europeanization and the Decline of Partisan Political Activity', presented at the 2003 General Conference of the European Consortium for Political Research, Marburg, Germany.

Katz, R. S. and Mair, P. (1995) 'Changing Models of Party Organization and Party Democracy: The Emergence of the Cartel Party', *Party Politics*, 1: 5–28.

Katzenstein, P. J. (1984) *Corporatism and Change: Austria, Switzerland and the Politics of Industry* (Ithaca, NY: Cornell University Press).

Katzenstein, P. J. (1985) *Small States in World Markets: Industrial Policy in Europe* (Ithaca, NY: Cornell University Press).

Kaufmann, D., Kraay, A., and Mastruzzi, M. (2006) 'Governance Matters: Aggregate and Individual Governance Indicators for 1996–2005', World Bank Policy Research Working Paper 4012 (Washington, DC: World Bank).

Kautto M. and Kvist J. (2002) 'Parallel Trends, Persistent Diversity—Nordic Welfare States in the European and Global Context', *Global Social Policy*, 2(2): 189–208.

Keane, J. (2015) 'Mediated Despotism. A World beyond Democracy', in J. Zielonka (ed.), *Media and Politics in New Democracies. Europe in a Comparative Perspective* (Oxford: Oxford University Press), 248–61.

Keating, M. (1997) 'The Political Economy of Regionalism', in M. Keating and J. Loughlin (eds), *The Political Economy of Regionalism* (London: Routledge), 17–40.

Keating, M. (1998a) 'Is There a Regional Level of Government in Europe?', in P. LeGalès and C. Lequesne (eds), *Regions in Europe* (London: Routledge), 11–29.

Keating, M. (1998b) *The New Regionalism in Western Europe: Territorial Restructuring and Political Change* (Cheltenham: Edward Elgar).

Keating, M. (2004) 'Introduction', in M. Keating (ed.), *Regions and Regionalism in Europe* (Cheltenham: Edward Elgar), xi–xv.

Keck, M. E. and Sikkink, K. (1998a) *Activists beyond Borders: Networks in International Politics* (Ithaca, NY: Cornell University Press).

Keck, M. E. and Sikkink, K. (1998b) 'Transnational Advocacy Networks in the Movement Society', in D. S. Meyer and S. Tarrow (eds), *The Social Movement Society: Contentious Politics for a New Century* (Lanham, MD: Rowman & Littlefield), 217–38.

Kegley, C. and S. L. Blanton (2014) *World Politics: Trend and Transformation 2014–2015* (Boston, MA: Wadsworth).

Kelley, J. (2012) *Monitoring Democracy. When International Election Observation Works, and Why It Often Fails* (Princeton, NJ and Oxford: Princeton University Press).

Kellstedt, P. M. and Whitten, G. D. (2013) *The Fundamentals of Political Science Research* (Cambridge: Cambridge University Press).

Kelly, M., Mazzoleni, G., and McQuail, D. (eds) (2004) *The Media in Europe: The Euromedia Research Group* (3rd edn) (London: Sage).

Keman, H. (1988) *The Development Toward Surplus Welfare: Social Democratic Politics and Policies in Advanced Capitalist Democracies (1965–1984)* (Amsterdam: CT Press).

Keman, H. (1990) 'Social Democracy and the Politics of Welfare Statism', *Netherlands Journal of Social Sciences*, 26(1): 17–34.

Keman, H. (1993a) 'Comparative Politics: A Distinctive Approach to Political Science?', in H. Keman (ed.), *Comparative Politics: New Directions in Theory and Method* (Amsterdam: VU Press), 31–57.

Keman, H. (ed.) (1993b) *Comparative Politics: New Directions in Theory and Method* (Amsterdam: VU Press).

Keman, H. (ed.) (2002a) *Comparative Democratic Politics: A Guide to Contemporary Theory and Research* (London: Sage).

Keman, H. (2002b) 'Comparing Democracies: Theory and Evidence', in H. Keman (ed.), *Comparative Democratic Politics: A Guide to Contemporary Theory and Research* (London: Sage), 32–61.

Keman, H. (2013) 'Political Science and History: Symbiosis or Synthesis?', in A. Zimmer (ed.), *Civil Societies Compared: Germany and the Netherlands* (Baden Baden: Nomos Verlaggesellschaft), 43–65.

Kendall-Taylor, A. and Frantz, E. (2015) 'How Democratic Institutions are Making Dictatorships More Durable', *Bloomberg View*, 7: 2015.

Kenworthy, L. (1999) 'Do Social-Welfare Policies Reduce Poverty? A Cross-National Assessment', *Social Forces*, 77(3): 1119–40.

Kenworthy, L. (2004) *Egalitarian Capitalism: Jobs, Incomes and Growth in Affluent Countries* (New York: Russell Sage Foundation).

Kerbo, H. R. (1982) 'Movements of "Crisis" and Movements of "Affluence". A Critique of Deprivation and Resource Mobilization Theories', *Journal of Conflict Resolution*, 26(4): 645–63.

Kerr, C., Dunlop, J. T., Harbison, F. H., and Myers, C. A. (1973) *Industrialism and Industrial Man* (London: Penguin).

Kershaw, I. (2001) *Hitler 1936–45: Nemesis* (London: Penguin).

Key, V. O., Jr (1964) *Politics, Parties, and Pressure Groups* (New York: Crowell).

Khanna, Parag (2016) 'A New Map for America', *New York Times*, 15 April (http://www.nytimes.com/2016/04/17/opinion/sunday/a-new-map-for-america.html?_r=0).

Kiernan, B. (2002) *The Pol Pot Regime: Race, Power, and Genocide in Cambodia under the Khmer Rouge, 1975–79* (New Haven, CT: Yale University Press).

King, A. (1973) 'Ideas, Institutions, and the Policies of Government: A Comparative Analysis', *British Journal of Political Science*, 3: 291–313.

King, A. (1975) 'Executives', in F. I. Greenstein and N. W. Polsby (eds), *Handbook of Political Science. V: Governmental Institutions and Processes* (Reading, MA: Addision-Wesley).

King, D. S. (1999) *In the Name of Liberalism: Illiberal Social Policy in the USA and Britain* (Oxford: Oxford University Press).

King, G. (1997) *A Solution to the Ecological Inference Problem* (Princeton, NJ: Princeton University Press).

King, G., Keohane, R. D., and Verba, S. (1994) *Designing Social Inquiry* (Princeton, NJ: Princeton University Press).

King, G., Rosen, O., and Tanner, M. A. (2004) *Ecological Inference: New Methodological Strategies* (Cambridge: Cambridge University Press).

King, G., Pan, J., and Roberts, M. E. (2013) 'How Censorship in China Allows Government Criticism but Silences Collective Expression', *American Political Science Review*, 107(2): 326–43.

King, P. (1982) *Federalism and Federation* (London: Croom Helm).

Kingdon, J. W. (2003) *Agendas, Alternatives, and Public Policies* (Harlow: Longman).

Kirchheimer, O. (1966) 'The Transformation of West European Party Systems', in J. LaPalombara and M. Weiner (eds), *Political Parties and Political Development* (Princeton, NJ: Princeton University Press).

Kirsch, H. and Welzel, C. (2019) 'Democracy Misunderstood: Authoritarian Notions of Democracy around the Globe', *Social Forces*, 98(1): 59–92, (https://doi.org/10.1093/sf/soy114).

Kitschelt, H. (1986) 'Political Opportunity Structures and Political Protest: Anti-Nuclear Movements in Four Democracies', *British Journal of Political Science*, 16: 57–85.

Kitschelt, H. (1994) *The Transformation of European Social Democracy* (Cambridge: Cambridge University Press).

Kitschelt, H. (1995) *The Radical Right in Western Europe* (Ann Arbor, MI: University of Michigan Press).

Kitschelt, H. (2001) 'Partisan Competition and Welfare State Retrenchment: When Do Politicians Choose Unpopular Policies?', in P. Pierson (ed.), *The New Politics of the Welfare State* (Oxford: Oxford University Press), 265–302.

Kitschelt, H. (2006) 'Movement Parties', in R. S. Katz and W. Crotty (eds), *Handbook of Party Politics* (London: Sage), 278–290.

Kitschelt, H., Marks, G., Lange, P., and Stephens, J. D. (eds) (1999) *Continuity and Change in Contemporary Capitalism* (Cambridge: Cambridge University Press).

Kitschelt, H., Katz, R. S.,and Crotty, W.(eds) (2006) *Handbook of Party Politics* (London: Sage).

Kittel, B. (1999) 'Sense and Sensitivity in Pooled Analysis of Political Data', *European Journal of Political Research*, 35: 225–53.

Kittel, B. (2006) 'A Crazy Methodology? On the Limits of Macroquantitative Social Science Research', *International Sociology*, 21(5): 647–77.

Kiyohara, S., Maeshima, K., and Owen, D. (2018) *Internet Election Campaigns in the United States, Japan, South Korea, and Taiwan* (Cham: Springer Palgrave).

Klandermans, B. (1997) *The Social Psychology of Protest* (Oxford: Blackwell).

Klandermans, B. and Staggenborg, S. (eds) (2002) *Methods of Social Movement Research* (Minneapolis, MN: University of Minnesota Press).

Kleider, H. (2018) 'Redistributive Policies in Decentralized Systems: Explaining the Effect of Decentralization on Subnational Welfare Spending', *European Journal of Political Research*, 57(2): 355–77.

Kleider, H., Röth, L., and Garritzman, J. L. (2018) 'Ideological Alignment and the Distribution of Public Expenditures', *West European Politics*, 41(3): 779–802.

Kleinman, M. (2001) *A European Welfare State? European Union Social Policy in Context* (London: Palgrave Macmillan).

Klingebiel, S. (2012) 'Aid—Dinosaur or Development Engine for Sub-Saharan Africa?' (https://www.die-gdi.de/uploads/media/BP_1.2012_.pdf).

Klingemann, H.-D. (1999) 'Mapping Political Support in the 1990s', in P. Norris (ed), *Critical Citizens* (New York: Oxford University Press).

Klingemann, H.-D., Volkens, A., Bara, J., Budge, I., and McDonald, M. (2006) *Mapping Policy Preferences II: Estimates for Parties, Electors, and Governments in Eastern Europe, European Union and OECD, 1990–2003* (supplemented with CD-ROM) (Oxford: Oxford University Press).

Klug, H. (2000) *Constituting Democracy: Law, Globalism, and South Africa's Political Reconstruction* (New York: Cambridge University Press).

Knill, C. (2001) *The Europeanisation of National Administration: Patterns of Institutional Change and Persistence* (Cambridge: Cambridge University Press).

Knill, C. (2005) 'Introduction: Cross-National Policy Convergence: Concepts, Approaches and Explanatory Factors', *Journal of European Public Policy*, 12(5): 764–74.

Knill, C. and Tosun, J. (2012) *Public Policy—A New Introduction* (Houndmills, Basingstoke: Palgrave Macmillan).

Knill, C., Tosun, J., and Bauer, M. W. (2009) 'Neglected Faces of Europeanization: The Differential Impact of the EU on the Dismantling and Expansion of Domestic Policies', *Public Administration*, 87(2): 519–37.

Knobloch-Westerwick, S., Liu, L., Hino, A., Westerwick, A., and Johnson, B. K. (2019) 'Context Impacts on Confirmation Bias: Evidence from the 2017 Japanese Snap Election Compared with American and German Findings', *Human Communication Research*, e-pub ahead of print, https://doi.org/10.1093/hcr/hqz005.

Kobach, K. W. (2001) 'Lessons Learned in the Participation Game', in A. Auer and M. Bützer (eds), *Direct Democracy: The Eastern and Central European Experience* (Aldershot: Ashgate), 292–309.

Kohler-Koch, B. and Quittkat, C. (2011) *Die Entzauberung partizipativer Demokratie. Zur Rolle der Zivilgesellschaft bei der Demokratisierung von EU-Governance* (Frankfurt am Main: Campus).

Kohler-Koch, B., De Biévre, D., and Maloney, W. (2008) 'Opening EU-Governance to Civil Society—Gains and Challenges', Connex Report Series No. 5 (http://www.mzes.uni-mannheim.de/projekte/typo3/site/index.php?id=641).

Kohnle-Seidl, R. and Eichhorst, W. (2008) 'Does Activation Work?', in W. Eichhorst, O. Kaufmann, and R. Kohnle-Seidl (eds), *Brining the Jobless into Work? Experiences with Activation Schemes in Europe and the US* (Heidelberg: Springer Verlag).

Kohring, M. and Goerke, A. (2000), 'Genetic Engineering in the International Media: An Analysis of Opinion-Leading Magazines', *New Genetics and Society*, 19(3): 345–63.

König, T., Tsebelis, G., and Debus, M. (eds) (2010) *Reform Processes and Policy Change: Veto Players and Decision-Making in Modern Democracies* (New York: Springer).

Kooiman, J. (2003) *Governing as Governance* (London: Sage).

Koopmans, R. (1992) *Democracy from Below: New Social Movements and the Political System in West Germany* (Boulder, CO: Westview).

Koopmans, R. (2001) 'Better Off by Doing Good: Why Antiracism Must Mean Different Things to Different Groups', in M. Giugni and F. Passy (eds), *Political Altruism? Solidarity Movements in International Perspective* (Lanham, MD: Rowman & Littlefield), 111–32.

Koopmans, R. (2004) 'Protest in Time and Space: The Evolution of Waves of Contention', in D. H. Snow, S. A. Soule and H. Kriesi (eds), *The Blackwell Companion to Social Movements* (Oxford: Blackwell Publishing), 19–46.

Koopmans, R. and Statham, P. (1999) 'Ethnic and Civic Conceptions of Nationhood and the Differential Success of the Extreme Right in Germany and Italy', in M. G. Giugni, D. McAdam, and C. Tilly (eds), *How Social Movements Matter* (Minneapolis, MN: University of Minnesota Press), 225–52.

Kornhauser, W. (1959) *The Politics of Mass Society* (Glencoe, IL: Free Press).

Korpi, W. (1983) *The Democratic Class Struggle* (London: Routledge & Kegan Paul).

Korpi, W. (1985) 'Economic Growth and the Welfare State: Leaky Bucket or Irrigation System?', *European Sociological Review*, 1(2): 97–118.

Korpi, W. (1989) 'Power, Politics, and State Autonomy in the Development of Social Citizenship: Social Rights during Sickness in Eighteen OECD Countries since 1930', *American Sociological Review*, 54(3): 309–28.

Korpi, W. (2002) 'The Great Trough in Unemployment: A Long-Term View of Unemployment, Strikes, and the Profit/Wage Ratio', *Politics and Society*, 30(3): 365–426.

Korpi, W. (2006) 'Power Resources and Employer-Centered Approaches in Explanations of Welfare States and Varieties of Capitalism', *World Politics*, 58(2): 167–206.

Korpi, W. and Palme, J. (1998) 'The Paradox of Redistribution and Strategies of Equality: Welfare State Institutions, Inequality, and Poverty in Western Countries', *American Sociological Review*, 63(5): 661–87.

Korpi, W. and Palme, J. (2003) 'New Politics and Class Politics in the Context of Austerity and Globalization: Welfare State Regress in Eighteen Countries, 1975–1995', *American Political Science Review*, 97(3): 425–46.

Kostiner, J. (ed.) (2000) *Middle East Monarchies: The Challenge of Modernity* (Boulder, CO: Lynne Rienner).

Krasner, S. (1984) 'Approaches to the State: Alternative Conceptions and Historical Dynamics', *Comparative Politics*, 16(2): 223–46.

Kreppel, A. (2001) *The Development of the European Parliament and Supranational Party System* (Cambridge: Cambridge University Press).

Kricheli, R., Livne, Y. and Magaloni, B. (2011) 'Taking to the Streets: Theory and Evidence on Protests under Authoritarianism', American Political Science Association 2010 Annual Meeting Paper.

Kriesi, H. (1991) 'The Political Opportunity Structure of New Social Movements: Its Impact on Their Mobilization', Discussion Paper FS III 91–103 (Berlin: Wissenschaftszentrum).

Kriesi, H. (1995) 'The Political Opportunity Structure of New Social Movements: Its Impact on Their Mobilization', in J. C. Jenkins and B. Klandermans (eds), *The Politics of Social Protest: Comparative Perspectives on States and Social Movements* (Minneapolis, MN: University of Minnesota Press), 167–98.

Kriesi, H. (1998) 'The Transformation of Cleavage Politics', *European Journal of Political Research*, 33(1): 165–85.

Kriesi, H. (2004) 'Political Context and Political Opportunity', in D. A. Snow, S. A. Soule, and H. Kriesi, H. (eds), *The Blackwell Companion to Social Movements*, Blackwell Companions to Sociology (Malden, MA: Blackwell), 67–90.

Kriesi, H. (2013) 'The Populist Challenge', *West European Politics* (forthcoming).

Kriesi, H. and Pappas, T. S. (eds) (2015) *European Populism in the Shadow of the Great Recession* (Colchester: ECPR-Press).

Kriesi, H., Koopmans, R., Duyvendak, J. W., and Giugni, M. G. (eds) (1995) *New Social Movements in Western Europe: A Comparative Analysis* (Minneapolis, MN: University of Minnesota Press).

Kriesi, H., Grande, E., Dolezal, M., Helbling, M., Höglinger, D., Hutter, S., and Wüest, B. (2012) *Political Conflict in Western Europe* (Cambridge: Cambridge University Press).

Krogslund, C. and Michel, K. (2014) 'A Larger-N, Fewer Variables Problem? The Counterintuitive Sensitivity of QCA', *Qualitative & Multi-Method Research*, 14(1): 25–33.

Krouwel, A. (2006) 'Party Models', in R. S. Katz and W. Crotty (eds), *Handbook of Party Politics* (London: Sage), 249–69.

Krugman, P. (1990) 'Policy Problems of a Monetary Union', in P. de Grauwe and L. Papademos (eds), *The European Monetary System in the 1990s* (London: Longman).

Kruse, S., Ravlik, M., and Welzel, C. (2019) 'Democracy Confused: When People Mistake the Absence of Democracy for Its Presence', *Journal of Cross-Cultural Psychology*, 50(3): 315–35, Doi: 10.1177/ 0022022118821437.

Kübler, D. (2015) 'De-Nationalization and Multi-Level Governance', in D. Braun, and M. Maggetti (eds), *Comparative Politics: Theoretical and Methodological Challenges* (Cheltenham Edward Elgar), 55–89.

Küchenhoff, E. (1967) *Möglichkeiten und Grenzen begrifflicher Klarheit in der Staatsformenlehre* (Berlin: Duncker & Humblot).

Kuhn, T. and Stoeckel, F. (2014) 'When European Integration Becomes Costly: The Euro Crisis and Public Support for European Economic Governance', *Journal of European Public Policy*, 21(4): 624–41.

Kühner, S. (2007) 'Country-Level Comparisons of Welfare State Change Measures: Another Facet of the Dependent Variable Problem within the Comparative Analysis of the Welfare State?', *Journal of European Social Policy*, 17(1): 5–18.

Kuhnle, S. (ed.) (2000) *Survival of the European Welfare State* (Abingdon: Routledge).

Kumlin, S. and Stadelmann-Steffen, I. (2016) 'Studying How Policies Affect People: Grappling with Measurement, Causality and the Micro–Macro Divide', in H. Keman and J. Woldendorp (eds), *Handbook of Research Methods and Applications in Political Science* (Cheltenham: Edgar Elgar), ch. 23.

Kuran, T. (1991) 'The East European Revolution of 1989: Is It Surprising That We Were Surprised?', *American Economic Review*, 81(2): 121–5.

Kurer, T. and Palier, B. (2019) 'Political Consequences of Technological Change', *Research & Politics*, 6(1): Special Issue.

Kurian, G., Longley, T. L. D., and Melia, T. O. (1998) *World Encyclopedia of Parliaments and Legislatures* (Washington, DC: Congressional Quarterly).

Kuruvilla, S., Lee, C. L., and Gallagher, M. E. (eds) (2011) *From Iron Rice Bowl to Informalization: Markets, Workers, and the State in a Changing China* (Ithaca, NY: Cornell University Press).

Kymlicka, W. (1998) *Finding Our Way: Rethinking Ethnocultural Dimensions in Canada* (Toronto: Oxford University Press).

Kymlicka, W. (1999) 'Citizenship in an Era of Globalization', in I. Shapiro and C. Hacker-Cordón (eds), *Democracy's Edges* (Cambridge: Cambridge University Press), 112–27.

Laakso, M. and Taagepera, R. (1979) 'Effective Number of Parties: A Measure with Application to West Europe', *Comparative Political Studies*, 12: 3–27.

Ladner, A., Keuffer, N., and Baldersheim, H. (2016) 'Measuring Local Autonomy in 39 Countries (1990–2014)', *Regional and Federal Studies*, 26(3): 321–57.

Ladner, A., Keuffer, N., Baldersheim, H., Hlepas, N., Swianiewicz, P., Steyvers, K., and Navarro, C. (2019) *Patterns of Local Autonomy in Europe* (London: Palgrave Macmillan).

Lancaster, T. and Lewis-Beck, M. (1989) 'Regional Vote Support: The Spanish Case', *International Studies Quarterly*, 33(1): 29–43.

Landman, T. (2003) *Issues and Methods in Comparative Politics: An Introduction* (Abingdon: Routledge).

Landman, T. and Carvalho, E. (2017) *Issues and Methods in Comparative Politics. An Introduction* (Abingdon and New York: Routledge).

Lane, E. (2008) *Globalization: The Juggernaut of the 21st Century* (Abingdon: Ashgate).

Lapuente, V., and Rothstein, B. (2014) 'Civil War Spain versus Swedish Harmony: The Quality of Government Factor', *Comparative Political Studies*, 47(10): 1416–41.

Laroche, P. (2016) 'Employment Relations in France', in G. J: Bamber, R.D. Lansbury, N. Wailes, and C. F. Wright (eds) *International and Comparative Employment Relations: National Regulation, Global Changes* (London: Sage), 153–78.

Larsen, C. A. (2002) 'Policy Paradigms and Cross-National Policy (Mis-)Learning from the Danish Employment Miracle', *Journal of European Public Policy*, 9(5): 715–35.

Lasswell, H. D. (1936) *Politics: Who Gets What, When, How* (New York: McGraw-Hill).

Lasswell, H. D. (1951) *Democratic Character* (Glencoe, IL: Free Press).

Lasswell, H. D. (1956) *The Decision Process: Seven Categories of Functional Analysis* (College Park, MD: University of Maryland Press).

Lasswell, H. D. (1960) *Psychopathology and Politics: A New Edition with Afterthoughts by the Author* (New York: Viking Press).

Lasswell, H. D. (1968) 'The Future of the Comparative Method', *Comparative Politics*, 1: 3–18.

Latham, E. (1965) *The Group Basis of Politics: A Study in Basing-Point Legislation* (New York: Octagon).

Lavenex, S. (2002) 'EU Enlargement and the Challenge of Policy Transfer', *Journal of Ethnic and Migration Studies*, 28(4): 701–21.

Laver, M., Benoit, K., and Garry, J. (2003) 'Extracting Policy Positions from Political Texts Using Words as Data', *American Political Science Review*, 97(2): 311–31.

Laver, M. and Hunt, W. B. (1992) *Policy and Party Competition* (London: Routledge).

Laver, M. and Schofield, N. (1990) *Multiparty Government* (Oxford: Oxford University Press).

Laver, M. and Shepsle, K. A. (1990) 'Coalitions and Cabinet Government', *American Political Science Review*, 84: 873–90.

Laver, M. and Shepsle, K. A. (1991) 'Divided Government: America is Not Exceptional', *Governance*, 4: 250–69.

Laver, M. and Shepsle, K. A. (eds) (1994) *Cabinet Ministers and Parliamentary Government* (Cambridge: Cambridge University Press).

Laver, M. and Shepsle, K. A. (1996) *Making and Breaking Governments: Cabinets and Legislatures in Parliamentary Democracies* (Cambridge: Cambridge University Press).

Law, D. and Versteeg, M. (2013), 'Sham Constitutions', *California Law Review*, 101: 863–950.

Lazardeus, S. G. (2015) *Cohabitation and Conflicting Politics in French Policymaking* (London: Palgrave Macmillan).

Lecours, A. and Moreno, L. (2003) 'Paradiplomacy: A Nation Building Strategy? A Reference to the Basque Country', in A.-G. Gagnon, M. Guibernau, and F. Rocher (eds), *The Conditions of Diversity in Multinational Democracies* (Montreal/Kingston: IRPP/McGill-Queen's University Press).

LeDuc, L. (2003) *The Politics of Direct Democracy: Referendums in Global Perspective* (Peterborough, Ontario: Broadview Press).

LeDuc, L., Niemi, R. G., and Norris, P. (eds) (2002) *Comparing Democracies 2* (London: Sage).

Lee, C. (2007) 'We Are All Comparativists Now: Why and How Single Country Scholarship Must Adapt and Incorporate the Comparative Politics Approach', *Comparative Political Studies*, 39: 1084–108.

Lee, C. C., Chan, J. M., Pan, Z., and So, C. Y. K. (2002) *Global Media Spectacle: News War Over Hong Kong* (New York: University of New York Press).

Lee Kaid, L. and Holtz-Bacha, C. (1994) *Political Advertising in Western Democracies: Parties and Candidates on Television* (London: Sage).

Lee Kaid, L. and Holtz-Bacha, C. (2004) *The Sage Handbook of Political Advertising* (London: Sage).

Leeke, M., Sear, C., and Gay, O. (2003) 'An Introduction to Devolution in the UK', Research Paper 03/84 (London: Parliament and Constitution Centre, House of Commons Library).

LeGrand, J. (1982) *The Strategy of Equality* (London: Allen & Unwin).

Lehmbruch, G. (1967) *Proporzdemokratie* (Tubingen: Mohr).

Lehner, F. and Homann, B. (1987) 'Consociational Decision-Making and Party Government in Switzerland', in R. S. Katz (ed.), *Party Governments: European and American Experiences* (Berlin: de Gruyter), 243–69.

Leibfried, S. and Pierson, P. (1995a) 'Semisovereign Welfare States: Social Policy in a Multitiered Europe', in S. Leibfried and P. Pierson (eds), *European Social Policy: Between Fragmentation and Integration* (Washington, DC: Brookings Institution).

Leibfried, S. and Pierson, P. (eds) (1995b) *European Social Policy: Between Fragmentation and Integration*. (Washington DC: Brookings Institution).

Lenaerts, K. (1990) 'Constitutionalism and the Many Faces of Federalism', *American Journal of Comparative Law*, 38: 205–63.

Lengauer, G., Donges P., and Plasser, F. (2014) 'Media Power in Politics', in B. Pfetsch (ed.), *Political Communication Cultures in Europe: Attitudes of Political Actors and Journalists in Nine Countries* (New York: Palgrave Macmillan), 171–95.

Lenschow, A., Liefferink, D., and Veenman, S. (2005) 'When Birds Sing: A Framework for Analysing Domestic Factors behind Policy Convergence', *Journal of European Public Policy*, 12(5): 764–74.

Léon, S. (2010) 'Who is Responsible for What? Clarity of Responsibilities in Multilevel States: The Case of Spain', *European Journal of Political Research*, 50(1): 80–109.

Léon, S. (2018) 'Muddling Up Political Systems? When Regionalization Blurs Democracy: Decentralization and Attribution of Responsibility', *Journal of Common Market Studies*, 56(3): 706–16.

León, S., Jurado, I. and Garmendia Madariaga, A. (2018) 'Passing the Buck? Responsibility Attribution and Cognitive Bias in Multilevel Democracies', *West European Politics*, 41(3): 660–82.

Léonard, E., Erne, R., Marginson, P., and Smismans, S. (2007) *New Structures, Forms and Processes of Governance in European Industrial Relation* (Brussels: Office for the Official Publications of the European Communities) (www.eurofound.europa.eu/publications/htmlfiles/ef0694.htm).

LeVan, A. (2011) 'Power Sharing and Inclusive Politics in Africa's Uncertain Democracies', *Governance*, 24: 31–53.

Levi, M. (2009) 'Reconsiderations of Rational Choice Theory in Comparative and Histrocial Analysis', in M. I. Lichbach and A. S. Zuckerman (eds), *Comparative Politics: Rationality, Culture and Structure* (2nd edn) (Cambridge: Cambridge University Press).

Levi-Faur, David (ed.) (2012) *The Oxford Handbook of Governance* (Oxford: Oxford University Press).

Levine, T. R., Weber, R., Hullett, C., Park, H. S., and Massi Lindsey, L. L. (2008) 'A Critical Assessment of Null Hypothesis Significance Testing in Quantitative Communication Research', *Human Communication Research*, 34: 171–87.

Levitsky, S. and Mainwaring, S. (2006) 'Organized Labor and Democracy in Latin America', *Comparative Politics*, 39(1): 21–42. Doi: 10.2307/20434019.

Levitsky, S. and Way, L. (2002) 'The Rise of Competitive Authoritarianism', *Journal of Democracy*, 13(2): 51–65.

Levitsky, S. and Way, L. (2010) *Competitive Authoritarianism: Hybrid Regimes after the Cold War* (New York: Cambridge University Press).

Levitsky, S. and Ziblatt, D. (2018) *How Democracies Die* (New York: Crown).

Levy, J. D. (1999) 'Vice into Virtue? Progressive Politics and Welfare Reform in Continental Europe', *Politics and Society*, 27(2): 239–74.

Lewin, A. Y., Kenney, M., and Murmann, J. P. (2016) 'China's Innovation Challenge: An Introduction', in A.Y. Lewin, M. Kenney, and J. P. Murmann (eds), *China's Innovation Challenge: Overcoming the Middle-Income Trap* (Cambridge: Cambridge University Press), 1–31.

Lewis, J. (1992) 'Gender and the Development of Welfare Regimes', *Journal of European Social Policy*, 2(3): 159–73.

Lewis, M. P., Simons, G. F., and Fennig, C. D. (eds) (2013) *Ethnologue: Languages of the World* (17th edn) (Dallas, TX: SIL International).

Lewis-Beck, C. and Lewis-Beck, M. (2016) *Applied Regression: An Introduction* (Los Angeles, CA: Sage).

Lichbach, M. I. (1995) *The Rebel's Dilemma, Economics, Cognition, and Society* (Ann Arbor, MI: University of Michigan Press).

Lieberman, E. S. (2005) 'Nested Analysis as a Mixed-Method Strategy for Comparative Research', *American Political Science Review*, 99(3): 435–52.

Lieberson, S. (1991) 'Small N's and Big Conclusions: An Examination of the Reasoning in Comparative Studies Based on a Small Number of Cases', in C. C. Ragin and H. Becker (eds), *What is a Case? Exploring the Foundations of Social Inquiry* (Cambridge: Cambridge University Press), 105–18.

Lijphart, A. (1968a) *The Politics of Accommodation: Pluralism and Democracy in the Netherlands* (Berkeley, CA: University of California Press).

Lijphart, A. (1968b) 'Typologies of Democratic Systems', *Comparative Political Studies*, 1(1): 3–44.

Lijphart, A. (1971) 'Comparative Politics and Comparative Method', *American Political Science Review*, 65: 682–93.

Lijphart, A. (1975) 'The Comparable-Cases Strategy in Comparative Research', *Comparative Political Studies*, 8: 158–77.

Lijphart, A. (1977) *Democracy in Plural Societies: A Comparative Exploration* (New Haven, CT: Yale University Press).

Lijphart, A. (1984) *Democracies: Patterns of Majoritarian and Consensus Government in Twenty-One Countries* (New Haven, CT: Yale University Press).

Lijphart, A. (ed.) (1992) *Parliamentary versus Presidential Government* (Oxford: Oxford University Press).

Lijphart, A. (1994) *Electoral Systems and Party Systems: A Study of Twenty-Seven Democracies, 1945–1990* (Oxford: Oxford University Press).

Lijphart, A. (1996) 'The Puzzle of Indian Democracy: A Consociational Interpretation', *American Political Science Review*, 90: 258–68.

Lijphart, A. (1999) *Patterns of Democracy: Government Forms and Performance in Thirty-Six Countries* (New Haven, CT: Yale University Press).

Lijphart, A. (2000) 'Varieties of Nonmajoritarian Democracy', in M. M. L. Crepaz, T. A. Koelble, and D. Wilsford (eds), *Democracy and Institutions: The Life Work of Arend Lijphart* (Ann Arbor, MI: University of Michigan Press).

Lijphart, A. (2008) *Thinking about Democracy: Power Sharing and Majority Rule in Theory and Practice* (Abingdon: Routledge).

Lijphart, A. (2012) *Patterns of Democracy: Government Forms and Performance in Thirty-Six Countries* (2nd edn) (New Haven, CT: Yale University Press).

Lijphart, A. and Waisman, C. (eds) (1996) *Institutional Design in New Democracies* (Boulder, CO: Westview Press).

Lilla, M. (2001) *The Reckless Mind* (New York: New York Review of Books).

Lilleker, D. G., Tenscher, J., and Štětka, V. (2015), 'Towards Hypermedia Campaigning? Perceptions of New Media's Importance for Campaigning by Party Strategists in Comparative Perspective', *Information, Communication and Society*, 18(7): 747–65.

Lin, C. (2017) 'Autocracy, Democracy, and Juristocracy: The Wax and Wane of Judicial Power in the Four Asian Tigers', *Georgetown Journal of International Law*, 48: 1063–144.

Lindbeck, A. and Snower, D. (1988) *The Insider–Outsider Theory of Unemployment* (Cambridge, MA: MIT Press).

Lindberg, L. N. (1963) *The Political Dynamics of Economic Integration* (Oxford: Oxford University Press).

Lindblom, C. E. (1959) 'The Science of Muddling Through', *Public Administration Review*, 19(2): 79–88.

Lindblom, C. E. (1977) *Politics and Markets: The World's Political-Economic Systems* (New York: Basic Books).

Lindblom, C. E. (2004) *Growing Public Social Spending and Economic Growth since the Eighteenth Century: Further Evidence* (Cambridge: Cambridge University Press).

Lindert, P. H. (2004) *Growing Public: Social Spending and Economic Growth since the Eighteenth Century* (Cambridge: Cambridge University Press).

Linz, J. (1964) 'The Case of Spain', in E. Allardt and Y. Littunen (eds), *Cleavages, Ideologies and Party Systems* (Helsinki: Westermarck Society), 291–342.

Linz, J. (1970) [1964] 'An Authoritarian Regime: Spain', in E. Allardt and S. Rokkan (eds), *Mass Politics* (New York: Free Press).

Linz, J. (1978) *The Breakdown of Democratic Regimes: Crisis, Breakdown and Equilibration* (Baltimore, MD: Johns Hopkins University Press).

Linz, J. (1990a) 'The Perils of Presidentialism', *Journal of Democracy*, 2: 131–45.

Linz, J. (1990b) 'Transitions to Democracy', *Washington Quarterly*, 13(3): 143–64.

Linz, J. (1992) 'Change and Continuity in the Nature of Contemporary Democracies', in G. Marks and L. Diamond (eds), *Reexamining Democracy: Essays in Honor of Seymour Martin Lipset* (Beverly Hills, CA: Sage).

Linz, J. (1994) 'Presidential or Parliamentary Democracy: Does it Make a Difference?', in J. Linz and A. Valenzuela (eds), *The Failure of Presidential Democracies. I: Comparative Perspectives* (Baltimore, MD: Johns Hopkins University Press).

Linz, J. and Stepan, A. (1996) *Problems of Democratic Transition and Consolidation: Southern Europe, South America, and Post-Communist Europe* (Baltimore, MD: Johns Hopkins University Press).

Linz, J. and Valenzuela, A. (eds) (1994) *The Failure of Presidential Democracies. I: Comparative Perspectives* (Baltimore, MD: Johns Hopkins University Press).

Linz, J. J. (2000) *Totalitarian and Authoritarian Regimes* (Boulder, CO: Lynne Rienner Publishers).

Lipset, S. M. (1959) 'Some Social Requisites of Democracy: Economic Development and Political Legitimacy', *American Political Science Review*, 53(1): 69–105.

Lipset, S. M. (1960) *Political Man: The Social Bases of Politics* (Garden City, NY: Doubleday).

Lipset, S. M. (1968) [1950] *Agrarian Socialism: The Cooperative Commonwealth Federation of Saskatchewanm: A Study in Political Sociology* (Garden City, NY: Doubleday).

Lipset, S. M. (1990) *Continental Divide: The Values and Institutions of the United States and Canada* (New York: Routledge).

Lipset, S. M. and Rokkan, S. (1967) 'Cleavage Structures, Party Systems, and Voter Alignments: An Introduction', in S. M. Lipset and S. Rokkan (eds), *Party Systems and Voter Alignments* (New York: Free Press), 1–64.

Lipsky, M. (1971) 'Street Level Bureaucracy and the Analysis of Urban Reform', *Urban Affairs Quarterly*, 6: 391–409.

Lipsky, M. (1980) *Street-Level Bureaucracy: The Dilemmas of Individuals in the Public Service* (New York: Russell Sage Foundation).

Ljungkvist, L. and Sargent, T. J. (1998) 'The European Employment Dilemma', *Journal of Political Economy*, 106(3): 514–50.

Llanos, M. and Marsteintredet, L. (2010) *Presidential Breakdowns in Latin America: Causes and Outcomes of Executive Instability in Developing Democracies* (Houndmills, Basingstoke: Palgrave Macmillan).

Lødemel, I. and Moreira, A. (2014) *Activation or Workfare? Governance and the Neo-Liberal Convergence* (Oxford: Oxford University Press).

Lohmann, S. (1994) 'The Dynamics of Informational Cascades: The Monday Demonstrations in Leipzig, East Germany, 1989–91', *World Politics*, 47(1): 42–101.

Lorwin, V. (1966a) 'Belgium: Religion, Class, and Language in National Politics', in R. A. Dahl (ed.), *Political Oppositions in Western Democracies* (New Haven, CT: Yale University Press), 147–87.

Lorwin, V. (1966b) 'Segmented Pluralism, Ideological Cleavages and Political Cohesion in the Smaller European Democracies', *Comparative Politics*, 3: 141–75.

Loughlin, J. (1986) 'Regionalist and Federalist Movements in Contemporary France', in M. Burgess (ed.), *Comparative Federalism and Federation* (London: Croom Helm), 76–98.

Loughlin, J. (1989) *Regionalism and Ethnic Nationalism in France: A Case Study of Corsica* (Florence: European University Institute).

Loughlin, J. (2004a) 'The "Transformation" of Governance: New Directions in Policy and Politics', *Australian Journal of Politics and History*, 50(1): 8–22.

Loughlin, J. (2004b) *Subnational Democracy in the European Union: Challenges and Opportunities* (Oxford: Oxford University Press).

Loughlin, J. (2007a) 'Les Nationalismes Britannique et Français Face aux Défis de l'Européanisation et de la Mondialisation', in A.-G. Gagnon, A. Lecours, and G. Nootens (eds), *Les Nationalismes Majoritaires Contemporains: Identité, Mémoire et Pouvoir* (Montréal: Québec Amérique), 193–215.

Loughlin, J. (2007b) *Subnational Government: The French Experience* (Basingstoke: Palgrave Macmillan).

Loughlin, J. and Martin, S. (2003) *International Lessons on Balance of Funding Issues: Initial Paper* (London: Office of the Deputy Prime Minister).

Loughlin, J. and Mazey, S. (eds) (1995) *The End of the French Unitary State? Ten Years of Regionalization in France* (London: Frank Cass).

Loughlin, J. and Peters, B. G. (1997) 'State Traditions, Administrative Reform and Regionalization', in M. Keating and J. Loughlin (eds), *The Political Economy of Regionalism* (London: Routledge), 41–62.

Loughlin, J., Lidstrom, A., and Hudson, C. (2005) 'The Politics of Local Taxation in Sweden: Reform and Continuity', *Local Government Studies*, 31(3): 334–68.

Loughlin, J., Hendriks, F., and Lidström, A. (eds) (2013a) *The Oxford Handbook of Subnational Democracy in Europe* (Oxford: Oxford University Press).

Loughlin, J., Kincaid. J., and Swenden W. (eds) (2013b) *Routledge Handbook of Regionalism and Federalism* (London: Routledge).

Lowi, T. (1964) 'American Business, Public Policy, Case Studies, and Political Theory', *World Politics*, 16: 677–715.

Lowi, T. (1969a) *The End of Liberalism: Ideology, Policy and the Crisis of Public Authority* (New York: W. W. Norton).

Lowi, T. (1969b) 'The Public Philosophy: Interest-Group Liberalism' in W. E. Connolly (ed.), *The Bias of Pluralism* (New York: Atheron Press), 81–122.

Lublin, D. (2014) *Minority Rules: Electoral Systems, Decentralization, and Ethnoregional Parties* (Oxford: Oxford University Press).

Lucas, R. E. (1972) 'Expectations and Neutrality of Money', *Journal of Economic Theory*, 4(2): 103–24.

Lucas, R. E. (1973) 'Some International Evidence on Output–Inflation Tradeoffs', *American Economic Review*, 63(3): 326–34.

Lück, J., Wessler, H., Wozniak, A., and Lycarião, D. (2018). 'Counterbalancing Global Media Frames with Nationally Colored Narratives: A Comparative Study of News Narratives and News Framing in the Climate Change Coverage of Five Countries', *Journalism*, 19(12): 1635–56.

Luebbert, G. M. (1991) *Liberalism, Fascism or Social Democracy: Social Classes and the Political Origins of Regimes in Interwar Europe* (Oxford: Oxford University Press).

Luhmann, N. (1970) *Soziologische Aufkldrung* (Cologne: Westdeutscher Verlag).

Luke, D. A. (2004) *Multilevel Modeling* (Thousand Oaks, CA: Sage).

Lukes, S. (1974) *Power: A Radical View* (London: Macmillan).

Lupia, A. and Johnston, R. (2001) 'Are Voters to Blame? Voter Competence and Elite Maneuvers in Referendums', in M. Mendelsohn and A. Parkin (eds), *Referendum Democracy: Citizens, Elites and Deliberation in Referendum Campaigns* (Houndmills, Basingstoke: Palgrave Macmillan), 191–210.

Lupia, A. and McCubbins, M. D. (1998) *Can Citizens Learn What They Need to Know?* (New York: Cambridge University Press).

Lupu, N. and Pontusson, J. (2011) 'The Structure of Inequality and the Politics of Redistribution', *American Political Science Review*, 105(2): 316–36.

Lustick, I. (1997) 'The Discipline of Political Science: Studying the Culture of Rational Choice as a Case in Point', *Political Science and Politics*, 30: 175–9.

Lusztig, M., James, P., and Kim, H., (2003) 'Signaling and Tariff Policy: The Strategic Multistage Rent-Reduction Game', *Canadian Journal of Political Science*, 36(4): 765–89.

Luxemburg, R. (2008) [1906] 'The Mass Strike, the Political Party and the Trade Unions' (https://www.marxists.org/archive/luxemburg/1906/mass-strike/).

Mackie, T. T. and Rose, R. (1991) *The International Almanac of Electoral History* (London: Macmillan).

Mackintosh, J. P. (1977) *The British Cabinet* (London: Stevens).

Macpherson, C. (1953) *Democracy in Alberta: The Theory and Practice of a Quasi-Party System* (Toronto: University of Toronto Press).

Macridis, R. (1955) *The Study of Comparative Government* (New York: Random House).

Maddison, A. (1991) *Dynamic Forces in Capitalist Development* (Oxford: Oxford University Press).

Maddison, A. (1995) *Monitoring the World Economy:1820–1992* (Paris: Organization for Economic Cooperation and Development).

Maddison, A. (2001) *The World Economy: A Millennial Perspective* (Paris: Development Centre of the OECD).

Madsen, P. K. (2002) 'The Danish Model of Flexicurity: A Paradise—With Some Snakes', in H. Sarfati and G. Bonoli (eds), *Labour Market and Social Protection Reforms in International Perspective: Parallel or Converging Tracks?* (London: Ashgate), 243–65.

Magaloni, B. (2006) *Voting for Autocracy: Hegemonic Party Survival and Its Demise in Mexico* (Cambridge: Cambridge University Press).

Magaloni, B. (2008) 'Credible Power-Sharing and the Longevity of Authoritarian Rule', *Comparative Political Studies*, 41(4–5): 715–41.

Maggetti, M. and Gilardi, F.(2016) 'Problems (and Solutions) in the Measurement of Policy Diffusion Mechanisms', *Journal of Public Policy*, 36(1): 87–107.

Magin, M., Podschuweit, N., Hassler, J., and Russmann, U. (2017) 'Campaigning in the Fourth Age of Political Communication. A Multi-Method Study on the Use of Facebook by German and Austrian Parties in the 2013 National Election Campaigns', *Information, Communication & Society*, 20(11): 1698–719.

Magleby, D. B. (1994) 'Direct Legislation in the American States', in D. Butler and A. Ranney (eds), *Referendums around the World: The Growing Use of Direct Democracy* (Houndmills, Basingstoke: Palgrave Macmillan), 218–57.

Magraw, R. (1992) *A History of the French Working Class*. Vol. 1: *The Age of Artisan Revolution1815–1871* (Oxford: Blackwell).

Mahler, G. (1998) 'Israel', in G. Kurian (ed.), *World Encyclopedia of Parliaments and Legislatures* (Washington, DC: Congressional Quarterly Press), 352–9.

Mahoney, C. and Baumgartner F. R. (2008) 'Converging Perspectives on Interest-Group Research in Europe and America', *West European Politics*, 31(6): 1251–71.

Mahoney, J. (2000) 'Strategies of Causal Inference in Small-N Analysis', *Sociological Methods & Research*, 28(4): 387–424.

Mahoney, J. (2003) 'Strategies of Causal Assessment in Comparative Historical Analysis', in J. Mahoney and D. -Rueschemeyer (eds), *Comparative Historical Analysis in the Social Sciences* (Cambridge: Cambridge University Press), 337–72.

Mahoney, J. (2012) 'The Logic of Process Tracing Tests in the Social Sciences', *Sociological Methods & Research*, 41(4): 566–90.

Mahoney, J. and Goertz, G. (2004) 'The Possibility Principle: Choosing Negative Cases in Comparative Research', *The American Political Science Review*, 98(4): 653–69.

Mahoney, J. and Rueschemeyer (eds) (2003) *Comparative Historical Analysis in the Social Sciences* (Cambridge: Cambridge University Press).

Mahoney, J. and Thelen, K. (eds) (2010*a*) *Explaining Institutional Change. Ambiguity, Agency, and Power* (Cambridge: Cambridge University Press).

Mahoney, J. and Thelen, K. (2010*b*) 'A Theory of Gradual Institutional Change', in J. Mahoney and K. Thelen (eds), *Explaining Institutional Change: Ambiguity, Agency, and Power* (Cambridge: Cambridge University Press), 1–37.

Mahoney, J., Kimball, E., and Koivu, K. L. (2009) 'The Logic of Historical Explanation in the Social Sciences', *Comparative Political Studies*, 42(1): 114–46.

Mainwaring, S. (1993) 'Presidentialism, Multipartism, and Democracy—the Difficult Combination', *Comparative Political Studies*, 26(2): 198–228.

Mainwaring, S., and Pérez-Liñán, A. (2013) *Democracies and Dictatorships in Latin America: Emergence, Survival, and Fall* (Cambridge: Cambridge University Press).

Mainwaring, S. and Shugart, M. S. (eds) (1997a) *Presidentialism and Democracy in Latin America* (Cambridge: Cambridge University Press).

Mainwaring, S., and Shugart, M. S. (1997b) 'Juan Linz, Presidentialism, and Democracy—A Critical Appraisal', *Comparative Politics*, 29(4): 449–71.

Mainwaring, S., Brinks, D., and Pérez-Liñán, A. (2007) 'Classifying Political Regimes in Latin America, 1945–2004', in G. Munck (ed.), *Regimes and Democracy in Latin America. Theories and Methods* (Oxford: Oxford University Press), 123–60.

Mair, P. (1995) 'Political Parties, Popular Legitimacy and Public Privilege', *West European Politics*, 18(3): 40–57.

Mair, P. (1996) 'Comparative Politics: An Overview', in R. E. Goodin and H.-D. Klingemann (eds), *A New Handbook of Political Science* (Oxford: Oxford University Press), 309–35.

Mair, P. (2002) 'Populist Democracy vs Party Democracy', in Y. Mény and Y. Surel (eds), *Democracies and the Populist Challenge* (Houndmills, Basingstoke: Palgrave Macmillan), 81–98.

Mair, P. (2006a) 'Party System Change', in R. S. Katz and W. J. Crotty (eds), *Handbook of Political Parties* (London: Sage), 63–73.

Mair, P. (2006b) 'Sistemi Partitici e Alternanza al Governo, 1950–1999', in L. Bardi (ed.), *Partiti e Sistemi di Partito* (Bologna: Il Mulino), 245–64.

Mair, P. (2006c) 'Ruling the Void: The Hollowing of Western Democracy', *New Left Review*, 42: 25–51.

Mair, P. (2007) 'Political Opposition and the European Union', *Government and Opposition*, 42(1): 1–17.

Mair, P. (2008) 'Concepts and Concept Formation', in D. della Porta and M. Keating (eds), *Approaches and Methodologies in the Social Sciences* (Cambridge: Cambridge University Press), 177–97.

Mair, P. and Biezen, I. van (2001) 'Party Membership in Twenty European Democracies, 1980–2000', *Party Politics*, 7(1): 5–21.

Maiz, R. and Losada, A. (2011) 'The Erosion of Regional Powers in the Spanish "State of Autonomies"' in F. Requejo and K.-J. Nagel (eds), *Federalism beyond Federations: Asymmetry and Processes of Re-symmetrisation in Europe* (Farnham: Ashgate), 81–107.

Majone, G. (1993) 'The European Community between Social Policy and Social Regulation', *Journal of Common Market Studies*, 31(2): 153–70.

Majone, G. (1994) 'The Rise of the Regulatory State in Europe', *West European Politics* 17(3): 77–101.

Majone, G. (1996) *Regulating Europe* (London: Routledge).

Mancini, P. and Hallin, D. C. (2012) 'Some Caveats about Comparative Research in Media Studies', in H. A. Semetko and M. Scammell (eds), *Sage Handbook of Political Communication* (Thousand Oaks, CA: Sage), 509–17.

Mandela, N. (1994) *Long Walk to Freedom* (London: Little Brown).

Manin, B. (1997) *The Principles of Representative Government* (Cambridge: Cambridge University Press).

Manners, I. (2002) 'Normative Power Europe: A Contradiction in Terms?', *Journal of Common Market Studies*, 40(2): 235–58.

Manoïlesco, M. (1936 [1934]) *Le Siècle du Corporatisme* (Paris: Felix Alcan).

Manow, P. (2004) 'The Good, the Bad, and the Ugly: Esping-Andersen's Regime Typology and the Religious Roots of the Western Welfare State', MPIfG Working Paper 3 (Bonn: Max-Planck-Institut für Gesellschaftsforschung).

Manow, P. (2015) 'Workers, Farmers and Catholicism: A History of Political Class Coalitions and the South-European Welfare State Regime', *Journal of European Social Policy*, 25(1): 32–49.

Manow, P., Palier, B., and Schwander, H. (eds) (2018) *Welfare Democracies and Party Politics: Explaining Electoral Dynamics in Times of Changing Welfare Capitalism* (Oxford: Oxford University Press).

Maor, M. and Gross, J. J. (2015) 'Emotion Regulation by Emotional Entrepreneurs: Implications for Political Science and International Relations', (https://www.researchgate.net/profile/Moshe_Maor/publication/275831564_Emotion_Regulation_by_Emotional_Entrepreneurs_Implications_for_Political_Science_and_International_Relations/links/5547cf470cf26a7bf4da987b.pdf).

March, J. G. and Olsen, J. P. (1984) 'The New Institutionalism: Organizational Factors in the Political Life', *American Political Science Review*, 78(3): 734–49.

March, J. G. and Olsen, J. P. (1989) *Rediscovering Institutions* (New York: Free Press).

March, J. G. and Olsen, J. P. (2008) 'Elaborating the "New Institutionalism"', in R. A. W. Rhodes, S. A. Binder, and B. A. Rockman (eds), *The Oxford Handbook of Political Institutions* (Oxford: Oxford University Press), 3–20.

Marchal, N., Neudert, L.-M., Kollanyi, B., and Howard, P. N. (2018) *Polarization, Partisanship and Junk News Consumption on Social Media during the 2018 US Midterm Elections* (Oxford Internet Institute: Data Memo).

Marchal, N., Kollanyi, B., Neudert, L.-M., and Howard, P. N. (2019) *Junk News during the EU Parliamentary Elections: Lessons from a Seven-Language Study of Twitter and Facebook* (Oxford Internet Institute: Data Memo).

Margetts, H. (2006) 'Cyber Parties', in R. S. Katz and W. Crotty (eds), *Handbook of Party Politics* (London: Sage), 528–35.

Marginson, P. (2015) 'Coordinated Bargaining in Europe: From Incremental Corrosion to Frontal Assault?', *European Journal of Industrial Relations* 21(2): 97–114.

Marginson, P. and Welz, C. (2015) 'European Wage-Setting Mechanisms under Pressure: Negotiated and Unilateral Change and the EU's Economic Governance Regime', *Transfer: European Review of Labour and Research*, 21(4): 429–50.

Markoff, J. (1996) *Waves of Democracy: Social Movements and Political Change* (Thousand Oaks, CA: Pine Forge Press).

Markoff, J. (1999) 'Where and When was Democracy Invented?', *Comparative Studies in Society and History*, 41(4): 660–90.

Marks, G. (1992) 'Rational Sources of Chaos in Democratic Transition', *American Behavioral Scientist*, 35: 397–421.

Marks, G. and Hooghe, L. (2004) 'Contrasting Visions of Multi-Level Governance', in Bache, I. and Flinders, M (eds), *Multi-Level Governance* (Oxford: Oxford University Press), 15–30.

Marks, G., Hooghe, L., and Blank, K. (1996) 'European Integration from the 1980s: State-Centric v. Multi-Level Governance', *Journal of Common Market Studies*, 34(3): 341–78.

Marks, G., Hooghe, L., and Schakel, A. H. (2008a) 'Patterns of Regional Authority', *Regional and Federal Studies*, 18(2–3): 165–80.

Marks, G., Hooghe, L., and Schakel, A. H. (2008b) 'Measuring Regional Authority', *Regional and Federal Studies*, 18(2–3): 111–20.

Markusen, A. (1987) *Regions: The Economics and Politics of Territory* (Lanham, MD: Rowman & Littlefield).

Marmor, T. L., Mashaw, J. L., and Harvey, P. L. (1990) *America's Misunderstood Welfare State: Persistent Myth, Enduring Realities* (New York: Basic Books).

Marsh, A. (1990) *Political Action in Europe and the USA* (Houndmills, Basingstoke: Palgrave Macmillan).

Marsh, M. (2007) 'Referendum Campaigns: Changing What People Think or Changing What They Think About?', in C. de Vreese (ed.), *The Dynamics of Referendum Campaigns* (Houndmills, Basingstoke: Palgrave Macmillan), 63–83.

Marshall, J. and Fisher, S. D. (2015) 'Compensation or Constraint? How Different Dynamics of Economic Globalization Affect Government Spending and Electoral Turnout', *British Journal of Political Science*, 45(2): 353–89.

Marshall, T. H. (1950) *Citizenship and Social Class, and Other Essays* (Cambridge: Cambridge University Press).

Marshall, T. H. (1965) *Class, Citizenship and Social Development* (New York: Anchor).

Martin, I. W. and Prasad, M. (2014) 'Taxes and Fiscal Sociology', *Annual Review of Sociology*, 40: 331–45.

Martin, J. P. (2000) *What Works among Active Labour Market Policies: Evidence from OECD Countries' Experiences*, OECD Economic Studies 30 (Paris: OECD).

Martin, L. and Simmons, B. (1998) 'Theories and Empirical Studies of International Institutions', *International Organization*, 52: 729–57.

Martin, L. W. and Vanberg, G. (2004) 'Policing the Bargain: Coalition Government and Parliamentary Scrutiny', *American Journal of Political Science*, 48: 13–27.

Martin, L. W. and Vanberg, G. (2011) *Parliaments and Coalitions* (Oxford: Oxford University Press).

Martínez-Gallardo, C. (2012) 'Out of the Cabinet: What Drives Defections from the Government in Presidential Systems?', *Comparative Political Studies*, 45(1): 62–90.

Martínez-Gallardo, C. and Schleiter, P. (2015) 'Choosing Whom to Trust: Agency Risks and Cabinet Partisanship in Presidential Democracies', *Comparative Political Studies*, 48(2): 231–64.

Marx, G. T. and Wood, J. L. (1975) 'Strands of Theory and Research in Collective Behavior', *Annual Review of Sociology*, 1: 363–428.

Marx, K. (1852) *Der 18. Brumaire des Louis Napoleon. Die Revolution* (New York: Deutsche Vereinsbuchhandlung).

Massey, D. (1978) 'Regionalism: Some Current Issues', *Capital and Class*, 6: 106–25.

Massicotte, L. (2008) 'Canada: Sticking to First-Past-the-Post, for the Time Being', in M. Gallagher and P. Mitchell (eds), *The Politics of Electoral Systems* (Oxford: Oxford University Press), 99–118.

Mattila, M. (2004) 'Contested Decisions: Empirical Analysis of Voting in the European Union Council of Ministers', *European Journal of Political Research*, 43(1): 29–50.

Mattoni, A. and Ceccobelli, D. (2018). 'Comparing Hybrid Media Systems in the Digital Age: A Theoretical Framework for Analysis', *European Journal of Communication*, 33(5): 540–57.

Mattson, I. (1995) 'Private Members Initiatives and Amendments', in H. Döring (ed.), *Parliaments and Majority Rule in Western Europe* (Frankfurt am Main: Campus), 448–87.

Mau, S. and Burkhardt, C. (2009) 'Migration and Welfare State Solidarity in Western Europe', *Journal of European Social Policy*, 19(3): 213–29.

Mayerhöffer, E. (2018). *Elite Cohesion in Mediatized Politics: European Perspectives* (London: Rowman & Littlefield International).

Mayhew, D. R. (1991) *Divided We Govern* (New Haven, CT: Yale University Press).

Mayntz, R. (1979) 'Public Bureaucracies and Policy Implementation', *International Social Science Journal*, 31(4): 633–45.

Mazmanian, D. and Sabatier, P. (1983) *Implementation and Public Policy* (Glenview, IL: Scott Foresman).

McAdam, D. (1982) *Political Process and the Development of Black Insurgency,1930–1970* (Chicago, IL: University of Chicago Press).

McAdam, D. (1996) 'Conceptual Origins, Current Problems, Future Directions', in D. McAdam, J. D. McCarthy, and M. N. Zald (eds), *Comparative Perspectives on Social Movements: Political Opportunities, Mobilizing Structures, and Cultural Framings* (Cambridge: Cambridge University Press), 23–40.

McAdam, D., McCarthy, J. D., and Zald, M. N. (eds) (1996) *Comparative Perspectives on Social Movements: Political Opportunities, Mobilizing Structures, and Cultural Framings* (Cambridge: Cambridge University Press).

McAdam, D., Tarrow, S., and Tilly, C. (2001) *Dynamics of Contention* (Cambridge: Cambridge University Press).

McBride, S. (1980) *Many Voices One World* (London: Kogan Page).

McCarthy, J. D. and Zald, M. N. (1977) 'Resource Mobilization and Social Movements: A Partial Theory', *American Journal of Sociology*, 82(6): 1212–41.

McCarthy, N. and Meirowitz, A. (2007) *Political Game Theory: An Introduction* (Cambridge: Cambridge University Press).

McClosky, H. and Brill, A. (1983) *Dimensions of Tolerance* (New York: Russell Sage).

McCutcheon, A. L. (1987) *Latent Class Analysis* (Thousand Oaks, CA, and London: Sage).

McDonald, M. D. and Budge, I. (2005) *Elections, Parties, Democracy* (Oxford: Oxford University Press).

McFaul, M. (2004) 'Democracy Promotion as a World Value', *Washington Quarterly*, 28(1): 147–63.

McGarry, J. and O'Leary, B. (2009) 'Must Pluri-National Federations Fail?', *Ethnopolitics*, 8(1): 5–26.

McKay, D. (1996) *Rush to Union: Understanding the European Federal Bargain* (Oxford: Clarendon Press).

McLean, I. (2000) 'Review Article: The Divided Legacy of Mancur Olson', *British Journal of Political Science*, 30(4): 651–68.

McMenamin, I. (2013) *If Money Talks, What Does it Say? Corruption and Business Financing of Political Parties* (Oxford: Oxford University Press).

McMillan, J. (1991) *Napoleon III* (Harlow: Longman).

McQuail, D. (1994) *Mass Communication Theory* (3rd edn) (London: Sage).

McQuail, D. (2005) *Mass Communication Theory* (5th edn) (London: Sage).

McQuail, D. (2009) *Media Performance: Mass Communications and the Public Interest* (London: Sage).

McQuail, D. (2010) *Mass Communication Theory* (6th edn) (London: Sage).

McRae, K. (1964) 'The Structure of Canadian History', in L. Hartz (ed.), *The Founding of New Societies* (New York: Harcourt, Brace & World).

McRae, K. (1974) *Consociational Democracy: Political Accommodation in Segmented Societies* (London: McClelland & Stewart).

Meardi, G. (2018) 'Economic Integration and State Responses: Change in European Industrial Relations since Maastricht', *British Journal of Industrial Relations*, 56(3): 631–55.

Meguid, B. (2005) 'Competition between Unequals: The Role of Mainstream Party Strategy in Niche Party Success', *American Political Science Review*, 99(3): 347–59.

Meguid, B. (2008) *Party Competition between Unequals* (New York: Cambridge University Press).

Meier, K. J. (2000) *Politics and the Bureaucracy: Policymaking in the Fourth Branch of Government* (New York: Harcourt College).

Meier, K. J. and Bohte, J. (2001) 'Structure and Discretion: The Missing Link in Representative Bureaucracy', *Journal of Public Administration Research and Theory*, 11: 455–70.

Mejia Acosta, A. and Meneses, K. (2019) 'Who Benefits? Intergovernmental Transfers, Subnational Politics and Local Spending in Ecuador', *Regional and Federal Studies*, 29(2): 219–47.

Mejia Acosta, A. and Tillin, L. (2019) 'Negotiating Universalism in India and Latin America: Fiscal Decentralization, Subnational Politics and Social Outcomes', *Regional and Federal Studies*, 29(2): 115–34.

Melucci, A. (1980) 'The New Social Movements: A Theoretical Approach', *Social Science Information*, 2: 199–226.

Melucci, A. (1995) 'The Process of Collective Identity', in H. Johnston and B. Klandermans (eds.), *Social Movements and Culture* (Minneapolis, MN: University of Minnesota Press), 41–64.

Meltzer, A. H. and Richard, S. F. (1981) 'A Rational Theory of the Size of Government', *Journal of Political Economy*, 89(5): 914–27.

Mény, Y., and Surel, Y. (eds) (2002) *Democracies and the Populist Challenge* (Houndmills, Basingstoke: Palgrave Macmillan).

Merkel, W. (2004) 'Embedded and Defective Democracies'. *Democratization* 11(5): 33–58.

Merkel, W. (2014) 'Is There a Crisis of Democracy?', *Journal of Democratic Theory*, 1(2): 1–25.

Merkel, W., Puhle, H.-J., Croissant, A., Eicher, C., and Thiery, P. (2003) *Defekte Demokratie* (Opladen: Leske & Budrich).

Merritt, R. and Rokkan, S. (eds) (1966) *Comparing Nations* (New Haven, CT: Yale University Press).

Merton, R. K. (1957) 'On Sociological Theories of the Middle Range', in R. K. Merton (ed.), *On Theoretical Sociology. Five Essays, Old and New* (New York: The Free Press), 39–72.

Meseguer Yebra, C. (2009) *Learning, Policy Making, and Market* (Cambridge: Cambridge University Press).

Meulemann, H. (2012), 'Information and Entertainment in European Mass Media Systems: Preferences for and Uses of Television and Newspapers', *European Sociological Review*, 28(2): 186–202.

Meyer, D. S. and Tarrow, S. (1998a) 'A Movement Society: Contentious Politics for a New Century', in D. S. Meyer and S. Tarrow (eds), *The Social Movement Society: Contentious Politics for a New Century* (Lanham, MD: Rowman & Littlefield), 1–28.

Meyer, D. S. and Tarrow, S. (eds) (1998b) *The Social Movement Society: Contentious Politics for a New Century* (Lanham, MD: Rowman & Littlefield).

Meyers, P. and Vorsanger, J. (2005) 'Street Level Bureaucracy', in B. G. Peters and J. Pierre (ed.), *Handbook of Public Administration* (London: Sage).

Mezey, M. (1979) *Comparative Legislatures* (Durham, NC: Duke University Press).

Mezgebe, D. (2015) 'Decentralized Governance under Centralized Party Rule in Ethiopia: The Tigray Experience', *Regional and Federal Studies*, 25(5): 473–90.

Michels, R. (1915) *Political Parties: A Sociological Study of the Oligarchical Tendencies of Modern Democracy* (London: Jarrold).

Michels, R. (1999) [1911] *Political Parties. A Sociological Study of the Oligarchical Tendencies of Modern Democracy* (New Brunswick, NJ: Transaction Publishers).

Milgrom, P. and Roberts, J. (1992) *Economics, Organization and Management* (Englewood Cliffs, NJ: Prentice-Hall).

Mill, J. S. (1843) [1959] *A System of Logic* (London: Longman), 55–89; also in *John Stuart Mill on Politics and Society* (London: Fontana, 1976).

Mill, J. S. (1859) 'M. de Tocqueville and Democracy in America', in *Dissertations and Discussions* (London: John W. Parker).

Miller, E. A. and Banaszak-Holl, J. (2005) 'Cognitive and Normative Determinants of State Policymaking Behavior: Lessons from the Sociological Institutionalism', *Publius*, 35(2): 191–216.

Miller, M. K. (2014) 'Elections, Information, and Policy Responsiveness in Autocratic Regimes', *Comparative Political Studies*, 48(6): 691–727.

Mills, C. W. (1956) *The Power Elite* (New York: Oxford University Press).

Milner, H. (1989) *Sweden: Social Democracy in Practice* (Oxford: Oxford University Press).

Minns, J. (2006) *The Politics of Developmentalism: The Midas States of Mexico, South Korea and Taiwan* (Houndmills, Basingstoke: Palgrave Macmillan).

Mitchell, D. (1990) 'Income Transfer Systems: A Comparative Study Using Microdata', Ph.D. dissertation (Canberra: Australian National University).

Mitchell, P. (2008) 'United Kingdom: Plurality Rule under Siege', in M. Gallagher and P. Mitchell (eds), *The Politics of Electoral Systems* (Oxford: Oxford University Press), 157–84.

Molina, O. and Rhodes, M. (2002) 'Corporatism: The Past, Present and Future of a Concept' *Annual Review of Political Science*, 5: 305–31.

Møller, J. (2007) 'The Gap between Electoral and Liberal Democracy Revisited: Some Conceptual and Empirical Qualifications', *Acta Politica*, 42(4): 380–400.

Montesquieu (1721) [1973] *Persian Letters* (Harmondsworth: Penguin).

Montesquieu, Charles de (1748) *De l'Esprit des Lois* (Geneva: Chatelain).

Moore, B. (1966) *Social Origins of Dictatorship and Democracy: Lord and Peasant in the Making of the Modern World* (Boston, MA: Beacon Press).

Morales, L. (2009) *Joining Political Organizations: Institutions, Mobilization, and Participation in Western Democracies* (London: European Consortium for Political Research Press).

Moravcsik, A. (1991) 'Negotiating the Single European Act: National Interests and Conventional Statecraft in the European Community', *International Organization*, 45(1): 19–56.

Moravcsik, A. (1993) 'Preferences and Power in the European Community: A Liberal Intergovernmentalist Approach', *Journal of Common Market Studies*, 31(4): 473–524.

Moravcsik, A. (1998) *The Choice for Europe: Social Purpose and State Power from Messina to Maastricht* (Ithaca, NY: Cornell University Press).

Moravcsik, A. (2002) 'In Defense of the "Democratic Deficit": Reassessing the Legitimacy of the European Union', *Journal of Common Market Studies*, 40(4): 603–34.

Morel, N., Palier, B., and Palme, J. (eds) (2012) *Towards a Social Investment Welfare State? Ideas, Policies and Challenges* (Bristol: Policy Press).

Moreno, L. (2001) *The Federalization of Spain* (London: Frank Cass).

Moreno, L. and Colino, C. (eds) (2010) *Diversity and Unity in Federal Countries* (Montreal: McGill-Queen's University Press).

Moreno, L., Arriba, A., and Servano, A. (1997) 'Multiple Identities in Decentralized Spain: The Case of Catelonia, Working Paper 97–06 (Madrid: Instituto de Estudios Sociales Avanzados (CSIC)).

Morgan, K. J. (2002) 'Forging the Frontiers between State, Church and Family: Religious Cleavages and the Origins of Early Childhood Education in France, Sweden, and Germany', *Politics and Society*, 30(1): 113–48.

Morgan, K. J. (2003) 'The Politics of Mothers' Employment', *World Politics*, 55(2): 259–89.

Morgan, K. J. (2006) *Working Mothers and the Welfare State: Religion and the Politics of Work–Family Policies in Western Europe and the States* (Stanford, CA: Stanford University Press).

Morgenstern, S. (2017) *Are Politics Local? The Two Dimensions of Party Nationalization around the World* (Cambridge: Cambridge University Press).

Morgenstern, S. and Nacif, B. (eds) (2002) *Legislative Politics in Latin America* (Cambridge: Cambridge University Press).

Morlino, L. (2012) *Changes for Democracy* (Oxford: Oxford University Press).

Morris, A. (1986) *The Origins of the Civil Rights Movement: Black Communities Organizing for Change* (New York: The Free Press).

Morrison, D. E. and Henkel, R. E. (eds) (2009) [1970] *The Significance Controversy* (New Brunswick and London: Aldine Transaction).

Morrison, K. M. (2014) *Nontaxation and Representation: The Fiscal Foundations of Political Stability* (Cambridge: Cambridge University Press).

Morton, R. B. and K. C. Williams (2010) *Experimental Political Science and the Study of Causality* (Cambridge: Cambridge University Press).

Moustafa, T. (2007) *The Struggle for Constitutional Power: Law, Politics, and Economic Development in Egypt* (Cambridge: Cambridge University Press).

Mudde, C. (2004) 'The Populist *Zeitgeist*', *Government and Opposition*, 39(3): 541–63.

Mudde, C. and Kaltwasser, C. R. (2013) 'Exclusionary vs Inclusionary Populism: Comparing Contemporary Europe and Latin America', *Government and Opposition*, 48(2): 1–28.

Mueller, D. C. (2003) *Public Choice III* (Cambridge: Cambridge University Press).

Muhhina, K. (2018) 'Administrative Reform Assistance and Democracy Promotion: Exploring the Democratic Substance of the EU's Public Administration Reform Principles for the Neighbourhood Countries', *Democratization*, 25(4): 673–91.

Mulaik, S. A. and Millsap, R. E. (2000) 'Doing the Four-Step Right', *Structural Equation Modeling*, 7(1): 36–73.

Mulherin, P. E. and Isakhan, B. (2019) 'The Abbott Government and the Islamic State: A Securitized and Elitist Foreign Policy Discourse', *Australian Journal of Political Science*, 54(1): 82–98.

Muller, E. N. (1979) *Aggressive Political Participation* (Princeton, NJ: Princeton University Press).

Muller, E. N. (1989) 'Distribution of Income in Advanced Capitalist States: Political Parties, Labour Unions, and the International Economy', *European Journal of Political Research*, 17(4): 367–400.

Muller, P. (1984) *Le Technocrate et le Paysan* (Paris: Éditions Ouvriéres).

Müller, W. C. (1994) 'Models of Goverment and the Austrian Cabinet', in M. Laver and K. A. Shepsle (eds), *Cabinet Ministers and Parliamentary Government* (Cambridge: Cambridge University Press).

Müller, W. C. and Narud, H. M. (eds) (2013) *Party Governance and Party Democracy* (New York: Springer).

Müller, W. C. and Strøm, K. (eds) (2000) *Coalition Governments in Western Europe* (Oxford: Oxford University Press).

Müller-Rommel, F. and Poguntke, T. (eds) (2002) *Green Parties in National Governments* (London: Frank Cass).

Munck, G. L. (2001) 'Game Theory and Comparative Politics: New Perspectives and Old Concerns', *World Politics*, 53(2): 173–204.

Munck, G. L. (2009) *Measuring Democracy* (Baltimore, MD: Johns Hopkins University Press).

Munck, G. L. and Snyder, R. (2007) 'Debating the Direction of Comparative Politics: An Analysis of Leading Journals', *Comparative Political Studies*, 40(1): 5–31.

Munck, G. L. and Verkuilen, J. (2002) 'Conceptualizing and Measuring Democracy—Evaluating Alternative Indices', *Comparative Political Studies*, 35(1): 5–34.

Mundell, R. (1961) 'A Theory of Optimal Currency Areas', *American Economic Review*, 51: 657–65.

Munger, M. C. (2000) *Analyzing Policy: Choices, Conflicts, and Practices* (New York: W. W. Norton).

Mungiu-Pippidi, A. (2005) 'The Unbearable Lightness of Democracy: Is Good Quality Democracy Possible in a Post-Communist Environment?', in L. Diamond and L. Morlino (eds), *Assessing the Quality of Democracy* (Baltimore, MD: Johns Hopkins University Press).

Mungiu-Pippidi, A. (2005) 'Freedom without Impartiality: The Viscious Circle of Media Capture', in P. Gross and K. Jakubowicz (eds), *Media Transformations in the Post-Communist world: Eastern Europe's Tortured Path to Change* (Lanham, MD: Lexington), 33–47.

Muñoz, J. and Guinjoan i Cesena, M. (2013) 'Accounting for Internal Variation in Nationalist Mobilization: Unofficial Referendums for Independence in Catalonia (2009–11)', *Nations and Nationalism*, 19(1): 44–67.

Murray, C. (1984) *Losing Ground: American Social Policy 1950–1980* (New York: Basic Books).

Musgrave, R. A. (1959) *The Theory of Public Finance* (New York: McGraw-Hill).

Myles, J. (1989) *Old Age in the Welfare State: The Political Economy of Public Pensions* (rev. edn) (Lawrence, KS: University Press of Kansas).

Myles, J. and Pierson, P. (2001) 'The Comparative Political Economy of Pension Reform', in P. Pierson (ed.), *The New Politics of the Welfare State* (Oxford: Oxford University Press), 305–33.

Myrdal, G. (1957) *Economic Theory and Underdeveloped Regions* (London: Gerald Duckworth).

Nairn, T. (1977) *The Break-Up of Britain: Crisis and Neo-Nationalism* (London: New Left Books).

Naisbitt, J. (1994) *The Global Paradox* (New York: Avon).

Naroll, R. (1968) 'Some Thoughts on Comparative Method in Cultural Anthropology', in H. M. Blalock and A. Blalock (eds), *Methodology in Social Research* (New York: McGraw-Hill), 236–77.

Narud, H. M. and Valen, H. (2008) 'Coalition Membership and Electoral Performance in Western Europe', in K. Strøm, W. C. Müller, and T. Bergman (eds), *Cabinets and Coalition Bargaining in Western Europe* (Oxford: Oxford University Press), 369–402.

Natali, D. (ed.) (2017) *The New Pension Mix in Europe* (Brussels: PIE-Peter Lang).

Naurin, D. and Wallace, H. (eds) (2008) *Unveiling the Council of the European Union: Games Governments Play in Brussels* (Palgrave: London).

Ndegwa, S. N. (1997) 'Citizenship and Ethnicity: An Examination of Two Transition Moments in Kenyan Politics', *American Political Science Review*, 91(3): 599–617.

Nechushtai, E. (2018). 'From Liberal to Polarized Liberal? Contemporary U.S. News in Hallin and Mancini's Typology of News Systems', *International Journal of Press/Politics*, 23(2): 183–201.

Needler, M. C. (1968) 'Political Development and Socioeconomic Development: The Case of Latin America', *The American Political Science Review*, 62(3): 889–97.

Neidhardt, F. (1994) 'Öffentlichkeit, öffentliche Meinung, soziale Bewegungen', in F. Neidhardt (ed.), *Öffentlichkeit, öffentliche Meinung, soziale Bewegungen*, Kölner Zeitschrift Sonderheft 34 (Opladen: Westdeutscher Verlag), 7–41.

Nenadović, M. (2012) 'An Uneasy Symbiosis: The Impact of International Administrations on Political Parties in Post-Conflict Countries', in P. Burnell and A. Gerrits (eds), *Promoting Party Politics in Emerging Democracies* (Abingdon: Routledge): 89–111.

Neuberger, C. (2019). 'Journalismus und Komplexität', in B. Dernbach, A. Godulla, and A. Sehl (eds), *Komplexität im Journalismus* (Cham: Springer), 31–9.

Neundorf, A., Ezrow, N., Gerschewski, J., Olar, R.G., and R. Shorrocks (2017) 'The Legacy of Authoritarian Regimes on Democratic Citizenship: A Global Analysis of Authoritarian Indoctrination, and Repression', presented at Midwest Political Science Association 2017, European Consortium for Poltical Research Joint Sessions 2017, European Political Science Association 2017.

Nevitte, N. (1996) *Decline of Deference* (Toronto: University of Toronto Press).

Newton, K. and van Deth, J. W. (2010) *Foundations of Comparative Politics* (Cambridge: Cambridge University Press).

Newton, K. and van Deth, J. W. (2016) *Foundations of Comparative Politics. Democracies of the Modern World* (Cambridge: Cambridge University Press).

Nickell, S. (1997) 'Unemployment and Labor Market Rigidities: Europe versus North America', *Journal of Economic Perspectives*, 11(3): 55–74.

Nickell, S. and Layard, R. (1999) 'Labour Market Institutions and Economic Performance', in O. Ashenfelter and D. Card (eds), *Handbook of Labour Economics* (Amsterdam: North Holland), 3029–84.

Nickell, S., Nunziata, L., and Ochel, W. (2004) 'Unemployment in the OECD since the 1960s: What Do We Know?', *Economic Journal*, 115(1): 1–27.

Nickerson, R. S. (2000) 'Null Hypothesis Significance Testing: A Review of an Old and Continuing Controversy', *Psychological Methods*, 5(2): 241–301.

Niedzwiecki, S. (2016) 'Social Policies, Attribution of Responsibility, and Political Alignments: Subnational Analysis of Argentina and Brazil', *Comparative Political Studies*, 49(4): 457–98.

Nielsen, J. H. (2016) 'Why Use Experiences in EU Studies?', *Comparative European Politics* 14(5): 626–44.

Nielsen, R. K. and Schrøder, K. C. (2014) 'The Relative Importance of Social Media for Accessing, Finding, and Engaging with News: An Eight-Country Cross-Media Comparison', *Digital Journalism*, 2(4): 472–89.

Nijeboer, A. (2005) 'The Dutch Referendum', *European Constitutional Law Review*, 1(3): 393–405.

Nikolenyi, C. (2004) 'Cabinet Stability in Post-Communist Central Europe', *Party Politics*, 10(2): 123–50.

Nisbet, E. C., Stoycheff, E., and Pearce, K. E. (2012). 'Internet Use and Democratic Demands: A Multinational, Multilevel Model of Internet Use and Citizen Attitudes about Democracy', *Journal of Communication* 62: 249–65.

Niskanen, W. A. (1971) *Bureaucracy and Representative Government* (Chicago, IL: Aldine Atherton).

Nolan, P. and Lenski, G. E. (1999) *Human Societies: An Introduction to Macrosociology* (New York: McGraw-Hill).

Nordlinger, E. A. (1977) *Soldiers in Politics: Military Coups and Governments* (Englewood Cliffs, NJ: Prentice-Hall).

Norris, P. (1999) 'Introduction: The Growth of Critical Citizens', in P. Norris (ed.), *Critical Citizens: Global Support for Democratic Government* (Oxford: Oxford University Press), 1–27.

Norris, P. (2000) *A Virtuous Circle: Political Communications in Postindustrial Societies* (Cambridge: Cambridge University Press).

Norris, P. (2001) *Digital Divide* (New York: Cambridge University Press).

Norris, P. (2002) *Democratic Phoenix: Reinventing Political Activism* (Cambridge: Cambridge University Press).

Norris, P. (2004) *Electoral Engineering: Voting Rules and Political Behaviour* (Cambridge: Cambridge University Press).

Norris, P. (2009) 'Comparing Political Communications: Common Frameworks or Babelian Confusion?', *Government and Opposition*, 44(3): 321–40.

Norris, P. (2012) *Democratic Governance and Human Security: The Impact of Regimes on Prosperity, Welfare and Peace* (New York: Cambridge University Press).

North, D. C. (1990) *Institutions, Institutional Change and Economic Performance* (Cambridge: Cambridge University Press).

North, D. C. (2010) *Understanding the Process of Economic Change* (Princeton, NJ: Princeton University Press).

Nowak, J. (2019) *Mass Strikes and Social Movements in Brazil and India: Popular Mobilisation in the Long Depression.* (Cham: Palgrave Macmillan).

Nulty, P., Theocharis, Y., Popa, S. A., Parnet, O., and Benoit, K. (2016) 'Social Media and Political Communication in the 2014 Elections to the European Parliament', *Electoral Studies*, 44: 429–44.

Nye, J. S., Jr (2001) 'Globalizations's Democratic Deficit', *Foreign Affairs*, 80: 2–6.

Nye, J. S., Jr (2002) *The Paradox of American Power* (Oxford: Oxford University Press).

Nye, J. S., Jr (2005) *Soft Power: The Means to Success in World Politics* (New York: Public Affairs).

O'Connor, J. (1973) *The Fiscal Crisis of the State* (New York: St Martin's Press).

O'Connor, J., Orloff, A., and Shaver, S. (1999) *States, Markets, and Families: Gender, Liberalism and Social Policy in Australia, Canada, Great Britain and the United States* (New York: Cambridge University Press).

O'Donnell, G. (1973) [1979] *Modernization and Bureaucratic Authoritarianism: Studies in South American Politics* (Berkeley, CA: Institute of International Studies / University of California).

O'Donnell, G. (1994) 'Delegative Democracy', *Journal of Democracy*, 5(1): 55–69.

O'Donnell, G. (1996) 'Illusions about Democracy', *Journal of Democracy*, (2): 34–51.

O'Donnell, G. and Schmitter, P. (1986) *Transitions from Authoritarian Rule: Tentative Conclusions about Uncertain Democracies* (Baltimore, MD: Johns Hopkins University Press).

O'Dwyer, C. (2006) *Runaway State-Building* (Baltimore, MD: Johns Hopkins University Press).

Oates, W. E. (1972) *Fiscal Federalism* (New York: Harcourt Brace Jovanovich).

Oates, W. (2005) 'Toward a Second-Generation Theory of Fiscal Federalism', *International Tax and Public Finance*, 12: 349–74.

Oberschall, A. (1973) *Social Conflict and Social Movements* (Englewood Cliffs, NJ: Prentice-Hall).

Obinger, H., Leibfried, S., and Castles, F. (eds) (2005) *Federalism and the Welfare State: New World and European Experiences* (Cambridge: Cambridge University Press).

Obinger, H., Schmitt, C., and Starke, P. (2013) 'Policy Diffusion and Policy Transfer in Comparative Welfare State Research', *Social Policy & Administration*, 47(1): 111–29.

Obinger, H., Petersen, K. and Starke, P. (eds) (2018) *Warfare and Welfare. Military Conflict and Welfare State Development in Western*

Countries (Oxford: Oxford University Press).

OECD (1994) *The OECD Jobs Study: Evidence and Explanations.* Part I: *Labour Market Trends and Underlying Forces of Change;* Part II: *The Adjustment Potential of the Labour Market* (Paris: OECD).

OECD (1997) *The OECD Jobs Strategy: Implementing the OECD Jobs Strategy. Member Countries' Experiences. and Making Work Pay: Taxation, Benefit, Employment and Unemployment* (Paris: OECD).

OECD (2000*a*) *OECD Historical Statistics 1999* (Paris: OECD).

OECD (2000*b*) *OECD Economic Outlook 68. December 2000* (Paris: OECD).

OECD (2006) *OECD Employment Outlook: Boosting Jobs and Incomes* (Paris: OECD).

OECD (2008*a*) *OECD Employment Outlook* (Paris: OECD).

OECD (2008*b*) *Growing Unequal? Income Distribution and Poverty in OECD Countries* (Paris: OECD).

OECD (2011*a*). *Divided We Stand. Why Inequality Keeps Rising* (Paris: OECD).

OECD (2011*b*) *Ministerial Advisors: Role, Influence and Management* (Paris: OECD).

OECD (2012) *Economic Policy Reforms* (Paris: OECD).

OECD (2014*a*) 'Africa Fact Sheet' (http://www.oecd.org/investment/investmentfordevelopment/47452483.pdf).

OECD (2014*b*) *Regional Outlook 2014: Regions and Cities: Where Policies and People Meet* (Paris: OECD).

OECD (2015*a*) *In It Together. Why Less Inequality Benefits All* (Paris: OECD).

OECD (2015*b*) *Economic Outlook98* (Paris: OECD).

OECD (2015*c*) 'OECD Social Expenditure Database' (http://www.oecd.org/social/expenditure.htm).

OECD (2018) *A Broken Social Elevator? How to Promote Social Mobility* (Paris: OECD).

OECD (2019*a*) *Under Pressure: The Squeezed Middle Class* (Paris: OECD).

OECD (2019*b*) 'Trade Union, Source and Method of the OECD Data on Trade Union Membership and Trade Union Density' (https://stats.oecd.org/index.aspx?DataSetCode=TUD).

OECD (2019*c*) 'OECD Income Distribution Database' (https://oe.cd/idd).

OECD (2019*d*) 'OECD Economic Outlook No. 105 (May 2019)' (http://stats.oecd.org).

Offe, C. and Wiesenthal, H. (1980) 'Two Logics of Collective Action', *Political Power and Social Theory*, 1: 67–115.

Offe, C. and Wiesenthal, H. (1985) 'Two Logics of Collective Action: Theoretical Notes on Social Class and Organizational Form', in C. Offe (ed.), *Disorganized Capitalism: Contemporary Transformations of Work and Politics* (Cambridge: Polity Press), 175–220.

Offer, A., Pechey, R., and Ulijaszek, S. (2010) 'Obesity under Affluence Varies by Welfare Regimes: The Effect of Fast Food, Insecurity, and Inequality', *Economics and Human Biology*, 8(3): 297–308.

Ohmae, K. (1993) 'The Rise of the Region State', *Foreign Affairs*, 72(2): 78–87.

Ohmae, K. (1995) *End of the Nation State: The Rise of Regional Economies* (London: HarperCollins).

Okun, A. M. (1975) *Equality and Efficiency: The Big Tradeoff* (Washington, DC: Brookings Institution Press).

Olson, D. (1980) *The Legislative Process: A Comparative Approach* (New York: Harper & Row).

Olson, M. (1965) *The Logic of Collective Action* (Cambridge, MA: Harvard University Press).

Onaran, Ö. and Boesch, V. (2014) 'The Effects of Globalization on the Distribution of Taxes and Social Expenditures in Europe: Do Welfare State Regimes Matter?', *Environment and Planning A*, 46(2): 373–97.

Opp, K. (1989) *The Rationality of Political Protest* (Boulder, CO: Westview Press).

Opp, K. (2009) *Theories of Political Protest and Social Movements. A Multidisciplinary Introduction, Critique and Synthesis* (London: Routledge).

Orbán, V. (2014) Full text of speech at Băile Tuşnad (https://budapestbeacon.com/full-text-of-viktor-orbans-speech-at-baile-tusnad-tusnadfurdo-of-26-july-2014).

Orloff, A. (1993) 'Gender and the Social Rights of Citizenship', *American Sociological Review*, 58(3): 303–28.

Ornstein, M. D. (1986) 'Regionalism and Canadian Political Ideology', in R. J. Brym (ed.), *Regionalism in Canada* (Richmond Hill, ON: Irwin), 47–88.

Ostrom, E. (2007) 'Institutional Rational Choice: An Assessment of the Institutional Analysis and Development Framework', in P. A. Sabatier (ed.), *Theories of the Policy Process* (2nd edn) (Boulder, CO: Westview Press), 21–64.

Ott, J. C. (2010) 'Good Governance and Happiness in Nations: Technical Quality Precedes Democracy and Quality Beats Size', *Journal of Happiness Studies*, 11(3): 353–68.

Oversloot, H. and Verheul, R. (2006) 'Managing Democracy: Political Parties and the State in Russia', *Journal of Communist Studies and Transition Politics*, 22(3): 383–405.

Page, E. and Goldsmith, M. (eds) (1987) *Central and Local Government Relations: A Comparative Analysis of West European Unitary States* (London: Sage).

Page, E. and Goldsmith, M. J. (eds.) (2010) *Changing Government Relations in Europe: From Localism to Intergovernmentalism* (London: Routledge).

Page, E. and Wright, V. (eds) (1999) *Bureaucratic Élites in Western European States* (Oxford: Oxford University Press).

Page, E. and Wright, V. (eds) (2007) *From the Active to the Enabling State* (Houndmills, Basingstoke: Palgrave Macmillan).

Palfrey, J., Zittrain, J., Deibert, R., and Rohozinski, R. (2008) *Access Denied: The Practice and Policy of Global Internet Filtering* (Cambridge, MA: MIT Press).

Palier, B. (ed.) (2010) *A Long Goodbye to Bismarck? The Politics of Welfare Reforms in Continental Europe* (Amsterdam: Amsterdam University Press).

Panebianco, A. (1988) *Political Parties: Organization and Power* (Cambridge: Cambridge University Press).

Panitch, L. (1980) 'Theorizations of Corporatism: Reflections on a Growth Industry', *British Journal of Sociology*, 31(2): 159–87.

Panke, D (2018) *Research Design and Method Selection: Making Good Choices in the Social Sciences* (London: Sage).

Papathanassopoulos, S., Coen, S., Curran, J., Aalberg, T., Rowe, D., Jones, P., Rojas, H., and Tiffen, R. (2013) 'Online Threat, but Television Is Still Dominant: A Comparative Study of 11 Nations' News Consumption', *Journalism Practice*, 7(6): 690–704.

Paquin, S. (2003) 'Paradiplomatie Identitaire et Diplomatie en Belgique Fédérale: Le Cas de la Flandre', *Revue Canadienne de Science Politique*, 36(3): 621–42.

Parkinson, C. N. (1958) *Parkinson's Law: The Pursuit of Progress* (London: John Murray).

Parsons, T. (1968) *The Structure of Social Action* (2nd edn) (New York: Free Press).

Paterson, M., Hoffmann, M., Betsill, M., and S. Bernstein (2014) 'The Micro Foundations of Policy Diffusion Toward Complex Global Governance: An Analysis of the Transnational Carbon Emission Trading Network', *Comparative Political Studies*, 47: 420–49.

Peck, J. and Zhang, J. (2013) 'A Variety of Capitalism … with Chinese Characteristics?', *Journal of Economic Geography*, 13(3): 357–96.

Pedersen, S. (1990) 'Gender, Welfare, and Citizenship in Britain during the Great War', *American Historical Review*, 95(4): 983–1006.

Pedersen, S. (1993) *Family Dependence and the Origin of the Welfare State, Britain and France, 1914–1945* (Cambridge: Cambridge University Press).

Peeters, P. (2007) 'Multinational Federations: Reflections on the Belgian State', in M. Burgess and J. Pinder (eds), *Multinational Federations* (Abingdon: Routledge), 31–49.

Pei, M. and Kasper, S. (2003) *Lessons from the Past: The American Record on Nation Building*, Policy Brief 24 (Washington, DC: Carnegie Endowment for International Peace).

Peng, I. and Wong, J. (2010) 'East Asia', in F. G. Castles, S. Leibfried, J. Lewis, H. Obinger, and C. Pierson (eds), *The Oxford Handbook of the Welfare State* (Oxford: Oxford University Press), 657–70.

Penner, E., Blidook, K., and Soroka, S. (2006) 'Legislative Priorities and Public Opinion: Representation of Partisan Agendas in the Canadian House of Commons', *Journal of European Public Policy* 13(7): 1006–20.

Pennings, P. (2016) 'Relating Theory and Concepts to Measurements: Bridging the Gap', in H. Keman and J. Woldendorp (eds), *Handbook of Research Methods and Applications in Political Science* (Cheltenham: Edward Elgar), ch. 4.

Pennings, P., Keman, H., and Kleinnijenhuis, J. (2006) *Doing Research in Political Science: An Introduction to Comparative Methods and Statistics* (2nd edn) (London: Sage).

Pérez-Liñán, A. (2007) *Presidential Impeachment and the New Political Instability in Latin America* (Cambridge: Cambridge University Press).

Pérez-Liñán, A., Schmidt, N., and Vairo, D. (2019) 'Presidential Hegemony and Democratic Backsliding in Latin America, 1925–2016', *Democratization*, 26(4): 606–25.

Perroux, F. (1950) 'Economic Space: Theory and Applications', *Quarterly Journal of Economics*, 64: 89–104.

Peters, B. G. (1998) *Comparative Politics: Theory and Methods* (Houndmills, Basingstoke: Palgrave Macmillan).

Peters, B. G. (2011) *Institutional Theory in Political Science: The New Institutionalism* (London: Continuum).

Peters, B. G. and Pierre, J. (eds) (2001) *Politicians, Bureaucrats, and Administrative Reform* (Abingdon: Routledge).

Peters, B. G., Pierre, J., and King, D. S. (2005) 'The Politics of Path Dependency: Political Conflict in Historical Institutionalism', *Journal of Politics*, 67(4), 1275–300.

Peters, B. G., Pierre, J., and Randma-Liiv, T. (2011) 'Global Financial Crisis, Public Administration and Governance: Do New Problems Require New Solutions?' *Public Organization Review*, 11(1), 13–27.

Peters, B. G., Schröter, E., and von Maravić, P. (2015) *Politics of Representative Bureaucracy: Power, Legit and Performance* (Cheltenham: Edward Elgar).

Peters, B. G. (2015) *Pursuing Horizontal Management: The Politics of Public Sector Coordination* (Lawrence: University Press of Kansas).

Peters, B. G. and Pierre, J. (2016) *Comparative Governance: Rediscovering the Functional Dimension of Governing* (Cambridge: Cambridge University Press).

Pevehouse, J. C. (2005) *Democracy from Above: Regional Organizations and Democratization* (Cambridge: Cambridge University Press).

Pfetsch, B. (2007), 'Government News Management: Institutional Approaches and Strategies in Three Western Democracies', in D. Graber and D. McQuail (eds), *The Politics of News; the News of Politics* (Washington: Congressional Quarterly Press), 71–97.

Pfetsch, B. and Heft, A. (2015), 'Theorizing Communication Flows within a European Public Sphere', in T. Risse (ed.), *European Public Spheres: Politics is Back* (New York: Cambridge University Press), 29–52.

Pfetsch, B. and Voltmer, K. (2012), 'Negotiating Control: Political Communication Cultures in Bulgaria and Poland', *International Journal of Press/Politics*, 17(4): 388–406.

Pfetsch, B., Adam, S., and Eschner, B. (2008), 'The Contribution of the Press to Europeanization of Public Debates. A Comparative Study of Issue Salience and Conflict Lines of European Integration', *Journalism*, 9(4): 465–92.

Pfetsch, B., Mayerhöffer, E., and Moring, T. (2014a) 'National or Professional? Types of Political Communication Culture across Europe', in B. Pfetsch (ed.), *Political Communication Cultures in Europe: Attitudes of Political Actors and Journalists in Nine Countries* (Houndmills, Basingstoke: Palgrave Macmillan), 76–102.

Pfetsch, B., Maurer, P., Mayerhöffer, E., and Moring, T. (2014b) 'A Hedge between Keeps Friendship Green—Concurrence and Conflict between Politicians and Journalists in Nine European Democracies', in M. J. Canel and K. Voltmer (eds), *Comparing Political Communication across Time and Space* (Houndmills, Basingstoke: Palgrave Macmillan), 172–91.

Piattoni, S. (2009) *The Theory of Multi-Level Governance: Conceptual, Empirical, and Normative Challenges* (Oxford: Oxford University Press).

Pichardo, N. A. (1997) 'New Social Movements: A Critical Review', *Annual Review of Sociology*, 23: 411–30.

Pierre, J. and Peters, B. G. (2000) *Governance, Politics and the State* (Houndmills, Basingstoke: Palgrave Macmillan).

Pierson, C. (2003) 'Learning from Labor? Welfare Policy Transfer between Australia and Britain', *Commonwealth and Comparative Politics*, 41(1): 77–100.

Pierson, P. (1994) *Dismantling the Welfare State? Reagan, Thatcher, and the Politics of Retrenchment* (New York: Cambridge University Press).

Pierson, P. (1995) 'Fragmented Welfare States: Federal Institutions and the Development of Social Policy', *Governance*, 8(4): 449–78.

Pierson, P. (1996) 'The Path to European Integration: A Historical Institutionalist Analysis', *Comparative Political Studies*, 29(2): 123–63.

Pierson, P. (1998) 'Irresistible Forces, Immovable Objects: Post-Industrial Welfare States Confront Permanent Austerity', *Journal of European Public Policy*, 5(4): 539–60.

Pierson, P. (2000) 'Increasing Returns, Path Dependence, and the Study of Politics', *American Political Science Review*, 94(2): 251–67.

Pierson, P. (2001a) 'Coping with Permanent Austerity: Welfare State Restructuring in Affluent Democracies', in P. Pierson (ed.), *The New Politics of the Welfare State* (Oxford: Oxford University Press) 411–56.

Pierson, P. (ed.) (2001b) *The New Politics of the Welfare State* (Oxford: Oxford University Press).

Pierson, P. (2003) 'Big, Slow-Moving and … Invisible: Macrosocial Processes in the Study of Comparative Politics', in J. Mahoney and D. Rueschemeyer (eds), *Comparative Historical Analysis in the Social Sciences* (Cambridge: Cambridge University Press), 177–207.

Pierson, P. and Skocpol, T. (2002) 'Historical Institutionalism in Contemporary Political Science', in I. Katznelson and H. V. Milner (eds), *Political Science: The State of the Discipline* (New York/Washington, DC: W. W. Norton/American Political Science Association), 693–721.

Piketty, T. (2014) *Capital in the Twenty-First Century* (Cambridge, MA: Belknap: Harvard University Press).

Piore, M. J. and Sabel, C. F. (1984) *The Second Industrial Divide: Possibilities for Prosperity* (New York: Basic Books).

Piper, N. and Uhlin, A. (eds) (2004) *Transnational Activism in Asia: Problems of Power and Democracy* (London: Routledge).

Pitigliani, F. (1933) *The Italian Corporative State* (London: King & Son).

Pitkin, H. (1967) *The Concept of Representation* (Berkeley, CA: University of California Press).

Piven, F. F. and Cloward, R. A. (1977) *Poor People's Movements: Why They Succeed, How They Fail* (New York: Pantheon).

Piven, F. F. and Cloward R. A. (1979) *Poor People's Movements: Why They Succeed, How They Fail* (New York: Vintage).

Pizzorno, A. (1978) 'Political Exchange and Collective Identity', in C. Crouch and A. Pizzorno (eds), *The Resurgence of Class Conflict in Western Europe since 1968, Vol. 2: Comparative Analysis* (London: Macmillan), 277–98.

Plasser, F. (2003) *Globalisierung der Wahlkämpfe. Praktiken der Campaign Professionals im weltweiten Vergleich* (Vienna: Facultas Universitätsverlag).

Plasser, F. (2008) 'Political Consulting Worldwide', in D. W. Johnson (ed.), *Handbook of Political Management* (New York: Routledge), 24–41.

Plasser, F. and Plasser, G. (2002) *Global Political Campaigning: A Worldwide Analysis of Campaign Professionals and Their Practices* (Westport, CT: Praeger).

Poggi, G. (1999) *The State: Its Nature, Development and Prospects* (Cambridge: Polity Press).

Poguntke, T. and Webb, P. (eds) (2005) *The Presidentialization of Politics* (Oxford: Oxford University Press).

Polanyi, K. (2001) [1944] *The Great Transformation: The Political and Economic Origins of Our Time* (Boston, MA: Beacon).

Pollack, M. A. (1997) 'Delegation, Agency and Agenda Setting in the European Community', *International Organization*, 51(1): 99–134.

Pollack, M. A. (2003) *The Engines of European Integration: Delegation, Agency, and Agenda Setting in the EU* (Oxford: Oxford University Press).

Polletta, F. (2001) 'Collective Identity and Social Movements', *Annual Review of Sociology*, 27: 283–305.

Polletta, F. (2006) *It Was Like a Fever: Storytelling in Protest and Politics* (Chicago, IL and London: University of Chicago Press).

Polsby, N. W. (1975) 'Legislatures', in F. I. Greenstein and N. Polsby (eds), *Handbook of Political Science* (Reading, MA: Addison-Wesley).

Pontusson, J. (1995) 'From Comparative Public Policy to Political Economy: Putting Institutions in their Place', *Comparative Political Studies*, 27: 117–47.

Pontusson, J. (2005) *Inequality and Prosperity: Social Europe vs Liberal America* (Ithaca, NY: Cornell University Press).

Pope Leo XIII (2010) [1891] 'Rerum Novarum. Encyclical of Pope Leo XIII on Capital and Labor' (http://www.vatican.va/holy_father/leo_xiii/encyclicals).

Popitz, H. (1992) *Phänomene der Macht* (2nd edn) (Tübingen: Mohr).

Popkin, S. L. (1979) *The Rational Peasant: The Political Economy of Rural Society in Vietnam* (Berkeley, CA: University of California Press).

Poppe, A., Leininger, J. and Wolff, J. (2019) 'Beyond Contestation: Conceptualizaing Negotiation in Democracy Promotion', *Democratization*, 26(5): 777–95.

Popper, K. R. (1971) [1962] *The Open Society and Its Enemies* (two volumes) (Princeton, NJ: Princeton University Press).

Porter, B. D. (1994) *War and Rise of the State: The Military Foundations of Modern Politics* (New York: Free Press).

Porter, M. E. (1990) *The Comparative Advantages of Nations* (New York: Free Press).

Posner, R. A. (2004) *Catastrophe: Risk and Response* (Oxford: Oxford University Press).

Post, R. (2000) 'Democratic Constitutionalism and Cultural Heterogeneity', Working Paper 2000–8 (Berkeley, CA: University of California at Berkeley, Institute of Governmental Studies).

Powell, G. B. (1982) *Contemporary Democracies: Participation, Stability and Violence* (Cambridge, MA: Harvard University Press).

Powell, G. B. (1986) 'American Voter Turnout in Comparative Perspective', *American Political Science Review*, 80(1): 17–43.

Powell, G. B. (2000) *Elections as Instruments of Democracy: Majoritarian and Proportional Vision* (New Haven, CT: Yale University Press).

Powell, W. W. (1991) 'Expanding the Scope of Institutional Analysis', in W. W. Powell and P. J. DiMaggio (eds), *The New Institutionalism in Organizational Analysis* (Chicago, IL: University of Chicago Press), 183–203.

Prasad, M. and Deng, Y. (2009) 'Taxation and the Worlds of Welfare', *Socio-Economic Review* 7: 431–57.

Prescott, T. and Urlacher, B.R. (2018) 'Case Selection and the Comparative Method: Introducing the Case Selector', *European Political Science*, 17(3): 422–36.

Pressman, J. L. and Wildavsky, A. (1973) *Implementation: How Great Expectations in Washington are Dashed in Oakland* (Berkeley, CA: University of California Press).

Preuß, U. (1996) 'The Political Meaning of Constitutionalism', in R. Bellamy (ed.), *Constitutionalism, Democracy, and Sovereignty* (Aldershot: Avebury Press).

Pryce, S. (1997) *Presidentializing the Premiership* (Houndmills, Basingstoke: Palgrave Macmillan).

Pryor, F. L. (1968) *Public Expenditure in Communist and Capitalist Countries* (London: Allen & Unwin).

Przeworski, A. (1991) *Democracy and the Market: Political and Economic Reforms in Eastern Europe and Latin America* (Cambridge: Cambridge University Press).

Przeworski, A. (2004a) 'Institutions Matter?', *Government and Opposition*, 39(4): 527–40.

Przeworski, A. (2004b) *States and Markets: A Primer in Politcial Economy* (Cambridge: Cambridge University Press).

Przeworski, A. and Limongi, F. (1997) 'Modernization: Theories and Facts', *World Politics*, 49(2): 155–83.

Przeworski, A. and Sprague, J. D. (1986) *Paper Stones: A History of Electoral Socialism* (Chicago, IL: University of Chicago Press).

Przeworski, A. and Teune, H. (1970) *The Logic of Comparative Social Inquiry* (New York: Wiley Interscience).

Przeworski, A. and Wallerstein, M. (1982) 'The Structure of Class Conflict in Democratic Capitalist Societies', *American Political Science Review*, 76(2): 215–38.

Przeworski, A., Alvarez, M. E., Cheibub, J. A., and Limongi, F. (2000) *Democracy and Development: Political Institutions and Well-Being in the World, 1950–1990* (Cambridge: Cambridge University Press).

Pülzl, H. and Treib, O. (2006) 'Policy Implementation', in F. Fischer, G. Miller, and M. Sidney (eds), *Handbook of Public Policy Analysis: Theory, Politics, and Methods* (Boca Raton, FL: CRC Press), 89–107.

Putnam, R. D. (1976) *The Comparative Study of Political Elites* (Englewood Cliffs, NJ: Prentice-Hall).

Putnam, R. D. (1993) *Making Democracy Work: Civic Traditions in Modern Italy* (Princeton, NJ: Princeton University Press).

Putnam, R. D. (1995) 'Tuning In, Tuning Out: The Strange Disappearance of Social Capital in America', *PS: Political Science and Politics*, 28(4): 664–83.

Putnam, R. D. (2000) *Bowling Alone: The Collapse and Revival of American Community* (New York: Simon & Schuster).

Putnam, R. D. (2015) *Our Kids. The American Dream in Crisis* (New York: Simon & Schuster).

Pye, L. (1968) 'Introduction', in L. Pye (ed.), *Political Culture and Political Development* (Princeton, NJ: Princeton University Press).

Quandt, T., Frischlich, L., Boberg, S., and Schatto-Eckrodt, T. (2019) 'Fake News', in T. P. Vos, F. Hanusch, D. Dimitrakopoulou, M. Geertsema-Sligh, and A. Sehl (eds), *The International Encyclopedia of Journalism Studies* (Oxford: Wiley-Blackwell) (10.1002/9781118841570.iejs0128).

Qvortrup, M. (2005) *A Comparative Study of Referendums: Government by the People* (2nd edn) (Manchester: Manchester University Press).

Radaelli, C. (2005) 'Diffusion Without Convergence: How Political Context Shapes the Adoption of Regulatory Impact Assessment', *Journal of European Public Policy*, 12(5): 924–43.

Rae, D. W. (1971) *The Political Consequences of Electoral Laws* (2nd edn) (New Haven, CT: Yale University Press).

Ragin, C. (1987) *The Comparative Method: Moving beyond Qualitative and Quantitative Strategies* (Berkeley, CA: University of California Press).

Ragin, C. (1992) '"Casing" and the Process of Social Inquiry', in C. Ragin and H. S. Becker (eds), *Exploring the Foundations of Social Inquiry* (Cambridge: Cambridge University Press), 217–26.

Ragin, C. (2000) *Fuzzy-Set Social Science* (Chicago, IL: The University of Chicago Press).

Ragin, C. (2004) 'Turning the Tables: How Case-Oriented Research Challenges Variable-Oriented Research', in H. E. Brady and D. Collier (eds), *Rethinking Social Inquiry* (Lanham, MD: Rowman & Littlefield), 123–38.

Ragin, C. (2008) *Re. designing Social Inquiry. Fuzzy Sets and Beyond* (Chicago, IL: University of Chicago Press).

Ragin, C. and Becker, H. S. (eds) (1992) *Exploring the Foundations of Social Inquiry* (Cambridge: Cambridge University Press).

Rahat, G. (2011) 'The Politics of Electoral Reform: The State of Research', *Journal of Elections, Public Opinion and Parties* 21(4): 523–43.

Rahat, G. and Hazan, R. Y. (2008) 'Israel: The Politics of an Extreme Electoral System', in M. Gallagher and P. Mitchell (eds), *The Politics of Electoral Systems* (Oxford: Oxford University Press), 333–52.

Rakove, J. N. (1996) *Original Meanings: Politics and Ideas in the Making of the Constitution* (New York: Knopf).

Ranney, A. (1962) *The Doctrine of Responsible Party Government* (Urbana, IL: University of Illinois Press).

Raschke, J. (1985) *Soziale Bewegungen. Ein historisch-systematischer Grundriß* (Frankfurt/New York: Campus).

Raunio, T. (2008) 'Finland: One Hundred Years of Quietude', in M. Gallagher and P. Mitchell (eds), *The Politics of Electoral Systems* (Oxford: Oxford University Press), 473–90.

Rawlings, R. (2001) 'Law, Territory and Integration: A View from the Atlantic Shore', *International Review of Administrative Sciences*, 67(3): 479–504.

Reed, M. and Wallace, M. (2015) 'Elite Discourse and Institutional Innovation: Making the Hybrid Happen in English Public Services', *Research in the Sociology of Organizations*, 43(S): 269–302.

Reed, S. R. (2008) 'Japan: Haltingly toward a Two-Party System', in M. Gallagher and P. Mitchell (eds), *The Politics of Electoral Systems* (Oxford: Oxford University Press), 277–94.

Reh, C., Héritier, A., Bressanelli, E., and Koop, C. (2013) 'The Informal Politics of Legislation: Explaining Secluded Decision Making in the European Union', *Comparative Political Studies*, 46(9): 1112–42.

Rehfeldt, U. (2009) 'La Concertation au Sommet Toujours d'Actualité Face à la Crise? Théorie du Néocorporatime et Analyse Comparée des Relations Professionnelles en Europe', *Chronique International de l'IRES*, 121 (November): 40–9.

Renwick, A. (2010) *The Politics of Electoral Reform: Changing the Rules of Democracy* (Cambridge: Cambridge University Press).

Renwick, A. (2014) 'Don't Trust Your Poll Lead: How Public Opinion Changes during Referendum Campaigns', in P. Cowley, and R. Ford (eds), *Sex, Lies and the Ballot Box: 50 Things You Need to Know about British Elections* (London: Biteback), 79–84.

Renwick, A. and Pilet, J-B. (2016) *Faces on the Ballot: The Personalization of Electoral Systems in Europe* (Oxford: Oxford University Press).

Requejo, F. (2005) *Multinational Federalismand Value Pluralism: The Spanish Case* (London: Routledge).

Requejo, F. and Nagel, K.-J. (eds), *Federalism beyond Federations: Asymmetry and Processes of Resymmetrisation in Europe* (Farnham: Ashgate).

Reynolds, A., Reilly, B., and Ellis, A. (2005) *Electoral System Design: The New International IDEA Handbook* (Stockholm: International IDEA).

Rhodes, M. (1998) 'Globalisation, Labour Markets and Welfare States: A Future of 'Competitive Corporatism?', in M. Rhodes and Y. Meny (eds), *The Future of European Welfare: A New Social Contract?* (London: Palgrave Macmillan), 178–203.

Rhodes, R. A. W. (1995) 'From Prime Ministerial Power to Core Executive', in R. A. W. Rhodes and P. Dunleavy (eds), *Prime Minister, Cabinet and Core Executive* (Houndmills, Basingstoke: Palgrave Macmillan).

Rhodes, R. A. W. (1997) *Understanding Governance: Policy Networks, Governance, Reflexivity and Accountability* (Buckingham: Open University Press).

Rhodes, R. A. W. and Dunleavy, P. (eds) (1995) *Prime Minister, Cabinet and Core Executive* (Houndmills, Basingstoke: Palgrave Macmillan).

Richardson, J. (ed.) (1982) *Policy Styles in Western Europe* (London: Allen & Unwin).

Richardson, J. (2018) *British Policy Making and the Need for a Post-Brexit Policy Style* (New York: Springer).

Rieger, E. and Leibfried, S. (1998) 'Welfare State Limits to Globalization', *Politics and Society*, 26(3): 363–90.

Rieger, E. and Leibfried, S. (2001) *Welfare State Mercantilism: The Relations between Democratic Social Policy and the World Market Order* (Frankfurt am Main: Suhrkamp).

Riggs, F. W. (1994) 'Thoughts about Neoidealism vs Realism: Reflections on Charles Kegley's ISA Presidential Address', *International Studies Notes*, 19(Winter): 1–6.

Riker, W. H. (1962) *The Theory of Political Coalitions* (New Haven, CT: Yale University Press).

Riker, W. H. (1964) *Federalism: Origin, Operation, Significance* (Boston, MA: Little, Brown).

Riker, W. H. (1982) *Liberalism against Populism* (San Francisco, CA: Freeman).

Riker, W. H. (1990) 'Political Science and Rational Choice', in J. E. Alt and K. A. Shepsle (eds), *Perspectives on Positive Political Economy* (Cambridge: Cambridge University Press), 163–81.

Rimlinger, G. V. (1971) *Welfare Policy and Industrialization in Europe, America and Russia* (New York: Wiley).

Ringen, S. (2006) *The Possibility of Politics: A Study in the Political Economy of the Welfare State* (Piscataway, NJ: Transaction Publishers).

Risse-Kappen, T. (1995) 'Bringing Transnational Relations Back In: Introduction', in T. Risse-Kappen (ed.), *Bringing Transnational Relations Back In: Non-State Actors, Domestic Structures,* and International Institutions (Cambridge: Cambridge University Press), 3–33.

Robeyns, I. (2011) 'The Capability Approach', in E. N. Zalta (ed.), *The Stanford Encyclopedia of Philosophy* (Stanford CA: Stanford University)

Robinson, W. (1950) 'Ecological Correlations and the Behavior of Individuals', *American Sociological Review*, 15: 351–7.

Robinson, W. I. (1996) *Promoting Polyarchy: Globalization, US Intervention and Hegemony* (Cambridge: Cambridge University Press).

Roche, W. K. and Cradden, T. (2003) 'Neo-Corporatism and Social Partnership', in M. Adshead and M. Millar (eds), *Public Administration and Public Policy in Ireland* (Abingdon: Routledge), 69–90.

Rodden, J. (2004) 'Comparative Federalism and Decentralization: On Meaning and Measurement', *Comparative Politics*, 36(4): 481–99.

Rodden, J. (2006) *Hamilton's Paradox: The Promise and Peril of Fiscal Federalism* (Cambridge: Cambridge University Press).

Rodgers, D. T. (2000) *Atlantic Crossings: Social Politics in a Progressive Age* (Cambridge, MA: Harvard University Press).

Rodrik, D. (1996) 'Why Do More Open Economies Have Bigger Governments?', NBER Working Paper Series 5537 (Cambridge: National Bureau of Economic Research).

Rodrik, D. (2017) 'Populism and the Economics of Globalization', paper, John F. Kennedy School of Government (Cambridge, MA: Harvard University).

Rodrik, D. (2018) 'Populism and the Political Economy of Globalization', *Journal of International Business Policy*, 1(1): 12–33.

Rodrik, D., Subramanian A., and Trebbi F. (2004) 'Institutions Rule: The Primacy of Institutions Over Geography and Integration in Economic Development', *Journal of Economic Growth*, 9: 131–65.

Roeder, P. D. (2009) 'Ethnofederalism and the Mismanagement of Conflicting Nationalisms', *Regional and Federal Studies*, 19(2): 203–19.

Rogers, E. M. (1995) *Diffusion of Innovations* (New York: Free Press).

Rogowski, R. (1989) *Commerce and Coalitions: How Trade Affects Domestic Political Alignments* (Princeton, NJ: Princeton University Press).

Rohlfing, I. (2012) *Case Studies and Causal Inference: An Integrative Framework* (Houndmills, Basingstoke: Palgrave Macmillan).

Rohrschneider, R. (2002) 'The Democratic Deficit and Mass Support for an EU-Wide Government', *American Journal of Political Science*, 46(2): 463–75.

Rokeach, M. (1960) *The Open and the Closed Mind* (New York: Basic Books).

Rokeach, M. (1968) *Beliefs, Attitudes and Values* (San Francisco: Jossey-Bass).

Rokkan, S. (1966) 'Norway: Numerical Democracy and Corporate Pluralism', in R. A. Dahl (ed.), *Political Oppositions in Western Democracies* (New Haven, CT: Yale University Press), 70–115.

Rokkan, S. (1970) *Citizens, Elections, Parties* (Oslo: Universitetsforlaget).

Rokkan, S. (1980) 'Territories, Centres and Peripheries: Toward a Geoethnic, Geoeconomic, Geopolitical Model of Differentiation within Western Europe', in J. Gottman (ed.), *Centre and Periphery: Spatial Variation in Politics* (Beverly Hills, CA: Sage), 163–204.

Rokkan, S. and Urwin, D. (eds) (1982) 'Introduction: Centres and Peripheries in Western Europe' in S. Rokkan and D. Urwin (eds), *The Politics of Territorial Identity: Studies in European Regionalism* (London: Sage), 1–17.

Rokkan, S. and Urwin, D. (1983) *Economy, Territory, Identity: Politics of West European Peripheries* (London: Sage).

Rolfe, M. (2012) *Voter Turnout: A Social Theory of Political Participation* (Cambridge: Cambridge University Press).

Romano, S. (1947) *Principii di Diritto Costituzionale Generale* (Milan: Giuffe).

Rose, R. (1969) 'The Variability of Party Government: A Theoretical and Empirical Critique', *Political Studies*, 17: 413–45.

Rose, R. (1976) *The Problem of Party Government* (Harmondsworth: Penguin).

Rose, R. (1991) 'What is Lesson-Drawing?', *Journal of Public Policy*, 11: 3–30.

Rose, R. (1993) *Lesson Drawing in Public Policy: A Guide to Learning across Time and Space* (Washington, DC: CQ Press).

Rose, R. and Chull Shin, D. (2000) 'Democratization Backward', *British Journal of Political Science*, 31: 331–75.

Rosenau, J. N. (1993) 'Citizenship in a Changing Global Order', in J. N. Rosenau and E.-O. Czempiel (eds), *Governance without Government: Order and Change in World Politics* (Cambridge: Cambridge University Press), 272–95.

Rosenfeld, M. (ed.) (1994) *Constitutionalism, Identity, Difference, and Legitimacy: Theoretical Perspectives* (Durham, NC: Duke University Press).

Rosenfeld, M. (2010) *The Identity of the Constitutional Subject* (London: Routledge).

Ross, F. (2000) '"Beyond Left and Right": The New Partisan Politics of Welfare', *Governance*, 13(2): 155–83.

Ross, M. H. and Homer, E. (1976) 'Galton's Problem in Cross-National Research', *World Politics* 29(1) 1–28.

Ross, M. L. (2001) 'Does Oil Hinder Democracy?', *World Politics*, 53(3): 325–61.

Rossi, P. H., Lipsey, M. W., and Freeman, H. E. (2004) *Evaluation: A Systematic Approach* (Thousand Oaks, CA: Sage).

Rothstein, B. (1998) *Just Institutions Matter: The Moral and Political Logic of the Universal Welfare State* (Cambridge: Cambridge University Press).

Rothstein, B. (2011) *The Quality of Government: Corruption, Social Trust, and Inequality in International Perspective* (Chicago, IL: University of Chicago Press).

Rothstein, B. (2013) 'Corruption and Social Trust: Why the Fish Roots from the Head Down', *Social Research*, 80(4): 1009–32.

Rothstein, B. (2015) 'Gulty as Charged? Human Well-Being and the Unsung Relevance of Political Science', in G. Stoker, B. G. Peters, and J. Pierre (eds), *The Relevance of Political Science* (New York: Palgrave), 101–23.

Rothstein, B. (2017) 'Solidarity, Diversity and the Quality of Government', in K. G. Banting and W. Kymlicka (eds), *The Strains of Committment: The Political Sources of Solidarity in Diverse Societies* (Oxford: Oxford University Press).

Rothstein, B. and Eek, D. (2009) 'Political Corruption and Social Trust—An Experimental Approach', *Rationality and Society*, 21(1): 81–112.

Rothstein, B. and Holmberg, S. (2014) 'Correlates of Corruption', QoG Working Paper (Gothenburg: The Quality of Government Institute, University of Gothenburg), 17.

Rousseau, J.-J. (1973) [1762] *The Social Contract: and Discourses* (London: Everyman), also (http://ebooks.adelaide.edu.au/r/rousseau/jean_jacques/r864s).

Rozell, M. J., Wilcox, C., and Madland, D. (2006) *Interest Groups in American Campaigns* (Washington, DC: CQ Press).

Rucht, D. (1994) *Modernisierung und Neue Soziale Bewegungen. Deutschland, Frankreich und USA im Vergleich* (Frankfurt am Main/New York: Campus).

Rucht, D. (2004) 'Movement Allies, Adversaries, and Third Parties', in D.A. Snow, S. A. Soule, and H. Kriesi (eds), *The Blackwell Companion to Social Movements* (Malden, Oxford, Carlton: Blackwell), 197–216.

Rucht, D. (2018) 'Exploring the Backstage: Preparation and Implementation of Mass Protests in Germany', *American Behavioral Scientist*, 61(13): 1678–702.

Rueda, D. (2005) 'Insider–Outsider Politics in Industrialized Democracies: The Challenge to Social Democratic Parties', *American Political Science Review*, 99(1): 61–74.

Rueschemeyer, D. (2003) 'Can One or a Few Cases Yield Theoretical Gains?', in J. Mahoney and D. Rueschemeyer (eds), *Comparative Historical Analysis in the Social Sciences* (Cambridge: Cambridge University Press), 305–36.

Rueschemeyer, D., Huber, E., and Stephens, J. D. (1992) *Capitalist Development and Democracy* (Cambridge: Polity Press).

Russett, B., Alker, H. R., Deutsch, K. W., and Lasswell, H. D. (1964) *World Handbook of Political and Social Indicators* (New Haven, CT: Yale University Press).

Rustow, D. (1955) *The Politics of Compromise: A Study of Parties and Cabinet Government in Sweden* (Princeton, NJ: Princeton University Press).

Rustow, D. A. (1970) 'Transitions to Democracy: Toward a Dynamic Model', *Comparative Politics*, 2(3): 337–63.

Saalfeld, T. (2008) 'Germany: Stability and Strategy in a Mixed-Member Proportional System', in M. Gallagher and P. Mitchell (eds), *The Politics of Electoral Systems* (Oxford: Oxford University Press), 209–30.

Saalfeld, T. (2013) 'Economic Performance, Political Institutions and Cabinet Durability in 28 European Parliamentary Democracies, 1945–2011', in W. C. Müller and H. M. Narud (eds), *Party Governance and Party Democracy* (New York: Springer).

Sabatier, P. A. (1988) 'An Advocacy-Coalition Framework of Policy Change and the Role of Policy-Oriented Learning Therein', *Policy Sciences*, 21: 129–68.

Sabatier, P. A. (1998) 'The Advocacy Coalition Framework: Revisions and Relevance for Europe', *Journal of European Public Policy*, 5(1): 98–130.

Sabatier, P. A. and Jenkins-Smith, H. (eds) (1993) *Policy Change and Learning* (Boulder, CO: Westview Press).

Sabetti, F. (2013) 'Civic Culture and Democracy', in C. Boix and S. Stokes (eds), *Handbook of Comparative Politics* (Oxford: Oxford University Press).

Sadurski, W. (2005) *Rights before Courts: A Study of Constitutional Courts in Postcommunist States of Central and Eastern Europe* (Dordrecht: Springer).

Sadurski, W. (2019) *Poland's Constitutional Breakdown* (Oxford: Oxford University Press).

Sager, F., Thomann, E., Zollinger, C., van der Heiden, N., and Mavrot, C. (2014) 'Street-Level Bureaucrats and New Modes of Governance: How Conflicting Roles Affect the Implementation of the Swiss Ordinance on Veterinary Medicinal Products', *Public Management Review*, 16(4), 481–502.

Saich, T. (2015) *Governance and Politics of China* (4th edn) (Basingstoke: Palgrave).

Sainsbury, D. (ed.) (1994) *Gendering Welfare States* (London: Sage).

Sainsbury, D. (ed.) (1996) *Gender and Welfare State Regimes* (Oxford: Oxford University Press).

Salgado, S., Strömbäck, J., Aalberg, T, and Esser, F. (2016) 'Interpretive Journalism', in C. de Vreese, F. Esser and D. Hopmann (eds), *Comparing Political Journalism* (London: Routledge).

Salisbury, R. H. (1969) 'An Exchange Theory of Interest Groups', *Midwest Journal of Political Science*, 13(1), 1–32.

Sanders, K. and Canel, M. J. (2013), 'Government Communication in 15 Countries. Themes and Challenges', in K. Sanders and M. J. Canel (eds), *Government Communication. Cases and Challenges* (London: Bloomsbury), 277–312.

Sandholtz, W. and Stone Sweet, A. (eds) (1998) *European Integration and Supranational Governance* (Oxford: Oxford University Press).

Sandholtz, W. and Zysman J. (1989) '1992: Recasting the European Bargain', *World Politics*, 42(1): 95–128.

Sandmo, A. (1991) 'Presidential Address: Economists and the Welfare State', *European Economic Review*, 35(2–3): 213–39.

Santen, R. v., Helfer, L., and Aelst, P. v. (2015) 'When Politics Becomes News: An Analysis of Parliamentary Questions and Press Coverage in Three West European Countries', *Acta Politica*, 50(1): 45–63.

Sartori, G. (1965) *Democratic Theory* (New York: Frederick Praeger).

Sartori, G. (1970) 'Concept Misformation in Comparative Politics', *American Political Science Review*, 65: 1033–53.

Sartori, G. (1976) *Parties and Party Systems: A Framework for Analysis* (Cambridge: Cambridge University Press).

Sartori, G. (ed) (1984) *Social Science Concepts* (Beverly Hills: Sage).

Sartori, G. (1986) 'The Influence of Electoral Systems: Faulty Laws or Faulty Method?', in B. Grofman and A. Lijphart (eds), *Electoral Laws and their Political Consequences* (New York: Agathon Press), 43–68.

Sartori, G. (1987) *The Theory of Democracy Revisited* (Washington, DC: CQ Press).

Sartori, G. (1991) 'Comparing and Miscomparing', *Journal of Theoretical Politics*, 3: 243–57.

Sartori, G. (1994) [1997] *Comparative Constitutional Engineering: An Inquiry into Structures, Incentives and Outcomes* (New York: New York University Press).

Saur, K. G. and Wresch, W. (1996) *Disconnected: Haves and Have-Nots in the Information Age* (New Brunswick, NJ: Rutgers University Press).

Savoie, D. (1986) *Regional Economic Development: Canada's Search for Solutions* (Toronto: University of Toronto Press).

Sbragia, A. M. (ed.) (1992) *Euro-Politics: Institutions and Policymaking in the 'New' European Community* (Washington, DC: Brookings Institution).

Scarpetta, S. (1996) 'Assessing the Role of Labour Market Policies and Institutional Settings on Unemployment: A Cross-Country Study', *OECD Economic Studies*, 26: 43–98.

Scarrow, S. E. (2003) 'Making Elections More Direct? Reducing the Role of Parties in Elections', in B. E. Cain, R. J. Dalton, and S. E. Scarrow (eds), *Democracy Transformed? Expanding Political Opportunities in Advanced Industrial Democracies* (Oxford: Oxford University Press), 44–58.

Schain, M. and Menon, A. (2007) *Comparative Federalism* (Oxford: Oxford University Press).

Schakel, A. H. (2013) 'Congruence between Regional and National Elections', *Comparative Political Studies*, 46(5): 631–62.

Schakel, A. H. (ed.) (2017) *Regional and National Elections in Eastern Europe. Territoriality of the Vote in Ten Countries* (Houndmills, Basingstoke: Palgrave Macmillan).

Schakel, A. H. (2019) 'Regional Spill-Over into Third-Order European Elections', unpublished paper.

Schakel, A. H. and Romanova, V. (2018) 'Towards a Scholarship on Regional Elections', *Regional and Federal Studies*, 28(3): 233–52.

Scharpf, F. W. (1984) 'Economic and Institutional Constraints of Full Employment Strategies: Sweden, Austria and Germany, 1973–1982', in J. H. Goldthorpe (ed.), *Order and Conflict in Contemporary Capitalism* (Oxford: Oxford University Press), 275–90.

Scharpf, F. W. (1987) *Sozialdemokratische Krisenpolitik in Europa* (Frankfurt am Main: Campus).

Scharpf, F. W. (1988) 'The Joint-Decision Trap: Lessons from German Federalism and European Integration', *Public Administration*, 66(3): 277–304.

Scharpf, F. W. (1997a) 'Economic Integration, Democracy and the Welfare State', *Journal of European Public Policy*, 4(1): 18–36.

Scharpf, F. W. (1997b) 'Employment and the Welfare State: A Continental Dilemma', MPIfG Working Paper 97/7 (Bonn: Max-Planck-Institut für Gesellschaftsforschung).

Scharpf, F. W. (1997c) *Games Real Actors Play: Actor-Centered Institutionalism in Policy Research* (Boulder, CO: Westview).

Scharpf, F. W. (1997d) 'Introduction: The Problem-Solving Capacity of Multi-Level Governance', *Journal of European Public Policy*, 4: 520–38.

Scharpf, F. W. (2000) 'Economic Changes, Vulnerabilities, and Institutional Capabilities', in F. W. Scharpf and V. A. Schmidt (eds), *Welfare and Work in the Open Economy. I: From Vulnerability to Competitiveness* (Oxford: Oxford University Press), 21–124.

Scharpf, F. W. and Schmidt, V. A. (eds) (2000) *Welfare and Work in the Open Economy* (Oxford: Oxford University Press).

Schattschneider, E. E. (1942) *Party Government* (New York: Holt, Rinehart & Winston).

Schattschneider, E. E. (1975) [1960] *The Semisovereign People: A Realist's View of Democracy in America* (London: Harcourt Brace Jovanovich).

Schattschneider, E. E. (1988) [1960] *The Semi-Sovereign People: A Realist's View of Democracy in America* (London/New York: Wadsworth/Holt, Rinehart & Winston).

Schedler, A (2006) (ed.) *Electoral Authoritarianism: The Dynamics of Unfree Competition* (Boulder, CO: Lynne Reiner).

Schedler, A. (2013) *The Politics of Uncertainty: Sustaining and Subverting Electoral Authoritarianism* (Oxford: Oxford University Press).

Scheinin, M. (ed.) (2001) *Welfare State and Constitutionalism: Nordic Perspectives* (Copenhagen: Nordic Council of Ministers).

Schenkkan, N. and Repucci, S. (2019) 'Democracy in Retreat', *Journal of Democracy*, 30(2): 110–14.

Scheppele, K. L. (2005) 'Democracy by Judiciary (or Why Courts can Sometimes Be More Democratic than Parliaments)', in W. Sadurski, M. Krygier, and A. Csarnota (eds), *Rethinking the Rule of Law in Post Communist Europe: Past Legacies, Institutional Innovations, and Constitutional Discourses* (Budapest: CEU Press).

Scheufele, D. and Tewksbury, D. (2006) 'Framing, Agenda Setting, and Priming: The Evolution of Three Media Effects Models', *Journal of Communication*, 57(1): 9–20.

Schimmelfennig, F. and Sedelmeier, U. (2005) *Europeanization of Central and Eastern Europe* (Ithaca, NY: Cornell University Press).

Schleiter, P. and Morgan-Jones, E. (2009) 'Citizens, Presidents and Assemblies: The Study of Semi-Presidentialism beyond Duverger and Linz', *British Journal of Political Science*, 39(4): 871–92.

Schlesinger, J. (1991) *Political Parties and the Winning of Office* (Ann Arbor, MI: University of Michigan Press).

Schlozman, K. L. (2002) 'Citizen Participation in America: What Do We Know? Why Do We Care?', in I. Katznelson and H. V. Milner (eds), *Political Science: The State of the Discipline* (New York: W. W. Norton and American Political Science Association).

Schmidt, M. G. (1982) *Wohlfahrtsstaatliche Politik unter bürgerlichen und sozialdemokratischen Regierungen* (Frankfurt am Main: Campus).

Schmidt, M. G. (1983) 'The Welfare State and the Economy in Periods of Economic Crisis', *European Journal of Political Research*, 11(1): 1–26.

Schmidt, M. G. (1998) *Sozialpolitik in Deutschland Historische Entwicklung und internationaler Vergleich* (Opladen: Leske & Budrich).

Schmidt, M. G. (2002) 'The Impact of Parties, Constitutional Structures and Veto Players on Public Policy', in H. Keman (ed.), *Comparative Democratic Politics. A Guide to Contemporary Theory and Research* (London: Sage).

Schmidt V. A. (2002) 'Does Discourse Matter in the Politics of Welfare State Adjustment?', *Comparative Political Studies*, 35(2): 168–93.

Schmitt, C., Lierse, H., Obinger, H., and Seelkopf, L. (2015) 'The Global Emergence of Social Protection Explaining Social Security Legislation 1820–2013', *Politics & Society*, 43(4): 503–24.

Schmitter, P. C. (1974) 'Still the Century of Corporatism?', *Review of Politics*, 36: 85–131; reprinted in P. C. Schmitter and G. Lehmbruch (eds) (1979) *Trends Towards Corporatist Mediation* (London: Sage), 7–52.

Schmitter, P. C. (1981) 'Interest Intermediation and Regime Governability in Contemporary Western Europe and North America' in S. Bergers (ed.), *Organizing Interests in Western Europe. Pluralism, Corporatism and the Transformation of Politics* (Cambridge: Cambridge University Press), 285–327.

Schmitter, P. C. (1989) 'Corporatism is Dead! Long Live Corporatism', *Government and Opposition*, 24: 131–57.

Schmitter, P. C. (1993) 'Comparative Politics', in J. Krieger (ed.), *The Oxford Companion to Politics of the World* (Oxford: Oxford University Press), 171–7.

Schmitter, P. C. (2008) 'The Design of Social and Political Research', in D. della Porta and M. Keating (eds), *Approaches and Methodologies in the Social Sciences* (Cambridge: Cambridge University Press, 263–95.

Schmitter, P. C. and Grote, J. R. (1997) 'The Corporatist Sisyphus: Past, Present and Future', European University Institute Working Paper SPS 97/4 (http://cadmus.iue.it/dspace/bitstream/1814/284/1/97_4.pdf).

Schmitter, P. C. and Karl, T. (1991) 'What Democracy Is and Is Not', *Journal of Democracy*, 2(3): 75–88.

Schmitter, P. C. and Lehmbruch, G. (eds) (1979) *Trends toward Corporatist Intermediation* (London: Sage).

Schmitter, P. C. and Trechsel, A. H. (eds) (2004) *The Future of Democracy in Europe: Trends, Analyses and Reforms* (Strasbourg: Council of Europe).

Schneider, C. Q. (2019) 'Macro-Qualitative Approaches', in W. Merkel, R. Kollmorgen, and H. J. Wagener (eds) *The Handbook of Political, Social, and Economic Transformation* (Oxford: Oxford University Press), 173–80.

Schneider, C. Q. and Grofman, B. (2006) 'It Might Look Like a Regression ... But It's Not', COMPASSS Working Paper (COMPASS).

Schneider, C. Q. and Rohlfing, I. (2013) 'Combining QCA and Process Tracing in Set-Theoretic Multi-Method Research', *Sociological Methods & Research*, 42(4): 559–97.

Schneider, C. Q. and Wagemann, C. (2012) *Set-Theoretic Methods for the Social Sciences* (Cambridge: Cambridge University Press).

Scholten, P. and Timmermans, A. (2010) 'Setting the Immigrant Policy Agenda: Expertise and Politics in the Netherlands, France and the United Kingdom', *Journal of Comparative Policy Analysis: Research and Practice* 12(5): 527–44.

Schuck, A. R. T., Vliegenthart, R., Boomgaarden, H., Elenbaas, M., Azrout, R., Spanje, J. v., and de Vreese, C. (2013) 'Explaining Campaign News Coverage: How Medium, Time and Context Explain Variation in the Media Framing of the 2009 European Parliamentary Elections', *Journal of Political Marketing*, 12(1): 8–28.

Schuck, A. R. T., Vliegenthart, R., de Vreese, C. (2016) 'Who's Afraid of Conflict? The Mobilizing Effect of Conflict Framing in Campaign News', *British Journal of Political Science*, 46(1): 177–94.

Schulz, W. (2008) 'Political Communication', in W. Donsbach (ed.), *The International Encyclopedia of Communication* (Cambridge, MA: Blackwell), 3671–82.

Schumpeter, J. A. (1943) *Capitalism, Socialism and Democracy* (New York: Harper & Row) (2nd edn 1947).

Schwab Cammarano, S. and Diez Medrano, J. (2014), 'Distant North–Conflictive South: Patterns of Interaction and Conflict', in B. Pfetsch (ed.), *Political Communication Cultures in Europe: Attitudes of Political Actors and Journalists in Nine Countries* (Houndmills, Basingstoke: Palgrave Macmillan), 271–86.

Schwartz, H. (2001) 'Round Up the Usual Suspects! Globalization, Domestic Politics, and Welfare State Change', in P. Pierson (ed.), *The New Politics of the Welfare State* (Oxford: Oxford University Press), 17–44.

Scobell, A. (2006) *Kim Jong Il and North Korea: The Leader and the System* (Darby, PA: DIANE Publishing).

Scruggs, L. (2002) 'The Ghent System and Union Membership in Europe, 1970–1996', *Political Research Quarterly*, 55(2): 275–97.

Scruggs, L. and Allan, J. (2006a) 'The Material Consequences of Welfare States: Benefit Generosity and Absolute Poverty in Sixteen OECD Countries', *Comparative Political Studies*, 39(7): 880–904.

Scruggs, L. and Allan, J. (2006b) 'Welfare State Decommodification in Eighteen OECD Countries: A Replication and Revision', *Journal of European Social Policy*, 16(1): 55–72.

Seawright, Jason and Gerring, John (2008) 'Case Selection Techniques in Case Study Research: A Menu of Qualitative and Quantitative Options', *Political Research Quarterly*, 61(2): 294–308.

Seeliger, R. (1996) 'Conceptualizing and Researching Policy Convergence', *Policy Studies Journal*, 24: 153–72.

Segura-Ubiergo, A. (2007) *The Political Economy of the Welfare State in Latin America: Globalization, Democracy, and Development* (New York: Cambridge University Press).

Seha, E. and Müller-Rommel, F. (2016) 'Case Study Analysis', in H. Keman and J. Woldendorp (eds), *Handbook of Research Methods and Applications in Political Science* (Cheltenham: Edward Elgar).

Seldon, S. C. (1997) *The Promise of Representative Bureaucracy* (Armonk, NY: Sharpe).

Semetko, H. and Tworzecki, H. (2018) 'Campaign Strategies, Media and Voters: The Fourth Era of Political Communication', in J. Fisher, E. Fieldhouse, M. Franklin, R. Gibson, M. Cantijoch, and C. Wlezien (eds), *The Routledge Handbook of Elections, Voting Behavior and Public Opinion* (New York: Routledge), 293–303.

Sen, A. (1999) 'Democracy as a Universal Value', *Journal of Democracy*, 10(3): 3–17.

Sen, A. (2010) *The Idea of Justice* (Cambridge MA: Harvard University Press).

Sen, A. (2011) 'Quality of Life: India vs. China', *New York Review of Books*, LVIII: 44–7.

Serdült, U. (2014) 'Referendums in Switzerland', in M. -Qvortrup (ed.), *Referendums Around the World: The Continued Growth of Direct Democracy* (Houndmills, Basingstoke: Palgrave Macmillan), 65–121.

Setälä, M. (1999) *Referendums and Democratic Government: Normative Theory and the Analysis of Institutions* (Houndmills, Basingstoke: Palgrave Macmillan).

Sevenans, J. and Vliegenthart, R. (2016) 'Political Agenda Setting in Belgium and the Netherlands: The Moderating Role of Conflict

Framing', *Journalism and Mass Communication Quarterly*, 93(1): 187–203.

Sewell, W. H. (1996) 'Historical Events as Transformations of Structures: Inventing Revolution at the Bastille', *Theory and Society*, 25: 841–81.

Shalev, M. (1983) 'The Social Democratic Model and Beyond: Two Generations of Comparative Research on the Welfare State', *Comparative Social Research*, 6: 315–51.

Shapiro, I. (2002) 'Problems, Methods, and Theories in the Study of Politics, or What's Wrong with Political Science and What to Do about It', *Political Theory*, 30(4): 588–611.

Shapiro, M. (1964) *Law and Politics in the Supreme Court: Studies in Political Jurisprudence* (Glencoe, IL: Free Press).

Shapiro, M. and Stone Sweet, A. (1994) 'The New Constitutional Politics of Europe', *Comparative Political Studies*, 26: 397–420.

Sharpe, L. (1993) *The Rise of Meso Government in Europe* (London: Sage).

Sharpe, L. and Newton, K. (1984) *Does Politics Matter? The Determinants of Public Policy* (Oxford: Clarendon Press).

Shaw, J. (1999) 'Post-National Constitutionalism in the EU', *Journal of European Public Policy*, 6(4): 579–97.

Shepsle, K. A. (2006) 'Rational Choice Institutionalism', in R. A. W. Rhodes, S.A. Binder, and B. A. Rockman (eds), *Oxford Handbook of Political Institutions* (Oxford: Oxford University Press), 23–38.

Shepsle, K. A. and Bonchek, M. S. (1997) *Analyzing Politics* (New York: W. W. Norton).

Shepsle, K. A. and Weingast, B. (1987) 'The Institutional Foundations of Committee Power', *American Political Science Review*, 81(1): 85–104.

Shils, E. (1975) *Center and Periphery: Essays in Macrosociology* (Chicago, IL: University of Chicago Press).

Shoemaker, P. J. and Cohen, A. A. (2006) *News Around the World* (Abingdon: Routledge).

Shore, C. (2013) *Building Europe: The Cultural Politics of European Integration* (London: Routledge).

Shugart, M. S. (2008) 'Comparative Electoral Systems Research: The Maturation of a Field and New Challenges Ahead', in M. Gallagher and P. Mitchell (eds), *The Politics of Electoral Systems* (Oxford: Oxford University Press), 25–56.

Shugart, M. S. and Carey, J. M. (1992) *Presidents and Assemblies* (Cambridge: Cambridge University Press).

Shugart, M. S. and Taagepera, R. (2017) *Votes from Seats: Logical Models of Electoral Systems* (Cambridge: Cambridge University Press).

Shugart, M. S. and Wattenberg, M. P. (eds) (2003) *Mixed-Member Electoral Systems: The Best of Both Worlds?* (Oxford: Oxford University Press).

Shugart, M. S., Valdini, M. E., and Suominen, K. (2005) 'Looking for Locals: Voter Information Demands and Personal Vote-Earning Attributes of Legislators under Proportional Representation', *American Journal of Political Science*, 49(2): 437–49.

Siaroff, A. (1999) 'Corporatism in Twenty-Four Industrial Democracies: Meaning and Measurement', *European Journal of Political Research*, 36: 175–205.

Siavelis, P. M. (2008) 'Chile: The Unexpected (and Expected) Consequences of Electoral Engineering', in M. Gallagher and P. Mitchell (eds), *The Politics of Electoral Systems* (Oxford: Oxford University Press), 433–52.

SIDA (2006) *Country Report 2006 Uganda* (Stockholm: Swedish International Development Cooperation Agency).

Sieder, R., Schjolden, L., and Angell, A. (2005) *The Judicialization of Politics in Latin America* (New York: Palgrave Macmillan).

Siegel, S. and Castellan, N. J., Jr (1988) *Nonparametric Statistics for the Behavioral Sciences* (New York: McGraw-Hill).

Silver, B. J. (2003) *Forces of Labor: Workers Movements and Globalization Since 1870* (Cambridge: Cambridge University Press).

Simeon, R. (1977) 'Regionalism and Canadian Political Institutions', in J. Meekison (ed.), *Canadian Federalism: Myth or Reality?* (Toronto: Methuen), 293.

Simmel, G. (1984) [1908] *Das Individuum und die Freiheit: Essays* [*The Individual and Freedom*] (Berlin, Germany: Duncker & Humblodt).

Simmons, B. A. and Elkins, Z. (2004) 'The Globalization of Liberalization: Policy Diffusion in the International Political Economy', *American Political Science Review*, 98: 171–89.

Simon, H. A. (1955) 'A Behavioral Model of Rational Choice', *Quarterly Journal of Economics*, 69(1): 99–118.

Simon, H. A. (ed.) (1957) *Models of Man: Social and Rational* (New York: Wiley).

Simons, G. F. and Fennig, C. D. (eds) (2018) *Ethnologue: Languages of the World* (21st edn) (Dallas, TX: SIL International) (http://www.ethnologue.com).

Simonton, D. K. (1993) 'Putting the Best Leaders in the White House: Personality, Policy and Performance', *Political Psychology*, 14: 537–48.

Singh, N. and Srinivasan, T. N. (2003) 'Can India Survive Globalization?' (http://www.project-syndicate.org/commentary/nsingh1).

Singh, P. (2015) 'Subnationalism and Social Development: A Comparative Analysis of Indian States', *World Politics*, 67(3): 506–62.

Sinnott, R. (2010) 'The Electoral System', in J. Coakley and M. Gallagher (eds), *Politics in the Republic of Ireland* (5th edn) (Abingdon: Routledge Press), 111–36.

Sinyai, C. (2006) *Schools of Democracy. A Political History of the American Labor Movement* (Ithaca, NY: Cornell University Press).

Skocpol, T. (1979) *States and Social Revolution: A Comparative Analysis of France, Russia and China* (Cambridge: Cambridge University Press).

Skocpol, T. (ed.) (1984) *Visions and Methods in Historical Sociology* (Cambridge: Cambridge University Press).

Skocpol, T. (1985) 'Bringing the State Back In: Strategies of Analysis in Current Research', in P. Evans, D. Rueschenmeyer, and T. Skocpol (eds), *Bringing the State Back In* (Cambridge: Cambridge University Press), 3–37.

Skocpol, T. (1992) *Protecting Soldiers and Mothers: The Political Origins of Social Policy in the United States* (Cambridge, MA: Belknap Press).

Skocpol, T. (2003) *Diminished Democracy: From Membership to Management in American Civic Life* (Norman, OK: University of Oklahoma Press).

Skocpol, T. and Amenta, E. (1986) 'States and Social Policies', *Annual Review of Sociology*, 12: 131–57.

Skocpol, T. and Orloff, A. S. (1986) 'Explaining the Origins of Welfare States: A Comparison of Britain and the United States, 1880s–1920s', in S. Lindenberg, J. S. Coleman, and S. Nowak (eds), *Approaches to Social Theory: Proceedings of the W. I. Thomas and Florian Znaniecki Memorial Conference on Social Theory* (New York: Russell Sage Foundation), 229–54.

Skocpol, T. and Somers, M. (1980) 'The Uses of Comparative History in Macrosocial Inquiry', *Comparative Studies in Society and History*, 22(2): 174–97.

Skocpol, T. and Williamson, V. (2012) *The Tea Party and the Remaking of Republican Conservatism* (Oxford: Oxford University Press).

Skoric, M. M., Zhu, Q., and Pang, N. (2016) 'Social Media, Political Expression, and Participation in Confucian Asia', *Chinese Journal of Communication*, 9(4): 331–47.

Slaughter, A.-M. (1997) 'The Real New World Order', *Foreign Affairs*, 76: 183–97.

Smeeding, T. M. (2005) 'Public Policy, Economic Inequality, and Poverty: The United States in Comparative Perspective', *Social Science Quarterly*, 86(Suppl.): 955–83.

Smeeding, T. M. and Gottschalk, P. (1999) 'Cross-National Income Inequality: How Great Is It and What Can We Learn From It?', *International Journal of Health Services*, 29(4): 733–41.

Smeeding, T. M., O'Higgins, M., and Rainwater, L. (1990) *Poverty, Inequality and Income Distribution in Comparative Perspective: The Luxembourg Income Study (LIS)* (New York: Harvester Wheatsheaf).

Smelser, N. J. (1962) *Theory of Collective Behavior* (New York: Free Press).

Smelser, N. J. (1966) 'Mechanisms of Change and Adjustment to Change', in J. Finkle and R. Gable (eds), *Political Development and Social Change* (New York: Wiley).

Smismans, S. (ed.) (2006) *Civil Society and Legitimate European Governance* (Cheltenham: Edward Elgar).

Smith, D. (1985) 'Party Government, Representation and National Integration in Canada', in P. Aucoin (ed.), *Party Government and Regional Representation in Canada* (Toronto: University of Toronto Press), 1–68.

Smith, J., Byrd, S., Reese, E. and Smythe, E. (eds) (2011) *Handbook on World Social Forum Activism* (Boulder, CO/London: Paradigm).

Smith, M. J. (1993) *Pressure, Power and Policy: State Autonomy and Policy Networks in Britain and the United States* (Pittsburgh, PA: University of Pittsburgh Press).

Smith, M. J. (1999) *The Core Executive in Britain* (Houndmills, Basingstoke: Palgrave Macmillan).

Smithies, A. (1941) 'Optimum Location in Spatial Competition', *Journal of Political Economy*, 49: 423–39.

Sniderman, P. (1975) *Personality and Democratic Politics* (Berkeley, CA: University of California Press).

Snow, D. A. and Benford, R. D. (1988) 'Ideology, Frame Resonance, and Participant Mobilization', in B. Klandermans, H. Kriesi, and S. Tarrow (eds), *From Structure to Action: Social Movement Participation Across Cultures* (Greenwich, CT: JAI Press), 197–217.

Snow, D. A., Rochford, E., Bourke, W., Steven, K. and Benford, R. D. (1986) 'Frame Alignment Processes, Micromobilization, and Movement Participation', *American Sociological Review*, 51(4): 464–81.

Snow, D. A., Soule, S. A., and Kriesi, H. (2004) *The Blackwell Companion to Social Movements*, Blackwell Companions to Sociology (Malden, MA: Blackwell).

Snyder, Richard (2001) 'Scaling Down: The Subnational Comparative Method', *Studies in Comparative International Development*, 36(1): 93–110.

Soja, E. (1989) *Postmodern Geographies: The Reassertion of Space in Critical Social Theory* (New York: Verso).

Somit, A. and Tanenhaus, A. (1964) *American Political Science: A Profile of a Discipline* (New York: Atherton).

Sørensen, G. (2001) *Changes in Statehood: The Transformation of International Relations* (Houndmills, Basingstoke: Palgrave Macmillan).

Sørensen, G. (2004) *The Transformation of the State: Beyond the Myth of Retreat* (Houndmills, Basingstoke: Palgrave Macmillan).

Sørenson, E. and Torfing, J. (2007) *Theories of Democratic Network Governance* (Houndmills, Basingstoke: Palgrave Macmillan).

Soroka, S., Andrew, B., Aalberg, T., Iyengar, S., Curran, J., Coen, S., Hayashi, K., Jones, P., Mazzoleni, G., Woong Rhee, J., Rowe, D., and Tiffen, R. (2013), 'Auntie Knows Best? Public Broadcasters and Current Affairs Knowledge', *British Journal of Political Science*, 43(4): 719–39.

Soss, J., Fording, R. C., and Schram, S. F. (2011) *Disciplining the Poor. Neoliberal Paternalism and the Persistent Power of Race* (Chicago, IL: University of Chicago Press).

Soysal, Y. N. (1994) *Limits of Citizenship: Migrants and Postnational Membership in Europe* (Chicago, IL: University of Chicago Press).

Spanish Center for Sociological Research (CSI Studies) (2019) Barometro Autonomico, 'Baròmetre d'Opinió Politica', 1a onad, Centre d'Estudis d'Opinió, Generalitat de Catalanya, No. 912, April 2019 (http://upceo.ceo.gencat.cat/wsceop/7008/Taules%20 estad%C3%ADstiques%20-919.pdf).

Spies, D. C. (2018) *Immigration and Welfare State Retrenchment* (Oxford: Oxford University Press).

Spruyt, H. (1994) *The Sovereign State and its Competitor: An Analysis of Systems Change* (Princeton, NJ: Princeton University Press).

Stan, S. (2005) *L'Agriculture Roumaine en Mutation. La Construction Sociale du Marché* (Paris: Éditions CNRS).

Stan, S., Helle, I., and Erne, R. (2015) 'European Collective Action in Times Of Crisis', *Transfer: European Review of Labour and Research*, 21(2): 131–9.

Starke, P. (2006) 'The Politics of Welfare State Retrenchment: A Literature Review', *Social Policy and Administration*, 40(1): 104–20.

Starke, P., Obinger, H., and Castles, F. G. (2008) 'Convergence Towards Where: In What Ways, If Any, Are Welfare States Becoming More Similar?', *Journal of European Public Policy*, 15(7): 975–1000.

Stasavage, D. (2011) *States of Credit: Size, Power, and the Development of European Polities* (Princeton, NJ: Princeton University Press).

Steenbergen, M. and Marks, G. (2007) 'Evaluating Expert Judgments', *European Journal of Political Research*, 46: 347–66.

Steiner, J. (1974) *Amicable Agreement versus Majority Rule: Conflict Resolution in Switzerland* (Chapel Hill, NC: University of North Carolina Press).

Steinmo, S., Thelen, K., and Longstreth, F. (eds) (1992) *Structuring Politics: Historical Institutionalism in Comparative Analysis* (Cambridge: Cambridge University Press).

Stepan, A. (1971) *The Military in Politics: Changing Patterns in Brazil* (Princeton, NJ: Princeton University Press).

Stepan, A. C. (2015) *The Military in Politics: Changing Patterns in Brazil* (Princeton, NJ: Princeton University Press).

Stepan, A. C. and Skach, C. (1993) 'Constitutional Frameworks and Democratic Consolidation: Parliamentarism versus Presidentialism', *World Politics*, 46(1): 1–22.

Stepan, A. C., Linz, J. J., and Yadav, Y. (2011) *Crafting State-Nations: India and Other Multinational Democracies* (Baltimore, MD: Johns Hopkins University Press).

Stephens, J. D. (1979) *The Transition from Capitalism to Socialism* (Champaign, IL: University of Illinois Press).

Stephens, J. D. (2005) 'Economic Internationalization and Domestic Compensation: Northwestern Europe in Comparative Perspective', in M. Glatzer and D. Rueschemeyer (eds), *Globalization and the Future of the Welfare State* (Pittsburgh, PA: University of Pittsburgh Press), 49–74.

Stevenson, G. (1980) 'Canadian Regionalism in Continental Perspective', *Journal of Canadian Studies*, 15(2): 16–27.

Stiglitz, J. (2010) *Freefall: Free Markets and the Sinking of the Global Economy* (London: Penguin Group).

Stohr, W. (ed.) (1990) *Global Challenge and Local Response: Initiatives for Economic Regeneration in Contemporary Europe* (London: Continuum Publishing).

Stoker, G., Peters, B. G., and Pierre, J. (eds) (2015) *The Relevance of Political Science* (New York: Palgrave Macmillan).

Stolleis, M. (2003) 'Judicial Review, Administrative Review, and Constitutional Review in the Weimar Republic', *Ratio Juris*, 16(2): 266–80.

Stone, A. (1990) *The Birth of Judicial Politics in France: The Constitutional Council in Comparative Perspective* (Oxford: Oxford University Press).

Stone, D. (2005) *Capturing the Political Imagination: Think Tanks and the Policy Process* (London: Frank Cass).

Stone Sweet, A. (1999) 'Judicialization and the Construction of Governance', *Comparative Political Studies*, 32(2), 147–84.

Stone Sweet, A. (2000) *Governing with Judges: Constitutional Politics in Europe* (Oxford: Oxford University Press).

Stone Sweet, A. (2002) 'Constitutional Courts and Parliamentary Democracy', *West European Politics*, 25: 77–100.

Stone Sweet, A. (2012), 'Constitutional Courts', in M. Rosenfeld and A. Sajo (eds), *Oxford Handbook of Comparative Constitutional Law* (Oxford: Oxford University Press).

Stone Sweet, A. and Brunell, T. (2013) 'Trustee Courts and the Judicialization of International Regimes: The Politics of Majoritarian Activism in the ECHR, the EU, and the WTO', *Journal of Law and Courts*, 1: 61–88.

Stone Sweet, A. and Mathews, J. (2008) 'Proportionality Balancing and Global Constitutionalism', *Columbia Journal of Transnational Law*, 47: 73–165.

Stone Sweet, A. and Mathews, J. (2017) 'Proportionality and Rights Protection in Asia: Hong Kong, Malaysia, South Korea, Taiwan—Whither Singapore?', *Journal of the Singapore Academy of Law*, 29: 774–99.

Stone Sweet, A. and Mathews, J. (2019) *Proportionality Balancing and Constitutional Governance* (Oxford: Oxford University Press).

Stone Sweet, A. and Thatcher, M. (2002) 'The Politics of Delegation: Non-Majoritarian Institutions in Europe', *West European Politics*, 25(1): 1–22.

Storper, M. (1995) 'The Resurgence of Regional Economies, Ten Years Later: The Region as a Nexus of Untraded Interdependencies', *European Urban and Regional Studies*, 2(3): 191–221.

Stouffer, S. A. (1955) *Communism, Conformity and Civil Liberties* (New York: Doubleday).

Strang, D. and Meyer, J. (1993) 'Institutional Conditions for Diffusion', *Theory and Society*, 22: 487–511.

Strang, D. and Soule, S. A. (1998) 'Diffusion in Organizations and Social Movements: From Hybrid Corn to Poison Pills', *Annual Review of Sociology*, 24: 265–90.

Strange, S. (1996) *The Retreat of the State: The Diffusion of Power in the World Economy* (Cambridge: Cambridge University Press).

Streeck, W. (1996) 'Neo-Voluntarism: A European Social Policy Regime?', in G. Marks, F. W. Scharpf, P. C., and W. Streeck (eds), *Governance in the European Union* (London: Sage).

Streeck, W. (2006) 'The Study of Organised Interests: Before "The Century" and After', in C. Crouch and W. Streeck (eds), *The Diversity of Democracy: Corporatism, Social Order and Political Conflict* (Cheltenham: Edward Elgar), 3–45.

Streeck, W. and Schmitter, P. C. (eds) (1985) *Private Interest Government: Beyond Market and State* (London: Sage).

Streeck, W. and Schmitter, P. C. (1991) 'From National Corporatism to Transnational Pluralism: Organized Interests in the Single European Market', *Politics and Society*, 19(2): 133–64.

Streeck, W. and Thelen, K. (2005) 'Introduction: Institutional Change in Advanced Political Economies', in W. Streeck and K. Thelen (eds), *Beyond Continuity: Institutional Change in Advanced Political Economies* (Oxford: Oxford University Press), 1–39.

Strøm, K. (1990) *Minority Government and Majority Rule* (Cambridge: Cambridge University Press).

Strøm, K. and Swindle, S. M. (2002) 'Strategic Parliamentary Dissolution', *American Political Science Review*, 96: 575–91.

Strøm, K., Müller, W. C., and Bergman, T. (eds) (2003) *Delegation and Accountability in Parliamentary Democracies* (Oxford: Oxford University Press).

Strøm, K., Müller, W. C., and Bergman, T. (eds) (2008) *Cabinets and Coalition Bargaining: The Democratic Life Cycle in Western Europe* (Oxford: Oxford University Press).

Strøm, K., Müller, W. C., and Smith, D. M. (2010) 'Parliamentary Control of Coalition Governments', *Annual Review of Political Science*, 13: 517–35.

Strömbäck, J. and Lee Kaid, L. (2008) *The Handbook of Election News Coverage* (Abingdon: Routledge).

Suleiman, E. N. (2003) *Dismantling Democratic States* (Princeton, NJ: Princeton University Press).

Summers, L. (2014) 'U. S. Economic Prospects: Secular Stagnation, Hysteresis, and the Zero Lower Bound', *Business Economics*, 49(1), 65–73. Delivered as 'IMF Economic Forum: Policy Responses to Crises', speech at the IMF Fourteenth Annual Research Conference, Washington, DC, 9 November 2013.

Sundberg, J. (1987) 'Exploring the Basis of Declining Party Membership in Denmark: A Scandinavian Comparison', *Scandinavian Political Studies*, 10(1), 17–38.

Surel, Y. (2000) 'The Role of Cognitive and Normative Frames in Policy-Making', *Journal of European Public Policy*, 7(4): 495–512.

Svolik, M. W. (2012) *The Politics of Authoritarian Rule* (Cambridge: Cambridge University Press).

Swank, D. (2001) 'Political Institutions and Welfare State Restructuring: The Impact of Institutions on Social Policy Change in Developed Democracies', in P. Pierson (ed.), *The New Politics of the Welfare State* (Oxford: Oxford University Press), 197–237.

Swank, D. (2002) *Global Capital, Political Institutions, and Policy Change in Developed Welfare States* (Cambridge: Cambridge University Press).

Swank, D. and Hicks, A. (1985) 'The Determinants and Redistributive Impacts of State Welfare Spending in the Advanced Capitalist Democracies, 1960–1980', in N. J. Vig and S. E. Schier (eds), *Political Economy in Western Democracies* (New York: Holmes & Meier), 115–39.

Swenden, W. and Maddens, B. (eds) (2009) *Territorial Party Politics in Western Europe* (New York, NY: Palgrave Macmillan).

Swenson, P. (2002) *Capitalists against Markets* (Cambridge: Cambridge University Press).

Swenson, P. (2004) 'Varieties of Capitalist Interest: Power, Institutions, and the Regulatory Welfare State in the United States and Sweden', *Studies in American Political Development*, 18: 1–29.

't Hart, P. (1990) *Groupthink in Government* (Amsterdam: Swets & Teitlinger).

Taagapera, R. and Shugart, M. (1989) *Seats and Votes: The Effects and Determinants of Electoral Systems* (New Haven, CT: Yale University Press).

Tajfel, H. and Turner, J. C. (1979) 'An Integrative Theory of Intergroup Conflict', in S. Worchel and W. G. Austin (eds), *The Social Psychology of Intergroup Relations* (Chicago, IL: Nelson-Hall), 33–47.

Tallberg, J. (2006) *Leadership and Negotiation in the European Union* (Cambridge: Cambridge University Press).

Tansy, O. (2015) 'Questioning "Autocracy Promotion"', *APSA Comparative Democratization*, 13(1): 1–7.

Tansey, O. (2016) 'The Problem with Autocracy Promotion', *Democratization*, 23(1): 141–63.

Tarrow, S. (1977) *Between Center and Periphery: Grassroots Politicians in Italy and France* (New Haven, CT: Yale University Press).

Tarrow, S. (1983) 'Struggling to Reform: Social Movement and Policy Change During Cycles of Protest', Western Societies Program, Occasional Paper No. 15 (Ithaca, NY: Cornell University).

Tarrow, S. (1988) 'Old Movements in New Cycles of Protest: The Career of an Italian Religious Movement', *International Social Movement Research*, 1: 281–304.

Tarrow, S. (1989) *Democracy and Disorder: Protest and Politics in Italy 1965–1975* (Oxford: Claredon Press).

Tarrow, S. (1991) 'Aiming at a Moving Target: Social Science and the Recent Rebellions in Eastern Europe', *PS: Political Science and Politics*, 24 (1): 12–20.

Tarrow, S. (1994) *Power in Movement: Social Movements, Collective Action and Politics* (Cambridge: Cambridge University Press).

Tarrow, S. (1996) 'States and Opportunities: The Political Structuring of Social Movements', in D. McAdam, J. D. McCarthy, and M. N. Zald (eds), *Comparative Perspectives on Social Movements: Political Opportunities, Mobilizing Structures, and Cultural Framings* (Cambridge: Cambridge University Press), 41–61.

Tarrow, S. (2005) *The New Transnational Activism* (New York: Cambridge University Press).

Tatham, M. (2014). 'Limited Institutional Change in an International Organization: The EU's Shift Away from "Federal Blindness"', *European Political Science Review*, 6(91): 210–45.

Taylor, C. (1993) 'The Deep Challenge of Dualism', in A.-G. Gagnon (ed.), *Quebec: State and Society* (2nd edn) (Toronto: University of Toronto Press), 82–95.

Taylor, C. L. and Hudson, M. C. (1972) *World Handbook of Political and Social Indicators* (2nd edn) (New Haven, CT: Yale University Press).

Taylor, C. L. and Jodice, D. A. (1983) *World Handbook of Political and Social Indicators* (3rd edn) (New Haven, CT: Yale University Press).

Taylor, P. (1982) 'Intergovernmentalism in the European Communities in the 1970s: Patterns and Perspectives', *International Organization*, 36(4): 741–66.

Taylor, V. (1989) 'Social Movement Continuity: The Women's Movement in Abeyance', *American Sociological Review*, 54(5): 761–75.

Teorell, J. (2010) *Determinants of Democratization: Explaining Regime Change in the World, 1972–2002* (Cambridge: Cambridge University Press).

Tepe, S. (2006) 'When and How Does Electoral Competition Moderate Religious Parties?', paper presented at the 2006 Annual Meeting of the American Political Science Association, Philadelphia, PA.

Teulings, C. and Baldwin, R. (eds) (2015) *Secular Stagnation: Facts, Causes and Cures* (London: CEPR Press).

Thaler, K. M. (2017) 'Nicaragua: A Return to Caudillismo', *Journal of Democracy*, 28(2): 157–69.

Thatcher, M. and Stone Sweet, A. (eds) (2002) *The Politics of Delegation: Non-Majoritarian Institutions in Europe,* special issue of *West European Politics*, 25(1): 1–219.

The Economist (2013) 'Coming Home', 29 October (http://www.economist.com/news/special-report/ 21569570-growing-number-american-companies-are-moving-their-manufacturing-back-united).

Thelen, K. A. (1999) 'Historical Institutionalism in Comparative Politics', *Annual Review of Political Science*, 2: 369–404.

Thelen, K. A. (2004) *How Institutions Evolve: The Political Economy of Skills in Germany, Britain, the United States, and Japan* (Cambridge: Cambridge University Press).

Thelen, K. A. (2014) *Varieties of Liberalization and the New Politics of Social Solidarity* (Cambridge: Cambridge University Press).

Thelen, K. A. and Steinmo, S. (1992) 'Historical Institutionalism in Comparative Politics', in S. Steinmo, K. Thelen, and F. Longstreth (eds), *Structuring Politics: Historical Institutionalism in Comparative Analysis* (Cambridge: Cambridge University Press), 1–32.

Therborn, G. (1977) 'The Rule of Capital and the Rise of Democracy', *New Left Review*, 103: 3–42.

Therborn, G. (1989) '"Pillarization" and "Popular Movements": Two Variants of Welfare State Capitalism: The Netherlands and Sweden', in F. G. Castles (ed.), *The Comparative History of Public Policy* (Cambridge: Polity Press), 192–241.

Thies, M. F. (2001) 'Keeping Tabs on Partners: The Logic of Delegation in Coalition Governments', *American Journal of Political Science*, 45: 580–98.

Thomann, E., Hupe, P., and Sager, F. (2018) 'Serving Many Masters: Public Accountability in Private Policy Implementation', *Governance*, 31(2): 299–319.

Thomson, E. P. (1963) *The Making of the English Working Class* (London: Gollancz).

Tierney, S. (2014) *Constitutional Referendums: The Theory and Practice of Republican Deliberation* (Oxford: Oxford University Press).

Tillin, L., Deshpande, R., and Kailash, K. K. (2015) 'Introduction: Comparing the Politics of Welfare Across Indian States', in Tillin, L., Deshpande, R. and Kailash, K. K. (eds) *Politics of Welfare: Comparison across Indian States* (Oxford: Oxford University Press), 1–39.

Tilly, C. (1978) *From Modernization to Revolution* (New York: Random House).

Tilly, C. (1984) *Big Structures, Large Processes, Huge Comparisons* (New York: Russell Sage Foundation).

Tilly, C. (1986) 'European Violence and Collective Action since 1700', *Social Research*, 53(1): 159–84.

Tilly, C. (1990) *Coercion, Capital, and European States AD990–1990* (Oxford: Blackwell).

Tilly, C. (1995) 'Contentious Repertoires in Great Britain, 1758–1834', in M. Traugott (ed.), *Repertoires and Cycles of Collective Action* (Durham, NC and London: Duke University Press), 15–42.

Tilly, C. and Tarrow, S. (2015) *Contentious Politics* (2nd edn, fully revised and updated) (New York: Oxford University Press).

Tilly, C., Tilly, L., and Tilly, R. (1975) *The Rebellious Century, 1830–1930* (Cambridge, MA: Harvard University Press).

Timmermans, A. I. (2003) *High Politics in the Low Countries* (Aldershot: Ashgate).

Timmermans, A. I. (2006) 'Standing Apart and Sitting Together: Enforcing Coalition Agreements in Multiparty Systems', *European Journal of Political Research*, 45: 263–83.

Titmuss, R. M. (1958) *Essays on the Welfare State* (London: Allen & Unwin).

Titmuss, R. M. (1974) *Social Policy: An Introduction* (ed. B. Abel-Smith and K. Titmuss) (New York: Pantheon Books).

Tocqueville, A. de (1961) [1835] *De la Démocratie en Amérique, Oeuvres Complètes*, Vol. 1 (Paris: Gallimard).

Tocqueville, A. de (2006a) [1835] *Democracy in America*, Vol. 1, Project Gutenberg ebook (http://www.gutenberg.org/etext/815).

Tocqueville, A. de (2006b) [1840] *Democracy in America*, Vol. 2, Project Gutenberg ebook (http://www.gutenberg.org/etext/816).

Tolbert, C. J., Lowenstein, D. H., and Donovan, T. (1998) 'Election Law and Rules for Using Initiatives', in S. Bowler, T. Donovan, and C. Tolbert (eds), *Citizens as Legislators* (Columbus, OH: Ohio State University Press), 27–54.

Tönnies, F. (1955) [1887] *Community and Association* (London: Routledge and Kegan Paul).

Tosun, J. (2013) *Environmental Policy Change in Emerging Market Democracies: Central and Eastern Europe and Latin America Compared* (Toronto: University of Toronto Press).

Tosun, J. and Croissant, A. (2016) 'Policy Diffusion: A Regime-Sensitive Conceptual Framework', *Global Policy*, 7(4): 534–40.

Tosun, J. and de Moraes Marcondes, M. (2016) 'Import Restrictions and Food Safety Regulations: Insights from Brazil', *Latin American Policy*, 7(2): 377–98.

Tosun, J. and Hartung, U. (2018) 'Decentralising Competences in Multi-Level Systems: Insights from the Regulation of Genetically Modified Organisms', *West European Politics*, 41(3): 803–23.

Tosun, J., Koos, S., and Shore, J. (2016) 'Co-Governing Common Goods: Interaction Patterns of Private and Public Actors', *Policy and Society*, 35(1): 1–2.

Toubeau, S. (2018) 'Restructuring the State: Mainstream Responses to Regional Nationalism', *Publius*, 48(1): 76–101.

Touraine, A. (1974) *The Post-Industrial Society. Tomorrow's Social History: Classes, Conflicts and Culture in the Programmed Society* (London: Wildwood House).

Trahan, L., Stuebing, K. K., Hiscock, M. K., and Fletcher, J. M. (2014) 'The Flynn-Effect: A Meta Analysis', *Psychological Bulletin*, 140: 1332–60.

Trampusch, C. and Palier, B. (2016) 'Between X and Y: How Process Tracing Contributes to Opening the Black Box of Causality', *New Political Economy*, 21(5): 437–54.

Transparency International (2008) *Global Corruption Report 2008: Corruption in the Water Sector* (Cambridge: Cambridge University Press).

Traxler, F., Blaschke, S., and Kittel, B. (2001) *International Labour Relations in Internationalized Markets: A Comparative Study of Institutions, Change and Performance* (Oxford: Oxford University Press).

Traxler, F. and Unger B. (1994) 'Industry or Infrastructure? A Cross-national Comparison of Governance, Its Determinants and Economic Consequences in the Dairy Sector', in J. R. Hollingworth, P. C. Schmitter, and W. Streeck (eds), *Governing Capitalist Economies: Performance and Control of Economic Sectors* (Oxford: Oxford University Press), 183–214.

Treisman, D. (2007) *The Architecture of Government: Rethinking Political Decentralization* (Princeton, NJ: Princeton University Press).

Tremewan, C. (2006) 'Welfare and Governance: Public Housing under Singapore's Party-State', in R. Goodman, H. Kwon, and G. White (eds), *The East Asian Welfare Model* (London: Routledge), 95–12.

Triandis, H. C. (1995) *Individualism and Collectivism* (Boulder, CO: Westview Press).

Trigilia, C. (1991) 'The Paradox of the Region: Economic Regulation and the Representation of Interests', *Economy and Society*, 20(3): 306–27.

Troeltsch, E. (1922) [1961] *Der Historismus und seine Probleme* (Aalen: Scientia).

True, J. L., Jones, B. D., and Baumgartner, F. R. (2007) 'Punctuated-Equilibrium Theory: Explaining Stability and Change in American Policymaking', in P. A Sabatier (ed.), *Theories of the Policy Process* (2nd edn) (Boulder, CO: Westview Press).

Truman, D. B. (1971) [1951] *The Governmental Process: Political Interests and Public Opinion* (New York: Knopf).

Tsebelis, G. (1990) *Nested Games: Rational Choice in Comparative Politics* (Berkeley, CA: University of California Press).

Tsebelis, G. (1994) 'The Power of the European Parliament as a Conditional Agenda-Setter', *American Political Science Review*, 88(1): 128–42.

Tsebelis, G. (1995) 'Decision Making in Political Systems: Veto Players in Presidentialism, Parliamentarism, Multicameralism and Multipartism', *British Journal of Political Science*, 25: 289–325.

Tsebelis, G. (2000) 'Veto Players and Institutional Analysis', *Governance*, 13: 441–74.

Tsebelis, G. (2002) *Veto Players: How Political Institutions Work* (Princeton, NJ: Princeton University Press).

Tsebelis, G. and Money, J. (1997) *Bicameralism* (Cambridge: Cambridge University Press).

Tukey, J. W. (1977) *Exploratory Data Analysis* (Boston, MA: Addison-Wesley).

Turner, R. A. and Killian, L. (1987) *Collective Behavior* (3rd edn) (Englewood Cliffs, NJ: Prentice-Hall).

Turner, R. H. (1969) 'The Theme of Contemporary Social Movements', *British Journal of Sociology*, 20: 390–405.

Tushnet, M. (2009) *Weak Courts, Strong Rights: Judicial Review and Social Welfare Rights in Comparative Constitutional Law* (Princeton, NJ: Princeton University Press).

Uleri, P. V. (1996) 'Introduction', in M. Gallagher and P. V. Uleri (eds), *The Referendum Experience in Europe* (Houndmills, Basingstoke: Palgrave Macmillan), 1–19.

Umbers L. M. (2018) 'Compulsory Voting: A Defence', *British Journal of Political Science*, Doi: 10.1017/S0007123418000303.

Umbricht, A. and Esser F. (2014) 'Changing Political News? Long-Term Trends in American, British, French, Italian, German and Swiss Press Reporting', in R. Kuhn and R. Kleis Nielsen (eds),

Political Journalism in Transition: Western Europe in a Comparative Perspective (London: I. B. Tauris), 195–218.

Umbricht, A. and Esser, F. (2016) 'The Push to Popularize Politics: Understanding the Audience-Friendly Packaging of Political News in Six Media Systems since the 1960s', *Journalism Studies*, 17(1): 100–21.

UN (United Nations) (1997) *World Investment Report 1997* (New York: United Nations).

UNCTAD (United Nations Conference on Trade and Development) (1993) *World Investment Report 1993: Transnational Corporations and Integrated International Production* (New York: United Nations).

UNDP (United Nations Development Programme) (2005) *Human Development Report 2005* (New York: Oxford University Press).

UNDP (2006) *Human Development Report: Beyond Scarcity: Power, Poverty and the Global Water Crisis* (New York: United Nations Development Program).

UNDP (2011) *Human Development Report 2011* (Houndmills, Basingstoke: Palgrave Macmillan).

UNDP (2014) *Human Development Report 2014* (New York: United Nations Development Programme).

UNDP (2015) *Democratic Governance Focus Areas* (New York: United Nations Development Programme).

United Nations Population Division. (2015) 'Trends in International Migration, 2015', *Population Facts*, 4: 1–4.

United States Agency for International Development (USAID) (2013) 'Strategy on Democracy, Human Rights and Governance' (http://pdf.usaid.gov/pdf_docs/pdacx557.pdf).

Urwin, D. (1998) 'Modern Democratic Experiences of Territorial Management: Single Houses, But Many Mansions', *Regional and Federal Studies*, 8(2): 81–110.

Uslaner, E. M. (2002) *The Moral Foundations of Trust* (New York: Cambridge University Press).

Valeriani, A. and Vaccari, C. (2016) 'Accidental Exposure to Politics on Social Media as Online Participation Equalizer in Germany, Italy, and the United Kingdom', *New Media and Society*, 18(9): 1857–74.

Van Aelst, P., and Aalberg, T. (2011) 'Between Trust and Suspicion. A Comparative Study of the Relationship between Politicians and Political Journalist in Belgium, Norway and Sweden', *Javnost—The Public*, 18(4): 5–20.

Van Aelst, P. and Walgrave, S. (eds) (2017) *How Political Actors Use the Media. A Functional Analysis of the Media's Role in Politics* (Cham: Macmillan Palgrave).

Van Aelst, P., Brants, K., van Praag, P., de Vreese, C., Nuytemans, M., and van Dalen, A. (2008) 'The Fourth Estate as Superpower? An Empirical Study of Perceptions of Media Power in Belgium and the Netherlands', *Journalism Studies*, 9(4): 494–511.

Van Aelst, P., Shehata, A., and Dalen, A. V. (2010) 'Members of Parliament: Equal Competitors for Media Attention? An Analysis of Personal Contacts between MPs and Political Journalists in Five European Countries', *Political Communication*, 27(3): 310–25.

Van Dalen, A., Albaek, E., and de Vreese, C. (2011) 'Suspicious Minds: Explaining Political Cynicism among Political Journalists in Europe', *European Journal of Communication*, 26(2): 147–62.

Van Dalen, A., Berganza, R., Hanitzsch, T., Amado Adiana, B., Beatriz, J. B., Seizova, S., Skovsgaard, M., and Steindl, N. (2019) 'Trust: Journalists' Confidence in Public Institutions', in Th. Hanitzsch, F. Hanusch, J. Ramaprasad, and S. de Beer Arnold (eds), *Worlds of Journalism. Journalistic Cultures around the Globe* (New York: Columbia University Press), 233–58.

van der Eijk, C. and Franklin, M. (eds) (1996) *Choosing Europe? The European Electorate and National Politics in the Face of Union* (Ann Arbor, MI: University of Michigan Press).

van der Velden, S., Dribbusch, H., Lyddon D., and Vandaele, K. (eds) (2007) *Strikes around the World, 1968–2005: Case Studies of 15 Countries* (Amsterdam: Aksant).

Van Deth, J. W. (ed.) (1998a) *Comparative Politics: The Problem of Equivalence* (London: Routledge).

Van Deth, J. (1998b) 'Equivalence in Comparative Political Research', in Jan van Deth (ed.), *Comparative Politics. The Problem of Equivalence* (London and New York: Routledge), 1–19.

Van Deth, J. W. and Scarbrough, E. (1995) *The Impact of Values* (Oxford: Oxford University Press).

Van Evera, S. (1997) *Guide to Methods for Students of Political Science* (Ithaca, NY: Cornell University Press).

Van Kersbergen, K. (1995) *Social Capitalism: A Study of Christian Democracy and the Welfare State* (London: Routledge).

Van Kersbergen, K. (2002) 'The Politics of Welfare State Reform', *Swiss Political Science Review*, 8(2): 1–19.

Van Kersbergen, K. and Vis, B. (2014) *Comparative Welfare State Politics. Development, Opportunities, and Reform* (Cambridge: Cambridge University Press).

Van Kersbergen, K. and Vis, B. (2015) '"Three Worlds" Typology: Moving Beyond Normal Science?', *Journal of European Social Policy*, 25(1): 111–23.

Van Oorschot, W. (2006) 'Making the Difference in Social Europe: Deservingness Perceptions among Citizens of European Welfare States', *Journal of European Social Policy*, 16(1): 23–42.

Van Spanje, J. and de Vreese, C. (2014). 'Europhile Media and Eurosceptic Voting: Effects of News Media Coverage on Eurosceptic Voting in the 2009 European Parliamentary Elections', *Political Communication*, 31: 325–54.

Van Thiel, S. (2006) 'Styles of Reform: Differences in Quango Creation between Policy Sectors in the Netherlands', *Journal of Public Policy*, 26(2): 115–39.

Van Waarden, F. (1995) 'Persistence of National Policy Styles', in B. Unger and F. van Waarden (eds), *Convergence or Diversity?* (Aldershot: Ashgate), 333–72.

Van Wersch, J. and de Zeeuw, J. (2005) 'Mapping European Assistance', Working Paper 36 (The Hague: Netherlands Institute of International Relations).

Vanderhill, R. (2013) *Promoting Authoritarianism Abroad* (Boulder: Lynne Rienner).

Vanhanen, T. (1997) *Prospects of Democracy: A Study of 172 Countries* (New York: Routledge).

Varju, M. and Chronowski, N. (2015) 'Constitutional Backsliding in Hungary', *Tijdschrift voor Constitutional Law*, 3: 296–310.

Varone, F. Ingold, K., and Fischer, M. (2019) 'Policy Networks and the Roles of Public Administrations', in *Swiss Public Administration* (London: Palgrave Macmillan), 339–53.

Vennesson, P. (2008) 'Case Studies and Process Tracing: Theories and Practices', in D. della Porta and M. Keating (eds), *Approaches and Methodologies in the Social Sciences* (Cambridge: Cambridge University Press), 223–39.

Verba, S. (1985) 'Comparative Politics: Where Have We Been, Where Are We Going?', in H. J. Wiarda (ed.), *New Directions in Comparative Politics* (Boulder, CO: Westview Press) 26–38.

Verba, S., Schlozman, K. L., and Brady, H. (1995) *Voice and Equality: Civic Voluntarism in American Politics* (Cambridge, MA: Cambridge University Press).

Verma, S. K. and Kumar, K. (eds) (2003) *Fifty Years of The Supreme Court of India: Its Grasp and Reach* (New Delhi: Oxford University Press).

Vilar, P. (1977) *Catalunya en la Espana moderna* (Barcelona: Ed. Critica).

Vile, M. J. C. (1967) *Constitutionalism and the Separation of Powers* (Oxford: Oxford University Press).

Vis, B. and van Kersbergen, K. (2007) 'Why and How Do Political Actors Pursue Risky Reforms?', *Journal of Theoretical Politics*, 19(2): 153–72.

Vis, B., Woldendorp, J., and Keman, H. (2007) 'Do Miracles Exist? Economic Performance of Nineteen OECD Democracies 1975–1999', *Journal of Business Research*, 60: 531–8.

Vliegenthart, R. and Damstra, A. (2019) 'Parliamentary Questions, Newspaper Coverage, and Consumer Confidence in Times of Crisis: A Cross-National Comparison', *Political Communication*, 36(1): 17–35.

Vliegenthart, R. and Skovsgaard, M. (2017). 'Too Powerful or Just Doing Their Job? Explaining Differences in Conceptions of Media Power among Politicians and Journalists', in P. Van Aelst and S. Walgrave (eds), *How Political Actors Use the Media: A Functional Analysis of the Media's Role in Politics* (London: Palgrave Macmillan) (85–103).

Vliegenthart, R., Walgrave, S., Baumgartner, F., Bevan, S., Breunig, C., Brouard, S., Bonafont, L., Grossman, E., Jennings, W., Mortensen, P., Palau, A., Sciarini, P., and Tresch, A. (2016) 'Do the Media Set the Parliamentary Agenda? A Comparative Study in Seven Countries', *European Journal of Political Research*, 55(2): 283–301.

Vogel, D. J. (1995) *Trading Up: Consumer and Environmental Regulation in a Global Economy* (Cambridge, MA: Harvard University Press).

Volcansek, M. (ed.) (1997) *Law above Nations: Supranational Courts and the Legalization of Politics* (Gainesville, FL: University of Florida Press).

Volkens, A., Bara, J., Budge, I., McDonald, M. S., and Klingemann, H.-D. (2013) *Mapping Policy Preferences from Texts III: Statistical Solutions for Manifesto Analysts* (Oxford: Oxford University Press).

Voltmer, K. (ed.) (2006) *Mass Media and Political Communication in New Democracies* (Abingdon: Routledge).

Voltmer K. (2013) *The Media in Transitional Democracies. Contemporary Political Communication* (Cambridge: Polity Press).

Vowe, G. and Henn, P. (eds) (2016) *Political Communication in the Online World* (London: Routledge).

Vowles, J. (2008) 'New Zealand: The Consolidation of Reform?', in M. Gallagher and P. Mitchell (eds), *The Politics of Electoral Systems* (Oxford: Oxford University Press), 295–312.

Waddington, J. and Conchon, A. (2015) *Board Level Employee Representation in Europe: Priorities, Power and Articulation* (London: Routledge).

Wagemann, C. (2012) *Breakdown and Change of Private Interest Governments* (Abingdon: Routledge).

Wagschal, U. (2000) 'Besonderheiten der gezügelten Sozialstaaten', in U. Wagschal and H. Obinger (eds), *Der gezügelte Wohlfahrtsstaat. Sozialpolitik in reichen Industrienationen* (Frankfurt am Main: Campus), 37–72.

Waldner, D. (2011) 'Process Tracing: Its Promise and Its Problems', paper presented at the Research Group on Qualitative and Multi-Method Analysis, Syracuse University, Syracuse (NY).

Waldner, D. (2012) 'Process Tracing and Causal Mechanisms', in H. Kincaid (ed.), *The Oxford Handbook of Philosophy of Social Science* (New York, NY: Oxford University Press), 65–84.

Walgrave, S., Varone, F., and Dumont, P. (2006) 'Policy with or without Parties? A Comparative Analysis of Policy Priorities and Policy Change in Belgium, 1991 to 2000', *Journal of European Public Policy*, 13(7): 1021–38.

Walker, I. and Smith, H. J. (2001) *Relative Deprivation: Specification, Development, and Integration* (Cambridge: Cambridge University Press).

Walker, N. (1996) 'European Constitutionalism and European Integration', *Public Law*(Summer): 266.

Wallerstein, I. (1979) *The Capitalist World Economy* (Cambridge: Cambridge University Press).

Wallis, J. J. and Oates, W. E. (1988) 'Decentralization in the Public Sector: An Empirical Study of State and Local Government', in Rosen, H. S. (ed.), *Fiscal Federalism Quantitative Studies* (Chicago, IL: University of Chicago Press), 5–32.

Walton, J. K. and Seddon, D. (2008) *Free Markets and Food Riots: The Politics of Global Adjustment* (Cambridge, MA: John Wiley & Sons).

Waltz, K. N. (1999) 'Globalization and Governance', *PS: Political Science and Politics*, 32(4): 693–700.

Wang, G., Goonasekera, A., and Servaes, J. (eds) (2000) *The New Communications Landscape: Demystifying Media Globalization* (Abingdon: Routledge).

Wannop, U. (1997) 'Regional Planning and Urban Governance in Europe and the USA', in M. Keating and J. Loughlin (eds), *The Political Economy of Regionalism* (London: Routledge), 139–70.

Warshaw, S. A. (1996) *Powersharing: White House Cabinet Relations in the Modern Presidency* (Albany, NY: State University of New York Press).

Wattenberg, M. P. (2006) *Is Voting for Young People?* (New York: Pearson).

Watts, R. (1996) *Comparing Federal Systems in the 1990s* (Kingston, Ontario: Institute of Intergovernmental Relations, Queen's University).

Watts, R. (1998) 'Federalism, Federal Political Systems, and Federations', *Annual Review of Political Science*, 1: 117–37.

Watts, R. (2008) *Comparing Federal Systems* (Kingston, Ontario: Institute of Intergovernmental Relations, Queen's University).

Way, L. (2015) 'The Limits of "Autocracy Promotion": The Case of Russia in the "Near Abroad"', *European Journal of Political Research*, 54(4): 691–706.

Weaver, D. (1998) *The Global Journalist* (New York: Hampton Press).

Weaver, D. H. and Willnat, L. (eds) (2012) *The Global Journalist in the Twenty-First Century* (New York: Routledge).

Weaver, R. K. and Rockman, B. A. (1993) 'Assessing the Effects of Institutions', in R. K. Weaver and B. A. Rockman (eds), *Do Institutions Matter? Government Capabilities in the United States and Abroad* (Washington, DC: Brookings Institution), 1–41.

Weber, E. (1976) *Peasants into Frenchmen* (Stanford, CA: University of Stanford Press).

Weber, M. (1920) *Gesammelte Aufsätze zur Religionssoziologie* (Tübingen: Mohr).

Weber, M. (1922) Wirtschaft und Gesellschaft (Tübingen: Mohr).

Weber, M. (1947) *The Theory of Social and Economic Organization* (New York: Free Press).

Weber, M. (1978) *Economy and Society: An Outline of Interpretative Sociology* (Berkeley, CA: University of California Press), first published in 1922 in German.

Weiler, J. H. H. (1991) 'The Transformation of Europe', *Yale Law Journal*, 100: 2403–83.

Weiler, J. H. H., Haltern, U., and Mayer, F. C. (1995) 'European Democracy and its Critique', *West European Politics*, 18(4): 4–39.

Weingast, B. R. (1995) 'The Economic Role of Political Institutions: Market-Preserving Federalism and Economic Development', *Journal of Law and Economic Organization*, 11: 1–31.

Weingast, B. R. (2002) 'Rational Choice Institutionalism', in I. Katznelson and H. V. Milner (eds), *The State of the Discipline* (New York/Washington, DC: W. W. Norton/American Political Science Association), 660–92.

Weingast, B. R., Shepsle, K. A., and Johnsen, C. (1981) 'The Political Economy of Benefits and Costs: A Neoclassical Approach to Distributive Politics', *Journal of Political Economy*, 89(4): 642–64.

Weiss, L. (1998) *The Myth of the Powerless State* (New York: Cornell University Press).

Wejnert, B. (2014) *Diffusion of Democracy: The Past and Future of Global Democracy* (New York: Cambridge University Press).

Weller, M. and Nobbs, K. (eds.) (2010) *Asymmetric Autonomy and the Settlement of Ethnic Conflicts* (Philadelphia, PA: University of Pennsylvania Press).

Wells, P. (1998) 'Quebecers? Canadians? We're Proud to be Both', *The Gazette*, 4 April 1998.

Welzel, C. (2007) 'Are Levels of Democracy Influenced by Mass Attitudes?', *International Political Science Review*, 28 (4): 397–424.

Welzel, C. (2010) 'How Selfish Are Self-Expression Values: A Civicness Test', *Journal of Cross-Cultural Psychology*, 41(March): 2–23.

Welzel, C. (2013) *Freedom Rising: Human Empowerment and the Quest for Emancipation* (New York: Cambridge University Press).

Welzel, C. and Inglehart, R. (2010) 'Values, Agency, and Well-Being: A Human Development Model', *Social Indicators Research*, 97(1): 43–63.

Welzel, C., Inglehart, R., and Deutsch, F. (2005) 'Social Capital, Voluntary Associations, and Collective Action', *Journal of Civil Society*, 1: 121–46.

Wen, D. (2005) *China Copes with Globalization* (San Francisco, CA: International Forum on Globalization).

Western, B. (1997) *Between Class and Market: Postwar Unionization in the Capitalist Democracies* (Princeton, NJ: Princeton University Press).

Wettstein, M., Esser, F., Schutz, A., Wirz, D., and Wirth, W. (2018) 'News Media as Gatekeepers, Critics, and Initiators of Populist Communication: How Journalists in Ten Countries Deal with the Populist Challenge', *International Journal of Press/Politics*, 24(3): 476–95.

Weyland, K. (2005) 'Theories of Policy Diffusion: Lessons from Latin American Pension Reform', *World Politics*, 57(2): 262–95.

Weyland, K. (2006) *Bounded Rationality and Policy Diffusion: Social Sector Reform in Latin America* (Princeton, NJ: Princeton University Press).

Weyland, K. (2017) 'Autocratic Diffusion and Cooperation: the Impact of Interests vs Ideology', *Democratization*, 28(7): 1235–52.

Weyland, K. G. (2014) *Making Waves: Democratic Contention in Europe and Latin America since the Revolutions of 1848* (Cambridge: Cambridge University Press).

Wheare, K. (1963) *Federal Government* (4th edn) (Oxford: Oxford University Press).

Whiteley, P., Clarke, H. D., Sanders, D., and Stewart, M. C. (2012) 'Britain Says NO: Voting in the AV Ballot Referendum', *Parliamentary Affairs*, 65: 301–22.

Wiard, V. (2019). 'News Ecology and News Ecosystems', in *Oxford Research Encyclopedia on Communication* (Oxford: Oxford University Press), 1–19, Doi: 10.1093/acrefore/9780190228613.013.847.

Wibbels, E. (2006) 'Madison in Baghdad? Decentralization and Federalism in Comparative Politics', *Annual Review of Political Science*, 9: 165–88.

Wildavsky, A. (1964) *The Politics of the Budgetary Process* (Boston, MA: Little, Brown).

Wildavsky, A. B. (1987) *Speaking Truth to Power: The Art and Craft of Policy Analysis* (New Brunswick, NJ: Transaction Books).

Wilensky, H. L. (1975) *The Welfare State and Equality: Structural and Ideological Roots of Public Expenditures* (Berkeley, CA: University of California Press).

Wilensky, H. L. (1981) 'Leftism, Catholicism, and Democratic Corporatism: The Role of Political Parties in Recent Welfare State Development', in P. Flora and A. J. Heidenheimer (eds), *The Development of Welfare States in Europe and America* (Piscataway, NJ: Transaction Publishers), 345–82.

Wilensky, H. L. and Lebeaux, C. N. (1965) *Industrial Society and Social Welfare: The Impact of Industrialization on the Supply and Organization of Social Welfare Services in the United States* (New York: Macmillan).

Wilkinson, R. G. and Pickett, K. (2009) *The Spirit Level: Why More Equal Societies Almost Always Do Better* (London: Allen Lane).

Wilkinson, R. and Pickett, K. (2010) *The Spirit Level. Why Equality is Better for Everyone* (London: Penguin Books).

Williams, M. (1998) *Voice, Trust and Memory: Marginalized Groups and the Failings of Liberal Representation* (Princeton, NJ: Princeton University Press).

Wilson, C. and Dunn, A. (2011) 'Digital Media in the Egyptian Revolution: Descriptive Analysis from the Tahrir Data Sets', *International Journal of Communication*, 5: 1248–72.

Wilson, G. K. (1990) *Interest Groups* (Oxford: Basil Blackwell).

Wilson, J. (1983) 'On the Dangers of Bickering in a Federal State: Some Reflections on the Failure of the National Party System', in A. Kornberg and H. Clarke (eds), *Political Support in Canada: The Crisis Years* (Durham, NC: Duke University Press), 171–222.

Wilson, J. Q. (1973) *Political Organizations* (Beverly Hills, CA: Sage).

Wilson, J. Q. (1989) *Bureaucracy* (New York: Basic Books).

Wilson, J. Q. (1995) *Political Organizations* (Princeton, NJ: Princeton University Press).

Wilthagen, T. (1998) *Flexicurity: 'A New Paradigm for Labour Market Policy Reform?'*, WZB Discussion Paper (Berlin: FSI).

Wilthagen, T. and Tros, F. (2014) 'The Concept of "Flexicurity": A New Approach to Regulating Employment and Labour Markets', *Transfer*, 20(1): 166–86.

Wilthagen, T., Tros, F., and van Lishout, H. (2003) 'Towards "Flexicurity": Balancing Flexicurity and Security in EU Member States', paper presented at the 13th World Congress of IIRA, Berlin.

Windhoff-Héritier, A. (1980) *Politikimplementation: Ziel und Wirklichkeit politischer Entscheidungen* (Königstein: Anton Hain).

Winter, D. G. (2013) 'Personality Profiles of Political Elites', in L. Huddy, D. O. Sears, and J. Levy (eds), *Oxford Handbook of Political Psychology* (2nd edn) (Oxford: Oxford University Press).

Wiseman, N. (1981) 'The Pattern of Prairie Politics', *Queen's Quarterly*, 88: 298–315.

Witt, M. A. (2016) 'The Road Ahead for China: Implications from South Korea's Experience', in A.Y. Lewin, M. Kenney, and J. P. Murmann (eds), *China's Innovation Challenge: Overcoming the Middle-Income Trap* (Cambridge: Cambridge University Press), 87–107.

Wittfogel, K. (1957) *Oriental Despotism* (New Haven, CT: Yale University Press).

Wolfe, C. (2013) *Before the Law; Humans and Other Animals in a Biopolitical Frame* (Chicago, IL: The University of Chicago Press).

Wolin, S. S. (1989) *The Presence of the Past: Essays on the State and the Constitution* (Baltimore, MD: Johns Hopkins University Press).

World Bank (2001) *World Development Report 2002: Building Institutions for Markets* (Washington, DC: The World Bank).

World Bank (2006) *World Development Report 2006* (New York: Oxford University Press).

World Bank (2010) 'Escaping the Middle-Income-Trap', in *World Bank East Asia Pacific Economic Update 2010, Vol. 2. Robust Recovery, Rising Risk* (Washington, DC: The World Bank).

Wren, A. (ed.) (2013) *The Political Economy of the Service Transformation* (Oxford: Oxford University Press).

Wright, J. (2008) 'Do Authoritarian Institutions Constrain? How Legislatures Affect Economic Growth and Investment', *American Journal of Political Science*, 52(2): 322–43.

Wright, J. and Escribà-Folch, A. (2012) 'Authoritarian Institutions and Regime Survival: Transitions to Democracy and Subsequent Autocracy', *British Journal of Political Science*, 42(2): 283–309.

Wriston, W. B. (1992) *The Twilight of Sovereignty: How the Information Revolution is Transforming our World* (New York: Charles Scribner's Sons).

Wroe, A. (2016) 'Economic Insecurity and Political Trust in the United States', *American Politics Research*, 44(1): 131–63.

Wyler, R. (2012) *Schweizer Gewerkschaften und Europa* (Münster: Westfälisches Dampfboot).

Yap, P. (2015) *Constitutional Dialogue in Common Law Asia* (Oxford: Oxford University Press).

Yap, P. (2017) *Courts and Democracies in Asia* (Cambridge: Cambridge University Press).

Young, A. and Wallace, H. (2000) *Regulatory Politics in the Enlarging European Union: Weighing Civic and Producer Interests* (Manchester: Manchester University Press).

Young, L. and Archer, K. (eds) (2002) *Regionalism and Party Politics in Canada* (Don Mills, Ontario: Oxford University Press).

Youngs, R. (eds) (2010) *The European Union and Democracy Promotion* (Baltimore, MD: Johns Hopkins University Press).

Yu, L. (2006) 'Understanding Information Inequality: Making Sense of the Literature of the Information and Digital Divides', *Journal of Librarianship and Information Science*, 38(4): 229–52.

Zacher, M. V. (1992) 'The Decaying Pillars of the Westphalian Temple: Implications for International Order and Governance', in J. N. Rosenau and E.-O. Czempiel (eds), *Governance without Government: Order and Change in World Politics* (Cambridge: Cambridge University Press), 58–102.

Zakaria, F. (1997) 'The Rise of Illiberal Democracy', *Foreign Affairs*, 76(6): 22–43.

Zakaria, F. (2007) *The Future of Freedom: Illiberal Democracy at Home and Abroad*. New York: W.W. Norton & Co.

Zaller, J. R. (1992) *The Nature and Origin of Mass Opinion* (Cambridge: Cambridge University Press).

Zielonka, J. (2018) *Counter-Revolution. Liberal Europe in Retreat* (Oxford: Oxford University Press).

Zohlnhöfer, R., Herweg, N., and Rüb, F. (2015) 'Theoretically Refining the Multiple Streams Framework: An Introduction', *European Journal of Political Research*, 54(3): 412–18.

Zuber, C. (2011) 'Understanding the Multinational Game: Toward a Theory of Asymmetrical Federalism', *Comparative Political Studies*, 44(5): 546–71.

Zuber, C. and Szöcsik, E. (2019) 'The Second Edition of the EPAC Expert Survey on Ethnonationalism in Party Competition—

Testing for Validity and Reliability', *Regional and Federal Studies*, 29(1): 91–113.

Zürn, M. (1998) *Regieren jenseits des Nationaalstaates: Globalisierung und Denationalisierung als Chance* (Frankfurt am Main: Suhrkamp).

Other sources

Afrobarometer (2002) Afrobarometer data, round 1 (see web links).

American National Election Studies (2004) American National Election Study 2004 (see web links).

CAWP (2006) Center for American Women and Politics (see web links).

CSES (2006) Comparative Study of Electoral Systems (see web links).

Comparative Study of Electoral Systems (2001) 'CSES Module 1: 1996 –2001' (http://www.cses.org).

Comparative Study of Electoral Systems (2005) 'CSES Module 2: 2001–2006' (http://www.cses.org).

Corporate Europe Conservatory (http://www.corporateeurope.org).

Elections in Euskadi (2006) (see the Online Resource Centre).

Environomics Research Institute for Surveys (in partnership with the Mowat Centre, the Canada West Foundation, the Centre' d'Analyse politique: Constitution et fédéralisme, the Institute for Research on Public Policy, and the Brian Mulroney Institute of Government (2019) *Confederation of Tomorrow 2019 Survey* (https://www.environicsinstitute.org/projects/project-details/confederation-of-tomorrow---2018).

European Values Study Group and World Values Survey Association (2006) 'European and World Values Surveys Four-Wave Integrated Data File, 1981–2004(V.20060423)' (http://www.worldvaluessurvey.org).

Eurostat (2019) Database (https://ec.europa.eu/eurostat/web/income-and-living-conditions/data/database).

EUSTAT (2006) Instituto Vasco de Estadística (see web links).

Foreign Policy and Kearney, A. T. (2006) 'The Globalization Index', *Foreign Policy*, November/December: 26–36.

Freedom House (2006) *Freedom in the World 2006: The Annual Survey of Political Rights and Civil Liberties* (Lanham, MD: Rowman & Littlefield).

Freedom House (2012) *Freedom in the World 2012* (New York: Freedom House).

Freedom House (2019). *Freedom in the World 2019* (https://freedomhouse.org/report/freedom-world/freedom-world-2019).

German Marshall Fund of the US (2005) *Transatlantic Trends 2005* (http://gmfus.org).

IDEA (2006) International Institute for Democracy and Electoral Assistance, 'Voter Turnout' (http://www.idea.int/vt).

International Labour Organization (2006) 'Statistics of Trade Union Membership: Data for 47 Countries Taken Mainly from National Statistical Publications'.

Inter-Parliamentary Union (2006) 'Women in National Parliaments' (http://archive.jpu.org).

NILT (2004) Northern Ireland Life and Times Survey 2004.

Scottish Social Attitudes Surveys (2014) National Centre for Social Research (http://www.natcen.ac.uk/media/563071/ssa-2014-has-the-referendun-campaign-made-a-difference.pdf), 8.

You GOV (2018) *Future of England Survey* (https://d25d2506sfb94s.cloudfront.net/cumulus_uploads/document/s7ot5ydjnu/FOE_Scotland_June18_Results_w.pdf).

Index